T... for international relations, from authors you trust and respect.

World Politics: Trend and Transformation is the best selling text for the International Relations course. This text has been translated into a multitude of languages and is now the leading book in the European Union, the People's Republic of China, Taiwan, South Korea, Russia, Brazil, Israel, Croatia, Serbia, and many other countries around the world. This powerful, informative text appeals to global citizens, and for good reason.

On every page, you'll find engaging narrative and exemplary scholarship that conveys a balanced and realistic sense of world politics today. Fascinating coverage of contemporary developments and historical trends give students a compelling perspective on political change. By analyzing both historical and contemporary trends and developments, **World Politics** resists the temptation to overly simplify global politics. Presenting material in a thought-provoking yet accessible manner, Kegley and Wittkopf prepare students to assess the possibilities for the global future and the potential impact on their lives.

Long trusted and relied upon, **World Politics: Trend and Transformation** remains a timely book that explores the constantly evolving theories and issues that confront countries, and looks at the image of the United States as perceived through the eyes of other countries. Faced with thought-provoking questions raised by the text, students are challenged to think about critical issues such as global welfare, international economics, ecology, human rights, global governance, global conflict, the changing face of terrorism, national security, warfare, and approaches to peace.

Accompanied by an unparalleled selection of online and multimedia resources!

Turn the page! Your PREVIEW begins here ▶

About the distinguished authors

Charles W. Kegley, Jr., is the Pearce Professor of International Relations at the University of South Carolina. A graduate of the American University and Syracuse University, and a Pew Faculty Fellow at Harvard University, Kegley serves on the Board of Trustees of the Carnegie Council on Ethics and International Affairs and is a past president of the International Studies Association (1993-94). Kegley has held faculty appointments at Georgetown University, the University of Texas, Rutgers University, the People's University of China, and the Graduate Institute of International Studies, Geneva. Recently published among his four dozen books are *The New Global Terrorism* (2003); *Controversies in International Relations Theory* (1995); and, with Gregory A. Raymond, *The Imperiled Imperium: The Consequences of Post 9/11 American Foreign Policy at Home and Abroad* (2005), *The Global Future* (2005), *From War to Peace* (2002); *Exorcising the Ghost of Westphalia* (2002); *How Nations Make Peace* (1999); *A Multipolar Peace? Great-Power Politics in the Twenty-First Century* (1994); and *When Trust Breaks Down: Alliance Norms and World Politics* (1990). He has also published his primary research in many scholarly journals.

Eugene R. Wittkopf is the R. Downs Poindexter Distinguished Professor of Political Science at Louisiana State University. A graduate of Valparaiso and Syracuse Universities, Wittkopf has held appointments at the University of Florida and the University of North Carolina at Chapel Hill. Wittkopf is author of *Faces of Internationalism: Public Opinion and American Foreign Policy* (1990); coeditor of *The Future of American Foreign Policy* (4th edition, 2004); and *The Domestic Sources of American Foreign Policy: Insights and Evidence* (2004). He has also published extensively in many scholarly journals. In 1997, he received the highest award given by Louisiana State University in recognition of faculty contributions to research and scholarship when he was awarded the LSU Distinguished Research Master of Arts, Humanities, and Social Sciences. Wittkopf served as coauthor of the first six editions of *World Politics*, for which his professional contributions to the development of this book are appreciatively acknowledged.

Kegley and Wittkopf have both been recipients of the Distinguished Scholar Award in Foreign Policy of the International Studies Association. Together, Kegley and Wittkopf have coauthored and edited more than twenty texts, including *American Foreign Policy: Pattern and Process* (6th edition, 2003); *The Global Agenda* (6th edition, 2001); *The Future of American Foreign Policy* (1992); *The Nuclear Reader* (2nd edition, 1989); and *The Domestic Sources of American Foreign Policy* (1988).

"This is a great text for teaching the Intro course. It covers all the major areas and gives students enough to do additional work later. The support material is very helpful if you are just starting. You are also not limited and can use this with most readers and ancillary texts."
— Michael D. Kanner,
    University of Colorado Boulder

"The chapters are lucidly organized, with relevant and useful pedagogy. Each device is extremely useful, and will greatly aid students in understanding and appreciating the materials. I particularly like the controversy boxes, which are thoughtfully done, the "world wide web" features, and the very timely literature presented on the further readings sections. I feel that the controversy boxes offer great starting points for student class presentations and debates."
— Shalendra D. Sharma,
    University of San Francisco

Helpful new features, streamlined coverage, and the latest information on today's hot issues make this powerful text even better!

- This text has been **fully updated** to include the most recent available indicators of global trends and the most recent events on the international scene, including consideration of the controversial superpower status now held and acted upon by the United States. *See page 4.*

- **Over three-dozen new maps, tables, photographs, and figures** broaden the book's coverage, provoke interest, and enable students to visualize ideas. *See page 8.*

- **New pedagogy** includes updated **Controversy Boxes** developed to capture the most pertinent issues being debated in world politics today. *See page 9.*

- **Revised Glossary terms** in the margins have been expanded to provide a "high definition" listing of the key terms used to discuss and analyze International Politics. *See page 9.*

- **The book has been consolidated to 15 chapters** to match the number of weeks in a typical semester. Chapters 12 and 13 of the previous edition, which covered military power, national security, counter-terrorism, strategic bargaining, and economic sanctions as instruments of influence have been abridged and merged into a single chapter called "Military Power, Coercive Diplomacy and National Security."

- **Technology Integration:** A new technology icon now appears in the margin of the text to direct students to online resources directly related to the material presented. These resources include interactive maps, simulations, and case studies previously provided on the CD-ROM and now thoroughly revised and updated for the new edition in an online format.

- **A new, richly designed website**—freely available to students who purchase a new copy of the text—includes updated and additional resources previously provided on CD-ROM, including simulations, data exercises, and mapping exercises. *See page 11.*

- **A compelling final chapter leaves students with a lot to think about:** *Ten Questions About Twenty-First-Century Global Prospects. See page 9.*

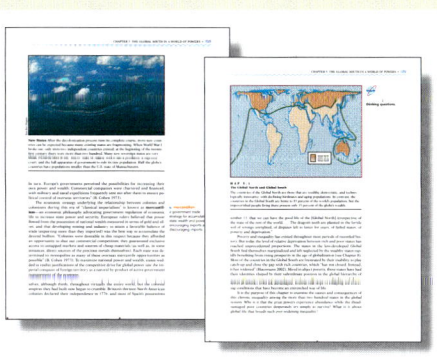

3

Rapid global changes require the most accurate and timely information.

Dramatic geopolitical changes make it essential that your students have the most modern and current text available, particularly in this era of globalization and extensive media coverage. To ensure you have the text you need and the timely information your students deserve, Kegley and Wittkopf have revisited every passage and integrated the latest analysis with the most current information available as the book went to press.

The end result? A book that presents indicators of global trends and clear, precise coverage of the most important issues on the global agenda. Kegley and Wittkopf present the latest information on:

- Cross-national levels of human development
- The latest changes in the status of women as indexed by the gender empowerment measure (GEM)
- Demographic projections of likely population changes, including aging and de-population
- National levels of globalization and interdependence
- The growing international health crisis
- Threats to the preservation of the environment such as global warming and the decline in biodiversity
- U.S. and global military expenditures
- The latest information on the magnitude of the international arms trade
- Trends in international trade and in foreign direct investment (FDI)
- The activities of more than 31,000 NGOs (non-governmental organizations)
- The frequency of civil wars
- The expansion of the community of liberal democracies
- Changes in human rights legislation, in arms control and disarmament agreements
- The latest available figures on the frequency of international terrorist acts
- International crises since 1919
- The proliferation of weapons of mass destruction and nuclear proliferation
- The expansion of the European Union to 25 countries and of NATO to 26 members
- U.N. peacekeeping operations
- Global refugee crisis

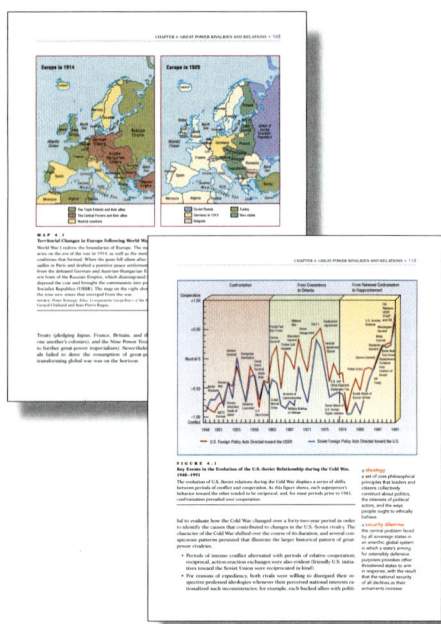

Thought provoking coverage of human rights and ethics inspires student to not only think, but also take action.

Chapter 7, *Humanitarian Challenges and the Protection of Human Rights*, challenges students to consider each individual human being in relation to the global forces that shape their experiences. This eye-opening chapter gives the issues of human security, human rights, and gender equity the highlighted treatment they deserve as these issues assume rapidly increasing significance in domestic and international political consideration. An important objective of the book is to **help students become informed scholars and citizens** capable of interpreting world affairs, while sensitizing them to their responsibility to think more critically about the moral implications of global circumstances and policies designed to alleviate human suffering.

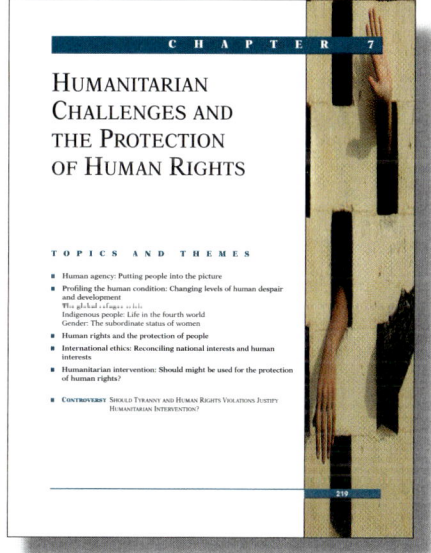

An **expanded discussion of ethics** examines the moral principles involved in the humanitarian challenge of protecting the human rights and civil liberties of all people—including refugees and displaced persons.

This **compelling** chapter underscores the critical importance of human beings in the overall scheme of world politics, while illustrating the ways in which each person's encounter is impacted by shifting social, political, religious, and linguistic institutions and traditions.

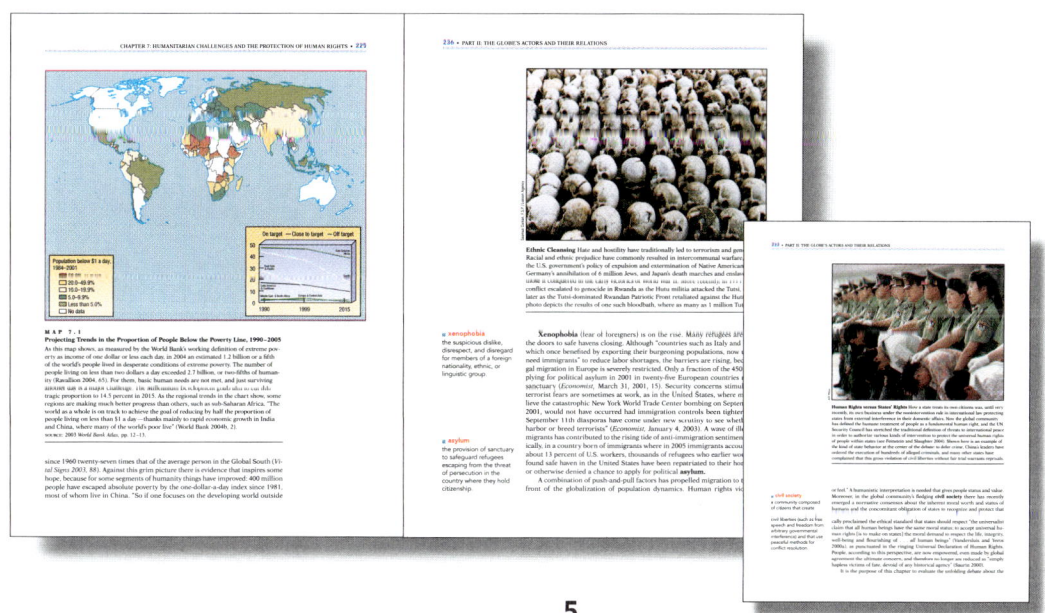

Fully updated and streamlined materials examine the most significant issues and help students understand and anticipate future trends in global politics.

In the Tenth Edition, the authors explore the dynamics of the twenty-first century political arena, and how existing and emerging global players interact to shape world politics. Students learn about the **rivalries and relationships** that drive decisions, and the increasing importance and influence of the Latin American, African and Asian countries in defining political issues.

Fully updated to reflect recent political developments on the international scene, the authors delve into the superpower status now held and acted upon by the United States, and the ramifications this situation has on global perception and receptivity to U.S. policies and actions.

In-depth analysis address such pivotal groups as the **World Trade Organization** and the **International Monetary Fund**—what they are, how they're organized—and provide the information students need to understand these seemingly "faceless" intergovernmental organizations that wield such influence. The book also examines the controversial nonstate actors that increasingly find themselves under attack as symbols of the problems attributed to globalization and rules established by global institutions.

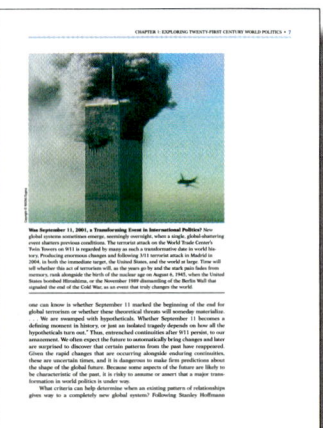

With **Global Terrorism** one of the most prominent issues today, the authors provide a comprehensive and thorough study of the convoluted issues of terrorism throughout the text. They examine the impact of 9/11 and the war on Iraq, the George W. Bush Administration's response and use of preemptive force, the role of military capability in determining an actor's range of policy options, the policy debate that preceded the decision to invade Iraq, and the way bureaucracy influenced that decision.

Provocative discussions about the ramifications of terrorism as a response to poverty and human rights violations, in the context of globalization, and as a factor in the relations between global powers culminate in the challenging question "Can the War Against Global Terrorism Be Won?"

Updated coverage of alternative theories provides students with an important perspective on the manner in which countries interact.

The dynamics of international relations are framed by **time-tested theories of realism and liberalism** in the Tenth Edition.

In addition, the authors push the envelope, building on those theoretical departures and exploring or integrating **new reconstructed theories**, such as the outlooks provided by constructivism and feminist theory.

By expanding these theories to include more contemporary approaches, the authors can relate them more explicitly to concrete global issues and encourage students to appreciate the contribution of political theory to understanding international relations.

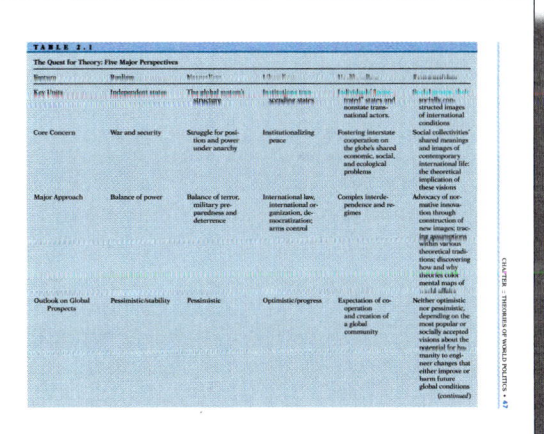

Global perspectives and issues come alive with vivid maps and illustrations.

Over three-dozen new maps, tables, photographs, and figures broaden the book's coverage, provoke interest, and enable students to visualize global ideas and issues. In the Tenth Edition, some of the events and issues illustrated in maps and figures include:

- The number of deaths due to terrorism
- Military spending by the US and the world
- International crises
- Peacekeeping operations
- Military interventions
- The arms trade
- Global health crisis
- Global warming and the Kyoto Accord
- The US Superpower status and the newly re-elected Bush Administration recommitment to assertive unilateralism and the global response to that aggressive policy
- Foreign aid

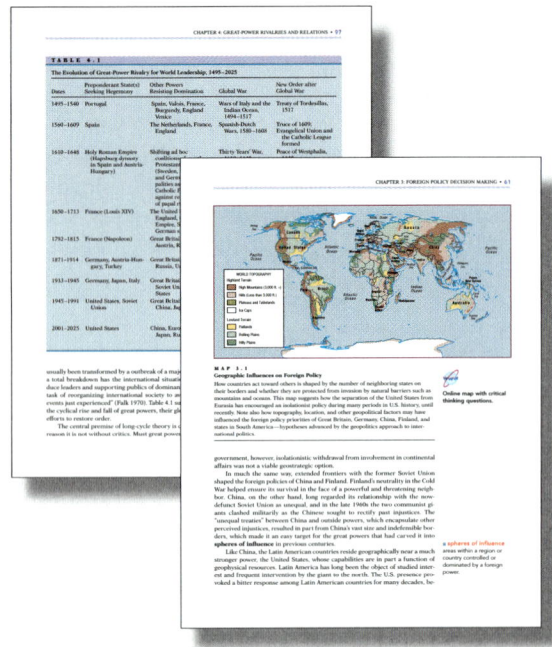

All the new maps and illustrations in the Tenth Edition introduce **relevant and timely topics** and each image includes a detailed caption that conveys its relationship to the larger issues discussed in the book.

Food for Thought
To further stimulate classroom discussion, a diverse selections of topics are presented:

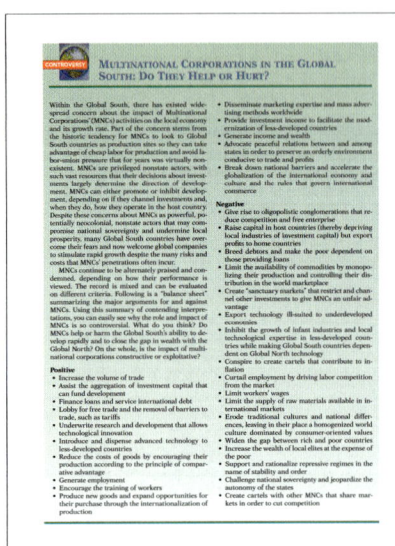

- The war in Iraq
- Ethnic cleansing
- Nationalism vs. patriotism
- Economic sanctions in coercive diplomacy
- Multinational corporations
- The global refugee crisis
- Failed states collapsing from civil wars
- The indigenous peoples of the Fourth World
- The gap between the rich and poor
- Ethics and statecraft
- Immigration
- "Just war" theory in international law
- Displaced peoples
- The "clash of civilizations"
- Recent adaptations in theories of foreign policy decision making
- The role of religion in international relations
- Employment outsourcing and transnational labor dilemmas and trends
- The "end of history"

Time-tested pedagogy combines with new features to facilitate comprehension.

In every chapter, you'll find thought provoking and updated **Controversy** Essays that outline the debate over essential issues. Each **Controversy** identifies a major topic with opposing positions. These essays deal with emerging issues, encourage students to consider rival viewpoints, and help them develop their own opinions.

New Controversy Boxes have been developed to callout and capture the liveliest issues being debated in world politics today, and offer excellent starting points for class discussions or research papers. Topics include:
- Policy and Personality: Do Leaders Make a Difference?
- Was Ideology the Primary Source of East-West Conflict?
- Does High Military Spending Decrease Human Security?
- Is it Ethical to Wage a Preemptive War to Prevent an Adversary's Potential Aggression?
- Should Tyranny and Human Rights Violations Justify Humanitarian Intervention?

Research citations within the text underline the book's careful documentation of recent research and data. All key terms in the text are presented in a **marginal glossary**, a tool used by the authors to introduce the new vocabulary that students will need to understand and interpret the language and concepts used both by policy makers and scholars to discuss international relations. Each chapter ends with suggested readings on the topics covered.

Revised Glossary terms in the margins have been expanded to provide a "high definition" listing of the key terms used to discuss and analyze International Politics, helping students to focus on key points.

A thought-provoking final chapter challenges students to think how today's political stage will impact the world's future—and their own lives.

Chapter 15, *Ten Questions About Twenty-First-Century Global Prospects*, concludes with a series of questions that stimulate critical thinking about the trends and issues identified in the book and the dilemmas the pose for the global future. These questions have been updated to reflect the events of the last two years. The discussion represents the most recent assessments of global prospects, while relating these "big picture" questions to specific ongoing issues in international relations.

Unparalleled technology integration and resources keep your students up-to-date with the rapidly changing global arena.

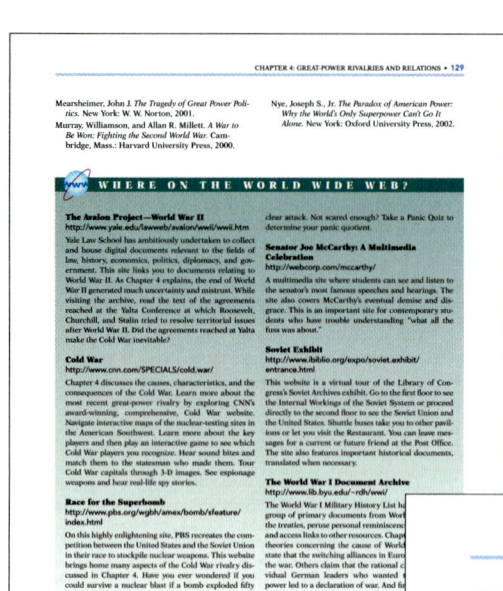

The Tenth Edition connects your students to powerful **multimedia teaching and learning tools** with thorough integration. At the end of each chapter, you'll find **Where on the World Wide Web?** links that lead students beyond the text to the borderless world of the Internet. These sections have been updated and expanded to list trustworthy major websites that student can explore for more information on the topics discussed in each chapter. Each Web listing is accompanied by a description of the site, as well as activities and research that students can pursue. The text also features a marginal icon that directs students to online resources directly related to the material presented in the text.

Also at the end of each chapter, **InfoTrac® College Edition** exercises are presented, as well as a listing of the most current and relevant articles available on the database.

Web-based resources take your course outside the classroom.

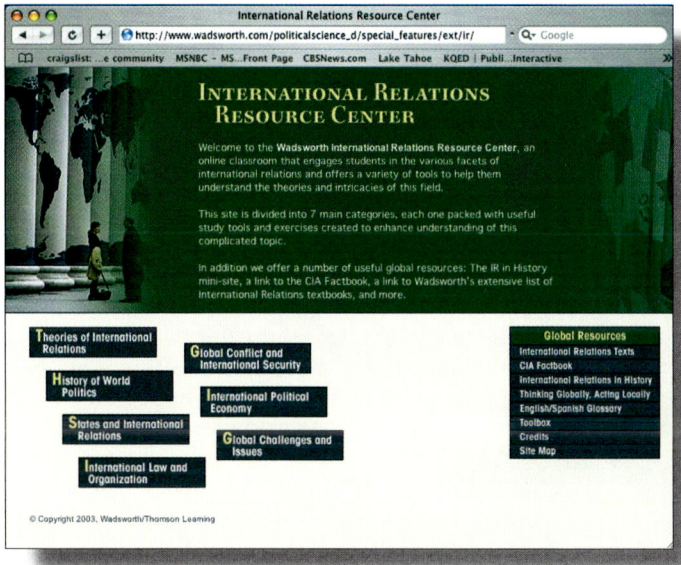

The Wadsworth International Relations Resource Center

http://politicalscience.wadsworth.com/ir

This outstanding site features, *InfoTrac® Reader*, Internet exercises, *MicroCase®* exercises, web links, simulations, *CIA Factbook*, an International Relations in History section, and more!

The World Politics Book Companion Website

http://politicalscience.wadsworth.com/kegley10

When you adopt *World Politics: Trend And Transformation,* you and your students will have access to a rich array of teaching and learning resources that you won't find anywhere else. Integrated with the text, this website provides chapter-by-chapter tutorial quizzes, audio flash cards, interactive maps, simulations, internet activities, links to useful web sites and news sources, and other resources related to the International Relations course referenced in the book's "*Where in the World Wide Web?*"

Bring topics to life with dynamic and interactive lectures.

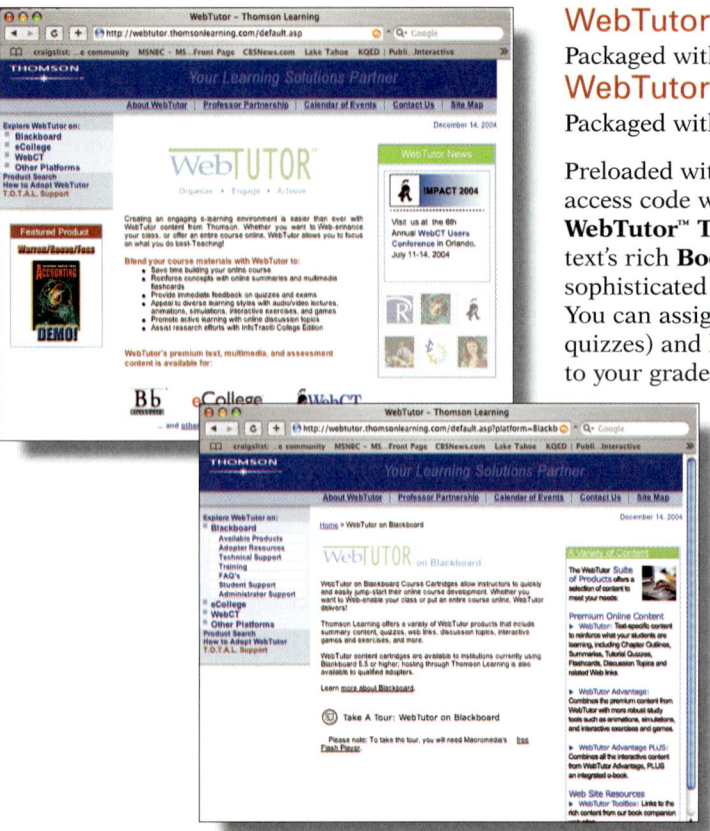

WebTutor™ ToolBox for WebCT™
Packaged with the text, use 0-495-04550-0
WebTutor™ ToolBox for Blackboard®
Packaged with the text, use 0-495-04554-3

Preloaded with content and available via a free access code when packaged with this text, **WebTutor™ ToolBox** pairs all the content of this text's rich **Book Companion Website** with sophisticated course management functionality. You can assign materials (including online quizzes) and have the results flow automatically to your grade book. **WebTutor ToolBox** is ready to use as soon as you log on—or you can customize its preloaded content by uploading images and other resources, adding weblinks, or creating your own practice materials. Students only have access to student resources on the website. Instructors can enter an access code for password-protected Instructor Resources.

Multimedia Manager with Instructor's Resources: A Microsoft® PowerPoint® Tool

This one-stop lecture and class preparation tool makes it easy for you to assemble, edit, publish, and present custom lectures for your course, using Microsoft *PowerPoint*. The **Multimedia Manager** lets you bring together text-specific lecture outlines and art from the book, along with video and animations from the Web or your own materials—culminating in a powerful, personalized, media-enhanced presentation. The **CD-ROM** also contains a full **Instructor's Manual, Test Bank, CNN® Video Clips** and other instructor resources. 0-534-60485-4

Teaching tools animate classroom discussion and debate.

CNN® Today Video: America's New War: CNN looks at Terrorism

This great discussion starter includes 16 two- to five-minute segments featuring CNN news footage, commentator remarks, and speeches dealing with terrorist attacks on U.S. targets throughout the world. Topics include: anthrax and biological warfare, new security measures, Osama bin Laden, Al Quaeda, asset freezing, homeland defense, new weapons of terrorism, and the Arab-American response to recent events. Ask your local representative about our video policy by adoption size.
Volume 1: 0-534-16805-1
Volume 2: 0-534-61600-3

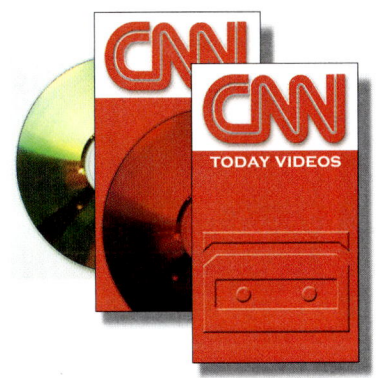

Wadsworth Political Science Video Library

Choose from this library's varied selection of videos to enrich your lectures and extend discussions of text material. Some of the relevant topics examined in these videos include: *The Global Neighborhood*, *NAFTA*, and *Killing in the Congo*. Available to qualified adopters; policy based on adoption size. Please contact your local representative for details.

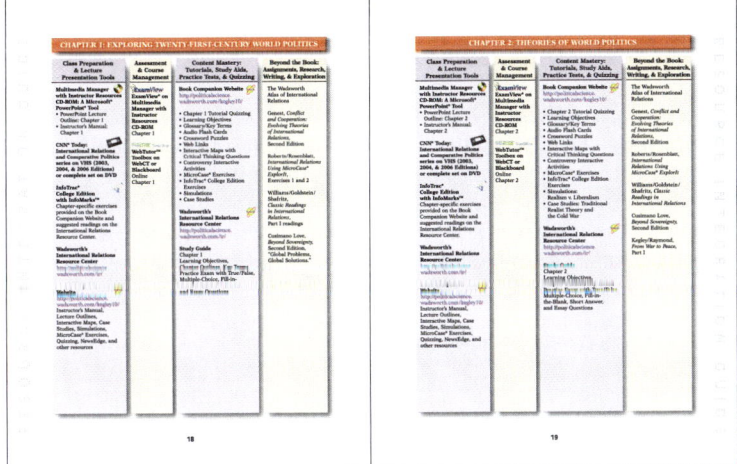

Instructor's Edition...featuring the Resource Integration Guide

The **Instructor's Edition** includes an essential tool for instructors... the *Resource Integration Guide*. This guide links every chapter's outline—topic by topic—to instructional ideas and corresponding supplement resources. At a glance, you'll see which specific videos, PowerPoint® slides, test questions and lecture suggestions are appropriate for each key chapter topic. The *Resource Integration Guide* starts on page 18. 0-534-60484-6

These resources help guide students toward success!
Package any of the resources below with the text

STUDENT RESOURCES

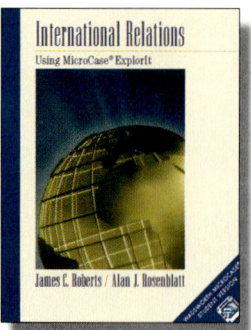

INTERNATIONAL RELATIONS: AN INTRODUCTION USING MICROCASE® EXPLORIT
Authors James C. Roberts of Towson University and Alan Rosenblatt of Stateside Associates created this workbook to explore important concepts, theories, and phenomena in International Relations using real data sets. Each chapter is organized around examples that focus on a set of concepts or theories. The workbook contains 12 computer-based assignments and includes software and nine data sets.
0-534-57385-1
To package with text: 0-495-04552-7

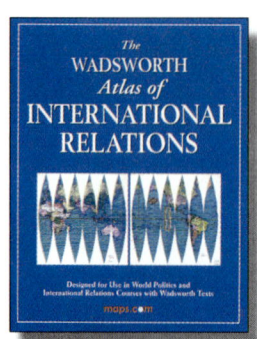

WADSWORTH ATLAS OF INTERNATIONAL RELATIONS
Fifty-one maps chosen by the authors of our texts reflect the major topics covered in the course.
0-534-61793-X
To package with text: 0-495-04551-9

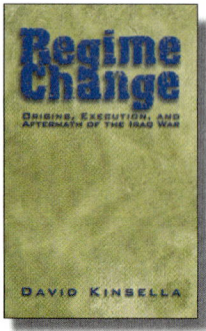

REGIME CHANGE: ORIGINS, EXECUTION, AND AFTERMATH OF THE IRAQ WAR
This supplement, *available FREE when ordered with any Wadsworth text*, is written by David Kinsella. The book provides an overview of the recent war with Iraq, including its origins in the failed policy of containment following the Gulf War, the political and legal debate over regime change, the conduct of Operation Iraqi Freedom, and the challenges of postwar stabilization and reconstruction. Includes a short bibliographic essay for further reference.
0-534-64337-X
To package with text: 0-495-04553-5

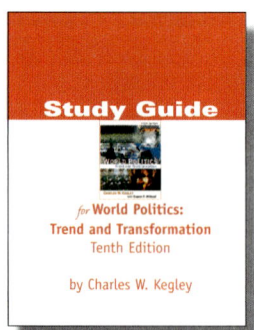

NEW! Study Guide
This helpful new Study Guide is available and features chapter outlines, chapter summaries, key term definitions, fill-in-the-blank chapter reviews, and practice test questions.
0-495-00494-4
To package with text: 0-495-04582-9

Additional options will further broaden your students' horizons.

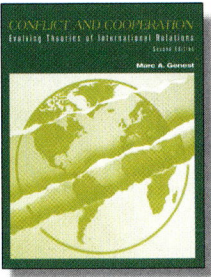

Conflict and Cooperation: Evolving Theories of International Relations, Second Edition
By Mark A. Genest
0-534-50690-9. ©2004

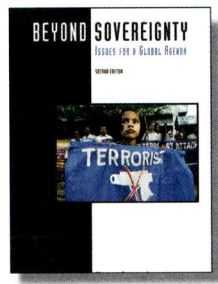

Beyond Sovereignty: Issues for a Global Agenda, Second Edition
By Maryann Cusimano Love
0-534-60893-0. ©2003

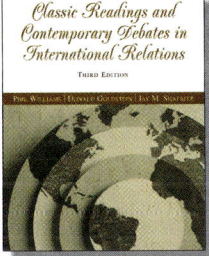

Classic Readings and Contemporary Debates in International Relations, Third Edition
By Phil Williams, Donald M. Goldstein, and Joy M. Shafritz
0-15-505543-7. ©1999
Watch for a new edition of this title, available in May, 2005!
ISBN: 0-534-63189-4

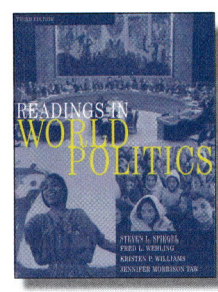

Readings in World Politics
By Steven L. Spiegel, Jennifer Morrison Taw, Fred L. Wehling, and Kristen Williams
0-15-506055-4. ©2005

And, don't forget! If you're looking for a briefer text for this course, consider:

The Global Future: A Brief Introduction to World Politics
By Charles W. Kegley, Jr. and Gregory A. Raymond
0-534-53693-X. ©2005

A briefer version of Kegley's best-selling *World Politics*, Kegley and Raymond's concise paperback textbook continues to offer balance, scholarship, and attention to current developments. Written in a clear, accessible style that speaks to students with a wide range of backgrounds and abilities, this textbook provides a set of concepts and analytical tools to help them understand contemporary events and emerging global trends. With an emphasis on engaging students in the latest international developments, *The Global Future* encourages them to think critically about contemporary issues and form their own opinions on how to address the pressing security, economic, and environmental problems of the twenty-first century.

STUDENT RESOURCES

From Ivy League universities to community colleges...

Only a text this trusted and respected would be used at the Citadel, United States Defense Colleges, and the Air Force Academy—as this text has! Previous editions of this book have been adopted by the following schools:

Abilene Christian University
Agnes Scott College
Albright College
Albuquerque Tech-Voc Institute
American River College
Anne Arundel Community College
Arizona State University
Athens State College
Augusta State University
Baton Rouge Community College
Baltimore City Community College
Benedict College
Birmingham Southern College
Boise State University
Bowling Green State University
Brescia College
Brewton Parker College
Brigham Young University
Broward Community College
Bucknell University
Collegeins College
Cabrini College
Caldwell College
California Polytechnic State University, San Luis Obispo
California State University, Fullerton
California State University, Hayward
California State University, Long Beach
Cameron University
Central Connecticut State University
Central Lakes Community College
Central Michigan University
Central Washington University
Century College
Chaffey College
Chapman University
Chattanooga State Technical College
City College of New York
Claremont Graduate School
Coastal Carolina Community College
College of Lake County
College of Saint Rose
College of San Mateo
College of the Redwoods
College of the Siskiyous
Colorado Northwestern Community College
Colorado Northwestern

Colorado State University Pueblo
Columbia College
Columbia Greene Community College
Columbia University
Concordia University
CUNY Hunter College
Daemen College
De Paul University
DeSales University
Delaware County Community College
Des Moines Area Community College
Diablo Valley College
Dickinson College
Dickinson State University
Dominican University
Dordt College
Dowling College
Drake University
Drew University
Duke University
Eastern Illinois University
Eastern Mennonite University
Eastern Michigan University
Eastern Oregon University
Elizabeth City State University
Elizabethtown Community College.
Emory University
Fairleigh Dickenson University
Fairmont State College
Fashion Institute of Technology
Fayetteville State University
Ferrum College
Finlandia University
Florida Atlantic University
Florida International University
Fort Lewis College
Front Range Community College
Ft. Hays Kansas State University
Gavilan College
George Mason University
George Washington University
Georgetown University
Georgia Military College
Grossmont College
Guilford Tech Community College
Hamilton College
Harford Community College

Hillsborough Community College
Hiram College
Honolulu Community College
Howard University
Humboldt State University
Humphreys College
Ivy Tech State College
Idaho State University
Indian Hills Community College
Iowa Lakes Community College
Iowa State University
James Sprunt Community College
Johnson County Community College
Kansas State University
Kapiolani Community College
Kennesaw College
Kent State University
La Grange College
Lake Michigan College
Lenoir-Rhyne College
Lewis and Clark College
Lincoln College, Normal
Lincoln University
Linfield College
Long Island University
Loyola Marymount University
Loyola University
Lyndon State College
Macomb Community College
Maria College
Marymount College
Mercer University
Miami University
Miami University
Mid-Plains Community College
Middle Tennessee State University
Millsaps College
Milwaukee Area Tech College
Minneapolis Community College
Monroe Community College
Morningside College
Morris College
Muskingum College
Napa College
Nazareth College of Rochester
New College
Nicholls State University
Northeastern Illinois University

This forward-thinking text has been used by thousands of students at institutions around the globe!

Northeastern University
Northern Arizona University
Northern Illinois University
Northwest Nazarene University
Oakton Community College
Ohio University
Oklahoma City Community College
Oklahoma State University
Pace University
Pennsylvania State University
Pfeiffer College
Piedmont Virginia Community College
Pima Community College
Queens College CUNY
Quinnipac University
Randolph Macon College
Regis College
Regis University
Rock Valley College
Roger Williams University
Rogers State College
Rollins College
Rose-Hulman Institute of Technology
Rosemont College
Rutgers, New Brunswick
Rutgers, Newark
Sacramento City College
Saint Ambrose College
Saint Olaf College
Salem State College
San Antonio College
San Diego State University
San Joaquin Delta College
Santa Clara University
Seton Hall University
Shawnee State University
Shepherd College
Shippensburg University
Sierra Nevada College
Skyline College
Soka University
Southern Nazarene University
Southwest Missouri State University
St. John's University
St. Lawrence University
St. Leo College
St. Louis University
St. Mary's College of California
St. Mary's University
St. Vincent College
St. Anselms College
State University of West Georgia
Suffolk Community College
Suffolk County Cmty College

Syracuse University
Tacoma Community College
Temple University
Texas A&M University
Texas Christian University
Texas Southern University
Tidewater Community College
Towson State University
Trinity Christian College
Triton College
Truman State University
Union County College
University of Alabama
University of Arizona
University of California
University of Central Arkansas
University of Central Oklahoma
University of Colorado
University of Dayton
University of Delaware
University of Florida
University of Georgia
University of Hawaii at Manoa
University of Houston-Downtown
University of Kansas
University of Louisville
University of Massachusetts
   At Lowell
University of Massachusetts
University of Miami
University of Minnesota
University of Missouri
University of New Hampshire
University of New Haven
University of North Texas
University of Northern Iowa
University of Oklahoma
University of Pennsylvania
University of Pittsburgh
University of Scranton
University of South Carolina
University of Southern Maine
University of Tennessee
University of Texas at Dallas
University of Utah
University of Wisconsin
University of Maryland
University of Houston
University of Central Florida
University of Colorado
University of Houston
University of Judaism
University of Maine
University of Memphis

University of Mississippi
University of Montevallo
University of New Hampshire
University of New Orleans
University of South Florida
University of St. Thomas
University of Texas
University of the South
University of Vermont
University of Washington
University of Wisconsin
University of Saint Mary
University of West Alabama
   at Livingston
Utah State University
Valdosta State University
Vanderbilt University
Villanova University
Western Iowa Tech
Wake Forest University
Washington State University
Wayne State University
Wellesley College
Wells College
Wenatchee Valley College
West Virginia University
West Virginia Wesleyan College
Western Illinois University
Western State College of Colorado
Wheaton College
Wheaton College
Whitworth College
Wichita State University
Widener University
Willamette University
Wilson College
Xavier University
Yale University
York College

Turn the page to begin utilizing the RESOURCE INTEGRATION GUIDE created to help you organize all the resources we offer!

17

CHAPTER 1: EXPLORING TWENTY-FIRST-CENTURY WORLD POLITICS

Class Preparation & Lecture Presentation Tools	Assessment & Course Management	Content Mastery: Tutorials, Study Aids, Practice Tests, & Quizzing	Beyond the Book: Assignments, Research, Writing, & Exploration
Multimedia Manager with Instructor Resources CD-ROM: A Microsoft® PowerPoint® Tool • PowerPoint Lecture Outline: Chapter 1 • Instructor's Manual: Chapter 1 **CNN® Today: International Relations and Comparative Politics** series on VHS (2003, 2004, & 2006 Editions) or complete set on DVD **InfoTrac® College Edition with InfoMarks™** Chapter-specific exercises provided on the Book Companion Website and suggested readings on the International Relations Resource Center. **Wadsworth's International Relations Resource Center** http://politicalscience.wadsworth.com/ir/ **Book Companion Website** http://politicalscience.wadsworth.com/kegley10/ Instructor's Manual, Lecture Outlines, Interactive Maps, Case Studies, Simulations, MicroCase® Exercises, Quizzing, NewsEdge, and other resources	**ExamView® on Multimedia Manager with Instructor Resources CD-ROM** Chapter 1 **WebTutor™ Toolbox on WebCT or Blackboard** Online Chapter 1	**Book Companion Website** http://politicalscience.wadsworth.com/kegley10/ • Chapter 1 Tutorial Quizzing • Learning Objectives • Glossary/Key Terms • Audio Flash Cards • Crossword Puzzles • Web Links • Interactive Maps with Critical Thinking Questions • Controversy Interactive Activities • MicroCase® Exercises • InfoTrac® College Edition Exercises • Simulations • Case Studies **Wadsworth's International Relations Resource Center** http://politicalscience.wadsworth.com/ir/ **Study Guide** Chapter 1 Learning Objectives, Chapter Outlines, Key Terms, Practice Exam with True/False, Multiple-Choice, Fill-in-the-Blank, Short Answer, and Essay Questions	The Wadsworth Atlas of International Relations Genest, *Conflict and Cooperation: Evolving Theories of International Relations,* Second Edition Roberts/Rosenblatt, *International Relations Using MicroCase® ExplorIt,* Exercises 1 and 2 Williams/Goldstein/Shafritz, *Classic Readings in International Relations,* Part I readings Cusimano Love, *Beyond Sovereignty,* Second Edition, "Global Problems, Global Solutions."

CHAPTER 2: THEORIES OF WORLD POLITICS

Class Preparation & Lecture Presentation Tools

Multimedia Manager with Instructor Resources CD-ROM: A Microsoft® PowerPoint® Tool
- PowerPoint Lecture Outline: Chapter 2
- Instructor's Manual: Chapter 2

CNN® Today: International Relations and Comparative Politics series on VHS (2003, 2004, & 2006 Editions) or complete set on DVD

InfoTrac® College Edition with InfoMarks™
Chapter-specific exercises provided on the Book Companion Website and suggested readings on the International Relations Resource Center.

Wadsworth's International Relations Resource Center
http://politicalscience.wadsworth.com/ir/

Book Companion Website
http://politicalscience.wadsworth.com/kegley10/
Instructor's Manual, Lecture Outlines, Interactive Maps, Case Studies, Simulations, MicroCase® Exercises, Quizzing, NewsEdge, and other resources

Assessment & Course Management

ExamView
ExamView® on Multimedia Manager with Instructor Resources CD-ROM Chapter 2

WebTutor™ ToolBox on WebCT or Blackboard
Online Chapter 2

Content Mastery: Tutorials, Study Aids, Practice Tests, & Quizzing

Book Companion Website
http://politicalscience.wadsworth.com/kegley10/
- Chapter 2 Tutorial Quizzing
- Learning Objectives
- Glossary/Key Terms
- Audio Flash Cards
- Crossword Puzzles
- Web Links
- Interactive Maps with Critical Thinking Questions
- Controversy Interactive Activities
- MicroCase® Exercises
- InfoTrac® College Edition Exercises
- Simulations: Realism v. Liberalism
- Case Studies: Traditional Realist Theory and the Cold War

Wadsworth's International Relations Resource Center
http://politicalscience.wadsworth.com/ir/

Study Guide
Chapter 2
Learning Objectives, Chapter Outlines, Key Terms, Practice Exam with True/False, Multiple-Choice, Fill-in-the-Blank, Short Answer, and Essay Questions

Beyond the Book: Assignments, Research, Writing, & Exploration

The Wadsworth Atlas of International Relations

Genest, *Conflict and Cooperation: Evolving Theories of International Relations,* Second Edition

Roberts/Rosenblatt, *International Relations Using MicroCase® ExplorIt*

Williams/Goldstein/Shafritz, *Classic Readings in International Relations*

Cusimano Love, *Beyond Sovereignty,* Second Edition

Kegley/Raymond, *From War to Peace,* Part I

CHAPTER 3: FOREIGN POLICY DECISION MAKING

Class Preparation & Lecture Presentation Tools

Multimedia Manager with Instructor Resources CD-ROM: A Microsoft® PowerPoint® Tool
- PowerPoint Lecture Outline: Chapter 3
- Instructor's Manual: Chapter 3

CNN® Today: International Relations and Comparative Politics series on VHS (2003, 2004, & 2006 Editions) or complete set on DVD

InfoTrac® College Edition with InfoMarks™
Chapter-specific exercises provided on the Book Companion Website and suggested readings on the International Relations Resource Center.

Wadsworth's International Relations Resource Center
http://politicalscience.wadsworth.com/ir/

Book Companion Website
http://politicalscience.wadsworth.com/kegley10/
Instructor's Manual, Lecture Outlines, Interactive Maps, Case Studies, Simulations, MicroCase® Exercises, Quizzing, NewsEdge, and other resources

Assessment & Course Management

ExamView® on Multimedia Manager with Instructor Resources CD-ROM
Chapter 3

WebTutor™ Toolbox on WebCT or Blackboard
Online Chapter 3

Content Mastery: Tutorials, Study Aids, Practice Tests, & Quizzing

Book Companion Website
http://politicalscience.wadsworth.com/kegley10/
- Chapter 3 Tutorial Quizzing
- Learning Objectives
- Glossary/Key Terms
- Audio Flash Cards
- Crossword Puzzles
- Web Links
- Interactive Maps with Critical Thinking Questions
- Controversy Interactive Activities
- MicroCase® Exercises
- InfoTrac® College Edition Exercises
- Simulations
- Case Studies

Wadsworth's International Relations Resource Center
http://politicalscience.wadsworth.com/ir/

Study Guide
Chapter 3
Learning Objectives, Chapter Outlines, Key Terms, Practice Exam with True/False, Multiple-Choice, Fill-in-the-Blank, Short Answer, and Essay Questions

Beyond the Book: Assignments, Research, Writing, & Exploration

The Wadsworth Atlas of International Relations

Genest, *Conflict and Cooperation: Evolving Theories of International Relations,* Second Edition

Roberts/Rosenblatt, *International Relations Using MicroCase® ExplorIt,* Exercises 3 and 5

Williams/Goldstein/Shafritz, *Classic Readings in International Relations,* Part II readings

Cusimano Love, *Beyond Sovereignty,* Second Edition

CHAPTER 4: GREAT-POWER RIVALRIES AND RELATIONS

Class Preparation & Lecture Presentation Tools	Assessment & Course Management	Content Mastery: Tutorials, Study Aids, Practice Tests, & Quizzing	Beyond the Book: Assignments, Research, Writing, & Exploration
Multimedia Manager with Instructor Resources CD-ROM: A Microsoft® PowerPoint® Tool • PowerPoint Lecture Outline: Chapter 4 • Instructor's Manual: Chapter 4 **CNN® Today: International Relations and Comparative Politics series on VHS (2003, 2004, & 2006 Editions) or complete set on DVD** Then and Now: A Comparison of Foreign Policy During the Cold War and the War on Terror, The End of the Arms Race?, Transatlantic Relations **InfoTrac® College Edition with InfoMarks™** Chapter-specific exercises provided on the Book Companion Website and suggested readings on the International Relations Resource Center. **Wadsworth's International Relations Resource Center** http://politicalscience.wadsworth.com/ir/ **Book Companion Website** http://politicalscience.wadsworth.com/kegley10/ Instructor's Manual, Lecture Outlines, Interactive Maps, Case Studies, Simulations, MicroCase® Exercises, Quizzing, NewsEdge, and other resources	**ExamView®** on Multimedia Manager with Instructor Resources CD-ROM Chapter 4 **WebTutor™ Toolbox on WebCT or Blackboard** Online Chapter 4	**Book Companion Website** http://politicalscience.wadsworth.com/kegley10/ • Chapter 4 Tutorial Quizzing • Learning Objectives • Glossary/Key Terms • Audio Flash Cards • Crossword Puzzles • Web Links • Interactive Maps with Critical Thinking Questions • Controversy Interactive Activities • MicroCase® Exercises • InfoTrac® College Edition Exercises • Simulations • Case Studies **Wadsworth's International Relations Resource Center** http://politicalscience.wadsworth.com/ir/ **Study Guide** Chapter 4 Learning Objectives, Chapter Outlines, Key Terms, Practice Exam with True/False, Multiple-Choice, Fill-in-the-Blank, Short Answer, and Essay Questions	The Wadsworth Atlas of International Relations Genest, *Conflict and Cooperation: Evolving Theories of International Relations*, Second Edition Roberts/Rosenblatt, *International Relations Using MicroCase® ExplorIt* Williams/Goldstein/Shafritz, *Classic Readings in International Relations*, Part VI readings Cusimano Love, *Beyond Sovereignty*, Second Edition Stoessinger, *Why Nations Go to War*, Chapters 1 and 2 Kegley/Raymond, *From War to Peace*, Part III

CHAPTER 5: THE GLOBAL SOUTH IN A WORLD OF POWERS

Class Preparation & Lecture Presentation Tools

Multimedia Manager with Instructor Resources CD-ROM: A Microsoft® PowerPoint® Tool
- PowerPoint Lecture Outline: Chapter 5
- Instructor's Manual: Chapter 5

CNN® Today: International Relations and Comparative Politics series on VHS (2003, 2004, & 2006 Editions) or complete set on DVD
India's Hopes for Peace, AIDS in the Third World, Indonesia: Islam and Democratization, Liberia: Then and Now, Venezuelan Politics, Cambodian Sweat Shops

InfoTrac® College Edition with InfoMarks™
Chapter-specific exercises provided on the Book Companion Website and suggested readings on the International Relations Resource Center.

Wadsworth's International Relations Resource Center
http://politicalscience.wadsworth.com/ir/

Book Companion Website
http://politicalscience.wadsworth.com/kegley10/
Instructor's Manual, Lecture Outlines, Interactive Maps, Case Studies, Simulations, MicroCase® Exercises, Quizzing, NewsEdge, and other resources

Assessment & Course Management

ExamView® on Multimedia Manager with Instructor Resources CD-ROM
Chapter 5

WebTutor™ Toolbox on WebCT or Blackboard
Online Chapter 5

Content Mastery: Tutorials, Study Aids, Practice Tests, & Quizzing

Book Companion Website
http://politicalscience.wadsworth.com/kegley10/

- Chapter 5 Tutorial Quizzing
- Learning Objectives
- Glossary/Key Terms
- Audio Flash Cards
- Crossword Puzzles
- Web Links
- Interactive Maps with Critical Thinking Questions
- Controversy Interactive Activities
- MicroCase® Exercises
- InfoTrac® College Edition Exercises
- Simulations
- Case Studies

Wadsworth's International Relations Resource Center
http://politicalscience.wadsworth.com/ir/

Study Guide
Chapter 5
Learning Objectives, Chapter Outlines, Key Terms, Practice Exam with True/False, Multiple-Choice, Fill-in-the-Blank, Short Answer, and Essay Questions

Beyond the Book: Assignments, Research, Writing, & Exploration

The Wadsworth Atlas of International Relations

Genest, *Conflict and Cooperation: Evolving Theories of International Relations,* Second Edition

Roberts/Rosenblatt, *International Relations Using MicroCase® ExplorIt,* Exercise 11

Williams/Goldstein/Shafritz, *Classic Readings in International Relations*

Cusimano Love, *Beyond Sovereignty,* Second Edition

CHAPTER 6: NONSTATE ACTORS IN THE INTERSTATE SYSTEM

Class Preparation & Lecture Presentation Tools

Multimedia Manager with Instructor Resources CD-ROM: A Microsoft® PowerPoint® Tool
- PowerPoint Lecture Outline: Chapter 6
- Instructor's Manual: Chapter 6

CNN® Today: International Relations and Comparative Politics series on VHS (2003, 2004, & 2006 Editions) or complete set on DVD
Transatlantic Relations, Extremists 101, European Union Summit, Turkey–European Union Relations

InfoTrac® College Edition with InfoMarks™
Chapter-specific exercises provided on the Book Companion Website and suggested readings on the International Relations Resource Center.

Wadsworth's International Relations Resource Center
http://politicalscience.wadsworth.com/ir/

Book Companion Website
http://politicalscience.wadsworth.com/kegley10/
Instructor's Manual, Lecture Outlines, Interactive Maps, Case Studies, Simulations, MicroCase® Exercises, Quizzing, NewsEdge, and other resources

Assessment & Course Management

ExamView® on Multimedia Manager with Instructor Resources CD-ROM
Chapter 6

WebTutor™ Toolbox on WebCT or Blackboard
Online Chapter 6

Content Mastery: Tutorials, Study Aids, Practice Tests, & Quizzing

Book Companion Website
http://politicalscience.wadsworth.com/kegley10/
- Chapter 6 Tutorial Quizzing
- Learning Objectives
- Glossary/Key Terms
- Audio Flash Cards
- Crossword Puzzles
- Web Links
- Interactive Maps with Critical Thinking Questions
- Controversy Interactive Activities
- MicroCase® Exercises
- InfoTrac® College Edition Exercises
- Simulations
- Case Studies: The European Union in Historical Perspective

Wadsworth's International Relations Resource Center
http://politicalscience.wadsworth.com/ir/

Study Guide
Chapter 6
Learning Objectives, Chapter Outlines, Key Terms, Practice Exam with True/False, Multiple-Choice, Fill-in-the-Blank, Short Answer, and Essay Questions

Beyond the Book: Assignments, Research, Writing, & Exploration

The Wadsworth Atlas of International Relations

Genest, *Conflict and Cooperation: Evolving Theories of International Relations*, Second Edition

Roberts/Rosenblatt, *International Relations Using MicroCase® ExplorIt*

Williams/Goldstein/Shafritz, *Classic Readings in International Relations*, Part III readings

Cusimano Love, *Beyond Sovereignty*, Second Edition "Intergovernmental Organizations and Trans-sovereign Problems: The New Battleground," "Nongovernmental Organizations: Politics Beyond Sovereignty," and "MNCs: Power and Responsibility"

Magstadt, *The European Union Today: A Quest for Unity Amidst Diversity*

CHAPTER 7: HUMANITARIAN CHALLENGES AND THE PROTECTION OF HUMAN RIGHTS

Class Preparation & Lecture Presentation Tools

Multimedia Manager with Instructor Resources CD-ROM: A Microsoft® PowerPoint® Tool
- PowerPoint Lecture Outline: Chapter 7
- Instructor's Manual: Chapter 7

CNN® Today: International Relations and Comparative Politics series on VHS (2003, 2004, & 2006 Editions) or complete set on DVD
Amnesty International Report, The Plight of Arab Minorities in Israel, Aid for Somalian Refugees, Coming Home: Afghan Refugees Returning to a War-Torn Nation, Cambodian Sweat Shops

InfoTrac® College Edition with InfoMarks™
Chapter-specific exercises provided on the Book Companion Website and suggested readings on the International Relations Resource Center.

Wadsworth's International Relations Resource Center
http://politicalscience.wadsworth.com/ir/

Book Companion Website
http://politicalscience.wadsworth.com/kegley10/
Instructor's Manual, Lecture Outlines, Interactive Maps, Case Studies, Simulations, MicroCase® Exercises, Quizzing, NewsEdge, and other resources

Assessment & Course Management

ExamView® on Multimedia Manager with Instructor Resources CD-ROM
Chapter 7

WebTutor™ Toolbox on WebCT or Blackboard
Online Chapter 7

Content Mastery: Tutorials, Study Aids, Practice Tests, & Quizzing

Book Companion Website
http://politicalscience.wadsworth.com/kegley10/

- Chapter 7 Tutorial Quizzing
- Learning Objectives
- Glossary/Key Terms
- Audio Flash Cards
- Crossword Puzzles
- Web Links
- Interactive Maps with Critical Thinking Questions
- Controversy Interactive Activities
- MicroCase® Exercises
- InfoTrac® College Edition Exercises
- Simulations
- Case Studies: Genocide in Rwanda

Wadsworth's International Relations Resource Center
http://politicalscience.wadsworth.com/ir/

Study Guide
Chapter 7
Learning Objectives, Chapter Outlines, Key Terms, Practice Exam with True/False, Multiple-Choice, Fill-in-the-Blank, Short Answer, and Essay Questions

Beyond the Book: Assignments, Research, Writing, & Exploration

The Wadsworth Atlas of International Relations

Genest, *Conflict and Cooperation: Evolving Theories of International Relations,* Second Edition

Roberts/Rosenblatt, *International Relations Using MicroCase® ExplorIt*

Williams/Goldstein/Shafritz, *Classic Readings in International Relations*

Cusimano Love, *Beyond Sovereignty,* Second Edition "Leaving Home: The Flow of Refugees"

CHAPTER 8: GLOBALIZATION AND THE PROSPECTS FOR GLOBAL GOVERNANCE

Class Preparation & Lecture Presentation Tools

Multimedia Manager with Instructor Resources CD-ROM: A Microsoft® PowerPoint® Tool
- PowerPoint Lecture Outline: Chapter 8
- Instructor's Manual: Chapter 8

CNN® Today: International Relations and Comparative Politics series on VHS (2003, 2004, & 2006 Editions) or complete set on DVD
Kaliningrad: Russian Enclave, Fujimori Extradition, AIDS in the Third World, Counting the Cost: Financing AIDS Research

InfoTrac® College Edition with InfoMarks™
Chapter-specific exercises provided on the Book Companion Website and suggested readings on the International Relations Resource Center.

Wadsworth's International Relations Resource Center
http://politicalscience.wadsworth.com/ir/

Book Companion Website
http://politicalscience.wadsworth.com/kegley10/
Instructor's Manual, Lecture Outlines, Interactive Maps, Case Studies, Simulations, MicroCase® Exercises, Quizzing, NewsEdge, and other resources

Assessment & Course Management

ExamView
ExamView® on Multimedia Manager with Instructor Resources CD-ROM
Chapter 8

WebTutor ToolBox
WebTutor™ Toolbox on WebCT or Blackboard
Online Chapter 8

Content Mastery: Tutorials, Study Aids, Practice Tests, & Quizzing

Book Companion Website
http://politicalscience.wadsworth.com/kegley10/
- Chapter 8 Tutorial Quizzing
- Learning Objectives
- Glossary/Key Terms
- Audio Flash Cards
- Crossword Puzzles
- Web Links
- Interactive Maps with Critical Thinking Questions
- Controversy Interactive Activities
- MicroCase® Exercises
- InfoTrac® College Edition Exercises
- Simulations: The Spread of AIDS and HIV
- Case Study: Globalization and the Mexican Peso Crisis

Wadsworth's International Relations Resource Center
http://politicalscience.wadsworth.com/ir/

Study Guide
Chapter 8
Learning Objectives, Chapter Outlines, Key Terms, Practice Exam with True/False, Multiple-Choice, Fill-in-the-Blank, Short Answer, and Essay Questions

Beyond the Book: Assignments, Research, Writing, & Exploration

The Wadsworth Atlas of International Relations

Genest, *Conflict and Cooperation: Evolving Theories of International Relations*, Second Edition

Roberts/Rosenblatt, *International Relations Using MicroCase® ExplorIt*

Williams/Goldstein/Shafritz, *Classic Readings in International Relations*,

Cusimano Love, *Beyond Sovereignty*, Second Edition
"The Cyberthreat Continuum" and "The Global Drug Trade vs. The Nation-State: Why the Thugs Are Winning"

CHAPTER 9: MARKETS AND MONEY IN THE GLOBAL POLITICAL ECONOMY

Class Preparation & Lecture Presentation Tools

Multimedia Manager with Instructor Resources CD-ROM: A Microsoft® PowerPoint® Tool
- PowerPoint Lecture Outline: Chapter 9
- Instructor's Manual: Chapter 9

CNN® Today: International Relations and Comparative Politics series on VHS (2003, 2004, & 2006 Editions) or complete set on DVD
Business with Iran, China's Changing Role in the International Landscape

InfoTrac® College Edition with InfoMarks™
Chapter-specific exercises provided on the Book Companion Website and suggested readings on the International Relations Resource Center.

Wadsworth's International Relations Resource Center
http://politicalscience.wadsworth.com/ir/

Book Companion Website
http://politicalscience.wadsworth.com/kegley10/
Instructor's Manual, Lecture Outlines, Interactive Maps, Case Studies, Simulations, MicroCase® Exercises, Quizzing, NewsEdge, and other resources

Assessment & Course Management

ExamView®
ExamView® on Multimedia Manager with Instructor Resources CD-ROM
Chapter 9

WebTUTOR ToolBox
WebTutor™ Toolbox on WebCT or Blackboard
Online Chapter 9

Content Mastery: Tutorials, Study Aids, Practice Tests, & Quizzing

Book Companion Website
http://politicalscience.wadsworth.com/kegley10/

- Chapter 9 Tutorial Quizzing
- Learning Objectives
- Glossary/Key Terms
- Audio Flash Cards
- Crossword Puzzles
- Web Links
- Interactive Maps with Critical Thinking Questions
- Controversy Interactive Activities
- MicroCase® Exercises
- InfoTrac® College Edition Exercises
- Simulation: Caribbean Banana Exporters Association
- Case Study: Globalization and the Mexican Peso Crisis

Wadsworth's International Relations Resource Center
http://politicalscience.wadsworth.com/ir/

Study Guide
Chapter 9
Learning Objectives, Chapter Outlines, Key Terms, Practice Exam with True/False, Multiple-Choice, Fill-in-the-Blank, Short Answer, and Essay Questions

Beyond the Book: Assignments, Research, Writing, & Exploration

The Wadsworth Atlas of International Relations

Genest, *Conflict and Cooperation: Evolving Theories of International Relations*, Second Edition

Roberts/Rosenblatt, *International Relations Using MicroCase® ExplorIt*, Exercise 10

Williams/Goldstein/Shafritz, *Classic Readings in International Relations*, Part I, "The Radical Tradition and the Roots of International Political Economy"

Cusimano Love, *Beyond Sovereignty*, Second Edition

CHAPTER 10: POPULATION PRESSURE, RESOURCE DEPLETION, AND THE PRESERVATION OF THE GLOBAL ENVIRONMENT

Class Preparation & Lecture Presentation Tools

Multimedia Manager with Instructor Resources CD-ROM: A Microsoft® PowerPoint® Tool
- PowerPoint Lecture Outline: Chapter 10
- Instructor's Manual: Chapter 10

CNN® Today: International Relations and Comparative Politics series on VHS (2003, 2004, & 2006 Editions) or complete set on DVD
World Hunger, Transatlantic Relations, Earth Summit, AIDS in the Third World, Counting the Cost: Financing AIDS Research

InfoTrac® College Edition with InfoMarks™
Chapter-specific exercises provided on the Book Companion Website and suggested readings on the International Relations Resource Center.

Wadsworth's International Relations Resource Center
http://politicalscience.wadsworth.com/ir/

Book Companion Website
http://politicalscience.wadsworth.com/kegley10/
Instructor's Manual, Lecture Outlines, Interactive Maps, Case Studies, Simulations, MicroCase® Exercises, Quizzing, NewsEdge, and other resources

Assessment & Course Management

ExamView®
ExamView® on Multimedia Manager with Instructor Resources CD-ROM
Chapter 10

WebTutor™ ToolBox
WebTutor™ Toolbox on WebCT or Blackboard
Online Chapter 10

Content Mastery: Tutorials, Study Aids, Practice Tests, & Quizzing

Book Companion Website
http://politicalscience.wadsworth.com/kegley10/
- Chapter 10 Tutorial Quizzing
- Learning Objectives
- Glossary/Key Terms
- Audio Flash Cards
- Crossword Puzzles
- Web Links
- Interactive Maps with Critical Thinking Questions
- Controversy Interactive Activities
- MicroCase® Exercises
- InfoTrac® College Edition Exercises
- Simulation: The Spread of AIDS and HIV
- Case Study: International Regulation of Intentional Discharges of Oil into the Ocean

Wadsworth's International Relations Resource Center
http://politicalscience.wadsworth.com/ir/

Study Guide
Chapter 10
Learning Objectives, Chapter Outlines, Key Terms, Practice Exam with True/False, Multiple-Choice, Fill-in-the-Blank, Short Answer, and Essay Questions

Beyond the Book: Assignments, Research, Writing, & Exploration

The Wadsworth Atlas of International Relations

Genest, *Conflict and Cooperation: Evolving Theories of International Relations*, Second Edition

Roberts/Rosenblatt, *International Relations Using MicroCase® ExplorIt*, Exercise 10

Williams/Goldstein/Shafritz, *Classic Readings in International Relations*

Cusimano Love, *Beyond Sovereignty*, Second Edition
"Ecological Interdependence and the Spread of Infectious Disease" and "The Nature of the Nature Problem: Environmental Interdependencies"

RESOURCE INTEGRATION GUIDE

CHAPTER 11: THE FACE OF TWENTY-FIRST-CENTURY ARMED CONFLICT

Class Preparation & Lecture Presentation Tools	Assessment & Course Management	Content Mastery: Tutorials, Study Aids, Practice Tests, & Quizzing	Beyond the Book: Assignments, Research, Writing, & Exploration
Multimedia Manager with Instructor Resources CD-ROM: A Microsoft® PowerPoint® Tool • PowerPoint Lecture Outline: Chapter 11 • Instructor's Manual: Chapter 11 **CNN® Today: International Relations and Comparative Politics series on VHS (2003, 2004, & 2006 Editions) or complete set on DVD** Then and Now: A Comparison of Foreign Policy During the Cold War and the War on Terror; Sharon's Choices: Decision Making in the Israeli-Palestinian Conflict, The Roadmap to Peace **American's New War: CNN® Looks at Terrorism** **InfoTrac® College Edition with InfoMarks™** Chapter-specific exercises provided on the Book Companion Website and suggested readings on the International Relations Resource Center. **Wadsworth's International Relations Resource Center** http://politicalscience.wadsworth.com/ir/ **Book Companion Website** http://politicalscience.wadsworth.com/kegley10/ Instructor's Manual, Lecture Outlines, Interactive Maps, Case Studies, Simulations, MicroCase® Exercises, Quizzing, NewsEdge, and other resources	**ExamView®** **ExamView® on Multimedia Manager with Instructor Resources CD-ROM** Chapter 11 **WebTutor™ ToolBox** **WebTutor™ Toolbox on WebCT or Blackboard** Online Chapter 11	**Book Companion Website** http://politicalscience.wadsworth.com/kegley10/ • Chapter 11 Tutorial Quizzing • Learning Objectives • Glossary/Key Terms • Audio Flash Cards • Crossword Puzzles • Web Links • Interactive Maps with Critical Thinking Questions • Controversy Interactive Activities • MicroCase® Exercises • InfoTrac® College Edition Exercises • Simulation: Presidential Response to Catastrophic Terrorism • Case Study: Genocide in Rwanda **Wadsworth's International Relations Resource Center** http://politicalscience.wadsworth.com/ir/ **Study Guide** Chapter 11 Learning Objectives, Chapter Outlines, Key Terms, Practice Exam with True/False, Multiple-Choice, Fill-in-the-Blank, Short Answer, and Essay Questions	The Wadsworth Atlas of International Relations Genest, *Conflict and Cooperation: Evolving Theories of International Relations,* Second Edition Roberts/Rosenblatt, *International Relations Using MicroCase® ExplorIt* Williams/Goldstein/Shafritz, *Classic Readings in International Relations,* Part V, "The Nature and Origins of War" Cusimano Love, *Beyond Sovereignty,* Second Edition "Networked Terror" Stoessinger, *Why Nations Go to War,* Chapter 9 Mayer, *9-11: The Giant Awakens* Kinsella, *Regime Change: Origins, Execution, and Aftermath of the Iraq War*

CHAPTER 12: MILITARY POWER, COERCIVE DIPLOMACY, AND NATIONAL SECURITY

Class Preparation & Lecture Presentation Tools

Multimedia Manager with Instructor Resources CD-ROM: A Microsoft® PowerPoint® Tool
- PowerPoint Lecture Outline: Chapter 12
- Instructor's Manual: Chapter 12

CNN® Today: International Relations and Comparative Politics series on VHS (2003, 2004, & 2006 Editions) or complete set on DVD
North Korea and the International Atomic Energy Agency, Extremists 101, Then and Now: A Comparison of Foreign Policy During the Cold War and the War on Terror, Oil Politics: Sanctions Against Iraq, The End of the Arms Race?, China's Changing Role in the International Landscape, India's Hopes for Peace

InfoTrac® College Edition with InfoMarks™
Chapter-specific exercises provided on the Book Companion Website and suggested readings on the International Relations Resource Center.

Wadsworth's International Relations Resource Center
http://politicalscience.wadsworth.com/ir/

Book Companion Website
http://politicalscience.wadsworth.com/kegley10/
Instructor's Manual, Lecture Outlines, Interactive Maps, Case Studies, Simulations, MicroCase® Exercises, Quizzing, NewsEdge, and other resources

Assessment & Course Management

ExamView®
ExamView® on Multimedia Manager with Instructor Resources CD-ROM
Chapter 12

WebTutor™ ToolBox
WebTutor™ Toolbox on WebCT or Blackboard
Online
Chapter 12

Content Mastery: Tutorials, Study Aids, Practice Tests, & Quizzing

Book Companion Website
http://politicalscience.wadsworth.com/kegley10/

- Chapter 12 Tutorial Quizzing
- Learning Objectives
- Glossary/Key Terms
- Audio Flash Cards
- Crossword Puzzles
- Web Links
- Interactive Maps with Critical Thinking Questions
- Controversy Interactive Activities
- MicroCase® Exercises
- InfoTrac® College Edition Exercises
- Simulation
- Case Study

Wadsworth's International Relations Resource Center
http://politicalscience.wadsworth.com/ir/

Study Guide
Chapter 12
Learning Objectives, Chapter Outlines, Key Terms, Practice Exam with True/False, Multiple-Choice, Fill-in-the-Blank, Short Answer, and Essay Questions

Beyond the Book: Assignments, Research, Writing, & Exploration

The Wadsworth Atlas of International Relations

Genest, *Conflict and Cooperation: Evolving Theories of International Relations*, Second Edition

Roberts/Rosenblatt, *International Relations Using MicroCase® ExplorIt*, Exercise 8

Williams/Goldstein/Shafritz, *Classic Readings in International Relations*, Part V, "International Crisis," "Nuclear Deterrence," and Part VII

Cusimano Love, *Beyond Sovereignty*, Second Edition "Nuclear Smuggling"

Mayer, *9-11: The Giant Awakens*

Kinsella, *Regime Change: Origins, Execution, and Aftermath of the Iraq War*

CHAPTER 13: THE REALIST ROAD TO SECURITY THROUGH ALLIANCES, ARMS CONTROL, AND THE BALANCE OF POWER

Class Preparation & Lecture Presentation Tools

Multimedia Manager with Instructor Resources CD-ROM: A Microsoft® PowerPoint® Tool
- PowerPoint Lecture Outline: Chapter 13
- Instructor's Manual: Chapter 13

CNN® Today: International Relations and Comparative Politics series on VHS (2003, 2004, & 2006 Editions) or complete set on DVD
The Roadmap to Peace; Cuba, the European Union, and the United States: Engagement or Isolation?; Then and Now: A Comparison of Foreign Policy During the Cold War and the War on Terror; The End of the Arms Race?; Transatlantic Relations; India's Hopes for Peace; China's Changing Role in the International Landscape

InfoTrac® College Edition with InfoMarks™
Chapter-specific exercises provided on the Book Companion Website and suggested readings on the International Relations Resource Center.

Wadsworth's International Relations Resource Center
http://politicalscience.wadsworth.com/ir/

Book Companion Website
http://politicalscience.wadsworth.com/kegley10/
Instructor's Manual, Lecture Outlines, Interactive Maps, Case Studies, Simulations, MicroCase® Exercises, Quizzing, NewsEdge, and other resources

Assessment & Course Management

ExamView®
ExamView® on Multimedia Manager with Instructor Resources CD-ROM
Chapter 13

WebTutor™ ToolBox
WebTutor™ Toolbox on WebCT or Blackboard Online
Chapter 13

Content Mastery: Tutorials, Study Aids, Practice Tests, & Quizzing

Book Companion Website
http://politicalscience.wadsworth.com/kegley10/

- Chapter 13 Tutorial Quizzing
- Learning Objectives
- Glossary/Key Terms
- Audio Flash Cards
- Crossword Puzzles
- Web Links
- Interactive Maps with Critical Thinking Questions
- Controversy Interactive Activities
- MicroCase® Exercises
- InfoTrac® College Edition Exercises
- Simulation
- Case Study

Wadsworth's International Relations Resource Center
http://politicalscience.wadsworth.com/ir/

Study Guide
Chapter 13
Learning Objectives, Chapter Outlines, Key Terms, Practice Exam with True/False, Multiple-Choice, Fill-in-the-Blank, Short Answer, and Essay Questions

Beyond the Book: Assignments, Research, Writing, & Exploration

The Wadsworth Atlas of International Relations

Genest, *Conflict and Cooperation: Evolving Theories of International Relations*, Second Edition

Roberts/Rosenblatt, *International Relations Using MicroCase® ExplorIt*

Williams/Goldstein/Shafritz, *Classic Readings in International Relations*

Cusimano Love, *Beyond Sovereignty*, Second Edition

Mayer, *9-11: The Giant Awakens*

Kinsella, *Regime Change: Origins, Execution, and Aftermath of the Iraq War*

CHAPTER 14: THE LIBERAL INSTITUTIONAL PATHS TO PEACE

Class Preparation & Lecture Presentation Tools

Multimedia Manager with Instructor Resources CD-ROM: A Microsoft® PowerPoint® Tool
- PowerPoint Lecture Outline: Chapter 14
- Instructor's Manual: Chapter 14

CNN® Today: International Relations and Comparative Politics series on VHS (2003, 2004, & 2006 Editions) or complete set on DVD
Fujimori Extradition; Cuba, the European Union, and the United States: Engagement or Isolation?; The International Criminal Court; Transatlantic Relations; India's Hopes for Peace

InfoTrac® College Edition with InfoMarks™
Chapter-specific exercises provided on the Book Companion Website and suggested readings on the International Relations Resource Center.

Wadsworth's International Relations Resource Center
http://politicalscience.wadsworth.com/ir/

Book Companion Website
http://politicalscience.wadsworth.com/kegley10/
Instructor's Manual, Lecture Outlines, Interactive Maps, Case Studies, Simulations, MicroCase® Exercises, Quizzing, NewsEdge, and other resources

Assessment & Course Management

ExamView
ExamView® on Multimedia Manager with Instructor Resources CD-ROM
Chapter 14

WebTutor ToolBox
WebTutor™ Toolbox on WebCT or Blackboard
Online Chapter 14

Content Mastery: Tutorials, Study Aids, Practice Tests, & Quizzing

Book Companion Website
http://politicalscience.wadsworth.com/kegley10/

- Chapter 14 Tutorial Quizzing
- Learning Objectives
- Glossary/Key Terms
- Audio Flash Cards
- Crossword Puzzles
- Web Links
- Interactive Maps with Critical Thinking Questions
- Controversy Interactive Activities
- MicroCase® Exercises
- InfoTrac® College Edition Exercises
- Simulations
- Case Studies: The Decision to Intervene in Bosnia

Wadsworth's International Relations Resource Center
http://politicalscience.wadsworth.com/ir/

Study Guide
Chapter 14
Learning Objectives, Chapter Outlines, Key Terms, Practice Exam with True/False, Multiple-Choice, Fill-in-the-Blank, Short Answer, and Essay Questions

Beyond the Book: Assignments, Research, Writing, & Exploration

The Wadsworth Atlas of International Relations

Genest, *Conflict and Cooperation: Evolving Theories of International Relations*, Second Edition

Roberts/Rosenblatt, *International Relations Using MicroCase® ExplorIt*, Exercise 9

Williams/Goldstein/Shafritz, *Classic Readings in International Relations*

Cusimano Love, *Beyond Sovereignty*, Second Edition

Kegley/Raymond, *From War to Peace*, Part V

Mayer, *9-11: The Giant Awakens*

Kinsella, *Regime Change: Origins, Execution, and Aftermath of the Iraq War*

Magstadt, *The European Union Today: A Quest for Unity Amidst Diversity*

CHAPTER 15: TEN QUESTIONS ABOUT TWENTY-FIRST-CENTURY GLOBAL PROSPECTS

Class Preparation & Lecture Presentation Tools

Multimedia Manager with Instructor Resources CD-ROM: A Microsoft® PowerPoint® Tool
- PowerPoint Lecture Outline: Chapter 15
- Instructor's Manual: Chapter 15

CNN® Today: International Relations and Comparative Politics series on VHS (2003, 2004, & 2006 Editions) or complete set on DVD
China-Tibet Relations, China's Changing Role in the International Landscape, International Criminal Court, Transatlantic Relations, India's Hopes for Peace, Sharon's Choices: Decision Making in the Israeli-Palestinian Conflict, Roadmap to Peace, Aid for Somalian Refugees, AIDS in the Third World, Counting the Cost: Financing AIDS Research, Cambodian Sweat Shops

InfoTrac® College Edition with InfoMarks™
Chapter-specific exercises provided on the Book Companion Website and suggested readings on the International Relations Resource Center.

Wadsworth's International Relations Resource Center
http://politicalscience.wadsworth.com/ir/

Book Companion Website
http://politicalscience.wadsworth.com/kegley10/
Instructor's Manual, Lecture Outlines, Interactive Maps, Case Studies, Simulations, MicroCase® Exercises, Quizzing, NewsEdge, and other resources

Assessment & Course Management

ExamView® on Multimedia Manager with Instructor Resources CD-ROM
Chapter 15

WebTutor™ Toolbox on WebCT or Blackboard
Online Chapter 15

Content Mastery: Tutorials, Study Aids, Practice Tests, & Quizzing

Book Companion Website
http://politicalscience.wadsworth.com/kegley10/
- Chapter 15 Tutorial Quizzing
- Learning Objectives
- Glossary/Key Terms
- Audio Flash Cards
- Crossword Puzzles
- Web Links
- Interactive Maps with Critical Thinking Questions
- Controversy Interactive Activities
- MicroCase® Exercises
- InfoTrac® College Edition Exercises
- Simulations
- Case Studies

Wadsworth's International Relations Resource Center
http://politicalscience.wadsworth.com/ir/

Study Guide
Chapter 15
Learning Objectives, Chapter Outlines, Key Terms, Practice Exam with True/False, Multiple-Choice, Fill-in-the-Blank, Short Answer, and Essay Questions

Beyond the Book: Assignments, Research, Writing, & Exploration

The Wadsworth Atlas of International Relations

Genest, *Conflict and Cooperation: Evolving Theories of International Relations,* Second Edition

Roberts/Rosenblatt, *International Relations Using MicroCase® ExplorIt*

Williams/Goldstein/Shafritz, *Classic Readings in International Relations*

Cusimano Love, *Beyond Sovereignty,* Second Edition

Kegley/Raymond, *From War to Peace*

Stoessinger, *Why Nations Go to War*

Mayer, *9-11: The Giant Awakens*

Kinsella, *Regime Change: Origins, Execution, and Aftermath of the Iraq War*

www.wadsworth.com

www.wadsworth.com is the World Wide Web site for Thomson Wadsworth and is your direct source to dozens of online resources.

At *www.wadsworth.com* you can find out about supplements, demonstration software, and student resources. You can also send email to many of our authors and preview new publications and exciting new technologies.

www.wadsworth.com
Changing the way the world learns®

TENTH EDITION

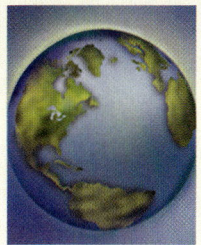 # WORLD POLITICS
Trend and Transformation

CHARLES W. KEGLEY, JR.
University of South Carolina

with

EUGENE R. WITTKOPF
Louisiana State University

Australia • Canada • Mexico • Singapore • Spain
United Kingdom • United States

DEDICATION

To our wives, Debra and Barbara, for their loving support of our endeavor in and through this book to make the world, through education, a better, safer, and more just world for future generations.

World Politics: Trend and Transformation, Tenth Edition
Charles W. Kegley, Jr., University of South Carolina
with Eugene R. Wittkopf, Louisiana State University

Publisher: Clark Baxter
Senior Development Editor: Stacey Sims
Editorial Assistant: Cheryl Lee
Technology Project Manager: Michelle Vardeman
Senior Marketing Manager: Janise Fry
Advertising Project Manager: Kelley McAllister
Project Manager, Editorial Production: Katy German
Art Director: Maria Epes
Print Buyer: Doreen Suruki

Permissions Editor: Sarah Harkrader
Production Service: Jamie Armstrong, G&S Book Services
Text Designer: Patricia McDermond
Photo Researcher: Linda Sykes
Copy Editor: Kathleen Fields
Cover Designer: Brian Salisbury
Cover Image: Corbis, Getty Images
Cover Printer: Phoenix Color Corp
Compositor: G&S Book Services

© 2006 Thomson Wadsworth, a part of The Thomson Corporation. Thomson, the Star logo, and Wadsworth are trademarks used herein under license.

ALL RIGHTS RESERVED. No part of this work covered by the copyright hereon may be reproduced or used in any form or by any means—graphic, electronic, or mechanical, including photocopying, recording, taping, Web distribution, information storage and retrieval systems, or in any other manner—without the written permission of the publisher.

Printed in the United States of America
1 2 3 4 5 6 7 09 08 07 06 05

For more information about our products, contact us at:
Thomson Learning Academic Resource Center
1-800-423-0563

For permission to use material from this text or product, submit a request online at
http://www.thomsonrights.com.
Any additional questions about permissions can be submitted by email to
thomsonrights@thomson.com.

© 2006 Thomson Learning, Inc. All Rights Reserved. Thomson Learning WebTutor™ is a trademark of Thomson Learning, Inc.

Library of Congress Control Number: 2004115438
ISBN 0-534-60220-7

Thomson Higher Education
10 Davis Drive
Belmont, CA 94002-3098
USA

Asia (including India)
Thomson Learning
5 Shenton Way
#01-01 UIC Building
Singapore 068808

Australia/New Zealand
Thomson Learning Australia
102 Dodds Street
Southbank, Victoria 3006
Australia

Canada
Thomson Nelson
1120 Birchmount Road
Toronto, Ontario M1K 5G4
Canada

UK/Europe/Middle East/Africa
Thomson Learning
High Holborn House
50–51 Bedford Road
London WC1R 4LR
United Kingdom

Latin America
Thomson Learning
Seneca, 53
Colonia Polanco
11560 Mexico
D.F. Mexico

Spain (including Portugal)
Thomson Paraninfo
Calle Magallanes, 25
28015 Madrid, Spain

Brief Contents

Controversy Boxes and Maps	xvii
Preface	xix
About the Authors	xxix

PART I: TREND AND TRANSFORMATION IN WORLD POLITICS — 1

1	Exploring Twenty-First-Century World Politics	2
2	Theories of World Politics	26

PART II: THE GLOBE'S ACTORS AND THEIR RELATIONS — 55

3	Foreign Policy Decision Making	56
4	Great-Power Rivalries and Relations	94
5	The Global South in a World of Powers	131
6	Nonstate Actors in the Interstate System	168
7	Humanitarian Challenges and the Protection of Human Rights	219

PART III: THE POLITICS OF GLOBAL WELFARE — 259

8	Globalization and the Prospects for Global Governance	260
9	Markets and Money in the Global Political Economy	300
10	Population Pressure, Resource Depletion, and the Preservation of the Global Environment	348

PART IV: MANAGING GLOBAL CONFLICT — 397

11	The Face of Twenty-First-Century Armed Conflict	398
12	Military Power, Coercive Diplomacy, and National Security	441
13	The Realist Road to Security through Alliances, Arms Control, and the Balance of Power	498
14	The Liberal Institutional Paths to Peace	528

PART V: THE PROBLEMATIC TWENTY-FIRST CENTURY — 571

15	Ten Questions about Twenty-First-Century Global Prospects	572
	References	R-1
	Photo Credits	C-1
	Index	I-1

Contents

Controversy Boxes and Maps	xvii
Preface	xix
About the Authors	xxix

PART I: TREND AND TRANSFORMATION IN WORLD POLITICS — 1

CHAPTER 1
EXPLORING TWENTY-FIRST-CENTURY WORLD POLITICS — 2

The Investigative Challenge	5
How Perceptions Influence Images of Reality	9
The Nature and Sources of Images	9
The Role of Images in World Politics	13
Breaking the Global Puzzle into Parts: Interpreting at Different Levels of Analysis	14
The Book's Approach: Actors, Issues, and Their Interactions	16
Facing the Future: Key Questions to Confront at the Dawn of the New Millennium	17
Are States Obsolete?	17
Is Globalization a Cure or a Curse?	18
What Will Be the Consequences of America's Superpower Status?	19
Will Geo-Economics Supersede Geopolitics?	20
What Constitutes Human Well-Being on an Ecologically Fragile Planet?	21
Key Terms	23
Suggested Reading	23
Where on the World Wide Web?	23
InfoTrac® College Edition	25

CHAPTER 2
THEORIES OF WORLD POLITICS — 26

Understanding World Politics	28
The Elusive Quest for Theory	28
The Evolution of Theoretical Inquiry	29
Liberalism	29
The Liberal Worldview	30
The Liberal Reform Program	31
Realism	33
The Realist Worldview	33
Realism in the Nuclear Age	35

The Limitations of Realism	35
The Neorealist or "Structural" Extension of Realism	38
The Neoclassical Extension of Realism	39
Neoliberalism	40
Transnational Interdependence as a Neoliberal Counter Worldview to Realism	42
International Regimes	44
Alternative Theories	45
Theorizing about Theory: The Constructivist Conception	46
Key Terms	52
Suggested Reading	52
Where on the World Wide Web?	53
InfoTrac® College Edition	54

PART II: THE GLOBE'S ACTORS AND THEIR RELATIONS — 55

CHAPTER 3
FOREIGN POLICY DECISION MAKING — 56

The Emergence of the Modern State System	58
The Global and Domestic Determinants of States' Foreign Policy Behavior	59
Geopolitics	60
Military Capabilities	62
Economic Conditions	63
Type of Government	65
The Unitary Actor and Rational Decision Making	69
States as Unitary Actors?	69
Policy Making as Rational Choice	69
Impediments to Rational Choice	72
The Bureaucratic Politics of Foreign Policy Decision Making	78
Bureaucratic Efficiency and Rationality	78
The Limits of Bureaucratic Organization	78
Attributes of Bureaucratic Behavior	82
The Consequences of Bureaucratic Policy Making	85
The Role of Leaders in Foreign Policy Decision Making	86
Leaders as Makers and Movers of World History	86
Factors Affecting the Capacity to Lead	88
Refinements to the History-Making Individuals Model	91
Constraints on Foreign Policy Making: Problems and Prospects	91
Key Terms	91
Suggested Reading	92

Where on the World Wide Web?	92
InfoTrac® College Edition	93

CHAPTER 4
GREAT-POWER RIVALRIES AND RELATIONS — 94

The Quest for Great-Power Hegemony	96
The First World War	98
The Causes of World War I	98
The Consequences of World War I	102
The Second World War	104
The Causes of World War II	104
The Consequences of World War II	109
The Cold War	110
The Causes and Evolutionary Course of the Cold War	111
The Consequences of the Cold War	119
The Future of Great-Power Politics: A Cold Peace?	119
America's Unipolar Moment in History	119
From Unipolarity to Multipolarity?	123
Responding to Multipolarity's Challenge	126
Key Terms	128
Suggested Reading	128
Where on the World Wide Web?	129
InfoTrac® College Edition	130

CHAPTER 5
THE GLOBAL SOUTH IN A WORLD OF POWERS — 131

The Colonial Origins of the Global South's Plight	135
The First Wave of European Imperialism	138
The Second Wave of European Imperialism	140
Colonialism, Self-Determination, and Decolonization in the Twentieth Century	142
North and South Today: Worlds Apart	144
Theoretical Explanations of Underdevelopment	147
Classical Economic Development Theory	147
Two Structural Theories: Dependency Theory and World Systems	147
Closing the Gap? The Global South's Prospects	149
The Global South's Foreign Policy Response to a World Ruled by the Great Powers	151
In Search of Power	152
The Search for Wealth in a Globalized World	154
Trade, Aid, Investment, Debt Relief—or Nothing?	157

The Future Role of the Global South	164
Key Terms	164
Suggested Reading	165
Where on the World Wide Web?	165
InfoTrac® College Edition	167

CHAPTER 6
NONSTATE ACTORS IN THE INTERSTATE SYSTEM — 168

Nonstate Actors, Intergovernmental Organizations (IGOs), and Nongovernmental Organizations (NGOs): An Introduction	170
Global Intergovernmental Organizations (IGOs)	173
The United Nations	173
The Organization of the United Nations: System and Structure	176
Other Prominent Global IGOs: The World Trade Organization, the World Bank, and the International Monetary Fund	181
The European Union as a Model Regional IGO: A Rite of Passage for "Euroland"?	187
Other Regional IGOs	192
Nongovernmental Organizations (NGOs)	194
Nonstate Nations: The Indigenous Ethnic Groups of the Fourth World	196
Religious Movements	202
Multinational Corporations and Transnational Banks	206
Are NGOs Capable of Transforming World Politics?	211
Nonstate Actors: Saviors or Stranglers of the State?	214
Key Terms	216
Suggested Reading	216
Where on the World Wide Web?	217
InfoTrac® College Edition	218

CHAPTER 7
HUMANITARIAN CHALLENGES AND THE PROTECTION OF HUMAN RIGHTS — 219

Putting People into the Picture	221
How Does Humanity Fare? Assessing the Human Condition	223
Measuring Human Development and Human Security	227
Political and Economic Preconditions for Human Development	229
Human Development in the Age of Globalization	231
The Global Refugee Crisis	233
Indigenous Peoples: Precarious Life in the Fourth World	237
Fourth World Reactions to Human Rights Violations	238
The Threat of State Disintegration to Human Security	239

Gender Politics: The Subordinate Status of Women and Its Consequences	240
Human Rights and the Protection of People	244
International Ethics: Reconciling National Interests and Human Interests	247
Key Terms	256
Suggested Reading	256
Where on the World Wide Web?	257
InfoTrac® College Edition	258

PART III: THE POLITICS OF GLOBAL WELFARE — 259

CHAPTER 8
GLOBALIZATION AND THE PROSPECTS FOR GLOBAL GOVERNANCE — 260

What Is Globalization?	264
The Global Information Age	265
The Media: Markets or Monopoly?	271
Global Health or Global Infection?	275
Global Migration	278
The Globalization of Finance	280
The Globalization of Trade	283
Globalization and the State: What Future?	295
Key Terms	297
Suggested Reading	298
Where on the World Wide Web?	298
InfoTrac® College Edition	299

CHAPTER 9
MARKETS AND MONEY IN THE GLOBAL POLITICAL ECONOMY — 300

The Global Context for Interpreting Contemporary World Economic Change	302
The Shadow of Past Commercial Policy Philosophy	303
The Clash between Liberal and Mercantile Values	305
Hegemony: A Precondition for Economic Order and Free Trade?	311
The Changing Free-Trade Regime	317
Monetary Matters: Can Financial Regimes Promote Growth?	320
The Nuts and Bolts of Monetary Policy	322
The Bretton Woods Monetary System	325
The End of Bretton Woods	327
Floating Exchange Rates	328
Reforming the International Financial Architecture?	329

From Currency Concerns to Trade Troubles	332
Emerging Unilateral Trade Policies	332
The Fate of Free Trade: Triumph or Trouble in a Global Age?	339
Premises for a Future Global Economy	342
Global Economic Destiny?	342
Playing Games with Prosperity on a Global Scale: Tricks-of-the-Trade Debate	343
Key Terms	344
Suggested Reading	345
Where on the World Wide Web?	346
InfoTrac® College Edition	347

CHAPTER 10
POPULATION PRESSURE, RESOURCE DEPLETION, AND THE PRESERVATION OF THE GLOBAL ENVIRONMENT   348

Population Change as a Global Political Challenge	350
Understanding Growth Rates: The Persian Chessboard	350
The Demographic Divide between Global North and Global South	353
Population Momentum	353
From Population Explosion to Population Implosion— A Demographic Transition?	356
New Plagues? The Global Impact of Tuberculosis and HIV/AIDS	357
The International Response to Population Issues	360
Food Fights: The Clash of Optimists and Pessimists	361
A Prescription for Optimism or Pessimism?	364
Environmental Security and Sustainable Development	365
The Ecopolitics of Energy	368
The Global Politics of Oil Supply and Consumption	368
Running on Empty: Is Energy Security an Elusive Goal?	369
The Ecopolitics of the Atmosphere	375
Climate Change	375
Climate-Change Culprits	378
Ozone Protection	380
The Ecopolitics of Forests and Biodiversity	382
Shrinking Forests and Dust Bowls	382
Biodiversity	384
Toward Preservation: The International Response	387
Trade, the Environment, and Sustainable Development	390
Toward Sustainability?	392
Key Terms	394
Suggested Reading	394
Where on the World Wide Web?	395
InfoTrac® College Edition	396

PART IV: MANAGING GLOBAL CONFLICT — 397

CHAPTER 11
THE FACE OF TWENTY-FIRST-CENTURY ARMED CONFLICT — 398

Continuities and Change in Armed Conflict	400
Rival Theories of the Causes of Aggression	403
The First Level of Analysis: Individuals' Human Nature	403
The Second Level of Analysis: States' Internal Characteristics	406
The Third Level of Analysis: Cycles of War and Peace in the Global System	413
Armed Conflict within States	420
The Characteristics of Civil War	420
The Causes of Civil War	422
The International Dimensions of Internal War	426
Terrorism	427
Key Terms	438
Suggested Reading	439
Where on the World Wide Web?	439
InfoTrac® College Edition	440

CHAPTER 12
MILITARY POWER, COERCIVE DIPLOMACY, AND NATIONAL SECURITY — 441

Power in International Politics	443
The Elements of State Power	443
Distinguishing Power from Capabilities	445
The Changing Character of World Power	448
The Pursuit of Military Capabilities	451
Trends in Military Spending	452
Changes in Military Capabilities	453
Trends in the Weapons Trade	454
Trends in Weapons Technology	460
Military Strategy in the Nuclear Age	467
Compellence	468
Deterrence	468
Preemption	470
The Uses and Limits of Coercive Diplomacy	473
Military Intervention	474
Economic Sanctions	476
The Great Powers' National Security Strategies	481
The U.S. Superpower Embraces a Revolutionary New Security Strategy	481
Russia Adjusts to Its New Geostrategic Circumstances	485

China's Global Clout and Security Posture	486
Japan's Search for a Strategy	488
Germany and the European Union Search for a Strategic Vision	490
The Search for Security in an Insecure World	492
Key Terms	495
Suggested Reading	495
Where on the World Wide Web?	496
InfoTrac® College Edition	497

CHAPTER 13
THE REALIST ROAD TO SECURITY THROUGH ALLIANCES, ARMS CONTROL, AND THE BALANCE OF POWER — 498

The Impact of Alliances on National and Global Security	501
Realpolitik Assumptions of Balance-of-Power Theory	503
Managing the Balance through a Concert of Great Powers	507
Stabilizing Power Balances through Arms Control	507
Arms Control versus Disarmament	508
Bilateral Arms Control and Disarmament	508
Multilateral Arms Control and Disarmament	510
The Problematic Future of Arms Control and Disarmament	512
Balancing Power in the Contemporary Global System	515
Models of the Balance of Power in the Twenty-First Century	516
World Domination by the U.S. Superpower, or a Multipolar Future of Balance-of-Power Competition?	518
Key Terms	525
Suggested Reading	526
Where on the World Wide Web?	526
InfoTrac® College Edition	527

CHAPTER 14
THE LIBERAL INSTITUTIONAL PATHS TO PEACE — 528

International Law and World Order	529
Law at the International Level: Core Principles	531
The Limitations of the International Legal System	533
The Relevance of International Law	535
The Legal Control of Warfare	537
International Organizations and World Order	547
The United Nations and the Preservation of Peace	547
Regional Security Organizations and Conflict Management	554
Political Integration: The Functional and Neofunctional Paths to Peace	556
World Federalism: A Single Global Government	556
Functionalism	558
Neofunctionalism	560

Political Disintegration	563
A Democratic Peace: Can Votes Stop Violence?	564
Liberal Institutions and World Order: From Security to Stability?	566
Key Terms	567
Suggested Reading	568
Where on the World Wide Web?	569
InfoTrac® College Edition	570

PART V: THE PROBLEMATIC TWENTY-FIRST CENTURY — 571

CHAPTER 15
TEN QUESTIONS ABOUT TWENTY-FIRST-CENTURY GLOBAL PROSPECTS — 572

Toward the Future: Critical Questions at the Start of the New Millennium	574
1. Should Global Interests Be Placed Ahead of National Interests?	574
2. If War between States Is Obsolete, What Is the Purpose of Military Power?	575
3. Can the New Global Terrorism Be Contained?	578
4. Will Separatist Conflict within States Lead to Hundreds of New States?	581
5. Will the Great Powers Intervene to Protect Human Rights?	581
6. Will Globalization Tie the World Together or Tear It Apart?	583
7. Is Realism Still Realistic and Is Liberalism Still Too Idealistic?	585
8. Is the World Preparing for the Wrong War?	587
9. Is This the "End of History"?	588
10. Is There a Reordered Global Agenda?	589
A New World Order or New World Disorder?	590
Key Terms	593
Suggested Reading	593
Where on the World Wide Web?	593
InfoTrac® College Edition	594
References	R-1
Photo Credits	C-1
Index	I-1

Controversy Boxes and Maps

CONTROVERSY BOXES

Chapter 1	Should We Believe What We See? The Organization of Observations and Projections of Global Realities 10	**Chapter 8**	Does Globalization Mean the End of the Age of States? 266
			Is Globalization Helpful or Harmful? 288
Chapter 2	Can Behavioral Science Advance the Study of International Relations? 37	**Chapter 9**	Globalization's Growing Pains: Is the World Trade Organization a Friend or Foe? 320
	Neoliberalism versus Neorealism: Which Theory Makes the Most Reasonable Assumptions? 41	**Chapter 10**	How Many People Can Earth Support? 362
	What's Missing in Realist Theories of Interstate Relations? The Feminist Critique 43	**Chapter 11**	Does Nationalistic Love of Country Cause War with Foreign Nations? 414
Chapter 3	Are Democracies Deficient in Foreign Affairs? 66		Can the War against Global Terrorism Be Won? 437
	Policy and Personality: Do Leaders Make a Difference? 90	**Chapter 12**	Does High Military Spending Lower Human Security? 450
Chapter 4	Was Ideology the Primary Source of East-West Conflict? 112		Is It Ethical to Wage Preemptive War to Prevent an Adversary's Potential Aggression? 472
	Why Did the Cold War End Peacefully? 118	**Chapter 13**	Do the Advantages of Alliances Outweigh the Disadvantages? 502
Chapter 5	Multinational Corporations in the Global South: Do They Help or Hurt? 161		Is a Unipolar, Bipolar, or Multipolar System the Most Stable? Three Schools of Thought on the Relationship of Polarity and International Peace 524
Chapter 6	Are Religious Movements Causes of War or Sources of Transnational Harmony? 204		
Chapter 7	Should Tyranny and Human Rights Violations Justify Humanitarian Intervention? 250	**Chapter 14**	Was the War in Iraq a Just War? 541

xvii

MAPS

World Map Inside Cover
Map 1.1 Mercator Projection 11
Map 1.2 Peter's Projection 11
Map 1.3 Orthographic Projection 11
Map 3.1 Geographic Influences on Foreign Policy 61
Map 3.2 The Map of Freedom: The Location of Democratically Governed Countries 67
Map 4.1 Territorial Changes in Europe following World War I 103
Map 4.2 World War II Redraws the Map of Europe 105
Map 4.3 The Emerging Centers of Power in the Twenty-First-Century Global Hierarchy 121
Map 5.1 The Global North and Global South 133
Map 5.2 The Great North-South Divide in Wealth and Population 136
Map 5.3 Global Imperialism, 1914 138
Map 6.1 The UN's Headquarters and Global Network 178
Map 6.2 The Indigenous Cultures of the Fourth World 198
Map 6.3 The World's Major Civilizations: Will Their Clash Create Global Disorder? 200
Map 6.4 Major Religions of the World 201
Map 7.1 Projecting Trends in the Proportion of People Below the Poverty Line, 1990–2015 225
Map 7.2 The Map of Human Development 230
Map 8.1 The International Flow of Finance Capital 282
Map 8.2 The World Trade Organization Goes Global 283
Map 9.1 Ranking Countries by Their Economic Freedom 335
Map 9.2 The Volume of Trade Flows between Major Trade Partners 337
Map 10.1 Death in the Prime of Life: The Most Seriously AIDS-Affected Countries, 2000–2005 359
Map 10.2 Global Warning about Global Warming: Who's to Blame? 378
Map 10.3 Loss of Forest and Ground to Deserts 385
Map 10.4 Measuring Environmental Sustainability and Locating Biodiversity Bastions and Endangered Biodiversity Hot Spots 388
Map 11.1 Demographic Stress and the Likelihood of Civil War 423
Map 11.2 The Dance of Death in the Middle East's Cauldron of Terror—the West Bank Flash Point 432
Maps 12.1 and 12.2 Two Measures of Military Power Potential: State Wealth and Size of National Armies 446
Map 12.3 Nuclear-Weapon Armed Countries, Today and Tomorrow 463
Maps 12.4 and 12.5 Vulnerable to Sanctions—Countries Dependent on Trade and Energy Imports 478
Map 13.1 Trick or Treaty? Can Arms Control Treaties Arrest the Proliferation of Weapons? 514
Map 13.2 The Enlarged NATO in the New Geostrategic Balance of Power 521
Map 14.1 UN Peace Missions since 1948 552
Map 14.2 From Few to Many: The Expansion of the European Union, 1951–2005 561

PREFACE

As the twenty-first century begins to unfold, much discussion centers on the prospects in the new millennium for a "new world order." Talk about possible global transformations continues in frenzied proportions, buoyed by the hope that the peace between states and rising prosperity within them during the 1990s will persist, alongside concern that terrorism and violence might prove to be the century's dominant characteristics. Many people set their sights on the promise of a stable global future—and many others on the dread of chronic global instability. Expectations of peace were abruptly shattered on September 11, 2001, when a shocked world witnessed the terrorist destruction of the World Trade Center in New York. Almost immediately, visions of world politics shifted as a new mood of doom and gloom set in about the probability that, rather than peace, the twenty-first century would be colored by the resumption of past patterns of global violence.

Our age does not have, as yet, a name. True, we are in a post–Cold War, post–twentieth-century, post–September 11 phase. But those labels do not adequately describe the period of transition through which world history is moving. We do not yet possess sufficient confidence about the likely characteristics of the future to predict how later generations will classify the defining characteristics of world affairs in our present period of history. Rapid, sweeping changes in world politics pose enormous challenges to policymakers, scholars, and especially students. Without a single overriding issue such as the Cold War or the continuing threat of global terrorism to structure thinking about global affairs, little agreement exists about which dimensions of world politics will characterize the twenty-first century.

The tenth edition of *World Politics: Trend and Transformation* is intended to provide the framework students need to put changes and continuities into perspective. The book combines the latest available information with contemporary debates in international relations to prepare students to assess the possibilities for the global future and its potential impact on their lives. *World Politics* aims to provoke such critical thinking by presenting a picture of the evolving relations among global actors, the historical developments that affect those actors' relationships, and the salient contemporary global trends that those interactions produce. The major theories scholars use to explain the dynamics underlying international relations—realism, liberalism, and their variants—frame our study. At the same time, this book incorporates the reconstructed theories newly advanced to interpret contemporary developments (such as constructivism and feminist theory) and resists the temptation to oversimplify world politics with a superficial treatment that would mask complexities and distort realities.

OVERVIEW OF THE BOOK

To help students make sense of political complexities, *World Politics* is organized into five parts. Part I introduces the central issues and major theories in the study of international relations. Part II identifies the major actors in the global arena and discusses the processes by which those actors make decisions. An added chapter focuses on people as important agents in international relations. Part III looks at issues of global welfare and the various global trends reshaping prevailing conditions for humanity. It discusses the impact of globalization on international trade and economic relations and on the linkage between population demographics and the ecological environment, whose preservation is necessary for the saga of the human story to continue. Global conflict is the subject of Part IV, including warfare, terrorism, national security, arms races, and rival approaches to peace. The text concludes with Part V, in which ten questions provoked by presently developing trends in world politics are posed to stimulate further thinking about the global future.

CHANGES IN THE TENTH EDITION

Content and Organization

Many global changes have taken place in the two years since the publication of the ninth edition. They required revisiting every passage of the manuscript and integrating the latest developments with the most current information available as the book went to press. This edition incorporates the most recent available indicators of global trends and addresses the most important issues on the global agenda, ranging from human development and the empowerment of women to the number of terrorist acts and peacekeeping operations in progress, and from fluctuations in foreign direct investments by multinational corporations to changes in the globalized political economy. In addition, coverage has been expanded to take account of new departures in theory that attempt to interpret recent global developments.

Without identifying every modification in the new edition, attention is drawn to the most important changes in each chapter. Those familiar with previous editions will immediately note some prominent organizational modifications, following the advice of users of past editions: (1) Chapters 12 and 13 were merged and abridged to put related topics together and thereby to reduce further the number of chapters to fifteen (to more closely match the number of weeks in a typical semester); (2) the revised chapter on people as actors on the global stage, and the human rights issues surrounding the place of people on the planet, has been repositioned in Part II to more properly treat people as players and participants in the global drama, alongside states and nonstate actors; (3) the Global South's less-developed countries are now positioned following the Global North's great powers on whom the former are so dependent. Chapter 6 introduces nonstate actors (such as multinational corporations and terrorist networks). Thematically, stress has been added to the causes and consequences of the predominant hegemonic position of the United States, and the controversies that that superpower status (and preemptive unilateralism) has created as the George W. Bush administration begins its second term in office, pledging to continue the hard-edged approach to national security that it practiced in its first term; and (4) new Controversy boxes capture the most lively issues being debated in world politics today, with increased attention given to ethical dilemmas and moral problems. In addition, new key terms have been added, with glossed definitions of the concepts in the margins, in response to the popularity of this "high definition" feature of *World Politics* as a pedagogical aid to build students' familiarity with the terminology used to discuss international issues. Perusal of the changes in individual chapters will pinpoint how these changes, and others, have been implemented, in this silver anniversary of the leading international relations textbook, to keep it recent, relevant, and rigorous as a cutting-edge introduction to world politics. In particular, the following salient revisions and modifications in each chapter are noteworthy for instructors who have used previous editions of the text for their students. (Of course, the entire text has been updated to keep abreast of the most important changes in world politics since the ninth edition was released in March 2003.)

- Chapter 1, "Exploring Twenty-First-Century World Politics," has been revised to further highlight the impact of perception on the social construction of images and theories of international relations. The five questions that conclude the chapter anticipate future trends in global politics and have been updated to account for recent changes in a global system rife with controversy. A new question centers on the issues created by the military superpower status of the United States, which has no rival to counterbalance American unilateralism. Some of these questions are revisited in greater length and from alternate perspectives in the final chapter.

- Chapter 2, "Theories of World Politics," builds on the two major theoretical interpretations of world politics, the realist and liberal traditions, by expanding coverage of constructivism in theoretical inquiry and by linking theory more explicitly to concrete global issues. Students are thereby encouraged to appreciate the contribution of political theory to an understanding of international relations.

- Chapter 3, "Foreign Policy Decision Making," more instructively illuminates the obstacles to rational choice facing both state and nonstate actors, such as international organizations and multinational corporations, when they make policy choices to cope with changing international circumstances. New case material introduces the impediments to rational decision making presented by "bureaucratic politics" and interagency competition, featuring the groupthink failures in the U.S. intelligence community that undermined the U.S. capacity to prevent the Al Qaeda terrorist network's destruction of the World Trade Center on September 11, 2001, and its failure to generate sound intelligence about weapons of mass destruction in Iraq or to anticipate the chaos that followed the U.S.-led invasion of Iraq.

- Chapter 5 (Chapter 6 in the ninth edition), "The Global South in a World of Powers," examines the implications of the wide gap between an impoverished and youthful Southern Hemisphere and a wealthy and aging Northern Hemisphere. It explores in greater depth the ways in which globalization may be marginalizing the Global South, and expands coverage of the strategies Global South countries use to arrest their disadvantaged circumstances vis-à-vis the rest of the world—namely, by following the examples of newly industrialized economies that have liberated themselves from dependence on, and now challenge, the dominant Global North.

- Chapter 6, "Nonstate Actors in the Interstate System," better emphasizes the profound and sometimes harmful impact that IGOs and NGOs, such as powerful multinational corporations, have on conditions in many countries. New analyses of both the World Trade Organization and the International Monetary Fund better cover the activities and impact of these global actors, which increasingly find themselves under attack as symbols of the problems attributed to globalization and to the rules created by global institutions. Moreover, there is a new discussion on how the push and pull among IGO and NGO nonstate actors exerts pressure for globalization, while countervailing coalitions among them lessen their influence over sovereign states.

- Chapter 7, "Humanitarian Challenges and the Protection of Human Rights," further pulls together material formerly scattered throughout the previous editions dealing with the individual in relation to the global forces that shape his or her experiences. In looking at world politics through a lens that gives each individual primacy, the chapter, now placed in Part II, which covers the actors in international relations, isolates the so-called individual level of analysis in order to punctuate its importance in the overall scheme of world history. At the same time, this point of view captures the ways in which each person's encounter with the world is mediated by social, political, religious, and linguistic institutions and traditions. The chapter gives the issues of human security and human rights, such as gender equality, the special, separate treatment they deserve. These issues assume increasing significance in comparison to traditional concerns about entire countries' national security (without regard for the security of welfare of the people living in them). This chapter also offers new discussions of ethics—the moral principles that speak to the challenge of protecting the human rights and civil liberties of people such as refugees and displaced persons.

- Chapter 8, retitled "Globalization and the Prospects for Global Governance," introduces the problems and politics of global welfare issues examined in the next two chapters. The potential decline in states' sovereign power is considered as a global trend, not only in the liberal democracies of the Global North but also in the "failed states" of the Global South. The revised chapter now highlights the growing controversies between winners and losers in the process of globalization by addressing the intensifying popular backlash against it. The new chapter reviews divided opinions about whether globalization will breed new and stronger institutions for global governance.

- Chapter 9, now titled "Markets and Money in the Global Political Economy," addresses newly evolving perspectives in commercial liberalism, mercantilism, and hegemonic stability theory to evaluate whether sustained prosperity, free trade, and the management of hypercurrency volatility, banking crises, and rising debt will continue and, if so, if the liberal international economic order will erode. The chapter pays attention to the influence of a globalized marketplace on international and national economic conditions. It also puts new emphasis on the hegemonic supremacy of the United States as the dominant player in the international political economy, whose position and recent new protectionist policies raise questions about the preservation of the liberal trade regime.

- Chapter 10, "Population Pressure, Resource Depletion, and the Preservation of the Global Environment," stresses the direct linkage between population growth pressure and the question of how the global ecology might be preserved through sustainable growth. Also explored are the opportunities and problems associated with the "birth dearth" in the aging Global North compared with the continuing population explosion in many Global South countries as they relate to the problematic status of recently negotiated legal regimes to control global warming and common environmental problems associated with biotechnology and genetic engineering.

- Chapter 11, now titled "The Face of Twenty-First-Century Armed Conflict," has been updated to examine the so-called new age of global terrorism in the aftermath of September 11 and the chronic violence in the Iraqi war, with an updated interpretation of the causes, characteristics, and control of armed conflict in its various manifestations. The chapter also covers recent changes in the incidence of all types of warfare, specifically expanding discussion of the wave of internal rebellions in failing states and of genocide in Sudan, the Ivory Coast, or elsewhere.

- Chapter 12, now titled "Military Power, Coercive Diplomacy, and National Security," consolidates most of the material previously covered in Chapter 13 from the ninth edition, and its merger punctuates the new military doctrines that have been promulgated by the United States and the other great powers to wage a worldwide war against global terrorism and to prevent the use of weapons of mass destruction, and the shifting distribution of military expenditures to pursue those goals. The so-called revolution in military technologies that makes new methods of warfare available is also discussed, and the chapter introduces the latest declassified estimates of the global distribution of arms sales. Also included in the revision is a discussion of the radical U.S. strategic shift from deterrence to preemptive prevention of violence by attacking potential aggressors before they can undertake anticipated military actions, and changes in the use of economic sanctions as a method of coercive diplomacy.

- Chapter 13, retitled "The Realist Road to Security through Alliances, Arms Control, and the Balance of Power," has been refocused to sharpen awareness of the similarities and differences in the realist and liberal approaches to world order. Incorporated is coverage of NATO's expansion by seven new members in 2004 and the U.S.-Russian SORT nuclear weapons reduction agreement, as well as the changing laws giving increased license to humanitarian military intervention.

- Chapter 14, "The Liberal Institutional Paths to Peace," reexamines, in light of the post–9/11 war against terrorism and the war in Iraq, the controversies surrounding the possibility of preserving peace by promoting the enlargement of the coalition of liberal democratic states, which have seldom if ever waged war against one another. Also added is a new assessment of the European Union's expansion to twenty-five members.

- Chapter 15, "Ten Questions about Twenty-First-Century Global Prospects," concludes with a series of questions designed to generate critical thought about the trends and issues identified in the preceding chapters and the dilemmas they pose for the global future. The section on the controversies surrounding the means for containing global terrorism has been updated in light of the war in Iraq and its aftershocks, as has the reconstruction of rival theories to explain these and other changes that have recently occurred. These ten questions have been revised thoroughly, and the discussion presents the most recent assessments of the global prospect, while relating them to enduring issues in international relations.

Design and Pedagogy

This tenth edition of *World Politics* features a refashioned interior design, including the following pedagogic improvements to make the intellectual journey through world politics easier than ever for students.

- **Reduced number of chapters.** A reorganization of the table of contents, including the merger of two chapters and the repositioning of some topics, makes a more orderly and organized presentation of topics. The instructor is not required to follow the book's presentation in sequence from start to end, however, because each chapter and part is self-contained.

- **Revised chapter Topics and Themes.** Each chapter begins with a new outline of major topics that correspond to the chapter headings and titles of featured sections. By breaking each topic into separate components, students can more easily navigate each chapter.

- **Updated Controversy boxes.** As a sense of change grips much of the world, discourse about international relations gives rise to questions that inspire intense new debate, such as rival hypotheses about the causes of global terrorism and contending prescriptions for combating it. Each Controversy box identifies a major issue for which there are opposing positions. The essays, four newly written to deal with new issues, encourage students to consider rival viewpoints and develop their own opinions. Addressing both classic dilemmas in international affairs and the most heated current debates, Controversy boxes offer excellent starting points for class debates or research papers.

- **Comprehensive marginal glosses.** Responding to the popularity of the marginal glosses introduced in the seventh edition, marginal glosses for *all* key terms in the text are provided, and the number of key concepts introduced has been increased to expand students' understanding of concepts that they will use to interpret world politics for the rest of their lives. For complex terms with multiple meanings, the marginal glosses provide the explanation that is most relevant to the topic being discussed.

- **Expanded, up-to-date map and illustration program.** More than three dozen new or revised maps, tables, photographs, or figures broaden the book's coverage, provoke interest, and enable students to visualize the ideas that now command attention. The new photographs and illustrations have been selected with an eye toward introducing the timeliest topics, including a detailed caption that identifies the picture and explains its relevance to the larger issues discussed in the text.

- **Updated Where on the World Wide Web? listings.** Responding to the new and rapidly changing information available on the Internet, the Where on the World Wide Web? section at the end of each chapter has been updated and expanded to list major websites that students can explore for further information on the topics being discussed. Each web listing is accompanied by a lively annotation describing the site's contents and suggesting activities and research that students can pursue on the site.
- **InfoTrac® College Edition.** Four months of FREE anywhere, anytime access to InfoTrac® College Edition, the online library, is automatically available with this book. The new and improved InfoTrac® College Edition puts cutting-edge research and the latest headlines at readers' fingertips, giving access to an entire online library for the cost of one book. This fully searchable database offers more than twenty years' worth of full-text articles (more than 10 million) from almost 4,000 diverse sources, such as academic journals, newsletters, and up-to-the-minute periodicals including *Foreign Affairs, International Security, Foreign Policy, World Politics, Time, Newsweek, Science,* and *USA Today.* A listing of the most current articles from the database relevant to the subject matter appears at the end of each chapter.
- **Revised list of suggested reading.** To bring the most recent scholarship and commentary to the attention of students for further study, a thoroughly revised list of authoritative books and articles appears at the end of each chapter, incorporating groundbreaking, recently published research into this inventory of essential books and journals.

SUPPLEMENTS

Instructor's Resource Manual with Test Bank

An *Instructor's Resource Manual with Test Bank* supports the tenth edition of *World Politics.* The manual includes chapter outlines to guide lectures; thematic guides suggesting a variety of approaches to covering each chapter's material; learning objectives; suggested readings for instructors; creative teaching aids for each chapter, including simulations, teaching cases, and multimedia offerings; and a test bank containing more than five hundred new or revised essay and multiple-choice questions. A computerized version of the test bank and manual is also available on CD-ROM.

The Wadsworth Political Science Resource Center at http://politicalscience.wadsworth.com

Here you will find information on how to better surf the web, links to general political websites, a career center, issues in the news, a monthly current events quiz, and more—including the following materials:

- *Citizen's Survival Guide*
- *Spanish Equivalents for Important Terms*
- *Terrorism: An Interdisciplinary Perspective*

Book Companion Website at
http://politicalscience.wadsworth.com/kegley10/

Offering a rich array of teaching and learning resources, this site includes tutorial quizzing, InfoTrac® College Edition activities, Internet exercises, web links, and instructor resources. It also includes updated resources from the CD-ROM that accompanied the book in the previous edition. Those resources include access to online MicroCase exercises that allow you to work with actual data, map exercises exploring the current demographic information of selected countries, historical maps and related exercises that supply context for the events of today, Internet research activities, and more.

ACKNOWLEDGMENTS

Many people have contributed to making the tenth edition the most timely and useful version of *World Politics* since the book was first published in 1981. In addition to those whose assistance helped establish *World Politics* as the field's leading text in its previous editions, the special assistance and advice of those who have contributed specifically to this edition is acknowledged.

We greatly appreciate the constructive comments and suggestions offered by reviewers. In particular, we express our gratitude to the professional scholars who provided blind reviews, including Chad Atkinson, University of Illinois at Urbana–Champaign; James A. Mitchell, California State University at Northridge; Michael D. Kanner, University of Colorado at Boulder; Shalendra D. Sharma, University of San Francisco; and Michael J. Siler, California State University, Los Angeles. Also extremly valuable were the blind reviews provided for the ninth edition, by Don Caldwell and Kevin D. Archer, Point Loma Nazarene College; Steve Chan, University of Colorado at Boulder; Paul Christensen at Boston College; David A. Dickson, University of Memphis; Deborah Gerner, University of Kansas; Deborah Moore Haddad, Ohio University; Virginia Haufler, University of Maryland; Clinton G. Hewan, Northern Kentucky University; Richard D. Hughes, California State University at Sacramento; Matthias Kaelberer, University of Northern Iowa; William W. Newman, Virginia Commonwealth University; Thomas Oatley, University of North Carolina at Chapel Hill; Iraj Paydar, Shoreline Community College; Richard Price, University of Minnesota; Neil Richardson, University of Wisconsin at Madison; Lt. Col. Skip Shackelford, U. S. Air Force Academy; Scott Tollefson, Kansas State University; and Stephen Wrage, U.S. Naval Academy.

Appreciation is also expressed to Gordon Smith, Roger Coate, and Donald Puchala—directors of the Walker Institute of International Studies at the University of South Carolina—whose support was instrumental in the preparation of this and the previous edition. In addition, to be thanked for advice and data are Richard F. Grimmett at the Congressional Research Office, Ted Robert Gurr at the University of Maryland, Ruchi Anand at the American Graduate School of International Relations and Diplomacy in Paris, Margaret G. Hermann at Syracuse University, Jeffrey Pickering at Kansas State University, Gregory A. Raymond at Boise State University, Eytan Gilboa at Bar-Ilan University in Israel, Susan McChucheon and Joseph Reap at the U.S. Department of State, Jonathan

Wilkenfeld at the University of Maryland, Marilea Polk Fried of Kluwer Academic Publishers, Rodney Tomlinson at the U.S. Naval Academy, Matthias Kranke at the University of Tier, Jonah Heilman at the University of Pennsylvania, John Candido at La Trobe University, and David Sylvan and Urs Luterbacher of the Graduate Institute of International Studies (GIIS) in Geneva. Particularly helpful at the same GIIS in Geneva was the advice and feedback of advanced doctoral students, including especially Flore-Anne Bourgeois, Navitri Putri, Joseph Marques, Ignacio de la Rassilla, Héctor Alcantara Palacios, Abigail Diaz de Leon, Abril Frayre, Aline Bailat, Allison Kerwin, Anna Brach, Anne-Kathrin Glatz, Ann-Kristin Sjöberg, Assia Alexieva, Bethany Webster, Brianna Dieter, Byoung-Soo Shon, Céline Furi, Elli Kytömäki, Emily Fox, Facundo Perez Aznar, Gérald Demartet, Grace Schatz, Ha Eun Seong, Heather Wipfli, James Pope, Jason Powers, Jennifer Wallace, Kate Lawrence, Katja Maria Fluckiger, Lana Srzic, Lisé Mackie, Marie-Béatrice Morin, Matthew Pountney, Michael Jaxa-Chanmiec, Mutaz Qafisheh, Paolo Sissa, Patrick Kalas, Sophie Zellmeyer, Stéphanie Pezrad, Thomas Messerli, Thomas Venema, Thorsten Wetzling, Véronique Barbelet, and Xavier Gillaume. Also helpful was the input provided by students at the University of South Carolina, both advanced graduates and undergraduates. The following deserve special thanks: Fahrettin Sumer, Young-Hoon Song, Sally Hansen, Anne "Marshall" Tobelmann, Chris Dixon, Daniel Walsh, Julie Loggins, Kimberly Bjorn, Kristen McGreogor, Maka Bashai, Manisha Patel, Nathan Hill, Nick Mathews, Ray Coble, Raymond Lloyd, Richard Egan, Ryan Curran, Sam-Sang Jo, T. Moss, William Baugh, Ye Zheng, and Zatch Pouchprom.

We are also grateful to John Soares, who diligently collected sites for the Where on the World Wide Web? sections, to Julie L. Mueller at the University of Delaware, for revising the *Instructor's Resource Manual with Test Bank,* and to Erich Saphir at Pima Community College–West for preparing the *Study Guide.*

Deserving of special gratitude are our highly skilled, dedicated, and helpful editors at Wadsworth: Senior Developmental Editor Stacey Sims and Executive Editor David Tatom, who exercised extraordinary professionalism in guiding the process that brought this edition into print, assisted by the project management of Katy German, Permissions Editor Sarah Harkrader and Photo Researcher Linda Sykes. Assistant Editor Rebecca Green and Technology Project Manager Michelle Vardeman worked diligently together in developing the online resources that accompany the new edition. In addition, the always helpful and accommodating Jamie Armstrong, Jessie Hunnicutt, and the rest of the staff at G&S Book Services, as well as Kathleen Fields, our diligent copyeditor, contributed immeasurably to the preparation, polish, and production of the book; all were extraordinary.

Prof. Kegley also wishes to thank those professorial colleagues in the Fulbright American Studies Institute, which he codirected with Don Puchala in 2003 and 2004. Their advice and insights proved invaluable. These scholars include Muhammad Mujeeb Afzal (Pakistan), Anak Agung Perwitha Banyu (Indonesia), Maryna Bessonova (Ukraine), Paul-Henri Bischoff (South Africa), Giulia Caccamo (Italy), María Engracia Cortez-Angulo (Mexico), Rogelio I. Espiritu (Philippines), Galal Ibrahim Fakirah (Yemen), Vladislav V. Froltsov (Belarus), Sabah A. R. Hammad (Iraq), Abubakar Eby Hara (Indonesia), Masaki Hirata (Japan), Heidi Hudson (South Africa), Arhur Ituassu (Brazil), Noam Kochavi (Israel), Lidya Kos-Stanic (Croatia), Gildas Le Voguer (France),

Anindya Jyoti Majumdar (India), Daad Bou Malhab (Lebanon), Mamdouh Mahmoud Mastafa Mansour (Egypt), Aap Neljas (Estonia), Aloysius-Michaels Nnabugwu Okolie (Nigeria), Aida Maria Silverio Pinto Pegado (Angola), Andrei Victorovich Repnevski (Russia), Rafael Inglesias San Jose (Mexico), Norma Breda Dos Santos (Brazil), Dragan R. Simic (Serbia and Montenegro), Sapam Rajendra Singh (India), Alina-Daniela Stanescu (Romania), Farzana Gul Taj (Pakistan), Ta Minh Tuan (Vietnam), Bulent Ugrasiz (Turkey), Leendert Johannes Maria Verhofstad (The Netherlands), Rashed Uz Zaman (Bangladesh), and Zhenjiang Zhang (China). Also helpful were the insights provided by speakers at the 2003 and 2004 Fulbright American Studies Institutes on U.S. Foreign Policy, including especially Don Fowler (past Chair of the Democratic National Committee); Linda P. Brady (Dean of Liberal Arts, North Carolina State University); Dan Caldwell (Pepperdine University); Jerel Rosati, William P. Kreml, Janice Love, Peter Sederberg, Brad Gomez, and Hal French (all of the University of South Carolina); Paula L'Ecuyer (Iraqi desk, U.S. Department of State); Darren Van Tassel (Georgia State University); Patrick Garvey and Marisha Singh (U.S. Senate Committee Foreign Relations); U.S. Senator Fritz Hollings; Col. Levi Rushing Martin; Joel Rosenthal (President, Carnegie Council on Ethics and International Affairs); Gregory Treverton and Glenn Robinson (RAND Corporation, Santa Monica); Matt Bryza (U.S. National Security Council); Josh Wash and David Rudd (Democratic National Committee); Raphael Danzinger (American Israeli Public Affairs Committee); Mitchell Reiss (Policy Planning Office of the U.S. Department of State); Jo Husbands and Lois Peterson (National Academy of Sciences); and Harriet Fulbright.

Beyond the Wadsworth staff and their associates, we are pleased to acknowledge the enormous contribution made to the many revisions in word processing providing by Young-Hoon Song, as well as assistance provided by Maria Anastasiou, Byongok Han, Amanda Cunningham, Daniel Sabia, Dona Roy, Holli Buice, Linda Logan, Long Wang, Mary Schwartz, Min Ye, Polly Brown, Robert J. Palmer, Sallie Buice, and Ye "Kitty" Zheng.

Charles W. Kegley, Jr.
with
Eugene R. Wittkopf

Wilkenfeld at the University of Maryland, Marilea Polk Fried of Kluwer Academic Publishers, Rodney Tomlinson at the U.S. Naval Academy, Matthias Kranke at the University of Tier, Jonah Heilman at the University of Pennsylvania, John Candido at La Trobe University, and David Sylvan and Urs Luterbacher of the Graduate Institute of International Studies (GIIS) in Geneva. Particularly helpful at the same GIIS in Geneva was the advice and feedback of advanced doctoral students, including especially Flore-Anne Bourgeois, Navitri Putri, Joseph Marques, Ignacio de la Rassilla, Héctor Alcantara Palacios, Abigail Diaz de Leon, Abril Frayre, Aline Bailat, Allison Kerwin, Anna Brach, Anne-Kathrin Glatz, Ann-Kristin Sjöberg, Assia Alexieva, Bethany Webster, Brianna Dieter, Byoung-Soo Shon, Céline Furi, Elli Kytömäki, Emily Fox, Facundo Perez Aznar, Gérald Demartet, Grace Schatz, Ha Eun Seong, Heather Wipfli, James Pope, Jason Powers, Jennifer Wallace, Kate Lawrence, Katja Maria Fluckiger, Lana Srzic, Lisé Mackie, Marie-Béatrice Morin, Matthew Pountney, Michael Jaxa-Chanmiec, Mutaz Qafisheh, Paolo Sissa, Patrick Kalas, Sophie Zellmeyer, Stéphanie Pezrad, Thomas Messerli, Thomas Venema, Thorsten Wetzling, Véronique Barbelet, and Xavier Gillaume. Also helpful was the input provided by students at the University of South Carolina, both advanced graduates and undergraduates. The following deserve special thanks: Fahrettin Sumer, Young-Hoon Song, Sally Hansen, Anne "Marshall" Tobelmann, Chris Dixon, Daniel Walsh, Julie Loggins, Kimberly Bjorn, Kristen McGreogor, Maka Bashai, Manisha Patel, Nathan Hill, Nick Mathews, Ray Coble, Raymond Lloyd, Richard Egan, Ryan Curran, Sam-Sang Jo, T. Moss, William Baugh, Ye Zheng, and Zatch Pouchprom.

We are also grateful to John Soares, who diligently collected sites for the Where on the World Wide Web? sections, to Julie L. Mueller at the University of Delaware, for revising the *Instructor's Resource Manual with Test Bank,* and to Erich Saphir at Pima Community College–West for preparing the *Study Guide.*

Deserving of special gratitude are our highly skilled, dedicated, and helpful editors at Wadsworth: Senior Developmental Editor Stacey Sims and Executive Editor David Tatom, who exercised extraordinary professionalism in guiding the process that brought this edition into print, assisted by the project management of Katy German, Permissions Editor Sarah Harkrader and Photo Researcher Linda Sykes. Assistant Editor Rebecca Green and Technology Project Manager Michelle Vardeman worked diligently together in developing the online resources that accompany the new edition. In addition, the always helpful and accommodating Jamie Armstrong, Jessie Hunnicutt, and the rest of the staff at G&S Book Services, as well as Kathleen Fields, our diligent copyeditor, contributed immeasurably to the preparation, polish, and production of the book; all were extraordinary.

Prof. Kegley also wishes to thank those professorial colleagues in the Fulbright American Studies Institute, which he codirected with Don Puchala in 2003 and 2004. Their advice and insights proved invaluable. These scholars include Muhammad Mujeeb Afzal (Pakistan), Anak Agung Perwitha Banyu (Indonesia), Maryna Bessonova (Ukraine), Paul-Henri Bischoff (South Africa), Giulia Caccamo (Italy), María Engracia Cortez-Angulo (Mexico), Rogelio I. Espiritu (Philippines), Galal Ibrahim Fakirah (Yemen), Vladislav V. Froltsov (Belarus), Sabah A. R. Hammad (Iraq), Abubakar Eby Hara (Indonesia), Masaki Hirata (Japan), Heidi Hudson (South Africa), Arhur Ituassu (Brazil), Noam Kochavi (Israel), Lidya Kos-Stanic (Croatia), Gildas Le Voguer (France),

Anindya Jyoti Majumdar (India), Daad Bou Malhab (Lebanon), Mamdouh Mahmoud Mastafa Mansour (Egypt), Aap Neljas (Estonia), Aloysius-Michaels Nnabugwu Okolie (Nigeria), Aida Maria Silverio Pinto Pegado (Angola), Andrei Victorovich Repnevski (Russia), Rafael Inglesias San Jose (Mexico), Norma Breda Dos Santos (Brazil), Dragan R. Simic (Serbia and Montenegro), Sapam Rajendra Singh (India), Alina-Daniela Stanescu (Romania), Farzana Gul Taj (Pakistan), Ta Minh Tuan (Vietnam), Bulent Ugrasiz (Turkey), Leendert Johannes Maria Verhofstad (The Netherlands), Rashed Uz Zaman (Bangladesh), and Zhenjiang Zhang (China). Also helpful were the insights provided by speakers at the 2003 and 2004 Fulbright American Studies Institutes on U.S. Foreign Policy, including especially Don Fowler (past Chair of the Democratic National Committee); Linda P. Brady (Dean of Liberal Arts, North Carolina State University); Dan Caldwell (Pepperdine University); Jerel Rosati, William P. Kreml, Janice Love, Peter Sederberg, Brad Gomez, and Hal French (all of the University of South Carolina); Paula L'Ecuyer (Iraqi desk, U.S. Department of State); Darren Van Tassel (Georgia State University); Patrick Garvey and Marisha Singh (U.S. Senate Committee Foreign Relations); U.S. Senator Fritz Hollings; Col. Levi Rushing Martin; Joel Rosenthal (President, Carnegie Council on Ethics and International Affairs); Gregory Treverton and Glenn Robinson (RAND Corporation, Santa Monica); Matt Bryza (U.S. National Security Council); Josh Wash and David Rudd (Democratic National Committee); Raphael Danzinger (American Israeli Public Affairs Committee); Mitchell Reiss (Policy Planning Office of the U.S. Department of State); Jo Husbands and Lois Peterson (National Academy of Sciences); and Harriet Fulbright.

Beyond the Wadsworth staff and their associates, we are pleased to acknowledge the enormous contribution made to the many revisions in word processing providing by Young-Hoon Song, as well as assistance provided by Maria Anastasiou, Byongok Han, Amanda Cunningham, Daniel Sabia, Dona Roy, Holli Buice, Linda Logan, Long Wang, Mary Schwartz, Min Ye, Polly Brown, Robert J. Palmer, Sallie Buice, and Ye "Kitty" Zheng.

Charles W. Kegley, Jr.
with
Eugene R. Wittkopf

ABOUT THE AUTHORS

CHARLES W. KEGLEY, JR., is the Pearce Professor of International Relations at the University of South Carolina. A graduate of the American University and Syracuse University, and a Pew Faculty Fellow at Harvard University, Kegley serves on the Board of Trustees of the Carnegie Council on Ethics and International Affairs and is a past president of the International Studies Association (1993–94). Kegley has held faculty appointments at Georgetown University, the University of Texas, Rutgers University, the People's University of China, and the Graduate Institute of International Studies, Geneva. Recently published among his four dozen books are *The New Global Terrorism* (2003); *Controversies in International Relations Theory* (1995); and, with Gregory A. Raymond, *The Imperiled Imperium: The Consequences of Post–9/11 American Foreign Policy at Home and Abroad* (2006), *The Global Future* (2005), *From War to Peace* (2002); *Exorcising the Ghost of Westphalia* (2002); *How Nations Make Peace* (1999); *A Multipolar Peace? Great-Power Politics in the Twenty-First Century* (1994); and *When Trust Breaks Down: Alliance Norms and World Politics* (1990). He has also published his primary research in many scholarly journals.

EUGENE R. WITTKOPF is the R. Downs Poindexter Distinguished Professor of Political Science at Louisiana State University. A graduate of Valparaiso and Syracuse Universities, Wittkopf has held appointments at the University of Florida and the University of North Carolina at Chapel Hill. Wittkopf is author of *Faces of Internationalism: Public Opinion and American Foreign Policy* (1990); coeditor of *The Future of American Foreign Policy* (4th edition, 2004); and *The Domestic Sources of American Foreign Policy: Insights and Evidence* (2004). He has also published extensively in many scholarly journals. In 1997, he received the highest award given by Louisiana State University in recognition of faculty contributions to research and scholarship when he was awarded the LSU Distinguished Research Master of Arts, Humanities, and Social Sciences. Wittkopf served as coauthor of the first six editions of *World Politics*. His professional contributions to the development of this book are appreciatively acknowledged.

Kegley and Wittkopf have both been recipients of the Distinguished Scholar Award in Foreign Policy of the International Studies Association. Together, Kegley and Wittkopf have coauthored and edited a number of leading texts, including *American Foreign Policy: Pattern and Process* (6th edition, 2003, with James A. Scott); *The Global Agenda* (6th edition, 2001); *The Future of American Foreign Policy* (1992); *The Nuclear Reader* (2nd edition, 1989); and *The Domestic Sources of American Foreign Policy* (1988).

PART I
TREND AND TRANSFORMATION IN WORLD POLITICS

The world has moved into a new century and new millennium. How are we to think about the global future? Part I introduces you to the study of world politics in a period of rapid change. It opens a window on the many trends that are unfolding, some of them in contrary directions, whose combined force may transform many aspects of international relations that, only recently, we expected to persist.

Obstacles exist to understanding world politics accurately. Chapter 1 explains how our perceptions of global realities can lead to distortions and provides a framework for getting beyond these barriers. Within this framework, major influences on ever-changing international conditions are divided into three categories—the individual, the state, and the global "levels of analysis." Chapter 2 introduces the major theories that scholars have developed over the years to help policymakers and citizens better describe, explain, and predict the evolving nature of international relations. Such theories are important, because they are the tools that can help us construct more accurate images of the complexity of world politics and better interpret emerging trends and transformations.

CHAPTER 1

Exploring Twenty-First-Century World Politics

TOPICS AND THEMES

- The challenge of investigating international affairs
- How perceptions influence images of reality
- Different levels of analysis: Individual, state, and the global system
- The book's approach: Actors, issues, and their interactions
- Facing the future: Key questions to confront

- **CONTROVERSY** SHOULD WE BELIEVE WHAT WE SEE? THE ORGANIZATION OF OBSERVATIONS AND PROJECTIONS OF GLOBAL REALITIES

Global warming is blamed for the blazing heat waves and droughts that have swept the globe, like that pictured here in Allahabud, India, in August 2002. Arresting global warming is a global issue.

This could prove to be a most interesting world, one that recalls the old Chinese curse, "may you live in interesting times."

—ROBERT JERVIS, political scientist, 2003

The world is at a critical juncture, and so are you. . . . Go ahead and make your plans . . . and don't stop learning. But be open to the detours that lead to new discoveries.

—KOFI ANNAN, UN secretary general, 2003

Picture yourself returning home from a two-week vacation on an island where you had no access to the news. When you departed—March 1, 2004—you were haunted by memories of the horrifying events of September 11, 2001. On that dreadful day nearly thirty months earlier, terrorists instilled fear worldwide when they destroyed the Twin Towers of the World Trade Center in New York City and hit the Pentagon. On your departure, a sense of vulnerability still haunted you as you went through tight airport security under the anxious eyes of "homeland security" forces placed at airports to prevent future terrorist attempts. You wondered once anew how and why, in today's world, such an astonishingly terrible assault happened to create a transforming "date with history," arguably as momentous as the historical turning point when the surprise bombing of Pearl Harbor by the Japanese on December 7, 1941, drew the United States into World War II.

Your vacation allowed you to take a break from the realities of today's often frightening world. It permitted you to experience peace and quiet. Now, however, upon your return, you cannot help but to become curious about what happened while you were away. As you pick up the newspapers piled outside your door, headlines catch your eye. They tell you that many events occurred in the short time you were gone. For starters, headlines inform you that the continuing U.S. military occupation of Iraq is not going well, and that local opposition

3

has taken the lives of another eight U.S. soldiers, bringing the American death toll to 553 since the Iraq invasion began on March 20, 2003. Next, you read that President George W. Bush has repeated his pledge that the United States will pursue its global war on terror until complete victory is achieved. Then, in a hasty effort to catch up on the latest news of the day, you turn to CNN to learn from live television broadcasts what is happening now. The news is shocking. Terrorists struck Madrid three days earlier, in what was labeled Europe's "3/11," killing more than two hundred passengers commuting by train to work. Now you witness the sad spectacle of a million mourners marching in grief and anger as the dead were being buried, while Spain pushed on with a national election. Terror was back! British Prime Minister Tony Blair appears on the TV screen warning that more terrorism "is not a matter of if, but when." To prove his grim prediction and illustrate how quickly events occur, with Blair's words barely out of his mouth CNN announces in "breaking news" that eight bystanders have been killed in a double-suicide terrorist bombing in what was believed to have been a secure area in Israel. But there is more bad news about the spread of violence elsewhere. Civil war is now breaking out in another failed state. You hear that a *coup d'état* has driven Haitian President Jean-Bertrand Aristide into exile and that he is blaming the United States for engineering his downfall and for undermining democracy in the process. The broadcast also reports that a large contingent of American peacekeeping troops, along with members of the French, Canadian, and Chilean militaries, are being sent as an advance UN "multinational interim force" to "secure and stabilize the country, facilitate humanitarian aid, and establish law and order." The operation, you hear, is expected to take years. This report is next followed by coverage of the elections being staged in Russia, with President Vladimir Putin projected to win reelection, even though the broadcast notes that whereas Putin is personally popular in Russia, concerns were rising that his increasing repression of civil liberties could spell the death of true democratization. Then, there is news of still more violence. You learn that the semi-autonomous region of Tbilisi is attempting to break away from Georgia and that both the Georgian government and Russia are vowing to militarily intervene to squash the revolt.

Alarmed by this sequence of reports of serial killings, you turn off the TV and connect to the Internet to learn what has been happening in the financial world. The news for you is both good and bad, given your beliefs. You are heartened by China's announcement that its communist leaders have decided to give constitutional protection to citizens' private property—a huge step in cementing capitalism in that country. However, the sobering news is that the value of your country's currency, the U.S. dollar, has fallen rapidly against foreign currencies. The stock market has dropped dramatically because of the 3/11 terrorist tragedy in Madrid. Also, the U.S. trade deficit has reached a record $43 billion and is expected to rise further in part because the American Congress has just authorized a huge $2.4 trillion fiscal spending spree for the next year that will require the country to borrow at least $45 billion a month from abroad to cover the expense. Worse still, America is not alone, you discover. Argentina, on the verge of economic collapse, will be rescued for the time being by a hefty loan from the International Monetary Fund, and South Korea's economy is being badly shaken by the government's impeachment of President Roh. Finally, you are reminded that it is not just countries that are experiencing anxiety—the Internet cites a new UN report that informs you of the depth of human suffering throughout the world by documenting that hundreds of millions of people are forced to endure lives of such abject poverty that their misery defies comprehension. Welcome back to the real world! Vacations are designed to allow people to "vacate" or escape from everyday worries, but there is no real escape from the world's problems.

The scenario just described is not hypothetical. The events outlined above actually occurred on March 14, 2004, and in the days leading up to it. Undoubtedly, many individuals experienced fear and confusion during this turbulent period. But it is uncomfortably not so different from others. Putting this information about unfolding events together, you cannot help but be reminded that the world matters and that those changes in it affect your circumstances and future powerfully. The "news" you received is not really new, because it echoes many old stories from the past about the growing sea of turmoil sweeping contemporary world circumstances. Nevertheless, the temptation to wish that this depressing kind of chaotic world would just go away is overwhelming. If only the unstable world would stand still long enough for a sense of predictability and order to prevail. Alas, that does not appear likely. You cannot escape the world or control its turbulence, and you cannot single-handedly alter its character.

We are all a part of the world, and the world is an integral part of each of us. Hence, if we are to live adaptively amid the fierce winds of global change, we must face the challenge of discovering the dynamic properties of world politics. As Italian leader Giuseppe Mazzini counseled in 1848, "Great things are achieved by guessing the direction of one's century." Because every person is influenced increasingly by world events, all can benefit by investigating how the global system works and how the process of globalization is remaking this century's political and economic world. Only through learning how our own decisions and behavior contribute to the global condition, as well as those of powerful state governments and nonstate transnational actors, and how all people and groups in turn are heavily conditioned by changes in world politics, can we address what U.S. President Bill Clinton in 1993 defined as "the question of our time—whether we can make change our friend and not our enemy."

THE INVESTIGATIVE CHALLENGE

The American poet Walt Whitman wrote in 1888, "I say we had best look at our times and lands searchingly, like some physician diagnosing some deep disease." His advice is as timely today as it was then. We must search to find, diagnosing our perceptions of our times in order to best understand the political convulsions that confront the globe's more than 6 billion people every day. How can we anticipate what lies in store for the global future? At the beginning of the twenty-first century, we were engulfed in futurist talk. We were forced to use unfamiliar language—"new century," "new millennium," "new world"—and to speculate, What will the new world be like? Will it be different? As global conditions change, will the human victims and beneficiaries change in the process? Or will the patterns of the past endure?

To visualize our probable human destiny, we must look beyond the confines of our immediate time. It is important to appreciate the impact of previous ideas and events on current realities. As philosopher George Santayana cautioned,

"Those who cannot remember the past are condemned to repeat it." Similarly, British Prime Minister Winston Churchill advised, "The farther backward you look, the farther forward you are likely to see." Thus, to understand the dramatic changes in world politics today and to predict how they will shape the future, we will view them in the context of a long-term perspective that examines how the **global political system**—the patterns of interaction among international political actors—has changed and how some of its fundamental characteristics have resisted change. What do evolving diplomatic practices suggest about the current state of world politics? Are the episodic shock waves throughout the world clearing the way for a truly new twenty-first-century world order? Or will many of today's dramatic disruptions ultimately prove temporary, mere spikes on the seismograph of history?

■ **global political system**
the patterns of political interaction among actors in the global arena.

We invite you to explore these questions with us. To begin our search, let us explore how the differences between continuities, changes, and cycles in world history can help us orient our effort.

Every historical period is marked to some extent by change. Now, however, the pace of change seems more rapid and its consequences more profound than ever. To many observers, the cascade of events today implies a revolutionary restructuring of world politics. Numerous integrative trends point to that possibility. The countries of the world are drawing closer together in communications, ideas, and trade, as the integration of national economies has produced a globalized market, forming interdependent bonds among countries and cultures. Globalization is changing the way the world works. Likewise, disintegrative trends are shaking the globe and restructuring the way it operates. The proliferation of conventional and unconventional weapons, global environmental deterioration, and the resurgence of nationalism and ethnic conflict all portend a restructuring marked by disorder. The opposing forces of integration and disintegration point toward a **transformation** in world politics as extensive and important as the system-disrupting convulsions following World Wars I and II and the **Cold War** between the United States and the former Soviet Union and its allies.

■ **transformation**
a change in the characteristic pattern of interaction among the most active participants in world politics of such magnitude that it appears that one "global system" has replaced another.

■ **Cold War**
the forty-two-year rivalry between the United States and the Soviet Union, as well as their competing coalitions, between 1949 and 1991, which sought to contain each other's expansion through an arms race and win worldwide predominance for capitalism (U.S.) or communism (USSR).

Distinguishing meaningful transformations (true historical watersheds) from temporary changes (sudden changes that at first shock and scare everyone, but then, with the passage of time, fade in importance) is difficult. The moment of transformation from one system to another is not immediately obvious. Still, certain times are especially likely candidates. Major turning points in world politics usually have occurred at the ends of major wars, which typically disrupt or destroy preexisting international arrangements. In the twentieth century, World Wars I and II and the end of the Cold War stimulated fundamental breaks with the past and set in motion major transformations, providing countries with incentives to rethink seriously the premises underlying their interests, purposes, and priorities. Similarly, many concluded that the terrorist attacks on September 11, 2001 (9/11), produced a fundamental transformation in world affairs. Indeed, many felt that 9/11 changed everything, perhaps forever. In U.S. President George W. Bush's words, "Night fell on a different world," adding later, "This is our life now. . . . The battle's just begun."

Despite all that appears radically different since the 9/11 terrorist attacks in 2001 and 3/11 in 2004, much also remains the same in world politics. In fact, as political journalist Robert J. Samuelson noted on the first anniversary of 9/11, "What is most striking about the past year is how little has changed. . . . What no

Was September 11, 2001, a Transforming Event in International Politics? New global systems sometimes emerge, seemingly overnight, when a single, global-shattering event shatters previous conditions. The terrorist attack on the World Trade Center's Twin Towers on 9/11 is regarded by many as such a transformative date in world history, producing enormous changes in both the immediate target, the United States, and the world at large. Time will tell whether this act of terrorism and the following 3/11 terrorist attack in Madrid in 2004, will, as the years go by and the stark pain fades from memory, rank alongside the birth of the nuclear age on August 6, 1945, when the United States bombed Hiroshima, or the November 1989 dismantling of the Berlin Wall that signaled the end of the Cold War, as an event that truly changes the world.

one can know is whether September 11 marked the beginning of the end for global terrorism or whether these theoretical threats will someday materialize. . . . We are swamped with hypotheticals. Whether September 11 becomes a defining moment in history, or just an isolated tragedy depends on how all the hypotheticals turn out." Thus, entrenched continuities after 9/11 persist, to our amazement. We often expect the future to automatically bring changes and later are surprised to discover that certain patterns from the past have reappeared. Given the rapid changes that are occurring alongside enduring continuities, these are uncertain times, and it is dangerous to make firm predictions about the shape of the global future. Because some aspects of the future are likely to be characteristic of the past, it is risky to assume or assert that a major transformation in world politics is under way.

What criteria can help determine when an existing pattern of relationships gives way to a completely new global system? Following Stanley Hoffmann

(1961), we will proceed by assuming that we have a new international system when we have a new answer to one of three questions: (1) *What are the system's basic units?* (e.g., states or supranational institutions for global governance); (2) *What are the predominant foreign policy goals that these units seek with respect to one another?* (e.g., territorial conquest or material gain through trade); and (3) *What can these units do to one another with their military and economic capabilities?*

These criteria might lead us to conclude that a new system has now emerged. First, new trade partnerships have been forged in Europe, the cone of South America, North America, and the Pacific Rim, and these trading blocs may behave as unitary, or independent, nonstate actors as they compete with one another. Moreover, international organizations, such as the World Trade Organization and the European Union, now sometimes flex their political muscles in contests with individual states, and transnational religious movements, such as Islamic fundamentalism, challenge the **global system** itself—a system that international law still defines as composed primarily of **states** consisting of various nationality groups who perceive themselves as unified by a common language, culture, or ethnic identity. At the same time, some states have disintegrated into smaller units. In 1991, the former Soviet Union fragmented into fractious political entities searching for national identity and autonomy. Other national units could disintegrate as well—peacefully, like the former Czechoslovakia, or violently, like the former Yugoslavia.

Second, territorial conquest is no longer the predominant goal of most states' foreign policies. Instead, their emphasis has shifted from traditional military methods of exercising influence to economic means. Meanwhile, the ideological contest between democratic capitalism and the Marxist-Leninist communism of the Cold War era no longer comprises the primary cleavage in international politics, and a major new axis has yet to become clear, even though many conclude that 9/11 and 3/11 mark the beginning of a new age dominated by a global war between terrorists and those who resist them, and still others conclude that the rise of United States to the status of the globe's sole superpower marks a new age punctuated by other states' efforts to resist U.S. domination.

Third, the proliferation of weapons technology has profoundly altered the damage that enemies can inflict on one another. Great powers alone no longer control the world's most lethal weapons. Increasingly, however, the great powers' prosperity depends on economic circumstances throughout the globe, reducing their ability to engineer growth.

The profound changes in recent years of the types of actors (units), goals, and capabilities have dramatically altered the power ranking of states that define the structure of international politics. Still, the hierarchies themselves endure. The *economic hierarchy* that divides the rich from the poor, the *political hierarchy* that separates the rulers from the ruled, the *resource hierarchy* that makes some suppliers and others dependents, and the *military asymmetries* that pit the strong against the weak—all still shape the relations among states, as they have in the past. Similarly, the perpetuation of international **anarchy**, in the absence of institutions to govern the globe and continuing chronic national insecurity still encourage preparations for war and the use of force without international mandate. Thus change and continuity coexist, with both forces simultaneously shaping contemporary world politics.

■ **global system**
the predominant patterns of behaviors and beliefs that prevail internationally to define the major worldwide conditions that influence heavily human and national activities.

■ **state**
an independent, territorially defined community in the global system administered by a sovereign government.

■ **anarchy**
a condition in which the units in the global system are subjected to few if any overarching institutions to regulate their conduct.

The interaction of constancy and change makes it difficult to predict whether the future will bring a wholly new and different international system. What is clear is that this interaction will determine future relations among global actors. This, perhaps, explains why **cycles** so often appear to characterize world politics: Periodic sequences of events occur that resemble patterns in earlier periods. Because the emergent global system shares many characteristics with earlier periods, historically minded observers may experience déjà vu—the illusion of having already experienced something actually being experienced for the first time.

The challenge, then, is to observe unfolding global realities objectively in order to describe and explain them accurately, and hence to understand their future impact. This requires appreciating how our images of reality shape our expectations. It also requires a set of tools for analyzing the forces of constancy and change that affect our world. Thus, the remainder of this chapter will briefly examine the role that images of reality play in our understanding of world politics, and then will identify some of the key questions that will be explored. Chapter 2 will examine the theoretical perspectives emphasized in this book to interpret trends and transformations in world politics.

■ **cycles**
the periodic reemergence of conditions similar to those that existed previously.

HOW PERCEPTIONS INFLUENCE IMAGES OF REALITY

We already hold mental images of world politics, although we may not have attempted to explicitly define our perceptions about the world in our subconscious. But whatever our level of self-awareness, our images perform the same function: they simplify "reality" by exaggerating some features of the real world while ignoring others. Thus we live in a world defined by our expectations and images.

These mental pictures, or perceptions, are inevitably distortions, as they cannot fully capture the complexity and configurations of even physical objects, such as the globe itself (see Controversy: Should We Believe What We See?). Thus many of our images of the world's political realities may be built on illusions and misconceptions. Even images that are now accurate can easily become outdated if we fail to recognize changes in the world. Indeed, the world's future will be determined not only by changes in the "objective" facts of world politics but also by the meaning that people ascribe to those facts, the assumptions on which they base their interpretations, and the actions that flow from these assumptions and interpretations—however accurate or inaccurate they might be.

The Nature and Sources of Images

The effort to simplify one's view of the world is inevitable and even necessary. Just as cartographers' projections simplify complex geophysical space so we can better understand the world, each of us inevitably creates a "mental map"—a habitual way of organizing information—to make sense of a confusing abundance of information. Although mental maps are neither inherently right nor wrong, they are important because we tend to react according to the way the world appears to us rather than the way it is. How we *view* the world (not what it is really like) determines our attitudes, our beliefs, and our behavior. Political

CONTROVERSY

SHOULD WE BELIEVE WHAT WE SEE?
The Organization of Observations and Projections of Global Realities

Many people assume that "seeing is believing" without questioning whether the ways they have organized their perceptions are accurate. But is there more to seeing than meets the eye? To view and interpret reality, do we perceive in ways that may produce a biased distortion? Students of perceptual psychology think so. They maintain that seeing is not a strictly passive act: what we observe is partially influenced by our preexisting values and expectations (and by the visual habits reinforced by the constructions society has inculcated in us about how to view objects). Students of perception argue that "what you see is what you get" and that two observers looking at the same object might easily see different realities. To illustrate this, perceptual psychologists are fond of displaying the drawing below, which, depending on how the viewer looks at it, can be seen as either a goblet or two faces opposing each other. Both images are possible.

This principle has great importance for investigation of international relations, where, depending on one's perspective, people can vary greatly on how they will view international events, actors, and issues. From competing images often arise intense disagreements.

To appreciate the kind of controversies that can result from the fact that different people can easily see different realities when they look at the same thing from different perspectives, consider something as basic as viewing objectively the location and size of the continents in the world. There exists a long-standing controversy among cartographers about the "right" way to map the globe, that is, how to make an accurate projection. The accuracy of their rival maps matter politically because they shape how people view what is important. All maps of the globe are distorted, because it is impossible to perfectly represent the three-dimensional globe on a two-dimensional piece of paper. The difficulty cartographers face can be appreciated by trying to flatten an orange peel. You can only flatten it by separating pieces of the peel that were joined when it was spherical. Cartographers who try to flatten the globe on paper, without "ripping it" into separate pieces, face the same problem. Although there are a variety of ways to represent the three-dimensional object on paper, all of them involve some kind of distortion. Thus cartographers must choose among the imperfect ways of representing the globe by selecting those aspects of the world's geography they consider most important to describe accurately, while making adjustments to other parts.

Cartographers' ideas of what is most important in world geography have varied according to their own global perspectives. These three maps (Maps 1.1, 1.2, and 1.3) depict the distribution of the Earth's land surfaces and territory, but each portrays a different image. Each is a model of reality, an abstraction that highlights some features of the globe while ignoring others. In examining these three ways of viewing and interpreting the globe, evaluate which projection you think is best. Which features of global reality are most worthy of emphasizing to capture an accurate picture? What does your answer reveal about your values and view of the world?

MAP 1.1
Mercator Projection

This Mercator projection, named for the Flemish cartographer Gerard Mercator, was popular in sixteenth-century Europe and presents a classic Eurocentric view of the world. It mapped the Earth without distorting direction, making it useful for navigators. However, distances were deceptive, placing Europe at the center of the world and exaggerating the continent's importance relative to other landmasses. Europe appears larger than South America, which is twice Europe's size, and two-thirds of the map is used to represent the northern half of the world and only one-third the southern half. Because lines of longitude were represented as parallel rather than convergent, this projection also greatly exaggerates the size of Greenland and Antarctica.

MAP 1.2
Peter's Projection

In the Peter's projection, each landmass appears in correct proportion in relation to all others, but it distorts the shape and position of the Earth's landmasses. In contrast with most geographic representations, it draws attention to the less-developed countries of the Global South, where more than three-quarters of the world's population lives today.

MAP 1.3
Orthographic Projection

The orthographic projection, centering on the mid-Atlantic, conveys some sense of the curvature of the Earth by using rounded edges. The sizes and shapes of continents toward the outer edges of the circle are distorted to give a sense of spherical perspective.

Online maps with critical thinking questions

leaders, too, are captives of this tendency. As Richard Ned Lebow (1981) warns, "Policymakers are prone to distort reality in accord with their needs even in situations that appear . . . relatively unambiguous."

Most of us—policymakers included—look for information that reinforces our preexisting beliefs about the world, assimilate new data into familiar images, mistakenly equate what we believe with what we know, and deny information that contradicts our expectations. We process information using **schematic reasoning;** that is, we rely on learned ways of psychologically perceiving new information and we interpret it in light of our memories (Rosenberg 1988). We use information shortcuts both to make political judgments and to help orient our attitudes and opinions toward specific events and policy issues. A schema thus aids in the organization of information and shapes our perceptions of the world.

We assemble and organize information about the world to help us simplify it. This is necessary "to cope with an extraordinarily confusing world by structuring views about specific foreign policies according to [our] more general and abstract beliefs" (Hurwitz and Peffley 1987). Our preexisting values and beliefs encourage us to accept some images as accurate while rejecting from consciousness others that are incongruent with our prior beliefs, a psychological conflict known as **cognitive dissonance** (see Festinger 1957). The mind selects, screens, and filters what it perceives. Thus our view of world politics depends not only on what happens in the world but also on how we interpret and internalize those events; **constructivism** informs us that our mental maps inevitably help to shape our attitudes about, and images of, global issues. Several factors influence our perceptions of international relations:

- our psychological needs, drives, and dispositions (e.g., trust or mistrust), which are ingrained in our personalities as a result of early childhood experiences
- our general views of international affairs (e.g., tolerance or fear of cultural diversity) as filtered through the socialization or learning we receive as children
- the images of international realities advanced by the most popular and powerful groups, comprised of leaders and scholars throughout the world, which present core ideas for discussion that offer a compelling, socially constructed shared worldview about the meaning and nature of international life
- our images of world history as shaped by the teachers and the books to which we are exposed
- opinions about world affairs expressed by our frequent associates, such as close friends
- attitudes stated by policymakers, political pundits, and others whose expertise we respect
- the positions we occupy and the various **roles** we perform (student, parent, bureaucrat, policymaker, diplomat, etc.)

Tolerance of ambiguity and receptivity to new ways of organizing thinking vary among individuals and personality types. Some people are receptive to diversity and therefore better able than others to revise perceptual habits to accommodate new realities. Nevertheless, to some extent, we are all prisoners of

■ **schematic reasoning**
the process of reasoning by which new information is interpreted according to a memory structure, a *schema*, that contains a network of generic scripts, metaphors, and simplified characterizations of observed objects and phenomena.

■ **cognitive dissonance**
the general psychological tendency to deny discrepancies between one's preexisting beliefs (cognitions) and new information.

■ **constructivism**
a scholarly approach to inquiry emphasizing the importance of agents (people and groups) and the shared meanings they construct to define their identities, interests, and institutions—understandings that influence their international behavior.

■ **role**
the position a person holds that has behavior-shaping expectations about how each role is to be performed.

the perceptual predispositions that have shaped us and that in turn shape our attitudes, beliefs, and images of world politics. This is why political **ideologies** tend to develop and to attract adherents, who join groups to express their common beliefs.

The Role of Images in World Politics

We must be careful not to assume automatically that what applies to individuals applies to entire countries, and we should not equate the beliefs of leaders, such as heads of states, with the beliefs of the people under their authority. Still, leaders have extraordinary influence, and leaders' images of historical circumstances often predispose them to behave in particular ways toward others, regardless of "objective" facts. For instance, the loss of 26 million Soviet lives in the "Great Patriotic War" (as the Russians refer to World War II) created an exaggerated fear of foreign invasion, which caused a generation of Soviet policymakers to perceive U.S. defensive moves with considerable suspicion and often alarm. Similarly, the founders of the United States viewed eighteenth-century European power politics as corrupt, contributing to two seemingly contradictory tendencies later evident in U.S. foreign policy: (1) America's isolationist impulse (its disposition to withdraw from world affairs), and (2) its determination to reform the world in its own image. The former led the country to reject membership in the League of Nations after World War I; the latter gave rise to the U.S. globalist foreign policy since World War II, which committed the country to active involvement nearly everywhere on nearly every issue. Most Americans, thinking of their country as virtuous, have difficulty understanding why others sometimes regard such far-reaching international activism as arrogant or threatening; they see in active U.S. interventionism only good intentions. As President Jimmy Carter once lamented, "The hardest thing for Americans to understand is that they are not better than other people."

Because leaders and citizens are prone to ignore or reinterpret information that runs counter to their beliefs and values, mutual misperceptions often fuel discord in world politics, especially when relations between countries are hostile. Distrust and suspicion arise as conflicting parties view each other in the same negative light—that is, as **mirror images** develop. This occurred in Moscow and Washington during the Cold War. Mirror-imaging is a property of nearly all **enduring rivalries**—long-lasting contests between opposing groups, such as Christianity against Islam during the Crusades, and Israel and Palestine, and the United States and Al Qaeda today, where both sides demonize the image of their adversary while perceiving themselves as virtuous. Self-righteousness often leads one party to view its own actions as constructive but its adversary's responses as negative and hostile. When this occurs, conflict resolution is extraordinarily difficult, as the Cold War and the recurrent ethnic conflicts and acts of global terrorism illustrate. Thus fostering peace is not simply a matter of expanding trade and other forms of transnational contact, or even of bringing political leaders together in international summits. Rather, it is a matter of changing deeply entrenched beliefs.

Although our constructed images of world politics are resistant to change, change is possible. Overcoming old thinking habits sometimes occurs when we experience punishment or discomfort as a result of clinging to false assumptions. As Benjamin Franklin once observed, "The things that hurt, instruct."

■ **ideology**
a set of core philosophical principles that a group of leaders and citizens collectively holds about politics, the interests of political actors, and the ways people ought to ethically behave.

■ **mirror images**
the tendency of states and people in competitive interaction to perceive each other similarly—to see others the same hostile way others see them.

■**enduring rivalries**
prolonged competition fueled by deep seated mutual hatred that leads opposed actors to feud and fight over a long time without resolution of their conflict.

Dramatic events in particular can alter international images, sometimes drastically. The Vietnam War caused many Americans to adjust their previous images about the use of force in contemporary world politics. The defeat of the Third Reich and revelations of Nazi atrocities committed before and during World War II caused the German people to confront their past as they prepared for a democratic future imposed by the victorious allies. The use of atomic bombs against Japan in the waning days of World War II caused many to confront the horrors of modern warfare and the immorality of weapons of mass destruction. More recently, the unexpected collapse of communist rule in the Soviet Union and Eastern Europe prompted policymakers and political commentators alike to reexamine their assumptions about foreign policy priorities in a new, post–Cold War system. Often such jolting experiences encourage us to construct new mental maps, perceptual filters, and criteria through which we may interpret later events and define situations.

As we shape and reshape our images of world politics and its future, we need to think critically about the foundations on which our perceptions rest. Are they accurate? Are they informed? Might they be adjusted to gain greater understanding and empathy? Rethinking our images is one of the major challenges we face in confronting contemporary world politics. Can we avoid prejudice—prejudging what we see based on misguided opinions, like a person with his or her nose pressed against the mirror trying to see their own body? Rethinking our images is one of the major challenges we face in confronting contemporary world politics.

BREAKING THE GLOBAL PUZZLE INTO PARTS: INTERPRETING AT DIFFERENT LEVELS OF ANALYSIS

To predict which forces will dominate the future, we also must recognize that many forces are operating at the same time. No trend or trouble stands alone; all interact simultaneously. The future is influenced by many determinants, each connected to the rest in a complex web of linkages. Collectively, these may produce stability by limiting the impact of any single disruptive force. If interacting forces converge, however, their combined effects can accelerate the pace of change in world politics, moving it in directions not possible otherwise.

Many international relations scholars agree that world politics can best be understood by first separating the multiple pieces of the puzzle into different categories, or levels, for analytic purposes. Most conventionally, investigators focus on one (or more) of *three* levels. Known as **levels of analysis,** this classification distinguishes: (1) individuals, (2) states as global actors, and (3) the entire global system.

The **individual level of analysis** refers to the personal characteristics of humans, including those responsible for making important decisions on behalf of state and nonstate actors, as well as ordinary citizens whose behavior has important political consequences. Here, for example, we may properly locate the impact of individuals' perceptions on their political attitudes, beliefs, and behavior, and explore the question of why each person is a crucial part of the

■ **levels of analysis**
the different aspects of and agents in international affairs that may be stressed in interpreting and explaining global phenomena, depending on whether the analyst chooses to focus on "wholes" (the complete global system and large collectivities) or on "parts" (individual states or people).

■ **individual level of analysis**
an analytical approach that emphasizes the psychological and perceptual variables motivating people, such as those who make foreign policy decisions on behalf of states and other global actors.

Globalization's Seeds of Change? At a time in world history rife with collapsing failed states, a worldwide war to combat terrorism, and ethnic wars within states and by state governments against minorities living within their national borders, many have pinned their hopes for future peace and prosperity on the effects of "globalization"—the expansion of international trade and the integration of the global economy. That aspiration and expectation is captured by this photo showing two happy Chinese people celebrating in June 2002 China's new membership in the World Trade Organization (WTO), a symbol of and catalyst for globalization. Critics, of course, see the WTO as a sinister force breeding inequality and the loss of national identity.

global drama and why the study of world politics is relevant to our lives and future.

The **state level of analysis** consists of the authoritative decision-making units that govern states' foreign policy processes and the internal attributes of those states (e.g., their type of government, level of economic and military power, and number of nationality groups), which both shape and constrain leaders' foreign policy choices. The processes by which states make decisions regarding war and peace and their capabilities for carrying out those decisions, for instance, fall within the state level of analysis.

The **global level of analysis** refers to the interactions of states and nonstate actors on the global stage whose behaviors ultimately shape the international political system and the levels of conflict and cooperation that characterize world politics. The capacity of rich states in the **Global North** to dictate the choices of poor states in the **Global South** falls properly within the global level of analysis. So does the capacity (or incapacity) of the UN to maintain peace.

Examples abound of the diverse ways in which global trends and issues are the product of influences at each level of analysis. Protectionist trade policies by an importing country increase the costs to consumers of clothing and cars and reduce the standard of living of citizens in the manufacturing states. Such policies are initiated by a *state* government (national level) but diminish the quality of life of *people* living both within the protectionist country and those living

■ **state level of analysis**
an analytical approach that emphasizes how the internal attributes of states influence their foreign policy behaviors.

■ **global level of analysis**
analyses that emphasize the impact of worldwide conditions on foreign policy behavior and human welfare.

■ **Global North**
a term used to refer to the world's wealthy, industrialized countries located primarily in the Northern Hemisphere.

■ **Global South**
a term now often used instead of "Third World" to designate the less-developed countries located primarily in the Southern Hemisphere.

abroad (individual level) and reduce the level of *global* trade while threatening to precipitate retaliatory trade wars. Of course, for some developments and issues, factors and forces emanating primarily from one or two particular levels provide more analytical leverage than do those from the other level(s). Accordingly, as we confront specific global issues in subsequent chapters, we will emphasize those levels of analysis that provide the most informative lens for viewing them. In the next section, we outline the path to discovery that *World Politics* will pursue.

THE BOOK'S APPROACH: ACTORS, ISSUES, AND THEIR INTERACTIONS

In part because world politics is complex and our images of it are often discordant, scholars differ in their approaches to understanding the contemporary world. In this book, we adopt a multilevel, multi-issue perspective that frames the investigation by looking at: (1) the characteristics, capabilities, and interests of the principal "actors" in world politics (states and various nonstate participants in international affairs); (2) the principal welfare and security issues—the key issues—on the **global agenda;** and (3) the patterns of cooperation and contention that influence the interactions between and among actors and issues. As we probe these interactions, we will discover why **politics**—the exercise of influence to affect the distribution of particular values, such as power, prestige, or wealth—is the most pervasive and controversial aspect of international affairs.

A multilevel, multi-issue perspective is useful not only because it takes into account the interaction of constancy and change in world affairs but also because it avoids dwelling on any particular events, countries, individuals, or transitory phenomena whose long-term significance is likely to diminish. Instead, the perspective seeks to identify behaviors that cohere into general global patterns—trends and transformations that measurably affect global living conditions. To portray contemporary global circumstances, we explore world politics by placing particular events into a larger, long-term theoretical context, providing the conceptual tools and theories that will enable us to interpret subsequent developments.

Our journey into the dynamics of world politics begins in Chapter 2 with an overview of the major realist and liberal theoretical traditions that scholars and leaders use most to interpret world politics, as well as interpretations informed by constructivism that give us a theoretical account of how both realism and liberalism are socially constructed sets of assumptions about how best to view world politics. This provides the intellectual background for the description, explanation, and prediction of the issues and developments that are treated in the remaining chapters.

Chapter 3 begins the analysis of actors, issues, and their interactions with a close examination of foreign policy decision-making processes *within* states, which remain the principal actors in world politics. Chapter 3 also covers the individual level of analysis, as we consider the role of leaders in making foreign policy. But the bulk of the chapter addresses how other forces at the state or domestic level can constrain the impact of individuals.

We will then turn our attention to each of the types of actors in world politics and examine how their characteristics and capabilities affect their inter-

■ **global agenda**
the primary issues, problems, and controversies on which states and humanity concentrate their attention and to which they allocate resources.

■ **politics**
to Harold Lasswell, the study of "who gets what, when, how and why?"

ests and influence in the world. **Great powers** (those wealthy countries with the biggest militaries) are the focus of attention in Chapter 4. In Chapter 5, we incorporate into the picture the place of the weaker states, that is, the less-developed countries of the Global South, explaining how the fate of this group of states is shaped by their relations with great powers and with nonstate actors and international institutions active in world politics. Then, in Chapter 6, we extend the account to cover two groups of **nonstate actors** (intergovernmental organizations—IGOs—on the one hand and nongovernmental organizations—NGOs—such as transnational ethnopolitical movements, religions, and multinational corporations on the other). This coverage describes how these actors interact with states and increasingly challenge the supremacy of all states, including even the great powers, by either transcending or subverting states' sovereign control over their destinies. In Chapter 7, "Humanitarian Challenges and the Protection of Human Rights," we discuss the role of individuals in the advancement of human welfare and human development, so as to put people, and the individual level of analysis, into the equation of actors engaging in international activity (and sadly, sometimes as subjects and victims of the powerful state and nonstate organizations that often determine peoples' fate).

The next group of chapters properly falls within the global level of analysis. Here we shift attention to global issues and inquire into how the characteristics, capabilities, and interests of the principal actors in world politics affect interactions and outcomes of the principal welfare and security issues on the global agenda. Welfare issues—the so-called **low politics** of problems relating to economics, population, and the environment—are the subjects of Chapters 8 through 10, topics that have assumed center stage in discussions of world politics in the age of globalization. Next, in Chapters 11 through 14, we examine the so-called **high politics** of security issues—the threat of armed conflicts through war and terrorism that traditionally have commanded primary attention on the global agenda, as well as the major approaches to the prevention of war and the preservation of peace. In the final chapter, Chapter 15, we offer contending perspectives about the probable shape of the global future.

■ **great powers**
the most powerful countries, militarily and economically, in the global system.

■ **nonstate actors**
all transnationally active groups other than states, such as organizations whose members are states, and nongovernmental organizations whose members are individuals and private groups from more than one state.

■ **low politics**
a category of global issues related to the economic, social, demographic, and environmental relations between governments and people.

■ **high politics**
issues related to the military, security, and political relations of states.

FACING THE FUTURE: KEY QUESTIONS TO CONFRONT AT THE DAWN OF THE NEW MILLENNIUM

Chapter 15 concludes our inquiry into the trends and transformations comprising contemporary world politics. It draws on the ideas and information presented in earlier chapters in order to address ten questions on the global issues that will dominate political discourse during the next decade. We anticipate those questions here by posing several that will also inform our inquiry in the chapters that follow.

Are States Obsolete?

The territorial state has been the primary actor in world politics for nearly four centuries. Resurgent nationalism and civil warfare throughout the world attest to the continuing quest by national independence movements for self-

■ **state sovereignty**
under international law, the status of states as equals in that, within their territory, a state's government is subject to no higher external authority.

governance and statehood, because the principal motive of most nationalistic separatist movements is to become a sovereign independent state—to achieve **state sovereignty.** The disintegration of failed states and the creation of new members of the international community in recent years account for the expansion of the number of UN member states from 166 in 1991 to 191 in 2005 following the admission of Switzerland and East Timor. If today's fragile failed states break into even smaller separate states, with various nationalities within them gaining independence and becoming sovereign states, the UN could have 400 to 500 members in the twenty-first century. Some estimate that the number of independent states in the global system could grow from 210 in 2005 to more than 800 by the year 2025. Others wonder if states will fade from the global scene in the twenty-first century, with globally engaged "citistates" assuming their place by the year 2100 as the organizing principle for world affairs (Peirce 2000).

In some respects, the territorial state is flourishing because it is still needed to provide military security, give people identity, raise taxes, provide safety nets for the needy, and protect the environment. At the same time some states are failing to adequately meet such traditional goals as providing for the poor, generating economic growth, preventing pollution, maintaining domestic stability, or countering terrorism. In fact, many have proclaimed "the end" of state sovereignty and its supreme authority in the face of growing challenges from home and abroad. To them, "The one trend that is sure to dominate the coming . . . quarter-century is the decline of the power of the state" (Zakaria 1999) because "a wide variety of forces has made it increasingly difficult for any state to wield power over its people and address issues it once considered its sole prerogative" (Stanley Foundation 1993).

"While states may not be about to exit from the political stage, and while they may even continue to occupy center stage, they do seem likely to become vulnerable and impotent" (Rosenau 1995). The question to be confronted is if "even where sovereignty still appears intact, states [can any] longer . . . retain sole command of what transpires within their own territorial boundaries. . . . The notion of the nation-state as a self-governing, autonomous unit appears to be more a normative claim than a descriptive statement" (Held et al. 1999, 8–9). As global trends put pressure for the transformation of world politics, the question is whether the state can cope with the challenges it now faces. Auguste Comte, a nineteenth-century French political philosopher, argued that societies create institutions to address problems and meet human needs. When these institutions are no longer able to perform these functions, they disappear. Today, as the managerial capabilities of states fail to inspire confidence, we must ask if states have a future.

■ **globalization**
the integration of states through increasing contact, communication, and trade, creating a holistic, single global system in which the process of change increasingly binds people together in a common fate.

■ **interdependence**
when the behavior of international actors greatly affects others with whom they have contact, and the parties to the exchange become mutually sensitive and vulnerable to the others' actions.

Is Globalization a Cure or a Curse?

Globalization has become a popular shorthand term to describe in general the internationalization and integration of the global community into a single society without barriers and national boundaries. Most observers would see globalization as "the increasing scale and importance of exchanges of people, products, services, capital, and ideas across international borders" (Auguste 1999). In addition, globalization is often seen as the culmination of what a quarter of a century ago was commonly called **interdependence**—the increasing degree since the mid-1970s to which the quality of life within states was rapidly and visibly becoming dependent on conditions in other states.

Interdependent globalization lies at the heart of the external challenges states now face. As the range of global issues has expanded and the integration of national economies has created a worldwide market and global culture, globalization in a borderless world has reduced states' ability to govern their affairs. Mutual vulnerabilities have reduced states' autonomy by curtailing their control of their own national fates, and globalization has erased the traditional distinctions between what is national and what is international, what is private and what is public, and what is domestic and what is foreign.

From an optimistic perspective, an awareness of the common destiny of all, alongside the declining ability of many sovereign states to cope with global problems through national means, will energize efforts to put aside interstate competition. According to this reasoning, conflict will recede as humanity begins to better recognize how little protection national borders and oceans provide it against the multiple challenges arising from the global revolution in travel, communications, and trade—shared problems that can only be managed through collective, multilateral cooperation. Globalization is creating a strong web of constraints on the foreign policy behavior of those plugged into the network of global transactions. Consequently, because globalization makes it imperative that states cooperate, we should welcome the continued tightening of interstate linkages.

From a more pessimistic point of view, the irreversible process of globalization will not lead to transnational collaboration, but to competition. Regardless of how compelling the need or how rewarding the benefits, increased contact and the trend toward an integrated single society of states will breed enmity, not amity. According to this view, globalization empowers advantaged states but constrains the prospects of weak states, producing new inequalities in a highly stratified global hierarchy in which the gap between the wealthy and the poor continues to widen. Because its benefits will not be distributed equally, globalization will likely generate conflict between winners and losers. Intertwined economies will sour relations more often than sweeten them. Under conditions of fierce competition, scarcity, and resurgent nationalism, the temptation may be irresistible to seek isolation from the assault of globalization on national identity and autonomy by creating barriers to trade and other transactions. The temptation to achieve political benefits by military force will also continue: "Interdependence promotes war as well as peace." (Waltz, 2000). Thus the tightening web of globalization foretells danger as well as opportunity.

What Will Be the Consequences of America's Superpower Status?

The United States sits at the apex of global power, without a rival. It is so powerful militarily, economically, and technologically that it reigns supreme, with resources so concentrated in its hands that it may possess a greater proportion of the world's wealth and military capability than any other previous **hegemon** or global leader in recorded history.

What this means is that the United States is now "unbound," "unburdened by the restraints that other world powers face" (Daalder and Lindsay 2003). America is a "colossus" (Ferguson 2004b), an "empire" (Bacevich 2003) re-

■ hegemon
a state so powerful that it has the capacity to control world politics and create rules for others to follow.

garded widely as an imperial or dominant power intent on preserving its superpower status and exerting influence seemingly at will over enemies and other states (Lifton 2004; Newhouse 2003).

This circumstance presents the United States with a critical choice: global domination or global leadership guided by principle (Brzezinski 2004). The decision is destined to be profound and consequential. It will not only determine how the United States will fare (Chomsky 2004) but also how the future fortunes (or misfortunes) of all humanity will unravel. America's monopoly of global power will color our collective global future, for better or for worse. How the United States harnesses its power for global purposes might well determine human destiny.

A question to be confronted and a controversy under debate is whether the United States can wisely use its power to advance both its own national interests as well as the welfare of the global community. Some people believe that the United States has embarked on an assertive and defiant independent course in international affairs that ignores the interests and concerns of the rest of the world and uses its power to unilaterally do whatever it pleases, with or without the support of the rest of the global community. Some critics, such as former policymaker in the Reagan administration Clyde Prestowitz (2003), even maintain that the United States has stepped outside the boundaries of international law by acting as a law unto itself and playing by its own rules, becoming in the process a "rogue nation." Others (e.g., Eland 2004) believe that America's overwhelming power has paradoxically left it weaker and more vulnerable to criticism and attack from overseas; according to this view, post–9/11 America is in the grip of fear, blinded by the terrorist threats it faces—an empire terrified and reactively self-destructive (Barber 2003). An extension of this perspective sees the United States "at war with [itself,] squandering its chance to build a better world" (Hirsh 2003).

What to do with, and about, American hegemony, presents dilemmas for the world, as seen in the wave of "anti-Americanism" (Revel 2004) that has swept the globe. "America unbound" (Daalder and Lindsay 2003) as a global empire ensures that whatever the American superpower colossus does internationally will affect powerfully every global issue and trend discussed in this book. This includes the possibility that in the long run, the end of the American era might result (Kupchan 2003) if the U.S. empire eventually disappears, as all previous empires eventually have in the past, partly because imperialism (Harvey 2004) generates the "sorrows of empire" (C. Johnson 2004). On the other hand, some believe that the United States will use its supreme might wisely and justly and not sacrifice its chance to build a better world, even though the American superpower is certain to "fascinate and infuriate the world" (Hertsgaard 2003).

The consequences of American preponderance and position atop the global pyramid of power thus for America could be huge. In America's hands global destiny will reside. This prevailing circumstance can shape the global future, and we will need to evaluate carefully the impact of America's future foreign policy choices on world politics and on America's ultimate place in the world.

Will Geo-Economics Supersede Geopolitics?

Throughout modern history, states have competed with one another militarily for position and prominence in the hierarchy of international power. For more than three centuries, world politics has been largely a record of preparing for, waging, and recovering from interstate war. Military might was equated with prestige and influence, and military conquest became the means to economic as well as political preeminence.

In the view of some, the battlefield in world politics has shifted to economic issues. National destinies will be determined by commercial competition, not military conquest. If issues of **geo-economics** (the distribution of wealth) become more important than conventional issues of **geopolitics** (the distribution of political and military power), will states' foreign policies also change? If wealth is converted into political muscle, nationalistic pride can give rise to competition and self-assertiveness. But economic interdependence and tight commercial relationships can also collapse into trade disputes and political rivalry. Nevertheless, the apparent shift of priorities to the economics of world politics is certain to alter the future distribution of global power. This shift is also likely to decrease the barriers of long-standing state borders.

What Constitutes Human Well-Being on an Ecologically Fragile Planet?

The worldwide quest for **human rights** requires people and governments to define and distinguish the fundamental values to which they are entitled. Throughout history, many have placed money and prosperity as their first priority. However, that value preference has been challenged, and the once-popular **limits-to-growth proposition**—the belief that the world cannot forever increase its productive capacity—has been replaced by the maxim of sustainability. Sustainability emphasizes "the growth of limits" in the global ecology (the total pattern of relations between organisms and their environment on Earth). Thus **sustainable development** means learning to live off Earth's interest without encroaching on its capital, in order that the planet can continue to provide the means to life that makes possible the pursuit of other values such as political freedom and religious principles.

Gross national product (GNP)—the total monetary value of goods and services produced in a state during a specified period, usually a year—is the common measure of states' relative economic well-being. It is an index of relative standards of living "closely bound up with human welfare. . . . Human welfare has dimensions other than the economic one. But it is widely held that the economic element is *very* important, and that the stronger the economy the greater the contribution to human welfare" (Daly and Cobb 1989). Indeed, many states' values are highly materialistic; money is perceived as a means to a secure and happy national existence—almost a human rights entitlement. To the inhabitants of most Global South less-developed countries, growth in GNP may mean more food, better housing, improved education, and an increased standard of living. However, affluent people in the Global North already enjoy these basic amenities; therefore, additional income usually allows them to satisfy comparatively trivial needs. When basic needs are fulfilled, conspicuous consumption and greed pose a danger to other values.

The global impact of population growth, as well as the continued quest for economic growth, are great. People consume, and the more people there are, the greater will be levels of consumption, depletion of the world's resources, and pollution—and the higher will be the toll on Earth's ecological system. Unbridled exploitation and consumption, in the ever-enduring quest for a higher standard of living that neglects the needs of future generations, will ultimately prove self-

■ **geo-economics**
the relationship between geography and the economic conditions and behavior of states that define their levels of production, trade, and consumption of goods and services.

■ **geopolitics**
the relationship between geography and politics and their consequences for states' national interests and relative power.

■ **human rights**
political rights and civil liberties recognized internationally as inalienable for individuals in all countries.

■ **limits-to-growth proposition**
the theory that Earth's capacity to support life has natural limits and that if important resources such as fresh water are depleted, many will perish.

■ **sustainable development**
economic growth that does not deplete the resources needed to maintain growth.

■ **gross national product (GNP)**
the total monetary value of goods and services produced in a state during a specified period.

Looking beyond Earth's Problems As we consider the future, we must ask ourselves whether technological innovation is inevitably the answer to our concerns. Although we are now able to send satellites into space and receive photos from planets we will never visit, we remain unable to eliminate hatred or aggression, or to achieve peace on earth.

destructive. As Mikhail Gorbachev, the last president of the Soviet Union, warned in 1988, we must halt "humanity's aggression against nature."

These ideas challenge the core values of Western civilization. Although sustainable development is an attractive goal, even it will be hard to realize. Sustainable economic welfare requires economic growth managed to limit natural resource depletion and environmental damage, while protecting people's rights of leisure and liberty. But can this kind of growth in a finite world proceed infinitely? How long can finite energy sources sustain uncontrolled consumption before automobiles sputter to a stop, industries grind to a halt, and lights go out? How many pollutants can the atmosphere absorb before irreparable environmental damage results? And how many people can a delicately balanced ecosystem support?

Understanding today's world requires a willingness to confront complexity. A true but complicated idea always has less chance of success than a simple but false one, the French political sociologist Alexis de Tocqueville cautioned in 1835. The challenge is difficult but the rewards warrant the effort. Humankind's ability to chart a more rewarding future is contingent on its ability to entertain complex ideas, to free itself from the sometimes paralyzing grip of the past, and to develop a questioning attitude about rival perspectives on international realities. On that hopeful yet introspective note, we begin our exploration of world politics in a new millennium.

KEY TERMS

global political system	mirror images	low politics
transformation	enduring rivalries	high politics
Cold War	levels of analysis	state sovereignty
global system	individual level of analysis	globalization
state	state level of analysis	interdependence
anarchy	global level of analysis	hegemon
cycles	Global North	geo-economics
schematic reasoning	Global South	geopolitics
cognitive dissonance	global agenda	human rights
constructivism	politics	limits-to-growth proposition
role	great powers	sustainable development
ideology	nonstate actors	gross national product (GNP)

SUGGESTED READING

Cornish, Edward. *Futuring: The Exploration of the Future*. Bethesda, Md.: World Future Society, 2004.

Dower, Nigel. *An Introduction to Global Citizenship*. New York: Columbia University Press, 2003.

Friedman, Thomas L. *Longitudes and Attitudes: Exploring the World after September 11*. New York: Farrar, Straus and Giroux, 2002.

Held, David, and Anthony McGrew, eds. *The Global Transformations Reader*, 2nd ed. Cambridge, U.K.: Polity Press/Blackwell, 2003.

Holsti, K. J. *Taming the Sovereigns: International Change in International Politics*. New York: Cambridge University Press, 2004.

Holsti, Ole R., Randolph M. Siverson, and Alexander L. George, eds. *Change in the International System*. Boulder, Colo.: Westview Press, 1980.

Kegley, Charles W., Jr., and Gregory A. Raymond *The Global Future*. Belmont, Calif: Wadsworth/Thomson Learning, 2005.

Kegley, Charles W., Jr., and Eugene R. Wittkopf, eds. *The Global Agenda: Issues and Perspectives*, 6th ed. New York: McGraw-Hill, 2001.

Krugman, Paul. *The Great Unraveling: Losing Our Way in the New Century*. New York: W. W. Norton, 2003.

Mazarr, Michael J. *Global Trends 2005: An Owner's Manual for the Next Decade*. London: Palgrave, 2001.

Rochester, J. Martin. *Between Two Epochs. What's Ahead for America, the World, and Global Politics in the 21st Century*. Upper Saddle River, N.J.: Prentice Hall, 2002.

Worldwatch Institute. *State of the World 2005*. New York: W. W. Norton, 2005.

WHERE ON THE WORLD WIDE WEB?

The World Wide Web's (WWW or web) features make it a powerful tool for providing access to global information sources. Using the web, you have instant access to documentation of important international events and agreements. Online information is current and often more complex than traditional sources. It quickly reflects the changing nature of international events. The web's global reach also permits users to locate opinions and perspectives from individuals across the United States and around the world. Many from the interna-

WHERE ON THE WORLD WIDE WEB? (continued)

tional community post their work on the web. Every day more sources become available online as individuals and institutions discover the wonders of the web.

The "Where on the World Wide Web?" sections that accompany each chapter provide you with interesting web links to explore. Through this investigation, you will become an active participant in the globalization of world information (see Chapter 8 for a discussion of the Internet's role in the globalization process). You will also gain a greater understanding of the concepts and terms discussed in *World Politics*.

As you begin to examine the trends and transformation of world politics, it is important that you understand the evolution of international events and keep abreast of the ever-changing world of international politics. The web links listed here will help you analyze current events.

American Journalism Review News Link
http://www.newslink.org/news.html

If you are interested in "going to the source" for your news, check out the *American Journalism Review*'s website. This site provides links to electronic newspapers from the United States and all over the world. Even campus papers are accessible through this site. You can read the news in a foreign language or try to find an English version. You may want to compare the same news story found in different newspapers around the world to see how different countries interpret the same event. Note that you can also access numerous radio and television broadcasts from this site.

CNN Interactive World News
http://www.cnn.com/WORLD/

Surf the website of the news organization that changed the way world news is reported by providing constant, minute-by-minute coverage of breaking news stories from around the world. CNN's World News main page is divided according to world region and reports the top stories in each area. During the course of a week, compare and contrast the content of the top stories from each region. Do you see a pattern in the type of news stories reported for each area? Also look for excerpts from international editions of *Time* magazine.

Foreign Affairs Online
http://www.people.virginia.edu/~rjb3v/rjb.html

This comprehensive website has been specifically designed to assist students and other individuals interested in international law, international relations, and U.S. foreign policy. It has links to general references, map resources, foreign states, the United Nations system, international organizations, international legal entities, think tanks, and media resources. It also has numerous links that discuss important aspects of the "digital divide." This is an important gateway to numerous international affairs resources on the web, so you may want to bookmark it.

National Geographic Society
http://www.nationalgeographic.com/maps/index.html

Publisher of the popular *National Geographic* magazine, the Society has created an impressive webtool called the MapMachine Online Atlas, one of the best interactive map sets on the web. Viewers can choose many different types of interactive maps. The Atlas Maps identify 191 independent states and provide a brief overview of each state. A quick click anywhere on the map gives key geographic, demographic, and economic data. As Chapter 1 explains, all maps focus on specific features while ignoring others, which leads to distortions. Compare the MapMachine maps with those found in the "Controversy: Should We Believe What We See? The Organization of Observations and Projections of Global Realities" in this chapter. Are the "dynamic" maps more accurate representations of reality? What distortions do they depict?

National Public Radio Online
http://www.npr.org/

As an alternative to reading the news, access National Public Radio Online. This site lets you listen to the top news stories and is updated every hour. You can also search the entire site for stories of particular interest from a variety of NPR radio shows. You may also want to take a minute to cruise the discussion area and give your thoughts on the headline stories. An added feature allows you to find the program schedule and streaming audio of your local NPR station.

New York Times on the Web
http://www.nytimes.com/

"All the news that's fit to print" is available online following a free registration. International news stories are easily accessed by clicking on the "International" news category. Keep in mind that the *Times* is a news source produced in the United States and may have American biases. While you read the news stories, think of ways in which they may have an "American slant."

University of Texas Library Online Map Collection
http://www.lib.utexas.edu/maps/index.html

If you've ever wondered exactly where Rwanda, Kosovo, Taiwan, or Pakistan is, this site can help. The Perry-Castañeda Library Map Collection of the University of Texas at Austin is an extensive collection of electronic maps. It features regional as well as state maps according to political and shaded relief criteria. When reading about a specific country in your textbook, make sure you can locate the country and identify its neighbors. This will give you a better understanding of international events.

INFOTRAC® COLLEGE EDITION

George, Alexander L. "Knowledge for Statecraft," *International Security* (Summer 1997).

Rothkopf, David J. "Cyberpolitik: The Changing Nature of Power in the Information Age," *Journal of International Affairs* (Spring 1998).

Selle, Robert R. "Yen for Adventure—and Geopolitics," *World and I* (April 2002).

Hoffmann, Stanley. "Clash of Globalizations," *Foreign Affairs* (July August 2002).

For more articles, enter:
"political science" in the Subject Guide, and then go to subdivision "analysis"
"political science research" in the Subject Guide
"international relations" in the Subject Guide, and then go to subdivision "analysis"

Go to http://politicalscience.wadsworth.com/kegley10 to access additional resources related to this chapter.

CHAPTER 2

THEORIES OF WORLD POLITICS

TOPICS AND THEMES

- Thinking theoretically to interpret global issues
- The liberal orientation
- The realist orientation
  The neorealist extension of realism
  The neoclassical extension of realism
- The neoliberal revision of liberalism
  Feminist theory
  Transnational interdependence
  International regimes
- Alternative theories
  Behavioralism
  Postmodern deconstructivism
- Theorizing about Theory: The Constructivist Conception

- **CONTROVERSY** CAN BEHAVIORAL SCIENCE ADVANCE THE STUDY OF INTERNATIONAL RELATIONS?
- **CONTROVERSY** NEOLIBERALISM VERSUS NEOREALISM: WHICH THEORY MAKES THE MOST REASONABLE ASSUMPTIONS?
- **CONTROVERSY** WHAT'S MISSING IN REALIST THEORIES OF INTERSTATE RELATIONS? THE FEMINIST CRITIQUE

One of the authors of your text, Charles Kegley, lectured in Poland in 2001 on the future of the theoretical study of world politics. His challenge was the same as yours—interpreting theoretically the meaning of a changing world for the global citizens facing the turbulent interconnectedness of the twenty-first century.

It's important that we take a hard, clear look . . . not at some simple world, either of universal goodwill or of universal hostility, but the complex, changing, and sometimes dangerous world that really exists.

—JIMMY CARTER, U.S. president, 1980

What is going on? This is the big question that international relations pundits, both academics and practitioners, have scrambled to answer, apparently with little success so far, concerning the reconfiguration of the international system after [2001].

—CORNELIA BJOLA, Canadian political scientist, 2003

Imagine yourself the newly elected president of the United States. You are scheduled to deliver the State of the Union address on your views of the current world situation and your foreign policy to deal with it. You face the task of both defining those aspects of international affairs most worthy of attention and explaining the reasons for their priority. To convince citizens these issues are important, you must present them as part of a larger picture of the world. Therefore, based on your perceptions of world politics, you must identify a general framework from which to consider global issues. You must, in short, think *theoretically*. At the same time, you must be careful, because your interpretations will necessarily depend on your assumptions about international realities that your citizens might find questionable. The effort to explain the world, predict new global problems, and sell others on a policy to deal with them is bound to result in controversy because even reasonable people often see realities differently.

When leaders face these kinds of intellectual challenges, they fortunately benefit from the existence of a body of theoretically informed ideas from which they can draw guidance. In this chapter we distinguish among the major theoretical perspectives policymakers and scholars use to interpret international relations. Since perceived "realities" of international affairs that these theories seek to explain influence the content of the theories, we will examine how perceived changes in underlying international conditions have shaped various theories. In addition, our review of contending political theories will identify the intellectual heritage that informs this book.

UNDERSTANDING WORLD POLITICS

Social scientists construct different theories to make international events understandable. Over time, a **paradigm,** or dominant way of looking at a particular subject, such as international relations, arises and influences judgments regarding which characteristics of the subject are most important, what puzzles need to be solved, and what analytic criteria should govern investigations. These paradigms or "fundamental assumptions scholars make about the world they are studying" (Vasquez 1997) tend eventually to be revised in order to explain new developments in world affairs. Thus, the theories that guide the thinking of policymakers and scholars in different historical circumstances tell us much about world politics itself.

- **paradigm**
derived from the Greek *paradeigma*, meaning an example, a model, or an essential pattern; a paradigm structures thoughts about an area of inquiry.

The Elusive Quest for Theory

Throughout history, paradigms have been revised or abandoned when their assertions have failed to mirror the prevailing patterns of international behavior. Major wars have been especially potent in bringing about significant changes in the theoretical interpretation of world affairs. "Every war . . . has been followed in due course by skeptical reassessments of supposedly sacred assumptions" (Schlesinger 1986) and has influenced "what ideas and values will predominate, thereby determining the ethos of succeeding ages" (Gilpin 1981). Three such system-transforming wars dominated the twentieth century: World War I, World War II, and the Cold War. Each has shaped policymakers' perceptions of world politics, and each has provided lessons critical to developing policy programs that can best preserve world order in the twenty-first century.

This chapter will concentrate on the two core perspectives that throughout history have most influenced thinking about international affairs and that continue to guide theorizing: liberalism and realism and their neoliberal and neorealist variants that have commanded a large following in the last two decades. In addition, we shall ground these two major theoretical traditions in the approach known as **constructivism.** Constructivism is used to explain how *all* paradigms depend for their acceptance on the extent to which theoreticians and other groups reach general agreement, or an *intersubjective consensus,* on the most meaningful ways to define in detail the core concepts of international affairs and communicate these shared images and understandings. Constructivism provides a lens for examining intellectual fads—that is, the formulations that make particular theoretical interpretations socially accepted and popular.

- **constructivism**
a liberal-realist theoretical approach advocated by Alexander Wendt that sees self-interested states as the key actors in world politics, whose actions are determined by the ways states socially "construct" and then respond to the meanings they give to world politics so that as their definitions change, cooperative practices can evolve.

The Evolution of Theoretical Inquiry

When the formal study of international relations began at the dawn of the twentieth century, the world abounded with optimism. Many people believed that peace and prosperity had taken root and would persist. The Hague peace conferences in 1899 and 1907 had inspired hope of controlling arms and sparing Europe another series of wars like those between 1848 and 1870. Moreover, numerous individuals—including the Scottish American industrialist Andrew Carnegie, who gave much of his fortune to the cause of world peace—assumed that as industrialization progressed and the costs and risks of war increased, the chance of protracted war among the great powers would decline dramatically (see also Angell 1910).

In those tranquil times, students of international relations studied history to glean insight on the events of the day. The study of international relations consisted mainly of commentary about personalities and events, past and present. Rarely did scholars seek to generalize theoretically about the lessons of history or about the principles or "laws" that might account for states' characteristic responses to similar stimuli or influences. Sir Halford Mackinder (1919) and Alfred Thayer Mahan (1890) were exceptions. Both sought to generate theoretical propositions pertaining to the influence of geographic factors on national power and international politics—efforts that laid the foundations for the study of political geography, which survives today as an important **geopolitical** approach to world politics (see S. Cohen 2003).

The large-scale death and destruction that World War I exacted from 1914 to 1918 destroyed the sense of security that had made the **current history approach** popular. This catastrophic war was a painful lesson that stimulated the search for knowledge to address contemporary policy problems in a theoretical context. However interesting descriptions of recent or past wars might be, they were of doubtful use to a world in search of ways to prevent wars of mass destruction. For those purposes, policymakers and scholars needed a **theory**—a statement attempting to account for general phenomena or patterns rather than explaining unique or individual circumstances—that could reliably predict war and instruct leaders on the best policies to prevent it.

LIBERALISM

World War I initiated a paradigmatic revolution in the study of international relations, in which several perspectives competed for attention. While the current history approach continued to claim some disciples in the waning days of World War I, after Russia's Bolshevik Revolution, Marxist-Leninist thought became increasingly influential, with its critique of capitalism's creation of inequality, class conflict, and imperialistic war. In the 1930s, with the rise of Adolf Hitler in Germany, national socialism (or fascism) also challenged conventional European thinking about world politics. Nazism, the German variant of national socialism, was particularly provocative. Not only did Nazism glorify the role of the state (as opposed to that of the individual) in political life, it also championed war as an instrument of national policy.

■ **geopolitics**
the relationship between geography and politics and its consequences for states' national interests and relative power.

■ **current history approach**
a focus on the description of contemporary and particular historical events rather than theoretical explanations to explain broader patterns of international relations.

■ **theory**
a set of hypotheses postulating the relationship between variables or conditions, advanced to describe, explain, or predict phenomena and make prescriptions about how positive changes ought to be engineered to realize particular goals and ethical principles.

Pioneers in the Liberal Quest for World Order A product of the Enlightenment, Scottish philosopher David Hume (left) tried to temper his realist concern that reason is a "slave of the passions" by embracing the liberal faith in wealth-generating free markets and free trade that could cohesively bind people together to create a peaceful civil society. Influenced by David Hume and Jean-Jacques Rousseau, Immanuel Kant (right) in *Perpetual Peace* (1795) helped to redefine modern liberal theory by advocating global (not state) citizenship, free trade, and a federation of democracies as a means to peace.

- **liberalism**
a paradigm predicted on the hope that the application of reason and universal ethics to international relations can lead to a more orderly, just, and cooperative world, and that international anarchy and war can be policed by institutional reforms that empower international organizations and laws.

- **politics**
to liberal idealists, the search for agreement about shared values to foster cooperation within the global community.

- **idealism**
post–World War I movement inspired by the liberal theoretical tradition which believed that the pursuit of ideals like world peace could change the world by reducing the disorder often exhibited in world politics.

The Liberal Worldview

Emerging as dominant, however, was a perspective known as **liberalism.** At the core of liberalism is an emphasis on the impact ideas have on behavior, the equality, dignity, and liberty of the individual, and the need to protect people from excessive state regulation. Liberalism views the individual as the seat of moral value and virtue and asserts that people should be treated as ends rather than means. It emphasizes ethical principles over the pursuit of power and institutions over capabilities as forces shaping interstate relations, and defines **politics** at the international level more as a struggle for consensus than a struggle for power and prestige.

Because advocates of liberalism were inspired by their interest in ideals, after World War I they are sometimes referred to as advocates of **idealism,** even though they were a diverse group within the larger liberal tradition. Post-World War I idealism, as argued by such scholars and policymakers as Alfred Zimmerman, Norman Angell, James T. Shotwell, and Woodrow Wilson, derived from ancient liberal philosophy and has been interpreted variously in different periods. These idealists drew their philosophy from such liberal thinkers as Immanuel Kant, Richard Cobden, Thomas Jefferson, James Madison, John Stuart Mill, John Locke, David Hume, Jean-Jacques Rousseau, and Adam Smith (see Doyle 1997, Howard 1978, and Zacher and Matthew 1995).

Collectively, post-World War I liberal idealism believed "the pen is mightier than the sword" and embraced a worldview that emphasized the power of ideas and ideals in controlling global destiny, based on the following beliefs:

1. Human nature possesses a "good" or altruistic drive that makes people capable of compassion and collaboration through reason and ethically inspired education.
2. The fundamental human concern for others' welfare makes progress possible.
3. Sinful or wicked human behavior, such as violence, is the product not just of flawed people but of evil institutions that encourage people to act selfishly and to harm others.
4. War and international anarchy are not inevitable and war's frequency can be reduced by strengthening the institutional arrangements that encourage its disappearance.
5. War is a global problem requiring collective or multilateral efforts, rather than independent, national, or unilateral efforts, to control it.
6. Reforms must be inspired by a compassionate ethical concern for the welfare and security of all people, and this humanitarian motive requires the inclusion of morality in statecraft guided by a primary concern for human rights and civil liberties.
7. International society must reorganize itself in order to eliminate the institutions that make war likely, and states must reform their political systems so that democratic governance and civil liberties within states can protect human rights and help pacify relations among states.

While not all liberal idealists subscribed to each of these tenets with equal conviction, they shared a moralistic, optimistic, and universalistic image of international affairs and believed it possible to replace competitive states with a global community regulated by institutions of global governance.

The Liberal Reform Program

Although liberal idealists after World War I differed significantly in their prescriptions for reforming the international political system (see Herz 1951), they generally fell into one of three groups. The first group advocated creating international institutions to replace the anarchical and war-prone balance-of-power system, characterized by coalitions of independent states formed to wage war or to defend a weaker coalition partner from attack. In place of this unregulated competitive system, idealists sought to create a new one based on **collective security.** This approach dealt with the problem of war by declaring any state's aggression an aggression against all who would act in concert to thwart the aggressor. The League of Nations was the institutional embodiment of collective security through international organization, reflecting simultaneously the liberal idealists' emphasis on international institutions and the possibility of international cooperation for global problem solving.

A second group emphasized the use of legal processes such as mediation and arbitration to settle disputes and avoid armed conflict. This facet of the idealists' policy prescriptions was illustrated by the creation in 1921 of the Permanent

■ **collective security**
a security regime agreed to by the great powers that sets rules for keeping peace, guided by the principle that an act of aggression by any state will be met by a collective response from the rest.

Court of International Justice to litigate interstate conflicts and by the ratification of the **Kellogg-Briand Pact** of 1928, which "outlawed" war as an instrument of national policy.

A third group followed the biblical injunction that because "those who live by the sword die by the sword," states should beat their swords into plowshares, and accordingly they sought disarmament as a means to ending war. This orientation was exemplified by efforts during the 1920s, such as those negotiated at the Washington and London naval conferences, to secure arms control and disarmament agreements.

Several corollary ideas gave definition to the liberals' emphasis on encouraging global cooperation through international institutions, law, and disarmament. These included:

- the need to substitute attitudes that stressed the unity of humankind for those that stressed parochial national loyalties to independent sovereign states
- the importance of individuals—their essential dignity and fundamental equality throughout the course of history, and the corollary need to place the protection and promotion of human rights and freedom ahead of national interests and state autonomy
- the use of the power of ideas through education to arouse world public opinion against warfare
- the promotion of free international trade in place of states' economic competition
- the replacement of secret diplomacy by a system of "open covenants, openly arrived at"
- the termination of interlocking bilateral alliances and the power balances they sought to achieve

In seeking a more peaceful world, some liberal reformers promoted the ideal of **self-determination**—giving nationalities the right through voting to become independent **states**—as a means to redraw the globe's political geography to make the borders of each **nation** conform to ethnic groupings. Related to this was U.S. President Woodrow Wilson's call for democratic domestic institutions. "Making the world safe for democracy," this liberal believed, would also make it secure and free from war, because democracies historically have almost never waged war against one another. Wilson's celebrated Fourteen Points speech to Congress in 1918 proposed the creation of the League of Nations and, with it, the pursuit of other liberal idealists' aims such as free trade to create wealth and a global harmony of states' interests. This speech, perhaps better than any other statement, expressed the idealistic sentiments of the liberal worldview and program.

Although a tone of idealism dominated policy rhetoric and academic discussions during the interwar period, with the exception of the League of Nations and the precedent-setting Washington Naval Disarmament Treaties, little of the liberal reform program was ever seriously attempted, and even less of it was achieved. When the winds of international change again shifted and the Axis powers pursued world conquest, enthusiasm for liberal idealism as a worldview receded.

■ **Kellogg-Briand Pact**
a multilateral treaty negotiated in 1928 that outlawed war as a method for settling interstate conflicts.

■ **self-determination**
the principle that the global community is obligated to give nationalities their own governments.

■ **state**
a legal entity with a permanent population, a well-defined territory, and a government capable of managing sovereign authority over the nations or nationality groups living within its legal borders.

■ **nation**
a collection of people who, on the basis of ethnic, linguistic, or cultural affinity, perceive themselves to be members of the same group.

REALISM

The drive for global conquest that led to World War II provoked strong criticism of the liberal idealist paradigm. Critics blamed the outbreak of war on what they believed to be the so-called idealists' naive legalistic and moralistic assumptions about the possibility of peace and progress through human aspiration, and alleged that idealists were utopians who neglected the harsh realities of power politics and humans' innate compulsion to put their personal welfare ahead of the welfare of others (Carr 1939). The lessons the critics drew from the period between World War I and II led many to construct a revised set of perceptions and beliefs.

Advocates of the new, ascendant paradigm known as **realism,** or **realpolitik** as a specific philosophy, emerged to frame an intellectual movement whose message reads like the antithesis of idealism. Among the principal prophets of this new worldview were E. H. Carr (1939), George F. Kennan (1951, 1954), Hans J. Morgenthau (1948), Reinhold Niebuhr (1947), and Kenneth W. Thompson (1960). Realism deserves careful scrutiny because its socially constructed worldview continues to guide much thought about world politics.

The Realist Worldview

As a political theory, realism can trace its intellectual roots to the ancient Greek historian Thucydides and his account of the Peloponnesian Wars between Athens and Sparta (431–404 B.C.E.), the writings of Kautilya (minister to the Maurya emperor of India more than two thousand years ago), and especially the sixteenth-century political thought of the Italian theorist Niccolò Machiavelli and the seventeenth-century English philosopher Thomas Hobbes.

Realism, as applied to contemporary world politics, views the state, which should answer to no higher political authority, as the most important actor on the world stage. Moreover, conflicts of interests among states are assumed to be inevitable. Realism also emphasizes the ways in which the anarchical nature of international politics dictate the choices that foreign policymakers, as rational problem solvers who must calculate their interest in terms of power, must make. (See Chapter 3 for discussion of the "rational" actor.)

Within the realist paradigm, the purpose of statecraft is national survival in a hostile environment. To this end, no means are more important than the acquisition of **power,** and no principle is more important than **self-help.** In this conception, **state sovereignty,** a cornerstone of international law, gives heads of state the freedom—and responsibility—to do whatever is necessary to advance the state's interests and survival.

To the hard-core realist, respect for moral principles is a wasteful and dangerous interference in the rational pursuit of national self-advantage. To these proponents of power politics, questions about the relative virtues of the values within this or that ideological or religious system cannot be allowed to interfere with sound policy making. A state's philosophical or ethical preferences are neither good nor bad—what matters is whether they serve its self-interest. Thus, the game of international politics revolves around the pursuit of power: acquiring it, increasing it, projecting it, and using it to bend others to one's will. At the extreme, realism appears to accept war as normal and rejects morality as it pertains to relations between individuals.

Simulation: Realism versus Liberalism

■ **realism**
a paradigm based on the premise that world politics is essentially and unchangeably a struggle among self-interested states for power and position under anarchy, with each competing state pursuing its own national interests.

■ **realpolitik**
the theoretical outlook prescribing that countries should prepare for war in order to preserve peace.

■ **power**
the factors that enable one actor to manipulate another actor's behavior against its preferences.

■ **self-help**
the principle that in anarchy actors must rely on themselves.

■ **state sovereignty**
under international law, the principle that the governments of states are subject to no higher external authority.

Realist Pioneers of Power Politics In *The Prince* (1532) and *The Leviathan* (1651) Niccolò Machiavelli and Thomas Hobbes, respectively, emphasized a political calculus based on interest, prudence, power, and expediency above all other considerations. This formed the foundation of what became a growing body of modern realist thinking that accepts the drive for power over others as necessary and wise statecraft.

At the risk of oversimplification, realism's message can be summarized in the form of ten assumptions and related propositions:

1. People are by nature narrowly selfish and ethically flawed and cannot free themselves from the sinful fact that they are driven to watch out for themselves and compete with others for self-advantage.
2. Of all people's evil ways, none are more prevalent, unchangeable, or dangerous than their instinctive lust for power and their desire to dominate others.
3. The possibility of eradicating the instinct for power is a hopeless utopian aspiration.
4. International politics is—as Thomas Hobbes put it—a struggle for power, "a war of all against all."
5. The primary obligation of every state—the goal to which all other national objectives should be subordinated—is to promote its **national interest** and to acquire power for this purpose.
6. The anarchical nature of the global system dictates that states acquire sufficient military capabilities to deter attack by potential enemies and to exercise influence over others; hence, states should acquire arms and "prepare for war to keep peace," and not be hesitant to use arms, since "might makes right."

■ **national interest**
the goals that states pursue to maximize what is selfishly best for their country.

7. Economics is less relevant to national security than is military might; economic growth is important primarily as a means of acquiring and expanding state power and prestige.
8. Allies might be sought increase a state's ability to defend itself, but their loyalty and reliability should not be assumed and commitments to allies should be repudiated if it is no longer in a state's national interests to honor them.
9. States should never entrust the task of self-protection to international security organizations or international law and should resist efforts to regulate international behavior through global governance.
10. If all states seek to maximize power, stability will result by maintaining a **balance of power,** lubricated by shifts in the formation and decay of opposing alliances.

■ **balance of power** the theory that peace and stability are most likely to be maintained when military power is distributed to prevent a single hegemon or bloc from controlling the world.

Realism in the Nuclear Age

The dour and pessimistic realist thinking that dominated policy making and academic discourse in the 1940s and 1950s fit the needs of a pessimistic age. World War II, the onset of rivalry between the United States and the Soviet Union, the expansion of the Cold War into a global struggle between East and West, the stockpiling of nuclear weapons, and the periodic crises that threatened to erupt into global violence all confirmed the realists' emphasis on the inevitability of conflict, the poor prospects for cooperation, and the divergence of national interests among incorrigibly selfish, power-seeking states.

The realists' constructed picture of international life appeared particularly persuasive after World War II, given the prevailing patterns of conflictual interstate relations. States and their incessant competition were accordingly seen as the defining elements of global reality; all other aspects of world politics became secondary. At the same time, the view that a threatening global environment demanded that foreign policy take precedence over domestic problems also appeared cogent; the global level of analysis was emphasized as a determinant of the behavior and policies of states and individual decision makers (Vasquez and Elman 2003).

As the historical imperatives of "power politics" required unceasing attention to the threat of war, the logic of realpolitik asserted that military security was the essence of world politics.

Case Study: Traditional Realist Theory and the Cold War

The Limitations of Realism

However persuasive the realists' constructed image of the essential properties of international politics, their contentions and conclusions were frequently at odds and even contradictory.

> Critics . . . noted a lack of precision and even contradictions in the way classical realists use such concepts as "power," "national interest," and "balance of power." They also see possible contradictions between the central descriptive and prescriptive elements of classical realism. On the one hand, as Hans Morgenthau put it, nations and their leaders "think and act in terms of interests defined as power," but on the other, diplomats are urged to exercise prudence and self-restraint, as well as to recognize the legitimate na-

tional interests of other nations. Obviously, then, power plays a central role in classical realism. But the correlation between the relative power balance and political outcomes is often less than compelling, suggesting the need to enrich analyses with other variables. (O. Holsti 2001, 125)

Once analysis moved beyond the belief that people are wicked and the rhetoric requiring that foreign policy serve the national interest, important questions remained: What policies best serve the national interest? Do alliances encourage peace or instability? Do arms promote national security or provoke costly arms races and war? Are states more prone to act aggressively when they are strong or weak? Are the interests of states better served through competition or through cooperation? If humankind is unchanging, then how do we explain the observable evolution and transformation of the global system? Indeed, how do we explain the growth of collaborative multilateral institutions, economic expansion, and states' observable willingness to abide by ethical principles and agreements rather than to exploit others ruthlessly when the opportunity arises?

Because many of the assumptions of the realist paradigm were not testable, realism began to be questioned (Waltz 2000; Vasquez and Elman 2003). Realism offered no criteria for determining what data were significant and what epistemological rules to follow to interpret relevant information. Even the policy recommendations that purportedly flowed from its logic were often divergent. For example, realists themselves were sharply divided as to whether U.S. intervention in Vietnam served American national interests and whether nuclear weapons contributed to international security.

A growing number of critics also pointed out that realism did not account for significant new developments in world politics. For instance, it could not explain the creation of new liberal trade and political institutions in Western Europe in the 1950s and 1960s, where the cooperative pursuit of mutual advantage rather than narrow self-interest appeared to dominate (at least in economic, if not always in military, affairs). Other critics began to worry about realism's tendency to disregard ethical principles and about the material and social costs that some of its policy prescriptions seemed to impose, such as retarded economic growth resulting from unrestrained military expenditures. Consequently, by the end of the 1960s, realism found itself bombarded by criticism, especially by advocates of **behavioral science,** who sought to replace realist thought and polemics with theories tested against evidence (see Controversy: Can Behavioral Science Advance the Study of International Relations?).

■ **behavioral science**
the application of scientific methods to the study of international behavior.

Despite realism's shortcomings, much of the world continues to think about world politics in the language constructed by realists, especially in times of global tension. This happened, for example, in the early 1980s when the Cold War competition between the United States and the Soviet Union entered an embittered new phase, and their arms race accelerated. Because realism provides great insight into the drive for national security through military means, it tends to be used to explain such phenomena as the outbreak of bloody wars in the 1990s between the new states emerging from the former Yugoslavia and the 9/11 and 3/11 terrorist attacks on the United States and Spain, respectively, in 2001 and 2004, with the U.S. war in Iraq a catalyst to the resurrection of realism.

Two schools of thought within the realist theoretical tradition have recently arisen to overcome realism's recognized limitations and to reconstruct it as a general theory: "neorealism" and "neoclassical realism." In its explanation for

Simulation: Can People Learn from History?

CONTROVERSY: CAN BEHAVIORAL SCIENCE ADVANCE THE STUDY OF INTERNATIONAL RELATIONS?

How should scholars construct theories to interpret international behavior? The answer to that question has never been satisfactorily resolved, and the long-standing debate about how best to construct theories of international relations continues today. Some scholars, known as advocates of "postmodern **deconstructivism**," challenge the ability of intellectuals to provide a satisfactory theoretical account of why states and people act as they do in international relations. These scholars devote their efforts to criticizing and "deconstructing" the theories of world politics to expose their inherent limitations. Most scholars remain motivated by the theoretical quest to interpret and comprehend the complexities of international relations, and challenge the pessimistic view that world politics defies meaningful understanding, despite the obstacles and limits to knowledge. What do you think? Is the scientific analysis of patterns of international relations a reasonable undertaking? Or are explanations of international relations impossible, as deconstructionists argue? In formulating your opinion, take into consideration the progression of this intellectual debate over the past five decades.

This evolving epistemological controversy took an important step in the 1960s and early 1970s when dissatisfaction with realism's shortcomings intensified and a movement known as **behavioralism** arose to challenge realism, which the behavioralists called "traditionalism," as well as other speculative and abstract interpretations of international relations not based on systematic evidence. Behavioralism was not a new theory of international relations so much as a new method of studying it, based largely on the application of scientific methods to the study of global affairs (see Knorr and Rosenau 1969; Knorr and Verba 1961).

Behavioralism advances principles and procedures for investigating international phenomena to reach generalizations or statements about international regularities that hold across time and place. Science, the behavioralists claim, is primarily a generalizing activity. From this perspective—a view consistent with that of many "traditional" realists and liberals—a theory of international relations should state the relationship between two or more variables that specifies the conditions under which the relationship(s) hold and explain why the relationship(s) should hold. To uncover such theories, behavioralists lean toward using comparative cross-national analyses rather than case studies of particular countries at particular times. Behavioralists also stress the need for data about the characteristics of countries and how they behave toward one another. Hence, the behavioral movement encourages the comparative and quantitative study of international relations (see, for example, Rosenau 1980; Singer 1968).

What makes behavioralism innovative is its attitude toward the purposes of inquiry: replacing subjective beliefs with verifiable knowledge, supplanting impressions and intuition with testable evidence, and substituting data and reproducible information for mere opinion. In this sense, behavioralists embrace liberalism's "high regard for modern science" and its "attacks against superstition and authority" (J. Hall 2001). In place of appeals to the "expert" opinion of authorities, behavioral scientists seek to acquire knowledge cumulatively by suspending judgments about truths or values until they have sufficient evidence to support them. They attempt to overcome the tendency of traditional inquiry to select facts and cases to fit preexisting hunches. Instead, all available data, those which contradict as well as those which support existing theoretical hypotheses, are to be examined. Knowledge, they argue, would advance best by theorists assuming a cautious, skeptical attitude toward any empirical statement. The slogans "Let the data, not the armchair theorist, speak," and "Seek evidence, but distrust it" represent the behavioral posture toward the acquisition of knowledge.

Although some behavioral research speaks directly to the moral issues that differentiate realism and liberalism, it is sometimes criticized for neglecting the ethical aspects of poverty, hunger, violence, and other global problems. This accusation led to a **postbehavioral movement** that called for a new research agenda that would focus on new issues (see D. Easton 1969). Nonetheless, postbehavioralists rarely have recommended discarding scientific methods, despite the harsh criticism of behavioral science by "postmodern deconstructionists."

■ **neorealism**
a theoretical account of states' behavior that explains it as determined by differences in their relative power instead of by other factors, such as their values, types of government, or domestic circumstances.

■ **structural realism**
a theory that emphasizes the influence of the world power structure on the behavior of the states within the global hierarchy, defined primarily by the distribution of power.

■ **neotraditional realism**
a body of recent realist theorizing that departs from neorealism by emphasizing the motives behind states' foreign policies more than global structure and that focuses on the internal influences on states' external behavior instead of the global determinants of states' foreign behavior.

■ **deconstructivism**
the postmodern theory that the complexity of the world system renders precise description impossible, and that the purpose of scholarship is to understand actors' hidden motives by deconstructing their textual statements.

■ **behavioralism**
an approach to the study of international relations that emphasizes the application of scientific methods to test hypotheses against evidence.

why interstate conflict persists, **neorealism** emphasizes the anarchic nature of global society without governance rather than the traditional realist emphasis on the unceasing lust for power inherent in human nature. For this reason, neorealism is sometimes referred to as **structural realism** because it emphasizes the potent influence of the global distribution of military power on states' behavior within it. The second reconstructed version of realism, known as **neotraditional realism,** reacted against the limitations of structural realism by returning to the original roots of realism, which placed considerable emphasis on the ways leaders of states made foreign policy decisions.

The Neorealist or "Structural" Extension of Realism

In his influential book *Theory of International Politics* (1979), the pioneer of neorealism, Kenneth N. Waltz, set out to convert the loose and disjointed body of realist thought into a formal, "rigorous, deductive systemic theory of international politics" (Keohane 1986b), Neorealism dismisses explanations developed at the individual and state levels of analysis and argues that explanations at the global system level are sufficient to account for the main trends in world politics. As Waltz (1995) expressed his neorealist conceptualization of the determinants of international behavior, "international structure emerges from the interaction of states and then constrains them from taking certain actions while propelling them toward others."

In neorealism, as in realism, anarchy or the absence of central institutions above states is the most important and enduring property of the structure of the system. States remain the primary actors, acting according to the principle of self-help and seeking to ensure their own survival. Thus, it is the neorealists' view that states do not differ in the tasks they face, only in their capabilities. Capabilities define the position of states in the system, and the distribution of capabilities defines the structure of the *global* system and shapes the ways the units in that system interact with one another.

Power also remains a central concept in neorealism. However, the quest for power is not considered an end in itself, as in realism; nor does it derive from human nature. Instead, states always pursue power as a means of survival. As Waltz (1979) explains, the "means fall into two categories: internal efforts (moves to increase economic capability, to increase military strength, to develop clever strategies) and external efforts (moves to strengthen and enlarge one's own alliance or to weaken and shrink an opposing one)." Furthermore, because the instinct for survival drives states, neorealism asserts that balances of power form automatically, regardless of whether "some or all states consciously aim to establish and maintain a balance, or whether some or all states aim for universal domination" (Waltz 1979). Once the global system is formed, its structure "becomes a force that the units may not be able to control; it constrains their behavior and interposes itself between their intentions and the outcomes of their actions" (Ruggie 1983).

Although neorealists recognize that states' goals sometimes "fluctuate with the changing currents of domestic politics, are prey to the vagaries of a shifting cast of political leaders, and are influenced by the outcomes of bureaucratic struggles," they contend that such factors as whether governments are democracies or dictatorships tell little about the process whereby states come to pursue the goal of balancing power with power. Instead, framed at the **global level of**

analysis, "structural constraints explain why the [same] methods are repeatedly used despite differences in the persons and states who use them" (Waltz 1979).

> In its stress on the structure of the international system, that is, the state of anarchy among sovereign states, [neo]realism attaches little or no importance to what is going on inside states—what kind of regimes are in power, what kind of ideologies prevail, what kind of leadership is provided. According to [neo]realists, the foreign policies of all states are basically driven by the same systemic factors—they are like so many billiard balls, obeying the same laws of political geometry and physics. (Harries 1995, 13)

Neorealist theory also helps to explain why the prospects for international cooperation and change often appear so dim and why states are naturally wary of others and compete. The anarchical structure of the system compels states to be sensitive to their *relative position* in the distribution of power.

> When faced with the possibility of cooperating for mutual gain, states that feel insecure must ask how the gain will be divided. They are compelled to ask not "Will both of us gain?" but "Who will gain more?" If an expected gain is to be divided, say, in the ratio of two to one, one state may use its disproportionate gain to implement a policy intended to damage or destroy the other. Even the prospect of large absolute gains for both parties does not elicit their cooperation so long as each fears how the other will use its increased capabilities. (Waltz 1979, 105; see also Snidal 1993)

Barriers to global cooperation therefore result not from the parties' negative attitudes toward the potential costs of collaboration but rather from the insecurity that the ruthlessly competitive system of **anarchy** breeds. "The condition of insecurity—at the least, the uncertainty of each about the other's future intentions and actions—works against their cooperation" (Waltz 1979), as does states' fear of dependence on others.

The Neoclassical Extension of Realism

Alongside neorealism, another group of realists who share a dim view of cooperation in world politics has arisen, advocating what is called "neotraditional realism." This theoretical movement seeks to transcend Waltzian neorealism's exclusive focus on the global level of analysis, which they argue incorrectly neglects classical realism's attention to the determinants of foreign policy at the individual and state levels of analysis (see Vasquez 1998). To neoclassical theorists the sources of states' foreign policy choices are best explained not by changes in the global structure, but by leaders' perception of national interests and capabilities. Leaders instead of states are the primary actors in international relations, and what matters is their perceptions that the global distribution of power is changing, more than whether real shifts are actually occurring. Hence, "a new breed of realist scholars have embraced the richer formulation of traditional, pre-Waltzian realists, who focus more on foreign policy than systemic phenomena. While not abandoning Waltz's insights about international structure and its consequences, neoclassical realists have added [factors at the state and individual levels of analysis] such as domestic politics . . . , state power and intentions, and statesmen's perceptions of the relative distribution of capabilities . . . to better explain historical puzzles and foreign policy decision making" (Schweller 1999).

■ **postbehavioral movement**
an approach to the study of international relations that calls for increased attention to the policy relevance of scientific research.

■ **global level of analysis**
analyses of world politics that emphasize the impact of worldwide conditions on the behavior of states and nonstate and other international actors.

■ **anarchy**
a system made up of competitive interacting actors in the absence of supervisory governing institutions to regulate the units' competition.

Many scholars and policymakers disagree with the view of the neorealists and the neoclassical realists about the prospects for international cooperation. They point out that the record suggests that patterns can change and that increased interdependence can lead to even higher levels of cooperation. This expectation lies behind the so-called neoliberal challenge to realism and neorealism (Doyle and Ikenberry 1997; Kegley 1995).

NEOLIBERALISM

In the last decade of the twentieth century, satisfaction with realism and neorealism began to fall. Arguing that it was time for a new, more rigorous liberal alternative to realism, critics pointed to several shortcomings: (1) power-politics perspectives failed to predict the peaceful end of the Cold War and international social change in general; (2) research suggested that the "underlying theory of war and peace [of realism and neorealism was] flawed" (Vasquez 1993) because realists "oversimplified the concept of power and misunderstood the lessons of history" (Kober 1990); and (3) it appeared that realism's approach would "not be an adequate guide for the future of international politics" (Jervis 1992), because the broadened global agenda included many questions and problems that realist theory could not cover. The problems of AIDS, environmental deterioration, global warming, economic underdevelopment, and the globalization of trade and markets were among those for which the realistic approach was seen as deficient.

"Some students of international politics," Kenneth Waltz (2000) complains, "believe that realism is obsolete. They argue that although realism's concepts of anarchy, self-help, and power balancing may have been appropriate to a bygone era, they have been changed by changed conditions and eclipsed by better ideas. New times call for new thinking, changed conditions require revised theories or entirely new ones." Among these scholars, Fareed Zakaria (1992–1993) asked, "is realism finished?", Jeffrey Legro and Andrew Moravcsik (1999) questioned "is anybody still a realist?", and Patrick James (1993) proclaimed that neorealism was "a research enterprise in crisis." In addition, as Waltz notes, many critics went beyond calling for a revision and replacement of realist theorizing by advocating that "the recovery of liberalism" (Little 1993) be treated as a theoretical goal in international relations. This view gained a following among policymakers. For example, in accord with Francis Fukuyama's conclusion (1992b) that there were "good reasons for examining aspects of the liberal international legacy once again," U.S. President Bill Clinton in 1995 maintained that "In a world where freedom, not tyranny, is on the march, the cynical calculus of pure power politics simply does not compute. It is ill-suited to the new era."

In light of this growing sentiment, in the early 1990s **neoliberalism** emerged, a new approach to world politics that concentrates on the ways international organizations and other nonstate actors promote international cooperation. This analytic departure goes by several labels including "neoliberal institutionalism" (Grieco 1995), "neoidealism" (Kegley 1993), and "neo-Wilsonian idealism" (Fukuyama 1992a).

Neoliberalism seeks to build theories of international relations by giving the basic tenets of classical liberalism and post-World War I liberal idealism a fresh

■ **neoliberalism**
a perspective that accounts for the way international institutions promote global change, cooperation, peace, and prosperity through collective programs for reforms.

> **CONTROVERSY**
>
> ## NEOLIBERALISM VERSUS NEOREALISM
> ### Which Theory Makes the Most Reasonable Assumptions?
>
> The issues dividing neoliberal and neorealist theorizing center on the different assumptions they make about the following six topics (David Baldwin, 1993, 4–8). Looking at the world, which set of assumptions do you think is the most accurate for interpreting twenty-first-century world politics?
>
> - *The Nature and Consequences of Anarchy.* Whereas everyone recognizes that the global system is anarchical because effective institutions for global governance are lacking, neorealists argue that anarchy does not matter much and in fact may be preferable to the restraints of world government. Neoliberals see anarchy as a big problem that can be reformed through the creation of strong global institutions.
> - *International Cooperation.* Although neorealists and neoliberals agree that international cooperation is possible, neorealists think cooperation is difficult to sustain whereas neoliberals believe cooperation can be expected because collaboration produces rewards that reduce the temptation to selfishly compete.
> - *Relative versus Absolute Gains.* Both neorealists and neoliberals are concerned with relative gain as well as absolute gain. Neorealists believe that the desire to get ahead of their competitor by obtaining relative gains is the primary motive, while neoliberals believe that states are motivated by the search for opportunities to cooperate that will produce absolute gains for all parties to the cooperative exchange.
> - *Priority of State Goals.* Both national security and national economic prosperity are seen as important state goals by neorealists and neoliberals, but neorealists stress security as the most important, while neoliberals believe states place a greater priority on economic welfare.
> - *Intentions versus Capabilities.* Contemporary neorealists maintain that the distribution of states' capabilities is the primary determinant of their behavior and international outcomes. Neoliberals maintain that states' intentions, interests, information, and ideals are more influential than is the distribution of capabilities.
> - *Institutions and Regimes.* Both neorealists and neoliberals recognize that states have created a variety of new international regimes and institutions to regulate their relations since World War II. Neoliberals believe that institutions such as the World Trade Organization create norms that are binding on their members and that change patterns of international politics. On the other hand, neorealists emphasize that organizations like the UN are arenas where states carry out their traditional competition and political rivalry for influence.

examination. Taking heart in the international prohibition, through community consensus, of such previously entrenched practices as slavery, piracy, dueling, colonialism, the slaughter of certain animals, and unrestrained exploitation of the planet's ecology, neoliberalism emphasizes the prospects for progress, peace, and prosperity. Studies of regional integration—processes whereby sovereign states might be politically unified—began to flourish in the 1950s and 1960s, paving the way for the new liberal theories that emerged in the 1990s. The expansion of trade, communication, information, technology, and immigrant labor propelled Europeans to sacrifice portions of their sovereign independence to create a new political community out of previously separate units. These developments were outside of realism's worldview, creating conditions that made the call for a theory grounded in the liberal tradition convincing to many who had previously been skeptical of realism.

Neoliberalism departs from neorealism on many assumptions (see Controversy: Neoliberalism versus Neorealism). In particular, neoliberalism focuses on the ways in which influences such as democratic governance, public opinion, mass education, free trade, liberal commercial enterprise, international law and organization, arms control and disarmament, collective security and multilateral diplomacy, and ethically inspired statecraft can improve life on our planet. Because they perceive change in global conditions as progressing over time, haltingly but still in the same trajectory, through cooperative efforts, neoliberal theorists maintain that the ideas and ideals of the liberal legacy could describe, explain, predict, and prescribe international conduct in ways that they could not during the conflict-ridden Cold War.

Like realism and neorealism, neoliberalism does not represent a cohesive intellectual movement or school of thought. Neoliberals operate from different assumptions, examining different aspects of the processes through which international change and cooperation might be promoted. Some, like neorealists, embrace a structural theory that examines the characteristics of the global system. Others concentrate on the characteristics of the units and subunits that comprise it, such as types of governments (democracies or dictatorships) and the leaders who govern states. Still other neoliberals give primary attention to the influence of international institutions such as the UN and nonstate actors such as multinational corporations. All neoliberals, however, share an interest in probing the conditions under which the convergent and overlapping interests among otherwise sovereign political actors may result in cooperation.

To illuminate these similarities and differences among neoliberals, consider two theoretical perspectives that paved the way for neoliberalism's acceptance and are a part of its orientation: "transnational interdependence" and "international regimes." For the sake of brevity, we have selected only these two examples from among the many other divergent strands within neoliberal theorizing (see Zacher and Matthew 1995) such as **feminist theory** and its critique of previous theorizing in general and realism in particular (see Tickner 2002, Chapter 7, and, in particular, Controversy: What's Missing in Realist Theories of Interstate Relations?).

Transnational Interdependence as a Neoliberal Counter Worldview to Realism

In the 1970s, a new analytical perspective known as "transnational relations" arose to question realism's key assumption that states are the only important actors on the global stage. With **complex interdependence** as its central concept, this theoretical departure advanced a "synthesis of liberal and realist perspectives [by] constructing a way of looking at world politics that helps us understand the relationship between economics and politics, and patterns of institutionalized international cooperation." It asked how under conditions of complex interdependence world "politics would be different than under realist conditions" (Keohane and Nye 2001a) and answered by arguing that differences were substantial because sweeping changes in international relations fostered by technological innovations and the information revolution were increasingly challenging realism's oversimplified view of world politics.

Emphasizing the growing importance of **nonstate actors,** such international organizations like the United Nations and emerging nongovernmental organizations (NGOs) like multinational corporations and transnationally tied human rights advocacy groups, the transnational interdependence perspective anticipated what is now called **globalization.** States were becoming increas-

■ **feminist theory**
a body of scholarship that emphasizes gender in the study of world politics.

■ **complex interdependence**
a theory stressing the complex ways in which the growing ties among transnational actors make them vulnerable to each other's actions and sensitive to each other's needs.

■ **nonstate actors**
all transnationally active groups other than states, such as organizations whose members are states (IGOs) and nongovernmental organizations (NGOs), whose members are individuals and private groups from more than one state.

■ **globalization**
the integration and growing interdependence of states through their increasing contact and trade. This creates a single united global society within a single culture in order to tie people together in a common fate, thereby reducing the capacity of states to control their national destinies.

> **CONTROVERSY**
>
> ## WHAT'S MISSING IN REALIST THEORIES OF INTERSTATE RELATIONS?
> ### The Feminist Critique
>
> Many scholars are dissatisfied with existing theories of world politics because nearly all fail, in their opinion, to give sufficient attention to certain important factors and forces. No theory can possibly cover everything comprehensively; however, if a theory ignores a key variable or issue in the effort to simplify, that theory will fail to capture the true complexity of international relations. Yet people disagree about what is essential. Determining which features should be emphasized is controversial, because certain questions are more interesting to some than others (as the debate between realists and liberals illustrates).
>
> Do you think mainstream realism and liberalism ignore any crucial factors in world politics? To stimulate your thinking about what is essential and what has potentially been ignored, consider the issue of gender. Until recently, most theories paid little attention to this variable, and thus failed to account for such crucial trends as the chronic and widening inequalities in income and freedom between men and women.
>
> Feminist theory, a body of scholarship that emphasizes the importance of gender as a factor in world politics, arose in the 1960s in response to the pronounced realist depersonalization of its accounts of foreign policy. In particular, feminist theory attacked the exclusion of women in discussions about public and international affairs as well as the injustice and unequal treatment of women this prejudice caused. The mainstream realist literature underestimated or ignored the plight and contributions of women, treating differences in men's and women's status, beliefs, and behaviors as unimportant. Gender roles were also ignored, along with the evidence that sexism is a pillar of the war system (Caprioli 2004). In the realists' masculine image of sovereign rulers, "Fame, wealth, and women were prizes to be won in battle. For the typical prince, war was a means to reputation and glory" (Tickner 2002). In the feminist critique, a remedy for this problem was to give women the prominence and power in policy making that traditional practices denied them (see Mazur 2002).
>
> As feminist theory crystallized, it moved away from focusing on a history of discrimination against women and began to direct much of its criticism at realism. In particular, many gender studies alleged that realism, formulated and dominated by males, ignored the human roots of global conditions and promoted an essentially masculine interpretation of international relations that was inattentive to human rights and rife with rationales for aggression.
>
> Derived in part from liberal principles supportive of fair play, justice, and the philosophical acceptance of love over power, feminist theory moved beyond this initial critique of realism's bias to chart an independent theoretical course (Enloe 2001). This perspective has focused on the performance of women as leaders of government and as members of infantry combat units (Regan and Paskeviciute 2003), as well as on the plight of women in business and in the less-developed countries of the Global South.
>
> Perhaps of greatest influence, however, has been feminist theory's rejection of the realist preoccupation with states' military strategies in favor of developing strategies for world security (see Tickner 2002). In this sense, feminist theory, like neoliberalism generally, is motivated by the quest for discovering paths to greater international cooperation. In liberating conventional theory from its narrow focus, can feminist theory open a window on the full range of international activity and point the way toward a fuller appreciation of the ways in which human beings influence global conditions?

ingly dependent on, sensitive to, and mutually vulnerable to one another in ways that were eroding their sovereign control and independence. To supplement realism's account for only state-to-state relations and to develop a more complex model of global change, the transnational perspective broadened realism's narrow view of world politics as centered on states' military capabilities and the use of force by highlighting the multiple channels through which both state and nonstate actors were visibly engaging in active transnational contact and communication worldwide. Transnational interdependence thus represented a holistic conception of world politics as the sum of its many interacting parts in a global society (see O. Holsti 2001).

Robert O. Keohane and Joseph S. Nye's (1977, 2001a) *Power and Interdependence* is the definitive treatise on the new extensions of liberalism. It paved the way for attempts to account for the growing willingness of states to see their interests served by the creation of international regimes, or the norms for behavior that are created when multinational cooperation becomes institutionalized and actors expect them to be followed, even though this necessitates a sacrifice of sovereignty.

Transnational interdependence has become a central component of the neoliberal perspective and continues to be widely used to interpret cooperative agreements between states under the continuing conditions of anarchy and fear of dependence and exploitation.

International Regimes

Although the global system is still characterized by anarchy, its nature is more properly conceptualized as an ordered anarchy and the world as a whole as an "anarchical society" (Bull 2002), because cooperation, not conflict, is often the observable outcome of relations among states.

Given this reality, the question arises: How can **international regimes** based on coordinated cooperation be established and preserved? Interest in this question derives from "a desire to understand the extent to which mutually accepted constraints affect states' behaviors" (Zacher 1987), alongside the quest to devise strategies for creating a less disorderly "world order."

Regimes are institutionalized or regularized patterns of cooperation with respect to a given issue or problem according to established rules. Because the international regime perspective necessarily looks primarily at global institutions and the ways in which norms influence states to behave according to more global than national interests, it is perhaps best viewed as an attempt to reconcile liberal and realist theories (Haggard and Simmons 1987).

The global trade and monetary rules created during and after World War II are vivid examples of international regulatory regimes. These rules, as well as particular sectors within the trade system, have been the focus of considerable inquiry from regime analysts. Together, the trade and monetary regimes constituted a Liberal International Economic Order (LIEO) that limited government intervention in the world political economy and otherwise facilitated the free flow of goods and capital across national boundaries. The General Agreement on Tariffs and Trade (GATT) that preceded the World Trade Organization (WTO) and the International Monetary Fund (IMF) played important institutional roles in the LIEO and reconfirmed the importance of international institutions in fostering transnational cooperation (see Chapter 9 for elaboration).

Most regime analyses focus on the low politics arena of economic and humanitarian relationships; until recently, relatively few "security regimes" (Adler and Barnett 1998; Buzan and Weaver 2003) had emerged in the realm of **high politics** dealing with the peaceful management of military competition. Early exceptions were the nuclear nonproliferation regime and the regime that the United States and the Soviet Union used to manage their crises (see George

■ **international regimes**
a concept constructed to explain the benefits to actors supporting particular rules to regulate a specific international problem, such as disposal of toxic wastes.

■ **high politics**
geostrategic issues of national and international security that pertain to matters of war and peace.

1986). The pressures of globalization have since fostered the creation of regimes in widening areas of international conduct. This is likely to accelerate efforts to grapple theoretically with the causes and consequences of multilateral approaches to collective problem solving.

ALTERNATIVE THEORIES

Having studied the liberal and realist traditions, keep in mind that this coverage is very selective. At least six additional major schools of thought regarding particular aspects of world politics also deserve attention, and each will be introduced along with still other theoretical subspecialties linked to them in later chapters where they best help to interpret the topic covered. First, as explained in Chapter 3, decision-making theory accounts for the ways leaders and administrators seek to make policy choices rationally, and the limits to this aspiration. Second, as introduced in Chapter 4, long-cycle theory seeks to explain the historical ebb and flow of world politics, global leadership, and systemwide war (Modelski and Thompson 1996). The rise and fall of the great powers and empires is its central concern. Third, dependency theory, first treated in Chapter 5, examines the pattern of dominance and dependence that characterizes the un-

Free At Last? For most of recorded history, women were deprived of the basic human right of voting in elections, as is explained by feminist theory, an extension of neoliberal theorizing. With recent reforms, that situation has begun to change, as shown in this photo of Somaliland women singing as they line up to cast their ballots for the first time on May 31, 2001, at a polling station in Hargeisa, Somalia, during a referendum on the constitution.

> **low politics**
>
> the category of global issues related to the economic, social, demographic, and environmental aspects of relations between governments and people.

equal relationship between the world's rich and poor states (P. Evans 2001). Fourth, to understand how cooperation among states often arises to deal with shared global problems primarily in the realm of **low politics** (Chapters 8–10), hegemonic stability theory, a hybrid of liberal–neorealist theory (Gill 2001b), examines what happens when a clearly predominant state, a "hegemon," exercises leadership and control of the global system by setting and enforcing the rules governing international trade, finance, investment, and other issues such as environmental regulation. Fifth, to expand this coverage and move to other topics dealing with global security, "world-system theory" looks at system dynamics from a long-term, structural perspective, emphasizing its economic underpinnings to explain the Western capitalist societies' rise to dominance and the lack of economic development in many other geographic areas (Chapters 5–10) and their military repercussions (Chapter 11) (see Wallerstein 2004). Sixth, to systematically organize inquiry about how states fit into international phenomena from diverse levels of analysis, advocates of the comparative study of foreign policy seek to probe the similarities and differences in states' international circumstances, national attributes and capabilities, foreign policy decision-making processes, and individual policymakers (see Hermann and Sundelius 2006). Still other streams of theorizing within both the liberal and realist traditions will be introduced in those chapters that address directly the problems investigated.

THEORIZING ABOUT THEORY: THE CONSTRUCTIVIST CONCEPTION

To understand our changing world and to make reasonable prognoses about the future, we must begin by arming ourselves with an array of information and conceptual tools, entertaining rival interpretations of world politics, and questioning the assumptions on which these contending worldviews rest. Because there are a great (and growing) number of alternative, and sometimes incompatible, ways of organizing theoretical inquiry about world politics, the challenge of capturing the world's political problems cannot be reduced to any one simple yet compelling account, such as the five major theoretical traditions stressed here (see Table 2.1). Each paradigmatic effort to do so in the past, whether derived from liberalism or from realism, has ultimately been abandoned as developments in world affairs eroded its continuing relevance. Although grand theories fade with the passage of time, they often regain their attractiveness when global transformations make them useful once again. In fact, world politics is so resistant to clear, comprehensive, and convincing analysis that some advocates of so-called **deconstructionism** contend that international complexity defies description, explanation, and prediction (see Controversy: Can Behavioral Science Advance the Study of International Relations?). Deconstructionists share the philosophical view that all peoples' conceptions of global realities are relative to their understandings and that, because there is no objective principle, the validity of which is independent of one's own personal point of view, any interpretation is as valid as any other, and there is no point in attempting to develop a shared conception of the world.

> **deconstructionism**
>
> a postmodern theory postulating that the complexity of the world system renders precise description impossible, and that the purpose of scholarship is to understand actors' motives by deconstructing their statements recorded in published texts.

TABLE 2.1
The Quest for Theory: Five Major Perspectives

Feature	Realism	Neorealism	Liberalism	Neoliberalism	Constructivism
Key Units	Independent states	The global system's structure	Institutions transcending states	Individuals' "penetrated" states and nonstate transnational actors.	Social groups, their socially constructed images of international conditions
Core Concern	War and security	Struggle for position and power under anarchy	Institutionalizing peace	Fostering interstate cooperation on the globe's shared economic, social, and ecological problems	Social collectivities' shared meanings and images of contemporary international life: the theoretical implication of these visions
Major Approach	Balance of power	Balance of terror, military preparedness and deterrence	International law, international organization, democratization, arms control	Transnational interdependence and regimes	Advocacy of normative innovation through construction of new images; tracing assumptions within various theoretical traditions; discovering how and why theories color mental maps of world affairs
Outlook on Global Prospects	Pessimistic stability	Pessimistic	Optimistic/progress	Expectation of cooperation and creation of a global community	Neither optimistic nor pessimistic, depending on the most popular or socially accepted visions about the potential for humanity to engineer changes that either improve or harm future global conditions

(continued)

TABLE 2.1 (continued)

Feature	Realism	Neorealism	Liberalism	Neoliberalism	Constructivism
Motives of Actors	National interests; zero-sum competition; security; power	Power, prestige, and advantage (relative gains) over other states	Collaboration; mutual aid; meeting human needs	Global interests (absolute gains); justice; peace and prosperity; liberty; morality	Contingent upon the socially constructed explanations about the basic drives of international actors in various epochs
Central Concepts	Anarchy; power; national interests; balance of power; polarity	Structural anarchy; rational choice; arms races; changes in distribution of military capabilities	Collective security; world order; law; integration; international organization	Transnational relations; law; free markets; interdependence; integration; liberal republican rule; human rights; gender	Ideas; identities; ideals; images—all as socially constructed by various groups
Policy Prescriptions	Increase national power; resist reduction of national autonomy	Preserve nuclear deterrence; avoid disarmament and supernational organizations	Institutional reform	Develop regimes and promote democracy and multilateral international institutions to coordinate collective responses to global problems	Broaden understanding of the ways international actors construct their images of international relations to clarify the limitations of rival theoretical interpretations and the policies on which they are based

Most other scholars continue to struggle in the pursuit of theory and knowledge about international affairs. For example, scholars adhering to **chaos theory** attempt to find new methods for modeling the kind of turbulent global change that is occurring in the world. However, because there exists no single general-purpose theory able to account for all questions regarding international relations, a number of scholars have returned to reconsider the basic questions of **epistemology** that are fundamental to evaluating the relative value and validity of rival theoretical frameworks. How do we know what to believe? What principles of analysis can lead us to recognize the strengths and weaknesses of various theories? How do we separate fact from fiction and sense from nonsense? What is the relative descriptive accuracy and explanatory power of different theories, and how much confidence should be placed in their explanations of world politics? To what extent, in short, should we accept the perspective of *any* theory, such as realism or liberalism, and the claims all such theories make about what should count as knowledge of international affairs?

Increasingly, many students of international relations have turned to **constructivist theory** to interpret both international life and the various substantive theories others have built to help understand international affairs. Strictly speaking, "constructivism is not a theory of international politics"; rather, it helps to "clarify the differences and relative virtues" of alternative theories (Wendt 2000). Beyond that, constructivism provides a lens for thinking critically about how theories of international relations can be constructed, and the kinds of premises and assumptions that are reasonable for any theorist to make as a starting point for explaining world politics. Constructivism follows Alexander Wendt's argument, therefore, that

> students of international politics must answer these questions, at least implicitly, since they cannot do their business without making powerful assumptions about what kinds of things are to be found in international life, and how they are related, and how they can be known. These assumptions are particularly important because no one can "see" the state or international system. International politics does not present itself directly to the senses, and theories of international politics often are contested on the basis of ontology [ideas about the nature of existence] and epistemology, i.e., what the theorist "sees." (Wendt 2000, 5)

Constructivism thus provides a pathway to theoretical interpretation by reminding students that perceptions about world politics must be organized for inquiry to be conducted, that is, first put together in a manner that identifies what is believed important, matters most, and is worthy of observation and analysis (recall Controversy: Should We Believe What We See?, Chapter 1, pp. 10–11).

Constructivism is best seen as a conceptualization of international affairs— a way of organizing perceptions about the subject—as a first step to investigating international phenomena theoretically and to evaluating more formal existing streams of theorizing. It attempts to bridge the gap between neoliberal and neorealist theories by accepting many key assumptions shared by both approaches while critically rejecting realism's failure to pay attention to the powerful role of ideas and norms in world politics. Constructivists emphasize the importance of shared ideas and understandings that are developed among actors on the world stage through their interactions. These shared experiences

■ **chaos theory**
the application of mathematical methods to identify underlying, episodically recurring patterns in rapidly changing and seemingly unconnected relationships (as many global phenomena appear) in order to better interpret complex reality.

■ **epistemology**
the philosophical examination of how knowledge is acquired and the analytic principles governing the study of phenomena.

■ **constructivist theory**
a liberal-realist theoretical approach advocated by Alexander Wendt that sees self-interested states as the key actors in world politics; their actions are determined not by anarchy but by the ways states socially "construct" accepted images of reality and then respond to the meanings they give to power politics, so that as their definitions change, cooperative practices can evolve.

define their interests, identities, and images of the world in which they interact (Wendt 2000; see also Hopf 1998; Onuf 1989 and 2002, and Adler 2002). Constructivism is helpful because it reminds us that how we think about the world matters. All theories are necessarily socially constructed based on communication among the agents in international relations, as seen by the advent of the so-called "realist-constructivist dialogue" (Barkin 2003; Jackson 2004). These constructions of shared meanings through social learning provide states and other actors with the mental models of international politics on which they act. This method of viewing international politics represents a welcome theoretical departure, because it reminds us that shared images influence the ways actors in the global arena see themselves and behave (Checkel 1998). Further, this emphasis on subjective beliefs helps us appreciate that the practices in statecraft and the identities of global actors or agents are products of shared ideas rather than, as the realists would have it, simply products of the objective or material structure of the international system. As the twenty-first century unfolds, it is likely to become increasingly popular to interpret world politics from a constructivist theory that focuses on the collective norms and culture of people and state actors. Those shared norms will define their reality and influence their relations within that constructed vision.

Note the underlying premises that have made constructivism so popular. It is hard to argue against the principle that international reality is defined by the ways people construct their images of it (Onuf 2002). Our visions are derived from our point of view, because all people are intellectual prisoners of the collective conceptions of the world. All conceptions and theories are shaped by the social pressures within groups for those groups' members to construct similar images or worldviews, ones that define global reality for them and provide a springboard for theoretical interpretation. Moreover, awareness of the influence of these socially constructed sets of collective images of world affairs, their inherent subjectivity, and their inability to fully capture global realities contributes to appreciation of the limits of valid theoretical interpretation and accurate representation of our subject matter. Constructivism cautions us to be skeptical of all claims of truth.

In addition, constructivism opens a window to insightful analysis. It brings to inquiry the possibility of learning through analysis, from which policymakers can construct more accurate pictures of international realities and use them to engineer change. Beginning with a stress on the power of ideas, constructivists counter, for example, structural realism's failure to overlook "what is often a more determinant factor, namely, the intersubjectively sharpened ideas that shaped behavior by constituting the identities and interests of actors" (Copeland 2000). The socially accepted ideas, norms, and values held by powerful state and nonstate actors are seen as making a difference in constructing an international consensus about the rules that should govern international society. For individuals, popular ideas shape people's self-images, sense of identity, and expectations about their purpose and roles in life; for the world writ large, leading ideas condition prevailing belief in each age about the global condition and the prospects for humanity to escape the problems posed by competing states in an anarchic arena. When a new consensus materializes about norms—what is legal and illegal—the modified shared global culture prepares the way for a **transformation** in world politics. Because "reality is in the eye of the beholder," agreement on the redefinition of reality enables the pattern of international re-

■ **transformation**
a change in the characteristic pattern of interaction among the most active participants in world politics of such magnitude that it appears that one "global system" has replaced another.

Defending Reason against Deconstructionist Criticism Pope John Paul II is shown here signing the "Fides et Ratio" encyclical in October 1998 that defends using reason to discover bedrock truths. Arguing that faith and reason are not incompatible, the statement describes deconstructionism as a nihilistic philosophy that breeds skepticism because it questions our ability to know anything for certain and rejects "the pursuit of truth through reason." Yet in a bewildering, complex world, it is easy to appreciate why some theoreticians give up the effort to discover the underlying principles of world politics, claiming that the challenge is hopeless.

lations to change from one epoch to another. Thus, "Changing attitudes toward slavery and racial and other forms of discrimination are illustrative of [constructivist] phenomena to which proponents of this approach point" (Dougherty and Pfaltzgraff 2001).

As we seek to understand the changing global conditions, we must be humble in recognizing the limitations of our understandings of world politics and at the same time inquisitive about its character. The task of interpretation is complicated because the world is itself complex. Donald Puchala theoretically framed the challenge in 2005 by observing to the authors:

> Conceptually speaking, world affairs today can be likened to a disassembled jigsaw puzzle scattered on a table before us. Each piece shows a fragment of a broad picture that as yet remains indiscernible. Some pieces depict resurgent nationalism; others show spreading democracy; some picture genocide; others portray prosperity through trade and investment; some picture nuclear disarmament; others picture nuclear proliferation; some indicate a reinvigorated United Nations; others show the UN still enfeebled and ineffective; some describe cultural globalization; others predict clashing civilizations.
>
> How do these pieces fit together, and what picture do they exhibit when they are appropriately fitted?

All theories are maps of possible futures. Theories can guide us in fitting the pieces together to form an accurate picture. However, in evaluating the usefulness of any theory to interpret global conditions, the historical overview in this chapter suggests that it would be wrong to oversimplify or to assume that a particular theory will remain useful in the future. Nonetheless, as the American poet Robert Frost observed in 1911, any belief we cling to long enough is likely to be true again someday, because "most of the change we think we see in life is due to truths being in and out of favor." So in our theoretical exploration of world politics, we must critically assess the accuracy of our impressions, avoiding the temptation to embrace one worldview and abandon another without any assurance that their relative worth is permanently fixed.

KEY TERMS

paradigm
constructivism
geopolitics
current history approach
theory
liberalism
politics
idealism
collective security
Kellogg-Briand Pact
self-determination
state
nation
realism
realpolitik
power
self-help
state sovereignty
national interest
behavioral science
neorealism
structural realism
neotraditional realism
deconstructivism
behavioralism
postbehavioral movement
global level of analysis
anarchy
neoliberalism
feminist theory
complex interdependence
nonstate actors
globalization
international regimes
high politics
low politics
deconstructionism
chaos theory
epistemology
constructivist theory
transformation

SUGGESTED READING

Campbell, John L., and Ovek Pederson, eds. *The Rise of Neoliberalism and Institutional Analyses.* Princeton, N.J.: Princeton University Press, 2001.

Carlsnaes, Walter, Thomas Risse, and Beth A. Simmons, eds. *Handbook of International Relations.* London: Sage, 2002.

Dougherty, James E., and Robert L. Pfaltzgraff, Jr. *Contending Theories of International Relations,* 5th ed. New York: Addison Wesley-Longman, 2001.

Elman, Colin, and Miriam Fendius Elman, eds. *Progress in International Relations Theory: Appraising the Field.* Cambridge, Mass.: MIT Press, 2003.

Ferguson, Yale H., and Richard W. Mansbach. *The Elusive Quest Continues: Theory and International Politics.* Upper Saddle River, N.J.: Prentice Hall, 2003.

Genest, Marc A. *Conflict and Cooperation: Evolving Theories of International Relations,* 2nd ed. Belmont, Calif.: Wadsworth/Thomson Learning, 2004.

Haslam, Jonathan. *No Virtue Like Necessity: Realist Thought in International Relations since Machiavelli.* New Haven, Conn.: Yale University Press, 2002.

Kegley, Charles W., Jr., ed. *Controversies in International Relations Theory: Realism and the Neoliberal Challenge.* New York: St. Martin's Press, 1995.

Maoz, Zeev, Alex Mintz, T. Clifton Morgan, Glenn Palmer, and Richard J. Stroll, eds. *Multiple Paths to Knowledge in International Relations.* Lexington, Mass.: Lexington Books, 2004.

Puchala, Donald J., ed. *Theory and History in International Relations.* New York: Rutledge, 2004.

Snyder, Jack. "One World, Rival Theories." *Foreign Policy* (November–December 2004): 53–62.

Wendt, Alexander. *Social Theory of International Politics.* Cambridge: Cambridge University Press, 2000.

WHERE ON THE WORLD WIDE WEB?

Contemporary Philosophy, Critical Theory, and Postmodern Thought
http://www.carbon.cudenver.edu/~mryder/itc_data/postmodern.html

The University of Colorado at Denver's School of Education has created a website that helps students understand the ideas behind critical theory and postmodern thought. Read about the main authors of postmodern thought and then access their works.

Data on the Net
http://odwin.ucsd.edu/idata/

Try your hand at being a behavioral social scientist. The University of California at San Diego has created a gateway website from which you can browse the collection of several hundred Internet sites of numerous social science statistical data. On the home page, type in a topic area that interests you and receive data that is relevant to your topic area. The site also contains gateways to more than eighty social science websites.

Feminist Theory Website
http://www.cddc.vt.edu/feminism/

The Center for Digital Discourse and Culture at Virginia Tech University hosts the award-winning Feminist Theory Website. This site provides one of the most extensive lists of research materials and information for students, activists, and scholars interested in women's conditions and struggles around the world, with a staggering 5,425 bibliographical entries and 593 links to other Internet sites. Its stated goals are to encourage research and dialogue between individuals in different countries around the world. True to its international focus, the site can be accessed in English, Spanish, or French. Those interested can read complete bibliographies from various fields as well as obtain information on women's movements and activities anywhere in the world. As noted in this chapter, much literature on world politics has ignored the plight and contributions of women. This website will undoubtedly contribute to remedying this situation.

Niccolò Machiavelli
http://www.philosophypages.com/ph/macv.htm

The writings of Niccolò Machiavelli (1469–1527) are often cited as the base of realist thinking in international relations. As this chapter explains, the realist worldview is primarily concerned with a state's drive for power. Visit this site for a complete informational resource on Machiavelli's life and times. There is also a link to his famous book on how to rule, *The Prince*, which you can read online.

President Woodrow Wilson
http://www.fordham.edu/halsall/mod/1918wilson.html

As Chapter 2 notes, Woodrow Wilson's celebrated Fourteen Points speech before a joint session of Congress on January 8, 1918, "expressed the sentiments of the liberal world view and program." Take a moment to read the Fourteen Points. In retrospect, did Wilson's speech aim to prevent another war or to establish American international dominance in a new world order? Which philosophy do you think underlies current U.S. foreign policy, liberalism or realism?

Chaos Theory
http://en.wikipedia.org/wiki/Chaos_theory

Chaos theory has exciting implications for many academic disciplines, including political science and the study of international relations. Visit this Wikipedia site for a clear explanation of the theory and its implications. How do mathematics and physics figure into chaos theory? How can chaos theory affect global politics?

INFOTRAC® COLLEGE EDITION

Legro, Jeffrey W., and Andrew Moravcsik. "Is Anybody Still a Realist?" *International Security* (Fall 1999).

Jervis, Robert. "Realism, Neoliberalism, and Cooperation." *International Security* (Summer 1999).

Kurth, James. "Inside the Cave: The Banality of I.R. Studies." *The National Interest* (Fall 1998).

Hoffmann, Stanley. "The Crisis of Liberal Internationalism." *Foreign Policy* (Spring 1995).

For more articles, enter:
"realism theory" in Keywords.
"neorealism" in Keywords.
"liberalism" in the Subject Guide, and then go to subdivision "international aspects."
"socialism" in the Subject Guide, and then go to "international aspects."

Go to http://politicalscience.wadsworth.com/kegley10 to access additional resources related to this chapter.

PART II

THE GLOBE'S ACTORS AND THEIR RELATIONS

Shakespeare wrote that "all the world's a stage and all the men and women merely players." When it comes to international politics, not just people but also organizations, groups, and countries have a variety of roles to play on the global stage. Part II identifies the major actors in world politics today and describes the roles they perform, the policies they pursue, and the predicaments they face.

Each chapter in Part II focuses on a prominent type of global actor. We begin with states (Chapter 3), using them to show the processes all transnational actors use to make foreign policy decisions. We also identify the factors that sometimes interfere with the actors' ability to make rational choices about their interests and policies. In Chapter 4 special attention is given to the actors with the greatest military and economic capabilities—the great powers. Next, Chapter 5 deals with the weaker, economically less-developed countries, known collectively as the Global South because the majority of them are located in the Earth's Southern Hemisphere, whose fates are shaped so much by the great powers and by multilateral institutions and actors. In Chapter 6, we examine the growing role of nonstate actors—intergovernmental organizations such as the United Nations and European Union and nongovernmental organizations of private actors such as Greenpeace and Amnesty International—whose members actively work for global change. This broad category also includes multinational corporations, ethnopolitical groups, and religious movements. Finally, we explore how all these actors and their activities profoundly affect the welfare and basic rights of all humanity—the more than 6 billion humans who struggle in the world to realize the ideals promised in the U.S. Declaration of Independence: life, liberty, and the pursuit of happiness.

CHAPTER 3

FOREIGN POLICY DECISION MAKING

TOPICS AND THEMES

- The emergence of the modern state system
- The global and domestic determinants of states' foreign policy behavior
- The unitary actor and rational decision making
- The bureaucratic politics of foreign policy decision making
- The role of leaders in foreign policy decision making
- Constraints on foreign policy making: Problems and prospects

- **CONTROVERSY** ARE DEMOCRACIES DEFICIENT IN FOREIGN AFFAIRS?
- **CONTROVERSY** POLICY AND PERSONALITY: DO LEADERS MAKE A DIFFERENCE?

U.S. President George W. Bush addressing the United Nations on September 10, 2002, giving the multilateral world body an ultimatum by warning the Security Council to authorize UN military action against Saddam Hussein.

Foreign policy is the system of activities evolved by communities for changing the behavior of other states and for adjusting their own activities to the international environment.

—GEORGE MODELSKI, political scientist, 1962

Much of the anguish of foreign policy results from the need to establish priorities among competing, sometimes conflicting, necessities.

—HENRY A. KISSINGER, former U.S. secretary of state, 1999

In studying world politics we typically use the term **actor** to refer to the agents who are the globe's primary performers. These transnational players include countries (for example, the United States and Japan), international organizations (the United Nations, or UN, and the Nordic Council), as well as nonstate actors such as nongovernmental international organizations (the World Wildlife Federation), indigenous nationalities (the Kurds in Iran, Iraq, and Turkey), multinational corporations (Wal-Mart and Sony), and terrorist groups (the Al Qaeda global network).

The conventional image is that of a stage on which players in the global drama act out their assigned roles. The leading actors dominate center stage, and the supporting players move along the periphery. Whatever their relative capacity to influence the global condition, add their decisions together and consider their impact on the decisions each and every one of us—the marginal players who constitute the mass of the Earth, humanity, human beings—make every day, which in countless ways make a small contribution to the trends that transform world politics. People, too, are global actors.

We will discuss each type of actor in later chapters, but here we will focus on countries, usually called "states." We particularly emphasize the ways states make foreign policy decisions designed to cope with challenges from abroad.

■ **actor**
an individual, group, state, or organization that plays a major role in world politics.

The processes by which states decide on foreign policy will illuminate as well the factors that influence how all the other categories of transnational actors make foreign policy choices. States demand primary attention, however, because international law gives them special status as the principal holders of economic and military capabilities in world affairs, and assigns to states alone the legal right to use armed force.

THE EMERGENCE OF THE MODERN STATE SYSTEM

As a network of relationships among independent territorial units, the modern state system was born with the Peace of Westphalia in 1648, which ended the Thirty Years' War in Europe. Thereafter, European rulers refused to recognize the secular authority of the Roman Catholic Church, replacing the system of papal governance in the Middle Ages with geographically and politically separate states that recognized no superior authority. The newly independent states all gave to rulers the same legal rights: territory under their sole control, unrestricted control of their domestic affairs, and the freedom to conduct foreign relations and negotiate treaties with other states. The concept of **state sovereignty**—that no other actor is above the state—captures these legal rights.

The Westphalian system still colors every dimension of world politics and provides the terminology used to describe the primary units in international affairs. Although the term *nation-state* is often used interchangeably with "state" and "nation," technically the three are different. A **state** is a legal entity that enjoys a permanent population, a well-defined territory, and a government capable of exercising sovereignty. A **nation** is a collection of people who, on the basis of ethnic, linguistic, or cultural affinity, so construct their reality as to primarily perceive themselves to be members of the same group. Thus the term *nation-state* implies a convergence between territorial states and the psychological identification of people within them. However, in employing this familiar terminology, we should exercise caution because this condition is relatively rare; there are few independent states comprising a single nationality. As we shall explain in Chapter 6, most states are populated by many nations, and some nations are not states. These "nonstate nations" are ethnic groups, such as Native American tribes in the United States, Sikhs in India, or Basques in Spain, composed of people without sovereign power over the territory in which they live.

When we speak generically about **foreign policy** and the decision-making processes that produce it, we mean the goals that officials heading states (and other transnational actors) seek abroad, the values that underlie those goals, and the means or instruments used to pursue them. To begin our inquiry into how foreign policy choices are made, we first consider the setting for states' choices and the circumstances outside national borders that make such choices necessary. Here we examine how states' national attributes influence their foreign policy behavior. Then, we look at decision making as a rational process before considering two ways of viewing national decision making: the bureaucratic politics and the history-making individual models.

■ **state sovereignty**
a state's supreme authority to manage internal affairs and foreign relations.

■ **state**
an independent legal entity with a government exercising supreme authority over the territory and population it governs.

■ **nation**
a collectivity whose people see themselves as members of the same group because they share the same ethnicity, culture, or language.

■ **foreign policy**
the decisions governing authorities make to realize international goals.

THE GLOBAL AND DOMESTIC DETERMINANTS OF STATES' FOREIGN POLICY BEHAVIOR

Geostrategic location, military might, economic prowess, and system of government are all variables that affect foreign policy choices. Still, due to the diversity of states, as well as their different locations and positions within the contemporary global system, it is difficult to generalize about the influence of any one factor or combination of factors. To determine the relative impact of specific factors under different circumstances, we must first distinguish between the global and internal influences on policy choices. Note the **levels of analysis** pictured in Figure 3.1.

In classifying the determinants not only of states' foreign policies but also of trends in world politics generally, the levels-of-analysis concept introduced in Chapter 1 helps to describe the multiple influences on decision-making processes. Recall that states and the global system make up two distinct levels: the state level encompasses domestic characteristics, and the global or international system level encompasses interstate relations and changes in these relations over time. Although these two traditionally discrete realms have become increasingly

■ **levels of analysis**
the different aspects of and agents in international affairs that may be stressed in interpreting world politics and explaining global phenomena, depending on whether the analyst chooses to focus on "wholes" (the complete global system and large collectivities) or on "parts" (individual states or people).

FIGURE 3.1
The Major Sources of States' Foreign Policy Decisions: Influences at Three Levels

The factors that shape states' foreign policies and the decisions of all others global actions can be categorized at three basic levels. At the global level are those structural features of the international system such as the prevalence of civil wars and the extent of trade interdependence. At the state level are internal or domestic influences such as the state's type of government or the opinions of its citizens. At the individual level are the characteristics of leaders—their personal beliefs, values, and personality. All three levels simultaneously affect decisions, but their relative weight usually depends on the issues and circumstances at the time of decision.

■ **intermestic**
a concept used to describe those issues confronting a state that are simultaneously international and domestic.

■ **globalization**
the accelerating process by which increasing interstate interconnectedness has eroded the traditional distinction between states' domestic and international affairs.

■ **states' attributes**
state characteristics that shape foreign policy behavior, such as its size, wealth, and the extent to which its leaders are accountable to its citizens in comparison with other states.

■ **isolationism**
a foreign policy aiming to withdraw from active global participation in order to distance a country from foreign dangers.

fused in what is called **intermestic** decision making, as the need for leaders to coordinate their domestic and foreign policies has increased with the **globalization** of international relations, this categorical distinction is still useful for purposes of analysis.

Global or "external" influences on foreign policy include all activities occurring beyond a state's borders that structure the choices its officials and the people they govern make. Such factors as the content of international law, the number of military alliances, destruction of forests and animal species, and the changing levels of international trade sometimes profoundly affect the choices of decision makers. Internal or "domestic" influences, on the other hand, are those that exist at the level of the state, not the global system. Here, attention focuses on variations in **states' attributes,** such as military capabilities, level of economic development, and types of government, that may influence different actors' foreign policy choices. Examples of both types of influences follow.

Geopolitics

One of the most important influences on a state's foreign policy behavior is its location and physical terrain. The presence of natural frontiers, for example, may profoundly guide policymakers' choices (see Map 3.1). Consider the United States, which has prospered because vast oceans separate it from Europe and Asia. The advantage of having oceans as barriers to foreign intervention, combined with the absence of militarily powerful neighbors, permitted the United States to develop into an industrial giant and to safely practice **isolationism** for more than 150 years. Consider also mountainous Switzerland, whose topography has made neutrality an attractive foreign policy option.

Similarly, maintaining autonomy from continental politics was for centuries an enduring theme in the foreign policy of Great Britain, an island country whose physical separation from Europe served historically as a buffer separating it from entanglement in major-power disputes on the Continent. Preserving this protective shield was a long-standing priority for Britain and helps to explain why the country has been so hesitant in the past quarter century to accept full integration in the European Union (EU) (see Chapter 14).

Most countries are not insular, however; they have many states on their borders, denying them the option of noninvolvement in world affairs. Germany, which is located in the geographic center of Europe, historically has found its domestic political system and foreign policy preferences profoundly affected by its geostrategic position. Germany in the twentieth century struggled through no less than six major radical changes in governing institutions, each of which pursued very different foreign policies: (1) Kaiser Wilhelm II's empire, (2) the Weimar Republic, (3) Adolf Hitler's authoritarian dictatorship and imperialistic wars seeking to establish a Thousand-Year Reich to rule the world; its two post–World War II successors, (4) the capitalist Federal Republic in West Germany, and (5) the communist German Democratic Republic in East Germany; and, finally, (6) a reunited Germany after the end of the Cold War, now committed to liberal democracy and full integration in the European Union. Each of these governments was preoccupied with its relations with neighbors but responded to the opportunities and challenges presented by Germany's position in the middle of the European continent with different foreign policy goals. For each

MAP 3.1
Geographic Influences on Foreign Policy

How countries act toward others is shaped by the number of neighboring states on their borders and whether they are protected from invasion by natural barriers such as mountains and oceans. This map suggests how the separation of the United States from Eurasia has encouraged an isolationist policy during many periods in U.S. history, until recently. Note also how topography, location, and other geopolitical factors may have influenced the foreign policy priorities of Great Britain, Germany, China, Finland, and states in South America—hypotheses advanced by the geopolitics approach to international politics.

Online map with critical thinking questions

government, however, isolationistic withdrawal from involvement in continental affairs was not a viable geostrategic option.

In much the same way, extended frontiers with the former Soviet Union shaped the foreign policies of China and Finland. Finland's neutrality in the Cold War helped ensure its survival in the face of a powerful and threatening neighbor. China, on the other hand, long regarded its relationship with the now-defunct Soviet Union as unequal, and in the late 1960s the two communist giants clashed militarily as the Chinese sought to rectify past injustices. The "unequal treaties" between China and outside powers, which encapsulate other perceived injustices, resulted in part from China's vast size and indefensible borders, which made it an easy target for the great powers that had carved it into **spheres of influence** in previous centuries.

Like China, the Latin American countries reside geographically near a much stronger power, the United States, whose capabilities are in part a function of geophysical resources. Latin America has long been the object of studied interest and frequent intervention by the giant to the north. The U.S. presence provoked a bitter response among Latin American countries for many decades, be-

■ **spheres of influence** areas within a region or country controlled or dominated by a foreign power.

■ **imperialism**
intentional imposition of one state's power over another, traditionally through territorial conquest, but more recently through economic domination, denying the victim population freedom to have a voice in the conquering regime's decisions.

■ **geopolitics**
the theoretical postulate that states' foreign policies are determined by their location, natural resources, and physical environment.

cause they could not compete on an equal footing with the U.S. economic and military powerhouse. Their foreign policy of resistance to so-called Yankee **imperialism** was driven by their vulnerable circumstances. Understandably, many other poor Global South countries without many resources also see that, given their weak geo-economic condition, their foreign policy goals should be geared to opposing imperialism—what former Egyptian President Gamal Abdel Nasser defined as "the subjugation of small nations to the interests of the big ones."

History is replete with other examples of geography's influence on states' foreign policy goals. This is why geopolitical theories are valuable. The **geopolitics** school of realist thought and political geography generally stresses the influence of geographic factors on state power and international conduct (S. Cohen 2003). Illustrative of early geopolitical thinking is Alfred Thayer Mahan's *The Influence of Sea Power in History* (1890), which maintains that control of the seas shaped national power and foreign policy. States with extensive coastlines and ports enjoyed a competitive advantage. Later geopoliticians, such as Sir Halford Mackinder (1919) and Nicholas Spykman (1944), stressed that not only location but also topography, size (territory and population), climate, and distance between states are powerful determinants of individual countries' foreign policies. The underlying principle behind the geopolitical perspective is self-evident: Leaders' perceptions of available foreign policy options are influenced by the geopolitical circumstances that define their states' place on the world stage.

Geopolitics is only one aspect of the global environment that may influence foreign policy. In other chapters we will discuss additional global factors. Here, we comment briefly on three internal attributes of states that influence their foreign policies: military capabilities, level of economic development, and type of government.

Military Capabilities

The realist proposition that states' internal capabilities shape their foreign policy priorities is supported by the fact that states' preparations for war strongly influence their later use of force (see Levy 2001; Vasquez 1993). While all states may seek similar goals, their ability to realize them will vary according to their military capabilities.

Because military capabilities limit a state's range of prudent policy choices, they act as a mediating factor on leaders' national security decisions. For instance, since the 1980s Libyan leader Muammar Qaddafi repeatedly provoked the United States through anti-American and anti-Israeli rhetoric and by supporting various terrorist activities. Qaddafi was able to act as he did largely because neither bureaucratic organizations nor a mobilized public existed in Libya to constrain his personal whims and militaristic foreign policy preferences. However, Qaddafi was doubtlessly more highly constrained by the outside world than were the leaders in the more militarily capable countries toward whom his anger was directed. Limited military muscle compared with the United States precluded the kinds of belligerent behaviors he threatened to practice—and in fact may have led to his deference to foreign pressure in his decision in 2004 to end his quest for weapons of mass destruction and to allow inspectors to verify that no efforts to acquire those weapons were underway.

Conversely, Saddam Hussein, the Iraqi dictator, made strenuous efforts to build Iraq's military might (partly with the help of U.S. arms sales) and by 1990 had built the fourth-largest army in the world. Thus the invasion of Kuwait became a feasible foreign policy option. In the end, however, even Iraq's impressive military power proved ineffective against a vastly superior coalition of military forces, headed by the United States. The 1991 Persian Gulf War forced Saddam Hussein to capitulate and withdraw from the conquered territory. Eleven years thereafter, in 2002 when the anti-Iraq coalition crumbled after its attempted enforcement of UN sanctions failed, Iraq was now defiant.

The U.S. president, George W. Bush, newly elected by a narrow margin in a contested election, claimed that Iraq was poised to militarily confront its primary enemy, the United States. Bush asserted that Iraq's potential military muscle was sufficient to give Saddam Hussein the capabilities to threaten its more powerful foe, although later evidence could not be supplied to support that claim. Thus, military might as a determinant of national security policy was underscored once again when President Bush chose to face the challenge that still existed after his father lost the White House to Bill Clinton in 1992: how to deter Saddam Hussein from arming himself with nuclear warheads and other weapons of mass destruction and possibly sharing them with terrorists to attack the United States and its allies. The potency of military capabilities as a driving influence on foreign policy decisions was made apparent in March 2003 when Bush announced a "new Bush doctrine" and launched a war against Iraq to remove Hussein from office by undertaking an unprovoked preemptive, or preventive, military attack on an enemy state to coerce regime change.

It was not surprising that Bush's Iraq policy at once met with staunch criticism at home and abroad, even from members of his own administration and political party, because a preemptive attack without prior aggressive provocation would have, and did, violate the established norm in international law prohibiting a premeditated attack to prevent an anticipated action (Gardner 2003). As former U.S. Secretary of State Henry Kissinger warned at the time, the danger is that every country could conclude that preemption is an acceptable practice; he counseled, "we cannot have a doctrine of pre-emption for all eternity" that would encourage any state to attack any adversary that it felt was threatening it. Nevertheless, this episode of preemptive showdown with Iraq illustrates well how real or imagined shifts in the balance of military capabilities between enemies can serve as a determinant of foreign policy decisions. In this case, the United States launched a war, despite the fact that the Bush administration had to later acknowledge that, despite its previous claims, the U.S. inspectors could not find evidence that Iraq had really developed weapons of mass destruction, or that it had been involved in the 9/11 terrorist attacks. Perceptions of Iraq's military capability and terrorist motives, not reality, guided U.S. decisions.

Economic Conditions

The level of economic and industrial development a state enjoys affects the foreign policy goals it can pursue. Generally, the more economically developed a state is, the more likely it is to play an activist role in the global political economy. Rich states have interests that extend far beyond their borders and typically possess the means to pursue and protect them. Not coincidentally, states that enjoy industrial capabilities and extensive involvement in international trade also tend to be militarily powerful—in part because military might is a function of economic capabilities.

The Burden of Foreign Policy Choice for Global Leadership George W. Bush was inaugurated on January 20, 2001, facing the awesome challenge of constructing a new U.S. foreign policy for the turbulent twenty-first century. In 2002, while pursuing his "war on global terror" in the wake of the 9/11 terrorist attacks, he confronted his most severe foreign policy crisis—how to reconcile competing values in dealing with Iraqi dictator Saddam Hussein. His decision to invade Iraq in 2003 came to be questioned and even criticized by many at home and abroad in the months that followed, but these doubts did not prevent the wartime president from winning re-election in November 2004. (No U.S. President has ever lost a re-election while a U.S. war was being waged.)

■ **gross national product (GNP)**
measure of a state's production of goods and services within a given period of time.

The United States today stands out as a superpower precisely because it benefits from a combination of vast economic and military capabilities, including extensive nuclear weapons capabilities. This enables the United States to practice unrestrained globalism; its "imperial reach" and interventionist behavior are seemingly unconstrained by limited wealth or resources. For this reason, **gross national product (GNP)** is often used in combination with other factors to identify great powers and by itself is an important element in predicting the extensiveness of states' global interests and involvements.

Although economically advanced states are more active globally, this does not mean that their privileged circumstances dictate adventuresome policies. Rich states are often "satisfied" ones that have much to lose from the onset of revolutionary change or global instability and that usually perceive the status quo as best serving their interests (Wolfers 1962). As a result, they often forge international economic policies to protect and expand their envied position at the pinnacle of the global hierarchy.

Levels of productivity and prosperity also affect the foreign policies of the poor states at the bottom of the hierarchy. Some dependent states respond to their economic weakness by complying subserviently with the wishes of the rich on whom they depend. Others rebel defiantly, sometimes succeeding (despite their disadvantaged bargaining position) in their resistance of efforts by great powers and powerful international organizations to control their international behavior.

Thus generalizations about the economic foundations of states' international political behavior often prove inaccurate. Although levels of economic development vary widely among states in the global system, they alone do not determine foreign policies. Instead, leaders' perceptions of the opportunities and constraints that their states' economic resources provide may more powerfully influence their foreign policy choices.

Type of Government

A third important attribute affecting states' international behavior is their political system. Although neorealism predicts that all states will act similarly to protect their interests, a state's type of government demonstrably constrains important choices, including whether threats to use military force are carried out. Here the important distinction is between **constitutional democracy** (representative government) on one end of the spectrum and **autocratic rule** (authoritarian or totalitarian) on the other.

In neither democratic (sometimes called "open") nor autocratic ("closed") political systems can political leaders survive long without the support of organized domestic political interests, and sometimes the mass citizenry. But in democratic systems those interests are likely to be politically potent, spread beyond the government itself, and active in their pressure on the government to make policy choices that benefit them. Public opinion, interest groups, and the mass media are a more visible part of the policy-making process in democratic systems. Similarly, the electoral process in democratic societies more meaningfully frames choices and produces results about who will lead than typically occurs in authoritarian regimes, where the real choices are made by a few elites behind closed doors. In short, in a democracy, public opinions and preferences may matter and, therefore, differences in who is allowed to participate and how much they exercise their right to participate are critical determinants of foreign policy choices.

Compare, for example, the foreign policy of Saudi Arabia, controlled by a king and royal family, with that of Switzerland, governed by a multiparty democratic process. In the former, foreign policy decisions have sometimes been bold and unexpected, as exemplified by the Saudi royal family's revolutionary policies in summoning U.S. military forces to its territory during the 1991 Persian Gulf War, in contravention of long-standing Arab policies designed to prevent Western encroachments against Muslim lands. In Switzerland, where voting and mass political participation heavily influence decisions about Switzerland's international activities, the government has pursued the policy of neutrality without deviation since 1815, and, as an indicator of its traditional foreign policy independence, did not join the UN until September 2002.

The proposition that domestic stimuli, and not simply international events, are a source of foreign policy is not novel. In ancient Greece, for instance, the realist historian Thucydides observed that what happened within the Greek city-states often did more to shape their external behavior than what each did to the others. He added that Greek leaders frequently concentrated their efforts on influencing the political climate within their own polities rather than on managing relations with other Greek city-states. Similarly, leaders today sometimes make foreign policy decisions for domestic political purposes—as, for example, when bold or aggressive acts abroad are intended to influence election outcomes at home or to divert public attention from economic woes. This is sometimes called the "scapegoat" phenomenon or the **diversionary theory of war** (Levy 1989b; Mitchell and Prins 2004).

Some see the intrusion of domestic politics into foreign policy making as a disadvantage of democratic political systems that undermines their ability to deal decisively with crises or to bargain effectively with less democratic adversaries and allies (see Controversy: Are Democracies Deficient in Foreign Af-

■ **constitutional democracy**
government processes that allow people through their elected representatives to exercise power and influence the state's policies.

■ **autocratic rule**
a system of authoritarian or totalitarian government where unlimited power is concentrated in a single person.

■ **diversionary theory of war**
the contention that leaders initiate conflict abroad as a way of increasing national cohesion at home by diverting national public opinion away from controversial domestic issues.

> ### CONTROVERSY
> ### ARE DEMOCRACIES DEFICIENT IN FOREIGN AFFAIRS?
>
> History suggests that democracies enjoy faithful allies and lose fewer wars than do nondemocracies, but, despite these achievements, democracies may make foreign policy choices in ways that are less rational and efficient than autocracies (see Siverson and Emmons 1991). For this reason, one realist thesis argues that democracies are decidedly inferior to nondemocratic regimes. Does the nature of democratic rule help or hinder those governments' capacities to realize their goals under anarchy? In evaluating this controversy, consider the views of a leading realist American policymaker, George F. Kennan, who advanced the following thesis:
>
>> I sometimes wonder whether a democracy is not uncomfortably similar to one of those prehistoric monsters with a body as long as this room and a brain the size of a pin. He lies there in his comfortable primeval mud and pays little attention to his environment; he is slow to wrath—in fact, you practically have to whack his tail off to make him aware that his interests are being disturbed; but, once he grasps this, he lies about him with such blind determination that he not only destroys his adversary but largely wrecks his native habitat. You wonder whether it would not have been wiser for him to have taken a little more interest in what was going on at an earlier date and to have seen whether he could not have prevented some of these situations from arising instead of proceeding from an undiscriminating indifference to a holy wrath equally undiscriminating. (Kennan 1951, 59)
>
> Against this criticism of democratic governments' tendency to react without foresight or moderation in foreign policy, defenders of liberal democratic governance such as Immanuel Kant, Thomas Jefferson, and Woodrow Wilson have argued just the opposite: that giving people power through the ballot and a voice in the making of foreign policy decisions restrains leaders in those countries from extreme or excessive choices, such as initiating a war on a whim. Thus, to liberals, democratization makes a positive contribution, enabling the leader of a democracy to bargain successfully with nondemocracies, because other states know that democratic governments are likely to have the support of the people and to honor their agreements.
>
> What do you think? Are democratic procedures for making foreign policy decisions an aid or a handicap? What arguments and evidence can you provide to support your general conclusion about this timeless controversy?

fairs?). Democracies are subject to inertia. They move slowly on issues, because so many disparate elements are involved in decision making and because officials in democracies are accountable to public opinion and must respond to pressure from a variety of domestic interest groups (groups mobilized to exercise influence over the future direction of their country's foreign policies, especially on issues highly important to them). A crisis sufficient enough to arouse the attention and activity of a large proportion of the population may need to erupt in order for large changes in policy to come about. As the French political sociologist Alexis de Tocqueville argued in 1835, democracies may be inclined to "impulse rather than prudence" because they overreact to perceived external dangers once they recognize them. "There are two things that a democratic people will always find difficult," de Tocqueville mused, "to start a war and to end it." In contrast, authoritarian governments can "make decisions more rapidly, ensure domestic compliance with their decisions, and perhaps be more consistent in their foreign policy" (Jensen 1982). But there is a cost: Nondemocracies "often are less effective in developing an innovative foreign policy because

MAP 3.2
The Map of Freedom: The Location of Democratically Governed Countries

Throughout most of modern history, the majority of states were ruled autocratically and the people living in them were not free. However, since the mid-1970s, an increasing number of states have undertaken political reforms leading to democratic governance and civil liberties. This map shows the location when the year 2004 ended (1) the eighty-eight "free" countries whose governments provide their citizens with a high degree of political and economic freedom and safeguard basic civil liberties, (2) the fifty-five "partly free" electoral democracies, and (3) the forty-nine "not free" states, where citizens' human rights and liberties are systematically abused or denied. Liberal democratic peace theory predicts that if the trend toward the spread of liberty worldwide continues so that democracy really, as some assert, has "established itself as a universal norm" (Muravchik 2002), then peaceful relations among the growing community of the liberal democracies is to be expected.

SOURCE: Adapted from annual surveys by Freedom House (2004, at www.freedomhouse.org).

of subordinates' pervasive fear of raising questions." In short, the concentration of power and the suppression of public opposition can be dangerous as well as advantageous.

The impact of government type on foreign policy choice has taken on great significance following the rapid conversion of many dictatorships to democratic rule. These liberal government conversions have occurred in three successive "waves" since the 1800s (Huntington 1991). The first wave occurred between 1878 and 1926 and the second between 1943 and 1962. The third wave began in the 1970s when a large number of nondemocratic countries began to convert their governments to democratic rule. In a remarkable global transformation from past world history, the once radical idea that democracy is the ideal form of decision making triumphed. Today, as the year 2005 began, according to Freedom House three-fourths of the world's countries were fully or partially democratic (see Map 3.2).

This sea change has prompted widespread speculation that we may be witnessing the **end of history**—meaning "the end of mankind's ideological evolution and the universalization of Western liberal democracy as the final form of government" (Fukuyama 1989; Mandelbaum 2002). If this trend continues, the contagious expansion of democratic states could transform the war-prone pattern of past international relations.

The recent growth of democracy has emboldened neoliberals to predict that a **democratic peace** will develop—that a twenty-first century increasingly dominated by liberal democracies will be a safer century. Their reasons for this prophecy vary (see also Chapters 11 and 14) but rely on the logic that Immanuel Kant outlined in his 1795 treatise *Perpetual Peace*. Kant believed democracies would act very differently than nondemocracies in their foreign relations: they would form a separate peace with each other. The basis for this prediction rested on Kant's recognition that in democracies leaders are accountable to the public, and that because ordinary citizens have to supply the soldiers and bear the human and financial cost of imperialistic policies, they would constrain leaders from initiating foreign wars (especially against other liberal democracies similarly constrained by norms and institutions that respect compromise and civil liberties). From this reasoning derived the neoliberal democratic peace argument that liberal democracies are natural forces for international peace.

Much empirical evidence supports the proposition at the core of **neoliberalism** that, as stated in 1994 by President Bill Clinton, "Democracies don't attack each other." Whereas liberal democracies fight wars often with nondemocracies, in the last two centuries there have been no major wars waged by one democracy against another (Russett 2001). This fact poses a serious challenge to the realist assumption that when it comes to war, liberal democracies are no different from illiberal states (since both, realism avers, act on their perceptions of their national interests, not their ideologies, and will respond to similar external threats with the same kind of military responses). The overall record shows that, contrary to realism's premise, the type of government and, more specifically, whether leaders are accountable to opposition groups through multiparty elections, strongly influence foreign policy goals (see Kegley and Hermann 2002). Many developments in world politics examined in Chapters 11 through 14 will draw further attention to the internal roots of external behavior.

Having described the international settings to which policymakers respond and the internal factors that influence their decisions, we now turn to how foreign policy decisions are reached. We begin with the rational model of decision making.

■ **end of history**
the thesis advanced by Francis Fukuyama that because liberal democracy and a market economy are the only workable options for modern societies, the contest with centrally planned governance has ended.

■ **democratic peace**
the theory that although democratic states sometimes wage wars against other states, they do not fight one another.

■ **neoliberalism**
a perspective that accounts for the way international institutions promote global change, cooperation, peace, and prosperity through collective reform approaches.

THE UNITARY ACTOR AND RATIONAL DECISION MAKING

According to realist theorizing, the primary goal of foreign policy is to ensure state survival. From this viewpoint, strategic calculations about national security are the primary determinants of policymakers' choices. Domestic politics and the process of policy making itself are of secondary concern.

States as Unitary Actors?

Realism emphasizes that changes at the **global level of analysis** determine state action. It assumes that foreign policy making consists primarily of adjusting the state to the pressures of an anarchical world system whose essential properties will not vary. Accordingly, it presumes that all states and the individuals responsible for their foreign policies confront the problem of national survival in similar ways. Thus all decision makers are essentially alike in their approach to foreign policy making:

> If they follow the [decision] rules, we need know nothing more about them. In essence, if the decision maker behaves rationally, the observer, knowing the rules of rationality, can rehearse the decisional process in his own mind, and, if he knows the decision maker's goals, can both predict the decision and understand why that particular decision was made. (Verba 1969, 225)

Because realists believe that leaders' goals and their corresponding approach to foreign policy choices are the same, the decision-making processes of each state can be studied as though each were a **unitary actor**—a homogenous or monolithic unit with few or no important internal differences that affect its choices. One way to picture this assumption is to think of states as billiard balls and the table on which they interact as the global system. The balls (states) continuously clash and collide with one another, and the actions of each are determined by its interactions with the others, not by what occurs inside it. According to this realist view, the leaders who make foreign policy, the types of governments they head, the characteristics of their societies, and the internal economic and political conditions of the states they lead are unimportant.

Policy Making as Rational Choice

The decision-making processes of unitary actors that determine national interests are typically described as rational. We define rationality or **rational choice** here as purposeful, goal-directed behavior exhibited when "the individual responding to an international event . . . uses the best information available and chooses from the universe of possible responses that alternative most likely to maximize his [or her] goals" (Verba 1969). Scholars describe rationality as a sequence of decision-making activities involving the following intellectual steps:

1. *Problem Recognition and Definition.* The need to decide begins when policymakers perceive an external problem and attempt to define objectively its distinguishing characteristics. Objectivity requires full information about the actions, motivations, and capabilities of other actors as well as the character of the international environment and trends within it. The search for

■ **global level of analysis**
an analytical approach to world politics that emphasizes the impact of worldwide conditions on the behavior of states, IGOs, NGOs, and other international actors.

■ **unitary actor**
a transnational actor (usually a sovereign state) assumed to be internally united, so that changes in its domestic opinion do not influence its foreign policy as much as do the decisions that actor's leaders make to cope with changes in its global environment.

■ **rational choice**
decision-making procedures guided by careful definition of situations, weighing of goals, consideration of all alternatives, and selection of the options most likely to achieve the highest goals.

information must be exhaustive, and all the facts relevant to the problem must be gathered.

2. *Goal Selection.* Next, those responsible for making foreign policy choices must determine what they want to accomplish. This disarmingly simple requirement is often difficult. It requires the identification and ranking of *all* values (such as security, democracy, and economic prosperity) in a hierarchy from most to least preferred.

3. *Identification of Alternatives.* Rationality also requires the compilation of an exhaustive list of *all* available policy options and an estimate of the costs associated with each alternative.

4. *Choice.* Finally, rationality requires selecting the single alternative with the best chance of achieving the desired goal(s). For this purpose, policymakers must conduct a rigorous means-ends, cost-benefit analysis guided by an accurate prediction of the probable success of each option.

Policymakers often describe their own behavior as resulting from a rational decision-making process designed to reach the "best" decision possible. Indeed, some past foreign policy decisions do reveal elements of this idealized process, described well by former U.S. Secretary of State Henry Kissinger when he observed that

> an effective decision-making process must . . . reflect well-thought-out policy choices—that is, they must answer these questions: What are we trying to achieve, or what are we trying to prevent? What consequences do we expect from this decision, and what steps do we have in mind for dealing with them? What is the cost of the proposed action? Are we willing to pay that price, and for what length of time? (Kissinger 1999, 1067)

The 1962 Cuban Missile Crisis, for example, illustrates several ways in which the deliberations of key U.S. policymakers conformed to a rational process (Allison and Zelikow 1999). Once Washington discovered the presence of Soviet missiles in Cuba, President John F. Kennedy formed a crisis decision-making group and charged it to "set aside all other tasks to make a prompt and intensive survey of the dangers and all possible courses of action." Six options were ultimately identified: do nothing; exert diplomatic pressure; make a secret approach to the Cuban leader Fidel Castro; invade Cuba; launch a surgical air strike against the missiles; or blockade Cuba. Before the group could choose among these six, it had to prioritize goals. Was removal of the Soviet missiles, retaliation against Castro, or maintaining the balance of power the objective? Or did the missiles pose little threat to vital U.S. interests? Until it was determined that the missiles posed a serious threat to national security, "do nothing" remained an option.

Once the advisers agreed that their goal was removing the missiles, their discussion turned to evaluating a surgical air strike versus a blockade. They eventually chose the latter because of its presumed advantages, including the demonstration of firmness it permitted the United States and the flexibility about further choices it allowed both parties.

President Bill Clinton's decision to commit the United States to participate in and lead NATO's military intervention in Kosovo following acts of genocide by Yugoslavian dictator Slobodan Milosevic's Serbian troops against the Albanian Kosovar minority in 1999 is often cited as another example of crisis decision making that conforms in part to the model of rational choice. After carefully weighing various options, a single choice from among the identified alternatives was selected: air strikes and massive bombardment to force Yugoslavia to stop the human slaughter, to surrender, and to accept NATO's military occupation of Kosovo. Whether the decision proved wise was highly debated, but few observers doubted that the Clinton administration had attempted, in collective consultation with its NATO allies, to reach what they thought was the "best" decision through a rational policy-making process.

The elusive quest for rational decision making was also illuminated in the crises that the second Bush administration faced. Most members of the closed circle of George W. Bush's U.S. advisers in September 2001 claimed that they were faithfully following the rules for rational choice in their declared war against "global terrorism" following 9/11 and in their decision to attack Iraqi dictator Saddam Hussein. For example, the administration in the latter case launched a campaign in public diplomacy to persuade all states that it was in their best interest to recognize the imminent danger posed by the possibility that Iraq was illegally obtaining weapons of mass destruction, and took its argument to the UN. The message was clothed in the language of deliberate logical choice to convince skeptics that the costs and benefits of all options had been carefully weighed.

However, like beauty, rationality often lies in the eye of the beholder, and reasonable, clear-thinking people can disagree and often do disagree about the facts and about the wisdom of foreign policy goals. Note that counterarguments of Bush's war planning were also couched in terms of rationality—criticisms that attacked the premises on which Bush's big plans for a major war were based. For example, one Australian observer complained that "unless Bush can mount a more persuasive case that Saddam is uniquely dangerous, Iraq's overthrow by force would send a powerful message that might is right and that the United States alone determines the rules of the game. This would be a repudiation of norms that have governed the conduct of international relations for the past half-century" (Dupont 2002). At home, critics also questioned the rationality of the decision process. Republican Senator Chuck Hagel, for instance, praised the president's September 10, 2001, ultimatum as an important first step in the decision process, which cast the confrontation with Iraq as a multilateral global issue and not a bilateral fight.

However, at the time Hagel worried that Bush failed to address the important questions required of a rational choice: If we invade Iraq, what allies will we have? Who governs after Saddam? What is the objective? Have we calculated the consequences, particularly the unintended consequences? What does [a war with Iraq] mean for the unfinished work with Afghanistan? For the Israeli-Palestinian conflict? For the tenuous truce between nuclear-armed India and Pakistan? . . . I support the Bush administration policy of regime change in Iraq [but] we must recognize, however, there are no easy, risk-free options. . . . Sending young men and women into war should never be taken lightly. Elected leaders should ask tough questions before sending them into a situation that may result in the ultimate sacrifice" (Broder 2002). To many throughout the world, these critical concerns voiced in March 2002 later proved prophetic, as the cost in lives and money mounted and allies' support for the U.S. intervention in Iraq declined (despite the dramatic capture of Saddam Hussein and the end of his tyranny).

This debate in the fall of 2002 demonstrated (as constructivism warns) that rationality is a decision-making goal to which all international actors aspire but that it is difficult to determine when the criteria for rational choice have been met. This raises the question; What are the barriers to rationality?

Impediments to Rational Choice

Despite the apparent application of rationality in these crises, rational choice is often more an idealized standard than an accurate description of real-world behavior. Theodore Sorenson—one of President Kennedy's closest advisers and a participant in the Cuban missile deliberations—has written not only about the steps policymakers in the Kennedy administration followed as they sought to follow the process of rational choice but also about how actual decision making often departed from it. He described an eight-step process for policy making that is consistent with the model we have described: (1) agreeing on the facts; (2) agreeing on the overall policy objective; (3) precisely defining the problems; (4) canvassing all possible solutions; (5) listing the possible consequences that flow from each solution; (6) recommending one option; (7) communicating the option selected; and (8) providing for its execution. But he explained how difficult it is to follow these steps, because

> each step cannot be taken in order. The facts may be in doubt or dispute. Several policies, all good, may conflict. Several means, all bad, may be all that are open. Value judgments may differ. Stated goals may be imprecise. There may be many interpretations of what is right, what is possible, and what is in the national interest. (T. Sorensen 1963, 19–20)

Despite the virtues rational choice promises, the impediments to its realization in foreign policy making are substantial, which is why an eminent historian concluded a "phenomenon noticeable throughout history regardless of place or period is the pursuit by governments of policies contrary to their own interests" (Tuchman 1984). In fact, **bounded rationality** is typical (Simon 1997, Kahneman 2003). Some of the barriers that make errors in foreign policy so common are human, deriving from deficiencies in the intelligence, capability, and psychological needs and aspirations of foreign policy decision makers. Others are organizational, since most decisions require group agreement about the national interest and the wisest course of action. Reaching agreement is not easy, however, as reasonable people with different values often disagree about goals, preferences, and the probable results of alternative options. Thus the impediments to rational policy making are not to be underestimated.

Scrutiny of the actual process of decision making reveals other hindrances. Available information is often insufficient to recognize emergent problems accurately, resulting in decisions made on the basis of incomplete information. Moreover, the available information is often inaccurate, because the bureaucratic organizations political leaders depend on for advice screen, sort, and rearrange it. Compounding the problem is decision makers' susceptibility to **cognitive dissonance**—they are psychologically prone to block out dissonant, or negative, information and perceptions about their preferred choice and to look instead for information that justifies that choice. This explains why policymakers sometimes pay little heed to warnings and overlook information about dangers, so that they repeat their past intellectual mistakes.

■ **bounded rationality**
the concept that decision makers' capacity to choose the best option is often constrained by many human and organizational obstacles.

■ **cognitive dissonance**
the general psychological tendency to deny discrepancies between one's preexisting beliefs (cognitions) and new information.

Diplomatic Ties—Rituals in a Global Diplomatic Culture Israeli Prime Minister Yitzhak Rabin, Egyptian President Hosni Mubarak, Jordan's King Hussein, U.S. President Bill Clinton, and the Palestine Liberation Organization's Yasser Arafat made history by signing an accord in September 1995 to expand Palestinian self-rule on the West Bank. The peacemaking agreement was reached through step-by-step bargaining to realize common objectives presumably carefully decided upon by rational choice. Fateful diplomatic ties, like neckties, can sometimes go askew, despite the best intentions. Five months later, the celebratory mood of the moment vanished when Rabin was assassinated by a terrorist as punishment for his act of courage, and the accord collapsed.

In addition, determining what goals best serve national interests is difficult, especially in the realm of foreign policy, where risk is high and there is much uncertainty. Decision making often revolves around the difficult task of choosing among values, so that the choice of one option means the sacrifice of others. Further, there is seldom a sufficient basis for confidently making choices, which is why so many decisions seem to produce bad unintended consequences.

How can we best choose the maximum alternative rationally, so that we can be certain that we have the best option, until we have considered all the options? Simply put, we can't, which is why we seldom consider each and every possible choice when making decisions. As an alternative, we irrationally figure **opportunity costs.** "Instead of calculating opportunity cost as the value of the single most attractive foregone alternative, we seem to assemble an idealistic composite of all the foregone [because] a wider range of slightly inferior options can make it harder to settle for the one you're happy with" (C. Caldwell 2004). People tend to avoid the challenge of searching for options to realize priority goals. This accounts for the tendency for after-the-fact decisions to frequently take later reevaluation. Decision makers are then disappointed to discover that what they thought they wanted was not nearly as valuable as other things they had not even considered. "Being a good decision-maker means you're good at making

■ **opportunity costs**
the kinds of sacrifices that sometimes result when the decision to select one option means that the opportunity to realize gains from other options is lost.

externalities
the negative side effects that result from choices, such as inflation resulting from runaway government spending.

policy agenda
the changing list of problems or issues to which governments pay special attention at any given moment.

satisficing
the tendency for decision makers to choose the first satisfactory option rather than searching further for a better alternative.

behavioral science
an approach to the testing of propositions against evidence generated by scientific methods to construct theories of human and international behavior.

prospect theory
the social psychological theory that international decision making is constrained by formed opinions and tendencies to overreact in crises, that decisions tend to be made based on the perceived prospects of choices to fulfill objectives, and that for policymakers, a crucial consideration in taking risks is the perceived prospects for avoiding losses and realizing big gains.

decisions, but it doesn't mean you make good decisions" summarizes this aspect of human choice (C. Caldwell 2004).

There seldom exists a confident basis for making foreign policy decisions. Alongside uncertainty, many decisions tend to produce bad unintended consequences—what economists call **externalities.** Furthermore, decision makers' inability to rapidly gather and digest large quantities of information constrains their capacity to make informed choices. Because policymakers work with overloaded **policy agendas** and short deadlines, the search for policy options is seldom exhaustive. "There is little time for leaders to reflect," observes former U.S. Secretary of State Henry Kissinger (1979). "They are locked in an endless battle in which the urgent constantly gains on the important. The public life of every political figure is a continual struggle to rescue an element of choice from the pressure of circumstance." In the choice phase, then, decision makers rarely make value-maximizing choices. Instead of selecting the option with the best chance of success, they typically end their evaluation as soon as an alternative appears that seems superior to those already considered. Herbert Simon (1957) describes this as **satisficing** behavior. Rather than "optimizing" by seeking the best alternative, decision makers are routinely content to choose the first option that meets minimally acceptable standards. Because they frequently face such difficult choices that make it impossible to choose without compromising competing preferences, often only choices that appear "good enough" and available are selected; costs and benefits are not carefully calculated. In short, decision makers are prone to rush to judgment. They rapidly estimate whether rival options are good or bad, react to these hastily constructed classifications, and then are content to settle with the relatively good as opposed to the best.

This construction of how decision making actually occurs in the real world is an extension from psychology using the methods of **behavioral science** (recall Chapter 2) to make observations from experiments about how people perceive and misperceive risks when making choices under conditions of uncertainty. This theoretical approach was pioneered by Daniel Kahneman (2003), who won the 2002 Nobel Prize in economics, and his collaborator, Amos Tversky.

They demonstrated that, contrary to the basic assumptions conventionally made about decision makers as rational, people and leaders usually do not behave rationally. Rather, more often than not, they avoid small risks and take wild gambles, and they have great difficulties abandoning formed opinions stemming from past decisions. They instead routinely engage in what behavioral economists call "confirmation bias." They psychologically need to discredit information that casts doubt on the original choice and seek information that confirms the wisdom of the previous choice.

From this emerged what is known today as **prospect theory.** It has had wide applications in international relations, with its "focus on individual political leaders" and the "strong shift away from the unitary actor assumption that has long characterized the study of international conflict, particularly by realists" (Levy 2003). Looking at leaders' behaviors when making foreign policy decisions, prospect theory informs us that leaders are not different from most people. Leaders have no monopoly on rationality. Like people everywhere, they tend to overvalue certainty to give themselves "peace of mind," often at an exorbitant price. They don't calculate the consequence of choices; they feel worse about losing than they do about gaining, even if both choices produce the same outcome. "Most of us," Daniel Kahneman concludes, "find losses roughly twice as painful as we find gains pleasurable" (*New York Times Magazine,* June 8, 2003, 34). Prospect theory reminds us that people despise the idea of losing and deviate from the expected utility theory which states that people make choices rationally with the purpose of maximizing gains. Instead, their primary motive is to avoid loss and the humiliation that a loss produces. So they avoid taking risks to realize gains by readily taking large risks to avoid losses from previous decisions, hating to lose more than they like to win (Levy 2003). Given this mentality, decision makers are likely to "frame," or construct, a definition of the boundaries of options for a given choice. They accept risk by reconsidering on the basis of hindsight the accumulating costs of previous decisions. At the same time they are eagerly and recklessly prone to taking big risks when gambling to achieve future gains. The result is that most people make decisions in ways that, in the last analysis, do not promote their own welfare; they consciously make decisions that counter their long-term interests. People decide irrationally.

According to prospect theory, decision makers make decisions by "framing" their choices by remembering from their past experience a critical "reference point" about probable gains and losses, and in so doing overvalue what they already possess or have decided. This results in the "observed tendency toward status-quo choices" (Levy 1997).

Prospect theory suggests that leaders do not make decisions according to the rational-choice model; they let their needs and expectations affect when they will be receptive to taking risks and when they will be psychologically reluctant to take the risk of making policy changes to achieve gains. One implication of this theory and evidence is that when leaders strike out by taking risks to initiate bold new foreign policy directions, they will have great difficulty admitting and correcting those choices if they later prove to be mistaken. Like investors who take big risks in the hope of making big profits but hold losing investments too long, policymakers view the prospects of new policies hopefully but cling to failed policies long after their deficiencies have become apparent. This—along with people's tendency to select the option that looks preferable judging by some past reference point rather than one with better prospects for future gains—may account for leaders' reluctance to make and implement corrective policy decisions for fear of public criticism (Bostdorff 1993).

Many studies from political psychology and "behavioral economics" demonstrate that most individuals do not behave like "rational choice" models of decision making. They do not cautiously evaluate all available options and choose the optimal solution. Instead, they tend to use "rules of thumb" that permit them to make quick choices to simplify complexities. These "decision rules" create biases and miscalculations in peoples' decision making.

Four psychological propensities reduce the bases for confidence in the rational model of foreign policy decision making. All of these were illustrated by the choices made by George W. Bush's administration that led to the war in Iraq (see Dowd 2004; J. Mann 2004). First, there is evident what is known as *confirmation bias*. When people embrace a set of assumptions, they are prone to look for information that confirms that view and disregard evidence that contradicts it. For example, the Bush administration readily believed the false reports of Iraqi exiles and others who told them that Saddam Hussein still had weapons of mass destruction. They disregarded the views of UN weapons Inspector Hans Blix and claimed that such observers were too cautious or naïve, when in fact those views were accurate. Second, foreign policy makers are inclined toward *overconfidence,* thinking they are smarter and better than others; they are overly confident about their own general knowledge and ability to assess intelligence reports (as seen in George W. Bush's assertion that he could not recall a single mistake he had made in office). A third problem, known as *anchoring,* is the tendency to become fixated on a particular aspect of a decision without considering the relationship of the choice to previous and present events. For example, the Bush administration assumed that because Saddam Hussein had had weapons of mass destruction in the past he therefore still possessed them (Bush might have been anchored on his father's "error" in not removing Saddam Hussein from power in the first Gulf War). Finally, there is what is known as *loss aversion* or the so-called sunk-costs propensity for people to cling to failing past choices because to correct a poor decision would force them to admit they had made a mistake. Instead, they persist in a losing strategy in the hope that they will ultimately be proven wise. The Bush administration thus was unwilling to consider withdrawing U.S. forces from occupied Iraq because that would suggest their own fallibility and that their error had cost many lives and much money. Leaders, in short, are human, and like ordinary citizens are vulnerable to the same nonrational impulses that lead to decisions that do not produce the best results.

The assumption that states are unitary actors partially explains the discrepancy between the theory and practice of rational decision making. Most leaders must meet the often incompatible demands of domestic politics and external diplomacy, and it is seldom possible to make policy decisions that respond rationally to both sets of goals. Domestic policy traditionally referred to governmental decisions affecting people's behavior within the state's borders and foreign policy to external relations. However, in an age of globalization and state interdependence, it is often difficult to know where domestic policy ends and foreign policy begins. Policies at home often have many consequences abroad. Similarly, foreign activities usually heavily influence a state's internal condition. This is why many leaders are likely to fuse the two sectors in contemplating policy decisions.

To better capture the way most leaders proceed as they make policy decisions, Robert Putnam coined the phrase **two-level games.** Challenging the assumptions of realism, he asserted that leaders should formulate policies simultaneously in both the diplomatic and domestic arenas and should make those choices in accordance with the rules dictated by the "game."

■ **two-level games**
a concept referring to the growing need for national policymakers to make decisions that will meet both domestic and foreign goals.

> At the national level, domestic groups pursue their interests by pressuring the government to adopt favorable policies, and politicians seek power by constructing coalitions among these groups. At the international level, national governments seek to maximize their own ability to satisfy domestic pressures, while minimizing the adverse consequences of foreign developments. Neither of the two games can be ignored by central decision makers so long as their countries remain interdependent, yet sovereign. (Putnam 1988, 434)

In addition to the complications undermining the separation of foreign and domestic decision making, states are administered by individuals with varying beliefs, values, preferences, and psychological needs, and such differences generate disagreements about goals and alternatives that are seldom resolved through

TABLE 3.1

Foreign Policy Decision Making in Theory and Practice

Ideal Rational Process	Actual Common Practice
Accurate, comprehensive information	Distorted, incomplete information
Clear definition of national interests and goals	Personal motivations and organizational interests shape choices about national goals
Exhaustive analysis of all options	Limited number of options considered; none thoroughly analyzed
Selection of optimal course of action for producing desired results	Course of action selected by political bargaining and compromise
Effective statement of decision and its rationale to mobilize domestic support	Confusing and contradictory statements of decision, often framed for media consumption
Careful monitoring of the decision's implementation by foreign affairs bureaucracies	Neglect of the tedious task of managing the decision's implementation by foreign affairs bureaucracies
Instantaneous evaluation of consequences followed by correction of errors	Superficial policy evaluation, uncertain responsibility, poor follow-through, and delayed correction

tidy, orderly, rational processes. These procedures may be better described as **muddling through,** or making incremental policy changes through small steps (Lindblom 1979). As one former U.S. policymaker put it, "Rather than through grand decisions or grand alternatives, policy changes seem to come through a series of slight modifications of existing policy, with new policy emerging slowly and haltingly by small and usually tentative steps, a process of trial and error in which policy zigs and zags, reverses itself, and then moves forward" (Hilsman 1967).

Despite the image that policymakers seek to project, the actual practice of foreign policy decision making is an exercise that lends itself to miscalculations, errors, and fiascoes. Policymakers tend to "avoid new interpretations of the environment, to select and act upon traditional goals, to limit the search for alternatives to a small number of moderate ones, and finally to take risks which involve low costs" (Coplin 1971). Thus, although policymakers can sometimes absorb new information quickly under great pressure and take calculated risks through deliberate planning, more often the degree of rationality "bears little relationship to the world in which officials conduct their deliberations" (Rosenau 1980). Indeed, **constructivism** advances a conception of decision makers as those individuals greatly shaped by the socially accepted shared understandings of national interests and foreign policy within their own policy making community and culture, and that these dominating ideas inevitably reduce their capacity to make fully rational choices.

Although rational foreign policy making is more an ideal than a reality, we can still assume that policymakers aspire to rational decision-making behavior, which they may occasionally approximate. Indeed, as a working proposition, it is useful to accept rationality as a picture of how the decision process *should* work as well as a description of key elements of how it *does* work (see Table 3.1).

■ **muddling through**
the tendency for leaders to make foreign policy decisions by trial-and-error adjustments in an attempt to cope with challenges.

■ **constructivism**
a scholarly approach to inquiry emphasizing the importance of agents (people and groups) and the shared meanings they construct to define their identities, interests, and institutions—understandings that influence their behavior.

THE BUREAUCRATIC POLITICS OF FOREIGN POLICY DECISION MAKING

Picture yourself as a head of state charged with managing your country's relations with the rest of the world. To make the right choices, you must seek information and advice, and you must see that the actions your decisions generate are carried out properly. Who can aid you in these tasks? Out of necessity, you must turn to those with the expertise you lack.

In today's world, states' extensive political, military, and economic relations require dependence on large-scale organizations. Leaders turn to these organizations for information and advice as they face critical foreign policy choices. Although this is more true of great powers than of small states, even those without large budgets and complex foreign policy bureaucracies seldom make decisions without the advice and assistance of many individuals and administrative agencies (Korany 1986). Organizations perform vital services, enhancing the state's capacity to cope with changing global circumstances.

In the United States, for instance, the State Department, Defense Department, and Central Intelligence Agency are all key participants in the foreign policy machinery. Other agencies also bear responsibility for specialized aspects of U.S. foreign relations, such as the Treasury, Commerce, and Agriculture Departments. Similar agencies characterize the foreign affairs machinery of most other major powers, whose governments face many of the same foreign policy management challenges as the United States.

Bureaucratic Efficiency and Rationality

Bureaucratic management of foreign relations is not new. However, with the internationalization of domestic politics during the twentieth century, the growth of large-scale organizations to manage foreign relations has spread. Bureaucratic procedures based on the theoretical work of the German social scientist Max Weber are commonplace, primarily because they are perceived to enhance rational decision making and efficient administration.

Bureaucracies increase efficiency and rationality by assigning responsibility for different tasks to different people. They define rules and standard operating procedures that specify how tasks are to be performed; they rely on record systems to gather and store information; they divide authority among different organizations to avoid duplication of effort; and they often lead to meritocracies by hiring and promoting the most capable individuals. Bureaucracies also permit the luxury of engaging in forward planning designed to determine long-term needs and the means to attain them. Unlike heads of state, whose roles require attention to the crisis of the moment, bureaucrats are able to consider the future as well as the present. The presence of several organizations can also result in **multiple advocacy** of rival choices (George 1972), thus improving the chance that all possible policy options will be considered.

The Limits of Bureaucratic Organization

What emerges from our description of bureaucracy is another idealized picture of the policy-making process. Before jumping to the conclusion that bureaucratic decision making is a modern blessing, however, we should emphasize that

■ **bureaucracies**
the agencies, regulatory commissions, and departments that conduct the functions of a central government.

■ **multiple advocacy**
the concept that better and more rational choices are made when decisions are reached in a group context, which allows advocates of differing alternatives to be heard so that the feasibility of rival options receives critical evaluation.

the foregoing propositions tell us how bureaucratic decision making should occur; they do not tell us how it does occur. The actual practice and the foreign policy choices that result show that bureaucracy produces burdens as well as benefits.

Consider again the 1962 Cuban Missile Crisis, probably the single most threatening crisis in the post–World War II era. The method that U.S. policymakers used in orchestrating a response is often viewed as having nearly approximated the ideal of rational choice. From another decision-making perspective, however, the missile crisis reveals how decision making by and within organizational contexts sometimes compromises rather than facilitates rational choice.

In Graham Allison's well-known book on the missile crisis, *Essence of Decision* (1971), he identifies two elements in the **bureaucratic politics model** (see also Allison and Zelikow 1999; D. Caldwell 1977; C. Hermann 1988). One, which he calls "organizational process," reflects the constraints that organizations and coalitions of organizations in **policy networks** place on decision makers' choices. The other, "governmental politics," draws attention to the "pulling and hauling" that occurs among the key participants and **caucuses** of aligned bureaucracies in the decision process.

One way in which large-scale bureaucratic organizations contribute to the policy-making process is by devising **standard operating procedures (SOPs)** —established methods to be followed in the performance of designated tasks. For example, once the Kennedy administration opted for a naval quarantine of Cuba, the Navy could carry out the president's decision according to previously devised procedures. These routines, however, effectively limit the range of viable policy choices. Rather than expanding the number of policy alternatives in a manner consistent with the logic of rational decision making, what organizations are prepared to do shapes what is and is not considered possible. In the Cuban crisis, a surgical air strike was seen as preferable to the blockade, but when the Air Force confessed that it could not guarantee complete success in taking out the missiles, the alternative was dropped.

Governmental politics, the second element in the bureaucratic politics model, is related to the organizational character of foreign policy making in complex societies. Not surprisingly, participants in the deliberations that lead to policy choices often define issues and favor policy alternatives that serve their organization's needs. "Where you stand depends on where you sit" is a favorite aphorism reflecting these bureaucratic imperatives. Consequently, many students of governmental politics observe that professional diplomats typically favor diplomatic approaches to policy problems, while military officers routinely favor military solutions.

Because the players in the game of governmental politics are responsible for protecting the nation's security, they are "obliged to fight for what they are convinced is right." The consequence is that "different groups pulling in different directions produce a result, or better a resultant—a mixture of conflicting preferences and unequal power of various individuals—distinct from what any person or group intended" (Allison 1971). Rather than being a value-maximizing process, then, policy making is itself an intensely competitive game of **politics.** Thus one explanation of why states make the choices they do lies not in their behavior vis-à-vis one another but within their own governments. And rather than presupposing the existence of a unitary actor, "it is necessary to identify

■ **bureaucratic politics model**
a description of decision making that sees foreign policy choices as based on bargaining and compromises among government agencies.

■ **policy networks**
leaders and organized interests (such as lobbies) that form temporary alliances to influence a particular foreign policy decision.

■ **caucuses**
informal groups that individuals in government join to promote their common interests.

■ **standard operating procedures (SOPs)**
rules for reaching decisions about particular types of situations.

■ **politics**
the exercise of influence in bargaining situations.

Collective Decision Making During crises that threaten a country's national security, decisions usually are made by the head of state and a small group of advisers rather than by large-scale bureaucracies. Here, in October 2002, George W. Bush and advisers in the White House "Situation Room" make plans for war against Iraq.

the games and players, to display the coalitions, bargains, and compromises, and to convey some feel for the confusion" (Allison 1971). From this perspective, the decision to blockade Cuba was as much a product of who favored the choice as of any inherent logic that may have commended it. Once Robert Kennedy (the president's brother and the attorney general), Theodore Sorensen (the president's special counsel and "alter ego"), and Secretary of Defense Robert McNamara united behind the blockade, how could the president have chosen otherwise?

Governmental politics—fighting among insiders within an administration and the formation of factions to carry on battles over the direction of foreign policy decisions—are chronic in nearly every country (but especially in democracies accepting of participation by many people in the policy-making process). Consider again the United States. Splits among key advisers over important foreign policy choices have been frequent. For example, under Presidents Nixon and Ford, Secretary of State Henry Kissinger fought often with James Schlesinger and Donald Rumsfeld, who headed the Department of Defense, over strategy regarding the Vietnam War; Jimmy Carter's national security adviser, Zbigniew Brzezinski, repeatedly engaged in conflicts with Secretary of State Cyrus Vance over the Iran hostage crisis; and under Ronald Reagan, Caspar Weinberger at Defense and George Shultz at State were famous for butting heads on most policy issues. Such conflicts are not necessarily bad because they force each side to better explain its viewpoint, and this allows heads of state the opportunity to weigh their competing advice before making decisions. However, battles among advisers can lead to paralysis and to rash decisions that produce poor results.

That possibility became evident more recently, in the fall of 2002, when serious divisions within George W. Bush's own administration developed over how and why the president's goal was to wage war against Saddam Hussein in Iraq. Fissures became transparent as key officials opened a debate in public over how best to invade another country, or even the wisdom of an invasion as opposed to the continuation of containment through diplomacy. On one side emerged an influential cabal of superhawks, the so-called get-Saddam hard-liners eager to use America's overwhelming military power and unconcerned about the reactions of long-time U.S. allies to such an unilateral military undertaking. Beating the war drums were Defense Secretary Donald Rumsfeld and his Deputy Paul Wolfowitz, supported by Vice President Dick Cheney and Chair of the Pentagon Defense Policy Board Richard Perle, as well as House Majority Whip Tom Delay, a conservative Republican congressman.

Opposing a military invasion to solve a political problem was Secretary of State Colin Powell, who rejected a preemptive strike without provocation to overthrow a foreign leader whose acquisition of weapons of mass destruction and support for the 9/11 terrorist attacks had not been established. Backing Powell was a coalition of unlikely critics of the president's war goals. It included Dick Armey, the top Republican House Majority Leader, who warned that "if we try to act against Saddam Hussein, as obnoxious as he is, without proper provocation, we will not have the support of other nation states [and] an unprovoked attack on another nation would not be consistent with what we have been as a nation or what we should be as a nation."

Weighing in on the critique was the secretary of state in the first Bush administration, Larry Eagleburger, who counseled that no action should be taken until proof was presented that Saddam has his finger on the trigger of nuclear or other weapons of mass destruction. The first President Bush's most trusted national security advisers, Brent Scowcroft and James A. Baker III, also sided with the doves in the battle for the president's ear, with Mr. Scowcroft arguing that "Saddam's goals have little in common with the terrorists who threaten us" and that the Iraqi leader would not risk nuclear blackmail because he is a "power hungry survivor" who knows America's response would be devastating.

In one way or another, those questioning President George W. Bush's war plans all reflected Colin Powell's qualms, based on his experience as a general in the U.S. Army, about the unacceptable costs of an ill-considered war. As Powell (the only combat veteran among Bush's senior aides) wrote in *My American Journey* (1995), "Many of my generation, the career captains, majors, and lieutenant colonels seasoned in [the Vietnam] war, vowed that when our turn came to call the shots, we would not acquiesce in half-hearted warfare for half-baked reasons that the American people could not understand or support."

As rumors of war spread and the intergovernmental debate between these two opposed groups of policymakers and advisers intensified, the national security policy-making decision process fell into disarray. The battle in Washington dominated the headlines, and the president had difficulty fulfilling the promise he made in his January 2002 State of the Union address: "We'll be deliberate." Looking askance at what he termed "the Babel over Babylon," Fareed Zakaria

(2002b), the former editor of *Foreign Affairs,* summarized the disturbing way in which a major foreign policy decision about war was unfolding, and the bureaucratic bases for its clumsy processes, when he concluded that "the reason for this seeming irrationality is that the real target of Cheney's and Rumsfeld's efforts is not Saddam Hussein but Colin Powell. Their strategy is a bureaucratic one, designed to box in a colleague rather than Iraq's dictator. Parlor politics have trumped power politics in the Bush administration." "There's no question that the world would be a better place without Saddam's regime," observed Samuel R. Berger, President Bill Clinton's national security adviser, "[but] if we don't do this operation right, we could end up with something worse. We need to be clear and open about the stakes, the risks and the costs that genuine success—meaning a more secure America and a more secure world—will require." In the aftermath of the decision to invade Iraq, critics feared that those concerns were valid, and that the Iraq war threatened to undermine both American and international security (Eland 2004; C. Johnson 2004; Kegley and Raymond 2005b). The obstacles to this kind of calculated rational decision making are illuminated further by examining more closely the characteristics of bureaucratic behavior.

Attributes of Bureaucratic Behavior

In addition to their influence on the policy choices of political leaders, bureaucratic organizations possess several other characteristics that affect decision making. One view proposes that bureaucratic agencies are parochial and that every administrative unit within a state's foreign policy-making bureaucracy seeks to promote its own purposes and power. Organizational needs, such as large staffs and budgets, come before the state's needs, sometimes encouraging the sacrifice of national interests to bureaucratic interests, as bureaucrats come to see their own interests as the state's. Bureaucracies fight for survival, even when their usefulness has vanished.

> Programs that don't concoct some new argument or other for their continuing indispensability also tend to survive. This is because of [an] immutable law of government: even the most anachronistic, abysmal, extravagant and counterproductive government program will do at least one thing that is hard to assault. (Greenfield 1995)

Bureaucratic parochialism breeds competition among the agencies charged with foreign policy responsibilities. Far from being neutral or impartial managers, desiring only to carry out orders from the head of state, bureaucratic organizations frequently take policy positions designed to increase their own influence relative to that of other agencies. Characteristically, they are driven to enlarge their prerogatives and expand the conception of their mission, seeking to take on other units' responsibilities and powers.

The tragic surprise terrorist attack on September 11, 2001, provides a telling example of these ascribed characteristics of bureaucratic politics. 9/11 was regarded by many as the worst intelligence failure since Pearl Harbor. U.S. intelligence agencies filed numerous reports before 9/11 indicating that terrorists were planning to attack the United States, and that the use of hijacked airliners as weapons was a strategy. Two months before September 11, a CIA briefing warned President Bush, "We believe that bin Laden will launch a significant terrorist attack against U.S. or Israeli interests in the coming weeks. The attack will be spectacular and designed to inflict mass casualties."

Alarmed U.S. citizens asked why, with an enormous army of agencies gathering intelligence, weren't the multitude of messages and warnings about the attack on September 11 on the World Trade Center and the Pentagon translated in time to prevent the disaster? Why weren't those dots connected? Why were the warnings ignored?

The answer at first accepted by most analysts was that America's chaotic system of intelligence was paralyzed by the morass of cross-cutting bureaucracies responsible. They engaged in turf battles with one another and did not share the vital information that arguably could have identified the Al Qaeda plot and prevented it. The problem was miscommunication and noncommunication; the signals about the attack were not forwarded to the executive branch in time. Why? Morton Abramowitz, a former assistant secretary of state in the Reagan administration, offered this explanation:

> Three features pervade the making of foreign policy in Washington today: massive overload, internal warfare and the short term driving out the long term. These problems exist in every administration. They are worse in [that of George W. Bush]. Moreover, while the clash of views is healthy and often produces better policy, this foreign policy team is beset by internal wars. . . . War is fought daily in the high-level bureaucratic trenches; ideology is very much in play. And that infighting has accentuated stasis or inconsistencies in both policies and rhetoric. (Abramowitz 2002, 6)

As the horror of 9/11 persisted, so did interest in and concern about what became a key issue in the 2004 presidential campaign: Who did what before September 11, 2001, to disrupt the Al Qaeda terrorist network operation? A congressional bipartisan commission was created to investigate what had gone wrong, in order to make needed corrections in the way the U.S. government makes decisions for national security and counterterrorism. The 9/11 Commission (2004) produced a new set of explanations for why so many opportunities to head off the 9/11 disaster were missed.

The Commission did not center blame on the inadequacies and infighting of the country's "alphabet soup" of agencies fighting terror, such as the CIA and FBI. Instead, the Commission pointed its criticism at the growing complaints (J. Mann 2004; Woodward 2004) about the inaction of the Bush administration and on the White House's pre–9/11 downplaying or ignoring of the loud and clear warnings submitted by U.S. intelligence bureaucracies of the true, imminent dangers of a likely terrorist attack.

The Bush inner circle had been warned repeatedly throughout 2001 that Al Qaeda was on the verge of orchestrating a large and possibly catastrophic attack on the United States. But it failed to take action in response to those requests before 9/11. Testifying before the Commission on March 24, 2004, President Bush's former counterterrorism chief, a Republican official who had directed America's counterterrorism for more than ten years, Richard A. Clarke (2004), reported that the Bush administration was negligent. Why? Because, Clarke explained, the president and his key advisers did not regard terrorism as an "urgent" threat before 9/11 and failed to heed the warnings. As Mr. Clarke explained on NBC's *Meet the Press*, "The Bush White House was preoccupied with Iraq and deserves 'a failing grade'" for its pre–September 11 terrorism planning because "they never got around to doing anything. They held interim meetings but they never actually decided anything before September 11" (*Wall Street Journal Europe,* March 31, 2004, p. 8).

This failure was in large part because the top Bush administration officials were distracted by their obsession with Iraqi dictator Saddam Hussein and accordingly their cognitive dissonance prevented them from appreciating the true extent of Al Qaeda's threat. The Bush administration's chief advisers ignored evidence that did not square with their prior belief that Saddam's Iraq was the real danger that should be dealt with.

In this case, the failure of the U.S government to protect its citizens might have been more due to the unwillingness of American leadership to listen to the warnings of its national security bureaucracies than to what CIA Director George Tenet testified to the 9/11 Commission. There, he blamed a chronic bureaucratic problem—a government throughout many years "racing from threat to threat without addressing systematic problems in stopping, determining or disrupting" global terrorism.

What decision making immediately before and after 9/11 revealed is the crippling effects of bureaucratic struggles and the inability of presidents to either control them or to seize the contributions to rational choice that such bureaucracies can provide if and when presidents resist the intelligence and help that bureaucracies can provide.

Consider the case where every U.S. president must seek to manage hundreds of competing agencies and subagencies, each of which are habitually loath to share information with one another for fear of compromising "sources and methods." Each agency competes with its rivals and engages in finger-pointing and scapegoating as a blood sport. Moreover, as FBI Special Agent Coleen Rowley testified, "There's a mutual-protection pact in bureaucracies. Mid-level managers avoid decisions out of fear a mistake will sidetrack their careers while a rigid hierarchy discourages agents from challenging superiors. There is a saying: 'Big cases, big problems; little cases, little problems; no cases, no problems.' The idea that inaction is the key to success manifests itself repeatedly" (Toner 2002).

All presidents have found these types of problems difficult to control, and few students of public administration believe that they automatically can be overcome through massive reorganization and restructuring. That is why critics of President George W. Bush's creation of a new Department of Homeland Security remain doubtful about its prospects for infusing greater rationality into national security policy in general and counterterrorism in particular. Sympathizing with the fact that "Mr. Bush is somewhat in the position of trying to steer an 80,000-ton supertanker with nothing more substantial than a sail boat rudder," George Melloan (2002a) noted that through the creation of the massive Homeland Security Department, President Bush was "no doubt hoping that in the process he could rationalize some of those [decision-making] efforts [but that] given the national tendency of bureaucrats to expand their remits, he will be lucky if he doesn't end up with more duplication and dead-weight than he has now." That may be why U.S. Secretary of Defense Donald Rumsfeld was moved to warn that "the Department of Defense cannot meet the challenges of the future with an organization anchored in the past. . . . We must change to meet the security challenges . . . not only on the battlefield, but also in the bureaucracy."

When put into perspective, we discern some key properties of bureaucratic politics. Among them, we see especially that bureaucratic organizations seek to protect their own interests. They attempt to reduce interference from and penetration by the political leaders to whom they report as well as from other government agencies. Because knowledge is power, a common device for promoting organizational exclusivity is to hide inner workings and policy activities from others. The "invisible government" operating within the U.S. National Security Council during the Reagan administration illustrates this syndrome. Lieutenant Colonel Oliver North used his authority as a staff member of the council to orchestrate a secret arms-for-hostages deal with the Iranian government, in what became popularly known as the Iran-Contra Affair (even though the U.S. State Department classified Iran as an enemy sponsor of international terrorism).

The natural inclination of professionals who work in large organizations is to adapt their outlook and beliefs to those prevailing where they work. As constructivism would illuminate, every bureaucracy develops a shared mind-set, or dominant way of looking at reality, akin to the **groupthink** characteristic that small groups often develop (Janis 1982). An institutional mind-set, or socially constructed consensus, discourages creativity, dissent, and independent thinking; it encourages reliance on standard operating procedures and deference to precedent rather than the exploration of new options to meet new challenges. This results in policy decisions that rarely deviate from conventional preferences.

■ **groupthink**
the propensity for members of a group to accept and agree with the group's prevailing attitudes, rather than speaking out for what they believe.

Or does it? Consider again the parallels between the mind-sets that led to ruinous U.S. interventions during the 1960s in Vietnam and later again in the early 2000s in Iraq. In both, we observe "self-justifying bureaucrats . . . blundering into escalating chaos [using] rationality without facts to intimate bureaucratic dissenters." The most powerful decision makers at both times acted from "too much loyalty to the office instead of to the national interest. This groupthink led in both cases to a sour credibility gap" in Vietnam that was "echoed by the President George W. Bush 'mission accomplished' happy talk after the fall of Saddam." But there was "no real White House debate about the domino theory, which as a promise for preemptive war in Vietnam was as intellectually suspect as the preemptive doctrine the Bush administration selectively applied to justify its invasion of Iraq." U.S. Secretary of Defense Donald Rumsfeld explained in a 2004 interview the hold of groupthink on decisions in both Vietnam and Iraq: "We were wrong. But we had in our minds a mindset that led to action" (Rich 2004).

Groupthink follows this conclusion. It is often cited by scholars as a process governing policy decision making that leads to riskier choices and extreme policies that ultimately miserably fail than likely would have been made by individuals without the pressures of peer groups (Janis 1982).

The Consequences of Bureaucratic Policy Making

A corollary of the notion that bureaucracies are often self-serving and guardians of the status quo is the idea that they defy directives by the political authorities they are supposed to serve. To thwart unpopular demands by authorities, bureaucracies often slow down and act inefficiently. At other times, bureaucratic sabotage is direct and immediate, again as vividly illustrated by the Cuban Missile Crisis. While President Kennedy sought to orchestrate U.S. action and bargaining, his bureaucracy in general, and the Navy in particular, were in fact controlling events by doing as they wished.

> [The bureaucracy chose] to obey the orders it liked and ignore or stretch others. Thus, after a tense argument with the navy, Kennedy ordered the blockade line moved closer to Cuba so that the Russians might have more time to draw back. Having lost the argument with the president, the navy simply ignored his order. Unbeknownst to Kennedy, the navy was also at work forcing Soviet submarines to surface long before Kennedy authorized any contact with Soviet ships. And despite the president's order to halt all provocative intelligence, an American U-2 [spy] plane entered Soviet airspace at the height of the crisis. When Kennedy began to realize that he was not in full control, he asked his secretary of defense to see if he could find out just what the navy was doing. McNamara then made his first visit to the navy command post in the Pentagon. In a heated exchange, the chief of naval operations suggested that McNamara return to his office and let the navy run the blockade. (Gelb and Halperin 1973, 256)

Bureaucratic resistance is not the only inertial force promoting status quo foreign policies. The dynamics of governmental politics, which reduce policy choices to a political tug of war, also retard the prospects for change. From the perspective of the participants, decision making is a high-stakes political game in which differences are often settled at the least common denominator instead of by rational cost-benefit calculations. As former U.S. Secretary of State Henry Kissinger described the process:

> Each of the contending factions within the bureaucracy has a maximum incentive to state its case in its most extreme form because the ultimate outcome depends, to a considerable extent, on a bargaining process. The premium placed on advocacy turns decision making into a series of adjustments among special interests—a process more suited to domestic than to foreign policy. . . . The outcome usually depends more on the pressure or the persuasiveness of the contending advocates than on a concept of overall purpose. (Kissinger 1969, 268)

THE ROLE OF LEADERS IN FOREIGN POLICY DECISION MAKING

The course of history is determined by the decisions of political elites. Leaders and the kind of leadership they exert shape the way in which foreign policies are made and the consequent behavior of states in world politics. "There is properly no history, only biography" is the way Ralph Waldo Emerson encapsulated the view that individual leaders move history.

Leaders as Makers and Movers of World History

This **history-making individuals model** of policy decision making equates states' actions with the preferences and initiatives of the highest government officials. We expect leaders to lead, and we assume new leaders will make a dif-

■ **history-making individuals model**
an interpretation that sees foreign policy decisions that affect the course of history as products of strong-willed leaders acting on their personal convictions.

ference. We reinforce this image when we routinely attach the names of leaders to policies—as though the leaders were synonymous with the state itself—as well as when we ascribe most successes and failures in foreign affairs to the leaders in charge at the time they occur. The equation of U.S. foreign policy with the **Nixon Doctrine** in the 1970s, the **Reagan Doctrine** in the 1980s, the **Clinton Doctrine** in the 1990s, and the **Bush Doctrine** in the 2000s are recent examples.

Citizens are not alone in thinking that leaders are the decisive determinants of states' foreign policies and, by extension, world history. Leaders themselves seek to create impressions of their own self-importance while attributing extraordinary powers to other leaders. The assumptions they make about the personalities of their counterparts, consciously or unconsciously, in turn influence their own behavior (Wendzel 1980), as political psychologists who study the impact of leaders' perceptions and personalities on their foreign policy preferences demonstrate (see the journal *Political Psychology*).

One of the dilemmas that leader-driven explanations of foreign policy behavior poses is that history's movers and shakers often pursue decidedly irrational policies. The classic example is Adolf Hitler, whose ruthless determination to seek military conquest of the entire European continent proved disastrous for Germany. How do we square this kind of behavior with the logic of realism? That theory says that survival is the paramount goal of all states and that all leaders engage in rational calculations that advance their countries' aspirations for self-advantage. But this theory can't account for the times when the choices leaders make ultimately prove counterproductive. If the realists are correct, even defects in states' foreign policy processes cannot easily explain such wide divergences between the decisions leaders sometimes make and what cold cost-benefit calculations would predict.

We can explain this divergence in part by distinguishing between procedural rationality and instrumental rationality (Zagare 1990). **Procedural rationality** is the foundation of the realists' billiard ball image of world politics. It views all states as acting similarly because all decision makers engage in the same "cool and clearheaded ends-means calculation" based on a careful weighing of all possible alternative courses of action. **Instrumental rationality** is a more limited view. It simply maintains that individuals have preferences and, when faced with two or more alternatives, they will choose the one they believe will yield the preferred outcome.

The implications of these seemingly semantic differences are important. The idea of instrumental rationality demonstrates that rationality does not "connote superhuman calculating ability, omniscience, or an Olympian view of the world," as is often assumed when the rational-actor model we have described is applied to real-world situations (Zagare 1990). They also suggest that an individual's actions may be rational even though the process of decision making and its product may appear decidedly irrational. Why did Libya's leader, the mercurial Muammar Qaddafi, repeatedly challenge the United States, almost goading President Ronald Reagan into a military strike in 1986? Because, we can postulate, Qaddafi's actions were consistent with his preferences, regardless of how "irrational" it was for a fourth-rate military power to take on the world's preeminent superpower. This and many other examples serve as a reminder of the importance of the human factor in understanding how decisions are made. Temptation, lack of self-control, anger, fear of getting hurt, religious conviction, bad

■ **Nixon Doctrine**
President Richard Nixon's position that U.S. allies should bear a greater share of the burden for their defense.

■ **Reagan Doctrine**
the Reagan administration's pledge of U.S. support for anticommunist insurgents who sought to overthrow Soviet-supported governments.

■ **Clinton Doctrine**
the Clinton administration's policy of active engagement in world affairs to support enlargement of the peaceful liberal democratic community.

■ **Bush Doctrine**
the unilateral policies of the George W. Bush administration proclaiming that the United States will make decisions only to meet America's perceived national interests, not to concede to other countries' complaints or to gain their acceptance.

■ **procedural rationality**
a method of decision making based on having perfect information and carefully weighing all possible courses of action.

■ **instrumental rationality**
a conceptualization of rationality that emphasizes the tendency of decision makers to compare options with the ones previously considered and then select the one that has the best chance of success.

habits, and overconfidence all play a part in determining why people make the kinds of decisions they do.

Factors Affecting the Capacity to Lead

Despite the popularity of the history-making individuals model, we must be wary of ascribing too much importance to individual leaders. Their influence is likely to be subtler, a probability summarized by U.S. President Bill Clinton in 1998 when he observed, "Great presidents don't do great things. Great presidents get a lot of other people to do great things." Henry Kissinger in a commencement address at the University of South Carolina in May 1985 urged against placing too much reliance on personalities:

> [There is] a profound American temptation to believe that foreign policy is a subdivision of psychiatry and that relations among nations are like relations among people. But the problem [of easing protracted conflicts between states] is not so simple. Tensions . . . must have some objective causes, and unless we can remove these causes, no personal relationship can possibly deal with them. We are [not] doing . . . ourselves a favor by reducing the issues to a contest of personalities.

Most leaders operate under a variety of political, psychological, and circumstantial constraints that limit what they can accomplish and reduce their control over events. In this context, Emmet John Hughes (1972), an adviser to President Dwight D. Eisenhower, concluded that "all of [America's past presidents] from the most venturesome to the most reticent have shared one disconcerting experience: the discovery of the limits and restraints—decreed by law, by history, and by circumstances—that sometimes can blur their clearest designs or dull their sharpest purposes." Abraham Lincoln in 1864 summarized his presidential experience with the conclusion, "I have not controlled events, events have controlled me."

The question at issue is not whether political elites lead or whether they can make a difference. They clearly do both. But leaders are not in complete control, and their influence is severely constrained. Thus personality and personal political preferences do not determine foreign policy directly. The relevant question, then, is not whether leaders' personal characteristics make a difference, but rather under what conditions their characteristics are influential. As Margaret G. Hermann has observed, the impact of leaders is modified by at least six factors:

> (1) what their world view is, (2) what their political style is like, (3) what motivates them to have the position they do, (4) whether they are interested in and have any training in foreign affairs, (5) what the foreign policy climate was like when the leader was starting out his or her political career, and (6) how the leader was socialized into his or her present position. World view, political style, and motivation tell us something about the leader's personality; the other characteristics give information about the leader's previous experiences and background. (M. Hermann 1988, 268)

The impact of leaders' personal characteristics on their state's foreign policy generally increases when their authority and legitimacy are widely accepted by citizens or, in authoritarian or totalitarian regimes, when leaders are protected from broad public criticism. Moreover, certain circumstances enhance individuals' potential influence. Among them are new situations that free leaders from conventional approaches to defining the situation; complex situations involving many different factors; and situations without social sanctions, which permit freedom of choice because norms defining the range of permissible options are unclear (DiRenzo 1974).

A leader's **political efficacy** or self-image—that person's belief in his or her own ability to control events politically—combined with the citizenry's relative desire for leadership, will also influence the degree to which personal values and psychological needs govern decision making (DeRivera 1968). For example, when public opinion strongly favors a powerful leader, and when the head of state has an exceptional need for admiration, foreign policy will more likely reflect that leader's inner needs. Thus Kaiser Wilhelm II's narcissistic personality allegedly met the German people's desire for a symbolically powerful leader, and German public preferences in turn influenced the foreign policy that Germany pursued during Wilhelm's reign, ending in World War I (Baron and Pletsch 1985).

Other factors undoubtedly influence how much leaders can shape their states' choices. For instance, when leaders believe that their own interests and welfare are at stake, they tend to respond in terms of their private needs and psychological drives. When circumstances are stable, however, and when leaders' egos are not entangled with policy outcomes, the influence of their personal characteristics is less apparent.

The amount of information available about a particular situation is also important. Without pertinent information, policy is likely to be based on leaders' personal likes or dislikes. Conversely, the more information leaders have about international affairs, the more likely they are to engage in rational decision making (Verba 1969).

Similarly, the timing of a leader's assumption of power is significant. When an individual first assumes a leadership position, the formal requirements of that role are least likely to restrict what he or she can do. That is especially true during the "honeymoon" period routinely given to new heads of state, during which time they are relatively free of criticism and excessive pressure. Moreover, when a leader assumes office following a dramatic event (a landslide election, for example, or the assassination of a predecessor), he or she can institute policies almost with a free hand, as "constituency criticism is held in abeyance during this time" (M. Hermann 1976).

A national crisis is a potent circumstance that increases a leader's control over foreign policy making. Decision making during crises is typically centralized and handled exclusively by the top leadership. Crucial information is often unavailable, and leaders see themselves as responsible for outcomes. Not surprisingly, great leaders (e.g., Napoleon Bonaparte, Winston Churchill, and Franklin D. Roosevelt) customarily emerge during periods of extreme tumult. A crisis can liberate a leader from the constraints that normally would inhibit his or her capacity to control events or engineer foreign policy change.

History abounds with examples of the seminal importance of political leaders who emerge in different times and places and under different circumstances to play critical roles in shaping world history. Mikhail Gorbachev dramatically illustrates an individual's capacity to change the course of history. Many experts believe that the Cold War could not have been brought to an end, nor Commu-

■ **political efficacy**
the extent to which policymakers' self-confidence instills in them the belief that they can effectively make rational choices.

CONTROVERSY

POLICY AND PERSONALITY: DO LEADERS MAKE A DIFFERENCE?

Some theorists, such as proponents of **neorealism**—embrace the assumption of rationality and assume that any leader will respond to a choice in the same way: the situation structures the reaction to the existing costs and benefits of any choice. But does this assumption square with the facts? What do we know about the impact of people's perceptions and values on the way they view choices? Political psychology and constructivism tell us that the same option is likely to have different value to different leaders. Does this mean that different leaders would respond differently to similar situations?

Consider the example of Richard Nixon. In 1971, Americans took to the streets outside the White House to protest the immorality of Nixon's massive bombing of Vietnam. His reaction to this perceived threat was to shield himself from the voice of the people, without success, as it happened. Nixon complained that "nobody can know what it means for a president to be sitting in that White House working late at night and to have hundreds of thousands of demonstrators charging through the streets. Not even earplugs could block the noise."

Earlier, on a rainy afternoon in 1962, John F. Kennedy faced a similar citizen protest. Americans had gathered in front of the White House for a Ban the Bomb demonstration. His response was to send out urns of coffee and doughnuts and invite the leaders of the protest to come inside to state their case, believing that a democracy should encourage dissent and debate.

Nixon saw protesters as a threat; Kennedy saw them as an opportunity. This comparison suggests that the type of leader can make a difference in determining the kinds of choices likely to be made in response to similar situations. More important than each president's treatment of the protesters, however, was whether he actually changed his policy decisions based on the protests. Although Kennedy was hospitable to protesters, he did not ban nuclear weapons; in fact, military spending under Kennedy grew to consume half of the federal budget. Many would protest that Kennedy alone could not be expected to eliminate nuclear weapons—that the zeitgeist was dominated by fear of the Soviet Union and intense concern for national security. The protesters in 1971, however, were more in keeping with the spirit of the times. Although they alone may not have persuaded Nixon to alter his policies in Vietnam, widespread protest and discontentment with the war, as well as America's inability to win, eventually prompted Nixon to order the gradual withdrawal of U.S. troops, ending American participation in the Vietnam War. These outcomes suggest that leaders are captive to zeitgeist, or larger forces that drive international relations in their times.

What do you think? Did Kennedy and Nixon choose courses of action that reflected who they were as individuals? Or would any president in their respective eras have made similar choices?

■ **neorealism**
theoretical account of states' behavior as determined by differences in their relative power.

nist Party rule in Moscow terminated and the Soviet state set on a path toward democracy and free enterprise, had it not been for Gorbachev's vision, courage, and commitment to engineering these revolutionary, system-transforming changes. Ironically, those reforms led to his loss of power when the Soviet Union imploded in 1991.

Refinements to the History-Making Individuals Model

Having said that the history-making individuals model may be compelling, we must be cautious and remember that leaders are not all-powerful determinants of states' foreign policy behavior. Rather, their personal influence varies with the context, and often the context is more influential than the leader (see Controversy: Policy and Personality: Do Leaders Make a Difference?). The "great person" versus **zeitgeist** ("spirit of the times") debate is pertinent here, as constructivist theorists like to observe. At the core of this enduring controversy is the question of whether certain times are conducive to the emergence of leaders or whether famous leaders would have an impact whenever and wherever they lived (see Greenstein 1987). That question may be unanswerable but at least reminds us that multiple factors affect states' foreign policy decisions. The history-making individuals model alone appears too simple an explanation of how states react to challenges from abroad.

■ **zeitgeist**
the "spirit of the times," or the dominant cultural norms assumed to influence the behavior of people living in particular periods.

CONSTRAINTS ON FOREIGN POLICY MAKING: PROBLEMS AND PROSPECTS

Can states (and for that matter, other transnationally active players on the world stage) respond to the demands that external challenges and internal politics simultaneously place on their leaders? For many reasons, that capability is increasingly strained.

Foreign policy choice occurs in an environment of uncertainty and multiple, competing interests. On occasion, it is also made in situations when policymakers are caught by surprise and a quick decision is needed. Preoccupied with sunk costs, short-run results, and postdecisional rationalization, the stress these conditions produce impairs leaders' cognitive abilities and may cause them to react emotionally rather than analytically.

The trends and transformations currently unfolding in world politics are the products of countless decisions made daily throughout the world. Some decisions are more consequential than others, and some actors are more important than others. Throughout history, great powers such as the United States have at times stood at the center of the world political stage, possessing the combination of natural resources, military might, and the means to project power worldwide that earned them great-power status. How such major powers have responded to one another has had profound consequences for the entire drama of world politics. To better understand this, we turn our attention next to this set of actors and to the dynamics of great power rivalry on the world stage.

KEY TERMS

actor
state sovereignty
state
nation

foreign policy
levels of analysis
intermestic
globalization

states' attributes
isolationism
spheres of influence
imperialism

geopolitics
gross national product (GNP)
constitutional democracy
autocratic rule
diversionary theory of war
end of history
democratic peace
neoliberalism
global level of analysis
unitary actor
rational choice
bounded rationality
cognitive dissonance
opportunity costs
externalities
policy agendas
satisficing
behavioral science
prospect theory
two-level games
muddling through
contructivism
bureaucracies
multiple advocacy
bureaucratic politics model
policy networks
caucuses
standard operating procedures
(SOPs)
politics
groupthink
history-making individuals model
Nixon Doctrine
Reagan Doctrine
Clinton Doctrine
Bush Doctrine
procedural rationality
instrumental rationality
political efficacy
neorealism
zeitgeist

SUGGESTED READING

Allison, Graham, and Philip Zelikow. *Essence of Decision: Explaining the Cuban Missile Crisis,* 2nd ed. New York: Longman, 1999.

Hagan, Joe D., and Margaret G. Hermann. *Leaders, Groups, Coalitions: Understanding the People and Processes in Foreign Policymaking.* Boston: Blackwell, 2001.

Hermann, Charles F., Charles W. Kegley, Jr., and James N. Rosenau, eds. *New Directions in the Study of Foreign Policy.* Boston: Allen & Unwin, 1987.

Hermann, Margaret G., and Bengt Sundelius, eds. *Comparative Foreign Policy Analysis: Theories and Methods.* Upper Saddle River, N.J.: Prentice Hall, 2005.

Hey, Jeanne A.K., ed. *Small States in World Politics: Explaining Foreign Policy Behavior.* Boulder, Colo.: Lynn Rienner, 2003.

Kahneman, Daniel. "Maps of Bounded Rationality." *American Economic Review* 93 (December 2003): 1449–1475.

Kegley, Charles W., Jr., and Gregory A. Raymond. *From War to Peace: Fateful Decisions in International Politics.* Boston: Bedford/St. Martin's, 2002.

Kubalkova, Vendulka, ed. *Foreign Policy in a Constructed World.* London: M. E. Sharpe, 2001.

Levy, Jack S. "Prospect Theory, Rational Choice, and International Relations." *International Studies Quarterly* (March 1997): 87–112.

Snyder, Richard C., H. W. Bruck, Burton Sapin, and Valerie M. Hudson. *Foreign Policy Decision Making* (*Revisited*). London: Palgrave, 2003.

't Hart, Paul, Eric K. Stern, and Bengt Sundelius, eds. *Beyond Groupthink: Political Group Dynamics and Foreign Policy-Making.* Ann Arbor: University of Michigan Press, 1997.

Wittkopf, Eugene R., Charles W. Kegley, Jr., and James M. Scott. *American Foreign Policy: Pattern and Process,* 6th ed. Belmont, Calif.: Wadsworth/Thomson Learning, 2003.

WHERE ON THE WORLD WIDE WEB?

Cuban Missile Crisis
http://library.thinkquest.org/11046/
The Cuban Missile Crisis brought the superpowers to the brink of nuclear war. This site provides an in-depth account and analysis of the crisis and the actors and issues involved. Read dossiers of the primary players, hear segments of the ExComm meeting, and see U-2 spy plane photos. At the end, take an online quiz to see how well you understand the crisis.

Freedom, Democracy, Peace; Power, Democide, and War
http://www.hawaii.edu/powerkills/

The democratic peace theory presented in Chapter 3 contends that while democracies do fight wars with nondemocracies, they do not fight wars with one another. Political scientist Rudolph J. Rummel has devoted his career to researching the causes and conditions of collective violence and war with a view toward helping bring about their resolution or elimination; he supports the democratic peace proposition. Visit his website to analyze his work. What evidence do you think supports the democratic peace proposition? How persuasive are his arguments? Caution: Some of the pictures on the site contain graphic violence.

Freedom House
http://www.freedomhouse.org/

Founded by Eleanor Roosevelt and Wendell Willkie, this nonprofit organization focuses on threats to peace and democracy. Each year since 1972, Freedom House has published comparative ratings for countries and territories around the world, evaluating levels of political rights and civil liberties. Map 3.2 in your text uses data on the spread of democratic liberty throughout the world provided by Freedom House. Examine specific countries' freedom ratings. Which have radically improved? Why do you think this is so?

The Presidents: PBS's *The American Experience*
http://www.pbs.org/wgbh/amex/presidents/

This inclusive website features some of the most prominent U.S. presidents of the twentieth century, including Theodore Roosevelt, Franklin Roosevelt, Dwight Eisenhower, Harry Truman, John Kennedy, Lyndon Johnson, Richard Nixon, Ronald Reagan, and Bill Clinton. Sections focus on the U.S. foreign policy achievements of each president. Chapter 3 introduces the history-making individuals model of government that equates a state's foreign policy with the preferences and initiatives of the highest government officials. Familiarize yourself with the foreign policy achievements of some U.S. presidents. Do you believe the history-making individuals model is a legitimate explanation of foreign policy? What are the limits to the model?

Francis Fukuyama
http://www.sais-jhu.edu/faculty/fukuyama

Francis Fukuyama developed the "end of history" concept discussed in this chapter. He is closely associated with the democratic peace concept and has been a provocative thinker and writer for over two decades. This is his own website. Here you can read a brief biography of his career and peruse a list of his publications, some of which you can read online. How has Professor Fukuyama blended both government service and an academic career? What are Professor Fukuyama's thoughts on important issues and trends affecting global politics?

INFOTRAC® COLLEGE EDITION

Meagher, Michael R. "In an Atmosphere of National Peril: The Development of John F. Kennedy's World View." *Presidential Studies Quarterly* (Summer 1997).

Pious, Richard M. "The Cuban Missile Crisis and the Limits of Crisis Management." *Political Science Quarterly* (Spring 2001).

Hoekstra, Douglas J. "Presidential Beliefs and the Reagan Paradox." *Presidential Studies Quarterly* (Summer 1997).

Jervis, Robert. "Understanding the Bush Doctrine." *Political Science Quarterly* (Fall 2003).

For more articles, enter:
"John F. Kennedy" in the Subject Guide, and then go to subdivision "military policy"
"Ronald Reagan" in the Subject Guide, and then go to subdivision "military policy"
"George W. Bush" in the Subject Guide, and then go to subdivision "military policy"
"bureaucratic politics" in Keywords

Go to http://politicalscience.wadsworth.com/kegley10 to access additional resources related to this chapter.

CHAPTER 4

GREAT-POWER RIVALRIES AND RELATIONS

TOPICS AND THEMES

- The quest for great-power hegemony
  Long-cycle theory
  Hegemonic stability theory
- The causes and consequences of World War I
  Structuralism
  Rational choice and great-power relations
- The causes and consequences of World War II
- The causes and consequences of the Cold War
- The future of great-power politics

- **CONTROVERSY** WAS IDEOLOGY THE PRIMARY SOURCE OF EAST-WEST CONFLICT?
- **CONTROVERSY** WHY DID THE COLD WAR END PEACEFULLY?

The "Big Three" (Winston Churchill, Franklin Roosevelt, and Joseph Stalin) discuss peace at Yalta, 1945.

The United States has been described as bestriding the world like a colossus. Looking more closely, we see that U.S. dominance varies across realms and that many relationships of interdependence go both ways. . . . Over the longer term, we can expect globalization itself to spread technological and economic capabilities and thus reduce the extent of U.S. dominance.

—JOSEPH S. NYE, JR., former U.S. undersecretary of state, 2002

It is the United States that sets the agenda for the world: other countries have to respond to whatever policies the United States pursues. [America's] dominant position imposes a unique responsibility . . . because only the United States is in a position to bring about systemic improvement [and] very little can be done in the way of international cooperation without American leadership or at least active participation.

—GEORGE SOROS, world-renowned financier and philanthropist, 2004

Who's number one? Who's gaining on the leader? What does it mean for the future if the strongest is seriously challenged for predominant position?

These are the kinds of questions sports fans often ask when the rankings of the top teams are adjusted after the preceding week's competition. World leaders also adopt what former U.S. Secretary of State Dean Rusk once called a "football stadium approach to diplomacy." And many people throughout the world habitually make comparisons of countries, asking which states are the biggest, strongest, wealthiest, and most militarily powerful and evaluating which states are rising and which are falling relative to one another. When making such rankings, both groups are looking at world politics through the lens of realism. They see a globe of competitors, with winners and losers in an ancient contest for supremacy. And they look most closely at the shifting rankings at the very top of the international hierarcy of power—at the rivalry and struggle among the "great powers." Moreover, they picture this conflict as continual. As Arnold J. Toynbee's (1954) famous cyclical theory of history explains: "The most emphatic punctuation in a uniform series of events recurring in one repetitive cycle after another is the outbreak of a great war in which one power that has forged ahead of all its rivals makes so formidable a bid for world domination that it evokes an opposing coalition of all the other powers."

Toynbee's conclusion lies at the center of realism. The starting point for understanding world politics, elaborates Hans J. Morgenthau (1985), the leading post–World War II realist theorist, is to recognize that "all history shows that nations active in international politics are continuously preparing for, actively involved in, or recovering from organized violence in the form of war." Cycles of war and peace colored twentieth-century world politics, with three global wars breaking out. World Wars I and II were fought with fire and blood; the Cold War was fought by less-destructive means but with equal intensity. Each of these three global wars set in motion major transformations in world politics, and have set the stage for the unfolding twenty-first century. In this chapter we explore the causes and consequences of these past great-power rivalries and their implications for the future. By examining their origins and impact, we can better anticipate whether in the twenty-first century the great powers will again fail to control their rivalries, and the world will once again experience the dangerous possibility of another global war.

THE QUEST FOR GREAT-POWER HEGEMONY

Great-power war was not unique to the twentieth century. Changes in the balance of power over the past five hundred years have regularly preceded war's outbreak (see Chapter 11). For this reason, the relationship between the great powers' rise and fall and global instability is a core concern in theories of world politics.

■ **long-cycle theory**
a theory that focuses on the rise and fall of the leading global power as the central political process of the modern world system.

■ **hegemon**
a single, overwhelmingly powerful state that exercises predominate influence over the global system.

One viewpoint, **long-cycle theory,** seeks to explain why over the past five centuries periods of war have been followed by periods of peace, with shifts in the cycle usually occurring in concert with changes in the major states' relative power (see Chase-Dunn and Anderson 2005; Modelski and Thompson 1999). During this long cycle, each global war led to the emergence of a victorious **hegemon,** a dominant global leader capable of dictating the rules governing the conduct of international political and economic relations. With its acquisition of unrivaled power, the hegemon reshapes the existing system by creating and enforcing rules to preserve its own dominant position, exercising power to maintain, for its own benefit, order in the global system.

Hegemony characteristically imposes an extraordinary tax on the world leader, which must bear the costs of maintaining economic and political order while protecting its position and preserving its empire. In time, as the weight of global responsibilities takes its toll, new rivals rise to challenge the increasingly vulnerable world leader. Historically, this struggle for power has set the stage for another global war, the demise of one hegemon and the ascent of another.

Long-cycle theory also draws attention to the fact that world politics has

TABLE 4.1

The Evolution of Great-Power Rivalry for World Leadership, 1495–2025

Dates	Preponderant State(s) Seeking Hegemony	Other Powers Resisting Domination	Global War	New Order after Global War
1495–1540	Portugal	Spain, Valois, France, Burgundy, England Venice	Wars of Italy and the Indian Ocean, 1494–1517	Treaty of Tordesillas, 1517
1560–1609	Spain	The Netherlands, France, England	Spanish-Dutch Wars, 1580–1608	Truce of 1609; Evangelical Union and the Catholic League formed
1610–1648	Holy Roman Empire (Hapsburg dynasty in Spain and Austria-Hungary)	Shifting ad hoc coalitions of mostly Protestant states (Sweden, Holland) and German principalities as well as Catholic France against remnants of papal rule	Thirty Years' War, 1618–1648	Peace of Westphalia, 1648
1650–1713	France (Louis XIV)	The United Provinces, England, the Hapsburg Empire, Spain, major German states, Russia	Wars of the Grand Alliance, 1688–1713	Treaty of Utrecht, 1713
1792–1815	France (Napoleon)	Great Britain, Prussia, Austria, Russia	Napoleonic Wars, 1792–1815	Congress of Vienna and Concert of Europe, 1815
1871–1914	Germany, Turkey, Austria-Hungary,	Great Britain, France, Russia, United States	World War I, 1914–1918	Treaty of Versailles creating the League of Nations, 1919
1933–1945	Germany, Japan, Italy	Great Britain, France, Soviet Union, United States	World War II, 1939–1945	Bretton Woods, 1944; United Nations, Potsdam, 1945
1945–1991	United States, Soviet Union	Great Britain, France, China, Japan	Cold War, 1949–1991	NATO/Partnerships for Peace, 1995; World Trade Organization, 1995
2001–2025	United States	China, European Union, Japan, Russia	A cold peace or hegemonic war, 2010–2025?	A new security regime to preserve world order.[i]

usually been transformed by an outbreak of a major, general war. "Only after such a total breakdown has the international situation been sufficiently fluid to induce leaders and supporting publics of dominant nations to join seriously in the task of reorganizing international society to avoid a repetition of the terrible events just experienced" (Falk 1970). Table 4.1 summarizes five hundred years of the cyclical rise and fall of great powers, their global wars, and their subsequent efforts to restore order.

The central premise of long-cycle theory is disarmingly simple, and for this reason it is not without critics. Must great powers rise and fall as if by the law of gravity—what goes up must come down? There is something disturbingly deterministic in a proposition that implies that global destiny is beyond policymakers' control. Fundamental hypotheses are difficult to confirm. Long-cycle theorists disagree on whether economic, military, or domestic factors produce these cycles, as well as about their comparative influence in different historical epochs. Still, long-cycle theory provokes questions about whether this entrenched cycle can be broken. It also invites critical consideration of **hegemonic stability theory.** That theory assumes that a stable world order requires a dominant global leader to punish aggressors who challenge the status quo and prevent the explosive competition of **enduring rivalries** between competing great powers from escalating into a major systemwide war. Many great powers have become entangled in long-term struggles "to occupy the same territory, control the same markets, or monopolize overlapping positions of influence [and] in the process they [have] become competitors for these objectives" (W. Thompson 1999b). The persisting clashes between Britain and France (1066–1904), France and Germany (1815–1955), and the United States and Japan (1905–1945) are examples of enduring rivalries that historically have produced significant interstate conflict. Long-cycle theory and hegemonic stability theory enable us to see the dynamics of great-power rivalries "from the standpoint of the present, future, and the past . . . to better understand all the other things that happen in international relations" (W. Thompson 1999b). For this purpose, this chapter inspects the three great-power wars of the twentieth century and the lessons these uncontained rivalries suggest for the twenty-first century.

■ **hegemonic stability theory**
a body of theory that maintains that the establishment of hegemony for global dominance by a single great power is a necessary condition for global order in commercial transactions and international military security.

■ **enduring rivalries**
prolonged competition between great powers or other pairs of countries whose perpetual conflicting interests often lead to war.

THE FIRST WORLD WAR

World War I rumbled onto the global stage when a Serbian nationalist seeking to free his ethnic group from Austrian rule assassinated Archduke Ferdinand, heir to the Hapsburg throne of the Austrian-Hungarian Empire, at Sarajevo in June 1914 (the same location where NATO's 1999 peacekeeping intervention in the former Yugoslavia was centered). This assassination sparked a series of moves and countermoves by states and empires distrustful of one another's intentions in the two months that followed, shattering world peace.

Before the assassination, two hostile alliances had already formed, pitting Germany, Austria-Hungary, and the Ottoman Empire against France, Britain, and Russia. The strategic choices of the two alliances culminated in World War I. By the time the first major European war in the previous century had ended, nearly 10 million people had died, three empires had crumbled, new states had been born, seven decades of communist rule in Russia had begun, and the world geopolitical map had been redrawn in ways that paved the way for the rise of Adolf Hitler in Nazi Germany.

The Causes of World War I

How can such a catastrophic war be explained? The multiple answers converge around structural neorealist explanations, which hold that World War I was inadvertent, not the result of anyone's master plan. It was a war bred by uncertainty and circumstances beyond the control of those involved, one that people

Might Makes Fright As the globe's reigning hegemon, the United States finds its militant unilateralism provoking protest and resistance throughout the world. American military might generates fright abroad, and fright often generates aggression rooted in anger. In November 2004, French President Jacques Chirac asserted that the U.S.-led war in Iraq was "without question increasing terrorist revolts worldwide by angered Muslims, rather than reducing the threat." Shown here is one example: demonstrators in Iran—long a bitter enemy of Iraq—protesting, in August 2004, a U.S. military attack in Najef, Iraq, home to one of the holiest Muslim shrines. This protest was followed by a burst of anti-American rallies, where protesters burned U.S. President George W. Bush in effigy, along with an American flag. Such protests continue to spread against the concentration of power in the hands of the United States and its leader, a newly re-elected President Bush focused on using U.S. military power in coercive diplomacy against enemies such as Iran that have sought to acquire weapons of mass destruction.

---

neither wanted nor expected. Some revisionist historians, using **counterfactual reasoning** (Ferguson 1999), regard World War I (and other great-power wars) as far from inevitable. One called World War I "a tragic and unnecessary conflict . . . because the train of events that led to its outbreak might have been broken at any point during the five weeks of crisis that preceded the first clash of arms, had prudence or common goodwill found a voice" (Keegan 1999).

Structuralism. Structuralism, a neorealist theory, sees the changing distribution of power within the global system as the primary factor determining states' behavior. The power distribution determines whether coalitions will form and peace will prevail. Many historians find a structural interpretation framed at the **global level of analysis** convincing because on the eve of World War I the great powers' prior rearmament efforts as well as their alliances and counteralliances (the Triple Alliance of Germany, Austria-Hungary, and Italy, initiated in 1882 and renewed in 1902, and the Entente Cordiale between Britain and France, forged in 1904) created a momentum that, along with the pressures cre-

■ **counterfactual reasoning**
speculations about historical events and developments that ask how the world might have changed had certain momentous foreign policy choices not been taken or had other conditions prevailed.

■ **structuralism**
the neorealist proposition that states' behavior is shaped primarily by changes in the properties of the global system, such as shifts in the balance of power, instead of by individual heads of states or by changes in states' internal characteristics.

■ **global level of analysis**
an analytical approach to world politics that emphasizes the impact of worldwide conditions on the behavior of states, IGOs, NGOs, and other international actors.

ated by the mobilization of armies and arms races, dragged European statesmen toward war (Tuchman 1962).

A related element in the structuralist explanation focuses on the nineteenth century, when Britain dominated world politics. An island country isolated by temperament, tradition, and geography from continental affairs, Britain's sea power gave it command of the world's shipping lanes and control of a vast empire stretching from the Mediterranean to Southeast Asia. This dominance helped to deter aggression. However, Germany would mount a challenge to British power.

After becoming a unified country in 1871, Germany prospered and used its growing wealth to create a formidable army and navy. With strength came ambition and resentment of British preeminence. As the predominant military and industrial power on the European continent, Germany sought to compete for international position and status. As Kaiser Wilhelm II proclaimed in 1898, Germany had "great tasks outside the narrow boundaries of old Europe." With Germany ascendant, the **balance of power** shifted as Germany's rising power and global aspirations altered the European geopolitical landscape.

Germany was not the only newly emergent power at the turn of the century, however. Russia was also expanding and becoming a threat to Germany. The decline in power of the Austrian-Hungarian Empire, Germany's only ally, heightened Germany's fear of Russia, as seen by its extreme reaction to Archduke Ferdinand's assassination. Germany, fearing an unfavorable shift in the balance of power in the event of a long war, became convinced that a short, localized, and victorious war was possible. Accordingly, while the advantages seemed clear-cut, Germany gave Austria-Hungary a "blank check" to crush Serbia, which proved to be a serious miscalculation.

To Germany's imperial rulers, the risk involved in the blank check made sense from the viewpoint of preserving the Austrian-Hungarian Empire. The disintegration of the empire would have left Germany isolated, without an ally. Unfortunately for Germany, its guarantee provoked an unexpected reaction from France and Russia. The two powers joined forces to defend the Slavs. Britain then abandoned its traditional "splendid isolation" and joined France and Russia in the Triple Entente in opposing Germany and its allied Central powers. The immediate objective was to defend Belgian neutrality. The war later expanded across the ocean when in April 1917 the United States, reacting to German submarine warfare, entered the conflict. For the first time ever, war became truly global in scope.

This chain reaction and the rapidity of escalation that led to World War I fit the interpretation that it was an "inadvertent war." Simply put, European leaders were not in full control of their own fate. Still, historians ask why they miscalculated so badly. Did they simply fail to recognize their primary interest in successfully managing the crisis? If so, was this because their alliances gave them a false sense of assurance, blinding them to danger and dragging them into a conflict that was not a part of anyone's design?

Rational Choice. Rational choice theory provides an alternative interpretation of World War I. From this perspective, framed at the **individual level of analysis**, the war's outbreak was a result of German elites' preference for a war with France and Russia in order to consolidate Germany's position on the Continent, confirm its status as a world power, and divert domestic attention from

■ **balance of power**
the tendency for opposed coalitions to form so that the distribution of military power is "balanced" to prevent any single power or bloc from dominating others.

■ **individual level of analysis**
an analytical approach to the study of world politics that emphasizes the psychological and perceptual origins of the foreign policy behaviors of international actors, with special attention to leaders.

its internal troubles (Kaiser 1990). The people gathered at the Imperial Palace in Berlin are believed to have pushed Europe over the brink.

If the **rational choice** model of decision making (see Chapter 3) offers an accurate interpretation, then World War I is best seen as a consequence of the purposive goal of rival great powers to compete against one another for global power, a drive that realists believe is an "iron law of history." It resulted from "an attempt by Germany to secure its position before an increasingly powerful Russia had achieved a position of equality with Germany (which the latter expected to happen by 1917)" (Levy 1998b).

As these rival interpretations suggest, the causes of World War I remain in dispute. Structural explanations, which emphasize the global distribution of power, and rational choice explanations, which direct attention to the calculations and goals of particular leaders, partially help us to understand the sequences that produced the world's first truly global war. We must, however, consider additional factors that, in association with these underlying causes, led to the outbreak of the globe's first world war.

Other Explanations. At the **state level of analysis,** some historians argue that domestic factors within countries were influential causes. In particular, many view the growth of **nationalism,** especially in southeastern Europe, as having created a climate of opinion that made war likely. Different groups began to champion their own state above all others. As nationalistic feelings intensified, they aroused long-suppressed ethnic and national hatreds, which strained European statesmen's ability to avoid war.

Domestic unrest inflamed these nationalistic passions, as did the pressure for war exerted by munitions makers who played on nationalistic sentiments. The Austrian-Hungarian Empire's reaction to the assassination crisis suggests that the potency of national passions fed Austria-Hungary's diabolic image of the enemy, its hypersensitivity about the preservation of the empire, and its overconfidence in its military capabilities.

The Germans and Russians were also driven by intense nationalism, an uncritically passionate, patriotic love of country that caused them to make serious miscalculations. Germany's insensitivity to others' feelings prevented it from understanding "the strength of the Russians' pride, their fear of humiliation if they allowed the Germans and Austrians to destroy their little protégé, Serbia, and the intensity of Russian anger at the tricky, deceptive way the Germans and Austrians went about their aggression" (R. White 1990).

Despite these national passions, World War I would not likely have unfolded without Anglo-German commercial rivalry, the Franco-Russian alliance, Germany's blank check to Austria-Hungary, and—perhaps most important—the formation of two entangling alliances. "One cannot conceive of the onset of World War I without the presence of the Triple Entente, which existed as an alliance of ideologically dissimilar governments" uniting Britain, France, and Russia (Midlarsky 1988). Consequently, the division of the multipolar balance-of-power system that drew the growing number of great-power contenders into two opposed coalitions so as to create conditions of **bipolarity**—and the absence of a single hegemon able to maintain order—may have made war inevitable, even though "political leaders in each of the great powers . . . preferred a peaceful settlement" of their differences (Levy 1990–91).

■ **rational choice**
the theory that decision makers choose on the basis of what they perceive to be the best interests for themselves and their states, based on their expectations about the relative usefulness of alternative options for realizing goals. Sometimes called "expected-utility theory," this model derives from realist theories.

■ **state level of analysis**
an analytical approach to the study of world politics that emphasizes how the internal attributes of states influence their foreign policy behaviors.

■ **nationalism**
a mindset glorifying a particular state and the nationality group living in it, which sees the state's interests as a supreme value.

■ **bipolarity**
a global system with two dominant centers of power, or poles, countering each other.

The Consequences of World War I

World War I destroyed both life and property and changed the face of Europe (see Map 4.1). In its wake, three empires—the Austrian-Hungarian, Russian, and Ottoman (Turkish)—collapsed, and in their place the independent states of Poland, Czechoslovakia, and Yugoslavia emerged. In addition, the countries of Finland, Estonia, Latvia, and Lithuania were born. The war also contributed to the overthrow of the Russian czar in 1917 by the Bolsheviks. The emergence of communism under the leadership of Vladimir Lenin produced a change in government and ideology that would have geopolitical consequences for another seventy years.

Despite its costs, the coalition consisting of Britain, France, Russia, and (later) the United States and Italy defeated the threat of domination posed by the Central powers (Germany, Austria-Hungary, Turkey, and their allies). Moreover, the war set the stage for a determined effort to build a new global system that could prevent another war.

> For most Europeans, the Great War had been a source of disillusionment. . . . When it was all over, few remained to be convinced that such a war must never happen again. Among vast populations there was a strong conviction that this time the parties had to plan a peace that could not just terminate a war, but a peace that could change attitudes and build a new type of international order. . . .
>
> For the first time in history, broad publics and the peacemakers shared a conviction that war was a central problem in international relations. Previously, hegemony, the aggressive activities of a particular state, or revolution had been the problem. In 1648, 1713, and 1815, the peacemakers had tried to resolve issues of the past and to construct orders that would preclude their reappearance. But in 1919 expectations ran higher. The sources of war were less important than the war itself. There was a necessity to look more to the future than to the past. The problem was not just to build a peace, but to construct a peaceful international order that would successfully manage all international conflicts of the future. (K. Holsti 1991, 175–176; 208–209)

World War I evoked revulsion for war and theories of **realism** that justified great-power competition, arms races, secret alliances, and balance-of-power politics. The deadly cost of this war led the peacemakers gathered at the Versailles Palace outside Paris to question realpolitik assumptions about the rules of statecraft. They sought instead to guard against the threat of another world war and global domination through a reformed program rooted in **liberalism** that sought to construct political and commercial cooperation among the great powers.

The two decades following World War I were the high point of liberal idealism. That liberal philosophy was given expression in Woodrow Wilson's "Fourteen Points" address, the creation of the League of Nations, the Five Power Treaty (signed by Japan, Britain, France, Italy, and the United States at the Washington Naval Conference in February 1922 that put a ceiling on the building and modernization of large warships), the **Kellogg-Briand Pact** (which in 1928 legally prohibited war as an instrument of foreign policy), the Four Power

■ **realism**
the school of thought that maintains that because interstate competition is natural, states should compete and prepare for war in order to avoid it.

■ **liberalism**
the school of thought that argues that progress and peace are possible through institutional reforms that control international anarchy.

■ **Kellogg-Briand Pact**
a multilateral treaty negotiated in 1928 that outlawed war as a method for settling interstate conflicts.

MAP 4.1
Territorial Changes in Europe following World War I

World War I redrew the boundaries of Europe. The map on the left shows state boundaries on the eve of the war in 1914, as well as the members of the two major opposing coalitions that formed. When the guns fell silent after the war, the victors met at Versailles in Paris and drafted a punitive peace settlement that stripped vast territories from the defeated German and Austrian-Hungarian Empires as well as from the western front of the Russian Empire, which disintegrated in the Bolshevik Revolution that deposed the czar and brought the communists into power in the new Union of Soviet Socialist Republics (USSR). The map on the right shows the new borders in 1920, with the nine new states that emerged from the war.

SOURCE: From *Strategic Atlas, Comparative Geopolitics of the World's Powers*, revised edition, by Gerard Chaliand and Jean-Pierre Ragau. Reprinted by permission of HarperCollins Publishers, Inc.

Treaty (pledging Japan, France, Britain, and the United States not to attack one another's colonies), and the Nine Power Treaty (that placed China off limits to further great-power imperialism). Nevertheless, the liberal idealists' proposals failed to deter the resumption of great-power rivalry. Another system-transforming global war was on the horizon.

THE SECOND WORLD WAR

Although it lost World War I, Germany did not lose its desire for global status and influence. On the contrary, Germany's aspirations intensified. Thus conditions were ripe for the second great-power war of the twentieth century, as Germany again pursued an aggressive course.

Global in scope, World War II was a struggle for power cast in the image of realism. It pitted a fascist coalition striving for world supremacy—the Axis trio of Germany, Japan, and Italy—against an unlikely "grand alliance" of four great powers that united despite their incompatible ideologies—communism in the case of the Soviet Union and democratic capitalism in the case of Britain, France, and the United States.

The world's fate hinged on the outcome of this massive effort to meet the Axis threat of world conquest and restore the balance of power. The Allied powers achieved success in a six-year ordeal, but at a terrible cost: each day 23,000 lives were lost, as the war resulted in the death of 53 million people worldwide (for an account of the campaigns that "called so many to pay the ultimate price for victory" to prevent the German and Japanese regimes "founded on racial superiority, slavery, and genocide" from imposing their values on the rest of humanity, see Murray and Millett 2000).

The Causes of World War II

Several factors revived Germany's hegemonic ambitions. Domestically, German nationalism inflamed latent **irredentism** and rationalized the expansion of German borders both to regain provinces previously lost in wars to others and to absorb Germans living in Austria, Czechoslovakia, and Poland. The rise of **fascism**—the Nazi regime's ideology championing racism, flag, fatherland, nationalism, and imperialism—animated this renewed imperialistic push and preached the most extreme version of realism, **machtpolitik** (power politics), to justify the forceful expansion of the German state and the other Axis powers aligned with Germany. "Everything for the state, nothing outside the state, nothing above the state" was the way Italy's dictator, Benito Mussolini, constructed his understanding of the fascist political philosophy, in a definition that embraced the extreme realist proposition that the state was supreme—entitled to rule by force every dimension of human life.

Germany also resented the punitive terms imposed by the victors of World War I (France, Great Britain, Italy, Japan, and the United States). Reflecting French demands, the harsh Peace of Paris (the Versailles treaty) insisted on the destruction of Germany's armed forces, the loss of territory (such as Alsace-Lorraine, which Germany had absorbed following the Franco-Prussian war of 1870–1871), and the imposition of heavy reparation payments to compensate the Allies for the damage that German militarism had exacted. In addition, the Austrian-Hungarian Empire was splintered into divided political units.

Not only was the Peace of Paris punitive, more significant and painful it prevented Germany's reentry into the global system as a coequal member. Germany was denied membership in the League of Nations until 1926. As a result of its exclusion, Germany sought to recover by force its perceived rightful status as a great power.

■ **irredentism**
a movement by an ethnonational group to regain control of lost territory by force so that the new state boundaries will no longer divide the group.

■ **fascism**
a far-right ideology that promotes extreme nationalism and the establishment of an authoritarian society built around a single party with dictatorial leadership.

■ **machtpolitik**
the German realist philosophy in statecraft that sees the expansion of state power and territory by use of armed force as a legitimate goal.

MAP 4.2
World War II Redraws the Map of Europe

The Axis coalition of great powers, composed of Germany, Italy, and Japan, sought to conquer and divide the world in World War II and almost succeeded. The map on the left shows the extent of German expansion in Europe at the height of its aggression in 1943, when Nazi Germany occupied Europe from the Atlantic Ocean and Baltic Sea to the Soviet Union's borders. The map on the right shows the new configuration of Europe after the "Grand Coalition" of Allied forces—Great Britain, the United States, and the Soviet Union—defeated the Axis's bid for supremacy. The Allies partitioned Germany into four sections occupied by British, French, Russian, and American troops and carved out other territorial changes that returned to the Soviet Union most of the land that it had lost at the end of World War I. Later, Germany was divided into two independent countries, the Federal Republic of Germany (West Germany) and the German Democratic Republic (East Germany).

SOURCE: Europe in 1945 from *Strategic Atlas, Comparative Geopolitics of the World's Powers,* revised edition, by Gerard Challand and Jean-Pierre Rageau. Reprinted by permission of HarperCollins Publishers, Inc.

Online map with critical thinking questions

isolationism
a policy of withdrawing from active participation with other actors in world affairs and instead concentrating state efforts on managing internal affairs.

appeasement
a strategy of making concessions to an aggressor state without retaliation in the hope that, satisfied, it will not make additional claims on the territory of its neighbors.

colonialism
the rule of a region by an external sovereign power.

Proximate Causes. Why did the victorious great powers permit German rearmament? A key reason was that Britain's hope for Anglo-American collaboration to maintain world order vanished when the United States repudiated the Versailles peace treaty and retreated to a policy of **isolationism,** withdrawing from active international involvements. As a result, Britain and France each fought for its own advantage in the treatment of Germany. While France wanted to deter Germany's readmission as an accepted member of the international community and prevent its recovery, Britain, in contrast, preferred to preserve the new balance of power by encouraging German rearmament and revival as a counterweight against the chance that France or the Soviet Union might dominate continental Europe.

Acquiescence to German rearmament and other militaristic maneuvers led to the policy of **appeasement,** or pacifying potential aggressors with concessions. Adolf Hitler, the German dictator who by the mid-1930s controlled Germany's fate, pledged not to expand German territory by force. He betrayed that promise in March 1938 when he forced Austria into union with Germany (the *Anschluss*). Shortly thereafter he demanded the annexation of the German-populated area of Sudetenland in Czechoslovakia. Fear of further German expansion led to the September 1938 Munich Conference attended by Hitler, British Prime Minister Neville Chamberlain, and leaders from France and Italy (Czechoslovakia was not invited). Based on the erroneous conviction that appeasement would halt further German expansionism and lead to "peace in our time," Chamberlain and the others agreed to Hitler's demands.

Rather than satisfying Germany, appeasement whetted its appetite and that of the newly formed fascist coalition of Germany, Italy, and Japan, which aimed to overthrow the international status quo. Japan, disillusioned with Western liberalism and the Paris settlements, and suffering economically from the effects of the Great Depression of the 1930s, embraced militarism. In the might-makes-right climate that Germany's imperialistic quest for national aggrandizement helped to create, Japanese nationalists led their country on the path to imperialism and **colonialism.** Japan's invasions of Manchuria in 1931 and China proper in 1937 were followed by Italy's absorption of Abyssinia in 1935 and Albania in 1939, and both Germany and Italy intervened in the 1936–1939 Spanish civil war on the side of the fascists, headed by General Francisco Franco, while the Soviet Union supported antifascist forces.

After Germany occupied the rest of Czechoslovakia in March 1939, Britain and France formed an alliance to protect the next likely victim, Poland. They also opened negotiations with Moscow in hopes of enticing the Soviet Union to join the alliance, but failed. Then, on August 23, 1939, Hitler, a fascist, and the Soviet dictator, Joseph Stalin, a communist, stunned the world with the news that they had signed a nonaggression pact, promising not to attack one another. Now confident that Britain and France would not intervene, Hitler invaded Poland. Britain and France, honoring their pledge to defend the Poles, declared war on Germany two days later. World War II began.

The war expanded rapidly. Hitler next turned his forces to the Balkans, North Africa, and westward, as the mechanized German troops invaded Norway and marched through Denmark, Belgium, Luxembourg, and the Netherlands. The German army swept around the Maginot line, the defensive barrier on the eastern frontier that France boasted could not be breached. Within six weeks France surrendered, even though Germany's forces were measurably inferior to those of France and its allies (only deficient French decision-making practices and overconfidence in technology enabled the German surprise attack to succeed—see May 2000). The alarming and nearly bloodless German victory forced the British to evacuate a nearly 340,000-strong expeditionary force from the French beaches at Dunkirk. Paris itself fell in June 1940. Meanwhile, to keep the United States from participating in the looming war, in September 1940 Japan forged the Tripartite Pact with Germany and Italy that pledged the three Axis powers to come to one another's aid if attacked by another nonbelligerent great power, such as the United States.

In the months that followed, the German air force, the Luftwaffe, pounded Britain in an attempt to force it into submission as well. Instead of invading Britain, however, the Nazi troops launched a surprise attack on the Soviet Union, Hitler's former ally, in June 1941. On December 7, 1941, Japan launched a surprise assault on the United States at Pearl Harbor. Almost immediately, Germany also declared war on the United States. The unprovoked Japanese assault and the German challenge ended U.S. aloofness and isolationism, enabling President Franklin Roosevelt to forge a coalition with Britain and the Soviet Union to oppose the fascists.

Underlying Causes. Many historians regard the reemergence of **multipolarity** in the global power distribution as a key factor in the onset and expansion of World War II. The post–World War I global system was placed "at risk when the sovereign states, which were its components, became too numerous and unequal in power and resources, particularly when (as happened after 1919) the great powers were reduced in number and new, lesser states proliferated" (Calvocoressi, Wint, and Pritchard 1989). In 1914, Europe had only twenty-two key states, but by 1921 the number had nearly doubled. When combined with resentment over the Versailles treaty, the Russian Revolution, and the rise of fascism, the increased number of states and the resurgence of nationalistic revolts and crises made "the interwar years the most violent period in international relations since the Thirty Years' War and the wars of the French Revolution and Napoleon" (K. Holsti 1991).

The collapse of the international economic system during the 1930s also contributed to the war. Great Britain found itself unequal to the leadership and regulatory roles it had performed in the world **political economy** before World War I. Although the United States was the logical successor, its refusal to exercise leadership hastened the war. "The Depression of 1929–1931 was followed in 1933 by a world Monetary and Economic Conference whose failures—engineered by the United States—deepened the gloom, accelerated nationalist trade **protectionism,** and promoted revolution" (Calvocoressi, Wint, and Pritchard 1989). In this depressed global environment, heightened by deteriorating economic circumstances at home, Germany and Japan sought solutions through **imperialism** abroad.

The League of Nations' failure to mount a collective response to the acts of aggression symbolized the weak institutional barriers to war. When Germany withdrew from the League of Nations in 1933, followed by Italy in 1937, war clouds gathered and the League of Nations was powerless to dispel them.

The Soviet Union's invasion of neutral Finland in 1939 provoked public indignation. In a final act of retaliation, the League of Nations expelled the Soviet Union, but the burden of defense fell on the shoulders of the victim. Ninety thou-

■ **multipolarity**
the distribution of global power into three or more great-power centers, with other states allied with one of the rivals.

■ **political economy**
a field of study that focuses on the intersection of politics and economics in international relations.

■ **protectionism**
barriers of foreign trade, such as tariffs and quotas, that protect local industries from competition for the purchase of the products local manufacturers produce.

■ **imperialism**
the policy of expanding state power through the conquest and/or military domination of foreign territory.

The Rise of Hitler and German Nationalism
In the 1930s the nationalistic ideologies of national socialism and fascism—realist philosophies that regarded the state as supreme, accepted dictatorship, and called for expansion at the expense of neighboring countries—took root in Germany and Italy. Consistent with the realist view that states have an inherent right to expand, Adolf Hitler's propaganda experts staged dramatic political rallies to glorify the German Führer ("leader," shown here at a fascist rally with Italy's Benito Mussolini), persuade the German people of the need to persecute the Jews, and expand German borders by armament and aggression.

sand fiercely independent Finns gave their lives in the victorious "Winter War" over the Soviet invaders while the rest of the astonished world watched.

At the state level of analysis, psychological forces also led to World War II. These included "the domination of civilian discourse by military propaganda that primed the world for war," the "great wave of hypernationalism [that] swept over Europe [as] each state taught itself a mythical history while denigrating that of others," and the demise of democratic governance (Van Evera 1990–91).

In the final analysis, however, the importance of leaders stands out. The war would not have been possible without Adolf Hitler and his plans to conquer the world by force. World War II arose primarily from German aggression. Professing the superiority of Germans as a "master race" and virulent anti-Semitism and anticommunism, Hitler chose to wage war to create an empire that he believed could resolve once and for all the historic competition and precarious coexistence of the great powers in Europe by eliminating Germany's rivals.

> The broad vision of the Thousand-Year Reich was . . . of a vastly expanded—and continually expanding—German core, extending deep into Russia, with a number of vassal states and regions, including France, the Low Countries, Scandinavia, central Europe, and the Balkans, that would provide re-

sources and labor for the core. There was to be no civilizing mission in German imperialism. On the contrary, the lesser peoples were to be taught only to do menial labor or, as Hitler once joked, educated sufficiently to read the road signs so they wouldn't get run over by German automobile traffic. The lowest of the low, the Poles and Jews, were to be exterminated. . . .

To Hitler . . . the purpose of policy was to destroy the system and to reconstitute it on racial lines, with a vastly expanded Germany running a distinctly hierarchical and exploitative order. Vestiges of sovereignty might remain, but they would be fig leaves covering a monolithic order. German occupation policies during the war, whereby conquered nations were reduced to satellites, satrapies, and reservoirs of slave labor, were the practical application of Hitler's conception of the new world order. They were not improvised or planned for reasons of military necessity. (K. Holsti 1991, 224–25)

A brutal war fought at terrible human cost, World War II was much more than a hegemonic struggle. Why and how the war was fought, at great sacrifice, may be best seen as springing from an epic clash between divergent ideologies—between one conception of civilization founded on moral values against another philosophy seeking to destroy it. In both the European and Pacific fronts, the Allies faced an enemy whose ideologies, "founded on racial superiority, slavery, and genocide" (Murray and Millett 2000), sustained a war longer than the mere pursuit of personal, national gain would, from a purely rational choice perspective, seem to justify. World War II was fought over ethical values for which people were willing to die.

The Consequences of World War II

Having faced ruinous losses in Russia and a massive Allied bombing campaign at home, Germany's Thousand-Year Reich lay in ruins by May 1945. By August, the U.S. atomic bombing of Hiroshima and Nagasaki forced Japan to end its war of conquest as well, and brace itself, after its shattering defeat followed by six years of U.S. military occupation, to meet the challenge of "starting over" by socially constructing acceptance of new values.

The Allied victory over the Axis redistributed power and reordered borders, resulting in a new geopolitical terrain. The Soviet Union absorbed nearly six hundred thousand square meters of territory from the Baltic states of Estonia, Latvia, and Lithuania, and from Finland, Czechoslovakia, Poland, and Romania—recovering what Russia had lost in the 1918 Treaty of Brest-Litovsk after World War I. Poland, a victim of Soviet expansionism, was compensated with land taken from Germany. Germany itself was divided into occupation zones that eventually provided the basis for its partition into East and West Germany. Finally, pro-Soviet regimes assumed power throughout Eastern Europe (see Map 4.2, p. 105). In the Far East, the Soviet Union took the four Kurile Islands—or the "Northern Territories," as Japan calls them—from Japan, and Korea was divided into Soviet and U.S. occupation zones at the thirty-eighth parallel.

What is more important than these dimensions of the peace settlement is the system-transforming impact of the Allied victory. "World War II brought an end to the great-power rivalries of Europe, to the extension of much of those rivalries to much of the world through imperialism, and to European dominance of the world's economic development and culture" (Murray and Millett 2000). In the immediate wake of World War II one global system ended, but the defining characteristics of the transformed new system had not yet become clear.

The prevailing sense of confusion amid chaos after the war generated much uncertainty and mistrust. The agreements governing goals, strategy, and obligations that had guided the Allied effort began to erode even as victory neared. Victory only magnified the great powers' growing distrust of one another's intentions in an environment of ill-defined borders, altered allegiances, power vacuums, and economic ruin.

The "Big Three" leaders—Winston Churchill, Franklin Roosevelt, and Joseph Stalin—met at the **Yalta Conference** in February 1945 to design a new world order, but the vague compromises they reached concealed the differences percolating below the surface. Following Germany's unconditional surrender in May, the Big Three (with the United States now represented by Harry Truman) met again in July 1945 at Potsdam. The meeting ended without agreement, and the facade of Allied unity began to fade.

World War II, like previous great-power wars, paved the way for a transformation in world politics. Allied collaboration after the war to create a new international organization to manage the postwar international order gave birth to the United Nations (UN). Consistent with the expectation that the great powers would cooperate to manage world affairs, China was promised a seat on the UN Security Council along with France and the Big Three. The purpose of the Security Council was to guarantee that all of the dominant states would share responsibility for preserving peace.

After the war, the United States and the Soviet Union remained the two great powers that were still strong, with the capacity to impose their will. The vanquished, Germany and Japan, fell from the ranks of the great powers. The other major-power victors, especially Great Britain, had exhausted themselves and also slid from the apex of the world-power hierarchy. Thus, as Alexis de Tocqueville had foreseen in 1835, the Americans and Russians now held in their hands the destinies of half of mankind. In comparison, all other states were dwarfs. In this atmosphere, observers of various ideological persuasions began to debate whether the twentieth century would become "the American century" or "the Russian century." In what eventually became known as the Cold War, Washington and Moscow used the fledgling UN not to keep the peace but to pursue their competition with each other. As the third and last great-power war of the twentieth century, the Cold War and its lessons still cast shadows over today's geostrategic landscape.

■ **Yalta Conference** the 1945 summit meeting among Franklin D. Roosevelt, Joseph Stalin, and Winston Churchill to resolve postwar territorial issues and voting procedures in the United Nations to collectively manage world order.

THE COLD WAR

The second great war of the twentieth century not only had brought about a bipolar system dominated by two superstates, the United States and the Soviet Union, it also hastened the disintegration of the great colonial empires assembled by imperialist states in previous centuries, thereby emancipating many peoples from foreign rule. The emergent global system, unlike earlier ones, featured a bipolar distribution of power consisting of many sovereign states outside the European core area that were dominated by the two most powerful. In addition, the advent of nuclear weapons radically changed the role that threats of warfare would play in world politics. Out of these circumstances grew the competition between the United States and the Soviet Union for hegemonic leadership.

The Causes and Evolutionary Course of the Cold War

The origins of the twentieth century's third hegemonic battle for domination are debated because the historical evidence lends itself to different interpretations (see Gaddis 1997). Several postulated causes stand out. The first is advanced by realism: the **Cold War** resulted from the **power transition** that propelled the United States and the Soviet Union to the top of the international hierarchy, which made each naturally suspicious of the other and their rivalry inescapable. Circumstances gave each superpower reasons to fear and to struggle against the other's potential global leadership and encouraged each superpower competitor to carve out and establish dominant influence in its own **sphere of influence,** or specified area of the globe.

A second interpretation holds that the Cold War was simply an extension of the superpowers' mutual disdain for each other's professed beliefs about politics and economics. U.S. animosity toward the Soviet Union was stimulated by the 1917 Bolshevik Revolution, which brought to power a government that embraced the Marxist critique of capitalistic imperialism. U.S. fears of Marxism stimulated the emergence of anticommunism as an opposing ideology. Accordingly, the United States embarked on a missionary crusade of its own to contain and ultimately remove the atheistic communist menace from the face of the earth.

Similarly, Soviet policy was fueled by the belief that capitalism could not coexist with communism. The purpose of Soviet policy, therefore, was to push the pace of the historical process in which communism eventually would prevail. However, Soviet planners did not believe that this historical outcome was guaranteed. They felt that the capitalist states, led by the United States, sought to encircle the Soviet Union and smother communism in its cradle, and that it was the Soviet obligation to resist. As a result, ideological incompatibility may have ruled out compromise as an option (see Controversy: Was Ideology the Primary Source of East-West Conflict?). Although the adversaries may have viewed "ideology more as a justification for action than as a guide to action," once the interests that they shared disappeared, "ideology did become the chief means which differentiated friend from foe" (Gaddis 1983).

A third explanation describes the Cold War as rooted in psychological factors, particularly in the superpowers' misperceptions of each other's motives. In this (constructivist) view, conflicting interests and ideologies were secondary to misunderstandings. Mistrustful actors are prone to see only virtue in their own actions and only malice in those of their adversaries. When such **mirror images** exist, hostility is inevitable (Bronfenbrenner 1971). Moreover, when perceptions of an adversary's evil intentions are socially constructed and become accepted as truth, **self-fulfilling prophecies** can develop. Prophecies are sometimes self-fulfilling because the future can be affected by the way it is anticipated. This tendency is illustrated by arms races: mistakenly fearing that a rival is preparing for an offensive war, a potential victim then arms in defense, thereby provoking the fearful rival to fulfill the prophecy by defensively building more weapons. The

■ **Cold War**
the forty-two-year (1949–1991) rivalry between the United States and the Soviet Union, as well as their competing coalitions, which sought to contain each other's expansion and win worldwide predominance.

■ **power transition**
a narrowing of the ratio of military capabilities between great-power rivals that is thought to increase the probability of war between them.

■ **sphere of influence**
a region of the globe dominated by a great power.

■ **mirror images**
the tendency of states and people in competitive interaction to misperceive each other—to see enemies the opposite favorable way they see themselves.

■ **self-fulfilling prophecy**
the tendency for one's expectations to evoke behavior that helps to make the expectations become true.

> **CONTROVERSY**
>
> ## WAS IDEOLOGY THE PRIMARY SOURCE OF EAST-WEST CONFLICT?
>
> Cold War America was gripped by a "great fear" not simply of the Soviet Union but of communism. Senator Joseph McCarthy led the most infamous hunt for communist sympathizers in government, Hollywood production companies blacklisted supposed communist sympathizers, and average American citizens were often required to take loyalty oaths at their offices. Everywhere, communism became synonymous with treasonous, un-American activity. As the nuclear arms race escalated and the U.S. government took military action to contain the Soviet Union, its justification was almost always expressed in terms of ideology. The threat, as the population learned to perceive it, was that of an atheistic, communistic system that challenged the fundamental American principles of democratic capitalism, and that according to the **domino theory,** which states that communism was driven to knock over one country after another, Soviet communism was inherently expansionistic. The other side also couched its Cold War rhetoric in terms of ideology, objecting to the imperialistic, capitalist system that the Soviets said America planned to impose on the whole world.
>
> Some would argue that fear of the other side's world dominance may have been more important in the Cold War than pure ideology. Both the American and the Soviet governments may have entered the Cold War to secure their relative power in the world order as much as to protect pure principles. After all, the United States and the Soviet Union had managed to transcend differing ideologies when they acted as allies in World War II. After World War II, however, a power vacuum drew them into conflict with each other, and as they competed, ideological justifications surfaced.
>
> All people have a psychological need to clarify their values and define them through the lens of an **ideology** or a belief system that expresses their convictions and enables them to explain what is of interest to them. Realism, liberalism, and Marxism-Leninism are all examples of such ideologies of international politics. Ideologies help us to interpret life and its meaning and are for that reason indispensable for organizing thought and values. But commitment to an ideology may at times cause hatred and hostility. Institutional proponents of particular ideologies are prone to perceive other ideologies competitively—as challenges to the truth of their own ideology's core beliefs. However, ideology can also become an excuse for less noble ambitions or for general fears. Although scholars are still debating the causes of the Cold War, we need to ask whether it was, in fact, an ideological contest over ideas in which the two governments proselytized about communism and capitalism to win peoples' hearts and minds, or a more general contest for power.
>
> What do you think? Was the Cold War really an ideological contest between international communism and the free-market capitalism espoused by the liberal democracies, or were there other, more powerful forces involved? In considering your opinion, take into account the end of the Cold War, in which the Soviet communistic system crumbled. Communist theoretician Vladimir Lenin described the predicament that he perceived to underlie the Cold War—prophetically, it turned out—when he predicted: "As long as capitalism and socialism exist, we cannot live in peace; in the end, either one or the other will triumph—a funeral dirge will be sung either over the Soviet Republic or over world capitalism."

■ **domino theory**
a metaphor popular during the Cold War that predicted that if one state fell to communism, its neighbors would also fall in a chain reaction, like a row of falling dominoes.

result is a classic illustration of the **security dilemma,** as each enemy's efforts to increase its own security by arming actually leads to a decline in security on both sides.

Additional factors beyond those rooted in divergent interests, ideologies, and images undoubtedly combined to produce this explosive Soviet-American hegemonic rivalry. To sort out the relative causal influence at the start of the Cold War and to grasp more completely the primary causes driving the dynamics of this great-power rivalry (and others in general), scholars have found it use-

FIGURE 4.1
Key Events in the Evolution of the U.S.-Soviet Relationship during the Cold War, 1948–1991

The evolution of U.S.-Soviet relations during the Cold War displays a series of shifts between periods of conflict and cooperation. As this figure shows, each superpower's behavior toward the other tended to be reciprocal, and, for most periods prior to 1983, confrontation prevailed over cooperation.

■ **ideology**
a set of core philosophical principles that leaders and citizens collectively construct about politics, the interests of political actors, and the ways people ought to ethically behave.

■ **security dilemma**
the central problem faced by all sovereign states in an anarchic global system in which a state's arming for ostensibly defensive purposes provokes other threatened states to arm in response, with the result that the national security of all declines as their armaments increase.

ful to evaluate how the Cold War changed over a forty-two-year period in order to identify the causes that contributed to changes in the U.S.-Soviet rivalry. The character of the Cold War shifted over the course of its duration, and several conspicuous patterns persisted that illustrate the larger historical pattern of great-power rivalries.

- Periods of intense conflict alternated with periods of relative cooperation; reciprocal, action-reaction exchanges were also evident (friendly U.S. initiatives toward the Soviet Union were reciprocated in kind).
- For reasons of expediency, both rivals were willing to disregard their respective professed ideologies whenever their perceived national interests rationalized such inconsistencies; for example, each backed allies with politi-

cal systems antithetical to its own when the necessities of power politics seemed to justify doing so.

- Both rivals consistently made avoidance of all-out war their highest priority. Through a gradual learning process involving push and shove, restraint and reward, tough bargaining and calm negotiation, the superpowers created a **security regime.**

■ **security regime** norms and rules for interaction agreed to by a set of states to increase their security.

These characteristics become visible when we inspect the evolution of the superpowers' relationship by dividing the Cold War into three chronological phases, shown in Figure 4.1.

Confrontation, 1948–1962. A brief postwar period of wary Soviet-American friendship soon gave way to mutual antagonism when the Cold War began. In this short period until 1949 of **unipolarity**—one characterized by a single dominant power center in the global system—the United States alone possessed the capacity to devastate its adversaries with the atomic bomb.

■ **unipolarity** a condition in which an international system has a single dominant power hegemon capable of dominating all other states.

Despite this restraining factor, all pretense of collaboration rapidly vanished as the superpowers' vital security interests collided in countries outside their clearly defined respective spheres of influence. At this critical juncture, George F. Kennan, then a diplomat in the American embassy in Moscow, sent to Washington his famous "long telegram" assessing the sources of Soviet conduct. Kennan's ideas were publicized widely in 1947, when the influential journal *Foreign Affairs* circulated his views in an article he published that was signed "X" to conceal his identity as its author. In this article, Kennan argued that Soviet leaders forever would feel insecure about their political ability to maintain power against forces both within Soviet society and in the outside world. Their insecurity would lead to an activist—and perhaps aggressive—Soviet foreign policy. However, the United States had the power to increase the strains under which the Soviet leadership would have to operate, which could lead to a gradual mellowing or final end of Soviet power. Thus, Kennan concluded: "In these circumstances it is clear that the main element of any United States policy toward the Soviet Union must be that of a long-term, patient but firm and vigilant *containment* of Russian expansive tendencies" (Kennan 1947, emphasis added).

■ **Truman Doctrine** the declaration by President Harry S Truman that U.S. foreign policy would use intervention to support peoples who allied with the United States against communist external subjugation.

Soon thereafter, President Harry S Truman made Kennan's assessment the cornerstone of American postwar foreign policy. Provoked in part by violence in Turkey and Greece, which he and others believed to be communist inspired, Truman declared, "I believe that it must be the policy of the United States to support free peoples who are resisting attempted subjugation by armed minorities or by outside pressures." Eventually known as the **Truman Doctrine,** this statement defined the strategy that the United States would pursue for the next forty years, over Kennan's objections (1967, 361). This strategy, called **containment,** sought to prevent the expansion of Soviet influence by encircling the Soviet Union and intimidating it with the threat of a military attack.

■ **containment** a strategy to prevent a great power rival from using force to alter the balance of power and increase its sphere of influence.

A seemingly endless series of new Cold War crises soon followed. They included the communist coup d'état in Czechoslovakia in 1948; the Soviet blockade of West Berlin in June of that year; the communist acquisition of power on the Chinese mainland in 1949; the outbreak of the Korean War in 1950; the Chinese invasion of Tibet in 1950; and the on-again, off-again Taiwan Straits crises that followed. Nonetheless, superpower relations began to improve in the 1950s. After the Soviets broke the U.S. atomic monopoly in 1949, shifts in the balance of power prompted a movement away from confrontation. The risks of massive destruction necessitated restraint and changed the terms of the struggle. In particular, both superpowers began to expend considerable resources recruiting allies, promising to protect new client states from external attack through a strategy known as **extended deterrence.** Thus the Cold War expanded across the entire globe, producing a distribution of military power characterized by bipolarity, with the United States and its allies at one pole and the Soviet Union and its allies at the other.

Because the Soviet Union remained strategically inferior to the United States, Nikita Khrushchev (who succeeded Stalin upon his death in 1953) pursued a policy of **peaceful coexistence** with capitalism. Even so, the Soviet Union at times cautiously sought to increase its power in places where opportunities appeared to exist. As a result, the period following Stalin's death saw many Cold War confrontations, with Hungary, Cuba, Egypt, and Berlin becoming the flash points.

A dark shadow loomed over hopes for superpower peace. As the arms race accelerated, the threats to peace multiplied. In 1962, the surreptitious placement of Soviet missiles in Cuba set the stage for the greatest test of the superpowers' capacity to manage their disputes—the Cuban Missile Crisis. The superpowers stood eyeball to eyeball. Fortunately, one (the Soviet Union) blinked, and the crisis ended. This painful "catalytic" learning experience both reduced enthusiasm for waging the Cold War by military means and expanded awareness of the suicidal consequences of a nuclear war.

From Coexistence to Détente, 1963–1978. The growing threat of mutual destruction, in conjunction with the growing parity of American and Soviet military capabilities, made coexistence or nonexistence appear to be the only alternatives. Given this equation, finding ways to coexist became compelling. At the American University commencement exercises in 1963, U.S. President John F. Kennedy explained why tension reduction had become necessary:

> Today, should total war ever break out again—no matter how—our two countries would become the primary targets. It is an ironical but accurate fact that the two strongest powers are the two in the most danger of devastation. . . . We are both caught up in a vicious and dangerous cycle in which suspicion on one side breeds suspicion on the other and new weapons beget counterweapons.
>
> In short, both the United States and its allies, and the Soviet Union and its allies, have a mutually deep interest in a just and genuine peace and in halting the arms race. . . .
>
> So let us not be blind to our differences, but let us also direct attention to our common interests and to the means by which those differences can be resolved. And if we cannot end now our differences, at least we can help make the world safe for diversity.

Kennedy signaled a shift in how the United States hoped thereafter to bargain with its adversary, and the Soviet Union reciprocally expressed its interest in more cooperative relations. That movement took another step forward following Richard Nixon's election in 1968. Coached by his national security adviser, Henry A. Kissinger, President Nixon initiated a new approach to Soviet relations that in 1969 he officially labeled **détente.** The Soviets also adopted this

■ **extended deterrence**
a great power's commitment to its allies to use its military might to prevent them from being attacked by an enemy.

■ **peaceful coexistence**
Soviet leader Nikita Khrushchev's 1956 doctrine that war between capitalist and communist states is not inevitable and that inter-bloc competition could be peaceful.

■ **détente**
in general, a strategy of seeking to relax tensions between adversaries to reduce the possibility of war.

Easing Tensions: U.S.-Soviet Détente As East-West tension waned, cooperation increased during the détente phase of U.S.-Soviet relations in the late 1960s. A considerable part of this departure from past confrontation was due to compromises at the bargaining table. Pictured here, President Richard Nixon, one of the architects of the U.S. **"linkage" strategy** along with Secretary of State Henry Kissinger, is toasting with Soviet Premier Leonid Brezhnev and fellow dignitaries at their meeting to discuss approaches to relaxing tensions between the superpowers.

■ **linkage strategy**
a set of assertions that claim leaders should take into account another country's overall behavior when deciding whether to reach agreement on any one specific issue so as to link cooperation to rewards.

■ **Strategic Arms Limitations Talks (SALT)**
two sets of agreements reached during the 1970s between the United States and the Soviet Union that established limits on strategic nuclear delivery systems.

■ **Carter Doctrine**
President Jimmy Carter's declaration of U.S. willingness to use military force to protect its interests in the Persian Gulf.

term to describe their policies toward the United States, and relations between the Soviets and Americans "normalized." Arms control stood at the center of the dialogue surrounding détente. The **Strategic Arms Limitation Talks (SALT),** initiated in 1969, sought to restrain the threatening, expensive, and spiraling arms race by limiting the deployment of antiballistic missiles. As Figure 4.1 shows, cooperative interaction became more commonplace than hostile relations. Visits, cultural exchanges, trade agreements, and joint technological ventures replaced threats, warnings, and confrontations.

From Renewed Confrontation to Rapprochement, 1979–1991. Despite the careful nurturing of détente, its spirit did not endure. In many respects, the Soviet invasion of Afghanistan in 1979 led to détente's demise. As President Jimmy Carter viewed it, "Soviet aggression in Afghanistan—unless checked—confronts all the world with the most serious strategic challenge since the Cold War began." In retaliation, he advanced the **Carter Doctrine** declaring America's willingness to use military force to protect its access to oil supplies from the Persian Gulf. In addition, he attempted to organize a worldwide boycott of the 1980 Moscow Olympics and suspended U.S. grain exports to the Soviet Union.

Relations deteriorated dramatically thereafter. President Ronald Reagan and his Soviet counterparts (first Yuri Andropov and then Konstantin Chernenko) delivered a barrage of confrontational rhetoric. Reagan asserted that the

Soviet Union "underlies all the unrest that is going on" and described the Soviet Union as "the focus of evil in the modern world." The atmosphere was punctuated by Reagan policy adviser Richard Pipes's bold challenge in 1981 that the Soviets would have to choose between "peacefully changing their communist system . . . or going to war." Soviet rhetoric was equally unrestrained and alarmist.

As talk of war increased, preparations for it escalated. The arms race resumed feverishly, at the expense of addressing domestic economic problems. The superpowers also extended the confrontation to new territory, such as Central America, and renewed their public diplomacy (propaganda) efforts to extol the virtues of their respective systems throughout the world. The **Reagan Doctrine** pledged U.S. support for anticommunist insurgents who sought to overthrow Soviet-supported governments in Afghanistan, Angola, and Nicaragua. In addition, American leaders spoke loosely about the "winability" of a nuclear war through a "prevailing" military strategy that included the threat of a "first use" of nuclear weapons in the event of conventional war. Relations deteriorated as these moves and countermoves took their toll. The new Soviet leader, Mikhail Gorbachev, in 1985 summarized the alarming state of superpower relations by fretting that "The situation is very complex, very tense. I would even go so far as to say it is explosive."

However, the situation did not explode. Instead, prospects for a more constructive phase improved greatly following Gorbachev's advocacy of "new thinking" in order to achieve a **rapprochement,** or reconciliation, of the rival states' interests. He sought to settle the Soviet Union's differences with the capitalist West in order to halt the deterioration of his country's economy and international position. Shortly thereafter, Gorbachev embarked on domestic reforms to promote democratization and the transition to a market economy, and proclaimed his desire to end the Cold War contest. "We realize that we are divided by profound historical, ideological, socioeconomic, and cultural differences," he noted in 1987 during his first visit to the United States. "But the wisdom of politics today lies in not using those differences as a pretext for confrontation, enmity, and the arms race." Soviet spokesperson Georgi Arbatov elaborated, informing the United States that "we are going to do a terrible thing to you—we are going to deprive you of an enemy."

Surprisingly, to many adherents of **realism** who see great-power contests for supremacy as inevitable and strategic surrender or acceptance of defeat an impossibility, the Soviets did what they promised: they began to act like an ally instead of an enemy. The Soviet Union agreed to end its aid to and support for Cuba, withdrew from Afghanistan and eastern Europe, and announced unilateral reductions in military spending. Gorbachev also agreed to two new disarmament agreements: the START treaty (Strategic Arms Reduction Treaty) for deep cuts in strategic arsenals, and the Conventional Forces in Europe (CFE) treaty to reduce the Soviet presence in Europe. In addition, the Soviet Union liberalized its emigration policies and permitted greater religious freedom.

The pace of steps to rapprochement then accelerated, and the "normalization" of Soviet-American relations moved rapidly. The Cold War—which began in Europe and centered on Europe for forty-two years—began to crumble in 1989 when the Berlin Wall came down and truly ended there in 1991 when the Soviet Union dissolved, accepted capitalist free-market principles, and initiated democratic reforms. To nearly everyone's astonishment, the Soviet Union acquiesced in the defeat of communism, the reunification of Germany, and the disintegration of its east European bloc of allies, the Warsaw Pact (see Contro-

■ **Reagan Doctrine**
a U.S promise to support anticommunist insurgents attempting to overthrow governments backed by the Soviet Union.

■ **rapprochement**
in diplomacy, a policy seeking to reestablish normal relations between enemies.

■ **realism**
the theory that states are unitary global actors in relentless competition with one another for position and power in the international hierarchy.

> **CONTROVERSY**
>
> # WHY DID THE COLD WAR END PEACEFULLY?
>
> How history is remembered is important because those memories shape future decisions about the management of great-power rivalries. Why did the Cold War end without the use of armed force? That question remains a puzzle that still provokes much controversy, in part because the Cold War's abrupt end came as such a surprise to most observers and, in the unanticipated outcome, also undermined confidence in the adequacy of conventional realist theories that argued that no great power would ever accept without a fight the loss of position to another hegemonic rival.
>
> What do you think? What was the cause of the Cold War's collapse? In considering your view on this issue, take into account some divergent opinions (see Herrmann and Lebow 2004).
>
> From one perspective, the policies George Kennan recommended in his famous "X" article now appear prophetic. In his version of nonmilitary containment, Kennan anticipated that this would "promote tendencies which must eventually find their outlet in either the breakup of or the gradual mellowing of Soviet power." Many believe that this was precisely what did happen, albeit more than forty years later!
>
> Neorealists, in contrast, emphasize the contribution that nuclear weapons, the West's superior military power, and extended deterrence through alliances made to forcing the Soviet Union's surrender. In 1991, for example, an adviser to U.S. President Reagan, Richard Perle, articulated the realist view in his contention that people "who argued for nuclear deterrence and serious military capabilities contributed mightily to the position of strength that eventually led the Soviet leadership to choose a less bellicose, less menacing approach to international politics."
>
> Liberals and neoliberals voice another interpretation about causes, as Ted Galen Carpenter (1991) did when he observed that many Russian demonstrators "who sought to reject communist rule looked to the American system for inspiration. But the source of that inspiration was America's reputation as a haven for the values of limited government, not Washington's $300-billion-a-year military budget and its network of global military bases."
>
> Although no consensus has materialized about the ways in which these factors individually or in combination put an end to the Cold War, a fundamental question resides at the center of this postmortem. Did military containment force the Soviet Union into submission? Or did Soviet leaders succumb to the inherent political weaknesses of communism, which caused an internal economic malaise that left them unable to conduct an imperial policy abroad or retain communist control at home? In other words, was the end of Communist Party rule accepted because of the intimidation of U.S. military strength? Or was the outcome produced by other political and economic influences within the Soviet Union, as suggested in 1991 by Georgi Arbatov, director of the USSR's Institute for the USA and Canada Studies. Arbatov countered the realist view "that President Reagan's 'tough' policy and intensified arms race . . . persuaded communists to 'give up' [calling it] 'sheer nonsense.' Quite the contrary this policy made the life for reformers, for all who yearned for democratic changes in their life, much more difficult. . . . The [communist hard-line] conservatives and reactionaries were given predominant influence. . . . Reagan made it practically impossible to start reforms after Brezhnev's death (Andropov had such plans) and made things more difficult for Gorbachev to cut military expenditures." But even Reagan himself rejected this view, describing himself graciously as a supporting actor. "Mr. Gorbachev deserves most of the credit," Reagan declared (Matlock 2004).
>
> Sorting out the contribution of different causes to ending the Cold War will doubtless intrigue historians for decades, just as determining the causes for its onset has done. The lessons drawn from this forty-two-year drama remain important because they affect how leaders are likely to manage new great-power rivalries throughout the twenty-first century.

versy: Why Did the Cold War End Peacefully?). The conclusion of the enduring rivalry between East and West, and with it the end of the seventy-year ideological dispute as well, was such a history-transforming event that, without serious opposition to liberal capitalism, the *end of history* was proclaimed by Francis Fukuyama (1992b). "Liberalism seemed to have triumphed—not merely capitalism but democracy and the rule of law, as represented in the West, and particularly in the United States" (Keohane and Nye 2001a).

The collapse of the Cold War suggested something quite different from the lesson of the twentieth century's two world wars, which had implied that great-power rivalries are necessarily doomed to end in armed conflict. The Cold War was different; it came to an end peacefully, as a combination of factors contributed at various stages in the Cold War's evolution to transform a global rivalry into a stable, even cooperative, relationship. This suggests that it is sometimes possible for great-power rivals to reconcile their competitive differences without warfare.

The Consequences of the Cold War

Though locked in a geostrategic rivalry made worse by antagonistic ideologies and mutual misperceptions, the United States and the Soviet Union avoided a fatal showdown. In accepting the devolution of their empire, Russian leaders made the most dramatic peaceful retreat from power in history. The end of the Cold War altered the face of world affairs in profound and diverse ways. With the dissolution of the Soviet Union in 1991, no immediate great-power challenger confronted American hegemonic leadership. However, a host of new security threats emerged, ranging from rogue states to terrorist networks. As the turbulent twenty-first century began to unfold, after the bipolar Cold War world of clearly defined adversaries vanished, a shadowy world of ill-defined allegiances and cross-cutting relationships appeared, in which the problem of distinguishing friends and foes grew.

THE FUTURE OF GREAT-POWER POLITICS: A COLD PEACE?

Rapid, unanticipated changes in world politics such as the abrupt end of the Cold War in 1991 and the equally surprising 9/11 terrorist attacks in 2001 create uncertainty about the global future. To optimists, the collapse of communism signified a transformation in world politics—a historical watershed—by ushering onto the global stage the **end of history,** "the end of mankind's ideological evolution and the universalization of Western liberal democracy as the final form of government" (Fukuyama 1989). To pessimists, these sea changes suggested not history's end but its resumption of contests for power and opposition over contested ideas and ideologies. Both groups recognized that Cold War bipolarity had been superseded by **unipolarity**—a hegemonic configuration of power with one predominant superstate that presented new and difficult challenges. And in the aftermath of 9/11, America acted on the accelerating achievement in the 1990s of supreme military strength to start a bold mission to eliminate terrorism from the face of the earth.

America's Unipolar Moment in History

Unipolarity refers to the concentration of power in a single preponderant state. At present, in a historical "moment" in world history (Krauthammer 2003), the United States now stands alone at the summit of the international hierarchy. It

■ **end of history**
Francis Fukuyama's thesis that the philosophy of economic and political liberalism has triumphed throughout the world, ending the contest between market democracies and centrally planned governance.

■ **unipolarity**
a condition in which an international system has a single dominant power hegemon capable of dominating all other states.

is the only country with the military, economic, and cultural assets to be a decisive player in any part of the world it chooses. Its military is not just stronger than anybody else's, it is stronger than everybody else's, with defense expenditures in 2005 exceeding all other countries combined. Complementing America's military might is its awesome economic strength. With less than 5 percent of the global population, the United States accounts for almost a third of the global gross domestic product and two-fifths of the entire world's combined spending on research and development. Further, America wields enormous "soft power" (Nye 2004b) because it is the hub of global communications and popular culture, through which its values spread all over the world. In the words of former French Foreign Minister Hubart Vedrine, the United States is not simply a superpower, it is a "hyperpower."

This rare confluence of military, economic, and cultural power gives the United States what might appear to be an extraordinary ability to shape the global future to its will. This is why America's unique position atop the global pyramid of power, the world's sole superpower, tends to be seen as an empire (Bacevich 2003), a preponderant power with the ability to act independently without restraint, as some advise for America (R. Kaplan 2002). Such overwhelming power can easily tempt leaders to act. Rather than working in concert with others, independent action may seem attractive to a strong, self-confident dominant hegemon that need not be worried about being hamstrung by quibbling lesser powers. Whereas other countries must address international problems through global organizations to be effective, the United States has the capability to "go it alone" even in the face of strident criticism from abroad.

This strategy has its costs, however; imperial empires also experience sorrows (C. Johnson 2004). Acting alone may appear attractive and useful, but it erodes international assistance on issues, such as combating global terrorism, where the United States badly needs cooperative support from others. And because the naked exercise of power "infuriates" the rest of the world (Hertsgaard 2003), beating an imperialistic path to rule the world by domination wins few admirers (Brzezinski 2004). The question is how the United States will use its power, and for what purposes, if the U.S. hegemon is bent on global dominance (Chomsky 2004) as it persues an apocalyptic confrontation with the rest of the world (Lifton 2004). Or, instead, might America use its supreme strength to work with others to build a just and secure world order?

The choices the United States makes will have profound consequences for the global future, for good or for evil. Those choices will also greatly shape America's own destiny. There is a "price" for being an empire (Ferguson 2004b), and ill-conceived choices could easily undermine American security and welfare both at home and abroad (Kegley and Raymond 2005b). Invincibility does not automatically mean invulnerability. On the contrary, unsurpassed strength could easily breed hostile resistance to an America using all its might to "end evil" in the world (Frum and Perle 2004), generating opposition and enemies threatened by American imperialism (Harvey 2004; Newhouse 2003). Indeed, to some, such as former Reagan policymaker Clyde Prestowitz (2003), the United States has already crossed the boundaries in abusing its power through defiant unilateralism, becoming a hated and feared "rogue nation," acting as an international outlaw by its own rules and in the process breeding a wave of "anti-Americanism" (Boyle 2004; Revel 2004).

Whatever foreign policy choices George W. Bush makes in his second term,

MAP 4.3
The Emerging Centers of Power in the Twenty-First-Century Global Hierarchy

To estimate which countries are the most powerful and which are relatively weak, analysts frequently rely on the size of states' economies, because that measure predicts the power potential of each state (that is, their relative capacity to project power and exercise global influence). The map pictures the proportionate economic clout of the leading great powers (measured by purchasing power parities), showing the United States, China, Japan, India, and Germany as today's leading economic powerhouses. Figure 4.2 on page 122 projects the probable rank order of the largest economic powerhouses by the year 2020, and postulates that in the short-term future the global hierarchy of power will look quite different from today, with China at the apex of economic power.
SOURCE: *Economist* (2002), 24.

the status of being a superpower, the single "pole," or center, of power without a real challenger, has fated the United States with heavy and grave responsibilities. Overwhelming power, observed former Secretary of State Henry Kissinger in 2001, "evokes nearly automatically a quest by other societies to achieve a greater voice . . . and to reduce the relative position of the strongest." If Washington neglects the politics of compromise and consensus building, it could find itself isolated at the very time that it is most in need of friends.

FIGURE 4.2
Projection of the Fifteen Largest Global Economies by 2020

Using purchasing power parities (PPPs) to account for differences in countries' price levels, the World Bank forecasts the probable size of the largest economies. The projections show that the rank order of the largest economic powerhouses by 2020 will be substantially different from today's. The political and military consequences are not predicted, but long-cycle theory postulates that the economic changes will breed political and even military conflict.
SOURCE: McGranahan (1995), 59; see also World Bank (2005b).

United States=100

Country	
China	~140
United States	100
Japan	~45
India	~32
Indonesia	~30
Germany	~25
South Korea	~23
Thailand	~20
France	~18
Taiwan	~17
Brazil	~17
Italy	~16
Russia	~16
Britain	~15
Mexico	~13

While the United States may hold an unrivaled position in the world today, in the long run unipolarity is very unlikely to endure. No previous hegemon has maintained primacy indefinitely. As Map 4.3 and Figure 4.2 show, the long-term economic trajectories based on differential national growth rates point to a world in which first China is likely to overtake the United States (see Casetti 2003 for projections), followed by another day when a united Europe and perhaps other great powers will eventually also challenge American financial preeminence (see Nye 2004a; Wallerstein 2002) and result in "the end of the American era" (Kupchan 2003; Todd 2003). At the same time, the United States will find it costly to maintain military dominance. Aside from major deployments in Afghanistan and Iraq, U.S. forces are positioned abroad in more than seventy countries along an arc of global instability reaching from the Balkans to the Caucasus, through the Gulf of Arden to the Korean Peninsula in Asia, and in Haiti (*Economist*, March 20, 2004, 34). **Imperial overstretch,** the gap between internal resources and external commitments, has bedeviled every previous leading great power (Kennedy 1987). Throughout history, hegemons repeatedly have defined their security interests more broadly that other states only to slip from the pinnacle of power by reaching beyond their grasp. "The problem in defense spending," former U.S. President Dwight Eisenhower concluded, "is to figure out how far you should go without destroying from within what you are trying to de-

■ **imperial overstretch**
the phrase coined by Paul Kennedy to capture the historic tendency for hegemons to sap their own strength through costly imperial pursuits and military spending that weaken their economies in relation to their rivals'.

A New Global Hegemon? China is a rising economic giant that many expect to become the globe's wealthiest country. In the West this has generated the fear that as China becomes a modern military power it will seek hegemony and use force to cause trouble abroad. Shown here are Chinese Peoples' Liberation Army soldiers marching with bayoneted rifles while performing official honor guard duties at a welcoming ceremony in Beijing—a show of strength at Tiananmen Square by the Chinese army, and a symbol of China's potential to project power.

fend from without." Excessive costs to preserve America's empire by military means could prove to be "the bubble of American supremacy" (Soros 2003).

From Unipolarity to Multipolarity?

If some combination of U.S. imperial overstretch alongside rising economic and military expense by America's chief challengers transforms the current distribution of global power, as many believe inevitable (Kaplan 2002), a number of scholars and policymakers predict that a **multipolar** system will emerge. Some of the states frequently mentioned as potential members of a future **power balance** known as multipolarity will include the United States, China, the European Union, Japan, and a reinvigorated Russia. Because multipolar systems include several comparatively equal great powers, they are complex. When we take into account the interplay of military and economic factors, such circumstances of great powers competing as equals are also fraught with uncertainty. Differen-

■ **multipolarity**
a global system with more than two dominant power centers.

■ **power balance**
a divison of global military and economic capabilities among more than one center or dominant superpower.

tiating friend from foe becomes especially difficult when allies in military security may be rivals in trade relationships.

Predicting what cleavages and partnerships will develop among the great powers in the future twenty-first-century multipolar system will be difficult because it will be hard to foresee what will become the next major axis of conflict. Competition could emerge from any pair of great powers, but it may be restricted to one sphere of interaction. For example, the United States, Japan, and China today are highly competitive in their commercial relations, but nevertheless they also display continuing efforts to manage their security relations collaboratively (as shown by their cooperation in fighting terrorism).

Such cross-cutting axes of conflict and cooperation will affect the stability of any future multipolar system. Throughout history different types of multipolar systems have existed, some of which have experienced more stability than others. The most unstable have possessed rigid, polarized alignments, such as during the period prior to the outbreak of World War I (Kegley and Raymond 1994). **Polarization** is dangerous because it usually focuses adversaries' attention on a single threat, making it more likely that minor disagreements will become magnified into larger tests of will. A system where great powers compete in one sphere of activity but cooperate elsewhere has the potential to prevent any given issue from separating into opposing coalitions. Great-power conflict would be frequent, but as long as security and economic disputes did not overlap, they would not necessarily divide the system into two antagonistic camps. Under these circumstances, the danger of polarization could be managed if the great powers develop international rules and institutions to manage their fluid, mixed-motive relationships.

The diffusion of wealth predicts the likely intensification of great-power political competition. Throughout history, changes in comparative economic advantage have preceded political competition. When multipolarity has existed, economic rivals have struggled to protect their wealth and have competed politically for economic position, with military conflict usually following **power transitions.**

A "new cold war" could emerge between any pair of great powers, such as between the globe's two major contenders for supremacy, the United States and China, if their competition escalates and they practice containment to prevent their rival's quest for hegemony. However, this kind of armed rivalry need not develop; cooperation could increase instead. Quite different and inconsistent political types of great-power relations could emerge in the economic and military spheres. There is the probability of economic rivalry growing under the pressures of **globalization,** whereas the likelihood of security cooperation for many of these same relationships is also high. For example, the United States, Japan, and China exhibit conflict in their commercial relations but nevertheless cooperate to manage their security relations (as shown by their collaboration in fighting terrorism). Table 4.2 presents a projection of the kind of cross-cutting bilateral relationships that could develop among the great powers in the twenty-first century. It estimates the probability of military cooperation and economic conflict between any pair of the five major powers.

Awareness of these different possibilities of cross-cutting axes of conflict and cooperation may have been behind former U.S. Secretary of State Lawrence

■ **polarization**
the formation of competing coalitions or blocs composed of allies that align with one of the major competing poles, or centers, of power.

■ **power transitions**
the dangerous period when a great power is challenged by the rise of rivals.

■ **globalization**
the integration of states' economies into a tightening web of interdependence as global trade expands.

TABLE 4.2

The New Great-Power Chessboard: Simultaneously Unfolding Military and Economic Rivalries

	Military Rivalry						Economic Rivalry				
	United States	Japan	European Union	Russia	China		United States	Japan	European Union	Russia	China
United States	—					United States	—				
Japan	L	—				Japan	H	—			
European Union	M	M	—			European Union	H	H	—		
Russia	M	H	H	—		Russia	L	L	M	—	
China	H	H	H	M	—	China	H	H	M	M	—

Note: The symbols H = high, M = medium, and L = low signify the likelihood of bilateral relationships that may develop in the twenty-first century.

How the great powers will align militarily and economically in the twenty-first century is difficult to predict. A wide variety of strategic and trade relationships are possible. To complicate the task of prediction, in the first decade of the twenty-first century the paradox exists that many of the pairs of great powers that are the most active trade partners are also the greatest military rivals. This table depicts the bilateral great-power relationships in their military and economic dimensions and illuminates the question of whether economic cooperation will help to reduce potential military competition.

Eagleburger's warning about the best way to steer the great powers through the ocean of perils:

> The issue: . . . is how well the United States accomplishes the transition from overwhelming predominance to a position more akin to a "first among equals" status, and how well America's partners—Japan and Western Europe—adapt to their newfound importance. The change will not be easy for any of the players, as such shifts in power relationships have never been easy.

Few observers see advantages resulting from the emerging situation. As former U.S. Secretary of State Henry A. Kissinger warns, this poses a serious challenge because "the United States has very little experience with a world that consists of many powers and which it can neither dominate nor from which it can simply withdraw in isolation."

Yet, we have no way of knowing whether the future will resemble the gloomy history of multipolar systems. Patterns and practices can change, and it is possible for policymakers to learn from previous mistakes and avoid repeating them. What is crucial is how the great powers react to the eventual emergence of a new multipolar global system. The grand strategies each of the powers forge to adapt to such new circumstances of shared power will be critical. Depending on the national security policies they embrace, they could shape a peaceful future. What are the options in the menu of choice?

RESPONDING TO MULTIPOLARITY'S CHALLENGE

What, then, can the great powers do to prevent the resumption of their rivalry? What security policies should they pursue in order to avoid the dangers of shared power and rapid transitions in their position and strength in the great-power hierarchy?

The answers are highly uncertain. As we will discuss in Chapters 12–14, debate about the methods of guaranteeing international security in Washington, Beijing, Tokyo, Brussels, and Moscow today revolves around four basic options. Each is actively under consideration, and each will become more or less practical, prudent, or problematic for each great power depending on the circumstances that materialize in tomorrow's multipolar world.

Unilateralism represents one option for a great power's strategy. Acting alone is especially attractive for a self-confident great power assured of its independent strength. With sufficient power, a potential hegemon can be self-reliant. Unilateralism can involve isolationism; an attempt to exert hegemonic leadership; a strategy of **selective engagement** that concentrates external involvements on vital national interests; or an effort to play the role of a "balancer" that skillfully backs one side or another in a great-power dispute, but only when necessary to maintain a military equilibrium between the other great-power disputants. At the extreme, unilateralism can lead the global leader to play the role of international bully, seeking to run the world. More commonly, unilateralism derives from the desire for control over the flexible conduct of a great power's foreign relations, independent of control by or pressure from other great powers. This was the primary motive behind European leaders' commitment to forge a common policy on security and defense to give the EU a "capacity for autonomous action," enabling it to act independently, without U.S. approval or support. To implement the goal of acting unilaterally, the EU has built its own independent "Eurocorps" military force. Likewise, the **Bush Doctrine** also captures the spirit and motives of unilateral approaches. That doctrine defiantly rejects "the liberal internationalist view of the world [that] the U.S. is merely one among many—a stronger country, yes, but one that has to adapt itself to the will and the needs of 'the international community.'" Instead, the U.S. administration under President George W. Bush constructed the view that "America is no mere international citizen. It is the dominant power in the world, more dominant than any since Rome. Accordingly, America is in a position to reshape norms, alter expectations and create new realities. How? By unapologetic and implacable demonstrations of will" (Krauthammer 2001).

Cultivation of a specialized relationship with another great power, similar to that between Great Britain and the United States, illustrates a second approach that some pairs of great powers might pursue. Many kinds of strategic bilateral partnerships can develop in a climate of fear, even between powers that have suffered from frosty relations in the recent past. For example, asserting that "no country should claim hegemony for itself or pursue policy from positions of strength and monopolize international affairs," Moscow and Beijing announced their agreement to warm relations by joining together to counterbalance the United States as the world's lone superpower. China also strengthened its new

■ **unilateralism**
an approach that relies on self-help, independent strategies in foreign policy.

■ **selective engagement**
a great-power grand strategy using economic and military power to influence only important particular situations, countries, or global issues by striking a balance between a highly interventionist "global policeman" and an uninvolved isolationist.

■ **Bush Doctrine**
the unilateral grand strategy of the George W. Bush administration to preserve a unipolar world under U.S. hegemony by keeping U.S. "military strength beyond challenge" by any other great power.

alliance with Russia to counterbalance the perceived threat of a U.S.-EU-Japanese attempt to squeeze the country from both east and west. Such dances among global giants, with the rapid formation and expansion of short-term specialized relationships among pairs of great powers in a climate of suspicion, is exactly the kind of national security maneuvering many expect to occur in the twenty-first century under conditions of multipolarity. Still other types of specialized relations between pairs of great powers could follow, at various levels of mutual support and commitment. There are several variants of this strategic option, including informal understandings, cooperation (sometimes termed an **entente**), and alliances formalized by treaties.

A third strategy under consideration is construction of a **concert,** or a cooperative agreement among the great powers to manage the global system jointly and to prevent international disputes from escalating to war. The Concert of Europe, at its apex between 1815 and 1822, is the epitome of previous great-power efforts to pursue this path to peace. The effort to build a great-power coalition to wage a war against global terrorism following 9/11 is a more recent example of **multilateralism** to construct a concert through collective approaches.

Finally, some policymakers recommend that today's great powers unite with the lesser powers in constructing a true system of **collective security.** The principles rationalizing the formation of the League of Nations in 1919 exemplify this multilateral approach to peace under conditions of multipolarity, as has the pledge by Russia to cooperate with NATO to build a twenty-first-century security partnership.

Whichever combination of approaches predominates in the strategies forged to prevent great-power rivalries from escalating to war in a multipolar future, it is clear that the choices the great powers make about war and peace will determine the fate of the world. To realists, there is every reason for concern. Even though to the liberal point of view the growth of interdependent globalization can act as a barrier to war, realists warn that "interdependence promotes war as well as peace. . . . Given the expectation of conflict, and necessity of taking care of one's interests, one may wonder how any state with the economic capability of a great power can refrain from arming itself with the weapons that have served so well as the great deterrent" (Waltz 2000). This prospect for a coming great-power arms race does not bode well for a twenty-first-century peace, because major changes in a number of great powers and their relative power are probable, and throughout history rapid changes in the great powers' balance of power have been followed by war.

> Our generation, therefore, so far as political realism is concerned, is wandering in a zone of historical ambiguity, a political no-man's-land between, on the one hand, the state system with its balance-of-power politics now rendered globally lethal by nuclear weapons and, on the other, an evolving world order; between a fatally flawed nation-state traditionalism and a newer globalism that is powerless in its infancy. Under these circumstances political realism must detach itself from time-honored links to the balance-of-power state system and find a new mooring. (Gulick 1999, 17)

The future is largely in the hands of the great powers, because "powerful states make the rules" (Keohane and Nye 2001a). What kinds of rules and insti-

■ **entente**
an agreement between states to consult if one is attacked by another party.

■ **concert**
a cooperative agreement among great powers to manage jointly the international system.

■ **multilateralism**
cooperative approaches to managing shared problems through collective and coordinated action.

■ **collective security**
a security regime agreed to by the great powers setting rules for keeping peace, guided by the principle that an act of aggression by any state will be met by a collective response from the rest.

tutions will they create, and will their creations increase or decrease the prospects for global security? In Chapter 5, we examine the impact of the great powers on the weak states whose security and welfare depend so heavily upon them, that is, the countries in the Global South.

KEY TERMS

long-cycle theory
hegemon
hegemonic stability theory
enduring rivalries
counterfactual reasoning
structuralism
global level of analysis
balance of power
individual level of analysis
rational choice
state level of analysis
nationalism
bipolarity
realism
liberalism
Kellogg-Briand Pact
irredentism
fascism
machtpolitik
isolationism
appeasement
colonialism

multipolarity
political economy
protectionism
imperialism
Yalta Conference
Cold War
power transition
sphere of influence
mirror images
self-fulfilling prophecy
security dilemma
domino theory
ideology
security regime
unipolarity
Truman Doctrine
containment
extended deterrence
peaceful coexistence
détente
linkage strategy

Strategic Arms Limitation Talks (SALT)
Carter Doctrine
Reagan Doctrine
rapprochement
realism
end of history
unipolarity
imperial overstretch
multipolarity
power balance
polarization
power transitions
globalization
unilateralism
selective engagement
Bush Doctrine
entente
concert
multilateralism
collective security

SUGGESTED READING

Bacevich, Andrews J., ed. *The Imperial Tense.* Chicago: Ivan R. Dee/Rowman and Littlefield, 2003.

Chase-Dunn, Christopher, and E. N. Anderson, eds. *The Historical Evolution of World Systems.* London: Palgrave, 2005.

Ferguson, Niall. *Colossus: The Price of America's Empire.* New York: Penguin Press, 2004.

Herrmann, Richard K., and Richard Ned Lebow, eds. *Ending the Cold War: Interpretations, Causation, and the Study of International Relations.* London: Palgrave MacMillan, 2004.

Kadera, Kelly M. *The Power-Conflict Story: A Dynamic Model of Interstate Rivalry.* Ann Arbor: University of Michigan Press, 2001.

Kegley, Charles W. Jr., and Gregory A. Raymond. *The Imperiled Imperium: America's Role on the Global Stage.* Cambridge, U.K.: Oxford University Press, 2005.

Kegley, Charles W. Jr., and Gregory A. Raymond. *A Multipolar Peace? Great-Power Politics in the Twenty-First Century.* New York: St. Martin's Press, 1994.

Kennedy, Paul. *The Rise and Fall of the Great Powers.* New York: Random House, 1987.

Lemke, Douglas, ed. "Symposium on Extensions of the Power Transition Theory," *International Interactions* 29 (October–December 2003): 269–364.

Mearsheimer, John J. *The Tragedy of Great Power Politics*. New York: W. W. Norton, 2001.

Murray, Williamson, and Allan R. Millett. *A War to Be Won: Fighting the Second World War*. Cambridge, Mass.: Harvard University Press, 2000.

Nye, Joseph S., Jr. *The Paradox of American Power: Why the World's Only Superpower Can't Go It Alone*. New York: Oxford University Press, 2002.

WHERE ON THE WORLD WIDE WEB?

The Avalon Project—World War II
http://www.yale.edu/lawweb/avalon/wwii/wwii.htm

Yale Law School has ambitiously undertaken to collect and house digital documents relevant to the fields of law, history, economics, politics, diplomacy, and government. This site links you to documents relating to World War II. As Chapter 4 explains, the end of World War II generated much uncertainty and mistrust. While visiting the archive, read the text of the agreements reached at the Yalta Conference at which Roosevelt, Churchill, and Stalin tried to resolve territorial issues after World War II. Did the agreements reached at Yalta make the Cold War inevitable?

Cold War
http://www.cnn.com/SPECIALS/cold.war/

Chapter 4 discusses the causes, characteristics, and the consequences of the Cold War. Learn more about the most recent great-power rivalry by exploring CNN's award-winning, comprehensive, Cold War website. Navigate interactive maps of the nuclear-testing sites in the American Southwest. Learn more about the key players and then play an interactive game to see which Cold War players you recognize. Hear sound bites and match them to the statesman who made them. Tour Cold War capitals through 3-D images. See espionage weapons and hear real-life spy stories.

Race for the Superbomb
http://www.pbs.org/wgbh/amex/bomb/sfeature/index.html

On this highly enlightening site, PBS recreates the competition between the United States and the Soviet Union in their race to stockpile nuclear weapons. This website brings home many aspects of the Cold War rivalry discussed in Chapter 4. Have you ever wondered if you could survive a nuclear blast if a bomb exploded fifty miles away? Nuclear Blast Mapper will analyze the "zones of destruction" for any location. If you survived the blast, find out if you would survive the fallout. Then, take a virtual tour of a secret government bunker maintained as shelter for lucky congressmen in case of a nuclear attack. Not scared enough? Take a Panic Quiz to determine your panic quotient.

Senator Joe McCarthy: A Multimedia Celebration
http://webcorp.com/mccarthy/

A multimedia site where students can see and listen to the senator's most famous speeches and hearings. The site also covers McCarthy's eventual demise and disgrace. This is an important site for contemporary students who have trouble understanding "what all the fuss was about."

Soviet Exhibit
http://www.ibiblio.org/expo/soviet.exhibit/entrance.html

This website is a virtual tour of the Library of Congress's Soviet Archives exhibit. Go to the first floor to see the Internal Workings of the Soviet System or proceed directly to the second floor to see the Soviet Union and the United States. Shuttle buses take you to other pavilions or let you visit the restaurant. You can leave messages for a current or future friend at the Post Office. The site also features important historical documents, translated when necessary.

The World War I Document Archive
http://www.lib.byu.edu/~rdh/wwi/

The World War I Military History List has assembled a group of primary documents from World War I. Read the treaties, peruse personal reminiscences, see photos, and access links to other resources. Chapter 4 puts forth theories concerning the cause of World War I. Some state that the switching alliances in Europe brought on the war. Others claim that the rational choices of individual German leaders who wanted to consolidate power led to a declaration of war. And finally, many assert that state factors, such as the rise of nationalism in Germany, were responsible for the war. After reading the documents in the archive, which theories do you think best explain the advent of World War I?

INFOTRAC® COLLEGE EDITION

Howard, Michael. "The Great War." *The National Interest* (Summer 2001).

Skidelsky, Robert. "Imbalance of Power (History of the Grand Alliance during World War II)." *Foreign Policy* (March 2002).

Brooks, Stephen G., and William C. Wohlforth. "Power, Globalization, and the End of the Cold War: Reevaluating a Landmark Case for Ideas." *International Security* (Winter 2000).

Waltz, Kenneth N. "Structural Realism after the Cold War." *International Security* (Summer 2000).

For more articles, enter:
"World War, 1914–1918" in the Subject Guide
"World War, 1939–1945" in the Subject Guide
"cold war" in the Subject Guide

Go to http://politicalscience.wadsworth.com/kegley10 to access additional resources related to this chapter.

CHAPTER 5

THE GLOBAL SOUTH IN A WORLD OF POWERS

TOPICS AND THEMES

- The politics of marginalization: the Global South in the international hierarchy
- Global North and Global South today: worlds apart
- The colonial origins of the Global South's plight
- Theoretical explanations of underdevelopment
- Closing the gap? The Global South's prospects
- The Global South's foreign policy response to a world ruled by the great powers
- The Global South's problematic future

- **CONTROVERSY** MULTINATIONAL CORPORATIONS IN THE GLOBAL SOUTH: DO THEY HELP OR HURT?

131

At the G-8 Summit in Alberta, Canada, in June 2002, Nigerian President Olusegun Obasanjo is invited to meet with the great-power leaders, in a gesture to open up to Global South participation in international decision making controlled by the Global North.

No one has developed a magic formula for how to make countries grow. . . . Growth economics suggests that poor countries have a hard time closing the income gap on rich countries at a rate greater than 2 percent per year, even under the best of circumstances. Catch-up—when it happens—takes generations.

—KENNETH ROGOFF, former director of research at the International Monetary Fund, 2004

In this unified world, poverty is our collective enemy. We must fight it because it is morally repugnant, and because its existence is like a cancer— weakening the whole of the body, not just the parts directly affected.

—JAMES D. WOLFENSOHN, president of the World Bank, 2002

Earth is divided into two hemispheres, north and south, at the equator. This artificial line of demarcation is, of course, meaningless except for use by cartographers to chart distance and location on maps. However, this divide captures a basic fact: the countries of the world are unequal, and this inequality can be viewed in a least a hundred different ways (Sutcliffe 2002). And it is not by coincidence that the hierarchy that separates rich and poor states, the weak and the strong, is located on either side of the equator (see Map 5.1).

Life for the countries in the Northern Hemisphere is very different from that in the Southern Hemisphere. The disparities between the "haves" and the "have nots" are profound, and for many Global South states the gap is growing. The division in status and power in this highly stratified society of states is a continuing issue on the global agenda—for which solutions must be found if the world is to experience a peaceful and stable future. As the ancient Greek political philosopher Aristotle warned, "wide differences in income are a source of war." The urgent moral need to reduce poverty and the war it breeds was argued in 2002 by British Prime Minister Tony Blair: "One illusion has been shattered on Sep-

MAP 5.1
The Global North and Global South
The countries of the Global North are those that are wealthy, democratic, and technologically innovative, with declining birthrates and aging populations. In contrast, the countries in the Global South are home to 85 percent of the world's population, but the impoverished people living there possess only 15 percent of the globe's wealth.

tember 11: that we can have the good life of the [Global North] irrespective of the state of the rest of the world. . . . The dragon's teeth are planted in the fertile soil of wrongs unrighted, of disputes left to fester for years, of failed states, of poverty and deprivation."

Poverty and inequality has existed throughout most periods of recorded history. But today the level of relative deprivation between rich and poor states has reached unprecedented proportions. The states in the less-developed Global South find themselves marginalized and left neglected by the wealthy states rapidly benefiting from rising prosperity in the age of globalization (see Chapter 8). Most of the countries in the Global South are frustrated by their inability to play catch-up and close the gap with rich countries, which "has not closed. Instead, it has widened" (Hausmann 2002). Mired in abject poverty, these states have had their identities shaped by their subordinate position in the global hierarchy of power. They find themselves reduced in their self-image to thinking of themselves as distinct from the advantaged, without real hope of escaping the crushing conditions that have become an entrenched way of life.

It is the purpose of this chapter to examine the causes and consequences of this chronic inequality among the more than two hundred states in the global system. Why is it that the great powers experience abundance while the disadvantaged poor countries desperately try simply to survive? What is it about global life that breeds such inequality?

■ **global level of analysis**
an analytical approach to world politics that emphasizes the impact of worldwide conditions on the behavior of states, IGOs, NGOs, and other international actors.

■ **structural realism**
a theory associated with neorealism that emphasizes the influence of the structure of world power on the behavior of the states within it.

■ **state level of analysis**
an analytical approach to the study of world politics that emphasizes how the internal attributes of states explain their foreign and domestic policy behaviors.

■ **individual level of analysis**
an analytical approach to the study of world politics that emphasizes the importance of individual people as agents or actors on the international stage, with special attention to leaders.

Most analysts begin to address this question at the **global level of analysis.** The popularity of this approach derives from the fact that the relative power and position of each state in the global system is assumed to be potently determined by changes in the system's hierarchical structure. How groups of states such as those in the less-developed Global South unfavorably fare in comparison with those in the advanced industrialized economies of the Global North is not believed to be accidental. Following the logic of **structural realism,** the global system is seen as having properties built into it that account for the inability of most Global South countries to engineer self-sustained growth and development at rates that would enable them to close the gap with the wealthy states.

As a preface to our inquiry, let us briefly elaborate on the reasoning underlying this perspective. It needs to be underscored that this chapter investigates the above question about international inequalities by inspecting the Global South states as international actors in world politics—that is, at both the global and the **state level of analysis.** Later, in Chapter 7, we will look at the human dimensions of welfare issues by inspecting peoples' inequalities as they exist both across the entire globe as well as within particular states. There, at the **individual level of analysis,** we will focus on humanitarian concerns and the barriers to human development and human rights.

Part of the basis for the resentment, envy, and sense of exploitation that the Global South countries feel stems from the fact that the modern state system, of which they are members, was created by the great powers in the 1648 Peace of Westphalia following the Thirty Years' War in Europe. Today's less-developed countries had no voice in creating the rules and the global institutions that govern both them and all sovereign states. The rules and laws that still cast their shadow over international affairs more than 350 years after Westphalia were constructed by the most powerful actors on the world stage, the so-called great powers. Those great powers constructed a system to serve their parochial self-interests by creating rules that would not only help them regulate their relationships with one another but also, and more important, enable them to conduct diplomacy in ways that would preserve their predominant positions at the top of the global pyramid of power, even at the expense of deterring the rise of less-powerful states seeking to join them (see Kegley and Raymond 2002a).

Indeed, the international organizations that have over time grown in number and influence (see Chapter 6) were created by the great powers to benefit themselves, but not necessarily all state members of the global community at large. Thus, to understand the origins and persistence of the inequalities of states in international society, we must make no mistake about the modern global system's most defining characteristic: it was initially, and remains, a socially constructed reality *by, of,* and *for* the powerful states, designed primarily to serve their interests and needs. The overarching motive was not the creation of a global civil society inspired by values of justice, but, in the realist construction, inspired by self-interest defined by power. The global system is understandably, given these assumptions, not designed as a system for equals; nor did the great powers design the global system with an eye to preventing the victimization of the weak and disadvantaged. In this sense, therefore, the inequalities that today divide into a class system the rich from the poor, and the mighty from the defenseless in terms of military capabilities, are part of a much longer historical pattern. It is important to look at the plight and predicament of the

Global South countries by first recognizing the long-term global forces that have created the position of weakness from which they now struggle to escape.

We begin by taking into consideration the legacy and impact of **colonialism** on the **indigenous peoples** whose territories were colonized by European imperial conquerors. These conquerors arbitrarily drew borders around their new territorial possessions without regard for the ethnic and linguistic divisions within the native populations they subjugated. Almost all the now independent sovereign states in the Southern Hemisphere were at one time colonies, including such contemporary powerhouses as the United States.

THE COLONIAL ORIGINS OF THE GLOBAL SOUTH'S PLIGHT

Despite their legal status as independent entities, sovereignty could not erase the colonial heritage and vulnerabilities that the former colonies faced. Indeed, the new poor states born after World War II were thrust to the international periphery, dominated by the wealthy great powers at the core of the transformed international system following the Second World War. The term **Third World** was first used to distinguish the growing number of newly independent but economically less-developed states that tended to share a colonial past from those states that identified with either the East or the West in the Cold War struggle, but it soon took on largely economic connotations. The Third World had failed to advance toward levels of economic development comparable to those of the **First World** industrialized great powers, like Europe, North America, and Japan. The so-called **Second World** consisting of the Soviet Union and its allies in other communist countries was distinguished by a communist ideological commitment to planned economic policies rather than reliance on market forces to determine the supply and demand for goods and services. Today the states comprising the former Second World have almost totally vanished from the global scene, with liberalism triumphant and nearly all states committed to free-market capitalism. The Second World describes the handful of "countries in transition" that have yet to join the World Trade Organization and accept its rules of free markets and free governments.

The term *Third World* carries Cold War baggage that makes it no longer useful. Today the terms **Global North,** which refers to what was previously known as the First World, and **Global South,** which refers to the rest of the world, are popular. As always, the placement of particular states within these categories is sometimes problematic. Considerable diversity exists within the countries of the Global South, even though it is common to describe them as a single group quite distinct from the similarly diverse great powers. Generally, four major dimensions differentiate the Global North and South: politics, technology, wealth, and demography.

States comprising the Global North are democratic, technologically inventive, wealthy, and aging, since their societies tend toward zero population growth (see Map 5.2). Some states in the Global South share many of these characteristics, but none shares them all. Saudi Arabia is rich but not democratic; China is aging but only a fraction of its slow-growing population has recently be-

■ **colonialism**
the rule of a region by an external sovereign power.

■ **indigenous peoples**
the native ethnic and cultural inhabitant populations within countries ruled by a government controlled by others, referred to as the "Fourth World."

■ **Third World**
a Cold War term to describe the developing countries of Africa, Asia, the Caribbean, and Latin America.

■ **First World**
the relatively wealthy industrialized countries that share a commitment to varying forms of democratic political institutions and developed market economies, including the United States, Japan, the European Union, Canada, Australia, and New Zealand.

■ **Second World**
during the Cold War, the group of countries, including the Soviet Union, its then-Eastern European allies, and China, that embraced central planning to propel economic growth.

■ **Global North**
a term used to refer to the world's wealthy, industrialized countries located primarily in the Northern Hemisphere.

■ **Global South**
a term now often used instead of "Third World" to designate the less-developed countries located primarily in the Southern Hemisphere.

MAP 5.2
The Great North-South Divide in Wealth and Population
If the countries in the globe were redrawn to reflect the size of their economies and populations, as shown here, huge differences would be visible. Most of the wealth is in the Global North, and most of the people are in the Global South. If prevailing trends persist as expected, the disparities will continue to preserve the existing division between rich and poor.
SOURCE: Adapted from data collected by the World Bank in its annual *World Development Report* (World Bank 2005b, 256–57).

Population

come wealthy; India is democratic but burdened with an enormous and growing population; and Singapore is both wealthy and technologically innovative, with a comparatively modest population growth rate, but is not democratic. Beyond these are many states that are not democratic, technologically innovative, or wealthy, but that are experiencing rapid population growth that increasingly strains overtaxed social and ecological systems. These, the **least developed of the less-developed countries** (LLDCs) are sometimes described today as the "Third World's Third World." Many, but not all, are in Africa, south of the Sahara.

The Global South is home to more than 85 percent of the world's people but commands less than 15 percent of its wealth. These disparities, illustrated in Map 5.2, underlie the long-festering "North-South conflict" more than do political and technological differences. Relations between the wealthy north and the poor south have been governed by struggle because of the fears and resentments that differences in status and unequal opportunities to compete economically naturally arouse. These conflicts are likely to intensify if globalization does not reduce the rich-poor gap.

The emergence of the Global South as an identifiable international actor is a distinctly contemporary phenomenon. Although most Latin American countries were independent before World War II, not until then did the floodgates of decolonization first open. In 1947, Great Britain granted independence to India and Pakistan, after which **decolonization**—the freeing of colonial peoples from their dependent status—gathered speed. Since then, a profusion of new sovereign states have joined the global community, nearly all carved from the British, Spanish, Portuguese, Dutch, and French empires built under colonialism four hundred years ago.

Today, few colonies exist, and the decolonization process is complete. However, the effects persist. Most of the ethnic national conflicts now so prevalent have colonial roots, as the imperial powers drew borders within and between their domains with little regard for the national identities of the indigenous peoples. (The divisions among these "nonstate nations" to this day undermine the sense of solidarity so important to the political stability of many multiethnic

■ **least developed of the less-developed countries (LLDCs)**
the most impoverished members in the Global South.

■ **decolonization**
the achievement of sovereign independence by countries that were once colonies of the great powers.

MAP 5.3
Global Imperialism, 1914

The ten major imperial powers competed for colonies throughout the globe in the present-day Global South, and on the eve of World War I their combined territories covered much of the world.

Global South countries.) Similarly, the staggering poverty facing Global South countries is partly a product of imperial pasts, when the European powers exploited their overseas territories. Although European powers have largely renounced political claims to their former colonies, the Global North maintains an active economic presence in many countries of the Global South. Thus, as viewed through the eyes of nationalist leaders in many of the emerging states, the disparity between the rich North and the poor South is the consequence of **neocolonialism** (or **neoimperialism**—unequal trade exchanges through which the advantaged exploit the disadvantaged by penetrating the latter's markets and by institutionalizing economic processes for this purpose).

■ **neocolonialism (neoimperialism)**
the economic rather than military domination of foreign countries.

The First Wave of European Imperialism

The first wave of European empire building began in the late fifteenth century, as the Dutch, English, French, Portuguese, and Spanish used their naval power to militarily conquer territories for commercial gain. As scientific innovations made the European explorers' adventures possible, merchants followed in their wake, "quickly seizing upon opportunities to increase their business and profits.

New States After the decolonization process runs its complete course, more new countries can be expected because many existing states are fragmenting. When World War I broke out, only sixty-two independent countries existed; at the beginning of the twenty-first century there were more than two hundred. Many new sovereign states are very small. Pictured here is the "micro" state of Nauru, which has a president, a supreme court, and the full apparatus of government to rule its tiny population. Half the globe's countries have populations smaller than the U.S. state of Massachusetts.

In turn, Europe's governments perceived the possibilities for increasing their own power and wealth. Commercial companies were chartered and financed, with military and naval expeditions frequently sent out after them to ensure political control of overseas territories" (B. Cohen 1973).

The economic strategy underlying the relationship between colonies and colonizers during this era of "classical imperialism" is known as **mercantilism**—an economic philosophy advocating government regulation of economic life to increase state power and security. European rulers believed that power flowed from the possession of national wealth measured in terms of gold and silver, and that developing mining and industry to attain a favorable balance of trade (exporting more than they imported) was the best way to accumulate the desired bullion. "Colonies were desirable in this respect because they afforded an opportunity to shut out commercial competition; they guaranteed exclusive access to untapped markets and sources of cheap materials (as well as, in some instances, direct sources of the precious metals themselves). Each state was determined to monopolize as many of these overseas mercantile opportunities as possible" (B. Cohen 1973). To maximize national power and wealth, states wedded to realist justifications of the competitive drive for global power saw the imperial conquest of foreign territory as a natural by-product of active government management of the economy.

By the end of the eighteenth century the European powers had spread themselves, although thinly, throughout virtually the entire world, but the colonial empires they had built now began to crumble. Britain's thirteen North American colonies declared their independence in 1776, and most of Spain's possessions

■ **mercantilism**
a government trade strategy for accumulating state wealth and power by encouraging exports and discouraging imports.

in South America won their freedom in the early nineteenth century. Nearly one hundred colonial relationships worldwide were terminated in the half-century ending in 1825 (Bergesen and Schoenberg 1980, 236).

As Europe's colonial empires dissolved, belief in the mercantilist philosophy also waned. As the Scottish political economist Adam Smith argued in his 1776 treatise, *The Wealth of Nations,* national wealth grew not through the accumulation of precious metals but rather from the capital and goods they could buy. Smith's ideas about the benefits of the "invisible hand" of the unregulated domestic and international marketplace laid much of the intellectual foundation for **classical liberal economic theory.** Following the thinking of Smith and other liberal free-trade theorists, faith in the precepts of **laissez-faire economics** (minimal government interference in the market) gained widespread acceptance (see also Chapter 9). European powers continued to hold numerous colonies, but the prevailing sentiment was now more anti- than pro-imperial.

The Second Wave of European Imperialism

Beginning in the 1870s and extending until the outbreak of World War I, a second wave of imperialism washed over the world as Europe, joined later by the United States and Japan, aggressively colonized new territories. The portion of the globe that Europeans controlled was one-third in 1800, two-thirds by 1878, and four-fifths by 1914 (Fieldhouse 1973, 3). As illustrated in Map 5.3, in the last twenty years of the nineteenth century Africa fell under the control of seven European powers (Belgium, Britain, France, Germany, Italy, Portugal, and Spain), and in all of the Far East and the Pacific, only China, Japan, and Siam (Thailand) were not conquered. But China was divided into **spheres of influence** by the foreign great powers that carved China into separate zones of commerce, which the great powers individually controlled and exploited for profit. Japan itself also imperialistically occupied Korea and Formosa (Taiwan). Elsewhere, the United States expanded across its continent, acquired Puerto Rico and the Philippines in the 1898 Spanish-American War, extended its colonial reach westward to Hawaii, leased the Panama Canal Zone "in perpetuity" from the new state of Panama (an American creation), and exercised considerable control over several Caribbean islands, notably Cuba. The preeminent imperial power, Great Britain, in a single generation expanded its empire to cover one-fifth of the earth's land area and comprised perhaps one-fourth of its population (B. Cohen 1973, 30). As British imperialists were proud to proclaim, it was an empire on which the sun never set.

Having abandoned their earlier acquired empires, why did most of the great powers—and those that aspired to great-power status—engage in this expensive and often vicious competition to control other peoples and territories? What explains the new imperialism? The answers are rooted in economics and politics.

With the Industrial Revolution, capitalism grew, emphasizing the free market, private ownership of the means of production, and the accumulation of wealth. Theorists following Karl Marx, who called themselves adherents of **communism,** saw imperialism's aggressive competition as caused by capitalists' need for profitable overseas outlets for their surplus ("finance") capital. One of the adherents was the Soviet leader Vladimir Lenin, who made distinctive contributions to the communist thinking later described as **Marxism-Leninism.**

In his famous 1916 monograph *Imperialism, The Highest Stage of Capital-*

■ **classical liberal economic theory**
a body of thought based on Adam Smith's ideas about the forces of supply and demand in the marketplace, emphasizing the benefits of minimal government regulation of the economy and trade.

■ **laissez-faire economics**
the philosophical principle of free markets with little governmental regulation.

■ **spheres of influence**
the area dominated by a great power.

■ **communism**
an ideology maintaining that if society is organized so that every person produces according to his or her ability and consumes according to his or her needs, a community without class distinctions will emerge, sovereign states will no longer be needed, and imperial wars of colonial conquest will vanish from history.

■ **Marxism-Leninism**
communist theory as derived from the writings of Karl Marx, Vladimir Lenin, and their successors, which criticizes capitalism as a cause of class struggle, the exploitation of workers, colonialism, and war.

Karl Marx Challenges Imperialism Pictured on the left is the German philosopher Karl Marx (1818–83), whose revolutionary economic theory argued that "the history of all hitherto existing society is the history of class struggle." Imperial conquest of colonial peoples could only be prevented, Marx warned, by humanity's shift from a capitalist to a socialist economy and society. Pictured on the right is the kind of imperialistic activity that provoked his wrath: ruthless, aggressive, and bent on acquiring property for profit, Britain's nineteenth-century imperial forces marched into battle to seize foreign territory.

---

ism, Lenin argued that military expansion abroad was produced by the "monopoly stage of capitalism." Lenin concluded that the only way to end imperialism was to abolish capitalism. Classical or liberal economists, on the other hand, regarded the new imperialism not as a product of capitalism as such but rather as "a response to certain maladjustments within the contemporary capitalist system which, given the proper will, could be corrected" (B. Cohen 1973). What the two perspectives shared was the belief that economics explained the new imperialism: "The fundamental problem was the presumed material needs of advanced capitalist societies—the need for cheap raw materials to feed their growing industrial complexes, for additional markets to consume their rising levels of production, and for investment outlets to absorb their rapidly accumulating capital" (B. Cohen 1973). Thus, from both the Marxist and classical liberal perspectives, the material needs of capitalist societies explained their imperial drive.

World-system analyses, like Marxist theories, also embrace an economic explanation. **World-system theory** postulates that a single capitalist world economy emerged during the "long 16th century" from 1450 to 1640, which created a world division of labor separating "core" (industrial) areas from those in the

■ **world-system theory**
a theory that claims the perpetual and widening inequity among states is explained by capitalism's international division of labor and production, which over time allows the wealthy core countries to become richer while the peripheral states supplying raw materials and cheap labor become poorer.

globe's (nonindustrial) "periphery" (see Wallerstein 2004). Northwest Europe first emerged as the core. As the Industrial Revolution proceeded, the core states exchanged manufactured goods for raw agricultural and mineral materials secured at bargain prices by taking advantage of willing sellers and cheap labor in the colonial territories at the periphery.

This perspective emphasizes colonization as the principal method for imperial control over foreign lands. After 1870 colonies effectively became occupation zones in which a small number of European sojourners coerced an indigenous population into production for the global economy (Boswell 1989).

Political factors also explain the new imperialism. In his seminal 1902 book, *Imperialism*, British economist J. A. Hobson argued that the jockeying for power and prestige between competitive empires had always characterized the great powers' behavior in the European balance-of-power system, and that imperialism through overseas expansion was simply a global extension of this inter-European competition for dominance inspired by the **realpolitik** theoretical premise that all states have an unquenchable thirst for more and more power.

■ **realpolitik**
the realist theoretical perspective emphasizing the drive for power as the primary motive in international politics.

By the 1800s Britain emerged from Europe's perpetual conflict as the world's leading power. By 1870, however, British hegemony was on the wane. Germany emerged as a powerful industrial state, as did the United States. Understandably, Britain tried to protect its privileged global position in the face of growing competition from the newly emerging core states, and its efforts to maintain the status quo help to explain the second wave of imperial expansion—especially in Africa, whose partition served the imperial powers at the expense of local populations.

The British-sponsored laissez-faire system of free trade promoted rapid economic growth in a number of colonial territories, but economic development elsewhere proceeded even more rapidly. Western Europe, North America, Australia, and New Zealand were able to complete their industrial revolutions during this period and to advance as industrial societies. Thus the gap between the world's rich and poor countries began to widen.

Colonialism, Self-Determination, and Decolonization in the Twentieth Century

■ **self-determination**
the liberal doctrine that people should be able to determine the government that will manage their affairs.

■ **liberalism**
the body of theoretical thought that stresses the importance of ideals, ideas, and institutions to generate progress, prosperity, and peace.

The climate of opinion turned decidedly anti-imperial when the 1917 Versailles peace settlement that ended World War I embraced the principle of national **self-determination** advocated by U.S. President Woodrow Wilson. Self-determination derived from **liberalism** meant that indigenous nationalities would have the right to decide which authority would represent and rule them. Wilson and others who shared his liberal convictions believed that freedom of choice would lead to the creation of states and governments content with their territorial boundaries and therefore less inclined to make war. In practice, however, the attempt to redraw states' borders to separate nationality groups was applied almost exclusively to war-torn Europe, where six new states were created from the territory of the former Austrian-Hungarian Empire (Austria, Czechoslovakia, Hungary, Poland, Romania, and the ethnically divided Yugoslavia). Other territorial adjustments were also made in Europe, but the proposition that self-determination should be extended to Europe's overseas empires did not receive serious support.

Still, the colonial territories of the powers defeated in World War I were not simply parceled out among the victorious allies, as had typically happened in the past. Instead, the territories controlled by Germany and the Ottoman Empire were transferred under League of Nations auspices to countries that would govern them as "mandates" pending their eventual self-rule. Many of these territorial decisions gave rise to subsequent conflicts such as in the Middle East and Africa after, for example, the League of Nations called for the eventual creation of a Jewish national homeland in Palestine and arranged for the transfer of control over South-West Africa (now called Namibia) to what would become the white minority regime of South Africa.

The principle implicit in the League of Nations mandate system gave birth to the idea that "colonies were a trust rather than simply a property to be exploited and treated as if its peoples had no rights of their own" (S. Easton 1964). This set an important precedent for the negotiations after World War II, when territories of the defeated powers placed under the United Nations (UN) trusteeship system were not absorbed by others but were promised eventual self-rule, and support for self-determination gained momentum. The decolonization process accelerated in 1947, when the British relinquished political control of India and Pakistan. War eventually erupted between these newly independent states as each sought to gain control over disputed territory in Kashmir, in 1965 and 1971, and again as the nuclear-armed states clashed in 2002. Violence also broke out in Indochina and Algeria in the 1950s and early 1960s as the French sought to regain control over colonial territories they had held before World War II. Similarly, bloodshed followed closely on the heels of independence in the Congo when the Belgians granted their African colony independence in 1960, and it dogged the unsuccessful efforts of Portugal to battle the winds of decolonization that swept over Africa as the 1960s wore on.

Despite these political convulsions, decolonization for the most part was not only extraordinarily rapid but also remarkably peaceful. This may be explained by World War II's having sapped the economic and military vitality of many of the colonial powers. World-system analysts contend that a growing appreciation of the costs of empire also eroded support for colonial empires (Strang 1990, 1991). Regardless of the underlying cause, colonialism became less acceptable in a world increasingly dominated by rivalry between East and West. The Cold War competition for political allies and the fear of large-scale warfare gave the superpowers incentives to lobby jointly for the liberation of overseas empires. Decolonization "triumphed," as Inis Claude (1967) explains, "largely because the West [gave] priority to the containment of communism over the perpetuation of colonialism."

The UN also contributed to the "collective delegitimization" of colonialism. With colonialism already in retreat, in 1960, Global South states took advantage of their growing numbers in the UN General Assembly to secure passage of the historic Declaration on the Granting of Independence to Colonial Countries and Peoples. "The General Assembly proclaimed that the subjection of any people to alien domination was a denial of fundamental human rights, contrary to the UN Charter, and an impediment to world peace and that all subject peoples had a right to immediate and complete independence. No country cast a vote against this anticolonial manifesto. . . . It was an ideological triumph" (Riggs and Plano 1994).

As the old order crumbled—and as the leaders in the newly emancipated territories discovered that freedom did not translate automatically into autonomy, economic independence, and domestic prosperity—the conflict between the rich Global North and the emerging states of the Global South began. And it continues today. While some see future international struggle as centered on a **clash of civilizations** (Huntington 1996), others argue that on account of cascading **globalization** a "civilizational clash" is "not so much over Jesus Christ, Confucius, or the Prophet Muhammad as it is over the unequal distribution of world power, wealth, and influence, and the perceived historical lack of respect accorded to small states and peoples by larger ones" (Fuller 1995). The widening gap between the developed and the developing world spells global turmoil in the future, as suggested by those (Crenshaw 2003) who trace the post–9/11 global terrorism to international inequalities.

■ **clash of civilizations**
Samuel Huntington's controversial thesis that in the twenty-first century the globe's major civilizations will conflict with one another, leading to anarchy and warfare similar to that resulting from conflicts between states over the past five hundred years.

■ **globalization**
the integration of states through increasing contact, communication, and trade to create a holistic, single global system in which the process of change increasingly binds people together in a common fate.

NORTH AND SOUTH TODAY: WORLDS APART

The Global South is sometimes described today as a "zone of turmoil" in large measure because, in contrast with the Global North where "peace, wealth, and democracy" prevail, most of the world's people live amid "poverty, war, tyranny, and anarchy" (Singer and Wildavsky 1993). A particularly noteworthy difference is that the states in the Global North are democratic and rarely fight one another, whereas in the Global South, violent conflict remains rife both within and among many states.

Democracy has spread rapidly and widely since the 1980s, becoming the preferred mode of governance throughout much of the Global South. However, some of the Global South's recent additions to the liberal democratic community have governments whose commitment to regular elections and human rights are fragile. Furthermore, many Global South countries lack well-developed domestic market economies based on entrepreneurship and private enterprise. Nonetheless, because the Global North's history suggests that free markets spawn the large middle class that is a precondition for free governments (Mazarr 1999), the continuing expansion of Global South market economies under capitalism appears likely to hasten democratization, although the continued enlargement of the liberal democratic community is not guaranteed.

Differences in technological capabilities also separate North and South. Typically, Global South countries have been unable to evolve an indigenous technology appropriate to their own resources and have been dependent on powerful Global North multinational corporations (MNCs) (see Chapter 6) to transfer technical know-how. This means that research and development expenditures are directed toward solutions of the Global North's problems, with technological advances seldom meeting the needs of the Global South. And in the information age, technology has not been distributed equally geographically: the highest density of computer connections to the Internet is in the Global North (see World Bank 2004a and Chapter 8).

The fact that 85 percent of the world's population is poor is both a reflection and cause of these unequally distributed resources. To measure the disparities, the World Bank differentiates the "low-income," "lower middle income," and "upper middle income" economies in **developing countries,** whose **gross national income (GNI)** in 2004 averaged $6,102 billion, from the "high-income" **developed countries,** which averaged $25,384 billion for each state (World Bank 2004b, 252). Among the developing countries, wide variations in economic performance (growth and inflation rates, debt burdens, and export prices, for example) and international circumstances (such as the availability of oil and other fuels) are evident.

Numbers paint pictures and construct images, and the data on the division between Global North and Global South point to brutal disparities and inequalities. When we compare the differences on some key indicators differentiating low- and middle-income countries from high-income countries, at the peak of development, we discover huge gaps (see Table 5.1).

This picture darkens even more when focus is shifted to the plight of the poorest in the low-income developing countries. More than 2.6 billion people (two-fifths of humanity) live in one of the 63 countries at the bottom of the global hierarchy, the LLDCs, where, typically, **barter** of one agricultural good for another (rather than money) is used for economic exchanges. These countries are not emerging or reemerging to break the chains of their destitution; they are falling behind the other Global South countries.

The low-income LLDCs are not participants in the global market: they account for less than 0.3 percent of world trade, and their meager exports are largely confined to inexpensive primary products, including food stuffs (cocoa, coffee, and tea), minerals (copper), hides, and timber. Because these low-income countries consume most of what they produce, theirs is typically a subsistence economy, and the prospects for change are dim, because most of these least-developed countries have been bypassed by direct foreign investment and ignored by foreign aid donors (World Bank 2005b).

High rates of population growth since 1990 have contributed to the widespread poverty of LLDCs. Likewise, it will take only twenty-five years for the LLDCs' total population to double, compared with two and a half centuries for the Global North. LLDCs' economic growth rates in the recent past have averaged less than 0.1 percent each year. Growth rates elsewhere have almost uniformly been higher. This is a powerful reason why the rich minority gets richer while the poorest of the poor will likely become even poorer.

Despite wide differences, a daunting scale of misery and marginalization thus is evident across the Global South, from which only a fraction of its countries have begun to escape. For most Global South countries, the future is bleak, and the opportunities and choices most basic to freedom from fear and poverty are unavailable. The aggregate pattern underlying global trends in the last twenty years shows that more than sixty countries today are worse off than they were and are falling ever further behind the levels achieved by the countries in the Global North. When we consider that nearly all the population growth in the twenty-first century will occur in the Global South, the poorest countries cut off from circulation in the globalized marketplace, it is hard to imagine how the gap can close, and how the soil of poverty can be prevented from producing terrorism and civil war.

This tragic portrayal of unspeakable despair for so many Global South states raises the basic theoretical question: Why does the Global South, at this historical juncture, suffer from such dismal destitution?

■ **developing countries**
a category used by the World Bank to designate those countries with an average GNI (in 2002) each year below $25,383 billion.

■ **gross national income (GNI)**
a measure of the production of goods and services within a given time period, which is used to delimit the geographic scope of production. GNI measures production by a state's citizens or companies, regardless of where the production occurs. An alternative measure is gross domestic product (GDP), which measures production occurring within the territory of a state, regardless of the national identity of the producers.

■ **developed countries**
a category used by the World Bank to designate those countries with a GNP (in 2000) above $631 billion annually.

■ **barter**
the exchange of one good for another rather than the use of currency to buy and sell items.

TABLE 5.1

Two Worlds of Development: An International Class Divide

Characteristic	Developing Global South	Developed Global North
Number of countries/economies	152	55
Population (millions)	5,236	965
Population density (people for each km^2)	53	31
Women in policy positions (%)	6	16
Land area (thousands of km^2)	101,510	32,365
GNI ($ billions)	6,102	26,310
Average growth rate of the domestic economy, 1990–2002 (%)	2.8	1.7
Foreign direct investment ($ millions)	185,390	727,130
Net foreign direct investment inflows (% of GDP)	2.5	1.9
Official development assistance received ($ millions)	55,150	10,030
Exports ($ billions)	1,748	6,350
Exports (% of GDP)	33	22
Imports (% of GDP)	30	19
Average years of citizen's schooling	6.5	10
Telephone mainlines per 1,000 people	96	584
Mobile phones per 1,000 people	51	532
Cellular subscribers per 1,000 people	101	653
Internet servers	5,573	115,650
Internet users per 1,000 people	40.9	445.8
Life expectancy at birth	64.5	78
Population living in cities (%)	41	79
Urban population (%)	41.4	77.8
Roads paved (%)	32	93
Number of motor vehicles per 1,000 people	60	610
Personal computer per 10,000 people	20	393
Television sets per 1,000 people	185	641
Research and development (R&D) expenditure (% of GNP, 1990–2002)	0.6	2.6
Researchers in R&D per million people	384	3,449
Electricity capacity per person (kWh)	1,035	88
Carbon dioxide emission (% of world total)	36.9	47.8
Armed forces	14,203,000	4,440,000

Where people live on the earth influences how they live. As this information shows, the situation is much more favorable—and the quality of life is relatively advantageous—in the developed countries of the Global North than it is in the Southern Hemisphere, where nearly all the Global South countries are located. As the World Bank predictions in the attatched figure show, global trends indicate that the discrepancy between the rich and the poor will continue through the year 2050.

SOURCES: World Bank (2004a and 2004b) and UNDP (2004), *Human Development Report 2004*.

World GDP, $trn, 1995 $
- Low- and middle-income countries
- High-income countries

Forecast: 2050, 2015
2000
1960

THEORETICAL EXPLANATIONS OF UNDERDEVELOPMENT

Why has the Global South lagged so far behind the Global North in its comparative level of well-being and **development**? And why have the development experiences even within the Global South differed so widely?

The diversity evident in the Global South invites the conclusion that underdevelopment is explained by a combination of factors within developing countries and in their relationships with the Global North. Some theorists explain the underdevelopment of most developing economies alongside the escape of others by looking primarily at differences among Global South states. Other theorists focus on the position of developing countries in the global political economy. We shall briefly discuss three variants on these interpretations: classical economic development theory, structuralist theories of dominance and dependence, and neoclassical theory.

■ **development**
the processes through which a country increases its capacity to meet its citizens' basic human needs and raise their standard of living.

Classical Economic Development Theory

Based on the definition of development—as constructed in the West—as increases in income, liberal economic development theories of **modernization** first emerged in the early post-World War II era. They argued that the major barriers to development were posed by the Global South countries' own internal characteristics. To overcome these barriers, most classical theorists recommended that the wealthy countries supply various "missing components" of development, such as investment capital through foreign aid or private foreign direct investment.

Once sufficient capital was accumulated to promote economic growth, these liberal theorists predicted that its benefits would eventually "trickle down" to broad segments of society. In this way, everyone, not just a privileged few, would enjoy the benefits of rising affluence. Walt W. Rostow, an economic historian and U.S. policymaker, formalized this theory in his influential book *The Stages of Economic Growth* (1960). He predicted that traditional societies beginning the path to development would inevitably pass through various stages by means of the free market and would eventually "take off" to become similar to the mass-consumption societies of the capitalist Global North. Even though the rich are likely to get richer, it was argued, as incomes in the world as a whole grow, the odds increase that a preindustrialized economy will grow faster and eventually reduce the gap between it and richer countries. That prognosis and the policies on which it was based were ultimately rejected by the impoverished Global South. Leaders there did not buy the classical liberal argument that the Global North became prosperous and assumed control of global economic power because their open societies concentrated on work, invention, skill, and investment in schools and tools to make them winners in the global marketplace (see Landes 1998; Thurow 1999). Economists in the Global South were persuaded by the rival structural theories that attribute the Global South's plight to the links between developing countries and the global political economy.

■ **modernization**
a view of development popular in the Global North's liberal democracies that argues that wealth is created through efficient production, free enterprise, and free trade, and that countries' relative ability to create wealth depends on technological innovation and education more than on natural endowments such as climate and resources.

Two Structural Theories: Dependency Theory and World Systems

Two prongs of structuralism merit attention, as both locate the causes and potential cures of most developing countries' persistent underdevelopment in their positions of dependence on the dominant great powers. The first is dependency

■ **dependency theory**
a theory that less-developed countries are exploited because global capitalism makes them dependent on the rich countries that create exploitative rules for trade and production.

theory and its liberal variant, called "dualism." The second, which we have already introduced, is world-system theory.

Dependency theory builds on Lenin's theory of imperialism but goes beyond it to account for changes that have occurred since Lenin first wrote his Marxist interpretation of capitalism as a cause of inequality and domination. Its central proposition is that the relationship between the advanced capitalist societies at the core of the world political economy and the developing countries at the periphery is exploitative, and that the underdevelopment of the Global South has been caused by world capitalism's impact: the division of the globe into two halves, one modern and the other backward.

Although the dependency theory literature is vast and arouses many controversies (see Caporaso and Levine 1992; P. Evans 2001), dependency theorists all reject Rostow's stages-of-growth thesis, arguing that underdevelopment "is not a stalled stage of linear development, a question of precapitalism, retarded or backward development, but rather a [product of the less-developed countries'] structural position in a hierarchical world division of labor" (Shannon 1989). In short, the Global South's underdevelopment results from its subordinate position in a world political economy dominated by capitalistic industrialized great powers.

Andre Gunder Frank (1969) wrote a definitive structural interpretation of chronic underdevelopment in Latin America; he argued that "the now-developed countries were never underdeveloped, though they may have been undeveloped." The reason, he asserted, was colonialism—the historical expansion of the capitalist system that "effectively and entirely penetrated even the apparently most isolated sectors of the underdeveloped world."

Other theorists—frequently called *dependentistas*—share Frank's concern about the "enslavement" of the Global South by the capitalist Global North. "The relation of interdependence between two or more economies, and between these and world trade," Theotonio Dos Santos (1970) argues, "assumes the form of dependence when some countries (the dominant ones) can expand and can be self-sustaining, while others (the dependent ones) can do this only as a reflection of that expansion, which can have either a positive or a negative effect on their immediate development." Hence, **dependency** is seen as resulting from a situation "in which the economy of certain countries is conditioned by the development and expansion of another economy to which the former is subjected."

■ **dependency**
a condition of retarded economic growth believed to result from the Global South's subordination and structural exploitation by the Global North's advanced capitalistic market economies, making the Global South especially vulnerable to the business cycles of expansion and contraction.

Dependent countries are vulnerable to penetration by outside forces. Dependency theorists argue that the overseas branches of giant multinational corporations (MNCs) headquartered in the Global North are the primary agents of neocolonial penetration because they transfer profits from the penetrated societies to the penetrators. Foreign investment—whether private or in the form of aid from other governments—is also an instrument of penetration. Technological dependence and "cultural imperialism," through which Global South societies become saturated with ideas and values alien to their indigenous cultures, are among the consequences. Once penetration by advanced capitalist states has occurred, continues the dependency theory argument, the inherently unequal exchanges that bind the exploiters and the exploited are sustained by elites within the penetrated societies, who sacrifice their country's welfare for personal profit.

■ **dualism**
the separation of a country into two sectors, the first modern and prosperous centered in major cities, and the second at the margin, neglected and poor.

The argument that a privileged few benefit from dependency at the expense of their societies is logically similar to **dualism.** Dualism refers to the existence of two separate economic and social sectors operating side by side. Dual societies typically have a rural, impoverished, and neglected sector operating alongside an urban, developing, or advanced sector—but with little interaction between the two. Thus whatever growth occurs in the industrial sector in dual societies "neither initiates a corresponding growth process in the rural sector nor generates sufficient employment to prevent a growing population in the stagnant sectors" (H. Singer and Ansari 1988). MNCs contribute to dualism by promoting "the interests of the small number of well-paid modern-sector workers against the interests of the rest by widening wage differentials . . . and worsen the imbalance between rural and urban economic opportunities by locating primarily in urban areas and contributing to the flow of rural-urban migration" (Todaro 2002).

World-system theorists share dependency theorists' view that the world is divided into a core (the advanced capitalist states), a periphery (the developing states), and a semiperiphery composed of ascending countries climbing from the periphery and declining countries falling from the ranks of the wealthy core. However, they take a longer-term structural perspective on the emergence of disparities between the two (in terms of classes, much as Karl Marx did).

For world-system theory a critical issue is the core-periphery distinction. "Within the world division of labor, core states specialize in the production of the most 'advanced' goods, which involves the use of the most sophisticated technologies and highly mechanized methods of production ('capital-intensive' production). [This means] that core states specialize in the production of sophisticated manufactured goods." Within the periphery, on the other hand, economic activities "are relatively less technologically sophisticated and more 'labor intensive.' . . . For most of the modern era, production for export was concentrated on raw materials and agricultural commodities" (Shannon 1989). Historically, states on the periphery have also been militarily inferior to core states and less well-organized administratively, which limited their ability to compete with the capitalist states.

World-system theorists cannot easily explain the industrialization now taking place in the periphery's emerging markets. To account for this, they have coined the term "semiperiphery" to accommodate geographic areas or countries, such as the **newly industrialized countries (NICs),** that are moving toward becoming **newly industrialized economies (NIEs)** in an intermediate position between the core and the periphery. Dependency theorists also have difficulty explaining these countries' growth. To interpret this anomaly, they sometimes use the term **dependent development** to describe the industrial development of peripheral areas in a system otherwise dominated by the Global North. The term suggests the possibility of either growing or declining prosperity, but not outside the confines of a continuing dominance-dependence relationship between North and South.

Closing the Gap? The Global South's Prospects

Is it possible for the Global South to escape the vicious cycle of poverty? When we look at the situation from the perspective of the poorest of the poor countries, the prospects appear dismal. However, there is a basis for optimism that can be found if you broaden the picture and see the conspicuous exceptions to the general pattern of persistent poverty. Destitution is not necessarily permanent. Al-

■ **world-system theorists** adherents of a theory that claims there is an international division of labor in which core states specialize in the capital-intensive production of sophisticated manufactured goods and peripheral states concentrate on the labor-intensive production of raw materials and agricultural commodities.

■ **newly industrialized countries (NICs) and newly industrialized economies (NIEs)** the most prosperous members of the Global South, which have become important exporters of manufactured goods as well as important markets for the major industrialized countries that export capital goods.

■ **dependent development** the industrialization of peripheral areas within the confines of the dominance-dependence relationship between North and South, which enables the poor to become wealthier without ever catching up to the core Global North countries.

though many Global South countries appear to be mired in persistent poverty, some Global South countries have managed to break the chains of underdevelopment. By pursuing bold paths for growth, they have seen their fortunes rise and are poised to enter the ranks of the advanced Global North economies. The ability for some developing countries to escape the syndrome that still affects the rest of the Global South suggests that others can succeed as well.

Consider one category of Global South states whose relative wealth contrasts sharply with the LLDCs' poverty: those Global South states that have fossil fuels to consume and export. The sixteen developing-country exporters of oil and other fuels, and especially the twelve members of the Organization of Petroleum Exporting Countries (OPEC), have escaped the LLDCs' grim fate. Notably, OPEC members Kuwait, Qatar, and the United Arab Emirates have risen to the high-income group's standards of living rivaling those of Global North countries.

Another category of Global South countries that inspires hope are the emerging or "middle-income" economies, or the so-called newly industrialized economies (NIEs), particularly in Asia, that have experienced even greater success than the oil-exporting countries. Their achievement lies in moving beyond the export of primary products to the export of manufactured goods. Today the NIEs are among the largest exporters of manufactured goods and the most prosperous members of the Global South, and have climbed from the periphery into the **semiperiphery.** The so-called **Asian Tigers** (South Korea, Singapore, Taiwan, and Hong Kong) have taken advantage of comparatively low wage rates to aggressively promote export-led economic growth. Pursuing strategies similar to the imperial powers of the past, the governments' neomercantilist practices include protecting infant industries from foreign competition and providing financial incentives for manufacturing industries. Spectacular economic growth has followed. With their population growth generally in check, the Asian Tigers have joined the ranks of the world's wealthiest states, and still other "new tigers" such as India have emerged as exports and foreign investment have stimulated a booming economy, fueled by the **outsourcing** of jobs from the labor-costly core to the skilled workers abroad able to perform the same labor well and at less expense to the home corporation.

Neither geography nor current levels of economic performance identify well the emerging markets with the greatest potential. What most distinguishes these countries engineering an economic revolution is that their governments have stabilized the value of their currencies, brought inflation under control, and privatized the businesses once owned by the government. In addition, many opened themselves to foreign investment. This change in philosophy about the causes of and cures for underdevelopment formerly prevalent throughout the Global South was a concession in Global South thinking, pressure inspired by **neoliberalism** to reform such powerful global IGOs as the World Bank and the International Monetary Fund.

> [The NIEs believed that for] competitive free markets to flourish, privatizing state-owned enterprises, promoting free trade and export expansion, welcoming investors from developed countries, and eliminating the plethora of government regulations and price distortions in . . . product and financial markets, both economic efficiency and economic growth will be stimulated. . . . [They concluded that] what is needed, therefore, [was] not a

■ **semiperiphery**
to world-system theorists, countries midway between the rich "core," or center, and the poor "periphery" in the global hierarchy, at which foreign investments are targeted when labor wages and production costs become too high in the prosperous core regions.

■ **Asian Tigers**
the four Asian NIEs that experienced far greater rates of economic growth during the 1980s than the more advanced industrial societies of the Global North.

■ **outsourcing**
the transfer of jobs by a corporation usually headquartered in a Global North country to a Global South country able to supply trained workers at lower wages.

■ **neoliberalism**
a perspective that accounts for the way international institutions promote global prosperity through reforms such as the creation of free markets and acceptance of free trade.

reform of the international economic system or a restructuring of dualistic developing economies or an increase in foreign aid or attempts to control population growth or a more effective central planning system. Rather, it [was] simply a matter of promoting free markets and laissez-faire economics within the context of permissive governments that allow the "magic of the marketplace" and the "invisible hand" of market prices to guide resource allocation and stimulate economic development. (Todaro 1994, 85–86)

The success of the free-market practices of the Asian NIEs in elevating themselves from the rest of the Global South inspired faith in the neoclassical theorists' export-led strategies for NIEs' economic growth and encouraged others to emulate their strategies. The neoclassical predictions that market economies will thrive where government management of the market is minimal, and their argument that entrepreneurial success is more likely to occur where basic democratic political freedoms are protected, led to widespread acceptance of liberal theory, which appeared triumphant (Mandelbaum 2002). Because success is often its own reward, these reforms heightened cries for additional reforms in the Global South countries in order to remove still other obstacles standing in the way of economic growth. These include pressure by the UN, the International Monetary Fund, and the World Bank for poor countries to pay more attention to attacking corruption and to protecting the environment and speeding up transitions toward fuller democratic governance—based on the liberal ethical premise that, properly understood, development is contingent upon the increase of freedom and civil liberties (Bhagwati 2004).

The achievements of the NIEs and the emerging markets alongside the stagnant or plummeting financial fate of the poorest Global South countries provoke policy questions: Despite these differences and the inequalities between Global South states, is there a commonality, a consensus, that unites them as a group? Does the Global South share a socially constructed collective vision around which they have built a common posture? How have the weak responded to the situation they inherited—being vulnerable states among the strong? How have the relatively powerless sought to deal with the great powers, on whom they have been dependent? The Global South countries are situated in a global system at the bottom of the global pyramid of power, facing mighty great powers as well as the influential **nonstate actors** that the great powers have created (IGOs, such as the United Nations, see Chapter 6). What strategies have the Global South countries forged to deal with their perceived exploitation resulting from having had to struggle from a position of weakness in a world of powers?

■ **nonstate actors**
all transnationally active groups other than states, such as organizations whose members are states (IGOs) and nongovernmental organizations (NGOs) whose members are individuals and private groups from more than one state.

THE GLOBAL SOUTH'S FOREIGN POLICY RESPONSE TO A WORLD RULED BY THE GREAT POWERS

The vast political, economic, and social differences separating North and South indicate that the Global South is "weak, vulnerable, and insecure—with these traits being the function of both domestic and external factors" (Ayoob 1995). Coping with this insecurity has long been a primary foreign policy goal of Global South states, and efforts to overcome these insecurities have often brought the Global South into contention with the Global North. Ironically, the end of the Cold War reduced the great powers' security interests in providing economic aid to Global South countries. Without foreign assistance, the Global South is now experiencing a burst of new armed conflicts (see Chapter 11). The globalization of finance and trade threatens to further expand the economic vulnerabilities of many poor Global South states.

As realists insist, power and wealth are states' core motives and are realized through military and economic prowess. Strategies designed to maximize power and prosperity continue to preoccupy foreign policy thinking in the Global South, where different states take different approaches to increasing prosperity. Let us examine how the Global South countries are pursuing their objectives, particularly in their relationships with the Global North.

In Search of Power

The states emerging after World War II struggled on separate tracks to find a foreign policy approach that could provide them with the power and prosperity they lacked. The **nonaligned states** were determined to strike a neutral course in the Cold War contest, while a broader group (including, for example, many Latin American states allied with the United States that had secured independence in the nineteenth century) concentrated their efforts more directly on severing their economic dominance by and dependence on the Global North.

Nonalignment. The nonalignment movement began in 1955, when twenty-nine Asian and African countries met in Bandung, Indonesia, to devise a strategy to combat colonialism. In 1961 leaders from twenty-five countries, mostly former colonies, met in Belgrade, Yugoslavia, where they created a lasting political coalition, the **Non-Aligned Movement (NAM),** whose membership would later grow to more than one hundred countries.

Because the new states sought to avoid entrapment in the Cold War, they tried through nonalignment to maximize their own gains while minimizing their costs. The strategy energized both the United States and the Soviet Union to renew their efforts to woo the uncommitted Global South "neutrals" to their own network of allies. The Cold War competitors became willing players in a bipolar **zero-sum** contest where one side's gains were the other's losses, often offering economic and military aid to win friends and influence allies.

The Cold War's end ended much of the competitive rationale for providing foreign aid and eroded the bargaining leverage nonalignment had provided the Global South. As a strategy, nonalignment "died" with the Cold War. The original justification for nonalignment no longer exists. But the passions for the improvement of the Global South behind it live on.

The challenge facing the nonaligned states today is how to promote their interests in a world where few listen to their voices. The nonaligned Global South can complain, but its bargaining power to engineer institutional reforms is limited. This weakness is displayed in the UN, where the most influence the Global South has mustered has symbolically been to delay serious proposals to make Germany and Japan permanent members of the Security Council by insisting that a nonaligned state or one of the larger developing countries (such as Brazil, India, Indonesia, Mexico, or South Africa) also be given a seat among the mighty. Weak states have some vocal power in numbers, but no clout or control.

■ **nonaligned states**
countries that do not participate in military alliances with rival blocs for fear that formal alliance will lead them to unnecessary involvement in war.

■ **Non-Aligned Movement (NAM)**
a group of more than one hundred newly independent, mostly less-developed states that joined together as a group of neutrals to avoid entanglement with the superpowers' competing alliances in the Cold War and to advance the Global South's common interests in economic cooperation and growth.

■ **zero-sum**
the perception in a rivalry that if one side gains, the other side loses.

Thus, the Global South worries that the future holds the feared prospect that only even-newer forms of great-power imperialism will continue to destroy any Global South hopes for progress.

Zones of Turmoil. These concerns are rooted in past experience: many developing countries felt betrayed and invaded when they became the battleground on which the superpowers conducted covert activities, paramilitary operations, and proxy wars. The Global South became the world's killing fields; more than 90 percent of the inter- and intrastate conflicts and 90 percent of the casualties in the past half-century occurred within it (see Chapter 11). The threat of civil war continues. More than 133 wars have erupted in the Global South since 1945, and most of these occurred after the Cold War ended in 1989 (Gleditsch 2004, 253–57). The danger of anarchy and violence *within* Global South countries has reached epidemic proportions. The Global South is a zone of danger, populated by many **failed states** that do not have governments strong enough to preserve domestic order.

Paradoxically, part of the insecurity facing Global South countries is due to the fact that most are multiethnic societies composed of a variety of **nonstate nations,** or nationality groups. Many of these suffer from a history of hatred and conflict with one another. Maintaining cooperation among competing ethnonational groups is difficult, especially because many of these nonstate actors, such as Palestine, are actively seeking independence in order to acquire statehood as new sovereign states. The potential for failed states in many Global South states is great, which is why many experts predict that by the middle of the twenty-first century there may exist as many as five hundred states.

The chief cause of concern about Global South political instability resides not from the potential for separatist activist groups within Global South countries to undermine central governments by challenging their sovereignty or, more dangerous still, by waging open rebellion. Although this is a serious problem, it is compounded exponentially by the scourge of poverty. "Poverty and conflict are not unrelated," warned Nitin Desai and Jayantha Dhanapala, both undersecretaries at the United Nations. "They often reinforce each other. Poverty is a potent catalyst for conflict and violence within and among states, particularly at a time when poor countries and peoples are increasingly aware of the relative affluence of others." The relationship between underdevelopment and war (see Lemke 2003) is explosive in the information age under conditions of globalization, where knowledge of vast differentials in wealth is now news everyplace (see Chapter 8).

As with many other aspects of the Global South's conditions, those states' capacity to contain domestic violence, in a borderless globe of interdependence, rests largely in the hands of the great powers. The Global South countries must face the task of deciding the fateful question of whether they dare call upon the great powers and the international organizations those powers dominate for help when violence, terrorism, and anarchy prevail and collapsing Global South countries require external **military intervention** to restore order. The cry for assistance poses risks, because where there is outside involvement there tends to follow outside influence, some of which may be unwelcome. There is a fine line between external involvement and interference. On top of this concern, it was not clear (until the United States in 2002 asserted the right to unilaterally take preemptive military intervention in dangerous Global South trouble spots

■ **failed states**
countries whose governments have so mismanaged policy that their citizens, in rebellion, threaten to disintegrate the state.

■ **nonstate nations**
national or ethnic groups struggling to obtain power and/or statehood.

■ **military intervention**
overt or covert use of force by one or more countries that cross the borders of another country in order to affect the target country's government and policies.

■ **doctrine**
the guidelines a state or an alliance specifies to identify the conditions under which it will use military power and armed force for political purposes abroad.

such as Iraq to eliminate the threat) that the great powers had sufficient interests in getting involved in Global South civil wars. They still have not agreed to a **doctrine** to guide great-power decisions about when, where, why, and how the great powers should collectively become involved within Global South borders where violence, terrorism, and ethnic cleansing are occurring.

Arms Acquisitions. Faced with seemingly endless conflict at home or abroad, it is not surprising that the Global South has joined the rest of the world's quest to acquire modern weapons of war—including in some cases (China, India, North Korea, Pakistan) nuclear weapons. As a result, the burden of military spending (measured by the ratio of military expenditures to GNP) is highest among those least able to bear it. In the Global South military spending typically exceeds expenditures on health and education; impoverished states facing ethnic, religious, or tribal strife at home are quite prepared to sacrifice expenditures for economic development in order to acquire weapons.

Few Global South states produce their own weapons. Weak Global South governments, paralyzed by fears of separatist revolts, have invested increased proportions of their country's modest national budgets in arms rather than seek to reduce poverty by reallocating scarce revenues from the military to social and economic development. Most Global South countries have increased their military spending to purchase arms produced in the Global North at higher rates than their wealthy Global North counterparts do (Grimmett 2004).

What makes the Global South's militarization so counterproductive is that the Global South's national security has fallen while the Global North is a "zone of peace," with few threats from other rich and democratic states. The contrast is most paradoxical with respect to the sale of weapons. The Global North sells most of its arms to the unstable Global South states, most of whom pose the greatest threat to world order. Since 1996, most arms transfers have been delivered to the Global South (Grimmett 2004). Therefore, in responding to a world of powers, the Global South appears to be increasing its dependence for arms purchases on the very same rich states whose military and economic domination they historically have most feared and resented.

■ **import-substitution industrialization**
a strategy for economic development that centers on the local country's businesses to produce products that customarily have been purchased from foreign importers.

■ **export-led industrialization**
a growth strategy that concentrates on developing domestic export industries capable of competing in overseas markets.

The Search for Wealth in a Globalized World

The persistent underdevelopment of most developing states underlies their drive for greater wealth, a better life for their people, and a higher position in the hierarchy of global power. Breaking out of their dependent status and pursuing their own industrial development remains their greatest foreign policy priority.

To this end, some Global South states (particularly those in Latin America) have pursued development through an **import-substitution industrialization** strategy designed to encourage domestic entrepreneurs to manufacture products traditionally imported from abroad. Governments (often dictatorships) have been heavily involved in managing their economies and in some cases became the owners and operators of industry.

Import-substitution industrialization eventually fell from favor, in part because manufacturers often found that they still had to rely on Global North technology and even component parts to produce goods for their domestic markets. The recent preference is for **export-led industrialization,** based on the realization that "what had enriched the rich was not their insulation from imports (rich countries do, in fact, import massively all sorts of goods) but their success in manufactured exports, where higher prices could be commanded than for [Global South] raw materials" (Sklair 1991).

As exemplified by the NIEs, the shift toward export-led growth strategies has transformed many Global South countries from being suppliers of raw materials into manufacturers of products already available in the Global North. Thus a new international division of labor is emerging as production, capital, labor, and technology are increasingly integrated worldwide and decision making has become transnational. The old ideas of national independence, self-reliance, and self-sufficiency have been discarded as states' economies have become increasingly tied together in webs of interdependence. The lessons of China and India have not been lost, suggesting that full participation in the integrated global marketplace is the best road out of poverty. As David Dollar and Aart Kraay (2004) of the World Bank observe, if we put China and India into the overall North-South equation, "the long-term global trend toward greater inequality prevailed for at least 200 years [but since about 1975] it has stabilized and possibly even reversed. The chief reason for the change has been the accelerated growth of two large and initially poor countries: China and India, whose openness to foreign trade and investment made their fast growth possible."

Not all Global South economies are positioned to survive in this highly competitive globalized market. Many of the least-developed countries remain heavily dependent on raw materials and other primary products for their export earnings. Some of the NIEs have not moved beyond the dependent development stage, as their export goods are in the old, declining industries of the Global North, whose technology is easily transferred to the semiperiphery. While some benefit from such global economic integration and prosper, others remain immune from the alleged benefits of globalization, and are especially vulnerable to recessions in the global economy.

How to cope with dominance and dependence remains a key Global South concern. As they search for status and economic security, let us next evaluate the Global South's key strategies in their relations with the Global North.

A New International Economic Order? The emerging Global South countries were born into a political-economic order with rules they had no voice in creating. Beginning in the 1950s they began to seek the means to control their own economic futures, centering their efforts on the UN, where their growing numbers gave them greater influence than they could otherwise command. In the 1960s they formed a coalition of the world's poor, the **Group of 77** (known in diplomatic circles simply as the **G-77**), and used their voting power to convene the UN Conference on Trade and Development (UNCTAD). UNCTAD later became a permanent UN organization through which the Global South expresses its interests concerning development issues.

A decade later the G-77 (then numbering more than 120 countries) again used its UN numerical majority to push for a **New International Economic Order (NIEO)** to counter the **Liberal International Economic Order (LIEO)** championed by the United States and the other capitalist powers since World War II. Motivated by the oil-exporting countries' rising bargaining "commodity power," the Global South sought to compel the Global North to abandon practices perceived as perpetuating their dominance and dependence. Later, the heated debate shifted as the Global South began to petition collectively for a re-

■ **Group of 77 (G-77)** the coalition of Third World countries that sponsored the 1963 Joint Declaration of Developing Countries calling for reforms to allow greater equity in North-South trade.

■ **New International Economic Order (NIEO)** the 1974 policy resolution in the UN that called for a North-South dialogue to open the way for the less-developed countries of the Global South to participate more fully in the making of international economic policy.

■ **Liberal International Economic Order (LIEO)** the set of regimes created after World War II designed to promote monetary stability and reduce barriers to the free flow of trade and capital.

distribution of world wealth. Not surprisingly, the Global North rejected the South's reform efforts, and the North-South exchange gradually degenerated into a dialogue of the deaf.

The Global South's determination to revise the existing rules gradually lost momentum as the movement failed to keep its unity and enthusiasm. The flame still flickers, however. At a critical World Trade Organization meeting in September 2003 in Cancún, Mexico, for example, the poor countries united in refusal to be pressured by the rich Global North countries, led by the emergence of a powerful bloc of developing countries including China, India, and Brazil. "Not only were we able to keep our unity," Brazilian Foreign Minister Celso Amorim cheered, "we were a permanent actor in the negotiations." As a result, despite differences the Global South stuck together to demand major concessions from richer countries, including the slashing of foreign subsidies. The Doha world trade round collapsed, with the WTO facing marginalization as many countries turned to bilateral deals.

Hence Global South muscle flexing is not over in the history of the struggle between rich and poor states. Many NIEO issues remain on the global agenda. However, for Global South countries, the critical choice is a philosophical one that each must make individually. To what extent should the state manage its country's international economic transactions? The liberal philosophy underlying the LIEO represents one option—that of limited government intervention. The alternative is advocated by "economic nationalists" in the mercantilist spirit of realism, which recommends using the power of the state to manage economic policy for active competition with other states in order to advance national interests and power. "The nationalist considers relative gain to be more important than mutual gain [and seeks] to change the rules or regimes governing international economic relations in order to benefit themselves disproportionately with respect to other economic powers" (Gilpin 2001). Clearly that competitive viewpoint remains popular in many Global South countries (as well as some in the Global North), even as privatization and a return to market mechanisms rather than state-run enterprises have become widely accepted for generating growth. As we will discover in Chapter 9, the tension between liberalism and mercantilism applies broadly to core contemporary issues in the global political economy.

Regional Trade Regimes. With the failure of reform envisioned by the NIEO, the integration of Global South countries into the globalization process will occur according to the rules dictated by the Global North. Are there alternatives? Can regional arrangements enable Global South states to take advantage of growing economic interdependence to achieve their development goals?

To promote growth through regional economic agreements, in the 1990s the global economy began to subdivide into three "trade blocs"—one in Europe, with the European Union (EU) as its hub; a second in the Americas, with the United States at the center; and a third in East Asia, with Japan and China dominant. Consider some recent developments:

- *In the Americas:* The North American Free Trade Agreement (NAFTA), formalized in 1993, brought Canada, Mexico, and the United States into a single free-trade area whose market size rivals that of the EU to create a hemisphere-wide free-trade area, in which tariffs among member countries are eliminated.

- *Also in the Americas:* The Mercosur agreement, which links Argentina, Brazil, Paraguay, and Uruguay (Latin America's largest trade bloc), hopes to incorporate the Andean Group (Bolivia, Colombia, Ecuador, Peru, and Venezuela) into its free-trade union.
- *In Asia:* The association of Asia-Pacific Economic Cooperation (APEC), an informal forum created in 1989 and now including twenty-one countries that has committed itself to creating a free-trade zone during the next twenty-five years.
- *Also in Asia:* The members of the Association of Southeast Asian Nations (ASEAN), first established in 1967 by Brunei, Indonesia, Malaysia, the Philippines, Singapore, and Thailand and now including Vietnam, agreed to set up a free-trade area.
- *In Africa:* The Southern African Development Community (SADC), formed in 1980, has pledged to develop a free-trade area and common currency.

Will the lofty expectations of these regional politico-economic groups be realized? In the past, political will and shared visions have proven to be indispensable elements in successful regional trade **regimes.** Economic complementarity is another essential component, as the goal is to stimulate greater trade among the members of the free-trade area, not simply between it and others. If one or more members export products that each of the others wants, the chances of the regime's success are greater; if, on the other hand, they all tend to export the same products or to have virtually no trade with one another (typically the case in Africa), failure is more likely.

Prospects for the success of regional trade regimes seem greatest when Global South countries cobble their futures to Global North states—but, complain Global South leaders, on terms that the Global North dictates. That conclusion hardly bodes well for regional economic agreements as an effective method for balancing the North-South relationship.

Trade, Aid, Investment, Debt Relief—or Nothing?

The developing countries have long pleaded for "trade, not aid" to improve their global position, turning to the NIEs' experience to support the view that access to the Global North's markets is critical to Global South economic growth. But many Global South countries have not improved their lot, often for two major reasons. First, market access has become increasingly difficult because domestic pressure groups in Global South countries have lobbied their governments to reduce the imports of other countries' products that compete with their own industries. Trade may be preferred to aid, but political barriers often interfere with free trade. Second, the character and distribution of foreign aid have changed as criticism of its effectiveness and effects has risen. Consequently, levels of foreign aid have stagnated. **Foreign aid** comes in a variety of forms and is used for a variety of purposes. Some aid consists of outright grants of money, some of loans at concessional rates, and some of shared technical expertise. Although most foreign aid is **bilateral** and is termed **official development assistance (ODA)**—meaning the money flows directly from one country to another—an increasing portion is now channeled through global IGO institutions such as the World Bank, and hence is known as "multilateral aid." Moreover, the

■ **regimes**
the rules agreed to by two or more states, aimed at working collectively on shared problems, even at the short-term risk of suffering relative losses, which are offset by the expectation that all parties will benefit and realize absolute gains.

■ **foreign aid**
economic assistance in the form of loans and grants provided by a donor country to a recipient country for a variety of purposes.

■ **bilateral**
interactions between two transnational actors, such as treaties they have accepted to govern their future relationship.

■ **official development assistance (ODA)**
grants or loans to countries from other countries, usually channeled through multilateral aid organizations, for the primary purpose of promoting economic development and welfare.

FIGURE 5.1
Ranking the Biggest Official Aid Donors
Official development assistance (ODA) from Global North donors has not grown over the past decade at a pace commensurate with the rich Global North's rates of global economic growth. In 2003 their foreign aid to the needy Global South increased by 3.9 percent above 2002 to $68.5 billion, after years of gradually declining giving since the 1990s (World Bank 2004b). Most of the official giving goes to the "have something" wealthier emerging Global South countries instead of the "have not" poorest in the Global South. The bar graph displays the net official aid of the top Global North aid donors in 2003, representing 0.25 percent of the donor's combined GDP. The United States, with the globe's largest economy, gave the most ($15.8 billion), but as a share of its GDP its aid budget is the world's smallest. Only a handful of donors give the 0.7 percent of their national incomes set by UN resolutions as an international target.
SOURCE: Data from the Organization for Economic Cooperation and Development cited in the *Economist*, May 1, 2004, p. 104.

Net Official Foreign Aid ($billion) as Percentage of GDP

Country	Billions of dollars
Norway	2.0
Denmark	1.7
Netherlands	4.1
Luxembourg	0.2
Sweden	2.1
Belgium	1.9
Ireland	0.5
France	7.3
Switzerland	1.3
Britain	6.2
Finland	0.6
Germany	6.7
Canada	2.2
Spain	2.0
Australia	1.2
New Zealand	0.2
Portugal	0.3
Greece	0.4
Japan	8.9
Austria	0.5
Italy	2.4
United States	15.8

purposes of aid are as varied as its forms. Commonly stated foreign aid goals include not only the reduction of poverty through economic development but also human development, environmental protection, reduced military spending, enhanced economic management, the development of private enterprise, increased power for women, the promotion of democratic governance and human rights, and humanitarian disaster relief and assistance to refugees. However, security objectives traditionally have figured prominently as motives of donors in the allocation of both economic aid and military assistance, and still do. For example, the United States continues to target Israel and Egypt as major recipients to symbolize friendship, maintain a balance of power, and tilt the scales toward peace in the Middle East. And security was the primary motive behind the doubling of the U.S. foreign assistance budget following 9/11, to provide funds for use in the global war on terrorism.

The assumption that development will support other goals, such as fostering solidarity among allies and promoting commercial advantage, free markets, or democratization, still underpins most donors' assistance programs. Today, however, many of these traditional justifications are under widespread attack in numerous donor countries (see Figure 5.1). Overall global official development assistance has in fact declined since peaking in 1991 (World Bank 2005b, 263).

Many aid donors have become frustrated with the slow growth rates of many of the Global South recipients and impatiently have grown doubtful of the effectiveness of their aid programs, despite strong evidence that foreign aid has made a positive difference (Easterbrook 2002). Critics particularly resent what they perceive to be an entrenched state of mind in many Global South cultures that stands in the way of development, which—while bemoaning poverty—at the same time condemns the profit motive, competition, and consumerism at the heart of the spirit of capitalism. "The revolution of economic development occurs when people go on working, competing, inventing, and innovating when they no longer need to be rich," argues Mariano Grondona, an Argentinian political scientist, in a statement that expresses the Global North's faith in hard work, economic competition, and individual entrepreneurial creativity as necessary cultural values crucial to progress and prosperity (in Samuelson 2001b).

The shift to market-oriented models has led many donors to conclude that foreign aid is no longer as needed and may even be detrimental. The emergent climate of opinion, moreover, has spawned more "conditionality," or demands that recipient countries must meet to receive aid. Almost one-fourth of official development assistance is "tied, meaning that the procurement contracts were limited to the donor country or a group of countries. Driven by domestic political interests," donors are playing a **two-level game** that "goes against the very free-market principles that most donors are trying to encourage in developing countries and results in inefficient use of aid. It has been estimated that tying aid reduces its value by 15–30 percent" (World Bank 2001, 200).

On top of this practice of tying aid, donors are highly selective in choosing the countries they target for assistance, especially when they treat foreign aid as a subsidy for their domestic corporations producing exports. Although most donors distribute aid to the poorer countries, "currently about a third of aid goes to middle-income countries, whose average GNP per capita is roughly six times that of low-income countries," and considerable sums are even contributed to high-income countries (World Bank 2001, 196). The result is that the poorest of the poor Global South countries (where the incidence of poverty is greatest) are receiving the least assistance and are suffering the most from the recent declines in foreign aid. Their resentment is reflected in the LLDCs' socially constructed image of foreign aid from rich countries, which sees it as a moral obligation, as repayment for years of unequal exchange perpetuated through colonialism and imperial rule.

Recently, however, many Global South leaders have joined Global North critics of foreign aid, interpreting it as an instrument of neocolonialism and neoimperialism and resenting the conditionality criteria for receiving aid imposed by the International Monetary Fund and other multilateral institutions, and they have joined the chorus of experts advocating trade and investment as substitutes for aid. Without lobbying, it appears unlikely that aid will expand above the current low level of only 0.9 percent of all Global South developing countries' combined gross national income (World Bank 2004b, 251, 253).

"There is a widely held fiction that masses of money are poured into aid. In fact, industrialized countries spend roughly one quarter of one percent of their gross domestic product for assistance to the world's poor countries," argued James D. Wolfensohn, the World Bank president, when he urged the Global North to recognize that greater foreign aid can contribute directly to the Global North's national security by helping to combat such problems as drug trafficking, climate change, and civil war. His viewpoint was embraced when in 2003 the United States announced the Millennium Challenge Account Initiative. This, U.S. Secretary of State Colin Powell declared, was part of the U.S. national se-

■ **two-level game**
a concept referring to the growing need for national policymakers to make decisions that will meet both domestic and foreign goals.

■ **foreign direct investment (FDI)**
an investment in a country involving a long-term relationship and control of an enterprise by nonresidents and including equity capital, reinvestment of earnings, other long-term capital, and short-term capital as shown in balance of payments accounts.

■ **externalities**
the unintended side effects of choices that reduce the true value of the original decision, such as trade protectionism against foreign imports increasing the costs of goods to consumers and stimulating inflation.

curity strategy "to provide the largest increase in U.S. development assistance since the Marshall Plan. By 2006 it would represent an increase of 50 percent over the core development assistance funding level in 2002. From 2006 onward, the U.S. would invest $5 billion per year additionally." The rationale was explained as using America's "great power for good" by targeting "only countries that govern justly, invest in their people and encourage economic freedom." The expectation was that recipients would be those countries that actively supported the U.S. global war against terrorism. If this initiative is fully funded, it would help restore foreign aid to a prominent place on the global agenda.

In addition to foreign aid, another tactic sitting center stage in the Global South's strategies for escaping destitution and stagnant economic growth has been to encourage multinational corporations (MNCs) to funnel an increasing share of their **foreign direct investment (FDI)** into its countries, thereby increasing its export earnings to gain a greater share of global trade. This strategy for economic growth has always been the target of critics who question whether the investment of capital by multinational corporations (and, to a lesser extent, private investors) into local or domestic business ventures is really a financial remedy. The strategy has always been controversial, because there are many hidden costs, or **externalities,** associated with permitting corporations controlled from abroad to set up business within the host state for the purpose of making a profit. Who is to be the ultimate beneficiary, the foreign investor or the states

Not the Choice of a New Generation Many nationalists blame multinational corporations for the problems of their countries' economies and social conditions. Foreign firms often face a backlash. In 1995, Hindu nationalists in India—the world's largest democracy—protested economic reforms that would open the country's borders to liberal trade and investment. These and other opponents pledged to drive some of the world's best-known brands out of the Indian market.

CONTROVERSY

MULTINATIONAL CORPORATIONS IN THE GLOBAL SOUTH: DO THEY HELP OR HURT?

Within the Global South, there has existed widespread concern about the impact of multinational corporations' (MNCs) activities on the local economy and its growth rate. Part of the concern stems from the historic tendency for MNCs to look to Global South countries as production sites so they can take advantage of cheap labor for production and avoid labor-union pressure that for years was virtually nonexistent. MNCs are privileged nonstate actors, with such vast resources that their decisions about investments largely determine the direction of development. MNCs can either promote or inhibit development, depending on if they channel investments and, when they do, how they operate in the host country. Despite these concerns about MNCs as powerful, potentially neocolonial, nonstate actors that may compromise national sovereignty and undermine local prosperity, many Global South countries have overcome their fears and now welcome global companies to stimulate rapid growth despite the many risks and costs that MNCs' penetrations often incur.

MNCs continue to be alternately praised and condemned, depending on how their performance is viewed. The record is mixed and can be evaluated on different criteria. Following is a "balance sheet" summarizing the major arguments for and against MNCs. Using this summary of contending interpretations, you can easily see why the role and impact of MNCs is so controversial. What do you think? Do MNCs help or harm the Global South's ability to develop rapidly and to close the gap in wealth with the Global North? On the whole, is the impact of multinational corporations constructive or exploitative?

Positive
- Increase the volume of trade
- Assist the aggregation of investment capital that can fund development
- Finance loans and service international debt
- Lobby for free trade and the removal of barriers to trade, such as tariffs
- Underwrite research and development that allows technological innovation
- Introduce and dispense advanced technology to less-developed countries
- Reduce the costs of goods by encouraging their production according to the principle of comparative advantage
- Generate employment
- Encourage the training of workers
- Produce new goods and expand opportunities for their purchase through the internationalization of production
- Disseminate marketing expertise and mass advertising methods worldwide
- Provide investment income to facilitate the modernization of less-developed countries
- Generate income and wealth
- Advocate peaceful relations between and among states in order to preserve an orderly environment conducive to trade and profits
- Break down national barriers and accelerate the globalization of the international economy and culture and the rules that govern international commerce

Negative
- Give rise to oligopolistic conglomerations that reduce competition and free enterprise
- Raise capital in host countries (thereby depriving local industries of investment capital) but export profits to home countries
- Breed debtors and make the poor dependent on those providing loans
- Limit the availability of commodities by monopolizing their production and controlling their distribution in the world marketplace
- Create "sanctuary markets" that restrict and channel other investments to give MNCs an unfair advantage
- Export technology ill-suited to underdeveloped economies
- Inhibit the growth of infant industries and local technological expertise in less-developed countries while making Global South countries dependent on Global North technology
- Conspire to create cartels that contribute to inflation
- Curtail employment by driving labor competition from the market
- Limit workers' wages
- Limit the supply of raw materials available in international markets
- Erode traditional cultures and national differences, leaving in their place a homogenized world culture dominated by consumer-oriented values
- Widen the gap between rich and poor countries
- Increase the wealth of local elites at the expense of the poor
- Support and rationalize repressive regimes in the name of stability and order
- Challenge national sovereignty and jeopardize the autonomy of states
- Create cartels with other MNCs that share markets in order to cut competition

FIGURE 5.2
Foreign Direct Investments in the Global South

Since the early 1990s most Global South countries have aggressively competed with their wealthy Global North counterparts to become the targets for capital investments from abroad to encourage their economic growth. They have made many advances in their quest to capture a larger share of the world proportion, and were the recipients of 28 percent of the world total of $653 billion in 2003, or $186 billion. However, the bulk of this Global South foreign direct investment (FDI) remained concentrated in the "have some" emerging markets of the Global South, which averaged between 1993 and 2003 $194 billion (reflecting the total 1996–98 surges of more than $300 billion each year, after which it fell with the decline in global FDI and the world economy generally). FDI inflows to the Global South, like the Global North, are expected to "bottom out" in 2005 from the peak $1.4 trillion in 2000, and then rise again. The figure to the right breaks apart the regional percentage of estimated FDI inflows into each major region in 2004, when the Global South's FDI entire share of 28 percent was only twice that of the U.S. economic giant alone.

SOURCE: United Nations Conference on Trade and Development, www.un.org, June 4, 2004; see also www.OECDobserver.org, June 7, 2004, and Institute of International Finance April 15, 2004, 1)

Regional FDI Share, 2004
- Central and Eastern Europe 5%
- Asia and the Pacific 16%
- EU 56%
- $653bn
- USA 14%
- South America and the Caribbean 7%
- Africa 2%

in which the investments are made? Considerable risks are entailed, as are a number of trade-offs among competing values (see Controversy: Multinational Corporations in the Global South: Do They Help or Hurt?).

The primary danger with this strategy is the potential for foreign investments to lead to foreign control, the erosion of sovereign governments' capacities to regulate the economy within their borders, and the probability that the multinational foreign investors will not invest their profits locally but channel them abroad for new investments or disburse them as dividends for their wealthy Global North shareholders (see Chapters 8 and 9). However, despite the risks, many developing countries have relaxed restrictions in order to attract foreign investors, with emphasis placed less on liberalizing investment restrictions and encouraging open domestic economic competition than on offering tax and cash enticements and opportunities for joint ventures. This has stimulated a recent surge in the flow of capital investments to the Global South (see Figure 5.2). However, keep in mind that over three-fourths of all FDI is channeled to the Global North, and the poorest Global South countries (the LLCDs) benefit from only 0.2 percent of investments from abroad (World Bank 2005b, 263).

The impact of this new infusion of foreign investments in the developing countries has been substantial, given the relatively small economies of the Global South. It has paved the way for emerging markets in the Global South to expand their rates of economic development despite the resistance of local industries in the Global South threatened by the competition and critics who have complained about the income inequalities that the investments are causing. Such fears and consequences notwithstanding, an intensified push among the

Global South developing countries to compete for foreign investment capital in order to liberate themselves from dependence and destitution seems likely.

The prospects for either foreign aid or for foreign direct investments to contribute to the future development of, and relief of poverty in, the Global South will depend on a number of other factors. Foremost is the extent to which the staggering level of debt facing many Global South countries can be managed and the decisive role that global economic growth and Global North leadership play in the creation of Global South debt (see Reuveny and Thompson 2004).

In 2001 the World Bank identified fifty-seven Global South countries, more than 80 percent of them in Africa, as burdened by "unsustainable debt" and in need of relief, noting that "many heavily indebted poor countries spend as much as a fifth of their annual budgets on debt service. . . . [B]ecause this is often more than the amount spent on social programs, debt servicing is viewed by many as a severe impediment to improving the lives of the world's poor" (World Bank 2001, 201). "Inspired by the biblical concept of Jubilee—to cancel external debt to the poorest," explained World Bank President James D. Wolfensohn in 2001, "religious leaders, rock stars and concerned men and women all over the world have galvanized public action and inspired official policy."

Debt relief—to slash the amount owned by these fifty-seven countries by more than two-thirds—is reflective of the changing attitudes toward the poorest Global South countries by the great powers and the multilateral institutions that the great powers have created, such as the World Bank. Attempting to compensate for the fact that only about 1 percent of official development lending is directed to the Global South (Cox 2003, 234), global institutions distributed more than $56 billion in relief to the financially distressed Global South countries, $11 for each person in 2002 (World Bank 2002a, 362). The Jubilee 2000 movement for the cancellation of crushing debt targets the seventy-seven **heavily indebted poor countries (HIPCs),** which owe a total of about $419 billion (about half is "bilateral" debt owed to governments, a third to international lending organizations, and the rest to private banks and other creditors [World Bank 2002a, 266]). It was predicated on the proposition that "the development of debt means the death of development" (Michael 2001, 78). Part of the motive was driven by compassion and part by the economic self-interests of the Global North, which see in debt relief a pragmatic method for arresting the collapse of the LLDCs' economies that pose a substantial threat to the continued growth of the entire world economy in the age of interdependent globalization.

It was enlightened awareness of the magnitude of this threat that prompted the Group of Eight (G-8) wealthy industrialized democracies to launch their program to assist the heavily indebted poor countries (HIPCs) with debt relief. The World Bank's "Enhanced HIPC Initiative," with an allocated $128 billion for 2002, and the International Monetary Fund's "Poverty Reduction and Growth Facility" (PRGF) are the primary products of this attempt to reduce the widening disparities between the Global North and Global South. Whether these programs will succeed will depend on the degree to which the Global South countries can undertake, with minimal corruption, the often painful liberalizing political reforms for democratic governance that are widely seen as a requirement for sustained economic growth (D. Kim and Wolfensohn 1999). Other parts of the equation include the prospects for still other reforms—such as implementation of the thirty-member Organization for Economic Cooperation and Development's proposed Corporate Conduct Code for Third World Nations,

■ **heavily indebted poor countries (HIPCs)**
the subset of countries identified by the World Bank's Debtor Reporting System whose ratios of government debt to gross national product are so substantial that they cannot meet their payment obligations without experiencing political instability and economic collapse.

■ **Fourth Way**
a strategy proposed for development in the Global South emphasizing government subsidies to help citizens contribute to growth within a free-trade market economy.

or the performance of Latin America's proposed **Fourth Way** alternative to neoliberalism, calling for increases in government funding for social services and education to foster economic growth, while accepting market economies, privatization of state-run corporations, global economic integration, and free trade.

THE FUTURE ROLE OF THE GLOBAL SOUTH

It is useful to remember the historical trends underlying the emergence of the Global South as an actor on the global stage, rather than rely on analysts' socially constructed concepts that became popular and shaped its identity. Those states that came to regard themselves as its members share important characteristics. Most were colonized by people of another race, experienced varying degrees of poverty and hunger, and felt powerless in a world system dominated by the affluent countries that once controlled them and perhaps still do. Considerable change occurred among the newly emergent states as post–World War II decolonization proceeded, but much also remained the same. Thus, the concept *Third World* continues to describe a state of mind that still galvanizes the Global South as it seeks to overcome the disorder and destitution that afflict so many people living there.

The relationships between the world's developed and developing countries will no doubt continue to change, but exactly how remains uncertain. A turn inward, toward isolationist foreign policies, in the Global North could lead to a posture of "benign neglect" of the Global South. Conversely, a new era of North-South cooperation could commence, dedicated to finding solutions to common problems ranging from commercial to environmental and security concerns. Elements of both approaches are already evident.

The Global South remains a set of global actors dominated by the great powers. That domination is funneled in part through the powerful international organizations like the United Nations and the World Bank that the great powers have created. To understand world politics and the roots of changes in international affairs, we need to inspect the impact of these influential intergovernmental organizations, or IGOs, as actors in the global arena. And to complete the picture, we also need to inspect the thousands of nongovernmental organizations, or NGOs, whose presence and pressure as nonstate actors are also transforming international politics, for both the Global North and the Global South. It is to those actors that we turn in Chapter 6.

KEY TERMS

global level of analysis
structural realism
state level of analysis
individual level of analysis
colonialism
indigenous peoples
Third World

First World
Second World
Global North
Global South
least developed of the less-
 developed countries (LLDCs)
decolonization

neocolonialism (neoimperialism)
mercantilism
classical liberal economic theory
laissez-faire economics
spheres of influence
communism
Marxism-Leninism

world-system theory
realpolitik
self-determination
liberalism
clash of civilizations
globalization
developing countries
gross national income (GNI)
developed countries
barter
development
modernization
dependency theory
dependency
dualism
world-system theorists
newly industrialized countries (NICs)
newly industrialized economies (NIEs)
dependent development
semiperiphery
Asian Tigers
outsourcing
neoliberalism
nonstate actors
non-aligned states
Non-Aligned Movement (NAM)
zero-sum
failed states
nonstate nations
military intervention
doctrine
import-substitution industrialization
export-led industrialization
Group of 77 (G-77)
New International Economic Order (NIEO)
Liberal International Economic Order (LIEO)
regimes
foreign aid
bilateral
official development assistance (ODA)
two-level game
foreign direct investment (FDI)
externalities
heavily indebted poor countries (HIPCs)
Fourth Way

SUGGESTED READING

Braveboy-Wagner, Jacqueline Anne, ed. *The Foreign Policies of the Global South.* Boulder, Colo.: Lynne Rienner, 2003.

Green, December, and Laura Luehrmann. *Comparative Politics of the Third World.* Boulder, Colo.: Lynne Rienner, 2004.

Griffiths, Robert J., ed. *Developing World 04/05.* Guilford, Conn.: McGraw-Hill/Dushkin, 2005.

Kohli, Atul. *State-Directed Development: Political Power and Industrialization in the Global Periphery.* Cambridge: Cambridge University Press, 2005.

Landes, David S. *The Wealth and Poverty of Nations: Why Some Are So Rich and Some So Poor.* New York: Norton, 1998.

Packenham, Robert A. *The Dependency Movement: Scholarship and Politics in Dependency Studies.* Cambridge, Mass.: Harvard University Press, 1992.

Petras, James. *The New Development Politics.* Willison, Vt.: Ashgate, 2004.

Rapley, John. *Understanding Development: Theory and Practice in the Third World,* 2nd ed. Boulder Colo.: Lynne Rienner, 2003.

Sutcliffe, Bob. *100 Ways of Seeing an Unequal World.* London: Zed Books, 2002.

Todaro, Michael P. *Economic Development,* 8th ed. New York: Addison Wesley, 2002.

Weatherby, Joseph N., et al. *The Other World: Issues and Politics of the Developing World,* 6th ed. New York: Allyn & Bacon/Longman, 2004.

World Bank. *World Development Report 2005.* Washington, D.C.: World Bank, 2005.

WHERE ON THE WORLD WIDE WEB?

The Age of Imperialism
http://www.smplanet.com/imperialism/toc.html
Chapter 5 begins with a discussion of European imperialism and its effects on the Global South. To extend your analysis of imperialism, review the Small Planet's website. Recommended by the History Channel, this site chronicles American expansion in the Pacific, the Spanish-American War, the Boxer Rebellion, and U.S. intervention in Latin America. See historic photos of the battleship *Maine,* maps of the regions, and portraits

WHERE ON THE WORLD WIDE WEB? (*continued*)

of the participants. Read letters, anti-imperialist essays from the past, and cartoons. You can even download movie clips.

Many U.S. citizens have trouble understanding the plight of the Global South. Use the following websites to familiarize yourself with these countries and the problems they face. Your might choose a country from each of the following regions: Latin America, Asia, Africa, and the Middle East. Using the websites listed here, compare and contrast each of the countries in terms of political and economic structures. Keep the following questions in mind: What type of government does each country have? Which industrial revolution has it experienced? What primary goods does each country import and export? Based on your findings, can you identify the biggest obstacles for each country in the development process?

African Studies WWW
http://www.sas.upenn.edu/African_Studies/AS.html

The University of Pennsylvania's African Studies Center has created a website that provides extensive links to country-specific information as well as a bulletin board that lists current events and important documents. You can also find a list of upcoming academic conferences on Africa. A multimedia archive allows you to view African sculptures. Check out the Alligator Head from Nigeria. Why is the Standing Male Figure from Zaire impaled on so many blades?

Asian Studies WWW Virtual Library
http://coombs.anu.edu.au/
WWWVL-AsianStudies.html

This global collaborative project provides bibliographic and hypertext access to scholarly documents, resources, and information systems concerned with or relevant to Asian Studies. The Asian Studies WWW Virtual Library website is divided according to global, regional, and country-specific areas. It provides a wealth of information on the region as well as specific countries. Look for links to various e-journals and online newsletters covering Asian topics. This site is well monitored, and each link is checked for its accuracy and content.

The Center for Middle Eastern Studies
http://menic.utexas.edu/menic/

The Middle East Network Information Center at the University of Texas at Austin is an inclusive source for general as well as country-specific information. Read about various countries' history, culture, business, energy resources, and government. View maps and scan the newspapers of the region. Learn more about Islam, Judaism, and Christianity and how these religions interact in the region. Click the News and Media link and hear Arabic spoken on numerous radio stations.

Political Database of the Americas
http://www.georgetown.edu/pdba/

A joint project of Georgetown University, the Organization of American States, and the Canadian Foundation for the Americas, this database provides documentary and statistical political information on Latin America, including constitutions; electoral laws; political parties; legislative, executive, and judicial branch information; local governance; and election data. Look in the Links section to find websites of newspapers and embassies and consulates.

The following Web sites provide general information on international development.

United Nations Conference on Trade and Development (UNCTAD)
http://www.unctad.org/

From the UNCTAD home page, go to the Least Developed Countries sub-site and investigate the backgrounds of the countries that the United Nations has deemed the poorest in the world. Examine the various programs UNCTAD has for helping the least developed countries. Which ones do you think have the best chance of succeeding? Why?

United Nations Development Programme (UNDP)
http://www.undp.org/

This United Nations branch helps countries in their efforts to achieve sustainable human development. As discussed in Chapter 5, the fulfillment of basic human needs (food, water, clothing, shelter, sanitation, health care, employment, and dignity) are important measures of a country's development level. The UNDP focuses its efforts on assisting countries in the Global South to design and carry out national development programs. Examine the various projects of the UNDP. Which ones have had the greatest impact on development? What are some recent news events about the activities of the UNDP?

U.S. Agency for International Development (USAID)
http://www.usaid.gov/

USAID is the federal government agency that implements foreign economic and humanitarian assistance programs to advance the political and economic interests of the United States. It assists countries recovering from disaster, trying to escape poverty, and engaging in democratic reforms. On the home page you can choose regions from the Where section. Now you are able to explore U.S. aid efforts in each country of the world. What are the U.S. aid priorities in each region? Do you think aid should be tied to advancing U.S. interests or should it be given to the needy without strings attached? What has the USAID been doing in Iraq and Afghanistan?

Virtual Library on International Development
http://w3.acdi-cida.gc.ca/Virtual.nsf/

This Canadian site outlines international development issues by topic, region, country, and organization. You can click on the outlines to discover links to organizations, news, and resources. The reference desk advises you of upcoming conferences and events related to international development and links you to libraries, periodicals, and reports of value in the study of international development.

INFOTRAC® COLLEGE EDITION

Streeten, Paul. "Beyond the Six Veils: Conceptualizing and Measuring Poverty." *Journal of International Affairs* (Fall 1998).

Bhagwati, Jagdish. "The Poor's Best Hope—Trading for Development." *The Economist (US)*, June 22, 2002.

Kremer, Michael, and Seema Jayachandran. "Odious Debt: When Dictators Borrow, Who Repays the Loan?" *Brookings Review* (Spring 2003).

Kahl, Colin. "Demographic Change, Natural Resources, and Violence: The Current Debate." *Journal of International Affairs* (Fall 2002).

For more articles, enter:

"International Monetary Fund" in the Subject Guide, and then go to subdivision "evaluation"

"World Bank" in the Subject Guide, and then go to subdivision "economic policy"

"developing countries" in the Subject Guide

Go to http://politicalscience.wadsworth.com/kegley10 to access additional resources related to this chapter.

CHAPTER 6

NONSTATE ACTORS IN THE INTERSTATE SYSTEM

TOPICS AND THEMES

- Nonstate actors: What are IGOs and NGOs?
- Global IGO actors
  The United Nations
  The World Trade Organization, the World Bank, the International Monetary Fund, and other global IGOs
- The European Union and other regional IGOs
- NGOs on the world stage
  Nonstate nations and the indigenous ethnic groups of the Fourth World
  Religious movements
  Multinational corporations and transnational banks
  Reevaluating NGOs' capacity to transform world politics
- Nonstate actors: Saviors or stranglers of the state?

- **CONTROVERSY** ARE RELIGIOUS MOVEMENTS CAUSES OF WAR OR SOURCES OF TRANSNATIONAL HARMONY?

The 30th World Economic Forum for the rich elite of businesses, governments, and a few advocacy groups including 2,100 participants from 94 countries met in the snowbound resort of Davos, Switzerland, in January 2004 to plan the global future. At the same time, as shown here, 80,000 people from more than 100 countries gathered at "anti-Davos," the annual World Social Forum in Bombay, India, to raise their voices in protest against the inequalities of global capitalism, unfair global trade, the monopoly of big business, and a long list of causes such as antiwar and antidiscrimination.

Any reform of the United Nations has to take into account of the new face of danger. If it fails to do so, the world may go its all too possible disastrous way without the United Nations.

—Brian Urquhart, senior UN administrator, 2004

No reason exists why—in addition to states—nationalities, diasporas, religious communities and other groups should not be treated as legitimate actors. . . . In the emerging global politics, however, state sovereignty and authority are withering and no alternative, such as some system of world government, is about to fill the vacuum.

—Samuel P. Huntington, realist theoretician, 2001

T he 1648 Peace of Westphalia, which ended the Thirty Years' War, also ended the secular authority of the pope by creating sovereign and independent territorial states. The history of world politics for the past 350 years has largely been a chronicle of interactions among states that remain the dominant political organizations in the world. States' interests, capabilities, and goals significantly shape world politics. However, the supremacy of the state has been severely challenged in recent years. Increasingly, world affairs are being influenced by intergovernmental organizations that transcend national boundaries—global international organizations such as the United Nations (UN) and regional organizations such as the European Union (EU). Such international organizations often carry out independent foreign policies and therefore can be considered global actors in their own right (Verbeek 2006). In addition, there exist many ways that individual people band together as coalitions of private citizens to play influential roles in international affairs. Religions, nationalities based on ethnic and linguistic heritages, and multinational corporations are examples of nongovernmental organizations. Diverse in scope and purpose, these nonstate actors push their own agendas and increasingly exert global influence.

FIGURE 6.1

The Number of States, IGOs, and NGOs since 1900

The number of independent states has increased greatly since 1900—especially since the decolonization movement began after World War II—but the number of intergovernmental organizations (IGOs) and especially nongovernmental organizations (NGOs) has grown even more rapidly.

SOURCE: Figures for states are based on the Correlates of War (COW) project at the University of Michigan (http://pss.la.psu.Edu/intsys.html); IGOs and NGOs from *Yearbook of International Organizations 2003/2004*, vol. 4 (2004, p. 576), and moving averages from selected prior volumes.

■ **intergovernmental organizations (IGOs)** institutions created and joined by states' governments, which give them authority to make collective decisions to manage particular problems on the global agenda.

■ **nongovernmental organizations (NGOs)** transnational organizations of private citizens maintaining consultative status with the UN; they include professional associations, foundations, multinational corporations, or simply internationally active groups in different states joined together to work toward common interests.

NONSTATE ACTORS, INTERGOVERNMENTAL ORGANIZATIONS (IGOs), AND NONGOVERNMENTAL ORGANIZATIONS (NGOs): AN INTRODUCTION

There are two principal types of nonstate actors: **intergovernmental organizations (IGOs),** whose members are states, and **nongovernmental organizations (NGOs),** whose members are private individuals and groups. Both types existed prior to the twentieth century and both are now pervasive. The Union of International Organizations, which maintains comprehensive, up-to-date information on both types, records that their numbers increased sharply during the nineteenth century, as international commerce and communications grew alongside industrialization. In 1909, there were 37 IGOs and 176 NGOs. By 1960 there were 154 IGOs and 1,255 NGOs, and at the start of 2005 these numbers had risen to 238 and 31,138 respectively (see Figure 6.1).

IGOs are purposely created by states to solve shared problems. This gives the IGOs whatever authority they possess for the purposes states assign them. In this sense, IGOs are more important than NGOs because their members are

TABLE 6.1

A Simple Classification of Intergovernmental Organizations (IGOs)

Geographic Scope of Membership	Range of Stated Purpose	
	Multiple Purposes	Single Purpose
Global	United Nations World Trade Organization UNESCO Organization of the Islamic Conference	World Health Organization International Labor Organization International Monetary Fund Universal Postal Union
Interregional, regional, subregional	European Union Organization for Security and Cooperation in Europe Organization of American States Organization of African Unity League of Arab States Association of Southeast Asian Nations	European Space Agency Nordic Council North Atlantic Treaty Organization International Olive Oil Council International North Pacific Coffee Organization African Groundnut Council

states and, as such, are a product of the *interstate* system at the **global level of analysis** that decisions by states have produced.

In interpreting the spectacular growth of IGOs, keep in mind that identifying these nonstate actors is not easy. In principle, IGOs are defined not only by the fact that their members are the governments of states but also by their permanence and institutional organization; IGOs meet at relatively regular intervals and have specified procedures for making decisions and a permanent secretariat or headquarters staff. If these definitional criteria were relaxed, an additional 4,802 highly active international bodies ("special type") would qualify for inclusion as IGOs (as would more than 42,867 other highly active nongovernmental associations that share characteristics with NGOs) (*Yearbook of International Organizations, 2003/2004*, vol. 4, 578). IGOs vary widely in size and purpose. Only thirty-two qualify as "intercontinental organizations" and only thirty-four are, like the UN, "universal membership" IGOs. The rest, accounting for more than 72 percent of the total, are limited in their scope and confined to particular regions. Table 6.1 illustrates these differences. The variation among the organizations in each subcategory is great, particularly with single purpose, limited-membership IGOs. The North Atlantic Treaty Organization (NATO), for example, is primarily a military alliance, while others, such as the Organization of American States (OAS), promote both economic development and democratic reforms. Still, most IGOs concentrate their activities on specific economic or social issues of special concern to them, such as the management of trade or transportation.

The expansion of IGOs has created a complex network of overlapping international organizations that cooperate with one another to deal with a wide range of global issues. They support one another to work, for example, on issues as varied as trade, defense, disarmament, economic development, agriculture,

■ **global level of analysis**

an analytical approach to world politics that emphasizes the impact of worldwide conditions on the behavior of states, IGOs, NGOs, and other international actors.

Grassroots Recruitment for Global Change NGOs are nonprofit, grassroots groups that advocate a wide variety of causes in order to set the global agenda in ways consistent with their ideology. In this advertisement, the Earthjustice Legal Defense Fund seeks to protect endangered species of plants and animals. More than thirty-one thousand NGOs are active throughout the globe.

health, culture, human rights, the arts, illegal drugs, tourism, labor, women's plight, education, debt, the environment, crime, humanitarian aid, civilian crisis relief, telecommunications, science, globalization, immigration, and refugees.

NGOs also differ widely. Due to their number and diversity, they are even more difficult than IGOs to classify. Like IGOs, some NGOs merge with other NGOs and others cease to operate actively, so the numbers are constantly changing. When the year 2005 began, the Union of International Associations categorized the major "conventional" NGOs as split, with 7 percent as "universal," almost 16 percent as "intercontinental," and the vast majority, 77 percent, as "regionally oriented." Functionally, NGOs span virtually every facet of political, social, and economic activity in an increasingly borderless globalized world, ranging from earth sciences to health care, language, history, culture, theology, law, ethics, security, and defense.

> Non-governmental organizations are not a homogeneous group. The long list of acronyms that has accumulated around NGOs can be used to illustrate this. People speak of NGOs, INGOs (International NGOs), BINGOs (Business International NGOs), RINGOs (Religious International NGOs), ENGOs (Environmental NGOs), QUANGOs (Quasi-Non-Governmental Organizations—i.e., those that are at least partially created or supported by states), and many others. Indeed, all these types of NGOs and more are among those having consultative status at the UN. Among the NGOs . . . are the Academic Council on the UN System, the All India Women's Conference, the Canadian Chemical Producers Association, CARE International, the World Young Women's Christian Association, the World Wide Fund for Nature International, the World Wide Fund for Nature (Malaysia), the Union

of Arab Banks, the Women's International League for Peace and Freedom, the World Energy Council, the World Federation of Trade Unions, and the World Veterans Association. Thus it is difficult to generalize about NGOs at the UN. (Stephenson 2000, 270)

In general, the socially constructed image of NGOs widely accepted throughout the world is highly positive: humanitarian movements dedicated to improving the human condition rather than seeking to benefit themselves at the expense of others. However, some NGOs arguably unite people for collective action in ways that can harm others. Nonetheless, most commentary emphasizes the helpful role that NGOs perform; most mobilize about needed changes in the global system, as they see it, rather than resist changes. An example is the World Bank's definition of NGOs as "private organizations that pursue activities to relieve suffering, promote the interests of the poor, protect the environment, provide basic social services, or undertake community development."

In general, the term *NGO* can be applied to all nonprofit organizations that are independent of government. It thus is also customary to think of NGOs as intersocietal organizations that contribute to negotiations between and among states in the hope of reaching agreements for global governance on nearly every issue of international public policy. NGOs link the global society by forming networks to advocate for policy changes. For this purpose, many NGOs interact formally with IGOs. For instance, more than one thousand NGOs actively consult with various agencies of the extensive UN system, maintain offices in hundreds of cities, and hold parallel conferences with IGO meetings to which states send representatives. Such partnerships between NGOs and IGOs enable both types to work (and lobby) together in pursuit of common policies and programs. That said, many IGOs work for, and are heavily financed by, rich corporations and some state governments, which also fund NGOs that support their interests.

Although widespread geographically, NGOs are most active in the advanced Global North industrial democracies. "This is so because open political systems, ones in which there is societal pluralism, are more likely to allow their citizens to participate in nongovernmental organizations, and such [democratic governments] are highly correlated with relatively high levels of economic development" (Jacobson 1984).

In this chapter, we will discuss some prominent and representative IGOs, including the UN, the EU, and various other regional organizations, and investigate the impact of NGOs, including ethnic nationalities and indigenous peoples, religious movements, and multinational corporations. The chapter's purpose is not simply to describe these nonstate actors but to provoke you to question the extent to which their activities undermine states' continuing autonomy. Thus, the focus throughout will be on state governments' capacity to manage global change and the role of nonstate actors in that process.

GLOBAL INTERGOVERNMENTAL ORGANIZATIONS (IGOs)

The United Nations

The United Nations (UN) is the best-known global organization. What distinguishes it from most other IGOs is its nearly universal membership, including today 191 independent states from every region (see Figure 6.2). The UN's nearly

FIGURE 6.2

The Changing Membership of the United Nations, 1945–2005

As the figure on the left shows, the UN's membership has seen episodic bursts of growth from 51 states in 1945 to 191 in 2005 with the admission of Switzerland and newly independent East Timor (the world's 210th sovereign state). During nearly six decades of expansion, the United Nations has increasingly included Global South countries (see figure on right). This shift has influenced the kinds of interests and issues the UN has confronted, expanding the global agenda from the priorities of the great powers in the Global North to include those important to the developing states in the Global South.
SOURCE: United Nations.

fourfold growth from the fifty-one states that joined it at the UN's birth in 1945 has been spectacular, but the admission process has from the start been governed by political conflicts that show the extent to which the organization reflects the relationships of the five great powers that created it and govern it through veto authority in the Security Council.

In principle, any sovereign state accepting the UN's regulations and principles can join, but the great powers have often let **realpolitik** political considerations dictate which countries were admitted. During the Cold War, both the United States and the Soviet Union prevented countries aligned with their adversary from joining, and the controversy has continued about Taiwan ever since. In the 1970s the United States recognized the communist government in China and engineered the transfer of the "China seat" from the so-called Republic of China in Taiwan. Because China insists that Taiwan in not an independent state but instead a rebel province of the mainland, Taiwan cannot rejoin the world organization. Similar political barriers stand in the way of Palestine gaining UN admission by gaining its statehood.

■ **realpolitik**
the realist theoretical outlook prescribing that countries should put their own national interests above concern for the global community.

The UN's Purposes. In addition to its nearly universal membership, and its pervasive **politics** mirroring world politics, the UN is also a multipurpose organization. Article 1 of the UN Charter defines the UN's objectives as centered on:

- maintaining international peace and security
- developing friendly relations among nations based on respect for the principle of equal rights and the self determination of peoples
- achieving international cooperation in solving international problems of an economic, social, cultural, or humanitarian character and in promoting and encouraging respect for human rights and for fundamental freedoms for all
- functioning as a center for harmonizing the actions of nations in the attainment of these common ends

Peace and security figured prominently in the thinking of the great powers responsible for creating the UN and its predecessor, the League of Nations. Following each twentieth-century global war, world leaders created new institutions to keep peace. The liberal conviction that war is not inevitable but can be controlled by reforming the international **anarchy** that encourages it inspired both efforts. The first, the League of Nations, sought to prevent a recurrence of the catastrophic First World War by replacing the balance-of-power system with one based on **collective security.** When the League failed to restrain Germany, Japan, and Italy during the 1930s, it collapsed. At the start of World War II, the U.S., British, and Russian allies began planning for a new international organization, the United Nations, not to subject themselves to the control of others but to achieve goals such as preserving the postwar peace after victory, which could not be realized unilaterally by any one power acting alone (Gaddis 2004). However, faith in the UN's ability quickly eroded. The world organization soon became paralyzed by the unforeseen **Cold War** conflict between the United States and the Soviet Union. But in 1991 when Russia renounced communism, the UN was freed from paralysis and, reborn, returned to its original mission.

The UN has sought from its birth to combine the dual goals of preserving peace and improving the quality of life for humanity. These twin missions have carried the UN into nearly every corner of the complex network of interstate relations. The UN's conference machinery has become permanent: it has provided a mechanism for the management of international conflict, and increasingly the UN has become involved in a broad range of global welfare issues.

The UN's Expanding Agenda. The history of the UN reflects the fact that both rich countries and developing countries have successfully used the organization to promote their own foreign policy goals, and this proud record has bred hopes throughout the world that the UN will be able to manage an ever changing and growing agenda. The UN Millennium Summit attended in September 2000 by 150 world leaders, which led to the ratification of nearly three hundred treaties and conventions, made explicit the UN's **ideology** as expressed in its "six fundamental values" essential to international relations in the twenty-first century: freedom, equality, solidarity, tolerance, respect for nature, and a sense of shared responsibility.

However, the UN's ambitions may exceed its meager resources. The UN has been asked to address an expanding set of pressing military and nonmilitary problems, and its plate is full. Consider the wide array of world conferences that

■ **politics**
the exercise of influence in attempts to get others to bend to one's will.

Simulation: The Rights of the Child

■ **anarchy**
an absence of governmental authority, or an absence at the global level of a supranational authority to regulate relations between states.

■ **collective security**
a security regime created by the great powers that sets rules for keeping peace, guided by the principle that an act of aggression by any state will be met by a collective response from the rest.

■ **Cold War**
the forty-two-year rivalry between the United States and the Soviet Union, as well as their competing coalitions, which sought to contain each other's expansion through an arms race and win worldwide predominance for capitalism (U.S.) or communism (USSR).

■ **ideology**
a set of core philosophical principles that a group of leaders and citizens collectively hold about politics, the interests of political actors, and the ways people ought to ethically behave.

the organization has been asked to address since the 1970s: human environment (1972, 2002), law of the sea (1973), population (1974, 1984, 1994, 1999), food (1974, 1976), women (1975, 1980, 1985, 1995), human settlements (1976, 2003), basic human needs (1976), water (1977, 2002), desertification (1977), disarmament (1978, 1982, 1988), racism and racial discrimination (1978, 2002), technical cooperation among developing countries (1978), agrarian reform and rural development (1974, 1979), science and technology for development (1979), new and renewable sources of energy (1981), least-developed countries (1981), aging (1982, 2004), the peaceful uses of outer space (1982), Palestine (1947, 1982), the peaceful uses of nuclear energy (1983), the prevention of crime and the treatment of offenders (1985), drug abuse and illicit trafficking in drugs (1987, 1990, 1998), the protection of children (1990, 2004), the environment and economic development (1992, 2002), transnational corporations (1992, 2004), indigenous peoples (1992, 1994), internationally organized crime (1994), the human rights responsibilities of transnational corporations (2004), social development (1995), housing (1996), human rights (1993, 1997), global warming (1992, 1997, 2002), international trafficking of children for prostitution and slavery (2000, 2004), and principles for world order (2000). These conferences provide a summary of the most important problems facing the global community and show how urgent needs compete with one another for attention. They also suggest how resistant to solution so many of these problems are, given the repetition with which some issues resurface.

The UN's agenda has grown over time, and it is certain that the number of issues and problems on the global agenda that the UN will be asked to manage will continue to grow in variety and complexity. In response to the demands that have been placed upon it, the United Nations has evolved over its more than fifty-year life into a vast administrative machinery, with offices and staff not only in the UN Headquarters in New York but also in centers spread throughout the globe (see Map 6.1, p. 178). To estimate the capacity of the United Nations to meet the huge burdens that the UN has been asked to carry across many issues, it is useful to explore how the United Nations is organized.

The Organization of the United Nations: System and Structure

The UN's limitations are perhaps rooted in the ways it is organized for its ambitious and wide-ranging purposes. The Security Council is one of six principal organs established by the UN Charter. The others are the General Assembly, the Economic and Social Council, the Trusteeship Council, the Secretariat, and the International Court of Justice. In the General Assembly—the only organ that represents all member states—decision making follows the principle of majority rule, with no state given a veto.

The Security Council, crafted by the great powers to allow them to jointly manage the world and protect their top-dog position within it (Gaddis 2004), is singularly permitted by the UN Charter to initiate actions, including especially the use of force. The General Assembly can only make recommendations. The founders of the UN did not foresee that this limited mandate would later be expanded to allow the General Assembly to participate with the Security Council in managing security. The General Assembly, which has grown in numbers and importance, has assumed wider responsibilities and is now the primary body for addressing security as well as social and economic problems. The growth of

Meeting Place for the World The United Nations Headquarters in New York (pictured here) is home to the Security Council, the General Assembly, the Secretariat, and a variety of departments and other agencies. The UN has evolved over its life into a huge bureaucracy with an equally huge global agenda.

the General Assembly's power may not be sufficient, however. As Secretary-General Kofi Annan noted, the original UN design is outdated: it "reflects the world of 1945 and not the economic and political realities of today," and this failure to adapt to changing times lies at the core of complaints that the UN is unprepared to control the threats facing humanity in the twenty-first century.

That inadequacy is not necessarily permanent, however. Look at the UN's history. In response to the challenge of managing the world's many problems, the UN has adaptively evolved into an extraordinarily complex network of overlapping institutions, some of which (the UN Children's Fund or UNICEF or the United Nations University, for example) fulfill their mission in part through NGOs. The UN has also increasingly come to rely on the many NGOs that are not under its formal authority. This collaboration blurs the line between governmental and nongovernmental functions, but UN-NGO cooperation helps the UN's mission. In the process, the UN has become not one organization but a decentralized conglomerate of countless committees, bureaus, boards, commissions, centers, institutes, offices, and agencies scattered around the globe, with each of its many specialized activities managed from offices in various cities (see Map 6.1).

If any of these various units in the UN's widespread family occupies a central role in the UN's overall structure, it is the General Assembly. Countries in the Global South—seizing advantage of their growing numbers under the one-state, one-vote rules of the General Assembly—have guided UN involvement in directions of particular concern to them. This has reflected the enormous growth of diverse affiliated agencies created to address the full array of the world's problems and needs. Today, a coalition of the less-developed Global South countries constituting three-fourths of the UN and led by the **Group of 77** previously nonaligned states, along with the "Fifth Committee" (which deals with the UN budget), seeks to resist domination by the Global North and to protest that the UN

■ **Group of 77 (G-77)**
a coalition of the world's poor countries formed in 1964 to press for concessions from wealthy Global North states.

MAP 6.1

The UN's Headquarters and Global Network

The United Nations has sought since its creation to address the continuously expanding problems on the global agenda. To reduce the gap between aspiration and accomplishment, as shown on this map the United Nations has spread its administrative arm to every corner of the globe in order to fulfill its expanded mission of serving what UN Secretary-General Kofi Annan has called "a noble experiment in human cooperation."
SOURCE: *The UN Handbook*.

ignores economic and social needs and fails to respect the Global South's special interests. The Global South's power in numbers gives it enormous clout.

North-South differences over perceived priorities are most clearly exhibited in the heated debate over the UN's budget. This controversy centers on how members should interpret the organization's charter, which states that "expenses of the Organization shall be borne by the members as apportioned by the General Assembly."

The UN budget consists of three distinct elements: the core budget, the peacekeeping budget, and the budget for voluntary programs. States contribute to the voluntary programs and some of the peacekeeping activities as they see fit. The core budget and other peacekeeping activities are subject to assessments.

The precise mechanism by which assessments have been determined is complicated, but, historically, assessments were generally allocated according to states' capacity to pay. Although this formula is under attack in many wealthy states, it still governs. Thus the United States, which has the greatest resources, contributes over 20 percent of the UN's core budget (and is also the primary contributor to UN peacekeeping and voluntary programs, contributing 24 percent of the UN's total 2004–2005 budget), whereas the poorest 70 percent of the UN's members pay the minimum (0.01 percent), contributing only $13,000 annually. By this agreement the richest states paid more than three-fourths of the UN's $3.16 billion regular 2004–2005 budget.

Resistance to this budgetary formula for funding UN activities has always existed. It has grown progressively worse, in large part because when the General Assembly apportions expenses, it does so according to majority rule. The problem is that those with the most votes (the less-developed countries) do not have the money, and the most prosperous countries do not have the votes. Wide disparities have grown, adhering to the principle that UN expenses should be appropriated according to members' capacity to pay—a rule by Resolution 55/B that applies until 2007. The ten largest contributors command only ten votes but pay 82 percent of the cost. At the other end of the spectrum, the poorest members paid only 18 percent of the UN budget but command 176 votes. This deep imbalance has led to many fierce financial disputes between the more numerous Global South developing countries that wield considerable influence over the kinds of issues on which the UN's attention and resources are focused and the great powers' concern about the UN's priorities, administrative efficiency, and expenses. The wealthy members charge that the existing budget procedures institutionalize a system of taxation without fair representation. The critics counter with the argument that the great-power members should bear financial responsibilities commensurate with their wealth and influence.

At issue, of course, is not simply money, which is paltry (averaging less than fifty-four cents for each person in the world each year). Differences in images of what is important and which states should have political influence are the real issues. Poor states argue that need should determine expenditure levels rather than the other way around. Major contributors, sensitive to the amounts asked of them and the purposes to which the funds are put, do not want to pay for programs they oppose. For years the United States has been the most vocal about its dissatisfaction, and in 2004, while seeking UN support in its war in Iraq and against global terrorism generally, it was in arrears, owing $1.2 billion. This debt by the American superpower was 72 percent of the UN's regular annual budget.

Even though the Global South countries have usually managed to set the agenda in the General Assembly, like the United States they also are not paying their assessments on time; in 2004 these other members accounted for 53 percent of the total unpaid $2.3 billion owed to the UN.

In response to persisting cash flow crises and rising complaints about the UN's "bloated bureaucracy" and inefficient administration, Secretary-General Kofi Annan undertook what he called "bold reforms—the most extensive and far-reaching reforms in the history of the Organization." His initiative consolidated the programs under his control, reduced costs, corrected corruption and waste, and reassigned administrative responsibilities to different units in order to make the UN more efficient. These massive reforms cut the Secretariat's administrative costs by one-third, from 38 percent of the core budget to 25 percent, and put the savings into a development fund for poor countries. The assessments of some Global North members were also adjusted: the United States pays

24.5 percent of the core budget, and Japan now pays 8.9 percent, Germany, 8.3 percent; Great Britain, 5.9 percent; France, 5.9 percent; Italy 4.7, percent; Canada, 2.7 percent; and Spain, 2.4 percent. But China, with the globe's fastest growing economy, pays only 1.9 percent, barely outpacing Mexico's and the Republic of Korea's 1.8 percent. The reorganization merged the score of disparate programs into five categories and created the UN's first deputy secretary-general position. The new budget for the 191 members puts the UN financial house on a firmer if leaner foundation.

The future of the UN nonetheless remains uncertain. However, many supporters feel optimistic about the organization's long-term prospects. Past crises (such as charges in 2004 of corruption in the UN administration of the Iraqi "Oil-for-Food" program, fueled by reports that Iraq illegally collected billions of dollars from oil surcharges and kickbacks) have been overcome, and the UN's many important previous contributions to world peace and development have given most countries a large stake in its survival. The great gap between the mandates that the UN's members ordered, and the means they allowed for fulfilling them, may yet be closed. Failure would spell disaster.

In contemplating the UN's future agenda, it is sobering to reflect that Kofi Annan (under attack for failing to manage the Oil-for-Food program) warned that "The global agenda has never been so varied, so pressing or so complex. It demands of the international community new approaches, new resources and new commitments." It is also sobering, given the UN's history, to recall that the agenda of issues that the UN is asked to address is likely to continue to be controversial and divisive. The UN is likely to remain an arena for heated exchanges among its diverse members, and the lack of consensus is likely to compromise the organization's capacity to forge new approaches and generate new resources to solve new global problems.

That said, the United Nations may be much maligned, but it is much needed. "The United Nations is everybody's whipping boy" notes Jonathan Power (2004), "but it is revealing how in a crisis—and Iraq is but the latest example—the big powers can run to it and find a solution. When the antagonists have talked or fought themselves into a corner they often tend to crawl back to the body that they were not long ago denouncing, to find an exit from the horrors that confront them. But then a few years later they seem to have forgotten the experience." It was that tendency that prompted President Luis Ignacio Lula da Silva of Brazil to warn against attempts to ignore UN authority in war, only to turn to the world body for help afterward, proclaiming, "The United Nations was conceived to do more than simply clear away the rubble of conflicts that it was unable to prevent."

In the twenty-first century, the UN is likely to continue to play an active role in areas both of social and economic enhancement and of peace and security. As we will examine in Chapter 14, however, the prospects for future UN peacekeeping are uncertain, and the capacity for the globe's most powerful IGO to engineer progress in the social and economic realm is also likely to be severely tested. The challenge will be great, because the UN is expected to serve the economic and social development needs of 191 states and 6 billion people with less money than the annual budget for New York City's police department. In the final analysis, the UN can be no more than the mandates and power that the member states give to it. As one high-level UN civil servant, Brian Urquhart, described the world's political dilemma, "Either the UN is vital to a more stable and equitable world and should be given the means to do the job, or peoples and governments should be encouraged to look elsewhere. But is there really an alternative?"

Other Prominent Global IGOs: The World Trade Organization, the World Bank, and the International Monetary Fund

Beyond the UN, literally hundreds of other IGOs are active internationally. Less than 15 percent are truly global, including as members every independent state. Unlike the UN, most IGOs include as members a large but incomplete list of today's sovereign states. In addition, the most influential, visible, and controversial IGOs usually have less-formal procedures in place to make policy decisions. To round out the sample, we look briefly at three of the most prominent of these other IGOs, all of which are specialized in their focus on the international political economy: the World Trade Organization, the World Bank, and the International Monetary Fund.

In each example, note that these nonstate global actors were created by the great powers for the purposes of their sponsors in response to the great powers' need for a stable international economic order, even at the voluntary sacrifice of sovereignty. IGOs such as the UN and these other IGOs "involve multilateral cooperation leading to the formation of international **regimes** on a global level . . . to achieve gains [states] want [which require] they cooperate" (Keohane and Nye 2001a). To design governing institutions on a world—and human—scale, IGOs are representative of a partial step by states toward that goal. However, "states retain many of their present functions," and stand as obstacles to full-scale global governance, even if "effective governance of a partially—and increasingly—globalized world will require more extensive international institutions . . . to promote cooperation and help resolve conflict" (Keohane 2002).

■ **regimes**
norms, rules, and procedures for cooperative interaction agreed to by a set of states.

The World Trade Organization. After World War II, the United States prepared a preliminary blueprint for the International Trade Organization (ITO). The organization was to be one of three major institutions—along with the World Bank and the International Monetary Fund—to support the postwar world economy. Like the Bank and the Fund, as first conceived the ITO was to function as a specialized agency within the overall framework of the UN. While early negotiations for the anticipated ITO were going on, many states urged an immediate attack on trade barriers through an ad hoc conference that would function as a temporary arrangement until the ITO came into operation. Meeting in Geneva in 1947, twenty-three states negotiated a vast number of **bilateral** tariff concessions that were written into a final act called the General Agreement on Tariffs and Trade (GATT), which became a less-ambitious regime to guide trading practices.

■ **bilateral**
relationships or agreements between two states.

The failure of the ITO nonetheless had given impetus to the GATT approach and led to the establishment of substitute international machinery. Unlike the ITO, GATT was based on executive agreements rather than a treaty, which meant that U.S. participation in GATT did not require U.S. Senate ratification.

GATT settlement procedures for dealing with tariff barriers to trade were sorely strained when world economic conditions took a turn for the worse, and these problems helped galvanize support for a stronger, more official IGO to address the rising economic threats to global trade and prosperity. This worldwide recession set the stage for the eventual passage of GATT and the birth of the

G-7
a group of the major most-advanced industrialized democracies, composed of the United States, Britain, France, Japan, Germany, Canada, and Italy, that meets in regular economic summit conferences; now known as the G-8 with the addition of Russia.

nonintervention norm
a fundamental international legal principle, now being challenged, that traditionally has defined as illegal external interference in the domestic affairs of a sovereign state.

rational choice
the theory that decision makers choose on the basis of what they perceive to be the best interests of themselves and their states, based on their expectations about the relative usefulness of alternative options for realizing goals. Sometimes called "expected utility theory," it was derived from realist theories.

World Trade Organization (WTO). The Uruguay Round of GATT deliberations that began in 1986 was significantly affected by the passing of the Cold War and the fall of communism in Russia and Eastern Europe. All these newly capitalist states undertook economic reforms and applied for GATT membership. Like all other major decisions creating today's key IGOs, the WTO's creation was supported by the United States and the world's other dominant economic actors in the **G-7** (Japan, Germany, Great Britain, France, Canada, and Italy). The Uruguay Round of the negotiations concluded in 1993 when the GATT members agreed to replace their temporary organization with a permanent World Trade Organization (WTO). The WTO began operations on January 1, 1995. The United States became a charter member of the new organization, and countries not yet members such as China, which later joined in 2002, were put on "fast track" for WTO membership.

The World Trade Organization was not exactly the ITO envisaged immediately following World War II, but it is nevertheless the most ambitious undertaking yet launched to regulate world trade. Unlike GATT, which functioned more as a coordinating secretariat, the World Trade Organization (WTO) is a full-fledged intergovernmental organization with a formal decision-making structure at the ministerial level. Organized as a fair-trade policeman, WTO is mandated to manage disputes arising from its trading partners. Functioning equally in overseeing trade in manufactures and agricultural commodities, the WTO was given authority for enforcing rules, which gives it the character of a court, and since 1995 the rules of the WTO authorize third parties to adjudicate conflicts among the WTO's 147 members.

"Ensuring trade flows as smoothly, predictably and as freely as possible" is the WTO's declared central purpose. However, the World Trade Organization has consistently sought to expand this agenda and the IGO's powers to lower trade barriers and thereby raise living standards through new initiatives. The WTO hopes to move well beyond the goals of reducing tariffs in agriculture, services, and traditional sectors to such areas as intellectual property rights. The present goal of the WTO is to transcend the existing matrix of free-trade agreements between pairs of countries and within particular regions or free-trade blocs and replace them with an integrated and comprehensive *worldwide* system of liberal or free trade.

Quite understandably, this liberal agenda poses a threat to some states, their sovereignty, and their perceived inability to successfully compete in the global capitalistic marketplace. At the heart of the complaint is the charge that the WTO undermines the traditional rule of law prohibiting interference in sovereign states' domestic affairs, including management of economic practices *within* the states' territorial jurisdiction. The WTO does indeed spark controversy because it undermines the **nonintervention norm** established at the 1648 Peace of Westphalia, for the WTO does in fact compromise and protract the conventional freedom given to sovereign states. However, the WTO, it should be kept in mind, developed as a result of agreements powerful states reached to voluntarily surrender some of their sovereign decision-making freedom, under the conviction that this pooling of sovereignty was a **rational choice** that would produce greater gains than losses. Even so, the WTO seems destined to remain an IGO target for criticism precisely because the WTO's authority comes, particularly to some states, at what is perceived as a high cost, namely, the reduction of a state's ability of regulate economic activities by businesses within their domestic economy.

The clout of the WTO is also somewhat uncertain and is widely perceived in the Global South as greater than probably actually exists. True, the WTO's purpose was to replace GATT with a permanent, highly administrated, and efficient IGO to pursue the same goals of liberalizing and expanding world trade. In fact "the Dispute Settlement process within the WTO gives it the strongest enforcement capacity of all international organizations" (J. Smith and Moran 2001). However, even though the WTO holds unprecedented responsibilities for administrating those multilateral trade agreements its members approve, the WTO cannot by itself manufacture its own agreements and does not possess the supranational authority to regulate any state's substantive economic policies. The WTO is only a formal institutional home available for member states to negotiate and implement the treaties that they voluntarily accept. The philosophy guiding the WTO is predicated and dependent on the vision its members have chosen to support—that open markets and free governments competing in global trade without discrimination contribute to the welfare of all countries. The continuation of that constructed vision depends, in the last analysis, on the willingness of the states that are members to abide by that philosophy. In addition, it would be inaccurate to characterize the WTO as a democratic IGO:

> In theory, the WTO was to promote greater democracy and transparency in global trade negotiations by allowing each member country a single vote in contrast to the financially weighted voting system used in the World Bank and the International Monetary Fund (IMF). In practice, however, there is little evidence of democracy within the WTO operations. The United States, the European Union (EU), Canada, and Japan (dubbed "the Quad") have routinely hammered out agreements in informal, "green room" meetings, named after the site of these secret conferences at the WTO's general headquarters. The Quad then uses its considerable economic and political influence to build "consensus" around these decisions made without participation from the full WTO membership. (J. Smith and Moran 2001, 69)

Like most IGOs, therefore, the WTO is an organization dominated by the great powers.

The World Bank. Created in July 1944 at the United Nations Monetary and Financial Conference held in Bretton Woods, New Hampshire, which was attended by forty-four countries, the World Bank was at first designed to support reconstruction efforts after the Second World War and to assist in "the development of productive facilities and resources in less developed countries." The International Bank for Reconstruction and Development (IBRD) and the International Development Association (IDA) were the twin IGO institutions created at the conference, but the term *World Bank* was coined as a shorthand way to informally refer to the IBRD alone.

From its inception, the International Bank for Reconstruction and Development was intended to be the central unit in UN lending operations. Within the UN system, the agencies of the World Bank group, along with the International Monetary Fund, are responsible for most of the capital aid transfers to the developing countries. Coordination between the World Bank agencies and the IMF is provided by the World Bank/IMF Development Committee. The committee functions both as an advisory body to the two boards of governors and as an action body to encourage "foreign capital flows of all kinds" to the developing states. Its membership includes twenty-two finance and development ministers from the boards of governors.

Administratively the World Bank is an IGO run according to its Articles of Agreement, which proclaim that "all the powers of the Bank shall be vested in the Board of Governors, consisting of a governor and an alternate appointed by each member in such manners as it may determine." A governor customarily is a member country's minister of finance, its central bank, or an equivalent official. The board cannot delegate decisions on many matters such as modifying the Bank's capital stock, suspending the Bank's operations and redistributing its assets, or allocating the Bank's net income. The Board of Governors delegates responsibility for the routine operations of the Bank to its twenty-four directors of its executive board. The five countries with the largest number of shares in the World Bank's capital stock (the United States, Germany, Japan, France, and the United Kingdom) appoint their own executive directors, and the remaining executive directors are either appointed (Saudi Arabia), elected by their states (China, Russia, and Switzerland), or elected by groups of countries.

The Bank's president is also selected by the executive directors and is the chairman of the executive board, but cannot vote unless it is needed to break a tie vote. The president acts as a CEO in charge of the Bank's operating staff and is responsible, with the approval of the executive director, for the organization, appointment, and dismissal of the Bank's administrative staff. The Articles of Agreement state that the president and staff of the Bank "owe their duty entirely to the Bank and to no other authority." During its first fifty years, the Bank has had ten presidents.

The World Bank's organization consists not only of the president but also three managing directors, a general counsel and senior vice president for Management and Personnel Services, and fourteen vice presidents (six responsible for the Bank's regions: Africa, East Asia and Pacific, South Asia, Europe and Central Asia, Middle East and North Africa, and Latin America and Caribbean). The Articles of Agreement require the president to "pay due regard to the importance of recruiting personnel on as wide a geographical basis as possible" and require that the Bank's principal office be located in the territory of the member holding the largest number of Bank shares. Because the United States has more shares than any other member, the Bank's headquarters are in Washington, D.C. The Bank also has offices in New York (the World Bank Mission to the United Nations), Paris (the European Office), London, and Tokyo. Seven regional missions, fifty-nine resident missions, and a number of smaller offices exist to administratively support the central offices.

Unlike the United Nations, which has a one country/one vote system, the World Bank has a system of weighted voting. Each member is entitled to 250 votes and receives one additional vote for each share held in the Bank's capital stock. The number of shares allocated is based on a quota so that the richer countries contribute to more shares than the poorer countries. This system recognizes the differences among members' holdings and is intended to protect the interests of the great powers that make more substantial contributions to the World Bank's resources. If a country's economic situation changes over time, its quota is adjusted and its allocation of shares and votes changes accordingly.

That said, the United States still has veto power and exercises, with the other economic powerhouses, preponderant influence over the Bank's decisions.

The World Bank is run by bankers to present the image that its board of governors seeks to project as a guardian of financial interests. The World Bank's loan criteria are aimed at protecting its creditors' interests. This constructed image of itself as a beacon of hope and help and a barrier against the collapse of global capitalism is prudent for its success, since most of the World Bank's loan funds are obtained not from governments but from borrowing in private capital markets. Loan applicants must use a "project" approach, which requires the applicant to demonstrate that the loan will finance a rationally planned undertaking that will contribute to the productive and earning capacity of the recipient country. The World Bank, like all banks, must lend funds that promise to make a return for its creditor investor countries in order to ensure their continuing support. For many years, the World Bank therefore frowned on loans for social projects, like building hospitals and schools or for slum clearance. Historically it also was reluctant to provide general-purpose loans, or loans to meet rising debt or to resolve balance-of-payment problems; but this has declined in recent years. In fact, the World Bank's lending policies underwent substantial modification in the latter half of the 1980s and 1990s when it began to encourage economic growth in major debtor Global South countries. This was a departure from policy in the World Bank's traditional use of funds for "self-liquidating projects" generating revenues large enough to service the debtor's debt payments. Today, the World Bank bases its loaning policies on the capacity of the recipient country's entire economy to produce enough growth to repay the loans provided for that purpose. On average, World Bank loans have financed only 25 percent of the cost of projects; to provide the balance, other investors are now required to support the World Bank.

Over the years both the self-image and operations of the World Bank have changed—from a strictly financial IGO to that of a development agency dedicated to solving problems of economic and political development and, recently, environmental sustainability. Instead of remaining aloof and merely passing judgment on loan applications, the World Bank now assists states in their development planning, helps prepare project proposals, and provides training for senior development officials. Its economic survey missions actively monitor the resource and investment potential of member countries and determine priorities for country and regional projects. The World Bank has also participated increasingly in consortium arrangements for financing private lending institutions. It has demonstrated repeatedly that it is also dedicated to the promotion of political development, defined as liberal democratic governance, by its recent insistence on democratic reforms as a condition for economic assistance. Like the G-8, the World Bank has a clear and consistent commitment to **liberalism;** it is an active promoter of both free trade and free governments.

Despite its increased pace of activity, the World Bank has never been able to meet all the needs for financial assistance of the developing states. The repayment of loans in hard currencies has imposed serious obstacles on impoverished and indebted borrowing states of the Global South that do not benefit from revenues through active participation in global trade. Many developing states are currently overstraining their debt-servicing capacities, and new loans could easily exacerbate the world debt crisis (see Chapter 5). Moreover, since economic activity is habitually controlled predominantly by private companies in many

■ **liberalism**
a paradigm predicated on the hope that the application of reason and universal ethics to international relations can lead to a more orderly, just, and cooperative world, and that international anarchy and war can be policed by institutional reforms that empower organizations and international laws for global governance.

developing Global South states, making loans to relatively small firms without government guarantees is risky, although it is widely regarded as essential to economic development. This has led some critics to conclude that whereas the World Bank has functioned effectively as an international bank, it has failed as an IGO (especially to critics who fondly recall the early post–World War II years when the developing countries fought vigorously to have the UN create a major capital grants institution, but lost the battle). The deficiencies of the World Bank, however, have been partly offset by the establishment of another lending IGO, the International Monetary Fund.

The International Monetary Fund. Prior to World War II, the globe had suffered from the absence of institutional mechanisms to manage orderly rules for the exchange of money across borders. As that world war neared its end, the United States led the Allies in creating the International Monetary Fund (IMF) (alongside the World Bank) at the 1944 Bretton Woods Conference for this goal. The IMF sought a multilateral solution to a multilateral problem—guarding against the continuation of the selfishly competitive "beggar-thy-neighbor" practices of currency restrictions and devaluations at others' expense that had destroyed the world economy in the 1930s. Cast in the mold of commercial liberalism, the IMF sought to create a global institution to maintain currency-exchange stability, primarily for orderly currency relations among the wealthy powers but secondarily as a lender of last resort for poor as well as rich countries experiencing financial crises.

Those were the IMF's origins. Since then, the global marketplace has expanded and with that growth has come the increasingly economic interdependence of all states, or **globalization** through the integration of national economies. As a result, the conditions in which the IMF were created have vanished, and with global transformations the IMF has evolved to perform new roles.

The IMF is now one of the sixteen specialized agencies within the UN system. Each IMF member is represented on its governing board, which meets annually to fix general policy. Day-to-day business is conducted by a twenty-two-member executive board chaired by a managing director who is also administrative head of a staff of approximately two thousand employees. The primary purpose of the IMF is stabilizing international monetary exchange rates. This powerful financial IGO derives its operating funds from its member states. Contributions (and thus voting strength) are based on a country's national income, monetary reserves, and trade balance. The IMF's voting thus is weighted according to a state's monetary contribution to the IMF, giving a larger voice to the wealthier states.

In addition to stabilizing exchange rates in order to facilitate international trade, the chief aims of the IMF, as set forth in its Articles of Agreement, include:

- promoting international monetary cooperation
- facilitating the expansion of international trade
- promoting exchange stability
- establishing a multilateral system of payments
- fostering members' confidence in the IMF
- allocating the resources available
- shortening the duration of, and reducing the degree of disequilibrium in, members' balances of payments

■ **globalization**
the integration of states, through increasing contact, communication, and trade, to create a holistic, single global system in which the process of change increasingly binds people together in a common fate.

The regime underlying the IMF assigns it the task of performing as a pooling arrangement, based on the requirement that all members will contribute to a common bank of monetary reserves from which they can draw to overcome short-term deficits in their balance of payments. In this regard, the IMF is designed to serve as a lender of last resort when one of its members is threatened by an economic downturn that could destroy its economy. Contributions are based on a quota system set according to a state's national income, gold reserves, and other factors affecting each member's ability to contribute. In this way, the IMF operates like a credit union that requires each of its 185 member countries to contribute to a common pool of funds from which it can borrow when the need arises. This is the cooperative spirit of liberalism in practice.

The IMF, as a standard practice, usually attaches conditions to large borrowings to ensure that the problems that produced the large deficit are remedied. The IMF has been subjected to considerable criticism for exercising the power given it to specify such often-strict financial conditions for its loans. The IMF's expanded power to include terms of conditionality has also been used to demand environmental protection and democratization, including empowerment of women in the members' political system. Critics contend that in so expanding its original mandate, the IMF has deviated from its charter, which called for making lending decisions strictly on economic bases.

Like the other major IGOs created by the great powers, the IMF is resented by the less powerful, who find that the IMF's beneficial intentions are betrayed by the domination and inequalities its programs, crafted by the great economic powers, have caused for the least-developed Global South countries most in need. As seen in Chapter 5, the Global South often looks at the great powers who manage IGOs like the IMF as operating from a double standard.

THE EUROPEAN UNION AS A MODEL REGIONAL IGO: A RITE OF PASSAGE FOR "EUROLAND"?

The tug of war between individual states and groups of states within the UN, the World Bank, and the IMF are reminders of an underlying principle that IGOs are run by the states that join them. This severely inhibits the IGOs' ability to rise above interstate competition and independently pursue their own purposes. Because they cannot act autonomously and lack the legitimacy and capability for independent global governance, universal IGOs are often viewed more as instruments of their state members' foreign policies and arenas for debate than as independent nonstate actors.

When states dominate universal international organizations like the UN, the prospects for international cooperation decline because, as **realism** emphasizes, states are fearful of multilateral organizations that compromise their vital national interests. This limits IGOs' capabilities for multilateral decision making to engineer global change.

A rival hypothesis—that cooperation among powerful states is possible and that international organizations help produce it—emerges from **neoliberal theory**. This viewpoint is especially pertinent to the European Union (EU). The EU is a good example of the powerful (global) role played by some regional IGOs. In many respects the EU is unique, if for no other reason than that it stands as the

■ **realism**
a theory based on the premise that world politics is essentially and unchangeably a struggle among self-interested states for power and position under anarchy, with each competing state pursuing its own national interests.

■ **neoliberal theory**
a philosophy that maintains that peaceful change with prosperity can be encouraged through multilateral cooperation in institutions that knit the states and peoples of the world together into a true global community.

■ **security community**
a group of states whose high level of institutionalized collaboration results in the settlement of disputes by compromise rather than by force.

■ **Third Way**
an approach to governance advocated primarily by many European leaders who, while recognizing few alternatives to liberal capitalism, seek to soften the cruel social impact of free-market individualism by progressively allowing government intervention to preserve social justice and the rights of individuals to freedom from fear of the deprivations caused by disruptions in the global economy.

globe's greatest example of peaceful international cooperation producing an integrated **security community** with a single economy and a common currency. The EU is also dedicated to liberal democratic governance and shares a preference for free-market capitalism tempered in Europe's search for **Third Way** values such as compassion for human suffering. Moreover, the EU, or what has become known as "Euroland," is not, strictly speaking, a freestanding supranational organization for the collective management of European domestic and foreign affairs. The EU coexists with a large number of other European IGOs, in which it is nested and with which it jointly makes decisions. Of these, the Organization for Security and Cooperation in Europe (OSCE) and the Council of Europe stand as regional institutions of equal European partners, free of dividing lines, designed to manage regional security and promote the human rights of minorities through democratization. In this overlapping network of European IGOs, the EU nonetheless is prominent as the primary example of a powerful organization that has transformed itself from a single- to a multiple-purpose nonstate actor.

The process of European integration began with the creation of the European Coal and Steel Community (ECSC) in 1951, the European Atomic Energy Community (Euratom) in 1957, and the European Economic Community (EEC) in 1957. They centered initially on trade and development. Since the late 1960s, the three have shared common organizational structures, and, in successive steps, have enlarged their mission as they came to be called "the European Community." Its membership grew and its geographical scope also broadened as the EU expanded in a series of waves to encompass fifteen countries by 1997: Belgium, France, Germany, Italy, Luxembourg, and the Netherlands (the original "six"); Denmark, Ireland, and the United Kingdom (which joined in 1973); Greece (1981); Portugal and Spain (1986); and Austria, Finland, and Sweden (1995). In May 2004, the EU reached a new milestone in its path toward enlargement when it formally admitted ten new members (the Czech Republic, Slovakia, Estonia, Hungary, Latvia, Lithuania, Malta, Poland, Slovenia, and the Greek-controlled part of Cyprus). This bold enlargement added 75 million people to create the globe's biggest free-trade bloc, and transformed the face of Europe by ending the continent's division (that enlargement process could continue if, as expected by most members, Bulgaria, Romania, and possibly even Turkey also join as a result of negotiations currently underway).

The idea of a single Europe remains compelling for many Europeans who are haunted by the specter of European nationalities and states that have been fighting one another ever since the Pax Romana collapsed eighteen hundred years ago. Peace is in Europe's future, providing that civil wars and unrest, such as that threatened by Ukraine's December 2004 election crisis, do not terminate this ambitious experiment in the integration of formerly separated countries.

And change can generate disunity. The enlargement of the EU has been a long-standing goal. "The agenda is not new—deepen in order to widen, widen in order to deepen, and reform in order to do both—but its scope and urgency are" (Serfaty 2003). EU enlargement through eastward expansion has presented the organization with a host of troublesome questions, compounded by the fact that the ten new members, whose combined economies are less than 10 percent of the entire EU's, have different (poorer) economies and (smaller populations) demographics than the previous fifteen EU members, and therefore have different needs and interests that can make reaching agreement on policy decisions increasingly difficult. The distinction made by U.S. Defense Secretary Donald

FIGURE 6.3
The European Union's Governmental Structure
The EU is a complex organization, with different responsibilities performed by various units. This figure charts the principal institutions and the relationships among them that collectively lead to EU decisions and policies.
SOURCE: *Economist*, Oct. 23, 1999, p. 16.

Rumsfeld between the "old" Europe (the West) and the "new" Europe (the East) underscored the probability of some of EU divisions on the horizon, since the new members supported the American war in Iraq and the Western members, with the exception of Great Britain, opposed the military invasion. If Germany, France, and the other Benelux countries join together to oppose the smaller less developed new members, a "club within a club" could split the EU into two opposed coalitions, and if East-West frictions coincide with new tensions between the big and the small EU members, collective decision making will be immeasurably more complicated. How is the EU organized to avoid this outcome?

EU Organization and Management. The EU's institutional structure has changed over time, as the organization has grown and expanded its authority over its members, to transform the EU toward governance beyond the nation-state. The principal institutions for governance, as shown in Figure 6.3, include a Council of Ministers, the European Commission, a European Parliament, and a Court of Justice. The EU's central administrative unit, the Council of Ministers, consists of cabinet ministers drawn from the EU's member states, who participate when the most important decisions are made. In this respect, the EU is an association of states similar to the UN. But the EU is more than this, as evidenced by the "enlargement" of the EU's authority over its twenty-five members, which has grown so that the EU is truly much more than the sum of its parts.

The Council of Ministers represents the governments of the EU's member states and retains final authority over the policy-making decisions. The council sets general policy guidelines for the **European Commission,** which consists of thirty commissioners (two each from Britain, France, Germany, Italy, and Spain, and one each from the remaining twenty member states). Commissioners are nominated by EU member governments and must be approved by the European Parliament. Headquartered in Brussels, the European Commission was created to construct common economic policies for the original six member states and to oversee their administration. Today the primary functions of the European Commission are to propose new laws for the EU, oversee EU treaties, and execute the decrees of the European Council. A professional staff of seventeen thousand civil-service "Eurocrats" assist the commission's administrative bureaucracy in proposing and directing decision making (by majority vote) for the EU and the Council of Ministers. The commission proposes legislation, implements EU policies, and represents the European Union in international trade negotiations. It also manages the EU's budget, which, in contrast with most international organizations, derives part of its revenues from sources not under the control of member states.

The European Parliament represents the political parties and public opinion within Europe. It has existed from the beginning of Europe's journey toward political unification, although at its creation this legislative body was appointed rather than elected and had little power. That is no longer the case. The European Parliament is now chosen in a direct election by the citizens of the EU's member states. Its more than 600 deputies debate issues at the monumental glass headquarters in Brussels and at a lavish Strasbourg palace in the same way that democratic national legislative bodies do. The European Parliament shares authority with the Council of Ministers representing member governments, but the Parliament's influence has increased over time. The deputies elected through universal suffrage pass laws with the council, approve the EU's budget, oversee the European Commission, and can overturn its acts. This last element in the Parliament's authority gives it substantial clout, which it has not been hesitant to exercise. For example, in July 1999 the Parliament accused the previous group of commissioners of cronyism and corruption and forced their resignation.

The European Court of Justice in Luxembourg has also grown in prominence and power as European integration has gathered depth and breadth. From the start, the court was given responsibility for adjudicating claims and conflicts among EU governments as well as between those governments and the new institutions the EU created. The court interprets EU law for national courts and rules on legal questions that arise within the EU's institutions and hears and rules on cases concerning individual citizens. The fact that its decisions are binding distinguishes the European Court of Justice from most other international tribunals.

■ **European Commission**
The executive organ administratively responsible for the European Union.

IGO Governance in Action Shown here is the hemi-cycle of the European Parliament in Brussels, Belgium, where EU Parliament members representing twenty-five countries make collective decisions. To shape Europe's future, they now allocate a budget exceeding $100 billion that comes from import duties, a 1.4 percent sales tax, and a portion of each members' gross national product.

EU Decision-Making Challenges. In practice, two decision-making procedures have been followed for the adoption of EU directives and regulations: consultation and cooperation. Which of the two procedures is followed to adopt regulations depends on the nature of the proposal under consideration, with the principal difference being that the European Parliament plays a greater role in the cooperative than in the consultive process. Under both procedures, however, the thirty commissioners of the European Commission in Brussels have been the driving force in European integration. But it must be noted that the process of EU collective decision making is difficult to characterize, because a variety of different procedures are usually operative at the same time, and they vary depending on the activity that is under consideration. Moreover, on some issues negotiations tend to proceed in a step-by-step process whereas on other issues decisions are the product of bargains reached by coalitions of members, in which the proposal stage is critical to the outcome (Selck 2004).

The political unification of Europe has been built step-by-step as the EU has marched toward ever greater unity. Moving beyond the nation-state toward a single integrated European federation has not been smooth, and disagreement persists over the extent to which the EU should become a single, truly united superstate, a "United States of Europe." Debate continues also over how far and how fast such a process of **pooled sovereignty** should proceed, and about the

■ **pooled sovereignty**
legal authority granted to an IGO by its members to make collective decisions regarding specified aspects of public policy heretofore made exclusively by each sovereign government.

natural geographical limits to the EU's "enlargement"—its ultimate membership and boundaries. These issues will be debated in the future, and only time will tell how they will be resolved (see Chapter 14). That said, the EU represents a remarkable success story in the history of international relations. Who would have expected that competitive states that have spent most of their national experiences waging war against one another would consolidate, put their clashing ideological and territorial ambitions aside, and construct a "European-ness" identity built on unity and confederated decision making? The EU has moved above the nation-state as a supranational regional organization pledged to giving the EU dominion over its twenty-five members' internal affairs and control over common foreign and military policies, while at the same time developing a sense of solidarity and belonging among the region's peoples, and emerging as a new superpower (Reid 2004).

Other Regional IGOs

Since Europe's 1950s initiatives toward economic and political integration, more than a dozen regional IGOs have been created in various other parts of the world, notably among states in the Global South. Most seek to stimulate regional economic growth, but many have drifted from that original single purpose to pursue multiple political and military purposes as well. The major regional organizations include:

- the Asia Pacific Economic Cooperation (APEC) forum, created in 1989 as a gathering of twelve states without a defined goal. APEC's membership has grown to twenty-one countries (including the United States). APEC has planned at its summits to establish free and open trade and investments in the region for developed countries by 2010 and for developing member countries by 2020.

- the North Atlantic Treaty Organization (NATO), a military alliance created in 1949 primarily to deter the Soviet Union in Western Europe. The security IGO has expanded its membership to twenty-six countries and broadened its mission to promote democratization and to police civil wars and terrorism outside its traditional territory within Europe. The United States and Canada are also members.

- the Association of Southeast Asian Nations (ASEAN), established in 1967 by five founding members to promote regional economic, social, and cultural cooperation. In 1999 it created a free-trade zone among its ten Southeast Asian members as a counterweight outside the orbit of Japan, China, the United States, and other great powers so that ASEAN could compete as a bloc in international trade. ASEAN's expansion has created an identity crisis, with fears of new divisions between the older and wealthy "haves" and the newer and less-wealthy "have not" members, which include Vietnam, Laos, Cambodia, and the impoverished Myanmar (formerly Burma). ASEAN today struggles with political, economic, and environmental problems that beset the region and that cannot be managed without the combined efforts of this regional IGO.

- the Caribbean Community (CARICOM), established in 1973 as a common market to promote economic development and integration among its fourteen country and territory members.

- the Council of Arab Economic Unity (CAEU), established in 1964 from a 1957 accord to promote trade and economic integration among its ten Arab members.
- the Economic Community of West African States (ECOWAS), established in 1975 to promote regional economic cooperation among its fifteen members.
- the Organization of the Islamic Conference (OIC) was established in 1969 to promote Islamic solidarity and cooperation by coordinating a large number of activities among fifty-seven Islamic states (plus the Palestine Liberation Organization). While not technically a regional IGO, the OIC orchestrates preventive diplomacy, does not condone the use of terrorism, and is not concerned with promoting fundamentalist Islamic religious principles.
- the Latin American Integration Association (LAIA), also known as Asociación Latinoamericana de Integración (ALADI), established in 1980 to promote and regulate reciprocal trade among its twelve members.
- the Southern African Development Community (SADC), established in 1992 to promote regional economic development and integration and to alleviate poverty among its fourteen members.
- the South Asian Association for Regional Cooperation (SAARC), established in 1985 to promote economic, social, and cultural cooperation and respect for sovereign territorial independence and non-interference in states' internal affairs among its seven members.

As these examples illustrate, most IGOs are organized on a regional rather than global basis. The governments creating them usually concentrate on one or two major goals (such as liberalizing trade or promoting peace within the region) instead of attempting through collective action to address at once the complete range of issues that they face in common, such as environmental protection and democratization, in addition to economic and security cooperation. Africa illustrates this tendency at the regional level. Within strife-torn Africa, fragile states have created a complex myriad network of regional IGOs, with multiple, cross-cutting memberships. Some are large multipurpose groups such as the Economic Community of Western African States (ECOWAS), the Common Market for Eastern and Southern Africa (COMESA), the Economic Community of Central African States (CEEAC), the Southern African Development Community (SADC), and the Arab Maghreb Union (AMU). Alongside these are many smaller organizations such as the Economic Community of the Great Lakes Countries, the Mano River Union, and the EAC.

It is hazardous to generalize about organizations so widely divergent in membership and purpose alongside many other, older IGOs whose function is to perform particular missions, such as the International Telecommunication Union founded in 1865, the World Meteorological Organization (1873), the Universal Postal Union (1874), the International Labour Organization (1919), and the International Civil Aviation Organization (1944). Regional IGOs seek to coordinate their programs, but none has managed to collaborate at a level that begins to match the institutionalized collective decision making achieved by the EU. The particular reasons why many regional IGOs sometimes fail and are often ineffective vary, but at bottom all IGOs are limited by national leaders' reluctance to make politically costly choices that would undermine their personal popularity at home and their governments' sovereignty. Nonetheless, these attempts at regional cooperation demonstrate many states' acceptance of the fact that they cannot individually resolve many of the problems that confront them collectively.

Because the state is clearly failing to manage many transnational policy problems, ironically it finds itself acting as the primary agent of the same cooperative management efforts that are eroding the state's power. Collective problem solving through the growth and expanding power of IGOs is likely to continue. Globalization and the force of a shrinking, borderless world are increasing the influence of international institutions; in turn, IGOs' expanding webs of interdependence are infringing on the power of states and changing the ways in which they network on the global stage. These IGOs and processes promise to transform world politics, which is why the thesis that the state is in retreat and its power to govern is eroding is so commonly voiced (see Paul, Ikenberry, and Hall 2003).

Another set of agents in the transnational transformation and globalization of world politics are nonstate actors such as NGOs, ethnonational movements, and multinational corporations, which are also highly active and increasingly influential. We now turn our attention to their behavior and impact.

NONGOVERNMENTAL ORGANIZATIONS (NGOs)

If you are like many other people in the world, there is at least one problem and possibly more that is of great concern to you. You would like to see the world change. How can you help make the world a better place? You are likely to realize that you cannot engineer global changes all by yourself. However, you probably recognize that other people share your concerns and that by joining together with other, like-minded people in the world your collective voices can give you a means of exercising influence.

In today's world, increasing numbers of people have found that through joining private interest groups they can participate in the global system and lobby to influence international decision making. They have joined as members of one or more nongovernmental organizations (NGOs), of which there are more than thirty-one thousand now in existence worldwide. NGOs are private international actors whose members are not states but are instead volunteers drawn from the populations of two or more states who have formed organizations to promote their shared interests and ideals in order to influence the policies of state governments and intergovernmental organizations (IGOs).

These NGOs tackle many global problems, seeking changes in the world for causes such as disarmament, women's rights, environmental protection, and human rights. Most of them pursue objectives that are highly respected and constructive and therefore do not provoke controversy or arouse much opposition. For example, NGOs such as Amnesty International, the International Chamber of Commerce, the International Red Cross, Save the Children, the World Wildlife Federation, and Global Youth Connect (which supports young people who are victims of human rights abuses) enjoy widespread popular support. Others, however, are more controversial because they push for changes that, were they to succeed, would threaten the interests of other groups who have a stake in preserving the status quo. For example, NGOs such as the Union of Concerned Sci-

NGOs: New Gods Overseas More than thirty-one thousand NGOs exist and are influential activists pursuing their own agendas—and publicity—throughout the globe. Increasingly, they work together with IGOs such as the United Nations, and because they are often respected, rich state governments have increasingly turned to NGOs to perform services such as distributing foreign aid or providing humanitarian relief.

entists and Doctors Without Borders are among the 1,230 international peace organizations (*Yearbook of International Organizations, 2002/2003*, vol. 5, 319) interested in reducing military spending, and this threatens the budgets of members of the "military industrial complex" whose jobs and income depend on continued high government spending on defense. Hence, many NGOs work at cross-purposes in a competitive struggle to redefine the global agenda.

What makes NGOs increasingly prominent on the world stage is that their bargaining activities have led to the successful creation of **regimes,** or new sets of rules that help to regulate some important transnational problems. NGOs "are now influencing decisions and helping to set agendas that were once determined solely by governments and corporations, from policies on international trade and investment to initiatives on literacy, international aid, and human rights. . . . NGOs have used their flexibility, small scale, technical expertise, and connections to the grass roots to spark something of an 'organization revolution'—forging an effective middle ground between the state and the free market" (*Vital Signs 1999*). At the same time, the demands of NGOs have shaken the sovereign control by state governments over their foreign policies. The challenge to states by minority racial or religious NGOs has been especially severe in fragile or failing states where revolt by NGOs has led to the collapse of the state, and even in some strong states NGO pressure has led to the **devolution** of the central government's power. NGOs are making borders porous and states vulnerable both to external pressures and to challenges from within their boundaries. As NGOs rise in numbers and influence, a key question to contemplate is whether what may be termed a "nongovernmental global society" will materialize to override

■ **regimes**
norms, rules, and procedures for interaction agreed to by a set of states.

■ **devolution**
states' granting of political power to minority ethnopolitical national groups and indigenous people in particular national regions under the expectation that greater autonomy will curtail their quest for independence as a new state.

■ nonstate nations
national or ethnic groups struggling to obtain power and/or statehood.

■ unitary actor
a transnational actor (usually a sovereign state) assumed to be internally united, so that changes in its internal circumstances do not influence its foreign policy as much as do the decisions that actor's leaders make to cope with changes in its global environment.

■ constructivism
a scholarly approach to inquiry emphasizing the importance of agents (people and groups) and the shared meanings they construct to define their identities, interests, and institutions—understandings that influence their international behavior.

■ nationalism
a mind-set glorifying a particular state and the nationality group living in it that sees the state's national interests as a supreme value.

■ ethnopolitical groups
people whose identity is primarily defined by their sense of sharing a common ancestral nationality, language, cultural heritage, and kinship ties.

■ ethnicity
perceptions of likeness among members of a particular racial or linguistic grouping leading them to act prejudicially toward outsiders in other kinship or cultural groups.

the traditional global system centered on sovereign states, and, if so, whether this structural transformation will democratize, or disrupt, global governance.

Let us look at the major NGOs to better evaluate if they are contributing to the erosion of state sovereignty and whether their impact spells promise, or peril, for the future of world politics. Today a small subset of increasingly active and self-assertive major nonstate actors receive the most attention and provoke the most controversy. To simplify our task, we will focus on three of the most visible politically active types of NGO nonstate actors: ethnopolitical groups or **nonstate nations,** religious movements, and multinational corporations.

Nonstate Nations: The Indigenous Ethnic Groups of the Fourth World

The images of the all-powerful state and of governments as sovereign and autonomous rulers of unified nations are not very realistic. These images exaggerate the extent to which the state resembles a **unitary actor,** as realists often ask us to picture it. In truth, the unitary actor conception is misleading, because many states are divided internally and are highly penetrated from abroad, and few states are tightly unified and capable of acting as a single body with a common purpose.

Although the state unquestionably remains the most visible actor in world affairs, as **constructivism** emphasizes, **nationalism** and nationality should be seen as potent cultural factors defining the core loyalties and identities of many people that influence how states act. Many people pledge their primary allegiance not to the state and government that rules them but rather to a politically active minority group with which they most associate themselves. One broad category of such national groups is **ethnopolitical groups** whose members share a common nationality, language, cultural tradition, and kinship ties. They view themselves as members of their nationality or ethnic group first and of their state only secondarily. **Ethnicity** is socially constructed, in that members of an ethnic or racial group learn to see themselves as members of that group and accordingly perceive their identity as determined by their inherited membership at birth. That perception is likely to be strongly reinforced when recognized by other ethnic groups. Hence, ethnicity is in the eye of the beholder—a constructed identity. "A basic definition might be a group of humans who share significant elements of culture and who reproduce themselves socially and biologically" (T. Hall 2004).

Ethnic nationalism (people's loyalty to and identification with a particular ethnic nationality group) in world affairs reduces the relevance of the unitary state. Many states are divided, multiethnic and multicultural societies made up of a variety of politically active groups that seek, if not outright independence, a greater level of regional autonomy and a greater voice in the domestic and foreign policies of the state. "Nearly three quarters of the world's larger countries (116 of 161) have politically significant minorities," and 275 minority groups comprising one-sixth of the world's population are at risk from persecution worldwide (Gurr 2001, 175). Relations between **ethnic groups** are a key element in the equation of relations between NGOs and the state, as contact is customarily widespread between groups who define their identity by their common ancestry. These ethnic divisions and the lack of unity within states make thinking of international relations as exclusively homogeneous interactions between uni-

Indigenous Peoples Organize Many subnational groups of nations and indigenous peoples reside on the territory of existing states that govern them.

fied states—the realist "billiard ball model"—dubious. "The multiethnic state is 'normal' in the statistical sense [and] this deepens the puzzle of the chimera of the ethnically homogeneous nation-state" (T. Hall 2004).

The Fourth World in World Politics. **Indigenous peoples** are the ethnic and cultural groups that were native to a geographic location now controlled by another state or political group. The globe is populated by an estimated six thousand separate indigenous nations, each of which has a unique language and culture and strong, often spiritual, ties to an ancestral homeland. In most cases indigenous people were at one time politically sovereign and economically self-sufficient. Today there are an estimated 300 million indigenous people, more than 5 percent of the world's population, scattered in more than seventy countries; some have placed the number as high as 650 million (Center for World Indigenous Studies 2002). This segment of global society is conventionally referred to as the **Fourth World** to heighten awareness of the poverty and deprivation that confront many native or tribal indigenous peoples.

It is difficult to differentiate the distinct nonstate nations making up the Fourth World's individual indigenous peoples. One common measure, regarded by social scientists as the best index of the number of distinct cultures, is the number of spoken languages. By this count, there are potentially as many indigenous peoples or cultures as there are known living languages—6,800. However, because "unprecedented numbers of languages are endangered," so, too, are indigenous peoples; indigenous cultures and "languages die for a number of reasons—war, genocides, disease, low birth rates, government writ. But globalization may now pose the biggest threat of all. As the world becomes more intertwined, many of those who speak minority languages, especially the young,

■ **ethnic nationalism**
devotion to a cultural, ethnic, or linguistic community within an existing state.

■ **ethnic groups**
a group of people of the same nationality who share a common culture, set of ancestors, or language.

■ **indigenous peoples**
the native ethnic and cultural inhabitant populations within countries ruled by a government controlled by others, referred to as the "Fourth World."

■ **Fourth World**
a term used to recognize the native national groups residing in many so-called united states who, although often minorities, occupied the state's territory first and refuse to accept domination, seeking instead to create a new state for themselves by splitting existing states or to gain greater political freedom to govern themselves.

MAP 6.2
The Indigenous Cultures of the Fourth World

More than five thousand indigenous peoples live in many countries throughout the globe and are concentrated regionally. As Julian Burger of the UN's Office of the High Commissioner for Human Rights noted in 1999, "All over the world indigenous peoples are asserting their cultural identity, claiming their right to control their futures, and struggling to regain their ancestral lands." To protect their human rights and national identity, Fourth World groups have organized meetings, such as the World Conference of Indigenous Peoples in Rio de Janeiro, Brazil, in May 1992. As a result of their lobbying, the UN named 1993 the International Year of the World's Indigenous Peoples. Many minority groups and indigenous peoples long denied self-determination are seeking to govern themselves by pursuing independence through separatist movements. If every major "racial or ethnic group won independence," U.S. President Bill Clinton observed in October 1999, "we might have 800 countries in the world."

Note: Colors indicate regional concentrations of indigenous peoples.
SOURCE: Julian Burger, United Nations. Adapted from "Vanishing Cultures" by Wade Davis, *National Geographic*, August 1999, pp. 66–67. NG Maps/NGS Image Collection.

Online map with critical thinking questions

often begin to regard their native tongues as economic and social liabilities and stop using them. Of the 6,800 known living languages, more than 400 are believed to be on the verge of extinction (defined as having just a few remaining speakers, all of them elderly), about a quarter of them are used by fewer than 1,000 people, and probably half will be gone by the end of the twenty-first century" (Ostler 2003, 30).

What is striking about the Fourth World's indigenous peoples is the extent to which the groups are widely scattered within many of the globe's pluralistic states. Many indigenous peoples have spread geographically across today's existing state boundaries, through migration, by peoples choosing to move from their homeland, and through forced exodus, as refugees escaping from the persecution by states or from environmental destruction that has made their homeland incapable of supporting life. These dispersions have erased the capacity of most states to assert that their country is populated by a single ethnic nationality (see Map 6.2). Thus, indigenous peoples such as the sizeable Kurdish mi-

MAP 6.3
The World's Major Civilizations: Will Their Clash Create Global Disorder?
According to the controversial thesis of Samuel P. Huntington, global war is bred today primarily by a "clash of civilizations." This map shows the location of the world's major civilizations, according to Huntington—the Sinic or Chinese, Japanese, Hindu, Islamic, Buddhist, Western, Latin American, the Orthodox Christians in Eastern Europe and Russia, African, Sinic/Western in the Philippines, and Hindu/Islamic in India. Critics of this thesis point out that no "civilization" is homogeneous in language, beliefs, or attitudes, and that the characteristics of any civilization fail to predict how people identified with it will act—as shown by the tendency for most clashes to be *within* a civilization or religion, between extremists and those who oppose them, rather than between civilizations.
SOURCE: Huntington (1999b, 17).

■ **cultural domains** groups that share a common intellectual heritage and values and do not recognize national borders when they define their identities and loyalties.

■ **clash of civilizations** political scientist Samuel Huntington's controversial thesis that in the twenty-first century the globe's major civilizations will conflict with one another, leading to anarchy and warfare similar to that resulting from conflicts between states over the past five hundred years.

norities of Turkey, Iraq, and Syria have members living in more than one of the globe's existing independent states. Linked together by common ancestry across national borders, these peoples form transnational **cultural domains** that share a common heritage and place higher value on ideals other than patriotic loyalty to particular states. Our world is composed of at least eight distinct transnational cultural communities, including European, Chinese, Russian, Hispanic, Islamic, Hindu, and both Black African and South African identities (Chaliand and Rageau 1993, 37). And, as a popular extension of this pessimistic thesis, Samuel P. Huntington (1996, 2001a) predicted that a **clash of civilizations** would occur between or among the seven or eight major "universalistic civilizations," such as a world war between the West and Islam (see Map 6.3). He stresses the constructivist interpretation that people identify with, and organize their activities around, the cultural values in their separate civilization, not their state, and forecasts that conflict between such NGO-centered transnational

MAP 6.4
Major Religions of the World

People everywhere seek a power higher than themselves to give meaning and purpose to their lives, and many accept one or another of the world's major religions for this purpose. There are compelling reasons for the quest, in an otherwise rootless and chaotic world, because life for many people is shallow without a deity to respect and a religious code of conduct to follow. This map shows where the world's major religious affiliations have attracted a dominant following. The chart on the bottom right provides an estimate of the number of people who adhere to the four largest religions in the world today—Buddhism, Christianity, Hinduism, and Islam. High birthrates in Asia and Africa make Islam the world's fastest growing major religion.

SOURCE: Adapted from *National Geographic,* August 1999 supplement: NG Maps/NGS Image Collection.

Online map with critical thinking questions

groupings is likely. That prediction proved rather prophetic on September 11, 2001, when the Al Qaeda terrorist network attacked the United States to vent the anger of its extremist Islamic members against the West (see Chapters 1, 3, and 11; Howell 2003). "What recent events demonstrate is that ethnicity, and race [and cultural conflict] are issues that are not disappearing and becoming less important. . . . Recent processes of global change, often glossed under the term globalization, are rapidly changing the contexts under which ethnic [and cultural] conflict arises [which] are no longer, if they ever were, entirely local"

(T. Hall 2004). That proposition suggests the need to turn from ethnic groups as NGOs to consider how religious movements operate as transnationally active NGOs.

Religious Movements

In theory, religion would seem a natural worldwide force for global unity and harmony. Yet millions have died in the name of religion. The Crusades between the eleventh and fourteenth centuries were originally justified by Pope Urban II in 1095 to combat Muslim aggression, but the fighting left millions of Christians and Muslims dead and, "in terms of atrocities, the two sides were about even [as both religions embraced] an ideology in which fighting was an act of self sanctification" (*Economist,* January 5, 1996). Similarly, the "not so holy wars" in the religious conflicts during the Thirty Years' War (1618–48) between Catholics and Protestants killed nearly one-fourth of all Europeans.

Many of the world's more than 6 billion people are affiliated in some form with a **religious movement**—a politically active organization based on strong religious convictions. At the most abstract level, a religion is a system of thought shared by a group that provides its members an object of devotion and a code of behavior by which they can ethically judge their actions. This definition points to commonalities across the great diversity of organized religions in the world, but it fails to capture that diversity. The world's principal religions vary greatly in the theological doctrines or beliefs they embrace. They also differ widely in the size of their followings, in the geographical locations where they are most prevalent (see Map 6.4), and in the extent to which they engage in political efforts to direct international affairs.

These differences make it risky to generalize about the impact of religious movements on world affairs. Those who study religious movements comparatively note that a system of belief provides religious followers with their main source of identity, and that this identification with and devotion to their religion springs from the natural human need to find a set of values with which to evaluate the meaning of life and the consequences of choices. Unfortunately this need sometimes leads believers of a religious creed to perceive the values of their own religion as superior to those of others, which often results in intolerance. The proponents of most organized religious movements believe that their religion should be universal—that is, accepted by everyone throughout the world. To confirm their faith in their religious movement's natural superiority, many organized religions actively proselytize to convert nonbelievers to their faith, engaging in evangelical crusades to win over nonbelievers and followers of other religions. Conversion is usually achieved by persuasion through missionary activities. But at times conversion has been achieved by the sword, tarnishing the reputations of some international religious movements (see Controversy: Are Religious Movements Causes of War or Sources of Transnational Harmony?).

In evaluating the impact of religious movements on international affairs, it is important to distinguish carefully the high ideals of doctrines from the activities of the people who head these religious bodies. The two realms are not the same, and each can be judged fairly only against the standards they set for themselves. To condemn what large-scale religious movements sometimes do administratively when they abuse the principles of the religions they manage does not mean that the principles themselves deserve condemnation. Moreover, many

■ **religious movement**
a set of beliefs, practices, and ideas administered politically by a religious group to promote the worship of its conception of a transcendent diety or its principles for conduct.

The Fusion of Church and State Religion, politics, and violence are seldom seen as contributing to one another. But in many countries, religious bodies are supported by the armies of the state and the state supports the transnational activities of religious movements. Consider South America, for instance, where the powerful Roman Catholic Church has often worked hand in hand with the governments the church supports. At the same time, proponents of "liberation theology" have joined forces with revolutionary groups in the so-called Marxist-Catholic alliance to bring about reforms in the repressive governments they oppose.

students of international relations draw a causal linkage between the activities of religious movements and the outbreak of political conflict and terrorism, arguing that religions powerfully condition how people react to the members of other cultures and faith with whom they come into contact (Juergensmyer 2003; Haynes 2004). But this does not apply to all religions. Consider the Hindu ideology of tolerance of different religions, which teaches that there are many paths to truth and accepts pluralism among diverse populations. Similarly, Buddhism preaches pacifism, as did early Christianity, which prohibited Christians from serving in the armies of the Roman Empire (later, by the fourth century, only Christians were permitted to serve when church and state became allies). But, notwithstanding the propensity for religious institutions to subordinate their beliefs to the state in order to survive and to increase public popularity, some observers maintain that otherwise pacificist and humanitarian religions at times are inclined to oppose each other violently, despite their professed doctrines of tolerance. When they do, religious movements become sources of international aggression, especially when they become radical, heavily involved in political action on a global scale, and fanatically dedicated to the promotion of their cause. The leaders of **extreme militant religious movements** are convinced that those

■ **extreme militant religious movements** politically active organizations based on strong religious convictions, whose members are fanatically devoted to the global promotion of their religious beliefs.

CONTROVERSY

ARE RELIGIOUS MOVEMENTS CAUSES OF WAR OR SOURCES OF TRANSNATIONAL HARMONY?

After 9/11, debate about the impact of religion on international conflict intensified, because many believed that the terrorist attacks were motivated by religious fanatics in the Islamic Al Qaeda global terrorist organization. As a result, the "religious roots of terrorism" (Juergensmeyer 2003) and of religious opposition to democracy in the Global South (Shah 2004) have received much attention, as have religions and religious bodies acting as NGO global actors more generally (Haynes 2004).

"To do harm, to promote violence and conflict in the name of religion," said Pope John Paul II in Egypt after fighting between Christians and Muslims led to bloodshed in 2000, "is a terrible contradiction and a great offense against God. But past and present history give us many examples of such misuse of religion." Yet it is difficult to understand the religious origins of violence because most people equate religion with peace, compassion, and forgiveness, not hatred or intolerance. Indeed, because high ideals inspire the believers of nearly all the world's major religious movements, many of the principles religions espouse are very similar and conducive to peaceful relations between people. They all voice respect and reverence for the sanctity of life and acceptance of all people as equal creations of a deity, regardless of race or color. These are noble ideals. Religions speak to universal principles, across time and place—to enduring values in changing times. Moreover, they recognize no boundaries for their eternal validity—no north, south, east, or west—but only true virtue wherever found and the relevance of moral precepts (e.g., the prohibition of killing and the value of working for the betterment of humankind throughout the world).

If all the world's great religious movements espouse universalistic ideals, why are those same religions increasingly criticized as sources of international conflict—of exclusivism, hatred, terror, and war? This, in the age of religious conflict and political violence, is a boiling controversy. What do you think?

In evaluating the role of religious NGOs in international affairs, consider first the view of sociologists of religion who contend that religious hostility results from the fact that universalistic religions are managed by organizations that often adopt a particularistic and dogmatic outlook (see Juergensmeyer 2003). The virtues that religions uphold ironically can become weapons against those who do not hold such views. Followers of a religion may conceive the world and history through an ideological lens that views one deity protecting a single people against inferior others and, in an effort to believe in unshakable doctrines, reject the attempt to separate what they wish to be true from what they or other religions think to be true. This constructed reality inspires an ethic that justifies violence, plunder, and conquest, in part because outsiders tend to be seen as threatening rivals whose loyalty and allegiance to other deities represents a challenge to their own religion's claim of universal worldwide applicability. In a word, religious movements often practice intolerance—disrespect for diversity and the right of people to freely embrace another religion's beliefs. The next logical step is for fanatics to paint these imagined enemies as evil, unworthy of mercy, and to justify brutal violence against them.

However, using this violence as an argument against religion is controversial. It is dangerous to accept stereotypes of religious groups as responsible for relentless barrages of terrorism. Paganistic and atheistic societies recognizing no higher deity have equally long histories of waging violent wars against external enemies and their own people. Meanwhile, many religions perform ably the mission of peace making, and in fact most religious bodies have historically coexisted peacefully for centuries.

It is important for you to weigh objectively the evidence about the impact of religious NGOs on world affairs. In so doing, take into account the impact of this controversy on theories of world politics and world order. The inclination of extremist religious movements to evoke prejudice and aggression has led some realist theorists of international politics to conclude that such movements are more a menace than a pacific influence. Observing that most wars have been fought in the name of religion, these realist critics ask the world to acknowledge the viciousness and mean-spiritedness of followers who betray their religion's humanistic and global values by championing a style of religious thought that denies that morality is about nourishing life, not destroying it. What do you think?

who do not share their convictions must be punished, and that compromise is unacceptable.

While not all radical religious movements involved in politics are alike, they share certain similar characteristics:

1. Militant religious political movements tend to view existing government authority as corrupt and illegitimate because it is secular and not sufficiently rigorous in upholding religious authority or religiously sanctioned social and moral values.
2. They attack the inability of government to address the domestic ills of the society in which the movement exists. In many cases the religious movement substitutes itself for the government at the local level and is involved in education, health, and other social welfare programs.
3. They subscribe to a particular set of behavior and opinions that they believe political authority must reflect, promote, and protect in all governmental and social activities. This generally means that government and all of its domestic and foreign activities must be in the hands of believers or subject to their close oversight.
4. They are universalists: unlike ethnic movements, they tend to see their views as part of the inheritance of everyone who is a believer. This tends to give them a trans-state motivation, a factor that then translates their views on legitimacy of political authority into a larger context for action. In some cases, this means that international boundaries are not recognized as barriers to the propagation of the faith, even if this means they resort to violence.
5. They are exclusionists: they relegate all conflicting opinions on appropriate political and social order to the margins—if they do not exclude them altogether. This translates as second-class citizenship for any nonbeliever in any society where such a view predominates.
6. Finally, they are militant, willing to use coercion to achieve the only true end. (Shultz and Olson 1994, 9–10)

Although militant religious movements are not the only nonstate actors whose ideologies and activities may contribute to violence, many experts believe that they tend to stimulate five specific types of international activities. The first is **irredentism**—the attempt by a dominant religion or ethnic group to reclaim previously possessed territory in an adjacent region from a foreign state that now controls it. The NGO group often rationalizes the use of force for this purpose. The second is **secession**, or **separative revolts**—the attempt by a religious (or ethnic) minority to break away from an internationally recognized state in a secessionist or separative revolt. Third, militant religions tend to incite migration, the departure of religious minorities from their countries of origin to escape persecution. Whether they move by force or by choice, the result, a fourth consequence of militant religion, is the same: the emigrants create **diasporas**, or communities that live abroad in host countries but maintain economic, political, and emotional ties with their homelands (Sheffer 2003). Finally, a fifth effect of militant religions is **international terrorism** in the form of support for radical coreligionists abroad (Homer-Dixon 2005; Sageman 2004).

If we critically inspect the compound consequences of the activities of militant religious movements, we come away with the impression that religious movements not only bring people together but also divide them. Religious

■ **irredentism**
efforts by an ethnonational or religious group to regain control of territory by force so that existing state boundaries will no longer separate the group.

■ **secession, or separative revolts**
a religious or ethnic minority's efforts, often by violent means, to gain independent statehood by separating territory from an established sovereign state.

■ **diasporas**
the migration of religious or ethnic groups to foreign lands despite their continuation of affiliation with the land and customs of their origin.

■ **international terrorism**
the use of terrorism against targets in other countries.

movements often challenge state authority, and religion-driven separatism can tear countries apart. Against this prophecy, we must contemplate another dimension of the sometimes close connection between religions and states: Many states actively support particular religions while repressing minority religions. States and religions are closely allied in many countries, with each reinforcing the other's power through many channels of contact, communication, and cooperation.

In the information age of disappearing borders, money matters, and this makes multinational corporations also increasingly influential as nonstate actors connecting cash flow and people together globally in ways that may be eroding the sovereignty that states have previously taken as an unchanging given.

Multinational Corporations and Transnational Banks

■ **multinational corporations (MNCs)** business enterprises headquartered in one state that invest and operate extensively in other states.

■ **globalization** the integration of states, through increasing contact, communication, and trade, to create a holistic, single global system in which the process of change increasingly binds people together in a common fate.

■ **foreign direct investment (FDI)** an investment in a country involving a long-term relationship and control of an enterprise by nonresidents and including equity capital, reinvestment of earnings, other long-term capital, and short-term capital as shown in the balance of payments.

Multinational corporations (MNCs)—business enterprises organized in one society with activities in another growing out of direct investment abroad—are a third major type of NGO. MNCs have grown dramatically in scope and potential influence with the **globalization** of the world political economy since World War II (see Chapters 8 and 9). As a result of their growing resources of power, MNCs have provoked both animosity and enthusiastic acceptance. As advocates of liberal free trade and as active contributors to the globalization of world politics, MNCs generate both credit for the positive aspects of free trade and globalization and blame for their costs.

The immense and growing size of MNCs make these corporate NGOs—sometimes called transnational corporations (TNCs)—objects of concern and controversy. MNCs cast a shadow over global trade, cross-border investments, and production, because together they account, according to the United Nations, for approximately one-fourth of world economic production, two-thirds of the world's exports, and one-third of the stock of all **foreign direct investment (FDI)**, formally defined by the IMF as "ownership of assets in one country by residents of another for purposes of controlling the use of those assets." The value of foreign direct investment, and thus the importance of MNCs in the global economy, has grown dramatically in the last twenty years, and this trend has expanded MNCs' influence and reach: "There are approximately 63,459 parent firms that together own a total of 689,520 foreign affiliates [and] employ some 86 million people worldwide" (Oatley 2004, 176). This penetration and profile positions the biggest MNCs to propel changes in relations between countries and within them. Consider Wal-Mart, with annual sales of more than $250 billion and 1.3 million employees, which every week attracts 100 million customers in its 49,000 stores worldwide. Wal-Mart buys $7.5 billion worth of goods directly from China each year, and another $7.5 billion from China's suppliers (*Economist*, April 17, 2004, 67).

In the past, MNCs were headquartered almost exclusively in the United States, Europe, and Japan, and their common practice was to make short-term investments in the Global South's plants, sales corporations, and mining operations, reflected in the fact that in the late 1900s about 80 percent of all MNCs' employees worked in the developing countries, where wages were lower, to bolster corporate profits at the parent headquarters. But no longer. "More and more multinationals will shift the operation and control of key business functions away from their home office [to transfer] white-collar professionals. . . . A growing number of companies are setting up regional headquarters or relocating specific headquarter functions elsewhere. . . . [In fact,] 829 headquarter operations of multinationals were relocated between January 2002 and March 2003, nearly a quarter of them in developing countries" (Hindle 2004, 97–98). Such outsourcing of management to locations where wages and costs are lower but skills are substantial is likely to continue, accelerating the consolidation of the global economy into a seamless integrated web. This outsourcing is now eagerly welcomed by the developing countries of the Global South, where once MNC domination was resisted, as a means to economic growth. The spread of digital information technology contributes to this rapid dispersion of MNCs' managers worldwide.

MNC expansion has been facilitated by **transnational banks (TNBs)**, another type of global NGO whose revenues and assets are primarily generated by financial transactions in the international economy. TNBs have become major forces in the world political economy. They have contributed to the globalization process that has led to financial integration worldwide at the same time that globalization has made international banks critical to global economic stability (as illustrated by the collapse of lending following occasional banking crises and the costs of recapitalizing, reorganizing, or liquidating insolvent banks by countries). At the start of 2000, the combined assets of the world's twenty largest banks exceeded $425 trillion, a staggering figure attesting to the consolidation of the highly profitable control of financial resources in a highly globalized economy. The major banks in the world have formed strategic alliances and have been merging rapidly with banks abroad to expand, with an eye toward maximizing their already huge revenues. The mergers among some of the largest TNBs from the United States, the eurocurrency area, and Japan and Britain are a sign of global banking's slow but steady consolidations.

The TNBs funnel trade and help to reduce the meaning of states' borders by making each state's economy dependent on other states' economies through the transfer of capital through international loans and investments. "The current environment of the MNC in the era of globalization is thus one of emergent alliances and coalitions across a broad array of actors" (Katzenstein and Lenway 2001). Together, TNBs and MNCs redistribute wealth and income in the world economy, contributing to the economic development of some states and the stagnation of others.

One feared consequence in the Global South is that the TNBs advance the rich Global North at the South's expense, because 77 percent of foreign direct investment is funneled into the richest countries with the poorest countries typically receiving very little (World Bank 2005a, 263). Like MNCs, therefore, TNBs spread the rewards of globalization unequally and inequitably, increasing wealth for a select group of countries and marginalizing the others.

Through their loans to the private sector, TNBs have made capital highly mobile and expanded the capacity of MNCs to lead the way in reducing differences across countries' tastes, lifestyles, and consumer products sold. As MNCs have grown in scope and power, concern has understandably been raised about whether their efforts to remove state barriers to foreign investments and trade is undermining the ability of seemingly sovereign states to control their own economies and therefore their own fates and cultures.

The benefits and costs attributed to MNCs as they have risen to a position of prominence since World War II have been many and complex. This has

■ **transnational banks (TNBs)**
the globe's top banking firms, whose financial activities are concentrated in transactions that cross state borders.

made them highly controversial nonstate actors, especially in the Global South where people frequently see MNCs as the cause of exploitation and poverty (see Chapter 5).

MNCs are seen as increasingly influential NGOs because the world's giant producing, trading, and servicing corporations have become the primary agents of the globalization of production. Table 6.2 captures their importance in world politics, ranking firms by annual sales and states by GNI. The profile shows that of the world's top one hundred economic entities, among the top fifty multinationals account for only fourteen, but in the next fifty, they account for forty. MNCs' financial clout thus rivals or exceeds that of most countries.

Wealth and power remain highly concentrated; the big seem to get bigger. "The 100 largest MNCs account for more than 15 percent of total foreign assets controlled by all MNCs, and for 22 percent of their total sales." Equally revealing is the geographical concentration of economic resources: "The 50 largest MNCs from developing countries control only $105 billion of foreign assets, less than 10 percent of the assets controlled by the 50 largest MNCs based in the advanced industrialized countries" (Oatley 2004, 171).

In addition to their global reach and economic power, MNCs' involvement in the domestic political affairs of local or host countries is also a controversial issue. In some instances this concern has extended to MNCs' involvement in the domestic politics of their home countries, where they actively lobby their governments for more liberal trade and investment policies that will enhance the profitability of their business activities abroad. In turn, both host and home governments have sometimes used MNCs as instruments in their foreign policy strategies. Perhaps the most notorious instance of an MNC's intervention in the politics of a host state occurred in Chile in the early 1970s when International Telephone and Telegraph (ITT) tried to protect its interests in the profitable Chiltelco telephone company by seeking to prevent the election of Marxist-oriented Salvador Allende as president and, once Allende was elected, pressured the U.S. government to disrupt the Chilean economy. Eventually Allende was overthrown by a military dictatorship. More recently, the huge profits and activities of corporate giant Halliburton to rebuild the infrastructure of Iraq in 2004 after the U.S. occupation provoked widespread complaints that this MNC was exploiting the circumstances to line its pockets, at U.S. taxpayers' expense.

Because MNCs assist in promoting free trade and are active participants in the process by which governments have reached agreements on rules liberalizing economic transactions in the global marketplace, it is tempting to conclude that MNCs are a threat to state power. However, this interpretation overlooks the fact that at the same time MNCs have grown in size, the regulatory power of states has grown.

> Only the state can defend corporate interests in international negotiations over trade, investment, and market access. Agreements over such things as airline routes, the opening of banking establishments, and the right to sell insurance are not decided by corporate actors who gather around a table; they are determined by diplomats and bureaucrats. Corporations must turn to governments when they have interests to protect or advance. (Kapstein 1991–92, 56)

Still, the blurring of the boundaries between internal and external affairs adds potency to the political role that MNCs unavoidably play as nonstate actors at the intersection of foreign and domestic policy. The symbolic invasion of national

TABLE 6.2

Countries and Corporations: A Ranking by Size of Economy and Revenues

Rank	County/Corporation	GNP/Revenues (Billions of Dollars)	Rank	County/Corporation	GNP/Revenues (Billions of Dollars)
1	United States	10207.9	51	VOLKSWAGON	98.6
2	Japan	4323.9	52	NIPPON TELEGRAPH & TELEPHONE	98.2
3	Germany	1876.3	53	Egypt, Arab Rep.	97.6
4	United Kingdom	1510.8	54	ING GROUP	95.9
5	France	1362.1	55	CITIGROUP	94.7
6	China	1234.2	56	Ireland	90.3
7	Italy	1100.7	57	INTERNATIONAL BUSINESS MACHINES	89.1
8	Canada	702.0	58	Singapore	86.1
9	Mexico	597.0	59	Malaysia	86.1
10	Spain	596.5	60	Philippines	82.4
11	India	494.8	61	AMERICAN INTERNATIONAL GROUP	81.3
12	Brazil	494.5	62	SIEMENS	80.5
13	Korea, Rep.	473.0	63	CARREFOUR	79.8
14	Australia	384.1	64	Colombia	79.6
15	Netherlands	377.6	65	HITACHI	76.4
16	Russian Federation	306.6	66	HEWLETT-PACKARD	73.1
17	Switzerland	263.7	67	HONDA MOTOR	72.3
18	WAL-MART STORES	263.0	68	MCKESSON	69.5
19	Belgium	237.1	69	U.S. POSTAL SERVICE	68.5
20	BRITISH PETROLEUM	232.6	70	VERIZON COMMUNICATIONS	67.8
21	Sweden	231.8	71	ASSICURAZIONI GERNERALI	66.8
22	EXXON MOBILE	222.9	72	SONY	66.4
23	ROYAL DUTCH/SHELL GROUP	201.7	73	Chile	66.3
24	GENERAL MOTORS	195.3	74	MATSUSHITA ELECTRONIC INDUSTRIAL	66.2
25	Austria	192.1	75	NISSAN MOTOR	65.8
26	Saudi Arabia	186.8	76	NESTLE	64.4
27	Poland	176.6	77	HOME DEPOT	64.8
28	Norway	175.8	78	BERKSHIRE HATHAWAY	63.9
29	Turkey	173.3	79	NIPPON LIFE INSURANCE	63.9
30	Hong Kong, China	167.6	80	ROYAL AHOLD	63.5
31	FORD MOTOR	164.5	81	DEUTSCHE TELECOM	63.2
32	Denmark	162.6	82	PEUGEOT	61.4
33	DAIMLERCHRYSLER	156.6	83	Pakistan	60.9
34	Argentina	154.0	84	ALTRIA GROUP	60.7
35	TOYOTA MOTOR	153.1	85	METRO	60.7
36	Indonesia	149.9	86	AVIVA	59.7
37	GENERAL ELECTRIC	134.2	87	ENI	59.3
38	Finland	124.2	88	MUNICH RE GROUP	59.1
39	Greece	123.9	89	CREDIT SUISSE	59.0
40	Thailand	123.3	90	STATE GRID	58.3
41	TOTAL	118.4	91	HSBC HOLDINGS	57.6
42	ALLIANZ	114.9	92	BNP PARIBAS	57.3
43	South Africa	113.4	93	VODAFONE	56.8
44	CHEVRONTEXACO	112.9	94	CARDINAL HEALTH	56.8
45	Iran, Islamic Rep.	112.9	95	FORTIS	56.7
46	AXA	111.9	96	STATE FARM INSURANCE	56.1
47	Portugal	109.1	97	Czech Republic	56.0
48	Israel	105.2	98	SINOPEC	55.1
49	Venezuela, RB	102.3	99	SAMSUNG ELECTRONICS	54.4
50	CONOCOPHILLIPS	99.5	100	Peru	54.0

By integrating production and marketing their products worldwide, MNCs are dominating the global economy. As a result, MNCs rival many countries in wealth and are translating that income into influence as NGO actors. The value of MNC global mergers and acquisitions rose five-fold in the 1990s, to more than $3.6 trillion in 2000 (*Economist*, January 27, 2001, 61). This trend suggests that "every day the line between companies and countries blurs a bit more . . . as the walls around the world disappear. . . . The sheer size and power that some of these companies are amassing" leaves few ways to prevent "big monopolies from overwhelming consumers and preventing big business from overwhelming democratic government," observers Thomas Friedman (2000).

SOURCE: MNC revenues, *Fortune* (July 26, 2004), p. 163; countries GNI, World Bank, *World Development Indicators 2004*, pp. 14–16. This table was prepared by Daniel R. Sabia III and Young-Hoon Song.

borders by MNCs can be expected to arouse the anger of many local nationalists who fear the loss of income, jobs, and control to foreign corporate interests. Because multinationals often make decisions over which national political leaders have little control, their growing influence appears to be contributing to the erosion of the global system's major organizing principle—that the state alone should be sovereign. "The growth of trade within MNCs reduces states' control by making it more difficult to collect taxes" (M. Wolf 2001). Because "the reach and influence of multinationals, large and small, is far greater than the official statistics suggest [and] the relationship between governments and multinationals is characterized by a complex distribution of benefits," states have every reason to feel that MNCs are stripping away their sovereign control inasmuch as "multinational corporations increasingly demand the freedom they need to optimize their operations across borders" (Stopford 2001). And in fact, in some respects states *are* losing control of their national economies as MNCs merge with one another and, in the process, cease to remain tied to any one parent state or region.

"Who owns whom?" cannot be answered anymore because the MNCs are truly multinational and therefore connected to no single country. "Half of Xerox's employees work on foreign soil and less than half of Sony's employees are Japanese. More than 50 percent of IBM's revenues originate overseas; the same is true for Citigroup, ExxonMobil, DuPont, Procter & Gamble, and many other corporate giants. Joint ventures no longer are merely a domestic decision. Corning obtains one half of its profits from foreign joint ventures with Samsung in Korea, Asahi Glass in Japan, and Ciba-Geigy in Switzerland" (Weidenbaum 2004, 26–27). How can any single state manage such multinational giants when no country can claim that an MNC is "one of ours"?

Controlling the resulting webs of corporate interrelationships, joint ventures, and shared ownership for any particular state purpose is nearly impossible. Part of the reason is that about 30 to 40 percent of world trade in goods and services occurs *within* multinationals, from one branch to another (Oatley 2004, 171). Joint production and **strategic corporate alliances** to create temporary phantom "virtual corporations" undermine states' ability to identify the MNCs they seek to control. "There is widespread concern that MNCs are becoming truly 'stateless' [as] the explosion of strategic alliances is transforming the corporate landscape" with more than ten thousand strategic alliances estimated to be forged each year recently (Stopford 2001, 74–75). "You can't find targets any more, and if you aim at a target you often find it's yourself," observes Richard J. Barnet, coauthor of *Global Reach* (Barnet and Müller 1974).

The multinationals' potential long-run influence is depicted in *Global Dreams: Imperial Corporations and the New World Order:*

> By acquiring earth-spanning technologies, by developing products that can be produced anywhere and sold everywhere, by spreading credit around the world, and by connecting global channels of communication that can penetrate any village or neighborhood, these institutions we normally think of as economic rather than political, private rather than public, are becoming the world empires of the twenty-first century. The architects and managers of these space-age business enterprises understand that the balance of power in world politics has shifted in recent years from territorially bound governments to companies that can roam the world. As the hopes and pretensions of government shrink almost everywhere, these imperial

■ **strategic corporate alliances**
cooperation between multinational corporations and foreign companies in the same industry, driven by the movement of MNC manufacturing overseas.

corporations are occupying public space and exerting a more profound influence over the lives of ever larger numbers of people. (Barnet and Cavanagh 1994, 14)

As multinational corporations play increasingly larger roles in world politics, the community of sovereign states will be forced to confront the many issues raised by an economic and business sector that has turned global. How will they respond? Assessing the future requires a theoretical examination of contemporary thinking regarding the MNCs and the other types of NGOs.

Are NGOs Capable of Tranforming World Politics?

"In global politics, interest group pluralism is growing" as citizens increasingly participate in NGOs in order to gain power "in the global institutions that shape people's daily lives" (Falk and Strauss 2001). Inspired by this trend, many people see NGOs as a democratic force in world politics that can empower individuals by giving them a voice in the decisions leading to transformations in international affairs. NGOs, many believe, can exert influence over the direction of global conditions. This viewpoint maintains that "alongside the necessary and imperfect interstate institutional framework, there is developing an informal political process that supplements the formal process of cooperative relations among states. . . . These organizations and the multiple channels of access across borders," Robert Keohane and Joseph Nye (2001a) explain, "are able to put increasing leverage on states. . . . The combination of private, transgovernmental, and transnational actors is creating an incipient, albeit imperfect, civil society at the global level."

Is this liberal **constructivist** image of the processes by which trends and transformations in world politics are determined realistic or exaggerated? Are NGOs influential? Or is a rival hypothesis—that NGOs remain relatively powerless in global governance—more accurate?

What is clear is that networks of transnational activists have formed NGOs at an accelerating rate, and through their pressure have performed an educational service that has demonstratively contributed to the emergence of a global **civil society**.

These networks of social movements have altered the international culture by reshaping values about international conduct (Barnett and Finnemore 2004). Further, they have registered some dramatic successes in their efforts to bring about global changes, as seen by the agreements reached on the International Criminal Court, the Kyoto Protocol on global warming, and the Landmine Convention. That said, skeptics warn that the NGOs' power has been exaggerated on some issues like the environment and human rights and is very weak on others, such as national security. The tendency for reform movements to mobilize groups aimed at countering and resisting the reforms undermines the capacity of a network to push history forward rapidly in a particular direction. But even more striking is the failure of NGOs to become "a serious rival to the power and processes of the state"; their goals of transforming the dominant processes of policy making and structure of corporate capitalism have not met with success (Price 2003). Indeed, it could be argued that NGOs, some well financed by states, MNCs, and IGOs, "have tended to reinforce rather than counter existing power structures" (Stephenson 2000).

■ **constructivist**
a scholarly approach to inquiry emphasizing the importance of agents (people and groups) and the shared meanings they construct to define their identities, interests, and institutions— understandings that influence their international behavior.

■ **civil society**
a community that embraces shared norms and ethnical standards to collectively manage problems without coercion and through peaceful and democratic procedures for decision making aimed at improving human welfare.

According to this thesis, world politics is still controlled by states—especially the great powers; it is a world ruled by the powerful, in which nonstate actors have little real influence. Even the United Nations, so this assessment concludes, "still represents a predominately state-centric approach to global governing at a time when this approach is being questioned and undermined" (Knight 2000; Opello and Rosow 2004).

Seen through the spectacles of **realism,** the critical choices that direct global destiny are made by the most powerful states. Global governance is not a product of the values and interests of the world's more than 6 billion people at large, organized into tens of thousands of nongovernmental organizations; it is dominated by a privileged minority, namely, the great powers, which possess the means to see that the most important global policy decisions are made to protect their national interests.

Juxtaposed to this conclusion is an alternative explanation: Whereas individuals do influence international policy by organizing themselves into groups to petition powerful governments on behalf of their shared interests and values, their individual efforts are compromised by the opposition of other NGOs resisting the first group of NGOs' endeavors to push international relations in a particular direction. Skeptics also point out that many NGOs represent powerful vested interests that work secretly behind the scenes to lobby for global policies that protect both the powerful through private commercial interests and the great powers who are their primary clients, at the expense of collective interests. Thus, the question is raised, Precisely how influential and effective are grassroot NGOs in their efforts to lobby the powerful for new global rules and **regimes** that put human welfare and the collective interests of all humanity above particular, parochial national interests? Studies of the impact of NGO pressure on global policy making suggest some conclusions that reduce confidence in the expectation that NGO pressure can lead to far-reaching reforms, even transformations, in the conduct of international relations:

- Interest group activity operates as an ever present, if limited, constraint on global policy making, but the impact *varies with the issue* and their influence is weakest on the most important problems on the global agenda.

- Similarly, the occasions when private NGOs are most influential are rare. The influences are greatest with respect to a particular issue—such as nuclear nonproliferation—when in the interest of the great powers.

- As a general rule, NGOs are relatively weak in the **high politics** of international security, because states remain in control of defense policy and are relatively unaffected by external NGO pressures. Conversely, the NGOs' clout is highest with respect to issues in **low politics,** such as protecting endangered species (e.g., whales) or combatting global warming, which are of concern to great and small powers alike.

- The influence between state governments and NGOs is reciprocal, but it is more probable that government officials manipulate transnational interest groups than that NGOs exercise influence over governments' foreign policies.

- Single-issue NGO interest groups have more influence than large general-purpose organizations.

- NGOs sometimes seek *inaction* from governments and maintenance of the

---

■ **realism**
a paradigm based on the premise that the state is the only really important actor and that world politics is essentially and unchangeably a struggle among self-interested states for power and position under anarchy, with each competing state pursuing its own national interests.

■ **regimes**
norms, rules, and procedures for interaction agreed to by a set of states.

■ **high politics**
geostrategic issues of national and international security that pertain to matters of war and peace.

■ **low politics**
the category of global issues related to the economic, social, demographic, and environmental aspects of relations between governments and people.

status quo; such efforts are generally more successful than efforts to bring about major changes in international relations. For this reason NGOs are often generally seen as agents of policy continuities.

The foregoing characteristics of NGO efforts to redirect global policy suggest that the mere presence of such groups, and the mere fact they are organized with the intent of persuasion, does not guarantee their penetration of the global policy-making process. On the whole, NGOs have participation without real power and involvement without real influence, given that the ability of any *one* to exert influence is offset by the tendency for *countervailing powers* to materialize over the disposition of any major issue. That is, as any particular coalition of NGOs works together on a common cause and begins to be powerful, other groups threatened by the changes advocated tend to spring up to balance it. When an interest group seeks vigorously to push policy in one direction, other nonstate actors—aroused that their established interests are being disturbed—are stimulated to push policy in the opposite direction. Global policy making consequently resembles a taffy pull: every nonstate actor attempts to pull policy in its own direction while resisting the pulls of others, with the result that often it appears that the quest for consensus proves elusive and the international community's posture toward many global problems fails to move in any single direction.

This balance process between opposing actors helps to account for the reason why so few global issues are resolved. Competition stands in the way of consensus, and contests of will over international issues are seldom settled. No side can ever claim permanent victory, for each decision that takes international policy in one direction merely sets the stage for the next round of the contest, with the possibility that the losers of the moment will be winners tomorrow. The result is usually a kind of continuous battleground over the primary issues on the global agenda, from which materializes no permanent resolution of the struggle. The debate and contests between those wishing to make protection of the environment a global priority and those placing economic growth ahead of environmental preservation provides one among many examples.

As the world grows more interdependent and transactions across state borders increase through the movement of people, information, and traded products, it is likely that world politics nonetheless will be increasingly affected by the activities of both IGO and NGO nonstate actors. Even though nonstate actors are unlikely to join together in a common cause to pressure the international community for radical reforms, their activities (however divided) are likely to challenge the ironlike grip that sovereign states have exercised for more than 350 years in determining the global system's architecture and rules. Ever since the Peace of Westphalia in 1648, states—and especially great powers—have ruled supreme. Nonstate actors were largely pawns at the states' mercy, to be moved at the states' will.

However, states' grip over trends in world politics *has* weakened, and nonstate actors are flexing their muscles in ways that directly challenge states' sovereign control over both their foreign and domestic policies (Alesina and Spolaore 2003). Despite their diversity and divisions, nearly all nonstate actors are animated by a desire to protest the existing organizational apparatus of international relations, in the hope that their voice will produce institutional and legal reforms. Are the pillars of the Westphalian system beginning to crumble, as some believe (see Falk and Strauss 2001; Kegley and Raymond 2002a)? Let us conclude our introduction to nonstate actors with some observations about the rise of nonstate actors and the potential challenge they may make to the states in the global system.

NONSTATE ACTORS: SAVIORS OR STRANGLERS OF THE STATE?

As it becomes increasingly misleading "to view the world as consisting of territorial units each exerting supreme authority within its borders" (Falk 2001b), an accurate conceptualization of contemporary world politics must acknowledge the growing influence of NGOs and IGOs as partners and independent actors. Having observed their diversity and wide-ranging impact, one generalization certainly is apt: nonstate actors will continue to be widely seen as posing a threat to the overriding prominence of states in the management of world affairs. Czech President Václav Havel voiced this sentiment in July 1999 when he argued, "There is every indication that the glory of the nation-state as the culmination of every national community's history . . . has already passed its peak [and] that human beings are more important than the state. In this new world, people—regardless of borders—are connected in millions of different ways: through trade, finance, property, and information."

IGOs and NGOs are both seeking to change the face of international affairs and reshape the global agenda (as a coalition of 160 NGOs from all regions did in October 1998 when they met in Toronto to control the shipment of small arms that they believed were causing misery and destruction worldwide). These global actors were collectively interested in turning the world of states upside down (Clegg 1999).

The question for the future is whether the nation-state system will survive, given the challenges from IGOs, NGOs, and the gales of globalization to their continuing domination. Consider one among many assessments:

> Even if a few states can still defend their territory against an invading army, not even the most powerful can protect its people and cities against a devastating surprise attack by guided missiles, and none can control the flow of images and ideas that shape human tastes and values. The globalized "presence" of Madonna, McDonald's, and Mickey Mouse make a mockery of sovereignty as exclusive territorial control. A few governments do their best to insulate their populations from such influences, but their efforts are growing less effective and run counter to democratizing demands that are growing more difficult to resist. . . . Interdependence and the interpenetration of domestic and international politics, the mobility and globalization of capital and information, and the rising influence of transnational social movements and organizations are among the factors that make it anachronistic to analyze politics as if territorial supremacy continues to be a generalized condition or a useful fiction. In particular, sovereignty, with its stress on the inside/outside distinction as between domestic and international society, seems more misleading than illuminating under current conditions. (Falk 2001b, 790–91).

Rage against Rising Institutional Symbols of Interdependence In the recent past, the meetings attended by finance ministers at such powerful IGOs as the World Bank or the International Monetary Fund drew little interest or publicity. Now, with increasing criticism of the globalization of national economies, these meetings are in the limelight. A backlash against the rising power of multinational corporations—the primary force driving the interdependence of the international economy—is evident, and the major financial IGOs are the most convenient target for protests against IGOs and MNCs, which are increasingly perceived to act like governments. This image is expressed by those who typically portray MNCs as "inherently exploitative . . . globetrotting sweatshop operators, indifferent polluters, and systematic tax evaders" (Stopford 2001). Seen here is one recent outburst, when the meeting of the World Trade Organization mobilized a broad-based coalition of NGOs to challenge this global trend perceived to threaten nationalistic values.

This by no means indicates that the era of state dominance is over, however (see Paul, Ikenberry, and Hall 2003). States retain a (near) monopoly on the use of coercive force in the global system, and they continue to shape the transnational interactions of nonstate actors. The state still molds the activities of nonstate actors more than its behavior is molded by them. It "may be anachronistic, but we have yet to develop an alternative form of societal organization that is able to provide its members with both wealth and power" (Kapstein 1991–92). It is also true that "a gain in power by nonstate actors does not necessarily translate into a loss of power for the state" (Slaughter 1997). We must conclude that whereas it would be premature to abandon the focus on the state in world politics, it would be equally mistaken to exaggerate the state's power as a determinant of the globe's fate and dismiss the expanding role that nonstate actors are playing within the tightening web of interdependent globalization that is eroding the power of states. We cannot ignore the shifts occurring "away from the state—up, down, and sideways—to supra-state, sub-state, and, above all nonstate actors—new players that have multiple allegiances and global reach" (Slaughter 1997). In the new globalized market, it is difficult to distinguish corporations, countries, and other actors in an era of collapsing states and reemergent nations. This is particularly true for the mass of humanity comprising ordinary people everywhere. It is to the circumstances of these individuals, in a world dominated by great powers, authoritarian **Global South** states, powerful global institutions, and huge corporations, to which we turn in the next chapter.

■ **Global South**
a term now often used instead of "Third World" to designate the less-developed countries located primarily in the Southern Hemisphere.

KEY TERMS

intergovernmental organizations (IGOs)
nongovernmental organizations (NGOs)
global level of analysis
realpolitik
politics
anarchy
collective security
Cold War
ideology
Group of 77 (G-77)
regimes
bilateral
G-7
nonintervention norm
rational choice
liberalism
globalization
realism

neoliberal theory
security community
Third Way
European Commission
pooled sovereignty
regimes
devolution
nonstate nations
unitary actor
constructivism
nationalism
ethnopolitical groups
ethnicity
ethnic nationalism
ethnic groups
indigenous peoples
Fourth World
cultural domains
clash of civilizations
religious movement

extreme militant religious movements
irredentism
secession, or separative revolts
diasporas
international terrorism
multinational corporations (MNCs)
globalization
foreign direct investment (FDI)
transnational banks (TNBs)
strategic corporate alliances
constructivist
civil society
realism
regimes
high politics
low politics
Global South

SUGGESTED READING

Barnett, Michael, and Martha Finnemore. *Rules for the World: International Organizations in Global Politics.* Ithaca, N.Y.: Cornell University Press, 2004.

Bomberg, Elizabeth, and Alexander Stubb, eds. *The European Union: How Does It Work?* Oxford, UK: Oxford University Press, 2003.

Dallmayr, Fred. *Dialogue among Civilizations.* London: Palgrave Macmillan, 2004.

Hall, Anthony J. *The American Empire and the Fourth World.* Montreal: McGill-Queen's University Press, 2004.

Haynes, Jeff. "Religion and International Relations: What Are the Issues?" *International Politics* 41 (September 2004): 451–462.

Hilhorst, Dorothea. *The Real World of NGOs: Dis-*

courses, *Diversity and Development*. London: Palgrave, 2003.

Karns, Margaret P., and Karen Mingst. *International Organizations: The Politics and Processes of Global Governance*. Boulder, Colo.: Lynne Rienner, 2004.

Paul, T. V., G. John Ikenberry, and John A. Hall, eds. *The Nation-State in Question*. Princeton, N.J.: Princeton University Press, 2003.

Pease, Kelly-Kate. *International Organizations: Perspectives on Governance in the Twenty-First Century*. Upper Saddle River, N.J.: Prentice Hall, 2003.

Shapiro, Michael T. *Methods and Nations: Cultural Governance and the Indigenous Subject*. New York: Routledge, 2004.

Wallace, William, and Daphne Jostelin, eds. *Nonstate Actors in World Politics*. London: Palgrave, 2002.

Weiss, Thomas G., David P. Forsythe, and Roger A. Coate. *The United Nations and Changing World Politics*, 4th ed. Boulder, Colo.: Westview, 2004.

WHERE ON THE WORLD WIDE WEB?

European Union
http://europa.eu.int/index.htm

The EU is an IGO with regional membership and multiple purposes. Chapter 6 characterizes the authority structure of the EU as one of pooled sovereignty, under which the member states grant the EU legal authority to make some collective decisions for them. After entering the Europa website, explore the main institutions of the EU. What is the European Commission and what are its powers and duties? How does the Court of Justice differ from the UN's International Court of Justice? How many political groupings are represented in the European Parliament? How might these divisions affect the formation of a unified EU foreign policy?

International Monetary Fund
http://www.imf.org/

The International Monetary Fund (IMF) is an IGO with global membership that was created to promote international monetary cooperation and to facilitate the expansion and balanced growth of international trade by promoting exchange stability. It does this by making monetary resources temporarily available to its members. Choose two or three countries of interest to you and see how they have interacted with the IMF. Examine the "What's New" section. What are the main issues discussed here? Which countries or groups of countries are affected? What is the most current information on the size and sources of IMF finances?

North Atlantic Treaty Organization
http://www.nato.int/

The North Atlantic Treaty Organization (NATO) is a military alliance that includes the European states, the United States, and Canada. It was originally formed to protect Europe from the Soviet threat after World War II. Since the end of the Cold War, it has been restructured; it now has an auxiliary membership, the Partnership for Peace (PfP). To see PfP's membership, click on the "Partnerships" link from the NATO home page and then click on the Partnership for Peace link. What characteristics do the PfP member countries share? Although once a regional collective defense organization, NATO has had to redefine its mission since the end of the Cold War. NATO's involvement in Bosnia was the first venture into new terrain. Many question whether it is appropriate for an organization designed for mutual self-protection from external attack to be involved in policing civil wars in Europe. What do you think?

Organization of American States
http://www.oas.org/

The Organization of American States (OAS) is a multipurpose IGO with regional members from North and South America. It is the "region's premier forum for multilateral dialogue and concerted action." The OAS is concerned with issues such as democracy, human rights, trade, environment, and education. Explore one of these challenges by selecting "Key OAS Issues" from the "About the OAS" drop-down menu. How might the United States and other hemispheric countries differ in their views of the challenge and the best way to solve it?

United Nations
http://www.un.org/

The United Nations (UN) is an IGO with global membership that performs multiple purposes. The UN website is organized according to the organization's primary concerns: peace and security, international law, humanitarian affairs, economic and social develop-

WHERE ON THE WORLD WIDE WEB? (continued)

ment, and human rights. Chapter 6 has introduced you to the major UN organs—the General Assembly, the Security Council, Economic and Social Council, and Secretariat. Which organs focus on which areas of concern? Examine the "Daily Briefing" link. What are some important events involving the UN?

World Health Organization
http://www.who.int/

The main goal of the World Health Organization (WHO) is the attainment by all peoples of the highest possible level of health. It defines health as the "state of complete physical, mental, and social well-being and not merely the absence of disease or infirmity." The WHO has been hailed as one of the best examples of how an international organization can benefit the world community. Review the WHO's major achievements and the challenges it faces. Do you think it is possible for the WHO to achieve its goals? Do you agree with its expanded definition of health that includes social well-being? What is WHO doing to combat AIDS/HIV?

The World Trade Organization
http://www.wto.org/

The World Trade Organization (WTO) is an IGO with a global membership and multiple purposes. Its mission is to ensure that trade flows between states as smoothly, predictably, and freely as possible. Decision making within the WTO is by consensus among all 147 member countries. Trade agreements are then ratified by members' legislatures. The WTO also uses a dispute settlement process that focuses on interpreting agreements and ensuring that member countries' trade policies follow them. Click on "WTO News" and "Trade Topics." What important issues is the WTO currently addressing?

Academic Info Religion
http://www.academicinfo.net/religindex.html

Many American students are unfamiliar with the belief systems of non-Western religions. Do you know the differences between Lamaistic and Theravada Buddhists? Find out by visiting the Academic Info Religion website. This site links you with Internet resources for the study of the world's religions. Read passages from the Koran and the Old and New Testaments. Compare and contrast Taoist, Zen, Mormon, Hindu, Gnostic, and Nag Hammadi texts. If your tastes lean more toward mythology and alchemy, you will find them here, too.

INFOTRAC COLLEGE EDITION

Albright, Madeleine K. "United Nations." *Foreign Policy* (September–October 2003).

Huebner, David, and Raja Haddad. "UN-Paid Dues: The Costs of Cooperation." *Harvard International Review* (Summer 2002).

Calleo, David. "A Choice of Europes." *The National Interest* (Spring 2001).

Peang-Meth, Abdulgaffar. "The Rights of Indigenous Peoples and Their Fight for Self-Determination." *World Affairs* (Winter 2002).

For more articles, enter:

"United Nations" in the Subject Guide, and then go to subdivision "management"

"Europe" in the Subject Guide, and then go to subdivision "politics and government"

"indigenous peoples" in the Subject Guide

Go to http://politicalscience.wadsworth.com/kegley10 to access additional resources related to this chapter.

CHAPTER 7

Humanitarian Challenges and the Protection of Human Rights

TOPICS AND THEMES

- Human agency: Putting people into the picture
- Profiling the human condition: Changing levels of human despair and development
  The global refugee crisis
  Indigenous people: Life in the Fourth World
  Gender: The subordinate status of women
- Human rights and the protection of people
- International ethics: Reconciling national interests and human interests
- Humanitarian intervention: Should might be used for the protection of human rights?

- **Controversy** Should Tyranny and Human Rights Violations Justify Humanitarian Intervention?

The elusive pursuit of freedom is shown by these death-row inmates crying for freedom from Iraq's Abu Ghraib prison in 2002, when Saddam Hussein was still in power. Following the American invasion of Iraq to liberate the Iraqi people from such violations of human rights, U.S. military occupation forces, CIA agents, and "outsourced" private U.S. contractors went berserk in 2004 and used the same prison to threaten and carry out rape, electrocution, and dog attacks on Iraqi prisoners, committing war crimes condemned by the International Red Cross that enraged Iraqi Muslims, the U.S. leadership, and the world.

Recognition of the inherent dignity and of the equal and inalienable rights of all members of the human family is the foundation of freedom, justice and peace in the world.

—Universal Declaration of Human Rights, 1948

Over the next twenty-five years, about two billion people will be added to the global population, but only fifty million of them will be in the richer countries. The vast majority will be born with the prospect of growing up in poverty and disillusioned with a world that they will inevitably view as inequitable and unjust. Terrorism is often bred in places where a fast-growing youth population sees hope as more of a taunt than promise.

—JAMES WOLFENSOHN, president of the World Bank, 2004

When we think about international relations, we are inclined to think about the most influential actors and agents that engage in transnational activities—the sovereign states that are regarded as the great powers (Chapter 4), the weaker states of the Global South (Chapter 5), and the global institutions or IGOs that states create (Chapter 6), the general products of countries' decisions made by state agents that produce global trends, such as the accelerating pace of globalization that so profoundly shapes the way the world works. From this perspective, world politics revolves around relations between states and intergovernmental organizations, and most other agents or actors are taken into view only to the degree to which they influence the relationships among the mighty state and nonstate global actors.

The predominant state-centric constructed image of the forces and factors that drive world affairs is helpful in understanding some properties of international relations, such as dynamics of war and economic conditions that propel the rise and fall of the great powers in their rivalry to attain hegemony. However, such a simplifying construction fails to capture the role played by human agency—by the people comprising the human race. Peoples' individual choices are consequential because they combine to produce in countless ways global trends and thereby contribute to transformations shaping the common fate of all people.

If you, as a student of international affairs, are to develop a more complete comprehension of the forces behind the prevailing trends in world politics, it is important to ask the question, How do humans—that is, ordinary individual people—act as agents of global change? What conception of human agency should be constructed? In short, to borrow the famous phrase in Karl Marx's *Capital*, the story of the world is *de te fibula narrator*—"this story is about you."

PUTTING PEOPLE INTO THE PICTURE

Until relatively recently, in the unfolding evolution of the international history of the theoretical study of world politics, the faceless billions of everyday people were neglected. That past theoretical legacy, in this tradition, pictured the mass of humanity as marginalized victims, or left them invisible by painting peoples' fates as controlled by forces over which hapless people have little influence. Fernand Braudel (1973) wrote that "when I think of the individual, I am always inclined to see him imprisoned within a destiny in which he himself has little hand, fixed in a landscape in which the infinite perspectives of the long-term stretch into the distance both behind and before."

When thinking about world affairs, people—the average person—long have been relegated to a mere "subject" whom rulers were traditionally permitted to manipulate to advance their states' interests. "For millennia, human beings saw nothing odd about slavery, about selling and disposing of persons as if they were things" (Ignatieff 2001a).

That vision has been rejected throughout the world. A consensus now supports the view that people are important, that they have worth, and that therefore **ethics** and **morality** belong in the study of international relations. As defined by Ronald Dworkin (2001), "Ethics includes convictions about what kinds of lives are good or bad for a person to lead, and morality includes principles about how a person should treat other people." These principles apply to interstate relations, and are at the heart of all analyses of human rights in world politics.

That consensus notwithstanding, many observers embrace the traditional assumptions of **realism** that vast global forces make people powerless. Realists recognize that people participate politically, but claim they have no real power, because an invisible set of powerful forces described as the "system" gives most human beings only superficial involvement without real influence.

This denigration of the importance and influence of individual human agency today seems increasingly strange, because classic thinking about the world has long concentrated on people and on the essential character of human nature. As the anthropologist Robert Redfield (1962) argued, "Human nature is itself a part of the method [of all analysis]. One must use one's own humanity as a means to understanding. The physicist need not sympathize with his atoms, nor the biologist with his fruit flies, but the student of people and institutions must employ [one's] natural sympathies in order to discover what people think

■ **ethics**
criteria for evaluating right and wrong behavior and the motives by individuals and groups.

■ **morality**
principles about the norms for behavior that should govern actors' interactions.

■ **realism**
the view that states are the most important global actors and that they are relentless competition with one another for position and prosperity in the international hierarchy, dedicated to the promotion of their own interests at the expense of other states.

Human Rights versus States' Rights How a state treats its own citizens was, until very recently, its own business under the nonintervention rule in international law protecting states from external interference in their domestic affairs. Now the global community has defined the humane treatment of people as a fundamental human right, and the UN Security Council has stretched the traditional definition of threats to international peace in order to authorize various kinds of intervention to protect the universal human rights of people within states (see Feinstein and Slaughter 2004). Shown here is an example of the kind of state behavior at the center of the debate: to deter crime, China's leaders have ordered the execution of hundreds of alleged criminals, and many other states have complained that this gross violation of civil liberties without fair trial warrants reprisals.

■ **civil society**
a community composed of citizens that create institutions that protect civil liberties (such as free speech and freedom from arbitrary governmental interference) and that use peaceful methods for conflict resolution.

or feel." A humanistic interpretation is needed that gives people status and value. Moreover, in the global community's fledging **civil society** there has recently emerged a normative consensus about the inherent moral worth and status of humans and the concomitant obligation of states to recognize and protect that status (Fields and Lord 2004). Morality matters, because most states have publically proclaimed the ethical standard that states should respect "the universalist claim that all human beings have the same moral status; to accept universal human rights [is to make on states] the moral demand to respect the life, integrity, well-being and flourishing of . . . *all* human beings" (Vandersluis and Yeros 2000a), as punctuated in the ringing Universal Declaration of Human Rights. People, according to this perspective, are now empowered, even made by global agreement the ultimate concern, and therefore no longer are reduced as "simply hapless victims of fate, devoid of any historical agency" (Saurin 2000).

It is the purpose of this chapter to evaluate the unfolding debate about the human prospect, the role of humans as actors on the global stage, and the ethics of **human rights.** Given "the increasing willingness to regard concern for human rights violations as acceptable justification for various kinds of international intervention, ranging from diplomatic and economic **sanctions** to military action, in the domestic affairs of states," we shall investigate the challenges posed by that lofty humanitarian ideal rooted in **liberalism** in order to explain why "the doctrine of human rights is a political construction intended for certain political purposes and to be understood against the background of a range of general assumptions about the character of the contemporary international environment" (Beitz 2001).

As described in Chapter 10, there are now more than 6 billion people on the face of the earth, and world population is growing. Between 2 and 4 billion more people will be added to the planet's population between now and the last quarter of the twenty-first century. With these numbers come concerns. Will humanity be valued, and human welfare and rights protected?

These are critical questions. Where does humanity fit into the prevailing and most popular **paradigms** or theoretical orientations that policymakers and scholars construct about what matters in world politics, such as neorealism and neoliberalism? For the most part, classical realism worships the state and its rulers' sovereign freedom and, except for building its image of international reality from a pessimistic conception of human nature, ignores the role of leaders and the NGOs people form (see Chapter 2). Liberals attach more importance to humans, following the ethical precept of the German philosopher Immanuel Kant that people should be treated as ends and not means, and that therefore peoples' human rights should be safeguarded. **Feminist theory** goes further, countering realist logic by making humanity the primary **level of analysis** (Sylvester 2002; see Chapter 2).

HOW DOES HUMANITY FARE? ASSESSING THE HUMAN CONDITION

"Man is born free, and everywhere he is in chains," the French political philosopher Jean Jacques Rousseau bemoaned in his famous 1762 book, *Social Contract.* Times have since changed. But in many respects Rousseau's characterization of the human condition remains valid. How should we evaluate the depth of human deprivation and despair against this fact? Can the poorest proportion of humanity sever the chains of their disadvantages, so as to realize their human potential and obtain the high ideals of human security, freedom, and dignity?

There are many reasons for conceiving of individuals as objects for concern and compassion. Among them, the inequalities and disparities evident in people's standards of living cannot help but to evoke sympathy for the plight of most people, but especially for those in the less-developed Global South countries. One American college student painfully learned this during his first visit to South America, where he found a reality far different from his own experience growing up in the southern United States. He was moved to write:

> I spent the first 24 years of my life in South Carolina. When I left . . . for Colombia [South America], I fully expected Bogotá to be like any large U.S.

■ **human rights**
the political rights and civil liberties recognized by the international community as inalienable and valid for individuals in all countries by virtue of their humanity.

■ **sanctions**
punitive actions by one global actor against another to retaliate for its previous objectionable behavior.

■ **liberalism**
a theory predicated on the hope that the application of reason and universal ethics to international relations can lead to a more orderly, just, and cooperative world, and that international anarchy and war can be policed by institutional reforms that empower organizations and international laws for global governance to protect human rights.

■ **paradigm**
derived from the Greek *paradeigma*, meaning an example, a model, or an essential pattern; a paradigm structures thoughts about an area of inquiry.

■ **feminist theory**
a body of scholarship emerging from the social feminist movement to promote the political equality of women with men, critiquing sexual biases and challenging gender roles that encourage female subordination and warfare.

■ **level of analysis**
the focus on which inquiry centers, depending on whether analysis concentrates on individuals, states, or the global system.

city, only with citizens who spoke Spanish. When I arrived there I found my expectations were wrong. I was not in the U.S., I was on Mars! I was a victim of culture shock. As a personal experience this shock was occasionally funny and sometimes sad. But after all the laughing and the crying were over, it forced me to reevaluate both my life and the society in which I live.

Colombia is a poor country by American standards. It has a per capita GNP of $550 and a very unequal distribution of income. These were the facts that I knew before I left.

But to "know" these things intellectually is much different from experiencing first-hand how they affect people's lives. It is one thing to lecture in air conditioned classrooms about the problems of world poverty. It is quite another to see four-year-old children begging or sleeping in the streets.

It tore me apart emotionally to see the reality of what I had studied for so long: "low per capita GNP and maldistribution of income." What this means in human terms is children with dirty faces who beg for bread money or turn into pickpockets because the principle of private property gets blurred by empty stomachs.

It means other children whose minds and bodies will never develop fully because they were malnourished as infants. It means street vendors who sell candy and cigarettes 14 hours a day in order to feed their families.

It also means well-dressed businessmen and petty bureaucrats who indifferently pass this poverty every day as they seek asylum in their fortified houses to the north of the city.

It means rich people who prefer not to see the poor, except for maids and security guards.

It means foreigners like me who come to Colombia and spend more in one month than the average Colombian earns in a year.

It means politicians across the ideological spectrum who are so full of abstract solutions or personal greed that they forget that it is real people they are dealing with.

Somewhere within the polemics of the politicians and the "objectivity" of the social scientists, the human being has been lost. (Wallace 1978, 15–16)

Despite wide differences that enable a proportion of humanity to enjoy unprecedented standards of living, a daunting scale of poverty and misery is evident throughout the world (see Map 7.1), from which only a small fraction of people in many countries have begun to escape. One indicator is money. As measured by the World Bank's common standard of one dollar a day in 2004, 1.2 billion people were living in extreme poverty, and another fifth of humankind—an additional 1.5 billion people—were seeking to survive on two dollars a day (Ravallion 2004, 65). Income inequality from which many other difficulties and disputes result is a serious global problem. And that problem is growing: "In the gross sense of inequality as the gap between the richest and the poorest citizens of the world, global inequality has increased dramatically since World War II, continuing a macro trend of the previous hundred and perhaps thousand years." And "there is some evidence that the forces of globalization in trade, investment and the labor forces are working to increase" the gap between rich and poor *people,* much as it appears to widen gap between the wealthy Global North and poor Global South countries (Babones and Turner 2004; see Chapter 5). One estimate calculates that the income of the average person in the Global North grew since 1960 twenty-

MAP 7.1
Projecting Trends in the Proportion of People Below the Poverty Line, 1990–2015

As this map shows, as measured by the World Bank's working definition of extreme poverty as income of one dollar or less each day, in 2004 an estimated 1.2 billion or a fifth of the world's people lived in desperate conditions of extreme poverty. The number of people living on less than two dollars a day exceeded 2.7 billion, or two-fifths of humanity (Ravallion 2004, 65). For them, basic human needs are not met, and just surviving another day is a major challenge. The Millennium Development goals aim to cut this tragic proportion to 14.5 percent in 2015. As the regional trends in the chart show, some regions are making much better progress than others, such as sub-Saharan Africa. "The world as a whole is on track to achieve the goal of reducing by half the proportion of people living on less than $1 a day thanks mainly to rapid economic growth in India and China, where many of the world's poor live" (World Bank 2004b, 2).
SOURCE: 2003 *World Bank Atlas*, pp. 12–13.

---

seven times that of the average person in the Global South (*Vital Signs 2003*, 88). Against this grim picture there is evidence that inspires some hope, because for some segments of humanity things have improved: 400 million people have escaped absolute poverty by the one-dollar-a-day index since 1981, most of whom live in China. "So if one focuses on the developing world outside China, the number of poor has changed very little. . . . The number of poor has fallen in Asia, but risen elsewhere. It has roughly doubled in Africa," where one in three of the world's poorest live (Ravallion 2004, 65; see also World Bank 2005b, 256–259).

Consumption patterns show other discrepancies. The division between the rich and the poor is a growing source of resentment and conflict (T. Hall 2004). Only about one-fifth of the globe's wealthiest people consume "anywhere from two-thirds to nine-tenths of its resources. The proportions reflect the figures given in the United Nations' regular *Human Development Report*, which show the richest fifth of humanity having, for example, 90 percent of all Internet accounts, 74 percent of all phone lines, and 82 percent of all export markets" (McGurn 2002, 23). "The poorest 20 percent of the world's population receives only 0.2 percent of global commercial bank lending, 1.3 percent of global investment, 1 percent of global trade and 1.4 percent of global income" (Saurin 2000, 208). Nearly one of every five people in the world live in extreme poverty (UNDP 2004, 129). A select few are thriving, and the rest are barely surviving: "the world's three richest individuals are now worth more than the forty-eight poorest nations" (Easterbrook 2002, 17). Crushing poverty for one-half of humanity against rising abundance for a small minority is a recipe for hopelessness, desperation, and violence such as terrorism and even suicidal martyrdom.

Another indicator besides the absence of income and available resources is the deplorable conditions in which many humans live. For many people the future is bleak, resembling how in 1651 the realist English political philosopher Thomas Hobbes described life—"solitary, poor, nasty, brutish, and short." The opportunities and choices most basic to freedom from fear and poverty are unavailable for most people in the Global South's developing countries experiencing much slower rates of development and human security than in the Global North, and the prospects of the "have-nots" are plummeting.

Much evidence captures the extreme suffering of people in many parts of the world, but especially in the low-income countries of the Global South where life has changed little from that of their ancestors. For example, life expectancy in the Global South averages less than sixty years, whereas in the Global North it is nearly eighty years. Human agony is also starkly evident in other respects. In the Global South, infant mortality rates are among the highest in the world; less than half of the adult population is literate (a proportion even lower among women); agriculture remains the dominant form of productive activity; and four out of every five people live in rural areas even as the world is undergoing rapid urbanization. World Bank President James Wolfensohn (2004, 6) captured the growing threat of global poverty by noting that "two billion people have no access to clear water; 120 million children never get a chance to go to school; over 40 million people in the developing countries are HIV-positive with little hope of receiving treatment for this dreadful disease. . . . So the world is at a tipping point: either we recommit to deliver on the goals, or the targets will be missed, the world's poor will be left even further behind—and our children will be left to face the consequences."

Given the serious deprivations in many aspects of life facing so many people, there are many reasons for humanitarian concerns. The denial to most humans of the inalienable rights to which all humans are presumably entitled— the "life, liberty, and the pursuit of happiness" of which the U.S. Declaration of Independence speaks—attests to the extent to which fundamental human rights are not being met. It is this problem that in 2002 prompted Mary Robinson, the

UN High Commissioner for Human Rights, to "call on global actors—corporations, governments and the international financial organizations—to join with globalized civil society and share responsibility for humanizing **globalization**."

To make the promotion of human rights the globe's major priority, a precise measure of human welfare is needed. How can human welfare—its level and the prospects for humanity's escape from poverty—best be gauged?

Measuring Human Development and Human Security

The human dimension of development first gained attention in the 1970s, partly in response to the growing popularity of the **dependency theory** advanced by Global South leaders who attributed persistent poverty to exploitation caused by dependent relationships of the less-developed countries with the wealthy Global North. It also was a reflection of the realization that more is not necessarily better. Advocates of a basic **human needs** perspective sought new ways to measure development beyond those focusing exclusively on economic indicators such as the average income for each person in each country. In 1990 Mahbud ul Haq, a famous social scientist, constructed for the United Nations Development Programme (UNDP) a **Human Development Index (HDI)** to measure states' comparative ability to provide for their citizens' well-being. Successive *Human Development Reports* have provoked fresh debate about the meaning of human development in international forums, including, for example, the 1995 World Summit for Social Development.

The HDI, as the UNDP most recently defines it, continues to seek to capture as many aspects of human development as possible in one simple, composite index and to rank human-development achievements. While no multiple-indicator index (a detailed set of statistical measures) can monitor progress in human development, the HDI comes close as an estimating procedure, by measuring "three dimensions of the development concept, living a long and healthy life, being educated and having a decent standard of living" (UNDP 2004).

The HDI is a more comprehensive measure than per capita income and has the advantage of directing attention from material possessions toward human needs. Income is only a means to human development, not an end. Nor is it the sum total of human lives. Thus, by focusing on aspects of human welfare beyond average income for each person—by treating income as a proxy for a decent standard of living—the HDI provides a more comprehensive picture of human life than income does. By this measure, the evidence provides a basic profile of the extent to which humanitarian aspirations are succeeding and failing.

The HDI ranges from 0 to 1. The HDI value for a country shows the distance that it has already traveled toward the maximum possible value of 1 and allows for comparison with other countries. The difference between the value achieved by a country and the maximum possible value shows how far it has to go; the challenge for every country is to find ways to reduce that discrepancy.

Look at the ability of countries to contribute to the human development of the people living within their borders, as measured by the HDI. We derive a revealing picture of the way personal welfare is provided (see Table 7.1 and Figure 7.1). These indicators show that consumption is not the same as human welfare, and that economic growth does not automatically produce human development. In fact, high consumption if not managed can produce inequalities and poverty that erode the capacity of people "to participate in the decisions that af-

■ **globalization**
the integration of states, through increasing contact, communication, and trade, to create a common global culture for all humanity.

■ **dependency theory**
a perspective that perceives the global economic system as responsible for the less-developed Global South countries' dependence on, and exploitation by, the wealthy Global North countries.

■ **human needs**
those basic physical, social, and political requirements, such as food and freedom, required for survival and security.

■ **Human Development Index (HDI)**
an index that uses life expectancy, literacy, average number of years of schooling, and income to assess a country's performance in providing for its people's welfare and security.

TABLE 7.1

Comparative Trends in Select Country's Advancement of Human Development, 1975–2002: Stories of Success and Stagnation

Country	HDI Rank 2002	HDI 2002	HDI 1975	Absolute Change
High Human Development (0.80–1.00) since 1975				
Ireland	10	0.94	0.81	0.13
Israel	22	0.91	0.79	0.12
Hong Kong (SAR)	23	0.90	0.76	0.14
Singapore	25	0.90	0.72	0.18
Korea, Rep. of	28	0.89	0.71	0.18
Chile	43	0.84	0.70	0.14
Medium Human Development (0.50–0.79) since 1975				
Malaysia	59	0.79	0.61	0.18
Colombia	73	0.77	0.66	0.11
Oman	74	0.77	0.49	0.28
Thailand	76	0.77	0.61	0.16
Turkey	88	0.75	0.59	0.16
Tunisia	92	0.75	0.52	0.23
China	94	0.75	0.52	0.23
Guyana	104	0.72	0.67	0.05
Indonesia	111	0.69	0.47	0.22
South Africa	119	0.67	0.66	0.01
Swaziland	137	0.52	0.52	0.00
Low Human Development (0.00–0.49) since 1975				
Pakistan	142	0.50	0.35	0.15
Congo	144	0.49	0.45	0.04
Zimbabwe	147	0.49	0.55	−0.06
Kenya	148	0.49	0.45	0.04
Nigeria	151	0.47	0.32	0.15
Senegal	157	0.44	0.32	0.12
Zambia	164	0.39	0.47	−0.08

SOURCE: United Nations Development Programme, *Human Development Report 2004*, pp. 143–146.

The Human Development Index (HDI) focuses on three measurable dimensions of human development: living a long and healthy life, being educated, and having a decent standard of living. Thus it combines measures of life expectancy, school enrollment, literacy, and income to allow a broader view of a country's development than does income alone (UNDP 2004). This chart captures changes since 1975 in various countries' HDI for the 177 countries for which data are available. Inspection of Table 7.1 shows countries' levels of human development are changing at different rates, depending on how their governments use resources for improving the lives of their citizens.

fect one's life and to enjoy the respect of others in the community. . . . The HDI can give a more complete picture of the state of a country's development than can income alone [since many countries] highlight the importance of policies that translate wealth into human development. In particular, well designed public policy and provision of services by governments, local communities and civil

FIGURE 7.1
Measuring Human Development: What Is Quality of Life?

Rank by HDI	Country	Rank by GDP per person*
1	Norway	2
2	Sweden	21
3	Australia	12
4	Canada	9
5	Netherlands	11
6	Belgium	13
8	United States	4
12	Britain	20
16	France	16
19	Germany	14
23	Hong Kong	17
27	Slovenia	30
34	Argentina	48
38	Hungary	41
40	Bahrain	36
52	Cuba	91
57	Russia	60
72	Brazil	63
77	Saudi Arabia	44
83	Philippines	105
94	China	99
109	Eq. Guinea	6
111	Indonesia	113
119	South Africa	53
127	India	117
147	Zimbabwe	122
166	Angola	128
177	Sierra Leone	176

Index: 0   0.2   0.4   0.6   0.8   1.0
*At PPP exchange rates

When using the Human Development Index to measure the human welfare and development of people within various populations, countries stack up somewhat differently than when using an aggregate measure such as the gross domestic product (GDP) per capita—the total each year of each country's production of goods and services as measured by the average amount of money for each person. "Norway is still the best place to live, according to the UN's annual Human Development Index. Sierra Leone is the country to avoid. The index takes into account life expectancy and education as well as GDP per person. So Equatorial Guinea, where life expectancy at birth is 49 years, is ranked 109th even though its oil riches mean that it apparently comes sixth in conventional comparison of GDP per person" (*Economist*, July 24, 2004, 92).

Compare the HDI rankings with those recorded for the GDP per person to see how closely the HDI and GDP indicators correspond. All measures of standards of living are controversial. Note, for example, a problem with the HDI is that "it does not include measures of the other aspects of human development such as leisure, security, justice, freedom, human rights and self-respect. It would be possible to register a high HDI in a zoo or even a well-run prison. And, although at low incomes illness often leads to death, the HDI has no independent indicator of morbidity, absence of which is surely one of the most basic needs. Life can be nasty, brutish, and long" (Streeten 2001).

SOURCE: UNDP (2004) as summarized by the *Economist*, July 24, 2004, 92. Copyright © 2004 by The Economist Newspaper Ltd. All rights reserved. Reprinted with permission. Further reproduction prohibited. www.economist.com.

society can advance human development even without high levels of income or economic growth" (UNDP 2004, 128).

Humanitarian goals for human development vary greatly in the countries of the world. Why is this the case? Let us consider several explanations.

Political and Economic Preconditions for Human Development

Many factors affect the extent to which people's human rights to live a good life are provided. Among them, one correlate stands out: political freedom—the degree to which countries rule themselves democratically and protect citizens' civil liberties. This is a potent determinant of human development. That is, where democracy thrives, there also thrives human rights and human development. Recall the states where democracy and political liberties exist (see Map 3.2, "The Map of Freedom," p. 67). That geographical profile from Freedom House's *Free-*

MAP 7.2
The Map of Human Development
This map measures the level of human development in the countries of the world, using the HDI scale. Note the wide variation. Although poorer Global South countries have made big gains in the past quarter century (following political reforms leading to greater democracy and economic reforms leading to free markets), a gap in peoples' quality of life and in their levels of human development is apparent and parallels to some degree the gap between the Global North and the Global South.
SOURCE: UNDP (2004, 139–47).

dom in the World survey recorded that at the start of 2005 less than half of the countries in the world, 46 percent, were "free," providing their citizens with a broad range of civil liberties in their political, civic, educational, cultural, ethnic, economic, and religious rights. In human terms, these liberties were experienced by 2.8 billion individuals, or 44 percent of the globe's population (Freedom House, 2004, freedomhouse.org). Now compare the location where people benefit from such freedom with Map 7.2, which shows the various levels of human development in countries across the globe. The two go hand in hand: where democracy flourishes, human development flourishes. But in autocratic governments not ruled by the will of the people, where government policies fail to recognize cultural identities and discourage diversity, human rights are denied and human development fails to occur (UNDP 2004).

Alongside democratization and respect for cultural liberty, rising economic prosperity also clearly helps the pace of human development, as shown by the selected illustrations in Figure 7.1 based on wealth for each person for countries based on **purchasing power parity (PPP)** exchange-rate comparisons. This is why levels of human development are generally highest in the Global North, where economic prosperity on average is also highest (as opposed to the low-income Global South). But the exceptions demonstrate the general rule that how countries organize themselves for governance, and their protection of the civil and cultural liberties of their populations, makes a crucial difference in achieving levels of human development.

Some question the trickle-down hypothesis (that if the rich first get richer eventually the benefits will trickle down to help the poor) while accepting the evidence that meeting basic human needs promotes long-term economic growth (Moon and Dixon 1992). Others maintain that redistributive policies to meet basic human needs or otherwise enhance human welfare and growth-oriented policies through trickle-down effects work at cross-purposes, because the latter can only be attained at the expense of the former. And many now recommend fostering human development through a **Third Way** strategy that combines the efficiency of a free enterprise capitalistic market with the compassion of governmental economic planning and regulation in an effort, through a fused administrative system, to produce the greatest good for the greatest number. Proponents agree that this mixed approach would enable a free market to generate rapid growth while providing a safety net for those most in need of assistance and that the formula is the best solution for engineering economic growth with a moral human purpose.

Human Development in the Age of Globalization

The rapid transfer of global capital and investment across borders that is integrating the world's economies has led to widespread speculation that **globalization** will provide a cure for the chronic poverty facing the majority of humanity. There exists "a widely shared image of globalization—a worldwide process of converging incomes and lifestyles driven by ever-larger international flows of goods, images, capital, and people as formidable equalizers [because] greater economic openness has made small parts of the changing world full-fledged members of the global village . . . so that globalized islands of prosperity are thriving in many developing nations" (Heredia 1999).

However, critics of globalization complain that it is the culprit: relative deprivation is caused by globalization, not cured by it. They see globalization as a part of the problem of human suffering, not the solution. To their constructed image of the consequences of cascading globalization, a more global economy increases inequality in some countries, particularly in the marginalized periphery of the Global South (Babones and Turner 2004). Other critics decry the "human harms" wrought by globalization, arguing that "nothing is more certain than the inequality and exploitation generated by a totally free market . . . and the inequalities that global capitalism generates are inequities because they violate the principles of egalitarian individualism. . . . This sin of globalization is thus both collective (an assault on the nation) and individual (injuring the nation's citizens), making it a severe violation of the global moral order" by creating "risks of injury and incapacitation that strike at the very being of human beings" (Boli, Elliott, and Bieri 2004). These complaints about the harmful impact of globalization to humanity point to the damage caused individuals by threats

■ **purchasing power parity (PPP)**
an index that calculates the true rate of exchange among currencies when parity—when what can be purchased is the same—is achieved; the index determines what can be bought with a unit of each currency.

■ **Third Way**
an approach to governance advocated primarily by European leaders who, while recognizing few alternatives to liberal capitalism, seek to soften the cruel social impact of free-market individualism by progressively allowing government intervention to preserve social justice and the rights of individuals to freedom from fear of the deprivations caused by disruptions in the global economy.

■ **globalization**
To David Held and Anthony McGrew, the emergence "of a single global economy transcending and integrating the world's major economic region.

to the environment and nature, local culture, jobs and labor, religion, and other values humans hold dear, but most center on economic deprivation and declining standards of living for the poorest. It is argued that globalization is not benefiting the people that need help most. Capital may flow more freely around the world, but it flows most slowly to the places and people where it is most scarce. A skeptical political economist from Mexico cautions: "Developing countries today are a much more heterogeneous group than [after World War II, but] globalization is not helping them become more equal. The poorest are not catching up with the fastest. . . . More and more people across the planet have become increasingly exposed to the amenities of the global marketplace, although mostly as permanent window shoppers and silent spectators. The large majority of humankind, however, is rapidly being left outside and far behind" (Heredia 1999). Stated differently, some critics disturbed by the widening gap between the rich and poor see "the race to the bottom caused by globalization, [with] the plight of the poor [expanding because they] are paying the price for everyone else's prosperity. 'One aspect is for sure in the globalization process: labor is suffering most'" (Rembert Weakland, cited in McGurn 2002).

Like the controversy about whether globalization brings benefits or misery (see Chapter 8), human development is an ideological and policy issue that colors much of the debate about the roots of global inequality and rival approaches for its alleviation. The general record of HDI changes presents an arresting picture of both unprecedented human progress and unspeakable human misery, of humanity's advance on several fronts alongside its retreat on others. The gap between rich and poor people continues. But that provides only a crude reflection of the simultaneously unfolding trends toward both progress and decline.

The past thirty years display a checked record, with some remarkable achievements in human development alongside daunting challenges that remain which warn how far progress must still travel in order for people to lead lives to their full potential. Despite some positive improvements many areas of human development remain in urgent need of remedy. Although progress in human development has occurred and will likely persist, so will trends toward declining human welfare, making the twenty-first century appear to be both the best of times and the worst of times. Thus, the future of world politics will be not only a struggle between the Global North and the Global South but also a contest between those who see global decline as inevitable and those who see global progress as possible.

In the wake of the 9/11 advent of global terrorism and, with it, the virtual globalization of terrorism, globalization holds the key to humanity's future. Globalization is forging greater interdependence, yet the world seems more fragmented—between rich and poor, between the powerful and the powerless, and between those who welcome the new global economy and those who demand a different course. The September 11, 2001, terrorist attacks on the United States cast new light on these divisions, returning strategic military alliances to the center of national policy making and inspiring heated debates on the danger of compromising human rights for national security (UNDP 2002). The realist view that human rights can be dismissed when paying primary attention to military security and counterterrorism was questioned by the ethicist Michael Ignatieff (2004a) when he astutely observed that "all the world's national security challenges come from regimes that are also human rights violators."

THE GLOBAL REFUGEE CRISIS

Another sign of concern about **human security** is expressed by the refugee crisis that now prevails. The vast majority of the world's population are either immigrants or the offspring of their immigrant parents or ancestors. Migration is pervasive, and it is politically controversial in many countries where existing, long-term residents are fearful of having foreigners as their neighbors. In Britain and France, for example, which continue to receive large numbers of immigrants from their former colonies, and also in Israel, which has absorbed a flood of immigrants, state governments struggling with absorbing tens of thousands of new migrants are frequently targets of nationalistic criticism. The Middle Eastern oil producers also have received large numbers of migrants in recent years. But the United States, historically a place of escape from religious and political persecution and a land of economic opportunity, is a special case. Its 1990s Commission on Immigration Reform aimed to reduce the flow of legal migrants to 175,000 annually. But that has not happened, as a flood of emigrants from Mexico (about 4,545,000 since the 1970s) has exploded the exodus, not counting the 8–10 million in 2003 (69 percent of total) illegal immigrants (Huntington 2004, 33–35). President George W. Bush granted these illegal Mexican residents immunity, as the inflow became a hot campaign issue in the 2004 presidential election. Some critics complained that Bush played a two-level game to win Mexican votes, and others that "the persistent flow of Hispanic immigrants threatens to divide the United States into two peoples, two cultures, and two languages" (Huntington 2004).

Refugees are individuals whose race, religion, nationality, membership in a particular social group, or political opinions make them targets of persecution in their own homelands and who migrate from their country of origin, unable to return to it. According to the UN High Commissioner for Refugees (UNHCR), the world's refugee population has grown each year since 1960, swelling to an all-time peak of more than 27 million in 1995. After that, the worldwide number of people "of concern" as refugees to the 145 countries that have signed the 1951 Geneva Refugee Convention has varied yearly with the advent of new wars and new tyrannies. At the start of 2005, the number was a staggering 20.6 million, or about 1 out of every 300 people throughout the world (see Figure 7.2). The total number of people "of concern" between 1960 and the start of 2005 exceed 440 million people seeking refuge and protection. This estimate does not count such categories as, at the start of 2005, 2.4 million "returnees" (former refugees who have returned to their homelands); 5.8 million "internally displaced people" living in situations similar to those of refugees but held hostage in their own countries and prevented from crossing borders to freedom; or the estimated additional 4–8 million children and women who are kidnapped yearly by crime rings in the sex-trafficking trade and smuggled across borders as captives for prostitution.

Refugees and displaced persons alike are often the victims of war. For example, the Persian Gulf War in 1991 created a refugee population of 5 million; genocide in Rwanda in 1994 drove more than 1.7 million refugees from their homeland; and 3.5 million Afghans sought asylum from terror in 2001. The persecution, **ethnic cleansing,** and armed conflict that accompanied the breakup of the former Yugoslavia uprooted nearly 3 million victims, moving Europe to the list of continents with large numbers of refugees—over 6 million—for the

■ **human security**
a concept that refers to the degree to which the welfare of individuals is protected and advanced, in contrast to national security which puts the interests of states first.

■ **refugees**
people who flee for safety to another country because of a well-founded fear of persecution.

■ **ethnic cleansing**
the extermination of an ethnic minority group by a state, in violation of international law since the mid-1990s, before which governments could treat the people within their territory as they wished.

FIGURE 7.2
The Chronic World Refugee Crisis

The number of refugees receiving assistance from the UN has risen exponentially in the last four and a half decades. More than 440 million people are estimated to have fled their home countires to avoid persecution or starvation, and approximately 11 million people on average each year seek "asylum"—the right to be recognized as bona fide refugees and receive legal protection and material assistance in a second state providing sanctuary. This mass exodus is a symptom of human rights abuses worldwide and a symbol of the globalization process that is creating a borderless world. Meanwhile, others estimate that since 1960 more than 70 million additional people have been internally displaced, living like refugees in their own countries.

SOURCE: Adapted from reprints of the United Nations High Commission for refugees (www.unncr.org).

first time since World War II. The U.S. war on terrorism in 2002 sought to root out the Taliban Al Qaeda terrorists in Afghanistan, but the conflict created what the UN termed a "major humanitarian catastrophe" for more than 3.6 million Afghan displaced people facing famine and freezing—in 2002 in excess of 30 percent of the global refugee population. At the start of 2005, Asia had the greatest number of people of concern, with nearly 9.4 million, followed by Africa with 4.6 million, and Europe with 4.4 million people (www.unhcr.org).

A large proportion of the world's refugees and displaced people flee their own homelands when ethnic and religious conflicts erupt in **failed states,** where governments have collapsed and no authority has gained acceptance to restore domestic law and order. In addition, human rights abuses provide a compelling explanation of why millions leave their homelands. "Refugees know that they cannot expect, at home, the protection of the police, access to a fair trial, redress of grievances through the courts, prosecution of those who violate their rights, or public assistance in the face of disaster. . . . Forcing people to flee is a violation of the human right to remain peacefully in one's home. The direct denial of other basic rights, including the rights of civilians not to be tar-

■ **failed states**
countries whose governments have so mismanaged policy that they have lost the loyalty of their citizens who, in rebellion, seek independence to create their own state.

Refugees on the Run on Desperate Roads That Lead Nowhere About 20 million refugees each year become homeless people in search of sanctuary. Shown here is the makeshift Moro Camp in Chad, where in late 2002 and early 2003 thousands of refugees from the central African Republic fled across the border when rebels attacked and pillaged villages following an attempted coup d'état. In 2004 Chad again became a place of escape when Sudan, whose Arab rulers have been fighting a twenty-year civil war against its rebellious black-African south, launched an ethnic cleansing campaign of murder, rape, and pillage that forced seven hundred thousand black African Sudanese to flee their villages (Kristof 2004, A9).

---

geted in military actions, often provides the immediate impetus for flight" (Newland 1994).

People also leave home in search of economic opportunity. Legal migrants—particularly young people in the **Global South** without productive employment—are among those leaving at record rates—mostly to Global North countries. Migration also is increasingly occurring *between* developing Global South countries.

Some leaving their home states are the best educated and most talented, causing a serious **brain drain,** but most are not. The majority of migrants take low-wage jobs shunned by local inhabitants. Typically this means migrants earn less than the citizens of those states but more than they would earn in their homelands when performing the same tasks. Host countries increasingly welcome migrants (as Europe did during the 1970s guest worker era) not only because they accept low wages for undesirable jobs but also because in many places the host pays little if anything for migrants' health, education, and welfare needs. On the other hand, the home (sending) countries sometimes encourage people to emigrate as a way of reducing unemployment or exporting unwanted elements of the population, such as criminals, or in the expectation that the emigrants will send much of their income back to their needy families in their homeland.

■ **Global South**
a term now often used instead of "Third World" to designate the less-developed countries located primarily in the Southern Hemisphere.

■ **brain drain**
the exodus of the most educated people from their home country to a more prosperous foreign country where the opportunities for high incomes are better, which deprives their homeland of the emigrants' ability to contribute to its economic development.

Ethnic Cleansing Hate and hostility have traditionally led to terrorism and genocide. Racial and ethnic prejudice have commonly resulted in intercommunal warfare, such as the U.S. government's policy of expulsion and extermination of Native Americans, Nazi Germany's annihilation of 6 million Jews, and Japan's death marches and enslavement of those it conquered in the early victories of World War II. More recently, in 1994 ethnic conflict escalated to genocide in Rwanda as the Hutu militia attacked the Tutsi, and later as the Tutsi-dominated Rwandan Patriotic Front retaliated against the Hutus. This photo depicts the results of one such bloodbath, where as many as 1 million Tutsis died.

■ **xenophobia**
the suspicious dislike, disrespect, and disregard for members of a foreign nationality, ethnic, or linguistic group.

Xenophobia (fear of foreigners) is on the rise. Many refugees are finding the doors to safe havens closing. Although "countries such as Italy and Ireland, which once benefited by exporting their burgeoning populations, now urgently need immigrants" to reduce labor shortages, the barriers are rising, because legal migration in Europe is severely restricted. Only a fraction of the 450,000 applying for political asylum in 2001 in twenty-five European countries received sanctuary (*Economist*, March 31, 2001, 15). Security concerns stimulated by terrorist fears are sometimes at work, as in the United States, where many believe the catastrophic New York World Trade Center attack on September 11, 2001, would not have occurred had immigration controls been tighter. "Since September 11th diasporas have come under new scrutiny to see whether they harbor or breed terrorists" (*Economist*, January 4, 2003). A wave of illegal immigrants has contributed to the rising tide of anti-immigration sentiments. Ironically, in a country born of immigrants where in 2005 immigrants accounted for about 13 percent of U.S. workers, thousands of refugees who earlier would have found safe haven in the United States have been repatriated to their homelands or otherwise denied a chance to apply for political **asylum.**

■ **asylum**
the provision of sanctuary to safeguard refugees escaping from the threat of persecution in the country where they hold citizenship.

A combination of push-and-pull factors has propelled migration to the forefront of the globalization of population dynamics. Human rights violations, environmental degradation, overpopulation, famine, war, and ethnonational clashes and **atrocities** within states—all *push* millions beyond their homelands. Migrants also are *pulled* abroad by the promise of political freedom elsewhere, particularly in the democratically ruled Global North countries. Indeed, the recent growth of immigration to the Global North from the Global South is related to the shrinking of the world (through revolutions in communication and transport) and the growing reach and absorptive power of global capitalism.

Shutting the door is increasingly viewed as a solution. This raises critical ethical issues. "Some states, especially leading industrial countries, have toughened their domestic refugee legislation and criteria for granting asylum" (www.unhcr.org). Where will the homeless, the desperate, the weak, and the poor find **sanctuary**—a safe place to live where human rights are safeguarded? Will the rich countries act with compassion or respond with indifference? And more broadly, what is the best way to view human security and reconcile it with **national security?** This choice may involve irreconcilable values, and this makes human security and human rights a highly debatable issue.

The conclusion is invited: the welfare and survival of everyday people are endangered, and the need for their protection is increasing. But that is not the end of the story. Other people suffer even more.

■ **atrocities**
brutal and savage acts against targeted citizen groups or prisoners of war, defined as illegal under international law.

■ **sanctuary**
a place of refuge and protection.

■ **national security**
a country's psychological freedom from fears that the state will be unable to resist threats to its survival and national values emanating from abroad or at home.

INDIGENOUS PEOPLES: PRECARIOUS LIFE IN THE FOURTH WORLD

As noted in Chapter 6, where we first addressed the topic of nonstate actors (NGOs), **indigenous peoples** are representative of one type of ethnic and cultural group that were once native to a geographic location now controlled by another state or political group. The globe is populated by an estimated 6,800 separate indigenous nations, each of which has a unique language and culture and strong, often spiritual, ties to an ancestral homeland. In most cases indigenous peoples were at one time politically sovereign and economically self-sufficient. There are today at least 300 million indigenous peoples constituting more than 5 percent of the world's population scattered in more than seventy countries; some estimate the number as high as 600 million (Center for World Indigenous Studies 2002; see also Map 6.2, p. 198). Recall that this segment of global society is conventionally referred to as the **Fourth World** to heighten awareness of the poverty and deprivation that confront many native or tribal indigenous peoples without a homeland or self-rule.

Many indigenous peoples believe to be persecuted because they feel that their livelihoods, lands, cultures, and lives are threatened. In part, these fears are inspired by the 130 million indigenous peoples who were slaughtered between 1900 and 1987 by state-sponsored **genocide** in their own countries (Rummel 1994). The tragedy is of a magnitude of staggering proportions.

> During the twentieth century there were not only two world wars but at least six major cases of genocide—the mass killing of Armenians by Turks in 1915, of Jews (and other groups such as the Gypsies) by Hitler, of Cambodians by the Khmer Rouge, of the Kurds of northern Iraq by Saddam Hussein, of the Tutsi of Rwanda by the Hutu, and of Croats, Muslims, and

■ **indigenous peoples**
the native ethnic and cultural inhabitant populations within countries ruled by a government controlled by others, referred to as the "Fourth World."

■ **Fourth World**
a term used to recognize the native national groups residing in many so-called united states who, although often minorities, occupied the state's territory first and refuse to accept domination, seeking instead to create a new state for themselves by splitting existing states or by gaining greater political freedom to govern themselves.

■ **genocide**
the deliberate extermination of an ethnic or minority group.

Case Study: Genocide in Rwanda

the Albanians of Kosovo by the Serbs. In all cases except the Kosovo Albanians, the international community and its Western leaders failed to act in time.

In 1948, halfway through this bloodiest of centuries, the United Nations General Assembly approved the text of the Genocide Convention, which outlaws the destruction by a government, in whole or in part, of a national, ethnic, racial, or religious group as such. Some forty years later the United States ratified the convention, and in the very last years of the century, the Hauge tribunal held hearings that led to the first conviction for genocide under the convention—of the Serb General Radislav Krstic for his part in the killings of Bosnians. Successive horrors have shamed governments into making some reluctant progress, but it is still far from certain that the nations of the world will act in time and with sufficient determination when genocide once again threatens some unfamiliar region. (Urquhart 2002, 12)

"The tragedy of the Nazi holocaust led a Polish jurist, Raphael Lemkin, to coin the word *genocide* from the Greek word *genos* (race, people) and the Latin *caedere* (to kill) and to begin action aimed at the international prohibition of genocide, which would in turn provide the necessary international legal basis for action against this crime. . . . Today . . . it is universally recognized that genocide is the gravest international crime and the most dangerous violation of human rights and that the international community is morally and politically responsible to take steps to prevent its occurrence and to punish persons responsible for crimes amounting to genocide" (Turk 2001).

Fourth World Reactions to Human Rights Violations

Aroused nationalists are now fighting back across the globe in rebellion against the injustice, misery, and prejudice they perceive states to have perpetrated against them (see Gurr et al. 2002). This is not to suggest that all indigenous minority groups are bent on tearing existing states apart, or on using violence to attain power. The members of many such **nonstate nations** are divided about objectives, and militants who are prepared to fight for independence are usually in a minority. In fact, most Fourth World indigenous movements only seek more representative clout in redirecting the policies and allocation of resources within existing states and are eliciting the support of NGOs and IGOs to pressure states to recognize their claims and protect their civil liberties and human rights. They strive to gain substate autonomy, not **sovereignty.**

A substantial number of indigenous movements in the last decade have successfully negotiated settlements resulting in **devolution**—the granting of political power to increase local self-governance by the state groups to ethnic and indigenous peoples, resulting in protagonists gaining concessions for greater local political power in exchange for accepting state sovereignty. Examples include the Miskitos in Nicaragua, the Gagauz in Moldova, and most regional separatists in Ethiopia and in India's Assam region. Yet, as suggested by the U.S. war against international terrorism after September 11, 2001, and the "perpetual crisis" and action-reaction chain of militant hostility between Israel and the Palestinians, resolving clashes between established and aspiring states through terror and other forceful methods represents an entrenched trend.

The potential levels of discontent were made clear by the alarming threat of

■ **nonstate nations**
national or ethnic groups struggling to obtain power and/or statehood.

■ **sovereignty**
the legal doctrine that states have supreme authority to govern their internal affairs and manage their foreign relations with other states and IGOs.

■ **devolution**
states' granting of political power to minority ethnopolitical national groups and indigenous people in particular national regions under the expectation that greater autonomy will curtail their quest for independence as a new state.

civil unrest painted by the official 2002 Communist Party's *China Investigation Report*, which warned that millions of Chinese are angered by rampant inequality, corruption, ethnic and religious conflicts, and the wrenching damage from China's end of its old state-run economy. It is difficult to foresee what will result from this and other cases of internal minority protests. One possibility is governmental devolution and the decentralization of state control to pacify nationalist separatist movements. Europe, today one of the world's most stable but ethnopolitically divided regions, could serve as a model for the twenty-first "devolution" century. However, from Kosovo to Kurdistan, and from Palestine to Afghanistan, we observe an alternative scenario: freedom fighters impatient with the map they have inherited, struggling to become an independent state. Fighting by oppressed minority groups and between tribal ethnic factions has spread. The chaos that engulfed Ukraine after the December 2004 election was condemned and a new election was scheduled provides a striking example of the pregnant threat to human rights posed by failed states.

In another even more gloomy scenario presenting grave dangers for humanity, a **clash of civilizations** will unfold to terrorize humanity (see Chapter 6). In the wake of the 9/11 terrorist attack by Islamic extremists on the United States, Huntington's thesis (1999a) appears convincing that "almost everywhere in the contemporary world people are espousing cultural and civilizational identities" and that **ethnocentrism** within a particular group that perceives itself as a special civilization threatens to undermine the ideal of universal human rights, applicable to all of humanity.

The Threat of State Disintegration to Human Security

Indigenous peoples are now highly mobilized because "they were largely pushed to inaccessible and unproductive lands by earlier waves of colonization [and] now find that even these lands are coveted by outsiders" (Watson 1997). In response, many today pursue **self-determination** to protect themselves and control the resources on their territories. This quest for greater self-governance can sometimes be achieved through the peaceful separation of formerly unified states. This happened in Czechoslovakia on December 31, 1992, when that country split peacefully through the so-called velvet divorce into the independent Czech Republic and Slovakia.

However, aroused nationalist passions are prone to escalate to violence. An extreme example is the bloody warfare that has racked the former Yugoslavia since 1991, when the Bosnian Serbs and Croats both committed atrocities in the name of **ethnic cleansing**—a program of genocide to murder the rival nationality. The war in Kosovo was its culmination. What Italian President Oscar Luigi Scalfaro described in 1997 as a new "danger of racial, religious, and tribal hatred" follows the tragic pattern of twentieth-century genocides. Genocide caused the death of 500,000 to 1,100,000 ethnic minorities in the Soviet Union between 1943 and 1947; 80,000 to 1,000,000 ethnic Chinese and communists in Indonesia between 1965 and 1966; and 100,000 to 282,000 Kurds in Iraq between 1984 and 1991 (Barbara Harff, as cited in Sadowaski 1998, 18).

The goal expressed in the UN Charter of promoting "universal respect for, and observance of, human rights and fundamental freedoms" for everyone is a challenge for many nationally diverse countries. Protecting the human rights and civil liberties of minority populations is inherently difficult. The divisions

■ **clash of civilizations**
political scientist Samuel Huntington's controversial thesis that in the twenty-first century the globe's major civilizations will conflict with one another, leading to anarchy and warfare similar to that resulting from conflicts between states over the past five hundred years.

■ **ethnocentrism**
a propensity to see one's nationality or state as the center of the world and therefore special, with the result that the values and perspectives of other groups are misunderstood and ridiculed.

■ **self-determination**
the doctrine that asserts nationalities have the right to determine what political authority will represent and rule them.

■ **ethnic cleansing**
the extermination of an ethnic minority group by a state government or rival majority ethnic group.

of most states into segregated fragments along ethnic and cultural lines are different from the political partitions that divided Korea, Vietnam, Germany, and China into separate states. The majority of states can be described as inherently fragile because they are composed of multiple nationalities that can splinter. Consider the degree to which minority groups compose many states: for example, the share of indigenous populations in Bolivia is 70 percent; Peru, 40 percent; Mexico, 12 percent; the Philippines, 9 percent; and Canada, 4 percent. Cultural diversity is also captured by the number of distinct languages spoken in "megadiversity" countries, of which Indonesia's 670 languages, Nigeria's 410, India's 380, Australia's 250, and Brazil's 210 are exceptional examples (Durning 1993, 83, 86). Such states are not culturally, linguistically, or politically "united."

Racism and intolerance are hothouses for fanatical **irredentism,** imperialism, and bloodshed. The inherent ethnocentrism underlying **ethnonationalism**—the belief that one's nationality is special and superior and that others are secondary and inferior—undermines the concept of human rights that "has attained increasingly broad support and is now firmly established under international law [and that stipulates] that human rights apply to everyone—by virtue of their humanity—everywhere, and at all times" (Clapham 2001). Nationalists are prone to marginalize and oppress "outside" nationalities, and to reject conciliation and compromise with them.

Although interethnic competition is a phenomenon that dates back to biblical times, it is a contemporary plague. According to *The Minorities at Risk Project* (see Gurr 1993, 2001), more than 450 ethnopolitical minority groups have been involved in serious, often violent, struggles since 1945, and there exist many risks of new and escalating ethnic wars of tribal terrorism and warfare.

To the extent that conflict within and between ethnically disunited and divided states becomes a major axis on which twenty-first-century world politics revolves, the advent of a new era of tribal terrorism spreading worldwide could unfold. Such a breakdown would destroy "the duty of all states to promote and protect human rights" the 1993 Vienna Declaration declared.

GENDER POLITICS: THE SUBORDINATE STATUS OF WOMEN AND ITS CONSEQUENCES

In population conferences during the twentieth century's final decade, the critical role of women was recognized as a human rights concern, and a global consensus emerged about the need to improve the status of women if human development was to progress. These conferences are signposts that increasingly depict women's controlling their own bodies and reproductive fate as a basic human right, recognizable under international law (see Table 7.2). The conferences have educated the world to the incontrovertible evidence that women's status in society, and especially their education, has an important influence on human development, and that women's treatment is a human rights issue that affects everyone.

As measured by the UN's **Gender Empowerment Measure (GEM),** women throughout the world continue to be disadvantaged relative to men across a broad spectrum of educational statistics, such as literacy rates, school and col-

---

■ **irredentism**
efforts by an ethnic or religious group to regain control of territory by force so that existing state boundaries will no longer separate the group.

■ **ethnonationalism**
a belief system valuing an ethnic or national community above other possible objects of devotion, such as a state, a religion, or the human community writ large.

■ **Gender Empowerment Measure (GEM)**
the UN Development Program's attempt to measure the extent of gender equality across the globe's countries, based on estimates of women's relative economic income, high-paying positions, and access to professional and parliamentary positions.

TABLE 7.2

Important Steps on the Path toward Human Rights and Women's Rights

Year	Conference	Key Passage or Issue of Treaty or Covenant
1968	United Nations International Conference on Human Rights (Teheran)	"Parents have a basic human right to decide freely and responsibly on the number and spacing of their children."
1974	World Population Conference (Bucharest)	"The responsibility of couples and individuals [should take] into account the needs to their living and future children, and their responsibilities towards the community."
1975	International Women's Year Conference (Mexico City)	"The human body, whether that of woman or man, is inviolable, and respect for it is a fundamental element of human dignity and freedom."
1979	Convention on the Elimination of All Forms of Discrimination against Women (Women's Convention, New York)	Article 12 calls on countries to "take all appropriate measures to eliminate discrimination against women in the field of health care in order to ensure, on a basis of equality of men and women, access to health care services, including those related to family planning."
1984	World Population Conference (Mexico City)	"Governments can do more to assist people in making their reproductive decisions in a responsible way. [Family planning is] a matter of urgency."
1992	United Nations Conference on Environment and Development (Rio)	Agenda 21 calls for "women-centered, women-managed, safe and accessible, responsible planning of family size and service."
1993	United Nations World Conference on Human Rights (Vienna)	The Vienna Declaration includes nine paragraphs on "The Equal Status and Human Rights of Women," and for the first time recognizes that "violence against women is a human-rights abuse."
1994	International Conference on Population and Development (Cairo)	ICPD Program of Action "reaffirms the basic human rights of all couples and individuals to decide freely and responsibility the number and spacing of children and to have the information, education, and means to do so."
1995	United Nations Fourth World Conference on Women (Beijing)	Sets a wide-ranging, ambitious agenda for promoting human development by addressing gender inequality and women's rights.
1999	United Nations Conference on World Population (The Hague)	Drafts recommendations on humane assistance for international family planning programs in light of the possibility that global population could start to decline late in the twenty-first century.
2002	World Summit on Sustainable Development (Johannesburg)	Drafts resolutions to combat abject and dehumanizing poverty, stressing the importance of reform to encourage gender equity and the rights of women in order to stimulate sustainable economic growth.
2004	NATO Conference on Trafficking in Humans (Brussels)	Seeks a convention to contain the growing problem of human trafficking and export of people across borders—particularly women and children.
2004	United Nations Conference on the Human Rights Obligations of Multinational Corporations (Geneva)	Opens debate to create a new code—the Human Rights Norms for Business—to impose human rights and gender equality obligations on "transnational companies and other businesses."
2004	United Nations Conference on Sexual and Reproductive Rights (New York)	Launches action plan to uphold women's "fundamental human rights including sexual and reproductive rights."

lege enrollments, and targeted educational resources. Women, for example, "account for 50–80 percent of the global refugee population" (*Vital Signs 2003*, 103). Women also enjoy less access to advanced study and training in professional fields, such as science, engineering, law, and business. In addition, within

Transforming the Gender Gap At times, circumstances for humans, especially women, can change quickly. Shown here is a telling case—new recruits in Kabul, Afghanistan, in Februry 2004 at a police training camp, women shedding one traditional **role** and accepting another.

SOURCE: *Foreign Affairs*, May–June 2004, p. 87.

■ **role**
the position a person holds and the expectations about how that position is to be performed that shapes the role-occupant's behavior.

■ **gender inequalities**
differences between men and women in opportunity and reward that are determined by the values that guide states' foreign and domestic policies.

occupational groups, they are almost always in less-prestigious jobs, they face formidable barriers to political involvement, and everywhere they receive less pay than men. Although these and other gender differences have narrowed in recent years, in most countries **gender inequalities** remain firmly rooted.

Indeed, gender inequalities—differences in living standards between men and women—remain widespread both within and across states, despite the measurable improvement in the daily lot and future prospects of millions of women during the past several decades. Although many facets of human development are improving, the prevalent worldwide gender gap remains especially wide throughout and within the Global South. "Significant gender disparities continue to exist, and in some places, to grow, in three regions: Southern Asia, the Middle East, and Sub-Saharan Africa" (Coleman 2004). Women's share of earned income in developing countries is less than a third of men's. Worse still, women account for a much smaller proportion of the nonagricultural workforce than men, and their pay in that sector for the same work is routinely less. Females hold fewer teaching positions at all levels of education and fewer Ph.D.'s, and their share of administrative and managerial jobs is minuscule. Much the same holds true in politics; "on average, women account for 15 percent of the world's parliamentary representatives. In fourteen countries, they comprise 30 percent or more; in sixty-five countries they account for 10 percent or less" (*Economist*, April 3, 2004, 106).

Furthermore, gender differences continue at the most basic levels of human development: more girls than boys die at a young age, and females' access to adequate health care is more restricted. Despite the fact that "since the eighteenth century feminists, scholars and activists have taken up the task of revealing just how much political life has been built on presumptions about femininity and masculinity . . . there is abundant evidence now that regimes and the states beneath them in fact have taken deliberate steps to sustain a sort of hierarchical gendered division of labor that provides them with cheapened, often completely unpaid, women's productive labor" (Enloe 2001). It is therefore easy to conclude that women remain victims of human rights abuse and discrimination nearly everywhere, as reflected in the grim statistic that "women and their dependent children constitute at least 70 percent of all current refugees [while] it is usually male refugees within [UN administered refugee] camps who presume to have authority, often using it to strengthen men's militias, while preventing women from gaining access to UN literacy classes" (Enloe 2001, 313). It was not until 2001 that "sexual enslavement" was established at The Hague as a war crime, a fact feminists point out as an example of the traditional disregard for women's human rights.

So-called gender myopia, denying the existence of the many barriers that deny women equal freedoms and privileges enjoyed by men, is pervasive, although the need to extend women equal human rights for economic growth is clear-cut: "Educating girls is the single most effective way to boost economic progress." What is also clear is that "robust democracy is exceedingly rare in societies that marginalize women" (Coleman 2004). These principle were recognized at the September 2002 Johannesburg World Summit on Sustainable Development. "The river of thought on human rights and development runs inexorably toward the emancipation of women everywhere, and the equality of men and women," notes the *State of the World 2002*, which warned sadly, "but eddies and rivulets carry the water backwards every day—as when pregnant girls are expelled from school, or when the genitals of young women are cut in a ritual destruction of their capacity for sexual pleasure."

Protecting women's rights is difficult because the issues touch deeply entrenched as well as widely divergent religious and cultural beliefs. In many Islamic countries, for example, women must hide their faces with veils in public, and women and men are often completely separated in social and religious activities. For many in liberal Western countries, these traditions are difficult to understand. On the other hand, Western conceptions of feminism and women's rights, typically focused on social, political, and economic equality of the sexes, are foreign to women elsewhere, where the issues are personal and the goals pragmatic: "access to capital, the right of inheritance, basic education for girls, a voice in the political establishment and medical systems that let them make choices, especially in reproductive health" (Crossette 1995).

In 1995, in Beijing, the UN convened its fourth World Conference on Women, the largest-ever gathering of women. Many of the issues regarding women's rights, along with the arguments provoked by differing religious and cultural traditions, surfaced during the conference as attention focused on gender issues. The concept of "gender empowerment"—the conviction that "only when the potential of all human beings is fully realized can we talk of true human development" (UNDP 1995)—gained acceptance as an **ideology** or lens through which to construct a view of the core issues on the global agenda.

Feminist theory is a departure from classical realist theory that seeks to rectify the ways conventional but distorted images of world politics are, as

■ **ideology**
a set of core philosophical principles that a group of leaders and citizens collectively hold about politics, the interests of political actors, and the ways people ought to ethically behave.

■ **constructivism**
a theoretical perspective emphasizing the extraordinary degree to which all interpretations—be they those advanced by realism, liberalism, behavioral science, or feminism—are shaped by the assumptions observers and scholars, policymakers and interpreters embrace about the hidden meanings embedded by the views of the groups with which they most closely identify.

■ **noncombatant immunity**
the legal principle that military force should not be used against innocent civilians.

■ **international regime**
the set of rules, norms, and decision-making procedures that coordinates state behavior within a given issue area.

constructivism informs us, socially constructed (see Chapter 2). The objective is to sensitize the world to the neglect of gender and the place of women in global society and to offer an alternative theoretical vision that empowers women and secures their basic human rights, while also challenging realist theories that honor the state and military power (Sylvester 2002; Tickner 2002).

HUMAN RIGHTS AND THE PROTECTION OF PEOPLE

Laws regulating the practices that sovereign states may use have changed rapidly in recent years. These restraints include the principles of discrimination and **noncombatant immunity,** which in times of war attempt to protect innocent civilians by restricting military targets to soldiers and supplies. The message of the 1949 Geneva Convention that even wars have limits has been strengthened. The delegates at that historic conference, whose focus was to make new rules for warfare, understood that the causes of war and the problems of peace are best dealt with separately. "For war to be as merciful as possible sparing noncombatants and, in particular, civilian populations it is best if the law that governs the rules of war be distinct from all possible political consideration. This principle, the separation between the causes of war and rules of war, became increasingly validated. . . . The world at large is so disgusted by acts of barbarity that governments and supranational bodies see it as their duty to intervene more and more to try to curb some of the more lurid atrocities that emerge here and there" (Sommaruga 1999).

This change in the rules of war is representative of a larger sea change in the international consensus about human rights. That phase has advanced from a mere slogan to a program of action. New humanitarian norms have now been accepted globally, which have created a human rights **international regime** backed by enforcement institutions. The human rights revolution has advanced moral progress by breaking states' monopoly on international affairs and over citizens (Ignatieff 2004b). In this sense, liberalism triumphed and realism was repudiated, for the human rights movement has rejected the harsh realist vision expressed by Thomas Hobbes, who argued in the seventeenth century that because world politics is "a war of all against all, the notions of right and wrong, justice and injustice have there no place." Moreover, international law has fundamentally revised the traditional realist protection of the state by redefining the relationship of states to humans. As Kofi Annan in 1999 defined the new conception of human rights, "States are now widely understood to be instruments at the service of their people, and not *vice versa*. At the same time . . . the fundamental freedom of each individual, enshrined in the Charter of the UN and subsequent international treaties—[has] been enhanced by a renewed and spreading consciousness of individual [human] rights. When we read the Charter today, we are more than ever conscious that its aim is to protect individual human beings, not to protect those who abuse them."

As a principle, human rights is a constructed liberal transnational ethical movement that supports the view that human beings should come first, ahead of other objects of identity such as the state. It recognizes humanity as members of

The Victimization of Children as the Ultimate Violation of Human Rights Women are not the only victims of the invisible forces that exploit the human rights of people. Another group of victims—to which every living human at one time belonged—is children. The UN Children's Fund estimates that some "200,000 children a year are trafficked in West and Central Africa. Girls are affected worst; most end up as domestic workers or prostitutes. Boys are forced to work on coffee or cocoa plantations or as fishermen" (*Time*, April 30, 2001, 39). Shown here is one tragic case: a starving farmer in Afghanistan, Akhtar Mohammed, watching his ten-year-old son, Sher, whom he traded to a wealthy farmer in exchange for a monthly supply of wheat. "What else could I do?" he asked. "I will miss my son, but there was nothing to eat."

---

the human community, in anticipation of the creation of a global civil society. Hence, a cosmopolitan vision is embraced:

- "Citizenship is not a condition that requires a state in the first instance; citizenship is a social status that requires mutual recognition of human moral worth" (Vandersluis and Yeros 2000a).
- People are valuable and equally entitled to certain "inalienable" rights, and therefore *everyone* deserves protection from the denial of those basic fundamental rights by virtue of their moral status as human beings and autonomous individuals, interconnected throughout the globe.

- Human rights are *universal*. Universality "means that human rights apply to everyone by virtue of their humanity—everywhere and at all times" (Clapham 2001).
- Human rights obligate all actors on the world stage to observe, respect, and protect these rights; this includes states, so that even they have clear duties that transcend borders and sovereign rights, because a moral demand is made "to respect the life, integrity, well-being and flourishing of others [and this ethical obligation] applies to all human beings" (Vandersluis and Yeros 2000a).

The persecution of individuals responsible for human rights violations in times of war attests to this accountability, which is now accepted in international law as a normative change that greatly reduces the traditional right of rulers to commit crimes against humanity in the name of defending the state: "states are no longer able to treat their citizens as they think fit" (Held and McGrew 2001).

When on December 10, 1948, the UN General Assembly proclaimed the Universal Declaration of Human Rights, it took a giant step in defining these rights and the liberal philosophy that inspired that declaration. "The declaration establishes a broad range of civil and political rights, including freedom of assembly, freedom of thought and expression, and the right to participate in government. The declaration also proclaims that social and economic rights are indispensable, including the right to education, the right to work, and the right to participate in the cultural life of the community. In addition, the preamble boldly asserts that 'it is essential, if man is not to be compelled to have recourse, as a last resort, to rebellion against tyranny and oppression, that human rights should be protected by the rule of law'" (Clapham 2001). These rights have since been codified and extended in a series of treaties, such as the 1981 African Charter of Human and Peoples Rights and the 1993 second Vienna World Conference on Human Rights. As one authority, Charles R. Beitz, summarizes:

> Together these documents, which often are referred to collectively (and . . . misleadingly) as the International Bill of Rights, constitute an authoritative catalog of internationally recognized human rights.
>
> There are various ways to classify the rights enumerated in these documents. For our purposes it is useful to think of internationally recognized human rights as falling roughly into five categories, although it is less important to agree about categories than to appreciate the scope and detail of the enumerated rights.
> 1. Rights of the person refer to life, liberty, and security of the person; privacy and freedom of movement; ownership of property; freedom of thought, conscience, and religion, including freedom of religious teaching and practice "in public and private;" and prohibition of slavery, torture, and cruel or degrading punishment.
> 2. Rights associated with the rule of law include equal recognition before the law and equal protection of the law; effective legal remedy for violation of legal rights; impartial hearing and trial; presumption of innocence; and prohibition of arbitrary arrest.
> 3. Political rights encompass freedom of expression, assembly, and association; the right to take part in government; and periodic and genuine elections by universal and equal suffrage.

4. Economic and social rights refer to an adequate standard of living; free choice of employment; protection against unemployment; "just and favorable remuneration;" the right to join trade unions; "reasonable limitation of working hours;" free elementary education; social security; and the "highest attainable standard of physical and mental health."
5. Rights of communities include self-determination and protection of minority cultures. (Beitz 2001, 271)

INTERNATIONAL ETHICS: RECONCILING NATIONAL INTERESTS AND HUMAN INTERESTS

From any perspective, the scale of the chronic poverty, political victimization, and suffering that afflicts such a large proportion of humanity cannot but provoke compassion and outrage. Only the most heartless can feel indifferent about the extent of suffering documented in this chapter. True, some observers are not alarmed by the growing absolute and relative inequalities that exist across a variety of measures of the human condition; but few are so callous as to feel no empathy with the plight of billions of hapless victims throughout the world. When we look at the way ordinary people live in the real world, almost no one would conclude that the basic human rights defined above through consensus in the international community are being protected. There is great distance between the high ideal of human rights and its realization.

The policy question facing the world is what steps can and should be taken to alleviate human suffering and to safeguard human rights. Agreement has yet to be reached on the extent to which the international community has a responsibility to react, to respond, and to intervene in order to protect human rights and rebuild broken humans. As the International Commission on Intervention and State Sovereignty noted in its December 2001 report, *The Responsibility to Protect*, the policy challenge is of great magnitude:

> Millions of human beings remain at the mercy of civil wars, insurgencies, state repression and state collapse. This is a stark and undeniable reality, and it is at the heart of all the issues with which this Commission has been wrestling. What is at stake here is not making the world safe for big powers, or trampling over the sovereign rights of small ones, but delivering practical protection for ordinary people, at risk of their lives, because their states are unwilling or unable to protect them.
>
> But all this is easier said than done. There have been as many failures as successes, perhaps more, in the international protective record in recent years. There are continuing fears about a "right to intervene" being formally acknowledged. If intervention for human protection purposes is to be accepted, including the possibility of military action, it remains imperative that the international community develop consistent, credible and enforceable standards to guide state and intergovernmental practice.

The search for agreement about the principles that should guide a **regime** "to establish clearer rules, procedures and criteria for determining whether,

■ **regime**
norms, rules, and procedures for interaction agreed to by a set of states.

Cruel and Unusual, or Simply Usual? The UN Human Rights Commission holds annual sessions that deal with accusations that some UN members are violating the human rights provisions enacted by international treaties. Shown in this photo is the kind of human rights abuse that some countries practice: a person being punished according to Saudi Arabia's Islamic laws.

■ **humanitarian intervention**
the use of peacekeeping troops by foreign states or international organizations to protect endangered people from gross violations of their human rights and from mass murder.

when and how to intervene" to protect human rights has proven elusive. The global community has not yet agreed upon a set of legal justifications for **humanitarian intervention** to protect civilians. The major paradox is this: "In major arenas of international politics concerns about human rights are more prominently expressed than ever before, and there is some reason to believe that these concerns increasingly motivate action. Yet, within contemporary political thought human rights are often regarded with suspicion" (Beitz 2001).

Advocating the protection and promotion of human rights is one thing high on the agenda of liberalism; yet taking the steps necessary for these goals is resisted by realists, who see the promotion and protection of state sovereignty as a priority. Hence, the promotion of human rights is primarily a *political* problem on the global agenda. The issue is not whether there exists a compelling human need and moral obligation to express concerns about populations at risk of slaughter, ethnic cleansing, starvation, or persecution; the issue is about how and if to forge a just response, when any response will comprise an interference in the internal or domestic affairs of a sovereign state. Humanitarian intervention is destined to remain inherently controversial (see Controversy: Should Tyranny and Human Rights Violations Justify Humanitarian Intervention?).

However, the mandate to permit intervention for humanitarian purposes appears to be growing in strength. The rationale for acceptance of humanitarian intervention to protect human rights has been advocated by the executive director of the NGO, Amnesty International:

> Here is the grandpappy of "realism," diplomat George Kennan: "I would like to see [the U.S.] government gradually withdraw from its public advocacy of democracy and human rights. . . . I don't think any such questions should enter into our diplomatic relations with other countries. If others [private parties] want to advocate changes in their conditions, fine—no objection. But not the State Department or the White House. They have more important things to do."
>
> "Realists" regard the pursuit of rights as an unnecessary, sometimes even a dangerous extravagance, often at odds with our national interest. What they seem rarely to garner is that in far more cases than they will allow, defending human rights is a prerequisite to *protecting* that interest. What we require is not less realism but a more expansive, sophisticated, comprehensive form of it—a "new realism" for an interconnected age. . . .
>
> Fortunately the connection between human rights and national interest is becoming more clear to an ever-expanding circle of observers. As *The Economist*, that bastion of respect for capitalist values, editorialized not too long ago, "Morality is not the only reason for putting human rights on the West's foreign-policy agenda. Self-interest also plays a part. Political freedom tends to go hand in hand with economic freedom, which in turn tends to bring international trade and prosperity. And governments that treat their own people with tolerance and respect tend to treat their neighbors in the same way. Dictatorships unleashed the First and Second World Wars, and most wars before and since." (Schulz 2001, 13, 14)

Humanitarian intervention "refers to a range of unilateral or collective actions taken by the international community to provide assistance to the population of a target state experiencing unacceptable and persistent levels of human suffering caused by natural disaster, deliberate government policy, or state collapse" (Malaquias 2001). The decision to engage in humanitarian intervention will always be controversial, because it will raise very big questions about the legitimacy of intervention in a sovereign state: Was the cause just, and were the human rights violations committed sufficiently serious to make outside involvement necessary? The answers will always be uncertain. However, human rights has gained the stature of accepted international law. As a result, we can expect human rights to receive continuing attention, as long as people continue to be in need of help when they are caught in emergency situations such as the threat of famine or genocide:

> There is a determination to ensure that states and governments are held accountable for failing to live up to their international obligations. We care about rights because we care about each other. The language of human rights obligations is the simplest way to express that sense of sympathy and outrage. Concerned citizens will continue to demand change as long as the inherent dignity of any human being remains threatened, unprotected, and unrealized. (Clapham 2001, 370)

We most vividly see the rising importance assigned ethically to human rights protection in international legislation in one area where, traditionally, these rights were more blatantly ignored: the conduct of war. The change has

CONTROVERSY: SHOULD TYRANNY AND HUMAN RIGHTS VIOLATIONS JUSTIFY HUMANITARIAN INTERVENTION?

Imagine yourself an American on a vacation in a foreign country. You find yourself unjustly imprisoned on accusations that you were transporting illegal drugs, spying for your government, trafficking in the practice and sale of children for prostitution, you name it. You are innocent and you are angry! Your human right to basic civil liberties has been violated. To make matters incredibly worse, you discover that the jail in which you are incarcerated is full of thousands of political prisoners held, and abused, by their guards, who are employed by a military dictatorship that claims the sovereign right to treat all accused lawbreakers any way they want. Never in the authorities' explanation is mention made of human rights, such as trial by a jury of peers and prohibition against the cruel punishment of prisoners.

What can you do? You are an innocent victim. Do you, and for that matter the hundreds of other possibly innocent victims in prison with you, have any hope?

For centuries, the answer was that your fate was hopeless. You had no power. Power was monopolized by state governments, which could do anything and everything to protect and promote their self-interests by preempting potential threats to their self-preservation. That code of conduct, enshrined in the 1648 Westphalian treaties drafted by realists, proclaimed that state authority was sacrosanct and sacred, and that people and their human rights were subservient. For the state and its rulers, anything goes toward subjects within a sovereign country's territory.

However, there is protection: recently, international law has radically changed. "For nearly sixty years after the creation of the Universal Declaration of Human Rights in 1948, there [was] still no international consensus about when [human] rights violations in one state justify other states to interference" (Ignatieff 2004a). But no longer. Now protecting human rights in foreign states has become legal for the first time under international law. The law has been "updated 'to close the gap between legality and legitimacy' [so that] rules and international law [now have been changed] to permit armed intervention for humanitarian protection" (Slaughter 2004b). This is hope for justice!

Or is it? An ideology that helps to protect your human rights also undermines the national interests of sovereign states, such as your powerful country—the United States. What may be beneficial for you may be harmful to your country, which cited the sovereign right to imprison suspected culprits of the 9/11 ter-

■ **noncombatants** those not engaged in fighting during wartime such as teachers and children, who, like soldiers, are often exposed to harm.

■ **war crimes** acts performed during war that the international community defines as illegal crimes against humanity, such as atrocities committed on an enemy's prisoners of war and civilians or the state's own minority population.

been sparked in great measure by the fact that **noncombatants**—that is, innocent civilians and ordinary people not engaged in fighting—have become the primary victims in warfare. In recent years, the ratio of civilians to soldiers killed in wars has reversed the historic pattern: today ninety civilian casualties result for every ten military losses (Pfaff 1999, 8).

To prevent the horror of civilian casualties and contain the mass slaughter that increasingly has taken place inside national frontiers, the global community, in revulsion, has made a radical revision in the rule of international law. For the first time, international law holds leaders of countries accountable for **war crimes** as war criminals. Traditionally, international law prohibited leaders from allowing their militaries to undertake actions in violation of certain principles accepted by the international community, including the protection of innocent noncombatants. However, when violations occurred, there was little that could be done except to condemn such actions. Another weakness was that traditional international law did not hold government leaders to the same standards to which it held soldiers and military officers who committed atrocities against enemy civilians and captured soldiers. Although international law set rorist attacks without right to legal defense or jury in its military prison in Guantánamo, Cuba, and to imprisonment and, it was later discovered, inhumane treatment, of captives in Iraq—to the outrage of the global community. But the United States claimed its right to ignore international humanitarian law on the grounds of "necessity" in times of warfare—this time a war against faceless terrorists.

Here you are forced to ask, Was that right? Moral? Legal? Should you defend the proclaimed might of your country to do as it pleases in times of alleged war, when that defense will compromise your ability to defend your complaint that your imprisonment was an immoral violation of your basic human rights and civil liberties by a sovereign state, and that complaint will undermine the case that your own government has championed? So you have a tough issue to face: how to reconcile your understandable love of country and its claimed sovereign national interests against your personal need to be shielded by a global code of state conduct that puts the human rights of all on an equal footing?

You do not have much power when you are imprisoned. The choice is philosophical, however. "The conflict between human rights and state sovereignty divides the two intervening states [in occupied Iraq], Britain and America, from much of the world. If the Iraq experiment fails it will also determine the future likelihood of interventions—and the use of human rights to justify them—for years to come" (Ignatieff 2004a).

This is a major issue on the global agenda. How would you choose? Keep in mind that your choice between the alternatives of external humanitarian intervention to protect human rights and continuing support for the prohibition of intervention in the internal affairs of other states could matter, if many also agree with you. So which do you put first, country or all of humanity? And as you contemplate this hypothetical controversy, keep in mind the entrenched defense of the traditional right of states to be protected against foreign intervention—even for humanitarian purposes—not only by the globe's reigning hegemon, the United States, which has placed national security ahead of humanitarian protection and has a long history of supporting state terrorists and dictators to protect America's security interests (see Gareau 2004). Likewise, many other states, especially the weak and relatively less defenseless governments in the Global South, also vigorously resist humanitarian interference within their borders. They maintain that opposition to resist humanitarian intervention within their borders is legal, and that movement against the nonintervention norm is not in their interests, either: "Antipathy on the part of Third World states is directly connected to [the Global South's] concerns from the erosion of sovereignty, which it considers to be bedrock on which international order rests" (Ayoob 2004). The rising China, on this point, agrees vehemently with the Global South and the United States.

---

standards for both individuals and states, leaders were free from jurisdiction under the doctrine of "sovereign immunity," even when their commands flouted the laws of war. Though they might behave as criminals, leaders were treated with respect because they were the people with whom the global community had had to negotiate to settle conflicts.

While many people and states still commit war crimes without facing punishment, the resumption of war crime tribunals in 1993 signaled to would-be perpetrators the global community's intolerance for these atrocities. In 1999, the prosecutor's office of the UN's International Criminal Court (ICC) indicted seventy-seven people and arrested seven for crimes in Bosnia. Building on this step, a permanent world criminal court was created in The Hague to try leaders for the most terrible of mass crimes, especially acts of genocide such as those occurring in ethnopolitical conflicts. Thus a goal the UN had pursued for half a century became a reality: the world community now has an international court with teeth, through a treaty approved by almost all states.

Moreover, heads of state are now held accountable for war crimes against humanity, removing the protection they had received under traditional international law. Ever since the ICC's founding statute, a head of state can be charged with war crimes committed at any time the leader was in office; even a sitting head of state can now be indicted for war crimes. In fact, Slobodan Milosevic of Yugoslavia and President General Augusto Pinochet of Chile were indicted in 1999, and, in September 2002, Milosevic, the ex-Yugoslavian president, faced prosecutors at The Hague, who accused him of war crimes as the mastermind behind the genocide planned to wipe out Bosnia's Muslims in the 1991–95 wars. (Milosevic portrayed Serbs as victims of ethnic aggression and claimed his policies had aimed at peace, not war.) The criminalization of rulers who have been alleged sponsors of state terrorism raises the legal restraints on the initiation and conduct of war to an all-time high, despite the continuing refusal of the United States to adhere to this treaty.

The global community has impressively expanded its legal protection of human rights. As Table 7.3 shows, a large number of conventions have been enacted in the last fifty years that have steadily endowed individuals with power, rights, and respect—rights ensuring that people are treated as worthy of the freedom and dignity traditionally granted by international law to states and rulers. "The old assumption that national sovereignty trumps all other principles in international relations is under attack as never before; . . . the age of human rights is upon us. In these post-communist, postmodern times, human rights seem to have become the dominant moral narrative for thinking about world affairs. No longer does national sovereignty provide blanket protection for human rights abusers. In the eyes of many Western intellectuals, there is a New World Moral Order—one ruled by ideals like civil society, humanitarianism and, first and foremost, human rights" (Rieff 1999, 67).

That said, the persistence of horrendous atrocities and human suffering makes a mockery of the standards for a just global civil society called for by the Universal Declaration of Human Rights. "As with most declarations of faith, their adherents—first and foremost governments—have frequently failed to live up to them [even though] practically all governments say they accept the basic code of conduct these declarations expound. The continuing effort to achieve and maintain those standards is the frontier between civilization and barbarism" (Urquhart 2001).

"Moral universalism is a late and vulnerable addition to the vocabulary of mankind" (Ignatieff 2001b). The humanitarian vision to promote human rights and to provide a moral shield against man's proverbial "inhumanity to man" remains a huge challenge on the global agenda. To now put people first is to live up to high ideals, and the world has a long way to go to achieve that aspiration. Eleanor Roosevelt was an early champion of human rights, and it was her energetic leadership that was largely responsible for global acceptance in 1948 by nearly all governments of the Universal Declaration of Human Rights. Her noble pursuit shows that one person can make a difference in transforming world politics. In thinking about humans and humanity, we can profit by the inspiration of her nightly prayer: "Save us from ourselves and show us a vision of a world made new." Former U.S. President Jimmy Carter in 2003 wrote that "for most of the world's people the glittering opportunities of the new century are beyond reach. . . . The problems may seem insurmountable, but they are not. We have the tools; we have brilliant dedicated people to find answers. All we need is a sense of sharing and the will to change. The will can grow from understanding. Once we care, we can change."

TABLE 7.3

Legal Steps in the Development of International Human Rights Protection: Some Major Conventions

Year	Convention
1948	Universal Declaration of Human Rights
1948	International Convention on the Prevention and the Punishment of the Crime of Genocide
1948	Freedom of Association and Protection of the Right to Organize Convention
1949	Convention for the Suppression of the Traffic in Persons and of the Exploitation of the Prostitution of Others
1949	Geneva Convention for the Amelioration of the Condition of the Wounded and Sick in Armed Forces in the Field
1949	Geneva Convention for the Amelioration of the Condition of Wounded, Sick and Shipwrecked Members of Armed Forces at Sea
1949	Geneva Convention relative to the Treatment of Prisoners of War
1949	Geneva Convention relative to the Protection of Civilian Persons in Time of War
1949	Right to Organize and Collective Bargaining Convention
1950	Convention for the Suppression of the Traffic of Persons and the Exploitation of the Prostitution of Others
1950	Statute of the Office of the United Nations High Commissioner for Refugees
1951	Convention relating to the Status of Refugees
1951	Convention (No.100) concerning Equal Remuneration for Men and Women Workers for Work of Equal Value
1952	Convention on the International Right of Correction
1953	Convention on the Political Rights of Women
1953	Protocol amending the 1926 Slavery Convention
1954	Convention relating to the Status of Stateless Persons
1955	Standard Minimum Rules for the Treatment of Prisoners
1956	Supplementary Convention on the Abolition of Slavery, the Slave Trade, and Institutions and Practices Similar to Slavery
1957	Convention concerning the Abolition of Forced Labour
1957	Convention on the Nationality of Married Women
1958	Convention concerning Discrimination in respect of Employment and Occupation
1959	Declaration of the Rights of the Child
1960	Convention against Discrimination in Education
1961	Convention on the Reduction of Statelessness
1962	Convention on Consent to Marriage, Minimum Age for Marriage and Registration of Marriages
1963	United Nations Declaration on the Elimination of All Forms of Racial Discrimination
1964	Employment Policy Convention
1965	International Convention on the Elimination of All Forms of Racial Discrimination
1965	Recommendation on Consent to Marriage, Minimum Age for Marriage and Registration of Marriages
1965	Declaration on the Promotion among Youth of the Ideals of Peace, Mutual Respect and Understanding between Peoples
1966	International Covenant on Civil and Political Rights
1966	Optional Protocol to the International Covenant on Civil and Political Rights
1966	International Covenant on Economic, Social and Cultural Rights
1966	Declaration of the Principles of International Cultural Co-operation
1966	Protocol relating to the Status of Refugees
1967	Convention on the Elimination of All Forms of Discrimination against Women
1967	Declaration of Territorial Asylum
1967	Declaration on Territorial Asylum
1968	Proclamation of Teheran

(continued)

TABLE 7.3 *(continued)*

Year	Document
1968	Convention on the Non-Applicability of Statutory Limitations to War Crimes and Crimes Against Humanity
1969	Inter-American Convention on Human Rights
1969	Declaration on Social Progress and Development
1971	Worker's Representatives Convention
1971	Declaration on the Rights of Mentally Retarded Persons
1973	International Convention on the Suppression and Punishment of the Crime of Apartheid
1973	Principles of International Co-Operation in the Punishment of War Crimes and Crimes against Humanity
1974	Declaration on the Protection of Women and Children in Emergency and Armed Conflict
1974	Universal Declaration on the Eradication of Hunger and Malnutrition
1974	Recommendation concerning Education for International Understanding, Co-operation and Peace and Education relating to Human Rights and Fundamental Freedoms
1975	Declaration on the Protection of All Persons from Being Subjected to Torture and Other Cruel, Inhuman or Degrading Treatment or Punishment
1975	Declaration on the Use of Scientific and Technological Progress in the Interests of Peace and for the Benefit of Mankind
1975	Declaration on the Rights of Disabled Persons
1976	International Covenant on Economic, Social, and Cultural Rights
1976	International Covenant on Civil and Political Rights
1976	Optional Protocol to the International Covenant on Civil and Political Rights
1977	Protocols on Humanitarian Law for International Armed Conflicts and Noninternational Armed Conflicts
1977	Protocol (I and II) Additional to the Geneva Conventions of 12 August 1949, and relating to the Protection of Victims of International Armed Conflicts
1978	Declaration on Fundamental Principles concerning the Contribution of the Mass Media to Strengthening Peace and International Understanding, to the Promotion of Human Rights and to Countering Racialism, Apartheid and Incitement to War
1978	Declaration on Race and Racial Prejudice
1978	Convention concerning Protection of the Right to Organize and Procedures for Determining Conditions of Employment in the Public Service
1979	Code of Conduct for Law Enforcement Officials
1979	Convention on the Elimination of All Forms of Discrimination against Women
1981	Covenant of Civil and Political Rights
1981	Declaration on the Elimination of All Forms of Intolerance and of Discrimination Based on Religion or Belief
1981	Convention concerning the Promotion of Collective Bargaining
1982	Principles of Medical Ethics relevant to the Role of Health Personnel, particularly Physicians, in the Protection of Prisoners and Detainees against Torture and Other Cruel, Inhumane or Degrading Treatment or Punishment
1984	Convention against Torture and Other Cruel, Inhumane, or Degrading Treatment or Punishment
1984	Safeguards Guaranteeing Protection of the Rights of Those Facing the Death Penalty
1984	Declaration on the Right of Peoples to Peace
1985	International Convention against Apartheid in Sports
1985	United Nations Standard Minimum Rules for the Administration of Juvenile Justice
1985	Declaration of Basic Principles of Justice for Victims of Crime and Abuse of Power
1985	Basic Principles on the Independence of the Judiciary
1985	Declaration on the Human Rights of Individuals Who are not Nationals of the Country in which They Live
1986	Declaration on Social and Legal Principles relating to the Protection and Welfare of Children, with special reference to Foster Placement and Adoption Nationally and Internationally
1986	Declaration on the Right to Development

1988	Body of Principles for the Protection of All Persons under Any Form of Detention or Imprisonment
1988	Convention concerning Employment Promotion and Protection against Unemployment
1989	Second Optional Protocol to the International Covenant on Civil and Political Rights, Aiming at the Abolition of the Death Penalty
1989	Convention on the Rights of the Child
1989	Principles on the Effective Prevention and Investigation of Extra-legal, Arbitrary and Summary Executions
1989	Convention concerning Indigenous and Tribal Peoples in Independent Countries
1990	Basic Principles for the Treatment of Prisoners
1990	Basic Principles on the Use of Force and Firearms by Law Enforcement Officials
1990	Basic Principles on the Role of Lawyers
1990	Guidelines on the Role of Prosecutors
1990	Model Treaty on the Transfer of Proceedings in Criminal Matters
1990	Model Treaty on the Transfer of Supervision of Offenders Who Have Been Conditionally Sentenced or Conditionally Released
1990	United Nations Rules for the Protection of Juveniles Deprived of Their Liberty
1990	United Nations Standard Minimum Rules for Non-Custodial Measures
1990	United Nations Guidelines for the Prevention of Juvenile Delinquency
1990	Guidelines for the Regulation of Computerized Personal Data Files
1990	International Convention on the Protection of the Rights of All Migrant Workers and Members of Their Families
1991	Convention on the Prevention and Suppression of Genocide
1991	Principles for the Protection of Persons with Mental Illness and the Improvement of Mental Health Care
1992	Declaration of Principles of International Law on Compensation to Refugees
1992	Declaration on the Rights of Persons Belonging to National or Ethnic, Religious or Linguistic Minorities
1992	Declaration on the Protection of All Persons from Enforced Disappearance
1993	Vienna Convention on Human Rights
1993	Declaration on the Elimination of Violence against Women
1994	African Convention on Human and Peoples' Rights
1997	Universal Declaration on the Human Genome and Human Rights
1999	Declaration on the Right and Responsibility of Individuals, Groups and Organs of Society to Promote and Protect Universally Recognized Human Rights and Fundamental Freedoms
2000	Convention Prohibiting Trafficking of Women and Children for Prostitution
2000	International Convention for the Suppression of the Financing of Terrorism
2000	Optional Protocol to the Convention on the Elimination of Discrimination against Women
2000	Optional Protocol to the Convention on the Rights of the Child on the Involvement of Children in Armed Conflicts
2000	Optional Protocol to the Convention on the Rights of the Child on the Sale of Children, Child Prostitution and Child Pornography
2000	Principles on the Effective Investigation and Documentation of Torture and Other Cruel, Inhumane or Degrading Treatment or Punishment
2002	Optional Protocol to the Convention against Torture and other Cruel, Inhumane or Degrading Treatment or Punishment

This inventory of some of the major conventions since the Universal Declaration of Human Rights was proclaimed in 1948 documents the extraordinary growth of human rights legislation.

In the chapters that follow in Part III, we will examine the primary issues of the politics of global welfare, helping us to better understand the world as it presently exists and contemplate as caring citizens of a global society the prospects for a transformed world—a world made new.

KEY TERMS

ethics
morality
realism
civil society
human rights
sanctions
liberalism
paradigm
feminist theory
level of analysis
globalization
dependency theory
human needs
Human Development Index (HDI)
purchasing power parity (PPP)
Third Way
globalization
human security

refugees
ethnic cleansing
failed states
Global South
brain drain
xenophobia
asylum
atrocities
sanctuary
national security
indigenous peoples
Fourth World
genocide
nonstate nations
sovereignty
devolution
clash of civilizations
ethnocentrism

self-determination
ethnic cleansing
irredentism
ethnonationalism
Gender Empowerment Measure (GEM)
role
gender inequalities
ideology
constructivism
noncombatant immunity
international regime
regime
humanitarian intervention
noncombatants
war crimes

SUGGESTED READING

Beitz, Charles R. "Human Rights as a Common Concern," *American Political Science Review* 95 (June 2001): 269–282.

Brysk, Alison, and Gershon Shafir, eds. *People out of Place: Globalization, Human Rights, and the Citizenship Gap.* New York: Routledge, 2004.

Coleman, Isobel. "The Payoff from Women's Rights." *Foreign Affairs* (May–June 2004): 80–95.

Felice, William F. *The Global New Deal: Economic and Social Human Rights in World Politics.* Lanham, Md.: Rowman and Littlefield, 2003.

Fields, A. Belden, and Kristen Milord, eds. *Rethinking Human Rights for the New Millennium.* London: Palgrave, 2004.

Franck, Thomas M. "Are Human Rights Universal?" *Foreign Affairs* 80 (January/February 2001): 191–204.

Gready, Paul, ed. *Fighting for Human Rights.* New York: Routledge, 2004.

Kardam, Nükel. "The Emerging Global Gender Equality Regime from Neoliberal and Constructivist Perspectives in International Relations." *International Feminist Journal of Politics* 6 (March 2004): 85–109.

Lauren, Paul Gordon. *The Evolution of International Human Rights: Visions Seen.* Philadelphia: University of Pennsylvania Press, 1999.

Schulz, William F. *In Our Own Best Interest: How Defending Human Rights Benefits Us All.* Boston: Beacon, 2001.

Tickner, J. Ann. *Gendering World Politics: Issues and Approaches in the Post-Cold War Era.* New York: Columbia University Press, 2002.

United Nations Development Programme (UNDP). *Human Development Report 2005.* New York: Oxford University Press, 2005.

WHERE ON THE WORLD WIDE WEB?

Amnesty International
http://www.amnesty.org/

Amnesty International (AI) is an international non-governmental organization (NGO) with a global reach and a specific purpose. Its activities are concentrated on prisoners around the world who are detained solely for their beliefs, color, sex, ethnic origin, language, or religion. Amnesty International advocates the release of all prisoners of conscience, the availability of a fair and prompt trial for political prisoners, and the abolishment of the death penalty, torture, and other cruel and inhumane treatment of prisoners. What are some of the issues of current concern to Amnesty International? What recent news events involve the rights of prisoners?

Business and Human Rights Resource Centre
http://www.business-humanrights.org/

The Business and Human Rights Resource Centre is a UK-based organization that works in conjunction with Amnesty International. It seeks to shed light on how businesses around the world treat their workers. To that end it provides a wide array of resources that document the human rights practices of businesses, both positive and negative. Investigate a specific company and find out how it treats workers. Compare two countries regarding worker rights.

University of Minnesota Human Rights Library
http://www1.umn.edu/humanrts/

The Human Rights Library at the University of Minnesota contains more than eighteen thousand documents related to human rights, including numerous primary sources such as UN treaties and U.S. documents. It also contains links to more than four thousand websites concerned with human rights. It is an excellent source for investigating human rights anywhere in the world.

Overseas Development Institute
http://www.odi.org.uk

Located in London, the Overseas Development Institute is a think tank that focuses on human rights and economic development. It seeks to coordinate the use of applied research in the formulation of practical policy advice. What are ODI's current areas of interest regarding humanitarian issues?

Fourth World Documentation Project
http://www.cwis.org/fwdp/fwdp.html

The Center for World Indigenous Studies created this website to document and make available important materials relating to the social, political, strategic, economic, and human rights problems that indigenous peoples face. The site is organized according to region and has links to international agreements and resolutions. Pick the region that interests you most and investigate a specific indigenous group.

NativeWeb
http://www.nativeweb.org

NativeWeb has both a resource center and a community center. Research the native peoples of the world by clicking on the "Resource Center" link, or click the "Communities" link to discuss current issues on the message board. You can also participate in an online chat.

NetAid
http://www.netaid.org

NetAid is a new effort to use the unique networking capabilities of the Internet to promote development and alleviate extreme poverty across the world. NetAid issues periodic calls to action on items of urgency and focuses attention on what works. Read about efforts aimed at ending hunger, helping refugees, saving the environment, securing human rights, and relieving debt. This site also suggests actions you can take to address some of these issues.

The United Nations and the Status of Women: Setting the Global Gender Agenda
http://www.un.org/Conferences/Women/PubInfo/Status/Home.htm

Table 7.2 chronicles thirty-five years of progress on women's rights. As you can see, the UN and its programs have provided the most important international forums on women's rights. This website explains the major UN programs that advance women's rights, including the Committee on the Elimination of Discrimination against Women, UN Actions for Women, Commission on the Status of Women, Women in Development, and the Convention on the Elimination of All Forms of Discrimination against Women. What specific actions are these committees and commissions taking to promote women's rights?

WHERE ON THE WORLD WIDE WEB? (continued)

United Nations High Commissioner for Refugees
http://www.unhcr.ch/

Any study of human rights requires that one consider migration. The UN High Commissioner for Refugees leads and coordinates international action for the worldwide protection of refugees and the resolution of refugee problems. This website offers a wealth of information on refugees and is a good place to start examining the issues involved. The "Protecting Refugees" link describes one of the fundamental aspects of the UN-HCR. The "Statistics" link gives you current numbers on refugees worldwide as well as by country. Explore the "News" link to examine important current topics.

INFOTRAC® COLLEGE EDITION

Monshipouri, Mahmood. "The Road to Globalization Runs through Women's Struggle: Iran and the Impact of the Nobel Peace Prize." *World Affairs* (Summer 2004).

Zakaria, Fareed. "Islam, Democracy, and Constitutional Liberalism." *Political Science Quarterly* (Spring 2004).

Litvin, Daniel. "Memo to the President." *Foreign Policy* (November–December 2003).

Schulz, William, Robin Fox, and Francis Fukuyama. "The Ground and Nature of Human Rights: Another Round." *The National Interest* (Summer 2002).

For more articles, enter:

"indigenous peoples" in the Subject Guide, and then go to subdivision "economic aspects"

"refugees" in the Subject Guide, and then go to subdivision "care and treatment"

"human rights" in the Subject Guide, and then go to subdivision "analysis"

Go to http://politicalscience.wadsworth.com/kegley10 to access additional resources related to this chapter.

PART III

THE POLITICS OF GLOBAL WELFARE

What factors most affect the welfare of the world's people? World politics may be played out on a large stage, but with the expansion of international commerce and communication, a new era of globalization has arisen, knitting the world into a tight web of interdependence. Money, goods, and people travel across national borders at an accelerating pace. The effects of globalization are felt locally because to an increasing extent what happens in one place influences what happens every place, and how people live any one place affects how people live everywhere else. The chapters in Part III draw attention to issues of global welfare throughout the world—and the ways that state-to-state relations and global institutions are transforming humanity's living standards and future prospects. This section explores the global condition and its human impact in the twenty-first century, looking at the ways in which globalization is transforming international relations (Chapter 8), how changes in international trade and monetary affairs affect world politics (Chapter 9), and how the relationship between population demographics and the earth's ecological system (Chapter 10) influence human and global prosperity—the quality of life, the degree of liberty, and the expectation of security.

CHAPTER 8

GLOBALIZATION AND THE PROSPECTS FOR GLOBAL GOVERNANCE

TOPICS AND THEMES

- What is globalization?
- The globalization of communications in the information age
- The globalization of contagious disease through transnational contact
- The globalization of finance
- The globalization of trade
- The globalization of production
- Globalization and widening inequalities?
- Globalization, the state, and global governance: What future?

- **CONTROVERSY** DOES GLOBALIZATION MEAN THE END OF THE AGE OF STATES?
- **CONTROVERSY** IS GLOBALIZATION HELPFUL OR HARMFUL?

The first McDonald's franchise opens in Lebanon.

What is globalization? The short answer is that globalization is the integration of everything with everything else. A more complete definition is that globalization is the integration of markets, finance, and technology in a way that shrinks the world from a size medium to a size small. Globalization enables each of us, wherever we live, to reach around the world farther, faster, deeper, and cheaper than ever before and at the same time allows the world to reach into each of us farther, faster, deeper, and cheaper than ever before.

—THOMAS FRIEDMAN, political journalist, 2002

In the post–9/11 world, the rich and poor worlds are linked as never before— by economics and trade, migration, climate change, disease, drugs, conflict and, yes, terrorism. We know that elections are won and lost on local issues—that is true for every country. But it is global issues . . . that will shape the world our children live in.

—JAMES WOLFENSOHN, World Bank president, 2004

Stock prices tumble as foreign investors sell investments across borders with lightning speed, while your parents fret about their ability to meet their bills. Industrial and financial tycoons merge their multinational companies to form a global business colossus, and you discover that your local bank is now controlled overseas and your new employer is headquartered abroad and plans to restructure by cutting the workforce. As the Federal Reserve System lowers U.S. interest rates, skittish currency traders sell billions of dollars and buy euros. Another U.S. manufacturer shifts production overseas, substituting foreign workers without trade unions for local union workers. A bomb explodes in your hometown, and a friend's family member dies from the violence believed caused by foreign terrorists. Meanwhile, clad in Levi Jeans no longer produced in the

United States and Calvin Klein shirts made in China, university students in Istanbul chat with friends in America on cellular phones as they sip raki in a local bar, while the music of Bono from U2 plays in the background.

What in the world is going on? The answer: globalization. Capital, commerce, advanced technology, and information are spreading worldwide at record speeds, producing the complexity and chaos associated with what is today widely known as **globalization.** "Globalization" is a shorthand for a cluster of interconnected phenomena that together are transforming world politics. It is used to describe, alternatively, a process, a policy, a predicament, and the product of vast, invisible international forces producing massive changes worldwide. Most would probably agree that globalization is a permanent trend leading to a global phenomenon.

Globalization is a hot topic. Money, goods, people, technology, and ideas are moving across national borders at an accelerating pace. As the world is rapidly becoming interconnected, linked tighter and tighter into a single, integrated global community and market, globalization is transforming world affairs profoundly.

This interdependence creates both possibilities and problems. On the one hand, globalization is uniting the world and generating unprecedented new levels of wealth. On the other hand, globalization is making national boundaries and state governments less important and, by creating some winners and many losers, it is also producing greater inequalities. Globalization is leading to the simultaneous integration and disintegration of states, to the growth of some states' power and the erosion of many other states' authority, and few global actors know how to adaptively respond to the force of globalization's changes.

It is understandable, therefore, that globalization is so controversial. It is a small world, after all; but is that good or bad? People cannot seem to agree. In fact, there is even disagreement about what globalization is, even if the word *globalization* "has become the most ubiquitous in the language of international relations [and] has spawned a new vocabulary: *globaloney* (why all the hype when the global economy was more integrated in the age of Queen Victoria?); *globaphobia* (the new, mainly mistaken, backlash); *globeratti* (the members of the international nongovernmental organizations [NGOs] who travel around the world from conference to conference, except when they are on the Internet mobilizing for the next conference), and so on" (Ostry 2001). In addition to trying to agree on what globalization encompasses is the larger issue about globalization's consequences. Consider one assessment:

> Days of speeches at the World Economic Forum [in Davos] and at the counter-gathering in Porto Alegre, Brazil, about the benefits and evils of globalization benumb the brain. Has globalization triumphed? Is it threatened by a backlash of which demonstrations and their suppression are the precursors? Or is everyone thinking at cross-purposes?
>
> Is the globalization divide just a replay of the North-South debate of two decades ago? Or perhaps yet another divide is emerging, with most of Asia opting out of what it sees as an acrimonious ideological debate that slows progress on pragmatic trade issues.
>
> In one corner are those who seem to believe that globalization is an ideology to be preached rather than the consequence of other, mostly beneficial forces—technological change plus the efforts of major countries to reduce

■ **globalization**
according to the International Monetary Fund, "the increasingly close international integration of markets both for goods and services and for capital."

barriers to the movement of goods, money and ideas. They are under the illusion that it is new, but globalization has been proceeding in fits and starts, with occasional major setbacks, for centuries. Nor is it measured by Internet penetration.

Many assume that globalization represents the triumph of the market, without stopping to think of how every nation, not least America, in practice views the market as a tool, not an ideology, which domestically is submitted to a moral and income distribution framework determined by society.

In the other corner are those who complain bitterly about all manner of evils that they attribute to globalization. These critics are divided between those in rich countries who fear its impact on them and those who attack it because it is, sometimes with good reason, passing them by. If they get beyond anger they often end up proposing solutions in line with the liberalization that contributes to globalization. (Bowring 2001, 8)

Try to construct an objective evaluation of these and other competing views of globalization. We ask you to contemplate two very different possible futures for world politics as a result of the globalization process that is so differently interpreted. That is, you will be forced to compare two forecasts for the global future. In one optimistic scenario, **neoliberal theory** sees sovereignty at bay as the globalization of markets and cultures transcends contemporary geopolitical boundaries and erodes the meaning of national identity, creating "global citizens" who assign loyalty to the common interests of all peoples. In the other, more pessimistic forecast, states will compete with one another to attain or retain the trappings of independence from and control over the homogenizing forces now sweeping the world. This competition will divide the world even as countries become more alike, making some wealthy and stable but others poorer and fragile.

Globalization stems from "the onrush of economic and ecological forces that demand integration and uniformity and that mesmerize the world with fast music, fast computers, and fast food—with MTV, Macintosh, and McDonald's pressing nations into one commercially homogenous global network: one McWorld tied together by technology, ecology, communications, and commerce" (Barber 1995). Such forces imply nothing less than a redistribution of global economic power "which will increasingly translate into a redistribution of political power" (Schwab and Smadja 1996).

In this and the next two chapters we will examine the diverse forces propelling the rapid globalization now sweeping the world. This chapter will look primarily at the economic influence of international trade, investment, finance, and production and their impact on markets, growth, and global governance. Chapter 9 broadens the coverage to encompass the implications of globalization for the new international political economy, and Chapter 10 examines the demographic (population) and ecopolitical (environmental) dimensions of a globalizing world. Together, all three chapters force consideration of how globalization is likely to affect the **human security** of people and their human rights (recall Chapter 7), as well as, at the **state level of analysis,** the well-being of countries in the Global North and the Global South. This evaluation will force consideration of the prospects for the continuation of states as sovereign and independent actors against the tide toward a cosmopolitan world culture and an emerging

■ **neoliberal theory**
a philosophy that maintains that peaceful change with prosperity can be encouraged through cooperation in institutions that knit the states and peoples of the world together into a true global community.

■ **human security**
a concept that refers to the degree to which the welfare of individuals is protected and advanced, in contrast to national security, which puts the interests of states first.

■ **state level of analysis**
an analytical approach to the study of world politics that emphasizes how the internal attributes of states explain their foreign policy behaviors.

The World at One's Fingertips The revolution in telecommunications has contributed to "the death of distance," as virtually instantaneous communications are possible nearly everywhere. Here, in a remote and desolate region of northern Kenya, a Samburu warrior makes a call on his cellular telephone.

global polity with institutions for global governance (see Controversy: Does Globalization Mean the End of the Age of States?). It will also force interpretation of the prospects for international cooperation and conflict. Before inspecting globalization's consequences—whether globalization is best seen as a plot by profit-hungry megacorporations to exploit workers and despoil the environment, a return to colonialism, a magic cure-all for economic problems, the last step in the creation of world government, or any number of potential possibilities—we must first inspect globalization's causes.

WHAT IS GLOBALIZATION?

■ **global village**
a popular image used to describe the growth of awareness that all people share a common fate, stemming from a macro perspective that the world is an integrated and interdependent whole.

Rapid and unrestrained communication is a hallmark of the **global village**—a metaphor used by many futurologists to portray a world in which borders will vanish and the world will become a single community. The major source of this global transformation is the growing speed and flow of communications. In the "age of global televison" (Gilboa 2003), the meaning of "home" and "abroad" and of "near" and "distance" vanishes, promoting changes in people's images of community and their own identity. Will cellular phones and other means of transnational communication portend consensus, and, perhaps, an integrated global village? Or is the vision of such a global village, in which shared information breeds understanding and peace, pure mythology? Worse, will the virus of interconnectiveness within globalization do away with private life, erasing what remains of identity, individualism, and independence?

The Global Information Age

Cellular phones are becoming available worldwide, enabling many in the world who have never before made a phone call to communicate instantly with others. The "wireless world" of mobile or cellular phones that use radio waves rather than installed lines is growing almost 50 percent yearly, allowing communication between rural areas in developing Global South countries and "wired" Global North countries, where connected telephone lines are already abundant. The globe is linked directly by more than 1 billion fixed-line telephone lines and now for the first time even more cellular phone subscribers, and the number of mobile subscribers worldwide has multiplied greatly by people making wireless connections to the Internet, bridging the communications divide between the rich and the poor (*Vital Signs 2003,* 60). As might be expected in a globalized world, the volume of international communications has increased proportionately. "The death of distance as a determinant of the cost of communications will probably be the single most important economic force shaping society in the first half of the [twenty-first] century," according to the *Economist* (September 30, 1995, 5–6). "It will alter, in ways that are only dimly imaginable, decisions about where people live and work; concepts of national borders; patterns of international trade. Its effects will be as pervasive as those of the discovery of electricity."

Computers are another significant agent of globalization. No area of the world and no arena of politics, economics, society, or culture is immune from the pervasive influence of computer technology. Even victims of ethnopolitical conflict and natural disasters in the most remote corners of the world are connected to others by the laptop computers that relief workers from the International Red Cross and Red Crescent Societies bring with them.

More than 250 million computers are in use today; more than 95 percent are personal computers (PCs), which have replaced the mainframes of yesteryear. Their number is growing by the millions annually, propelled by miniaturization. Microprocessors in today's PCs are incredibly small and growing more powerful at a phenomenal rate. "Computers owe their growth and impact to a phenomenon dubbed Moore's Law (after Gordon Moore, the founder of Intel), which says that computing power and capacity double every eighteen months. This exponential growth has led to the digital revolution."

The freedom people enjoy with personal computers without government intervention is most apparent on the Internet. Individuals routinely "surf the Net" without constraints, creating a global, electronic web of people, ideas, and interactions—a **cyberspace**—unencumbered by state borders. The Internet is the functional equivalent of the "information superhighway" telecommunications specialists have long anticipated and promised.

Use of the Internet has grown—fueled by the growth of personal computers in homes and businesses—from less than 100,000 Internet hosts in 1988 to more than 172 million hosts connecting 689 million people in 2002 (*U.S. News & World Report,* April 22, 2002, 69). Most experts estimate that the Internet will grow by at least 50 percent each year. The number of web pages is increasing nine times faster than world population, and Internet users are growing by more

■ **cyberspace**
metaphorical term used to describe the global electronic web of people, ideas, and interactions on the Internet, which is unencumbered by the borders of the geopolitical world.

> **CONTROVERSY**
>
> ## DOES GLOBALIZATION MEAN THE END OF THE AGE OF STATES?
>
> What does globalization today mean for the survival of the state? To some thinkers "it's the end of sovereignty [which] has seen the rise of the European state as the epitome of political organization. The twenty-first century will see the end of state sovereignty as we have known it" Howell (1998). According to this construction, states are "overwhelmed by globalization. . . . They have lost control of their economies and are powerless to deal with large-scale environmental problems. . . . The state is famously disparaged as being too small for the big things and too big for the small things. . . . If [a state's] industries are undermined [and] its resources controlled by foreigners, it has no hope succeeding in the pursuit of progress. The state will be weak, corrupted by foreign capital and unable to meet its responsibilities to ensure the welfare and liberties of its people" (Boli, Elliott, and Bieri 2004). But others believe that a backlash is under way against globalization that signals a renewed rise in the power of the state, and that the nation-state has "made a remarkable, unexpected recovery. . . . Globalizaton [is] in the middle of an accelerating political meltdown marked by astonishing levels of nationalist violence [as the world has] entered the post-globalization vacuum [with] the return of the idea of national power" (Saul 2004).
>
> Consider this debate as informed by the observations of journalist Neal R. Peirce, who attended the fiftieth Salzburg Seminar of global leaders in 1997 to contemplate the state's future in the face of transformative globalization. Peirce issued this provocative summary of the debate, which provides a good framework to consider rival ideas about globalization's causes, likely consequences, and probable impact on the survival of the nation-state.
>
>> Is the nation-state at the end of its 500-year run? Is it about to succumb to rapid-fire economic globalization, resurgent regions or to ethnic and tribal rivalries?
>>
>> Not entirely, say midcareer professionals from some 32 nations who came here in March [1997] to debate the nation-state's furture at the elegant 18th-century palace that has been the site of the Salzburg Seminar for 50 years.
>>
>> Whether from advanced or undeveloped, Western or Eastern nations, most participants agreed we'll still need nation-states to give people identity, raise taxes, provide social safety nets, protect the environment and guarantee internal security.
>>
>> But for a peek into the deep uncertainties of the 21st century and the astounding array of forces now undermining the nation-states, this conference was a remarkable tour de force.
>>
>> Leading the parade of transformative change are globalization and its accomplices. The computer and telecommunications revolutions enable instant worldwide communications to create new relationships, new economics, whether central governments like them or not.

than a million each week (Aaronson 2001, 545, 547). "In 1992, only 1 in 237 people worldwide used a mobile phone, and 1 in 778 used the Internet; the numbers have soared to 1 in 5 and 1 in ten, respectively" (*Vital Signs 2003*, 60).

The Internet is an engine for the conduct of business and the transfer of capital through e-commerce across borders. In this sense, although the entire world is being wired and connected, it is at different rates: The ratio of Global North to Global South Internet users is 17 to 1 (*Vital Signs 2003*, 60). Thus, geography still matters. The Internet has not liberated many in the Global South countries from their technological dependence on the places where almost all management of websites is located. Even if the Internet has made for the worldwide hypermobility of ideas and information, the so-called digital arms race has resulted in the concentration and control of intellectual property in the Global North in such international Internet bandwidth giants as the most-wired country in the world, Finland, and the globe's economic powerhouse, the United States. This is made especially evident with respect to global e-commerce, which

Multinational corporations now assemble goods from plants across the globe and have moved heavily into services, too—law, accounting, advertising, computer consultation—as if the world were borderless.

Financial markets are also globalized. Where nation-states once sought to set exchange rates, private traders now control currency flows—at a scarcely believable level of $1.5 trillion a day.

The nation-states fatefully shrank their own power by creating supernational institutions such as the United Nations, World Trade Organization and World Bank. Each creates its own cadres of civil servants unaccountable to any single state.

Now comes a rise of influential, globally active non-governmental organizations—the NGOs—ranging from Greenpeace to Amnesty International to animal rights groups. They got official UN recognition at the Rio Earth Summit in 1992; now they're negotiating to get a voice in official UN deliberations. Yet the NGOs, like multinationals, are mostly based in Europe and North America, feeding off cutting-edge technology, setting new global standards without much accountability to anyone.

Globalization is creating immense wealth. Yet countries unwilling or unequipped to become technologically connected—many in Africa today, for example—face "marginalization," another word for isolation and poverty.

At the Salzburg sessions there was real unease about globalization—a fear that the world order now emerging would be too cruel, too amoral, too exclusive in its power-wielding.

Anil Saldanha, a corporate executive from India, gave voice to these concerns.

"Man is not well," Mr. Saldanha said. "He is going through a process of insularity—insecurity, fright, fear. He doesn't know what's thrust on him. He must cope. So we need to look inward, to express our individuality, spirituality. If we do not put a human face on globalization, bring humanity to the forefront, we may not have far to go."

A global market does not create a global community, another speaker commented.

Yet the conference made it clear that the erosion of the nation-state is not only coming from above, it's creeping up from below.

One force is the rise of subnational regions impatient with the bureaucracy and unresponsiveness of large national governments. Nimble city-states—the "Asian tigers" of Hong Kong, Taiwan and Singapore, for example—have been recent models of success. In 1970, four U.S. states had trade offices abroad. Now virtually all do and all have official standing in the World Trade Organization.

Ethnic, racial and religious groups grasping for power are perhaps an even greater pressure from below. The end of the Cold War untapped myriad ethnic nationalistic tensions.

Indeed, we may end up with more nation-states. The United Nations had 166 member "states" in 1991. It now has 185 [now 191], and it could one day end up with 400 or more, just because of ethnic divisions. But how many will be viable nations? And what does the developed world do about the collapse of countries worlds removed from its sleek globalization?

New hybrid structures—African, Asian or Latin American emulations of the European Union, for example—may be needed.

Perhaps we'll see forms of community as unknown now as the nation-state was when it burst on the scene in the 16th century.

SOURCE: Peirce (1997), 9.

---

raises concerns. "Something like three-quarters of all e-commerce currently takes place in the United States. The country also accounts for 90 percent of commercial websites. Given that the Internet is, by its very nature, global in reach, theses two facts raise a vital question about e-commerce for the rest of the world: is America in general, and are American websites in particular, inevitably going to dominate it?" (*Economist*, February 26, 2000, 49).

Communication technologies are driving much of the globalization process and are the underlying force in the global race for knowledge in today's information age:

Communications technology set this era of globalization apart from any other. The Internet, mobile phones, and satellite networks have shrunk space and time. Bringing together computers and communications unleashed an unprecedented explosion of ways to communicate at the start of the 1990s. Since then tremendous productivity gains, ever-falling costs and rapidly growing networks of computers have transformed the computing and communications sector. If the automobile industry had the same productivity growth, a car today would cost $3. (UNDP 1999, 57–58)

If there's one constant that stands out, it is continuous change in technological innovation. The rapid pace of information technology (IT) development drives globalization. It can make today's methods of communicating look ancient in a few years, and in the process transform patterns in how people communicate and which countries lead (and prosper) and which follow. Consider what Thomas Friedman (2004) labels "the third great era of globalization," the

> convergence of a variety of software applications—from e-mail to Google, to Microsoft Office, to specially designed outsourcing programs—that, when combined with all those personal computers and bandwidth, made it possible to create global work-flow platforms. These work-flow platforms can chop up any service job—accounting, radiology, consulting, software engineering—into different functions and then, thanks to scanning and digitization, outsource each function to teams of skilled knowledge workers around the globe, based on which team can do each function with the highest skill at the lowest price. Then the project is reassembled back at headquarters into a finished product. Thanks to this new work-flow network, knowledge workers anywhere in the world can contribute their talents more than ever before, spurring innovation and productivity. But these same workers will be under more pressure than ever to constantly upgrade their skills. India and China are at the moment the primary beneficiaries of this technological face of globalization, supplying the skilled labor at low costs for services other countries cannot supply competitively and, in the process, creating an explosion of wealth in the middle classes of the world's two biggest nations, India and China, and giving both nations a huge stake in the success of globalization. (Friedman 2004b, 9)

To some enthusiasts, the advantages of the communications revolution are, through globalization, a blessing for humanity. Far-reaching changes "as the communications revolution turns digital promises . . . to connect everything to everything else, are creating . . . a tremendous force for human development for all those connected—by providing information, enabling empowerment, and raising productivity" (UNDP 1999). Enthusiasts see globalization as advantageous because the digital revolution reduces state governments' authority. Envisioning the information age as liberating, advocates for the promotion of globalization regard it as a leveling factor that allows small businesses to successfully compete in the global marketplace, empowering the globe's more than 31,000 nongovernmental organizations (NGOs) to bring a new lobbying power to previously silent voices on the global stage, allowing a diversity of voices and cultures to be heard. The Internet expands information and communication in ways that threaten dictatorial governments' rule, as China discovered when it once unsuccessfully sought to muzzle web networking by the Falun Gong religious movement.

Critics, on the other hand, complain that the growing electronic network has created a new global condition known as **virtuality.** Claude Moisy (1997) defines this as "the ability to create a fictitious world using one's computers." In such a world one can conceal one's true identity, which threatens to make the activities of international organized crime and terrorist groups easier, as illustrated by the

■ **virtuality**
imagery created by computer technology of objects and phenomena that produces a fictitious picture of actual things, people, and experiences.

FIGURE 8.1
The Digital Divide

International communication is making a global village, but the rate at which information is transferring is uneven in different regions. This figure taps the density with which communications occur in the world and captures what is meant by the so-called digital divide, the division of the technological "haves" in the Global North and the technological "have-nots" in the Global South. Note that the highest density of flows is shown in the darker shading across North America, Europe, and northeast Asia. The "digital divide" in the availability of the Internet is evident; the wealthy Global North is far more connected than are countries within the less-developed Global South, although the gap is rapidly closing in the emerging markets.
SOURCE: Flanagan, Frost, and Kugler (2001, 24).

global terrorist network Al Qaeda's use of computers to coordinate the destruction of the World Trade Center towers in New York on September 11, 2001.

Critics also warn that even as Internet use and commerce grow, the communications revolution is widening the gap between the rich and the poor, leading to the globalization of poverty and the destruction of local culture. They point to the probability that computer technology and communication are agents of rapid globalization, that accentuate the already wide differences in countries' abilities to shape (and be shaped by) a computer-driven world. As shown in Figure 8.1 for example, the spread of the Internet is heavily concentrated in the Global North to a handful of newly industrialized economies, primarily in Asia. Thus the communication revolution through computer technology suggests the peril that globalization will be increasingly uneven, benefiting the privileged countries while putting the rest at a great disadvantage. For example, the doors to the communication revolution for small entrepreneurs in developing countries remain closed, creating a **digital divide** where one-third of the world's 6 billion people have not yet gained access. The digital divide refers broadly to the access that people have to **information and communications technology (ICT)**. The demographic, economic, and social patterns that explain

■ **digital divide**
the division between the Internet technology-rich Global North and the Global South in the proportion of Internet users and hosts.

■ **information and communications technology (ICT)**
the technological means through which information and communications are transferred, such as through the World Wide Web.

The Internet and the Export of Mass Culture throughout the Globe As the Internet has expanded throughout the globe, in a wired world local customs and culture are becoming lost as the same language and messages are communicated around the world at the same time. "Mass culture is now exported from all over to all over [producing] a global hall of mirrors in which we do not always know what originated where" (Pells 2002). "Consider the word 'O.K.' How often do you use it? How often do you hear others use it? O.K. has found its way into the local vernacular of a vast number of languages—so much so that it may be the only word you will understand if you travel to foreign

---

the digital divide are not surprising. Because educational attainment is closely correlated with income and urban residence, level of education is the single most powerful determinant of ICT access and use.

The so-called digital divide remains deep. Yet the divide probably will close in the future because globalization has been more fierce in the spread of technology than originally thought, and "Current trends suggest that the divide is actually shrinking, not growing" (*Economist*, January 24, 2004). Increasingly the volume of digital communications evident in the United States is being matched not only elsewhere in the technologically sophisticated Global North but also in the Global South. But because education and income are in short supply in the Global South, it also is not surprising that the global digital divide closely tracks the inverse of the global demographic divide (see Figure 8.1).

ICT technologies hold great promise for many of the poorer countries of the world, since these technologies permit the Global South to "leapfrog" technologies in which the Global North invested heavily as they developed economically. Wireless phones, for example, enjoy both popularity and promise in many developing countries, where the cost of stringing line from pole to pole for traditional wired phones is often prohibitive. But because the individual, social, economic, and geographic factors that have created and perpetuated the digital countries. This is globalization in process. . . . We are becoming a soup of culture, politics, society, race and language sloshed into a large melting pot labeled 'humanity'" (Leow 2002). The Internet is the primary vehicle for the homogenization of the world through globalization that is erasing traditional identities. Above left is one example: new technology in Moorea. Above right is another example: the EasyEverything Internet Café in Paris, a crowded web bar that is jammed around the clock with eager customers passing information and ideas through e-mail around the world.

---

divide are complex, narrowing it will prove difficult. The Global North remains at present the primary beneficiary of the communications revolution. In particular the United States, where the Internet was developed, remains predominant in this electronic network, although "Denmark leads the world as the country most open to information technology. America ranks third" (*Economist*, November 20, 2004, 6). America's technological and information edge may not enable it to dominate the future world.

The Media: Markets or Monopoly?

Ours is often described as the information age, but a remarkably large portion of the information we receive is controlled by a small number of media sources. In the United States, despite more than twenty-five thousand media outlets, only a handful of merging multimedia giants now control most daily newspapers, magazines, television, books, and motion pictures. And as corporate America merges its media sources into ever larger and fewer units—as witnessed in Disney Corporation's buyout of the ABC broadcasting network, as well as Viacom's acquisition of the CBS broadcasting network and the giant spread of Verizon Communications—fewer and fewer corporate executives will control what Americans hear and see about the world around them. The world's population may become a captive audience to what a few telecommunication corporate giants choose to present as information. Although thousands of potential sources of information about politics, society, and culture are available, the influence of such media midgets is negligible compared to that of the giants. This gives the rich Global North and, in particular the United States, extraordinary power over the information people throughout the world receive, structuring what they believe and how they view the world.

The media's impact on the global diffusion of Western culture is widely seen as influential, as the handful of news and information agencies operate like a giant circulatory system, pumping ideas, information, and ideals from the wealthy center to the remote periphery in the Global South. This global reach is nowhere more striking than in the fact that the Internet reaches all over the world. The media's power is also attributed to CNN (Cable News Network), the twenty-four-hour news channel beamed around the world, and MTV, which has been called "one of the first global television channels [to give] rise to a global teenage culture linked through music" (Etheredge 1999). Indeed, the recent merger of giant telecommunications companies concentrates further the control of information in the hands of conglomerates. The January 2000 merger of America Online and Time Warner, for example, gave it enormous clout with financial resources one-fourth larger than the annual budget of France (*Harper's,* March 2000, 19). What Global South opponents of globalization complain about is not so much modernization and trade; rather, they oppose "corporate globalization" dictated by multinational corporations that, they contend, ignore the values and needs of the vast majority in the developing world.

The type of power the media wields over international affairs is, in fact, a specific and limited type of power. Scholarship shows that the media influence what people *think about* more than what they *think*. In this way, the media primarily functions to *set the agenda* of public discussion about public affairs instead of determining public opinion. In the process of **agenda setting** the media demonstrably shape international public policy. (see Gilboa 2002). For example, global broadcasts of thousands of marchers protesting for days Ukraine's fraudulent December 2004 election discredited the results, and worldwide protests led the Ukrainian parliament and supreme court to demand a new election. This example of the power of information technology in international politics aside, some people caution that this kind of "virtual diplomacy," possible because of the development of a "global brain" circulating common information through hundreds of communication satellites weaving an information web around the globe, has real limitations. One critic has described the impact of CNN and the media this way:

> In foreign policy circles these days one often hears that the advent of instantaneous and global technology has given the news media far greater influence in international relations than ever before, robbing diplomacy of its rightful place at the helm in the process. Observers of international affairs call it the CNN curve. . . . It suggests that when CNN floods the airwaves with news of a foreign crisis, it evokes an emotional outcry from the public to "do something." Under the spell of the CNN curve, goes this refrain, policymakers have no choice but to redirect their attention to the crisis at hand or risk unpopularity, whether or not such revision is merited by policy considerations. (Neuman 1995–1996, 109)

Control of television and other media sources by the hegemonic United States and a small number of European countries became the focus of hot dis-

■ **agenda setting**
the thesis that by their ability to identify and publicize issues, the communications media determine the problems that receive attention by governments and international organizations.

The Making of a Global Culture? Some people regard globalization as little more than the spread of the values and beliefs of the globe's reigning hegemon, the United States. Shown here is one example that fuels these images— a Santa Claus mannequin with a bicycle "sleigh" attempting to attract customers in downtown Hanoi, Vietnam—a predominantly Buddhist country still subscribing to communist principles emphasizing the greed of market capitalism and the class divisions it is believed to create. The sale of Christmas trees is also rising there, too.

pute with the Global South during the 1980s. Dissatisfied with the media coverage it received from Global North news agencies and resentful of G-8 domination of other forms of communication, Global South leaders demanded a **New World Information and Communication Order (NWICO)** to create a new regime with fair rules to right the imbalance of the information flows from Global North to Global South. The image of the Global South painted by such sources, they believed, fostered Northern values, such as consumerism and conspicuous consumption, that perpetuated the South's dependence on the North. As the North-South conflict brewed, the United States angrily withdrew from the United Nations Educational, Scientific, and Cultural Organization (UNESCO), in part as a rejection of its role in promoting the new communications order. (In September 2002, in an effort to galvanize multilateral support for a preemptive war against Iraq, the United States rejoined UNESCO.)

The NWICO has since receded on the global agenda, but the issues remain very much alive in NGOs concerned about the concentration of so much media power in so few hands. In 1995, Hollywood was able to beam the Academy Awards around the world to over a billion people, and American evangelist Billy Graham preached via electronic links to a similar number in more than 185 countries. The new global information infrastructure is "especially disturbing because dominance in 'global' products implies not just the ability to ship products around the world, but dominance in the export of culture. This dominance

■ **New World Information and Communication Order (NWICO)**
the controversial 1980 call by the less-developed Global South to combat what was termed "cultural imperialism" by circumscribing the news and information disseminated by the Western transnational news agencies.

provides the potential to displace indigenous culture with a tide of largely Western, largely consumerist, global conformity. Perhaps globalization is just a nice word that multinational corporations use to hide their efforts to infect the entire world with the cultural virus of commercialism" (Mowlana 1995).

Against this, many, such as British analyst Philippe Legrain (2003), think that despite America's hegemonic leadership at this point in history, "cultural globalization is *not* Americanization. It is a myth that globalization involves the imposition of Americanized uniformity, rather than an explosion of cultural exchange. . . . If critics of globalization were less obsessed with 'Cola-colonization,' they might notice a rich feast of cultural mixing that belies fears about Americanized uniformity. . . . For all the spread of Western ideas . . . globalization is not a one-way street. . . . Americans are [not] the only players in the global media industry. Of the seven market leaders that have their fingers on nearly every pie, four are American (AOL, Time Warner, Disney Viacom and News Corporation), one is German (Bertelsmann), one is French (Viendt), and one Japanese (Sony). . . . The biggest publisher in the English-speaking world is Germany's Bertelsmann, which gobbled up America's biggest publisher, Random House. . . . Bertelsmann publishes books by American writers, News Corporation broadcasts Asian news, Sony sells Brazilian music."

Whatever its true character, the nearly $1 trillion global telecommunications industry is without question the major vehicle for the rapid spread of ideas, information, and images worldwide. It also plays a role in the transfer of institutions and generation of income, as exhibited by the World Trade Organization's (WTO) World Telecom Pact. Issued by more than sixty countries, the accord to open the industry to the free market creates a new **regime** that ends government and private telecommunication monopolies in many states and has pumped new funds into the global economy by slashing phone costs to consumers and creating countless jobs. Estimating that liberalization could add $1 trillion, or 4 percent, to the value of world economic output over the next decade, WTO Director-General Renato Ruggiero in 1997 proclaimed that the accord "is good news for the international economy, it is good news for businesses and it is good news for the ordinary people around the world." That prediction proved to be on the mark. The WTO agreement on basic telecommunications services generated immediate results that exceeded expectations in four areas:

> market access, the adoption of regulatory principles, liberalization of foreign investment rules, and satellite offers. Market access soared. Fifty-nine countries agreed to adopt transparent, pro-competitive regulatory principles, representing 99 percent of the WTO telecommunications market. Forty-four countries agreed to permit significant inward foreign investment. Fifty countries guaranteed market access for all domestic and international satellite services and facilities. (Aaronson 2001, 543)

The success of the regime suggested the benefits perceived to result from international cooperation to conduct global transactions by rules. Advocates see global telecommunications as a vehicle for progress, liberating minds, expanding choices, penetrating societies closed to diplomatic communication, and creating a single, more united, homogenized "world culture" (Boli and Lechner 2004). Others disagree, however. They note that the airwaves can broadcast divisive messages as well as unifying ones, and that what is said is more important than how much is said.

■ **regime**
the rules agreed to by states to regulate their exchanges.

One counterpoint to the "McWorld" of transnational media consumerism is "Jihad"—a world driven by "parochial hatreds," not "universalizing markets" (Barber 1995). In this context, it is sobering to note that the Ayatollah Khomeini, author of the revival of Islamic fundamentalism that swept the shah of Iran from power in 1979, "combined his access to networks of mosques and bazaars with that of electronic communication and cassette tapes" to carry on a successful long-distance bid to create an Iranian theocracy (Mowlana 1995).

Hence, because globalized communications and information may be used as tools for conflict and revolution as well as for community and peace, the creation of a world without boundaries, where everybody will know everything about anybody's activities, will not necessarily be a better world. We must ask, would the world be better or worse if it were to become an increasingly impersonal place, with rootless individuals with declining connections to their own country's culture and history.

Global Health or Global Infection?

Humankind and the threat of disease have always coexisted uneasily. In the early 1990s, for example, in Kikwit, Zaire, the deadly Ebola virus—after lying dormant for twenty years—broke out and ravaged its victims with massive hemorrhaging and certain death. Globalization not only heightens awareness of health risks but actually multiplies them. Truck drivers in India are primary agents for the AIDS (acquired immune deficiency syndrome) epidemic in that country and elsewhere in Asia. Rapid urbanization in much of the world also contributes to the rapid spread of diseases. Growing numbers of refugees forced into unsanitary camps are ravaged by cholera and other diseases that can prove as deadly as the violence and terrorism they flee. Excessive population growth forces people to move into habitats where unknown microorganisms and killer viruses await them. Millions of airline travelers share cabin-sealed environments filled with the carriers of potentially fatal diseases. A shrinking globe, in short, has made the spread of disease across borders rapid and difficult to control (Chen, Leaning, and Narasimhan, 2003). Gar Harlem Brundtland, the World Health Organization's director-general from 1998 to 2003, summarizes well the so-called globalization of health and disease and the issues it has created:

> The reality is that public health is, as never before, a priority on the global agenda, for the simple reason that so many of the challenges we face now have a global impact, requiring global solutions and a global response. In an interconnected and interdependent world, bacteria and viruses travel almost as fast as email messages and money flows. There are no health sanctuaries. No impregnable walls between the world that is healthy, well-fed, and well-off, and another world that is sick, malnourished, and impoverished. Globalization has shrunk distances, broken down old barriers, and linked people together. It has also made problems half way around the world everyone's problem—the tenacity of the SARS virus and the public health and economic uncertainty it brings underscores this too well. Countries trying to grapple with new epidemics or collapsing under the weight of disease and malnutrition can now have a devastating impact on economies and societies around the globe. The way that we, as an international community, work to address current crises and prevent future ones will determine

whether we succeed or fail in our shared efforts to advance global development, growth, and peace. These global transformations must lead to a profound change in the way we think about health policy—locally, nationally, and internationally. (Brundtland 2003, 7)

The AIDS virus has become a symbol for the global spread of disease in a shrinking world. It is an epidemic, global in scope, with the number of people infected with HIV—the virus that causes AIDS—climbing to more than an estimated 70 million victims, making the HIV/AIDS epidemic "the world's most serious development crisis as well as the most devastating epidemic in history. The epidemic continues to spread, with over 15,000 new infestations every day, and an alarming acceleration in regions and countries hitherto spared" (UNDP Bureau for Development Policy, www.undp.org, December 11, 2004). The number is expected to rise further, despite the increasing availability of antiretroviral treatment in the Global North. One reason is that for the first time, women, who are biologically more vulnerable to the virus than males and are "two to four times more likely than men to become infected during unprotected vaginal sex," now account for half the people with HIV/AIDS" (*Vital Signs 2003*, 68).

AIDS strikes most virulently in the impoverished Global South among the youthful wage earners who are the foundation of the labor force, but it undermines economic growth everywhere on the planet. "Life expectancy is likely to fall to 35 years or less in the worst affected countries" (UNDP Bureau for Development Policy, www.undp.org, December 4, 2004). The human toll from AIDS-related disease has been most severe in sub-Saharan Africa, where the devastating disease accounts for three-quarters of the globe's HIV infections and is the leading cause of death, cutting life expectancy almost in half. The virus is not confined to any quarter of the globe, however; it travels across borders and throughout the world (alongside the increase in travel throughout the world).

Adding to the challenge of preventing international infectious diseases beyond HIV/AIDS is another problem brought on by rising globalization: As a result of underuse of antibiotics in the developing world and overuse in the developed world, viruses are developing stronger strains that are able to overcome standard antibiotics. A recent report (www.who.org, December 4, 2004) by the World Health Organization observes that "almost all infection diseases are slowly but surely becoming resistant to existing medicines." Acute respiratory infections such as pneumonia kill a million more people each year than does AIDS. Diarrheal diseases, tuberculosis, malaria, and measles combined with AIDS and respiratory infections account for 90 percent of total infectious disease deaths worldwide.

"Experts fret that globalization is increasing the risk of the spread of new diseases. Ebola, SARS [severe acute respiratory syndrome], Avian flu, and mad cow disease: We live in the shadow of new epidemics. The avian virus, for instance, might transmute... leading to transmit itself directly from human to human" (Bowring 2004). But humans are not the only victims of so-called borderless diseases, as was made evident in 2001 when the contagious foot-and-mouth disease swept through Europe, and Europeans desperately tried to seal their frontiers to a virus that spread with frightening speed, devastating livestock. As they pitched battle over how to respond, many noted that such epidemics in the European Union were increasingly difficult to contain because borders between countries had all but dissolved and it had been years since anybody needed a passport to travel between most European countries.

Does Globalization Make the Whole World Sick? With increasing contact among humanity growing with tourism and travel, many suspect that the same scientific innovations that make life for humanity healthier, safer, and pleasurable can also make life less secure and safe. One dimension of the debate is whether the globalized world is becoming more healthy. Shown here is one symptom of globalization's potential dangers: in Taipei, Republic of China, commuters alarmed by the global spread of infectious diseases take care to avoid infection as they travel to work.

Another unfortunate product of globalization has been the spread of diseases throughout the globe that are causing massive ecological destruction to the environment. As the World Conservation Union (an NGO that includes more than 78 states and over 10,000 scientists) warns, alien animal, plant, and insect invaders that cross national borders are doing irreparable damage to thousands of native species and, in the process, creating an enormous problem for the planet's environment and public health. In May 2001 the union used World Biodiversity Day to heighten awareness of the threat posed by this invasion, which it labeled "among the costliest and least understood aspects of globalization," proclaiming

> if this were an invasion from space, governments would be alarmed. But these are not extraterrestrials. They are ordinary animals, plants and insects that have escaped from their normal environment to wreak havoc someplace else.

Consider these examples:

- A poisonous brown tree snake from Australia and Indonesia has exterminated most of the native forest birds on Guam and is spreading

across the Pacific, sometimes by hopping a ride in the wheel well of aircraft.
- The Indian mongoose was introduced to the West Indies to control rats, but it has wiped out many native species of birds, reptiles and amphibians. It also carries rabies.
- Crazy ants, proliferating in Asia, are indirectly destroying the rain forest on Christmas Island by exterminating land crabs that play an important role in the ecosystem. In one 18-month period, the ants were estimated to have killed three million crabs.

Globalization is dramatically increasing the opportunities for plants and animals to get from where they form a normal part of the flora and fauna to other places where they can become destructive pests, weeds and parasites, either because people deliberately introduce new species such as exotic fish and plants, or because the invaders slip in aboard aircraft, ships and containers. (James 2001a, 1)

The globalization of health concerns is limited only by the extent to which contagious diseases, viruses, and infections respect state boundaries—which they don't. The world is too interconnected to isolate these threats to health in any location. Other kinds of communicative health problems cross national borders with increasing ease.

Consider the effect of narcotics. Many view narcotic use as a disease. The illicit use of drugs is widespread, hugely profitable, and difficult to control in a borderless world. Fueled by major production and distribution complexes in the Andes and Southeast and Southwest Asia (such as Northern Afghanistan, where opium production increased nineteen-fold since 2001 despite U.S. military occupation (*Harper's*, March 2004, 11), the narcotics trade generates an estimated $500 billion in profits each year for the criminal empires that traffic in illegal, black-market drugs. **International organized crime (IOC)** syndicates have taken advantage of the opportunities created by globalization. A borderless world has made it possible for IOCs to contribute to the corruption of governments, the spread of global terrorism, the growing trafficking of women and children for prostitution, and a whole host of other global problems (Berdal and Serrano 2002).

■ **international organized crime (IOC)**
crime syndicates specializing in the use of technology to cooperatively network with one another throughout the world.

Global Migration

The movement of populations across frontiers has reached unprecedented proportions, producing a **global migration crisis.** Nearly 20 million people in each year from 1998 to 2005 qualified for and received refugee assistance. As floods of people leave their homeland for another country each year, the crossnational movement has become a norm—so common that leaving one's native country has become almost an expectation. "The ease of travel and communication, combined with looser borders, gives rise to endless crisscrossing streams of wanderers and guest workers, nomadic adventures, and international drifters" (Hoffman 2000). Global travel and emigration have become routine in the global age. But the mass movement of people living abroad has raised a host of moral issues, such as the ethnic balance inside host countries, the meaning of citizenship and sovereignty, the distribution of income, labor supply, xenophobia, the impact of multiculturalism, protection of basic human rights and prevention of

■ **global migration crisis**
a crisis stemming from the growing number of people moving from their home country to another country, straining the ability of the host countries to absorb the foreign migrants.

exploitation, and the potential for large flows of migrants and refugees from **failed states** to undermine democratic governance and state stability (see Chapter 7). Particularly troubling is the moral inconsistency between liberal democracies that simultaneously defend the fundamental right of refugees to emigrate and the absolute right of sovereign states to control their borders.

It is not clear, in the absence of a true global civil society able to empower institutions to manage international trends such as cross-border migration, whether the problems and payoffs of globalization can be addressed. State governments are losing their grip on regulating the movement of foreigners inside their borders, and no multilateral IGOs for meaningful global governance exist to deal with the consequences of the escalating migration of people (and jobs!) around the globe. One characteristic is clear: there are both winners and losers through the globalization of migration. Globalization's impact is uneven, affecting conditions in some places favorably and in others harmfully. "While for some globalization has generated wealth and welfare," Juan Somavia, the director-general of the International Labor Organization, explained in 2003,

> many see it as a source of persistent inequality and social exclusion. Growing insecurity and a sense that the rules of the game are unfair have given rise to frustrations in the hearts of many individuals and their families. Questions of legitimacy and sustainability have led to increasingly acrimonious exchanges, most visible in the protests that regularly accompany major meetings of international financial and trade institutions. And what are people worried about? Jobs, to begin with.
>
> Official unemployment, which continues to rise, masks the even larger problem of underemployment and billions of people unable to work in ways that fully utilize their creativity or maximize their productive potential. The work of the poor is largely invisible. Far too much of women's work is still uncounted and undervalued. And the greatest failure of the current system is for young people who see no future (International Labour Office, 2004, 6).

For millions, a common approach to recovering hope for a future is to migrate, and this mass movement of people across borders for jobs has had many **externalities,** or unanticipated consequences, as seen in the huge flow of "remittances" or money that migrants earn while working abroad and then send to their families in their home countries. Remittances across borders are benefiting many poor Global South countries by providing foreign currency. "Every day, migrants working in rich countries send money to their families in the developing world. It's just a few hundred dollars here, a few hundred dollars there. [In 2002] these remittances added up to $80 billion, outstripping foreign aid and ranking as one of the biggest sources of foreign exchange for poor countries. Following a boom in the 1990s, this flow of money [is now] double the amount of foreign aid and ten times higher than net capital transfers (which is the bottom line after deducting all financial outflows, such as profit repatriation and interest payments). The principal beneficiaries are lower middle-income countries . . . which receive nearly half of all remittances worldwide. This flow of money is lifting entire countries out of poverty, creating new financial channels, and reshaping international politics" (Kapur and McHale 2003, 49). As money goes around the world at these growing remittance rates, the globalization of migration means the globalization of finance.

■ **failed states**
countries whose governments no longer enjoy support from their rebelling citizens and from displaced peoples who either flee the country or organize revolts to divide the state into smaller independent units.

■ **externalities**
the side effects produced by choices and behaviors in one activity that alter other conditions, for some beneficially and for others negatively.

THE GLOBALIZATION OF FINANCE

Global finance encompasses "all types of cross-border portfolio-type transactions—borrowing and lending, trading of currencies or other monetary claims, and the provision of commercial banking or other financial services. It also includes capital flows associated with foreign direct investment—transactions involving significant control of producing enterprises" (B. Cohen 1996). The **globalization of finance** refers to the increasing transnationalization or centralization of financial markets through the worldwide integration of capital flows. The central characteristic of the emerging consolidated system of financial arrangements is that it is not centered on a single state. Thus globalization implies the growth of a single, unified world market. While telecommunications specialists talk about the "death of distance," financial specialists talk about the "end of geography," which "refers to a state of economic development where geographic location no longer matters in finance" (O'Brien 1992).

Evidence of financial globalization abounds. Although trade has grown dramatically, since World War II, the volume of cross-border capital flows has increased even more. Financial flows now greatly exceed the volume of trade, and the gap continues to widen. Similarly, cross-border transactions in bonds and equities have increased at an astonishing rate over the past twenty years. In the mid-1990s, "$1,300 billion (roughly the equivalent of the French annual GNP) were being exchanged daily, compared to $18 billion at the beginning of the 1970s" (Pfetsch 1999, 3). "Each day well over a trillion dollars flows around the world, exceeding the volume of trade by 60 times" (Eizenstat 1999, 6).

Further evidence of financial globalization is the astonishing recent increases in the daily turnover on the foreign exchange market. On many days, private currency traders may exchange as much as $2 trillion to make profits through **arbitrage** on the basis of minute shifts in the value of states' currencies, and their activity continues to climb steadily. Consequently, interconnected markets require more than ever a reliable system of money to conduct business across borders while coping with an array of fluctuating national currencies. "It has become a well-known fact that the daily turnover on the currency markets now often exceeds the global stock of official foreign exchange reserves—so what chance have central banks in influencing exchange rates by buying and selling currency in the markets?" (*Economist,* September 10, 1997).

As the transnational economy becomes integrated, "most national central banks are now irrelevant [because] the world's money is essentially controlled by three key institutions: the U.S. Federal Reserve Board, the Bank of Japan, and the German Bundesbank, and global capital markets centered in London, Tokyo, and New York are facilitating increased internationalization in every area of finance" (Thurow 1998). As the market value of stock transactions increased fivefold between 1980 and 2005, a major change occurred: a rise or fall in the security market of any one state began to immediately cause similar changes in other countries' stock indexes. In addition, "derivatives" emerged, leading to new markets in which stocks are traded. Derivatives combine speculation in options and futures to hedge against volatility in financial markets, but they require no actual purchase of stocks or bonds. Derivatives account for trillions of dollars in cross-border transactions and are now estimated to be the most globalized financial market. Automated online trading for equity sales on the Internet in the emerging **digital world economy** has lowered the costs and increased the volume of such cross-border exchanges. It also contributed to the rise of

---

■ **globalization of finance**
the increasing transnationalization of financial markets.

Case Study: Globalization and the Mexicon Peso Crisis

■ **arbitrage**
the selling of one currency (or product) and purchase of another to make a profit on the changing exchange rates; traders ("arbitragers") help to keep states' currencies in balance through their speculative efforts to buy large quantities of devalued currencies and sell them in countries where they are valued more highly.

■ **digital world economy**
a system based largely on globalized electronic debt and credit systems.

global portfolio equity investments and nonbank credit flows through dedicated bond purchases to their highest levels in 2004—$225 billion—in the past seven years, the Institute of International Finance reported.

The computerization of financial transactions and contracts occurred at the same time that, since the 1970s, **commercial liberalism** and its advocacy of state deregulation of global investments and capital movements gained acceptance. States reduced their authority by relaxing their legal control over their economies and by opening their markets to foreign capital.

The predictable result of financial liberalization has been great increases in capital mobility—an exploding expansion of international financial transactions. According to the **capital mobility hypothesis,** the free or unregulated flow of money across borders has produced the globalization of finance.

Because the accelerating mobility of capital means that financial markets are no longer centered within states, the globalized financial system is not subject to regulation by any one state in particular. Most states are losing their capacity to control the flow and level of finance in their national economies. The expanded power of private markets and corporations no longer tied to any one country is "increasingly undermining state power itself and institutionalizing that of the global marketplace. . . . Having set up the conditions in which more open international financial markets were established in the 1970s and 1980s, [states] are now having difficulty controlling their own creations" (Cerny 1994). The accelerated mobility of capital has undermined the assumption of **realist theory** that states are autonomous, unitary actors capable of regulating their internal economic affairs. Globalization limits "the ability of governments to restrict—or even control—economic activity" (Thurow 1998).

The lightning speed of capital mobility has made national markets extremely volatile and vulnerable to sudden reversals caused by their dependence on foreign capital and the rapid flight of capital at the first sign of economic trouble. Capital mobility is at historically high levels (inspect Map 8.1, which in the figure on the right provides a profile of this global trend). As Map 8.1 shows, capital mobility has some unintended consequences, affecting adversely the developing countries of the Global South in comparison with the Global North. About 95 percent of finance capital flows from one rich country to another, rather than from the Global North to the Global South. However, the proportion of global finance capital directed to the Global South is rising in the early-twenty-first century, in response to developing countries' economic liberalization reforms, low interest rates worldwide, increasing liquidity through debt reductions, and the lowered costs of cross-border transportation and communication that has stimulated economic growth.

Hence, the globalization of finance and "capital flight" has resulted in inequalities. True, all countries are mutually vulnerable to rapid transfers of capital in an interdependent, globalized financial world. But the Global South is the most dependent and vulnerable. This circumstance suggests why bankers and economists have called for the creation of more reliable multilateral mechanisms for policy coordination to better manage the massive movement of cross-border capital. For instance, in 2004 Director-General Juan Somavia of the International Labour Organization called for a new compact of different institutions to steer globalization, which is "changing the policy landscape and distribution of power and gains" in order to better defend "social justice for all seekers of sustainable growth."

■ **commercial liberalism**
an economic theory advocating free markets and the removal of barriers to the flow of trade and capital as a locomotive for prosperity.

■ **capital mobility hypothesis**
the proposition that MNCs' movement of investment capital has led to the globalization of finance.

■ **realist theory**
the view that states are sovereign, unitary global actors in relentless competition with one another for position and prosperity in the international hierarchy, able to engineer policies to promote their own interests and to control conditions within their borders.

MAP 8.1

The International Flow of Finance Capital

Capital flows internationally through loans by commercial banks and private creditors and through foreign direct investments (FDI) in businesses located in countries different from those of the investors. The movement of capital across borders has greatly expanded since the 1950s, as the chart above shows. The long-term pattern since 1860 has been cyclical, rising until World War I, and then plummeting before climbing again after World War II with the steady expansion of the international economy. Another long-term trend is also evident: On the eve of World War I, about a quarter of the world stock of foreign capital was sent equally to both rich and poor countries (the other half flowed within each group), but today the Global South is the recipient of only about 5 percent of world finance capital, despite the Global South's impressive ninefold increase since 1990 (*Economist*, May 18, 2002, 27 and May 19, 2001, 104). This "financial divide," like the "digital divide," between the Global North and the Global South makes the international flow of finance capital look less globalized than regionalized.

SOURCE: Distribution of international flows of finance capital, International Monetary Fund indicators, 2004; capital mobility figure from the *Economist*, May 18, 2000, p. 27. Copyright © 2002 by The Economist Newspaper Ltd. All rights reserved. Reprinted with permission. Further reproduction prohibited.

MAP 8.2
The World Trade Organization Goes Global

At the start of 2005, 147 countries, or 70 percent of the world's 210 states, were members of the World Trade Organization, including 30 of the Global South's least developed countries. In addition, 30 "observers," including the Russian Federation, are poised to begin accession negotiations within five years if they are to gain formal membership. Headquartered in Geneva, the WTO feels it is often unfairly criticized by those whose constructed image fails to understand its mission and power. To clarify, the WTO explains that "there are a number of ways of looking at the WTO. It's an organization for liberalizing trade to promote economic growth. It's a forum for governments to negotiate trade agreements. It's a place for them to settle trade disputes. It operates a system of trade rules, a place where member governments go, to try to sort out the trade problems they face with each other through negotiations to lower trade barriers."

As the WTO is fond of saying, far from being antidemocratic it is "hyperdemocratic," because each and every WTO member has a veto over the rules. The WTO acts as a mere referee when members face trade disputes. In addition, the WTO has few resources. With a staff of only 530 and a budget of $78 million (about one-half of what the World Bank spends on travel), the WTO is a midget in the world of nonstate actors. As WTO Director Mike Moore pointed out in 2001, the World Wildlife Fund has three times the financial budget of the WTO.

SOURCE: World Trade Organization.

Online map with critical thinking questions

THE GLOBALIZATION OF TRADE

Technological changes have led to the integration of states' economic markets. However, the extraordinary pace at which the countries of the world have linked their markets can be attributed to more than the increased speed of transport and communication. The internationalization of markets at a global level, and the convergence of commodity prices across countries, have been driven by the worldwide reduction of tariff rates that has made the expansion of international trade possible.

After World War II, the General Agreement on Tariffs and Trade (GATT) was created by the international community, along with the IMF, the World Bank, and other international organizations. Based on the principles of multilateral cooperation, the GATT had a mandate to roll back tariffs from their prewar peaks and to continue reducing them in the future. The GATT was extremely successful in 1947 in the first Geneva Round in reducing tariffs by 35 percent. Successive rounds in the 1950s, 1960s (the Kennedy Round), and the 1970s (Tokyo Round) and the recent Uruguay Round have virtually eliminated tariffs on manufactured goods. The World Trade Organization (WTO), which succeeded GATT in 1994, is currently engaged in reducing nontariff barriers and protection, including in areas not covered by the GATT. (IMF 1997, 113)

The WTO has enlarged its membership, and the 147 countries that have agreed to adhere to its free-trade rules are spread across the globe, with other applicants eagerly seeking entry (see Map 8.2). If and when this expansion process is complete, the globalization of trade will escalate even further and faster.

In historical perspective, the globalization of trade serves as testimony to the wisdom of commercial liberalism, which held that trade liberalization to remove barriers to exports would permit the free trade crucial to growing prosperity. That liberal theory has been supported by experience. The reduction of tariff rates since World War II (see Chapter 9) has permitted international trade and world output to grow hand in hand. "In the half-century since the founding of the **General Agreement on Tariffs and Trade (GATT),** the world economy has grown six-fold, in part because trade has expanded 16-fold" (Micklethwait and Wooldrige 2001, 22). The expansion of global trade is expected to continue to accelerate further the integration of the world marketplace and thereby deepen the level of global interdependence. In Chapter 9 we will examine the dynamics underlying transformations in the world economy. Here we focus attention on the primary product—the rising globalization of trade interdependence.

In 1950, exports accounted for 8 percent of worldwide GDP, and in the fifty-five years since they have more than tripled. The impact of the rising volume of goods shipped from one country to another has been enormous, pushing economic growth to unprecedented levels. International trade has become increasingly important to all states, especially those that in the past were not concerned about exports. Now every state has become increasingly dependent on exports for economic growth and aggressively compete with other countries for a share of the growing international trade market. This has made states interdependent—the key defining characteristic of globalization.

Trade integration is the measure of the extent to which the growth rate in world trade increases faster than does the growth rate of world gross domestic product. As trade integration grows, so does globalization, because states' interdependence grows when countries' exports account for an increasing percentage of their gross domestic product. As Michael Mazarr (1999) explains, "Measuring global trade as a percentage of GDP is perhaps the simplest and most straightforward measure of globalization. If trade in goods and merchandise is growing faster that the world economy as a whole, then it is becoming more integrated."

Figure 8.2 records the remarkable extent to which trade integration has indeed become an entrenched and growing characteristic of world politics be-

■ **General Agreement on Tariffs and Trade (GATT)**
an international organization affiliated with the United Nations that was designed to promote international trade and tariff reductions, replaced by the World Trade Organization.

■ **trade integration**
economic globalization measured by the extent to which world trade volume grows faster than the globe's combined gross domestic product.

FIGURE 8.2
The Growth of Global Trade Integration, 1970–2008

When the percentage change each year in the volume of world trade grows faster than the annual rate of growth of the combined world economy, "trade integration," or international economic transactions, increases. The growth of world trade has far outpaced the growth of real world gross product (WGP), and the trend toward trade interdependence has been accelerating since 1970. Compare the two trends. On the left we observe that the annual percentage change of world trade has been growing on average almost 7 percent each year. On the right we see that the annual percentage change in world economic output has grown in close association with the growth of world trade, but at about half the same average rate. Trade integration has globalized economic interdependence by making countries' increasingly dependent on the expansion of trade with others for economic growth.

SOURCE: World Bank 2004, with projections from 2004 to 2008 (in shaded area) based on International Monetary Fund.

---

tween 1970 and 2008. As world trade has grown more rapidly than the world economy (and world population as well), the former has made the latter possible. Further, the increasing dependence of states' prosperity on exports with others binds the world together in a tightening web of mutual interdependence. States are increasingly dependent on the willingness of other states to import the goods they produce. This convergence of countries' economic fortunes ties the growth rates to the expansion of trade across countries to one another. One "externality" or effect is that all countries are vulnerable simultaneously to disruptions and downturns in the global economy. "Different economies' business cycles are becoming more closely correlated over time [because] increased trade causes economies to move more closely in step [so that] increasing globalization could lead to bigger economic booms and bursts" (*Economist*, September 28, 2002).

Countries differ in the degree to which their economies become integrated through trade in the global political economy. It is important to note that the pace of trade integration has been higher in the Global South than in the Global

FIGURE 8.3
The Global South in World Trade
In recent years, international trade has grown more rapidly than the production of goods and services. The Global South's contribution to world trade growth and its rising share of world imports reveal its growing importance to the world political economy.
SOURCE: World Bank (1995a), 58; UNDP (1999), 26.

North, reflecting the less-developed Global South's increasing contribution to world trade—a trend expected to continue (see Figure 8.3). This also means that the Global South is becoming increasingly important to growing economic prosperity in the Global North. Some Global South countries' imports matter more than others, inasmuch as differences exist in the extent to which Global South countries are participants in the global marketplace.

"The global economy created in the 1990s by the spread of markets . . . and more open trade have yet to prove that it distributes its fruits more evenly: the rich still get richer and the poor get poorer—only faster" (Hoagland 1999b). The differences among these groups reflect their historical experiences and the different strategies of development each has chosen (see Chapter 5). They also reflect changes in technology and consumer demands in a global economy. High-technology electronic goods (e.g., data-processing equipment, telecommunications equipment, and semiconductors and microprocessors) make up an increasing proportion of trade in manufactured goods. Here, the advanced Global North economies have cornered the market as the major suppliers, accounting for two-thirds of world exports in goods and services (World Bank 2005b). The United States and Japan lead the pack, followed by the European Union (EU) countries. However, globalization has altered these patterns, creating new winners in the creation of new products and in their command of the market.

Opportunity Lost? Globalization has transformed world production and employment patterns, moving both manufacturing and jobs across borders in response to MNCs' perceptions of changing investment opportunities. These changes have provoked various responses, many negative, because change frightens people and threatens established interests. On the left, Fiat automobiles manufactured by the Italian-based carmaker in Rio de Janeiro await export to Europe. Fiat is one of many European companies that have moved production to Brazil, whose economy leads the Mercosur free-trade bloc. The rich countries in the Global North fear that manufacturing is passing into the hands of the poor Global South countries where production is inexpensive, and some are lobbying against globalization. Globalization often wreaks havoc on local economies and leads to protests against the economic volatility it engenders, as shown at right in Brazil.

As noted, the Global South's share of global trade has grown (from 23 percent in 1985 to 28 percent in 2004) and is projected to expand in the future. The developing countries' share of global exports in manufactured products has also grown (increasing from 10 percent in 1980 to 27 percent in 2004. In this context the Global South's growth in the share of *new* products for exports is especially impressive; as a result of recent industrialization, the **newly industrialized economies (NIEs)** of the Global South have cornered about one-fifth of that portion of global trade (World Bank 2004b). Asia has taken the lead in developing new products; the three Asian tigers and the new "cubs"—Malaysia, Thailand, and especially India—account for almost two-thirds of this new export trade. Asian NIEs have been winners.

Trade in services also promises to make new winners. Because the United States enjoys comparative advantages in this area, it has been a strong advocate of bringing "services" under the liberalizing rules of the WTO. Trade in services has already expanded more than threefold since 1980, with the Global North reaping most of the benefits, even though the Global South has increased its share of this growing trade even more rapidly. The spread of information technology and the comparatively lower wage costs in developing economies are among the reasons why the World Bank predicts that developing countries will capture an increasing share of world trade in the first two decades of the twenty-first century. In the case of services, then, it appears that—at least for the time being—the Global North and Global South will both reap the growing profits from the globalization of trade.

■ **newly industrialized economies (NIEs)**
states such as Singapore and South Korea that have successfully grown into advanced industrialized societies. As wealthy countries, they are now members of the Global North and competitive players in global trade and investments, no longer in need of development assistance.

CONTROVERSY: IS GLOBALIZATION HELPFUL OR HARMFUL?

Many people recommend globalization as a form of international public policy, because they believe that its consequences are basically good for humankind. However, critics argue that globalization's costs far outweigh its benefits. As the pace of globalization has become a recognized force in world politics, it has also become a heated topic of debate. Globalization has hit a political speed bump, provoking intense critical evaluation of globalization's causes, characteristics, and consequences and inspiring fresh ethical examination of the elevated interdependence of countries and humans. The uncertain wisdom and morality of globalization may be the most discussed issue on today's global agenda. "While the war on terrorism has dominated the headlines, the great engine of globalization has kept moving, rewarding some, punishing others, but always keeping up the pressure by increasing human contact, communication and competition. For almost every country today, its primary struggle centers on globalization issues—growth, poverty eradication, disease prevention, education, urbanization, the preservation of identity" (Zakaria 2004).

To many students of international relations, globalization displays two faces, one positive and the other negative. To those whose perceptions focus on globalization's benefits, globalization is a blessing that should be promoted to deepen and widen its helpful effects, such as breaking down traditional divisions of humanity into races, nations, and cultures that are barriers to peace, prosperity, and justice. To others, globalization is a harmful phenomenon, breeding such things as global warming, and therefore a force to be resisted.

What do you think? Take any issue that is part of the debate and sort out the balance sheet of globalization's costs and benefits. For example, consider the charge that globalization has increased poverty and inequality. Is that true? Examine the evidence pre-

Trade as Aid to Help the Poor In April 2002 the aid agency Oxfam International launched an international "Make Trade Fair" campaign with a report on trade, globalization, and the fight against poverty entitled "Rigged Rules and Double Standards." Arguing that the United States and the European Union have betrayed their own free-trade principles by tilting the rules of the global trading system overwhelmingly to their advantage, Oxfam mounted this display in Hong Kong to urge fair trade rules for rich and poor countries alike, which Oxfam says can fight poverty better than aid or debt relief.

sented in Chapter 5 on the Global South, and the information in this chapter and Chapter 7 on the income inequity of human beings on the planet. Consider, too, the differences of opinion by policymakers and scholars and the theories of international relations (recall Chapter 2) that inform these divergent opinions. Conduct, in other words, the kind of evaluation that the International Labour Organization un-

It would be terribly inaccurate to picture trade globalization as a panacea for poverty, however. It is not proving to be a path to wealth for many developing countries. Globalization "has changed the distribution of these gains from trade. There are clear winners and losers, both between and within countries. More trade with developing countries hurts low-skilled workers while simultadertook in 2004. The World Commission on the Social Dimensions of Globalization noted that "the globalization debate is at an impasse," and assigned for itself the mission of providing "new thinking to break the deadlock and bridge the divide." Imagine yourself writing such a report. Do you think your research would agree or disagree with the findings of the World Commission? To frame your analysis, see if your evaluation would support or question the World Commission's conclusion:

> Globalization can and must change. The commission's report acknowledges globalization's potential for good—promoting open societies, open economies and freer exchange of goods, knowledge and ideas. But the commission also found deep-seated and persistent imbalances in the current workings of global economy that are ethically unacceptable and politically unsustainable.
>
> These imbalances are reflected in today's global economy.... The gap between people's income in the richest and poorest countries has never been wider, having risen from 50-to-1 in the 1960s to more than 120-to-1 today. Global unemployment is at its highest level ever. More than one billion people are either unemployed, underemployed or working poor. Clearly, globalization's benefits are out of reach for far too many people. (Somavia 2004, 6)

An alternative exercise would be to make an ethical assessment of the morality or immorality of globalization. This is what philosopher Peter Singer did in *One World: The Ethics of Globalization* (2004). In it, he applies as a criterion the utilitarian principle that it is a moral duty to maximize the happiness and welfare of all human beings and even animal welfare. Singer sees great benefits to the retreat of the doctrine of state sovereignty and the advance of the view that the entire world should be the unit of ethical analysis. Global interdependence encourages global thinking and a moral outlook because it promotes one's ethical responsibilities to act from awareness that there is only "one community," "one law," "one economy," and "one atmosphere." This is beneficial, to Singer, because globalization gives all of us great incentives to perform our utilitarian duty toward others; his conclusion springs from a UN report that observed, "In the global village, someone else's poverty very soon becomes one's own problem: illegal immigration, pollution, contagious disease, insecurity, fanaticism, terrorism." Under globalization, altruism and concern for others pay dividends, whereas narrow selfish behavior causes the selfish competitor to counterproductively harm. To this logic, globalization is beneficial. What do you think?

Or try one last thought experiment. Think like an economist. This is what the famous Harvard social scientist Jagdish Bhagwati did in writing *In Defense of Globalization* (2004). Would your similar economic analysis of globalization agree with his conclusions? Richard N. Cooper (2004) summarizes Bhagwati's liberal theoretical position and propositions thusly:

> Globalization is a buzzword that has no precise definition. It takes on many meanings, drawing both fervent support and fervent opposition. Indeed, the term is so imprecise that it is possible to be simultaneously for and against globalization.
>
> In *Defense of Globalization* focuses on its economic dimension, defined by Bhagwati as "diverse forms of international integration such as foreign trade, multinational direct foreign investment, movements of 'short-term' portfolio funds, technological diffusion, and cross-border migration." His main thesis is that economic globalization is an unambiguously good thing, with a few downsides that thought and effort can mitigate. His secondary thesis is that globalization does not need to be given a "human face"; it already has one. A thoughtful and objective evaluation, Bhagwati believes, will make this clear, and that is what he sets out to do.
>
> The book addresses a slate of charges against globalization; that it increases poverty, encourages child labor, harms women, threatens democracy, imperils culture, lowers wages, erodes labor standards, worsens the environment, and gives full reign to predatory corporations. Bhagwati also discusses capital market liberalization and international migration, before turning to fixes for globalization's downsides: improving governance, accelerating social agendas, and managing the speed of transitions. He concedes a few points to globalization's critics but, wielding logic and fact, demolishes most of the allegations made against it. His conclusion: that the world, particularly its poorest regions, needs more globalization, not less.... To the claim that globalization increases poverty, Bhagwati's response is, rubbish. (Cooper 2004, 152–53).

---

neously increasing the incomes of more highly skilled workers" (Held et al., 1999). A backlash to these growing inequalities has grown as many groups see themselves as victims of an integrated trade world (Broad 2002; Aaronson 2001). The Global South's poorer countries are not participating in the advantages that globalization is providing the winners. The losers, "poor countries and poor people," often find their interests neglected. The "Controversy: Is Globalization Helpful or Harmful?" frames the issues surrounding the painful costs of trade globalization for the Global South. While the shares of global exports of the Asian NIEs and the rapidly industrialized economies have increased since the late 1960s, the shares of most of the other Global South developing countries have not increased and in some cases have declined. If globalization is to continue, as appears highly likely, then perhaps in the long run globalization's success will depend on increased aid, investment, loans, and imports from the Global North to the Global South.

From a management point of view, traditionally MNCs' overseas operations were "appendages" of a centralized hub. The aim today, however, is to dismantle the hub by dispersing production facilities worldwide. MNCs are replacing national corporations, because the sales of large companies are now geared to the global market and a large proportion of their revenues are generated from sales outside the countries where they are headquartered. The growing globalization of production is transforming the international political economy. Once, it made sense to count trade in terms of flows between countries, and that analytic tradition continues because national account statistics are still gathered with states as the units of analysis. But increasingly that picture fails to portray realities. Countries do not really trade with each other, corporations do. And multinational corporations account for most of the trade trends. The globe's transnational corporations and their 689,520 foreign affiliates (Oatley 2004, 176) sell an estimated $10 trillion in goods and services across borders every year, and the United Nations Conference on Trade and Development (UNCTAD) estimates that together they are now responsible for about one-fourth of the world's production and two-thirds of the world's exports. What MNCs do transforms the distribution of world trade. And to compete for a share of the global trade profits, MNCs have increasingly moved their production and labor to countries located abroad from corporate headquarters. MNCs' have discovered that to export to another country it is necessary to relocate there. Placing production and management in an MNCs' regional foreign affiliate avoids tariffs and taxes, while allowing economies of scale by making trade between MNCs' worldwide branches possible. The result: almost a third of global trade is estimated to be between MNCs' cross-border affiliates. As the wave of MNC mergers unfolds, the globalization of trade seems destined to be taken to unprecedented heights. That rising clout will leave behind the validity of constructing images of trade patterns in terms of transactions between sovereign states.

MNCs are now the primary agents in the globalization of production. By increasingly forming **strategic corporate alliances** with companies in the same industry, and by merging with one another at a frenzied pace, MNCs have become massive NGOs rivaling states in financial resources (see Table 6.2, p. 209). These global actors have grown in influence also because many MNC parent companies are now linked with one another in **virtual corporations** and alliances of coownership and coproduction. These corporate networks of MNCs pursue truly global strategies for financial gain, often through long-term supplier agreements and licensing and franchising contracts, both using MNCs' international alliances and joint foreign direct investment strategies; today "almost half of what we call foreign trade actually involves transactions between different parts of the same company—between a domestic firm and its overseas subsidiaries or between a foreign firm and its domestic subsidiaries. In a geopo-

■ **strategic corporate alliances**
cooperation between MNCs and foreign companies in the same industry, driven by the movement of MNC manufacturing overseas.

■ **virtual corporations**
agreements between otherwise competitive MNCs, often temporary, to join forces and skills to coproduce and export particular products in the borderless global marketplace.

Child Labor in a Global System Globalization is sped not only by the rapid expansion of technology but by the availability of cheap labor in some countries, which take advantage of their peoples' low wages to make products highly competitive in the globalized marketplace. Here a child labors at near slave wages in Bangladesh, producing goods that cost less than those made where labor unions protect workers. Such practices have mercantilist nationalists and free-trade critics up in arms, even though open global markets encourage them.

litical sense, this is foreign commerce. To the company, however, these international flows of goods and services are internal affairs" (Weidenbaum 2004, 26). The outward flow of **foreign direct investment** (FDI) attributable to MNCs' 689,520 foreign affiliates has increased rapidly. As they funnel large financial flows across national borders, these global corporate conglomerates are integrating national economies into a single global market.

The impact of FDI on creating an interconnected global capital market extends beyond money. With it comes technology, managerial expertise, and most important now, employment opportunities. Jobs are desperately needed, and there exists in the age of globalization (and because of it?) a huge surplus of available labor. The lack of jobs is a worldwide problem, even in the Global North where so-called **underemployment** is widespread. The conditions are worse in the Global South, where the UN estimates that about one in six workers and one-third of the world's workforce was unemployed or underemployed in 2001, and predicts that at least 500 million new jobs will be needed in the next decade to accommodate new arrivals on the job market.

MNCs' investments are seen as an attractive potential cure to unprecedented levels of unemployment (although it is widely recognized that the growth of trade will not automatically create more employment and better wages). Not surprisingly, many Global South countries "are keener than ever" to seek MNC in-

■ **foreign direct investment (FDI)**
purchase of stock, property, or assets in another country, with a goal of long-term involvement in the economy of that country.

■ **underemployment**
a condition critics trace to trade globalization in which a large portion of the labor force only works part-time at low pay in occupations below their skill level.

FIGURE 8.4

The Ebb and Flow of Foreign Investments, 1990–2003: Is Globalization a Global North Phenomenon?

Most foreign direct investment (FDI) is controlled by powerful multinational corporations, and their recent "urge to converge" to create monster transnational conglomerates has enhanced their economic clout. Through megamergers, the economic titans target their investments primarily toward the rich and large Global North markets in Europe and North America (figure on right). The figure on the left shows the annual global level of FDI, in trillions of dollars, between 1990 and 2003. UNCTAD predicts that total global foreign direct investments will rebound sharply in 2004 and beyond, boosted by an improving global economy and higher corporate profits, after experiencing two consecutive declines in 2001 and 2002.

SOURCE: United Nations Conference on Trade and Development (UNCTAD), www.unctad.org.

vestment capital (Hindle 2004) and the other advantages they perceive will result from it, such as new jobs (see Chapter 5). Global South countries are now aggressively pursuing MNC investment to stimulate growth to achieve the same economic success achieved by the NIEs. Foreign capital is critical to this goal. In 1992, worldwide foreign direct investment was less than $175 billion; by 2000 it hit a record high of $1,400 billion, but as a result of the collapsing global economy thereafter fell each consecutive year almost by half, to $653 billion in 2003 (see Figure 8.4). For the Global South, FDI rose in 2003 to $182 billion—just about one-fifth above its peak level of $101 billion in 2000 (www.unctad.org). Most of this MNC investment in search of profits continues to flow into the Global North (72 percent in 2003) and secondarily into the NIEs, where China and India are increasingly seen as targets of opportunity. The continuing concentration of FDI in the Global South is self-interest.

Multinationals Making Money and Globalizing Trade. The international search for global markets by MNCs has paid off financially. Almost no country now prohibits their international production and product marketing. The result has been the expansion of choices available to consumers (and corporate profits to the MNC competition!). China—still officially a communist state whose ideology oppresses capitalism—has economically embraced commercial liberalization and open trade, which has led to rapid economic growth. Shown here are the payoffs, among others: a consumer contemplates the wide variety of foreign-manufactured cell phones in a Shanghai department store. China is now the biggest market of cell phones in the world, an indication of the link between globalization and transformation in world politics.

Profits are MNCs' primary motivation, and their investment returns are likely to be greatest in the Global North, where a combination of affluence and political stability reduces investment risks. Still, the Global South is the recipient of considerable and growing FDI. Although the amounts fluctuate yearly, at the start of the twenty-first century a growing number of developing countries were viewed as targets of investment opportunity, and inflows in 2002 totaled $182 billion (www.unctad.org).

Although MNCs are a key catalyst to trade integration and globalization, critics worry that MNCs have become too powerful for states to control:

> The formidable power and mobility of global corporations are undermining the effectiveness of national governments to carry out essential policies on behalf of their people. Leaders of nation-states are losing much of the control over their own territory they once had. More and more, they must conform to the demands of the outside world because the outsiders are already inside the gates. Business enterprises that routinely operate across borders are linking far-flung pieces of territory into a new world economy that by-

The Global Top 20 and Bottom 10

Country
Ireland
Singapore
Switzerland
Netherlands
Finland
Canada
United States
New Zealand
Austria
Denmark
Sweden
United Kingdom
Australia
Czech Republic
France
Portugal
Norway
Germany
Slovenia
Malaysia
Brazil
Kenya
Turkey
Bangladesh
China
Venezuela
Indonesia
Egypt
India
Iran

Legend:
- Political engagement
- Technological connectivity
- Personal contact
- Economic integration

FIGURE 8.5
Levels of Globalization

There are various ways to measure the extent to which countries are integrated in the globalization of the world. These levels, of course, affect different countries differently, depending upon the degree to which each state is involved in the various dimensions of "globalization." The globalization index calculates these levels yearly, in order to bring "globalization into sharper focus by assessing changes in its most important components, whether engagement in international relations and policymaking, trade and financial flows, or the movement of people, ideas, and information across borders" (*Foreign Policy*, January–February 2002). This chart scales and ranks the top 20 "globalized" countries in 2004 on four measures (top) as well as the world's "bottom 10" least globalized states (bottom).

SOURCE: Adapted from A. T. Kearney and the Carnegie Endowment of International Peace, as presented in "Measuring Globalization," *Foreign Policy* (March–April 2004): 54, 67. Used by permission.

passes all sorts of established political arrangements and conventions. (Barnet and Cavanagh 1994, 19)

Some corporate visionaries proudly extol the transnational virtues and the positive contribution they claim MNCs make by encouraging replacement of narrow nationalistic values with those of a truly global, cosmopolitarian culture. To the extent that this influence grows, MNCs' globalization of production and investment will lead to the transfer of people's loyalties from individual countries to the world as a whole. This trend undermines state sovereignty or its ability to exercise sovereignty in its internal affairs. The globalization of production builds bridges across the **politics** that divides states—providing a common ground for people to cooperate. This would fulfill the humanist vision of international harmony resulting from acceptance of everyone's shared humanity and destiny. "There are no longer any national flag carriers," in the words of Kenichi Ohmae, a Japanese management consultant. "Corporations must serve their customers, not governments."

■ **politics**
the effort by actors to resolve controversial issues against the wishes of the targeted affected actors.

GLOBALIZATION AND THE STATE: WHAT FUTURE?

Rapid globalization, fueled in large measure by technological revolutions, is almost certain to continue. Is globalization desirable, or despicable? The answer depends on the constructed images of the observers. Some observers concentrate their interpretation on the clear-cut advantages of globalization for creating wealth; others concentrate on the uneven and unequal benefits of globalization's effects and are understandably concerned about the failure of globalization to help at the same rate poor countries and poor people. Still a third set of observers construct their images around the problems that globalization presents to a global system that remains based on sovereign territorial states, and the failures that result from this tendency, which, without global governance, reduce the world's capacity to steer globalization in more rewarding directions.

We can expect the controversies about globalization's alleged virtues and vices, benefits and costs, to heighten as finance, population, trade, labor, and culture continue to converge globally. While globalization has narrowed the distance between the world's people, some have gained and others have lost ground. The global village is not likely to be an equally hospitable home for everyone. Levels of satisfaction with cascading globalization vary widely (see A. T. Kearney/*Foreign Policy* 2002), as do the levels to which countries and people are linked to globalization's multiple forces (see Figure 8.5). Winners in the game of trade and investment play down the costs of global integration, while protectionist critics of free trade and open capitalist markets deny globalization's benefits, and the debate about globalization's problematic impact has intensified without resolution as the debaters have hardened their positions without listening to the counterarguments.

The key question is really about fairness, **ethics,** and justice, not about the benefits of free trade, which both rich and poor countries recognize as they competitively seek to gain a larger share of the global export market. The evidence about the costs and payoffs is mixed, because globalization refers to different

■ **ethics**
criteria for distinguishing right from wrong in assessing an actor's behavior and the intentions that animated its behavior.

In Defense of Jobs at Home Free trade and globalization are seen as threats to the job security of some workers, who seek protection to preserve their employment in vulnerable, relatively uncompetitive sectors of the global market. In 1993, American workers demonstrated against the North American Free Trade Agreement (NAFTA). If such protests succeed around the globe, free-trade agreements are likely to unravel, and the pace of globalization will slow.

phenomena, the outcomes of which are open to constructivist interpretation. While many issues remain uncertain, it is clear that globalization is far from a win-win situation. Therefore, the debate will continue.

Is globalization eroding the ability of even the rich states to control their economic and political fortunes? To be sure, a world of vanishing borders challenges all territorial states, rich and poor alike. In an era of globalization, "one often hears that sovereignty is being undermined by the global market [and if] sovereignty is being steadily weakened, then we can eventually expect the state to no longer be the central form of political organization in the world" (Barkin 2001). However, states have proven themselves to be remarkably resilient since the time they were formally created by international law in 1648. States still rule and govern the institutions and laws that shape changes in the world economy, among whom the American superpower and the other G-8 economic powerhouses have the most power. They promote their preferences and policies, mostly liberal, that are spread across the globe to the followers (Simmons and Elkins 2004). This means that states, and particularly the most powerful states, are potentially more powerful than ever, even in the era of global interdependency. Globalization may even strengthen the economic clout of states. The age of big government is certainly not dead (Opello and Rosow 2004).

The expansion of governmental control over states' spending notwithstanding, globalization has arguably reduced the sovereign control of states over activities within their borders and their relations with other states and nonstate actors.

Globalization reduces the capacity of states to exercise political power over the territory in which private-sector nonstate actors operate. This loss of control probably means that globalization has reduced the state's monopoly over internal sovereignty, which was formerly a territorial area of exclusive control. The globalization of terrorism worldwide punctuates the declining capacity of state governments to protect citizens from external danger. Globalization suggests that everyone and everything is increasingly vulnerable to events everywhere, and that states' capabilities are on a weaker and weaker foundation. As U.S. policymaker Joseph S. Nye urged in 2001, "We need to think harder about norms and procedures for the governance of globalization. Denial of the problem . . . will not do. We need changes in processes."

A key issue is whether states can find a focal point, a norm, around which cooperation could coalesce. Liberal theorists, who focus on the mutual gains stemming from international cooperation, are optimistic about the possibilities. Realists and neomercantilists, who are concerned more with **relative gains** than **absolute gains**, are more pessimistic. But all accounts agree on one proposition: "that the communications and technology revolution that facilitate the flow of capital, information, and jobs across old national boundaries will force a redefinition of the role of states [because] the process of globalization is remaking the economic world and inevitably will reshape the political world as well" (Broder 1999).

This chapter began by asking whether globalization is the route to a global village—one free of conflict and intent only on improving villagers' welfare—or whether this is mere mythology. *Global pillage* is an alternative description of the probable consequences that will flow from cascading globalization. There is no limit to the dangers attributed to globalization. If globalization means anything, it means that the sturdiness of the global economy is vulnerable to shocks that can overturn it, and faith in globalization as a motor of progress is destined to collapse whenever the international market begins to melt. In addition, September 11, 2001 (9/11), and March 11, 2004 (3/11), show that terrorism has become another unpleasant manifestation of globalization and that as terrorism becomes global it can wreak havoc everyplace. The cost of rapidly accelerating globalization promoted primarily by growing international trade must be balanced by the benefits. Will the continuing economic trade-offs that result from the globalization of world trade spell eventual doom, or will it spell growth and the consolidation of a cosmopolitan global culture? The next chapter investigates possible answers to this question.

■ **relative gains**
a measure of how much some participants in an exchange benefit in comparison to others.

■ **absolute gains**
a measure of the degree to which all participants in an exchange become better off.

KEY TERMS

globalization
neoliberal theory
human security
state level of analysis
global village
cyberspace
virtuality
digital divide
information and communications technology (ICT)
agenda setting
New World Information and Communication Order (NWICO)
regime

international organized crime (IOC)
global migration crisis
failed states
externalities
globalization of finance
arbitrage
digital world economy
commercial liberalism
capital mobility hypothesis
realist theory
General Agreement on Tariffs and Trade (GATT)
trade integration

newly industrialized economies (NIEs)
strategic corporate alliances
virtual corporations
foreign direct investment (FDI)
underemployment
politics
ethics
relative gains
absolute gains

SUGGESTED READING

Baldwin, Robert E, and L. Alan Winters, eds. *Challenges to Globalization.* Chicago: University of Chicago Press, 2004.

Baylis, John, and Steve Smith, eds. *The Globalization of World Politics,* 2nd ed. New York: Oxford University Press, 2002.

Bello, Walden. *Deglobalization: Ideas for a New World Economy,* 2nd ed. London: Zed Books, 2005.

Bhagwati, Jagdish. *In Defense of Globalization.* New York: Oxford University Press, 2004.

Boli, John, and Frank L. Lechner. *World Culture.* London: Blackwell, 2004.

Kapstein, Ethan B. "Models of International Economic Justice," *Ethics and International Affairs* 18 (No. 2, 2004): 79–92.

Lechner, Frank L., and John Boli. *The Globalization Reader,* 2nd ed. London: Blackwell, 2004.

Nye, Joseph S., Jr. *Power in the Global Information Age: From Realism to Globalization.* New York: Routledge, 2004.

Pieterse, Jan Nederveen. *Globalization or Empire?* New York: Routledge, 2004.

Scholte, Jan Art. *Globalization: A Critical Introduction,* 2nd ed. London: Palgrave, 2004.

Singer, Peter. *One World: The Ethics of Globalization.* New Haven, Conn.: Yale University Press, 2002.

Wolf, Martin. *Why Globalization Works.* New Haven, Conn.: Yale University Press, 2004.

WHERE ON THE WORLD WIDE WEB?

LaborNet
http://www.labornet.apc.org/

LaborNet provides labor news from around the world, Internet services, and Internet training to those interested in workers' causes. Want to be a sympathetic striker? Click on the Strike Page and find out the who, what, where, and why of current strikes anywhere in the world. This website also has extensive links to international labor unions. Want to form a student union organization? This is the place to look for support and more information. It also gives a sense of how the Internet has contributed to the globalization of labor.

Migration Dialogue
http://migration.ucdavis.edu/

The University of California at Davis has created a website that "provides timely, factual and nonpartisan information and analysis of international migration issues." Most useful to you at this site is Migration News, which has up-to-date reports on migration issues in various states and regions of the world. Its archives allow you to search news by year and month, so you can track migration issues over time. Based on your exploration of the site's offerings, do you think there is a "global migration crisis"? How are the governments of various countries reacting to migration issues?

The Progress of Nations
http://www.unicef.org/pon99/

As described in this chapter, AIDS is a disease that has spread around the world through the process of globalization. The United Nations Children's Fund (UNICEF) has created a website that details the devastating impact of HIV/AIDS on children. Use this site to analyze the effects of AIDS on children in a variety of countries. Charts present a cross-country comparison of the number of children orphaned by AIDS and the impact it has had on their lives. What country's children are most affected by the AIDS epidemic?

International Forum on Globalization
http://www.ifg.org/

The International Forum on Globalization (IFG) is "an alliance of sixty leading activists, scholars, economists, researchers and writers formed to stimulate new thinking, joint activity, and public education in response to economic globalization." What are the major programs of the IFG? What does the organization say about the World Trade Organization? What problems does it identify with globalization?

The World Bank on Globalization
http://www1.worldbank.org/economicpolicy/globalization/

This website presents the World Bank's thinking about globalization and how it should be managed. How does the site define globalization? What problems does it identify with globalization? What solutions does it propose? Do you support these proposed solutions? Why or why not?

Institute for International Economics on Globalization
http://www.iie.com/research/globalization.htm

The Institute for International Economics is a nonprofit and nonpartisan research group based in Washington, D.C. It provides policy briefs and working papers in five areas of globalization: globalization and the environment, globalization and labor, issues and impact, migration, and the politics of globalization. This is a good site for detailed and authoritative information on globalization.

INFOTRAC® COLLEGE EDITION

Moller, J. Orstrom. "Wanted: A New Strategy for Globalization." *The Futurist* (January–February 2004).

Naim, Moises. "An Indigenous World: How Native Peoples Can Turn Globalization to Their Advantage." *Foreign Policy* (November–December 2003).

Taylor, Timothy. "The Truth about Globalization." *Public Interest* (Spring 2002).

Hoffmann, Stanley. "Clash of Globalizations." *Foreign Affairs* (July–August 2002).

For more articles, enter:
"globalization" in the Subject Guide, and then go to subdivision "analysis"
"globalization" in the Subject Guide, and then go to subdivision "evaluation"
"anti-globalization movement" in the Subject Guide

Go to http://politicalscience.wadsworth.com/kegley10 to access additional resources related to this chapter.

CHAPTER 9

MARKETS AND MONEY IN THE GLOBAL POLITICAL ECONOMY

TOPICS AND THEMES

- The importance of trade and currency exchange in a globalized political economy
- The global context for interpreting contemporary world economic change
  Past commercial philosophy
  Liberal versus mercantile values
  Hegemony: A precondition for economic order and free trade?
- The changing free-trade regime
- Monetary matters: Can regimes promote trade and growth?
- The fate of free trade: triumph or trouble?

- **CONTROVERSY** GLOBALIZATION'S GROWING PAINS: IS THE WORLD TRADE ORGANIZATION A FRIEND OR FOE?

Workers using sewing machines in Vietnam make sports clothes for European and U.S. markets.

Globalization . . . [is] no longer a buzzword: it has arrived. There is substantial evidence for an increasingly globalized marketplace. World trade is expanding much faster than world production and cross-border investments are growing at a more rapid rate than trade. People in one country are more likely to be affected by economic actions in other nations in many capabilities: as customers, entrepreneurs and investors, managers and taxpayers, and citizens. . . . Globalization is producing fundamental changes in business [and] on balance, globalization—warts and all—is working. Those "terrible" multinational enterprises are creating widespread wealth.

—MURRAY WEIDENBAUM, political economist, 2004

Efficiently functioning trade is an important prerequisite for a more stable and prosperous world. But such trade is not based on the rules of the poor. It is trade based on an agreed order that takes into account the weakest and systematically promotes their fuller integration. It facilitates access of less developed countries to foreign markets and thus to financial resources needed for development.

—VACLAV HAVEL, president of the Czech Republic, 2001

"Money makes the world go 'round," is an old saying. Today, more than ever, that adage is true at least in one sense. Money is moving around the world at a quickening pace, as purchases at home are made increasingly of goods produced abroad. You are a participant in this process that is integrating a globalizing marketplace. When you buy a sandwich, a sweater, a car, or the gasoline to make it run, the chances are exceedingly high that what you purchased was produced at least in part in a foreign land. Your transaction contributed to the movement of money across borders, because the purchase you made will ultimately affect the balance of payments and the cash position of your country in international currency accounts. Congratulations! You have become an actor on the world stage, and your actions have registered an international impact. As a result of your decision, money has moved around the world and the distribution of income and wealth globally has shifted in a small way.

This chapter is about trading places and money markets in the global system. We will look at the processes governing international economics, concentrating on how international trade and currency exchanges operate and affect national and human security. We thus look at a phenomenon as old as recorded history and inspect how it influences life in the twenty-first century. The quest for wealth is an ageless pursuit. Because it provides the means by which many other prized values can be realized, the successful management of economics lies at the center of how governments define their national interests. What practices (and underlying philosophies justifying them) should they embrace to regulate commercial and monetary activities within their borders? And what foreign economic policies should each state adopt to influence trading and financial exchanges with other states?

These are the principal concerns of **international political economy.** This **paradigm,** or, approach to study, is "concerned with the political determinants of international economic relations. International political economy tries to answer such questions as: How have changes in the international distribution of power among states affected the degree of openness in the international trading system? Do the domestic political economies of some states allow them to compete more effectively in international markets? Is the relative poverty of the [Global South] better explained by indigenous conditions in individual countries or by some attribute of the international economic system? When can international economic ties among states be used for political leverage?" (Krasner 2001).

To introduce these topics, this chapter will first examine the ways in which the global economic system has evolved. This will allow us to then investigate how trade and monetary activities today are creating new issues in the twenty-first century.

■ **international political economy**
the study of the intersection of politics and economics that illuminates the reasons why changes occur in the distribution of states' wealth and power.

■ **paradigm**
derived from the Greek *paradeigma*, meaning an example, a model, or an essential pattern; a paradigm structures thoughts about an area of inquiry.

THE GLOBAL CONTEXT FOR INTERPRETING CONTEMPORARY WORLD ECONOMIC CHANGE

Rapid changes in the world force people to think about and interpret world politics in fresh ways. Of all the many recent changes, perhaps none has been more profound and far-reaching than **globalization,** regarded by some as little more than a euphemism for capitalism (Petras and Veltmeyer 2004). The growth of states' economic interdependence can be viewed as the recent culmination of a trend that began more than a century ago, but its current level is unprecedented. Accordingly, basic ideas about states, markets, trade, and currency exchange are at the center of debate, and issues in international political economy are at the vortex of global discussion. The contests between the rich Global North and the

■ **globalization**
the increasingly close international integration of markets both for goods and services and for capital.

poor Global South, and between supplier and producer, have risen to prominence. While some might say (especially after 9/11) that the **high politics** governing national security remains a necessary preoccupation, most would also agree that **low politics,** where international economic issues such as inequalities are being negotiated, is of equal importance. The strong undercurrents in the latter are reshaping the former. International trade integration and the increasingly interlocked world economy compel attention to economic transactions. Today, high interest rates in one country lead to high interest rates in others, and a stock market free fall starting in New York will spread to Asia and London overnight. Depression abroad means recession at home. Inflation is shared everywhere, and it seems to be beyond the control of any single state. The balance of fiscal power is now as pertinent to national security and quality of life as the global balance of military power. These are some of the consequences of the growing international interdependence known as globalization (see Chapter 8).

Theories of political economy dating back to John Stuart Mill's *Principles of Political Economy* and Karl Marx's *A Contribution to the Critique of Political Economy* in the mid-nineteen century have been rediscovered. This reconsideration stems from the growing awareness that the conventional categories of politics and economics can no longer be separated, because now "much of politics is economics, and most of economics is politics" (Lindblom 1979).

In today's world, politics (states) and economics (markets) are merging. The relentless march in the volume of international commerce has made trade increasingly important to countries' economies and is expected to increase at an even faster rate through the year 2015 (Central Intelligence Agency 2002). Trade comprises a growing share of the global economy, now accounting for 40 percent of global domestic product, up from 20 percent in 1990 (World Bank 2005b). World trade is the most visible symbol of globalization and deserves our primary attention, but so do the dynamics of the floating **international monetary system,** through which foreign currencies and credits are calculated when capital moves across borders through trade, investments, foreign aid, and loans.

We need to first step backward to understand leading ideas about states' trade and monetary policies, which are rooted in past thinking. In this chapter we will focus on the critical role of the United States as an economic superpower in shaping the contest between liberalism and mercantilism underlying the different trade and monetary strategies states are pursuing in the quest for power and wealth.

The Shadow of Past Commercial Policy Philosophy

In July 1944, forty four states allied in war against the Axis powers met in the New Hampshire resort community of Bretton Woods. Their purpose was to devise new rules and institutions to govern international trade and monetary relations after World War II. As the world's preeminent economic and military power, the United States, played the leading role. Its proposals were shaped by its perception of the causes of the 1930s' economic catastrophe and its beliefs about the role the U.S. dollar and economy should play in the postwar world. The United States sought free trade, open markets, and monetary stability—all central tenets of what would become the "Bretton Woods system"—based on the

■ **high politics**
geostrategic issues of national and international security as related to war and peace.

■ **low politics**
the category of global issues related to the economic, social, demographic, and environmental aspects of relations between governments and people.

■ **international monetary system**
the financial procedures governing the exchange and conversion of national currencies so that they can be bought and sold for one another to calculate the value of currencies and credits when capital is transferred across borders through trade, investment, foreign aid, and loans.

■ **commercial liberalism**
an economic theory advocating free markets and the removal of barriers to the flow of trade and capital as a locomotive for prosperity.

■ **mercantilism**
the seventeenth-century theory preaching that trading states should increase their wealth and power by expanding exports and protecting their domestic economy from imports, a competitive strategy which is still advocated by some today.

■ **Liberal International Economic Order (LIEO)**
the set of regimes created after World War II, designed to promote monetary stability and reduce barriers to the free flow of trade and capital.

■ **interdependence**
a situation in which the behavior of international actors greatly affects others with whom they have contact, making all parties mutually sensitive and vulnerable to the others' actions.

theoretical premises of **commercial liberalism,** which advocates free markets with few barriers to private trade and capital flows.

Britain also played an important role at the conference. Led by John Maynard Keynes—whose theories about the state's role in managing inflation, unemployment, and growth influenced a generation of economic thinking throughout the capitalist world—the British delegation won support for the principle of strong government action by states facing economic problems. That ideology conforms less closely with liberalism than with the principles of **mercantilism,** which assigns states a greater role than markets in managing economic interactions and accepts protectionist trade policies to expand exports and to limit imports as a strategy for acquiring national wealth.

Despite these differences, the rules established at Bretton Woods reflected a remarkable level of agreement and governed international economic relations for the next twenty-five years, because they rested on three political bases. First, power was concentrated in the rich Western European and North American countries, which reduced the number of states whose agreement was necessary for effective management by restricting the potential challenges by Japan, the Global South, and the then-communist states of Eastern Europe and the Soviet Union. Second, the system's operation was facilitated by the dominant states' shared preference for an open international economy with limited government intervention. The onset of the Cold War helped cement Western unity, because a common external enemy led the Western industrial countries to perceive economic cooperation as necessary for both prosperity and military security. That perception promoted a willingness to share economic burdens. Third, Bretton Woods worked because the United States assumed the burdens of hegemonic leadership and others willingly accepted that leadership.

The political bases of the Bretton Woods system crumbled in 1972 when the United States suspended the convertibility of the dollar into gold and abandoned the system of fixed currency exchange rates at its core. Since then, as floating exchange rates and growing capital mobility have made monetary mechanisms unstable, more chaotic processes of international economic relations have materialized. Still, commercial liberalism's preference for market mechanisms over government intervention and the urge to privatize and otherwise reduce government regulation of markets has spread worldwide, since the Cold War collapsed, and multinational corporations (MNCs) are serving as a powerful pillar in support of the continuing strength of the liberal rules of the global trade regime. Thus it is still useful to characterize the contemporary international economic system as a **Liberal International Economic Order (LIEO)**—one based on such free market principles as openness and nondiscriminatory trade.

Although liberalization has spread worldwide as a policy principle (Simmons and Elkins 2004), not all states consistently support the liberal tenet that governments should not interfere by managing trade flows because they fear the potential costs of free trade. Commercial liberalism is under attack in many states, including some of liberalism's unenthusiastic proponents, which are pressured domestically to protect industries and employment at home. Globalization has not eliminated the urge to compete, because states fear that **interdependence** will compromise their sovereignty and security. Interdependence encourages states to maximize their gains through transborder transactions while minimizing their vulnerability. States' trade policies are naturally influenced by the selfish desire to increase the domestic benefits of international economic transactions and to lessen their adverse consequences, even if this will undermine the expansion of a global capitalist economy propelled by free trade.

The Clash between Liberal and Mercantile Values

How should states rationally cope in the globalized political economy to best manage economic change? The choices inspire different philosophies and policies. They force governments to attempt to reconcile the overriding need for states to cooperate with others in trade liberalization if they are to maximize their wealth with each state's natural competitive desire to put its own welfare first.

Most controversies in international political economy are ultimately reducible to the competing ideologies of liberalism and mercantilism, which represent "fundamentally different . . . conceptions of the relationships among society, state, and market" (Gilpin 2001). A comparison of the logic behind the two theoretical traditions can help us to appreciate why a reconciliation or balance is so hard to achieve, why particular protectionist domestic interests sacrifice collective prosperity in order to maximize their own parochial gains, and why others criticize mercantilism as self-defeating.

Commercial Liberalism. Commercial liberalism as a political **theory** explains economics by building on the presumption that humankind's natural inclination is to cooperate in order to increase prosperity and enlarge individual liberty under law. Consequently, it is closely related to liberal theory (described in Chapter 2), which is based on the assumption that individuals and groups usually make decisions on the basis of rational calculations through the application of intellect to analyze available facts. Commercial liberalism asserts that through mutually beneficial exchanges people can benefit and the problems of capitalism—boom-and-bust cycles, trade wars, and poverty—can be successfully managed. Commercial liberal theory has many roots and variations, but all liberal thinkers agree that the promotion of free international trade to lift the poor from poverty and to expand political liberties is one of the globe's "great causes" (see Bhagwati 2004).

Adam Smith, the eighteenth-century political economist who helped define the precepts of classical liberalism as well as modern-day economics, used the metaphor of the unregulated market's "invisible hand" to show how the collective or public interest can be served by humans' natural tendency to "truck, barter, and exchange" in pursuit of private gain. Hence the importance of "free" markets, which produce collective as well as private gain. David Ricardo, a nineteenth-century British political economist, added an important corollary to liberal thought as applied to the international economy. Ricardo demonstrated conclusively that when all states specialize in the production of those goods in which they enjoy a **comparative advantage** and trade them for goods in which others enjoy an advantage, a net gain in welfare for both states, in the form of higher living standards, will result. The principle of comparative advantage underpins commercial liberalism's advocacy of free trade as a method for capital accumulation. Material progress is realized and mutual gains are achieved, according to this principle, providing countries specialize in the production of what they can produce least expensively, are willing to purchase from other

■ **theory**
a set of conclusions derived from assumptions (axioms) and/or evidence about some phenomenon, including its character, causes, and probable consequences and their ethical implications.

■ **comparative advantage**
the concept in liberal economics that a state will benefit if it specializes in those goods it can produce comparatively cheaply and acquires through trade goods that it can only produce at a higher cost.

TABLE 9.1

Comparative Advantage and the Gains from Free Trade

Country	Worker Productivity per Hour		Before Specialization		Specialization, No Trade		Specialization with Trade	
	Camera	Computer	Camera	Computer	Camera	Computer	Camera	Computer
Japan	9	3	900	300	990	270	910	300
United States	4	2	400	200	320	240	400	210

countries goods that are costly for them to produce, and, in addition, do not restrict the flow of trade across borders.

Liberalism maintains that open markets and free trade are both advantageous and the engines of economic progress. As Benjamin Franklin summarized commercial liberal theory more than two centuries ago, "No nation was ever ruined by trade." Another way of expressing this idea is to say that each country should specialize in producing those goods in which it has the greatest comparative cost advantage or least comparative cost disadvantage, and trade with others. The assumption is that trade competition is good for all. Competition stimulates technological innovation to improve production efficiency in order to meet the competition for trade by other producers, and in the long run the world's output and income will increase and everyone's standard of living will rise, providing all abide by the rules of free trade and open markets. Commercial liberalism recognizes that in the short run free trade will result in unequal rewards for some and produce inequalities in countries' rate of growth, but argues that the long-term gains for all in a **laissez-faire economic** system of free markets are most important.

Why does free trade produce benefits for trade partners who specialize in the production of goods for which they each have comparative advantage? Consider a hypothetical illustration of Japan and the United States, each of which produces cameras and computers but with different worker productivity (output per hour) for each country, as shown in the first column of Table 9.1.

Clearly Japan has an absolute advantage in both products, as Japanese workers are more productive in turning out cameras and computers than the American workers are. Does this mean the two countries cannot benefit by trading with each other? If trade does occur, should each country continue to allocate its resources as in the past? The answer to both questions is no.

Each country should specialize in producing that item in which it has the greatest comparative cost advantage or least comparative cost disadvantage, and trade for others. Because Japan is three times more productive in cameras than computers, it should direct more of its resources into manufacturing that industry. One cost of doing so is lost computer output, but Japan can turn out three additional cameras for every computer given up. The United States, on the other hand, can obtain only two computers. Like their Japanese counterparts, American workers are also more productive in making cameras than computers. Still, U.S. resources should be directed to computers because the United States

■ **laissez-faire economics**
from a French phrase (meaning literally "let do") that Adam Smith and other commercial liberals in the eighteenth century used to describe the advantages of free-wheeling capitalism without government interference in economic affairs.

is at a smaller disadvantage compared with Japan in this area. If the United States specializes in computers and Japan in cameras and they trade with each other, each will benefit. The following scenario shows why.

Begin with one hundred workers in each industry without specialization or trade (second column). Next specialize production by shifting ten Japanese workers from computer to camera production and shifting twenty American workers from camera production to computers (third column). Then permit free trade so that eighty Japanese-manufactured cameras are exported to the United States and thirty U.S. computers are exported to Japan. With specialization *and* free trade, the benefits to both countries improve.

By shifting Japanese resources into the production of cameras and U.S. resources into computers and allowing trade, the same total allocations will cause camera and computer output to rise ten units each (fourth column). Resources are now being used more efficiently. Both countries realize benefits when each trades some of its additional output for the other's. Japan ends up with more cameras than before specialization and trade and the same number of computers, while the United States finds itself with more computers and the same number of cameras. More output in both countries means higher living standards.

Liberals such as Smith, Ricardo, and Franklin believed that markets work best when free of government interference. They reasoned that economic processes governing the production, distribution, and consumption of goods and services operate according to certain natural laws. They saw **politics** as necessary, if crass, and argued that while governments often performed their key tasks poorly, they had the capacity to overcome their historic proclivity to abuse power and could instead become engines for prosperity—providing they would not exercise a heavy hand in regulating the marketplace. Today people subscribing to these views are sometimes described as conservatives, not liberals. The tenets described here are those of "classical" liberalism. The hallmark of commercial liberal theory, then, is its commitment "to free markets and minimal state intervention. . . . Liberals believe economics is progressive and politics is regressive. Thus they conceive of progress as divorced from politics and based on the evolution of the market" (Gilpin 2001).

Transferred to the international level, these principles suggest that trade and other forms of economic relations "are a source of peaceful relations among nations because the mutual benefits of trade and expanding interdependence among national economies will tend to foster cooperative relations. . . . A liberal international economy will have a moderating influence on international politics as it creates bonds of mutual interests and a commitment to the status quo" (Gilpin 2001). Thus, trade liberalization is believed to produce many economic and political benefits: the removal of trade restrictions generates rapid export and economic growth because it promotes competition, improves resource allocations, reduces production costs, generates pressures for increased production efficiencies, attracts foreign capital and expertise, provides foreign exchange needed for imports, and promotes more equal access to scarce resources. Thus, "openness to trade promotes growth in a variety of ways. Entrepreneurs are forced to become increasingly efficient since they must compete against the best in the world to survive. Openness also affords access to the best technology and allows countries to specialize in what they do best rather than produce everything on their own. The fall of the [state-regulated communist economy of the] Soviet Union was in no small measure due to its failure to access cutting-edge

■ **politics**
the use of power by those in authority to exercise influence against subordinates and other authorities, and their reciprocal use for the same purpose.

technologies, compete against world-class producers, and specialize in production. Even as large an economy as the United States today specializes heavily in services, which account for 80 percent of total U.S. output" (Panagariya 2003, 21). These economic benefits to open trade are believed by liberals to produce another externality that is beneficial politically: free trade promotes democratic governance and the protection of citizens' human rights and civil liberties.

There is a fly in this liberal ointment, however. Although commercial liberal theory promises that the "invisible hand" will maximize efficiency so that everyone will gain, it does not promise that everyone will gain equally. Instead, "everyone will gain in accordance with his or her contribution to the whole, but . . . not everyone will gain equally because individual productivities differ. Under free exchange, society as a whole will be more wealthy, but individuals will be rewarded in terms of their marginal productivity and relative contribution to the overall social product" (Gilpin 2001). This applies at the global level as well: The gains from international trade are distributed quite unequally, even if the principle of comparative advantage governs. Globalization has not benefited middle-income countries as much as richer and poorer states (Garrett 2004). Commercial liberal theory ignores these differences, as it is concerned with **absolute gains** rather than **relative gains.** Other theorists, however, are more concerned with the distribution of economic rewards.

Mercantilism.
Mercantilism is an economic philosophy deeply entrenched in the long story of states' quest for power and wealth. Its theoretical underpinnings prompted Adam Smith to write his famous critique in *The Wealth of Nations,* and its practice prompted rebellious American colonists to dump British tea into the Boston harbor in 1773.

Mercantilism advocates government regulation of economic life to increase state power and security. An economic extension of realist theorizing, mercantilism emerged in Europe as the leading political economy philosophy after the decline of feudalism and helped to stimulate the first wave of Europe's imperialist expansion, which began in the fifteenth century. Accumulating gold and silver was seen as the route to state power and wealth, and imperialistically acquiring overseas colonies was seen as a means to that end.

While states no longer try to stockpile precious metals, many continue to intervene in the marketplace. In the contemporary context, then, **neomercantilism** refers to "a trade policy whereby a state seeks to maintain a balance-of-trade surplus and to promote domestic production and employment by reducing imports, stimulating home production, and promoting exports" (Walters and Blake 1992). Its advocates are sometimes called "economic nationalists." In their view, states must compete for position and power, and economic resources are the source of state power. From this it follows that "economic activities are and should be subordinate to the goal of state building and the interests of the state. All nationalists ascribe to the primacy of the state, of national security, and of military power in the functioning of the international system" (Gilpin 2001).

As an ideology of political economy, mercantilism shares much in common with political realism: Realists and mercantilists both see the state as the principal world actor; both view the global system as anarchical; and both dwell on the aggressively competitive drive of people and states for advantage. "Economic nationalists . . . stress the role of power in the rise of a market and the conflictual nature of international economic relations; they argue that economic inter-

■ **absolute gains**
a measure of the degree to which all participants in an exchange become better off.

■ **relative gains**
a measure of how much some participants in an exchange benefit in comparison to others.

■ **neomercantilism**
a contemporary version of classical mercantilism that advocates promoting domestic production and a balance-of-payment surplus by subsidizing exports and using tariffs and nontariff barriers to reduce imports.

dependence must have a political foundation and that it creates yet another arena of interstate conflict, increases national vulnerability, and constitutes a mechanism that one society can employ to dominate another" (Gilpin 2001).

While commercial liberals emphasize the mutual benefits of cooperative trade agreements, mercantilists are more concerned that the gains realized by one side of the bargain will come at the expense of the other. "The logical absurdity of all governments seeking a surplus at the same time was not perceived as a problem. Within a zero-sum world, there had to be winners and losers" (Mayall 2001). For mercantilists, relative gains are more important than both parties' absolute gains. An American economic nationalist, for instance, would complain about a trade agreement that promised the United States a 5 percent growth in income and the Chinese 6 percent. Although the bargain would ensure an eventual increase in U.S. living standards, its position compared with China's would erode. Indeed, projected over the long run, such seemingly small differences would eventually lead to China's replacement of the United States as the world's largest economy—an outcome declared in 2002 as highly unacceptable to American economic nationalists, as President Bush did when his new grand strategy proclaimed that preserving U.S. hegemonic supremacy was to be America's highest priority. Calculations such as these explain why achieving mutual gains through multilateral international cooperation often encounters stiff resistance from domestic groups seeking to protect their profits from foreign competition. It also explains why specific, negatively affected domestic producers lobby for mercantilist measures, and why they sometimes succeed against the unorganized interests of consumers who benefit from the lower cost of goods as a result of free trade.

Protectionism is the generic term used to describe a number of mercantilist policies designed to keep foreign goods out of a country and to subsidize the export of goods to encourage foreigners to buy domestically produced goods.

- **Beggar-thy-neighbor policies** seek to enhance domestic welfare by promoting trade surpluses that can be realized only at other countries' expense. They reflect a government's efforts to reduce unemployment through currency devaluations, tariffs, quotas, export subsidies, and other strategies that adversely affect its trade partners. These protective strategies encourage unequal exchanges between exporters and importers (see Chapter 5).
- **Import quotas** unilaterally specify the quantity of a particular product that can be imported from abroad. In the late 1950s, for example, the United States established import quotas on oil, arguing that they were necessary to protect U.S. national security. Hence the government, rather than the marketplace, determined the amount and source of imports.
- **Export quotas** result from negotiated agreements between producers and consumers and restrict the flow of products (e.g., shoes or sugar) from the former to the latter. An **orderly market arrangement (OMA)** is a formal agreement in which a country agrees to limit the export of products that might impair workers in the importing country, often under specific rules designed to monitor and manage trade flows. Exporting countries are willing to accept such restrictions in exchange for concessions on other fronts from the importing countries. The Multi-Fiber Arrangement (MFA) is an example of an elaborate OMA that restricts exports of textiles and apparel. It originated in the early 1960s, when the United States formalized earlier, in-

■ **protectionism**
a policy of creating barriers to foreign trade, such as tariffs and quotas, that protect local industries from competition.

■ **beggar-thy-neighbor policies**
the attempt to promote trade surpluses by trade policies that cause trade partners to suffer trade deficits.

■ **import quotas**
nontariff barriers to free trade that involve limits on the quantity of particular products that can be imported.

■ **export quotas**
barriers to free trade agreed to by two trading states to protect their domestic producers.

■ **orderly market arrangements (OMAs)**
voluntary export restrictions that involve a government-to-government agreement and often specific rules of management.

- **voluntary export restrictions (VERs)**
a protectionist measure popular in the 1980s and early 1990s, in which exporting countries agree to restrict shipments of a particular product to a country to deter it from imposing an even more onerous import quota.

- **nontariff barriers (NTBs)**
measures that discriminate against imports without direct tax levies and are beyond the scope of international regulation.

- **infant industry**
a newly established industry that is not yet strong enough to compete effectively in the global marketplace.

- **strategic trade policy**
an industrial policy that targets government subsidies toward particular industries so as to gain competitive advantage over foreign producers.

- **countervailing duties**
tariffs imposed by a government to offset suspected subsidies provided by foreign governments to their producers.

- **antidumping duties**
duties imposed to offset another state's alleged selling of a product at a price below the cost to produce it.

- **realism**
the theoretical tradition that operates from the assumption that competitive states seek self-advantage and are unlikely to cooperate.

formal **voluntary export restrictions (VERs)** negotiated with Japan and Hong Kong to protect domestic producers from cheap cotton imports. The quota system was later extended to other importing and exporting countries and then, in the 1970s, to other fibers, when it became the MFA.

- Import and export quotas are representative of a broader category of trade restrictions known as **nontariff barriers (NTBs),** which discriminate against imports without direct tax levies. They cover a wide range of creative government regulations designed to shelter particular domestic industries from foreign competition, including health and safety regulations, government purchasing procedures, subsidies, and antidumping regulations (to prevent foreign producers from selling their goods for less than they cost domestically).

- Among developing countries whose domestic industrialization goals may be hindered by the absence of protection from the Global North's more efficient firms, the **infant industry** argument is often used to justify mercantilist trade policies. According to this argument, tariffs or other forms of protection are necessary to nurture young industries until they eventually mature and lower production costs to compete effectively in the global marketplace. Import-substitution industrialization policies, once popular in Latin America and elsewhere, often depended on protection of infant industries (see Chapter 5).

- In the Global North, creating comparative advantages now motivates the use of what is known as **strategic trade policy** as a neomercantilist means of ensuring that a country's industries will remain competitive. Strategic trade is a form of government industrial policy that targets subsidies toward particular industries so they gain a competitive edge over foreign producers. Two protectionist strategies that are increasingly used are **countervailing duties,** the imposition of tariffs to offset alleged subsidies by foreign producers, and **antidumping duties** imposed to counter the alleged sale of products at below the cost of production.

Realist theory helps to account for states' impulse to practice mercantilist and neomercantilist protectionism. Recall that **realism** argues that states often shun cooperation, because international anarchy without global governance creates fear: Threatened states mistrust one another's motives. Moreover, in the self-help global system, states alone are responsible for their survival and well-being. As a result, uncertainty about others' expansionist aims encourages each state to spend "a portion of its effort, not forwarding its own good, but in providing the means of protecting itself against others" (Waltz 1979).

The insecurity that breeds competition rather than cooperation is often exhibited in international economic relations. Those who see states' power and wealth as inextricably linked conclude that "even if nation-states do not fear for their physical survival, they worry that a decrease in their power capabilities relative to those of other states will compromise their political autonomy, expose them to the influence attempts of others, or lessen their ability to prevail in political disputes with allies and adversaries" (Mastanduno 1991). Thus many states are "defensively positional actors" that seek not only to promote their domestic well-being but also to defend their rank (position) in comparison with others (see Grieco 1995; see also Schweller 2004).

The "relative gains" issue speaks to the difficulties of achieving international cooperation under anarchical conditions and explains why some domestic producers vigorously oppose liberal (open) international economies despite the fact that "the data show a definite statistical link between freer trade and economic growth" (World Trade Organization, www.wto.org, May 6, 2004). Different countries therefore practice dissimilar economic policies. Some endorse free trade, and others impose protectionist barriers; some see an unregulated market as the best method for protecting the greatest good for the greatest number, while others seek to tilt the playing field to their own advantage.

Hegemony: A Precondition for Economic Order and Free Trade?

Hegemonic stability theory, a blend of liberalism and mercantilism, holds that when a single state ascends to hold a preponderance of military and economic power such that a **hegemon** emerges, international economic stability based on liberal principles can materialize to alleviate the fears of nationalistic mercantilists. Unlike mercantilism, this realist worldview follows the logic of **long-cycle theory** (see Chapter 4) in viewing the balancing of power among competing actors in anarchy as the key to global economic order, but accepts the likelihood that order can best emerge at those phases in the long-term redistribution of global power when an all-powerful single hegemon uses its supremacy to enforce free-trade rules. Hegemonic stability theory thus "assumes that a liberal economic system cannot be self-sustaining but must be maintained over the long term through the actions of the dominant economy" (Gilpin 2001).

Hegemony is the ability to "dictate, or at least dominate, the rules and arrangements by which international relations, political and economic, are conducted" (Goldstein 1988). In the world economy it occurs when a single great power garners a sufficient preponderance of material resources so that it can dominate the international flow of raw materials, capital, and trade.

From its preponderant position, a hegemon is able to promote rules for the whole global system that protect the hegemon's own interests. Hegemons such as the United States (and Britain before it), whose domestic economies are based on capitalist principles, have championed liberal international economic systems, because their comparatively greater control of technology, capital, and raw materials has given them more opportunities to profit from a system free of mercantilist restraints. When they have enforced such free-trade rules, the hegemon's economies typically have served as "engines of growth" for others in the "liberal train."

However, historically, hegemons have also had special responsibilities. They have had to coordinate states' **macroeconomic** policies, manage the international monetary system to enable one state's money to be exchanged for others', make sure that countries facing balance-of payments deficits (imbalances in their financial inflows and outflows) could find the credits necessary to finance their deficits, and serve as lenders of last resort during financial crises. When the most powerful liberal states could not perform these tasks, they have often backtracked toward more closed (protected or regulated) domestic economies, and in doing so have undermined the open international system that was previously advantageous to them. This kind of departure historically has made tariffs, monetary regulations, and other mercantilist policies more widespread and thereby weakened or destroyed the LIEO regime. In short, hegemonic states not

■ **hegemonic stability theory**
the proposition that free trade and interstate peace depend on the existence of a predominant great power willing and able to use economic and military strength to promote global stability.

■ **hegemon**
a single, overwhelmingly powerful state that exercises predominant influence over other global actors.

■ **long-cycle theory**
the proposition based on the evidence that great powers rise to positions of hegemonic global leadership but eventually decline when their leadership is challenged by ascendant rivals.

■ **hegemony**
the ability of one state to lead in world politics by promoting its worldview and ruling over arrangements governing international economics and politics.

■ **macroeconomics**
the study of aggregate economic indicators such as GDP, the money supply, and the balance of trade that governments monitor to measure changes in the national and global economy.

Preparing the Pathways to Global Economic Recovery In the wake of the September 11, 2001, terrorist attacks in New York City, stock markets shut down as investor and consumer gloom spread quickly across the globe and the vulnerability of the United States undermined confidence in the capability of America to perform as an unchallenged hegemon in international economics to preserve the liberal system of free trade. The world economy enjoyed spectacular growth of almost 5 percent in 2000, but after 9/11 fears of a worldwide recession escalated. In order to avert a massive recession, prime ministers, bankers, and CEOs gathered in 2002 at the meeting of the World Economic Forum to talk about the most effective multilateral plans for propelling recovery, moving their annual conclave from Davos, Switzerland, to New York. Their goal: to signal their solidarity with the charred city, as terrorists still threatened to destroy the pillars of global capitalism. The terrorist attacks forced a major rethinking about how the global economy works and how to make the international economy resume its pace of growth since the early 1990s. Adding to the challenge is the continuing protest movement arrayed against globalization. Shown here are New York City police practicing to act as bodyguards to protect the participants at the 2002 World Economic Forum. "The success of the World Economic Forum, whose meetings began informally in 1982, attracted the criticism of those who objected to the economic and social values associated with Anglo-American-style capitalism [and in reaction in 2001] critics established an 'anti-Davos' to develop constructive alternatives to globalization" (Pfaff 2001a). The critics held their first counter-meeting in Porto Alegre, Brazil, at the same time that the annual Davos forum was scheduled.

only have had the greatest capacity to make a free-trade regime succeed but in the past they also have had the greatest responsibility for its effective operation and preservation. To interpret whether hegemonic stability theory is likely to hold in the future, a closer look at the theory's logic is useful.

The Hegemonic Pillars of Free Markets and Free Trade. Nearly all economic theories accept particular principles about the preconditions for fostering the free movement of goods across national borders. A core concept that informs discussion is that of public or **collective goods**—benefits that everyone shares and from which no one can be excluded selectively. National security is one such collective good that governments try to provide for all of their citizens, regardless of the resources that individuals contribute through taxation. In the realm of economic analysis, an open international economy permitting the relatively free movement of goods, services, and capital is similarly seen as a desirable collective good, inasmuch as it permits economic benefits for all states that would not be available if the global economy were closed to free trade.

According to hegemonic stability theory, the collective good of an open global economy needs a single, dominant power—a hegemon—to remain open and liberal. If a hegemon does not exist or is unwilling to use its power to provide this collective good, states will be tempted to take selfish advantage of the opportunities provided rather than contribute to maintaining the liberal international economy. A major way in which the hegemon pays may be to open its own market to less-expensive imported goods even if other countries "free ride" by not opening their own markets. And if enough states take this easy route, the entire structure may collapse.

The analogy of a public park helps us to clarify this principle. If there were no central government to provide for the maintenance of the park, individuals themselves would have to cooperate to keep the park in order (the trees trimmed, the lawn mowed, litter removed, and so on). But some may try to come and enjoy the benefits of the park without pitching in. If enough people realize that they can get away with this—that they can enjoy a beautiful park without helping with its upkeep—it will not be long before the once beautiful park looks shabby. Cooperation to provide a public good is thus hard to sustain.

This is also the case with the collective good of a liberal international economy, because many states that enjoy the collective good of an orderly, open, free market economy pay little or nothing for it. These are known as **free riders**. A hegemon typically tolerates free riders, partly because the benefits that the hegemon provides, such as a stable global currency, encourage other states to accept the leader's dictates. Thus both gain, much as liberalism sees the benefits of cooperation as a "positive-sum" outcome because both sides to a bargain stand to gain from their exchanges. If the costs of leadership begin to multiply, however, a hegemon will tend to become less tolerant of others' free riding. In such a situation cooperation will increasingly be seen as one-sided or **zero-sum** because most of the benefits come at the expense of the hegemon. Then the open global economy will crumble amid a competitive race for individual gain at others' expense.

Charles Kindleberger (1973) first theorized about the need for a preponderant liberal hegemon to maintain order and stability. In his explanation of the

■ **collective goods**
goods such as safe drinking water from which everyone benefits.

■ **free riders**
those who enjoy the benefits of collective goods but pay little or nothing for them.

■ **zero-sum**
an exchange in which what one competitor gains is lost by the other party to the exchange.

1930s Great Depression, Kindleberger concluded that "the international economic and monetary system needs leadership, a country which is prepared, consciously or unconsciously, . . . to set standards of conduct for other countries; and to seek to get others to follow them, to take on an undue share of the burdens of the system, and in particular to take on its support in adversity." Britain played this role from 1815 until the outbreak of World War I in 1914, and the United States assumed the British mantle in the decades immediately following World War II. In the interwar years, however, Britain was unable to play its previous leadership role, and the United States, although capable of leadership, was unwilling to exercise it. The void, Kindleberger concluded, was a principal cause of the "width and depth" of the Great Depression throughout the world in the 1930s.

A Globe without Hegemonic Leadership? Although hegemonic powers benefit from the liberal economic systems that their power promotes, the very success of liberalism eventually erodes the pillars that support it.

> Economic competition and the price mechanism drive the market economy toward ever higher levels of productive efficiency, economic growth, and the integration of national markets. In time, the market produces profound shifts in the location of economic activities and affects the international redistribution of economic and industrial power. The unleashing of market forces transforms the political framework itself, undermines the hegemonic power, and creates a new political environment to which the world must eventually adjust. With the inevitable shift in the international distribution of economic and military power from the core to rising nations in the periphery and elsewhere, the capacity of the hegemon to maintain the system decreases. Capitalism and the market system thus tend to destroy the political foundations on which they must ultimately rest. (Gilpin 1987, 77–78)

The leading economic power's ability to adapt is critical to maintaining its dominant position. Britain was unable to adapt and fell from its top-ranked position. Many wonder if the United States is destined, however imperial as a global empire it appears now in the so-called American Century (Eckes and Zeiler 2003, Kegley and Raymond 2005b), to ultimately suffer the same fate, not because of economic failure but because of the lack of political will to exercise leadership through concerted multilateral action (Prestowitz 2003). The United States now stands as an economic superpower, with few apparent ends in sight to economic dominance, the expected eventual rise of China to the position of the globe's largest economy and biggest population notwithstanding. However, the circumstances confronting the United States today are eroding its capacity to exercise hegemonic leadership.

The United States is a "'dependent colossus' [because] although globalization today reinforces American power, over time it promises to have the opposite effects" (Nye 2002a). At present, the United States has the largest economy, but no one predicts that its position of dominance will increase. The trajectories are moving in the opposite direction. The U.S. share of world output has fallen steadily since World War II ended. In 1947, the United States accounted for nearly 50 percent of the combined gross world product. By 1960, its share had slipped to 28 percent, by 1970 to 25 percent, and "by the 1990s to 20 percent or less—less than of what it had been at its peak and less than it was at the time of the Spanish-American War, when the United States first emerged as a world power" (D. White 1998, 42). Another symptom of the U.S. erosion in the international pecking order is that the U.S. share of world financial reserves has declined. The United States went from being the globe's greatest creditor country in 1980 to the world's largest debtor by 1990, and since then has become the biggest debtor in history. America's huge and growing current account deficit (what is owed to foreign creditors) has swelled, and it is a growing problem compounded by huge post–9/11 increases in U.S. military spending, alongside tax cuts that reduced federal revenue. At the end of 2004, the United States ran a $650 billion deficit in its current account balance (the balance of goods and services between America and the rest of the world), which is being covered by borrowing from private investors, most from overseas, and increasingly from foreign central banks at the rate of more than $45 billion each month. The central banks of China and Japan hold about $1 trillion in U.S. Treasury bonds and bills, almost a quarter of the publicly held U.S. debt (Ip 2004, 1). This U.S. dependence on the willingness of foreigners to provide the funds needed to pay the interest on U.S. debts leaves America vulnerable—especially if China and Japan stop buying U.S. bonds or sell them. The globe's greatest military power is also the globe's greatest debtor, with runaway spending expected to add $5 trillion over the next ten years to the cumulative U.S. deficit (Friedman 2004a, 5). A third symptom of U.S. vulnerability is the fact that the U.S. trade deficit at the start of 2003 reached the highest level ever. Finally, alongside these debt burdens and trade imbalances, U.S. investment in public infrastructure to stimulate future growth is lower than that of all the other G-8 industrialized powerhouses, a problem that ultimately will reduce America's capacity to compete with other economies because of its relatively low savings rate and shrinking support for public education, perhaps the most important long-term factor in economic growth (Ferguson 2004b). These trends suggest that the U.S. advantage as a hegemon and leader will not persist in the long run (Kegley and Raymond 2005b).

In many areas essential to lasting hegemony—control over capital, markets, and robust production—U.S. preponderance may continue to be as secure as ever. This makes less convincing Paul Kennedy's popular thesis (1987) that **imperial overstretch** was likely to cause America's fall from its preeminent position at the pinnacle of global economic power. As Kennedy argued in the late 1980s, "The United States now runs the risk that the sum total of [its] global interests and obligations is nowadays far larger than the country's power to defend them all simultaneously." This prediction derived from a principle suggested by past hegemonic experiences, namely "that a power that wants to remain number one for generation after generation requires not just military capability . . . but also a flourishing and efficient economic base, strong finances and a healthy social fabric, for it is upon such foundations that the country's military strength rests in the long term."

An undisputed hegemonic power typically can afford to be less concerned about its relative power position than others. It is therefore less likely to attempt to maximize its share of the global market than are aspiring hegemons or other

■ **imperial overstretch**
Paul Kennedy's thesis that hegemons decline because they make costly global commitments in excess of their ability to fulfill them.

economic powers threatened by an erosion in their relative power. As a hegemon's dominance erodes, however, its trade and other economic policies can be expected to become less benevolent (interested in general benefits for all) and more coercive (self-interested and exploitative) by putting relative gains ahead of absolute gains for the collective majority. The United States today is less willing to assume the burdens of maintaining the liberal international economic order it once championed, emphasizing competitiveness more than the acceptance of the burden of making sacrifices to maintain the stability of the global political economy.

The Problematic Consequences of Waning Hegemonic Leadership. What will happen if and when the U.S. hegemon's preponderant power persists, but its willingness to lead declines? Domestically we would expect the United States to abandon the torch of commercial liberalism as the forces of economic nationalism through trade protectionism gain politically. Internationally, hegemonic stability theory predicts that disorder will result, because hegemonic leadership is "the cement that holds the system together" (Gilpin 1987).

Have the institutions and rules put into place to govern the liberal order in the post–World War II era of unilateral American hegemony now taken on a life of their own? This view is the most convincing one to commercial liberals, who believe that the rise of a liberal international regime and embedded network of complementary institutions to support its open rules explains the persistence of economic order and growth, even if American willingness to engage in hegemonic leadership fades.

The power of that conviction resides in the fact that the commercial liberalism institutionalized in the original Bretton Woods system is now deeply entrenched. True, "America's defection could throw the process into reverse" (Bergsten 1997). However, even in the absence of a U.S. hegemon pushing for trade liberalization, and even in the face of the U.S. hegemon succumbing to the temptations of (free-riding) mercantilism (as the Bush administration did when it in 2002 imposed tariffs on steel imports to protect that fading sector), trade liberalization may now be too established for it to collapse. Does the free-trade regime have too many supporters, including powerful MNCs, for that regime to need a single hegemonic protector to preserve free trade as it did in the past two hundred years? To some optimists, institutionalized globalization has now progressed to a level that makes the continuation of a liberal trading system likely, because too many states and multilateral institutions have an enormous stake in its preservation. "Built-in restraints on imposing new trade barriers have never been greater" (Stokes 2000).

International regimes are created by states to devise rules for cooperation even under international anarchy. Most of the liberal international regimes (rules and institutions) that govern international trade today first developed after World War II when the United States was both dominant and willing to lead. "By providing more information, establishing mechanisms for monitoring and generating shared expectations, institutions can create an environment in which interstate cooperation is possible even without a single dominant leader" (Krasner 2001). The free-trade regime may no longer depend on the existence of an all-powerful hegemon.

To better probe that hypothesis and understand the likely future of global

■ **international regimes**
the set of rules, norms, and decision-making procedures that coordinates state behavior in such areas as international trade.

economics, let us now inspect how those international trade and monetary rules have evolved from mere pledges to liberalization to customary policy practices.

THE CHANGING FREE-TRADE REGIME

In the period immediately following World War II, when the United States became the world's new political hegemon, it simultaneously became the preeminent voice in international trade affairs. The liberal trading system the United States chose to promote rejected the zero-sum, beggar-thy-neighbor competitive economic nationalism widely seen as a major cause of the economic depression of the 1930s. Removing barriers to trade became a priority and led to the recurrent rounds of trade negotiations that cumulatively produced remarkable reductions in tariff rates. As the large U.S. market was opened to foreign producers, other countries' economies grew, and rising trade contributed to a climate that encouraged others to open their markets also.

That movement toward free trade progressed in a series of steps. At the time of the Bretton Woods negotiations, the United States at first envisioned a new International Trade Organization (ITO) that would seek lower restrictions on trade and set rules of commerce. The organization was stillborn, however. The proposed trading scheme, popularly known as the Havana Charter, failed to win the approval of the U.S. Congress: "Protectionists opposed the arrangement for being too liberal, and liberals were against it for being too protectionist. . . . Without U.S. support the ITO was dead" (Isaak 2000).

Without the ITO, the United States needed to find another institutional base from which to create and enhance a liberalized trade regime. It turned to the **General Agreement on Tariffs and Trade (GATT),** which, after its birth in the late 1940s, became the principal international organization designed to promote and protect free trade in the postwar LIEO.

GATT was never intended to be a formal institution with enforcement powers. Instead, a premium was placed on negotiations and reaching consensus to settle disputes among parties to the agreement, which was first and foremost a commercial treaty. As the trading system changed and disputes multiplied, though, GATT—under pressure from the United States—increasingly became involved in dispute settlement following increasingly legalistic procedures. Those rules put into law an evolving regime whose primary mission has been increasing free trade.

The emergence of a global free-trade regime is a history of starts and stops along the progressive path toward the reduction of barriers to the free flow of goods across national borders. Progress toward lower tariffs has encountered resistance along the way, but in 1994 the GATT sessions in the **Uruguay Round** of negotiations that had begun in 1986 culminated in the 1995 creation of the **World Trade Organization (WTO),** a new free-trade IGO with "teeth" (see Table 9.2 and Figure 9.1). That twenty-two thousand page agreement was the most comprehensive trade deal in history, covering everything from paper clips to potato chips to jet aircraft.

The WTO represents a breathtaking step in free-trade management, although it has also provoked much criticism (see Controversy: Globalization's

■ **General Agreement on Tariffs and Trade (GATT)**
an international organization affiliated with the United Nations that promotes international trade and tariff reductions, now the World Trade Organization.

■ **Uruguay Round**
the multilateral trade negotiations of GATT that began in 1986 and concluded in 1995 with the creation of the WTO.

■ **World Trade Organization (WTO)**
a multilateral agency that monitors the implementation of trade agreements and settles disputes among trade partners.

TABLE 9.2

Round and Round: A GATT-WTO Chronology

Date	Summary
1947	Birth of the GATT, signed by 23 countries on October 30 at the Palais des Nations in Geneva.
1948	The GATT comes into force. First meeting of its members in Havana, Cuba.
1949	Second round of talks at Annecy, France. Some five thousand tariff cuts agreed to; 10 new countries admitted.
1950–51	Third round at Torquay, England. Members exchange 8,700 trade concessions and welcome 4 new countries.
1956	Fourth round at Geneva. Tariff cuts worth $1.3 trillion at today's prices.
1960–62	The Dillon Round, named after U.S. Undersecretary of State Douglas Dillon, who proposed the talks. A further 4,400 tariff cuts.
1964–67	The Kennedy Round. Many industrial tariffs halved. Signed by 50 countries. Code on dumping agreed to separately.
1973–79	The Tokyo Round, involving 99 countries. First serious discussion of nontariff trade barriers, such as subsidies and licensing requirements. Average tariff on manufactured goods in the 9 biggest markets cut from 7 percent to 4.7 percent.
1986–93	The Uruguay Round. Further cuts in industrial tariffs, export subsidies, licensing, and customs valuation. First agreements on trade in services and intellectual property.
1995	Formation of WTO with power to settle disputes between members.
1997	Agreements concluded on telecommunications services, information technology, and financial services.
1999	The Millennium Round convenes at Seattle in November to organize for a new round of multilateral trade negotiations. Thousands demonstrate against globalization and trade liberalization, including numerous NGOs pressuring the WTO to advance their agendas.
2000	The WTO grows to 135 members, and more than 30 other states are applicants for membership. WTO opens new negotiations to revamp rules of trade on agricultural goods and services.
2001	WTO resumes discussions in Doha, Qatar, in hope that the remote setting will prevent protest disruptions from antiglobalization protestors. 142 states unsuccessfully chart a path for the world's biggest economies to deal cooperatively with regionalism between competitive trade blocs and to raise hopes for recovery.
2002	WTO convenes in New York. Later admits China and Taiwan to its membership, which grows to 145 members.
2005	The so-called development round of the Doha negotiations continue after abruptly collapsing at the Cancún session in 2003, but resolution is resisted by the new Global South's WTO members opposed to the WTO's "one size fits all" approach requiring transparency in government procurement and the elimination of bureaucratic red-tape barriers to the import of foreign exports for WTO's 147 members.

SOURCE: World Trade Organization annual reports; OECD (www.OECD.org/may5/2004).

Growing Pains: Is The World Trade Organization a Friend or Foe?). The WTO extended GATT's coverage to products, sectors, and conditions of trade not previously adequately covered. The WTO also enhanced previous dispute-settlement procedures by making the findings of its arbitration panels binding on the domestic laws of participating states (GATT's findings were not binding). Finally, the WTO deals with the problem of free riding by being available only to states that belong to the WTO, subscribe to all of the Uruguay Round agreements, and make market access commitments (under the old the WTO system, free riding

FIGURE 9.1
Round and Round: A GATT-WTO Chronology
The liberalization of the international trading system is the product of cooperative efforts within the framework of the General Agreement on Tariffs and Trade (GATT), as shown in this summary of the major GATT multilateral negotiating rounds since its creation in 1947 and the growth of trade among the WTO's members since 1985. The free-trade regime has greatly aided the expansion of global trade, which more than doubled in the last fifteen years of the twentieth century. Trade integration is expanding at a rapid rate; world trade has grown fourfold since 1970 and now accounts for about one-third of all countries' combined gross domestic product.
SOURCE: World Trade Organization annual reports; OECD (www.OECD.org/may5/2004).

was possible when some small states were permitted to benefit from trade liberalization without having to make contributions of their own).

The accord's acceptance was hailed as a big step toward keeping the liberal trade regime afloat in an increasingly competitive and globalized world economy. Today, three-fourths of the globe's countries derive at least a third of their national income from exports and by 2015 this percentage is expected to increase to about two-fifths for the world (Central Intelligence Agency 2002, 36). The WTO was reconfigured to guard against trade wars. The incentives for lowering barriers to free trade are powerful, since much evidence supports the liberal proposition that exports and imports contribute to higher standards of living. The creation of the WTO signaled a victory for liberalism and a setback for neomercantilist free riding. At the same time, this transforming treaty advanced globalization and multilateralism, because it "reduced the powers of all governments to regulate behavior and set independent economic policies" (Thurow 1998). Trade squabbles nonetheless continue despite overwhelming profits from trade liberalization. There are many tricks to free trade, and contentious issues inevitably cast the spotlight on the continuing frictions caused by a shrinking globe of competitive states. Free trade generates new jobs and wealth, but laissez-faire international capitalism also brings unprecedented risks.

> ## CONTROVERSY
>
> ## GLOBALIZATION'S GROWING PAINS
> Is the World Trade Organization a Friend or Foe?
>
> In late November 1999, the then 135-member countries of the World Trade Organization (WTO) and 30 additional observer states made final preparations to stage in Seattle what was billed as the Millennium Round on trade negotiations—the follow-up to the Uruguay Round of trade talks completed in 1993. At the time the mood was optimistic. The meeting promised to celebrate the free-trade regime for the global marketplace and the contributions that lower trade barriers arguably had made to the growth of international exports and, for many members (particularly the United States), their longest and largest peacetime economic expansion in the twentieth century. There appeared to be widespread recognition that
>
>> Every country in history that has raised its living standards—including the United States—has done so by hitching its wagon to the world economy. . . . During the past [fifty] years, the world has seen a massive reduction in trade barriers—and consequently the biggest and longest economic boon in history. Between 1950 and [2000], world exports of manufactured goods multiplied [sixteen-fold] and world economic output increased sixfold. All this has meant rising standards of living for people around the world, but most especially those in the West and the United States. (Zakaria 1998a, 40; Mickletwhait and Wooldridge 2001)
>
> A half-century of generally rising prosperity had generated a climate of enthusiasm for the power of free trade. Fears of imports tend to recede in good economic times, and, with the best decade ever, most leaders in the twilight of the twentieth century emphasized the sunnier side of free trade. Advocates share the liberal conviction that countries, companies, and consumers have much to gain by a globalized economy freed from restraints on the exchange of goods across borders. A world without walls promotes prosperity and welfare. Negotiators in 1999 expected added benefits from a new trade round that could slash tariffs and other trade barriers in agriculture, manufactured goods, and services.
>
> That mood and the seeming consensus on which it was based was shattered when the Seattle trade talks opened. An estimated fifty thousand to one hundred thousand protesters and grassroots anti-WTO activists, who differed widely in their special interests (the poor, environment, labor, women, indigenous people), joined hands to shout their common opposition to the general idea of globalization and free trade. A plane trailed a banner proclaiming "People Over Profits: Stop WTO" as part of what became known as "The Battle in Seattle" or, alternatively, the "Carnival against Capitalism." A tirade against open trade ensued, fueled by citizen backlash (Broad 2002; Aaronson 2001).
>
> The Seattle conference will be remembered as the moment when the debate over the benefits and costs of the globalized economy rose to the pinnacle of the global agenda. The immediate target of the demonstrations was the WTO; however, the organization itself was simply a convenient symbol of a much larger sea of discontent. The WTO protests—and the failure of the WTO conference attendees to compromise on tightly held positions and agree on even a minimal accord—exposed the deep divisions about the best ways to open global commerce and adopt new rules at a time of rapid change.
>
> Controversies about globalization, free trade, and global governance are multiple. At the core is the question of whether a globalized economy is inevitable and, if so, is it an antidote to suffering or an enemy of human welfare. The debates are explosive, because everyone is affected, but in quite different ways. Many enjoyed the 1990s boom years under liberalized trade engineered by the WTO's trade agree-

MONETARY MATTERS: CAN FINANCIAL REGIMES PROMOTE GROWTH?

States cannot always trade as they wish. The exports and imports depend on many factors, especially on changes in global demand and prices for the goods and services that countries' producers sell in the global marketplace. The mechanisms for setting the currency exchange rates by which the value of traded ments. But the celebration is confined largely to the top—the privileged, powerful, and prosperous. Many others see themselves as clear victims of an open global economy, as when a factory closes and workers lose their jobs. Those discontented with globalized free trade include a diverse coalition of protestors, many of whom harbor specific concerns about wages, the environment, and human rights issues. Labor leaders contend that the WTO is sacrificing worker rights; environmental groups complain that when green values collide with world commerce, environmental standards are left out of trade negotiations; and human rights activists accuse the WTO of serving the preferences of MNCs for erasing trade barriers in ways that fail to protect human security. In addition, enraged trade ministers from the Global South's developing countries see a Global North conspiracy in the WTO's efforts to adopt core labor standards, because the less-developed Global South views such high-sounding rules as a method to impose high tariffs on their products and take away the comparative advantages Global South developing nations enjoy with lower wage scales.

These, and other issues, continue as major controversies. What do you think? Is the WTO a valuable tool for improving global governance and human welfare, or a threat? Is the WTO and the free trade practices it promotes too strong or too weak? Does the WTO put corporate greed and profits above human needs and environmental protection, as critics charge? Or do you agree with WTO Director-General Mike Moore's defense of free trade, and his warning against what he called a "false debate" between people and the WTO, when he maintained, "Trade is the ally of working people, not their enemy. As living standards improve, so does education, health, the environment and labor standards." What direction should global trade take?

goods are priced heavily influence international trade. Indeed, the **monetary system** is crucial for international trade, for without a stable and predictable method of calculating the value of sales and foreign investments, those transactions become too risky, causing trade and investment activities to fall. As the World Bank argues, the success of international trade depends on the health of the financial system.

■ **monetary system**
a stable and predictable method for calculating the value of sales and foreign investments across national currencies.

The Nuts and Bolts of Monetary Policy

Monetary and financial policies are woven into a complex set of relationships between states and the global system, and, because monetary and currency issues have their own specialized technical terminology, they are difficult to understand. However, the essentials are rather basic:

> **Monetary policy** works on two principal economic variables: the aggregate supply of money in circulation and the level of interest rates. The **money supply** (currency plus commercial bank demand deposits) is thought to be directly related to the level of economic activity in the sense that a greater money supply induces expanded economic activity by enabling people to purchase more goods and services. This in essence is the *monetarist theory* of economic activity. Its advocates argue that by controlling the growth of the money supply, governments can regulate their nations' economic activity and control inflation. (Todaro 2000, 657)

To understand the importance of monetary policies as determinants of states' trade, growth rates, and wealth consider both why **exchange rates** (see Table 9.3) fluctuate daily, often widely, and the impact of these currency fluctuations. Money works in several ways and serves different purposes. First, money must be widely accepted, so that people earning it can use it to buy goods and services from others. Second, money must serve to store value, so that people will be willing to keep some of their wealth in the form of money. Third, money must act as a standard of deferred payment, so that people will be willing to lend money knowing that when the money is repaid in the future, it will still have purchasing power.

Governments attempt to manage their currencies to prevent inflation. Inflation occurs when the government creates too much money in relation to the goods and services produced in the economy. As money becomes more plentiful and thus less acceptable, it cannot serve effectively to store value or to satisfy debts or serve well as a medium of exchange.

Movements in a state's exchange rate occur in part when changes develop in peoples' assessment of the national currency's underlying economic strength or the ability of its government to maintain the value of its money. A deficit in a country's balance of payments, for example, would likely cause a decline in the value of its currency relative to that of others. This happens when the supply of the currency is greater than the demand for it. Similarly, when those engaged in international economic transactions change their expectations about a currency's future value, they might reschedule their lending and borrowing. Fluctuations in the exchange rate could follow.

Speculators—those who buy and sell money in an effort to make it—may also affect the international stability of a country's currency. Speculators make money by guessing the future. If, for instance, they believe that the Japanese yen will be worth more in three months than it is now, they can buy yen today and sell them for a profit three months later. Conversely, if they believe that the yen will be worth less in three months, they can sell yen today for a certain number of dollars and then buy back the same yen in three months for fewer dollars, making a profit. The globalization of finance now also encourages managers of investment portfolios to move funds from one currency to another in order to realize gains from differences in states' interest rates and the declining value of other currencies in the global network of exchange rates.

■ **monetary policy**
the decisions made by states' central banks to regulate the national economy and control inflation using policies such as changing the money supply and interest rates.

■ **money supply**
the total amount of currency in circulation in a state, calculated to include demand deposits, such as checking accounts in commercial banks, and time deposits, such as savings accounts and bonds, in savings banks.

■ **exchange rate**
the rate at which one state's currency is exchanged for another state's currency in the global marketplace.

TABLE 9.3

Currency Concerns: Concepts for Conversing about International Exchange Rates and Balance-of-Payments Issues

Term	Concept
Balance of Payments	A calculation summarizing a country's financial transactions with the external world, determined by the level of credits (export earnings, profits from foreign investment, receipts of foreign aid) minus the country's total international debts (imports, interest payments on international debts, foreign direct investments, and the like). A favorable balance of payments is achieved when a country's international credits exceed its national debits, as recorded in its current account (the market value of exports and imports with the rest of the world) and its capital account (the ratio of a country's private and foreign investments flowing into and outside the country).
Balance-of-Trade Deficit	A situation that results when a state buys more from abroad than it sells. The balance measures both the value of merchandise goods and services imported and exported. To correct a payments deficit, a country has available three basic but painful options: (1) its government can initiate deflationary policies at home by raising interest rates to tighten budgets; (2) it can restrict the outflow of money by imposing higher tariffs, import quotas, or other restrictions; or (3) it can borrow in capital markets or liquidate its foreign exchange reserves.
Central Bank	A state's major agency in charge of issuing its currency, managing its foreign resources, putting the government's monetary policies into practice, and acting as a bank for the government and for the state's commercial banks.
Devaluation	The lowering of the official exchange rate of one country's currency relative to the value of all other states' currencies, usually in the hope that the devaluation will encourage foreigners to purchase products through trade at the artificially reduced price.
Exchange Rate	The rate at which one state's currency is exchanged for another state's currency in the global marketplace. For 1 U.S. dollar, you might receive 1.5 Swiss francs or 9 Mexican pesos. Exchange rates are subject to rapid fluctuations, usually changing daily, though to small degrees. One day your 1 U.S. dollar might buy 1.51 Swiss francs and the next day 1.54 Swiss francs.
External Debt	"Debt owed by a country to non-residents repayable in foreign currency, goods and services" (UNDP 1999).
Fixed Exchange Rate	A system in which a government sets the value of its currency at a fixed rate for exchange in relation to another country's currency (usually the U.S. dollar) so that the exchange value is not free to fluctuate in the global money market.
Floating Exchange Rate	The system that replaced the Bretton Woods system of fixed exchange rates in the early 1970s, when the link between the dollar and gold was severed. Market forces, rather than government actions, are expected to adjust the relative value of states' currencies to reflect the underlying strengths and weaknesses of their economies. In principle, a floating exchange rate is based on the expectation that imbalances in states' payments to one another will more or less automatically adjust themselves, but in practice states have intervened frequently to ensure monetary stability and flexibility.
Managed Exchange Rate System	The kind of system constructed by the European Union (EU) when it created the single European currency, the euro. The European Monetary System (EMS) links the currencies of EU members whose governments pledge to stabilize currency values through government intervention if necessary.
Official Exchange Rate	The rate at which a state's central bank agrees to buy and sell its currency in exchange for a unit of another country's currency such as the U.S. dollar.

In the same way that governments try to protect the value of their currencies at home, they often try to protect them internationally by intervening in currency markets. Their willingness to do so is important to importers and exporters, who depend on orderliness and predictability in the value of the currencies they deal in to carry out transnational exchanges. Governments inter-

FIGURE 9.2
How to Tell a Real Bargain? Calculating the Cost of Goods in the Globe's Confusing Currency Exchange System

Countries must constantly estimate their current account trade balance with other countries, after trade transactions are made, because, in the U.S. case, the dollar has risen and fallen relative to the currencies of the other powers since 1980. The figure on the left shows the weighted average of the foreign exchange values of the U.S. dollar against a subset of the currencies of a large group of major U.S. trading partners. The value of the U.S. dollar declined since 1985 (making U.S. exports less expensive for people in many other countries to purchase), but rose seven straight years between April 1995 and 2001 as the world's (overvalued?) supercurrency, after which it fell 17 percent amid fears that America's current account deficit will rise by 2006 to $825 billion, or 6.4 percent of America's GDP (*Economist*, December 4, 2004, 71, 9).

Anyone traveling abroad soon finds the costs of items difficult to calculate in terms of the home currency and difficult to compare to what it would cost at home. In each case, it is necessary to convert the foreign price to one's local price by calculating the currency exchange rate, which can change daily and even hourly. One way of calculating exchange rates is by the purchasing power parity (PPP), which adjusts the price of goods to equalize their price across countries. The index on the right (p. 325) first formulated in the mid-1980s by the *Economist* displays the differentials according to one item, the price of a Big Mac sold by McDonald's in more than 120 countries. In the long run, countries' exchange rates should move toward rates that would equalize the prices of an identical basket of goods and services. This Big Mac PPP is the exchange rate at which hamburgers would cost the same in America as they would everyplace. Compare the index rate in December 2004; it shows that the euro then was 25 percent overvalued against the dollar and British Sterling was 20 percent overvalued, whereas the least expensive burger could be purchased for $1.26 in China against the U.S. price at $3.00 and therefore was 58 percent undervalued. To compare the size of countries' economies, the simplest method is to convert GDP into a common currency such as the U.S. dollar. But this method is misleading because it overlooks differences in *relative* prices, as the Big Mac index suggests, because non-tradable goods are usually less expensive in poor countries than in wealthy ones.

SOURCES: Major Currencies Index, U.S. Federal Reserve; Big Mac Index from the *Economist*, December 18, 2004, p. 162. Copyright © 2004 by The Economist Newspaper Ltd. All rights reserved. Reprinted with permission. Further reproduction prohibited.

	Local currency under (−)/over (+) valuation against the dollar (%)	Big Mac price* ($)
Switzerland		5.46
Denmark		4.97
Sweden		4.46
Euro area		3.75†
Britain		3.61
New Zealand		3.16
United States		3.00‡
Hungary		2.85
Turkey		2.80
Peru		2.74
Canada		2.60
Chile		2.56
Japan		2.50
Australia		2.46
Czech Republic		2.45
South Africa		2.44
South Korea		2.36
Taiwan		2.32
Singapore		2.19
Mexico		2.12
Poland		2.06
Brazil		1.99
Egypt		1.67
Argentina		1.60
Indonesia		1.57
Hong Kong		1.54
Thailand		1.52
Russia		1.49
Philippines		1.42
Malaysia		1.33
China		1.26

*At market exchange rate (December 13, 2004)
†Weighted average of member countries
‡Average of four cities

vene when countries' central banks buy or sell currencies to change the value of their own currencies in relation to those of others. Unlike speculators, however, governments are pledged not to manipulate exchange rates so as to gain unfair advantages, for states' reputations as custodians of monetary stability are valuable. Whether governments can affect their currencies' values in the face of large transnational movements of capital is, however, increasingly questionable. So is the value of any country's currency in relation to any other's (see Figure 9.2).

The Bretton Woods Monetary System

When the leaders of the capitalist West met at Bretton Woods, they were acutely aware of the need to create a reliable mechanism for determining the value of countries' currencies in relation to one another, and agreed to a set of concepts to define monetary and currency policy for conducting international trade and finance. Recognizing that a shared system and vocabulary was a necessary precondition for trade, and from it post–World War II economic recovery and prosperity, the negotiating parties agreed that the postwar monetary regime should be based on **fixed exchange rates** and assigned governments primary responsibility for enforcing its rules. In addition, they foresaw the need to create what later became the **International Monetary Fund (IMF),** to help states maintain equilibrium in their balance of payments and stability in their exchange rates with one another. The International Bank for Reconstruction and Development, known as the **World Bank,** was also created to aid recovery from the war.

Today the IMF and World Bank are important, if controversial, players in the global monetary and financial systems. They now share 141 of the same state members, and the primary mission of both IGOs is to serve as "lenders of last resort" when its member states face financial crises, providing those seeking assistance meet the often painful conditions requiring domestic adjustments to strengthen their economies. In the period immediately after World War II, these institutions commanded too little authority and too few resources to cope with the enormous devastation of the war. The United States stepped into the breach.

The U.S. dollar became the key to the hegemonic role that the United States eagerly assumed as manager of the international monetary system. Backed by a vigorous and healthy economy, a fixed relationship between gold and the dollar (pegged at $35 per ounce of gold), and the U.S. commitment to exchange gold for dollars at any time (known as "dollar convertibility"), the dollar became "as good as gold." In fact, others preferred dollars to gold for use in managing their balance-of-payments and savings accounts. Dollars earned interest, which gold did not; they did not incur storage and insurance costs; and they were needed to buy imports necessary for survival and postwar reconstruction. Thus a dollar-based system, with the dollar a universally accepted "parallel currency," was accepted in exchange markets as the reserve used by monetary authorities in most countries and by private banks, corporations, and individuals for international trade and capital transactions.

To maintain the value of their currencies, central banks in other countries either bought or sold their own currencies, using the dollar to raise or depress their value. Thus the Bretton Woods monetary regime was based on fixed exchange rates and ultimately required a measure of government intervention for its preservation.

To get U.S. dollars into the hands of those who needed them most, the Marshall Plan provided Western European states billions of dollars in aid to buy the U.S. goods necessary for rebuilding their war-torn economies. The United States also encouraged deficits in its own balance of payments as a way of providing **international liquidity** in the form of dollars.

In addition to providing liquidity, the United States assumed a disproportionate share of the burden of rejuvenating Western Europe and Japan. It supported European and Japanese trade competitiveness, permitted certain forms of protectionism (such as Japanese restrictions on importing U.S. products), and condoned discrimination against the dollar (as in the European Payments Union, which promoted trade within Europe at the expense of trade with the United States). The United States willingly incurred these leadership costs and others' free riding because subsidizing economic growth in Europe and Japan would widen the U.S. export markets and strengthen the West against communism's possible popular appeal.

■ **fixed exchange rates**
a system under which states establish the parity of their currencies and commit to keeping fluctuations in their exchange rates within narrow limits.

■ **International Monetary Fund (IMF)**
a financial agency with 185 members affiliated with the United Nations, formed in 1945 to promote international monetary cooperation, free trade, exchange rate stability, and democratic rule by providing financial assistance and loans to countries facing financial crises.

■ **World Bank**
also known as the International Bank for Reconstruction and Development (IBRD), the World Bank is the globe's major IGO for financing economic growth.

■ **international liquidity**
reserve assets used to settle international accounts.

Dealing with Economic Integration New skyscrapers—a symbol of economic growth—dot the skyline of Shanghai, the venue of the ninth meeting of the Asia-Pacific Economic Co-operation (APEC) forum held in July 2001 to respond to growing economic and trade interdependence in the region.

Although this system worked well with the United States operating as the world's banker, the costs grew as the enormous number of dollars held by others made the U.S. economy increasingly vulnerable to financial shocks from abroad. As the British had discovered before, U.S. leadership made devaluing the dollar without hurting U.S. allies difficult; nor could inflationary or deflationary pressures at home be managed without hurting allies abroad. This reduced the United States' ability to use the normal methods available to other states for dealing with the disruption caused by deficits in a country's balance of trade, such as adjusting interest and currency exchange rates.

The End of Bretton Woods

As early as 1960 it was clear that the dollar's top currency status could not be sustained by U.S. hegemony. A number of developments combined to destroy the monetary system, leading to a crisis in which the collapse of one country's economy and currency—in a modern version of the **commercial domino theory**—leads to "fiscal contagion" that spreads uncontrollably around the world, wreaking havoc on global capitalism. The fall of fiscal dominoes rippling through the world economy has become a common experience in a tightly interconnected international monetary system, in which capital and currency move instantaneously outside borders at the slightest sign of fiscal troubles. In any imploding

■ **commercial domino theory**
the notion that under conditions of globalization the depletion of one country's currency reserves panics investors worldwide and spreads like a contagious disease to other countries, which, in a chain reaction, witness the decline of their own currency reserves as the flight of capital also reduces the value of their currency.

national market, when one country's currency reserves are depleted, it sets in motion panic abroad as investors reduce their holdings and the flight of capital brings down other countries in a chain reaction (Sanger 1998). For the first time in history a single, integrated global economic system had emerged, and the deficiencies of global financial institutions with unstable fixed and floating currencies have become apparent. Not much is being done to revise and reform the shaky existing global financial architecture. In a world of increasingly mobile capital, volatility in capital flows threatens, in the absence of international financial regulation, to end the continuation of world economic growth.

"Much of the international relations literature concerned with prospects for international monetary reform can be read as a search for an alternative to hegemony as a basis for international monetary stability" (Eichengreen 2000). The need for a reformed system stems in large part from the failure of the United States to adjust its policies so it could continue to serve as a hegemonic stabilizing force in international finance or unilaterally regulate international monetary affairs (Underhill and Zhang 2003).

Floating Exchange Rates

After 1971, U.S. President Richard Nixon abruptly announced—without consulting with allies—that the United States would no longer exchange dollars for gold. With the price of gold no longer fixed and dollar convertibility no longer guaranteed, the Bretton Woods system gave way to a substitute system based on **floating exchange rates.** Market forces, rather than government intervention, now determine currency values. A country experiencing adverse economic conditions now saw the value of its currency fall in response to the choices of traders, bankers, and businesspeople. This was expected to make its exports cheaper and its imports more expensive, which in turn would pull its currency's value back toward equilibrium—all without the need for central bankers to support their currencies. In this way, it was hoped that the politically humiliating devaluations of the past could be avoided.

Those expectations were not met. Beginning in the late 1970s, escalating in the 1980s, and persisting through the 1990s, a rising wave of financial crises, both in currency and banking, occurred. These were and remain compounded by massive defaults by countries unable to make interest payments on their debts. This chronic problem in the crushing sea of circulating capital flows throughout the globe has strained the circulatory system of the international monetary process to the brink of collapse. About one-fifth of the world's countries have foreign debts in excess of $10 billion. This staggering debt load has made these countries vulnerable to external economic and political influence that compromises their capabilities to chart their future by themselves—as sovereign states are supposed to do. Even the most powerful are vulnerable. The reigning global hegemon, the United States, has entered this danger zone, borrowing from foreign creditors almost $11 trillion, or more than 6 percent of its GDP to cover the $2.5 trillion runaway deficit "big enough to have bankrupted any other country some time ago" (*Economist*, December 4, 2004, 9).

Financial crises have become increasingly frequent around the world as a result of the inability of states to manage debt, inflation, interest, and income in a volatile monetary system fraught with wild currency exchange rate gyrations. In the past forty years, more than one hundred major episodes of banking insolvency occurred in ninety developing and emerging countries. The financial

■ **floating exchange rates**
an unmanaged process where market forces and private investors rather than governments influence the relative rate of exchange for currencies between countries.

cost of these crises, in terms of the percentage of GDP lost, has been huge. The disastrous debts generated by banking and currency disruptions forced governments to suffer, on average between 1970 and 1997, direct loses of nearly 15 percent of their GDP for each crisis and more than a 5 percent decline in output growth after each crisis (World Bank 1999b, 126).

In response to the growing awareness of the extent to which the health of others' economies depended on the value of the U.S. dollar internationally (which in turn depended on the underlying strength of the U.S. economy), since 1985 the Group of Five (or G-5 great powers, the United States, Britain, France, Japan, and Germany) has adhered to the landmark agreement reached secretly at the Plaza Hotel in New York City, in which they pledged to collectively coordinate their economic policies through management of exchange rates internationally and interest rates domestically.

The **Group of Seven** (the **G-7,** consisting of the G-5 plus Canada and Italy) and the **G-8** (with the inclusion of Russia in 1997) has pledged to coordinate global monetary management. That promise has not been kept, and it is self-evident that the globe's leading economic powerhouses have not found common ground about the best ways to handle exchange rates and monetary and fiscal policies in order to sustain global trade and economic growth. "There is no detailed consensus on the right approach to international financial regulation; there is plenty of activity, but for the most part it is cooperation without conviction [about how to weigh] to costs and benefits of different kinds of capital mobility, and settling policies accordingly" (*Economist,* May 3, 2003).

In the absence of true collective management of global monetary conditions, it appears likely that the volume of world trade and the activities of currency speculators (who use sophisticated global electronic technologies and rely on thousands of "hedge funds" to make profits in currency trading) will increasingly determine national currency values. An average of at least $1.5 trillion in currency trading occurs each day—a transfer of capital greater than one-fourth of the world's average *weekly* level of international trade. International sales of stocks and bonds have mushroomed as well, and promise to rise through increased investor trading on the Internet. In the volatile world of increasingly mobile capital, wide fluctuations in national currencies' exchange rates have become common. The globalization of finance and the removal of barriers to capital flows across borders expose national economies to shocks, with little hope that such volatility will vanish.

■ **Group of Seven (G-7)/Group of Eight (G-8)**
a group of advanced industrialized democracies composed of the United States, Britain, France, Japan, Germany, Canada, and Italy that meets in regular economic summit conferences; since 1997, known as the G-8 with the addition of Russia.

Reforming the International Financial Architecture?

"No institution has worldwide responsibility for the arrangement of capital flows at present [although there does exist] an entire set of principles, standards and rules of relatively universal scope" (Berthelot 2001). Hardly anyone is happy with the prevailing weak and somewhat haphazard global financial architecture, but it appears that only when severe financial crises occur that threaten a global recession does sufficient pressure mount to engineer new reforms, beyond the cosmetic improvements in monitoring transactions and making money exchanges transparent in an attempt to control the money laundering practices of crime syndicates and terrorist groups.

Many proposals have been advanced for reforming the international monetary system to help cushion the aftershocks of the rapid movement of investment funds among countries that create booms and busts, such as the 1980s

Financial Empires without Umpires? Currency moves rapidly throughout the world, and in principle in a free global marketplace it should gravitate to any location where investors believe they can make a profit. The game is played according to rules, but it remains true that the rules and economic institutions to manage finance capitalism are created by the wealthy finance managers of powerful state governments that create the exchange-rate systems by which their currencies are adjusted to facilitate investments and trade. Monetary policies create currency dilemmas that sometimes unleash hostile feelings. For example, when finance ministers lower interest rates in ways that benefit a country with high unemployment, that shift breeds inflation in other countries with low unemployment. Some people opposed to the integration of international finance see monetary adjustments as a conspiracy designed to enrich the wealthy few at the expense of the many. Shown here are two examples. Top, Czech police pass under a protest banner reading "Money makes the world go round—but in which direction?" at the September 2000 annual economic summit of the IMF and the World Bank in Prague. Bottom, a scene of a protestor preparing to throw a firebomb at the G-8 Genoa summit in July 2001, where twenty thousand policemen pitched battles with demonstrators.

The Domino Effect in Global Finance When a country's banks go bankrupt and its economy collapses, foreign capital flees in panic. No worldwide central bank exists to cushion such crashes. Money problems in one country lead to money problems in others, provoking currency depreciations and plunges in stock prices at home and abroad. Here stunned brokers react to the January 1998 plummet of Hong Kong stocks that caused the key indexes elsewhere in Asia, London, Frankfort, New York, and Paris to fall. Described as "the worst international financial crisis in fifty years [which] took global finance to the edge of collapse" (Altman and Cutter 1999), since then no serious reforms have been implemented.

Latin American debt crisis and the global crisis that followed on the heels of the 1997–98 flight of capital from Asia. Some see reversion to the pre–World War I gold standard as preferable to the exchange rates with highly fluctuating currencies. Others recommend something like the Bretton Woods system of fixed but adjustable rates.

What these and other proposals seek is a mechanism for creating the currency stability and flexibility on which prosperity through trade depends. However, there is little agreement about how to bring about reforms. With global democratization, most governments face domestic pressures to sacrifice such goals as exchange rate stability for unemployment reduction, so it seems likely that floating exchange rates, with all their costs and uncertainties, are here to stay because almost no one wants to stop the fierce flow of money moving world wide in pursuit of the highest returns that almost universally are seen as stimulating growth. As one observer notes,

> The . . . leading powers in the world economy have too much of a stake in existing arrangements to show much appetite for reinventing the IMF or for charting a new Bretton Woods. For these actors, the IMF remains a preferred instrument for coping with financial crises. Hence, while the schemes for alternatives proliferate, the prospects are for incremental tinkering rather than wholesale restructuring. The prospects also tend to favor *ad hoc* case-by-case treatment of financial crises. (Babai 2001, 418)

That said, it is discomforting that the global currency regime is unstable and erratic and that the lack of an effective exchange mechanism to orchestrate adjustments causes such disruptions in a globalized marketplace in which states' economies are highly integrated. As long as the flow of trade across borders continues to expand, as is highly likely, the currency dilemmas facing the world are likely to intensify. Currency fluctuations and monetary instability are at the root of the difficulties, and the prevailing regime remains inadequate. No exchange rate system is perfect. Whether countries fix or float to manage their currencies, problems inevitably surface.

Some small steps to address short-term financing problems have been taken, such as the IMF's establishment of the Contingency Credit Line (CCL) to meet balance-of-payments problems arising from international financial contagion. However, these steps do not correct the major difficulties, and as Rubens Ricupero, secretary-general of UNCTAD, cautions, reform of the international financial architecture is needed: "Financial regulation is constantly struggling to keep up with financial innovation, and in this struggle, it is not always successful. . . . The key question is whether there exists a viable and appropriate exchange rate regime for developing economies when major reserve currencies are subject to frequent gyrations and misalignments, and when international capital exchanges are extremely unstable." In the meantime, the only option available for countries is the choice between "dollarization or regionalization" to weather currency and debt crises.

That conclusion was highlighted by the "solution" to the currency problem the European countries adopted in 2002, which severed dependence on the U.S. dollar in preference for a **regional currency union** to try to stabilize erratic exchange rate fluctuations. To this end, the European Union created the euro in the hopes that the creation of a single currency will make the European Union a single market for business, under the expectation that the euro promotes economic growth, cross-border investment, corporate innovation and efficiency, and political integration.

As innovative as the creation of the euro appears, it may not serve as a model for other countries and regions. The euro remains controversial even in Europe, especially among important EU states (Britain, Denmark, and Sweden so far have rejected it). The new common currency is much more than an economic change; to critics it is an ambitious *political* change designed to create a European superstate and thereby erase the individuality and economic and political sovereignty of European states (Reid 2004). This solution through currency integration in Europe can only been seen as a response to the domination of the United States in the global economy, where the U.S. dollar remains the global currency for settling international accounts. To many, globalization really means the "dollarization" of the international political economy. As long as U.S. economic and military supremacy continues, it is unlikely that the present free-floating exchange mechanism for currency exchanges valued in terms of the U.S. dollar will be overturned by creation of new global institutions accepting supranational management. This means that the debate over currency and monetary policies will remain as intense as ever, particularly in the turbulent arena of international trade.

■ **regional currency union**
the pooling of sovereignty to create a common currency (such as the EU's euro) and single monetary system for members in a region, regulated by a regional central bank within the currency bloc to reduce the likelihood of large-scale liquidity crises.

FROM CURRENCY CONCERNS TO TRADE TROUBLES

Emerging Unilateral Trade Policies

To anticipate the future, we can look at the **unilateral** strategies of individual countries and at the regional strategies of groups of countries or blocs.

■ **unilateral**
a state's policies to manage foreign policy problems independently through self-help measures.

FIGURE 9.3
To Tariff or Not to Tariff—That Is the Question

All states want the same thing—for other countries to purchase their exports and to protect domestic producers from foreign imports. These goals are incompatible if **reciprocity** is to prevail so that all countries treat international trade according to the same rules that allow goods to be traded without interference. To promote trade, the industrialized countries have greatly reduced tariffs, from the peak period of economic nationalism through protectionism in the 1940s to less than 5 percent today, as shown in the figure on the left. The reduction of tariffs has fostered the growth of trade, thus serving the liberal goal of open trade. However, as the figure on the right shows, the temptation to introduce barriers to free trade have been difficult to resist, and many countries have imposed various nontariff barriers to protect their domestic economies from external imports. According to the office of U.S. trade representative, in 2005 roughly sixty countries had established mechanisms for restricting trade with the rest of the world (not including the American economic superpower's own elaborate restrictions and anticompetitive policies and practices). Thus, the struggle between the liberal value of free trade and the mercantilist value of economic nationalism is far from over.

SOURCES: Office of the U.S. Trade Representative, with information on commercial restrictions on imports summarized by the *Economist,* April 7, 2001, p. 121. Copyright © 2001 by The Economist Newspaper Ltd. All rights reserved. Reprinted with permission. Further reproduction prohibited. www.economist.com

■ **reciprocity**
the norm that accepts the ethical prescription that actors should treat others as they themselves would wish to be treated, so that the same standards of conduct apply.

In the past, the United States led the way to the decline of protectionist tariffs in the industrialized world (see Figure 9.3). However, the United States has not consistently advocated free trade; in reaction to its increasingly shaky global position in the 1980s, it began to practice "aggressive unilateralism" by retaliating against states perceived to be engaging in unfair trade practices. The Omnibus Trade Act incorporated a bellicose "Super 301" provision that required the president to identify countries believed to be engaging in unfair trade practices and to force them to either negotiate remedies or face U.S. retaliation. This is symptomatic of the fragility of commitments to free trade, because almost all countries viewed the Super 301 provision as a clear violation of GATT rules. Since then, however, the United States has acted under the milder, less accusatory "ordinary" 301 legislation (which does not carry automatic retaliatory penalties), but has still initiated hundreds of complaints. Hence, free trade remains under challenge.

One of the reasons why the preservation of the free-trade regime is precarious is because the United States itself does not always live up to its own ideals and rhetoric. Many states complain bitterly that the United States imposes many elaborate restrictions on imports that undermine free competition through protectionist policies such as nontariff barriers. The United States has not supported free trade as enthusiastically as it claims to promote an open trading system. Like the other G-8 great powers, national interests are sometimes (increasingly?) put above collective ideals. Examples abound of tariff protectionism and its recent growth. For example, "the United States stabs a 244 percent tariff on sugar imports and 174 percent on peanuts, two products grown cheaply in poor countries . . . and the EU discourages beef imports with a tariff of 213 percent, while Japan limits wheat with a 353 percent charge and Canada restricts butter with a 360 percent tax" (Drozdiak 2001, 17). To free-trade liberals, the trade game is rigged, to the harm of everyone but especially the poor. Today, 1.2 billion people struggle below the poverty line on one dollar a day or less, while European Union and American cows are estimated to receive about two dollars apiece in government subsidies. The IMF anticipates that if all Global North rich country trade barriers and subsidies to agriculture were repealed, global welfare would expand about $120 billion. "The rigged game is sowing ever-greater resentment toward the United States, the principal architect of the global economic order. In the aftermath of 9/11, Americans have desperately been trying to win the hearts and minds of poor residents of the Muslim world. [America's] insincere free-trade rhetoric" undermines this political objective (*New York Times,* July 20, 2003, p. 10).

U.S. trade policy reflects twin instincts: to push for trade liberalization in foreign markets and to cushion the impact of imports on the U.S. economy and employment rate. The stakes are high; the Commerce Department estimates that one in five U.S. jobs are supported by trade. Awareness of this dependence was behind the George W. Bush administration's 2002 successful reestablishment of the president's **fast-track negotiating authority** from Congress (suspended in 1994) to permit the president to negotiate trade pacts that U.S. Congress could approve or reject but not change.

How U.S. trade partners and rivals view the American commitment to free trade will shape their own trade policies and whether they will choose free trade over protectionism. Tough negotiations and countercharges plague U.S–China exports as well as the relationships between many other active international trade partners.

Domestic economic policies also tend to shape many countries' foreign trade policies. Observe in this context how countries differ in the extent to which they regulate their national economies within their borders and the degree to which the level of economic freedom within states predicts the level of growth they experience as well as their willingness to open their domestic markets to foreign imports in order to elevate their citizens' standard of living. Over-

■ **fast-track negotiating authority**
a concession by the U.S. Congress permitting the president to negotiate reciprocal tariff-reduction agreements with other countries that, when granted, enable the United States to reach bilateral trade treaties more easily.

MAP 9.1
Ranking Countries by Their Economic Freedom

A consensus has developed about the principle that states with the most economic freedom experience the highest rates of economic growth. To **neoliberalism,** the free market promotes prosperity, and that hypothesis has been confirmed over the past two decades. According to this index, economic liberty expanded for the tenth straight year when, at the start of 2005, of 155 economies, 71 or 45 percent were either economically "free" or "mostly free," while 84 were still "mostly unfree" or "repressed." Economically free or liberal market economies also tend to be the most democratic and stable and, as a consequence, the safest environments for corporations and private investors to make investments.

SOURCE: The Heritage Foundation, *2004 Index of Economic Freedom* (www.heritage.org).

neoliberalism
a perspective that accounts for the way international institutions promote global cooperation and prosperity through reforms such as the creation of free markets and acceptance of free trade.

whelming evidence shows that economic freedom makes for prosperity; those countries that do not interfere with trade at home tend to have the highest average economic growth rates. Liberalism in domestic economic policy pays many financial, political, and security dividends. Compare the rankings of countries according to their economic freedom, and we see much evidence supporting the liberal view that open markets stimulate economic growth.

Refer to Map 9.1. We see strong evidence suggesting that the most economically free states grow their wealth at the fastest rates, by providing the best or safest environments for investments with the least risk. Free economies are the primary targets for global investment and trade (see Chapter 8). In addition, these open economies are the least corrupt and least prone to civil wars. This is because economically free countries also tend to be politically free, that is, ruled democratically with civil and legal ways for resolving conflicts, as opposed to economically repressed countries that also politically repress civil liberties and violate citizens' **human rights.**

human rights
the political rights and civil liberties recognized by the international community as inalienable and valid for individuals in all countries by virtue of their humanity.

Given these seemingly clear-cut economic advantages to free markets and free trade, it is difficult to understand why many governments protectively resist open markets. The answer lies in the fact that trade is profoundly treacherous, and appears in the eye of the beholder to be inherently unfair. Trade unions in wealthy Global North states complain that the lower wages of the Global South countries give them "unfair" advantage and, for their part, the less-developed Global South states complain that they cannot "fairly" compete against their more productive, technologically advanced Global North counterparts. This is why the age-old debate between free traders and mercantilists persists as a global issue in the brutally competitive globalized world economy.

Emerging Regional Tug-of-War Trade Policies? A recent trend has been to construct trade partnerships within particular regions and bilaterally between particular pairs of countries. The United States first experimented with the former approach in 1984, with the Caribbean Basin Initiative to reduce tariffs and provide tax incentives to promote industrialization and trade. This was soon followed in 1987 with free-trade agreements with Israel and Canada and in 1989 with the **North American Free Trade Agreement (NAFTA)** (signed by Canada, Mexico, and the United States in 1993). NAFTA's purpose was the most ambitious—to integrate the North American region. In addition, in 2001 the United States and thirty-three Western Hemispheric democracies took a bolder step when they pledged to build the **Free Trade Area of the Americas (FTAA)** in that region by 2005. This would create the globe's largest barrier-free trade zone, from the Arctic to Argentina, linking markets to 800 million people.

The successful Mercosur free-trade zone in South America is another example of a regional regime. Its six member countries—Argentina, Brazil, Paraguay, Uruguay, and later Chile and Bolivia increased the value of trade in 2002 to $16.5 billion from only $3.6 billion in 1991. The enlarged ten-member Association of Southeast Asian Nations (ASEAN) free-trade region is representative of yet another among the many multilateral regional trading blocs.

Many feel that NAFTA and other regional free-trade zones are consistent with the WTO's rules, and see regional trade agreements (RTAs) as catalysts to trade, since they provide tariff preferences or duty-free treatment to exports originating from the bloc's members. Others worry, however, that a division of the global marketplace into competing regional trade blocs is an obstacle to the integration of the entire global economy, and that they intensify competition between the three major trade blocs, ASEAN, NAFTA, and the EU. If trade-bloc rivalry intensifies, the result would be a cutthroat mercantile rivalry in which each bloc's fear and exclusion of the others splits the world into three or more competitive economic poles, or regional trade centers, and destroys the benefits that open world trade can provide for all.

Inspect Map 9.2, tracing the levels of trade flowing across and between the globe's regions. Intra-regional trade, the growing percentage of trade in exports within a trade bloc as a result of the major regional trade agreements, has been a recent trend. "The share of intra-regional exports as a percentage of regional bloc exports has been increasing since 1970 in most of the major regional trade blocs. Over 60 percent of the European Union exports are with other EU partners and over half of NAFTA exports are to other NAFTA partners. However, intra-regional export shares within the EU have remained nearly constant and

■ **North American Free Trade Agreement (NAFTA)**
an agreement that brings Mexico into the free-trade zone linking Canada and the United States.

■ **Free Trade Area of the Americas (FTAA)**
a set of rules to promote free trade among thirty-four democracies in North and South America.

Simulation: Caribbean Banana Exporters Association

MAP 9.2
The Volume of Trade Flows between Major Trade Partners

As world trade has grown dramatically in the past five decades, the volume of trade (the value of trade exports plus imports) between the major regions has spread unevenly. Although trade among Global South developing countries and regions has been increasing, still more than half of world trade flows between the three major regional trade blocs in the wealthy Global North countries. Most trade is concentrated *within* regional blocs, that is, between parties to regional trade agreements (RTAs) such as the European Union, NAFTA, or ASEAN.

Note: Flows of less than $30 billion are not shown.
SOURCE: World Bank (2003, 49).

those for NAFTA have shown an upward trend since 1970, well before NAFTA entered into force in 1994. Similar patterns can be identified for other major RTAs. MERCOSUR is an exception, where data show a sharp increase in intra-regional export shares after the agreement entered into force. [In general,] the data do not show that trade is increasingly becoming concentrated within regional RTAs" (World Trade Organization; www.wto.org, May 5, 2004, citing *World Trade Report 2003*, 5).

The conclusion is suggested that the globalization of trade integration throughout the world is progressing, despite opposition and resistance by some groups lobbying to keep trade close to their neighboring states within their own region. The removal of trade barriers sharpens competition and increases eco nomic growth, and trade flows to reward the competitors that produce the best products at the best price, wherever in the world they are located.

One of the major reasons why few states have succeeded in regional efforts to practice "discriminatory liberalization" is that it has proven counterproductive. "Rapid globalization has done nothing to undermine the confidence liberals have always placed in trade. No serious economist questions the case for international integration through flows of goods and services, though there is a lively argument over how integration through trade can be brought about" (Crook 2003, 3). One currently popular approach has been for countries to sign bilateral trade deals with both regional trade organizations outside their own region and with individual other states. They are racing to negotiate RTAs to gain access to trade, especially in the sizzling East Asia. The WTO describes this trend by reporting that "the vast majority of WTO members are party to one or more regional trade agreements. The surge in RTAs has continued unabated since the early 1990s. Some 250 RTAs have been notified to the GATT/WTO up to December 2002, of which 130 were notified after January 1995. Over 170 RTAs are currently in force; an additional 70 are estimated to be operational although not yet notified. By the end of 2005, if RTAs reportedly planned or already under negotiation are concluded, the total number of RTAs in force might well approach 300" (World Trade Organization, www.wto.org/region, May 6, 2004).

The impact seems destined to be a consequential transformation in global trade integration. "The international trading system is increasingly characterized by a complex network of preferential trade regimes, sitting side-by-side with the WTO multilateral trading system. We see a rise in cross-regional bilateral agreements, the growing involvement of countries that have traditionally remained outside regional agreements, the development of inter-linked (overlapping) agreement, and considerable variations in the design and content of RTAs. One-third of the FTAs [free trade agreements] currently under negotiation are among countries that belong to different geographical areas. All major countries are involved in cross-regional FTAs. . . . Countries that have traditionally remained outside regional agreements are now negotiating and joining RTAs." The proliferation of RTAs and the increasing bilateral free trade agreements has meant overlapping membership for many countries. "A large number of countries are now a party to two or more RTAs. For example, the EU has over 30 preferential trade agreements. Mexico is a member of NAFTA and has bilateral FTAs with Australia, EFTA, Japan, New Zealand and the United States. All these countries are involved in negotiating future agreements" (World Trade Organization, www.wto.org/regional, May 14, 2004).

This activity portends a large jump in the degree to which international trade is likely to expand as the web of trade agreements enlarges. The linkage between states throughout the world will open free trade to new levels, integrating more and more countries in cross-cutting agreements that tie them together. The WTO estimates that "43 percent of world merchandise trade now occurs under the umbrella of preferential-trade agreements" and predicts that "this share will increase as more RTAs are negotiated in the future. If all RTAs under negotiation at present are successfully concluded [by 2006] over 50 percent of world merchandise trade will occur among countries linked by preferential agreements" (World Trade Organization, www.wto.org, May 14, 2004, citing *World Trade Report 2003*, 48).

THE FATE OF FREE TRADE: TRIUMPH OR TROUBLE IN A GLOBAL AGE?

Since 1950 world trade has grown sixteen-fold, climbing above $8.2 billion in 2005 (World Trade Organization, www.wto.org, January 3, 2005). In the same period, gross world product has grown sevenfold, reaching $48.5 trillion. The exponential growth of trade has contributed measurably to the unprecedented rise in global economic prosperity. Reductions in barriers to free trade are expected to accelerate these trends if world trade continues, as in the past five decades, to expand three times faster than real world output (see Figure 9.4). The expected consequence is that **trade integration** will increasingly bind countries' economies ever more tightly in interdependent economic relationships, and thereby promote the further growth of globalization; one estimate predicts that by the year 2015 world trade will rise well above today's 40 percent of world GDP (Central Intelligence Agency 2002).

The projections assume that the process of liberalizing the global political economy will continue. Progress, however, remains problematic if the forces of neomercantilism also remain vibrant. Although hegemonic stability theory would predict that a U.S. leadership decline will inevitably be followed by the liberal trade regime's closure, a collapse of free trade is unlikely. The liberal trade regime may endure with the support of global institutions such as the WTO and liberal regional regimes such as FTAA and RTAs generally.

Many states see advantages in rejecting mercantilism and accepting instead the **most-favored-nation (MFN) principle,** now known as normal trade relations (NTR) (which holds that the tariff preferences granted to one state must be granted to all others exporting the same product), as well as the reciprocity norm (countries will reduce their own tariffs in return for another's reductions) and the **nondiscrimination rule** (goods produced at home and abroad are to be treated the same).

"The economic case for an open trading system is simple enough and rests largely on commercial common sense supported by evidence: the experience of world trade and economic growth since the Second World War," explains the World Trade Organization. Elaborating, it notes that

> The data show a definite statistical link between freer trade and economic growth. Economic theory points to strong reasons for the link. All countries, including the poorest, have assets—human, industrial, natural, financial—which they can employ to produce goods and services for their domestic markets or to compete overseas. Economics tells us that we can benefit when these goods and services are traded. Simply put, the principle of "comparative advantage" says that countries prosper first by taking advantage of their assets in order to concentrate on what they can produce best, and then by trading these products for products that other countries produce best. In other words, liberal trade policies—policies that allow the unrestricted flow of goods and services—sharpen competition, motivate innovation and breed success. They multiply the rewards that result from producing the best products, with the best design, at the best price. But success in trade is not static. The ability to compete well in particular products can shift from company to company when the market changes or new technologies make cheaper and better products possible. Producers are encouraged to adapt gradually and in a relatively painless way. They can focus on new products, find a new "niche" in their current area or expand into new areas.

■ **trade integration**
the difference between growth rates in trade and gross domestic product.

■ **most-favored-nation (MFN) principle**
unconditional nondiscriminatory treatment in trade between contracting parties guaranteed by GATT; in 1997, U.S. Senator Daniel Patrick Moynihan introduced legislation to replace with the term "normal trade relations (NTR)" to better reflect its true meaning.

■ **nondiscrimination rule**
a principle for trade that proclaims that goods produced at home and abroad are to be treated the same for import and export agreements.

FIGURE 9.4
Global Economic Prospects: The Growth of Trade and Wealth, 1950–2008

Since 1970, the volume of world trade has increased on average nearly 4 percent each year, and 6.5 percent between 1990 and 2000. Trade liberalization and liberal market reforms have spurred both trends upward. The top figure on the left charts this trade expansion in the global export of goods and of goods and services combined through 2004, with WTO projections extending the likely trend to 2008, when world trade in goods and services is expected to reach over $9 trillion. The bottom figure (left) of gross world product (GWP), following the same projections after 2004, suggests how the rise of wealth has likewise risen at the same time, with trade growth contributing to economic growth, which is expected to reach nearly $60 trillion by 2008. Although trade integration is deepening, the benefits of trade and an expanding economy are not evenly distributed. Some leading exporters of goods participate at much higher levels than others. Inspect the chart on the right, which ranks the fifteen leading exporting countries according to their level and shares of total merchandise trade. These fifteen trade leaders in 2003 captured two-thirds of the $6.3 trillion in global exports of goods in 2003.

Experience shows that competitiveness can also shift between whole countries. A country that may have enjoyed an advantage because of lower labour costs or because it had good supplies of some natural resources, could also become uncompetitive in some goods or services as its economy develops. However, with the stimulus of an open economy, the country can move on to become competitive in some other goods or services. This is normally a gradual process.

Nevertheless, the temptation to ward off the challenge of competitive imports is always present. And richer governments are more likely to yield to the siren call of protectionism, for short term political gain—through subsidies, complicated red tape, and hiding behind legitimate policy objectives such as environmental preservation or consumer protection as an excuse to protect producers" (World Trade Organization, www.wto.org, May 15, 2004).

And that temptation is proving harder and harder to resist, because many states play **two-level games** and succumb to domestic interest-group lobbying pressure to introduce trade barriers to protect local jobs and manufacturing, even if, according to liberalism, their relations with their trade partners will deteriorate and all will suffer in the long run if these trade partners retaliate with counter-protectionist tariffs. That would mean that the protectionist competitions would sacrifice the benefits free trade could otherwise provide to both. "Trade may be global," warn Ramesh Thakur and Steve Lee (2000), but "politics is still local." If neomercantilist thinking that "imports are bad but exports are good" spreads, the free-trade regime will lose its momentum.

The simultaneous pursuit of liberalism and mercantilism today shows states' determination to reap the benefits of interdependence while minimizing its costs. It also reveals the tension between states and markets, between the promise that everyone will benefit and the fear that the benefits will not be equally distributed. The absence of world government encourages each state to be more concerned with how it fares competitively in relation to other states—its relative gains—than collectively with its absolute gains. These simple yet powerful ideas shed light on the reasons why the United States, the principal advocate of free trade in the post–World War II era, has increasingly engaged in neomercantilism and protectionism and has not practiced what it has preached. It has undermined, given its stature as the globe's leading economic superpower best able to take responsibility for setting standards for free trade, the liberal regime. "Perhaps the greatest hypocrisy," writes Ian Campbell (2004) in criticizing America's "troubling protectionism . . . that evokes the mood of the 1930s . . . is that the United States, which preaches the merits of free trade more strongly than almost any other country, spends tens of billions of dollars to prevent its own markets from being free and has taken fresh measures to enable its own markets to discriminate against other countries' producers. The biggest blow to the Doha round was struck in 2002 when a new farm bill was passed [that] authorized in the words of the U.S. Trade representative, Robert Zoellick, 'up to

■ **two-level games**
the practice by countries to undertake policies that pay political dividends at the domestic level by winning votes and public approval that also have costs for the country's relations with other states at the global level.

Note: Trends since 2004 based on WTO projections.
SOURCES: Global trade trends from IMF as reported in *State of the World 2004*, p. 147, and growth of world product from OECD and IMF as reported in *Vital Signs 2003*, p. 45. Copyright 2004 and 2003 respectively from Worldwatch Institute. Top exporters from the *Economist*, April 10, 2004, p. 85. Copyright by The Economist Newspaper Ltd. All rights reserved. Reprinted with permission.

$123 billion in all types of food-stamp, conservation and farm spending over six years.' The U.S. position—and that of the European Union—is immoral. Developing countries that depend utterly on agriculture are forced to compete with a U.S. agricultural sector that is hugely subsidized.... What the United States and the European Union bring to trade meetings is not a willingness to do what is right but a determination not to give anything away."

Will this surge toward protectionism smother free trade and world prosperity? Or can the stalled global trade talks regain their former momentum by the leading exporters' willingness to eliminate their export subsidiaries? The stakes are high. At the Paris meeting of over thirty countries' trade ministers in May 2004, U.S. Trade Representative Robert Zoellick predicted that a new World Trade Organization agreement to lower protectionist barriers to free trade might give a $500 billion lift to the world economy (*International Herald Tribune*, May 14, 2004, 12).

Premises for a Future Global Economy

Six premises dictate the boundaries within which the global economy is likely to vary in the future.

1. Free trade contributes to economic growth, and trade protection reduces prosperity in the long run.
2. The future will depend heavily on the rules the leading economic powers choose to support to govern trade and monetary policy. The choices are between the contrasting philosophies of commercial liberalism without burdensome regulation and mercantilist and neomercantilist approaches that seek protectionism.
3. The position of the globe's largest economy, the United States, will likely remain pivotal in the equation, for how this hegemon makes economic policy will influence the direction in which others' trade and monetary policies are likely to move.
4. The activities of powerful and wealthy mobile MNCs in foreign investment and trade will increasingly determine economic flows; these activities and pressure for continuing trade liberalization are increasingly beyond the control of state governments, whose sovereign power is eroding.
5. Nonstate commercial and monetary actors (for example, transnational banks, many of which are negotiating mergers to consolidate their power) will provide much of the lubrication that can keep the global trade engine humming.
6. Globalization is likely to accelerate, and, as competition expands wealth and reduces the costs of both products and labor, the economic fate of the globe's 6 billion people will be tied together in increasingly interdependent ties, making the welfare of any one important to the welfare of all.

Global Economic Destiny?

The United States, Europe, and Japan have advocated quite different philosophies toward states and markets over the years, and their policies have evolved as their circumstances in the global economy have changed over time. At times, Japan has embraced mercantilism (even as it talked of liberalization), the United

States has touted liberalism (even as it practiced mercantilism), and Europe historically has stood midway between the two (but looked more inward than outward). Increasingly, economic nationalism "could propel the preeminent economic powers—and the rest of the world with them—into an era of 'real-economik,' in which parochial economic interests drive governments to pursue marginal advantage in an international system marked by growing interdependencies" (E. Peterson 1998).

Whether a collision of these contending capitalisms can be averted by revival of reductions in trade barriers may be the most critical question for the global future. And how the American hegemon responds will be determinative of the continuation, or erosion, of the free-trade regime that has engineered unprecedented economic growth since World War II. Will the U.S. hegemon retreat from its commitment to open trade by continuing the estimated $600 billion spent annually to support its trade deficit (*U.S. News and World Report*, March 22, 2004, 96)? Will it return to the policies based on the principle that a healthy global political economy necessitates a desire and willingness for all countries to be larger exporters *and* importers? Or will it choose to dominate instead of leading (Brzezinski 2004) by acting unilaterally and competitively, thereby provoking a new wave of creeping protectionism, discriminating trade blocs, and competitive tit-for-tat currency devaluations?

Playing Games with Prosperity on a Global Scale: Tricks-of-the-Trade Debate

International trade and finance can be likened to a global game of dominoes. If, and when, the globe's biggest economy (the United States) falters, how, in an integrated global system fraught with competition alongside connection, can other countries' economies stay aloft? Does global growth require a resurgence by the economic hegemon? In a U.S. downdraft, can the rest find the resources and policies to cushion themselves from the dynamic repercussions? In a global recession, how does any country obtain a parachute when the economic fate of everyone depends on the economic growth of everyone else? Sinking under conditions of interdependence is synchronized; so is ascendance in times of economic expansion for the world's biggest economies. This principle was underscored in 2004 when the World Bank warned that the global economy could not fly forever on a single engine—the U.S. economy.

The liberal trading agreements so slowly built up over five decades will be precarious, especially in the absence of support from the global hegemon, the United States. At risk is the entire edifice of prosperity that has materialized through the removal of barriers to trade. That liberal free-trade regime could collapse under further economic pressure. Merely contemplate the vulnerability of the liberal international economic order should international economic conditions worsen. The combination of a global slowdown, financial market volatility, staggering record-high U.S. trade imbalances and current account deficits financed by foreign central bank loans, and worldwide manufacturing over-capacity could easily bring about a global upsurge in protectionism, because protectionism breeds protectionism.

However, a new wave of mercantilism and trade wars is not preordained. A number of other important developments are also likely to influence the future direction of the world political economy, and these, in combination, are likely to sustain and strengthen the liberal free-trade regime that has contributed to global economic growth. World commerce has become globalized; global financial flows outstrip trade transactions within countries; and market forces almost everywhere are now being given a freer reign to determine economic outcomes. With trade growing rapidly in the absence of barriers, and with the expansion of free-trade areas and the escalating growth of cross-regional trade agreements (RTAs) and states bilateral open-trade agreements with regional blocs and with one another, pressure to preserve the liberal trade regime is expanding. Multinational corporations are increasingly playing a larger role in the continuing growth of commercial liberalism worldwide, and they are supported in this aspiration by the powerful WTO, the conversion of India and China to acceptance of freer trade, and the opening up of restrictive markets to exports. All these developments suggest that the prospects for the momentum of commercial liberalism to gain strength are promising.

Some theorists believe that the spread of liberal market philosophies will eliminate the need for new institutions to cope with the changed and changing world political economy. Others caution that the unregulated market should not be considered the ideal and universal arrangement for economic activity, because coordinating institutions are needed to manage sustained growth. The task of reaching agreement about economic principles is made more daunting by the absence of a true consensus about what the world political economy should look like, as the continuing contest between liberalism and mercantilism (as well as the conflict between rich and poor countries) illustrates. Furthermore, the globalization of commerce and finance increasingly seems to shape, rather than be shaped by, states' policies—thus challenging the sovereign prerogatives of states themselves.

If liberals are correct, the process of rapid globalization already occurring will hasten the trend toward interdependence and integration and, with that, the prospects for economic prosperity and political harmony. If mercantilists are right, however, an emerging era of geo-economics will increase states' vulnerability and thus the likelihood of political conflict and states' efforts to dominate others. What the future holds is hard to foresee, because the various rules for trade and currency are likely to change in the twenty-first century, and these changes will undercut the usefulness of past economic philosophies.

The world seems to be spinning out of control in a sea change of rapid globalization that hides the decisions that affect our daily lives. Globalization is entangling the functions of governments and markets and making it difficult to tell the difference between countries and corporations. In the next chapter we shall move from geo-economics to ecopolitics and examine how changes in world population and resources in a globalized planetary environment are also likely to transform world politics in the twenty-first century.

KEY TERMS

international political economy
paradigm
globalization
high politics
low politics
international monetary system
commercial liberalism
mercantilism

Liberal International Economic Order (LIEO)
interdependence theory
comparative advantage
laissez-faire economics
politics
absolute gains
relative gains
neomercantilism
protectionism
beggar-thy-neighbor policies
import quotas
export quotas
orderly market arrangements (OMA)
voluntary export restrictions (VERs)
nontariff barriers (NTBs)
infant industry
strategic trade policy
countervailing duties
antidumping duties
realism
hegemonic stability theory
hegemon
long-cycle theory
hegemony
macroeconomics
collective goods
free riders
zero-sum
imperial overstretch
international regimes
General Agreement on Tariffs and Trade (GATT)
Uruguay Round
World Trade Organization (WTO)
monetary system
monetary policy
money supply
exchange rate
fixed exchange rates
International Monetary Fund (IMF)
World Bank
international liquidity
commercial domino theory
floating exchange rates
Group of Seven (G-7)/Group of Eight (G-8)
regional currency union
unilateral
reciprocity
fast-track negotiating authority
neoliberalism
human rights
North American Free Trade Agreement (NAFTA)
Free Trade Area of the Americas (FTAA)
trade integration
most-favored-nation (MFN) principle
nondiscrimination rule
two-level games

SUGGESTED READING

Fligstein, Neil. *The Architecture of Markets.* Princeton, N.J.: Princeton University Press, 2004.

Gilpin, Robert, with Jean M. Gilpin. *Global Political Economy: Understanding the International Economic Order.* Princeton, N.J.: Princeton University Press, 2001.

Goddard, C. Roe, Patrick Cronin, and Kishore C. Dash, eds. *International Political Economy: State-Market Relations in a Changing Global Order,* 2nd ed. Boulder, Colo.: Lynne Rienner, 2003.

Greenfield, Liah. *The Spirit of Capitalism: Nationalism and Economic Growth.* Cambridge, Mass: Harvard University Press, 2003.

Grieco, Joseph M., and G. John Ikenberry. *State Power and World Markets: The International Political Economy.* New York: W.W. Norton, 2003.

Oatley, Thomas. *International Political Economy: Interests and Institutions in the Global Economy.* New York: Pearson Longman, 2004.

O'Brien, Robert, and Marc Williams. *Global Political Economy: Evolution and Dynamics.* London: Palgrave, 2004.

Peterson, V. Spike. *A Critical Rewriting of Global Political Economy,* New York: Routledge, 2003.

Petras, James, and Henry Veltmeyer. *A System in Crisis: The Dynamics of Free Market Capitalism.* London: Palgrave, 2004.

Phillips, Nicola, ed. *Globalizing Political Economy.* London: Palgrave, 2005.

Spero, Joan E., and Jeffrey A. Hart. *The Politics of International Economics,* 6th ed. Belmont, Calif.: Wadsworth/Thomson Learning, 2003.

Underhill, Geoffrey R. D., and Xiakoe Zhang, eds. *International Financial Governance under Stress: Global Structures versus National Imperatives.* Cambridge: Cambridge University Press, 2003.

WHERE ON THE WORLD WIDE WEB?

Exchange Rates
http://www.x-rates.com

There is no common international currency for carrying on financial transactions. Currency rates of exchange show the value of one country's currency in relation to another's. The Exchange Rates site allows you to compare currencies for thirty-seven different countries. Using this site, see how the euro, the currency of the European Union, is doing in relation to the U.S. dollar, or use the Custom Table to compare the U.S. dollar with all other currencies. For fun, you can click on Photos to see what a Belgian franc looks like, or you can even order foreign currencies before your trip abroad. You can also click on links that explain how and why people trade currencies.

Organisation for Economic Co-operation and Development
http://www.oecd.org/

The Organisation for Economic Co-operation and Development (OECD) began with the purpose of rebuilding war-ravaged economies after World War II and administering the distribution of the Marshall Plan's aid to Europe. Today, the OECD promotes policies that contribute to the expansion of world trade on a nondiscriminatory basis. It provides a forum in which governments of the twenty-nine member states can compare their experiences and further the principles of a market economy. From the OECD's home page, you can access the largest source of comparative statistical data on the industrialized countries. Look at the Frequently Requested Statistics, which is accessible from the home page. Also look at the "What's New" portion of the home page; it discusses recent activities of the OECD.

Trade Resources
http://www.usitc.gov/tr/tr.htm

According to its website, the U.S. International Trade Commission (USITC) is an "independent, nonpartisan, quasi-judicial federal agency that provides trade expertise to both the legislative and executive branches of government, determines the impact of imports on U.S. industries, and directs actions against certain unfair trade practices, such as patent, trademark, and copyright infringement." The USITC has created an information referral service for those seeking information related to international trade and investment. Interested in investing in a chemical company in Canada? Want to export tractors to Russia? This website provides Internet resources to help those interested in international trade and investment to obtain information on their client country, research various products, access trade assistance, understand patent law, or view international law.

U.S. Trade Representative
http://www.ustr.gov/

The Office of the U.S. Trade Representative (USTR) is responsible for "developing and coordinating U.S. international trade, commodity, and foreign direct investment policy, and leading or directing negotiations with other countries on such matters." Learn about the history of the U.S. Trade Representative, read speeches by the current representative and other past trade representatives, and scan the trade agreements the United States has with many other countries.

World Bank
http://www.worldbank.org/

The World Bank is the world's largest source of development assistance. The Bank was first created to aid European countries in their recovery from World War II. Today the Bank's mission is to help developing countries achieve stable, sustainable, and equitable growth. Its main focus is to help the poorest people and the poorest countries to grow economically. Explore this website to find out the eligibility requirements for borrowing money. What are some of the criteria? What are some of the recent actions of the World Bank? What does the site say about dealing with debt, especially that of Global South governments?

World Trade Organization
http://www.wto.org/

The World Trade Organization (WTO) is a multilateral, global intergovernmental organization (IGO). The WTO's main purpose is to administer trade agreements between countries, monitor trade policies, and provide technical assistance and training for developing countries. Unlike many international organizations, the WTO has a mechanism for settling international disputes with limited enforcement abilities. Search the site for information on how disputes are brought before the organization and how they are settled.

INFOTRAC® COLLEGE EDITION

Panagariya, Arvind. "International Trade: Think Again." *Foreign Policy* (November–December 2003).

Moss, Todd, and Alicia Bannon. "Africa and the Battle over Agricultural Protectionism." *World Policy Journal* (Summer 2004).

Heginbotham, Eric, and Richard J. Samuels. "Mercantile Realism and Japanese Foreign Policy." *International Security* (Spring 1998).

Sampson, Gary P. "The Environmentalist Paradox: The World Trade Organization's Challenges." *Harvard International Review* (Winter 2002).

For more articles, enter:
"mercantilism" in the Subject Guide
"World Trade Organization" in the Subject Guide
"International Monetary Fund" in the Subject Guide
"World Bank" in the Subject Guide

Go to http://politicalscience.wadsworth.com/kegley10 to access additional resources related to this chapter.

CHAPTER 10

POPULATION PRESSURE, RESOURCE DEPLETION, AND THE PRESERVATION OF THE GLOBAL ENVIRONMENT

TOPICS AND THEMES

- The tragedy of the global commons
- Global demographic trends
  Factors affecting population growth rates
  The epidemic and impact of HIV/AIDS
- How population policy colors world politics
- The international response to population issues
- Environmental security and sustainable development
  The ecopolitics of energy
  The ecopolitics of the atmosphere
  The ecopolitics of forests and biodiversity
- Trade, the environment, and sustainable development
- Toward sustainability

- **CONTROVERSY** HOW MANY PEOPLE CAN EARTH SUPPORT?

India's population reached 1 billion in August 1999 and the UN predicts that India will be the world's most populous country by 2050. Shown here is a railway station in Bombay, India, on the day world population reached 6 billion, October 12, 1999.

A host of contradictory demographic trends and measures will likely reshape the world during the next quarter century.

—NICHOLAS EBERSTADT, demographer, 2001

Today we abuse the Earth's resources. We feed on portions that belong to unborn generations. . . . Protection of the environment is a noble endeavor in itself. But the survival of the environment is also the strategic basis of human survival.

—THABO MBEKI, FERNANDO HENRIQUE CARDOSO, and GORAN PERSSON, presidents, respectively, of South Africa, Brazil, and Spain, 2002

"Chances are," notes an expert in **demography,** Jeffrey Kluger (2002, 25), "that you will never meet any of the estimated 247 human beings who were born in the past minute. In a population of six billion, 247 is a demographic hiccup. In the minute before last, however, there were another 247. In the minutes to come, there will be another, then another, then another. By next year at this time, all those minutes will have produced nearly 130 million newcomers in the great human mosh pit. That kind of crowd is very hard to miss." What will that crowd do in the long run to the planet's **carrying capacity**—the Earth's ability to support and sustain life? That concern has made population and environmental policy a central issue in world politics.

Increasing numbers of people are populating the planet, and globalization is bringing them closer together in an interdependent and crowded global village. Evidence strongly suggests that unrestrained population growth will result in environmental degradation and domestic strife (Population Action International 2003). This problem has made population and environmental policy a key political issue on the global agenda.

■ **demography**
the study of population changes, their sources, and their impact.

■ **carrying capacity**
the maximum number of humans and living species that can be supported by a given territory.

349

■ **tragedy of the commons**
a metaphor, widely used to explain the impact of human behavior on ecological systems, that explains how rational self-interested behavior by individuals may have a destructive collective impact.

The **tragedy of the commons** is a metaphor that highlights the potential impact of human behavior on the planet's resources and its delicately balanced ecological systems. First articulated in 1833 by English political economist William Foster Lloyd and later by contemporary human ecologist Garrett Hardin, the commons parable depicts a medieval English village, where the "green" was common property on which all villagers could graze their cattle. Freedom of access to the commons was a cherished village value. Sharing the common grazing area worked well as long as usage by individuals (and their cattle) didn't reduce the land's usefulness to everyone else. Assuming the villagers were driven by the profit motive and no laws existed to restrain their greed, herders had maximum incentive to increase their stock as much as possible. In the short run, the addition of one more animal would produce a personal gain whose costs would be borne by everyone. But in the long run the overgrazed green was destroyed. The lesson? "Ruin is the destination toward which all men rush," Hardin (1968) concluded, "each pursuing his own best interest."

This chapter uses the tragedy of the commons metaphor to explore how changes in demography, resources, and the environment influence the global future by examining how changes in world population affect the prospects for preserving for future generations the planet's ecology on which life itself depends.

POPULATION CHANGE AS A GLOBAL POLITICAL CHALLENGE

How many people can the Earth support? What are the costs of population growth to human freedom and welfare, and many environmental issues ranging from excessive fishing of the oceans to transboundary pollution caused when industries spew toxic wastes into the atmosphere? The right to produce children is a major unregulated freedom. "The most important aspect of necessity that we must now recognize," Hardin (1968) wrote in explaining the tragedy of the commons, "is the necessity of abandoning the commons in breeding. Freedom to breed will bring ruin to all. . . . The only way we can preserve and nurture other and more precious freedoms is by relinquishing the freedom to breed and . . . very soon. . . . Only so, can we put an end to this aspect of the tragedy of the commons."

■ **ethics**
the criteria by which right and wrong behavior and motives are distinguished.

■ **politics**
the exercise of influence in attempt to resolve controversial issues in one's favor.

Not everyone agrees with the **ethics** of Hardin's arguments. Some regard the freedom to parent as a human right. Others claim that controls on family size are unnecessary because the ultimate carrying capacity of the global ecosystem is unknown and the impact of unregulated population growth on human welfare and environmental quality remains uncertain. For this reason, **politics** governs debates about population policies. To understand why this issue has become so controversial, it is helpful to trace the global trends in population growth that have made the topic so problematic (see Figure 10.1).

Understanding Growth Rates: The Persian Chessboard

The rapid growth of world population is described by a simple mathematical principle the Reverend Thomas Malthus in 1798 noticed: unchecked, population increases in a geometric or exponential ratio (e.g., 1 to 2, 2 to 4, 4 to 8),

FIGURE 10.1
World Population Growth Projections to the Year 2050

In the twentieth century world population grew from less than 2 billion people to more than 6 billion, with each billion added in less time than the previous billion. World population is growing at 1.2 percent each year. Between 1.2 and 2.2 billion additional people will be living on the Earth by the middle of the twenty-first century, depending on how fast fertility rates (the number of babies born for each woman) fall (see figure on left) and life spans increase. The UN figure on the right sketches three potential scenarios for the future, showing that by 2050 world population is expected to be between 8 billion (low variant) and 11 billion (high variant), with the medium variant leading to about 9 billion.

SOURCE: United Nations Population Division (www.un.org/esa/population/unpop.htm, May 25, 2004).

---

whereas subsistence increases in only an arithmetic ratio (1 to 2, 2 to 3, 3 to 4). When population increases at such a geometric rate, the acceleration can be staggering. Carl Sagan illustrated this principle governing growth rates with a parable he termed "The Secret of the Persian Chessboard":

> The way I first heard the story, it happened in ancient Persia. But it may have been India, or even China. Anyway, it happened a long time ago. The Grand Vizier, the principal adviser to the King, had invented a new game. It was played with moving pieces on a board of 64 squares. The most important piece was the King. The next most important piece was the Grand Vizier— just what we might expect of a game invented by a Grand Vizier. The object of the game was to capture the enemy King, and so the game was called, in Persian, shahmat—shah for king, mat for dead. Death to the King. In Russia it is still called shakhmaty, which perhaps conveys a lingering revolutionary ardor. Even in English there is an echo of the name—the final move is called "checkmate." The game, of course, is chess.

As time passed, the pieces, their moves and the rules evolved. There is, for example, no longer a piece called the Grand Vizier—it has become transmogrified into a Queen, with much more formidable powers.

Why a king should delight in the creation of a game called "Death to the King" is a mystery. But, the story goes, he was so pleased that he asked the Grand Vizier to name his own reward for such a splendid invention. The Grand Vizier had his answer ready: He was a humble man, he told the King. He wished only for a humble reward. Gesturing to the eight columns and eight rows of squares on the board he devised, he asked that he be given a single grain of wheat on the first square, twice that on the second square, twice that on the third, and so on, until each square had its complement of wheat.

No, the King remonstrated. This is too modest a prize for so important an invention. He offered jewels, dancing girls, palaces. But the Grand Vizier, his eyes becomingly lowered, refused them all. It was little piles of wheat he wanted. So, secretly marveling at the unselfishness of his counselor, the King graciously consented.

When the Master of the Royal Granary began to count out the grains, however, the King was in for a rude surprise. The number of grains starts small enough: 1, 2, 4, 8, 32, 64, 128, 256, 512, 1,024. . . . . But by the time the 64th square is approached, the number becomes colossal, staggering. In fact the number is nearly 18.5 quintillion grains of wheat. Maybe the Grand Vizier was on a high fiber diet.

How much does 18.5 quintillion grains of wheat weigh? If each grain were 2 millimeters in size, then all the grains together would weigh around 75 billion metric tons, which far exceeds what could have been stored in the King's granaries. In fact, this is the equivalent of about 150 years of the world's present wheat production. (Sagan 1989, 14)

To picture in another way how growth rates unfold, consider how money deposited in a savings account grows as it earns interest not only on the original investment but also on the interest payments. If one of our ancestors had saved a mere ten dollars in the bank for us two hundred years ago, and it accrued a steady 6 percent annual interest, today we would all be millionaires! Population grows in the same way: It is a function of increases in the original number of people plus those accruing from past population growth. Thus a population growing at a 1 percent rate will double in sixty-nine years, while a population growing at a 2 percent rate will double in only thirty-five years. (The impact of different growth rates on doubling times can be easily calculated by dividing 69 by the percentage of growth.)

The story of population growth is told in its statistics: The annual rate of population growth in the twentieth century increased from less than 1 percent in 1900 to a peak of 2.2 percent in 1964. It has since dropped to about 1.2 percent. Despite the recent drop in rate, however, the absolute number of people *added* each year has continued to grow, from 16 million in 1900 to a peak of 87 million in 1990, and thereafter has declined to an additional 77 million new people in 2001, when global population expanded by adding the equivalent of another Germany. Plainly, the planet is certain to have many more people by the mid-twenty-first century, well beyond the 6.3 billion already roaming the planet. Yet the feared "population explosion" once believed certain to overwhelm the Earth's resources is now expected to be much less than previously predicted.

If a catastrophic population explosion is not necessarily assured and the probability of continuing population growth overwhelming a crowded planet is receding, why then does population remain such a political powder keg in world politics? The answers are numerous. Several salient features about population dynamics make demographic change the source of new global issues and problems.

The Demographic Divide between Global North and Global South

Population growth rates are not the same throughout the world. Population is growing much more rapidly in the developing Global South countries than in the wealthy countries in the Global North, and that trend is expected to continue. In fact, the population of the industrialized world is actually expected to decline. This "demographic divide," as projected in Figure 10.2, explains a large part of the problem making population such a hot political issue.

Because population growth is occurring in precisely those countries least able economically to support a growing number of people, global population cannot be expected to stabilize until it falls below replacement-level fertility in the developing countries. Between 2000 and 2005, the worldwide average number of children born to a woman during her lifetime—the total **fertility rate**—was around 2.7. However, these projections for the entire globe overlook the different rates for the rich and the poor. Although the world's population grew by 77 million people each year between 2000 and 2005, 95 percent of the continuing global population surge was added in the developing Global South, already home to 5.3 billion people, or more than 80 percent of the world (World Bank 2005b, 257). Hence, global population growth is the result of new births in the developing Global South, where the average fertility rate averaged 3.1 children for each mother (5.8 for the least-developed countries). In contrast, the wealthy, developed Global North's fertility rate has actually declined to 1.4 children for each woman, which is below **replacement-level fertility** (each couple replacing itself with 2.1 children). Fertility rates around the world, presently at 2.7, must fall to an average of 2.1 children for each woman in order to fall to replacement level. Yet, throughout much of the Global South, the preferred family size remains far in excess of the replacement level, especially in the poorest countries.

The developing countries' high fertility rates have important economic consequences. Almost all the problems in the North-South dispute can be traced to disparities in income and economic growth that are directly linked to the differentials in population growth rates. A brief look at these dynamics completes the picture of ongoing political conflict between the haves and the have-nots.

Population Momentum

The surge in the Global South's population in the twentieth century is easily explained as a combination of high birthrates and rapidly falling death rates. But to understand the population surge projected throughout the twenty-first century—when birthrates throughout the world will decline—we have to understand the force of population momentum, the continued growth of population for decades into the future because of the large number of women now entering

■ **fertility rate**
the average number of children born to a woman (or group of women) during her lifetime.

■ **replacement-level fertility**
one couple replacing themselves with two children, so that a country's population will remain stable if this rate prevails.

FIGURE 10.2
The New Demographics: The Global North–Global South Population Divide

Overpopulation is much feared, but the UN estimates that we can expect steady reductions of global population growth rates leading eventually to reductions in world population. Even though population changes are not expected to occur everyplace at the same pace, nearly all of the future population growth will take place in the Global South, especially the **least developed of the less-developed countries (LLDCs),** whereas a "birth dearth" in the Global North is expected to reduce the absolute number of people living there, as shown in the figure. Assuming continuing declines in fertility, Global South population is expected to rise to 8 billion in 2050 (in the absence of such declining birth rates, the less-developed countries will reach 11.5 billion by 2050, and by 2050 the Global North's population is anticipated to decline to 1.2 billion because fertility rates are likely to remain below replacement levels. Life expectancy is increasing. People everywhere are living longer. This growth in the proportion of elderly people is already affecting the size of each region's future population. When interpreting these projections, take into account the number of people within each country as controlled by geographical size, known as "population density." Some countries and regions are very crowded and others are not. For example, Singapore is the most congested country in the world, with 6,967 people for each square kilometer, and people in Australia are the least likely to bump into one another, with only three people for each square kilometer (World Bank 2005b, 256–57).

SOURCE: Adapted from the United Nations Population Division.

■ **least developed of the less-developed countries (LLDCs)**
the most impoverished member of the Third World in the Global South.

their childbearing years. Like the inertia of a descending airliner when it first touches down on the runway, population growth simply cannot be halted even with an immediate, full application of the brakes. Instead, many years of high fertility mean that more women will be entering their reproductive years than in the past. Not until the size of the generation giving birth to children is no larger than the generation among which deaths are occurring will the population "airplane" come to a halt.

Western Europe and sub-Saharan Africa illustrate the force of population momentum. Africa's demographic profile is one of rapid population growth, as each new age group (cohort) contains more people than the one before it. Thus, even if individual African couples choose to have fewer children than their parents, Africa's population will continue to grow because there are now more men and women of childbearing age than ever before. In contrast, Europe's population profile is one of slow growth, as recent cohorts have been smaller than preceding ones. In fact, Europe has moved beyond replacement-level fertility to become a "declining" population, described by low birthrates and a growing number of people who survive middle age. A product of an extended period of low birthrates, low death rates, and increased longevity, Europe is best described as an aging society, where the low birthrates and aging populations have caused alarm that the number of European newborns will not be sufficient to renew populations.

As the Global North generally ages, much of the Global South continues to mirror the sub-Saharan African profile: because each cohort is typically larger than the one before it, the number of young men and women entering their reproductive years will also continue to grow. The resulting differences in these demographic momentums will produce quite different population profiles in the developed and the developing worlds. Two examples illuminate the contrast. Germany has at present a low birthrate of 0.82 per woman and between now and the year 2030, people over 65 in the world's third-largest economy will account for almost half the adult population (compared with one-fifth in 2005). The net result will be that Germany's total population of 82 million will shrink to about 70 million and the number of working-age people will fall about 25 percent (from 40 million to 30 million). Seeing those with large incomes having children as an "opportunity cost," Germany is becoming a country with decreasing numbers of young people paying into pension systems that must support growing numbers of older people who, on average, will be in retirement for almost as many years as they worked to earn their pensions in the first place. (Throughout Europe, only two-fifths of men over age 55 still work.) In Germany, by 2035 every worker will support one retired person (Bernstein 2003, 3).

Similarly, the population of Japan, the world's second-largest economy, will peak in the year 2007 at 127 million. Given the Japanese birthrate of 1.27 per woman, by the year 2050 the proportion of children under 15 will fall below 11 percent of the 92–108 million total population (*Economist*, November 13, 2004, 45). "The figures are pretty much the same for most other developed countries—Italy, France, Spain, Portugal, the Netherlands, Sweden—and for a good many emerging ones, especially China. . . . The only developed country that has so far avoided this fate is America. But even there the birthrate is well below replacement level, and the proportion of older people in the adult population will rise steeply in the next 30 years" (Drucker 2001, 5). Thus, the population divide will grow; Japan, Europe, and the other Global North countries will become older and smaller while the United States is "getting older, to be sure, but also bigger. By 2050 the United States will be alone as the only developed country among the world's twenty most-populous countries" (Srodes 2001, 13).

From Population Explosion to Population Implosion— A Demographic Transition?

High rates of population growth are, simply put, punitive and painful, condemning low economic growth and increasing the likelihood of civil war (Population Action International 2003). How can the poor Global South escape the population explosion that in many developing countries is blocking their economic development?

One path out of this economic prison is reducing population by following the path known as **demographic transition.** That term was coined to describe the change that Europe and, later, North America experienced between 1750 and 1930, when high birthrates combined with high death rates were replaced by low birthrates and low death rates. The transition started when death rates began to fall due to rising prosperity and living standards in addition to improved disease control. Although the potential for substantial population growth was high, birthrates soon began to decline as well. During this phase of the demographic transition, the population growth rate slowed to less than 1.5 percent each year.

Demographic transition is now under way virtually everywhere in the world, but at much different rates in different countries and regions. As noted above, with the exception of about twenty-five states now at near replacement levels, the experience of the Global South differs greatly from that of Europe and North America, where death rates declined slowly. In most of the Global South, death rates have declined rapidly—the average life span of 65 is now only 13 years lower than the 78 years people in the Global North can expect to live (UNDP 2004, 171)—largely as a result of more effective public health "death control" programs introduced by the outside world. A population explosion inevitably followed.

There are two ways that changes in birth and death rates enable demographic transitions to develop. First, a decline in death rates can itself stimulate a decline in birthrates. When people begin to expect to live longer lives, couples begin "to realize that more of their children will live to adulthood, and therefore, to feel secure that they can have fewer births and still achieve their desired number of surviving children" (Lutz 1994). Second, demographic transitions are a by-product of **modernization,** which leads to value changes about the preferred size of family. In traditional low-income societies children are economic bonuses because they provide labor that contributes to family income; as modernization proceeds, children can become economic burdens, inhibiting social mobility and capital accumulation of wealth. "In most every country where people have moved from traditional ways of life to modern ones, they are choosing to have too few children to replace themselves" (Singer 1999). Modernization—and the improved nutrition and greater opportunities for women's education and employment that occurs with it (Engelhardt and Prskawetz 2004)—changes family values and drives fertility rates toward replacement level; a democratic transition then begins, followed by little or no population growth.

If these trends continue, they are certain to transform the world. Con-

■ **demographic transition**
an explanation of population changes over time that highlights the causes of declines in birth and death rates so that a country's population achieves a stable level.

■ **modernization**
a view of development popular in the Global North's liberal democracies which argues that wealth is created through efficient production, free enterprise, and free trade and that countries' relative ability to create wealth depends on technological innovation and education.

sider the impact of "graying" of the world presently occurring. A revolution in longevity is unfolding, with life expectancy at birth in 2005 worldwide at a record-high 66.9 years, and expected to rise by 2050 to 74.3 years. This is making for an increasingly aged world population. By 2015, over a third of the globe's expected 7.2 billion population are likely to be 65 or older (UNDP 2004, 142, 155). What are the consequences?

It was concern about this trend that propelled representatives from 160 countries to participate in Madrid at 2002 UN Second World Assembly on Aging. They sought to address the challenges posed by the evidence that the world's senior population (over the age of 65) had tripled over the past fifty years, and global aging is occurring at rates never seen before. At issue are almost cataclysmic predictions. If this prevailing trend continues, by 2050 the number of people older than 65 will again triple, to comprise four-fifths of humanity, and those approximately 5.7 billion would greatly outnumber the world's youths. The "oldest old," 80 years or more, is expected to increase even faster—more than fivefold by 2050 (UNPD 2004).

This unprecedented aging of the world could create economic problems of crisis proportions. With the percentage of taxpaying workers shrinking, the budgets of state governments (especially in the developed Global North where the number of elderly is already the highest) could be overwhelmed by attempts to provide retirement and health benefits for the elderly. In addition, dwindling birthrates, lengthening life spans, and early retirements could spell trouble for a worker-hungry Global North in need of immigrants to supply labor. Without migration, the UN notes, the Global North population would have started to decline in 2003 rather than 2025, and by 2050 would be 126 million less than the 1.2 billion under the assumption of continued migration (UNPD 2001). For example, to maintain its present workforce through the year 2050, Japan will require 30 million new immigrants (*Harper's*, June 2000, 23). The graying of world population does not leave the developing countries immune from the challenge, because in the Global South the pace of aging is faster than in the developed countries, with the proportion of the population over 65 rising to 35 percent in 2050. This gives the poorest societies less time to cope as they continue to simultaneously try to confront the scourges of poverty and disease.

Against this scenario, consider as well alternative ways of visualizing the global future. All projections are dangerous, because natural or human-made events can overturn the conditions that make for today's prevailing trends. For example, current projections could be overturned overnight by a nuclear war or a terrorist act of mass destruction with biological weapons, rendering obsolete today's life expectancy of nearly 80 years in the Global North. Other threats, such as the outbreak of a widespread, deadly contagious disease, also could produce a **population implosion**—a severe reduction in world population. We take a brief look at two examples of life-ending diseases of epidemic proportions.

New Plagues? The Global Impact of Tuberculosis and HIV/AIDS

Although infant and child mortality rates remain discouragingly high in much of the developing world, at least they are decreasing. On a global level, life expectancy at birth each year since 1950 has increased, climbing to 66.9 years by UN estimates. However, this trend in rising longevity could reverse if globally transmittable diseases cut into the extension of life spans made possible by improvements in health care, nutrition, water quality, and public sanitation.

■ **population implosion** a rapid reduction of population that reverses a previous trend toward progressively larger populations.

Simulation: The Spread of AIDS and HIV

■ **human immunodeficiency virus (HIV)**
a virus that can lead to acquired immune deficiency syndrome (AIDS).

■ **AIDS (acquired immune deficiency syndrome)**
an often fatal condition that can result from infection with the human immunodeficiency virus (HIV).

Throughout history the spread of bacteria, parasites, viruses, plagues, and diseases to various ecospheres, regardless of state borders, has suspended development or brought down once mighty states and empires. For example, drug-resistant strains of tuberculosis (TB) have developed recently, and whether at home or abroad TB knows no borders, since in our age of globalization the disease can be passed on with a sneeze or cough on an international flight. It is not possible to control the disease within a country if it continues to spread in other parts of the world. This could certainly curtail population growth, because "about one-third of the world's population is infected with the bacteria that causes TB—over two billion people, and TB will kill nearly two million" each year (Clyburn 2001, A9).

The grim possibility that virulent disease will diminish the world's population, and that we all share a common fate, is made no more evident than in the spread of the **human immunodeficiency virus (HIV)** that causes **AIDS (acquired immune deficiency syndrome).** Since the 1970s onset of the AIDS pandemic, the UN estimates that, in the words of UN Secretary-General Kofi Annan in November 2001 on the eve of World AIDS Day, "Every day more than 8,000 people die of AIDS. Every hour almost 600 people become infected. Every minute a child dies of the virus. Just as life and death go on after September 11, so must we continue our fight against the HIV/AIDS epidemic. Before the [9/11]

Can AIDS Be Stopped? As the AIDS epidemic has spread throughout the world and become a transnational health problem, the demand has increased for assistance to those afflicted with the deadly disease. Shown here is a demonstration in November 2001 outside South Africa's parliament demanding antiretroviral drugs to HIV-positive pregnant women to prevent the transfer of HIV from a mother to her child. In sub-Saharan Africa, women account for 57 percent of adult infections (*Economist*, December 4, 2004, 106).

MAP 10.1
Death in the Prime of Life: The Most Seriously AIDS-Affected Countries, 2000–2005.

AIDS brings death throughout the world to millions of working-age victims in their most productive and reproductive years, between the ages of 15 and 64. This map shows the severity of this mortality rate between 2000 and 2005, which is expected to worsen and spread, as an estimated 50 to 75 million will be affected worldwide by 2010 (Altman 2002, 1). The United Nations identifies 53 countries "AIDS affected with HIV prevalence at 1 percent or greater, plus Russia, the United States, India and China," and shown here are the "most seriously AIDS-affected countries with more than 20 percent of their reproductive age population infected with the virus [which are] now losing 10 to 18 percent of their working age population through premature death every five years" (Population Action International 2003, 63–64).

SOURCE: Data from United Nations Joint Programme on HIV/AIDS, 2002, as cited in Population Action International, *The Security Demographic* (2003, p. 63).

---

terrorist attacks, . . . tremendous momentum had been achieved in that fight. To lose it now would be to compound one tragedy with another."

Most health experts agree with Annan's warning that "in the ruthless world of AIDS there is no us and them" and that international solidarity is required to fight the disease which in a globalized planet spreads across national borders.

The circumstances are tragic and the tragedy is only expected to get worse. UN demographers estimate, for example, that in many of the "most seriously AIDS-affected countries" deaths are projected to overtake births and cause population decreases in the next few years" (Population Action International 2003, 64).

More than 90 percent of new infections occur in the Global South, but the contagion respects no borders and is a truly global epidemic, killing throughout the world (see Map 10.1). Are world death rates thus destined to rise in the future, reversing the upward trend in world population? The "age of AIDS" is a sobering reminder that population and power are heavily determined by natural phenomena in an era when what occurs anywhere often has consequences everywhere. The spread and control of infectious diseases such as AIDS, tuberculosis, malaria, Lassa fever, Ebola, and mad cow disease, have established themselves on the radar screen of policymakers throughout the world, and will not vanish from their sight anytime soon.

THE INTERNATIONAL RESPONSE TO POPULATION ISSUES

The world community convened its first World Population Conference to address the world's growing population in Bucharest in 1974. Many Global South delegates then concluded from Europe's and North America's demographic transitions that declining fertility rates flowed more or less automatically from economic growth and proposed policies that focused on economic development rather than population control. They called on the Global North for economic development assistance, reasoning that the population problem would then take care of itself. The slogan "Development is the best contraceptive" reflected the prevailing view.

A decade later, a second World Population Conference was held in Mexico City. By then, a new consensus had converged around the critical importance of family planning. However, the United States, previously a major advocate of this viewpoint, resisted this emerging global consensus, and argued that free market economies and technological innovations to offset shortages created by population growth should take precedence over such government interventions in population programs as the use of mandatory sterilization and abortion as approaches to family planning.

The debate between optimists and pessimists has continued. In 1994 the UN-convened International Conference on Population and Development (ICPD) in Cairo concluded that population stabilization could be achieved only in conjunction with efforts to promote **human development** and sustainable economic growth, supported by increases in **multilateral aid.** This conclusion was reaffirmed at the August 2002 Johannesburg World Conference on Sustainable Development. Despite the contentious issue of abortion rights, the precedent-setting 1994 Cairo agreement and the 2002 Johannesburg resolutions set standards regarding other issues of environmental quality, resource conservation, demographic sources of political instability and ethnic conflict, urbanization, and inequalities between the Global North and Global South. Prominent among the key objectives, a global consensus has crystallized on

- stabilizing population growth levels consistent with sustainable development
- focusing assistance programs on the unmet need and demand for family planning and reproductive health services
- preventing HIV/AIDS infection
- addressing women's health needs and protecting children
- advancing the economic, political, and social rights of women
- increasing male responsibility in family planning and childbearing

■ **human development** the extent to which humans' ability to develop to their individual potential is protected, such that they are provided with sufficient schooling, income, and opportunity to live a full life.

■ **multilateral aid** assistance provided through more than two states or other international actors for the purpose of collective action to combat perceived problems.

Specific goals to be achieved were set at both global conferences, which included access to primary school education, family-planning services, and reproductive health to improve rates on infant and child mortality, maternal mortality, and life expectancy.

The proposals of these precedent-setting world conferences were only recommendations, not binding on governments. Indeed, few could be expected to act on all of them, particularly given the enormous resources their realization demands. By 2005, global family-planning expenditures alone are expected to balloon to $15 billion, nearly double the amount spent in the early 1990s. Even greater sums will be required to meet the goals of increased access to primary education and to health care. Global South countries cannot be expected to meet these demands by themselves. Others—meaning governments in the Global North—will also be asked to contribute more. Since domestic political support for foreign aid among donor countries has declined since the early 1990s, however, large subsidies are unlikely.

Mounting a sustained effort to stem the growth of world population thus remains a formidable challenge. However, the goal itself is no longer in serious dispute, because most now agree with UN Secretary-General Kofi Annan's once controversial view, stated in 1999, that "we have to stabilize the population of this planet," inasmuch as the global community has agreed that the concurrent growth of human population and demands on the planet exceed some of the natural limits on the earth's carrying capacity. The world community now, in the age of globalization, has also begun to accept the once controversial view that the real problems are poverty and inequality. At the 1999 Hague conference, like the 2002 Johannesburg conference, more than one hundred countries convened to review the obstacles to carrying out the consensus commitment that first emerged at the 1994 Cairo conference, which emphasized the need to take a humane, noncoercive approach to population stabilization. In a comparatively short time, the "population problem" moved nearer to the top of the global agenda.

Food Fights: The Clash of Optimists and Pessimists

The impact of population growth centers on long-standing disputes in the so-called realm of **low politics.** In recent years, a new question has emerged: Is the planet running out of food? If world population grows to 9 billion and food supplies are depleted, many will be underfed and undernourished. Who will eat and who will starve?

This kind of question makes for a continuing international controversy, with **neo-Malthusians,** alarmed about potential food shortages, debating **cornucopians** who claim these pessimists' concerns are unwarranted (see Controversy: How Many People Can Earth Support?). History does not provide a clear answer. Furthermore, the range of opinion and conviction separating them is less clear than the labels suggest. As noted in Chapter 5, for example, the absolute gap in income between Global North and Global South continues, but the gap in human development between people in rich and poor countries has narrowed, and many optimists are counting on such technological miracles as genetically engineered crops to revolutionize farming and feed future generations. **Genetic engineering** develops hybrid seeds for new plants, and genetically modified or genetically engineered **transgenetic crops** are altered by inserting genes to develop a desired trait, such as herbicide tolerance or increased oil content. Unlike crop varieties developed through traditional plant breeding, trans-

■ **low politics**
the category of global issues related to the economic, social, demographic, and environmental aspects of relations between governments and people.

■ **neo-Malthusians**
pessimists who warn of the global ecopolitical implications of uncontrolled population growth.

■ **cornucoplans**
optimists who question limits-to-growth analyses and contend that markets effectively maintain a balance between population, resources, and the environment.

■ **genetic engineering**
research geared to discover seeds for new types of plant and human life for sale and use as substitutes for those produced naturally.

■ **transgenetic crops**
new crops with improved characteristics created artificially through genetic engineering that combines genes from species that would not naturally interbreed.

CONTROVERSY

HOW MANY PEOPLE CAN EARTH SUPPORT?

Are there limits to the size of world population beyond which humanity will perish? Two thousand years ago, when the earth had about the same number of people as the United States does today, few would have pondered that question. They do now, however, because with 8 to 10 billion people expected to live on the earth and consume what can be grown on it in the twenty-first century, the possibility has arisen that there will not be enough food to feed the world. If so, food scarcities will lead to famine and mass starvation, and countries will engage in "food fights" over agriculture products.

It is unclear whether this grim outcome will materialize, however. Demographic and environmental scientists are divided in their evaluations about the planet's future carrying capacity—the limits on its ability to supply the resources to sustain life on a planet teeming with a growing human population. The two major broadly defined groups of analysts approach these issues quite differently. Taking their name and orientation from Thomas Malthus and his classic 1798 *Essay on the Principle of Population*, the first group, neo-Malthusians, believes that world population is pushing against the earth's resources, straining its ability to meet the needs of this generation and the next. Sometimes called "growth pessimists," many neo-Malthusian ecologists point to a host of disconcerting facts about the present global condition: "Since Malthus wrote, the human population has grown by a factor of six, and total human energy use by a factor of one hundred or so.... The forest cover of the earth has been cut by a third and the area of undisturbed wetlands by half. The composition of the atmosphere has been altered by human-generated pollution. Hundreds of millions of people have starved to death; thousands of species have gone extinct" (Meadows 1993).

In contrast with the pessimism of neo-Malthusians, the second group, the cornucopians (many of

Genetic Engineering in Agriculture A Chinese farmer harnesses a transgenetic cow to produce milk and power.

whom are economists and otherwise known as "growth optimists"), emphasizes quite different global trends. Observing that global life expectancy has more than doubled since 1950 to 66.9 years, they conclude that rapid population growth has occurred not because human beings suddenly started breeding like rabbits but because they finally stopped dropping like flies. Despite the growth of global population from 1.6 billion in 1900 to more than 6.3 billion in 2005, cornucopians argue that "global health and productivity have exploded. Today human beings eat better, produce more, and consume more than ever.... Overpopulation is a problem that has been

genetics often contain genes from unrelated species—of plant, animal, bacteria, or other origin—with which the crop could not reproduce naturally. Despite lingering consumer unease, genetically modified crops "are gaining ground. In 2001 53 million hectares were planted with transgenetic crops, a 19 percent rise over the previous year. Thirteen countries now grow genetically modified soy-

Freak Food or Unfair Foreign Trade? A Greenpeace activist in France protests the import of genetically modified corn, which the United States produces for export around the globe.

misidentified and misdefined. The term has no scientific definition or clear meaning. The problems typically associated with over-population (hungry families, squalid and overcrowded living conditions) are more properly understood as issues of poverty." Although some blame dwindling natural resources for the reversals and catastrophes that have recently befallen heavily populated low-income countries, such episodes are directly traceable to the policies or practices of presiding governments (Eberstadt 1995).

What do you think? How do you line up on the divisions of opinion that follow? Note that some governments understandably view too many people as a problem and will seek to control population growth. Other countries are facing the threat of shrinking populations and see additional people as critical to their future. These differences in national needs make population policies highly contentious, especially because divergent population policies affect everyone and will determine whether technological advances will be sufficient for the earth to provide enough resources for its people. Some people have high hopes that genetically engineered agriculture will enable genetically modified or transgenetic livestock and crops to be developed to feed the world. Shown left (p. 362) is one example on which these "cornucopian" enthusiasts pin their hopes: a farmer in Tienman, China, cultivates a field using a new breed of cow developed by researchers in Africa that is strong enough to work in the field without reducing its capacity to produce milk or to breed. Critics of genetically modified crops, like the Greenpeace activist shown in the photo above vandalizing a field of transgenic corn in protest, complain that genetic engineering through biotechnology is dangerous because it is harmful to public health. "Far from being a solution to the world's hunger problem," complain some experts (Rosset 1999), "the rapid introduction of genetically engineered crops may actually threaten agriculture and food security."

beans, maize, corn, cotton or canola. America accounts for two-thirds of global production but China, South Africa and Australia are rapidly increasing their share" (*Economist*, January 19, 2002, 90). As the risk of plant and animal extinction escalates, scientists have turned to the desperate strategy of seeking to replicate them in surrogate forms through cloning.

■ **food security**
access by all people at all times to enough food for an active, healthy life.

Like the computer revolution, geneticists could revolutionize agriculture and transform the capability of the planet to feed the globe's growing population, increasing **food security.** However, the growing prevalence of commercially grown and globally marketed genetic agricultural production is a rising controversy on the global agenda and has met with considerable opposition from groups who feel that tampering with nature and life is immoral. Should scientists manipulate nature for human needs? Are gene-spliced plants and hormone-treated meat safe? Do transgenic foods created through genetic engineering contain allergens that cause serious allergic reactions that endanger health?

What makes population policy so difficult to forge is that some of the problems associated with demographic trends are declining, and others are growing worse. How is the globe responding?

Global environmental issues pose another controversy, one that engages the competing perspectives of optimistic cornucopians and pessimistic neo-Malthusians. Cornucopians adhere to the belief that if free markets and free trade are practiced, ecological imbalances that threaten humankind eventually will be corrected. For them, prices are the key adjustment mechanism that in time produce the greatest good for the greatest number of people. Neo-Malthusians, on the other hand, share more in common with economic **mercantilism,** which argues that free markets fail to prevent excessive exploitation of both renewable and nonrenewable resources, and that, accordingly, intervention by governing institutions is necessary (recall Chapter 9). More fundamentally, it requires rejecting the belief that the free market will always maximize social welfare, because neither an inexhaustible supply of natural resources nor "sinks" for disposing the wastes from consuming those resources are available.

■ **mercantilism**
a government trade strategy for accumulating state wealth and power by active government management of the state's economic, population, and environmental policies.

A Prescription for Optimism or Pessimism?

Neo-Malthusians and cornucopians paint quite different visions of our future. Might both be right? Rapidly expanding populations increase environmental degradation, poverty, and reproduction to hedge against the future. Economic development, on the other hand, encourages small families by stimulating reduced birthrates and hence declining rates of population growth. So, too, do government family-planning policies. Where each of us chooses to focus attention—dictated by our perceptual lens—will in turn frame our constructed images and our policy prescriptions.

The world community has made great strides in recent decades in recognizing the complex causes and consequences of rapid population growth. Whether it has the will and shared vision to cope with the problems and expand the possibilities for humanity remains to be seen. Meanwhile, an interdependent globalizing world promises that none will be immune to world population trends, even as the effects of population growth strain the natural environment on which we depend. Population politics are linked directly to the issue of protecting the planet's ecology, which we now examine.

ENVIRONMENTAL SECURITY AND SUSTAINABLE DEVELOPMENT

To explore global environmental challenges and responses to them, broadly described by the concept **ecopolitics**—the intersection of ecology and politics—we need to examine the linkage between the two. Ecology deals with the impact of human activity on the environment. Politics, as we have seen, is concerned with the exercise of power. Ecopolitics, then, centers on how political actors make choices to manage the impact of human behavior on their environments. Politics is a powerful force that permeates all dimensions of environmental and resource issues, ranging from the evaluation of scientific evidence to policy prescriptions for dealing with that evidence.

What is almost self-evident is that the ecological preservation of the global environment is required if any other values are to be achieved, for without the means to a healthy life no other values can be realized. Awareness of the importance of environmental protection has expanded greatly in recent years. When

■ **ecopolitics**
how political actors influence perceptions of, and policy responses to, changing environmental conditions, such as population density.

The View from Afar People on the planet collectively face many threats to survival, one of which is the threat posed by heat-trapping greenhouse gases that contribute to climate change and destructive global warming. Taken from a NASA global satellite surveillance system, this photo shows how integrated the globalized, borderless planet appears from outer space. NASA monitors the geophysical and biological conditions that will affect the earth's climate and the prospects for sustaining human life.

■ **realist theory**
the view that states are unitary global actors in relentless competition with one another for position and prosperity in the international hierarchy, dedicated to the promotion of their own interests at the expense of other states.

■ **high politics**
geostrategic issues of national and international security that pertain to matters of war and peace.

■ **neoliberalism**
a perspective that accounts for the way international institutions promote global change, cooperation, peace, and prosperity through collective reform approaches.

■ **politics of scarcity**
the view that the unavailability of resources required to sustain life, such as food, energy, or water, can undermine security in degrees similar to military aggression.

■ **environmental security**
a concept recognizing that environmental threats to global life systems are as important as the threat of armed conflicts.

■ **liberalism**
the school of thought that stresses the need for international cooperation through institutions to manage global problems and promote progress.

U.S. astronauts first viewed the Earth from the Apollo spacecraft, they remarked to millions of listeners about the "big blue marble" planet they saw through their small windows and how the clouds and continents flowed into one another without regard to the political boundaries humans had imposed on a pristine planet. Those images were often replayed. However, the improvement in space technology since the 1990s also enabled the world to see uncomfortable images—of atmospheric poisons that encircle the globe; of violent winter and summer storms pounding islands and continents with relentless fury; of massive holes in the ozone shield that protects humans from dangerous ultraviolet rays; of vanishing forests and widening deserts. Will the consumption habits and excessive toxic waste of industrialization cause irreparable environmental damage? There is no consensus on this question. Not surprisingly, then, there is no more consensus on how states ought to cope with ecological degradation than on how they should deal with the globalization of demographic changes and the economic and political transformations they cause.

Environmental issues are linked to other values that states prize, notably, security and economic and social well-being. "Security" means freedom from fear. It also means freedom from risk and danger. Because fear of a nuclear holocaust and other forms of violence such as terrorism have long haunted the world, security has been conventionally equated with "national security," the struggle for state power central to **realist theory** in the so-called realm of **high politics.** Today many analysts urge people to adopt a broader conception of what constitutes security at both the state and global levels. That rival view recommended by **neoliberalism** suggests that threats to national security should be defined as actions that reduce the quality of life for a country's inhabitants. This is the **politics of scarcity,** which predicts that future international conflict will likely be caused by resource scarcities—restricted access to food, oil, and water, for example—rather than by overt military challenges (see Klare 2001). Compelling as this unconventional viewpoint may be, scarcity continues to be studied primarily from a state-centric ecopolitical perspective.

Environmental security is a useful concept to broaden the definition of national security, pushing our vision beyond borders and their protection. Focusing on the transboundary character of challenges to preserving the global environment, it recognizes that threats by such phenomena as global warming, ozone depletion, and the loss of tropical forests and marine habitats can threaten the future of humankind just as much as can the threat of warfare using weapons of mass destruction. Because environmental degradation undercuts states' economic well-being and the quality of life all governments seek for their citizens, **liberalism** informs thinking about how states can cooperate with intergovernmental organizations (IGOs) and nongovernmental organizations (NGOs) to preserve the global environment. The effort by the neoliberal **epistemic community** to redefine *security* seeks to move beyond realism's popular state-centric conception of international politics, although the attempt to broaden the definition is understandably resisted by realists.

The dominant cornucopian social **paradigm** stressing the right to conspicuous consumption is under attack by environmental activists and think-tank experts such as Worldwatch, which question the dubious equation of consumption with happiness, noting that in today's consumer culture peoples' life satisfaction has not risen with their increasing wealth (*State of the World* 2004, 164–79). It is also under attack internationally. **Sustainable development** is now popularly perceived as an alternative to the quest for unrestrained growth. The movement began in earnest in 1972, when the UN General Assembly convened the first UN Conference of the Human Environment in Stockholm. Conferences have since been held on a wide range of environmental topics, with scores of treaties negotiated and new international agencies put into place to promote cooperation and monitor environmental developments.

The concept of sustainable development enjoys widespread support among governments and a broad range of NGOs that are particularly active in shaping the global environmental agenda. Its heritage is even more directly traceable to *Our Common Future*, the 1987 report of the World Commission on Environment and Development, popularly known as the "Brundtland Commission" after the Norwegian prime minister who chaired it. The commission concluded that the world cannot sustain the growth required to meet the needs and aspirations of the world's growing population unless it adopts radically different approaches to basic issues of economic expansion, equity, resource management, energy efficiency, and the like. Rejecting the "limits to growth" maxim popular among neo-Malthusians, it emphasized instead "the growth of limits." The commission defined a "sustainable society" as one that "meets the needs of the present without compromising the ability of future generations to meet their own needs."

A second milestone in the challenge to the dominant cornucopian social paradigm was the Earth Summit, which took place in Rio de Janeiro, Brazil, in 1992—the twentieth anniversary of the Stockholm conference. Formally known as the UN Conference on Environment and Development (UNCED), the meeting brought together more than 150 states, 1,400 nongovernmental organizations, and 8,000 journalists. Prior to the Earth Summit, environment and economic development had been treated separately—and often regarded as being in conflict with each other, as economic growth frequently imperils and degrades the environment. In Rio, the concept of sustainability galvanized a simultaneous treatment of environmental and development issues. That concept continued to be the key theme on environmental protection enthusiastically endorsed at the UN World Summit on Sustainable Development that concluded in early September 2002 in Johannesburg. These and other international conferences have punctuated the strong consensus behind the proposition that all politics—even global politics—are local, that what happens anyplace ultimately affects conditions everyplace, and accordingly that the protection of the Earth's environment is a primary international security issue.

Sustainability cannot be realized without substantial changes in the social, economic, and political practices throughout an increasingly interconnected world. Is that possible? Are individuals willing to sacrifice personal consumption for the common good? Will they sacrifice now to enrich their heirs? The tragedy of the commons provides little basis for optimism, whether applied to individuals or states, suggesting that greed and the striving for **relative gains** by some in the absence of strong international regulation leads to reductions in everyone's **absolute gains** and possibly to their destruction. Add to this that international anarchy without potent institutions for true global governance discourages states from cooperating with one another out of fear that some will gain more than others, and it becomes clear why environmental problems that cross national boundaries are seldom effectively managed.

To better understand the multiple tensions that global environmental problems pose in an anarchical world and how competition undercuts effective re-

■ **epistemic community**
a group of experts from around the world who, based on their knowledge, develop a shared understanding of a problem on the global agenda and a set of preferences for responding to it.

■ **paradigm**
derived from the Greek *paradeigma*, meaning an example, a model, or an essential pattern; a paradigm structures thoughts about an area of inquiry.

■ **sustainable development**
economic growth that does not deplete the resources needed to maintain growth.

■ **relative gains**
a measure of how much some participants in an exchange benefit in comparison with others.

■ **absolute gains**
a condition in which all participants in exchanges become better off.

sponses to them, consider next three interrelated clusters of problems on the global ecopolitical agenda: (1) oil and energy, (2) climate change and ozone depletion, and (3) biodiversity and deforestation. The clusters illustrate the problems and pitfalls that states and nonstate actors (IGOs and NGOs) face as they seek sustainable development of common properties and renewable resources.

THE ECOPOLITICS OF ENERGY

In April 1990, the average price for a barrel of internationally traded crude oil was less than $15. Five months later—stimulated by Iraq's invasion of the tiny oil sheikdom of Kuwait—it rose to more than $40. For the third time in less than two decades, the world suffered an oil shock when the price paid for the most widely used commercial energy source skyrocketed.

The 1990 Persian Gulf War was precipitated by the attempt of Iraq's Saddam Hussein to subjugate Kuwait and acquire its oil—an act of aggression—that culminated two decades of Middle Eastern turmoil during which oil disputes figured prominently. Concern about new oil wars, pitting buyers like the United States against Middle East sellers has persisted and grown since the U.S.-led "coalition of the willing" occupied Iraq in its 2003 war, which was followed by the highest world oil prices ever ($55 a barrel in late 2004, and possibly topping $100 if oil supply were disrupted; *Economist*, December 4, 2004, 76). The prospects for global prosperity and peace depend heavily on the preservation of order in the volatile Middle East. Ensuring access to the region's oil is especially critical to the Global North's economic fortunes, inasmuch as nearly all the cheaply extracted oil lies under the desert sands of a handful of countries around the Persian Gulf, and the Middle East is widely seen in the Global North as soil from which global terrorism is primarily growing.

The Global Politics of Oil Supply and Consumption

The importance of oil to the Global North generally and the United States in particular is evident from their disproportionate share of energy consumption. The average person living in Europe uses more than twice as much energy as people in the Global South, while Canada and the United States use more than six times as much. The differences parallel the gap between the globe's rich and poor countries apparent in so many other dimensions of the world.

Throughout the twentieth century, demand for and consumption of oil spiraled upward. An abundant supply of oil at low prices facilitated the recovery of Western Europe and Japan from World War II and encouraged consumers to use energy-intensive technologies, such as the private automobile. An enormous growth in the worldwide demand for and consumption of energy followed. Oil consumption hit a new all-time high of 70 million tons per day in 2005, when oil was still supplying about nine-tenths of the world's commercial energy and is expected by 2020 to climb to nearly 120 million barrels a day (Caruso 2003, 15). The industrialization of many emerging Global South economies has contributed to the growing demand, and the global shift to oil has been propelled by the aggressive production and promotion of a small group of multinational corporations (MNCs). Their operations encompass every aspect of the business, from exploration to the retail sales of products at their gas stations. Their search for, production of, and marketing of low-cost oil was for decades largely unhindered. Concessions from countries in the oil-rich Middle East and elsewhere were easy to get. And incentives for developing technologies for alternative energy sources, such as coal, were virtually nonexistent. Eventually, to maximize profits, the Organization of Petroleum Exporting Countries (OPEC) emerged as an important IGO **cartel.** Because the resources OPEC controls cannot be easily replaced, it has monopoly power. In March 1999 OPEC began to flex its economic muscles by cutting production to limit supplies. Oil prices tripled within a year, showing that OPEC could still make oil a critical global political issue—as it again did in 2004 in an effort to use oil prices as an instrument of **coercive diplomacy** to influence the course of the unfolding war on terrorism, particularly between Palestine and Israel.

■ **cartel**
an organization of the producers of a commodity that seeks to regulate the pricing and production of that commodity to increase revenue.

■ **coercive diplomacy**
the use of threats or limited armed force to persuade an adversary to alter its foreign and/or domestic policies.

Running on Empty: Is Energy Security an Elusive Goal?

Oil supplies assume great importance in world politics because oil is not being discovered at the same rate it is being used: "For every two barrels pumped out of the ground, the [giant oil companies] find less than one barrel to add to reserves. Production in the United States peaked thirty years ago. Russia peaked in 1987. North Sea production appears to be peaking now. [About] 70 percent of the oil consumed today was found twenty-five years ago or longer. . . . Meanwhile, demand for oil keeps moving up [and] the era of cheap and abundant oil is drawing to a close" (Quinn 2002, 43).

What strikes fear in the minds of those who study oil supplies against rising demand is the widespread "illusion" of petroleum plenty. "Petroleum reserves are limited. Petroleum is not a renewable resource and production cannot continue to increase indefinitely. A day of reckoning will come sometime in the future, the point at which increasing demand will mean a radical and painful readjustment globally to everyday life. . . . The world uses about 27 billion barrels of oil per year, meaning that 112 billion barrels—the proven oil reserves in Iraq, the second largest proven oil reserves in the world—will last a little more than four years at today's usage rates. In the future, 112 billion barrels will likely prove even shorter-lived" (Cavallo 2004, 20). What this foretells is future petroleum scarcities, and potentially sooner rather than later, as once predicted. "The International Energy Agency estimates the world's spare oil production capacity at about 2.5 million per day, almost all of it in the Gulf region. It also [predicted] that global oil demand in 2004 would be, on average, 2 million barrels per day higher than in 2003," Paul Krugman (2004, 9) warns, adding "if there is a major supply disruption the world will have to get by with less oil, and the only way that can happen in the short run is if there is a world economic slowdown. An oil-driven recession does not look at all far-fetched."

This alarming predicament suggests the "new geopolitics of oil" (Barnes, Jaffe, and Morse 2004) is likely to dominate world politics if world oil consumption rises as expected by 2020 to 120 million barrels each day (Caruso 2003, 15). To best characterize the present problem, it is less an issue of declining oil supplies than a question of how the oil producers will use their supplies in international bargaining with those oil-importing countries that are dependent and vulnerable to supply disruptions. The world does not now face the immediate threat of running out of oil; it faces instead the problem that oil reserves are concentrated in a small number of countries. Because OPEC members, who control approximately half of the world's oil reserves, are drawing down their reserves at half the average global rate, it seems almost inevitable that OPEC's share of the world oil market will grow. This means that OPEC is critical to global oil supply, the Middle East is critical to OPEC, and countries that depend on oil imports from this volatile, unstable source are highly vulnerable to disruptions—such as the United States (the percentage of whose oil from foreign suppliers exceeds 60 percent [*Harper's*, November 2001, 92] and whose oil inventories will hit a twenty-seven-year low in 2006).

OPEC's future role could change significantly, however, as its finances and political clout depend heavily on factors largely outside its control: changes in international demand (consumption) and supply. And we now may be witnessing the advent of a potentially historic juncture that could overturn the place of oil in the twenty-first-century's global political economy. Why? Largely because "world energy needs are projected to double in the next several decades, but no credible geologist foresees a doubling of world oil production, which is expected peak within the next few decades" (L. Brown and Flavin 1999, 6). "China's economic engine in particular is in desperate need of power from oil imports to keep its financial juggernaut moving forward; in terms of energy use it adds a middle-sized country every year" (Yardley 2004, 3). Between 2004 and 2010 China's oil consumption will double to 8 million barrels per day and its share of world oil consumption is expected by 2010 to climb beyond 9 percent, and its dependence makes China especially vulnerable because it imports two-thirds of its oil from the unstable Middle East, regarded as a bastion of American influence (Chandler 2004, 99).

How the world will meet its growing energy needs in the future is a critical economic, environmental, and political question. It places oil-producing countries in a powerful bargaining position. Consider the estimated proven reserves of oil in billions of dollars. "Saudi Arabia remains the kingpin of oil. It has a quarter of the world's proven reserves, about 262 billion barrels of oil, under its vast desert expanses. Add in the reserves held by the country's allies in the OPEC cartel, and the total is a whopping 815 billion barrels—some three-quarters of world reserves. In contrast, [in the 30 wealthy] OECD countries, which use much of the world's oil, have less than one-tenth of total reserves" (*Economist*, July 21, 2001, 88). This distribution of oil reserves means that "unless vast reserves are discovered outside the Middle East, global dependence on Persian Gulf oil will grow [and] this is a long-term problem [especially] for the United States in the wake of September 11 because for three decades Americans have only haphazardly tried to fortify themselves against a catastrophic cutoff of oil from the Middle East, which accounts for about a third of world production and two-thirds of known reserves" (Samuelson 2001a, A17).

The global energy system appears to be in the process of reinvention. Fossil fuel—coal, oil, and natural gas—provide 90 percent or more of industrialized countries' energy and 75 percent of energy worldwide. Petroleum, the most convenient and available energy source, now appears to be without an alternative. However, that seems destined to change in the wake of the events of September 11, 2001, the troubled war in Iraq, and the out-of-control rate at which China's sizzling economic growth requires the import of foreign supplies of oil to sustain its continued financial expansion and consumption. Technological, economic, cultural, and environmental changes suggest that the early stage of a major energy transformation is under way, forced by supply scarcities and demand increases.

"The broad outlines of a new energy system may now be emerging, thanks in part to a series of revolutionary new technologies and approaches. These developments suggest that our future energy economy may be highly efficient and decentralized, using a range of sophisticated electronics. The primary energy resources for this system may be the most abundant ones on Earth: the sun, the wind, and other renewable sources of energy [such as] hydrogen, the lightest and most abundant element in the universe." Humans only became dependent on nonrenewable finite stocks of fossilized fuel when Europeans began mining coal in the seventeenth century. For most of their existence, humans have relied on abundant renewable energy resources such as plants, sun, wind, and water to meet basic human needs for shelter, heat, cooking, lighting, and transportation. "Fossilized fuels . . . remaining energy is now equivalent to less than 11 days of sunshine. From a millennial perspective, today's hydrocarbon-based civilization is but a brief interlude in human history" (Flavin and Dunn 1999, 23).

The impact of such a global transformation would be huge, overturning the past 125-year pattern in world energy development and consumption. Could the era of "big oil" really be ending? That could be the case. A growing number of energy analysts and industry officials now argue that "two forces much more powerful than the fickle oil price are driving the [long-run shift from fossil fuels]: the rise of markets, and growing public alarm over global warming [and that] these twin forces . . . in time . . . may even make it yesterday's fuel" (Vaitheeswaron 2000, 89). This prophecy was captured in a remarkable speech in Houston in early 1999, when Mike Bowlin, chairman and CEO of the ARCO Oil Company, said, "We've embarked on the beginning of the Last Days of the Age of Oil." Bowlin went on to say that the world is moving "along the spectrum away from carbon and headed toward hydrogen and other forms of energy" (*Vital Signs 1999*, 48).

> Long before we completely run out of fossil fuels, however, the environmental and health burdens of using them may force us toward a cleaner energy system. Fossil fuel burning is the main source of air pollution and a leading cause of water and land degradation. Combustion of coal and oil produces carbon monoxide and tiny particles that have been implicated in lung cancer and other respiratory problems; nitrogen and sulfur oxides create urban smog, and bring acid rain that has damaged forests extensively. Oil spills, refinery operations, and coal mining release toxic materials that impair water quality. Increasingly, oil exploration disrupts fragile ecosystems and coal mining removes entire mountains. Although modern pollution controls have improved air quality in most industrial countries in recent decades, the deadly experiences of London and Pittsburgh are now being repeated in Mexico City, São Paulo, New Delhi, Bangkok, and many other cities in the developing world. Each year, coal burning is estimated to kill 178,000 people prematurely in China alone. (Flavin and Dunn 1999, 25)

This transformation portends a probable global shift from oil to unconventional sources (such as tar sands and shale) and renewable forms of energy. In the latter category, solar, tidal, and wind power, as well as geothermal energy and bioconversion are among the alternatives to oil most likely to become tech-

FIGURE 10.3

Phasing Out Fossil Fuels? The Potential for Renewable Energy to Supply the World's Energy Needs by the Year 2100

The global economy's need for energy continues to rise, requiring more energy than is ultimately available from nonrenewable resources. Rising demand is likely to change the current distribution of sources on which the world relies to meet its energy needs (left). As the Fossil Free Energy Scenario prediction (right) suggests, it would be possible to tap renewable sources to meet the world's entire energy needs by the end of the twenty-first century. For example, it is estimated that more than fifty Global South countries could produce as much energy from the biomass residues generated by sugar production as they presently obtain from oil; that less than 5 percent of the globe's small-scale hydropower has been exploited; and that land-based wind turbines could provide 20 million megawatt-hours of electricity each year—twice as much as the world consumed in 1987 (Crump 1998, 223). Renewable energy from replaceable sources also has the advantage of doing relatively little damage to the environment. Whether these sources of energy will actually be harnessed remains to be seen, because the relatively low financial cost of using the planet's nonrenewable resources (like oil, which takes millions of years to form) makes them economically attractive.

Note: Percentages do not equal 100 due to rounding errors.
SOURCE: Adapted from Crump (1998), 193 (left) and 223 (right).

nologically and economically viable. Their development would reduce dependence on oil from the volatile Middle East and reduce anxieties over possible scarcity. As Figure 10.3 shows, advocates of reliance on environmentally friendly, renewable energy supplies picture a radically different twenty-first century. They urge immediate planning for a new global "eco-economy, one that satisfies today's need without jeopardizing the prospects of future generations to meet theirs by altering how we light our homes, what we eat, where we live, how we use our leisure time, and how many children we have. It will give us a world where we are part of nature, instead of estranged from it" (Brown 2002).

Among known technologies, nuclear energy has often been championed as the leading alternative to fossil fuel dependence, and for that goal the United States allocated $15 billion for companies to build seven new nuclear power plants since its existing plants provide only 20 percent of America's electricity (Borenstein 2003, A5). But safety and financial problems have forced some countries to reduce their nuclear programs. Well-publicized nuclear accidents in the United States at the Three Mile Island nuclear power plant in Pennsylvania in 1979 and at Chernobyl in Ukraine in 1986 and no less than five major accidents between 1995 and 1999 at Japan's fifty-two nuclear power plants (which supply about a third of Japan's electricity) dramatized the potential dangers of nuclear power. Since then fears have not decreased, in part because 92 percent of U.S. nuclear power plants that were operating in 1996 had since broken U.S. federal safety regulations (*Harper's*, April 2001, 17). At Chernobyl, in 1986, catastrophe *did* strike. Thousands died; hundreds of thousands were forced to evacuate their homes; and the radioactive fallout—the equivalent of ten Hiroshima bombs—permanently poisoned agricultural land the size of the Netherlands. Radioactive fallout spread beyond Ukraine, multiplying the geographical scope and number of those ravaged by the catastrophe's long-term consequences and costs, with the environmental cleanup estimated to require billions of dollars and taking generations to complete.

Political support for nuclear power in Japan has steadily fallen after the series of accidents since 1995, and Green Party environmental activists throughout Europe have led a crusade to shut down nuclear power plants and reactors. The Greens' argument: Nuclear energy produces lethal wastes that endanger future generations for centuries because there is no way to render them harmless, and the meltdown of a nuclear reactor is a catastrophic possibility.

Concerns about the risks of nuclear power extend beyond safety. How and where to dispose of highly radioactive nuclear waste, for example, is an unresolved issue virtually everywhere. For example, at least fifty nuclear weapons are on the ocean's floor out of reach as a result of U.S. and Soviet accidents (*Harper's*, March 2004, 11). There are no safe procedures for handling toxic radioactive nuclear waste, some of which remains dangerous for hundreds of thousands of years. Ironically, after the Cold War ended, the problem compounded since dismantling both nuclear weapons and their production facilities required unavailable means and places of disposal. "Not in my back yard" (NIMBY) is a divisive cry on the global ecopolitical agenda; the Global North prefers to dump waste outside its own territory, and the Global South would prefer not to be the dump—but often is.

A related fear is that countries that do not now possess nuclear know-how might develop nuclear weapons. Most nuclear-energy-generating facilities continue to produce weapons-grade material, specifically highly enriched uranium and plutonium, which is a national security concern because nonnuclear countries may use it to develop nuclear weapons. It was this concern that prompted the United States (with the help of South Korea and Japan) to give North Korea—a longtime political-military adversary—nuclear reactors less susceptible to nuclear weapons production than those North Korea admitted in late 2002 that it was attempting to develop secretly.

The Unforgiving Cost of Nuclear Power Failure Using nuclear power to generate energy appears inexpensive and cost-efficient, but involves risks, not only increasing the probability of nuclear weapons proliferation but also the potential of producing damage of toxic poisons to the environment. Show here is the town of Pripyat, Ukraine, which was abandoned after the Chernobyl accident. Rather than learning from this lesson, and despite strong opposition from the public, in 2001 Russia prepared to open its borders to become the largest international repository for radioactive nuclear wastes, in the hope of earning $21 billion over the next two decades (Tyler 2001).

In a political world in which growing population means growing demand for energy, food, and other resources only the environment and technology can provide, the politics of scarcity becomes central. What countries do to try to meet their needs has consequences for everyone everyplace, because they automatically will influence how the global commons evolves and the prospects for preserving the global environment. For example, the World Resources Institute notes that global energy use has increased 70 percent since 1976 and is expected to increase at more than 2 percent annually for the next fifteen years. Even though this will provide people with more energy for services such as refrigeration and transportation, there is a costly externality—it will raise the greenhouse gas emissions that contribute to the danger of global warming about 50 percent (WRI 2004, www.wri.org, May 17, 2004). Let us look at the concerns that the linkage between energy use and environmental damage raise.

THE ECOPOLITICS OF THE ATMOSPHERE

The scores of government negotiators and nongovernmental representatives who converged on Rio de Janeiro in 1992 came in the wake of the hottest decade on record. For years scientists had warned that global warming—the gradual rise in world temperature—would cause destructive changes in world climatological patterns and that rising sea levels, melting glaciers, and freak storms would provoke widespread changes in the globe's political and economic systems and relationships. Perhaps because they had been burned by the chronic heat wave throughout the 1980s, negotiators agreed at Rio to a Framework Convention on Climate Change whose purpose was to address the human causes of climate change by reducing emissions of carbon dioxide and other greenhouse gases. Since then, fears have not subsided. The year 2001 was the warmest on record, and because of this, alongside hurricanes and tropical storms well above annual averages, the 2002 UN World Summit in Johannesburg included in its sixty-five-page plan for action heavy emphasis on controlling the sources of global warming.

In recent years, the world's top climate scientists have concluded that the extent of climate change is greater than once believed and furthermore, that evidence shows a discernible human influence. In response to many ecological alarm bells, the cry for greater attempts to curb the pollutants blamed for global warming has risen.

Climate Change

Major gaps in our knowledge of climate change remain, but few climate scientists think the world can afford to wait for answers. The changes are substantial and threatening. Most climatic scientists in this epistemic community of experts believe that the gradual rise in the earth's temperature, especially evident since the late eighteenth century when the invention of power-driven machinery produced the Industrial Revolution, is caused by an increase in human made gases that alter the atmosphere's insulating effects. The gas molecules, primarily carbon dioxide (CO_2) and chlorofluorocarbons (CFCs), form the equivalent of a greenhouse roof by trapping heat remitted from Earth that would otherwise escape into outer space. As these gases are released into the atmosphere they have created a **greenhouse effect** that has caused the global temperature to rise. As shown in Figure 10.4, the temperature on the Earth's surface has increased nearly a half degree since 1950; thirteen of the hottest years since record-keeping began in 1866 have occurred since 1987, with 2003 matching 1998 as the world's hottest average temperatures at 58.03 degrees Fahrenheit—1.03 degrees warmer than the 124-year world average.

The globe's temperature is now between 0.3 and 0.6 degrees Celsius higher than it was in 1880 and is projected to further increase by 3.6 degrees Celsius by 2100 if preventive action is not taken (Soroos 2001). Although CO_2 is the princi-

■ **greenhouse effect**
the phenomenon producing planetary warming when gases released by burning fossil fuels act as a blanket in the atmosphere, thereby increasing temperatures.

FIGURE 10.4
Rising Average Global Temperatures at the Earth's Surface since 1867

The World Meteorological Organization (WMO) monitors average global surface temperatures at thousands of sites around the world. Its records show that so-called global warming is not a myth. For nearly 140 years, the globe's temperature has seesawed up and down, usually by tiny fractions of degrees. But since the mid-1970s, the mercury has largely been on the rise, and the WMO predicts that the average global surface temperature could jump 3.6 degrees Celsius by the end of the twenty-first century—more than triple the rise of the past one hundred years.

Note: Five-year averages of global temperatures.
SOURCE: Intergovernmental Panel on Climate Change (IPCC), as cited by the World Resources Institute (www.wri.org, May 21, 2004).

pal greenhouse gas, concentrations of methane in the atmosphere are growing more rapidly. Methane gas emissions arise from livestock populations, rice cultivation, and the production and transportation of natural gas. To many scientists' alarm, the largest concentrations of methane are not in the atmosphere but locked in ice, permafrost, and coastal marine sediments. This raises the probability that warming will cause more methane to be released into the atmosphere, which would then accelerate the process because of methane's strong warming potential.

While some scientists believe that the rise in global temperature is part of the cyclical change the world has experienced for tens of thousands of years and that cold water needs to be poured on all the "hot air," finding that it is "a climate myth" (Kunzig 2003), that view has been steadily discredited. Since 1988, hundreds of atmospheric scientists from around the world organized several UN agencies to study global climate change. The team, known as the Intergovernmental Panel on Climate Change (IPCC), first conclusively stated in 1995 its belief that global climate trends are "unlikely to be entirely due to natural causes," that humans are to blame for at least part of the problem, and that the consequences are likely to be very harmful and costly. The implications were self-evident: Without significant efforts to reduce the emission of greenhouse gases, the increase in global temperatures by the year 2100 could be equivalent to that which ended the last ice age. Even at the lower end of the panel's estimates, the rise would be faster than any experienced in recorded human history.

Global climate change was elevated to the top of the international agenda (Luterbacker and Spinz 2001) as many countries expressed their appreciation of the need to respond to fresh evidence that temperatures were rising faster than previously thought—"faster and higher than most experts feared only a short time ago—faster, in fact than at anytime during the past 10,000 years" (James 2001b). According to the IPCC, global warming is not coming, it's here, and recent evidence suggests that a more dire climatic heating—a catastrophic abrupt climate change more dramatic than anything resembling the decades or even centuries of gradual change—is likely (*Harper's,* May 2004, 26).

> Many strange things are happening. The seasons are changing, rainstorms are becoming more intense, sea levels are rising, mighty glaciers are receding, the permafrost (by definition, the permanently frozen subsoil in the polar regions) is thawing, trees are flowering earlier, insects are emerging sooner, and so on. . . . More people are projected to be harmed than benefited by climate change, even for global mean temperature increases of less than a few degrees centigrade. (Herbert 2001, A7)

According to this constructed evidence generated in the spirit of **behavioralism** (see Chapter 2), the world has already entered a period of climatic instability likely to cause widespread economic, social, and environmental dislocations over the twenty-first century, because government leaders have not "responded to the problem with the sense of urgency that is called for [inasmuch as] carbon dioxide doesn't just float away in a day or two. It remains in the atmosphere for more than 100 years. The consequences of our failure to act will last for centuries" (Herbert 2001). The effects of continued temperature rises could be both dramatic and devastating:

- Sea levels could rise up to three feet, mostly because of melting glaciers and the expansion of water as it warms up. That will flood vast areas of low-lying coastal land, including major river deltas; most of the beaches on the U.S. Atlantic coast; part of China; and the Maldive Islands, the Seychelles, and the Cook and Marshall Islands. More than 1 million people could be displaced, and 30 million would be put at risk of at least one flood per year.
- Winters would get warmer and warm-weather hot spells (such as the 1995 summer heat wave that killed five hundred people in Chicago) would become more frequent and more severe.
- Rainfall would increase globally, but only the areas already prone to flooding would flood more often and more severely, with freak storms such as the 1997 El Niño surge of storms in the Pacific and the flooding in the Dakotas becoming more common. Since water evaporates more easily in a warmer world, drought-prone regions would become even dryer. As oceans heat, hurricanes, which draw their energy from warm oceans, would become even stronger.
- Entire ecosystems would vanish from the planet, and a hotter earth would drive some plants to higher latitudes and altitudes and require farmers to irrigate and change their crops and agriculture practices.
- The combination of flooding and droughts would cause tropical diseases such as malaria and dengue fever to flourish in previously temperate regions that were formerly too cold for their insect carriers.

■ **behavioralism**
an approach to the study of human and international behavior relying on scientific methods to test hypotheses to provide evidence about the questions investigated; the theory that is accepted is the one repeated tests have shown to be correct.

MAP 10.2
Global Warning about Global Warming: Who's to Blame?
This map shows the yearly carbon dioxide emissions in tons for each person in each country. The Kyoto Protocol of 2001 needed the support of countries accounting for 55 percent of greenhouse-gas emissions to come into force, and it received it by a vote of 190 to 1 (the United States). The United States, which is responsible for most greenhouse gases, claimed it wanted nothing to do with the treaty: "Other countries have chosen their path," one senior U.S. negotiator belched, "and our answer is still 'No'" (*Economist*, November 17, 2001). The fight against global warming persists despite the 2002 rejection of the Kyoto Protocol by the United States. President George W. Bush's stance infuriated "other nations, since the U.S. is by far the biggest polluter on the planet. With only 4 percent of the world's population, America produces 25 percent of the world's carbon dioxide from fossil fuels and 27 percent of its greenhouse gases" (www.worldwatch.org, May 17, 2004).

SOURCE: From *TIME*, April 9, 2001, p. 30–31. Copyright © 2001 TIME, Inc. Reprinted by permission.

Climate-Change Culprits

The politics of agreements to reduce the threat of global warming are divisive. The economics and financial stakes are enormous and almost every proposal generates stiff opposition. CO_2 emissions from the burning of fossil fuels have climbed steadily, rising fourfold since 1950. The high-income Global North states are the principal sources of global carbon emissions, accounting for three-fourths of global CO_2 emissions; the United States emits more CO_2 into the atmosphere than any other state, about 20 percent for each person of human-made sources of greenhouse gases behind global warming, using sixteen times as much energy per person as India (*Economist*, May 10, 2003, 90). In large measure because of its big buildings, millions of cars, and relatively inefficient industries, the U.S. CO_2 emissions for each person are nearly those in all Western Europe, and five times the world average (see Map 10.2). Elsewhere, China is a

Cold Comfort for Global Warming Global emissions of carbon dioxide and other greenhouse gases are rising and contributing to global warming. If the earth continues to heat, oceans will rise and land will be submerged. "Altogether, the ice cap has shrunk by 250 million acres, an area the size of California and New York combined" (*New Yorker*, November 17, 2003, 63). This meltdown raises the specter of collapsing ice shelves, disappearing glaciers, impermanent permafrost, and rising sea levels. Pictured here is the Bering Glacier at the edge of Vitus Lake in Alaska, which according to Greenpeace has shrunk about 40 feet in length during the past century due to global warming. An even more dramatic indicator of the effect of global warming began on January 31, 2002, when the Larsen B patch of floating ice shelf in Antarctica—thirty to forty miles across (the size of Rhode Island), weighing 500 billion tons and seven hundred feet thick—collapsed from warming temperatures in less than a month (Stott 2002). The U.S.-based National Snow and Ice Data Center described it as "the largest single event in a series of retreats by ice shelves in the peninsula over the last 30 years."

---

major and growing source of concern because coal emits more atmospheric pollutants than other fossil fuels, and three-fourths of China's energy for its fast-growing economy comes from coal. China now accounts for about 10 percent of all greenhouse gas emissions, making it the fastest-growing major contributor to global warming.

Coal is a major source of atmospheric sulfur and nitrogen oxides. These pollutants return to Earth, typically after traveling long distances, in the form of **acid rain,** which adds to the acidification of lakes, the corrosion of materials and structures, and the impairment of ecosystems. Acid rain is a serious problem in much of China. Because the oxides that cause it are also transboundary pollutants, China's domestic energy policies have become a major irritant in its relations with its neighbors, particularly South Korea and Japan. Nonetheless, China plans to increase the amount of coal it burns by nearly 900 million tons a year by 2010. Other Asian states are following in its path, including populous In-

■ **acid rain**
precipitation that has been made acidic through contact with sulfur dioxide and nitrogen oxides.

dia, which, like China, has sizable coal deposits. Already China and India account for 18 percent of global greenhouse emissions, and their combined share of CO_2 emissions is expected to grow. "Human activity has now added more than 200 billion tons of carbon to the atmosphere since 1950. Among industrial nations, responsible for 45 percent of global carbon emissions, output increased 8.1 percent between 1990 and 1998. The United States, the world's leading emitter with 27 percent of the overall total, saw output rise 11.8 percent between 1990 and 1998. . . . Developing countries held a 41 percent share of global carbon emissions, and saw a 39 percent rise in output between 1990 and 1998" (*Vital Signs 1999*, 60). Hence, global warming will remain a "hot topic" on the global agenda.

To combat the danger of accelerating global warming, more than 160 states signed the 1992 UN Framework Convention on Climate Change, which sought to contain greenhouse gases at levels to avoid threatening climate change and aimed to return emissions to 1990 levels. But that agreement did not go far enough, and most industrial countries missed their targets for reductions. When many predicted that yearly CO_2 emissions would climb about 50 percent by 2010—49 percent above 1990 levels, the 1997 Kyoto Protocol was reached, requiring 28 industrial countries to reduce their current greenhouse gas emissions by about 50 percent between the years 2008 and 2012. If it had been followed, the United States would have cut emissions by 7 percent, the European Union by 8 percent, and Japan by 6 percent; and the protocol asked China, India, and other developing economies to voluntarily set sizable reduction targets.

The UN's Framework Convention on Climate Change entered into force in 1994, and ten years later 179 countries had ratified that treaty (with only the United States, at the peak of its power and unilateral defiance of global opinion, refusing to sign it). For the first time, that convention required industrialized Global North states to cut emission of gases linked to global warming, and rescued the 1997 Kyoto Protocol. But the United States shocked the world when it refused go along, claiming the convention would hurt the U.S. economy. President George W. Bush labeled the treaty "fatally flawed," explaining, "We will work together, but it's going to be what's in the interest of our country, first and foremost." Bush's hard line stunned environmentalists who were exasperated and enraged by the fact the U.S. carbon dioxide emissions had risen 13 percent in the 1990s (*U.S. News & World Report*, March 26, 2001, 7). The Bush administration's rejection of global opinion outraged U.S. allies, such as the European Union and Japan, which ratified the Kyoto Treaty because they and all other countries calculated that the cost of slowing emissions to reduce the threat of climate change would be much lower than the staggering long-term costs of inaction.

Ozone Protection

The story of climate change is similar to states' efforts to cope with the depletion of the atmosphere's protective **ozone layer.** In this case, however, an international **regime** has emerged, progressively strengthened by mounting scientific evidence that environmental damage was directly caused by human activity.

Ozone is a pollutant in the lower atmosphere, but in the upper atmosphere it provides the earth with a critical layer of protection against the sun's harmful ultraviolet radiation. Scientists have discovered a marked depletion of the ozone

■ **ozone layer**
the protective layer of the upper atmosphere over the earth's surface that shields the planet from the sun's harmful impact on living organisms on the planet.

■ **regime**
norms, rules, and procedures for collective, cooperative action agreed to by a set of states.

layer—most notably an "ozone hole" over Antarctica that has grown larger than the continental United States, and they have conclusively linked the thinning of the layer to CFCs—a related family of compounds known as halons, hydrochlorofluorocarbons (HCFCs), methyl bromide, and other chemicals. Depletion of the ozone layer exposes humans to health hazards of various sorts, particularly skin cancer, and threatens other forms of marine and terrestrial life.

Scientists began to link halons and CFCs to ozone depletion in the early 1970s. Even before their hypotheses were conclusively confirmed, the **United Nations Environment Programme (UNEP),** a UN agency created in the aftermath of the 1972 Stockholm conference, sought some form of regulatory action. Despite scientific uncertainty and policy differences, the 1987 landmark Montreal Protocol on Substances that Deplete the Ozone Layer treaty was signed and "initiated dramatic declines in CFC output, which is many times below peak production years, the late 1980s." World CFC production between 1989 and 1999 declined 86 percent (*Vital Signs 2002*, 55). International cooperation for the construction of regimes sometimes works. However, in spite of reductions in CFCs over the past decade, the ozone hole over Antarctica continues to expand and under the current international regime depletion of the protective ozone shield is expected to accelerate before it begins to regenerate itself. Although production of CFCs in the Global North declined sharply in the 1990s as the largest producers (and consumers) prepared for their complete phase-out, production in the Global South surged, and increased demand for refrigerators, air conditioners, and other products using CFCs will offset the gains realized by stopping production in the Global North. Developed countries agreed to provide aid to help the developing countries adopt CFC alternatives, but have failed to provide all of the resources promised. Without this support, many in the Global South may not be able to keep their end of the global bargain. Meanwhile, a significant illegal trade in both virgin and recycled CFCs has emerged, threatening to further undermine the positive effects of the ozone regime.

Having scientific evidence and an active NGO epistemic community to actively popularize it, many believe, is what made the ozone initiative successful. Can it serve as a model for breakthroughs on other issues, notably climate change? Can environmental threats be given higher priority than vested interests? Again, consider the example of global warming. "There's a better scientific consensus on this than any other issue I know—except maybe Newton's second law of dynamics," observed D. James Baker of the U.S. National Oceanic Administration. "Man has reached the point where his impact on the climate can be as significant as nature's" (Warrick 1997).

Global efforts to avert the tragedy of the commons on atmospheric issues are inadequate. Continued conflicts are predicated on efforts to negotiate new treaties to protect forests and the earth's biological heritage. The same is true with respect to pollution in the world's mountains. The UN designated 2002 the International Year of Mountains, highlighting the importance of mountains as the source of rich plant and animal life and more than half the world's fresh water. Mountains and highlands cover about a quarter of the globe and are home to 10 percent of the world's population, or 60 million people. According to the UN, mountains are the "water towers of the world," supplying more than half of the world's population; but that supply is endangered, because twenty-three of the globe's armed conflicts in 2002 were being fought in mountainous areas, destroying the environment.

■ **United Nations Environment Programme (UNEP)** a UN agency created in 1972 to study environmental deterioration and propose regulations to protect the global environment.

THE ECOPOLITICS OF FORESTS AND BIODIVERSITY

Forests are critical in preserving the Earth's biodiversity and to protecting the atmosphere and land resources. For these reasons they have been a rising ecological issue on the global agenda. Some rules have emerged to guide international behavior in the preservation of **biodiversity,** but issues concerning forests have proven much more difficult to address.

■ **biodiversity**
the variety of life on earth.

Shrinking Forests and Dust Bowls

■ **deforestation**
the destruction of forests.

Trends since the 1980s point toward considerable **deforestation** in the United States and throughout much of the Global South. Worldwide, over the past eight thousand years the World Resources Institute estimates almost half of the forests that once covered the Earth have been converted for ranching farmland, pastures, and other uses, and that "one-fifth of the Earth's original forest remains in large, relatively natural ecosystems—what are known as 'frontier forests.'" Forest loss is most severe in the tropics of Asia (30 percent) and Africa and South America (20 percent), which add to the total loss for the world (about 22 percent) (www.wri.org, May 17, 2004). Destruction of tropical rain forests in such places as Brazil, Indonesia, and Malaysia is a matter of special concern, since much of the world's genetic heritage is found there.

Deforestation Destruction of the world's forests contributes to climate change through global warming and threatens the earth's biodiversity and genetic heritage. Lumbering for commercial purposes to meet the rising global demand for wood for building construction and for fuel exacts a toll on forests, but deforestation due to the expansion of agriculture to meet the needs of a growing population may be a more critical threat.

The representatives sent to the 1992 Earth Summit hoped to secure an easy victory on a statement of principle for global forest conservation. But opposition quickly developed to the principle that the global interest makes all countries responsible for protecting national forests. The Global South—led by Malaysia, a principal exporter of tropical wood products—objected especially vigorously to the socially constructed view that the world's forest were a common property resource, the "common heritage of mankind." These developing countries feared that legally accepting this view would enable the Global North to interfere with the local management of their tropical forest resources. In the end, the Earth Summit backed away from the goal of establishing international guidelines for trade in "sustainably managed" forest products. The situation today remains largely unchanged, even though the International Tropical Timber Organization (ITTO), dominated largely by the timber interests centered in the Global North, continues to be the principal global forum for addressing the transnational issue (of trade) in timber products.

Meanwhile, high population growth rates, industrialization, and urbanization increase pressure to farm forests and marginal land poorly suited to cultivation. This has led to deforestation and **desertification,** which turn an increasing portion of the earth's landmass into deserts useless for agricultural productivity or wildlife habitats. "The world is running out of fresh water. There's water everywhere, of course, but less than three percent of it is fresh, and most of that is locked up in polar ice caps and glaciers, unrecoverable for practical purposes. Lakes, rivers, marshes, aquifers, and atmospheric vapor make up less than one percent of the earth's total water, and people are already using more than half of the accessible runoff. Water demand, on the other hand, has been growing rapidly—it tripled worldwide between 1950 and 1990—and water use in many areas already exceeds nature's ability to recharge supplies. By 2025, the demand for water around the world is expected to exceed supply by fifty-six percent" (Finnegan 2002, 44). With rising population and consumption, "water availability is likely to become one of the most pressing and contentious resource issues of the twenty-first century. One third of the world's population lives in countries already experiencing moderate to high water stress, and that number could rise to two-thirds in the next thirty years without serious water conservation measures and coordinated watershed planning among water users" (WRI, www.wri.org, May 17, 2004).

Soil degradation has stripped billions of acres of the earth's surface from productive farming; 4 billion acres of top soil are estimated to erode worldwide each year (*Harper's,* June 2000, 23). Soil erosion and pollution are problems both in densely populated developing countries and in the more highly developed regions of mechanized industrial agriculture. "Since 1950, 11 percent of the planet's vegetation [approximately 2.9 billion acres], has suffered land degradation" (Crump 1998, 78). Map 10.3 shows the regions of the globe where desertification is occurring most rapidly. Based on previous trends, it has been estimated that an area of one-fourth to one-half of an American football field is deforested each time another person is added to the world population (J. Cohen 1995, 338). This means that the addition of another billion people will require as much as 2.5 million square kilometers of additional land for food production and other uses.

In the Global North, reforestation has alleviated some of the danger. This is not the case in many cash-starved Global South countries, however, which ea-

■ **desertification**
the creation of deserts due to soil erosion, overfarming, and deforestation, which converts cropland to nonproductive, arid sand.

From Farmland to Dustbowl Desertification has hit many areas hard, such as this once productive soil.

gerly sell timber for income and to make room for their growing populations, seemingly without concern for the long-term consequences of the destruction of their forests. The World Wide Fund for Nature (WWFN), a London-based environmental NGO, called 1997 "the year the world caught fire," complaining that more tropical forests were deliberately burned that year than in any other year in recorded history, 80 percent by multinational corporations (MNCs) clearing land for planting or development. Up to 12.4 million acres of forest were burned in Indonesia and Brazil alone in what the WWFN termed a "planetary disaster that is destroying our insurance for the future."

The clearing and burning of tropical rain forests to make room for farms and ranches is doubly destructive. From the viewpoint of climate change, green plants remove CO_2 from the atmosphere during photosynthesis. So, the natural processes that remove greenhouse gases are destroyed when forests are cut down, and, as the forests decay or are burned, the amount of CO_2 discharged into the atmosphere increases.

Biodiversity

Biodiversity, or biological diversity, is an umbrella term that refers to the earth's variety of life. Technically it encompasses three basic levels of organization in living systems: genetic diversity, species diversity, and ecosystem diversity. Until

MAP 10.3
Loss of Forest and Ground to Deserts

Deforestation and desertification are global phenomena, destroying vast stretches of green forests and fields and turning them into brown deserts. This map displays the extent to which certain regions are experiencing desertification or lost, degraded dry lands as the result of climate change and exploitative agricultural overgrazing and the lack of conservation efforts. Deforestation stems from the same by-products or externalities resulting from industrialization and the spread of urban suburbs to the countryside. Worldwide, each year more than 10 million acres of farmland are becoming unproductive deserts (Seck 1999, 9), and tropical forests in Central and South America, Africa, and Southeast Asia are being cleared at an alarming rate. The 1999 UN Convention to Combat Desertification (CCD) seeks to stop the spread of deserts, which now cover 2 million square miles inhabited by one-third of the world's population. All countries voted in favor of this treaty, with only the United States opposing it (www.un.org, June 2, 2004).

SOURCE: Originally developed from map located on U.S. Department of Agriculture website at www.nrcs.usda.gov.

Online map with critical thinking questions

---

recently, public attention has been focused almost exclusively on preserving species diversity, including old growth forests, tall grass prairies, wetlands, coastal habitats, and coral reefs.

Forests, especially tropical forests, are important to preserving biodiversity because they are home to countless species of animals and plants, many of them still unknown. Scientists believe that the global habitat contains between 8 and 10 million species. Of these, only about 1.5 million have been named, and most of them are in the temperate regions of North America, Europe, Russia, and Australia (Edwards 1995, 215). Destruction of tropical forests, where two-thirds to three-fourths of all species are believed to live, threatens the destruction of much of the world's undiscovered biological diversity and genetic heritage. There exists overwhelming, alarming evidence that environmental deterioration is destroying a wide range of living organisms. One study by scientists predicted in 2004 that global warming could drive to extinction up to 37 percent of all living species by the mid-twenty-first century (Gugliotta 2004, A6). Another study ominously concluded that "current extinction rates are 100 to 1,000 times higher than prehuman levels, and projected losses of habitat from land conversion . . . will probably push this rate higher still" (WRI, www.wri.org/trends, December 12, 2004).

Many experts worry that the globe is relentlessly heading toward major species extinction. Of the 242,000 plant species surveyed by the World Conservation Union, some 33,000, or 14 percent, are threatened with extinction, mainly as a result of clearing land for housing, roads, and industries. Others doubt the imminence of a massive die-out, estimating that only a small fraction of the earth's species have actually disappeared over the past several centuries. Indeed, optimistic cornucopians argue that species extinction may not be bad news, as new species may evolve that will prove even more beneficial to humanity (McKibben 1998).

Threats to biodiversity have implications for all species, some of which face increasing competition for survival from nonnative species entering their local habitats through the cross-border transportation facilitated by globalization. The problem parallels other threats to other collective-goods kinds of resources, but biodiversity's distributional characteristics also make it unique. In particular, because so much of the earth's biological heritage is concentrated in the tropics, the Global South has a special interest in this issue. Moreover, the Global South also has a growing concern about protecting its interest in the face of the recent surge of MNCs to reap profits from the sale of marketable products, based on the claim that the genetic character of the many species of plants and animals should be considered a part of the global commons and therefore available for commercial use by all, for their medical benefit.

The rapid growth of biotechnology has added incentives for preserving the earth's biological diversity so as to maintain a wide gene pool from which to develop new medical and agricultural products. MNCs in the Global North are major players in the so-called **enclosure movement** geared to privatize and merchandise the products derived from plant and animal genes that are the genetic bases for sustained life. In India, for example, products from the neem tree have been used for medicine, contraception, toiletries, timber, fuel, and insecticide. In 1985 U.S. and Japanese firms began patenting a variety of neem compounds that Indians never patented. Now, local Indian populations must compete with MNCs for neem-derived products, often at sharply higher prices.

Pharmaceutical companies in particular have laid claim to Global South resources. They actively explore plants, microbes, and other living organisms in tropical forests for possible use in prescription drugs. Ten of the globe's twenty-five top-selling drugs are derived from "natural biological sources" (UNEP www.un.org, December 10, 2004).

Biogenetical engineering of harvests threatens to disrupt established trade and profits because most transgenetically altered foods and crops (primarily

■ **enclosure movement**
the claiming of common properties by states or private interests.

soybeans, beef, corn, and cotton) derived from the Global South are produced in North America and later exported for sale abroad in other countries' grocery stores. For example, food suppliers increasingly must acquire primitive germ plasma (the genetic material containing hereditary information) from the Global South to produce genetically altered seeds for the international market. Such seeds are patented and as private property can be sold back to Global South consumers. Most genetically altered seeds require expensive additives such as chemical fertilizers and pesticides that often are environmentally as well as financially costly. To compound the problem, when farmers in the Global South rely on hybrid varieties and genetically altered seeds, the risk increases that old varieties will disappear.

Biogenetic engineering threatens to escalate the loss of global diversity. Biological resources—animal and plant species—are distributed unevenly in the world. Map 10.4 shows the location of major "biodiversity bastions" where more than half the earth's species are found, primarily tropical wilderness territories laden with plant and animal species covering only 2 percent of the land. It also shows the location of "biodiversity hot spots," where human activity threatens to disturb and potentially destroy many species that international law defines as **collective goods,** a resource for all humanity. According to the UN, about fifty thousand plant and animal species become extinct each year. This issue will intensify as the global community wrestles with the ethics of biodiversity preservation and management policies. The issue is also likely to influence and possibly poison relations between the Global North, where transgenetic crops are manufactured, and the Global South.

■ **collective goods**
goods such as safe drinking water from which everyone benefits.

TOWARD PRESERVATION: THE INTERNATIONAL RESPONSE

The 1992 Earth Summit in Stockholm was precedent setting because, from it, a separate convention on biodiversity set forth a comprehensive framework for preservation of biodiversity. As finally ratified by 161 countries, the agreement established guidelines for sharing the profits of biotechnology between the Global North and Global South and committed state governments to devise national strategies for conserving species and habitats, protecting endangered species, expanding protected areas and repairing damaged ones, and promoting public awareness of the need to protect the earth's heritage. Since then, the world has attempted to cooperate through concerted efforts to reach agreements and back them with ratified treaties to protect and sustain the global commons.

Given the growing threats to environmental protection that are now recognized, this response is understandable. As documented, there is ample evidence to mobilize for collective action, because there are strong reasons to believe that natural resources are running out. World population continues to grow at rates that threaten to leave less and less for humans to eat. Forests are vanishing and fish stocks are disappearing. The planet's air and water are becoming ever more polluted, as global warming exacerbates all of these alarming trends. The question facing the world is whether the response to date is adequate. International environmental treaties have grown exponentially in the last eighty-five years (see

MAP 10.4
Measuring Environmental Sustainability and Locating Biodiversity Bastions and Endangered Biodiversity Hot Spots

To the left is a ranking of select countries based on an "environmental sustainability index" that measures "dozens of variables that influence the environmental health of economies. One of the strongest determinants, besides wealth, seems to be good governance including a broad commitment to the rule of law" (*Economist*, March 16, 2002, 110). The map provides another picture of the "danger zones" throughout the globe, identifying the estimated number of plant and animal species that are endangered in these biodiversity "hot spots." Biodiversity has become a hot global issue, and the magnitude of the danger has spread geographically, because of biologically rich areas that human activity has disrupted or destroyed. "Scientists describe the current era as the greatest period of mass extinction since the disappearance of the dinosaurs. More than 800 species [of plants and animals] already have disappeared because of the degradation of their environments, and 11,000 more are threatened." (James 2002b, 1).

SOURCE: Environmental sustainability from the *Economist*, January 29, 2001, p. 126. Copyright © 2001 by The Economist Newspaper Ltd. All rights reserved. Reprinted with permission. Further reproduction prohibited. www.economist.com. Map adapted from *TIME*, Dec. 14, 1998, pp. 63–64. Used with permission.

Online map with critical thinking questions

ECOSYSTEM TYPES WITHIN HOT SPOTS
- Tropical rain forest
- Tropical dry forest
- Arid ecosystem
- Temperate forest
- Mediterranean ecosystem
- Grassland
- Desert
- Mangrove

- Biodiversity hot spot
- Tropical wilderness area

Caucasus 1,600
Indo-Burma 7,000
South-Central China Mountains 3,500
Philippines 5,832
Western India and Sri Lanka 2,180
Sundaland 15,000
Eastern Arc Mountains and Coastal Forest, Tanzania and Kenya 1,400
Wallacea 1,500
New Guinea and Adjacent Archipelago
Madagascar/Indian Ocean Islands 8,904
Southwestern Australia 4,331
New Caledonia 2,551
Micronesia and Polynesia 3,334
New Zealand 1,865
Floristic Region

Figure 10.5). However, many skeptics fear that these efforts are too little, too late, and that not enough is being done to save the global commons for future generations.

To be seen in the long-term is whether the state of the global ecological environment is in peril. Many question the ability of today's existing treaties to manage the environmental dangers they are meant to address. Some are weak and introduce expressions of concern without commanding necessary policy changes to remedy the various problems they identify. Of particular concern is the reluctant backing of the globe's superpower, the United States. Of the UN's thirty-one major global environmental agreements, the United States has only ratified ten (*Harper's*, August 2001, 16). Environmental protection activists worry that if the American hegemon refuses to lead, the prospects for strengthening the rules of the environmental preservation regime are dim. The decision by U.S. President George W. Bush in March 2001 that his administration would not regulate power plants' emissions of carbon dioxide, which contributes to global warming (reversing his 2001 campaign promise), and his refusal to ratify the Kyoto Protocol on global warming that was signed by 179 other countries (leaving the United States the only state not to participate in that agreement),

FIGURE 10.5
The Number of International Environmental Treaties since 1921: Protecting the Global Commons?
Recognizing the alarming trends toward environmental deterioration, the international community has taken a number of steps to address the major threats. Shown here is one inventory of the global rise of environmental protection treaties. Recent examples include the 2003 UN Framework Convention on Climate Change (UNFCCC), the UN Convention to Combat Desertification (UNCCD), the Basel Convention on the Control of Transboundary Movements of Hazardous Wastes and Their Disposal, the Stockholm Convention on Persistent Organic Pollutants, the Cartagena Protocol on Biosafety, and the Kyoto Protocol on Global Warming. As environmental problems have grown, so have efforts by the global community to legally contain their damage.
SOURCE: *State of the World 2000*, p. 201. Copyright 2000 Worldwatch Institute; after 1999 to 2005 based on the UN's Treaties in Force (2004–2005 are estimates).

heightened fears throughout the world that meaningful controls of threats to the environment will not materialize.

Trade, the Environment, and Sustainable Development

A contrast may be drawn between free trade and sustainable development. Do these values complement one another, or are they in conflict? The question is especially pertinent in a rapidly globalizing world in which trade increasingly links politics, economics, societies, and cultures in complex interdependencies (see Chapter 8).

Liberal economic theory argues that free trade produces benefits. If all states specialize in the production of goods in which they enjoy comparative advantages and trade them with others who enjoy advantages in other products, all will eventually prosper and new wealth will promote the means to correct past environmental degradation. Going even further, while acknowledging that "trade forces can hurt the global environment," they insist that "trade opening can bring environmental benefits as well [and] just as governments should not subsidize trade to help the environment, neither should they restrict it to avoid harming the environment" (Panagariya 2003, 28).

Environmentalists question commercial liberal economists' logic, especially

The Price of Progress? Smog, produced by the emissions of modern society, covers the city of Los Angeles.

because they see economic growth and environmental protection as goals at cross-purposes. They argue that the focus on profits and production ignores hidden social and environmental costs that ultimately make us poorer, not richer.

Beyond the issue of the gains from and costs of trade, environmentalists and liberal economists differ in their assessments of the wisdom of using trade to promote environmental standards. Liberal economists see such efforts as market distortions, while environmentalists view them as useful instruments for correcting market failures, such as markets' inability to compensate for the "**externalities**" of environmental exploitation (for example, atmospheric pollution by chemical companies). Some countries, however, particularly in the Global South, view the use of trade mechanisms to protect the environment as yet another way in which the rich states block entry into lucrative Global North markets to keep the Global South permanently disadvantaged.

■ **externalities**
the external and often unforeseen costs that derive from policy choices made to produce benefits.

Trade-offs must sometimes be made between goals that, in principle, all seem designed to increase human well-being. However, another interpretation maintains that trade encourages states to live beyond their means. According to some ecologists, trade magnifies the damaging ecological effects of production and consumption by expanding the market for commodities beyond state borders. Countries that have depleted their resource bases or passed strict laws to protect them can easily look overseas for desired products, in ways that shift the environmental stress of high consumption to someone else's backyard. These concerns provoked Leon Brittan, the European Union commissioner for external trade, in 1999 to argue that "the economic case for pursuing the process of trade liberalization is an overwhelming one. But it is impossible to ignore the fact that . . . there are widespread fears of the social and environmental consequences of the combination of liberalization and globalization."

The major issue is whether free trade and sustainable development are compatible or whether they work at cross-purposes. The path from the first Earth summits in Rio de Janeiro in 1992 and Johannesburg in 2002 has been paved with good intentions and high expectations about preserving the environment. However, pledges and promises about safeguarding the planet's ecology in the face of rising world population have *not* significantly improved conditions or expectations about the earth's capacity to expand economic growth while supporting life. When the Johannesburg World Summit on Sustainable Development concluded in September 2002, "threats [were] higher than ever to natural resources such as forests, fish, and clean water and air. The richest one-fifth of mankind—including wealthy minorities in poor countries—[were consuming] energy and resources at such a high rate that providing a comparable lifestyle to the rest of the world's population would require the resources of four planets the size of the earth" (James 2002b, 1). "Conditions are worse," UN Secretary-General Kofi Annan bemoaned, "than they were ten years ago."

To reverse this global circumstance, 180 countries in Johannesburg signed agreements to protect global resources such as biodiversity. However, there emerged no firm commitments to sustainable development that might reconcile the conflicts between financial growth and environmental protection. Also left unresolved were the conflicting interests that separated the profits of MNCs from the value of environmental protection, at a time when "the area covered by tropical forests [was] disappearing at the rate of four Switzerlands every year [and] the global forestry industry [was picking] up $35 billion subsidies every year" (James 2002b, 8).

What happens when everyone does the same thing? The tragedy of the commons suggests a bleak future. Is ruin the destination toward which humankind rushes?

TOWARD SUSTAINABILITY?

"Overall, there are considerable signs that the capacity of ecosystems to continue to produce many of the goods we depend on is declining," the World Resources Institute summarizes (www.wri.org, May 17, 2004). "This is not a sprint, it's a marathon," is how U.S. Secretary of State Colin Powell in 2002 described sustainable development. Although the goal of sustainable development remains distant and frustrations about lost opportunities high, government and nonstate actors' acceptance of the concept continues to inspire creative, environmentally sensitive responses. No one wants to live in an unhealthy polluted environment; quality of life matters, and matters a lot, for rich and poor alike. Think about your dreams—where you would like to visit, perhaps even live. Never to a place where environmental disaster is likely, the number of which is sadly increasing. At least 25 million people became "environmental refugees" ten years ago, "fleeing from hopelessly unlivable environments, and the number is expected to double by 2010, to nearly 8,500 each day" (Worldwatch *Vital Signs Facts,* from www.worldwatch.org. December 6, 2004). Want to be a tourist in those locations? What about the United States, if you are not already a U.S. citizen? It is also "suffering from many environmental problems. Most Americans have become aware of more crowding and stress . . . living in large American cities and encountering increased commuting delays because the number of people and hence cars is increasing faster than the number of freeway lanes," and the environment is collapsing with the possibly that a civilization as most have known it is ending (Diamond 2003).

Environmental decay seems to recognize few borders; it is a worldwide problem, for both poor and for rich countries. That transformation makes protection of the planetary environment a necessity, but the solutions are hard to find when many people put their personal advantage ahead of those of all humanity. "Earth provides enough to satisfy every man's need," the Indian peace activist Mohandas Gandhi explained, "but not every man's greed."

Differences between the rich Global North and the Global South will continue to spark controversy about such issues as the transfer of resources and technology needed to deal with climate change, ozone depletion, biodiversity, and a host of other specific problem areas. With growing populations and rising wealth, the Global South is beginning to face the same serious environmental challenges as the Global North, where consumption levels far exceed those of other states. However, one encouraging trend is that, as the industrialized countries move into the **information age** and their economies shift away from "dirty" manufacturing to much cleaner service-oriented activities, it is likely that the adverse environmental consequences of these advanced countries' economic activities will decline. Trade with other states, nevertheless, will ensure continuing pressures on global resources and the environmental burdens they pose.

Is the world ready for the sacrifices required for balancing the desire for economic growth with the need to protect the earth's regenerative capacity? Because, alongside expanding population growth pressures, "there are strong scientific indications of unsustainability, we must act on behalf of the future—even at the price of today's development. That may be expensive, so it is prudent to try to minimize those risks in the first place. Human ingenuity and a bit of luck have helped mankind stay a few steps ahead of the forces degrading the environment this past half century, the first full one in which the planet has been exposed to industrialization. In the [twenty-first century], the great race between development and degradation could well become a close call" (*Economist,* July 6, 2002, 18). "We need action at all levels—local, national, regional, and international—to promote sustainable development," warned Hans Christian Schmidt, Danish environmental minister, in 2002.

"The ability of states to regulate usage of the global common spaces in the

■ **information age**
the era in which the rapid generation and transfer of information globally through mass communication and the Internet is contributing to the globalization of knowledge.

twenty-first century has far-reaching consequences for the environment and for humankind" (Joyner 2001). In looking at the future, what is decided now will be crucial. Humankind is at a critical historical juncture. The path taken will determine the health of the planet for centuries. The stakes are high. All the pieces in the puzzle—population, environmental, technology policy, and preferences in lifestyles—must be worked on simultaneously, through a global effort, if humanity is to survive and if human security is to be enhanced.

Perhaps the most immediate consequence of rapid population growth alongside the economic expansion driving excessive energy demands and shrinking supplies of natural resources, predicts Michael T. Klare (2001; see also Population Action International 2003), will be a new era of "resource wars" in which future global conflicts will be increasingly fought over access to and supplies of vital natural resources and will occur less frequently over conflicts of interests and ideology in the struggle for power. That proposition serves as an introduction to the next arena in world politics on the global agenda that we shall consider in Part IV: the global character of armed conflict and its management.

KEY TERMS

demography
carrying capacity
tragedy of the commons
ethics
least developed of the less-
 developed countries (LLDCs)
politics
fertility rate
replacement-level fertility
demographic transition
modernization
population implosion
human immunodeficiency virus
 (HIV)
AIDS (acquired immune deficiency
 syndrome)
human development
mulilateral aid

low politics
neo-Malthusians
cornucopians
genetic engineering
transgenetic crops
food security
mercantilism
ecopolitics
realist theory
high politics
neoliberalism
politics of scarcity
environmental security
liberalism
epistemic community
paradigm
sustainable development
relative gains

absolute gains
cartel
coercive diplomacy
greenhouse effect
behavioralism
acid rain
ozone layer
regime
United Nations Environment
 Programme (UNEP)
biodiversity
deforestation
desertification
enclosure movement
collective goods
externalities
information age

SUGGESTED READING

Barnes, Joe, Amy Joffe, and Edward L. Morse. "The New Geopolitics of Oil," *The National Interest* (Winter 2004/Special Energy Supplement): 3–6.

Broadhead, Lee-Anne. *International Environmental Politics: The Limits of Green Diplomacy.* Boulder, Colo.: Lynne Rienner, 2003.

Brown, Lester R. *Plan B: Rescuing a Planet under Stress and a Civilization in Trouble.* New York: Norton, 2003.

Castles, Stephen, and Mark Miller. *The Age of Migration: International Population Movements in the Modern World,* 3rd ed. London: Palgrave Macmillan, 2004.

Dobkowski, Michael N., and Isidor Wallimann, eds. *On the Edge of Scarcity: Environment, Resources, Populations, Sustainability, and Conflict.* Syracuse, N.Y.: Syracuse University Press, 2002.

Firor, John, and Judith E. Jacobsen. *The Crowded Greenhouse: Population, Climate Change, and Creating a Sustainable World.* New Haven, Conn.: Yale University Press, 2004.

Friedmann, S. Julio, and Thomas Homer-Dixon. "Out of the Energy Box," *Foreign Affairs* 83 (November/December 2004): 72–83.

Hollander, Jack M. *The Real Crisis: Why Poverty, Not Affluence, Is the Environment's Number One Enemy.* Berkeley: University of California Press, 2003.

Klare, Michael T. *Resource Wars: The New Landscape of Global Conflict.* New York: Holtzbrinck Academic, 2002.

Longman, Phillip. "The Global Baby Bust," *Foreign Affairs* 83 (May/June 2004): 64–79.

Weart, Spencer R. *The Discovery of Global Warming.* Cambridge, Mass.: Harvard University Press, 2003.

Worldwatch Institute, *State of the World 2005.* New York: W. W. Norton, 2005.

WHERE ON THE WORLD WIDE WEB?

International Data Base
http://www.census.gov/ipc/www/idbnew.html

The U.S. Census Bureau offers you the chance to use their computerized bank of demographic data for all countries of the world. From their home page you can look at the Summary Demographic Data to see totals in population and rates of growth for each country. Click on "Population Pyramids" to compare countries according to their population pyramids. First, choose the United States. What age groups had the largest concentration of people in 2000? Does this change in the year 2025? What about in the year 2050 (when you will probably be retired)? Is there a big difference between male and female populations? Now, choose a country in Africa. How is the pyramid for this country different from the one for the United States? How does it change across time? What conclusions can you draw about the problems each of the countries may face given the number of citizens in different age categories in different time periods?

UNAIDS
http://www.unaids.org/

UNAIDS is a joint program of the UN and a leading advocate for worldwide action against HIV/AIDS. Its mission is to support and strengthen an expanded response to the global AIDS epidemic. UNAIDS devises programs that will prevent the spread of HIV, provide care and support for those affected by the disease, and alleviate the socioeconomic and human impact of the epidemic. Explore the HIV/AIDS epidemic by country and find out about the World AIDS Campaign. What effect do you think AIDS will have on population growth rates? How is the AIDS epidemic affecting economic development?

World POPClock Projection
http://www.census.gov/cgi-bin/ipc/popclockw

The U.S. Census Bureau's World Population Clock projects the world population every second of every day. Look at the number of people in the world. Then, hit the Reload button on the top of your web browser. How many more people were born in the time that it took you to *read* the number of people in the world? Click Reload again. How many more people were born?

Earth Times
http://www.earthtimes.org/

Earth Times is an independent international electronic newspaper devoted to reporting global and national issues relating to the environment, sustainable development, population, human rights, and current affairs. This award-winning site gives you up-to-date reports on and analyses of ecological issues. It is a good resource on current events.

Greenpeace
http://www.greenpeace.org/

Greenpeace is an international nongovernmental organization (NGO) committed to global environmental advocacy. Its operation focuses on protecting the oceans and forests, phasing out use of fossil fuels, and promoting renewable energies in order to stop climate change. Visit this site to see how a nongovernmental actor affects global environmental issues. Find out how you can become a cyberactivist!

WHERE ON THE WORLD WIDE WEB? (continued)

IISDnet
http://www.iisd.org/

The International Institute for Sustainable Development (IISD) has produced a website to help users learn about sustainable development, provide information on controversial topics, explore issues in environmental management, and show how businesses can turn sustainability into a competitive advantage. The site also includes a Sustainable Development Timeline, an especially interesting section. Find it by entering "sustainable development timeline" in the site's search engine. Here you can follow how our society has tried to integrate protection of the environment with the establishment of healthy societies and economies. Is there a specific event that you believe has crystallized global thinking on sustainable development? Which decade do you believe has seen the greatest advances? Follow some of the timeline links and read about the organizations that have been at the forefront of environmental protection.

Climate Change
http://www.nationalgeographic.com/

The National Geographic Society has an extensive website that covers many aspects of the interactions of humans with the environment. Enter the search terms "global warming" and "climate change" in the site's search engine. What are some sample articles that catch your interest? What are examples of climate change affecting a single animal or plant species? How is climate change affecting humans?

Rainforest Action Network
http://www.ran.org

The mission of the Rainforest Action Network is to protect the Earth's rain forests and support the rights of rain forest inhabitants through education, grassroots organizing, and nonviolent direct action. Visit the network's website and learn about the threats to rain forests and read about the campaigns that this group is waging. Learn what you can do to help protect the world's rain forests.

INFOTRAC COLLEGE EDITION

Gardner, Gary. "Religion and the Quest for a Sustainable World." *The Humanist* (March–April 2003).

Luke, Nancy, and Susan Cotts. "Reactions of Developing-Country Elites to International Population Policy." *Population and Development Review* (December 2002).

Lee, Kai N. "Searching for Sustainability in the New Century." *Ecology Law Quarterly* (February 2001).

Postel, Sandra L., and Aaron T. Wolf. "Dehydrating Conflict." *Foreign Policy* (September 2001).

For more articles, enter:
"population" in the Subject Guide, and then go to subdivision "economic aspects"
"population policy" in the Subject Guide
"global warming" in the Subject Guide

Go to http://politicalscience.wadsworth.com/kegley10 to access additional resources related to this chapter.

PART IV

MANAGING GLOBAL CONFLICT

The threat of violence and warfare casts a dark cloud throughout the globe. Humanity lives in fear of aggression from terrorists, a neighboring state, or even their own government, bent on persecuting its citizens because of their nationality or religion. National and international security—freedom from fear of a military attack—remains precarious in the twenty-first century. Millions of people are the victims of aggression, and millions more have had to flee as refugees seeking sanctuary from the ravages of war.

Part IV explores the changing character of armed conflict and war (Chapter 11), looking closely at the growing number of prolonged civil wars in failing states and episodic terrorist attacks throughout the globe that undermine national security and threaten human security. Chapter 12 addresses the national security strategies of states to provide for defense through military expenditures and to produce and import armaments. It discusses the new national security strategies of the great powers in an age of nuclear proliferation, global terrorism, and the rising danger posed by weapons of mass destruction, such as biological and chemical weapons. It also examines how states seek to coerce other states to agree to their demands or to refrain from behaving in an undesired way by such means as economic sanctions or military interventions. Finally, we consider the alternative paths to peace prescribed by the realist (Chapter 13) and liberal (Chapter 14) theoretical traditions.

CHAPTER 11

THE FACE OF TWENTY-FIRST-CENTURY ARMED CONFLICT

TOPICS AND THEMES

- The types of military conflict, past and present
- The causes of armed conflict: Rival theories
- Armed conflict within states: Civil wars, uncivil methods
- The new global terrorism

- **CONTROVERSY** DOES NATIONALISTIC LOVE OF COUNTRY CAUSE WAR WITH FOREIGN NATIONS?
- **CONTROVERSY** CAN THE WAR AGAINST GLOBAL TERRORISM BE WON?

The September 11, 2001, attacks are seen by the U.S. superpower to mark the start of a new age of international terrorism.

Mankind must put an end to war or war will put an end to mankind.
—John F. Kennedy, U.S. president, 1961

Violence only begets conditions that beget future violence.
—Former U.S. President Jimmy Carter, acceptance speech of the Nobel Peace Prize, 2002

In the calm summer of 2001, complacency had taken hold in the zone of peace and prosperity in the Global North, where many thoughtful observers, noting the disappearance of interstate war among the economic giants, began to ask if war was becoming obsolete. That mood and conclusion was shattered shortly thereafter on September 11 when international terrorists destroyed the Twin Towers of the World Trade Center in New York City. The 9/11 attack, the U.S.-led "coalition of the willing" war against Iraq that began in 2003, and the 3/11 terrorist attack in Madrid in 2004 all underscored the persisting tragedy of mass murder and violence. Whether these events marked a new chapter in human history remains to be seen. Was this a new type of warfare—nonterritorial networks of terrorists fighting against established territorial states—or was it a throwback to earlier millennia when that kind of war between states was frequent? Whatever the ultimate consensus, prior hopes for national, international, and human security had vanished. Few claimed they were safe. In daily conversations, a new vocabulary emerged to capture the threatening new realities. Students began to talk a new talk: bedrooms were "ground zero"—a total mess; a mean instructor—"He's a total terrorist"; a disciplined student—"*It* was total jihad." America's most frightening days had become slang and comic relief in an effort to alleviate the fear that violence would and could hurt anyone, anywhere, anytime—a new language to take horrific ideas and make them go away. Given the widespread occurrence of violence in today's world, it is little wonder that so many people think of international politics as the same thing as armed aggression.

war
a condition arising within states (civil war) or between states (interstate war) when actors use violent means to destroy their opponents or coerce them into submission.

conflict
discord, often arising in international relations over perceived incompatibilities of interest.

politics
activities aimed at getting another actor to do something it would not otherwise do.

armed conflict
combat between the military forces of two or more states or groups.

In *On War,* Prussian strategist Karl von Clausewitz advanced his famous dictum that war is merely an extension of diplomacy by other means—"a form of communication between countries," albeit an extreme form. This insight underscores the realist belief that **war** is an instrument for states to use to resolve their conflicts. War, however, is the deadliest instrument of conflict resolution, and its onset usually means that persuasion and negotiations have failed.

In international relations, **conflict** regularly occurs when actors interact and disputes over incompatible interests arise. In and of itself, conflict (like **politics**—the exercise of influence) is not necessarily threatening, because war and conflict are different. Conflict may be seen as inevitable and occurs when two parties perceive differences between themselves and seek to resolve those differences to their own satisfaction. Some conflict results whenever people interact and may be generated by religious, ideological, ethnic, economic, political, or territorial issues; therefore we should not regard it as abnormal. Nor should we regard conflict as necessarily destructive, since it can promote social solidarity, creative thinking, learning, and communication—all factors critical to the resolution of disputes and the cultivation of cooperation (Coser 1956). However, the costs of conflict do become threatening when the parties take up arms to settle their perceived irreconcilable differences. When that happens, violence occurs, and we enter the separate sphere of warfare.

This chapter explores the challenge that armed conflicts pose in world affairs, examining the character, causes, and magnitude of international violence, as well as changes in it over time. It investigates three primary ways that **armed conflict** most often occurs: *wars* between states, *civil wars* within states, and *terrorism*. The next chapters consider the ways in which states and other global actors are attempting to control this global problem.

CONTINUITIES AND CHANGE IN ARMED CONFLICT

behavioralism
the methodological research movement to incorporate rigorous scientific analysis into the study of world politics in order to base conclusions about patterns on measurement, data, and evidence rather than on speculation and subjective belief.

constructivism
a scholarly approach to inquiry emphasizing the importance of agents (people and groups) and the shared meanings they construct to interpret what is perceived to be occurring.

In a world seemingly experiencing constant change, one grim continuity stands out: war and violence, or, in the words of former UN Secretary-General Boutros Boutros-Ghali, a "culture of death." The description remains apt; since 1900 at least seven hundred armed conflicts have been waged, killing millions, creating hordes of refugees, and costing trillions of dollars of lost revenues, as well as untold human misery. The belief that "only the dead will see the end of war" is based on the fact that warfare has been an ugly, almost constant factor in a changing world. In the past 3,400 years, Chris Hedges (2003) calculates, "humans have been entirely at peace for 268 of them, or just 8 percent of recorded history."

Scientists who study war quantitatively from the perspective of **behavioralism** (see Bennett and Stam 2004) have attempted to estimate the frequency of armed conflicts and to ascertain if trends exist in the global system's level of violent conflicts. Different definitions and indicators produce somewhat different pictures of variations over time (as **constructivism** emphasizes they will; see Gleditsch 2004). Various measures converge on the basic trends and patterns, from different periods of measurement. In the long-term (over the past six hundred years), armed conflicts have been continual, with a general trend toward rising incidence. In the relative short-term (since 1950), however, the pattern has shown fewer, but more deadly, armed conflicts. The number of people killed by armed conflicts since World War II is probably twice that of the entire 1900s and perhaps seven times that of the 1800s (Kane 1995, 19; Sivard 1996, 7). Figure 11.1 records the continuities and changes for comparative purposes from these two observation periods. These inventories report in different ways what the mass media tell us: that violence and global insecurity are likely to remain core concerns in the twenty-first century.

The September 11, 2001, terrorist attacks and the war to counter global terrorism in Afghanistan and Iraq cast a dark shadow over public perceptions of the face of contemporary warfare. In the past, most armed conflicts were either between states or civil wars within an existing state. Indeed, between 1946 and 2003, a total of 229 armed conflicts broke out in 148 different locations, and since the Cold War began to thaw in 1989, 116 armed conflicts have occurred in 78 countries. Of those 116 conflicts, only seven were interstate wars between countries while the rest (109) were civil wars within states (20 of which had external intervention by other states) (Eriksson and Wallersteen 2004, 625–627). Until 9/11, most security analysts expected wars between states and, increasingly, civil wars within states, to remain the most common type of organized violence. But that expectation has been shattered. Now military planners face two unprecedented security challenges, described by former U.S. Secretary of State Henry Kissinger in November 2004: "terror caused by acts until recently considered a matter for internal police forces rather than international policy, and scientific advances and proliferation that allow the survival of countries to be threatened by developments entirely within another state's territory." Thus many future armed conflicts are probable, fought by irregular militia and private or semiprivate forces (such as terrorist networks) against the armies of states, or by "shadow warriors" commissioned by states as "outsourced" mercenaries or paid militants (Kibbe 2004) to carry out unpleasant tasks—fighting, interrogation of enemy captives, and assassinations that regular army state soldiers are prohibited from carrying out by the Geneva Convention (see Chapter 14). The characteristics of contemporary warfare appear to be undergoing major transformation, even though many of the traditional characteristics of armed conflict between states and within them continue. The general trends show that

- the proportion of countries throughout the globe engaged in wars has declined
- most wars now occur in the Global South, which is home to the highest number of states, with the largest populations, the least income, and the least stable governments
- the goal of waging war to conquer foreign territory has ceased to be a motive
- wars between the great powers are becoming obsolete; since 1945 the globe has experienced a **long peace**—the most prolonged period in modern history (since 1500) in which no wars have occurred between the most powerful countries.

■ **long peace**
long-lasting periods of great-power peace.

These changes raise questions about why wars occur. What ends motivate human beings to continue to resort to force, given the unspeakable casualties? The

FIGURE 11.1
Two Pictures of the Changing Frequency of Armed Conflicts

Armed conflict between states has been around for as long as sovereign states have existed, as the trend on the left based on one index inventorying 2,566 individual wars *for each decade* since the year 1400 indicates. It shows that the number dropped considerably in the late 1600s in the aftermath of the Thirty Years' War, but has risen sharply in the three centuries since, peaking in the 1960s. Measuring the frequency of armed conflicts each year since 1950 by "the application of different criteria for what constitutes an armed conflict," the trend on the right records a gradual increase in the frequency of armed conflicts until the peak in 1991 (54), after which a decline has taken root. Most of the 229 armed conflicts since 1946 have occurred in the poor and unstable Global South countries and have been long lasting (Eriksson and Wallensteen 2004, 631, 626). Armed conflicts arising from civil wars dominate the global landscape. "Since the 1950s, the number of interstate conflicts (warfare between the governments of two or more countries) has shown no upward or downward trend, while new civil conflicts since 1950 were almost four times higher at their peak in 1990 and since 1995 the incidence has averaged about 12 percent of the globe's countries" (Hegre 2004, 243).

SOURCES: Left: Adapted from "The Characteristics of Violent Conflict since 1400 A.D." by Peter Brecke. Used with permission. Right: University of Hamburg, presented in *Vital Signs 2003*, p. 75; data for 2002–2003 in Eriksson and Wallensteen (2004, 625).

The Wages of War In 2003 the United States ordered thousands of American soldiers to invade Iraq. The goal was deterrence—to disarm Iraq of alleged weapons of mass destruction, to force "regime change" by overthrowing Saddam Hussein, and to preemptively deter an attack on the United States. Many U.S. soldiers paid the ultimate sacrifice. Shown here in April 2004 is an American official unloading coffins of soldiers killed in Iraq.

question provokes a more fundamental set of related questions about the causes of aggression generally. Accordingly, it is useful to review contending theories about the sources from which armed conflicts arise.

RIVAL THEORIES OF THE CAUSES OF AGGRESSION

Throughout history efforts have been made to explain why people resort to violence. Inventories of war's origins (see Cashman 2000; Midlarsky 2000) invariably conclude that they are incomplete, in part because most agree that war is rooted in multiple sources at various **levels of analysis.** For our purposes, the most plausible causes are divided here into three major levels or categories: individuals, states, and the global system.

The First Level of Analysis: Individuals' Human Nature

In a sense, all wars originate from the decisions of the leaders of states or non-state actors such as terrorist organizations. Their choices ultimately determine whether armed conflict will occur (see Chapter 3). We must therefore consider the relationship of war to individuals and their choices, and for this, questions about human nature are central.

The repeated outbreak of war has led some, such as psychologist Sigmund Freud (1968), to conclude that aggression is an instinctive part of human nature

■ **levels of analysis**
the interpretation of the sources of international phenomena that looks separately at the influences of individuals, the characteristics of states, or the global system.

- **intraspecific aggression**
killing members of one's own species.

- **interspecific aggression**
killing members of species other than one's own.

- **realism**
the theory that states are driven to compete for power through war and imperialism because of human nature, which is flawed by the urge to engage in aggression.

- **pacifism**
the liberal idealist school of ethical thought that recognizes no conditions that justify the taking of another human's life, even when authorized by a head of state.

- **survival of the fittest**
a realist concept derived from Charles Darwin's theory of evolution that advises that ruthless competition is ethnically acceptable to survive, even if the actions violate moral commands not to kill.

- **nature versus nurture**
the controversy over whether human behavior is determined more by the biological basis of "human nature" than it is nurtured by the environmental conditions that humans experience.

- **socialization**
the processes by which people learn the beliefs, values, and behaviors that are acceptable in a given society.

that stems from humans' genetic programming and psychological makeup. Identifying *Homo sapiens* as the deadliest species, ethologists (those who study animal behavior in order to understand human behavior) such as Konrad Lorenz (1963) similarly argue that humankind is one of the few species practicing **intraspecific aggression** (routine killing of its own kind), in comparison with most other species, which practice **interspecific aggression** (killing only other species, except in the most unusual circumstances—cannibalism in certain tropical fishes being one exception). Ethologists are joined in their interpretation by those proponents of **realism** who believe that all humans are born with an innate drive for power that they cannot avoid, and that this instinct leads to competition and war. They therefore accept the sociological premise suggested by Charles Darwin's theories of evolution and natural selection: Life entails a struggle for survival of the fittest, and natural selection eliminates the traits that interfere with successful competition, such as **pacifism,** which rejects the right of people to kill in order to obtain power.

Many question these theories on both empirical and logical grounds. If aggression is an inevitable impulse deriving from human nature, then should not all humans exhibit this genetically determined behavior? Most people, of course don't; they ethically reject killing as evil and neither murder nor accept others' killing on behalf of the state or any other cause. In fact, at some fundamental, genetic level, argues Francis Fukuyama (1999a), human beings are built for consensus, not for conflict: "People feel intensely uncomfortable if they live in a society that doesn't have moral rules." In addition, liberal theory and behavioral social science research suggest that genetics fails to explain why individuals may be belligerent only at certain times. Social Darwinism's interpretation of the biological influences on human behavior can be countered by examining why people cooperate and act morally. As James Q. Wilson (1993) argues, Darwinian **survival of the fittest** realist theory overlooks the fact that "the moral sense must have adaptive value; if it did not, natural selection would have worked against people who had such useless traits as sympathy, self-control, or a desire for fairness in favor of those with the opposite tendencies."

Although the **nature versus nurture** controversy regarding the biological bases of aggression has not been resolved (see Nelson 1974; Ridley 2003), most social scientists now strongly disagree with this realist premise that humans are essentially selfish and aggressive and that people murder and kill because of their innate genetic drives to act out aggressively. Instead, war is interpreted as a learned cultural habit. Aggression is a propensity acquired early in life as a result of **socialization.** Therefore, aggression is a learned rather than a biologically determined behavior, and "violent human nature is a myth" (Murithi 2004). The 1986 *Seville Statement*, endorsed by more than a dozen professional scholarly associations, maintains that "it is scientifically incorrect" to say that "we have inherited a tendency to make war from our animal ancestors," "that war or any other violent behavior is genetically programmed into our human nature," "that humans have a 'violent brain,'" or "that war is caused by 'instinct' or any single motivation" (see Somit 1990). Ted Robert Gurr (1970) expresses the thesis, supported by behavioral research, that the "capacity, but not the need, for violence appears to be biologically entrenched in humans."

Individuals' willingness to sacrifice their lives in war out of a sense of duty to their leaders and country is one of history's puzzles. "The fog of war" is what the Russian author Leo Tolstoy and others have called the fact that people will give their lives in struggles, large and small, whose importance and purpose are sometimes not understood. Clearly, this self-sacrifice stems from learned beliefs that some convictions—such as loyalty to the state—are worth dying for. "It has been widely observed that soldiers fight—and noncombatants assent to war— not out of aggressiveness but obedience" (Caspary 1993). This, however, does not make human nature a cause of war, even if such learned habits of obedience taught in military training are grounds for participation in the aggression authorized by others, and even if at times the mass public's jingoistic enthusiasm for aggression against foreign adversaries encourages leaders to start wars.

Human nature is not a direct cause of interstate conflict. How then do we explain the enduring rivalries and the repetitive recourse to genocide in some areas? It is the bloody history of territories such as the Balkans that inspires anthropologists to inquire if territoriality drives human aggression. Could it be that the genocides occurring in Sudan and the Ivory Coast in 2005 stemmed from "an innate human aggression, inherited from our animal ancestors, to possess territory believed to be one's own"? Robert Ardrey (1966), the playwright turned anthropologist, advanced the proposition of human territorial aggression in *The Territorial Imperative*. The controversial best-seller argued that "the territorial instincts of animals apply equally to man. . . . Simply put, Mr. Ardrey's theory proposes that humans, like animals, are compelled by instinct to possess and defend territory they believe belongs exclusively to them" (Levingston 1999). The **territorial imperative** has been resurrected as a theory to account for the kinds of ethnic wars that rage across the globe in so many regions today, especially the war ravaged Middle East.

Also to be questioned is that **national character** drives certain nationalities to aggression. Countries sharing cultural values and identity can express these in different ways and can change. For example, Sweden and Switzerland, once warlike, have managed conflicts without warfare since 1809 and 1815, respectively. In fact, since 1500, one in five countries has never experienced war (Sivard 1991, 20). This suggests that other factors beyond the inborn collective traits of particular peoples better explain why certain countries tend to engage in organized violence. As Ralph Bunche, a U.S. policymaker, argued before the UN, "There are no warlike people—just warlike leaders." "The common people do not go to war of their own accord, but are driven to it by the madness of kings," St. Thomas More advised in the sixteenth century. Thus, war most often occurs because of the choices leaders make, not the preferences of their entire societies.

This idea introduces an important analytic problem. Can the characteristics of cultures and populations within countries in the aggregate, the sum of the parts, predict the behaviors of the individuals within those groups? No. To generalize from the whole to the part is to commit what demographers and statisticians call a logical **ecological fallacy**. Why? Because, unless all members of the same group are exactly alike, the characteristics of the collectivity (the entire state or culture, for example) do not safely predict the beliefs and behaviors of the individuals in the grouping. Do all Americans think alike? All Muslims? All Japanese or Chinese? Hardly. This is racial and cultural stereotyping at its worst. Rarely can we safely generalize from groups to individuals. Likewise, the opposite, what logicians call the **individualistic fallacy**, is also a mental error. We cannot generalize safely about the beliefs or behavior of individual leaders (Adolf Hitler of Nazi Germany, Joseph Stalin of the Soviet Union, George Bush of the United States, or Vladmir Putin of Russia) and ascribe them to the pre-

■ **territorial imperative**
the term coined by anthropologist Robert Ardrey to popularize the proposition that people and nations will defend to the death their territory, just like animals instinctively do.

■ **national character**
the collective characteristics ascribed to the people within a state.

■ **ecological fallacy**
the error of assuming that the attributes of an entire population—a culture, a country, or a civilization— are the same attributes and attitudes of each person within it.

■ **individualistic fallacy**
the logical error of assuming that the population that an individual person has legal authority to govern is representative of the people and opinions of the population governed, so that all of them are necessarily accountable for the vices and virtues (to be given blame or credit) of the leaders authorized to speak for them.

vailing preferences of the collective cultures and states that each of them headed. They are symbols, not samples. Their actions do not tell us much about the opinions and values of the pluralistic populations for whom they speak. Individual guilt is not collective guilt.

What should be obvious is that some of the foreign policy decisions by the leaders able to make them are immoral. Moreover, most of those decisions by countries' leaders are, in hindsight, less wise than mistaken; they fail to conform to the **rational choice** model of decision making (see Chapter 3). In addition, even intelligent leaders and moral leaders are sometimes prone to take unnecessarily high-risk decisions to wage war because they are pressured through **groupthink** by advisers representing large-scale bureaucracies. This observation about the influences on leaders' choices about war and peace directs attention to the domestic factors that encourage some states to engage in foreign aggression.

The Second Level of Analysis: States' Internal Characteristics

Conventional wisdom holds that variations in states' governments, sizes, ideologies, geographical locations, population dynamics, ethnic homogeneity, wealth, economic performance, military capabilities, and level of educational attainment influence whether they will engage in war. Drawing on the possibility suggested by Russian political theorist Peter Kropotkin in 1884 that "the word *state* is identical with the word *war*" and the evidence that war has contributed to the rise of the state (Kegley and Raymond 2002a), we need to examine some theories addressing the internal characteristics of states that influence leaders' choices regarding the use of force. Implicit in this approach to explaining armed conflict at the **state level of analysis** is the assumption that differences in the types or classes of states will determine whether they will engage in war. To argue that the prospects for war are influenced most heavily by national attributes and the types of leaders making policy decisions for states is to challenge the premise of **neorealism** that war's inevitability must be accepted (Hanson 2003), that global circumstances are the most powerful determinants of warfare, and that domestic factors have no influence.

Duration of Independence. New states, not long-lasting states, are the most likely to experience civil wars and engage in foreign wars. Newly independent countries typically go through a period of political unrest following their acquisition of **sovereignty,** as they struggle to resolve long-standing internal grievances and territorial disputes with their neighboring enemies—foreign disputes that frequently provoke great-power **intervention.** The high levels of civil wars and involvement in international conflicts in the Global South are linked to the fact that nearly all these less-developed countries have recently gained independence from colonialism, many through revolutions.

Cultural Determinants, Feminist Theory, and the Decay of Moral Constraints. Countries' behavior is strongly influenced by the cultural and ethical traditions of their peoples. In the state system governed by the rules championed by realism, moral constraints on the use of force do not command wide acceptance. Instead, most governments encourage their populations to glorify the state and to accept whatever decisions their leaders claim are necessary for national

---

■ **rational choice**
the assumption that decision makers make choices through cool-headed calculations of costs and benefits and pick the options that have the best chance of realizing preferred goals.

■ **groupthink**
the propensity for members of a decision-making group to accept and agree with the group's prevailing attitudes, rather than speaking out for what they believe would be the most rational choice.

■ **state level of analysis**
an analytical approach to the study of world politics that emphasizes how the internal attributes of states explain their foreign policy behaviors.

■ **neorealism**
the so-called structural version of realism that explains state conduct as a function of changes in the global system's structure, such as shifts in the distribution of states' military capabilities.

■ **sovereignty**
the legal doctrine that states have supreme authority to govern their internal affairs and manage their foreign relations with other states and IGOs.

■ **intervention**
external interference in a state's internal affairs.

security, including warfare against adversaries. Many scholars believe these kinds of cultural beliefs make violence more probable.

Advocates of the cultural origins of war argue that most people in most societies live an everyday experience of disengagement, or "numbness," which disinclines them to oppose their leaders' decisions to wage war. The modern state thus organizes its society to accept war and "builds a culture that affirms death" and accepts senseless carnage (Caspary 1993). In contrast, critics operating from the perspective of **feminist theories** of international relations argue that the foundation of war worldwide, alongside cultural numbing, is rooted in the masculine ethos of realism, which prepares people to accept war and to respect the warrior as a hero (see especially Enloe 2000 and Tickner 2002). Gender roles, they assert, supported by realist values contribute to the prevalence of militarism and warfare:

> According to feminist critics, international relations theory as it has evolved incorporates "masculinist" prejudices at each of its three levels of analysis: man, the state, and war. Realists are "androcentric" in arguing that the propensity for conflict is universal in human nature ("man"); that the logic and the morality of sovereign states are not identical to those of individuals ("the state"); and that the world is an anarchy in which sovereign states must be prepared to rely on self-help, including organized violence ("war"). Feminist theorists would stress the nurturing and cooperative aspects—the conventionally feminine aspects—of human nature; they would expose the artificiality of notions of sovereignty, and their connection with patriarchy and militarism; and they would replace the narrow realist emphasis on security, especially military security, with a redefinition of security as universal social justice. (Lind 1993, 37)

To feminists and other constructivist theorists about the causes of war who embrace a cultural interpretation, the penchant for warfare does not evolve in a vacuum but is produced by the ways in which societies shape their populations' beliefs and norms. Many governments, through the educational programs they fund in schools and other institutions, indoctrinate values in their political culture that condone the practice of war. Ironically, in a world of diverse national cultures, the messages of obedience and of duty to make sacrifices to the state through such **cultural conditioning** are common. States disseminate the belief that their right to make war should not be questioned and that the ethical principles of religious and secular philosophies prohibiting violence should be disregarded. Consequently, critics stress the existence of powerful institutions that prepare individuals to subconsciously accept warfare as necessary and legitimate.

Poverty. A country's level of economic development also affects the probability of its involvement in war. Indeed, "underdevelopment . . . is a statistically significant predictor of war" (Lemke 2003). As U.S. Secretary of Defense Robert S. McNamara explained in 1966, "there is no question but that there is evidence of a relationship between violence and economic backwardness."

Before we conclude that poverty always breeds war, however, we must note that the *most* impoverished countries have been the least prone to start wars with their neighbors. The poorest countries cannot vent their frustrations aggressively because they lack the military or economic resources to do so. This

■ **feminist theory**
a body of scholarship emerging from the social feminist movement to promote the political equality of women with men, critiquing sexual biases and challenging gender roles that encourage female subordination and warfare.

■ **cultural conditioning**
the impact of national traditions and societal values on the behavior of states, under the assumption that culture affects national decision making about issues such as the acceptability of aggression.

War's Human Impact Innocent noncombatants, especially children and women, are often the primary victims of military conflict in the Global South. At the May 2002 World Summit for Children, the United Nations estimated that about three hundred thousand children under the age of eighteen were made soldiers and forced to fight in wars in more than thirty countries (*Newsweek*, May 13, 2002, 28). Shown here (left) is the ten-year-old son of an Afghani police commissioner carrying an assault rifle nearly as tall as him. The protection of children and women from warfare has usually required humanitarian military intervention by an outside power. Shown on the right are a Somalian mother and child in 1997 waiting with other displaced people for relief supplies delivered by U.S. military aircraft to a refugee camp in Kenya.

---

does not mean that the poorest countries will always remain peaceful. If the past is a guide to the future, then the impoverished countries that develop economically will be those most likely to acquire arms and engage in future external wars. In particular, many studies suggest that states are likely to initiate foreign wars *after* sustained periods of economic growth—that is, during periods of rising prosperity, when they can most afford them (Cashman 2000). This signals danger if countries in the Global South develop rapidly and direct the new resources toward armament, as India and Pakistan chose to do by acquiring nuclear weapons in 1998, rather than investing in sustained development.

The New Geography of Conflict. "Location, location, location"—the geographical roots of armed conflict are now being recognized as an important influence on the probability of instability and warfare (Flint 2004). Geopolitical thinking has resurfaced as national security planners have assigned growing attention to the military consequences of a country's world position and topography. "Increased competition over access to major sources of oil and gas, growing friction over the allocation of shared water supplies, and internal warfare over valuable export commodities have produced a new geography of conflict, a reconfigured cartography in which resource flows rather than political and ideological divisions constitute the major fault lines" (Klare 2001; see also Cincotta, Engelman, and Anastasion 2003 and M. Ross 2004). The UN designated 2002 as the International Year of Mountains (partially because twenty-three of the twenty-seven armed conflicts that the UN identified as occurring in 2002 were being fought in mountainous areas) to address one dimension of the geographical impact on peace and war—how crippling poverty among mountain people and ecological destruction in the world's mountain ranges provide an environment conducive to the resource wars of the future.

Militarization. "If you want peace, prepare for war," realism counsels. It is questionable whether the acquisition of military power leads to peace or to war, but clearly most Global South developing countries agree with the realists' thesis that weapons contribute to their security. They have been by far the biggest customers in the robust global trade in arms and have built huge armies to guard against their neighboring states' potential aggression and to control their own citizens (see Chapter 12).

As Global South countries concentrate their budgets on equipping their militaries, many worry that war will become more frequent before it becomes less so. Militarization has *not* led to peace in the Global South. Will the curse of violence someday be broken there?

One clue comes from examination of the relationship between changes in military capabilities and war that occurred over centuries in Europe. During its transition to the peak of development, Europe was the location of the world's most frequent and deadly wars. The major European states armed themselves heavily and were engaged in warfare about 65 percent of the time in the sixteenth and seventeenth centuries (Wright 1942). Between 1816 and 1945, three-fifths of all interstate wars took place in Europe, with one erupting on average every other year (J. Singer 1991, 58). Not coincidentally, this happened when the developing states of Europe were most energetically arming in competition with one another. Perhaps as a consequence, the great powers—those with the largest armed forces—were the most involved in, and most often initiated, war (Cashman 2000). Since 1945, however, with the exception of war among the now-independent units of the former Yugoslavia, interstate war has not occurred in Europe. As the European countries moved up the ladder of development, they moved away from war with one another (internal conflict is another matter).

In contrast, the developing countries now resemble Europe prior to 1945. If the Global South follows the European pattern, the immediate future may well witness a peaceful, developed world surrounded by a violent, less-developed world.

Economic System. Does the character of states' economic systems influence the frequency of warfare? The question has provoked controversy for centuries. Particularly since Marxism took root in Russia following the Bolshevik Revolution in 1917, communist theoreticians claimed that capitalism was the primary cause of war—that capitalists practice imperialism and colonialism. They were fond of quoting Vladimir Lenin's 1916 explanation of World War I as a war caused by imperialistic capitalists' efforts "to divert the attention of the laboring masses from the domestic political crisis" of collapsing incomes under capital-

■ **communist theory of imperialism**
the Marxist-Leninist economic interpretation of imperialist wars of conquest as driven by capitalism's need for foreign markets to generate capital.

■ **laissez-faire economics**
free markets in which goods are exchanged within minimal management by the state.

ism. According to the **communist theory of imperialism,** capitalism produces surplus capital. The need to export it stimulates wars to capture and protect foreign markets. Thus **laissez-faire economics**—based on the philosophical principle of free markets with little governmental regulation of the marketplace—rationalized militarism and imperialism for economic gain. Citing the demonstrable frequency with which wealthy capitalist societies engaged in aggression, Marxists believed that the best way to end international war was to end capitalism.

Contrary to Marxist theory is commercial liberalism's conviction that free market systems promote peace, not war. Defenders of capitalism have long believed that free market countries that practice free trade abroad are more pacific. The reasons are multiple, but they center on the premise that commercial enterprises are natural lobbyists for world peace because their profits depend on it. War interferes with trade, blocks profit, destroys property, causes inflation, consumes scarce resources, and encourages big government and counterproductive regulation of business activity. By extension, this reasoning continues, as government regulation of internal markets declines, prosperity will increase (see Chapter 9) and fewer wars will occur.

The evidence for these rival theories is, not surprisingly, mixed. Conclusions depend in part on perceptions regarding economic influences on international behavior, in part because alternative perspectives focus on different dimensions of the linkage. This controversy was at the heart of the ideological debate between East and West during the Cold War, when the relative virtues and vices of two radically different economic systems—socialism and capitalism—were uppermost in people's minds.

The end of the Cold War did not end the historic debate about the link between economics and war. This basic theoretical question commands increasing interest, especially given the "shift in the relevance and usefulness of different power resources, with military power declining and economic power increasing in importance" (Huntington 1991).

■ **globalization**
the integration of states, through increasing contact, communication, and trade, to create a holistic, single global system in which the process of change increasingly binds people and states together in a common fate.

Globalization, through which the growing economic interdependence of countries has tightly linked states' growth rates, has intensified the debate about the relationship between trade and international armed conflict. Although "most leaders still cling to the long-standing belief that expanding economic ties will cement the bonds of friendship between and within nations that make resort to arms unfathomable," observe Katherine Barbieri and Gerald Schneider (1999), "in contrast, realist and Marxist critics reject the liberal view" that the opening of free market economies within states and increased levels of trade between them will produce peace (see Chapters 8 and 9). Even though substantial evidence exists to support "the liberals' belief that economic interdependence [and economic and political freedom] have important pacific benefits" (Oneal and Russett 1999), that conclusion is unlikely to be widely accepted by the many poor Global South countries who maintain that under interdependent globalization the wealthy will profit disproportionally from trade, at their expense.

■ **relative gains**
a situation in which some participants to an exchange benefit more than others.

This **relative gains** argument insists that conflict is produced because the benefits of economic exchanges are distributed unequally (the rich get richer and the poor get poorer), and trade-war disputes and even wars are likely to undermine world peace. In addition, the relationship between types of states' political systems, such as democracy and cooperation in international trade, remains an issue of theoretical and policy debate (Mansfield, Milner, and Rosendorff 2002; Dai 2002). The future will tell if free markets and free trade will generate international conflict or cooperation in the globalized twenty-first century. In the meantime, the effects of economic changes such as the globalization of the sale of products worldwide on peace and war continue to provoke interest. For instance, in a tongue-in-cheek extension of this neoliberal logic, columnist Thomas Friedman (1999) advanced the "Golden Arches Theory of Conflict Prevention"—that no two countries have fought a war once McDonald's was present in both countries. Friedman "attributes the phenomenon to the growth of a peaceable middle class. 'People in McDonald's countries didn't like to fight wars anymore. . . . They preferred to wait in line for burgers'" (Stross 2002).

Type of Government. Realist and especially neorealist theories discount the importance of government type as an influence on war and peace. Not so with liberalism, especially **neoliberal theories.** As noted in Chapter 2, the liberal tradition assigns great weight to the kinds of political institutions that states create to make policy decisions, and predicts that the spread of "free" democratically ruled governments will promote peaceful interstate relations. As Immanuel Kant in 1795 argued in *Perpetual Peace*, when citizens are given basic **human rights** such as choosing their leaders through ballots as well as civil liberties such as free speech and a free press, these democracies would be far less likely to initiate wars than would countries ruled by dictators and kings, because a government accountable to the people would be constrained by public opinion from waging war. Kant was joined by other liberal reformers, such as Thomas Jefferson, James Madison, and Woodrow Wilson in the United States—all of whom believed that an "empire of liberty" (as Madison pictured a growing community of liberal democracies) would be one freed of the curse of war, and that if democratic institutions spread throughout the world, the entire past pattern of belligerent international relations would be replaced by a new pacific pattern.

These liberal and neoliberal predictions have been fulfilled by the passage of time since they were first advanced. "We now have solid evidence that democracies do not make war on each other" (Russett 2001). Much research demonstrates that democracies resolve their differences with one another at the bargaining table rather than the battlefield, and that they are more likely to win wars than non-democracies (Choi 2004; Souva 2004). This pattern provides the cornerstone for the **democratic peace** proposition (Ray 1995) holding that, as Bruce Russett summarizes,

> Democracies are unlikely to engage in any kind of militarized disputes *with each other* or to let any such disputes escalate into war. They rarely even skirmish. Pairs of democratic states have been only one-eighth as likely as other kinds of states to threaten to use force against each other, and only one-tenth as likely actually to do so. Established democracies fought *no wars* against one another during the entire twentieth century.
>
> The more democratic each state is, the more peaceful their relations are likely to be. Democracies are more likely to employ "democratic" means of peaceful conflict resolution. They are readier to reciprocate each other's behavior, to accept third-party mediation or good offices in settling disputes, and to accept binding third-party arbitration and adjudication. Careful statistical analyses of countries' behavior have shown that democracies' relatively peaceful relations toward each other are not spuriously caused by some other influence such as sharing high levels of wealth, or rapid growth,

■ **neoliberal theories**
the "new" liberal theories stressing the critical impact of free governments and free trade in promoting peace and prosperity through democratically managed institutions, following the liberal world politics philosophies of Immanuel Kant, Thomas Jefferson, James Madison, and Woodrow Wilson.

■ **human rights**
the political rights and civil liberties recognized by the international community as inalienable and valid for individuals in all countries by virtue of their humanity.

■ **democratic peace**
the liberal theory that lasting peace depends on the deepening of liberal democratic institutions within states and their diffusion throughout the globe, given the "iron law" that democracies do not wage wars against one another.

FIGURE 11.2
The Advance of Electoral Democracy, 1700–2005

For 250 years since 1700, most choices about war were made by monarchs, despots, dictators, and autocrats. That has changed in a major global transformation, occurring in three "waves" in the growth of "electoral democracy" worldwide, with competitive and regular multi-party elections conducted openly without massive voting fraud (see Cederman and Gleditsch 2004), as the figure on the right shows. In 1974 only one in four countries were electoral democracies; today, the number has grown to 88 countries, or 46 percent (Freedom House 2005). Whether this dramatic transformation will produce peace is being tested.

SOURCES: Data for 1700–1950 based on *Global Trends 2005*, by Michael J. Mazarr, p. 107. Copyright © Michael J. Mazaar. Reprinted with permission of Palgrave Macmillan. Data for 1950–2005 based on Freedom House (2005).

or ties of alliance. The phenomenon of peace between democracies is not limited just to the rich industrialized states of the Global North. It was not maintained simply by pressure from a common adversary in the Cold War, and it has outlasted that threat. (Russett 2001, 235)

The growing recognition that ballots serve as a barrier against the use of bullets and bombs by one democracy against another has been inspired by the growth of democratic governance over the past two centuries (see Figure 11.2). "The last two decades of the twentieth century have been dubbed the 'third wave' of democratization, as dictatorial regimes fell in scores of countries. . . . In the 1980s and 1990s. . . . 81 countries took significant steps toward democracy" (UNDP 2002, 1, 14). There is no certainty that liberal democracy will become universal or that the continued growth of democracy will automatically produce a peaceful world order. The fact that leaders in elective democracies are accountable to public approval and electoral rejection does not guarantee that they will not use force to settle disputes with other democracies:

> It was, after all, the democratization of conflict in the nineteenth century that restored a ferocity to warfare unknown since the seventeenth century; the bloodiest war in American history remains the one fought between two (by today's standards flawed) democracies—the Civil War. Concentration camps appeared during another conflict between two limited democracies, the Boer War. World War I was launched by two regimes—Wilhelmine Germany and Austria-Hungary—that had greater representation and more equitable legal systems than those of many important states today. And even when modern liberal democracies go to war they do not necessarily moderate the scope of the violence they apply; indeed, sensitivity to their own casualties sometimes leads to profligate uses of firepower or violent efforts to end wars quickly. Shaky democracies fight each other all the time. . . . We must remind ourselves just how peculiar the wealthy and secure democracies of the West are, how painful their evolution to stability and the horror of war with each other has been. Perhaps other countries will find short-cuts to those conditions, but it would be foolish to assume they will. (E. Cohen 1998, 39)

■ **nationalism**
sentimental devotion to the welfare of one's own nation without concern for the common interest of all nations and states in the global community.

Nationalism. Nationalism—love of and loyalty to a nation—is widely believed to be the cauldron from which wars often spring (Van Evera 1994; see also Chapters 4 and 5). "The tendency of the vast majority of people to center their supreme loyalties on the nation-state," Jack S. Levy explains, is a powerful catalyst to war. When people "acquire an intense commitment to the power and prosperity of the state [and] this commitment is strengthened by national myths emphasizing the moral, physical, and political strength of the state and by individuals' feelings of powerlessness and their consequent tendency to seek their identity and fulfillment through the state, . . . nationalism contributes to war" (Levy 1989a).

The connection between nationalism and war has a long history originating in Europe 350 years ago when monarchical rulers such as Ferdinand and Isabella of Spain engaged in "state building" by forcibly constructing nationalism to mobilize and manage the population, which bred religious and political intolerance, the repression of minorities, and war (Marx 2003). The linkage between nationalism and war grew over time. English essayist Aldous Huxley saw nationalism as "the religion of the twentieth century"—when history's most destructive interstate wars were fought. This leads many to critique nationalism, although many defend it as a virtue that makes for unity and solidarity within a country (see Controversy: Does Nationalistic Love of Country Cause War with Foreign Nations?). Whatever its consequences, nationalism is widely seen as perhaps the most powerful force in today's world, an idea and **ideology** that animates the constructed images of many. This is why many social scientists, looking at the evidence constructed by **behavioralism** (recall Chapter 2), conclude that nationalistic sentiments promote the outbreak of war.

Most armed conflicts today are fed by nationalist sentiments that promote "war fever . . . accompanied by overt hostility and contempt toward a caricatured image of the enemy," out of which sadistic violence and genocide have historically emanated (Caspary 1993). And the danger could escalate. Nationalism's threat to world order led former Soviet President Mikhail Gorbachev to warn in May 1992 that "the demons of nationalism are coming alive again, and they are putting the stability of the international system to the test. Even the United States itself is not immune from the dangerous nationalism."

This discussion of the characteristics of states that influence their proclivity for war does not exhaust the subject. Many other potential causes internal to the state exist. But, however important domestic influences might be as a source of war, many believe that the nature of the global system is even more critical.

■ **ideology**
a set of beliefs about the importance of particular ideas and values that orders peoples' constructed images of reality to give meaning to their lives.

■ **behavioralism**
an approach to the study of human and international behavior using the methodologies of science to test theories against data to estimate their validity.

The Third Level of Analysis: Cycles of War and Peace in the Global System

Realism emphasizes that the roots of armed conflict rest in human nature. In contrast, neorealism sees war springing from changes at the **global level of analysis,** that is, as a product of the decentralized character of the global system that requires sovereign states to rely on **self-help** for their security.

> Although different realist theories often generate conflicting predictions, they share a core of common assumptions: The key actors in world politics are sovereign states that act rationally to advance their security, power, and wealth in a conflictual international system that lacks a legitimate governmental authority to regulate conflicts or enforce agreements.
>
> For realists, wars can occur not only because some states prefer war to peace, but also because of unintended consequences of actions by those who prefer peace to war and are more interested in preserving their posi-

■ **global level of analysis**
an analytical approach to world politics that emphasizes the impact of global conditions on foreign policy behavior.

■ **self-help**
the principle that in anarchy states in the global system must rely on themselves.

CONTROVERSY: DOES NATIONALISTIC LOVE OF COUNTRY CAUSE WAR WITH FOREIGN NATIONS?

What does *patriotism* mean? The most familiar definition is popularly expressed as "love for one's country." Often, it involves "love for the nation or nationality of the people living in a particular state," especially when the population of that state primarily comprises a single ethnonational racial or linguistic group. Because "love" for valued objects of affection, such as a person's homeland, is widely seen as a virtue, it is understandable why governments everywhere teach young citizens that love for country is a moral duty—it fosters a sense of political community. Nationalism encourages internal harmony and political stability, and thereby makes a positive contribution to civic solidarity and domestic peace. On these grounds, nationalism is not controversial. However, critics of nationalism find patriotism to be potentially dangerous in its extreme form. Superpatriots, these critics warn, are hypernationalists who measure their patriotism by the degree of hatred and opposition exhibited toward foreign nations and by the blind approval of every policy and practice of the "patriot's" own nation. In this sense, nationalistic patriotism can ignore transcendent moral principles such as the love for all humanity, even toward one's enemies, as preached by Jesus Christ in the Sermon on the Mount and other religious leaders such as Muhammad, the founder of Islam, and the legendary King Solomon in Judaism. If so, then is nationalistic superpatriotism sometimes a cause of war between nations? What do you think?

In contemplating your opinion about this controversial issue over values—about whether nationalism and internationalism are mutually exclusive, and whether nationalism makes for war by undermining justice under law for the world of nations—take into consideration the view of Karl Deutsch, a German-born immigrant and famous scholar who taught for many years at Harvard University. Deutsch, an authority on nationalism, described nationalism's linkage to armed conflict in these moving words:

> *Nationalism* is an attitude of mind, a pattern of attention and desires. It arises in response to a condition of society and to a particular stage in its development. It is a predisposition to pay far more attention to messages about one's own people, or to messages from its members, than to messages from or about any other people. At the same time, it is a desire to have one's own people get any and all values that are available. The extreme nationalist wants his people to have all the power, all the wealth, and all the well-being for which there is any competition. He wants his people to command all the respect and deference from others; he tends to claim all rectitude and virtue for it, as well as all enlightenment and skill; and he gives it a monopoly of his affection. In short, he totally identifies himself with his nation. Though he may be willing to sacrifice himself for it, his nationalism is a form of egotism written large. . . .
>
> Even if most people are not extreme nationalists, nationalism has altered the world in many ways. Nationalism has not only increased the number of countries on the face of the earth, it has helped to diminish the number of its inhabitants. All major wars in the twentieth century have been fought in its name. . . .
>
> Nationalism is in potential conflict with all philosophies or religions—such as Christianity—which teach universal standards of truth and of right and wrong, regardless of nation, race, or tribe. Early in the nineteenth century a gallant American naval officer, Stephen Decatur, proposed the toast, "Our country! In her intercourse with foreign nations, may she be always in the right, but our country, right or wrong." Nearly 150 years later the United States Third Army, marching into Germany following the collapse of the Nazi regime, liberated the huge concentration camp at Buchenwald. Over the main entrance to that place of torture and death, the Nazi elite guard had thoughtfully written, "My Country, Right or Wrong." (Deutsch 1974, 124–125)

In confronting the impact of nationalism on armed conflict, we need to recognize its dual character: It is a force that (1) binds nations and nationalities together in common bonds, and (2) divides nation against nation, nationality against nationality, and is used to justify armed conflicts against other nations.

tion than in enhancing it. Even defensively motivated efforts by states to provide for their own security through armaments, alliances, and deterrent threats are often perceived as threatening and lead to counteractions and conflict spirals that are difficult to reverse. This is the **"security dilemma"**—the possibility that a state's actions to provide for its security may result in a decrease in the security of all states, including itself. (Levy 1998b, 145)

International **anarchy** may promote war's outbreak, but it fails to provide a complete explanation of changes in the levels of war and peace over time or why particular wars are fought. To capture war's many structural determinants, we must consider how and why systems change. This requires us to explore the impact of the distribution of military capabilities, balances (and imbalances) of power, the number of alliances and international organizations, and the rules of international law. At issue is how these factors—the system's characteristics and institutions—combine to influence changes in war's frequency. We will examine many of these factors in Chapters 13 and 14. Here we focus on cycles of war and peace at the international level and the structural determinants of armed conflict.

Does Violence Breed Violence? The adage "violence breeds violence" reflects the notion that the seeds of future wars are found in past wars (see Walter 2004). From this perspective World War II was an outgrowth of World War I, the U.S. attack of Iraq in 2003 was an extension of the 1990 Persian Gulf War, and the successive waves of terrorism and war in the Middle East were seemingly little more than one war, with each battle stimulated by its predecessor. Because the frequency of past wars is correlated with the incidence of wars in later periods, war appears to be contagious and its future outbreak inevitable. If so, then something within the dynamics of world politics—its anarchical nature, its weak legal system, its uneven distribution of power, inevitable destabilizing changes in the principal actors' relative power, or some combination of structural attributes—makes the state system a war system.

Those believing in war's inevitability often cite the historical fact that war has been so repetitive. We cannot, however, safely infer that past wars have *caused* later wars. The fact that a war precedes a later one does not mean that it caused the one that followed. That is why many scholars reject the deterministic view that history is destiny, with outcomes caused by previous events. Instead, they embrace the **bargaining model of war,** which sees war as a product of rational choice. The decision to engage in warfare is part of the bargaining process that occurs between adversaries to settle disputes and disagreements "over scarce goods, such as the placement of a border, the composition of a national government, or control over national resources" (Reiter 2003; see also Filson and Werner 2002; Smith and Stam 2004).

War's recurrence throughout history does not necessarily mean we will always have it. War is not a universal institution; as we have seen, some societies have never known war, and others have been immune to it for prolonged periods. Moreover, since 1945 the outbreak of armed conflicts *between* states has greatly declined, despite the large increase in the number of independent countries. This indicates that armed conflict is not necessarily inevitable and that historical forces do not control people's freedom of choice or experiences.

Power Transitions. These trends notwithstanding, when changes have occurred in the major states' military capabilities, war has often resulted. Although not inevitable, war has been likely whenever competitive states' power ratios (the

■ **security dilemma**
the tendency of states to view the defensive arming of adversaries as threatening, and when they arm in response, everyone's security declines.

■ **anarchy**
at the global level, the absence of institutions for global governance with the power to enforce rules and regulate disputes between states to ensure that international relations are peaceful.

■ **bargaining model of war**
an interpretation of war's onset as a choice by the initiator to bargain through aggression with an enemy in order to win on an issue or to obtain things of value, such as territory or oil.

Nationalism's Dark and Deadly Past and Future Under the fascist dictatorship of Adolf Hitler, shown on the left, the Nazi government glorified the state and claimed that the German people were a superior race. What followed from this extreme form of nationalism was a ruthless German world war and campaign of genocide against the Jews and other ethnic minorities. U.S. troops under the command of General George Patton, shown on the right, are arriving to liberate the concentration camp at Buchenwald in May 1945, but not in time to save the lives of the prisoners the Nazi elite guard had put to death in the gas chambers. Millions of innocent victims perished from the hypernationalism that created a cultural climate permissive of war and genocide.

■ **power transition theory**
the theory that war is likely when a dominant great power is threatened by the rapid growth of a rival's capabilities, which reduces the difference in their relative power.

■ **structural realism**
a neorealist theory that emphasizes the influence of the structure of world power on the behavior of the states within the global system.

differentials between their capabilities) have narrowed. Dubbed the **power transition theory,** this explanation rooted in **structural realism** holds that

> an even distribution of political, economic, and military capabilities between contending groups of states is likely to increase the probability of war; peace is preserved best when there is an imbalance of national capabilities between disadvantaged and advantaged nations; the aggressor will come from a small group of dissatisfied strong countries; and it is the weaker, rather than the stronger, power that is most likely to be the aggressor. (Organski and Kugler 1980, 19)

During the transition from developing to developed status, emergent challengers can achieve through force the recognition that their newly formed military muscles allow them. Conversely, established powers ruled by risk-acceptant leaders are often willing to employ force to put the brakes on their relative decline. Thus when advancing and retreating states seek to cope with the changes in their relative power, war between the rising challenger(s) and the declining power(s) has become especially likely. For example, the rapid changes in the power and status that produced the division of Europe among seven great powers nearly equal in military strength are often (along with the alliances they nurtured) interpreted as the tinderbox from which World War I ignited.

As explained in Chapter 13, rapid shifts in the global distribution of military power have often preceded outbursts of aggression, especially when the new distribution nears approximate parity (equality) and thereby tempts the rivals to wage war against their hegemonic challengers. According to the power transition theory, periods in which rivals' military capabilities are nearly balanced create "the necessary conditions for global war, while gross inequality assures peace or, in the worst case, an asymmetric, limited war" (Kugler 2001). Moreover, transitions in states' relative capabilities can potentially lead the weaker party to start a war in order to either overtake its rival or protect itself from domination. Presumably, the uncertainty created by a rough equilibrium prompts the challenger's (usually unsuccessful) effort to wage war against a stronger opponent. Equally persistent is the power transition theory's observation that advantages have shifted from the attacker to the defender: "In earlier centuries the aggressor seemed to have a 50-50 chance of winning the war, but this no longer holds. The chances of the starter being victorious are shrinking. In the 1980s only 18 percent of the starters were winners" (Sivard 1991, 20). As in the past (e.g., Japan's attack and subjugation of China in 1931 and 1937), there are notable exceptions: "Since 1945, six out of twenty wars have secured decisive advantage for the initiator (the Vietnam, Six Day, Bangladesh, Yom Kippur/Ramadan, Falklands, and Persian Gulf wars)" (Ziegler 1995).

Cyclical Theories. If war is recurrent but not necessarily inevitable, are there other international factors besides power transitions that might also explain changes over time in its outbreak? The absence of a clear trend in its frequency since the late fifteenth century and its periodic outbreak after intermittent stretches of peace suggest that world history seesaws between long cycles of war and peace. This provides a third structural explanation of war's onset.

The more recent formal analysis of such cycles is known as **long-cycle theory**. As noted in Chapter 4, its advocates argue that cycles of world leadership and global war have existed over the past five centuries, with a "general war" erupting approximately once every century, although at irregular intervals (Hopkins and Wallerstein 1996; Wallerstein 2004; Modelski 1987b; Modelski and Thompson 1996). Long-cycle theory seeks to explain how an all-powerful invisible hand built into the global system's dynamics causes such peaks and valleys. Although this theory embraces many contending explanations (see Goldstein 1988), they converge on the proposition that some combination of systemic properties (economic, military, and political) produce the frequency with which major wars have erupted periodically throughout modern history.

Long-cycle theory draws its insights from the observation that a great power has risen to a hegemonic position about every hundred years. Using as a measure of dominance the possession of disproportionate sea power, we observe the rise of a single **hegemon** regularly appearing after particular hegemonic wars (see Figure 11.3). Portugal and the Netherlands rose at the beginning of the sixteenth and seventeenth centuries, respectively; Britain climbed to dominance at the beginning of both the eighteenth and nineteenth centuries; and the United States became a world leader at the end of World War II and regained its position of global supremacy after the Cold War ended in 1991. American military spending rose to exceed, by 2004, that of the rest of the world combined (see Chapter 12). During their reigns, these hegemonic powers monopolized military power and trade and determined the system's rules. Yet no previous hegemonic

■ **long-cycle theory**
an interpretation of world history that focuses on repeating patterns of interstate behavior, such as the outbreak of systemwide general wars at different intervals, after long periods during which other patterns (global peace) were dominant.

■ **hegemon**
a single dominant military and economic state that uses its unrivaled power to create and enforce rules aimed at preserving the existing world order and its own position in that order.

FIGURE 11.3
The Long Cycle of Global Leadership and Global War, 1494–2020
Over the past five hundred years, five great powers have risen to control the global system by dominating it. However, none of these hegemons (except Britain and the United States) has managed to reign for long. The past pattern shows that each leader's grip on top-dog status eventually has slipped, and in time new rivals have risen to challenge that leadership position by fighting a global war to settle the contest. The troubling question is whether this long cycle of war can be broken in the future or whether humankind will again experience a global war to determine which great power will lead, if China, as widely predicted, will surpass the economic and, someday, military capabilities of the reigning U.S. "empire."
SOURCE: Adapted from *Exploring Long Cycles* by George Modelski, ed., p. 6. Copyright © 1987 by Lynn Beinner Publishers. Reprinted by permission of the publisher.

power has retained its top-dog position perceptually (see Table 4.1, p. 97). In each cycle, overcommitments, the costs of empire, and ultimately the appearance of rivals led to the delegitimation of the hegemon's authority and to the deconcentration of power globally. As challengers to the hegemon's rule grew in strength, a "global war" has erupted after a long period of peace in each century since 1400. At the conclusion of each previous general war, a new world leader emerged dominant (Modelski 1978, 1987b), and the cyclical process began anew. As Brock Tessman and Steve Chan summarize and explain,

> The theory of power cycles contends that the growth and decline of national power holds the key to understanding the occurrence of extensive wars. Certain critical points in a state's power trajectory are especially dangerous occasions for such armed clashes [from which we can] derive expectations about the risk propensity of states during different periods in their power cycle. . . . Critical points tend to incline states to initiate deterrence confrontations and escalate them to war. . . . Changes in national power tend to follow a regular pattern of ascendance, maturation, and decline and . . . these trajectories reflect the major states' relative competitiveness in the in-

ternational system. When these states encounter an unexpected reversal in the direction or rate of change in their power trajectory, they are subject to various psychological impulses or judgmental challenges that increase the danger of extensive wars. The larger the number of major states that find themselves under the duress of such reversals, the greater the tendency for their disputes to become extensive wars. (Tessman and Chan 2004, 131)

Such deterministic theories have intuitive appeal. It seems plausible, for instance, that just as long-term downswings and recoveries in business cycles profoundly affect subsequent behaviors and conditions, wars will produce aftereffects that may last for generations. The idea that a country at war will become exhausted and lose its enthusiasm for another war, but only for a time, is known as the **war weariness hypothesis** (Blainey 1988). Italian historian Luigi da Porto expresses one version: "Peace brings riches; riches bring pride; pride brings anger; anger brings war; war brings poverty; poverty brings humanity; humanity brings peace; peace, as I have said, brings riches, and so the world's affairs go round." Because it takes time to move through these stages, alternating periods of enthusiasm for war and weariness of war appear to be influenced by learning and forgetting over time.

Cyclical theories of war's outbreak provoke much discussion. However, scholars attempting to construct a consensus about the existence of cycles of war and peace have failed to arrive at agreement. Their estimates diverge, because different measures of the frequency of war's outbreak construct rival pictures of the duration of periods of peace and war (compare Wright 1942, Richardson 1960a, and Sorokin 1937). What makes a true test for the presence of a cycle difficult is the increase in states' numbers over time, from about twenty-five during the 1816–48 Concert of Europe to over two hundred in the post–Cold War period. The ballooning number of independent states in the global system increases the probability of wars. However, the number of interstate wars between 1815 and 1991 has been fairly stable. The conclusion is offered therefore, that there is *not* a clear cycle operative in war's onset, and, given that, there is reason to doubt that the global system has properties that automatically produce recurrent cycles in wars (J. Singer 1981). The trends suggest, rather, that since the Congress of Vienna, war between states has been under way almost continuously. Although there were eighty-two years between 1816 and 1991 in which no new interstate wars began, there were in that period only twenty years in which no wars were being fought (Small and Singer 1982, 149; J. Singer 1991, 60–75). The available scientific evidence "suggests not so much that discrete wars come and go with some regularity, but that, with some level of such violence almost always present, there may be certain periodic fluctuations in the amount of that violence" (Small and Singer 1982). This characteristic draws attention to an abrupt recent development: Since 1989 war *between* states has nearly disappeared from the international scene. Through 2004 only seven interstate wars have been under way, including the U.S./Great Britain–led "coalition of the willing" attack of Iraq (Eriksson and Wallensteen 2004, 625–627). In contrast, the number of civil wars has increased dramatically.

Although the disappearance of war *between* states may be possible over the long run, armed conflict and violence persists *inside* established states. We now turn from our exploration of the multiple causes of armed conflicts between states to examine armed conflicts within states.

■ **war weariness hypothesis**
the proposition that fighting a major war is costly in terms of lost lives and income, and these costs greatly reduce a country's tolerance for undertaking another war until enough time passes to lose memory of those costs, at which time leaders tend to once again view a new war against a new enemy as a realistic option that will not provoke public opposition.

ARMED CONFLICT WITHIN STATES

■ **civil war**
war between factions within the same country.

Civil wars—wars within states—have erupted far more frequently than have wars between states. It is these armed struggles that most often capture news headlines worldwide.

The Characteristics of Civil War

There is a basis in fact for the above assertion. Between 1989 and the start of 2004, internal armed conflicts over government (civil wars) or over territory (state-formation conflicts) have been the most common by far. In this period, 109 civil wars erupted in comparison with only 7 between states. At the start of 2004, 26 civil wars were raging, and only 2 cross-border military conflicts were being fought worldwide.

Civil wars resulting in at least one thousand civilian and military deaths per year occurred 233 times between 1816 and 2004 (Small and Singer 1982; J. Singer 1991, 66–75; Eriksson and Wallensteen 2004; see also Gleditsch 2004). Their outbreak has been somewhat irregular. Although at least one civil war was begun in eighty-four of these years, over time civil war has become increasingly frequent (see Table 11.1). Of the civil wars since 1816, nearly three-fourths began after 1945, with a frequency steadily climbing each decade (almost half of the civil wars since the 1816 Congress of Vienna and the Cold War began to fade in 1989). However, this accelerating trend is, in part, a product of the increase in the number of independent states in the global system, which makes the incidence of civil war statistically more probable. Civil wars stem from similar emerging conditions, share defining characteristics (Sambanis 2004), and center around several salient issues:

- ethnic groups seeking greater autonomy or striving to create an independent state for themselves (such as the Kurds in Turkey and Chechens in Russia).
- internal battles fought to gain control of an existing state.
- "failed states" where the authority of a national government has collapsed and armed struggle has broken out between the competing ethnic militias, warlords, or criminal organizations seeking to obtain power and establish control of the state.
- impoverished states where there exists "a situation of individual hardship or severe dissatisfaction with one's current situation [and] the absence of any nonviolent means for change" (Walter 2004). As the World Bank (2003, 46) describes the syndrome, "Low-income countries, where about a billion people live, face greatest risk of civil war—about 15 times that of high-income countries."

Refer to Table 11.1, where we learn of another characteristic of civil war—the tendency for countries that have experienced one civil war to undergo two or more subsequent civil wars. They often re-erupt with seemingly endless repetition: since 1945, 36 percent of countries experiencing civil war followed it with another war (Walter 2004, 371). Moreover, the average duration of civil wars once they erupt has increased (Hegre 2004, 203–4). What this means is that the number of civil wars *under way* has exceeded the rate of civil war initiation. Civil wars dominate the global terrain because they start and re-ignite at

TABLE 11.1

The Frequency of 233 Civil Wars across Six Periods, 1816–2004

Period	Key System Characteristics	System Size (average number of states)	Number of Civil Wars Begun	Number (percentage) of Civil Wars Internationalized through Large-Scale Military Intervention
1816–48	Monarchies in Concert of Europe suppress democratic revolutions	28	12	3 (25%)
1849–81	Rising nationalism and civil wars	39	20	1 (5%)
1882–1914	Imperialism and colonization	40	18	3 (17%)
1915–45	World wars and economic collapse	59	14	4 (29%)
1946–88	Decolonization and independence for emerging Global South countries during Cold War	117	60	14 (23%)
1989–2004	Age of failed states and civil wars	196	109	20 (18%)
Totals			233	48 (21%)

SOURCES: Data for 1816–1988 courtesy of the Correlates of War project under the direction of J. David Singer and Melvin Small; data for 1989–2004 based on Eriksson and Wallensteen 2004; for another inventory see Gleditsch 2004.

a higher rate than they end, and they last longer. Consider examples of long-lasting and resumed civil wars in Afghanistan, Burundi, Colombia, Congo, Indonesia, Iran, Iraq, Ivory Coast, Liberia, Peru, Rwanda, Sri Lanka, and Sudan.

Also note the relationship that has materialized between civil wars and their "internationalization" through the military intervention of one or more foreign states. Since 1945 about one-fifth of the world's civil wars have experienced the intervention of outside actors seeking to influence their outcome (Eriksson and Wallensteen 2004, 626). Civil wars are not exclusively internal affairs—they attract global attention and, fairly often, external involvement. When others get involved, they globalize the conflict and in the process the civil wars cast their shadow over world politics.

Another noteworthy characteristic of civil wars is their severity. The number of lives lost in civil violence has remained high since the Napoleonic Wars ended in 1815. Casualty rates from civil wars show an alarming growth, especially since World War II. One symptom of the climbing lethality of civil rebellions is that seven of the fifteen most destructive civil wars since 1816 have occurred after World War II (Small and Singer 1982, 241). The cliché that "the most savage conflicts occur in the home" captures the ugly reality, as genocide and mass slaughter aimed at depopulating entire regions have become commonplace in recent civil wars. That grim reality was illustrated in Rwanda, where the Hutu government orchestrated a genocidal slaughter resulting in the murder of half a million people in a matter of weeks. Sudan provides another horrifying example of the mass slaughter of civilians that often occurs when governments seek to keep power by destroying minority opposition groups. The Arab-controlled Sudanese government, which seized power in 1989, suspended democracy and undertook a divide-and-destroy campaign of the predominately Christian and animist South. It made state-sponsored terrorism against civilians a policy that has resulted in the killing of staggering numbers and produced a mass exodus of over 500,000 refugees in 2004. At least 2.5 million people have perished and another 4 million have become displaced within this tragic killing land. The bloodbath by 2004 was described as the worst since World War II, but the great powers—preoccupied by the war in Iraq—failed to intervene to stop the killing.

A final noteworthy characteristic of civil wars is their resistance to negotiated settlement. Making peace among rival factions that are struggling for power, driven by hatred and poisoned by the inertia of prolonged killing that has become a way of life is difficult. Civil wars rarely result in the decisive victory of one faction over another. The pattern of civil wars is that domestic enemies are rarely able to end the fighting through negotiated compromise at the bargaining table; over half end on the battlefield (Walter 1997, 335).

The growing frequency, severity, length, and indeterminate conclusion of the civil wars are accounted for by the multiple causes of these prolonged domestic disputes raging across the globe.

The Causes of Civil War

Civil wars stem from a wide range of ideological, demographic, religious, ethnic, economic, social-structural, and political conditions. Civil war and revolution have simultaneously been defended as instruments of justice and condemned as the immoral acceptance of violent change. They contain ingredients of both. Those who engineered the American, Russian, and Chinese Revolutions claimed that violence was necessary to realize social change, political freedom, and independence; the powers from whom they sought liberation berated the immorality of their actions and methods.

Relative Deprivation. Among the sources of civil war, internal violence is a reaction to frustration and **relative deprivation**—people's perception that they are unfairly deprived of the wealth and status that they deserve in comparison with advantaged others (Gurr 1970). According to the United Nations, "some 359 million people (of the 578 million who belong to groups that face some form of cultural exclusion) are disadvantaged or discriminated against relative to others in the state in following their beliefs," and their frustration and anger often erupts in violence (UNDP 2004, 32). When people's expectations of what they deserve rise more rapidly than their material rewards, the probability of conflict grows. That, of course, applies to most of the countries in the Global South today, where the distribution of wealth and opportunities is highly unequal (see Chapter 5).

Demographic Stress. A number of demographic factors contribute to and collectively combine to precipitate civil wars. Among them several characteristics stand out as potent: "high proportions of young adults, rapid urban population growth, diminishing per capita supplies of cropland and fresh water, and high rates of death among working-age adults" (Cincotta, Engelman, and Anastasion 2003). Inspect Map 11.1. It shows the risk of civil war due to high levels of demographic and environmental stress between 2000 and 2010. Particularly

■ **relative deprivation** inequality between the wealth and status of individuals and groups, and the outrage of those at the bottom about their perceived exploitation by those at the top.

MAP 11.1
Demographic Stress and the Likelihood of Civil War
Where there are large numbers of unemployed youth concentrated in large cities and a lack of environmentally sustainable growth, the odds of civil war increase dramatically. Shown here are the projected locations of such demographic stress where the likelihood of civil war is expected to be high through the year 2010.
SOURCE: *Population Action International, The Security Demographic* (Washington D.C.: Population Action International 2003, 71. (Special Edition for Worldwatch Institutue *State of the World* Library Subscribers.)

influential as a catalyst to civil war is the presence of many young men: "Young men—out of school, out of work and charged with hatred—are the lifeblood of deadly conflict. Countries with a high proportion of adults under 30 have two and a half times the probability of experiencing a new outbreak of civil conflict as those with more mature age structures . . . and [high levels] of cropland or fresh water resources relative to population size" (Cincotta and Engleman 2004, 18).

Secessionist Revolts. The seeds of civil strife are often sown by national independence movements. "More than two thirds of all the armed combat in the world between 1945 and 1995 were manifestations of the state-creation enterprise" (K. Holsti 1995, 22). Violence often has been the means through which states have been given—or denied—birth.

Nationalistic Ethnic Hatred. U.S. President Bill Clinton observed in his June 7, 1994, speech before the French National Assembly that militant ethnic nationalism was "on the rise, transforming the healthy pride of nations, tribes, religious and ethnic groups into cancerous prejudice, eating away at states and leaving their people addicted to the political painkillers of violence and demagoguery." Much of the internal revolt and ethnic warfare currently sweeping the world is inspired less by political motives and economic aims than it is by deeply

Ethnic Warfare and Children Children have often been the major victims of civil strife. This photo, which received the World Press Award in 1985, depicts children caught in the ethnonational and religious civil war in Beirut, the capital of Lebanon—a country whose population is about two-thirds Muslim and one-fourth Christian, with each faction further divided into sects.

■ **ethnic warfare**
violence resulting from wars between two or more ethnic groups or from state-sponsored violence to terrorize or destroy an ethnic minority.

■ **displaced people**
people involuntarily uprooted from their homes but still living in their own countries.

■ **failing states**
those governments that are in danger of losing the loyalty of their citizens, who are rebelling against corruption and administrative failure, and, in the process, tearing the country into separate political parts.

rooted ethnic hatreds. Waged primarily by irregular militia and private gangs against their neighbors, extreme ethnonationalists are people who are prepared to kill and die in large numbers. Ethnonational clashes differ greatly from the anticolonial secessionist independence movements of the past. There is much evidence that intense identification with one's own nationality or ethnic group provokes civil war against a government, especially if it is repressive (Walter 2004). There are as many as five thousand separate "nations" or separate indigenous peoples living in existing countries (see Chapter 6), and many of these nonstate nations have members seeking to use violence and terrorism against other nationalities or a governing majority. Civil rebellion and **ethnic warfare** have reached epidemic proportions. In today's civil wars, the UN estimates that at least 90 percent of all killed are innocent noncombatants and over half the **displaced peoples**—refugees within their own countries—are women and children.

Failed States. Many fledgling governments are fragile and fall apart as they fail to effectively manage the regulatory power that international sovereignty gives them to govern affairs within their territorial borders. Mismanagement by government administration is causing an epidemic of **failing states** throughout the globe, as disarray, discontent, and disorder have mobilized desperate populations living in conditions of anarchy to rebel. The civil wars percolated by state failure have caused as many as 113 states to dissolve or fragment into separate units between 1955 and 1994 according to the U.S. Central Intelligence Agency's

"State Failure Task Force" report. In 2004 no less than another 22 states were "high-risk" countries vulnerable to destruction through civil rebellion against a feeble government.

The causes of state failure and civil disintegration are multiple, but failed states share some key characteristics. Among them, the CIA "State Failure Task Force" report finds the following:

- Democracy generally lowers the risk of state failure; autocracy increases it.
- Poor democracies, however, are more unstable than either rich democracies or poor nondemocracies, and poor democracies that do not improve living standards are exceptionally vulnerable.
- The best predictor of failure is high infant mortality.
- High levels of trade openness seem to inoculate any kind of regime against failure. States that have fair rules allowing a high degree of international trade gain stability.
- The existence of a "youth bulge"—a large proportion of young adults in the population—increases the risk of ethnic war because large pools of under-employed youths are easily mobilized into action.
- Mass killings are often associated with low levels of trade openness, in part, because countries with little foreign trade are usually of little concern to the international community. (Zimmerman 1996, 46)

Inasmuch as many of the 210 sovereign states in the world have one or more of these attributes, it is likely that failing states will grow as a problem in the globalized twenty-first century. The globe is speckled with many dangerous civil war flashpoints where countries are highly vulnerable to dissolution as a result of state failure, mismanagement, and civil revolt.

Economic Roots. The destabilization caused by rapid growth also helps to account for the ubiquity of internal war (Murdoch and Sandler 2004). In contrast with what intuition might suggest, civil violence often erupts in countries in which conditions are improving, not deteriorating. "Economic modernization," former U.S. Secretary of State Henry Kissinger stated, "leads to political instability rather than political stability." When modernization generates rising expectations that governments are unable to satisfy, civil war often follows. This is the essence of relative deprivation as a cause of internal violence, as people who feel they have been denied the resources they deserve are often inclined to use force in acts of rebellion (Gurr 1970).

Today, even in the period of democratization and economic growth through free trade and free markets, misery among those not sharing in the benefits is breeding revolt. This is made evident by the fact that 57 percent of the armed conflicts between 1990 and 1995 erupted in the poor countries ranking "low" on the UN **human development index (HDI;** see Chapter 7), and another 34 percent in the "medium-human-development" countries, in contrast to only 14 percent in the "high" countries providing relative prosperity, health and education for their citizens" (D. Smith 1997, 48, 50). It is therefore not surprising that "death rates from violence in poor countries are more than double the level in rich ones" (*Economist*, October 5, 2002, 98). As the UN High Commissioner for Refugees Sadaka Ogata concluded, "to establish a more peaceful, prosperous and secure world, poverty must be eliminated and income differentials reduced."

Case Study: Genocide in Rwanda

■ **human development index (HDI)**
an index that uses life expectancy, literacy, average number of years of schooling, and income to assess a country's performance in providing for its citizens' welfare and security.

The International Dimensions of Internal War

It is tempting to think of civil war as stemming exclusively from conditions within countries. However, external factors often influence internal rebellions. "Every war has two faces. It is a conflict both between and within political systems; a conflict that is both external and internal. [It is undeniable that] internal wars affect the international system [and that] the international system affects internal wars" (Modelski 1964).

Several phases have influenced the linkage between transformations in the global system and the incidence of civil war. First, the effects of imperialism, industrialization, nationalism, and ideology provoked the comparatively high levels of civil war between 1848 and 1870. Second, the breakup of the European colonial empires contributed to the frequent incidence of civil war between the end of World War II and the 1960s. And today, the discipline imposed by Cold War bipolarity has disappeared, reducing states' fear that turmoil within their borders will precipitate military intervention by the great powers.

Because the great powers have global interests, historically they have been prone to intervene militarily in civil wars to support friendly governments and to overthrow unfriendly ones. When they did, wars within states became internationalized. But today it is often difficult to determine where an internal war ends and another begins. As the information in Table 11.1 reveals, outside intervention in civil wars has been common, especially between 1946 and 2004, when 70 percent of all external participation in internal wars since 1816 took place. Since 1946, other states have militarily intervened in one-fifth of the civil wars that have erupted (Eriksson and Wallensteen 2004, 626). In the aftereffects of external intrusions, the targets' domestic societies have been transformed—those of both weak and powerful states (Midlarsky 2003).

Many analysts believe that domestic conflicts become internationalized because leaders who experience internal opposition are inclined to provoke an international crisis in the hope that their citizens will become less rebellious if their attention is diverted to the threat of external aggression. This proposition has become known as the **diversionary theory of war.** This theory is based on the expectation that external war will result in increased domestic support for political leaders. It draws a direct connection between civil strife and foreign aggression, maintaining that when leaders suffer conflict at home, they are prone to attempt to contain that domestic strife by waging a war against foreigners in the hope that the international danger will take citizens' attention away from their dissatisfaction with their home leadership. "To put it cynically, one could say that nothing helps a leader like a good war. It gives him his only chance of being a tyrant and being loved for it at the same time. He can introduce the most ruthless forms of control and send thousands of his followers to their deaths and still be hailed as a great protector. Nothing ties tighter the in-group bonds than an out-group threat" (Morris 1969).

It is logical for leaders to assume that national unity will rise when a foreign rivalry exists (Mitchell and Prins 2004), and strong temptations for them to seek to manage domestic unrest by initiating foreign adventures. Indeed, many political advisers have counseled this strategy, as the realist theorist Niccolò Machiavelli did in 1513 when he advised leaders to undertake foreign wars whenever turmoil within their state became too great. He was echoed by Hermann Goering, Adolf Hitler's Nazi adviser, when he instructed, "Voice or no voice, the people can always be brought to do the bidding of the leaders. That is easy. All

■ **diversionary theory of war**
the hypothesis that leaders initiate conflict abroad as a way of increasing national cohesion at home.

you have to do is tell them they are being attacked and denounce the pacifists for lack of patriotism." Similarly, in 1939 John Foster Dulles recommended before he became U.S. secretary of state that "the easiest and quickest cure of internal dissension is to portray danger from abroad."

Whether leaders actually start wars to offset domestic conflict remains a subject of debate. We cannot demonstrate that many leaders intentionally undertake diversionary actions to defend themselves against domestic opposition. Unpopular leaders may instead be highly motivated to exercise caution in foreign affairs and to avoid the use of force overseas in order to cultivate a reputation as a peacemaker; it is better to avoid further criticism that they are intentionally manipulative by addressing the domestic problems that cause civil unrest, rather than engaging in reckless wars overseas—especially unpopular wars that trigger protest demonstrations and reduce leaders' public opinion approval ratings. Hence, there is reason to question the linkage between civil unrest and interstate war initiation. "The linkage depends," Jack Levy (1989b) observes, "on the kinds of internal conditions that commonly lead to hostile external actions for diversionary purposes." Diversionary wars are undertaken by desperate leaders in desperate times, such as in an economic recession or a reelection that the opposition appears likely to win. In noncrisis times, however, when people take to the streets to protest a leader's domestic policies, most leaders are inclined to concentrate on the internal disturbances than they are to manufacture threats of a foreign war.

TERRORISM

Terrorism poses another alarming kind of contemporary violence. The instruments of terror are varied and the motivations of terrorists diverse, but "experts agree that terrorism is the use or threat of violence, a method of combat or a strategy to achieve certain goals, that its aim is to induce a state of fear in the victim, that it is ruthless and does not conform to humanitarian norms, and that publicity is an essential factor in terrorist strategy" (Laqueur 2003).

Some terrorist activities, such as the 1995 bombing of the U.S. federal government building in Oklahoma City, begin and end in a single country. Many, however, cross national borders. At the start of the twenty-first century, most terrorists targeted citizens and property in external countries, and because terrorist acts are spread throughout the globe, the risks are also widespread.

Terrorism is a tactic of the powerless against the powerful. Thus it is not surprising that political or social minorities and ethnic movements sometimes turn to acts of terrorism on behalf of their political causes (see Laqueur 2004). Those seeking independence and sovereign statehood, such as the Basques in Spain, typify the aspirations that animate terrorist activity. Religion also sometimes rationalizes the terrorist activities of extremist movements, such as the efforts of the Sikh groups who wish to carve out an independent state called Khalistan ("Land of the Pure") from Indian territory, and of the Islamic extremist group Hamas to destabilize Israel and sabotage a negotiated peace between Israel and its neighbors (Haynes 2004). In November 1995 a fanatical right-wing law student terrorist assassinated Israeli Prime Minister Yitzhak Rabin to derail the peace process in Palestine.

■ **terrorism**
premeditated politically motivated violence perpetrated against noncombatant targets by subnational groups or clandestine agents, usually intended to influence an audience.

Simulation: U.S. Presidential Response to Catastrophic Terrorism

In the industrialized and urbanized world, terrorism often occurs where discrepancies in income are severe and where minority groups feel deprived of the political freedoms and privileges enjoyed by the majority. Guerrilla warfare—normally associated with rural uprisings—is not a viable route to self-assertion, but terrorist tactics are.

Terrorism was well known in ancient times, as evident in the assassination of tyrants in ancient Greece and Rome, and killings by the Zealots in Palestine and the Hashashin of medieval Islam. In the nineteenth century, terrorism became associated with anarchist bombings and with murders and destruction of property by nationalist groups. The ethnic, political, or religious movements now practicing terrorism all seek to exact revenge against those states and cultures that each terrorist group perceives as its oppressor. Often the terrorists are the "international homeless" whose main objective is to obtain for themselves a territory and state they can control. Whereas religious fanaticism is responsible for many terrorist incidents, the primary goals of most terrorist groups are independence and statehood.

Terrorist groups may be thought of as an unconventional type of violent nonstate actor (or NGO) on the global stage. However, terrorist groups are difficult to identify, and it would be a mistake to lump all terrorist movements together. Today terrorism is a strategy practiced by a diverse group of movements, as seen by the fact that in 2004 the U.S. State Department identified thirty-five different organizations as worldwide terrorist groups.

The difference between nationalistic "freedom fighters," whose major complaint is that they lack a country, and governments claiming to protect freedom, often lies in the eye of the beholder. This problem makes the definition of a terrorist group less obvious and more controversial, as what most distinguishes terrorist groups from liberation movements is the outcome—which faction succeeds or fails in a political struggle for power. Keep in mind that those who are willing to use violence and terror outside the evolving rules of warfare tend to be condemned or praised, depending on whether those who condemn or praise accept or reject the terrorist's cause. Consider, for example, the observation that "the overwhelming demonizing and thought-deadening impact of the word 'terrorism' is precisely the charm of the word for its more cynical and unprincipled users and abusers [to describe] 'violence that I don't support.' Anyone who reads both the Western and the Arab press cannot help noticing that the Western press routinely characterizes as 'terrorism' virtually all Palestinian violence against Israelis (even against Israeli occupation forces within Palestine), while the Arab press routinely characterizes as 'terrorism' virtually all Israeli violence against Palestinians" (Whitbeck 2004).

The popularity of the slogan that "one person's terrorist is another's freedom fighter" notwithstanding, there is a difference. Terrorists are defined by the *means* (terror) they use, and freedom fighters by the *end* (civil liberty) they pursue. Because freedom can be fought for by moral and legal methods that respect the immunity of noncombatant targets, freedom fighters can operate differently from terrorists, who are prepared to use violence against unarmed civilians and to promote worthy causes by evil methods.

Although many terrorist groups today are undeniably seeking sovereignty, a broader definition of terrorism would acknowledge that many governments undertake terrorist acts, sometimes against their own people and sometimes by supporting terrorism against other established sovereign states (Crenshaw

2003). In fact, some states underwrite the activities of terrorist movements that advocate philosophies they embrace (or challenge the security of rival states). States have often financed, trained, equipped, and provided sanctuary for terrorists whose activities serve their foreign goals. The practice of such **state-sponsored terrorism** is among the charges that the United States leveled in 2002 against the so-called axis of evil—Iran, Iraq, and North Korea—as well as against Cuba, Libya, Sudan, and Syria. Similarly, others had previously accused the United States of sponsoring terrorist activities in Vietnam, Chile, El Salvador, Nicaragua, and elsewhere.

■ **state-sponsored terrorism** formal assistance, training, and arming of foreign terrorists by a state in order to achieve foreign policy goals.

Unsettling incidents of terrorism such as the 9/11 and 3/11 terrorist attacks provide conspicuous examples of the recurrent human tragedy and exemplify the potency of terrorism and the frustration and failure of efforts to contain it. Past acts of ruthless terrorism have been committed on a regular basis. Their primary purpose usually has been to produce alarm. To instill paralyzing fear—to terrorize—has unfortunately become a common way of expressing grievances and attempting to realize political objectives.

The inherently sadistic nature of violent terrorism can obscure terrorists' identity, making states appear blameless and dissimilar from revolutionary terrorists. However, an objective definition of terrorism as a strategy must acknowledge that *both* governments and countergovernment movements claim to seek liberty and both are labeled terrorists by their opponents.

> Those who are described as terrorists, and who reject that title for themselves, make the uncomfortable point that national armed forces, fully supported by democratic opinion, have in fact employed violence and terror on a far vaster scale than what liberation movements have as yet been able to attain. The "freedom fighters" see themselves as fighting a just war. Why should they not be entitled to kill, burn, and destroy as national armies, navies and air forces do, and why should the label "terrorist" be applied to them and not the national militaries? (C. O'Brien 1977, 56–57)

Perhaps the inherently subjective meaning of "terrorism" accounts for the American superpower's frequent use of the term in identifying the threats it perceives necessary to wage a global war against. "With the United States relying on the word to assert, apparently, a right to attack any country it dislikes, many people around the world understandably feel a genuine sense of terror (dictionary definition: 'a state of intense fear') as to where the United States is taking the rest of the world. [This explains why] most acts to which the word 'terrorism' is applied (at least in the West) are tactics of the weak, usually (although not always) against the strong. Such acts are not a tactic of choice but of last resort. The poor, the weak and the oppressed rarely complain about 'terrorism.' The rich, the strong and the oppressors constantly do" (Whitbeck 2004).

In addressing terrorism, we are dealing with a value-laden subject that resists precise definition and whose description is often motivated by the desire to condemn, not to offer detached evaluation. An objective analysis requires comparing different ways in which transnational actors threaten violence and extracting valid generalizations about the characteristics terrorists share with other actors and those that set them apart. A definition must balance the need to identify commonalities against the need to recognize unique features of individual cases. Should suicide Al Qaeda and Taliban bombers, Palestinian skyjackers, Zionist hit squads, Basque separatists, Irish revolutionaries, and South

American kidnappers be seen as similar? Are they properly classified with the insurgents who produced the American, French, and Russian Revolutions? Do their actions resemble the tactics of the Red Brigade, the Ku Klux Klan, the Roman Catholic Church during the Inquisition, or big-time drug-trafficking street gangs and networks of international organized crime? Were the methods of the African National Congress and the racist South African government it opposed both cases of terrorist actors? Was the "state terrorism" of Pol Pot, Adolf Hitler, Joseph Stalin, and Mao Tse-Tung a part of the same terrorist syndrome? Is an attack on a principle such as freedom of the press different from a terrorist attack on human life? And what about the nuclear deterrence strategies pursued by the United States and the Soviet Union during the Cold War, which relied on terror to prevent attack (see Chapter 12)? Where does one draw the line?

Whether some forms of terrorism are found acceptable will be shaped by the socially constructed images of it. As constructivist theorists remind us, what we see depends on what we look at, what we look for, what we expect to see, what we wish to see, and how we react to what we discern.

In this context, consider, for example, the seemingly simple question of whether global terrorism has increased in frequency since the 1960s. On the surface, this would appear to be an easy question to answer, yet estimates vary considerably. Indices select, screen, and filter what is perceived about the volume of international terrorism. For instance, the U.S. Department of State's Office of Counter-Terrorism—which employs the broad definition for international terrorism as any "premeditated, politically motivated violence perpetrated against noncombatant targets by subnational groups or clandestine agents, usually intended to influence an audience involving the citizens or territory of more than one country"—began to inventory the frequency of terrorist acts after terrorism first emerged as a significant international problem in the 1960s and grew to epidemic proportions in the 1970s and 1980s. Figure 11.4 shows the changing frequency of terrorism and its level of destruction in today's world, as measured by this account, which reveals that global terrorist activity had increased nearly threefold between 1968 and 1987, after which the number of incidents has gradually but erratically declined. International terrorist attacks during 2003 rose to 208 from the prior year of 205 separate terrorist acts worldwide. However, in three fateful years—1995, 1989, and 2001—the number of people killed by terrorists' acts rose dramatically: nearly three thousand people were killed as a result of the September 11 attack, the most lethal terrorist incident since World War II. This fourth wave of global terrorism continued to display its lethal face in 2004 when the latest phase of the Palestinian-Israeli conflict escalated and multiple suicide bombings by Islamic Jihad and Hamas (Islamic Resistance Movement) killed thousands, which provoked Israeli counterattacks, the building of a wall to divide territories, reoccupation of Palestinian villages and land, and executions of suspected terrorists and bombing of their hiding places. As the so-called war on terrorism suggests, the threat of increasing terrorism in the aftermath of 9/11 and 3/11 and the persistent suicide bombings in Iraq after its return to sovereignty in June 2004 is expected to continue, as is the rise of pirate attacks on ships, "bringing piracy-related deaths in 2004 to a 10-year global high" (Laqueur 2004; Nankivell 2004, 30).

Regardless of the total volume, global terrorist actions always exert a powerfully symbolic and dramatic impact, which heightens every time a major attack occurs. Until 9/11, terrorism was dismissed as a significant danger because

FIGURE 11.4
The Number of Terrorist Incidents throughout the Globe and the Changing Number of Casualties Caused by International Terrorism, since the Late 1960s

The frequency of international terrorist activity has changed over time since 1968, and the number of incidents each year has been between 174 (in 1968) and 666 (in 1987). These activities appear entrenched, but vary over time. Note also (bottom figure) the relatively modest toll of human life exacted by terrorism. No level is acceptable, but on average far fewer people die each year from terrorist acts than from the annual toll of U.S. homicides (25,000 Americans were murdered in 2004, and at the same time U.S. car accidents were claiming about 40,000 lives each year; in contrast in 2003 terrorists took the lives of only 35 U.S. citizens (U.S. Department of State 2004, 186). Statistically, it is said that a person is more likely to be struck by lightning than by an act of terrorism. Note, however, that casualty rates have begun to climb since 1995 and fears of mass destruction through terrorism have risen since 9/11.

SOURCE: Office of the Coordinator for Counter-Terrorism, U.S. Department of State.

MAP 11.2
**The Dance of Death in the Middle East's Cauldron of Terror—
the West Bank Flash Point**

The state of Israel was carved in 1948 from the former British Protectorate of Palestine —home of Muslim Arabs—and ever since a reign of tension and terror has prevailed in the disputed West Bank area that was excluded from the original settlement and taken from the Arab state of Jordan. Palestinians, numbering 2.4 million, call the West Bank home, but after the 1967 Six Day War Israel established a large number of settlements for 409,000 Israelis living there and, in 2001, built a 410-mile wall to bolster security to stem the wave of Palestinian suicide terrorist attacks. This map outlines the troubled West Bank and identifies the major arenas of terrorist and counterterrorist activities. In November 2004, for the first time in history, the Israeli parliament approved a plan to uproot Jewish settlements from lands claimed by Palestinians in Gaza for a future state.

even though international terrorism was increasingly lethal, global terrorism previously had seldom taken many lives. Nevertheless, terrorism at all times has commanded high attention because each spectacular terrorist act always has generated a powerful shock effect, elevated by its dramatic publicity in the news media. Consider one major flash point of today's terrorism—the Middle East (see Map 11.2).

The New Global Terrorism. September 11, 2001, forced people to rethink the meaning of terrorism and its previously marginal threat to global stability. The events of 9/11 seem destined to remain permanently etched in the minds and memories of everyone. Few, if any, will ever forget where they were when they first heard the horrendous news. In a single moment the world was forced to confront grim new realities. Instantaneously, those absent towers in New York became the symbol for the shapelessness of an apparent new world disorder.

"The prospect of another attack," warned U.S. Vice President Dick Cheney in 2002, "is not a matter of if, but when." The generation of fear was 9/11's primary product. That was precisely the terrorists' purpose behind this atrocious act. "America is full of fear," proclaimed a jubilant Osama bin Laden in the taped message he broadcast in anticipation of the U.S. response to his slaughter of thousands of innocent people. "They cry for their children," he gleefully asserted, while warning, "nobody in the United States will feel safe."

Provoking fear is an old game, and traditional forms of the old terrorism are far from dead. However, terrorism after September 11 is no longer a marginal menace in other countries to be watched on the evening news. 9/11 was a sadistic assault that exposed a previously complacent community's vulnerability to an enemy that recognized no moral restraints, that was relentless in pursuit of violence, and that claimed to be poised to strike anyone, anything, anywhere, anytime.

There *is* much that is new and therefore different about terrorism today from the terrorism of the late twentieth century, prior to September 11. The two epochs can be distinguished, which is why many observers have asserted that *everything* has changed and that September 11 likely will be remembered as "the day the world changed."

What arguably made September 11 a historic watershed ushering in a new age is that it marked the advent of new rules for a violent old game by the weak against the strong, now conducted by ideological terrorists acting transnationally to transform the international status quo. Prior to 9/11, the primary purpose of terrorism was publicity, to elicit attention and sympathy for the terrorist's cause. Accordingly terror was previously regarded as mainly theater, and it was often observed that "terrorists want a lot of people watching, not a lot of people dead." No longer. Terrorists began to engage in new practices for new purposes—seeking not simply to coerce changes in enemies' policies but to annihilate enemies: They now wanted a lot of people dead.

To U.S. President George W. Bush, "Night fell on a different world," marking not only, in his words, "the first war of the twenty-first century" but also inaugurating a defining era. "We have found our mission and our moment. . . . The way I view this is that we're fighting evil, and I don't see any shades of gray." In April 2002, before she became Bush's secretary of state, Condoleezza Rice, echoed his interpretation, declaring "an earthquake of the magnitude of 9/11 can shift the tectonic plates of international politics."

To be sure, there are many elements of truth in all these claims about the sea change that commenced. Does a new disease now stalk the face of the earth? If so, it raises unfamiliar issues. What is different today is that the new age of terrorism is

- global, in the sense that with the death of distance borders no longer serve as barriers to terrorism

Terrorist Weapons Terrorists have made "the human weapon," or suicide bombers, commonplace. Predicting who is willing to die as a "martyr" is difficult. Shown here (left) is an example—Raed Abdul Hamid Misk and his children days before he blew himself up on a Jerusalem bus. Shown also (right) is another symptom of terrorism's fury—Sunni Muslim insurgents celebrating their attack in April 2004 of an American military convoy outside Falluja, Iraq.

- lethal, because now terrorists have shifted their tactics from theatrical violent acts seeking to alarm for publicity to purposeful destruction of a target populated entirely by civilian noncombatants, to kill as many as possible for the purpose of instilling fear in as many people as possible
- waged by civilians without state sanction in ways and by means that erase the classic boundaries between terrorism and a declared war between states
- reliant on the most advanced technology of modern civilization to destroy through those sophisticated technological means the modern civilization seen as posing a threat to the terrorist's sacred traditions
- orchestrated by transnational nonstate organizations through global conspiratorial networks of terrorist cells located in many countries, involving unprecedented levels of communication and coordination (Sageman 2004)
- pursued by fanatical extremists to annihilate through maximal bloodshed rather than to persuade, by carrying out crimes against humanity by suicidal methods requiring the terrorists to sacrifice their own lives in acts that cannot be deterred or prevented through negotiated compromise
- driven by hatred of the target—by terrorists' desire to make the target suffer for what the target is, what it does, and the values for which the target stands

These changes will require a new compass to travel through the new global landscape, and new approaches to contain another wave of increasingly deadly global terrorism.

Counterterrorism. Disagreement about the character and the cause of global terrorism past, present, and future remains pronounced, and without agreement on these preliminaries, agreement on the best response to the new global terrorism is unlikely. Much like a disease that cannot be treated until it is first

Terrorist Mastermind The 9/11 terrorist attacks were coordinated by one man—Osama bin Laden, the wealthy Saudi expatriate, former CIA employee in the Afghan resistance against the Soviet Union, and zealous Islamic revolutionary who financed and organized the Al Qaeda terrorist network responsible for the September 11 attack. The question is whether terrorism is primarily the product of individual fanatics motivated by religious, political, and ideological beliefs, or whether it arises from other sources such as poverty (Kaminski 2002), religion (Rubenstein 2003), or a clash between opposed civilizations (Howell 2003).

accurately diagnosed, so the plague of the new terrorism cannot be prevented until it is first defined, and successful strategies of control are contingent upon understanding its causes. Hence, "While the resolve to do whatever necessary to combat terrorism will remain undiminished, a great debate has already begun: What exactly is to be done? The answer will depend in large measure on the answer to a prior question, "What happened [on September 11] and why?" (Talbott and Chanda 2002).

Those persuaded by one particular image of terrorism's character and primary causes are inevitably drawn to a particular set of policy recommendations, while those persuaded by a competing constructed image inevitably embrace an entirely different set of counterterrorist policy prescriptions and programs.

Consider the diametrically opposed views of whether repression or conciliation is the most effective remedy (see Controversy: Can the War against Global Terrorism Be Won?). Those advocating the former harsh approach see terrorism springing from the rational decisions of extremists to rely on political violence, and they advise prevention and even preemptive strikes that promise surgical attacks to kill terrorists, and failing that, swift and severe retaliation. In contrast are those who see terrorism rooted in frustrations with political oppression and deprivation; they recommend addressing these root causes in order to contain terrorism, taking as their point of departure the November 2, 1972, UN resolution that concluded: "measures to prevent international terrorism [require] study of the underlying causes of those forms of terrorism and acts of violence which lie in misery, frustration, grievance and despair." To those of this persuasion, long-term reforms and short-term conciliatory policies are proposed.

At issue therefore is how the line should be drawn between the legitimate and illegitimate uses of military force. The debate about methods for waging a **just war** against the new global terrorism revolves around a series of interconnected issues (see Wills 2004): Are the policies effective? Ethical? Compatible with other values such as the preservation of civil liberties and democratic procedures? Require multilateral (international) cooperation (or can they be engineered through unilateral, go-it-alone independent national solutions)? Can technology provide a barrier? Can global terrorism be addressed through legal or institutional procedures? What are the relative benefits and costs of counterterrorist measures defined by the categories prevention, protection, and prosecution?

- **just war**
the theory originating in the Middle Ages that identifies the conditions under which it is morally permissible, or "just," for a state to go to war and the methods by which a just war might be fought.

The dangers of stereotypes and the responses they rationalize show why the prospects are dim for eradicating terrorism through negotiated settlements and, conversely, also why combating terrorism through hard military operations tends to legitimize violence and thereby may inadvertently encourage further terrorist actions. The record of past efforts that have relied on these "solutions" reveals their deficiencies. Consider the impotence of promising punitive retaliation to acts of terrorism when those threats are not carried out: "although terrorists attacked U.S. interests more than 2,400 times between 1983 and 1998, the United States responded with overt military action only three times" (Reinares 2002, 92). Although most experts would agree that whereas "it is not possible to extirpate terrorism from the face of the globe," they share faith in the more modest goal—that "it should be possible to reduce the incidence and effectiveness of terrorism." Maintaining a proper balance between respect for freedom and a capacity for decisive resolute action will prove to be a substantial challenge in the "war" against the new global terrorism.

It is unlikely that the danger of terrorism will decline. Indeed, terrorism has become more deadly and harder to curb in the borderless globalized system that makes the practice of terrorism so effortless. The previous reasons for terrorist activity remain as strong as ever, and the **information age** makes transnational networking among terrorist groups convenient. The 2002 International Convention for the Suppression of the Financing of Terrorism adopted by 132 countries failed to curb terrorist activity, despite the best of intentions, in an increasingly interdependent world that facilitates the free movement of people and goods across national borders. Adding to the persistent threat is that contemporary terrorism has become more radicalized and more violent. "Any survey of the world map of terrorism—the part of the world where the most casualties occur—reveals not only growing fanaticism but also the growth of indiscriminate murder, the desire to exercise power, and sheer bloodlust. In recent years, terrorists have become less hesitant to inflict heavy casualties and cause physical destruction" (Laqueur 2001). Because terrorists now have available a variety of new tactics, such as the use of electronic threats to practice "cyberterrorism" and engage in "Netwar" strategies, the dangers are climbing. Terrorism today is the work of people willing to use weapons of mass destruction (WMD, the initials preferred to ABC for atomic, biological, and chemical weapons).

- **information age**
the era in which the rapid creation and global transfer of information through mass communication and the Internet is contributing to the globalization of knowledge.

International terrorism is certain to persist for still other reasons. One of the

CONTROVERSY: CAN THE WAR AGAINST GLOBAL TERRORISM BE WON?

In the wake of September 11, a new conventional wisdom has arisen—namely, in the words of U.S. Secretary of Defense Donald Rumsfeld, that "if the [United States] learned a single lesson from September 11, it should be that the only way to defeat terrorists is to attack them. There is no choice. You simply cannot defend in every place at every time against every technique. All the advantage is with the terrorist in that regard, and therefore you have no choice but to go after them where they are." This reflects the view that even if appeasement is tempting, the only way to respond is relentlessly and thoroughly.

Exactly what *is* the right thing to do to control the new global terrorism is likely to remain controversial. Many experts question the U.S. characterization of the problem and the ambitious crusade it promised to undertake, including skeptical allies on whom the United States is dependent if the antiterror war is to be won. To conduct a worldwide war requires an enduring commitment at high costs. That is why proposals for an effective and just response to the new global terrorism differ, as do recommendations about how the world can most effectively reduce the probability that September 11 will never be repeated.

What makes counterterrorism so controversial is that strategists often fail to distinguish different types of terrorist movements and their diverse origins. Therefore they construct counterterrorist strategies in the abstract—with a single formula—rather than tailoring approaches for dealing with terrorism's alternate modes. As one expert advises, "One lesson learned since September 11 is that the expanded war on terrorism has created a lens that tends to distort our vision of the complex political dynamics of countries" (Menkhaus 2002).

What do you think? If terrorism is the problem, and the goal is its complete eradication, how should those pursuing that quest proceed? In evaluating proposed controls in the fight against the latest wave of global terrorism, you will need to confront a series of incompatible clichés and conclusions: "concessions only encourage terrorists' appetite for further terrorism" as opposed to "concessions can redress the grievances that lead to terrorism," or "terrorism requires a long-term solution" as opposed to the claim that "terrorism cannot be cured but it can be prevented by preemption." Your search for solutions will necessarily spring from incompatible assumptions you make about terrorism's nature and sources, and these assumptions will strongly affect your conclusions about the wisdom or futility of contemplated remedies. Keep in mind that what may appear as a policy around which an effective counterterrorist program might be constructed could potentially only exacerbate the problem by provoking the very result your preferred plan was designed to solve: recourse to future terrorist actions. Counterterrorism is controversial because one person's solution is another person's problem, and the answers are often unclear. A counterterrorist program that may succeed in one location may backfire in another. Because promise and/or peril may result when the same countermeasure is deployed, what would you advise governments about the best methods of fighting terrorism?

---

most important and potent is the condition that Walter Laqueur terms **postmodern terrorism.** This phrase describes the globalized environment that today makes terrorism easy to practice, in part because it has become so "complex" (Homer-Dixon 2005). So-called postmodern terrorism is likely to expand because the globalized international environment without meaningful barriers allows terrorists to practice their ancient trade by new rules and methods, while at the same time encouraging state-sponsored terrorism as a substitute for warfare and making the most advanced countries the most vulnerable (Laqueur 2003). Another reason is the rapid spread of new weapons and technology, and their easy transport across borders, which provides unprecedented opportunities for terrorists to commit atrocities and to change their tactics in response to

■ **postmodern terrorism** to Walter Laqueur, the terrorism practiced by an expanding set of diverse actors with new weapons "to sow panic in a society, to weaken or even overthrow the incumbents, and to bring about political change."

successes in countering them. A third reason is the growing difficulty in a globalized system of detecting and deterring the attacks of disciplined globalized terrorist networks that are generously funded by international organized crime (IOC) syndicates to facilitate their profit in the narcotics trade (Berdal and Serrano 2002). And still another reason is the moral ambiguity that surrounds the activities of extremist militia, such as suicide bombers, who are glorified as religious martyrs. In addition, some of the mass media praise terrorists for their independent defiance of government authority.

Terrorists appear destined to be regarded either as hated villains or as honored heros, depending on the view of the observer. This ensures that terrorism is likely to remain a fixture of twenty-first-century politics and that violence will continue to cast its shadow over international relations.

Could it be that a world so ingenious in perpetrating violence also will learn that war and violence are too costly, too destructive to continue? If so, can it discover effective paths to sustained peace? Can "the transformation of the warfare state into the welfare state" (Ferguson 2001) progress on its winding road? The chapters that follow examine some of the methods for controlling military conflict that policymakers and concerned global citizens have proposed.

KEY TERMS

war
conflict
politics
armed conflict
behavioralism
constructivism
long peace
levels of analysis
intraspecific aggression
interspecific aggression
realism
pacifism
survival of the fittest
nature versus nurture
socialization
territorial imperative
national character
ecological fallacy
individualistic fallacy
rational choice

groupthink
state level of analysis
neorealism
sovereignty
intervention
feminist theory
cultural conditioning
communist theory of imperialism
laissez-faire economics
globalization
relative gains
neoliberal theories
human rights
democratic peace
nationalism
ideology
behavioralism
global level of analysis
self-help
security dilemma

anarchy
bargaining model of war
power transition theory
structural realism
long-cycle theory
hegemon
war weariness hypothesis
civil war
relative deprivation
ethnic warfare
displaced people
failing states
human development index (HDI)
diversionary theory of war
terrorism
state-sponsored terrorism
just war
information age
postmodern terrorism

SUGGESTED READING

Badey, Thomas J., ed. *Violence and Terrorism 05/06*, 8th ed. Dubuque, Iowa: McGraw-Hill Dushkin, 2005.

Bennett, Scott, and Allan C. Stam. *The Behavioral Origins of War*. Ann Arbor: University of Michigan Press, 2004.

Flint, Colin, ed. *The Geography of War and Peace*. New York: Oxford University Press, 2004.

Gilpin, Robert. *War and Change in World Politics*. Cambridge, Eng.: Cambridge University Press, 1981.

Harff, Barbara, and Ted Robert Gurr. *Ethnic Conflict in World Politics*, 2nd ed. Boulder, Colorado: Westview, 2003.

Holsti, Kalevi J. *War, the State, and the State of War*. New York: Cambridge University Press, 1996.

Kegley, Charles W., ed. *The New Global Terrorism: Characteristics, Causes, Controls*. Upper Saddle River, N.J.: Prentice Hall, 2003.

Nye, Joseph. *Understanding International Conflicts*, 5th ed. New York: Longman, 2005.

Sageman, Marc. *Understanding Terror Networks*. Philadelphia: University of Pennsylvania Press, 2004.

Schneider, Gerald, Katherine Barbieri, and Nils Petter Gleditsch, eds. *Globalization and Armed Conflict*. Lanham, Md.: Rowman and Littlefield, 2003.

Tilly, Charles. *The Politics of Collective Violence*. Cambridge: Cambridge University Press, 2003.

Walzer, Michael. *Arguing about War*. New Haven, Conn.: Yale University Press, 2004.

WHERE ON THE WORLD WIDE WEB?

CAIN Web Service
http://cain.ulst.ac.uk/index.html

The Conflict Archive on the Internet (CAIN) is a joint project of three educational institutions in the United Kingdom (the University of Ulster, the Queen's University of Belfast, and the Linen Hall Library) that seeks to provide information on the ongoing conflict in Northern Ireland, historically known as "the Troubles." There are links to descriptions of the key events and issues of this long-term conflict and background on society in Northern Ireland. The site also includes full-length articles and lectures on the conflict that would be good sources for a research paper. What main disputes have driven this conflict? What steps have been taken to resolve it? What are the prospects for a long-term peaceful resolution?

Dreams of Tibet
http://www.pbs.org/wgbh/pages/frontline/shows/tibet/

PBS Online offers this educational website devoted to issues surrounding Tibet and its quest for independence. View the chronology of Tibet's history starting in the year 600. Then read background about Tibetan Buddhism and find out who the Dalai Lama is. Peruse ten interviews, including those with Jamyang Norbu, a Tibetan author in exile; actor Richard Gere, who is a "Free Tibet" activist; and Martin Scorsese, who directed the movie *Kundun*, which was based on the biography of the Dalai Lama. The site includes excerpts from media articles and reports on the tense relationship between Tibet and the Chinese government. You can share your own thoughts in a discussion forum.

Incore
http://www.incore.ulst.ac.uk/cds/countries/index.html

The University of Ulster has developed an Internet guide for the Initiative on Conflict Resolution and Ethnicity that allows you to examine the most recent international conflicts and nationalist movements in detail. Clearly arranged by geographic location, this site offers information about conflicts around the globe. Read about the Kurds' quest for their own state and the conflict between Israelis and Palestinians. There are links to research sources, news sources, maps, nongovernmental organizations, and e-mail lists and newsgroups. You can also gather information according to theme. Want to know how war affects children? Visit the "Children and Conflict" link. Want to investigate the interaction of gender and war? Click the "Gender and Conflict" link.

WHERE ON THE WORLD WIDE WEB? (continued)

Institute for War and Peace Reporting
http://www.iwpr.net

Students of international relations often have a hard time getting up-to-date information from conflict areas that is not heavily censored by government agencies. The main goal of the Institute for War and Peace Reporting (IWPR) is to bring unbiased information on international conflicts to Internet users. An independent media resource, IWPR informs readers on international conflicts and supports media development in war-torn areas. Special reports provide in-depth analysis of conflict, media, and human rights issues in regions across the globe. Read reports from trouble spots as events unfold. There is also an extensive list of Internet links for those who want more information on the conflicts.

International Crisis Group
http://www.icg.org/

The International Crisis Group (ICG) is a private, multinational organization dedicated to understanding and responding to international crises. The organization's analysts conduct field research and prepare reports about ongoing conflicts that are used to make recommendations to states' decision makers. Currently, ICG has projects in most regions of the globe. Students who are interested in regional conflicts will find informed overviews of specific countries, reports on developments, and maps.

War Reporting
http://www.mediachannel.org/atissue/warpeace/

Mediachannel.org created this site, which explores the nature and dangers of being a journalist in a war zone. The site contains several first-person accounts from reporters, and it also has articles that examine "peace journalism" and the ethics of war reporting. Articles also cover media biases and government manipulation of the media in recent conflicts, including the 1991 Persian Gulf War and the continuing war in Iraq.

Terrorism Research Center
http://www.terrorism.com/

This site is a good source for research on terrorism and links to other web sources on terrorism. Look at the "Terrorist Profiles" for discussion and analysis of groups. Keep in mind that one group's "freedom fighters" may be another group's "terrorists."

INFOTRAC® COLLEGE EDITION

Gallagher, Tony. "After the War Comes Peace? An Examination of the Impact of the Northern Ireland Conflict on Young People." *Journal of Social Issues* (Fall 2004).

Serebriannikov, V. V. "On Cold and Hot Wars." *Military Thought* (March–April 2002).

Kagan, Donald. "A Look at the Great Wars of the Twentieth Century." *Naval War College Review* (Autumn 2000).

Bennett, D. Scott, and Allan C. Stam III. "The Duration of Interstate Wars, 1816–1985," *American Political Science Review* (June 1996).

For more articles, enter:

"war" in the Subject Guide, and then go to subdivision "analysis"

"war" in the Subject Guide, and then go to subdivision "causes of"

"terrorism" in the Subject Guide

Go to http://politicalscience.wadsworth.com/kegley10 to access additional resources related to this chapter.

CHAPTER 12

MILITARY POWER, COERCIVE DIPLOMACY, AND NATIONAL SECURITY

TOPICS AND THEMES

- Power in world politics
- The pursuit of military capability
- Military strategy in the nuclear age
- The uses and limits of coercive diplomacy
- The great powers' national security strategies

- **CONTROVERSY** DOES HIGH MILITARY SPENDING LOWER HUMAN SECURITY?
- **CONTROVERSY** IS IT ETHICAL TO WAGE PREEMPTIVE WAR TO PREVENT AN ADVERSARY'S POTENTIAL AGGRESSION?

The thriving international trade in the weapons of war and terrorism.

> *It is an unfortunate fact that we can only secure peace by preparing for war.*
> —JOHN F. KENNEDY, U.S. presidential candidate, 1960

> *Inflexible hard-line policies . . . are not likely to decrease the satisfaction of other states but are likely to lead to a negative response that leaves all concerned worse off.*
> —FRANK C. ZAGARE, political scientist, 2004

■ **self-help**
the principle that because in international anarchy all global actors are independent, they must rely on themselves to provide for their security and well-being.

■ **national security**
a country's capacity to resist external or internal threats to its physical survival or core values.

■ **coercion**
the threat or use of military force or economic sanctions as tools of punishment to change a target actor's policies against its will.

Armed conflicts are frequent and destructive. Whenever and wherever they break out, they incite tension and terror. These features explain why states are fixated on security threats and why preparing for defense is a nearly universal preoccupation. Because the anarchical global system encourages states to rely on **self-help** for protection, **national security**—a country's psychological freedom from fear of foreign aggression—is of paramount priority on policymakers' foreign policy agendas.

This chapter examines why states often respond to perceived threats by arming, and explores the use of military intervention and economic sanctions as tools of **coercion** to exercise control over foreign governments' policies and leaders. The place of power in the interdependent age of globalized world politics is first considered. Next, we evaluate states' efforts to reduce threats to their security, exploring trends in military spending (and their domestic socioeconomic consequences), the arms trade, and weapons technology, as well as the dilemmas that armament acquisitions create and the great powers' national security strategies. Later chapters will use this discussion to examine which paths to peace realists and liberals advocate for escaping the danger of war.

POWER IN INTERNATIONAL POLITICS

What is this abstraction called **power,** which realists assume to be states' primary objective? Most leaders schooled in realpolitik conventionally operate from the traditional assumption that power is something that gives states the ability to promote national interests, to win in international bargaining, and to shape the rules governing the global system. Leaders tend to view power primarily as a political phenomenon revolving around the capacity of one actor to persuade another to do what it otherwise would not. Thus, we will first evaluate this definition, which sees power as **politics**—the exercise of influence to control and dominate others. But we must keep in mind that power is an ambiguous concept (see Claude 1962; Kadera and Sorokin 2004) and therefore it is difficult to determine how states' power should be measured.

When we view power as the means to control, it is reasonable to ask, when **conflict** occurs, Who is stronger and who is weaker? to predict which party will get its way and which will be forced to make concessions. These considerations invite the more fundamental question, What enables states to achieve their goals?

THE ELEMENTS OF STATE POWER

To determine the comparative power of states, analysts usually rank them according to the capabilities or resources presumed necessary to achieve influence over others. For such purposes, multiple factors (most significantly, military and economic capability) measure countries' relative **power potential.** If we could compare each state's total capabilities, according to this logic, we could then rank them by their relative ability to draw on these resources to exercise influence. Such a ranking would reveal the global system's hierarchy of power, differentiating the strong from the weak, the great from the marginal.

Of all the components of state power, military capability is regarded by realists as the central element in states' power potential. "Throughout history, the decisive factor in the fates of nations has usually been the number, efficiency, and dispositions of fighting forces," they argue. "National influence bears a direct relationship to gross national strength; without that, the most exquisite statesmanship is likely to be of limited use" (German 1960). **Realism** assumes that the ability to coerce is more important than the ability to reward or to purchase; realists therefore reject the view of neoliberal strategic thinkers that under conditions of **globalization,** economic resources will be increasingly more critical to national strength and human security than military capability (Nye 2004b).

Following traditional thinking, one way to estimate the power potential of states is to compare the extent to which they spend money on acquiring military capabilities. Figure 12.1 presents a ranking that taps what most people would likely regard as the world's most "powerful" states, according to their expenditures to wage war.

Money is not the measure of a man, or of a country. Yes, a state can spend without concern for cost in an effort to reach the elusive goal of obtaining national security. But there is never a guarantee that bucks will translate into bangs. In the U.S. case, there is uncertainty whether the $1.75 trillion budgeted

■ **power**
the factors that enable one state to coerce another; to realists, arms and military capabilities are the most important factor in determining which state will win a dispute.

■ **politics**
the process by which important values are upheld or compromised when two or more actors become involved in a zero-sum conflict in which a gain for one party will create a partial or total loss for the other party.

■ **conflict**
discord, often arising in international relations over perceived incompatibilities of interest.

■ **power potential**
the relative capabilities or resources held by a state that are considered necessary to its asserting influence over others.

■ **realism**
a paradigm based on the premise that world politics is essentially and unchangeably a struggle among self-interested states for power and position under anarchy, with each competing state single-mindedly pursuing its own national self-advantage without altruistic concern for others or sentimental attachment to moral values.

■ **globalization**
the processes by which the countries of the world are becoming linked to one another economically, politically, and militarily in interdependent bonds.

FIGURE 12.1
The Military Race for Hegemony: How U.S. Military Spending Stacks Up against Its Primary Competitors

All states seek safety from foreign attack, and many spend large sums of their national budgets for arsenals and armies for that defensive purpose. States vary widely, however, in their military expenditures. As this figure shows, the globe's "sole superpower" is the biggest spender on armaments, with U.S. President George W. Bush's budget in 2004 for $399.1 billion to safeguard U.S. national security through military spending exceeding the next twenty countries' combined military expenditures. The U.S. increase in 2003 accounted for "almost half of the world total" (SIPRI 2004). In terms of military spending as a measure, the United States stands at the apex of global power, predominate and without rival as a true hegemonic superpower.

SOURCE: Adapted from data provided by the Center for Defense Information (http://www.cdi.org/budget/2004/world-military-spending.cfm).

---

by the newly re-elected George W. Bush administration for military spending between 2006 and 2009 (not counting expected additional appropriations to support U.S. forces in Iraq) will automatically increase U.S. safety or reach the fighting men and women in the field. The size of the defense budget does not matter as much as how wisely it is spent and whether it goes to the needs that really matter, such as protecting citizens from terrorist attacks with an effective homeland security system. As U.S. Secretary of State Condoleezza Rice summarized, "Power is nothing unless you can turn it into influence." For the U.S. military colossus (Ferguson 2004b), the issue is critical. What are the returns for the investment? It now costs the average U.S. citizen $1,211 for defense (as compared with $2.77 for international peacekeeping), and the anticipated U.S. increase now exceeds the gross domestic product of more than one-third of the globe's states (World Bank 2005b). The result has not paid large dividends, because the United States, by far the globe's greatest spender on defense, remains the primary target of terrorist attacks (Crenshaw 2003).

Power potential also derives from factors other than military expenditures. Among the so-called elements of power, analysts take into account such capabilities as the relative size of a state's economy, its population and territorial size, geographic position, raw materials, degree of dependence on foreign sources of materials, technological capacity, political culture and values, ideology, efficiency of governmental decision making, industrial productivity, volume of trade, savings and investment, educational level, national morale and internal solidarity, and especially "advances in technology and increases in social and economic transactions [that can] lead to a new world in which states, and their control of force, will no longer be important" (Keohane and Nye 2001b). For example, if power potential is measured by territorial size, Russia, twice as large as its closest rivals (Canada, China, the United States, Brazil, and Australia, in that order) would be the globe's most powerful country. Likewise, if power is measured by the UN's projections for countries' populations by the year 2025, China, India, the United States, Indonesia, Pakistan, Nigeria, and Brazil, in that order, would be the most powerful. In a similar comparison, the rankings of countries' expenditures on research and development (as a percentage of GDP) to fund future economic growth and military might would rank Israel, Sweden, Finland, Japan, Iceland, the United States, Switzerland, South Korea, and Germany as the countries with the brightest future (UNDP 2004, 252, 180). Clearly, strength is relative. The leading countries in some dimensions of power potential are not leaders in others, because power comes in many forms and the global spread of technology has made it increasingly difficult to distinguish between powerful and weak states.

For these reasons, there is little consensus on how best to weigh the various factors that contribute to military capability and national power; that is, there is no agreement as to what their relative importance should be in making comparisons, or what conditions affect the power potential of each factor. Although most analysts agree that states are not equal in their ability to influence others, few agree on how to rank their potential to exercise their power. Consider what divergent pictures of the global hierarchy emerge when the great powers' relative capabilities are ranked in other categories that realists also define as especially important, such as the size of each state's economy and/or armed forces (see Maps 12.1 and 12.2).

Distinguishing Power from Capabilities

Part of the difficulty of defining the elements of power is that their potential impact depends on the circumstances (in a bargaining situation between conflicting actors, for example) and especially on how leaders perceive those circumstances. Such judgments are subjective, as power ratios are not strictly products of measured capabilities. Perceptions also matter.

In addition, power is not a tangible commodity that states can acquire. It has meaning only in relative terms. Power is relational: A state can have power over some other actor only when it can prevail over that actor. Both actual and perceived strength determine who wins a political contest. To make a difference, an adversary must know its enemy's capabilities and willingness to mobilize those capabilities for coercive purposes. Intentions—especially perceptions of them—are critically important when making threats. The mere possession of weapons does not increase a state's power if its adversaries do not believe it will use them, or if they are willing to suffer huge damages to prevail.

Historically, those with the largest arsenals have not necessarily triumphed in political conflicts. Weaker states often successfully resist pressure from their

MAPS 12.1 AND 12.2
Two Measures of Military Power Potential: State Wealth and Size of National Armies

Many people look at economic indicators to measure national power, because a large economy provides the means for acquiring the military capabilities necessary for projecting political influence overseas. Indeed, wealth is a key measure of security and political clout in the global marketplace, because rich countries possess the means of exercising influence. The map on the left measures gross national income (GNI) across countries to estimate national levels of economic well-being and shows the vast differences in states' wealth that separate the rich from the poor (and the strong from the weak?). Another measure of power projection is the number of the personnel in uniform in states' armies, navies, and air forces. This map on the right shows the varying distribution of armed forces among the nations of the world. In the **information age,** where high-tech military equipment makes a huge difference, realists regard the size of a country's armed forces as critically important in conducting modern warfare.

SOURCE: National wealth, World Bank (2004a), 252–53; Armed forces personnel, UNDP (2004), 211–14.

Intractive map with critical thinking questions

■ **information age**
today's era in which mass communication and the Internet transfer information instantaneously throughout the globe.

military superiors. Although Vietnam was weak in the conventional military sense, it succeeded against a vastly stronger France and, later, United States. Similarly, U.S. superior military power did not prevent North Korea's seizure of the USS *Pueblo* in 1968, Iran's taking of American diplomats as hostages a decade later, or the Al Qaeda terrorist network's 9/11 attack. Indeed, the capacity

Total Armed Forces
- High (more than 1 million)
- Medium (500,000 to 1 million)
- Low (less than 500,000)
- No data

after June 2004 of a quasi-sovereign Iraq to move in directions that the U.S. superpower objected to but could not control underscored the weakness of superior military force in interstate bargaining. The Soviet Union's inability, prior to its disintegration, to control political events in Afghanistan, Eastern Europe, or even among its own constituent republics—despite an awesome weapons arsenal—shows that the impotence of military power is not particular to the United States. History is replete with examples of small countries that won wars or defended their independence against much more militarily powerful enemies. Think of Switzerland against the Hapsburg Empire, the Netherlands against Spain, and Greece against the Ottomans in the seventeenth century. In each case, intangible factors such as the will of the target population to resist a more powerful army and their willingness to die to defend the homeland were key elements in the capacity of a weaker state to defend itself against a much stronger military force—as Great Britain reluctantly recognized in 1781 when it concluded that the price of reclaiming the American colonies was too great.

Nonetheless, the quest for security through arms and the realist belief in military force remain widespread. Most policymakers assume that "while it could be a mistake to assume that political influence is proportional to military strength, it would be an even bigger mistake to deny any connection between the two" (Majeed 1991). Many believe that this is because military capability is a prerequisite to the successful exercise of **coercive diplomacy** through the threat of limited force. Perhaps it was this conviction that inspired U.S. President George W. Bush to assert that "a dangerous and uncertain world requires America to have a sharpened sword."

■ **coercive diplomacy**
the use of threats or limited armed force to persuade an adversary to alter its foreign and/or domestic policies.

The Changing Character of World Power

Military power is central in leaders' conceptualizations of national security. As noted in previous chapters, however, many analysts now argue that "the sources of power are, in general, moving away from the emphasis on military force and conquest that marked earlier eras. In assessing international power today, factors such as technology, external respect and reputation, education, and economic growth are becoming more important, whereas geography, population, and raw materials are becoming less important" (Nye 2004b). In part this is because military force has often proven ineffectual, notably against revisionist states and belligerent terrorist nonstate actors resisting pressure from abroad. Military superiority is especially questioned in the war against politically mobilized terrorist movements, where intelligence and communications are arguably as important in counterterrorism as are military capabilities. Moreover, awareness of the importance of trade competitiveness to national standing has directed increasing attention to the nonmilitary dimensions of national security.

If we compare military, political, and trade strategies as alternative methods for realizing national security in the era of globalization, policies emphasizing economic and trade approaches to national power begin to appear increasingly effective in acquiring political power and material advancement. Since 1945 only a handful of states have borne crushing military costs, while the others have gained a relative competitive edge by investing in research on the development of goods to export abroad and by conserving resources by relying on allies and global institutions to provide defense against potential threats. While the United States (which in 2005 accounted for almost half of world military expenditures) has spent two-thirds of its research and development budget on military programs since the mid-1980s, European countries spent two-thirds on development of new technologies for consumers and civilians at home and abroad, and Japan's civilian product research exceeded 99 percent of all its research (SIPRI 2004).

■ **opportunity costs**
the concept in decision-making theories that when the opportunity arises to use resources, what is gained for one purpose is lost for other purposes, so that every choice entails the cost of some lost opportunity.

■ **peace dividend**
the global savings from arms expenditure reductions made possible by the end of highly hostile international rivalries such as the Cold War.

Military expenditures extract other **opportunity costs** as well that retard economic growth and create fiscal deficits. According to the International Monetary Fund (IMF), "military spending crowds out both private and public investment." Had U.S. military outlays remained at the 1990 levels established at the end of the Cold War, the **peace dividend** would have exceeded $400 billion in the next decade and potentially could have been made available for other purposes. The United States failed to do this, however, unlike many other countries. In addition to sacrificing other economic opportunities, this argument continues, military spending has direct costs, because expensive equipment quickly becomes outdated in the face of rapid technological innovations. This creates the need for even-more sophisticated new weapons, the costs of which are staggering.

Yet development of expensive new weapons, such as improved stealth aircraft and many others geared to fight the last century's threats, continue apace at the expense of lost revenue for other investments. At a time of uncontested U.S. military superiority, it was concern about reckless runaway spending on unneeded weapons that led U.S. Secretary of Defense Donald Rumsfeld in 2002 to cancel the contract on the Army's expensive Crusader artillery program, even though Congress sought to fund its development.

Because "states can afford more 'butter' if they need fewer 'guns'" and eliminate plans to construct obsolete weapons, Richard Rosecrance (1997) notes, "the two objectives sometimes represent trade-offs: The achievement of one may

Who Pays for Defense? In many countries, military spending remains exceptionally high, and maintaining a large army comes at a high cost. Poor people often lose the most. One example is the United States. In October 1999, Stansfield Turner, a former director of the Central Intelligence Agency, complained that "since the dawn of the nuclear age, the government has spent more than $5.5 trillion on nuclear forces, more than on education, the environment and transportation combined. . . . Cutting back our current force of more than 12,000 nuclear warheads . . . could save billions for schools, health insurance for the many children who lack it, Head Start and other needed initiatives." However, that proposal was not accepted, in part because of what President Dwight Eisenhower termed "the military-industrial complex," which continues to shape national budgets in the United States and elsewhere. Children often suffer unmet needs or are put in harm's way. In fact, outside the United States, hundreds of thousands of children are required to be soldiers. Here some of the newly trained child-soldiers ride through the streets of Monrovia in Liberia in April 1996, taking up arms to wage war on behalf of their government sponsors.

diminish the realization of the other." The substantial costs of defense can erode national welfare—what policymakers hope to defend with military might. Conversely, commercial clout and trade competitiveness for national exports may contribute more than military might to national power in a globalized marketplace without barriers to trade; in that setting, trade bloc competition replaces the military and diplomatic struggles of the past (see Controversy: Does High Military Spending Lower Human Security?).

In addition to economic capability, other less-tangible sources of national power now figure more prominently in calculations regarding national defense, including the communications media empires' control of global information. "Political leaders and philosophers have long understood that power comes from setting the agenda and determining the framework of a debate. The ability to establish preferences tends to be associated with intangible power resources such as culture, ideology, and institutions" (Nye 1990). These intangible resources constitute *soft power*, in contrast with *hard power*, conventionally defined as "tangible resources like military and economic strength" (Nye 2004b). Soft power is "the ability to achieve goals through attraction rather than coercion . . . by convincing others to follow or getting them to agree to norms and institutions that produce the desired behavior" (Keohane and Nye 2001b). If soft power grows in relative importance in today's so-called information age, military force ratios will no longer translate into power potential in the way they once did.

CONTROVERSY

DOES HIGH MILITARY SPENDING LOWER HUMAN SECURITY?

Politics requires making hard choices about priorities and about how public funds should be spent. One such difficult choice is between "guns versus butter"—how to allocate scarce finances for military preparedness as opposed to meeting the human needs of citizens and enabling them to live a secure and long life. The former category looks to arms for **national security,** and the latter stresses **human security.** Neither goal can be pursued without making some sacrifice for the realization of the other.

The "guns versus butter" trade-off is a serious controversy in every country, and different countries deal with it in different ways. That difference is captured by the range in states' willingness to pay a heavy burden for defense: by grouping states according to the share of gross domestic product (GDP) they devote to the military and then juxtaposing this relative burden with their GDP. The **relative burden of military spending,** the ratio of defense spending to GDP, is the customary way in which the sacrifices that mil-

Military Expenditures as a Percentage of GDP
- High (more than 5%)
- Medium (2% to 5%)
- Low (less than 2%)
- No data

SOURCE: UNDP (2004), 202–5.

itary spending requires is measured. As the map to the left shows, there exist wide variations, with many countries allocating high proportions of their total GDP to defense and other countries choosing to spend their wealth on enhancing human security. Indeed, note that some comparatively wealthy states (Kuwait, Israel, and Brunei) bear a heavy burden, whereas other states that provide a high average income for their citizens (Japan, Austria, and Luxembourg) have a low defense burden. Likewise, the citizens of some very poor countries (Sierra Leone, Mozambique, and Chad) are heavily burdened, whereas those of others (Bhutan and Zaire) are not. Thus, it is difficult to generalize about the precise relationship between a country's defense burden and its citizens' standard of living, human development, or stage of development.

"The problem in defense spending," as U.S. President Dwight D. Eisenhower observed in 1956, "is to figure how far you should go without destroying from within what you are trying to defend from without." How much should a country sacrifice for national security? To many realists, the price is never too high. However, others question this argument and maintain that the cost of high military spending reduces the state's ability to provide for the human security of its citizens. Again, Eisenhower expressed this view when he observed, "The world in arms is not spending money alone. It is spending the sweat of its children." This position was also argued by Oscar Arias, the 1987 Nobel Peace laureate and former president of Costa Rica, who wrote in 1999 that "world leaders must stop viewing militaristic investment as a measure of national well-being. The sad fact is that half the world's governments invest more in defense than in health programs. If we channeled just $40 billion each year away from armies and into antipoverty programs in ten years all of the world's population would enjoy basic social services—education, health care and nutrition, potable water and sanitation. Another $40 billion each year over ten years would provide each person on this planet with an income level above the poverty line for his or her country."

The case of the United States, the globe's biggest spender on the military, speaks to Dr. Ariasa's proposition that high military spending reduces social welfare. Consider how the United States ranks on various nonmilitary indicators of human security:

U.S. Rank Compared to 175 Other States

Social Development	
Gender empowerment measure (GEM)	14
Human development (HDI)	8
Female and male literacy rate	4
GDP for each person	4
Economic—Social Standing	
Percent infants with low birthweight	49
Under-five mortality rate	30
Infant mortality rate (for each 100,000 live births)	30
Number of physicians for each person	27
Life expectancy	23
Human poverty	17
Public health expenditures for each person (% of GDP)	16
Public education expenditures for each person	14
Public education expenditures for each student	10
Maternal mortality rate	12

These rankings (UNDP 2004, 201–31) suggest that when expenditures for arms go up, so do disease, illiteracy, and poverty, and the rate of economic growth goes down (Ward, Davis, and Lofdahl 1995). That said, every country is in need of a strong defense for national security.

If you were a head of state, what budget priorities would you propose for your country's national security and your citizens' human security? How would you reconcile the need for defense with the need to provide for the common welfare? The choices you would make would be difficult, because they entail a necessary trade-off between competing values. For this reason military-spending decisions are highly controversial everywhere.

THE PURSUIT OF MILITARY CAPABILITIES

How people spend their money reveals their values. Similarly, how governments allocate their revenues reveals their priorities. Examination of national budgets discloses an unmistakable pattern: Although the sources of global political power may be changing, many states continue to seek security by spending substantial portions of their national treasures on arms.

■ **national security**
a country's psychological freedom from fear that the state will be unable to resist threats to its survival and national values emanating from abroad or at home.

■ **human security**
a concept that refers to the degrees to which the welfare of individuals is protected and advanced, in contrast to national security, which puts the interests of states first.

■ **relative burden of military spending**
a measure of the economic burden of military activities calculated by the share of each state's gross domestic product allocated to military expenditures.

Trends in Military Spending

States' willingness to purchase expensive weapons has kept world military spending high. Since the Cold War ended, world military spending has grown, with an increase of 18 percent since 2002, to reach $956 billion (in current U.S. dollars) in 2004. The amount of economic resources devoted to military activities is staggering when set in a global perspective. The overall level of world military spending in 2004 is ten times higher than official development assistance worldwide (SIPRI 2004).

Looking at the global military expenditures at the start of 2004, the total of $956 billion exceeded more than $1.7 million each minute. However, world military spending could have been even higher, had past levels continued. In fact, by 1998, it had declined by about a third since a peak of $1.35 trillion in 1987. Since 1998, however, expenditures have once again been rising, with the sharpest increases recorded by the United States, which has risen since 2002 to account for almost half of the global total at the beginning of 2004 (SIPRI 2004).

Measured in constant dollars adjusted for inflation, another impression of the global outlay emerges. The 2004 level shows an increase over past levels, 2.9 times that spent in 1960, 2.1 times that of the 1970 total, and 1.4 times the 1980 level. These increases appeared especially noticeable in the 1980s, but on closer inspection they extend the growth rates of world military expenditures exhibited throughout the entire twentieth century. Military spending has increased sixteen-fold since the mid-1930s. The growth rate exceeded that of world population, the rate of expansion of global economic output, expenditures for public health to protect people from disease, and prices (U.S. ACDA 2002; Sivard 1991, 1993, 1996).

These aggregate figures require interpretation, because the global total spent for arms and armies conceals widely varying trends for particular groups of countries. Historically, the rich countries have spent the most money on arms acquisitions, and this pattern has continued. As 2004 began, the Global North was spending $717 billion for defense, in contrast with the developing Global South's $239 billion. Thus the high-income developed countries' share of the world total was about 75 percent. However, when measured against other factors, the differences became clearer. The Global North spent an average of 2.2 percent of their GNIs on weapons, whereas the Global South spent an average 3.9 percent (at a relatively greater sacrifice of funding needed to promote human development and economic growth among the poor where it is most needed).

While these two groups' military spending levels were quite different, over time they are converging. Figure 12.2 reveals that the Global South's military expenditure in 1961 was about 7 percent of the world total, but by 2004 it had climbed threefold to approximately one-quarter. This trend indicates that poor states are copying the past costly military budgetary habits of the wealthiest states.

There are equally mixed regional and national variations in these levels and growth rates. The level of perceived threats in each region from potential or actual wars within (and, less frequently, between) states, and the spread of conventional and advanced weapons of mass destruction, exert a great impact on the rise or fall of states' levels of military spending. Similar variations are also exhibited in the rates of military expenditures across different regional organizations and military alliances.

FIGURE 12.2
Changes in the Levels of Military Expenditures since 1960, Global North and Global South

Global military budgets have fluctuated since 1960, with total expenditures worldwide peaking in 1987, after which they fell about a third, but have been rising in the wake of the 9/11 war on terrorism. As the trend lines show, the military budgets of the Global South's developing countries peaked in a 1982–86 plateau, then declined before rising again since 1993 to $239 billion in 2004—about one-fourth of the world's total (U.S. ACDA 2002; SIPRI 2004). The Global North's defense spending began to decline after the threat of interstate wars receded in the wake of the Cold War, but has risen generally as the huge U.S. military budget increases pulled the developed countries' aggregate total higher, in excess of $717 billion in 2004. U.S. spending has widened considerably the gap between the United States and its great-power partners. "The gap in military capacity is so staggering that even professor Paul Kennedy, author of the highly influential *The Rise and Fall of the Great Powers* [in 1987], has now recanted the America-in-decline theory he fathered in the late 1980s. Kennedy has been moved to express his awe at American resurgence: 'Nothing has ever existed like this disparity of power; nothing'" (in Krauthammer 2002).

SOURCES: 1961–95, U.S. ACDA (1971), 1; 1996–2004, SIPRI www.SIPRI.com.

Changes in Military Capabilities

The growing militarization of the Global South and of mobilized terrorist movements by nonstate actors manifests itself in other ways as well. Military capabilities are now more widespread than ever. Part of the reason is because weapons production capabilities are no longer concentrated in the industrial Global North. Global South countries and terrorist organizations are now in the business of manufacturing modern aircraft, tanks, and missiles. A parallel

FIGURE 12.3
Arms Deliveries to the Global North and Global South, 1996–2003

The continuing global arms trade has led to the globalization of military capabilities throughout the Global North and especially the Global South. Although the value of all arms deliveries worldwide fell to $28.7 billion in 2003 (the lowest total in decades), the shipments between 1996 and 2003 were a staggering $345 billion, and in that period the Global South accounted for more than three-fifths of these weapons purchases, or $210 billion (Grimmett 2004, 3, 54).
SOURCE: Grimmett (2004, 33).

change in the open and clandestine (secret) arms trade and in the destructiveness of modern weapons has accelerated the spread of military capabilities around the world.

Trends in the Weapons Trade

During the Cold War's forty-two-year period of tension, many states sought to increase their security through the purchase of arms produced by suppliers eagerly seeking allies and profits. In 1961, world arms trade was valued at $4 billion. The traffic in arms imports thereafter climbed rapidly and peaked in 1987 at $82 billion (U.S. ACDA 1997, 10, 100). The end of the Cold War did not end the arms trade, however. Since 1991, when the Cold War ended, and continuing through 2003 in the wake of the era of global terrorism that began on 9/11, the total value of all international arms deliveries was $395 billion (Grimmett 2004, 3).

A chief characteristic of the arms trade is the extent to which the less-developed Global South accounts for the bulk of global arms deliveries (see Figure 12.3). Between 1996 and 1999, the Global South was the recipient of 70 percent of global arms deliveries, and since then it has accounted for most of the traffic—59 percent in 2003 of all shipments (Grimmett 2004, 3–4). A persistant trend in a changing world, therefore, has been for the least stable Global South states to spend the largest percentages of their relatively small economies for purchase of the weapons of war.

Spurred by the developing countries' energetic search for armaments commensurate with those of the industrial countries, and their production of them for use at home and export abroad, the global arms trade has fueled the dispersion of military capability worldwide. Weapons delivered by major suppliers to developing countries between 1996 and 2003 included 5,402 tanks and self-propelled cannons, 3,922 artillery pieces, 1,312 supersonic combat aircraft, 15,174 surface-to-air missiles, and a large number of warships, submarines, antishipping missiles, and other technologically advanced weapons systems (Grimmett 2004, 67).

The major recipients of all global arms shipments remain heavily concentrated in a subset of major Global South arms purchasers: between 1996 and 2003, weapon deliveries to the top ten recipients as a group accounted for three-fourths of all deliveries in the Global South. All of the top ten were located in either Asia or the Near East, with Saudi Arabia leading that group, spending $6.1 billion and accounting for more than two-fifths of the total deliveries. In rank order of the value of their purchases, the other leading recipients of imported arms after Saudi Arabia were Taiwan, China, Egypt, South Korea, Israel, United Arab Emirates, Kuwait, India, and Pakistan (Grimmett 2004, 53, 62).

The regional distribution of arms deliveries seems to follow trends in the location of the world's flash points. At the turn of the twenty-first century, for example, the weapons trade gravitated toward the turbulent Near East region, which led the feverish rush to purchase arms, spending $105 billion (54 percent) of the global total between 1996 and 2003. With its numerous pairs of competitive states, the Near East is in an intense **arms race.** In the wake of the 1991 Persian Gulf War and the 2003 war against Iraq, rivalries endure between Israel and Palestine, Egypt and Libya, Iran and Iraq, Iran and Saudi Arabia, Iraq and Kuwait, Iraq and Syria, Iraq and Turkey, and Israel and Syria. These states' high level of activity in the global arms market has continued. Countries in the Near East accounted for only 11 percent of world arms imports in 1967, but that share rose to 51 percent between 2000 and 2003. Recent brutal violence in the Israeli-Palestinian conflict and increasing terrorist attacks from militant state and nonstate groups have pushed arms sales in that region to an all-time high. In addition, the area is likely to see increased arms transfers for the global "war on terrorism." The same situation exists in Asia, the region now ranked second in the value of arms deliveries, accounting for 43 percent ($35 billion) of all global shipments in the period between 2000 and 2003 (Grimmett 2004, 36–37).

It is difficult to predict future trends in arms purchases. As mentioned above, regular shifts in procurement have occurred rapidly in response to emergent wars and perceived threats, as well as the growing trend toward limiting arms purchases from abroad and instead placing greater emphasis on joint production of weapons with other countries (Grimmett 2004, 4). Each state's proportionate share of total weapons purchases is likely to change, depending on the location of the globe's next hot spots and each country's involvement in them. Similarly, aggregate levels of world arms imports are likely to be influenced by the performance of each state in the global economy. Levels of weapon imports activity fluctuate sharply from year to year—not only in unstable regions in countries where the risk of civil war and terrorism are high and in situations where pairs of enemy states are engaged in arms races but also especially in countries when, in a period of growth in the business cycle, financial resources become available for arms purchases.

Alongside changing demands of arms importers, it is also important to observe changes in the activities of arms *suppliers.* During the Cold War the superpowers dominated the arms export market. Between 1975 and 1989, the U.S.-Soviet share of global arms exports varied between one-half and three-fourths, and the United States alone had cornered 40 percent of the world arms export market when the Cold War ended (U.S. ACDA 1997, 19). In that period the two superpowers together "supplied an estimated $325 billion worth of arms and ammunition to the Third World" (Klare 1994, 139). But with the demise of the Soviet Union and the advent of the worldwide war on terrorism, the United States increased its supply of weapons worldwide to countries that agreed to be partners in the post–9/11 "coalition of the willing." The U.S. reemerged as the

■ **arms race**
the buildup of weapons and armed forces by two or more states that threaten each other, with the competition driven by the conviction that gaining a lead is necessary for security.

unrivaled "arms merchant of the world" (a phrase used by former U.S. President Jimmy Carter to deplore what he sometimes regarded while in office as an unsavory business). Between 1996 and 2003 the United States accounted for a higher proportion of worldwide contracts to sell arms than any other supplier, agreeing to weapons-export contracts exceeding $167 billion, or 49 percent of the $345 billion total worldwide in that period. These contracts, or agreements to purchase arms in the future, account for the suppliers' share of the arms that will eventually be *delivered*.

> Recently, from 2000–2003, the United States and Russia have dominated the arms market in the developing world, with the United States ranking first and Russia second each of the last four years in the value of arms transfer *agreements*. From 2000–2003, the United States made $35.8 billion in arms transfer agreements with developing nations [in *constant* 2003 dollars], 47 percent of all such agreements. Russia, the second leading supplier during this period, made over $21 billion in arms transfer agreements, or 28 percent.
>
> In 2003, the United States ranked first in arms transfer *agreements* with developing nations with over $6.2 billion or 45 percent of these agreements. Russia was second with $3.0 billion or 23 percent of such agreements. In 2003, the United States ranked first in the value of arms *deliveries* to developing nations at $6.3 billion, or 37 percent of all such deliveries. The United Kingdom ranked second at $4 billion or 24 percent of such deliveries. Russia ranked third at $3.4 billion or 19 percent of such deliveries. (Grimmett 2004, 5, 2)

In this fierce race for income through arms sales, between 2000 and 2003 the United States and Russia collectively made *agreements* for future sales of arms abroad that accounted for three-fourths of all the future arms transfer agreements by all suppliers. The U.S. monopoly on the arms trade in 2003 rose to 37 percent of all arms deliveries. The arms sale agreements already under contract assure that the arms trade will remain vigorous in the future, and that the United States will continue to be the largest exporter, followed by the other great powers.

Although the top ten major suppliers dominate the global arms market, the number of new suppliers has grown steadily, as more than seventy-five Global South countries now also produce arms for export at various levels of quantity and quality. Still, most of these are small producers struggling for a share of the lucrative conventional armaments trade. In fact, for the countries in the Global South, the struggle has not been very successful, considering their huge populations and combined economic clout; in 2003 they accounted for only 5.6 percent of world arms exports (Grimmett 2004, 82).

A consequence of the increased competition for arms markets is the relaxation of export controls. The UN Register of Conventional Arms, begun in 1991 to monitor the weapons exports and imports of countries, has not curbed their sale. Supplier diversification, as well as joint ventures among arms manufacturers in different countries, has ended many former solid supplier-consumer ties. Suppliers, it seems, are now eager to sell to any purchaser, and they continue the supply of weapons to both sides of a number of international disputes. Compounding the danger, moreover, is the illegal export of nuclear, ballistic missile, and chemical weapons technology.

Protecting National Security? Chinese missiles on display in Beijing.

The threat of terrorists acquiring weapons of mass destruction on the black market through covert suppliers poses a real danger, although the extent of the threat is impossible to gauge, because this flow of the arms trade is invisible. Nonetheless, the absence of evidence is not evidence of absence. Terrorists are widely believed to be actively searching for weapons of mass destruction. Consider this scenario: "It takes just a few kilograms of plutonium and less than 20 kilograms of highly enriched uranium to make a nuclear bomb [and] about 40 kilograms of weapons-usable uranium and plutonium have been stolen from poorly protected nuclear facilities in the former Soviet Union during the last decade. While most of that material has been retrieved, two kilos of highly enriched uranium taken from a research reactor in Georgia is still missing, and that's just for starters. The real amount of missing weapons-grade material [likely to be part of the illicit trafficking of nuclear material worldwide] could be 10 times higher than is officially known" (*USA Today* 130 [June 2002], 1).

Motives for the Arms Trade. Economic gain is an important rationale for foreign military sales, because producers sell arms abroad to subsidize their arms production at home. For example, the United States uses arms exports to offset its chronic balance-of-trade deficits and to ensure its lead in the lucrative arms business. In 1998, the United States assigned 6,493 full-time federal employees to handle U.S. arms deals and spent $477 million on promotional activities for U.S. arms dealers (*Harper's*, February 1998, 13). Following the disintegration of the Soviet Union, Russia sought to raise desperately needed hard

The Production of Weapons: Purchasing Protection or Protecting Profits? In the past five decades, the United States has invested heavily in the development of many new weapons such as the SR-71 Blackbird, shown here. Most are expensive. Consider for example Boeing's 767-200 tanker that was planned for the Air Force in 2002 with new weapons and enhanced air-to-ground capabilities as a new-generation fighter-attack jet. The manufacturer in 2002 sought a defense contract calling for $20 billion to be charged to the Air Force to lease one hundred of these refueling tankers, asking the Department of Defense to foot the bill for constructing the aircraft (at $150 million each), and pay $30 million to reconfigure each of the 767s for commercial use and ten years later *give* the planes back to Boeing. The controversial tanker deal was suspended, and several people were jailed for their part in it. It was this kind of cozy deal that reminded people of President Dwight Eisenhower's warning "of the perils of ignoring the influence of what he christened the military-industrial complex. Ike's words have been repeated endlessly, and there have been countless editorials decrying 'beltway bandits' and their predilection for waste, fraud, and abuse" (*U.S. News & World Report*, May 13, 2002).

■ **military-industrial complex**

the term coined by U.S. President Eisenhower to describe the coalition among arms manufacturers, military bureaucracies, and top government officials that promotes unnecessary defense expenditures for its own profit and power.

currency by selling at bargain-basement prices its one product mix still in demand—weapons.

The **military-industrial complex** is widely believed to exercise enormous power over defense budgets and arms sales agreements in the United States (Mount, Maier, and Freeman 2003; Fallows 2002). Arms manufacturers seek to increase their profits, and the best way of succeeding is by lobbying for military spending and the production and sale of new weapons. The same pressures are operative in many other countries' civilian sectors for the same purposes.

The end of almost all *interstate* wars since the early 1990s ironically in-

Weapons for Sale The global arms trade is big business, and it remains brisk in many regions where perceptions of threats are intense. The Middle East, which accounts for more than two-thirds of global arms sales, is a prime example. Shown here are buyers examining a model of a warship at a 1997 defense exposition in Saudi Arabia. These "arms bazaars" are a regular feature of the global weapons market.

---

creased states' incentives to sell arms merely for profit. Nonetheless, many states continue to sell arms (or make outright grants) for time-honored purposes: to support friendly governments, to honor allies' requests, and to cultivate cooperation. This was illustrated by U.S. arms export policy prior to and in the aftermath of the 1990 Persian Gulf War. The United States delivered 56 percent of the $101 billion in arms sold to the strife-torn Middle East between 1994 and 2001 (Grimmett 2002, 53, 5), allegedly for the purpose of anchoring allies and preserving the military balance of power in that explosive region. However, the profit motive, fueled in part by the desire of defense contractors to maintain income in an era in which many states are reducing their defense budgets, also continues to drive the for-profit sale of weapons across borders. As noted, an underground "black market" in weapons is flourishing and suggests that greed is behind many defense contractors' illegal participation in the global arms trade.

The Strategic Consequences of Arms Sales.   Whether the arming of other countries has accomplished all of its intended goals is open to dispute. During the Cold War, for example, the United States and the Soviet Union thought they could maintain peace by spreading arms to politically pivotal recipients. Between 1983 and 1987 the United States provided arms to fifty-nine less-developed countries while the Soviet Union supplied forty-two (Klare 1990, 12). Yet many of the recipients engaged in war with their neighbors or experienced internal rebellion. Of the top twenty arms importers in 1988, more than half "had governments noted for the frequent use of violence" (Sivard 1991, 17). The toll in lives from the wars in the Global South since 1945 exceeds tens of millions of people. Undoubtedly, the import of such huge arsenals of weapons aided this level of destruction. As the arms exporters "peddle death to the poor," they seldom acknowledge how this scouting for customers contradicts other proclaimed foreign policy goals. The U.S. arms export program, for example, undermines the current U.S. policy priority of promoting democracy, because no less than one-third (eighteen) of the recipients of U.S. arms exports were nondemocratic governments, which purchased $13.25 billion (41 percent) of the total U.S. arms sold ($32.43 billion) in 1993 (Blanton and Kegley 1997, 94–95).

The inability of arms suppliers to control the uses to which their military hardware will be put is troubling. "The concern is that friends can become foes, and secrets can be stolen" (J. Brown 1999). Loyalty is often a fragile commodity, and supplying weapons can backfire, as the United States discovered both when the weapons it sold to Iraq were used against U.S. forces by Saddam Hussein in the Persian Gulf War (Timmerman 1991) and when the Stinger missiles the United States supplied to Taliban forces resisting the Soviet Union's 1979 invasion in Afghanistan fell into the hands of terrorists later opposing the United States. Likewise, in 1982 Great Britain found itself shipping military equipment to Argentina just eight days before Argentina's attack on the British-controlled Falkland Islands, and in 1998 U.S. military technology sold to China was exported to Pakistan, making possible its nuclear weapons test.

Trends in Weapons Technology

The widespread quest for armaments has created a potentially explosive global environment. The description is especially apt when we consider not only trends in defense expenditures and the arms trade but also in the destructiveness of modern weapons.

Nuclear Weapons. Technological research and development has radically expanded the destructiveness of national arsenals. The largest "blockbuster" bombs of World War II delivered a power of ten tons of TNT. The atomic bomb that leveled Hiroshima had the power of over fifteen thousand tons of TNT. Less than twenty years later, the former Soviet Union built a nuclear bomb with the explosive force of fifty-seven megatons (million tons) of TNT. Since 1945 it is estimated that "more than 128,000 nuclear warheads had been built worldwide—all but 2 percent of them by the United States (55 percent) and the Soviet Union or Russia (43 percent)." Many have been dismantled, but in 2004 the global stockpile of nuclear warheads belonging to the world's eight known nuclear states exceeded thirty thousand. Since its 1986 peak, the global nuclear arsenal has declined by 50 percent (*Bulletin of the Atomic Scientists*, November–December 2004). Even after these cuts, those nuclear warheads available for a strike collectively had the explosive force of over 1.3 million Hiroshima bombs.

The use of such weapons could destroy not only entire cities and countries but, conceivably, the world's entire population. Albert Einstein, the Nobel Prize–winning physicist whose ideas were the basis for the development of nuclear weapons, was alarmed by the threat they posed. He professed uncertainty about the weapons that would be used in a third world war, but was confident that in a fourth they would be "sticks and stones." He warned that inasmuch as "the un-

Deadly Conventional Small-Arms Sales The exact extent of global trade in so-called light conventional weapons is unknown, but growing. Of the armed conflicts fought worldwide since 1990, 90 percent were fought exclusively with small arms (*Harper's*, January 2000, 11), and small arms kill three hundred thousand people each year (*International Herald Tribune*, October 28, 2002, 8). In reaction, the 1998 UN Register of Conventional Arms required that states' inventories and procurement of such weapons be reported. "Millions of the rifles now in the hands of the world's killers started out as legal weapons," Michael Renner (1999) warns. Shown here are M-16s from the El Salvadoran Battalion. This U.S.-trained unit massacred eight hundred civilians at El Mozote and murdered six Jesuit priests in San Salvador in 1989. During the Reagan-Bush years, the United States supplied El Salvador with thirty-three thousand M-16s (Lumpe 1999).

leashed power of the atom has changed everything save our modes of thinking . . . we thus drift toward unparalleled catastrophe."

At the start of 2005, the number of operational nuclear stockpiles of the five major powers were estimated to total about 19,600 strategic warheads. The U.S. arsenal then had 10,350 nuclear warheads, and Russia had about 8,400. In addition, France stockpiled an estimated 400 warheads; China had 400; Great Britain retained 200; India and Pakistan were believed to have 100 nuclear warheads between them; and Israel as many as 200. Thus, at the start of 2005 there were eight "official" members of the nuclear club—the United States, Russia, Great Britain, France, China, India, Pakistan, and Israel. Moreover, Iran and North Korea, in addition to as many as twenty-two other states (such as Brazil) or nongovernmental terrorist organizations, are generally believed the most likely to violate the spirit and law of the **Nuclear Nonproliferation Treaty (NPT)** by becoming members of the nuclear club (see Chapter 13). In short, the **proliferation** of arms is a serious global concern, because the so-called **Nth country problem** (the addition of new nuclear states) is expected to become an increas-

■ **Nuclear Nonproliferation Treaty (NPT)**
an international agreement that seeks to prevent horizontal proliferation by prohibiting nuclear weapons sales, acquisitions, or production.

■ **proliferation**
the spread of weapon capabilities from a few to many states in a chain reaction, so that an increasing number of states gain the ability to launch an attack on other states with devastating (e.g., nuclear) weapons.

■ **Nth country problem**
the addition of new nuclear states.

■ **horizontal nuclear proliferation**
an increase in the number of states that possess nuclear weapons.

■ **vertical nuclear proliferation**
the expansion of the capabilities of existing nuclear powers to inflect with their nuclear weapons increasing destruction.

ing likelihood. Both **horizontal nuclear proliferation** (the increase in the number of nuclear states) and **vertical nuclear proliferation** (increases in the capabilities of existing nuclear powers) are probable (Singh and Way 2004).

The obstacles to increased proliferation are fragile, as shown by the nuclear development programs of India and Pakistan in 1998 and the collapse of the nuclear-test ban's future following the U.S. rejection of the Comprehensive Test Ban Treaty (CTBT). The incentives to join the nuclear club and to acquire missiles and bombers for delivery are strong for several additional reasons.

First, the materials needed to make a nuclear weapon are widely available. This is partly due to the widespread use of nuclear technology for generating electricity. Today almost 440 nuclear-power and research reactors are in operation in forty-four countries throughout the world. In addition to spreading nuclear know-how, states could choose to reprocess the uranium and plutonium, which power plants produce as waste, for clandestine nuclear weapons production. In the early 2000s, commercial reprocessing reactors were producing enough plutonium to make as many as forty thousand nuclear weapons.

Second, the scientific expertise necessary for weapons development has spread with the globalization of advanced scientific training. "It will be possible to duplicate almost all past technology in all but the most forlorn of Third World backwaters, and much of the present state-of-the-art will be both intellectually and practically accessible" (Clancy and Seitz 1991–92).

Third, export controls designed to stop technology transfer for military purposes are weak. In addition, the leaks in nuclear export controls have weakened the antiproliferation regime (Krepon 2002). Conversion of peacetime nuclear energy programs to military purposes can occur either overtly or, as in the case of India and Pakistan, covertly. The safeguards built into the **nonproliferation regime** are simply inadequate to detect and prevent secret nuclear weapons development programs.

■ **nonproliferation regime**
rules to contain arms races so that weapons or technology do not spread to states that do not have them.

Fourth, nonnuclear weapons states have strong incentives to develop weapons similar to those of the existing nuclear club. They voice the complaint of former French President Charles de Gaulle, who argued that without an independent nuclear capability France could not "command its own destiny." Similarly, in 1960 Britain's Aneurin Bevan asserted that without the bomb Britain would go "naked into the council chambers of the world." And since 1993, North Korea has refused to allow monitoring of its five nuclear-power facilities, and has periodically vowed to convert its uranium for nuclear weapons.

Nuclear weapons serve as a symbol of status and power. Because of the widespread conviction rooted in realism that military might confers political stature, many countries, such as Iran in 2004, regard the Nuclear Nonproliferation Treaty as hypocrisy because it provides a seal of approval to the United States, Russia, China, Britain, and France for possessing nuclear weapons while denying it to all others. The underlying belief that it is acceptable to develop a nuclear capacity for deterrence, political influence, and prestige was expressed in 1999 by Brajesh Mishra, India's national security adviser, when he justified India's acquisition of nuclear weapons by asserting that "in the twenty-first century a new security order is likely to arise in the Asia-Pacific region, one in which India should be granted as much respect and deference by the United States and others as is China today."

It is unlikely that the nuclear threat will cease (see Map 12.3). "There's not

MAP 12.3
Nuclear-Weapon Armed Countries, Today and Tomorrow

Despite the great decline in the number of wars between states since the end of the Cold War (see Chapter 11), nuclear proliferation is a growing trend, as this map shows. Beyond the United States, Russia, Great Britain, France, China, India, Pakistan, and Israel, four new independent Soviet republics (Ukraine, Kazakhstan, Uzbekistan, and Georgia) still retain the nuclear weapons they acquired from the old Soviet Union. South Africa is believed to already possess the capacity to use nuclear warheads in wartime, and North Korea has pursued a uranium-enrichment program in violation of past agreements and in 2003 prepared to restart a nuclear reactor capable of producing weapons-grade plutonium. Six other countries have active nuclear-weapon development programs, which may include the capacity to manufacture and deliver these weapons of mass destruction—Argentina, Brazil, Iran, Libya, North Korea, and Taiwan. Nuclear proliferation means that nuclear deterrence will remain a key component of national strategy and coercive diplomacy.

SOURCE: Based on estimates from *Bulletin of the Atomic Scientists* (November–December 2004).

Intractive map with critical thinking questions

	U.S. forces		Russian forces	
	2002	2012	2002	2012
ICBMs	1,700	500	3,364	230*
SLBMs	2,784	1,440	1,868	616
Bombers	1,660	260	582	240
Total	6,144	2,200	5,814	1,086

*Depending on warhead load per missile

FIGURE 12.4
Caging the Nuclear Threat: The Rise and Fall of Deployed Strategic U.S. and Russian Warheads

The U.S.-Russian Moscow Treaty, or Strategic Offensive Reduction Treaty (SORT), of May 2002 promises to distance the former adversaries from the brink of nuclear destruction. Shown here is a comparison of their nuclear arsenals between 1946 and 2012, with the chart on the right breaking down both countries' forces according to their warhead deployments.

SOURCES: Arms Control Association and the Carnegie Endowment for International Peace (left); *The Economist,* May 18, 2002, p. 30 (right). Copyright © 2002 by The Economist Newspaper Ltd. All rights reserved. Reprinted with permission. Further reproduction prohibited. www.economist.com.

a snowball's chance in hell we'll eliminate all nuclear weapons from the face of the earth," explains Matthew Bunn, editor of *Arms Control Today*. "That genie is long since out of the bottle and there's no chance of ever getting him back in." Moreover, a world nearing nuclear disarmament would not end the threat, because even if every nuclear weapon were eliminated, the first country that built a handful of new nuclear weapons could blackmail everyone else.

That said, the most powerful nuclear states, the United States and Russia, took a bold step toward nuclear disarmament in May 2002 when they reached the Strategic Offensive Reductions Treaty (SORT), which pledged a reduction of their nuclear arsenals by two-thirds within the next ten years (see Figure 12.4). That reduction will greatly reduce the number of nuclear warheads in the world. Whether it will be followed by the other major powers remains to be seen. In the past, opportunities have been missed.

The opportunity for reducing deployments of strategic—that is, intercontinental—nuclear weapons was seized, when Presidents George W. Bush and Vladimir Putin signed the SORT accord in Moscow committing their countries to reducing their nuclear weapons from about 6,000 on each side to between 1,700 and 2,200 by the end of 2012. Neoliberal optimists cheered in the belief that the world would finally become a safer place as the danger of global annihilation showed promise of vanishing.

The continuing danger of annihilation was made evident at the same time in 2002 when India and Pakistan squared off against each other, poised for war in a standoff over Kashmir, the disputed province that has been the source of two of the three India-Pakistan wars since 1947. A deadly game of nuclear brinkmanship unfolded. The India-Pakistan confrontation illustrates the **security dilemma.** Both sides sought to increase their national security by increasing their armaments and by developing nuclear weapons in 1998, and these preparations for war had the opposite effect—neither side was more secure than they had been prior to their build up of war-making capabilities. This may account for the relaxation of tensions that began in 2004.

Technological Improvements and Weapons Delivery Capabilities. Advances in weapons technology have been rapid and extraordinary. Since the advent of the atomic age, with the "gravity bombs of 1945 . . . a whole warehouse of varied weapons, each with its own special purpose" has been created. These include:

> clean bombs; dirty bombs; bombs that burrowed into the earth, seeking underground command posts; bombs that went off undersea, seeking submarines; bombs that went off high over earth, to fry the brains of electrical devices with a huge shower of electromagnetic pulses; bombs that killed tank crews with radiation but didn't flatten towns or cities; bombs delivered by guidance so precise that they could destroy anything with a known location on or near the surface of the earth. . . . The results of this tireless invention were weapons powerful enough to threaten human life on the planet. (Powers 1994, 123)

Particularly deadly have been the technological refinements that enable states to deliver weapons from as far away as nine thousand miles to within one hundred feet of their targets in less than thirty minutes. The United States and Russia, for example, equipped their ballistic missiles with **multiple independently targetable reentry vehicles (MIRVs),** which enable a single missile to launch multiple warheads toward different targets simultaneously and accurately. One MIRV U.S. MX (Peacekeeper) missile could carry ten nuclear warheads—enough to wipe out a city and everything else within a fifty-mile radius. As a result of MIRVing before the superpowers agreed to the START II treaty to ban MIRVed intercontinental ballistic missiles, the world's combined nuclear inventory grew nearly three times larger than the number of nuclear warheads previously in existence.

Other technological improvements have led to steady increases in the speed, accuracy, range, and effectiveness of weapons. Laser weapons, nuclear-armed tactical air-to-surface missiles (TASMs), stealth air-launched cruise missiles (ACMs), and antisatellite (ASAT) weapons that can project force in and wage war from outer space have become a part of the military landscape. In addition, in development and in use by the United States in the Iraq War are the new high-tech **nonlethal weapons (NLWs)** made possible by the **revolution in military technology (RMT).** They include sounds, shocks, and stinks to disperse or incapacitate crowds (*Economist*, December 4, 2004). NLWs also deploy information-warfare squadrons to protect military computer networks from electronic sneak attacks; energy pulses to knock out or take down enemies without necessarily killing them; biofeedback, beamed electromagnetic and sonic wavelengths that can modify the human behavior of targets (for example, putting people to sleep through electromagnetic heat and magnetic radiation); and underground **smart bombs,** which at a speed of one thousand feet per second,

■ **security dilemma**
the propensity of armaments undertaken by one state for ostensibly defensive purposes to threaten other states, which arm in reaction, with the result that their national security declines as their arms increase.

■ **multiple independently targetable reentry vehicles (MIRVs)**
a technological innovation permitting many weapons to be delivered from a single missile.

■ **nonlethal weapons (NLWs)**
the wide array of "soft kill," low-intensity methods of incapacitating an enemy's people, vehicles, communications systems, or entire cities without killing either combatants or noncombatants.

■ **revolution in military technology (RMT)**
the sophisticated new weapons technologies that make fighting war without mass armies possible.

■ **smart bombs**
precision-guided military technology that enables a bomb to search for its target and detonate at the precise time it can do the most damage.

- **firebreak**
the psychological barrier between conventional wars and wars fought with weapons of mass destruction.

- **strategic weapons**
weapons of mass destruction that are carried on intercontinental ballistic missiles (ICBMs), submarine-launched ballistic missiles (SLBM)s, or long-range bombers and are capable of annihilating an enemy state.

- **virtual nuclear arsenals**
the next generation of "near nuclear" military capabilities produced by the revolution in military technology that would put strategic nuclear weapons of mass destruction at the margins of national security strategies by removing dependence on them for deterrence.

- **deterrence**
a preventive strategy designed to dissuade an adversary from doing what it would otherwise do.

- **information warfare (IW) or infowar tactics**
attacks on an adversary's telecommunications and computer networks to penetrate and degrade an enemy whose defense capabilities depend heavily on these technological systems.

can penetrate a buried bunker and, at the proper millisecond, detonate five hundred pounds of explosive to destroy an adversary's inventory of buried chemical and biological weapons. These technological advances in warfare make orthodox ways of classifying weapons systems as well as prior equations for measuring power ratios obsolete.

For decades, a **firebreak** has separated conventional from nuclear wars. The term comes from the barriers of cleared land that firefighters use to keep forest fires from racing out of control. In the context of modern weaponry, it is a psychological barrier whose purpose is to prevent even the most intensive forms of conventional combat from escalating into nuclear war. The danger is growing that the firebreak is being crossed from both directions—by a new generation of near-nuclear conventional weapons capable of levels of violence approximating those of a limited nuclear conflict and by a new generation of near-conventional **strategic weapons** capable of causing destruction similar to that of the most powerful weapons of mass destruction.

The precision and power of today's conventional weapons have expanded exponentially, at precisely the moment when the revolution in military technology is leading to "the end of infantry" because, in the computer age "the sky has eyes, bullets have brains, and victory will belong to the country whose military has the better data network" (P. Ross 1997). Note also that even as the nuclear powers retain the capacity to turn cities into glass, they (and now, terrorist groups) increasingly rely on a variety of new cyberstrategies to deter and demobilize enemies and are turning to **virtual nuclear arsenals** for **deterrence** of an adversary's attack. Examples include such futuristic weapons as the electromagnetic pulse (EMP) bomb, which can be hand delivered in a suitcase and can immobilize an entire city's computer and communications systems; computer viruses of electronic-seating microbytes that can eliminate a country's telephone system; and logic bombs that can confuse and redirect traffic on the target country's air and rail system. Also planned are **information warfare (IW)** or **infowar tactics** that deploy information-age techniques "to disrupt the enemy's economy and military preparedness, perhaps without firing a shot" (P. Ross 1997). One example of these is the U.S. Air Force's Commando Solo psychological operations plane, which can disrupt signals and insert in their place a "morphed" TV program, in which the enemy leader makes unpopular announcements on the screen that alienate him from his population.

Unconventional Biological and Chemical Weapons.

Biological and chemical weapons pose a special and growing threat, particularly in the hands of terrorists aiming for mass destruction rather than influencing public opinion. These unconventional weapons of mass destruction (WMD) are sometimes regarded as a "poor man's atomic bomb," because they can be built at comparatively little cost and cause widespread injury and death. Chemical weapons proliferation is especially of worldwide concern. In addition to the American hegemon, which led the way in building these weapons, twenty-four other countries are suspected to have produced chemical weapons (Stock and De Geer 1995, 340), and terrorists are widely perceived to be committed to acquiring and using them. Following the September 11, 2001, terrorist attacks on the United States, the spread of anthrax through the U.S. mail system was widely considered to be the work of Middle Eastern terror networks.

International law prohibits the use of chemical weapons; the 1925 Geneva

Protocol banned the use of chemical weapons in warfare, and the Chemical Weapons Convention (CWC), signed by 185 countries by 2004, required the destruction of existing stocks. However Iran's and Iraq's use of gas in warfare and Iraq's use of chemical weapons in 1989 against its own Kurdish people demonstrate the weaknesses of these legal barriers. In addition, many radical and extremist groups, often beyond the control of weak state governments, see chemical and biological weapons as a cheaper, effective means for practicing terrorism. The firebreak has been breached.

A pervasive sense of the loss of security haunts much of the world. The danger of nuclear annihilation has not disappeared with the U.S.-Russian agreement to drastically cut their nuclear warheads. In January 2005 the famous "doomsday clock" of the *Bulletin of the Atomic Scientists* showed that the world was only seven minutes from nuclear Armageddon—exactly the same amount of time as when the clock was originally set in 1947. The world is *not* a safer place with terrorists roaming around and plotting mass destruction (see Allison 2004).

What matters in the pursuit of national security is the *method* on which states rely to use the capabilities they have acquired. How can weapons (and economic resources) be used to promote national interests and exercise international influence? These questions require consideration of the types of strategies available. We look next at two categories: military strategy and economic trade sanctions.

MILITARY STRATEGY IN THE NUCLEAR AGE

The dropping of the atomic bomb on Japan on August 6, 1945, is the most important event distinguishing pre– from post–World War II international politics. In the blinding flash of a single weapon and the shadow of its mushroom cloud, the world was transformed from a "balance of power" to a "balance of terror" system. In the following decades, policymakers in the nuclear states had to grapple with two central policy questions: (1) whether they should use nuclear weapons; and (2) how to prevent others from using them. The search for answers has been critical, because the immediate and delayed effects of a nuclear war are terrifying to contemplate. Even a short war using a tiny fraction of any country's nuclear warheads would destroy life as we know it. The planet would be uninhabitable, because a **nuclear winter** would result, with devastating consequences: "Fires ignited in such a war could generate enough smoke to obscure the sun and perturb the atmosphere over large areas . . . [lowering] average planetary temperatures . . . [and darkening] the skies sufficiently to compromise green plant photosynthesis" (Sagan and Turco 1993, 369). It has been estimated that "the missiles on board a single [U.S.] SLBM submarine may be enough to initiate nuclear winter" (Quester 1992)—enough to end human existence.

■ **nuclear winter**
the expected freeze that would occur in the Earth's climate from the fallout of smoke and dust in the event nuclear weapons were used, blocking out sunlight and destroying plant and animal life that survived the original blast.

Although weapons of mass destruction have existed since World War II, the postures of the Americans and the Soviets toward them have evolved as technologies, defense needs, capabilities, and global conditions have changed. For analytical convenience, we can treat those postures in terms of three periods: compellence, deterrence, and preemption. The first began at the end of World War II and lasted until the Cuban Missile Crisis. U.S. nuclear superiority was the dominant characteristic of this period. The second began in 1962 and lasted until the breakup of the Soviet Union in 1991. Growing Soviet military capability was the dominant characteristic of this period, which meant that the United States no longer stood alone in its ability to annihilate another country without fear of its own destruction. The third phase began after the end of the Cold War, taking shape as the great powers began to revise their strategic doctrines in the light of new global threats.

Compellence

Countries that possess military preeminence often think of weapons as instruments in diplomatic bargaining. The United States, the world's first and for many years unchallenged nuclear power, adopted the strategic doctrine of **compellence** (Schelling 1966) when it enjoyed a clear-cut superiority over the Soviet Union. Military capabilities do not have to be used for them to be useful; a state may exercise influence over others simply by "demonstrating the quantity of force and highlighting the capability of, and intention to, use force" (Majeed 1991). The U.S. doctrine of compellence used nuclear weapons as tools of political influence, not for fighting but for convincing others to do what they might not otherwise do.

The United States sought to gain bargaining leverage by conveying the impression that it would actually use nuclear weapons. This posture was especially evident during the Eisenhower administration, when Secretary of State John Foster Dulles practiced **brinkmanship,** deliberately threatening U.S. adversaries with nuclear destruction so that, at the brink of war, they would concede to U.S. demands. Brinkmanship was part of the overall U.S. strategic doctrine known as **massive retaliation.** To contain communism and Soviet expansionism, it called for a **countervalue targeting strategy,** that is, aiming U.S. nuclear weapons at what the Soviets most valued—their population and industrial centers. The alternative is a **counterforce targeting strategy,** which targets an enemy's military forces and weapons, thus sparing civilians from immediate destruction.

Massive retaliation heightened fears in the Kremlin that a nuclear exchange would destroy the Soviet Union but permit the survival of the United States. In addition to augmenting their nuclear capabilities, Soviet leaders accelerated their space program and successfully launched the world's first satellite (*Sputnik*), thereby demonstrating Moscow's ability to deliver nuclear weapons beyond the Eurasian landmass. Thus the superpowers' strategic competition took a new turn, and the United States for the first time faced a nuclear threat to its homeland.

Deterrence

As U.S. nuclear superiority eroded, American policymakers began to question the usefulness of weapons of mass destruction as tools in political bargaining. They were horrified by the destruction that could result if compellence should provoke a nuclear exchange (see Frankel 2004). The nearly suicidal Cuban Missile Crisis of 1962 brought about a major change in American strategic thought, shifting strategic policy from compellence to **nuclear deterrence.**

Whereas compellence contains an offensive coercive threat aimed at persuading an adversary to relinquish something without resistance, deterrence

---

■ **compellence**
a method of coercive diplomacy usually involving an act of war or threat to force an adversary to make concessions against its will.

■ **brinkmanship**
the intentional, reckless taking of huge risks in bargaining with an enemy, such as threatening a nuclear attack, to compel submission.

■ **massive retaliation**
the Eisenhower administration's policy doctrine for containing Soviet communism by pledging to respond to any act of aggression with the most destructive capabilities available, including nuclear weapons.

■ **countervalue targeting strategy**
the bargaining doctrine that declares the intention to use weapons of mass destruction against an enemy's most valued nonmilitary resources, such as the civilians and industries located in its cities.

■ **counterforce targeting strategy**
targeting strategic nuclear weapons on particular military capabilities of an enemy's armed forces and arsenals.

■ **nuclear deterrence**
dissuading an adversary from attacking by threatening retaliation with nuclear weapons.

Nuclear Testing When informed of the possibility of designing a hydrogen bomb, U. S. President Truman asked, "What the hell are we waiting for?" Politicians hailed the nuclear weapon as a defensive force. However, scientists such as Robert Oppenheimer —who headed the Manhattan Project, which produced the atomic bomb—maintained that the hydrogen bomb was inherently immoral because it was a weapon of genocide that was so destructive that its use could not be restricted to military purposes. More than two thousand nuclear-weapons tests have occurred since 1945, and testing has continued. Pictured here is a 1995 French atomic test in the South Pacific of a nuclear bomb smaller than the hydrogen bomb that, in 1952, created a three-mile fireball one thousand times more powerful than the bombs used by the United States on Hiroshima and Nagasaki.

seeks to dissuade an adversary from undertaking some future action. At the heart of deterrence theory is the assumption that the defender has the ability to punish an adversary with unacceptably high costs if an attack is launched. The key elements of deterrence are: (1) *capabilities*—the possession of military resources that make threats of military retaliation plausible; (2) *credibility*—the belief that the actor is willing to defend its declared position; and (3) *communication*—the ability to send a potential aggressor the clear message that it will carry out its threat. Advocates of deterrence argue that it "will succeed if threatened costs can be communicated to the challenger, assessed by the challenger, and believed by the challenger" (Harknett 1994).

Ironically, the shift from compellence to deterrence stimulated rather than inhibited the U.S.-Soviet arms race. A deterrent strategy depends on the unquestionable ability to inflict intolerable damage on an opponent. It requires a **second-strike capability** that enables a country to withstand an adversary's first strike and still retain the ability to retaliate with a devastating counterattack. To ensure a second-strike capability and an adversary's awareness of it, deterrence rationalized an unrestrained search for sophisticated retaliatory capabilities. Any system that could be built was built because, as President Kennedy

■ **second-strike capability**
a state's capacity to retaliate after absorbing a first-strike attack with weapons of mass destruction.

■ **mutual assured destruction (MAD)**
a condition of mutual deterrence in which both sides possess the ability to survive a first strike and launch a devastating retaliatory attack.

explained in 1961, "only when arms are sufficient beyond doubt can we be certain without doubt that they will never be employed."

Policymakers coined the phrase **mutual assured destruction (MAD)** to describe the strategic balance that emerged between the United States and the Soviet Union after the Cuban Missile Crisis. Regardless of who struck first, the other side could destroy the attacker. Under these circumstances, initiating a nuclear war was irrational; the frightening costs outweighed any conceivable benefits. As Soviet leader Nikita Khrushchev put it, "If you reach for the push button, you reach for suicide." Safety, in former British Prime Minister Winston Churchill's words, was "the sturdy child of terror and survival the twin brother of annihilation."

As U.S.-Soviet relations evolved, debate in the United States over the best way to protect national security with nuclear weapons split into polar positions. Although MAD continued to dominate the thinking of some, others advocated **nuclear utilization theory (NUTs),** an approach whereby nuclear weapons would not simply play a deterrent role but could also be used in war. Such a posture was necessary, some U.S. policy advisers argued, because the Soviet Union was preparing to fight—and win—a nuclear war (Pipes 1977). Furthermore, advocates of NUTs argued that use of nuclear weapons would not necessarily escalate to an unmanageable, all-out nuclear exchange. Instead, they reasoned that it was possible to fight a "limited" nuclear war. By making nuclear weapons more usable, they argued, the United States could make nuclear threats more credible. Proponents of MAD, on the other hand, held that deterrence remained the only sane purpose for nuclear weapons and contended that any use of nuclear weapons—however limited initially—would surely escalate to an unrestrained exchange.

■ **nuclear utilization theory (NUT)**
a body of strategic thought that claimed deterrent threats would be more credible if nuclear weapons were made more usable.

A new shift in strategic thinking occurred in 1983 when U.S. President Reagan proposed building a space-based defensive shield against ballistic missiles. The **Strategic Defense Initiative (SDI),** or "Star Wars" as critics labeled it, called for the development of a defense against Soviet ballistic missiles using advanced space-based lasers to destroy weapons launched in fear, anger, or by accident. The goal, as President Reagan defined it, was to make nuclear weapons "impotent and obsolete." Thus SDI sought to shift U.S. nuclear strategy away from mutual assured destruction, which President Reagan deemed "morally unacceptable." However, the United States was unable to build a reliable ballistic missile defense during the remaining years of the Cold War.

■ **Strategic Defense Initiative (SDI)**
the so-called Star Wars plan conceived by the Reagan administration to deploy an antiballistic missile system using space-based lasers that would destroy enemy nuclear missiles before they could enter Earth's atmosphere.

Preemption

Despite uncertainties about the effectiveness of a ballistic missile defense system, even with technological advances, the United States has continued to proceed with its development. In the first Bush administration, the primary purpose was to protect the United States from a Soviet nuclear attack. However, when the Cold War ended in 1991, the original rationale for such a system faded as Washington and Moscow negotiated a series of historic arms control agreements. Other great powers also reduced the number of nuclear warheads in their arsenals. Worldwide, the total number of nuclear warheads was cut in half in 2005 to fewer than twenty-five thousand. As a consequence, the strategic nuclear balance is radically different today than it was during most of the second half of the twentieth century.

Was nuclear deterrence successful in bringing about this remarkable transformation? Some attribute the peaceful end of the Cold War to the effectiveness of the superpowers' deterrence strategies. The "Nobel Peace Prize," quipped historian Arthur Schlesinger, Jr., "should have gone to the atomic bomb." Others disagree. They point out that as plausible as this explanation sounds, it requires using **counterfactual reasoning** that begs the question of what would have happened after World War II had nuclear weapons not existed (Johansen 1991; Vasquez 1991). According to their line of reasoning, "although it can be argued that nuclear deterrence worked during the Cold War, we do not know that for sure. (The USSR may never have wished to invade Europe or to attack the United States with nuclear weapons.) It is very difficult to prove deterrent successes because that would require showing why an event did not occur" (Haffa 1992).

Regardless of its causes, the end of the Cold War has not brought strategic planning to a conclusion. New nuclear threats are on the horizon. This is why the United States has vigorously pushed forward with plans to develop an antiballistic missile system while simultaneously declaring a willingness to undertake preemptive action against emerging dangers. To justify its new strategy, the United States cites the proliferation of states with nuclear weapons (see Map 12.3) and the challenge of keeping fissile materials out of the hands of terrorists. The challenge is great, because illegal trafficking in the cross-border transport of the materials necessary to produce nuclear bombs is active, with more than four hundred confirmed incidents since 1993 (*Foreign Policy*, January–February 2002, 14).

"We face a threat with no precedent," President George W. Bush insisted during his commencement address at West Point on June 1, 2002. On the one hand, modern technology allows shadowy terrorist networks to launch catastrophic attacks against the United States. On the other hand, these networks cannot be dissuaded by the threat of punishment because they have no fixed territory or populace to protect. "We must take the battle to the enemy," he exhorted, "and confront the worst threats before they emerge."

Bush's call for acting preemptively against terrorists and the rogue states that harbored them became the major and most controversial cornerstones of the 2002 *National Security Strategy of the United States of America* (NSS). Building on the proposition that "nations need not suffer an attack before they can lawfully take action to defend themselves against forces that present an imminent danger," the report argued that the acquisition of weapons of mass destruction by global terrorists provided the United States with a compelling case for engaging in anticipatory self-defense. "Traditional concepts of deterrence will not work against a terrorist enemy whose avowed tactics are wanton destruction and the targeting of innocents; whose so-called soldiers seek martyrdom in death and whose most potent protection is statelessness." This requires, the security strategy document argued, the **rational choice** to be made that **preemptive war** for coercion, rather than deterrence, was necessary. As U.S. Secretary of Defense Donald Rumsfeld put it, "This isn't about punishment. We've got the wrong models in our minds if we're thinking about punishment. We're not. This isn't retaliation or retribution." The strategy calls for striking a menace before it uses aggression, with or without the support of allies and international institutions.

The Bush national security strategy has been called the most sweeping reformulation of U.S. defense policy in more than half a century (Gaddis 2002). Although under international law states have a legal right to defend themselves

■ **counterfactual reasoning**
thought experiments to consider the consequences that probably would have resulted had something happened that actually did not, such as speculating "what if Adolf Hitler had invaded Britain" or "what if John F. Kennedy had not been assassinated."

■ **rational choice**
the theory that decision makers choose on the basis of what they perceive to be in the best interests of themselves and their states, and select options according to their expectations about the relative usefulness of alternative means for the realization of their preferred goals. Sometimes called "expected-utility theory," this model derives from realist theories.

■ **preemptive war**
a quick first-strike attack that seeks to defeat an adversary before it can organize a retaliatory response.

CONTROVERSY

IS IT ETHICAL TO WAGE PREEMPTIVE WAR TO PREVENT AN ADVERSARY'S POTENTIAL AGGRESSION?

From the first recorded use of weapons by one society against another in human history, people have debated the ethical criteria by which a just war can be waged without violating the principle that it is morally wrong to kill. That debate has continued without a consensus emerging worldwide about the conditions under which it is morally acceptable to use armed force for political purposes. Experts in both defense and moral ethics remain divided as to the just means for containing aggression. International law also is divided (see Chapter 14).

Can war be stopped by waging it? Some realists believe so, arguing there are no moral limits: the ends justify the terrible means; might makes right; evil must be resisted; you can't negotiate with aggressors, so their aggression must be prevented. The savagery of war, of course, can never be justified to its victims. Critics argue that such strategies, which overlook the traditional right of innocent noncombatants to protection from genocide, violate international law and are crimes against humanity. Classic Christian and other pacifist theologians also condemn the extreme realist position that accepts evil methods, maintaining that a right intention does not automatically justify any means to achieve it.

The debate over the conditions justifying waging war to preserve peace heated up in 2002, when the Bush administration spelled out its grievances against Iraqi leader Saddam Hussein in attempting to justify why the United States planned a preemptive first strike to prevent Iraq from obtaining weapons of mass destruction for use against the United States. The United States invaded, asserting that Saddam was too irrational for deterrence. "We do not have the luxury of doing nothing," National Security Adviser Condoleezza Rice claimed. Critics questioned the logic and the morality. Germany's Chancellor Gerhard Schroeder barked that attacking an enemy simply because of what it might intend to do, to prevent its later aggression, was the same faulty argument Adolf Hitler had used in starting World War II. An attack also violates the established U.S. ban on assassination of foreign leaders, and the UN Charter's prohibition against waging war except in defense against an actual armed attack by an aggressor—not to remove another state's military capabilities. "Who can possibly argue that there is anything moral about killing other people's children?" the outraged British Minister Public Alice Mahon added. In planning a preemptive attack, critics claimed the Bush administration was ignoring the just war restraints against first strikes for either deterrence or revenge, and overturning 150 years of international law.

Protestors in Madrid, Spain, demonstrate against the U.S.-led preemptive strike against Iraq.

What do you think? Should the United States expect support for its radical new policy? If the U.S. actions are judged as justifiable, also ask what this means for others if they follow the same logic as that of the globe's reigning superpower. In the "categorical imperative," the German philosopher Immanuel Kant argued that when evaluating the morality of a decision, the question to ask is what would happen if everyone else acted on the same basis. What will the world be like if preemptive strikes become a universal norm and *all* states base their peace strategies on the claimed right to make war for preemptive purposes?

against aggression as well as imminent attacks, critics charge that beneath the language of military preemption lies a more radical policy of preventive war. In brief, a *preemptive* military attack entails the use of force to quell or mitigate an impending strike by an adversary. A *preventive* attack entails the use of force to eliminate any possible future strike, even if there is no reason to believe that the capacity to launch an attack currently exists. Whereas the grounds for preemption lie in evidence of a credible, imminent threat, the basis for prevention rests on the suspicion of an incipient, contingent threat (Kegley and Raymond 2004). Indeed, ethicists and legal experts, ever mindful of **just war theory,** question the morality and legality of preemptive war for preventive purposes. The U.S. posture has generated a heated debate (see Controversy: Is It Ethical to Wage Preemptive War to Prevent an Adversary's Potential Aggression?).

According to critics of the new Bush strategy, preventive uses of military force set a dangerous precedent. Predicting another state's future behavior is difficult because its leadership's intentions are hard to discern, information on long-term goals may be shrouded in secrecy, and signals of its policy direction may be distorted by background noise. If suspicions about an adversary become a justifiable cause for military action, then every truculent, self-indulgent leader will have a rough-and-ready pretext for ordering a first strike. In rebuttal, the Bush administration argues that waiting for nuclear threats to fully materialize is waiting far too long, and that preemption is a necessary doctrine suited for **asymmetrical warfare.**

The strategy of anticipatory self-defense thus raises anew timeless questions about the conditions under which, and the purposes for which, military force is justifiable. What does precaution warrant when nameless, faceless enemies are willing to engage in indiscriminate, suicidal attacks against noncombatants? How can force be used to influence an adversary's decision-making calculus? What are the conditions that affect the success of coercive diplomacy?

■ **just war theory**
the theory that identifies the criteria under which it is morally permissible, or "just," for a state to go to war and the methods by which a just war might be fought.

■ **asymmetrical warfare**
armed conflict between different types of enemies; one of which is much more militarily powerful than the other.

THE USES AND LIMITS OF COERCIVE DIPLOMACY

The strategy of **coercive diplomacy** employs threats or limited force to persuade an opponent to stop or cease pursuing an action already under way. The goal is to alter the target state's calculation of costs and benefits, so that it is convinced that acceding to another's demands will be better than defying them. This may be accomplished by delivering an **ultimatum** that promises an immediate and significant escalation in the conflict, or by issuing a warning and gradually increasing pressure on the target (Craig and George 1990).

Coercive diplomacy's reliance on the threat of force is designed to avoid the bloodshed and expense associated with traditional military campaigns. It seeks "to resolve without violence, or with only minimal violence, those conflicts that are too severe to be settled by ordinary diplomacy and that in earlier times would have been settled by war" (Snyder and Diesing 1977). Nevertheless, these attempts at intimidation carry some risk of war. Figure 12.5 shows the annual frequency between 1918 and 2001 of 433 international crises involving coercive efforts. Most of these crises were initiated by the great powers, roughly two thirds occurred in the Global South, and about one of every three led to war (Brecher 1993, 333, 476). Examples of violence that were preceded by a crisis in-

■ **coercive diplomacy**
an approach to bargaining between states engaged in a crisis in which threats to use arms are made to force an adversary to reach a compromise.

■ **ultimatum**
a demand that puts a time limit for the target to comply and a threat of punishment for resistance.

FIGURE 12.5
International Tension since World War I: The Annual Frequency of International Crises since 1918

On 433 occasions states confronted each other militarily between 1918 and 2001, in the hopes of forcing concessions. The frequency has varied over time, but its recurrence attests to states' compulsion to threaten each other with military force to get their way. In February 2000, the world witnessed another crisis when two enemies, India and Pakistan, amassed troops on their mutual border and spoke openly of nuclear war; and, of course, on September 11, 2001, the entire world went on alert in reaction to the terrorist destruction of the World Trade Center in New York.

SOURCE: Based on International Crisis Behavior (ICB) data, provided courtesy of Jonathan Wilkenfeld at the University of Maryland, and Michael Brecher.

clude World War I (1914), Kashmir (1948 and 2002), Suez (1956), Tibet (1959), the Bay of Pigs (1961), Goa (1961), Kuwait (1990), Yugoslavia (Kosovo, 1999), Macedonia (2001), and Afghanistan (2001).

Orchestrating the mix of threats and armed force can be done in various ways, from traditional **gunboat diplomacy** to sophisticated cruise missile strikes. We will focus on **military intervention,** the oldest and most common approach to military coercion.

Military Intervention

Intervention can come in many forms. States can intervene physically through direct entry into another country or indirectly with propaganda. They can act alone or in league with other states. Military intervention involves "opera-

■ **gunboat diplomacy**
a show of military force; historically naval force.

■ **military intervention**
overt or covert use of force by one or more countries that cross the border of another country in order to affect the target country's government and policies.

tions undertaken openly by a state's regular military forces within a specific foreign land in such a manner as to risk immediate combat" (Tillema 1994). Altogether, nearly 1,000 individual acts of military intervention were initiated between 1945 and 2001, resulting in 2.4 million fatalities (Tillema 2006). Excluded from this estimate are an unknown number of **covert operations.** Military interventions have often heightened international tension and led to war. Between 1816 and 2004, 48 cases of third-party military intervention in 233 civil wars occurred, with the result that 21 percent were transformed into interstate wars (see Table 11.1, p. 421). These statistics raise important questions about the use of military intervention for coercive diplomacy. Do interventions yield positive results, punishing regimes that violate human rights and calming war-torn societies? Or do they make matters worse? These questions have become among the most hotly debated issues in world politics as a result of the wave of **failed states.** In the wake of humanitarian interventions in Kosovo and East Timor in 1999, the great powers struggled unsuccessfully to reach consensus about the need to intervene in sovereign states when innocent civilians are victimized by tyrants, for such interventions undercut the principles of state sovereignty and the **nonintervention norm** in international law. UN Secretary-General Kofi Annan's plea in September 1999 for the permanent members of the Security Council to make a "new commitment to intervention" stirred up an already intense debate about military intervention, even in the name of morality, justice, and **human rights.**

Few question the necessity to stand up to genocide and intervene to protect the lives of persecuted peoples. However, many great powers remain reluctant to pledge unconditionally their willingness to uphold human rights anywhere they are violated. Instead, they practice selective engagement, picking and choosing when and where they will intervene. Regardless of humanitarian considerations, they generally avoid taking action when their interests appear to be served by noninvolvement—as the United States did between 2002 and 2004 when it sat on the sidelines as waves of terrorist violence and counterattacks took the lives of both Israeli and Palestinian civilians. On the other hand, the great powers insert themselves when their security appears at stake, as the United States has done recently in attempting to weaken terrorist networks with global reach. Since 1990 the U.S. Army has been deployed abroad three times as often as the number of "major" deployments in the entire period between 1946 and 1989 (*Harper's*, July 1999, 17). But public opposition to and international criticism of the U.S. military stands in the way of its practicing interventionism with abandon. As a result, many of the counterterrorist interventions in the future will likely be conducted in the shadows by covert and clandestine methods.

Policymakers today disagree about the appropriate use of military coercion. Research on coercive diplomacy suggests that its success depends upon the context of each specific situation. The following conditions are thought to favor the effective use of coercive diplomacy (George 1992; Art 2005):

- *Clarity of user objectives.* The coercing power's demands must be clearly understood by the target state.
- *Asymmetry of motivation favoring the user.* The coercing power must be more highly motivated than the target by what is at stake. Timing is critical. Military coercion tends to be effective when it occurs prior to the target making a firm commitment on the issue at hand, and when factions exist within the target state's government. It is far more difficult for a coercing

■ **covert operations** secret activities undertaken by a state outside its borders through clandestine means to achieve specific political or military goals with respect to another state.

■ **failed states** countries whose governments have so mismanaged policy that they have lost the loyalty of their citizens who, in rebellion, threaten to divide the state into separate countries.

■ **nonintervention norm** a fundamental international legal principle, now being challenged, that traditionally has defined interference by one state in the domestic affairs of another as illegal.

■ **human rights** the political rights and civil liberties recognized by the international community as freedoms to which all people are entitled, even though many such inalienable privileges are not universally protected by the laws of states.

power to undo something that has already been accomplished by the target state.

- *Opponent's fear of escalation and belief in the urgency for compliance.* The coercing power must create in the adversary's mind a sense of urgency for compliance with its demand. Two factors are important in affecting an adversary's perceptions: (1) the coercing power's reputation for successfully using armed force in the past, and (2) its capability to increase pressure to a level that the target would find intolerable. Coercion generally fails when the target has the ability to absorb the punishment delivered by the coercing state.

- *Adequate domestic and international support for the user.* In addition to having political support at home, the coercing power is helped when it also can count on support from key states and international organizations.

- *Clarity on the precise terms of settlement.* The coercing power must be able to articulate the specific conditions for ending the crisis, as well as give assurances that it will not formulate new demands for greater concessions once the target capitulates.

While these conditions improve the odds of successful coercive diplomacy, they do not guarantee success. National leaders who resort to coercive diplomacy start a process over which they have imperfect control. Given the uncertainties surrounding the use of armed force, states often employ nonmilitary methods to alter an opponent's behavior. Recalling an ambassador and terminating cultural or scientific exchanges are some of the ways states signal their displeasure. **Sanctions** through **boycotts** figure prominently in this regard, as an alternative to bombs and bullets for coercion. They are seen by many as so popular that they are "the main tool of coercive diplomacy" (Hoagland 1996) and "the most favored tool of diplomats" (Pound and El-Tahri 1994).

Economic Sanctions

When the Arab members of the Organization of Petroleum Exporting Countries (OPEC) placed an embargo on the shipment of oil to the United States and the Netherlands in 1973, their purpose was to alter these countries' policies toward the Arab-Israeli conflict. When the UN Security Council decided in August 1990 that the world organization should cease trade with Iraq, its purpose was to force the immediate and unconditional withdrawal of Iraq from Kuwait. Both are examples of the use of **economic sanctions**—"deliberate government actions to inflict economic deprivation on a target state or society, through the limitation or cessation of customary economic relations" (Leyton-Brown 1987).

Economic sanctions are an increasingly popular approach to convincing another state to desist from some unacceptable behavior. They include a broad array of instruments: withholding foreign aid, placing tariffs and quotas on imports from a targeted state, boycotting its products, declaring an embargo on the sale of goods to the target, and freezing assets it may have in international banks. To the extent that there is a degree of optimism today about the potential effectiveness of sanctions, it is likely because of the perception shared by many that broad multilateral sanctions helped to end the segregationist apartheid system in South Africa and opened the way for black majority rule. Since World War I, there have been 120 observable episodes of economic sanctions, 104 of which

■ **sanctions**
punitive actions by one state against another to retaliate for its previous objectionable behavior.

■ **boycotts**
concerted efforts, often organized internationally, to prevent relations such as trade with a state, to express disapproval or to coerce acceptance of certain conditions.

■ **economic sanctions**
the punitive use of trade or monetary measures, such as an embargo, to harm the economy of an enemy state in order to exercise influence over its policies.

Trade Interdependence and Sanctions In this photo, a tanker carrying natural gas leaves Qatar for Japan. Qatar, with huge gas reserves, hopes exports will transform its economy; Japan badly needs natural gas to propel its consumer-rich economy. Japan's dependence on foreign suppliers for desperately needed energy sources reduces its willingness to use economic sanctions to influence the policies of suppliers. The use of economic sanctions is often influenced by the relationships between commodity-dependent importers and commodity-wealthy exporters. In April 2002, Crown Prince Abdullah visited U.S. President George W. Bush at his Crawford, Texas, ranch and warned Bush that American support for Israel in Palestine undercut the war on terrorism, but promised that it would not use oil as a weapon.

---

have been enacted since World War II (Hufbauer, Schott, and Elliott 1990). The United States has relied heavily on economic sanctions during this period. By 1998, half the world's population lived in countries that had been placed under U.S. sanctions (*Harper's*, February 1998, 13).

The rationale for employing sanctions as instruments of influence stems largely from the fact that they avoid the dangers of using armed force. Military coercion can easily backfire, draining government budgets, producing undue casualties, and provoking widespread public criticism at home and abroad. In comparison, economic sanctions appear less risky and far less costly. Hence, "policymakers continue to use sanctions with increasing frequency" (Baldwin 2000).

Another reason for the rising use of economic sanctions is that today national economies are increasingly integrated through trade, which increases the dependence on others for their own prosperity. This circumstance makes sanctions that threaten targets with the loss of an export market more effective than

MAPS 12.4 AND 12.5
Vulnerable to Sanctions—Countries Dependent on Trade and Energy Imports

Many states find themselves subject to external coercion and vulnerable to manipulations by states that impose sanctions on them, especially if they are highly dependent on exports for their economic prosperity and/or imports for their commercial energy use. Sanctions through boycotts or embargoes, undertaken to coerce change in a trade-dependent or energy-dependent country's policies, can be devastating. The map on the left shows the great extent to which many countries are today dependent on trade, and in the globalized marketplace the level of states' dependence on exports for economic prosperity is growing. The map on the right shows the varying levels countries are dependent on foreign suppliers for their energy needs; note that only a small number of states are net exporters, with the rest dependent on and therefore vulnerable to manipulation by the foreign sources from which they import their energy—such as the Organization of Petroleum Exporting Countries (OPEC).

SOURCES: Economic dependence on exports, UNDP (2004), 192–95; energy dependence on imports, World Bank (2005a).

---

in the past, when countries could better withstand a foreign embargo. Likewise, countries dependent on imports from abroad for their basic needs are highly vulnerable to sanctions, since supply disruptions could bring their economies to a standstill (see Maps 12.4 and 12.5). Economic sanctions are also gaining proponents because more than sixty states are highly vulnerable "single-commodity-dependent economies" that derive at least 40 percent of their export revenues from foreign purchase of a single product (*Handbook of International Economic Statistics* 2000, 72–73). This high level of vulnerability makes sanctions appear

Net Energy Imports as a Percentage of Commercial Energy Use
- High (more than 70%)
- Medium (30% to 70%)
- Low (less than 30%)
- Major exporters of energy

potent enough to exercise influence according to the classic reasoning of James Madison and Thomas Jefferson, who advocated "peaceable coercion" against those foreign governments that would have to yield to American pressure because U.S. goods were essential to their prosperity.

Five major policy goals are customarily pursued by states when they adopt economic sanctions to pressure a foreign target:

- *compliance* ("to force the target to alter its behavior to conform with the initiator's preferences"), as in the case of the 1982 U.S. embargo of Libya, designed to force it to end its support of terrorism
- *subversion* ("to remove the target's leaders . . . or overthrow the regime"), as in the cases of the 1993–94 U.S. trade embargo against Haiti and the 2002 U.S. efforts to topple Saddam Hussein in Iraq
- *deterrence* ("to dissuade the target from repeating the disputed action in the future"), as in the case of the Soviet grain embargo by the United States
- *international symbolism* ("to send messages to other members of the world community"), as in the case of the British sanctions against Rhodesia after its unilateral declaration of independence in 1965
- *domestic symbolism* ("to increase its domestic support or thwart international criticism of its foreign policies by acting decisively"), as in the case of U.S. sanctions against Iran following its seizure of U.S. diplomats in 1979 (Lindsay 1986)

These multiple uses notwithstanding, it is rare for policymakers to advocate the use of economic sanctions without generating criticism. Critics invariably argue that they frequently do not work or fail to accomplish the objectives for which they were initiated (Haass 1997). To be sure, sanctions have a checkered history. At times they have succeeded, such as in the case of Libya, where after a decade of international pressure, Libyan dictator Muammar Qaddafi finally turned over to Western powers for trial two Libyans alleged to have blown up the Pan Am Flight 103 over Scotland in 1988 that killed all of its 280 passengers. Despite this and a few other successes, the historical record casts great doubt on the capacity of sanctions to work, even when used by the world's foremost powerful economic power, the United States. Between 1970 and 1990, "just 5 of 39 unilateral U.S. sanctions [achieved] any success at all" (K. Elliott 1998, 58). Conspicuous in the many cases where U.S. economic coercion through sanctions failed is the U.S. experience with Cuba. The United States placed sanctions on the Castro regime shortly after it came to power in 1960 and forged an alliance with the Soviet Union. In response, the United States banned all trade with Cuba and pressured other countries to do the same, hoping to overthrow the Castro regime. This goal was not realized. Castro has survived for more than forty-five years.

Cuba is often cited as perhaps the best example of the inherent obstacles to successful sanctions. Other such U.S. failures include the inability of the United States to impose a partial embargo on the sale of grain to the Soviet Union after its 1979 intervention in Afghanistan, as well as the inability of the Reagan administration in 1981 to use sanctions to stop Poland and the Soviet Union from building the trans-Siberian gas pipeline designed to bring Soviet energy into western European markets. These examples suggest that "sanctions are seldom effective in impairing the military potential of an important power, or in bringing about major changes in the policies of the target country" (Hufbauer, Schott, and Elliott 1990), and "have been absolutely ineffective in bringing about a change of government leadership within a target country" (Cortwright and Lopez 1995). Rather than effectively and efficiently achieving the foreign policy goals of compliance, subversion, or deterrence, economic sanctions serve an important symbolic function by publicizing unacceptable behavior by other states.

The limitations of economic sanctions as a tool of coercive diplomacy can be seen in the unsuccessful efforts to topple Iraqi dictator Saddam Hussein after the Persian Gulf War ended in 1991. Despite a UN embargo, Hussein was able to continue exporting oil on the black market through dummy corporations and to purchase weapons from foreign manufacturers. Meanwhile, ordinary Iraqis suffered. The death of more than six hundred thousand Iraqi children as a result of the economic sanctions (*Harper's*, November 2002, 13) led the UN to begin experimenting with so-called smart sanctions (Cortwright and Lopez 2002), which would target governmental elites, not innocent citizens.

The choice between military force and economic sanctions is always a difficult one, and there is every reason to expect states to continue to pursue both strategies when they are confronted with situations that seem to demand coercive measures. To make sanctions effective, and smart, it will be necessary to rectify those features that previously have made them a weak tool in statecraft. These include the following deficiencies:

- A typical response to economic coercion in the sanctioned society is a heightened sense of nationalism, a *laager* mentality (circle the wagons to face oncoming enemies), which stimulates resistance in the target state.

- Sanctions sometimes hurt the disempowered people they seek to help—the country's average citizens.
- Governments often act covertly to support the sanctioned state even as they publicly profess their support of sanctions.
- Sanctions are an invisible form of trade protectionism that interferes with liberal free trade and therefore profits.
- The credibility of the state(s) imposing sanctions is often low.
- Widespread and collective sustained cooperation from the international community and international organizations seldom materializes, and unilateral sanctions seldom succeed in a globalized market with many competitive suppliers of embargoed goods.

These limitations attributed to sanctions underscore why their use is often questioned whenever new sanctions are proposed for bargaining. Nonetheless, the impulse to use this tool is likely to remain strong because sanctions enable a leader to show leadership without suffering the criticism that tends to follow decisions to use military force.

In the pursuit of national security, the goals and plans of the most powerful states have the most impact. We conclude with an overview of the great powers' recent reformulations of their national security strategies and defense policies. We look first at the United States—the globe's uncontested military superpower—and how its actions heavily influence how the other major powers respond to both U.S. predominance and other security concerns.

THE GREAT POWERS' NATIONAL SECURITY STRATEGIES

The new age of global terrorism drives new strategic thinking, as defense planners in Washington, Moscow, Beijing, Tokyo, Berlin, and Brussels struggle to construct defense doctrines to manage the security threats on the horizon.

As noted in Chapter 4, the choices range between the extremes of isolationist withdrawal from participation in world affairs and active international engagement. The other choices need to be made between **unilateral** self-help actions on one end of the continuum, **multilateral** action with others on the other, and specialized **bilateral** alliances and ad hoc partnerships in between. And these choices force decisions to be made about honoring ideals without undermining self-interests: in short, to reconcile **liberalism** and realism.

What sort of national security response is most likely? We will look briefly at the emerging security policies of the five major great powers.

The U.S. Superpower Embraces a Revolutionary New Security Strategy

After September 11, U.S. global strategy shifted immediately, defining as its priorities military security, preservation of its premier position as world leader, and an assertive unilateralism that would do whatever served Amercan national interests. All other goals, including economic recovery and the promotion of

■ **unilateralism**
a go-it-alone, self-reliant strategy for dealing with threats from another actor or global problem.

■ **multilateralism**
a cooperative strategy of working with allies or with collective problem-solving institutions to face threats from another actor or global problem.

■ **bilateralism**
an intermediary strategy of working with a specific ally or in a specially created ad hoc partnership to face threats from another actor or global problem.

■ **liberalism**
a paradigm predicated on the hope that the application of reason and universal ethics to international relations can lead to a more orderly, just, and cooperative world, and that international anarchy and war can be policed by institutional reforms that empower organizations and international law for global governance.

such traditional U.S. ideals as free trade and human rights throughout the world (which also contribute, according to neoliberal thinking, to global prosperity and peace), were secondary. This preference about priorities will always be controversial, because three schools of thought about America's role in global affairs continue to divide U.S. policymakers:

> Neoisolationists want the U.S. to deal only with threats to America's physical security, political independence, and domestic liberty. They . . . argue that the U.S. should let other powers, and regional balances of power, take care of all the world's woes. Realists such as Henry Kissinger want the U.S. to continue to be the holder of the world balance of power, the arbiter of the main regional power groups, and the watchdog against all potential imperialistic troublemakers. Liberal internationalists want a greater role for multilateral institutions and more emphasis on human needs and rights, the environment and democracy. (Hoffmann 1992, 59)

Every post–9/11 U.S. administration's national security advisers will have to struggle to reconcile these divergent outlooks and to strike a balance among the need for self-help isolationism, the impulse to flex supreme U.S. military muscle in an activist push to run the world, and the desire to promote traditional U.S. liberal ideals such as human rights, democracy, and multilateral international cooperation. The quest is challenging because they entail a **zero-sum** trade-off among choices, in which one goal can only be pursued by compromising pursuit of others. For example, the United States cannot play the role of hegemonic superpower leading the world and also isolationistically withdraw from the costs of paying for foreign aid, regional collective security alliances, or UN peacekeeping missions; nor can the United States avoid looking hypocritical if it undertakes a massive military buildup at the same time that it preaches the ideals of arms control, disarmament, and nonproliferation for others.

The Bush administration sought to reconcile these partially incompatible goals by pursuing the priorities it identified in its revolutionary September 2002 *National Security Strategy of the United States of America:*

- wage, and win, the war against the worldwide network of terrorist organizations
- prevent any other great power from challenging the hegemonic position of the United States as the sole global superpower
- deter the use of nuclear, biological, or chemical weapons against the United States and its allies
- pursue "regime change" and disarmament in Iraq by all means necessary, including the preemptive use of military force, to overthrow Iraqi dictator Saddam Huessin
- attempt to recruit global support for U.S. military operations while, in those endeavors, preventing the United States from becoming isolated from those parts of the world opposed to U.S. operations overseas
- pursue the search for technological solutions to military problems through the development of smaller smart bombs, nonlethal weapons, and an improved ballistic missile defense system in outer space
- remain capable of using military interventions at the same time in at least two regions of strategic U.S. importance

■ **zero-sum**
competitive situations in which there is little room for compromise, because the gains from one choice or one goal require a loss for another.

- maintain U.S. technological superiority
- foster democratic values in other countries

The **Bush Doctrine** advocates "unabashed unilateralism [that aims] to re-shape norms, alter expectations and create new realities [by] unapologetic and implacable demonstrations of will" (Krauthammer 2001). This "go-it-alone" posture rejects the accommodation of American foreign policy to the wishes and interests of other countries in order for the United States to be seen as a good international citizen. Instead, the United States warns that it will venture forward as it chooses and will break the straightjacket imposed by multilateral treaties—on arms control, antiballistic missiles, biological weapons, nuclear testing, the landmine convention, the Kyoto treaty on global warming, and the international criminal court.

In the aftermath of the trauma of the September 11 terrorist attacks the United States quickly retreated from the bold unilateralism first asserted in the Bush Doctrine. After 9/11, the U.S. counterterrorism program required unrestrained global interventionism and needed the approval and assistance of allies and international organizations. Viewed in light of the **realpolitik** definition of its evolving defense doctrines, the United States is now especially committed to relying on military might while also attempting to build liberal ideals into the definition of its goals (as seen in the way Bush defined the war on terrorism as a war to defend liberty). U.S. national security policy after Bush's November 2004 re-election has reaffirmed the U.S. commitment to be prepared to wage two major wars simultaneously and to be able to intervene militarily around the world, while at the same time to deter an attack on the United States. For these objectives, the U.S. has increased its defense budget exponentially; newly re-elected George W. Bush pledged a record $447 billion in military spending in fiscal 2005 with further increases in future years. Power has been defined primarily in terms of military might and secondarily in terms of the promotion of high ideals such as free trade and free governments to secure a **democratic peace**.

The United States faces the awesome task of preserving U.S. predominance and its traditional reputation as a honorable peace-loving country that abides by moral principles. To some realists, American hegemonic leadership will require a warrior mentality and a pagan ethos. As the realist writer Robert D. Kaplan (2002) counsels, "the paramount question of world politics in the early twenty-first century will be the re-establishment of order," and for that crusade the United States will have to lead by using ruthless military methods as an imperial power that (like the Leviathan state envisioned by the realist Thomas Hobbes in the seventeenth century) crushes revisionist actors seeking to overturn the international status quo.

Neoliberals will have to live for a long time with these U.S. commitments, from which the next administration will have difficulty distancing itself. They want the U.S. empire to pursue a different set of goals and approaches, and warn that suppressing freedom by force can undermine the very order that an imperial hegemon hopes to preserve. The fact is that in the present stage of world history the United States is stronger militarily than it (or any other great power) has ever been in history. However, the U.S. homeland in the age of global terrorism arguably has never been less secure or more vulnerable (Kegley and Raymond 2005b). So the United States faces a supreme test about the policies that should guide and preserve its power and reduce its vulnerability. As neoliberal former

■ **Bush Doctrine**
the declaration that the United States intended to behave globally in terms of its perceived national self-interests, without the necessary approval of others and, as a corollary, would consider taking unilateral preemptive military action against any security threat such as Iraq to defeat it before it could attack the United States.

■ **realpolitik**
the theoretical outlook prescribing that countries should prepare for war in order to preserve peace.

■ **democratic peace**
the theory that, because democratic states do not fight each other, the diffusion of democratic governance throughout the world will reduce the probability of war.

Remote-Control Warfare? In the twenty-first century, the United States plans to preserve its commanding edge in military capabilities and combat the growing threat of insurgencies by building a new generation of technologically sophisticated new weapons, instead of attempting to build up an overpowering inventory of big bombs that are risky to use. A wide variety of weapons are under construction, ranging from thousand-pound bombs (the concrete, nonexplosive bombs the U.S. bombarded Iraq with in late 1999) to landmines. Some of the nonnuclear strategic weapons systems on the drawing boards "may be able to engage 1,500 targets in the first hour, if not minutes, of a conflict." Shown here is one example: "An artist's conception of an advanced unmanned aircraft system—one possibility for strategic strikes with conventional explosives" (Krepinevich and Kusiak 1998).

U.S. policymaker Joseph S. Nye wrote in 2002, the "paradox of American power" is that at the height of its military capabilities the United States is more dependent on others than ever, because the United States is most affected by globalization. "The world's only superpower can't go it alone, and it is imperative that the United States seek constructive relations with others, for it cannot by itself ensure success and stability." What is needed, Nye (2004b) concludes, is a new U.S. strategic vision, one that relies less on the traditional measures of "hard power" defined in terms of military capabilities and more on the type of "soft power" that emanates from the appeal of America's humanitarian values and culture and its free institutions.

Standing at the pinnacle of global power, the United States will have to struggle with the dilemma of occupying—and holding—its lonely unipolar position as the supreme superpower at the top of the global pyramid of power. It will have to avoid the extremes of isolationism and imperialism if it is to lead in the world, but resist the temptation to dominate others and thereby drive them into hostile resistance. Globalization precludes the possibility of redesigning the world to advance U.S. prominence. The U.S. standing among the community of nations remains high, and that is a source of influence; but the U.S. capacity to use military force to compel other countries to act as the United States wishes is low, and the prospects of eliminating an entrenched phenomenon like terrorism worldwide are low. The soft power that respect for U.S. ideals and ideas coupled with economic strength can provide can be the basis for the United States to fashion the globe into a prosperous and peaceful place, providing it leads by example rather than by force (Brzezinski 2004). Finding a global vision that balances realist interests with liberal ideals will be America's continuing greatest challenge.

In the chaotic twenty-first century, American leaders can be expected to adapt U.S. strategy to the unknown dangers that lurk beneath the surface of turbulent global geostrategic waters. Limits on America's capacity to foresee the future—and limits on resources to take a unilateral approach to managing the new millennium's multiple security threats—suggest that a coherent strategy resting on a clear vision is likely to prove an elusive goal for the United States in the future.

Given the overwhelming military predominance of the United States, it is understandable that the other great powers have constructed their national security policies to a large extent around their uncertain relationship with the U.S. hegemon. (Ironically, so have the global terrorist movements that have made the U.S. superpower their major enemy and primary target.) We next briefly look at the policies the other great powers have crafted, as they likewise attempt to deal with the prevailing reality of U.S. preponderance and with changes in both their national circumstances at home and in their region.

Russia Adjusts to Its New Geostrategic Circumstances

For Russia, perhaps its most important challenge is American predominance, power, and policy. Confronting the United States as an adversary remains a fight Russia does not want and could not win. As a consequence, Russia is building its new security policies around the effort to cultivate a strategic partnership with the United States and, secondarily, the North Atlantic Treaty Organization (NATO), which the United States dominates. Russian military weakness has also forced Russia to forge ever closer political and economic relations with its major trading partners in the enlarged twenty-five-member European Union. Russia has set its sights on integrating itself into the global institutions created by the United States and its allies in the West.

Much of this shift reflects Russia's precarious geostrategic circumstances. Russia's army has lost its roar amid continuing financial shortfalls, which have required the country to reduce its military spending to seven times less than that of the United States. Moreover, Russia has now dismantled much of the awesome strategic nuclear stockpile that formerly was the backbone of its defense and the symbol of its military might. Simply put, Russia is undergoing **power transition** of unprecedented pace and magnitude, and this has compromised its capacity to deal with the many separatist movements active in the remaining regions of its shrunken empire (such as in the explosive war in the breakaway republic of Chechnya and in Russia's southern rim, where Islamic terrorist bombings continue). Russia simply does not have the resources to be a global power.

To deal with the country's security predicament Russian President Vladimir Putin revised his original 1997 *Concept of National Security*. The new doctrine set the following priorities:

- cutting the Russian defense budget and nuclear arsenal even further and undertaking fundamental restructuring to eliminate entire branches of the armed services, and putting the savings from this defense conversion toward stimulating economic recovery
- creating smaller, more mobile, and technologically adept fighting forces to manage civil rebellions within Russia as well as along Russia's troubled southern borders in the "near abroad" and neighbors such as Ukraine
- preserving the boundaries of Russia's sphere of influence, which have steadily retreated, to hold them firmly at Ukraine's western border

■ **power transition**
a situation resulting from the rapid increase or deterioration in one state's military capabilities relative to a rival's, often provoking fears that lead to warfare.

■ **no first use**
the doctrine that a nuclear state would not be the first to use its strategic weapons in the event of a military attack by another state.

- repealing Mikhail Gorbachev's **no first use** pledge that Russia would not be the first to use nuclear weapons in the event of a conventional or nuclear attack—because Russia relies on its remaining nuclear warheads to repel a foreign aggressor

Vulnerable, Russia emphasizes a multilateral diplomatic approach to its many security problems and has isolationistically reduced the global scale of its international involvements. One example was the rejection of the previous strategy of building a countercoalition to balance what Russia had previously called a threat—U.S. hegemonial domination. Russia's doctrine now pursues the goal of **bandwagoning** by making Russia an alliance partner with the stronger United States and its European allies. In 2004 President Putin pushed hard toward closer relations with the West, and his efforts paid dividends when Russia gained full participation in NATO, the European Union redefined Russia as a market economy to smooth its way into the World Trade Organization, and Russia's new partners offered to import oil from Russia's vast supplies as a means of cementing Russia's cooperation in the new war on international terrorism.

■ **bandwagoning**
the tendency for weak states to seek alliance with the strongest power, irrespective of that power's ideology or form of government, in order to increase security.

China's Global Clout and Security Posture

China figures prominently in U.S. and Russian conceptions of security.

> The rise of China, if it continues, may be the most important trend in the world. . . . When historians one hundred years hence write about our time, they may well conclude that the most significant development was the emergence of a vigorous market economy—and army—in the most populous country of the world. This is particularly likely if many of the globe's leading historians and pundits a century from now do not have names like Smith but rather ones like Wu.
>
> China is the fastest growing economy in the world, with what may be the fastest growing military budget. It has nuclear weapons, border disputes with most of its neighbors, and a rapidly improving army that may—within a decade or so—be able to resolve old quarrels in its own favor. The United States has possessed the world's largest economy for more than a century, but at present trajectories China may displace it in the first half of the next century and become the number one economy in the world. (Kristof 1993, 59; see also R. Kaplan 1999)

China is now an economic giant, driven by the long-term goal of gaining respect and recognition as a great power. To that end, China has followed the realist script by attempting to harness its economic clout by modernizing its military. Since it abandoned Marxist-Leninist communism in the 1980s, China's economy has grown at a compound annual rate of about 10 percent; its GDP has quadrupled to over $1.7 trillion, making China the globe's sixth largest economy (World Bank, 2005b, 260). These resources thus enable China, formerly regarded as sleeping giant, to awaken and convert finances into military power to symbolize and possibly act upon its new rising status. And China's pledge to recover Taiwan by force if necessary has renewed anxieties about potential Chinese militarism.

However, China has far to go in order to become a military superpower. Its maritime and air capabilities remain antiquated, with only twenty DF-5 liquid-fueled ICMBs, no aircraft carriers, and only 3,500 jet fighters. China's defense spending is growing, but at $47 billion in 2004 is only 12 percent that of the

A Hegemonic Challenger on the March? China is an ascendant superpower with the capacity to intimidate its Asian neighbors and strike fear into distant great-power rivals, who suspect that its rise to the top rank among national economies will be followed by foreign aggressiveness. At the moment, China is not a serious challenger to U.S. supremacy. As this photo of Chinese soldiers suggests, China's military is more stylish pomp than it is a truly modern force able to credibly project power throughout the globe.

United States and inadequate for the major buildup required to rival the United States. Moreover, "the Chinese are not implementing these [military modernization] programs on a crash basis, and most of them will not bear fruit for years. Even then their military technology will lag far behind that of the United States" (Joffe 2001). Rather than building a modern military itself, China is allocating its military budget to purchase advanced arms from other suppliers, such as fighter aircraft and surface-to-air missiles from Russia and Israel.

China seeks to reduce other states' fears about its rising capabilities as the globe's most populous and fastest growing economy and repeatedly has asserted that it seeks peaceful relations with all. For example, China has ceased condemning the United States for pursuing the singular goal "the hegemonic domination of the world."

Like other great powers, China has struggled to find long-term solutions to its security problems. One direction is signaled by China's continuing arms buildup, its preservation of its modest strategic arsenal of nuclear weapons, and its feverish attempt to equip the globe's largest standing army of 2.27 million soldiers. The other direction is signaled by China's unrestrained efforts to increase further its diplomatic stature through continuing rapid economic growth. That path to security was made evident by the sacrifices China made in 2002 to successfully gain membership in the World Trade Organization, which necessitated opening China to foreign imports and expanding civil liberties through political reforms. China has cast its fate in this neoliberal direction, hoping to win the benefits of active participation in the global marketplace, and so far this strategy is paying huge benefits. Following membership in the World Trade Organization, foreign direct investment (FDI) in China has risen, on average, about 30 percent each year, and rapid economic growth following economic liberalization (from $106 billion in 1970 to $1.7 trillion in 2004) has emboldened China to act as a regional economic policy leader to promote greater cooperation and reduce neighbors' anxieties about its clout (Melloan 2002b, A17).

To find a safe place in the sun where it feels it belongs, China has defined its national security priorities through a strategy that seeks to

- deter a large-scale conventional or nuclear attack on China by any other great power, such as the United States
- develop the military force required to successfully invade Taiwan should negotiations fail to integrate with the mainland what China sees as a renegade province
- lobby to see that the traditional international legal rule prohibiting external interference in sovereign states' domestic affairs is respected, to safeguard against foreign intervention to punish China for disregard of its citizens' human rights, while at the same time developing the military capability to prevent U.S. intervention if Beijing decides to impose reunification with Taiwan by force

China's national security policies emphasize the importance of "maintaining good and friendly relations with all countries" and above all avoiding becoming the next target of a U.S.-led coalition assembled to contain its rise. Establishing normalized diplomatic relations with the United States and the other great powers is crucial to Chinese security, because the last thing China needs is to be regarded as an enemy facing a new U.S. **containment** policy in a new Cold War. Mistrust prevails whenever great-power rivals clash, and to the other great powers these Chinese proclamations inspire divergent reactions.

China's strategic situation is at a crossroads. As its vigorous rearmament and force-modernization program proceeds, the country's growing arsenal will position it to play a dominant military role in Asia and eventually the entire world. Napoleon Bonaparte counseled in 1803 that the world should "let China sleep" because, he predicted, when it awakens, "the world will tremble." China has now awakened. What it will do with its rapidly growing power remains to be seen.

Japan's Search for a Strategy

An emerging economic superpower in the 1990s and proudly the second richest country behind the United States, Japan has recently struggled to keep pace economically and has been overshadowed by China, the most expanding economy in the world. The future is clouded by Japan's aging and shrinking population and now-staggering national debts.

In the aftermath of World War II, Japan strictly adhered to the guidelines of the **Yoshida Doctrine,** in which Prime Minister Shigeru Yoshida argued that Japanese security policy should avoid international disputes, keep a low profile on divisive global issues, and concentrate on economic pursuits. That doctrine

■ **containment**
a term coined by U.S. policymaker George F. Kennan for deterring Soviet Russia's expansionist aims by counter-pressures, which has since become a general term used by strategists to describe the methods used to prevent an expanding great power from using its military muscles for expansionist hegemonic purposes.

■ **Yoshida Doctrine**
Japan's traditional security policy of avoiding disputes with rivals, preventing foreign wars by low military spending, and promoting economic growth through foreign trade.

remains timely, given the 1990s' "lost decade" in which the Japanese economy actually declined, undermining the country's ability to play a more active global role. Japan continues to stress words over deeds and to advocate a neoliberal foreign policy philosophy.

Despite economic restraints, Japan is expanding its global involvement. Prime Minister Kiichi Miyazawa's policy departures in 1992 presaged the new direction of Japan's security policies. Miyazawa won passage of the Peacekeeping Operations Bill, which enabled Japan to deploy a self-defense military force to participate in UN peacekeeping operations in Cambodia in 1992—the first use of Japanese armed forces abroad since World War II. Japan's acceptance of a large increase in its previous UN dues (almost 20 percent in 2005), its push for inclusion as a permanent member of the UN Security Council, and its rise to the top of the world's foreign aid donors also suggest growing Japanese international activism. Such policies have continued in 2005.

As a sign of the Japanese effort to discard its traditional isolationism and to be a player in world affairs, Japan increased defense expenditures to $42.6 billion in 2004. Japan still adheres to the policy of spending no more than 1 percent of its gross national product on defense and remains committed to its postwar constitution, which forbids remilitarization. However, after a half-century of strict pacifism, alarmed that its neighbors' arms races are disrupting the Asian balance of power, and jittery over North Korea's launch of a three-stage long-range missile over Japan in August 1998, Japan is reconsidering how military might can contribute to national security and global standing. Japan's Self-Defense Force is impressive, with 240,000 soldiers in uniform and the Pacific's largest navy. Although it does not have advanced offensive weapons such as long-range bombers and aircraft carriers, Japan has seventeen of the most sophisticated submarines in the world. Japan's air force and navy may still be numerically fewer than China's, but they are more advanced and are likely to remain so for a long time. This shift in strategy worries its neighbors, who remember well Japan's history as a feared military power. Postwar Japanese pacifism could, with this military clout, give way to resurgent militarism aimed at its simmering territorial disputes with both Russia and China. From the Japanese perspective, the country faces growing security concerns, which have intensified in troubled northeast Asia (especially North Korea) because the United States abruptly announced in June 2004 that it cut by a third its military presence in Asia so that those troops could be deployed elsewhere.

Japan has sought to adapt the country's national security policies in several ways. First, Japan's security strategy seeks to further tie the country into the web of multilateral global institutions (the UN, the WTO, the G-8) on which it increasingly depends for preservation of the world order that has made possible Japan's post–World War II prosperity. Second, Japan has stepped up its efforts to lead in foreign assistance to developing Global South countries; it perceives advancing the poor a profitable investment in its own advancement. Third, Japan seeks to tie its security closer to America's and in 1999 beefed up the Japanese-American military alliance treaty by giving Japanese forces new authority to provide logistic support to U.S. combat forces in the vaguely defined "area around Japan." Combinations of bilateralism and multilateralism have replaced Japan's traditional preference for unilateralism in foreign affairs.

More problematically, with its neighbors arming to the teeth, Japan has begun to have second thoughts about nuclear weapons. Alarmed by the rising power of China and anxious about the effectiveness of security guarantees from the United States, some of Japan's most powerful politicians have begun to consider breaking with a half-century-old policy of pacifism by acquiring nuclear weapons (French 2002). This potential reversal of traditional Japanese doctrine—the three nonnuclear principles never to own, produce, or allow nuclear weapons on Japanese territory—signals the possibility of a radical departure in Japan's posture toward its future military role in the world.

Germany and the European Union Search for a Strategic Vision

Germany has begun to show a new assertiveness now that most of the immense costs of reunifying and rebuilding the former German Democratic Republic in the east have been absorbed. Given its size, economic strength, and geographic location, the challenge for Europeans will be to find a way to absorb Germany within a broad European power-sharing arrangement. According to some analysts, however, Germany is too powerful to disappear into a wider European framework. It already accounts for nearly two-fifths of the European Union's (EU) gross national product. In addition, its share of the EU budget is twice the amount of Great Britain and France combined. Moreover, most European states' economies are heavily linked to Germany's economy and trade. This extraordinary economic clout ensures Germany's continued dominance within the enlarged twenty-five-member European Union. There is no other EU country capable of balancing the power of a united Germany. "Too big for Europe, too small for the world" describes Germany's place in continental affairs.

If Germany's economic strength and diplomatic independence continue to grow, one consequence will be greater competition with the United States and other trade rivals. Yet this is not likely to result in a renewed push to flex German military muscle—even though Germany has one of the largest armies in Europe (296,000 soldiers), and, at $24.9 billion in 2003, the seventh largest military budget in the world. Despite the parliamentary amendment to Germany's constitution that permitted German troops to take part in international peacekeeping operations (for example, Germany's armed forces made up the second-biggest contingent in NATO's 1999 peace force in Kosovo), an independent German military presence on the world stage is unlikely. Renewed militarism is even less likely. Germany's armed forces are still deeply entrenched in and constrained by the joint command in NATO and the European Union's joint Eurocorps armed force. Because Germany remains a fervent advocate of the nuclear nonproliferation regime, economic rivalry is unlikely to culminate in a future arms buildup. In fact, European states cashed in the so-called peace dividend after the Cold War ended and reduced their military budgets by large percentages. Total European military spending was once 60 percent of the U.S. allocation, but now it is about 40 percent of what the U.S. spends on defense, and the billions of dollars required for the EU to catch up with U.S. military technology stand as an enormous obstacle to the ability of a European force to act unilaterally without U.S. support through NATO.

German Chancellor Gerhard Schroeder recast Germany's traditional sense of its place on the international stage—economically powerful but militarily timid—when he announced that his country's post–World War II role as a secondary player had "irrevocably passed." He announced, "Germany needs to show a new international responsibility" as he called for a more muscular and independent German national security policy. Schroeder's advocacy of an expanded German global presence and his harsh criticism of U.S. President George W. Bush's invasion of Iraq proved critical to Schroeder's September 2004 reelection and popularity at home.

Europe regards itself as "a second federal, democratic superpower [and] in the longer term, Euroland can—and probably will—look beyond its immediate borders. To be sure, it is not a military superpower like the United States and may not be one for some time. But that reality is less significant than is often thought. The deployment of Euroland's mammoth economic resources can have a strategic impact" (M. Elliott 1998). Thus, a strong German aversion to militarism persists and is likely to shape Germany's security policies well into the twenty-first century. In this regard, German defense strategy differs from the posture the other great powers have assumed.

Further, Germany remains the most enthusiastic supporter of integration and institutional approaches to the preservation of peace. Its security strategy subscribes unflinchingly to the tenets of **neoliberal institutionalism:** Germany has cast its fate on the spread of international organizations, European unification, international law, disarmament, and the promotion of democracy, free markets, and free trade as the most effective strategy for ensuring that a twenty-first century peace will prevail. In that spirit, Germany is the leading proponent of the EU's quest to forge a common security policy, and Germany has been an enthusiastic supporter of the EU's decision to create an all-European expeditionary force of sixty thousand soldiers (over the U.S. protest that the European Rapid Reaction Force would reduce the need for NATO and would undermine the U.S.–European alliance). Despite U.S. objections, Europe is proceeding with its strategic vision, aiming no longer to be dependent on U.S. missiles for defense and willing to protest U.S. policies such as the U.S. preemptive strike against Iraq. As the realist analyst Fareed Zakaria characterizes the European mood,

■ **neoliberal institutionalism**
the neoliberal theory in international relations that advocates creating global institutions to promote peace and security among states.

> If it wants to be a global player in the Atlantic alliance, Europe needs a strike force that can fight with or without America. Europe has to get back into the business of making war. Since the end of the Cold War, every serious division between Europe and the United States has been over military action. Europeans simply do not believe in war anymore, largely because of their own experience. After an incredibly bloody past, Europe has moved beyond war—an amazing achievement. Within Western Europe, dialogue, cooperation and trade have made conflict between the allies a distant memory. But the Europeans have now projected this mentality—born of highly unusual circumstances—onto a very difficult world. They spend lavishly on aid and send negotiation teams around the globe peddling their kinder, gentler power. Even though many of them believe that Saddam Hussein is a dangerous aggressor, their solution is "anything but war." . . . With economies of roughly the same size ($8 trillion each), Europe spends only $140 billion on defense, compared with America's [$396] billion. Worse, Europe spends its money badly, maintaining large land armies (created to fight a Soviet invasion) rather than developing technology, logistics and strike forces, which are the needs of the present. The United States spends almost $30,000 per soldier on research and development, while Europe spends $4,000. Even af-

ter September 11, no European politician of note has urged a large increase in defense spending. (Zakaria 2002a, 35)

The core group of EU, NATO, and OSCE countries see nuclear weapons as legitimate and NATO's first use of nuclear weapons doctrine to deter an attack as necessary. The wisdom or folly of Germany's strategy—and the EU's bid to become a new superpower (Reid 2004)—will be tested by the consequences that flow from the "nuclearization" of the EU's approach to national security.

THE SEARCH FOR SECURITY IN AN INSECURE WORLD

Preparation for war continues to command support from defense planners as an approach to peace. Rationalized by realism, the quest is understandable in a world where states alone remain responsible for their own self-defense. As President Eisenhower once noted, "until war is eliminated from international relations, unpreparedness for it is well nigh as criminal as war itself."

The fears produced by visions of national vulnerability also explain why many defense planners base their plans on worst-case analyses of others' capabilities and intentions. The urge to arm is further stimulated by defense planners' influence in the policy-making process of most countries and the tendency of political leaders to adopt the vocabulary and concepts of their military advisers. A new arms race now appears to be under way as a consequence.

What breeds the competition between states that leads to preparation for war? The eighteenth-century French political philosopher Jean-Jacques Rousseau argued that "the state . . . always feels itself weak if there is another that is stronger. Its security and preservation demand that it make itself more powerful than its neighbors. It can increase, nourish, and exercise its power only at their expense. . . . Because the grandeur of the state is purely relative, it is forced to compare itself to that of the others. . . . It becomes small or great, weak or strong, according to whether its neighbor expands or contracts, becomes stronger or declines."

Although states ostensibly arm for defensive purposes, their military might is often perceived as threatening. Alarmed, their neighbors arm in response. Thus, as Rousseau observed, security is relative. Such fear and its reciprocated behaviors create a predicament known as the **security dilemma,** defined as what results when "each party's power increments are matched by the others, and all wind up with no more security than when the vicious cycle began, along with the costs incurred in having acquired and having to maintain their power" (Snyder 1984).

Some scholars also describe the dynamics of this arms competition as the **spiral model** (Jervis 1976). The imagery captures the tendency of defense-enhancing efforts to result in escalating arms races that diminish the security of all. Sir Edward Grey, British foreign secretary before World War I, described this process well:

The increase in armaments, that is intended in each nation to produce consciousness of strength and a sense of security, does not produce these effects. On the contrary, it produces a consciousness of the strength of other

■ **security dilemma**
the chronic distrust that actors living under anarchy feel because, without sanctions or regulatory rules, rivals will do anything, including arming and using aggression, to get ahead, with the result that all lose their security in a climate of mistrust.

■ **spiral model**
a metaphor used to describe the tendency of efforts to enhance defense to result in escalating arms races.

nations and a sense of fear. Fear begets suspicion and distrust and evil imaginings of all sorts, til each government feels it would be criminal and a betrayal of its own country not to take every precaution, while every government regards every precaution of every other government as evidence of hostile intent. (Grey 1925, 92)

Although the security dilemma affects all states, leaders still refuse to accept vulnerability. Searching for strength, they often proceed from the assumptions that (1) security is a function of power; (2) power is a function of military capability; and (3) military might is a measure of national greatness. Each of these suppositions is, of course, consistent with realpolitik.

Asking whether military preparedness endangers, rather than ensures, national security raises an uncomfortable question that challenges the prevailing approach to national security throughout much of the world's history. Yet many experts believe such questioning is justified. To their way of thinking, now that fears of great-power war have receded, the economic and ecological dimensions of national security have assumed relatively greater prominence, and in the twenty-first century, "security" should be defined more broadly so as to include both military and nonmilitary threats to human survival. Consider the argument made on behalf of a new definition of "national security":

> The concept of "security" must include protection against all major threats to human survival and well-being, not just military threats. Until now, "security"—usually addressed as "national security"—has meant the maintenance of strong military defenses against enemy invasion and attack. This approach may have served us well in the past, when such attack was seen as the only real threat to national survival; today, however, when airborne poisons released by nuclear and chemical accidents can produce widespread death and sickness (as occurred with the Bhopal and Chernobyl disasters), and when global epidemiological and environmental hazards such as AIDS and the "greenhouse effect" can jeopardize the well-being of the entire planet, this perspective appears increasingly obsolete. As individual economies become ever more enmeshed in the world economy, moreover, every society becomes more vulnerable to a global economic crisis. And, as modern telecommunications bring us all closer together, we are made acutely aware of the pain and suffering of those living under oppression, tyranny, and injustice.
>
> Given the fact that our individual security and well-being will depend to an ever-increasing extent on the world's success in mastering complex political, economic, environmental, and epidemiological problems, we must redefine "security" to embrace all of those efforts taken to enhance the long-term health and welfare of the human family. Defense against military aggression will obviously remain a vital component of security, but it must be joined by defenses against severe environmental degradation, worldwide economic crisis, and massive human suffering. Only by approaching the security dilemma from this multifaceted perspective can we develop the strategies and instruments that will be needed to promote global health and stability.
>
> Given the multiplicity of pressing world hazards, the concept of "national security" must be integrated with that of "world security." Until now, most people have tended to rely on the nation-state to provide protection

against external threats, and have viewed their own nation's security as being adversely affected by the acquisition of power and wealth of other nations. Thus, in the interests of "national security," nation-states have often engaged in a competitive struggle to enhance their own economic and military strength at the expense of other nations' capabilities. This us-versus-them, zero-sum competition for security is naturally biased toward unilateral solutions to critical problems, frequently entailing military and/or economic coercion. In today's interdependent world, however, the quest for security is rapidly becoming a positive-sum process, whereby national well-being is achieved jointly by all countries—or not at all. (Klare and Thomas 1991, 3)

Approaches to the study of national security now frequently advocate putting these nonmilitary dimensions of the problem into the picture (for example, Shultz, Godson, and Quester 1997). At issue is whether this new way of organizing perceptions of national security is an idea whose time has come.

It is an idea certain to be given close scrutiny, because a wide spectrum of problems has risen on political agendas, and the concerns of today's foreign policymakers are arguably different and more diverse than they were just a short time ago. Former U.S. Assistant Secretary of Defense Joseph Nye (2001) argues, "Power in the twenty-first century will depend on economic growth and mastering the information revolution, not on the brute nuclear force of the twentieth century. Nuclear weapons are not a power equalizer, and they cannot be used to blast one's way into an imagined great power club." Though the danger of nuclear weapons and inter- and intrastate warfare continues, it would be foolish to neglect the dangers posed by such emergent threats as trade-bloc competition, neomercantilism, trade protectionism, the continuing impoverishment of the least-developed countries, acid rain, deforestation, global warming, soaring population growth, the AIDS epidemic, international narcotic trafficking, the depletion of the earth's finite resources, and destruction of its protective ozone layer. These nonmilitary threats must command attention, as human survival may depend on addressing them.

However, the critical questions in an age of vulnerability to annihilation persist: How can states escape the prospect of destruction? How can they meet these emergent nonmilitary threats when the threat of warfare in a nationalistic age remains as pervasive as ever?

The security situation of the twenty-first century is unlikely to provide much room to maneuver. The world has yet to accept **common security** and nonoffensive defense, strategies that would eliminate offensive capabilities (Møller 1992). Many states still build weapons of attack for deterrence, even though conventional deterrence has failed frequently in the past. Moreover, contemporary deterrence theory remains based on the almost illogical premise that successful defense requires the continuing vulnerability of all states. Nonetheless, most believe that the threat system must be preserved to counter the threat and put more faith in the realist belief that for disputes to be resolved successfully it is safer to rely on the force of arms than on the force of arguments.

Thus, security may depend as much on the control of force as on its pursuit. The next chapter examines the ways in which the realist road to peace is pursued by national leaders persuaded that military approaches and coercive diplomacy provide the safest path to defense.

■ **common security**
a concept advocating replacing the notion of states competing with one another for their own national security with collective security to promote the security of all states.

KEY TERMS

- self-help
- national security
- coercion
- power
- politics
- conflict
- power potential
- realism
- globalization
- information age
- coercive diplomacy
- opportunity costs
- peace dividend
- national security
- human security
- relative burden of military spending
- arms race
- military-industrial complex
- Nuclear Nonproliferation Treaty (NPT)
- proliferation
- Nth country problem
- horizontal nuclear proliferation
- vertical nuclear proliferation
- nonproliferation regime
- security dilemma
- multiple independently targetable reentry vehicles (MIRVs)
- nonlethal weapons
- revolution in military technology (RMT)
- smart bombs
- firebreak
- strategic weapons
- virtual nuclear arsenals
- deterrence
- information warfare (IW) or infowar tactics
- nuclear winter
- compellence
- brinkmanship
- massive retaliation
- countervalue targeting strategy
- counterforce targeting
- nuclear deterrence
- second-strike capability
- mutual assured destruction (MAD)
- nuclear-utilizyation theory (NUTs)
- Strategic Defense Initiative (SDI)
- counterfactual reasoning
- rational choice
- preemptive war
- just war theory
- asymetrical warfare
- coercive diplomacy
- ultimatum
- gunboat diplomacy
- military intervention
- covert operations
- failed states
- nonintervention norm
- human rights
- sanctions
- boycotts
- economic sanctions
- unilateralism
- multilateralism
- bilateralism
- liberalism
- zero-sum
- Bush Doctrine
- realpolitik
- democratic peace
- power transition
- no first use
- bandwagoning
- containment
- Yoshida Doctrine
- neoliberal institutionalism
- security dilemma
- spiral model
- common security

SUGGESTED READING

Allison, Graham. *Nuclear Terrorism: The Ultimate Preventable Catastrophe*. New York: Henry Holt, 2004.

Barnett, Thomas P. *The Pentagon's New Map: War and Peace in the Twenty-First Century*. New York: G. P. Putnam's Sons, 2004.

Cortwright, David, and George A. Lopez, eds. *Smart Sanctions: Targeting Economic Statecraft*. Lanham, Md.: Rowman and Littlefield, 2002.

Eizenstat, Stuart E. *Do Economic Sanctions Work?* Washington, D.C.: The Atlantic Council, 2004.

Gaddis, John Lewis. *Surprise, Security, and the American Experience*. Cambridge, Mass.: Harvard University Press, 2004.

Hentz, James J., ed. *The Obligation of Empire: United States' Grand Strategy for a New Century*. Lexington: The University Press of Kentucky, 2004.

Jervis, Robert. *American Foreign Policy in a New Era*. New York: Routledge, 2005.

Knox, MacGregor, and Williamson Murray. *The Dynamics of Military Revolution, 1300–2050*. Cambridge: Cambridge University Press, 2001.

Lehneman, William J., ed. *Military Intervention: Cases in Context for the Twenty-First Century.* Lanham, Md.: Rowman and Littlefield, 2004.

Mandel, Robert. *Armies without States: The Privatization of Security.* Boulder, Colo.: Lynne Rienner, 2002.

Nye, Joseph S., Jr. *Soft Power: The Means to Success in World Politics.* Washington, D.C.: Public Affairs, 2004.

Powell, Robert. *In the Shadow of Power: States and Strategies in International Politics.* Princeton, N.J.: Princeton University Press, 2000.

WHERE ON THE WORLD WIDE WEB?

Arms Sales Monitoring Project
http://www.fas.org/asmp/

Concerned with the global production and trade of weapons, the Federation of American Scientists monitors arms transfers and makes data available to the public through this website. Click on "Sales Data." Which country is the biggest recipient of U.S. arms sales? See what was sold to whom and for how much. Why do you think that certain countries got freebies? Which American companies are the largest arms manufacturers? What are some important proposed weapons sales?

The Henry L. Stimson Center
http://www.stimson.org/

The Henry L. Stimson Center is a nonprofit, nonpartisan research center that concentrates on the intersection of national and international security policy and technology. It provides information on chemical and biological weapons, nuclear proliferation, and missile defense systems. It houses important international agreements and searches for ways to eliminate weapons of mass destruction. It is an excellent site for timely information. What are the most important current issues discussed at this site?

International Code of Conduct on Arms Transfers
http://www.basicint.org/WT/wtindex.htm

The British American Security Information Council (BASIC) is an independent research organization that analyzes government policies and promotes public awareness of defense, disarmament, military strategy, and nuclear policies. Because the United States and Great Britain are the suppliers of 80 percent of the world light arms trade, BASIC's main goal is to petition the two countries to create controls for weapons transfers. Visit this website to explore arms transfers and learn about initiatives such as Codes of Conduct and Multilateral Arms Control Regimes. Also examine BASIC's information on weapons of mass destruction (WMDs).

National Commission for Economic Conversion and Disarmament
http://www.webcom.com/ncecd/

The National Commission for Economic Conversion and Disarmament is a nonprofit public organization dedicated to public education on the need to transfer military resources to civilian use and the ways to accomplish this task. This website gives information on the costs associated with arms manufacturing and how monies can be better spent in other ways. What are some of the important arguments made in articles found on the site? What has been Washington's official view toward economic conversion and disarmament?

SIPRI Military Expenditure Country Graphs
http://databases.sipri.se/

The Stockholm International Peace Research Institute (SIPRI) monitors trends in military expenditures throughout the world. Its website lets you compare military expenditures and evaluate the economic burdens they pose. Choose three countries, one each from the Middle East, Far East, and Africa. How does their military spending compare with that of European countries? What conclusions can you draw?

A-Bomb WWW Museum
http://www.csi.ad.jp/ABOMB/index.html

Visit this Japanese website for eyewitness accounts of the impact the first atomic bomb had on Hiroshima. The site includes pictures from the Peace Memorial Museum in Hiroshima that show the effect of the bombing and stories from survivors, many of them deeply disturbing. The A-Bomb WWW Museum was created as a perpetual reminder of the horrors of using nuclear weapons. It welcomes e-mail responses from all around the world.

Atomic Bomb: Decision
http://www.dannen.com/decision/index.html

This website houses the available documents on the decision to use atomic bombs on the cities of Hiroshima and Nagasaki. Scan eyewitness accounts of the Trinity Test. Read what the individuals responsible for creating the bomb and for deciding to drop it had to say. See the official bombing order and hear an excerpt of President Truman's radio speech announcing the decision. Based on what you have read and heard, do you think the United States should have dropped the bomb?

Remembering Nagasaki
http://www.exploratorium.edu/nagasaki/index.html

A stunning website, Remembering Nagasaki presents the photographs of Japanese army photographer Yosuke Yamhata, who took pictures the day after the bomb was dropped. A public forum on issues related to the atomic age includes memories from people all over the world of the moment when they heard about the explosion of the bomb, discussion of the decision to drop the bomb, the question of how to tell history, and the ethical responsibilities of scientists. This is a truly fascinating site that explores the issues from all sides.

Russian Roulette
http://www.pbs.org/wgbh/pages/frontline/shows/russia/

PBS's famous *Frontline* series is online with a look at the safety and security of Russia's nuclear arsenal and the potential for accidental launch or diversion of its nuclear weapons. Take a look at Russia's nuclear complex. Compare and contrast U.S. and Russian nuclear arsenals and become familiar with nuclear smuggling incidents. Read interviews with policy experts, smugglers, scientists, analysts, and law enforcement agents, and analyze Russian and U.S. articles for further perspective. On the other hand, you may not want to look at this website at all. As a Russian proverb states, "the less you know the better you sleep."

INFOTRAC® COLLEGE EDITION

Pfiffner, James P. "Did President Bush Mislead the Country in His Arguments for War with Iraq?" *Presidential Studies Quarterly* (March 2004).

Rubin, James P. "Stumbling into War." *Foreign Affairs* (September–October 2003).

Cohen, Eliot. "General Strategies: How the United States Makes War." *Harvard International Review* (Fall 2003).

Barnett, Roger W. "What Deters? Strength, Not Weakness." *Naval War College Review* (Spring 2001).

For more articles, enter:

"international relations" in the Subject Guide, and then go to subdivision "analysis"

"war" in the Subject Guide, and then go to subdivision "analysis"

"national security" in the Subject Guide, and then go to subdivision "analysis"

"deterrence" in the Subject Guide

Go to http://politicalscience.wadsworth.com/kegley10 to access additional resources related to this chapter.

CHAPTER 13

THE REALIST ROAD TO SECURITY THROUGH ALLIANCES, ARMS CONTROL, AND THE BALANCE OF POWER

TOPICS AND THEMES

- Realism and the balancing of power
- Stabilizing power balances through arms control
- Models of power balances in the contemporary global system

- **CONTROVERSY** DO THE ADVANTAGES OF ALLIANCES OUTWEIGH THE DISADVANTAGES?
- **CONTROVERSY** IS A UNIPOLAR, BIPOLAR, OR MULTIPOLAR SYSTEM THE MOST STABLE?

A test of a nuclear bomb in 1954, when only two powers had nuclear capabilities. Today the capacity to wage war with weapons of mass destruction has spread to many countries, and the diffusion has transformed the global balance of power.

Critics of U.S. global dominance should pause and consider the alternative. If the United States retreats from its hegemonic role, who would supplant it? Not Europe, not China, not the Muslim world—and certainly not the United Nations. Unfortunately, the alternative to a single superpower is not a multilateral utopia, but the anarchic nightmare of a new Dark Age.

—NIALL FERGUSON, political historian, 2004

As nature abhors a vacuum, so international politics abhors unbalanced power. Faced by unbalanced power, states try to increase their own strength or they ally with others to bring the international distribution of power into balance.

—KENNETH N. WALTZ, neorealist theoretician, 2004

■ **security dilemma**
the propensity of armaments amassed by one state for ostensibly defensive purposes to be perceived by others as threatening, which drives the alarmed competitors to undertake as a counter-measure a military buildup that heightens both states' insecurities.

Imagine yourself as the next Secretary-General of the United Nations (UN). You face responsibility for fulfilling the UN's Charter to preserve world peace. Looking at the globe, you see that many countries have the capacity to annihilate their enemies with new weapons of mass destruction whenever they wish to unleash the military power in their states' arsenal. As a consequence, you see the **security dilemma** that has been created: Due to the escalating destructive power of modern weapons, most states' sense of national security has decreased, rather than increased, and the globe's more than 6 billion people live in fear that

TABLE 13.1

The Realist Road to Security: Assumptions and Policy Recommendations

The Realist Picture of the Global Environment

Primary global condition:	Anarchy; or the absence of authoritative governing institutions
Probability of system change/reform:	Low, except in response to extraordinary events such as 9/11 and 3/11
Prime actors:	States, and especially great powers
Principal actor goals:	Power over others, self-preservation, and physical security
Predominant pattern of actor interaction:	Competition and conflict
Pervasive concern:	National security
Prevalent state priorities:	Acquiring military capabilities
Popular state practice:	Use of armed forces for coercive diplomacy

Realist Policy Prescriptions	Premises
Prepare for war:	If you want peace, prepare for war.
Remain vigilant:	No state is to be trusted further than its national interest.
Avoid moralism:	Standards of right and wrong apply to individuals but not states; in world affairs amoral actions are sometimes necessary and can produce positive results.
Remain involved and actively intervene:	Isolationism is not an alternative to active global involvement.
Protect with arms:	Strive to increase military capabilities, and fight rather than submit to subordination.
Preserve the balance of power:	Do not let any state or coalition of states become predominant.
Prevent arms races from resulting in military inferiority with rivals:	Negotiate agreements with competitors to maintain a favorable military balance.

they will not see tomorrow. What course should you counsel the UN's 191 members to pursue?

Most states continue to reject **liberalism** and the neoliberal paths of peace, which recommend building institutions for world law, states' integration, and/or democratic governmental reforms (see Chapter 14). Rather, most states follow the realist road, seeing their viable choices as among three basic, time-honored options: States can (1) arm themselves; (2) form (or sever) alliances with other countries; or (3) negotiate arms control and disarmament agreements to reduce the threat of adversaries' weapons. Most leaders usually pursue various combinations of these military strategies.

Up to this point, our discussion of conflict and its management has followed a logical progression. Chapter 11 began by exploring why the frequency of war makes preparations for it so energetic. Chapter 12 examined the search for national security through the acquisition of military capabilities and assessed states' use of coercive diplomacy, both to realize their national goals abroad and to deter or preempt their rivals from aggression. We now concentrate on the other two military approaches to national security—the use of alliances and

■ **liberalism**
a paradigm predicated on the hope that the application of reason and universal ethics to international relations can lead to a more orderly, just, and cooperative world, and that international anarchy and war can be policed by institutional reforms that empower international organizations and law.

arms control to maintain a favorable balance of power and thereby enhance security. These approaches draw their inspiration primarily from the assumptions that realist theory makes about the most prudent paths to peace (see Table 13.1).

THE IMPACT OF ALLIANCES ON NATIONAL AND GLOBAL SECURITY

Alliances usually form when two or more states face a common security threat. They are formal agreements among states to coordinate their behavior by heeding realism's first rule of statecraft: to increase military capabilities. By acquiring allies, states increase their mutual armaments, which when facing a common threat, provides them with the means of reducing their probability of being attacked (**deterrence**), obtaining greater strength in case of attack (defense) while precluding their allies from alliance with the enemy (Snyder 1991).

These advantages notwithstanding, realists often see a downside and counsel against forming alliances, as Britain's Lord Palmerston did in 1848 when he advised that states "should have no eternal allies and no perpetual enemies." Their only duty is to follow their interests and whenever possible to rely on **self-help.**

The greatest risk to forming alliances is that they bind a state to a commitment that may later become disadvantageous. This is why "wise and experienced statesmen usually shy away from commitments likely to constitute limitations on a government's behavior at unknown dates in the future in the face of unpredictable situations" (Kennan 1984a). Because conditions are certain to change sooner or later and the usefulness of all alliances is certain to change once the common threat that brought the allies together declines, the realist tradition advises states not to take a fixed position on temporary convergences of national interests and instead to forge alliances only to deal with immediate threats.

When considering whether a new alliance is a **rational choice** in which the benefits outweigh the costs, heads of state usually recognize that allies can easily do more harm than good (see Controversy: Do the Advantages of Alliances Outweigh the Disadvantages?). Many realists advise states against forming alliances for defense, basing their fears on five fundamental flaws:

- Alliances enable aggressive states to combine military capabilities for aggression.
- Alliances threaten enemies and provoke the creation of counteralliances, which reduces the security for both coalitions.
- Alliance formation may draw otherwise neutral parties into opposed coalitions.
- Once states join forces, they must control the behavior of their own allies to discourage each member from reckless aggression against its enemies, which would undermine the security of the alliance's other members.
- The possibility always exists that today's ally might become tomorrow's enemy.

In a 1917 address to the U.S. Senate, President Woodrow Wilson proposed that "all nations avoid entangling alliances which would draw them into . . . a net

■ **alliances**
coalitions that form when two or more states combine their military capabilities and promise to coordinate their policies to increase mutual security.

■ **deterrence**
a preventive strategy designed to dissuade an adversary from doing what it would otherwise prefer to do.

■ **self-help**
reliance only on one's state for defense since under anarchy no state can depend on others—even allies—to come to its defense if attacked.

■ **rational choice**
a decision made by careful definition of the situation, weighing of goals, consideration of all alternatives, and selection of the options most likely to achieve the highest goals.

CONTROVERSY: DO THE ADVANTAGES OF ALLIANCES OUTWEIGH THE DISADVANTAGES?

When states make decisions about forging alliances, they must keep in mind the many risks of sharing their fate with other states. While realists generally see alliances as potentially beneficial, they caution that making a defense pact with an ally will also carry a heavy price (Weitsman 2004). Creating alliances will:

- foreclose options
- reduce the state's capacity to adapt to changing circumstances
- weaken a state's capability to influence others by decreasing the number of additional partners with which it can align
- eliminate the advantages in bargaining that can be derived from deliberately fostering ambiguity about one's intentions
- provoke the fears of adversaries
- entangle states in disputes with their allies' enemies
- interfere with the negotiation of disputes involving an ally's enemy by precluding certain issues from being placed on the agenda
- preserve existing rivalries
- stimulate envy and resentment on the part of friends who are outside the alliance and are therefore not eligible to receive its advantages

These potential dangers explain why alliance decisions are so controversial, even when advocates enthusiastically propose that another state be sought as an ally for mutual defense. The posture of leaders about the advantage or disadvantage of alliances has depended on their personal philosophy and the country's circumstances.

What do you think? What are the advantages of having alliance partners? In considering your options, look at the 1796 photo picturing George Washington, the first president of the United States, advising other leaders in American government that it should be the foreign policy of the United States to "steer clear of permanent alliances." He felt that whereas a state "may safely trust to temporary alliances for extraordinary emergencies" it is an "illusion . . . to expect or calculate real favors from nation to nation." Yet, almost every state is insecure in one way or another and is tempted to recruit allies to bolster its defense capabilities and protect its power as a united friend to adversaries that threaten it.

of intrigue and selfish rivalry." Wilson advocated as a substitute for alliances and counteralliances the idea of **collective security,** which would repel aggression by any state through a response from all other state orchestrated by multilateral institutions. In taking this position, which reflected Wilson's liberal belief that alliances and secret diplomacy transform limited conflicts into global wars with many participants, he underscored the difficulties and the dangers of making alliance decisions. Despite their uncertain usefulness, many states throughout history have chosen to ally because, the risks notwithstanding, the perceived benefits to security in a time of threat justified that decision.

■ **collective security**
a global or regional security regime agreed to by the great powers setting rules for keeping peace, guided by the principle that an act of aggression by any state automatically will be met by a combined military response from the rest.

To best picture how alliances affect global security, it is instructive to move from the state level of analysis, which views alliance decisions from the perspective of an individual state's security, to the global **level of analysis** (recall Chapters 1 and 3) by looking at the impact of alliances on the frequency of interstate war. This view focuses attention on the possible contribution of alliance formation to maintaining the balance of power.

Realpolitik Assumptions of Balance-of-Power Theory

The concept of a **balance of power** has a long and controversial history. Supporters envision it as a equilibrating process that maintains peace by counterbalancing any state that seeks military preponderance, distributing global power evenly through **alignments,** or shifts by neutrals to one or the other opposed coalitions. Critics deny its effectiveness, arguing that it breeds jealousy, intrigue, and antagonism. Part of the difficulty in evaluating these rival claims lies in the different meanings attributed to the concept (see Vasquez and Elman 2003; Claude 1962). While "balance of power" may be widely used in everyday discourse, there is confusion over precisely what it entails.

At the core of nearly all the various meanings of "balance of power" is the idea that national security is enhanced when military capabilities are distributed so that no one state is strong enough to dominate all others. If one state gains inordinate power, balance-of-power theory predicts that it will take advantage of its strength and attack weaker neighbors, thereby giving compelling incentive for those threatened to align and unite in a defensive coalition. According to the theory, their combined military might would deter (or, if need be, defeat) the state harboring expansionist aims. Thus for realists, laissez-faire competition among states striving to maximize their national power yields an international equilibrium, ensuring everyone's survival by checking hegemonic ambitions.

Balance-of-power theory is also founded on the realist premise that weakness invites attack and that countervailing power must be used to deter potential aggressors. Realists assume that the drive for expanded power guides every state's actions. It follows that all countries are potential adversaries, and each must strengthen its military capability to protect itself. Invariably, this reasoning rationalizes the quest for military superiority, because others pursue it as well. The reasons spring from the realist belief that a system revolving around suspicion, competition, and anarchy will breed caution; uncertainty makes for restraints on the initiation of war. Why? Because when all states are independent and as sovereign actors free to make rational choices designed to protect their national security interests in a climate of fear and mistrust, they have powerful incentive to realign to form coalitions that would lead to an approximately even distribution of power. Accordingly, a free-floating **security regime** underlying balance-of-power dynamics could curtail the natural temptation of any great power to imperialistically attempt to conquer the others. In classic balance-of-power theory, fear of a third party would encourage alignments, because those threatened would need help to offset the power of the mutual adversary. An alliance would add the ally's power to the state's own and deny the addition of that power to the enemy. As alliances combine power, the offsetting coalitions would give neither a clear advantage. Therefore, aggression would appear unattractive and would be averted.

■ **levels of analysis**
variables at the global, state, and individual levels that explain why transnational actors behave as they do in international relations.

■ **balance of power**
the theory that peace and stability are most likely to be maintained when military power is distributed to prevent a single hegemon or bloc from controlling the world.

■ **alignments**
the acceptance by a neutral state threatened by foreign enemies of a special relationship short of formal alliance with a stronger power able to protect it from attack.

■ **security regime**
norms and rules for interaction accepted by a set of states to cooperatively increase their mutual security.

■ **nonalignment**
a foreign policy posture in which states do not participate in military alliances with either of two rival blocs for fear that alliance will lead to involvement in an unnecessary war.

■ **size principle**
the propensity for competitors to form coalitions sufficient in size only to ensure victory, even if by a narrow margin, with the result that over time opposed alliances tend to remain roughly equal to one another.

To deter an aggressor, counteralliances were expected to form easily, because "free riders," states sitting on the sidelines, could not, as rational actors, risk **nonalignment.** If they refused to ally, their own vulnerability would encourage an expansionist state to attack them sooner or later. The result of these individual calculations, according to what is known as the **size principle,** is likely to be the formation of coalitions sufficient in size only to ensure victory, resulting in offsetting coalitions that are roughly equal in size (Riker 1962).

To balance power against power in opposed coalitions approximately equal in strength, realists recognize that what is required is for national actors to see the value of rapidly shifting alliances. This requires adherence to decision rules.

Rules for Rivals in the Balancing Process.
Although balancing is occasionally described as an automatic, self-adjusting process, most realists see it as the result of deliberate actions undertaken by national leaders to maintain an equilibrium among contending states. They see the balancing of power as produced by adherence to rules of action and reaction that states must follow. It is necessary for all leaders to constantly monitor changes in states' relative capabilities so policies about arms and allies can be adjusted to rectify imbalances of power. Choices must be made by rational, self-interested actors that recognize the trade-off of costs and benefits of strategic options. For example, some options, like expanding mililitary capabilities through armaments and alliances, attempt to add weight to the lighter side of the international balance. Others, such as negotiating limits on weaponry and spheres of influence, attempt to decrease the weight of the heavier side.

Various theorists have attempted to specify a set of rules that must be heeded in this constructed security regime in order for the balancing process to function effectively. What follows is a brief synthesis of these rules:

1. Stay vigilant. Constantly watch foreign developments in order to identify emerging threats and opportunities. Because international anarchy makes each state responsible for its own security, and states can never be sure of one another's intentions, self-interest encourages them to maximize their relative power. As Morton Kaplan (1957) writes: "Act to increase capabilities but negotiate rather than fight. . . . [At the same time, states should] fight rather than pass up an opportunity to increase capabilities."

2. Seek allies whenever you cannot match the armaments of your adversary. States align with each other when they adopt a common stance toward some shared security problem. An alliance is produced when they formally agree to coordinate their behavior under certain specified circumstances. The degree of coordination may range from a detailed list of military forces that will be furnished by each party in the event of war to the more modest requirement that they will consult with one another should hostilities erupt. According to balance-of-power theory, alliances are the primary means of compensating for an inability to keep up with a rival's arms acquisitions.

3. Remain flexible in making alliances. Formed and dissolved according to the strategic needs of the moment, alliances must be made without regard to cultural or ideological affinities. Because alliances are instrumental, short-term adjustments aimed at rectifying imbalances in the distribution of military capabilities, past experiences should not predispose states to accept or reject any potential partner. Nowhere is this better seen than in the

balancer role Great Britain once played in European diplomacy. From the seventeenth through the early twentieth centuries, the British shifted their weight from one side of the continental balance to the other, arguing that they had no permanent friends and no permanent enemies, just a permanent interest in preventing the balance from tipping either way (Dehio 1962). As described by Winston Churchill, Britain's goal was to "oppose the strongest, most aggressive, most dominating Power on the Continent.... [It] joined with the less strong Powers, made a combination among them, and thus defeated and frustrated the Continental military tyrant whoever he was, whatever nation he led."

4. Oppose any state that seeks hegemony. The purpose of engaging in balance-of-power politics is to survive in a world of potentially dangerous neighbors. If any state achieves absolute mastery over everyone else, it will be able to act with impunity. Under such circumstances, the territorial integrity and political autonomy of other states will be in jeopardy. By joining forces with the weaker side to prevent the stronger side from reaching preponderance, states can preserve their independence. As Joseph Nye (2005b) has put it: "Balance of power is a policy of helping the underdog because if you help the top dog, it may eventually turn around and eat you."

5. Be moderate in victory. "An equilibrium," argues Edward Gulick (1955), "cannot perpetuate itself unless the major components of that equilibrium are preserved." In the event of war, the winning side should not eliminate the defeated. Looking forward rather than backward, it should do as little damage as possible to those it has vanquished because yesterday's enemy may be needed as tomorrow's ally. Victors that couple firmness regarding their own interests with fairness toward the interests of others encourage defeated powers to work within the postwar balance of power. Similarly, states that win at the bargaining table can stabilize the balance of power by granting the other side compensation in return for its concessions.

These realist policy prescriptions urge states to check the ambitions of anyone who threatens to amass overwhelming power, because aspiring hegemons are a potential threat to everyone. Human beings, they argue, are by nature selfish and shortsighted, but balancing rival interests stabilizes their interactions. Weakness, realists insist, invites aggression. Thus when faced with unbalanced power, leaders of states should mobilize their domestic resources or ally with others to bring the international distribution of power back into equilibrium (Schweller 2004; Waltz 1979). The alarmed response by China and Russia after the September 2002 *National Security Strategy of the United States*, which announced that the country would do everything within its power to preserve forever America's supreme global primacy, illustrates the balancing process. Also illustrative was the resistance of Germany, France, and many other countries to the 2003 U.S. decision to launch a war of **preemption** to prevent Iraq from acquiring and using weapons of mass destruction—especially because evidence of Iraq's possession of such weapons, ties to the 9/11 terrorist attacks, or intention to wage war did not exist.

Difficulties with Balance of Power Systems.
Can balancing power further world order, as most realists believe? Critics of balance-of-power theory raise several objections to the proposition that balancing promotes peace. First, some

■ **balancer**
under a balance-of-power system, an influential global or regional great power that throws its support in decisive fashion to a defensive coalition. This role was often played by Great Britain in the eighteenth, nineteenth, and twentieth centuries.

■ **preemption**
a quick, first-strike attack that seeks to defeat an adversary before it can attack or organize a retaliatory response.

bandwagoning
the tendency for weak states to seek alliance with the strongest power, irrespective of that power's ideology or form of government, in order to increase security.

scholars argue that the theory's rules for behavior are contradictory (Riker 1962). On the one hand, states are urged to increase their power. On the other hand, they are told to oppose anyone seeking preponderance. Yet sometimes **bandwagoning** with (rather than balancing against) the dominant state can increase a weaker country's capabilities by allowing it to share in the spoils of a future victory. History suggests that states that are most content with the status quo tend to balance against rising powers more than do dissatisfied states.

A second objection to balance-of-power theory is that it assumes policymakers possess accurate, timely information about other states. As we have discussed in the previous chapter, "power" is an ambiguous concept. Tangible factors, such as the performance capabilities of the different types of weapons found in an adversary's inventory, are hard to compare. Intangible factors, such as leadership skills, troop morale, or public support for adventuresome or aggressive foreign policies, are even more difficult to gauge. Without a precise measure of relative strength, how can policymakers know when power is becoming unbalanced? Moreover, in an environment of secret alliances, how can they be sure who is really in league with whom? An ally who is being counted on to balance the power of an opponent may have secretly agreed to remain neutral in the event of a showdown; consequently the actual distribution of power may not resemble the constructed distribution imagined by one side or the other.

Problems in determining the strength of adversaries and the trustworthiness of allies leads to a third objection to balance-of-power theory: the uncertainty of power balances frequently causes defense planners to engage in worst-case analysis, which can spark an arms race. The intense, reciprocal anxiety that shrouds balance-of-power politics fuels exaggerated estimates of an adversary's strength, which prompts each side to expand the quantity and enhance the quality of its weaponry. Critics of realism warn that if a serious dispute occurs between states locked in relentless arms competition under conditions of mutually assured suspicions, the probability of war increases.

A fourth objection is that balance-of-power theory assumes that decision makers are risk averse—when confronted with countervailing power, they refrain from fighting because the dangers of taking on an equal are too great. Yet, as **prospect theory** illuminates, national leaders assess risk differently. Some are risk acceptant. Rather than being deterred by equivalent power, they prefer gambling on the chance of winning a victory, even if the odds are long. Marshaling comparable power against adversaries with a high tolerance for risk will not have the same effect as it would on those who avoid risks.

prospect theory
an interpretation of decision making that is based on the tendency of people to overreact to crises and that asserts that policymakers in particular are reluctant to make choices about anticipated gains but are inclined to take risks when making decisions about expected losses.

Finally, many people object to the balance-of-power theory because it has not been effective. If the theory's assumptions are correct, historical periods during which its rules were followed should also have been periods in which war was less frequent. Yet a striking feature of those periods is their record of warfare. Since the 1648 Peace of Westphalia created the global system of independent territorial states, the great powers have participated in a series of increasingly destructive general wars that threatened to engulf and destroy the multistate system. As Inis L. Claude (1989) soberly concludes, it is difficult to consider these wars "as anything other than catastrophic failures, total collapses, of the balance-of-power system. They are hardly to be classed as stabilizing maneuvers or equilibrating processes, and one cannot take seriously any claim of maintaining international stability that does not entail the prevention of such disasters." Indeed, the historical record has led some theorists to construct **hegemonic stability theory** as an alternative to the balance of power. This theory postulates that a single, dominant **hegemon** can guarantee peace better than military parity among competing great powers (Ferguson 2004a; Organski 1968).

Managing the Balance through a Concert of Great Powers

A significant problem with the balance-of-power system is its haphazard character. To bring order to the system, the great powers have occasionally tried to institutionalize channels of communication. The Concert of Europe that commenced with the Congress of Vienna in 1815 exemplified this strategy. In essence, it was "an exclusive club for the great powers" (Claude 1962).

The idea behind a concert is "rule by a central coalition" of great powers (Rosecrance 1992). It is predicated on the belief that the leading centers of power will see their interests advanced by collaborating to prevent conflict from escalating into war in those regions under their mutual jurisdiction. Although it is assumed that the great powers share a common outlook, concerts still allow "for subtle jockeying and competition to take place among them. Power politics is not completely eliminated; members may turn to internal mobilization and coalition formation to pursue divergent interests. But the cooperative framework of a concert, and its members' concern about preserving peace, prevent such balancing from escalating to overt hostility and conflict" (Kupchan and Kupchan 1992).

A common sense of duty is the glue that holds great-power concerts together. When a belief in mutual self-restraint dissipates, concerts unravel. "Friction tends to build as each state believes that it is sacrificing more for unity than are others," notes Robert Jervis (1985). "Each will remember the cases in which it has been restrained, and ignore or interpret differently cases in which others believe they acted for the common good." Overcoming this friction requires continuous consultation in order to reinforce expectations of joint responsibilities. Concert members should not be challenged over their vital interests, nor should they suffer an affront to their prestige and self-esteem (Elrod 1976). A "just" equilibrium among contending great powers bound together in a concert means more than an equal distribution of military capabilities; it includes recognition of honors, national rights, and dignity (Schroeder 1989).

While a concert framework can help manage relations among counterpoised great powers, the normative consensus underpinning this arrangement is fragile and easily eroded. As a result, realists have looked beyond concerts for other ways to steady vacillating power balances. One approach is to limit everyone's arsenals, especially with regard to those weapons that are seen as provocative and thus destabilizing.

■ **hegemonic stability theory** the argument that a dominant state is necessary to enforce international cooperation, maintain international rules and agreements, and keep the peace.

■ **hegemon** a single dominant military and economic state.

STABILIZING POWER BALANCES THROUGH ARMS CONTROL

Liberal reformers have often attacked the theory that power can be balanced to preserve world order. They have advocated instead the biblical prescription that states should beat their swords into plowshares. The destructiveness of today's

■ **arms control**
multilateral or bilateral agreements to contain arms races by setting limits on the number and types of weapons states are permitted.

■ **disarmament**
agreements to reduce or destroy weapons or other means of attack.

■ **bilateral agreements**
exchanges between two states, such as arms control agreements, negotiated cooperatively to set ceilings on military force levels.

■ **multilateral agreements**
cooperative compacts among many states to ensure that a concerted policy is implemented toward alleviating a common problem, such as levels of future weapons capabilities.

■ **Strategic Arms Limitation Talks (SALT)**
the negotiations begun in 1969 between the United States and the USSR to freeze offensive weapons at existing levels and promote balanced, verifiable limits on strategic nuclear weapons.

■ **Strategic Arms Reduction Treaty (START)**
the U.S.-Russian series of negotiations that began in 1993 and, with the 1997 START-III agreement ratified by Russia in April 2000, pledged to cut the nuclear arsenals of both sides by 80 percent of the Cold War peaks, in order to lower the risk of nuclear war by making a successful preemptive strike impossible.

weapons has inspired many people once again to take this tenet of liberal theory seriously. But this approach is not solely a liberal preserve. Many realists also see arms limitation as a way of stabilizing the balance of power. In fact, most policymakers who have negotiated such agreements have been realists who perceived these treaties as a prudent tool to promote their countries' security.

Arms Control versus Disarmament

Although the terms *arms control* and *disarmament* are often used interchangeably, they are not synonymous. **Arms control** refers to agreements designed to regulate arms levels either by limiting their growth or by restricting how they may be used. This is a far more common and less ambitious endeavor than **disarmament,** which is the reduction or elimination of weapons. Controlling war by reducing weapons inventories is hardly a novel idea. Yet until recently, states have generally failed to negotiate disarmament agreements. True, some countries in the past did reduce their armaments. For example, the Chinese states in 600 B.C.E. formed a disarmament league that produced a peaceful century for the league's members. Canada and the United States disarmed the Great Lakes region through the 1817 Rush-Bagot Agreement. Nonetheless, these kinds of achievements have been relatively rare in history. Most disarmament has been involuntary, the product of reductions imposed by the victors in the immediate aftermath of a war, as when the Allied powers attempted to disarm a defeated Germany after World War I.

In addition to differentiating between arms control and disarmament, we should also distinguish between **bilateral agreements** and **multilaterial agreements.** Because the former involves only two countries, they are often easier to negotiate and to enforce than are the latter, which are agreements among three or more countries. As a result, bilateral arms agreements tend to be more successful than multilateral agreements. By far the most revealing examples are the superpower agreements to control nuclear weapons. Let us briefly look at the record of Soviet-American negotiations before examining the checkered history of multilateral arms control and disarmament.

Bilateral Arms Control and Disarmament

The Cold War between the Soviet Union and the United States never degenerated into a trial of military strength. One of the reasons was the series of more than twenty-five arms control agreements Moscow and Washington negotiated in the wake of the Cuban Missile Crisis. Beginning with the 1963 Hot Line Agreement, which established a direct radio and telegraph communication system between the two governments, Soviet and American leaders reached a series of modest agreements aimed at stabilizing the military balance and reducing the risk of war. Each of these bilateral treaties lowered tensions and helped build a climate of trust that encouraged efforts to negotiate further agreements.

Perhaps the most important agreements between the superpowers were the **Strategic Arms Limitation Talks (SALT)** of 1972 and 1979; the **Strategic Arms Reduction Treaties (START)** of 1991, 1993, and 1997; and the **Strategic Offensive Reductions Treaty (SORT)** of 2002. The first two agreements stabilized the nuclear arms race, and the remaining agreements reduced the weapons in each side's inventory (see Figure 13.1.) When the Cold War ended in 1991,

FIGURE 13.1
Countdown to Strategic Parity: The Negotiated End of the U.S.-Russian Arms Race

After decades of rapidly building the number of nuclear warheads in their arsenals, the United States and Russia have, through a series of disarmament agreements, pledged to cut dramatically the number of nuclear warheads in their stockpiles. This has inspired most of the other nuclear powers to not increase the number of warheads they have deployed. Since its 1986 peak, the size of the two great powers' nuclear arsenal has declined by nearly 90 percent, and it will decline further by 2012 as a result of the Putin-Bush SORT. However, fears that disarmament will not continue have arisen, provoked by the U.S. commitment in 2005 to store rather than destroy its remaining Cold War warheads and to develop its "Stars Wars" missile defense plans, and by Putin's proud announcement that in 2005 Russia would deploy its new Bolava ballistic missile, "a weapon that not a single other nuclear power has or will have in the future" and that will "ring a bell for the Americans, forcing Washington to reassess its estimates" of Russia's great-power status. SOURCE: Based on data from Worldwatch data diskette, U.S. Arms Control Association *Fact Files* and *SIPRI Yearbooks*.

■ **Strategic Offensive Reductions Treaty (SORT)**
the U.S.-Russian agreement to reduce the number of strategic warheads to 1,700–2,200 for each country by 2012.

the United States had more than 9,500 nuclear warheads and Russia had about 8,000. However, the January 1993 agreement pledged to cut their combined arsenals to about 6,500. Even more dramatically, this agreement also affected the kinds of weapons each country could possess. Under its terms, Russia and the United States gave up all the **multiple independently targeted reentry vehicles (MIRVs)** on their land-based intercontinental ballistic missiles and reduced submarine-launched ballistic missile (SLBM) warheads to no more than 1,750.

The next major step occurred in May 2002 when Presidents George W. Bush and Vladimir Putin signed the SORT. This brief document calls for the two countries to cut their combined number of strategic nuclear warheads by two-thirds over the next ten years. Still, both parties were left with enough firepower to retain the deterrent threat of **mutual assured destruction** (see Chapter 12). In addition, the treaty contained no requirement to destroy warheads taken out of service, and permitted either side to withdraw from the agreement with three months' notice by citing "a supreme national interest." Hence, while this treaty signaled a step toward nuclear disarmament, it was regarded as mostly symbolic in importance (Mendelsohn 2002). That said, the success recently enjoyed by Russia and the United States inspires hope that negotiations can be expanded to include other states.

Multilateral Arms Control and Disarmament

There are many historical examples of multilateral arms control and disarmament efforts. As early as the eleventh century, the Second Lateran Council prohibited the use of crossbows in fighting. The 1868 St. Petersburg Declaration prohibited the use of explosive bullets. In 1899 and 1907, International Peace Conferences at The Hague restricted the use of some weapons and prohibited others. The leaders of the United States, Britain, Japan, France, and Italy signed treaties at the Washington Naval Conferences (1921–22) agreeing to adjust the relative tonnage of their fleets.

Nearly thirty major multilateral agreements have been signed since the Second World War (see Table 13.2). Of these, the 1968 Nuclear Nonproliferation Treaty (NPT), which prohibited the transfer of nuclear weapons and production technologies to nonnuclear weapons states, stands out as the most symbolic multilateral agreement, with 187 signatory parties. While adherence to the treaty, which promotes **nonproliferation,** or stopping the expansion of states possessing weapons of mass destruction (WMD), has been widespread, India and Pakistan have broken the NPT's barriers to become nuclear-weapons states. In addition, Israel is believed to have clandestinely produced nuclear weapons, and countries such as Iran and North Korea remain outside the NPT and are seeking to become nuclear-weapons states.

Similar problems plague other multilateral agreements. The 1993 Chemical Weapons Convention (CWC), for example, required all stockpiles of chemical weapons to be destroyed within ten years. However, the agreement lost some of its authority in 2001 when the Bush administration refused to accept the enforcement measures. This erosion of support for arms control caused UN Secretary-General Kofi Annan to warn that "much of the established multilateral disarmament machinery has started to rust."

■ **multiple independently targeted reentry vehicles (MIRVs)** the technological innovation that permits many nuclear warheads to be delivered from a single ballistic missile.

■ **mutual assured destruction (MAD)** a condition of mutual deterrence in which both sides in an arms race possess the ability to survive a first strike and launch a devastating retaliatory attack.

■ **nonproliferation** the commitment to no development of weapons or technology by countries that do not already possess them.

TABLE 13.2

Major Multilateral Arms Control Treaties since 1945

Date	Agreement	Number of Parties (2004)	Principal Objectives
1959	Antarctic Treaty	45	Prevents the military use of the Antarctic, including the testing of nuclear weapons
1963	Limited Test Ban Treaty	135	Prohibits nuclear weapons in the atmosphere, outer space, and underwater
1967	Outer Space Treaty	103	Outlaws the use of outer space for testing or stationing any weapons, as well as for military maneuvers
1967	Treaty of Tlatelolco	33	Creates the Latin America Nuclear Free Zone by prohibiting the testing and possession of nuclear facilities for military purposes
1968	Nuclear Nonproliferation Treaty	189	Prevents the transfer of nuclear weapons and nuclear-weapons-production technologies to nonnuclear weapons states
1971	Seabed Treaty	115	Prohibits the deployment of weapons of mass destruction and nuclear weapons on the seabed beyond a twelve-mile coastal limit
1972	Biological Weapons Convention	167	Prohibits the production and storage of biological toxins; calls for the destruction of biological weapons stockpiles
1977	Environmental Modifications Convention (Enmod Convention)	86	Bans the use of technologies that could alter the Earth's weather patterns, ocean currents, ozone layer, or ecology
1980	Protection of Nuclear Material Convention	106	Obligates protection of peaceful nuclear material during transport on ships or aircraft
1981	Inhumane Weapons Convention	99	Prohibits the use of such weapons as fragmentation bombs, incendiary weapons, booby traps, and mines to which civilians could be exposed
1985	South Pacific Nuclear Free Zone (Roratonga) Treaty	18	Prohibits the testing, acquisition, or deployment of nuclear weapons in the South Pacific
1986	Confidence-Building and Security-Building Measures and Disarmament in Europe (CDE) Agreement (Stockholm Accord)	54	Requires prior notification and mandatory on-site inspection of conventional military exercises in Europe
1987	Missile Technology Control Regime (MTCR)	35	Restricts export of ballistic missiles and production facilities
1990	Conventional Forces in Europe (CFE)	30	Places limits on five categories of weapons in Europe and lowers force levels
1990	Confidence- and Security-Building Measures Agreement	53	Improves measures for exchanging detailed information on weapons, forces, and military exercises
1991	UN Register of Conventional (CSBM) Arms	101	Calls on all states to submit information on seven categories of major weapons exported or imported during the previous year

SOURCE: Stockholm International Peace Research Institute, *SIPRI Yearbook 2004* (781–805).

(continued)

TABLE 13.2

(continued)

Date	Agreement	Number of Parties (2004)	Principal Objectives
1992	Open Skies Treaty	33	Permits flights by unarmed surveillance aircraft over the territory of the signatory states
1993	Chemical Weapons Convention (CWC)	185	Requires all stockpiles of chemical weapons to be destroyed within ten years
1995	Protocol to the Inhumane Weapons Convention	135	Bans some types of laser weapons that cause permanent loss of eyesight
1995	Treaty of Bangkok	10	Creates a nuclear-weapon-free zone in Southeast Asia
1995	Wassenaar Export-Control Treaty	33	Regulates transfers of sensitive dual-use technologies to nonparticipating countries
1996	ASEAN Nuclear Free Zone Treaty	10	Prevents signatories in Southeast Asia from making, possessing, storing, or testing nuclear weapons
1996	Comprehensive Test Ban Treaty (CTBT)	169	Bans all testing of nuclear weapons
1996	Treaty of Pelindaba	53	Creates an African nuclear-weapon-free zone
1997	Antipersonnel Landmines Treaty (APLT)	151	Bans the production and export of landmines and pledges plans to remove them
1999	Inter-American Convention on Transparency in Conventional Weapons Acquisitions	20	Requires all thirty-four members of the Organization of American States (OAS) to annually report all weapons acquisitions, exports, and imports
2000	Nuclear Non-Proliferation Treaty Review Conference		Attended by 155 of the 187 signatory states; consensus on the final communiqué was reached to continue support for the NPT treaty

The Problematic Future of Arms Control and Disarmament

The obstacles to arms control and disarmament are formidable. Critics complain that these agreements frequently regulate obsolete armaments or ones that the parties to the agreement have little incentive for developing in the first place. Even when agreements are reached on modern, sophisticated weapons, the parties often set ceilings higher than the number of weapons currently deployed, so they do not have to slash their inventories.

A second pitfall is the propensity of limits on one type of weapon system to prompt developments in another system. Like a balloon that is squeezed at one end but expands at the other, constraints on certain parts of a country's arsenal can lead to enhancements elsewhere. An example can be seen in the 1972 SALT I agreement, which limited the number of intercontinental ballistic missiles possessed by the United States and Soviet Union. Although the number of missiles was restricted, no limits were placed on the number of nuclear warheads that could be placed on each missile; consequently both sides began developing multiple independently targeted reentry vehicles (MIRVs). In short, the quantitative freeze on launchers led to qualitative improvements in their warhead delivery systems.

Also reducing faith in future meaningful arms control is the slow, weak, and ineffective ability of the global community to ban some of the most dangerous and counterproductive weapons. Consider the case of **antipersonnel landmines (APLs),** which cannot discriminate between soldiers and civilians. More than 100 to 300 million landmines are believed to be scattered on the territory of more than seventy countries (with another 100 million in stockpiles). In the mid-1990s there was about one mine for every fifty humans on earth, and each year they killed or maimed more than twenty-six thousand people—almost all of them civilians. In 1994, not a single state would endorse a prohibition on these deadly weapons. It took a peace activist, Jody Williams, to organize the International Campaign to Ban Landmines, which opened for signature in December 1997 the Convention on the Prohibition of the Use, Stockpiling, Production and Transfer of Antipersonnel Mines and Their Destruction. For her efforts, Williams received the Nobel Peace Prize. But the United States, Russia, and other great powers stubbornly resisted the APL convention until a coalition of NGO peace groups mounted sufficient pressure for them to produce this epic treaty (still without U.S. acceptance). Still, the challenge of enforcing the ban, now signed by 158 states, and the task of removing APLs remains staggering.

■ **antipersonnel landmines (APLs)** weapons buried below the surface of the soil that explode on contact with any person—soldier or citizen—stepping on them.

A final problem facing those advocating arms control and disarmament is continuous innovation. By the time limits are negotiated on one type of weapon, a new generation of weapons has emerged. Modern technology is creating an ever-widening range of novel weapons—increasingly smaller, deadlier, and easier to conceal.

Why do states often make decisions to arm that apparently imprison them in the grip of perpetual insecurity? On the surface, the incentives for meaningful arms control seem numerous. Significant controls would save money, reduce tension, reduce environmental hazards, and diminish the potential destructiveness of war. However, most countries are reluctant to limit their armaments because of the self-help system that requires each state to protect itself. Thus states find themselves caught in a vicious cycle summarized by two basic principles: (1) "Don't negotiate when you are behind. Why accept a permanent position of number two?" and (2) "Don't negotiate when you are ahead. Why accept a freeze in an area of military competition when the other side has not kept up with you?" (Barnet 1977).

Here policymakers read from the script of **realism,** which insists that national security is best protected by developing military capabilities and not by reducing armaments or military spending. Realists regard treaties to be dangerous in an anarchical world in which the promises of self-interested rivals cannot be trusted. Rather than putting faith in arms control treaties when threatened states turn to self-reliance and military preparedness. That propensity was exhibited in the first five months of the George W. Bush administration, when in January 2001 it announced that it would not send the treaty for establishing the International Criminal Court to the U.S. Senate for ratification, followed by the decision on March 28 to abandon the 1997 Kyoto Protocol on global warming, the May 1 decision to abrogate the 1972 Anti-Ballistic Missile Treaty, the July 21 threat to withdraw from a UN conference to impose limits on illegal trafficking of small arms, and the July 25 rejection of proposed enforcement measures for the 1972 Biological Weapons Convention.

■ **realism** a paradigm based on the premise that world politics is essentially and unchangeably a struggle among self-interested states for power and position under anarchy, with each competing state pursuing its own national interests by expanding military capabilities.

Bush showed his realist colors by rejecting faith in treaties. He was not alone in this regard, of course. But as leader of the global hegemon, his disregard for arms control set a standard for other states to follow. Especially troublesome to America's allies was the U.S. repudiation of the 1972 Anti-Ballistic Missile

MAP 13.1
Trick or Treaty? Can Arms Control Treaties Arrest the Proliferation of Weapons?

Hope was rising in 1999 that the testing of nuclear weapons, which had been declining since 1945 (see chart at bottom of map of the number of nuclear tests yearly), would stop if the forty-four nuclear-capable states ratified the Comprehensive Test Ban Treaty (CTBT). Those hopes dissolved that October when the U.S. Senate rejected the test ban, and in so doing opened the way for ambitious states like India and Pakistan to resume testing. Headlines compared the U.S. repudiation of the arms-control treaty to the same kind of partisan **intermestic** politics for domestic payoffs that prompted the U.S. rejection of the 1919 Treaty of Versailles (an isolationistic fear of multilateral treaties that arguably paved the road to World War II). The CTBT would have banned all nuclear test explosions worldwide for all time, created a multilateral global monitoring network to detect explosions and verify compliance, and allowed for on-site inspections of areas of clandestine nuclear testing. This map shows that twenty-six of the forty-four nuclear-capable states had ratified the treaty, fifteen had not ratified, and three had neither signed nor ratified, and shows the number of nuclear tests conducted by each of the eight nuclear states through 2004. With the CTBT's collapse, termed by arms-control expert Brent Scowcroft as a "pathetic blow to global arms control," the prospect of continued testing of nuclear weapons is high.

SOURCE: Arms Control Association; Stockholm International Peace Research Institute.

Online map with critical thinking questions

■ **intermestic**
those issues confronting a state that are simultaneously international and domestic, encouraging policymakers to play two-level games when making decisions.

(ABM) Treaty, regarded by many as the cornerstone of nuclear arms control. That announcement was the first time in modern history that the United States had renounced a major international accord, and it ignited fears that a global chain reaction of massive repudiations by other states of arms control agreements would follow. As Jack Mendelsohn, a U.S. delegate to the SALT I and SALT II treaty negotiations, complained in October 2002, "The Bush administration has been stunningly mute on the future of arms control [and] clearly believes that it has completed its arms control agenda.... By playing make-believe arms control . . . the Bush administration has sacrificed the security of structure and predictability for the putative virtues of flexibility and unilateralism."

The tendency of states to make improving their weapons a priority over controlling them is illustrated by the example of nuclear testing (see Map 13.1). The eight known nuclear states have conducted a total of 2,056 nuclear explosions in twenty-four different locations since 1945—an average of one test every ten days. Both China and the United States regularly conduct so-called zero-yield nuclear experiments and are suspected of conducting explosive tests so small that they can't be detected. Moreover, the partial test ban treaty of 1963, which prohibited atmospheric and underwater testing but not underground explosions, did not slow the pace of testing. Three-fourths of all nuclear tests took place after the ban went into effect.

In summary, arms control remains a murky policy area, and the past record suggests that we should not exaggerate its potential. As long as aggressive national leaders exist, it would be imprudent to disarm. Limits on weapons may confine the rivalry between states, but they do not remove the underlying source of the conflict. Arms, after all, are less causes of war than symptoms of political tension: People "do not fight because they have arms. They have arms because [they are afraid and] they deem it necessary to fight" (Morgenthau 1985).

BALANCING POWER IN THE CONTEMPORARY GLOBAL SYSTEM

The use of alliances and arms control to balance power has shifted over time in a series of redistributions. At one extreme have been periods in which a powerful state has tried to prevail over another state, which in response usually has built additional arms or sought allies to offset its adversary's strength. Over time, each increase in military capability by one side has provoked an increase by the other. If neither side yields, at times they have managed the spiraling crisis by negotiating arms control agreements. At the other extreme, a more fluid competition has emerged, with encroachments by one state against another also precipitating a quest for arms and allies. But rather than resulting in the formation of rigid, counterbalanced blocs, this kind of military confrontation has triggered many shifts by others to produce a kaleidoscope of overlapping alliances—a checkerboard of multiple great powers competing in balance-of-power politics.

To visualize these potential types of **global structure** and their causes and consequences, we conclude with an overview of the models of the range of balance-of-power distributions that have arisen since World War II, with an eye to the kinds of polarity structures that may develop in the twenty-first century's age of **globalization** dominated by American military supremacy. Having exam-

■ **global structure**
the defining characteristics of the global system—such as the distribution of military capabilities—that exist independently of all actors but powerfully shape their actions.

■ **globalization**
the integration of states through increasing contact, communication, and trade to create a holistic, single global system, which increasingly binds people together in a common fate.

ined how the balance of power is supposed to operate, we consider now how it actually has functioned in world politics during the last half century.

Models of the Balance of Power in the Twenty-First Century

Military power can be distributed in different ways—an idea scholars call **polarity.** Historically, these have ranged from highly concentrated power on one end of the continuum to highly dispersed distributions on the other. The former has included regional empires (e.g., the Roman Empire), while an example of the latter is the approximate equality of power held by the European powers at the conclusion of the Napoleonic Wars in 1815. Using the conventional ways historians separate turning points from one type of balance-of-power system to another, we identify four distinct periods of polarity. This evolution displays a **long cycle,** since the transformations went through four phases that conclude today the way the system began: (1) unipolarity, 1945–49; (2) bipolarity, 1949–91; (3) multipolarity 1991–2001; and (4) another unipolar system today with the United States again an unchallenged hegemon.

■ **polarity**
the degree to which the global system revolves around one or more extremely powerful states, or "poles," as power concentrates in a single (unipolar) center of power or is distributed between two (bipolar) main powers or among three or more (multipolar) great powers.

■ **long cycle**
an interpretation of world history that focuses on repeating patterns of interstate behavior, such as the outbreak of system-wide general wars at regular intervals, after long periods during which peace prevailed.

Unipolarity—the United States. Most countries were devastated by World War II. The United States, however, was left in a clearly dominant position, its economy accounting for about half the world's combined gross national product (GNP). The United States was also the only country with the atomic bomb and had demonstrated its willingness to use the new weapon. This underscored to others that it was without rival and incapable of being counterbalanced. The United States was not just stronger than *anybody*—it was stronger than *everybody*. In the period immediately following World War II, a unipolar distribution of power materialized, because power was concentrated in the hands of a single *hegemon* able to exercise overwhelming influence over all other states, either through leadership or through domination. So supremely powerful was the United States at that time that people spoke of a new "American Empire" ruling over an impoverished world ravaged by war. That hegemonic status was short lived, however, as an ascendant challenger to U.S. preponderance, the Soviet Union, soon began to undermine America's supremacy and hegemonic status.

The U.S. capacity to act unilaterally in pursuit of its interests and ideals underwent a decline over the next four decades, as the U.S. grip on global developments and its ability to influence others eroded.

■ **bipolarity**
the division of the balance of power into two coalitions headed by rival military powers, each seeking to contain the other's expansion.

■ **polarization**
the degree to which states cluster in alliances around the most powerful members of the global system.

Bipolarity—the United States and Russia. The recovery of the Soviet economy, the growth of its military capabilities, its maintenance of a large army, and growing Soviet-U.S. rivalry less than five years after the end of World War II gave rise to a new distribution of world power. The Soviets broke the U.S. monopoly on atomic weapons in 1949 and exploded a thermonuclear device in 1953, less than a year after the United States. This achievement symbolized the creation of the global **bipolarity.** Military capabilities became concentrated in the hands of two competitive "superpowers," whose capacities to massively destroy anyone made comparisons with the other great powers meaningless.

Power combined to form two opposing blocs or coalitions through **polarization** when states joined counterbalanced alliances. In interpreting these dynamics, it is important not to use the concepts of polarity and polarization interchangeably. They refer to two distinct dimensions of the primary ways in which military power is combined (or divided) at any point in time in the global system. When states independently build arms at home, their differential production rates change the system's *polarity*, or number of power centers (poles). In contrast, when states combine their arms through alliance formation, the aggregation of power through *polarization* changes the system's balance of power. A system with multiple power centers can be said to be moving toward a greater degree of polarization if its members form separate blocs whose external interactions are characterized by increasing levels of conflict while their internal interactions become more cooperative (Rapkin and Thompson with Christopherson 1989). Conversely, polarization decreases when the number of cross-cutting alignments expands. The concept of polarization is especially apt in this context because a *pole* suggests the metaphor of a magnet—it both repels and attracts.

The formation of the **North Atlantic Treaty Organization (NATO)**, linking the United States to the defense of Western Europe, and the Warsaw Pact, linking the former Soviet Union in a formal alliance with its Eastern European clients, were produced by this polarization process. The opposing blocs formed in part because the superpowers competed for allies and in part because the less-powerful states looked to one superpower or the other for protection. Correspondingly, each superpower's allies gave it forward bases from which to carry on the competition. In addition, the involvement of most other states in the superpowers' struggle globalized the East-West conflict. Few states remained outside the superpowers' rival alliance networks as neutral or nonaligned countries.

By grouping the system's states into two blocs, each led by a superpower, the Cold War's bipolar structure bred insecurity among all. The balance was constantly at stake. Each bloc leader, fearing that its adversary would attain hegemony, viewed every move, however defensive, as the first step toward world conquest. **Zero-sum** conflict prevailed as both sides viewed what one side gained as a loss for the other. Both superpowers attached great importance to recruiting new allies. Fear that an old ally might desert the fold was everpresent. Bipolarity left little room for compromise or maneuver and worked against the normalization of superpower relations (Waltz 1993).

Bipolarity first began to disintegrate in the 1960s and early 1970s when the opposed coalitions' internal cohesion eroded and new centers of power emerged. At the same time, weaker alliance partners were afforded more room for maneuvering, as illustrated by the friendly relations between the United States and Romania and between France and the Soviet Union. The superpowers remained dominant militarily, but this less rigid system allowed other states to perform more independent foreign policy roles.

Rapid technological innovation in the superpowers' major weapons systems was a catalyst in the dissolution of the Cold War blocs and the national strategy **doctrines** that the adversaries had constructed. Intercontinental ballistic missiles (ICBMs), capable of delivering nuclear weapons through space from one continent to another, lessened the importance of forward bases on allies' territory for striking at the heart of the adversary. Furthermore, the narrowed differences in the superpowers' arsenals loosened the ties that had previously bound allies to one another. The European members of NATO in particular began to question whether the United States would, as it had pledged, protect Paris or London by sacrificing New York. Under what conditions might Washington or Moscow be willing to risk a nuclear holocaust? The uncertainty

■ **North Atlantic Treaty Organization (NATO)**
a military alliance created in 1949 to deter a Soviet attack on Western Europe that now seeks to maintain peace and promote democracy.

■ **zero-sum**
the perception in a rivalry that what one side gains, the other side loses.

■ **doctrine**
the guidelines a great power embraces as a strategy to specify the conditions under which it will use military power and armed force for political purposes abroad.

■ **extended deterrence**
the protection received by a weak ally when a heavily militarized great power pledges to "extend" its capabilities to it in a defense treaty.

became pronounced while the pledge to protect allies through **extended deterrence** seemed increasingly insincere.

The movement toward democracy and market economies by some communist states in the late 1980s further eroded the bonds of ideology that had formerly helped these countries face their security problems from a common posture. The 1989 dismantling of the Berlin Wall tore apart the Cold War architecture of competing blocs. With the end of this division, and without a Soviet threat, the consistency of outlook and singularity of purpose that once bound NATO members together disappeared. Many perceived the need to replace NATO and the defunct Warsaw Pact with a new security arrangement. However, most leaders maintained that some configuration of a European defense architecture was still necessary to cement relationships and stabilize the rush of cascading events.

World Domination by the U.S. Superpower, or a Multipolar Future of Balance-of-Power Competition?

■ **power transition**
a change in the ratio of military capabilities between great power rivals that may either increase or decrease the probability of war between them.

■ **unipolarity**
a condition in which an international system has a single dominant power center, or pole, able to exercise supreme authority by its superior economic resources and military capability.

■ **Bush Doctrine**
the policy of assertive unilateral hegemonic leadership proclaimed by George W. Bush in 2001 as the policy principle that would guide American foreign policy, elaborated in the 2002 *National Security Strategy of the United States* pledging to maintain a unipolar world and to use preemptive warfare to prevent enemies' use of force.

Following the dissolution of the Soviet Union in 1991, a **power transition** occurred, prompting most analysts to conclude that a new era of **unipolarity** had arisen, with the United States emerging as the world's only superpower. A decade after the collapse of communism in Europe, columnist Charles Krauthammer (2002) proclaimed that "no country has been as dominant culturally, economically, technologically, and militarily in the history of the world since the Roman Empire." The question remained as to whether this would prove beneficial or damaging. Recall that to hegemonic stability theorists a unipolar concentration of power allows the global leader to police chaos and maintain international peace. Their faith in America as a well-intentioned peacekeeper was bolstered by President George W. Bush's pledge in 2001 that the U.S. role in the world would be "the story of a power that went into the world to protect but not possess, to defend but not to conquer."

Against this optimistic view currently runs a strong suspicion about the future stability of a unipolar world under U.S. management, in part by Bush's assertive **Bush Doctrine** pledging that the U.S. would unilaterally act however it wishes abroad, without the approval of others. This has stimulated criticism and backlash. Warns one critic, "It is virtually universal in history that when countries become hegemons . . . they tend to want everything their own way, and it never works" (Mathews 2000). Others condemn the shortsightedness of U.S. leadership, guided, as they see it, more by self-interests than by ideals and motivated more by a desire to preserve America's position as top dog and less to promote multilateral cooperation for peace and prosperity.

Regardless of whether the optimists or pessimists are correct, many policy analysts believe that U.S. preponderance cannot last long given the toll of "imperial overstretch" and the inevitability of differential economic growth rates that favor faster-growing challengers, especially if the United States forgets the dangers of imperial policies (Kupchan 2003; Ripsman 2004; Judis 2004). Other countries "will obstruct American purposes whenever and in whatever way they can, and the pursuit of American interests will have to be undertaken through coercion rather than consensus. Anti-Americanism will become the global language of political protest—the default ideology of opposition—unifying the world's discontents and malcontents, some of whom, as we have discovered, can

The Vestiges of Communist Power In 1998, only five countries (China, Cuba, Laos, North Korea, and Vietnam) remained members of the "communist bloc." In 1988, before the Cold War ended, that coalition consisted of fifteen countries. Pictured here is Cuba's Fidel Castro being assisted by Vietnam's General Secretary Do Muoi and a Vietnamese soldier at farewell ceremonies of a 1995 summit in Hanoi. The Cuban leader visited both China and Vietnam to observe how they had adapted Marxism to market economies. The meeting raised the question of whether communist ideology can still unify what remains of the communist bloc in a common coalition. Perhaps national self-interest rather than ideology will cement future alignments, as suggested by the pledge of Russian President Vladimir Putin to strengthen ties with Cuba, its former communist ally.

---

be very dangerous" (Zakaria 2002c; see also Revel 2004). Eventually, unipolarity will give way to a new configuration of power whose probable consequences are not clear. Some forecast the return of a bipolar pattern of direct opposition, with a new Sino-Russian bloc, European-Russian entente, or Sino-Japanese alliance countering the United States (Brzezinski 2004). Others see the emergence of a more complex multipolar pattern of balance-of-power competition, where the United States, China, Japan, Russia, and the European Union would constitute five centers of global power. According to this image of the future, as power becomes more equally distributed, each player will be increasingly assertive, independent, and competitive, leading to confusion about the identity of friends and foes.

The search for the capacity to compete on an equal footing with the other centers of power is characteristically strong when power becomes spread across three or more poles. With the effort by the European Union to enter the playing field alongside the United States, China, Japan, Russia, and other regional players like Brazil and India, the game of rivalry and balancing is becoming much different from the strategies and alignments that tend to materialize in unipolar and bipolar systems. As power becomes increasingly equally distributed, each player becomes assertive, independent, and competitive; diplomacy displays a nonideological, chesslike character; and conflict intensifies as each contender fears the power of its rivals. An enlarged global chessboard of multiple geostrategic relationships develops. A congested landscape leads to confusion about the identity of friends and foes. To make this setting even more confusing in multipolar systems, the interplay takes place simultaneously on two playing fields—the first military and the second economic (recall Table 4.2, p. 125). The major players align together against others on particular issues, as their interests dictate. Behind the diplomatic smiles and handshakes, one-time friends and allies begin to grow apart, formally "specialized" relations begin to dissolve, and former enemies forge friendly ties.

This competition under conditions of multipolarity is evident in the growing U.S.-Japan-EU trade-bloc rivalry on the economic battlefield (see Chapter 9). In addition, much counterbalancing and shifting in flexible and fluid alliances occurs, with the United States often casting itself in the role of balancer. For example, in December 2002, China and Russia signed a new friendship treaty, calling for a "multipolar world" to express resentment of U.S. global dominance even though Russia at the same time was also energetically pursuing full membership in NATO.

The evolution of the North Atlantic Treaty Organization (NATO) since the end of the Cold War reflects the shifting geopolitical landscape. At first, many observers felt that NATO would disappear along with its rival Warsaw Pact. The purpose for which NATO was created—containing Russian expansionism—no longer was relevant, because the threat no longer existed. However, NATO did not dissolve. It reinvented itself, changing its membership and its mission. In January 1994, NATO began to encourage bandwagoning by allowing four formerly communist bloc states (Poland, the Czech Republic, Slovakia, and Hungary) to join the alliance under the **Partnership for Peace (PfP)** plan. The PfP did not then give them the same guarantee of aid in the event of an attack that the existing full members were promised. But it became a pivotal step in the process of enlargement aimed at creating a peaceful, united, and democratic Europe. So too, did the **Euro-Atlantic Partnership Council (EAPC),** whose forty-six-member countries at the time served to help coordinate NATO's efforts to manage crises and provide for greater security in Europe. As Map 13.2 shows, after admitting Poland, the Czech Republic, and Poland in 1999, NATO took enlargement a big step forward in November 2002 when it undertook the biggest expansion in its fifty-three-year history. Bulgaria, Estonia, Latvia, Lithuania, Romania, Slovakia, and Slovenia were admitted as full members, joining the nineteen existing countries under NATO's security umbrella. The expansion stretches NATO's territory from the Baltic Sea to Russia's west coast to the Black Sea on Europe's southeastern rim. In addition, Russia has been invited to formally participate in full decision making on NATO security policies, which helps to reduce Russian fears that the alliance continues to perceive Russia as a potential enemy. NATO, a product of a bygone bipolar world, has become a new security IGO on the global stage, committed to defending its twenty-six members'

■ **Partnership for Peace (PfP)**
a plan proposed in 1993 by the United States that established limited military partnerships between NATO and the former Warsaw Pact countries.

■ **Euro-Atlantic Partnership Council (EAPC)**
a coordinating institution within NATO created in 1998 to manage the common political, military, financial, and security issues confronting Europe.

MAP 13.2
The Enlarged NATO in the New Geostrategic Balance of Power

The twenty-first-century geostrategic landscape has been transformed by NATO's expansion at the start of 2003 to twenty-six full members. An additional thirty-eight countries work as Partners for Peace in the Euro-Atlantic Partnership Council (EAPC). As shown in this map, NATO now casts its security umbrella across and beyond Europe in its endeavor to create a collective security regime including states that once were its enemies. If NATO succeeds in redefining itself as a coalition of liberal democracies fighting tyranny, terrorism, and a range of other economic and environmental problems, the transformation will defy the tendency for Europe's alliances to collapse after the defeat of a common adversary.

SOURCE: From *U.S. New and World Report*, July 14, 1997. Copyright © 1997, U.S. News & World Report, L.P. Reprinted with permission.

Rivalry among Allies Seeking to disarm and defuse European allies' anxieties about his plan for the United States to build a missile defense system, Bush proclaimed his administration's "new receptivity" to the European allies at the June 2001 NATO summit. However, French, German, and other Europeans were not persuaded, and a climate of mistrust among allies prevailed. Shown here is a June 2001 protest demonstration in Europe against the United States.

borders as though they were its own. Revitalized with a larger membership and a wider territorial reach, NATO seeks to orchestrate a cooperative approach to security among liberal democracies, as shown by NATO's agreement in June 2004 to help the United States train Iraqi militia for defense.

That search for a purpose stemmed from NATO's decision on September 13, 2001, to invoke for the first time NATO's mutual defense principle. It recognized the 9/11 terrorist attack as an attack on all NATO members and decided to act as a united coalition to punish those behind the atrocities. This action further helped dispel doubts about NATO's continuing usefulness and about whether NATO's cumbersome decision-making procedures permit the alliance to be used for fighting wars rather than peacekeeping missions. The advantages to enlargement are offset by the risk that expansion will reduce the alliance to a mere conference association for discussing security issues and will end its role as a military alliance in the global balance of power.

Critics of NATO's enlargement complain that this alliance undermines the security of the states it excludes. At times not only Russia but also China, Japan, and other powers have complained that the presence of a solidified military alliance in Europe without other strong military alliances to balance it poses a threat to global security. NATO asserts that these charges are unjustified because its new decision rules, giving every full member a veto over decisions regarding coercive military operations, remove the threat of a NATO preemptive strike. Other proponents of NATO and European Union enlargement claim that the maze of overlapping European security organizations (including the OSCE and the Council of Europe) are too cumbersome and slow to permit any of them to take decisive military actions outside their sphere of influence.

The innovative redesign of NATO and its expansion illustrate the grip that realist thinking exerts on national security policy as states and alliances seek to adjust to changes in the global distribution of military power. Coalitions form and dissolve in response to changes in security threats and national interests. One example is the division that developed between the United States and its NATO allies when nearly all the European states opposed the Bush administration's 2003 preemptive strike against Iraq. That episode of strained trans-Atlantic relationships shattered some of the enthusiasm for building a concert of great powers to wage a global war against terrorism. Alignments shifted again when friction grew between the United States and its closest allies over how to pursue the war on terrorism after President Bush condemned North Korea, Iran, and Iraq as an "axis of evil." As a measure of how sensitive particular issues can be among great powers, both the European Union's foreign affairs commissioner, Christopher Pattern, and the German foreign minister, Joschka Fischer, castigated President Bush for treating America's coalition partners as subordinate "satellites," and Russian President Vladimir Putin quickly joined their criticism of U.S. unilateralist disregard of the interests of America's would-be partners in the antiterrorist coalition. In a multipolar system, alignments can be fragile. Consider the response of French President Jacques Chirac to U.S. President George W. Bush's re-election in November 2004. Chirac, who was unhappy with the election's outcome, argued that a strong America reinforced the need for a stronger Europe "politically and economically" in an "ever more multipolar world"—a phrase Chirac and other European leaders use to describe a world with a superpower Europe (Reid 2004) to balance the U.S. giant.

Another indicator of continuing balance-of-power jockeying for global position and independence typical of emergent multipolarity was the decision by the European Union to create its own rapid deployment force so it can undertake military actions on its own, without the approval of the United States. The European reaction was a response to the growing recognition that U.S. power had grown so dramatically that it overshadowed everyone else combined. In short, history had cyclically begun to move toward the resurrection of a previous condition, as the second era of American unipolarity has begun to show signs that, sooner or later, the unipolar era of U.S. domination will end and a new multipolar era will begin (Kupchan 2003).

But it is difficult to confidently predict what the twenty-first century will look like and whether it will be chaotic or stable. Should a new multipolar world develop in the mid-twenty-first century, the probable consequences are here again unclear. The three different schools of thought on the relationship between polarity and global stability contend with one another (see Controversy: Is a Unipolar, Bipolar, or Multipolar System the Most Stable?). Because there is no real consensus on whether systems with a certain number of poles are more war prone than others, it would be imprudent to conclude that a new multipolar system will necessarily produce another period of warfare or of peace. But if the

> **CONTROVERSY**
>
> ## IS A UNIPOLAR, BIPOLAR, OR MULTIPOLAR SYSTEM THE MOST STABLE?
> ### Three Schools of Thought on the Relationship of Polarity and International Peace
>
> In the early twenty-first century, a long-standing debate has intensified about which type of polarity distribution—unipolar, bipolar, or multipolar—is the most capable of preventing large-scale war. What do you think? Consider the divided opinions about this issue, as represented by the arguments in three contending schools of thought.
>
> One interpretation holds that peace will occur when one hegemonic state acquires enough power to deter others' expansionist ambitions. This view maintains that the concentration of power reduces the chances of war because it allows a single superpower to maintain peace and manage the international system (Wohlforth 1999). The long peace under Britain's leadership in the 1800s (the Pax Britannica) and earlier, under the Roman Empire (the Pax Romana), offered support for the idea that unipolarity brings peace, and therefore inspires the hope that the twenty-first century under a Pax Americana will be stable as long as U.S. dominance prevails (Knickerbocker 1999).
>
> In contrast, a second school of thought (e.g., Waltz 1964) maintains that bipolar systems are the most stable. According to this line of reasoning, stability, ironically, results from "the division of all nations into two camps [because it] raises the costs of war to such a high level that all but the most fundamental conflicts are resolved without resort to violence" (Bueno de Mesquita 1975). Under such stark simplicities and balanced symmetries, the two leading rivals have incentives to manage crises so that they do not escalate to war.
>
> Those who believe that a bipolar world is inherently more stable than either its unipolar or multipolar counterparts draw support from the fact that in the bipolar environment of the 1950s, when the threat of war was endemic, major war did not occur. Extrapolating, these observers (e.g., Mearsheimer 1990) reason that because a new multipolar distribution of global power makes it impossible to run the world from one or two centers, disorder will result:
>
>> It is rather basic. So long as there [are] only two great powers, like two big battleships clumsily and cautiously circling each other, confrontations—or accidents—[are] easier to avoid. [With] the global lake more crowded with ships of varying sizes, fueled by different ambitions and piloted with different degrees of navigational skill, the odds of collisions become far greater. (House 1989, A10)
>
> A third school of thought argues that multipolar systems are the least war prone. While the reasons differ, advocates share the belief that polarized systems that either concentrate power, as in a unipolar system, or that divide the world into two antagonistic blocs, as in a bipolar system, promote struggles for dominance (see W. Thompson 1988; Morgenthau 1985). The peace-through-multipolarity school perceives multipolar systems as stable because they encompass a larger number of autonomous actors, giving rise to more potential alliance partners. This is seen as pacifying because it is essential to counterbalancing a would-be aggressor, as shifting alliances can occur only when there are multiple power centers (Deutsch and Singer 1964).
>
> Abstract deductions and historical analogies can lead to contradictory conclusions, as the logic underlying these three inconsistent interpretations illustrates. The future will determine which of these rival theories is the most accurate.

past truly is a reliable guide to the future, the distribution of global power will exert a strong influence on what kind of global system the world will experience.

Realists insist that the tragic struggle for security among great powers will continue (Mearsheimer 2001). The validity of this interpretation of the global future is still at issue, however. So, too, is the question of whether international security is best served by states' military search for their own national security or whether instead the pursuit of security through military means will sow the

Russia and China Seek to Balance U.S. Power When NATO approved formal enlargement in 1997, both Russia's and China's sense of security plummeted. In reaction, the old rivals, feeling excluded, repaired their broken alliance by agreeing to a new "strategic partnership" aimed at rearranging the global geostrategic chessboard. Russian Premier Vickor Cheknomyrdin (right) and Chinese President Jiang Zemin met in Moscow in April 1997 to negotiate the "new world order" joint statement, which called for creation of a new "multipolar" system cemented by a new Sino-Russian axis to counter the threat of global domination by the U.S. hegemonic superpower. This friendship treaty was renewed in 2002. The logic of balance-of-power politics rationalizes the formation of these kinds of strategic unions to check the growing influence of a rising great-power rival. The same thinking inspired the 1999 common defense treaty between Japan and the United States to offset the expanding military power of China.

seeds of the world's destruction. In the next chapter we will turn our attention away from the balance-of-power politics of realism and examine proposals by liberal theorists for harnessing international law and organizations to create a more peaceful world.

KEY TERMS

security dilemma
liberalism
alliances
deterrence
self-help

rational choice
collective security
levels of analysis
balance of power
alignments

security regime
nonalignment
sine principle
balancer
preemption

bandwagoning
prospect theory
hegemonic stability theory
hegemon
arms control
disarmament
bilateral agreements
multilateral agreements
Strategic Arms Limitation Talks (SALT)
Strategic Arms Reduction Treaty (START)
Strategic Offensive Reductions Treaty (SORT)
multiple independently targeted reentry vehicles (MIRVs)
mutual assured destruction (MAD)
nonproliferation
antipersonnel landmines (APLs)
realism
intermestic
global structure
globalization
polarity
long cycle
bipolarity
polarization
North Atlantic Treaty Organization (NATO)
zero-sum
doctrine
extended deterrence
power transition
unipolarity
Bush Doctrine
Partnership for Peace (PfP)
Euro-Atlantic Partnership Council (EAPC)

SUGGESTED READING

Diehl, Paul F., and Gary Goertz. *War and Peace in International Rivalry.* Ann Arbor: University of Michigan Press, 2000.

Ferguson, Niall. *Colossus: The Price of America's Empire.* New York: Penguin, 2004.

Hodge, Carl Cavanagh. *Atlanticism for a New Century: The Rise, Triumph, and Decline of NATO.* Upper Saddle River, N.J.: Prentice-Hall, 2005.

Kegley, Charles W., Jr., and Gregory A. Raymond. *A Multipolar Peace? Great-Power Politics in the Twenty-First Century.* New York: St. Martin's Press, 1994.

Kupchan, Charles A. *The End of the American Era.* New York: Knopf, 2003.

Larsen, Jeffrey A., ed. *Arms Control: Cooperative Security in a Changing Environment.* Boulder, Colo.: Lynne Rienner, 2002.

Lobell, Steven E. *The Challenge of Hegemony.* Ann Arbor: University of Michigan Press, 2003.

Magstadt, Thomas M. *An Empire if You Can Keep It: Power and Principle in American Foreign Policy.* Washington, D.C.: CQ Press, 2004.

Mearsheimer, John J. *The Tragedy of Great Power Politics.* New York: W. W. Norton, 2001.

Snyder, Glenn. *Alliance Politics.* Ithaca, N.Y.: Cornell University Press, 1997.

Vasquez, John A., and Colin Elman. *Realism and the Balancing of Power: A New Debate.* Upper Saddle River, N.J.: Prentice Hall, 2003.

Weitsman, Patricia A. *Dangerous Alliances: Proponents of Peace, Weapons of War.* Stanford, Calif.: Stanford University Press, 2004.

WHERE ON THE WORLD WIDE WEB?

Bulletin of the Atomic Scientists
http://www.bullatomsci.org/

After World War II, many of the scientists responsible for the production of the atomic bomb helped form a movement to control nuclear energy. In 1945, they founded the *Bulletin* to advocate international control of the means of nuclear production. Still published today, the *Bulletin* now appears online. Current and archived issues are available. Read brief or detailed histories of technological and political developments. Scan the "Nuclear Notebook" to get up-to-date facts and figures on the world's nuclear arsenals. Click on the "Clock" link to see how international tensions and nuclear developments have brought us alternatively closer to midnight or back from the brink. Where is the clock set now? What reasons are given for this setting?

Center for Nonproliferation Studies (CNS)
http://cns.miis.edu/index.htm

The Center for Nonproliferation Studies (CNS) at the Monterey Institute of International Relations is the largest nongovernmental organization in the United States devoted exclusively to research and training on nonproliferation issues. At this site you will find articles on featured topics as well as summaries of CNS projects. Its extensive electronic resources are organized according to region of the world, subject (nuclear, chemical, or biological weapons), and publication type. Which countries of the world are active in the production of weapons of mass destruction? Why do you think this is the case?

Federation of American Scientists
http://www.fas.org/

Students interested in examining international arms control treaties and related issues should visit the Federation of American Scientists' (FAS) website to find a comprehensive archive of nuclear, chemical, and biological arms control agreements. FAS is a privately funded nonprofit policy organization engaged in analysis and advocacy of science, technology, and public policy issues that concern global security. Topics such as arms sales monitoring, chemical and biological arms, space policy, and nuclear nonproliferation and disarmament are covered extensively. There is also a section covering the impact of information technologies.

NATO
http://www.nato.int/

The North Atlantic Treaty Organization's (NATO) website contains information on NATO's enlargement as well as a NATO chronology. What are some its important current activities? What opinions of NATO and its role are expressed in the latest edition of NATO Review?

United Nations Conference on Disarmament
http://www.unog.ch/disarm/disarm.htm

The UN Conference on Disarmament web page links to all the major international instruments on disarmament, from the 1949 Geneva Convention through the 1997 antipersonnel landmines convention. Read the texts of some of the most influential international agreements that seek to control or eliminate weapons of mass destruction. What main areas of disarmament have been covered in these agreements?

United Nations Demining Database
http://disarmament2.un.org/MineBan.nsf

Antipersonnel landmines (APLs) are internationally recognized as an inhumane and counterproductive weapon. In 1997, more than one hundred countries signed a treaty prohibiting the production of landmines and supporting the removal of those buried in the ground, but enforcing the treaty remains a challenge. This comprehensive site explores the issues involved with demining. Read about specific countries' problems demining their land and the origins of the mines found within their borders. See how many mines different countries have, the area contaminated, and the number of victims. Which countries have the greatest number of landmines? Why do you think this is so? Who are the biggest suppliers?

INFOTRAC® COLLEGE EDITION

Sokov, Nikolai. "The Russian Nuclear Arms Control Agenda after SORT." *Arms Control Today* (April 2003).

Kampmark, Binoy. "America's Nuclear Deterrence in the Age of Terrorism." *Contemporary Review* (April 2003).

Chace, James. "The Balance of Power." *World Policy Journal* (Winter 1998).

Jervis, Robert. "Arms Control, Stability, and Causes of War." *Political Science Quarterly* (Summer 1993).

For more articles, enter:

"balance of power" in the Subject Guide

"war" in the Subject Guide, and then go to subdivision "causes of"

"nuclear arms control" in the Subject Guide

Go to http://politicalscience.wadsworth.com/kegley10 to access additional resources related to this chapter.

CHAPTER 14

THE LIBERAL INSTITUTIONAL PATHS TO PEACE

TOPICS AND THEMES

- Liberalism and conflict management
- International law as a means to world order
- International organizations and world order: The UN and regional organizations
- Political integration: The functional and neofunctional paths to peace
- Democracy as a means to peace
- Liberal institutions and world order

- **CONTROVERSY** WAS THE WAR IN IRAQ A JUST WAR?

Liberal democracies give citizens the right of assembly and free speech and allow mass public participation in the policy-making process. Shown here are people exercising those rights in a protest demonstration in October 2002 against the U.S. plan to attack Iraq, which occurred five months later.

My first axiom: The quest for international security involves the unconditional surrender by every nation, in a certain measure, of its liberty of action, its sovereignty that is to say, and it is clear beyond all doubt that no other road can lead to such security.

—ALBERT EINSTEIN, scientist, 1932

No nation, no matter how powerful, can organize the international system by itself. . . . The goal of U.S. foreign policy must be to turn dominant power into shared responsibility—to conduct policy [with] a style less focused on imposing immediate policy prescriptions than achieving a common definition of long-range purposes.

—HENRY A. KISSINGER, former U.S. secretary of state, 2004

Since antiquity, the world has pursued two primary paths to peace. The realist road emphasizes *military* solutions; the liberal road emphasizes *political* solutions. This chapter examines four principal approaches to the control of armed conflict from the liberal theoretical tradition: international law, organization, integration, and democratization (see Table 14.1). Because all four stress institutions, these liberal paths are sometimes referred to collectively as **neoliberal institutionalism.** While they differ in their approach to security, they share a fear of states' historic tendency to make war.

INTERNATIONAL LAW AND WORLD ORDER

In 1984, the United States announced that it would unilaterally withdraw from the World Court's jurisdiction. This move followed Nicaragua's accusation that the U.S. Central Intelligence Agency had illegally attempted to "overthrow and

■ **neoliberal institutionalism**
the recent theoretical effort to explain how peace and prosperity instead of war might be created through law, global governance, and liberal democracies' cooperation to engineer international change

TABLE 14.1

Liberal Paths to International Security

Policy Prescriptions	Premises
Provide states rules of international law to regulate competition.	Interstate cooperation can be encouraged by creating rules for peaceful interaction.
Participate in the creation of international organizations.	If you want peace, prepare global institutions to keep it.
Practice collaboration to bind independent states together in integrated security communities.	Interdependence makes imperative uniting states and building a transnational civil society.
Promote the spread of democratic governance.	Countries that protect their own citizens' civil liberties do not wage war against other governments that also protect their citizens' human rights.
Provide education.	The pen is mightier than the sword, and education prepares people for democratic governance.
Prepare rules to facilitate free trade.	Trade protectionism is counterproductive to prosperity and peace.
Produce agreements to reduce armaments to levels that discourage war.	States get what they plan for—beat swords into plowshares.
Provide humanitarian assistance to the impoverished.	Rich states can help themselves only by helping poor people also.
Value principles more than power.	Principled moral behavior ultimately reaps higher rewards for all because it encourages reciprocity.

destabilize" the elected Sandinista government. Nicaragua charged that the United States had illegally mined its ports and supplied money, military assistance, and training to the rebel *contra* forces. The United States denied the tribunal's authority. In so doing, however, it was not acting without precedent; others had done so previously. Nonetheless, by thumbing its nose at the court and the rule of law it represents, had the United States, as some claimed, become an "international outlaw"? Or, as others asserted, had it acted within its rights?

The World Court supported the former view. In 1984, the court ruled against the United States as follows:

> The right to sovereignty and to political independence possessed by the Republic of Nicaragua, like any other state of the region or of the world, should be fully respected and should not in any way be jeopardized by any military and paramilitary activities which are prohibited by the principles of international law, in particular the principle that states should refrain in their international relations from the threat or the use of force against the territorial integrity or the political independence of any state, and the principle concerning the duty not to intervene in matters within the domestic jurisdiction of a state. (*New York Times*, May 11, 1984, 8)

Yet this ruling had little effect, as neither the court nor Nicaragua had any means to enforce it.

Events such as this have led many critics to conclude that international law is "weak and defenseless" (Fried 1971). Indeed, many experts—whether they are realists or liberals—skeptically ask whether international law is really law. There are many reasons to answer this question affirmatively. Although international law is imperfect, actors regularly rely on it to redress grievances (see Joyner 2001). Most of this activity falls within the realm of **private international law**—the regulation of routine transnational activities in such areas as commerce, communications, and travel. While largely invisible to the public, private international law is the locus for almost all international legal activities. It is where the majority of transnational disputes are regularly settled and where the record of compliance compares favorably with that achieved in domestic legal systems.

In contrast, **public international law** covers issues of relations between governments and the interactions of governments with intergovernmental organizations (IGOs) and nongovernmental organizations (NGOs) such as multinational corporations. Some believe that we should use the phrase *world law* to describe the mixture of public and private, domestic and international transactions that public international law seeks to regulate in an increasingly globalized world. However, it is the regulation of government-to-government relations that dominates the headlines in discussion of public international law. This area of activity also receives most of the criticism, for here, failures—when they occur—are quite conspicuous. This is especially true with respect to the breakdown of peace and security. When states engage in armed conflict, criticism of its shortcomings escalates. Israeli Ambassador Abba Eban lamented that "international law is that law which the wicked do not obey and the righteous do not enforce."

Because this chapter examines the capacity of public international law to control war, our discussion will address only the laws and institutional machinery created to manage armed conflict. That is, it will explore that segment of public international law popularly regarded as the most deficient.

Law at the International Level: Core Principles

Public international law is usually defined as the rules that govern the conduct of states in their relations with one another. The *corpus juris gentium* (the body of the law of nations) has grown considerably during the past four centuries, changing in response to transformations in international politics. An inventory of the basic legal principles relevant to the control of war reveals the contemporary character of the global system.

The Rules of International Law. No principle of international law is more critical than state sovereignty. **Sovereignty** means that no authority is legally above the state, except that which the state voluntarily confers on the international organizations it joins. In fact, as conceived by theoreticians schooled in the tradition of **realism** since the seventeenth century, the rules of international law were written to protect states and permitted states "a complete freedom of action" (Parry 1968) to preserve their sovereign independence.

Nearly every legal doctrine supports and extends the cardinal principle that states are the primary subjects of international law. Although the Universal De-

■ **private international law**
law pertaining to routinized transnational intercourse between or among states as well as nonstate actors.

■ **public international law**
law pertaining to government-to-government relations.

■ **sovereignty**
the legal doctrine that states have supreme authority to govern their internal affairs and manage their foreign relations with other states and nonstate actors.

■ **realism**
the theoretical tradition arguing that sovereign states are the most important global actors and should be unrestrained by law, principles of justice, or supranational organizations when making decisions regarding war and peace.

claration of Human Rights in 1948 expanded concern about states' treatment of individual people, states remain supreme. "Laws are made to protect the state from the individual and not the individual from the state" (Gottlieb 1982). Accordingly, the vast majority of rules address the rights and duties of states, not people. For instance, the principle of **sovereign equality** entitles each state to full respect by other states as well as equal protection by the system's legal rules. The right of independence also guarantees states' autonomy in their domestic affairs and external relations, under the logic that the independence of each presumes that of all. Similarly, the doctrine of **neutrality** permits states to avoid involvement in others' conflicts and coalitions.

Furthermore, the noninterference principle forms the basis for the **nonintervention norm**—that is, states' duty to refrain from uninvited involvement in another's internal affairs. This sometimes-abused classic rule gives governments the right to exercise jurisdiction over practically all things on, under, or above their bounded territory. (There are exceptions, however, such as **diplomatic immunity** for states' ambassadors from the domestic laws of the country where their embassies are located and **extraterritoriality,** which allows control of embassies on other states' terrain.)

In practice, domestic jurisdiction permits a state to enact and enforce whatever laws it wishes for its own citizens. In fact, international law was so permissive toward the state's control of its domestic affairs that, prior to 1952, "there was no precedent in international law for a . . . state to assume responsibility for the crimes it committed against a minority within its jurisdiction" (Wise 1993). A citizen was not protected against the state's abuse of human rights or **crimes against humanity.** Note also that international law permits states to set their own rules for citizenship. Two basic principles govern the way nationality and citizenship are conferred: under *jus soli,* citizenship is determined by the state in whose territory the birth took place; under *jus sanguinis,* citizenship is acquired by descent from a parent who is already a citizen of a state.

In addition, in earlier periods of modern international law, states were permitted to create whatever form of government they desired without regard to its acceptability to other states. This principle was expressed in the realpolitik language of the Treaty of Augsburg (1555) and the Westphalian treaties (1648), which made states all-powerful by recognizing the **divine right of kings.** This doctrine was reaffirmed in the 1943 Atlantic Charter's pledge of "the right of all people to choose the form of government under which they will live." However, the right of people to live under the liberties of democracy is increasingly being defined as an "entitlement" or a basic human right. At Geneva in 1999, states proclaimed that all individuals have a right to democracy, thereby revising international law through a United Nations resolution and by the same vote dealing "a severe blow to those countries which continue to deny their citizens not only democracy but other fundamental human rights" (Rubin 1999; see also Slaughter 2004a). International law still gives states the complete freedom to regulate economic transactions within their boundaries and empowers the state to draft those living on its soil into its armed forces to fight—and die, if necessary—to defend the state.

The Montevideo Convention of 1933 on the Rights and Duties of States summarizes the major components of **statehood.** A state must possess a permanent population, a well-defined territory, and a government capable of ruling its citizens and of managing formal diplomatic relations with other states. Essentially,

---

■ **sovereign equality**
the principle that states are legally entitled to equal protection under international law.

■ **neutrality**
the legal doctrine that provides rights and duties for states who remain nonaligned with adversaries during wartime.

■ **nonintervention norm**
the principle prohibiting one state from interfering in another state's internal affairs.

■ **diplomatic immunity**
the legal doctrine that gives a country's officials when abroad release from the local legal jurisdiction of the state when they are visiting or stationed (e.g., diplomats and ambassadors) to represent their own government.

■ **extraterritoriality**
the legal doctrine that allows states to maintain jurisdiction over their embassies in other states.

■ **crimes against humanity**
a category of activities, made illegal at the Nuremberg war crime trials, condemning states that abuse human rights.

■ **divine right of kings**
the realist doctrine that because kings are sovereign they have the right to rule their subjects authoritatively and are not accountable to the public because their rule is ordained by God.

the acquisition of statehood depends on a political entity's recognition as such by other states. Whether a state exists thus rests in the hands of other states; that is, preexisting states are entitled to extend **diplomatic recognition** to another entity. **De facto recognition** is provisional and capable of being withdrawn in the event that the recognized government is superseded by another. It does not carry with it the exchange of diplomatic representatives or other legal benefits and responsibilities. **De jure recognition,** on the other hand, extends full legal and diplomatic privileges from the granting state. This distinction emphasizes that recognition is a political tool of international law, through which approval or disapproval of a government can be expressed.

Other rules specify how treaties are to be activated, interpreted, and abrogated. International law holds that treaties voluntarily entered into are binding (*pacta sunt servanda*). However, it also reserves for states the right to unilaterally terminate treaties previously agreed to, by reference to the escape clause known as *rebus sic stantibus*. This is the principle that a treaty is binding only as long as no fundamental change occurs in the circumstances that existed when it was concluded.

Procedures for Dispute Settlement. In addition to these general principles, international law provides a wide variety of legal methods for states to resolve their conflicts. The laws of **negotiation** do not obligate states to reach agreement or to settle their disputes peacefully. They do, however, provide rules for several conflict resolution procedures, including:

- **mediation:** when a third party proposes a nonbinding solution to a controversy between two other states
- **good offices:** when a third party offers a location for discussions among disputants but does not participate in the actual negotiations
- **conciliation:** when a third party assists both disputing sides but does not offer any solution
- **arbitration:** when a third party gives a binding decision through an ad hoc forum
- **adjudication:** when a third party offers a binding decision through an institutionalized tribunal, such as a court

The Limitations of the International Legal System

Sovereignty and the legal principles derived from it shape and reinforce international anarchy. World politics is legally dependent on what governments choose to do with one another and the kinds of rules they voluntarily support. Throughout most of modern history, international law as constructed by realists was designed by states to protect the state and so made sovereignty the core principle to ensure states' freedom to act in terms of their perceived national interests.

To liberal theoreticians, putting the state ahead of the global community was a serious flaw that undermined international law's potential effectiveness. Many theorists consider the international legal system institutionally defective due to its dependence on states' willingness to participate. Because formal legal institutions (like those within states) are weak at the global level, critics make

■ **statehood** the legal criteria by which a country and its government become a state in the global community.

■ **diplomatic recognition** the formal legal acceptance of a state's official status as an independent country.

■ **de facto recognition** a government's acknowledgment of the factual existence of another state or government short of full recognition.

■ **de jure recognition** a government's formal, legal recognition of another sovereign government or state.

■ **negotiation** discussion between two or more parties with the goal of resolving perceived differences of interests and the conflicts they cause.

■ **mediation** a conflict-resolution procedure in which a third party offers a nonbinding solution to the disputants.

■ **good offices** the offering by a third party of a location for discussion among disputants.

■ **conciliation** a conflict-resolution procedure in which a third party assists both parties to a dispute but proposes no solution.

■ **arbitration**
a conflict-resolution procedure in which a third party makes a binding decision between disputants through a temporary ruling board created for that ruling.

■ **adjudication**
a conflict-resolution procedure in which a third party makes a binding decision about a dispute in an institutional tribunal.

■ **self-help**
unilateral actions undertaken by individual states without the aid of allies or multinational institutions to defend national interests.

the following points. First, in world politics no legislative body exists that is capable of making binding laws. Rules are made only when states willingly observe or embrace them in the treaties to which they voluntarily subscribe. There is no systematic method of amending or revoking treaties. Article 38 of the Statute of the International Court of Justice (or World Court) affirms this. Generally accepted as the authoritative definition of the "sources of international law," it states that international law derives from (1) custom; (2) international treaties and agreements; (3) national and international court decisions; (4) the writings of legal authorities and specialists; and (5) the "general principles" of law recognized since the Roman Empire as part of "natural law" and "right reason."

Second, in world politics no judicial body exists to authoritatively identify the rules accepted by states, record the substantive precepts reached, interpret when and how the rules apply, and identify violations. Instead, states are responsible for performing these tasks themselves. The World Court does not have the power to perform these functions without states' consent, and the UN cannot speak on judicial matters for the whole global community (even though it has recently defined a new scope for Chapter VII of the UN Charter that claims the right to make quasi-judicial authoritative interpretations of global laws).

Finally, in world politics there is no executive body capable of enforcing the rules. Rule enforcement usually occurs through the **self-help** actions of the victims of a transgression or with the assistance of their allies or other interested parties. No centralized enforcement procedures exist, and compliance is voluntary. The whole system rests, therefore, on states' willingness to abide by the rules to which they consent and on the ability of each to enforce through retaliatory measures the norms of behavior they value.

Consequently, states themselves—not a higher authority—determine what the rules are, when they apply, and how they should be enforced. This raises the question of greatest concern to liberal advocates of world law: When everyone is above the law, is anyone ruled by it? It was precisely this problem that prompted UN Secretary-General Kofi Annan in 1999 to push for abandonment of traditional "state sovereignty" and to substitute a new conceptualization "which would induce states to find greater unity in the pursuit of common goals and values. In the context of many of the challenges facing humanity today," he argues, "the collective interest is the global interest."

Beyond the barriers to legal institutions that sovereignty poses, still other weaknesses reduce confidence in international law. Critics and reformers usually cite these additional alleged deficiencies:

- *International law lacks universality.* An effective legal system must represent the norms shared by those it governs. According to the precept of Roman law, *ubi societas, ibi jus* (where there is society, there is law), shared community values are a minimal precondition for forming a legal system. Yet the contemporary international order is culturally and ideologically pluralistic and lacks consensus on common values, as evidenced by the peculating "clash of civilizations" (Berger and Huntington 2002) and the rejection by terrorists and others of the Western-based international legal order. The simultaneous operation of often incompatible legal traditions throughout the world undermines the creation of a universal, cosmopolitan culture and legal system (Bozeman 1994).

- *International law justifies the competitive pursuit of national advantage without regard to morality or justice.* As in any legal system, in international pol-

Formal institutions for rule enforcement do not guarantee compliance. No legal system can deter all of its members from breaking existing laws. Consequently it is a mistake to expect a legal system to prevent all criminal behavior or to assert that any violation of the law proves the inadequacy of the legal structure. Law is designed to deter crime, but it is unreasonable to expect it to prevent it.

Similarly, we should not view every breakdown of international law as confirming general lawlessness. Conditions of crisis strain all legal systems, and few, when tested severely, can contain all violence. Since 1500, more people have died from civil wars than from wars between sovereign states (Sivard 1991). Today, with street crime in cities worldwide at epidemic proportions and ethnic and religious warfare *within* countries exacting a deadly toll against hundreds of minority groups, states' domestic legal systems are patently failing to prevent killing. Thus, the allegedly "deficient" international legal system performs its primary job—inhibiting interstate violence—more effectively than the supposedly more sophisticated domestic systems. Perhaps, then, the usual criteria by which critics assess legal systems are dubious. Should they be less concerned with structures and institutions and more concerned with performance?

The Legal Control of Warfare

Liberal reformers often complain that law clearly fails in the realm of behavior most resistant to legal control—conflict management. If under international law, as fashioned by realist leaders, states are "legally bound to respect each other's independence and other rights, and yet free to attack each other at will" (Brierly 1944), international law may actually encourage war. The ethical and jurisprudential **just war doctrine** from which the laws of war stem shapes discussions of contemporary public international law (see Wills 2004). Because throughout history changes in international law have followed changes in the moral consensus about the ethics of using armed force in interstate relations, it is important to understand the origins of just war theory and the way it is evolving today, before reviewing contemporary changes in the legal rules of warfare, which have led to the formation of **security regimes**—sets of rules to contain armed conflict.

Just War Doctrine: The Changing Ethics Regarding the Use of Armed Force.
Many people are confused by international law because it both prohibits and justifies the use of force. The confusion derives from the just war tradition in "Christian realism," in which the rules of war are philosophically based on **morals** (principles of behavior) and **ethics** (explanations of why these principles are proper). In the fourth century, St. Augustine questioned the strict view that those who take another's life to defend the state necessarily violate the commandment "Thou shalt not kill." He counseled that "it is the wrong-doing of the opposing party which compels the wise man to wage just wars." The Christian was obligated, he felt, to fight against evil and wickedness. To St. Augustine, the City of Man was inherently sinful, in contrast to the City of God; thus in the secular world it was sometimes permissible to kill—to punish a sin by an aggressive enemy (while still loving the sinner) to achieve a "just peace." This realist logic was extended by Pope Nicholas I, who in 866 proclaimed that any defensive war was just.

■ **just war doctrine**
a doctrine regarding moral considerations under which war may be undertaken and how it should be fought once it begins.

■ **security regimes**
the norms and rules for interaction agreed to by a set of states to increase their security.

■ **morals**
principles clarifying the difference between good and evil and the situations in which they are opposed.

■ **ethics**
the branch of philosophy that deals with the sources, status, and justification of moral rules and how right and wrong behavior and motives should be distinguished.

War and the Birth of Modern International Law Enraged by the inhumane international conditions he witnessed during his lifetime, Dutch reformer Hugo Grotius (1583–1645) wrote *De Jure Belli et Pacis (On the Law of War and Peace)* in 1625 in the midst of the Thirty Years' War. His treatise called on the great powers to resolve their conflicts by judicial procedures rather than on the battlefield and specified the legal principles he felt could encourage cooperation, peace, and more humane treatment of people. Grotius consequently became known as the "founder of international law."

From this perspective evolved the modern just war doctrine as developed by such humanist reformers as Hugo Grotius, who challenged the warring Catholic and Protestant Christian powers in the Thirty Years' War (1618–48) to abide by humane standards of conduct and sought to replace the two "cities," or ethical realms, of Augustine with a single global society under law. For Grotius, a just war was one of self-defense or punishment for inflicted damages: "No other just cause for undertaking war can there be excepting injury received." For war to be moral it must be fought by just means without harm to innocent noncombatants. From this distinction evolved the modern version of just war doctrine, consisting of two categories of argument, *jus ad bellum* (the justice of a war) and *jus in bello* (justice in a war). The former sets the legal criteria by which a leader may wage a war. The latter specifies restraints on the range of permissible tactics to be used in fighting a just war.

These distinctions have been hotly debated since their inception. Drawing the line between murder and just war is a controversial task. Yet just war theory seeks to define these boundaries. According to this legal tradition, some circumstances in which lethal force may be justifiable are recognized under international law, which also provides guidelines for sanctioned coercive methods.

At the core of the just war tradition is the conviction that the taking of human life may be a "lesser evil" when necessary to prevent further life-threatening aggression (Ignatieff 2004b). St. Thomas More contended that the assassination of an evil leader responsible for starting a war was justified if it would prevent the taking of innocent lives. From this premise, a number of other principles follow. The criteria today include ten key ideas:

1. All other means to a morally just solution of conflict must be exhausted before a resort to arms can be justified.
2. War can be just only if employed to defend a stable political order or a morally preferable cause against a real threat or to restore justice after a real injury has been sustained.

War Crimes and the Loss of Global Legitimacy In May 2004 the American hegemon was scandalized when more than one thousand graphic digital photos of U.S. soldiers abusing Iraqis at the Abu Ghraib prison in Baghdad were televised worldwide. Respect for the United States, which had claimed that America invaded Iraq to bring liberty and law, plummeted to the lowest levels in thirty years, according to the U.S. Information Agency. President George W. Bush's statement that he "was sorry for the humiliation suffered by the Iraqi prisoners" and Secretary of Defense Donald Rumsfeld's apology that he felt "terrible . . . they're human beings" did not limit the damage caused by these war-crime violations of the Geneva Convention. The tragic episode showed how even a superpower is subject to the court of world opinion, as America's conduct created a crisis of U.S. legitimacy (R. Kagan 2004).

Those who play the game of international politics by recognized rules receive rewards, whereas states that ignore international law or opportunistically break customary norms pay costs for doing as they please. Other countries will be reluctant to cooperate with them. They must also fear retaliation by those victimized, as well as the loss of prestige. For this reason, only the most ambitious or reckless state is apt to flagrantly disregard accepted standards of conduct.

A primary reason why states value international law and affirm their commitment to it is that they need a common understanding of the "rules of the game." International law is an "institutional device for communicating to the policymakers of various states a consensus on the nature of the international system" (Coplin 1965). Law helps shape expectations, and rules reduce uncertainty and enhance predictability in international affairs. These communication functions serve every member of the global system.

itics what is legal is not necessarily moral. In fact, international law legitimizes the drive for hegemony and contributes to conflict (Lissitzyn 1963). The principle of self-help fails to check states' pursuit of power at others' expense; it is a concession to power. By accepting the unbridled autonomy of sovereign independence, international law follows the realists' "iron law of politics"—that legal obligations must yield to the national interest (Morgenthau 1985).

- *International law is an instrument of the powerful to oppress the weak.* In a voluntary consent system, the rules to which the powerful willingly agree are those that serve their interests. These rules therefore preserve the existing hierarchy (Friedheim 1965). For this reason, some liberal theorists claim that international law has bred the so-called **structural violence** resulting from the hierarchical organization of world politics in which the strong benefit at the expense of the weak (Galtung 1969). Enforcement is left "to the vicissitudes of the distribution of power between the violator of the law and the victim of the violation." Therefore, Hans J. Morgenthau (1985) concedes, "it makes it easy for the strong both to violate the law and to enforce it, and consequently puts the rights of the weak in jeopardy."

- *International law is little more than a justification of existing practices.* When a particular behavior pattern becomes widespread, it becomes legally obligatory; rules *of* behavior become rules *for* behavior (Hoffmann 1971). Eminent legal scholar Hans Kelsen's contention that states ought to behave as they have customarily behaved (see Onuf 1982) and E. Adamson Hoebel's dictum (1961) that "what the most do, others should do" reflect the **positivist legal theory** that when a type of behavior occurs frequently, it becomes legal. In fact, the highly regarded positivist legal theorists stress states' customary practices as the most important source from which laws derive in the absence of formal machinery for creating international rules. When the origins of international law are interpreted in this way, the actions of states shape law, not vice versa.

- *International law's ambiguity reduces law to a policy tool for propaganda purposes.* The vague, elastic wording of international law makes it easy for states to define and interpret almost any action as legitimate. "The problem here," observes Samuel S. Kim (1991), "is the lack of clarity and coherence [that enables] international law [to be] easily stretched, . . . to be a flexible fig leaf or a propaganda instrument." This ambivalence makes it possible for states to exploit international law to get what they can and to justify what they have obtained (Wright 1953).

■ **structural violence** the condition defined by Norwegian peace researcher Johan Galtung as the harm and injury caused by the global system's unregulated structure, which effectively allows strong states to victimize weak states that cannot protect themselves.

■ **positivist legal theory** a theory that stresses states' customs as the most important source of law.

The Relevance of International Law

Although international law has deficiencies, that should not lead to the conclusion that it is irrelevant or useless. States themselves find it useful and expend much effort attempting to shape its evolution. "The reality as demonstrated through their behavior," legal scholar Christopher Joyner (2001) observes, "is that states do accept international law as law and, even more significant, in the vast majority of instances they . . . obey it."

The major reason even the most powerful states adhere to international legal rules is because they recognize that adherence pays benefits that outweigh the costs of expedient rule violation. International reputations are important.

3. A just war must have a reasonable chance of succeeding in these limited goals.
4. A just war must be proclaimed by a legitimate government authority.
5. War must be waged for the purpose of correcting a wrong rather than for malicious revenge.
6. Negotiations to end a war must be in continuous process as long as fighting continues.
7. Particular members of the population, especially noncombatants, must be immune from intentional attack.
8. Only legal and moral means may be employed in prosecuting the war.
9. The damage likely to be incurred from a war may not be disproportionate to the injury suffered.
10. The final goal of the war must be to reestablish peace and justice.

These ethical criteria continue to color thinking about the rules of warfare and the circumstances under which the use of armed force is legally permissible. However, the advent of nuclear and chemical or biological weapons of mass destruction that would violate many of these principles has created a crisis of relevance in just war doctrine. Fuzzy circumstances have materialized with the innovations of the **revolution in military affairs (RMA)**. Because containment and prevention of violence have become the the chief purposes of arms and armies today, leaders and scholars are struggling to revise just war doctrine to deal with the new strategic realities of contemporary weapons and warfare, especially in light of post–9/11 global terrorism (J. Johnson 2005).

As Figure 14.1 shows, since World War I the international community has increasingly rejected the traditional legal right of states to use military force to achieve their foreign policy objectives. Just war theory reflects this continuing quest to place legal constraints on the use of armed force, in order to create a moral consensus about the conditions under which ends justify means, even though "today there is a sharp difference of opinion about the criteria that should be accepted" (von Glahn 1996). These differences became especially evident in the heated debate after the U.S. preemptive invasion on Iraq. Many condemned the U.S. attack as a legal breach of international law (Barber 2003; Boyle 2004), and argued that the U.S. counterterror war in general violated many principles of just war theory (Crawford 2003), making the American hegemon a "rogue nation" (Gareau 2004; Prestowitz 2003) or outlaw state. Others disagree (Elshtain 2003; J. Johnson 2003), making the legality of the use of force a hot issue, as even famous realists (Mearsheimer and Walt 2003) joined liberals in labeling the U.S. attack on Iraq "an unnecessary war" (see Controversy: Was the War in Iraq a Just War?).

The Hague conferences of 1899 and 1907 were early developments in shaping new attitudes toward the start of armed conflict. World War I, however, revealed more than any other event the dangers inherent in the fact that "under general international law, as it stood up to 1914, any state could at any time and for any reason go to war without committing an international delinquency" (Kunz 1960).

Until 9/11, legal injunctions increasingly restricted states' rights to resort to war. The doctrine of **military necessity** still accepts the use of military force as

■ **revolution in military affairs (RMA)**
the goal of seeking to increase military capabilities and effectiveness with new technology that does not rely on weapons of mass destruction, but makes novel ways of fighting possible.

■ **military necessity**
the legal doctrine asserting that violation of the rules of warfare may be excused during periods of extreme emergency.

FIGURE 14.1
The Legal Prohibition against Initiating Wars, 1815–2005

Legal restraints on the historic right of states to start a war *(jus ad bellum)* have fluctuated over time, but have grown steadily since World War I when the carnage prompted the global community to make wars of conquest illegal. Since 9/11 these legal prohibitions of the traditional right of states to initiate war have been questioned in the aftermath of the U.S. efforts to promote **preemption** as a legal right to repel the *potential* aggression of another state or nonstate terrorist network even before its threat of attack is imminent.

SOURCE: Adapted and updated from the Transnational Rules Indicators Project (TRIP), as described in Charles W. Kegley Jr. and Gregory A. Raymond, *When Trust Breaks Down* (Columbia: University of South Carolina Press, 1990).

■ **preemption**
a quick, first-strike attack that seeks in self-defense to defeat an adversary before it can undertake military action or can organize a retaliatory response.

■ **Bush Doctrine**
the declaration underscored in the 2002 *National Security Strategy of the United States* that the Bush administration would act unilaterally to preserve American unipolar predominance and, if necessary, undertake preemptive warfare to prevent as adversary's military action, without the approval of allies.

legal only as a last recourse for defense (Raymond 1999). However, even though the initiation of war is no longer licensed and the intention to make war is still a crime (labeling those who start a war "criminals"), the posture of a hegemonic superpower has the capacity to challenge this norm and change international law, because, as former U.S. diplomat Richard N. Cooper notes, "throughout history dominant states have shaped international law" (see Byers and Nolte 2003). The **Bush Doctrine** defending the legality of preemptive military strikes to prevent possible anticipated wars could make such preemption an accepted legal practice for the first time in three hundred years (Kegley and Raymond 2004).

CONTROVERSY: WAS THE WAR IN IRAQ A JUST WAR?

On February 5, 2003, U.S. Secretary of State Colin Powell delivered a lengthy address to the UN Security Council, charging Iraq with a breach of its disarmament obligations under UN Security Council Resolution 1441. American intelligence agencies, Powell asserted, had evidence that Saddam Hussein's regime possessed weapons of mass destruction. After emphasizing the gravity of the threat these weapons posed, Powell reminded his audience of the Iraqi leader's ruthlessness and warned that he would "stop at nothing until something stops him."

Over the next few weeks, U.S. President George W. Bush and other members of his administration reiterated these accusations. On March 17, Bush claimed that Iraq "continued to possess and conceal some of the most lethal weapons ever devised," and threatened military action if Saddam Hussein did not leave the country within forty-eight hours. When Hussein failed to comply, the United States and its "coalition of the willing" launched a series of precision air strikes and swarming ground attacks that quickly overwhelmed Iraqi defenses.

The Bush administration gave three primary justifications for its war against Iraq: (1) Saddam Hussein had weapons of mass destruction; (2) he had close ties with the Al Qaeda terrorist network; and (3) his removal from power would provide an opportunity to transform Iraq into a democratic regime, which would change the political atmosphere throughout the entire Middle East.

Yet 17 months after the president declared victory on May 1, 2003, from the flight deck of the USS *Abraham Lincoln*, American and coalition troops were locked in fierce fighting with Sunni insurgents in the central Iraqi city of Falluja, and with Shiite militia loyal to the firebrand cleric Muqtada al-Sadr in various southern cities. Though expected to be welcomed with rice and rose petals, the coalition forces came to be seen as occupiers rather than liberators. In a May 2004 poll of Iraqi public opinion sponsored by the U.S. Coalition Provisional Authority, more than 80 percent of those interviewed indicated that they had no confidence in the United States after the Abu Ghraib prison abuse scandal, and wanted Washington to withdraw its troops as soon as possible. Meanwhile, the much-touted Iraqi weapons of mass destruction had not been found, and the National Commission on Terrorist attacks upon the United States investigating the September 11 attacks reported in 2004 that it failed to discover any collaborative relationship between Saddam Hussein and Al Qaeda. In response, the Bush administration continued to insist that weapons of mass destruction might still be found, Saddam Hussein had numerous contacts with Al Qaeda, and that the construction of a democratic regime in Iraq was on track. The war had been "just," and the United States would stay the course.

What do you think? Drawing upon the criteria proposed by just-war theorists (e.g., Wills 2004; J. Johnson 2005), would you characterize the 2003 war against Iraq as a just war? Was it initiated for a just cause and with the right intentions? Was it undertaken as a last resort with the appropriate authorization? Did the good toward which the war aimed outweigh the harm caused by the fighting? Do you agree with Vice President Dick Cheney's claim that the "risks of inaction [were] far greater than the risk of action" (Woodward 2004)?

New Rules for Military Intervention. International law has recently begun to fundamentally revise its traditional prohibition against military intervention in the wake of the recent wave of terrorism by states against their own people. For humanitarian purposes, "the belief that governments have a right, even obligation, to intervene in the affairs of other states seems to have gained great currency" (Blechman 1995), and today international law has defined military intervention as a right and duty to alleviate human suffering, stop genocide and ethnic cleansing, and prevent the repression by states of basic human rights and civil liberties (Feinstein and Slaughter 2004; Finnemore 2003). The result has

FIGURE 14.2
The Changing Status of the Nonintervention Norm in International Law since 1820

Over time, the illegality of intervening in sovereign states has changed, as measured by changes in authoritative international law texts about the prevailing consensus regarding rules for international conduct in each period. Since 1960, international law has adopted an increasingly permissive posture toward this form of coercive diplomacy for a variety of purposes including humanitarian aid, preventing genocide, protecting civil liberties, promoting democracy through "reform interventions," and combating global terrorism.

SOURCE: From Transnational Rules Indicators Project, as originally measured in Kegley, Raymond, and Hermann (1998).

---

been the collapse of the Westphalian principle that what a state does within its own boundaries was its own business; international law has relaxed its restrictive definition of when the global community can legally use military intervention to make it increasingly permissive (see Figure 14.2). The world has made a choice on genocide, declaring organized savagery illegal: "The last fifty years have seen the rise of universal endorsed principles of conduct" defining humanitarian intervention as a legal right to protect **human rights** by punishing acts of genocide and by interpreting intervention as "a spectrum of possible actions ranging from mild diplomatic protest to military invasion, even occupation" (M. Smith 2000).

International law, it appears, develops most rapidly when global problems arise that require collective solutions and legal remedies. The acceptance of intervention arose in response to the atrocities that grew alongside genocide and the need to rewrite the rules to permit interventions in an attempt to contain a growing problem in which international law was traditionally weakest—the control of civil wars in failed states and **terrorism,** for which a global response was needed to prevent their spread:

■ **human rights**
the political rights and civil liberties recognized by the international community as inalienable and valid for individuals in all countries by virtue of their humanness.

■ **terrorism**
criminal acts and threats against a targeted actor for the purpose of arousing fear in order to get the target to accept the terrorists' demands.

Attention to terrorism has led to increased cooperation and spawned new branches of international law.... Terrorism, far from disrupting the legal and organizational structures of the world community, has prompted states to step up their mutual cooperation on criminal matters and devise mechanisms based on common interest, designed both to prevent terrorist groups from attacking innocent civilians or state officials, and, in case such attacks are carried out, to arrest the culprits and bring them to justice. Treaties which demand that states either extradite or prosecute those accused of terrorism committed outside their territory have multiplied and are now copied in fields such as money laundering, corruption, and drug trafficking. (Cassese and Clapham 2001, 411)

The Rules for War's Conduct and the Expansion of Human Rights Legislation. Laws regulating the methods that states may use in war (*jus in bello*) have also grown. These restraints include the principles of discrimination and **noncombatant immunity,** which attempt to protect innocent civilians by restricting military targets to soldiers and supplies. The laws of retaliation specify conditions under which certain practices are legitimate. One category of **coercive power, reprisals** (hostile and illegal acts permitted only if made in proportionate response to a prior hostile and illegal act), stipulates procedures for military occupations, blockades, shows of force, and bombardments. Another category, **retorsion** (hostile but legal retaliatory acts made in response to similar legal acts initiated by other states), provides rules for embargoes, boycotts, import quotas, tariffs, and travel restrictions to redress grievances.

The advent of a new set of legal justifications for military intervention to protect civilians is explained by the fact that noncombatants have become the primary victims in warfare. "World War I was mass-conscription, democratic war with a vengeance, but it still was limited in its direct effect on civilians. The ratio of soldiers to civilians killed between 1914 and 1918 is about 90-to-10. In World War II, the ratio was 50-to-50. In recent years, it has been 90 civilian casualties to every 10 military losses—a reversal of the World War I ratio" (Pfaff 1999, 8).

To prevent the horror of civilian casualties and contain the mass slaughter that increasingly has taken place, the global community has radically revised the rules of international law. For the first time international law holds leaders of countries accountable for war crimes as war criminals. Traditionally, international law prohibited leaders from allowing their militaries to undertake actions in violation of certain principles accepted by the international community, including the protection of innocent noncombatants. However, when violations occurred, there was little that could be done except to condemn such actions. Another weakness was that traditional international law did not hold government leaders to the same standards to which it held soldiers and military officers who committed atrocities against enemy civilians and captured soldiers. Although international law set standards for both individuals and states, leaders were traditionally free from jurisdiction under the doctrine of "sovereign immunity," even when their commands flouted the laws of war. Though they might behave as criminals, leaders were treated with respect because they were the people with whom the global community had to negotiate to settle conflicts.

While many people and states still commit war crimes without facing punishment, the resumption of war crime tribunals in 1993 signaled to would-be

■ **noncombatant immunity**
the legal principle that military force should not be used against innocent civilians.

■ **coercive power**
the use of threats and punishment to force changes in the target.

■ **reprisals**
the international legal practice of resorting to military force short of war in retaliation for losses suffered from prior illegal military actions.

■ **retorsion**
hostile but legal retaliatory acts.

544 • PART IV: MANAGING GLOBAL CONFLICT

UGANDA
Idi Amin

IRAQ
Saddam Hussein

HAITI
Jean-Claude Duvallier

UNITED STATES
George Bush
(Persian Gulf War)

BRITAIN
Margaret Thatcher
(Falklands/
Malvinas War)

YUGOSLAVIA
Slobodan Milosevic
(Convicted)

Identifying War Criminals In 1994, the UN Security Council got serious about prosecuting war criminals and created two special crimes tribunals in The Hague. Swiss criminal lawyer Carla del Ponte (left) was appointed in September 1999 as chief prosecutor for the UN's war crimes tribunals for Yugoslavia and Rwanda, in which eighty prisoners were tried. The principle that national leaders cannot get away with mass murder and torture was established after World War II at the Nuremberg and Tokyo war crimes trials, but the norm was not reinforced until the UN responded in 1999 to the genocide and state terrorism in Bosnia, Rwanda, and Tanzania by setting up special-purpose war crimes tribunals. The performance of these tribunals is believed critical to the credibility of the newly created International Criminal Court.

The question about precisely what behavior is proscribed for a head of state is creating a new controversy. International law still is unclear about the limits. At right are some past heads of state who potentially, according to *Time* (December 14, 1998, 42), could be called before courts to defend their use of arms, either against their own people or in foreign wars. In 2005 Slobodan Milosevic, the president of the former Yugoslavia, began facing a prolonged trial (see Lesser 2004) after his 2002 conviction as a criminal for starting three ethnic-cleansing wars. The management of this trial will heavily shape the future power of the International Criminal Court, which the United States vehemently opposed in an April 2002 reversal for fear that U.S. leaders, diplomats, and soldiers could be brought before the court. Also in 2005, the trial of the captured Saddam Hussein began in Iraq.

■ **International Criminal Court (ICC)**
a court established by the United Nations for indicting and administering justice to people committing war crimes.

■ **permanent world criminal court**
a standing international court to judge crimes against victimized groups, such as genocide against ethnic or religious groups.

perpetrators the global community's intolerance for these atrocities. In 1999, the prosecutor's office of the UN's **International Criminal Court (ICC)** indicted seventy-seven people and arrested seven for crimes in Bosnia. Building on this step, a **permanent world criminal court** was created in The Hague to try leaders for the most terrible of mass crimes—especially acts of genocide such as those perpetrated by terrorists. A goal the UN had pursued for half a century became a reality: the world community now has an international court with teeth, through a treaty signed by 191 states and ratified by 64 (and all major states except China, Iran, and the United States, which in May 2002 "unsigned" the ICC agreement by informing the UN that the United States was pulling out, to the dismay of U.S. allies). Moreover, heads of state are now held accountable for war crimes against humanity, removing the protection they had received under traditional international law. Ever since The Hague tribunal's 1997 founding statute, a head of state can be charged with war crimes committed at any time the leader was in office; even a sitting head of state can now be indicted for past war crimes. In fact, Slobodan Milosevic of Yugoslavia and President General Augusto Pinochet of Chile were indicted in 1999 (and in 2005 Saddam Hussein began facing trial in Iraqi courts under the same principles). The criminalization of rulers' **state-sponsored terrorism** raises the legal restraints on the initiation and conduct of war to an all-time high, widening the scope of acts now classified as **war crimes.**

Law's Contribution to Peace. Cynics who contend that international law is irrelevant to the control of war overlook several dimensions of law's character.

- International law is not intended to prevent all warfare. Aggressive war is illegal, but defensive war is not. It is a mistake, therefore, to claim that international law has broken down whenever war breaks out.
- Instead of doing away with war, international law preserves it as a sanction against breaking rules. Thus war is a device of last resort to punish aggressors and thereby maintain the system's legal framework.
- International law is an institutional substitute for war. Legal procedures exist to resolve conflicts before they erupt into open hostilities. Although they cannot prevent war, they sometimes make recourse to violence unnecessary by resolving disputes that might otherwise escalate to war.

The demonstrable capacity of pacific methods to reduce the frequency of war does not mean that international adjudicative machinery is well developed or functionally effective. Nowhere is this more evident than with the International Court of Justice (ICJ), known as the World Court, which was created after World War II as the highest judicial body on earth—the only international court with universal scope and general jurisdiction. The court is highly regarded in principle; 191 states are party to the statute of the court, and 64 have made declarations that they accept the court's compulsory jurisdiction. (This number includes the EU members, but not the United States.) In addition, more than three hundred bilateral or multilateral treaties provide for the World Court to have jurisdiction in the resolution of disputes arising from their application for a legal interpretation.

A weakness in the World Court is that it can make rulings only on disputes freely submitted by states exercising their sovereign rights; the court cannot rule on cases that states do not bring to it. Their sovereignty is protected, and many states have traditionally been hesitant to use the court because ICJ decisions are final—there is no opportunity to appeal. This is why between 1946 and 1991 states permitted the court to hear only 64 cases. However, the workload has expanded, as the ICJ reports: "whereas in the 1970s the court had only one or two cases in its docket at any one time, between 1990 and 1997 this number varied between nine and 13 [and] since then the number of cases has exceeded 20. As of July 2004, it stood at 25."

World order will depend to a considerable extent on the future uses to which states put international law. Alleged shortcomings of international law do not lie with the laws but with their creators—states and their continuing realpolitik

■ **state-sponsored terrorism**
formal assistance, training, and arming of foreign terrorists by a state in order to achieve foreign policy and/or domestic goals.

■ **war crimes**
acts performed during war that the international community defines as crimes against humanity, including atrocities committed against an enemy's prisoners of war, civilians, or the state's own minority population.

Saddam Hussein in Court The war crimes trial of Saddam Hussein in an Iraqi tribunal and other cases will similarly determine the status and strength of global legal institutions. In July 2004 a defiant and combative Saddam Hussein rebutted the Iraqi special court for trying him, claiming he was still Iraq's president and that the trial was an illegal political "theater" designed for President George W. Bush's reelection campaign. In December 2004, Saddam's lawyers claimed he had legal "immunity" because he was the legitimate Iraqi president.

dedication to preserving sovereignty as a legal right in order to protect states' independence and autonomy.

Crucial in determining the role that international law will play will be which trend shall prevail—whether states choose to strengthen international law or insist on continuing to resist the compulsory jurisdiction to the World Court and other international tribunals. One path is displayed by the United States, which in 2002 pledged it would continue to act in accordance to its so-called Connally amendment that reserves the U.S. right to determine which cases it will permit the World Court to hear. The U.S. preference is to try cases in U.S. courts and to let others use U.S. courts as global arbiters of global rights and wrongs. The latter use of American courts by foreigners to sue for human rights violations stems from the 1789 Alien Tort Claims Act written to fight piracy, and enables victims of torture, genocide, slavery, and war crimes throughout the world to try to get justice in court. The trend toward use of U.S. courts to conduct criminal prosecutions of foreign terrorists captured abroad is accelerating as the United States is transforming itself from "global policeman" to "global attorney" (Glaberson 2001; Slaughter 2004a). An example of this occurred in 2001 when five Chinese civilians sued Chinese Prime Minister Li Pong in an American court for his role in the 1989 crackdown in Beijing's Tiananmen Square, which killed hundreds of civilians. In July 2004 the U.S. Supreme Court upheld this old law by allowing victims of the Abu Ghraib prison abuses to sue the prison's private

U.S. contractors (*International Herald Journal,* July 3, 2004, A14). This ruling follows the tenet of liberal theory advanced by U.S. President Eisenhower, who counseled that it "is better to lose a point now and then in an international tribunal and gain a world in which everyone lives at peace under the rule of law." That approach has been accepted at the regional level, where the EU's twenty-five members have given the European Court of Human Rights the power to exercise authoritative jurisdiction, and in South America, where the Inter-American Court on Human Rights hears cases.

The global community could, in principle, follow Europe's lead and strengthen international law's capacity. Still, many barriers remain to creating, as John F. Kennedy expressed liberal theory's hope, "a new world of law, where the strong are just and the weak secure and the peace preserved." We next consider the role of international organizations in maintaining such a world peace.

INTERNATIONAL ORGANIZATIONS AND WORLD ORDER

Liberal theorists recommend the creation of international organizations as a second institutional path to peace. To understand this approach, we must also understand its theoretical underpinnings. The expectations about and performance of the UN exemplify those theoretical premises.

The United Nations and the Preservation of Peace

The UN's purposes are multiple; but, as Article I of the UN Charter signals, peace is primary:

- maintain international peace and security
- develop friendly relations among nations based on respect for the principle of equal rights and self-determination of peoples
- achieve international **cooperation** in solving international problems of an economic, social, cultural, or humanitarian character and in promoting and encouraging respect for human rights and for fundamental freedoms for all
- function as a center for harmonizing the actions of nations in the attainment of these common ends

■ **cooperation**
actions that maximize the collective well-being of the parties to the interaction

The UN Charter states that all members are required to "settle their international disputes by peaceful means." That said, on many occasions UN members have *not* honored that promise—taking up arms to resolve their differences on the battlefield. In addition, many members have militarily intervened in nonmembers' internal wars, and especially in the past two decades the UN has faced the difficult choice of what to do with the rampant outbreak of civil wars, ethnic or religious warfare, and terrorism in **failed states** (Krasner 2004). "Everywhere we work," lamented Secretary-General Boutros-Ghali in 1995, "we are struggling against the culture of death."

To evaluate the prospects for meeting the chronic challenge of controlling militarized conflict, it is important to understand how states have organized the UN to carry out the missions it has asked it to perform. Recall from Chapter 6 that the UN Charter divided authority and decision power into three separate or-

■ **failed states**
countries whose governments have so mismanaged policy that they have lost the loyalty of their citizens and face anarchy and revolution.

gans: The Security Council of fifteen members, the General Assembly of representatives of all 191 member states, and the Secretariat administrative staff under the secretary-general. This unwieldy structure enshrined the great powers on the Security Council with final authority over peacekeeping decisions, although the General Assembly attempted to expand its jurisdiction in matters of security when the Security Council was paralyzed by the great powers' use of vetoes during the Cold War. The end of the Cold War in 1991 allowed the UN to step up to the plate and begin to assume a greater role in attempting to police the cascade of civil wars that erupted. However, budgetary constraints have reduced the UN's capacity to play a more active security role.

There remains a huge gap between the UN's mandate to keep the peace and the resources that member states have provided as means to fulfill those objectives. Two basic approaches continue to be pursued. The first seeks to address the underlying social and economic roots of armed conflict (recall Chapter 11) by attempting to alleviate the human suffering that often causes aggression and terrorism. These efforts are carried out through the UN's "specialized agencies," such as the World Health Organization (WHO), the Food and Agriculture Organization (FAO), the International Labour Organization (ILO), the UN Educational Scientific and Cultural Organization (UNESCO), and many others. In addition, various UN programs operate to assist these efforts in the realm of **low politics,** such as the UN Development Programme (UNDP), the UN Children's Emergency Fund (UNICEF), the UN Conference on Trade and Development (UNCTAD), the World Food Programme (WFP), and many others. The second approach is more ambitious: taking on the task of directly bringing fighting under control, resolving armed conflicts when they arise, and maintaining the peace when the fighting stops. Let us look more closely at the UN's pursuit of that central goal.

Collective Security. **Collective security** is often viewed as a liberal alternative to the competitive balanced alliances that realists recommend. In a balance-of-power system, it is assumed that each state, acting in its own self-interest through self-help for its individual protection, will form coalitions offsetting others and that the resulting equilibrium will prevent war. In contrast, collective security asks each state to share responsibility for all other states' security. It "assumes that every nation perceives every challenge to the international order in the same way, and is prepared to run the same risks to preserve it" (Kissinger 1992). All states are to take joint action against any transgressor, and all are to act in concert. This presumes that the superior power of the entire community will deter those contemplating aggression or, failing this, that collective action will defeat any violator of the peace.

Pointing to the League of Nations' inability to put collective security into practice, realist critics attacked what they regarded as the illusory expectations on which liberal proponents had built the model. The league's failures stemmed from the U.S. refusal to join the organization; the other great powers' fear that the league's collective strength might be used against them; disagreement over objectively defining an instance of aggression in which all concurred; states' pervasive dread of inequities in sharing the risks and costs of mounting an organized response to aggression; and states' tendency to voice approval of the value of general peace but unwillingness to organize resistance except when their own security was threatened. In the final analysis, the theory's central fallacy was that

■ **low politics**
the category of global issues related to the economic, social, demographic, and environmental aspects of relations between governments and people.

■ **collective security**
a security regime agreed to by the great powers setting rules for keeping peace, guided by the principle that an act of aggression by any state will be met by a collective response from the rest.

it expected a state to be as anxious to see others protected as it was to protect itself. That assumption did not prove true in the period between World War I and World War II. As a result, the League of Nations never became a valid collective security system.

The architects of the UN were painfully aware of the league's disappointing experience. While they voiced support for collective security, their design restored the **balance of power** to maintain peace. The 1945 UN Charter permitted any of the Security Council's five permanent members (the United States, the Soviet Union, Great Britain, France, and China) to veto and thereby block any proposed enforcement action that any of them disapproved. Because the Security Council could act in concert only when the permanent members fully agreed, the UN Charter was a concession to states' sovereign freedom:

> In the final analysis, the San Francisco Conference must be described as having repudiated the doctrine of collective security as the foundation for a general, universally applicable system for the management of power in international relations. The doctrine was given ideological lip service, and a scheme was contrived for making it effective in cases of relatively minor importance. But the new organization reflected the conviction that the concept of collective security had no realistic relevance to the problems posed by conflict among the major powers. (Claude 1962, 164–65)

To further enhance the great powers' authority relative to the UN, the charter severely restricted the capacity of the General Assembly to mount collective action. The charter authorized it only to initiate studies of conflict situations, bring perceived hostilities to the attention of the Security Council, and make recommendations for initiatives to keep the peace. Moreover, it restricted the role of the secretary-general to that of chief administrative officer. Article 99 confined the secretary-general, and the working staff of the Secretariat created to aid that person, to alerting the Security Council to peace-threatening situations and to providing administrative support for the operations that the Security Council authorized.

Although the UN's structure compromises the organization's security mission, it is still much more than a mere debating society. It is also more than an arena for power politics. During the Cold War the UN fell short of many of the ideals its more ambitious founders envisioned, principally because its two most powerful members in the Security Council, the United States and the Soviet Union, did not cooperate. More than 230 Security Council vetoes were cast, stopping action of any type on about one-third of the UN's resolutions. In this period, UN action was only taken when a conflict was outside the East-West rivalry and did not involve either superpower, with decolonization disputes involving relatively small and weak countries receiving most of the UN's attention. Between 1945 and 1984 the UN attempted to mediate only 40 percent of the 319 interstate conflicts that erupted (Holsti 1988, 423). To put it mildly, the UN's peacemaking achievements during the Cold War were at best modest.

Like any adaptive institution, the UN found other ways to overcome the compromising legal restrictions and lack of great-power cooperation that inhibited its capacity to preserve world order. For example, in contrast to peace enforcement as in the Korean War, the UN undertook a new approach, termed **peacekeeping,** that aimed at separating enemies. The UN Emergency Force (UNEF), authorized in 1956 by the Uniting for Peace Resolution in the General

■ **balance of power**
the theory that peace and stability are most likely to be maintained when threatened states form a military coalition and thereby redistribute power to prevent any single great-power hegemon or bloc from dominating the global system.

■ **peacekeeping**
the efforts by third parties such as the UN to intervene in civil wars and/or interstate wars or to prevent hostilities between potential belligerents from escalating, so that by acting as a buffer a negotiated settlement of the dispute can be reached.

International Peacekeepers to the Rescue? In response to desperate pleas for help, the UN has selectively authorized peacekeeping forces to intervene. In September 1999, Australian soldiers marched off to lead the UN-authorized peacekeeping force in East Timor, where after voting four to one for independence from Indonesia, the people in East Timor were killed and raped in an act of state-sponsored terrorism. This mission restored a fragile order, and democracy was born.

- **preventive diplomacy**
diplomatic actions taken in advance of a predictable crisis to prevent or limit violence.

- **peacemaking**
the process of diplomacy, mediation, negotiation, or other forms of peaceful settlement that arranges an end to a dispute and resolves the issues that led to conflict.

- **peace building**
postconflict actions, predominantly diplomatic and economic, that strengthen and rebuild governmental infrastructure and institutions in order to avoid renewed recourse to armed conflict.

- **peace operations**
a general category encompassing both peacekeeping and peace enforcement operations undertaken to establish and maintain peace between disputants.

- **peace enforcement**
application of military force, or the threat of its use, normally pursuant to international authorization, to compel compliance with resolutions or sanctions designed to maintain or restore peace and order.

Assembly in response to the Suez crisis, was the first of many other peacekeeping operations. In addition, in 1960 Secretary-General Dag Hammarskjold sought to manage security through what he termed **preventive diplomacy** by attempting to resolve conflicts before they reached the crisis stage, in contrast to ending wars once they erupted. Likewise, in 1989 Secretary-General Javier Perez de Cuellar, frustrated with the superpowers' prevention of the UN to "play as effective and decisive a role as the charter certainly envisaged for it," pursued what was called **peacemaking** initiatives designed to obtain a truce to end the fighting so that the UN Security Council could then establish operations to keep the peace. UN Secretary-General Kofi Annan has since concentrated the UN's efforts on **peace building** by creating the conditions that make renewed war unlikely, while at the same time working on peace making (ending fighting already under way) and managing the UN's **peace operations** to police those conflicts where the threat of renewed fighting between enemies is high. These endeavors have emphasized **peace enforcement** operations, relying on UN forces trained and equipped to use military force if necessary without the prior consent of the disputants.

For more than four decades, the UN was a victim of superpower rivalry. However, the end of the Cold War removed many of the impediments to the UN's ability to lead in preserving peace. For example, the Security Council swung into action to authorize military coercion to force Iraq to withdraw from Kuwait, which it had invaded. This successful collective security initiative jump started

Superclerk to the World Running the United Nations as secretary-general is perhaps the most challenging job in the world. In 1997, that position changed hands, as Kofi Annan of Ghana (at right) replaced Boutros Boutros-Ghali. Annan undertook massive organizational reforms with reduced finances to increase the UN's efficiency, such as engineering the appointment of Louise Frechette (at left) as the UN's first deputy secretary-general. The popular Annan was elected to a second five-year term in 2002, but was personally criticized for the UN's "Oil-for-Food" scandal in which Saddam Hussein stole billions. However, the United States did not support calls for Annan's resignation. The secretary-general's 2004 blue-ribbon panel proposed 101 reforms for the UN, including increasing the Security Council from 15 to 24 states, with the possibility of expanding the number of veto-wielding countries to 11 to better reflect today's balance of power.

optimism for and use of the UN for peacekeeping leadership, and after 1990 the UN launched almost five times as many peacekeeping missions as it had in its previous forty years of its existence. On average, since 1990, it has managed fifteen operations each year (see Map 14.1).

Supporters of the UN as a peacekeeping organization still encounter resistance. The UN seems to have many critics because many countries make demands on the organization that cannot be met with existing resources and that other countries oppose. Countries call on the UN in times of need, but attack it when it fails to comply with the requests made. For example, in October 2002, U.S. President George W. Bush warned the UN to act quickly on Iraq or "face irrelevance." However, at the time, Russian, Chinese, and French opposition to the U.S. and British determination to use force against Iraq stiffened, and did not ease for another seven weeks until, after much diplomatic squabbling and rising U.S. criticism of the entire UN, the Security Council issued an **ultimatum** to Iraq that it prove it did not have weapons of mass destruction or face "serious consequences." (U.S. inspectors after the invasion were never able to find those weapons.)

The office of the secretary-general has undertaken many big organizational reforms to make the UN more efficient and to fulfill its humanitarian and security mandate, especially through intervention to stop horrific atrocities wherever and whenever they occur. However, critics voice concerns that the UN is inclined to practice **selective engagement** in sending peacekeeping forces primarily to those trouble spots where the Security Council's great powers have economic interest in securing access to resources such as oil and other products. There is

■ **ultimatum**
in strategic bargaining, a threat to a target that it comply with a demand or face punishment.

■ **selective engagement**
a state's or an IGO's choosing to intervene militarily in some situations but declining to do so in others.

MAP 14.1
UN Peace Missions since 1948

In its first forty years the UN undertook a mere thirteen peacekeeping operations. But since 1986 the UN has been much more active, sending Blue Helmet peacekeepers to forty-eight additional flash points throughout the globe. Since 1989, on average, the UN has had no less than sixteen operations under way each year (see figure on right) and in 2005 about half of the missions had been in operation for a least a decade. Budget constraints for peacekeeping operations have reduced the UN's capacity to fulfill the goals of its pathbreaking December 2004 report, *A More Secure World: Our Shared Responsibility*. "A country's level of democracy accounts for why and how much countries contribute to [UN peace operations] when competing with a host of alternative explanations derived from a realist and liberal perspective" (Lebovic 2004).

SOURCE: Based on data from the United Nations Department of Public Information.

```
Number of UN Peacekeeping Operations
```

Year	Operations
1989	10
1990	8
1991	11
1992	13
1993	17
1994	17
1995	17
1996	16
1997	15
1998	17
1999	17
2000	15
2001	15
2002	17
2003	16
2004	16
2005	14

"some evidence of a regional bias in the UN's selection of missions" but the UN nonetheless has attempted to "balance between the dictates of power and concerns of principle [because] one of the best predictors of UN interventions is the number of deaths in a conflict [which] speaks well of the UN's mission to address costly human suffering. On the other hand, the UN has not been evenhanded in how it responds to deaths. The UN acts more swiftly when the deaths occur in Europe than in Africa, and it acts more swiftly in Africa than in Asia" (Gilligan and Stedman 2003). Perhaps this peacekeeping focus is a product of limited financial restraints as much as it is the priorities of the Security Council's great powers. Peacekeeping expenditures have fallen from $3.4 billion in 1994 to $2.8 billion at the start of 2005, and in the same span total peacekeeping personnel fell from 78,000 in 1994 to 55,000 in 2005. UN peacekeeping operations remain understaffed, underfunded, and overwhelmed in responding to the surge of civil wars and failed states where "Blue Helmet" participation is needed. "The business of peacekeeping has been getting a lot tougher. Rich nations are putting their muscle where their immediate interests lie, leaving the job of patrolling in hardscrabble territory to their less financially capable UN colleagues" (Neack 2004). The UN is not empowered to achieve the high purposes for which it was created, and the aim of global collective security for all humanity cannot be met with inadequate capabilities. This weakness accounts for the UN's growing reliance on regional organizations and multiparty state alliances to step in the breach in situations where UN forces have not been given the support necessary to provide assistance.

The global **public goods** of peace, prosperity, sustainable development, and good governance cannot be achieved by any single country acting on its own. For the UN to succeed, the world community must match the demands made on it with the means given to it. The organization has to strike a balance between realism and idealism. The United Nations will be incapacitated if it alienates its most important members, in particular the United States. As John Bolton, the U.S. Secretary of State for Arms Control and International Security in the second Bush administration, wrote in 2001,

■ **public goods**
shared values from which everyone who has access to them benefits, such as safe drinking water and international peace, even if not everyone contributes to their creation or preservation.

> Only the United States can lead the United Nations effectively. . . . The UN neither has, nor should have, the capability for independent action. It follows that when [the U.S. hegemon entrusts] it with responsibility for an independent undertaking, the United States must understand that it alone can lead the effort to a successful conclusion. . . .
>
> In fact, this observation should lead logically to the question; what exactly is the United Nations? In practical terms, it is simply an agglomeration of member states, served (at least in theory) by a staff that has no power or autonomy—and no independent democratic or other political legitimacy—to act except as directed by the member governments. Thus understood, there really is no "United Nations;" there is no "there" there, only the shifting reflections of the several views of the members. The UN has no more legitimacy or permanence than those members, and especially the largest, most important members, choose to give it.

The UN must reflect the current realities of U.S. economic military predominance. However this poses a dilemma, because the organization also risks losing all credibility if it compromises core values. "Opponents of the United Nations, who have long argued that it should not act as a world government, will object. But, while less than perfect, the United Nations is the only global mechanism for effective collaboration in circumstances where states are reluctant or ill-placed to act alone" (DeVecchi and Helton 1999). The reasons underlying this assessment are summarized by the view expressed by a seasoned UN official, Brian Urquhart (1994), that,

> In the great uncertainties and disorders that lie ahead, the United Nations, for all its shortcomings, will be called on again and again, because there is no other global institution, because there is a severe limit to what even the strongest powers wish to take on themselves. . . . Either the UN is vital to a more stable and equitable world and should be given the means to do its job, or peoples and governments should be encouraged to look elsewhere. But is there really an alternative?

Actually, there is a conspicuous alternative. The great powers' reluctance to equip the UN to contain civil wars lends credence to the 1995 prophecy of Karel Kovanda (the Czech Republic's UN ambassador) that the "important issues are going to be taken care of by regional organizations . . . with the United Nations giving its blessings."

Regional Security Organizations and Conflict Management

If the UN reflects the lack of shared values and common purpose characteristic of a global community, perhaps regional organizations, whose members already share some interests and cultural traditions, offer better prospects. The kinds of wars raging today do not lend themselves to control by a worldwide body, because these conflicts are now almost entirely civil wars. The UN was designed to manage only international wars *between* states; it was not organized or legally authorized to intervene in internal battles *within* sovereign borders. This, however, is not the case for regional institutions; regional IGOs see their security interests vitally affected by armed conflicts within countries in their area or adjacent to it, and historically have shown the determination and discipline to police bitter civil conflicts "in their backyards." Hence, regional security organizations can be expected to play an increasingly larger role in the future security affairs of their regions.

The North Atlantic Treaty Organization (NATO) is the best-known regional security organization. Others include the Organization for Security and Cooperation in Europe (OSCE), the ANZUS pact (Australia, New Zealand, and the United States), and the Southeast Asia Treaty Organization (SEATO). Regional organizations with somewhat broader political mandates beyond defense include the Organization of American States (OAS), the League of Arab States, the Organization of African Unity (OAU), the Nordic Council, the Association of Southeast Asian Nations (ASEAN), and the Gulf Cooperation Council.

Although Article 51 of the UN Charter encourages the creation of regional organizations for collective self-defense, it would be misleading to describe NATO and the other regional organizations as a substitute collective security instrument for the UN. They are not. More accurately, **regional collective defense** regimes are designed to deter a potential common threat to the region's peace, one typically identified in advance.

Many of today's regional security organizations face the challenge of preserving consensus and solidarity without a clearly identifiable external enemy or common threat. Cohesion is hard to maintain in the absence of a clear sense of the alliance's mission. Consider NATO. The ambiguous European security setting is now marked by numerous ethnic and religious conflicts for which NATO was not originally designed to deal. Its original charter envisioned only one purpose—mutual self protection from external attack; it never defined policing civil wars as a goal. Consequently, until 1995, when NATO took charge of all military operations in Bosnia-Herzegovina from the UN, it was uncertain whether the alliance could adapt to a broadened purpose. Since that intervention, NATO *has* redefined itself, and in March 1999 it performed the same interventionary peacemaking assignment in Kosovo. Today, NATO is an enlarged alliance, with seven new members joining in 2002 (see Map 13.2, p. 521), and has transformed itself to become both a *military* alliance for security between states and within them and for containing the spread of global terrorism, as well as a *political* alliance for encouraging the spread of democracy. That said, the primary purpose remains putting NATO's twenty-six members under a security umbrella, with the promise that an attack on one would be considered an attack on all. This **collective security** clause was invoked for the first time after 9/11 when the Al Qaeda terrorist network attacked the United States. This reaffirmed NATO's commitment to the protection of its members' security. And in 2004 it expanded that mandate modestly by agreeing to help train Iraq's security forces after the United States restored sovereignty to an appointed Iraqi government, while 150,000 U.S. troops remained as occupation forces fighting to stabilize the chronic terrorism that took lives daily.

Likewise, in other regional mutual security systems, controversies among the coalition partners about the identity of "the enemy" and the conditions warranting intervention raise doubts about their capacity to engineer collective defense projects. These doubts are fueled by the history of regional organizations in peacemaking efforts. Between 1945 and 1984, of 291 high-intensity armed conflicts involving military units, less than one-fourth, or only 68, were handled by regional organizations (K. Holsti 1992, 353). This record suggests that although regional collective defense institutions were, to some extent, created to

■ **regional collective defense**
organizations and military alliances within a specific region created to preserve peace and security for their members collectively.

■ **collective security**
a security regime created by a group of allied states that sets rules for keeping peace, guided by the principle that an act of aggression against any member will be met by a collective response from the rest.

overcome the deficiencies of global institutions, they may not be able to perform that task any better than global institutions.

The overlapping memberships in Europe's major international organizations illustrate the obstacles to the maintenance of peace through regional organizations, because in that region their institutional development has been most rapid. Since World War II, Europe has built, in a series of steps, an increasing number of economic, political, and military organizations encompassing more and more countries throughout an enlarged geographic network of institutions. The overlapping architecture includes OSCE, NATO, EAPC, the Council of Europe, and the EU defense organizations. As Anne-Else Holjberg in NATO's Political Affairs Division complained "there is still a certain degree of rivalry between [these] different organizations," and the multilayered structure has made collective decision making difficult. The Kosovo, Iraq, and Ukraine crises exemplify the barriers to collective security that regional organizations face. These cases and others suggest that regional organizations have the capacity to bring conflict under control only when their members are in agreement. However, they also indicate that they often lack the consensus and political will to control controversial conflicts and require pressure from world public opinion, mobilized in global organizations such as the UN, to take action.

In the twenty-first century, regional collective defense institutions, assisted by unilateral peacekeeping forces from particular interested states, and now supported by mercenaries that regional organizations and states hire or "outsource" from private multinational corporations (Isenberg 2001; Neack 2004), may help to build a global security community in which the expectation of peace exceeds the expectation of war. The processes through which such transformations might occur are addressed by the functional and neofunctional approaches to peace within the constructed liberal paradigm.

POLITICAL INTEGRATION: THE FUNCTIONAL AND NEOFUNCTIONAL PATHS TO PEACE

■ **political integration** the processes and activities by which the populations of two or more states transfer their loyalties to a merged political and economic unit.

Political integration refers to either the process or the product of efforts to build new political communities and supranational institutions that transcend the state. Their purposes are to remove states' incentives for war and to engineer reform programs to transform international institutions from instruments of states to structures *over* them.

World Federalism: A Single Global Government

■ **world federalism** a reform movement proposing as a path to peace combining two or more previously independent countries to form single unified federal states, with the ultimate goal of creating federal institutions for global governance.

Integration in its various forms does not necessarily make a frontal attack on the state by proposing to replace it with some central authority. That radical remedy is represented by **world federalism,** a school of thought advocating the merger of previously sovereign states into a single integrated federal union. Federalists follow the liberal conviction of Albert Einstein "that there is no salvation for civilization, or even the human race, other than the creation of a world government."

The Interventionist Road to Peace? The chaos and killing in failed states provoke widespread concern, but until recently many states and IGOs have been reluctant to intervene militarily to keep the peace in civil wars outside their spheres of influence. NATO's 1999 humanitarian intervention in Kosovo is an exception—the first time the alliance used force "out of area" to prevent a campaign of state-sponsored terror against an ethnic minority. Here a British tank heading to the Kosovo border in 1999 is greeted by jubilant Islamic Albanian Kosovars thankful that NATO's KFOR (Kosovo Force) peacekeepers appeared on the scene to rescue them. The mission was supported by three hundred Eurocorps soldiers provided by the EU, made up largely of French and German officers, in what became the first mission of the EU's new Rapid Reaction Force of sixty thousand soldiers. NATO created its own rapid-reaction force "to fight anywhere in the world." Humanitarian military interventions could become frequent now that international law has relaxed traditional prohibitions against external interference in the internal affairs of an established state.

■ **absolute gains**
conditions in which all participants in exchanges become better off.

■ **relative gains**
conditions in which some participants in interactions benefit more than others.

■ **nationalism**
the feeling of loyalty to a particular state and/or nationality or ethnic group, to the exclusion of attachment to other states, universal religious values, or the collective welfare of all people.

Federalists reason that if people value an **absolute gain** such as humanity's survival more highly than **relative gains** such as an individual state's national advantage over its rivals, they will willingly transfer their loyalty to a supranational authority to dismantle the anarchical system of competitive territorial states that produces war. "World government," they believe, "is not only possible, it is inevitable," because it appeals to the patriotism of people who "love their national heritages so deeply that they wish to preserve them in safety for the common good" (Ferencz and Keyes 1991).

It is not surprising that ardent adherents to **nationalism** have vehemently attacked the revolutionary federalist "top-down" peace plan. Because it seeks to subvert the system of sovereign states, federalism threatens many entrenched interests. More abstractly, other critics reject the world federalists' proposition that governments are bad but people are good, wise, and enlightened (see Claude 1971). Likewise, they question the assumption that the need for changes will automatically lead to global institutional innovation.

Many of the globe's more than 31,000 **nongovernmental organizations (NGOs)** are sympathetic to peace plans that seek to reduce the capability of states to make wars. Some accept the bold view of NGOs like United World Federalists that still actively promote creation of a world government. Nevertheless, aversion to war and raised consciousness of its dangers have not mobilized widespread grassroots enthusiasm for this radical step. Other approaches to reforming the world political system have attracted more adherents.

Functionalism

Classical functionalism is a rival but complementary reform movement associated with liberalism. In contrast to federalism, **functionalism** is not directed toward creating a federal institution for global governance. Rather, it seeks to build "peace by pieces" through transnational organizations that emphasize the "sharing of sovereignty" instead of its surrender. Functionalism advocates a "bottom-up" evolutionary strategy for building cooperative ties and unity among states.

According to functionalists, technical experts, talking to one another throughout the world in their area of specialization as members of **epistemic communities,** rather than professional diplomats, are the best agents for building collaborative links across national borders. They see diplomats as being overly protective of their country's national interests at the expense of collective human interests. Rather than addressing the immediate sources of national insecurity, the functionalists' peace plan calls for transnational cooperation in technical (primarily social and economic) areas as a first step. Habits of cooperation learned in one technical area (such as medicine), they assume, will "spill over" into others—especially if the experience is mutually beneficial and demonstrates the potential advantages of cooperation in other areas (such as transportation and telecommunication).

To enhance the probability that cooperative endeavors will prove rewarding, the functionalist plan recommends that less-difficult tasks be tackled first. It assumes that successful mastering of one problem will encourage attacking other problems collaboratively. If the process continues unabated, the bonds among countries will multiply, because no state government would dare oppose a web of functional organizations that provide such clear-cut benefits to its citizens. Thus, "the mission of functionalism is to make peace possible by organizing particular layers of human social life in accordance with their particular requirements, breaking down the artificialities of the zoning arrangements associated with the principle of sovereignty" (Claude 1971). Its intellectual parent, David Mitrany (1966), argued in *A Working Peace System* (first published in 1943) that functionalism is based on self-interest.

> Functionalism proposes not to squelch but to utilize national selfishness; it asks governments not to give up sovereignty which belongs to their peoples but to acquire benefits for their peoples which were hitherto unavailable,

■ **nongovernmental organizations (NGOs)** transnational organizations of private citizens maintaining consultative status with the UN; they include professional associations, foundations, multinational corporations, and internationally active groups in different states joined together to work toward common interests.

■ **functionalism** the theory advanced by David Mitrany and others explaining how people can come to value transnational institutions (IGOs, integrated or merged states) and the steps to giving those institutions authority to provide the public goods (for example, security) previously supplied by their state.

■ **epistemic communities** scientific experts on a subject of inquiry such as global warming that are organized internationally as NGOs, brought together to communicate with one another and use their constructed understanding of "knowledge" to lobby for global transformations.

not to reduce their power to defend their citizens but to expand their competence to serve them. It intimates that the basic requirement for peace is that states have the wit to cooperate in pursuit of national interests that coincide with those of other states rather than the will to compromise national interests that conflict with those of others. (Claude 1971, 386)

Persuaded by the logic of this argument, farsighted liberals such as Jean Monnet applied functionalist theory to begin the process by which war-prone Europe began to form an integrated "security community" after World War II.

The permanent problem-solving organizations created in the 1800s, such as the Rhine River Commission (1804), the Danube River Commission (1857), the International Telegraphic Union (1865), and the Universal Post Union (1874), suggested a process by which states might cooperate to enjoy mutual benefits and hence to launch the more ambitious experiments that functionalists anticipated. Their lessons informed the early organizational **ideology** that also inspired the missions assigned to the UN's specialized agencies (such as the World Health Organization) and the growth of **intergovernmental organizations (IGOs)** and NGOs generally.

Functionalism, as originally formulated, did not pertain to **multinational corporations (MNCs),** the institutions some now consider the "dominant governance institutions on the planet" (Korten 1995). However, many now believe that MNCs' roles in the integration of states' economies and the globalization of world politics are consistent with functionalist logic. Individuals who manage global corporations often think and speak of themselves as a "revolutionary class," possessing a holistic, cosmopolitan, or supranational vision of the Earth that challenges traditional nationalism supporting state sovereignty (Barnet and Müller 1974). This ideology and the corresponding slogan "Down with borders" are based on the assumption that the world can be managed as a single, integrated market. From it comes a view of the world that sees global corporations as the primary catalysts to a borderless world opposed to governments that interfere unnecessarily with the free flow of capital and technology. According to this liberal perspective, MNCs' investments and trade promote the growing level of cooperation and compromise exhibited between otherwise competitive states that is creating the emerging global culture—a culture that is eroding state sovereignty as states' economies become interdependent and states' foreign policies become increasingly **intermestic** (simultaneously international and domestic).

Critics charge that as a theory of peace and world order, functionalism does not take into account some important political realities (Barbieri 2003). First, functionalism argues that poverty and the lack of public goods cause war. Critics counter that war may instead cause poverty and the lack of public goods. Addressing issues of poverty may not alleviate war, they also argue, especially if the rapid acquisition of wealth enables dissatisfied states to build armies for war.

Second, functionalism assumes that political differences among countries will be dissolved by the habits of cooperation learned by epistemic communities organized transnationally to cope with technical problems such as global warming, environmental deterioration, or contagious disease. The reality, say critics, is that technical cooperation is often more strongly influenced by politics than the other way around. The U.S. withdrawal in the 1980s from the International Labour Organization (ILO) and the UN Educational, Scientific, and Cultural Organization (UNESCO) because that hegemon then felt that those IGOs were too

■ **ideology**
a set of core philosophical principles collectively held about the ways people and governments ought to behave ethically and politically.

■ **intergovernmental organizations (IGOs)**
international organizations whose members are states, such as the World Trade Organization.

■ **multinational corporations (MNCs)**
business enterprises headquartered in one state that invest and operate extensively in other states.

■ **intermestic policies**
those issues confronting a state that are both local (domestic) and global (international).

politicized illustrated the primacy of politics (the U.S. re-entry in UNESCO after 9/11 in 2002 to seek UN support for antiterrorism punctuates the proposition, too).

As skeptics conclude, functionalists are naive to argue that technical (functional) undertakings and political affairs can be separated. If technical cooperation becomes as important to state welfare as the functionalists argue that it will, states will assume an active role in technical developments. Welfare and power cannot be separated, because the solution of economic and social problems cannot be divorced from political considerations. The expansion of transnational institutions' authority and competency at the expense of national governments and state sovereignty is, therefore, unlikely (Lentner 2004). Functionalism, in short, may be an idea whose time has passed.

Neofunctionalism

A new, albeit derivative, theory arose in the 1950s to question the assumption that ever-expanding functional needs for joint action to address property rights, health, technological change, and other shared problems would force the resolution of political disputes. Termed **neofunctionalism,** the reconstructed liberal theory sought to directly address the political factors that dominate the process of merging formerly independent states.

> *Neofunctionalism* holds that political institutions and policies should be crafted so that they lead to further integration through the process of . . . "the expansive logic of sector integration." For example, [the first] president of the ECSC [European Coal and Steel Community], [Jean] Monnet, sought to use the integration of the coal and steel markets of the six member countries as a lever to promote the integration of their social security and transport policies, arguing that such action was essential to eliminate distortions in coal and steel prices. [The] neofunctionalism of Monnet and others [had] as its ultimate goal . . . the creation of a federal state. (Jacobson 1984, 66)

Neofunctionalism thus proposes to accelerate the processes leading to new supranational communities by purposely pushing for cooperation in politically controversial areas, rather than by avoiding them. It advocates bringing political pressure to bear at crucial decision points to persuade opponents of the greater benefits of forming a larger community among formerly independent national members.

The European Integration Example. Europe has shown the world how neofunctionalism can work to create an integrated political community. In 2004, the **European Union (EU)** added ten European countries to the fifteen-country regional bloc (see Map 14.2). This enlargement created the globe's biggest free-trade area, swelling the EU to bring together under a single administrative umbrella more than 455 million people. The twenty-five EU members united nearly all the continent for the first time in history.

In order to speak with one voice and act collectively not only in economics but also in defense and foreign policy, the EU took a big step when it endorsed its **Common Foreign and Security Policy (CFSP),** which defined as the EU's objectives safeguarding "the common values, fundamental interests, and inde-

---

■ **neofunctionalism**
the revised functional theory explaining that the IGOs that states create to manage common problems provide benefits that exert new pressures for further political integration, the creation of additional IGOs, and the globalization of international relations in an expanding network of interdependence that reduces states' incentives to wage war.

■ **European Union (EU)**
a regional organization created by the merger of the European Coal and Steel Community, the European Atomic Energy Community, and the European Economic Community, called the European Community until 1993.

■ **Common Foreign and Security Policy (CFSP)**
the agreement reached by the European Union defining the goals in foreign and defense policy the EU pledges to jointly pursue.

European Union Expansion at a Glance

Belgium (1); **France** (2); **Germany** (3);
Italy (4); **Luxembourg** (5); **Netherlands** (6)

Denmark (7); **Ireland** (8); **U.K.** (9)

Greece (10)

1951 EU-6

1973 EU-9

1981 EU-10

Portugal (11); **Spain** (12)

Austria (13); **Finland** (14); **Sweden** (15)

Cyprus (16); **Czech Republic** (17)
Estonia (18); **Hungary** (19); **Latvia** (20);
Lithuania (21); **Malta** (22); **Poland** (23);
Slovakia (24); **Slovenia** (25)

1986 EU-12

1995 EU-15

2006 EU-25

MAP 14.2
From Few to Many: The Expansion of the European Union, 1951–2005

The European Union is a premier example of the formation and integrative growth of a supranational regional IGO. It has grown in six expansions from six members in 1951 to twenty-five in 2006, as shown here, and waiting in the wings are Turkey and others, such as Ukraine. Expansion has invigorated the drive for the EU to work together with NATO, the UN, and the international donor community to participate actively in international peacekeeping.

SOURCE: From Wall Street Journal Europe, May 3, 2004, p. A6. Reprinted by permission.

pendence of the Union," strengthening the EU's security, preserving "world peace and international security [as well as promoting] international cooperation to develop and consolidate democracy and the rule of law, and respect for human rights and fundamental freedoms." To fulfill these goals, the EU established the European Rapid Reaction Force, taking the next step toward becoming a military presence on the world stage capable of *unilateral* action (Reid 2004). This sixty thousand strong military force enables the EU to reduce both its dependence on the United States and U.S. domination of NATO.

The political unification of Europe represents an enormous achievement, overturning a past of chronic suspicion and warfare—the dark side of European history. Instead of competing, the EU has created a **security community** (Deutsch 1957) in which the expectation of war between states has vanished from one of the historically most violence-prone regions of the world. The sovereign state in Europe has lost ground, as "a serious sense of European citizenship, along with the rights that go with it, seems to be laying the basis of a supranational identity" (B. Cohen 2000). With unity has come greater efforts at collective security through a common European posture aimed at preventing armed conflicts (Rifkin 2004). Those aspirations inspire hopes that Europe will leave behind the tragic cycle of rivalry and mistrust that haunted it for centuries.

The Preconditions for Regional Integration.

The record of previous integrative experiments demonstrates that the factors promoting (or inhibiting) successful integration efforts are many and their mixture complex. It is not enough that two or more countries choose to interact cooperatively. Research indicates that the probability of such cooperative behavior resulting in integration is remote without geographical proximity, steady economic growth, similar political systems, supportive public opinion led by enthusiastic leaders, cultural homogeneity, internal political stability, similar experiences in historical and internal social development, compatible forms of government and economic systems, similar levels of military preparedness and economic resources, a shared perception of a common external threat, bureaucratic compatibilities, and previous collaborative efforts (Cobb and Elder 1970; Deutsch 1957). While not all of these conditions must be present for integration to occur, the absence of more than a few considerably reduces the chances of success. The integration of two or more societies—let alone entire world regions—is, in short, not easily accomplished.

European institution building nonetheless has served as a model for the application of the neofunctionalist approach to integration in other regions, including Africa, Asia, the Caribbean, and South America. However, current trends suggest that political integration may be peculiarly relevant to the Global North's advanced industrial democracies and the rapidly emerging economic giants of Asia, but of doubtful applicability to the Global South's less-developed countries. The record, moreover, indicates that even where conditions are favorable there is no guarantee that integration will proceed automatically. As noted, even in Europe high hopes have alternated with periods of disillusionment. When momentum has occurred, **spillover**—involving either the deepening of ties in one functional area or their expansion to another to ensure the members' satisfaction with the integrative process—has led to further integration. But there is no inherent expansive momentum in integration schemes. Thus, **spill-

■ **security community**
a group of states whose high level of noninstitutionalized collaboration results in the settlement of disputes by compromise rather than by force.

■ **spillover**
the propensity for successful integration across one area of cooperation between states to propel further integration in other areas.

■ **spillback**
the reversal of previous steps toward integration, reducing the number of sectors in which integrating states are engaged in cooperative exchanges.

back (when a regional integration scheme fails, as in the case of the East African Community) and **spillaround** (when a regional integration scheme stagnates, or its activities in one area work against integration in another, as occured in mid-2004 when elections throughout Europe suggested voter resistance to some aspects of further European integration) are also possible.

■ **spillaround**
the stagnation or encapsulation of regional integration activities.

Political Disintegration

The substantial difficulty that most regions have experienced in achieving a level of institution building similar to that of the EU suggests the magnitude of existing barriers to creating new political communities out of previously divided ones. Furthermore, the paradox that the planet is dividing precipitately and coming together reluctantly at the very same moment confounds predictions. We are witnessing a convulsive splintering of states, as hundreds of ethnic nationalities are currently seeking autonomy. Consider Europe, where in 1991 hypernationalism led to the creation of fifteen newly independent countries. Since then five additional European states have been created from the former Yugoslavia. Between 1990 and 1998, the global annual rate of new-country creation as a consequence of civil wars within states was 3.1 (Enriquez 1999, 30). Ironically, this fragmentation occurred in precisely the same period when elsewhere political units were reintegrating, as Hong Kong in 1997 and Macao in 2000 did when, after centuries of colonialism, they once again became a part of China.

The surge of ethnic and religious secessionist movements tearing countries apart in many of the globe's 209 currently separate states could multiply the number of independent countries to as many as 500 by the year 2025, according to UN estimates. With fewer than 25 countries ethnically homogeneous and with three thousand to five thousand **indigenous peoples** interested in securing a sovereign homeland, the prospects are high that **political disintegration** will continue, especially if the number of failed states where central governing institutions have imploded in a sea of chaos continues to rise (see Chapters 6 and 11). This division of the globe into more and more smaller states could be slowed if existing states accepted **devolution** (the granting of greater political power to quasi-autonomous regions), as many central governments have done for the purpose of containing separatist revolts. However, in many countries where governmental institutions are fragile, the leadership has refused to accept devolution and repressed by force the minority peoples seeking to share power. In these cases the hypernationalist quest for independence under the banner of the **self-determination** principle threatens to dismember some formerly integrated sovereign states, including such widely dissimilar states as Canada, Russia, Spain, South Africa, and the United Kingdom, where minorities (the proportion of a state's population made up by different ethnic, nationality, or racial groups) perceive themselves to be an oppressed subclass. About a third of the globe's countries contain restless, politically repressed minorities struggling at various levels for human rights and independence (see Allen and Leppnan 2004, 37; Gurr 2000, 2001). Such struggles and revolutions are not new, of course. The U.S. Civil War between 1861 and 1865, the thirty-year civil war in Ethiopia that enabled Eritrea to gain independence in 1991, and the 2004 electoral crisis that divided Ukraine remind us that states may either integrate into larger unions or disintegrate into smaller states. Hence, there is little reason to expect integrative pro-

■ **indigeneous peoples**
the native ethnic and cultural inhabitant populations within countries ruled by a government controlled by others, known as the "Fourth World."

■ **political disintegration**
the separation of a failed state into fragments to create two or more newly independent countries.

■ **devolution**
states' granting of political power to ethnic and religious groups and indigenous people under the expectation that greater autonomy for them in particular regions will reduce their quest for independence as a new state.

■ **self-determination**
the standard advocated strenuously in U.S. President Woodrow Wilson's "Fourteen Points" address that national and ethnic groups have a right to statehood so they can govern themselves as independent countries.

cesses, once under way, to automatically continue by the force of their own momentum. Globalization, uneven growth rates, and income inequalities could easily pull history in the opposite direction, toward the disintegration of states to create many new national flags.

A DEMOCRATIC PEACE: CAN VOTES STOP VIOLENCE?

Historically liberal theory has emphasized the need for *global* institutional reforms to promote peace. For this reason, liberalism is most closely identified with international law, organization, and integration. However, liberalism embraces a fourth institutional approach: that democratization is critical, because if states are ruled democratically the world will become more peaceful. (This liberal thesis runs directly counter to realism's assumption that states' forms of government do not influence their foreign policy very much, because all governments, realists maintain, will respond similarly to similar types of security threats.)

James Madison in 1792 voiced the liberal ideas underlying expectations about a **democratic peace** when he argued that "in the advent of republican governments [would be found] not only the prospect of a radical decline in the role played by war but the prospect as well of a virtual revolution in the conduct of diplomacy" (Tucker and Hendrickson 1990). Evidence generated by quantitative **behavioral** research (Bennett and Stam 2004) has convincingly demonstrated that there are sound reasons for accepting this liberal proposition. Studies have repeatedly shown that "well-established democracies have never made war on one another [and] republics and only republics have tended to form durable, peaceful leagues" (Weart 1994; see also Lipson 2003).

This lesson was not lost on leaders in democratic states seeking to find a principle on which to ground their national security policies. "Ultimately the best strategy to insure our security and to build a durable peace is to support the advance of democracy elsewhere," the 1994 *U.S. National Strategy* concluded. That **doctrine** was officially endorsed by the other major EU and NATO liberal democracies who members insist on states being democratically ruled as a condition for membership. In addition, the major international organizations have also endorsed the promotion of democracy as a policy priority, including the **Group of Eight (G-8)**, the World Bank, the International Monetary Fund (IMF), the Organization for Economic Cooperation and Development (OECD), and the Organization of American States (OAS).

The active promotion of democratic reforms in the past four decades has produced significant results. The reform-minded rhetoric to "export democracy" has been met with much action to back it up (Schraeder 2002). Since the mid-1970s freedom and civil liberties have grown in a series of transitions, and today the enlarged community of liberal democracies make up three-quarters of the globe's governments, ruled by free or partially free institutions (see Figure 14.3).

Skeptics grounded in realism question whether democracies can be counted on to put their liberal ideals for promoting liberties worldwide ahead of their narrow national interests by risking their soldiers' lives in humanitarian crusades in countries of low geopolitical importance. Needless to say, confidence in the liberal path to peace through democratization will remain shaky in a pre-

---

■ **democratic peace**
the theory that, because democratic states do not fight one another, the diffusion of democratic governance throughout the world will reduce the probability of war.

■ **behavioralism**
an approach to the study of international relations that emphasizes the application of scientific methods.

■ **doctrine**
the guidelines a state specifies to identify the conditions under which it will use power for political purposes abroad.

■ **Group of Eight (G-8)**
the major industrialized countries including Russia, whose leaders participate in annual summit conferences to set economic, political, and military goals for the global future.

FIGURE 14.3

Will a Freedom Fence Result from the Global Growth of Democratic Governance?

The number of free and partly free countries that are members of the community of democracies has increased as a percentage of the world's state governments since 1974 in fits and starts. As this figure shows, as the year 2005 began three-fourths of the countries in the world were either fully or partially democratic, according to Freedom House. Eighty-eight "free" countries had governments that provided their citizens with a high degree of political and economic freedom and civil liberties, and another fifty-five "partly free" countries had electoral governments. Despite terrorism and the political repression it spawns to reduce freedom, the number of countries at the start of 2005 gaining in civil liberties was double those that suffered setbacks. This inspires liberals' hopes that a global peace among democracies will continue to spread and deepen, even in difficult times of terrorism and tension.

SOURCE: Freedom House annual surveys.

carious globalized world where the institutional foundations of lasting peace are still fragile. Some have been provoked to predict that global politics will constrain democracy, rather than democratization taming world politics (Gilbert 2000; see also Chernoff 2004). Others fret that global terrorism will undermine the democratic project, observing that the war on terrorists such as Osama bin Laden (who believe they can change U.S. policy through terror) will force democratic states to suspend their civil liberties.

These doubts notwithstanding, past trends provide strong evidence to support the liberal tenet that democracy produces many benefits (Siegle, Weinstein, and Halperin 2004), including—beyond freedom, human rights, civil liberties, and prosperity—the capacity to deter wars within and between members of the democratic community of states (Huth and Allee 2003; Souva 2004). Therefore, providing that democratic states continue to abide by their past record of dealing with conflicts by compromise through negotiation, mediation, arbitration, and adjudication, the existing liberal democracies' efforts to enlarge their community could potentially usher in a major transformation of world politics. The hopes that Pope John Paul II expressed could make an ancient dream a reality: "No more war, war never again."

However, promise dictates neither performance nor destiny. As Prime Minister Ingvar Caarlsson of Sweden warned, "If we fail to nurture democracy—the most fundamental political project . . . we will never be able to realize our goals and the responsibilities which the future will call for."

LIBERAL INSTITUTIONS AND WORLD ORDER: FROM SECURITY TO STABILITY?

Liberal and neoliberal theories that focus on international law, organization, integration, and democratization see armed conflict as deriving from prevailing and deeply rooted institutional deficiencies. Neoliberal reformers believe that the current anarchical system is the problem, not the solution, because weak institutions make security scarce and global welfare subservient to national welfare. To change this, they advocate legal and institutional methods to pool sovereignty and reform the character of nondemocratic governments. Seeing the global system as underdeveloped and unstructured, advocates of these reforms believe that a rebuilt state system can best eliminate the roots of war. As one liberal scholar argues, global change requires innovation, because "during the coming decades global challenges will continue and may increase. . . . There is more and more of an overlap between national interests and global responsibilities. The task of multilateral diplomacy is to cope with new issues, new demands and new situations [through] 'shared responsibilities' and 'strengthened partnership'" (Kinnas 1997).

To liberal advocates, the big problems on the global agenda are ones that simultaneously affect many states. They cannot be meaningfully managed unilaterally; they are transnational and cannot be met effectively with a national response. With respect to such global issues as free trade, environmental degradation, global warming, the control of AIDS, the global refugee crisis, failed states, and civil wars, a multilateral cooperative approach may be required under conditions of interdependent globalization. In this context, President Martti Ahtisaari of Finland observed in 1999 that "the world has turned from mere coexistence to cooperation [and it has] succeeded in reaching beyond the boundaries of state sovereignty." Whether multilateral IGOs such as the UN, the democratically driven EU, and the liberal community of states at large can orchestrate their collective opposition to interstate and civil war through multilateral action will determine if this liberal path to peace will ultimately succeed.

The contributions of the expanding number of international institutions created in the twentieth century to this grand purpose were, until recently, rather modest. Despite some promising developments, armed conflict has been frequent. This is not surprising when states allocate less than two dollars for every man, woman, and child to the UN for humanitarian and security emergencies, while spending trillions in the aggregate for "defense"—with "homeland insecurity" often the disappointing product of these huge expenditures. However, the impact of multilateral management of strife-torn areas should not be minimized. As Inis L. Claude maintains,

> Particular *organizations* may be nothing more than playthings of power politics and handmaidens of national ambitions. But international *organization*, considered as an historical process, represents a secular trend toward the systematic development of an enterprising quest for political means of making the world safe for human habitation. It may fail, and peter out ignominiously. But if it maintains the momentum that it has built up in the twentieth century, it may yet effect a transformation of human relationships on this planet which will at some indeterminate point justify the assertion that the world has come to be governed—that mankind has become a community capable of sustaining order, promoting justice, and establishing the

conditions of that good life which Aristotle took to be the supreme aim of politics. (Claude 1971, 447–48, emphasis added)

Liberal institutionalists have appropriately raised various concerns about the capacity of independent and competing sovereign states to engineer a hopeful future for humanity. On balance, sovereign states have not used their foreign policies to create a safe and secure global environment in which their youth can survive and prosper. Instead, states have historically been instruments for making war with others, and recently national governments have proven ineffective at either preventing civil wars or commanding widespread loyalty and respect from their constituents. The global "crisis of confidence" in governments has resulted in the disintegration of failing states at the same time that these fragile states have become tied together in an interdependent globalized community. "Liberal internationalists see a need for international rules to solve states' problems, proclaim the end of the nation-state, [and see] transgovernmentalism rapidly becoming the most widespread and effective mode of international governance," said Anne-Marie Slaughter (1997, see also 2004a) in defining the contemporary currents of public opinion.

States are, to be sure, uniting by creating global institutions and a common culture to jointly protect themselves against the many shared problems they face. They appear to increasingly accept the once radical liberal view that, as Kofi Annan argues, "a new, broader definition of national interest is needed in the [twenty-first] century," which would unify states to work on common goals that transcend national interests.

Borders and oceans cannot isolate or insulate states from these threats to security; they can only be controlled in the global commons by a collective effort. It is for this reason that many intergovernmental organizations (IGOs) originally came into being, and it is the persistence of collective threats produced by an increasingly globalized world that makes IGOs durable. As the globe shrinks and borders less and less operate as barriers, we can predict that liberal paths to peace and prosperity will continue to find favor and policymakers will take seriously the call to help create what Swedish Foreign Minister Anna Lindh describes as "a global culture of conflict prevention." Similarly, in his Nobel Peace Prize acceptance speech, former U.S. President Jimmy Carter warned against the impulse to violence, as some realists recommend, to punish enemies for injuries perceived to have been inflicted: "War may sometimes be a necessary evil. But no matter how necessary, it is always an evil, never a good. We will not learn to live together in peace by killing each other's children." If pursued, will acceptance of the liberal belief that peace is best preserved through ethical policies (Lebow 2003) break the violent historical pattern? The world awaits an answer.

KEY TERMS

neoliberal institutionalism
private international law
public international law
sovereignty
realism
sovereign equality

neutrality
nonintervention norm
diplomatic immunity
extraterritoriality
crimes against humanity
divine right of kings

statehood
diplomatic recognition
de facto recognition
de jure recognition
negotiation
mediation

good offices
conciliation
arbitration
adjudication
self-help
structural violence
positivist legal theory
just war doctrine
security regimes
morals
ethics
revolution in military affairs (RMA)
military necessity
preemption
Bush Doctrine
human rights
terrorism
noncombatant immunity
coercive power
reprisals
retorsion
International Criminal Court (ICC)
permanent world criminal court
state-sponsored terrorism

war crimes
cooperation
failed states
low politics
collective security
balance of power
peacekeeping
preventive diplomacy
peacemaking
peace building
peace operations
peace enforcement
ultimatum
selective engagement
public goods
regional collective defense
collective security
political integration
world federalism
absolute gains
relative gains
nationalism
nongovernmental organizations (NGOs)
functionalism

epistemic communities
ideology
intergovernmental organizations (IGOs)
multinational corporations (MNCs)
intermestic policies
neofunctionalism
European Union (EU)
Common Foreign and Security Policy (CFSP)
security community
spillover
spillback
spillaround
indigenous peoples
political disintegration
devolution
self-determination
democratic peace
behavioralism
doctrine
Group of Eight (G-8)

SUGGESTED READING

Huth, Paul K., and Todd I. Allee. *The Democratic Peace and Territorial Conflict in the Twentieth Century.* Cambridge: Cambridge University Press, 2003.

Ignatieff, Michael. *The Lesser Evil: Political Ethics in an Age of Terror.* Princeton, N.J.: Princeton University Press, 2004.

Joyner, Christopher C. *International Law in the 21st Century.* Landam, Md.: Rowman and Littlefield, 2005.

Karns, Margaret P., and Karen A. Mingst. *International Organizations: The Politics and Processes of Global Governance.* Boulder, Colo.: Lynne Rienner, 2004.

Kegley, Charles W., Jr., and Gregory A. Raymond. *Exorcising the Ghost of Westphalia: Building World Order in the New Millennium.* Upper Saddle River, N.J.: Prentice Hall, 2002.

Long, William J., and Peter Brecke. *War and Reconciliation: Reason and Emotion in Conflict Resolution.* Cambridge, Mass.: MIT Press, 2003.

Malone, David M., ed. *The UN Security Council: From Cold War to the 21st Century.* Boulder, Colo.: Lynne Rienner, 2004.

Mandelbaum, Michael. *The Ideas that Conquered the World: Peace, Democracy, and Free Markets in the Twenty-First Century.* New York: Public Affairs Press, 2002.

Mansfield, Edward D., and Brian M. Pollins, eds., *Economic Interdependence and International Conflict.* Ann Arbor: University of Michigan Press, 2003.

Nolan, Cathal L., ed. *Ethics and Statecraft: The Moral Dimensions of International Affairs.* Westport, Conn.: Praeger, 2004.

Russett, Bruce, and John Oneal. *Triangulating Peace: Democracy, Interdependence, and International Organization.* New York: W. W. Norton, 2000.

Slaughter, Anne-Marie. *A New World Order.* Princeton, N.J.: Princeton University Press, 2004.

WHERE ON THE WORLD WIDE WEB?

Carnegie Council on Ethics and International Affairs
http://www.cceia.org/

The best inventory of global issues, with commentary and links to other websites dealing with each issue. What are the major foci of the Carnegie Council on Ethics and International Affairs? In what ways does this website represent the liberal and realist views of global politics?

Human Rights Watch
http://www.hrw.org/

Human Rights Watch (HRW) is an independent, nongovernmental organization dedicated to protecting the human rights of people around the world. To this end, the organization investigates and exposes human rights violations and holds abusers accountable. As this chapter notes, the international community has impressively expanded the human rights protection granted under international law. HRW challenges governments to respect these laws. Its website reports breaking news concerning human rights around the globe. The site delivers HRW reports on specific countries' human rights abuses. Which countries have the best and worst human rights records? Which countries are currently engaging in human rights abuses, and how is the international community responding?

The International Court of Justice
http://www.icj-cij.org/

The International Court of Justice (ICJ) is the principal judicial organ of the United Nations. Examine the court's statutes to find out who can bring cases before the court. Then read the biographies of the court's fifteen members. Finally, access the "Decisions" link to examine some of the ICJ's contentious cases. Which countries have brought the United States to court? What were the ICJ's rulings in those cases?

International Court of Justice Considers Genocide
http://oz.uc.edu/thro/genocide/index.html

Professor Howard Tolley of the University of Cincinnati has created an interactive website on which you can role-play the judge at the International Court of Justice when Bosnia brought charges against Yugoslavia in 1993. Explore the facts, research the law, and consider opposing arguments, and then make your judgement. How does it compare to the court's actual decision?

International Criminal Tribunal for the Former Yugoslavia (ICTY)
http://www.un.org/icty/

Established by the United Nations Security Council in 1993, the ICTY is mandated to prosecute persons responsible for serious violations of international humanitarian law committed in the territory of the former Yugoslavia since 1991. Visit this website to see who was indicted for war crimes and what judgment was rendered. What has happened with the case against Slobodan Milosevic, the former Yugoslavian leader? Do you believe that the international community's ability to punish individuals for war crimes will be a deterrent against future acts of genocide and inhumanity?

Fletcher-Ginn Multilaterals Project
http://fletcher.tufts.edu/multilaterals.html

The Fletcher School of Law and Diplomacy makes available the texts of international multilateral conventions and other instruments. It has a searchable database as well as a list of conventions organized by subject, such as the rules of warfare, the environment, cultural protection, and biodiversity. You can also view the Treaty of Westphalia and the League of Nations covenant. For thorough historical background on a subject, read the documents chronologically.

United Nations Peacekeeping Operations
http://www.un.org/Depts/dpko/dpko/index.asp

The United Nations has deployed numerous international military and civilian personnel to conflict areas to stop or contain hostilities and to supervise the carrying out of peace agreements. In what countries are UN peacekeepers currently located? Click on an ongoing mission and read about the profile, background, and facts and figures concerning the mission. Do the same thing for an older mission. Are there any similarities or differences?

Universal Declaration of Human Rights
http://www.un.org/Overview/rights.html

This chapter discusses the development of international human rights protections. Read the document that started it all—the Universal Declaration of Human Rights. Did you know that Eleanor Roosevelt, serving as a delegate to the United Nations, chaired the committee that produced this document? What are the most important provisions of the document?

INFOTRAC® COLLEGE EDITION

Himes, Kenneth R. "Intervention, Just War, and U.S. National Security." *Theological Studies* (March 2004).

Kurlantzick, Joshua. "Taking Multinationals to Court: How the Alien Tort Act Promotes Human Rights." *World Policy Journal* (Spring 2004).

Dellinger, Walter, and Samuel P. Fried. "Promoting the Rule of Law Abroad: How the U.S. Legal and Business Communities Can Help." *World Policy Journal* (Summer 2003).

Petersmann, Ernst-Ulrich. "Human Rights and the Law of the World Trade Organization." *Journal of World Trade (Law-Economics-Public Policy)* (April 2003).

For more articles, enter:

"just war doctrine" in the Subject Guide

"International Court of Justice" in the Subject Guide

"international law" in the Subject Guide, and then go to subdivision "evaluation"

Go to http://politicalscience.wadsworth.com/kegley10 to access additional resources related to this chapter.

PART V

THE PROBLEMATIC TWENTY-FIRST CENTURY

How are the trends that are emerging in world politics today likely to influence the global future? Will the twenty-first century find past approaches to world order useful, or will it reject past approaches as new questions that demand new answers arise?

Part V presents ten thought-provoking questions that ask how current trends in world politics are likely to have an impact on the early part of the twenty-first century. These questions, which expand on some of those originally introduced in Chapter 1, draw on ideas you have encountered as you have read this book. Thinking about possible answers will require you to analyze these ideas, looking ahead to the global future informed by your knowledge of the contemporary character of international relations and recently constructed images about how world politics works.

CHAPTER 15

Ten Questions about Twenty-First-Century Global Prospects

THEMES AND TOPICS

- Should global interests be placed ahead of national interests?
- If war between states is obsolete, what is the purpose of military power?
- Can the new global terrorism be contained?
- Will separatist conflict within states lead to hundreds of new states?
- Will the great powers intervene to protect human rights?
- Will globalization tie the world together or tear it apart?
- Is realism still realistic and is liberalism still too idealistic?
- Is the world preparing for the wrong war?
- Is this the "end of history"?
- Is there a reordered global agenda?

Global inequalities have widened the gap between rich and poor. The World Urban Forum in 2002 sought to instill awareness of the destitute in many cities worldwide, as shown here, to conceive of more sensible public policies, arguing that, ethically, the advantages of modern civilization ought to be within the grasp of all.

It is a new world and exceedingly dangerous. Everything is at stake. This is the first time in history the knowledge of how to make society-destroying weapons has been democratized. Today, small radical groups allied with small radical states can do the kind of damage to the world that in the past only a great strategically located industrialized power . . . could do.

—CHARLES KRAUTHAMMER, political journalist, 2004

Trend is not destiny.

—RENÉ DUBOS, French author, 1975

The opposing trends toward integration and fragmentation point toward a new global system—one whose character has yet to develop definition. Uncertainty and unpredictability define the contemporary mood. But one thing is certain: The seismic shifts under way will challenge the wisdom of old beliefs and orthodox visions. Because turmoil and turbulence govern contemporary international affairs, they require that we ask unconventional questions about conventional ideas. They push us to try to think four-dimensionally in order to perceive how political, military, market, and environmental pressures—intensified through globalization—are increasingly being brought to bear on the countries of the world, the people who reside in them, and their interactions.

Chapter 1 suggested that the investigative challenge to interpreting the future of world affairs would require the consideration of five controversial questions:

1. Are states obsolete?
2. Is globalization a cure or a curse?
3. What will be the consequences of America's superpower status?

4. Will geo-economics supersede geopolitics?
5. What constitutes human well-being on an ecologically fragile planet?

Answers to these questions are elusive. The conclusions boldly asserted by would-be prophets are not likely to prove definitive, because, as former UN Secretary-General Boutros Boutros-Ghali warns, "those caught up in revolutionary change rarely understand its ultimate significance." It is hard to recognize, and to describe, the bewildering array of problems that now confront humanity. UN Secretary-General Kofi Annan summarized in the December 2004 UN report, *A More Secure World*,

> We face a world of extraordinary challenges—and of extraordinary interconnectedness. We are all vulnerable to new security threats, and to old threats that are evolving in complex and unpredictable ways.... Six clusters [are salient]: economic and social threats, including poverty and deadly infectious disease; interstate conflict and rivalry; internal violence, including civil war, state collapse and genocide; nuclear, radiological, chemical and biological weapons; terrorism; and transnational organized crime.

Given this complex and dangerous environment, it is important to weigh plausible answers to these same five key questions as we attempt to prepare ourselves intellectually for understanding the problematic future of world politics.

This final chapter addresses ten additional questions about the future, based on the preceding discussion of the major trends currently unfolding in world politics.

TOWARD THE FUTURE: CRITICAL QUESTIONS AT THE START OF THE NEW MILLENNIUM

Leaders and policy analysts worldwide are debating a number of controversial issues that require policy choices. How these and other questions are answered will significantly shape world politics throughout the twenty-first century.

1. Should Global Interests Be Placed Ahead of National Interests?

What goals should states pursue? In earlier times, the answer was easy: The state should promote the internal welfare of its citizens, provide for defense against external aggression, and preserve the state's values and way of life. States followed a largely realist script, putting their national interests ahead of global interests. This meant competing with other states for power, position, and prestige, and above all else protecting the state from external attack by acquiring arms for defense. Working with other states on common problems or with many other countries in building multilateral institutions for global governance was secondary—to be considered only after national security was enhanced by acquiring military might and political clout.

Leaders pursue the same goals today, but their domestic and foreign policy options are increasingly limited. Many problems can be resolved only at the risk of worsening others. Under such conditions, the national quest for narrow **zero-sum** self-advantage and global position often carries prohibitively high costs.

■ **zero-sum**
a situation resulting when actors perceive their individual self-interest to be completely in conflict with a competitor's interests.

The historic tendency toward chauvinism (my country, right or wrong) in defining national interests can be counterproductive domestically as well as internationally. No country can long afford to pursue its own welfare in ways that reduce its competitors' security and welfare.

In the past, those who questioned the primacy of the national interest seldom found support. Few accepted the notion that the global community's "moral meaning is better expressed in the notion of a 'human community,' which exists prior to the sovereign state" (Hehir 2002). That is changing. As Margaret Mead (1968) noted, people are beginning to endorse the view that "substantially we all share the same atmosphere today, and we can only save ourselves by saving other people also. There is no longer a contradiction between patriotism and concern for the world." Former U.S. Secretary of State Cyrus Vance voiced a similar idea when he observed that "more than ever cooperative endeavors among nations are a matter not only of idealism but of direct self-interest."

E. H. Carr (1939), a British pioneer of **realism,** was convinced of the realism of idealism, maintaining that opposing the general interests of humankind does not serve any country's self-interest. Failing to recognize the plight of others can ultimately threaten one's own well-being—a view underscored by Martin Luther King, Jr., who urged that "injustice anywhere is a threat to justice everywhere." Indeed, it was largely enlightened awareness of the limitations of traditional notions of state sovereignty and the conventional ways in which states have defined their national interests that prompted UN Secretary-General Kofi Annan to warn: "The world has changed in profound ways . . . but I fear our conceptions of national interest have failed to follow suit. A new, broader definition of national interest is needed . . . which would induce states to find greater unity in the pursuit of common goods and values." These proposals put human interests and global security ahead of national interests and national security. If such conceptions, largely rooted in the legacy of **liberalism,** gain a wider following in world public opinion, will the collective concerns of all humanity begin to better compete with states' continuing competitive preoccupation with their own narrow national interests?

2. If War between States Is Obsolete, What Is the Purpose of Military Power?

Prevalent practices tend to wither away when they cease to serve their intended purpose, as the examples of slavery, dueling, and colonialism illustrate. Is war between states subject to these same forces? Since World War II, legal prohibitions against interstate military aggression have expanded, and war has occurred almost exclusively in the Global South. And since the end of the Cold War, military conflicts between states have neared the vanishing point. Even more impressively, the period since 1945 has been the longest span of great-power peace since the seventeenth century, raising expectations that large-scale wars between states will continue to decline and perhaps cease altogether. (This hope exists even as internal or civil wars and terrorism are on the rise and humanitarian concerns about genocide and war crimes increasingly require interventionary peacekeeping.) "For modern states the anticipated costs [of waging war], political and economic as well as human, generally exceed the benefits" (Mack 1996).

It is, of course, debatable whether the disincentives and dangers of using to-

■ **realism**
the orthodox theory of world politics based on the assumption that because humans are born to seek self-advantage, international politics is doomed to be an endless struggle for power involving war.

■ **liberalism**
the optimistic view that because humans are capable of compassion, cooperation, and self-sacrifice for collective gain, it is possible for world politics to progress beyond narrow competition and war.

day's destructive weapons are truly making war between states obsolete. Instead, this kind of war may eventually disappear in another, far more frightening way—because resorting to weapons of mass destruction will obliterate humankind. The puzzle, then, is when and by what means war will become obsolete. As Martin Luther King, Jr., put it, "The choice is either nonviolence or nonexistence."

In the past, military might enabled states to project power, exercise influence, and dominate others. Today, nuclear, biological, and chemical weapons of mass destruction make the use of military might by states against other states risky. Continuing arms proliferation raises new questions. Does the acquisition of more weapons increase **national security**—a psychological phenomenon? Or are preparations for war and defense responsible for the **security dilemma** that all countries face?

■ **national security**
a country's psychological freedom from fear that the state will be unable to resist threats to its survival and national values emanating from abroad or at home.

■ **security dilemma**
the propensity of armaments undertaken by one state for ostensibly defensive purposes to threaten other states, which arm in reaction, with the result that all arming states' national security declines as their arms increase.

Most leaders agree with the ancient Greek philosopher Aristotle, who argued that "a people without walls is a people without choice." Thus most accept the realist premise that preparing for war is necessary for peace, especially against terrorist groups. Yet the capacity to destroy does not always make for a convincing threat, especially against countries and transnational terrorists with the capacity to retaliate, whose citizens, not soldiers, would die in the largest numbers. Today, the threat of force often lacks credibility, especially against faceless and invisible nonstate terrorist groups willing to die for their cause. These movements' attacks cannot be deterred easily because there is not a territory to target, and they cannot be destroyed in preemptive strikes without a location to attack. Military power has become impotent by its very strength. And when military might no longer compels others' compliance, then weapons will have lost their traditional primary role as a basis, or substitute, for diplomacy.

No level of military might can guarantee a state's invulnerability. And states' primary security problem today is the rise of internal, not external, aggression, or an attack by a transnational terrorist network such as Al Qaeda, which is believed to operate within more than one hundred countries. Therefore, preparation for traditional warfare can be assessed only in terms of other consequences. Thresholds may exist, beyond which the addition of greater destructive power or the discovery of technologically revolutionary new kinds of lethal and nonlethal weapons are meaningless. Furthermore, excessive and financially costly preparations for war may leave a country heavily fortified with little left to defend, as U.S. President Eisenhower warned in 1961. To avoid debt and inflation, some states have adjusted to the diminishing usefulness of weapons by slashing their military budgets, inspired by their recognition that in the long run high military spending can reduce their industrial growth, weaken global economic competitiveness, and ultimately undermine the ability to satisfy citizens' cravings for a reasonable standard of living and a promising financial future.

Although immediate fears of another great-power conflict causing a world war have declined and further eroded justifications for acquiring military power, states' traditional quest for military advantage has not disappeared. Military spending by the United States, China, the European Union (EU), and other aspiring global powers is scheduled to climb, fueled by enormous expenditures for homeland defense against terrorist attacks. Another sign of the persistent belief that military power increases political influence and national security is found in the fact that the global trade in weapons is the world's largest industry. In addition, the proliferation of weapons of mass destruction continues, as In-

People Power? States continue to seek sovereignty and supremacy, but increasingly world politics is being transformed at the grassroots level by networks of nongovernmental organizations (NGOs)—people dissatisfied with states' definitions of national interests. Individuals have formed more than thirty-one thousand NGOs that advocate global changes and reforms. One such well-known NGO is Greenpeace, whose goal is to protect humanity from environmental degradation of the global commons. Shown here are Greenpeace members in action. NGOs have emerged as a major force to overcome global problems, such as war, famine, human rights abuse, gender inequality, and poverty, that many people feel are not being tackled effectively by states' governments and wish to see human interests reinterpreted as states' primary national interests.

---

dia's and Pakistan's nuclear weapons suggests, as does the pursuit of weapons of mass destruction by untold numbers of nonstate terrorist movements. The one predicament that nearly every state finds unacceptable is being vulnerable to foreign aggression or subject to other states' dictates. Consequently, the pursuit of military power is likely to continue at the same time that concerns about the social and financial costs of preparations to use military force in war are likely to rise.

If the power to destroy does not provide the power to control, then we can expect states' willingness to spend for destructive weapons to decline. But that may not happen if states follow the lead of the U.S. superpower **hegemon**, which accounts for nearly half the world's military expenditures and, with George W. Bush's November 2004 re-election, can be expected to continue widening the gap between itself and everyone else. The United States adheres to a traditional realist script that seeks military preponderance in order to act unilaterally, so that no other competitors are able to balance its power or resist its activities. This does not guarantee that the payoff of this gamble for destiny will succeed for America, or that other countries will join the United States in its massive investment in military force.

■ **hegemon**

a single state so powerful that it has the capabilities to try to control world politics and to create rules for others to follow.

One reason was stated by the 2002 *National Security Strategy of the United States* itself, which acknowledged that America was now "menaced less by fleets and armies than by catastrophic technologies in the hands of the embittered few [or] weak states like Afghanistan that compose as great a danger to our [U.S.] national interest as strong ones." If so, what advantages reside from costly weapons and missiles, when other less expensive methods of protecting homeland security can pay higher dividends? This is the question asked by those who challenge the realist proposition that overwhelming military might is required to play the game of international **politics** because it enables a military powerhouse to bend others to its will. Critics note that equation does not calculate. They add that reliance on military power for coercive diplomacy overlooks the advantages of multilateral diplomacy and **soft power**—"the ability to persuade rather than coerce." As Joseph S. Nye (2004a) explains, "Soft power arises from the attractiveness of a country's culture, political ideals and policies. . . . Legitimacy is also a form of power. Humans live not only by the sword, but also by the word." In America's case, soft power "means that others want what you want, and there is less need to use carrots and sticks . . . when America's policies are seen as legitimate in the eyes of others. . . . [When America's positions and practices are seen as attractive] other countries are more willing to co-operate on the solution of transnational issues." This insight reduces faith in push-and-shove military confrontation and the huge costs they require, and increases the probability that "soft power will become increasingly important in preventing terrorists from recruiting supporters from among the moderate majority and for dealing with the transnational issues that require multilateral cooperation for their solution."

■ **politics**
the pursuit and exercise of power to promote self-interests and goals.

■ **soft power**
the ability to exercise influence in world politics due to intangible resources such as moral authority and international respect for a state's culture, ideals, and institutions, as opposed to methods that rely on military might.

3. Can the New Global Terrorism Be Contained?

September 11, 2001, has been called by many people the day that changed the world—forever. The destruction of the World Trade Center and damage to the Pentagon by terrorists using hijacked airplanes as missiles shattered the prevailing illusion that terrorism was merely "theater" aimed primarily at shocking to gain attention; it was now aimed at killing large numbers. The goal of the Al Qaeda terrorist network spread across the globe and orchestrated by the former U.S. CIA client and Islamic extremist Osama bin Laden was to hit the enemy, and hard—to provoke widespread terror at the alarming thought that even more deadly acts were likely. As the Al Qaeda leader warned in a videotape aired four days before the U.S. national election on November 2, 2004, "there are still reasons to repeat what happened [on 9/11] because of injustices . . . by Israel and the United States."

September 11 gave birth to the new age of global terrorism, pitting nonterritorial terrorists against established territorial states to vent hatred and exact revenge for perceived past injustices. In the bull's-eye on their target is the globe's sole superpower, the United States, seen as a demonic global evil. Also on the screen are America's allies that also symbolize all that has gone wrong in the world, such as the loss of cultural traditions and religions by alien forces—globalization, consumerism, atheism, and modernization generally. In response, the United States launched a global war to eliminate all terrorists and their sponsors from the face of the earth.

Extricating terrorism from the world is, of course, an extremely ambitious goal. Terrorism has been practiced for more than three thousand years, and ending a practice that has been around since antiquity will require vast resources and unswerving perseverance. To fight a war against terrorism is to fight a phenomenon, not an adversary actor. It is like fighting the war on poverty and on drugs—a noble undertaking against a perpetual phenomenon resistant to control.

How does a fragile worldwide coalition committed to counterterrorism win this kind of war? Can it? Opinions diverge on the answers to both questions.

On one extreme are experts who maintain that terrorism cannot be eliminated unless the conditions that cause it are first corrected. To them, circumstances of misery, poverty, persecution, and marginalization are the preconditions that pave the way to the outbreak of terrorist acts, and alleviating the suffering and despair by desperate people and reducing their grievances is the only long-term solution. To root out terrorism is to repair the soil from which terrorism grows—the kinds of terrain that breed people willing to take high risks and even to die as martyrs in suicide missions. At another extreme are counterterrorist strategists who see the new terrorism perpetrated by maniacs and fanatics and who conclude that because these terrorist leaders are responsible for today's terrorism, the answer lies in militarily striking and destroying the people who organize terrorist movements. This is the posture that was advocated by many in the Bush administration who claimed it was necessary to attack Iraq and remove Saddam Hussein from power, because those presidential advisers (falsely) believed that the Iraqi dictator had stockpiled weapons of mass destruction and planned to someday use them. Intelligence never supported that claim (or, for that matter, the assertion that the Iraqi despot was involved in the Al Qaeda 9/11 attacks). Nonetheless, **preemptive war**—militarily attacking enemies and state sponsors of terrorism before they can strike—is now the U.S. superpower's declared strategic doctrine. In addition this policy forces all countries to take a position. In April 2002 Bush stated, "I laid out a doctrine [that] said if you harbor a terrorist, you're just as guilty as the terrorist; if you feed one or hide one, you're just as guilty as those who came and murdered thousands of innocent Americans."

Military approaches may be required in the short run, rationalized by the principle of **military necessity**. But killing such terrorists as Osama bin Laden does not mean that a new generation of terrorists will not arise, motivated by the same hostilities toward countries and cultures they believe are the enemies responsible for the problems they face. To defeat terrorism, the conditions that create terrorist movements must be transformed. Moreover, to successfully wage a war against worldwide terrorism, everyone recognizes that a broad-based international coalition of allies will be required. Global terrorism is a global problem that requires a global, multilateral approach.

Dividing the world into two camps—the just and the unjust, the good and the evil—is risky in the turbulent international world where friends and foes are hard to distinguish and where alignments on one global issue dissolve in the face of other issues and allegiances (see photo, p. 580). National interests are bound to conflict at times, even among allies united against a common enemy as threatening as global terrorism. This was illustrated when President Bush warned Russian President Vladimir Putin in May 2002 that the U.S.-Russian strategic partnership depended on Russian willingness to end arms sales to Iran, a ter-

■ **preemptive war**
a quick first-strike military attack that seeks to defeat an adversary before it can undertake aggression.

■ **military necessity**
the legal doctrine asserting that the violation of the rules against the initiation of warfare may be justified during periods of extreme emergency.

Might Makes Fright America's military supremacy and unilateral muscle flexing throughout the world has alarmed and angered even some of America's closest allies. As former U.S. Secretary of State Henry Kissinger warned after George W. Bush's November 2004 re-election, the United States today "acts as the trustee of global stability," but is seen as a bully cultivating a climate of fear. Shown here is one example: When Bush visited Canada in December 2004, protesters in that allied country made a statue of him to topple, just as U.S. troops and Iraqis toppled statues of Saddam Hussein after the U.S. Army overran Iraq. "Unilateralism for its own sake is self-defeating," Kissinger added. "The challenge for America is to reconcile consultation with vast power."

rorist state. "If Iran gets a weapon of mass destruction, deliverable by a missile, that's going to be a problem for all of us, including Russia," Bush warned.

Putting an immediate end to global terrorism is not regarded as likely in the near future, by whatever means. Not even U.S. policymakers are optimistic that the war on terrorism can be won quickly and without high risk and causalities. The threat will not vanish soon, as the March 2004, 3/11 terrorist attack in Madrid showed. As Bush warned, "there can be no lasting security in a world at the mercy of terrorists—for my nation, or for any nation." U.S. Vice President Dick Cheney underlined the danger in May 2002 when he declared that terrorists would strike again in the United States and that "it's not a matter of if, but when." "There will be another terrorist attack. We will not be able to stop it. It's something we all will have to live with," U.S. FBI Director Robert Mueller added. So it remains to be seen if the war on terrorism can ultimately be contained, but at present it is unlikely that the danger of global terrorism will recede.

4. Will Separatist Conflict within States Lead to Hundreds of New States?

Throughout world history, when distinct cultures have come into contact, either the collisions have sparked communication and a healthy respect for diversity or familiarity has bred contempt. When followers have embraced **ethnocentrism,** the view that their own group's values are inherently superior, animosity and disrespect for differences have been especially characteristic, and persecution and killing have often followed.

Civilizations such as those of both the Western and the Islamic traditions tend to think of themselves ethnocentrically, which is why Samuel Huntington (1996) predicts that a **clash of civilizations** will dominate world politics. Another possibility is the rise of ethnic clashes *within* states, between tribes and religions. An epidemic of violent conflicts has erupted already between nationalities whose identity is defined by a shared language, religion, or race that makes their members feel different from others. Most of these have involved the indigenous peoples of the **Fourth World** threatened with **state terrorism** and **ethnic cleansing.** The predictable result is that many civil wars have erupted that threaten to break existing states into many new separate states. East Timor's formal entry into the international community in 2002 as an independent sovereign state following four hundred years of Portuguese colonial rule and another twenty years of brutal occupation by Indonesia is another recent example of the state-formation trend under way. Between 1980 and 1998, more than thirteen new states on average were created *each year* (Enriquez 1999, 40).

Most of the globe's 210 independent countries are made up of many different nationality and ethnic groups, and it is not surprising that a large number of the globe's three- to five-thousand indigenous peoples and ethnic minorities are seeking **self-determination.** Rebellion is especially prevalent in **failing states** where governments have lost the support of the population, can no longer maintain law and order, and have massacred rebelling peoples instead of protecting their human rights. If every major "political and ethnic and religious group" won independence, President Bill Clinton warned in October 1999, "we might have eight hundred countries in the world, [perhaps even] eight thousand."

The dilemma created by the striving for independence around the globe is that it pits important values against one another. Sovereign independence and human rights are treasured, but so are prosperity and peace. How will these values be reconciled, if at all? Would the breakup of states into smaller units be a blessing or a burden to the long-term collective interests of humanity?

5. Will the Great Powers Intervene to Protect Human Rights?

Conflicts within countries are raging throughout the world. Many civilians are the targets of overt oppression and violence by the governments presumably created to preserve law and order in courts and through ballots. Of great concern is whether the moral outrage of the globe's major powers will be sufficient for them to make concerted peacekeeping and peacemaking interventions to end **human rights** abuses in those countries where standards of conduct accepted in international law have been blatantly disregarded. Atrocities in many failed states each year force a mass exodus of tens of millions of refugees and **dis-**

■ **ethnocentrism**
a propensity to see one's nationality or state as the center of the world and therefore special, with the result that the values and perspectives of other groups are misunderstood and ridiculed.

■ **clash of civilizations**
Samuel Huntington's prediction that conflict between the globe's major "civilizations" will dominate world affairs, leading to anarchy and warfare similar to that resulting from conflicts between states over the past five hundred years.

■ **Fourth World**
indigenous people or native ethnic and tribal groups who often live in poverty and deprivation within a state that occupies the land from which they originate.

■ **state terrorism**
formal assistance, training, and arming of terrorists by a state in order to achieve foreign and domestic policy goals.

■ **ethnic cleansing**
the extermination of an ethnic minority group by a state, in violation of international law.

■ **self-determination**
the doctrine that asserts nationalities have the right to determine what political authority will represent and rule them.

Ignoring Systematic Slaughter in Sudan? While global attention was riveted on crises in the Middle East and suicide bombings of American occupation forces in Iraq, a two-year genocidal war was waged by Omar el-Bashir's Arab government in an effort to eliminate black skin on the land it ruthlessly rules in Sudan. Like the inaction ten years earlier that allowed the ethnic cleansing in Rwanda, by early 2005 no humanitarian intervention had been launched to end the Sudanese bloodbath. Millions have been either killed or driven from their homes. Shown here is a Sudanese refugee after she and her family reached sanctuary on the Chad border after hiding for a year in a cave in Sudan's Darfur region. Called the worst genocide since the Holocaust, this campaign of slaughter raised deep concerns that the world's great powers intervene only when vital security interests or materials such as oil are threatened.

■ **failing states**
those governments that are in danger of losing the loyalty of their citizens, who are rebelling against corruption and administrative failure and in the process tearing the country into separate political parts.

■ **human rights**
the political rights and civil liberties recognized by the international community as inalienable and valid for individuals in all countries by virtue of their humanity.

■ **displaced people**
people involuntarily uprooted from their homes and forced either to flee outside their state or to seek sanctuary within their own countries.

■ **nonintervention norm**
a fundamental international legal principle, now being challenged, that traditionally has defined interference by one state in the domestic affairs of another as illegal.

placed people from their homes to seek safety. The global community is being put to a test of its true ideals and its capacity to defend them, at potentially high costs. Will a humanitarian concern for the victims targeted for extermination crystallize into a response? Or will the victims perish in a sea of indifference?

Human rights law now provides unprecedented protection in principle for people everywhere to live in freedom without fear. The traditional legal rule of state sovereignty and its corollary—the **nonintervention norm** prohibiting external interference in the internal affairs of states—has been revised. UN Secretary-General Kofi Annan described well the redefinition when he noted that "states are now widely understood to be instruments at the service of their people, and not vice versa. At the same time . . . the fundamental freedom of each individual, enshrined in the charter of the UN and subsequent international treaties—[has] been enhanced by a renewed and spreading consciousness of individual [human] rights. When we read the charter today, we are more than ever conscious that its aim is to protect individual human beings, not to protect those who abuse them."

Principle is one thing; the reality of human suffering another. Will the great powers in the globalized community back their expressed convictions with action to free humanity from the oppression of mass murder? Can the great powers agree on a **doctrine** for **humanitarian intervention** that defines when it is legitimate to militarily respond to gross violations of "human rights, wherever they take place, and also on ways of deciding what action is necessary, and when, and by whom"? The challenge, Kofi Annan elaborated, is to transcend traditional notions of sovereignty. Those old ideas remain an "obstacle to effective action in humanitarian crises" that still encourages states "to stand idly by while the horror unfolds," instead of taking military action to enforce international human rights law. If the global community truly recognizes that all people have rights that transcend national borders, and defines those human rights as the core of the community's "common global interests," then it will have to answer and act on the essential unresolved questions, "What is the common interest? Who shall define it? Who shall defend it? Under whose authority? And by what means of intervention?" True global governance will begin if a consensus can be reached on such monumental questions and if the world's commitment to humanitarian action worldwide is then backed by **collective security** action irrespective of region or state.

6. Will Globalization Tie the World Together or Tear It Apart?

Former Soviet President Mikhail Gorbachev observed in 1999, "Politics is being conducted in a terribly clumsy way everywhere." Why does it suddenly appear that the world and the states within it are spinning out of control? One answer is ascribed to **globalization,** a widely accepted socially constructed code word understood as a transforming force that is creating sweeping governance crises in a new age of increasing interdependent complexity. Globalization captures the idea that everyone and everything on the planet is now more closely connected than ever before, but on an institutional foundation that is shaky and unprepared for managing the massive adjustments brought on by accelerating worldwide changes. Most affected and at a loss are the so-called sovereign states, no longer able to exercise control over the economic, political, and environmental problems within their territories. States everywhere are experiencing a sense of lost **sovereignty** as they attempt to cope with the pressures originating outside their borders. Simply put, the communications and technology revolution has sped the flow of information, capital, people, and jobs across state boundaries, and the integration of the globe is forcing a redefinition—of historic proportions—of the role of states within this transformed, interconnected world.

The shrinking of distances and sharing of knowledge and ideas characteristic of a borderless world and common cosmopolitan culture have reduced old feelings of independence, identity, and autonomy and driven many states to surrender some of their sovereignty in order to benefit from collaborative participation in a competitive global marketplace. The message has been heard everywhere: borders and barriers cannot be revived in a nationalistic effort to close off a country in solitary isolation. "Join the world or become irrelevant" is the way Edward Ballador, a former French prime minister, described "the end of **nationalism**."

Many people feel that globalization is the whole world's problem. To be sure, it is not just a threat, but an opportunity as well. When everyone depends on

■ **doctrine**
a statement of the principles a state's leaders will follow when making decisions about solutions to anticipated national security problems, such as the conditions under which it will use military power and armed force for political purposes abroad.

■ **humanitarian intervention**
the use of peacekeeping troops by foreign states or international organizations to protect endangered people from gross violations of their human rights and from mass murder and starvation.

■ **collective security**
the principle that it is the responsibility of all states to act in concert to protect human security every place through united multilateral action.

■ **globalization**
the integration of states through increasing contact, communication, and trade to create a holistic, single global system in which the process of change increasingly binds people together in a common fate.

■ **sovereignty**
the legal doctrine that states have supreme authority to govern their internal affairs and manage their foreign relations with other states and IGOs.

■ **nationalism**
a mindset glorifying the nationalities of a people living in a state that holds loyalty to the state's national interests as a supreme value.

everyone else, they *must* work together. "People are recognizing that if there is a serious problem with the Brazilian economy," British Prime Minister Tony Blair counseled in 1999, "it develops into a serious problem for the British economy or the European economy or the American economy. It is similar with security problems." The challenge of globalization resides primarily in the fact that it reduces states' control over their national future and their capacity to govern, in conjunction with the pressing need to create stronger institutions of international governance to regulate the global system's integrated free market economy. The crisis of complexity makes it imperative that states work together and undertake bold departures from the **self-help** approaches of the past. "The only practical prospect for universal peace [and prosperity] must be more civilization" through globalization, and so to attain this goal "we should strive to create the largest social, economic, and political units possible, ideally one encompassing the whole world" (Keeley 1996). These observers see globalization optimistically as an unstoppable engine for unity and progress. They reason that people who trade have shared interests and fewer incentives to fight; by integrating countries' investments and consumers in the global economy, the capacity for troublemaking and warmaking among countries will be reduced. At the extreme is Thomas Friedman's (1999) celebratory view in his best-selling book *The Lexus and the Olive Tree: Understanding Globalization* that globalization is a **public good** to be promoted as a cause for human development because it will ultimately increase the wealth of everyone everywhere. Adds Francis Fukuyama (2002), "The September 11 terrorist attacks on the United States represent a serious detour, but in the end modernization and globalization will remain the central structuring principles of world politics."

There are in actuality serious questions about how future domestic and international problems will be addressed in such a globalized world without organized global governance. There are "many globalizations" operating in a culturally diverse world that affect different peoples differently (Berger and Huntington 2002). How will this complexity be managed? Can it be managed when so many people are not participating in the benefits of globalization and are threatened by it and anxious to reverse it? These questions were allegedly uppermost in the 9/11 suicide terrorists' minds, who sought to overturn their hated symbol of globalization's commercial culture, the United States (Howell 2003). These complaints are symptomatic, too, of the challenge of the minority groups' quest for autonomy from within and of the challenge of NGOs (such as Doctors without Borders and multinational corporations) from outside. Many observers blame globalization for leaders' confusion about how to react to the crisis of globalization's economic and social impact on those not benefiting. "We need to be concerned," Kofi Annan advised in October 2002, "about the gulf between insiders and outsiders in a globalized world . . . where the privileges of the few are painfully apparent to those multitudes who still yearn for liberty and opportunity."

To make globalization a green, clean, and compassionate process for engineering **sustainable development** for all humanity, a global **civil society** will require greater global governance to manage a world knit closer together. Globalization may have emasculated the sovereign power of states, but this same force has strengthened many governments (Lentner 2004; Opello and Rosow 2004). The question for the future is whether humanity can count on relatively powerless but growing NGOs at the grassroots level, now numbering more than

■ **self-help**
the principle that because in international anarchy all global actors are independent, they must rely on themselves to provide for their security and well-being.

■ **public good**
a shared value from which everyone who has access to the value benefits, such as safe drinking water, even if not everyone contributes to its creation or preservation.

■ **sustainable development**
economic growth that does not deplete the resources needed for future growth.

■ **civil society**
a community that embraces shared norms and ethical standards to collectively manage problems, without coercion and through peaceful and democratic procedures for making decisions to promote human welfare.

A Worldwide Integrated Market Today, products made anywhere are available for sale everywhere. Internet access is common worldwide, even in countries such as China that fear the growth of electronic underground journals that circulate information critical of state policies. Here a billboard advertises for a computer company in Shenzen, China. The information age is rapidly making every place more like every other place, in part because "Computing power has doubled every eighteen months for the last thirty years. . . . Similarly, growth of the Internet and the World Wide Web has been exponential. Internet traffic doubles every 100 days" (Keohane and Nye 2001b, 28).

thirty-one thousand, seeking through global public policy networks to assume responsibility for engineering human progress. If states do not respond to the challenge, can the world's people expect a new global architecture with accepted supranational global governance and global norms to crystalize? This may be the most important issue facing twenty-first-century world politics.

7. Is Realism Still Realistic and Is Liberalism Still Too Idealistic?

Since the eve of World War II, leaders and scholars alike have constructed their thoughts and images almost exclusively from the perspective of realism. Their reliance on realism to explain and predict international developments was understandable. Finding a fertile ground in which to flourish during the conflict-ridden fifty-year period between 1939 and 1989, realism accounted for, better than any other theoretical perspective, the great powers' prevailing lust for power, the appetite for imperial expansion and struggle for hegemony, the all-consuming arms race, and the obsession with military security.

At least until the shattering events of 9/11, and still after it, however, a window opened to expose quite different dimensions of world politics that were previously neglected. In the peaceful and prosperous 1990s the global agenda shifted from geopolitics to geo-economics to deal less with great-power competition for hegemony and more with the rising issues of transnational interdependence such as global warming, trade balances, and environmental protection. Welfare, not warfare, was the primary concern, and liberal institutional multilateral cooperation using "smart power" instead of military force was ascendant (Nossel 2004). As a consequence of these changing issues commanding the world's concern, the realist image of states as unitary rational actors looked increasingly archaic. In the borderless global village, nongovernmental organizations (NGOs) composed of private citizen groups have flexed their muscles and raised their voices, and they are being heard and are orchestrating changes in people's values. "More and more," observed Espen Barth Eide of the Norwegian Foreign Policy Institute in 1997, "the global agenda is being set by others . . . rather than [by] superpowers and governments."

To a number of theorists, the broadened and transformed global agenda goes beyond what realism can be expected to address accurately. To their minds, realist preoccupations threaten to mask the deeper political, economic, and social challenges in international affairs. Many critics are disturbed by realism's failure to anticipate the democratic revolutions that accompanied the Cold War's end, the voluntary retreat of the Soviet Union, and global change and cooperation generally. "The wisdom [that] calls itself 'realism,'" scolded Harvard University's Stanley Hoffmann (in Friedman 1993), "is utter nonsense today." Perhaps it was this sentiment that prompted Jeffrey Legro and Andrew Moravcsik (1999) to ask, "Is anybody still a realist?" If these critics of realism's receding accuracy and relevance are correct, then pressure will mount for a new theoretical approach that places less emphasis than realism, neorealism, and **neotraditional realism** on conflict in world politics and on military power and self-help to maintain international stability.

What a new theory will or should look like is not presently obvious, as challengers to realism differ in their prescriptions. Yet many agree with the general view that "it is time for a new, more rigorous idealist alternative to realism" (Kober 1990) and that "there are good reasons for examining aspects of the liberal international legacy once again" (Fukuyama 1992a) by giving Woodrow Wilson's liberal vision "the fair test it has never received" (Gaddis 1990; see also McNamara and Blight 2001). A number of scholars and policymakers have advocated **neoliberalism** for interpreting world politics and the transformed conditions of globalization. Such a new liberal approach emphasizes the transnational interdependence that drives cooperation in international affairs; it attaches importance to global governance, international law, and high ideals such as the promotion and protection of human rights and democracy as methods for reforming international anarchy and weapons proliferation and for creating a world order guided by a shared global consensus about international morality. This liberal perspective places a greater value on ethical principles than on power, on ideals rather than national self-interest (see Lebow 2003).

To the extent that global tensions recede and global harmony and cooperation prevail over warfare, neoliberalism is likely to grow increasingly popular as a way to describe and explain international relations. However, if the world experiences a new arms race and even another war between highly armed adversaries, then liberalism will once again be perceived as too idealistic and optimistic, as it was when World War II began. Should a major war break out between old enemies, such as between India and Pakistan, or if the United States continues to unilaterally confront the world through domination (Bacevich 2003), rely on preemptive military attacks, and dedicate itself to preserving predominate hegemony at all costs (Brzezinski 2004), a climate of continuing heightened global tension will propel the resurgent popularity of realism and neorealism as theories of international security. That resurgence of realism was already highly evident in the wake of 9/11 and the war against international terrorism, and the interpretation that realism constructs of world affairs is certain to regain many adherents if terrorists use weapons of mass destruction to carry out their deadly goals. Realism accounts for violence and the absence of security better than any rival theoretical perspective focusing on humanity's cooperation in such areas as trade.

In all probability, twenty-first-century world politics will continue to display

■ **neotraditional realism**
a body of recent realist theorizing that departs from neorealism by stressing foreign policy more than international structure and that focuses on the internal influences on states' external behavior instead of the global determinants of states' foreign behavior.

■ **neoliberalism**
a theoretical perspective that accounts for the way international institutions promote global change, cooperation, peace, and prosperity through collective reform approaches.

combinations of both conflict and cooperation, unity and disunity, order and disorder. Should those dual properties simultaneously characterize the future of world politics, a synthesis of the rich insights of both realism and liberalism will be needed to capture the divergent trajectories. A reconstructed theory of world politics that fuses the most useful and reasonable assumptions of neorealist and neotraditional realist theories of international politics with those of neoliberalism may provide the intellectual framework needed to understand and guide policy making in the global future. At the moment, "in liberal democracies, realism is the theory that everyone loves to hate" for its disregard of global institutions and law and its seeming acceptance of the amoral imperial pursuit of domination and empire. But some realists call for moderation and prudent resistance to the U.S. drive for power, arguing that "the move toward empire must be halted immediately" (Snyder 2004). Thus realism still speaks to many of the issues that define contemporary power politics, "creatively reassessing how its principles relate to the post-9/11 world." Realism can remain relevant as it accommodates itself to liberal principles in its world view, which, as Jack Snyder (2004) points out, even George W. Bush attempted to do by promising "to fight terror by spreading liberal democracy to the Middle East" and claiming "that skeptics 'who call themselves realists . . . have lost contact with a fundamental reality' that 'America is always more secure when freedom is on the march.'"

8. Is the World Preparing for the Wrong War?

To preserve peace, one must prepare for war. That remains the classical realist formula for national security. But would states not be wiser to prepare to conquer the conditions that undermine prosperity, freedom, and welfare? "War for survival is the destiny of all species," observes philosopher Martin J. Siegel (1983). "In our case, we are courting suicide [by waging war against one another]. The world powers should declare war against their common enemy—the catastrophic and survival-of-the-fittest forces that destroyed most of the species of life that came before us."

Increasingly, fewer world leaders are succumbing to the single-mindedness of preparing to compete with other states. President François Mitterrand of France warned in 1983 that "together we must urgently find the solutions to the real problems at hand—especially unemployment and underdevelopment. This is the battlefield where the outlines of the [future] will be drawn." India's Prime Minister Indira Gandhi predicted that "either nuclear war will annihilate the human race and destroy the earth, thus disposing of any future, or men and women all over must raise their voices for peace and for an urgent attempt to combine the insights of different civilizations with contemporary knowledge. We can survive in peace and goodwill only by viewing the human race as one, and by looking at global problems in their totality." These prescriptions adhere to a fundamental premise, as expressed by Martti Ahtisaari, the former president of Finland: "To deal with the great security challenges of our time, including population growth, the spread of weapons of mass destruction, crime, environmental degradation and ethnic conflicts, we must resolutely adopt new methods of managing change and building global security."

These rhetorical positions doubtless reflect the problems and self-interests the leaders faced at home and abroad. Nonetheless, they reveal a minority view.

■ **human security**
a concept that refers to the degree to which the welfare of individuals is protected and advanced, in contrast to national security, which puts the interests of states first.

The war of people against people goes on. **Human security** remains precarious, as a large percentage of humanity faces famine, poverty, and a denial of basic human rights; millions are threatened by genocide and terrorism sponsored by their own governments. Humankind may consequently self-destruct, not because it lacks opportunities, but because of its collective inability to see and to seize them. "Perhaps we will destroy ourselves. Perhaps the common enemy within us will be too strong for us to recognize and overcome," the eminent astronomer Carl Sagan lamented. "But," he continued, "I have hope. . . . Is it possible that we humans are at last coming to our senses and beginning to work together on behalf of the species and the planet?"

9. Is This the "End of History"?

To many observers, the history of world affairs is the struggle between tyranny and liberty. The contest has taken various forms since antiquity: between kings and mass publics; despotism and democracy; ideological principle and pragmatic politics. Labels are misleading and sometimes dangerous. However, they form the vocabulary of diplomacy and inform theoretical discussion of governance and statecraft. History, in this image, is a battle for hearts and minds. It is an ideological contest for the allegiance of humankind to a particular form of political, social, and economic organization.

With the defeat of fascism in World War II and the collapse of the international communist movement a generation later, it has become fashionable to argue that we have witnessed the end of a historic contest of epic proportions—and thus the triumph of liberalism and what Francis Fukuyama called the **end of history:**

■ **end of history**
the thesis that the philosophy of economic and political liberalism has triumphed throughout the world, ending the contest between market democracies and centrally planned governance.

> The twentieth century saw the developed world descend into a paroxysm of ideological violence, as liberalism contended first with the remnants of absolutism, then bolshevism and fascism, and finally an updated Marxism that threatened to lead to the ultimate apocalypse of nuclear war. But the [twentieth] century that began full of self-confidence in the ultimate triumph of Western liberal democracy seems at its close to be returning full circle to where it started: . . . to the unabashed victory of economic and political liberalism. (Fukuyama 1989, 3; see also Fukuyama 1999b)

The abrupt repudiation of communism has raised expectations that history has indeed "ended," in the sense that liberal democratic capitalism has triumphed throughout most of the world. Liberals, inspired by the belief that "liberal democracy and a market-oriented economic order are the only viable options for modern societies" (Fukuyama 1999b; see also Fukuyama 2004), are heartened by the doubling since the mid-1980s of the number of countries practicing multiparty elections and capitalism at home and in foreign trade. World order, they believe, can best be created by free governments practicing free trade. As Woodrow Wilson argued, making the world "safe for democracy" would make the world itself safe. From this liberal perspective, the diffusion of democratic capitalism bodes well for the future of world politics.

A less reassuring possibility is that history has not "ended" and that the battle between totalitarian and democratic governance is not truly over. There remain many democracies ruled by one-party despots who, although elected, disregard constitutional limits on their power and deny their citizens basic political freedoms and religious and economic human rights. Many governments continue to abuse fundamental civil liberties and freedoms. This persistence of leaders not accountable to the electorate suggests that we may not be witnessing history's end. Like previous turning points in history, tomorrow may signal history's resumption: the return to the ageless search for barriers against the resurgence of tyranny, nationalism, and terrorism and war. Especially to followers of realpolitik, the most salient feature of world politics—the relentless competitive struggle for power under international anarchy—is permanent, and they take as evidence the continuing efforts of terrorist movements to use violence against such despised targets as the United States and the republic for which it stands. There is not assurance that the global community has moved beyond tyranny or interstate competition and militarized conflict. As former Soviet President Mikhail Gorbachev warned in 1992, "A major international effort will be needed to render irreversible the shift in favor of a democratic world—and democratic for the whole of humanity, not just half of it."

10. Is There a Reordered Global Agenda?

The paradox of contemporary world politics is that a world liberated from the paralyzing grip of the Cold War must now face a series of challenges every bit as threatening and as potentially unmanageable. Globalization has simultaneously enlarged the responsibilities and expanded the issues to be confronted. In a prosperous and stable period of history, when confidence in peace and economic growth was high, and his administration was still in office, U.S. President Bill Clinton found it necessary to warn that "profound and powerful forces are shaking and remaking our world. And the urgent question of our time is whether we can make change our friend and not our enemy."

The changes in recent years have spawned transnational threats to world order, in addition to the resurgence of nationalism, ethnic conflict, failed states, and separatist revolts. These include acid rain, AIDS and other contagious diseases, drug trafficking, international organized crime, ozone depletion, climate change, obstacles to gender equality, energy and food insecurity, desertification and deforestation, financial crises and collapsing economies, and neomercantile trade protectionism.

The potential impact of these additional threats is formidable, as emerging trends suggest that nonmilitary dangers will multiply alongside the continuing threat of arms and armed conflicts in civil wars, as well as interstate wars in particular regions and terrorism almost any place and at any time in the world. As distance and borders cease to be barriers in the global village, low politics is becoming high politics; conversely, as weapons cut across state boundaries and reduce human security, whenever bombs and bullets are fired, killing people and degrading the environment, high politics has become low politics. Accordingly, the distinction between **high politics** (war and peace) and **low politics** (economic and other issues of human welfare) may disappear. How will humanity set priorities for action in a system crowded with so many interrelated issues and problems, all of which require attention if peace and prosperity with justice is to prevail?

■ **high politics**
geostrategic issues of national and international security that pertain to matters of war and peace.

■ **low politics**
the category of global issues related to the economic, social, demographic, and environmental aspects of relations between governments and people.

A NEW WORLD ORDER OR NEW WORLD DISORDER?

Previously established patterns and relationships have been obliterated. Something revolutionary, not simply new, appears to be unfolding. This book has focused on global change. It has identified the most important changes under way that are potentially leading to transformations in world politics. Change, as we have seen, can be abrupt or slow. It moves constantly, but at its own pace, and history reminds us that the evolutionary direction of global change is uncertain. Many trends are unfolding at the same time, and their impact in combination can move the world along an unexpected trajectory. In addition, trends can reverse themselves, and each trend that moves forward advances at its own rate. Some trends move incredibly slowly in an evolutionary process that can only result in dramatic transformations over many centuries, where others exhibit short bursts of rapid change, interrupted by long periods of stasis or continuity. Many examples of reversible, interrupted, and constant trends exist, as you have learned in this book's survey. It is in their mix that the future will be shaped.

To appreciate their diverse ways of combining, we must construct our images by using memories of the past and by being inspired by visions of the future. In 1775, an American revolutionary, Patrick Henry, underscored the importance of history, observing that he had "but one lamp by which my feet are guided, and that is the lamp of experience. I know of no way of judging the future but by the past." Decades later, in 1848, another patriot, the Italian political leader Guiseppe Mazzini, stressed the importance of futurist thinking when he similarly observed, "great things are achieved by guessing the direction of one's century." All of us need both perspectives, constructed with keen awareness that our images of history and of the future must avoid the temptation to see ourselves and our own country as we wish to be seen without taking into account how differently others might view us and our state.

From the early part of the twenty-first century, it now appears that the collective impact of the divergent trends under way is signaling a major transformation in world politics. Yet, juxtaposed against the revolutionary is the persistent—the durability of accepted rituals, existing rules, established institutions, and entrenched customs that resist the pull of the momentous recent changes in world politics. Persistence and change coexist uneasily, and it is this mixture that makes the future so uncertain. The twin forces of integration and disintegration, continuity and change, create a mood of both confidence and disorientation. As Australia's Prime Minister John Howard put it in 1997, "In one sense, you are a remarkably lucky generation, but in another sense you have been born into a period of social and technological change . . . and economic evolution."

The outcomes of two races will determine the difference between the world that is and the world that will be. The first is the race between knowledge and oblivion. Ignorance stands in the way of global progress and justice. Advances in science and technology far outpace resolution of the social and political problems they generate. Building the knowledge to confront these problems may therefore present the ultimate challenge. "The splitting of the atom," Albert Einstein warned, has "changed everything save our modes of thinking, and thus we drift toward unparalleled catastrophe. Unless there is a fundamental change in

Picturing Global Destiny Globalization "implies a holistic worldview and a rejection of the traditional realist paradigm. A globalist perspective embraces a much wider range of important international actors than realism does and addresses a much broader range of issues, as well as expanding the definition of existing concepts such as security" (Sheehan 1996). This view of a globe without borders is captured by this photo taken of the eastern Mediterranean from the Earth-orbiting space shuttle *Columbia*. It pictures an integrated world community, in which humanity shares a common destiny. It also captures the kinds of threats confronting humanity in a globalized world, where problems do not stop at borders. According to scientists studying this photo, the difference in visibility in this panorama suggests that a pollution event near the Black Sea contaminated the atmosphere.

[our] attitudes toward one another as well as [our] concept of the future, the world will face unprecedented disaster."

"Knowledge is our destiny," philosopher Jacob Bronowski declared. If the world is to forge a promising future, it must develop more-sophisticated knowledge. Sophistication demands that we see the world as a whole, as well as in terms of its individual parts. We must overcome the temptation to picture others according to our images of ourselves and to project onto others our own aims and values. We must discard belief in a simple formula for a better tomorrow and resist single-issue approaches to reform. Toleration of ambiguity, even the pursuit of it, is essential.

Realpolitik Definitions of Good versus Evil In the 1980s, when the United States saw Iran as a great threat, it embraced the realpolitik belief that "an anomie of my enemy is my friend," and provided Hussein with arms and aid to assist Iraq in its eight-year war with Iran (Timmerman 1991). The United States saw Hussein as a heroic, reasonable friend, sympathetic to secular Western culture and willing to fight against Islamic extremists. Later, after the Persian Gulf War, U.S. realpolitik pictured Hussein as part of the "axis of evil" in the world, and in 2003 launched Operation Iraqi Freedom. Shown at right, an unidentified man in Washington, D.C., looks at the front pages of international newspapers announcing Saddam Hussein's capture on December 15, 2003. After Hussein's capture, he condemned America as evil and its war as illegal. His trial began in 2005; meanwhile, the mayhem in Iraq continued.

The future of world politics also rests on the outcome of a race between states' ability to cooperatively act in concert and their historic tendency to compete and fight. Paraphrasing a line from William Shakespeare's *Julius Caesar*, U.S. National Security Adviser Samuel Berger, noting in 1997 that it was time for the international community to get beyond settling conflicts by force, said, "I come not only to praise the post–Cold War era, but to bury it." Only concerted international cooperation can avert slipping back into military conflicts guided by the belief that "might alone makes right." Because "policymakers have a deep-seated penchant for putting off hard choices as long as possible" (George 2000), the world's political will to implement the reforms necessary to meet global challenges is uncertain.

The future is cloudy, but it is ours to shape. The moving words of President John F. Kennedy thus describe a posture we might well assume: "However close we sometimes seem to that dark and final abyss, let no man of peace and freedom despair. For he does not stand alone. . . . Together we shall save our planet or together we shall perish in its flames. Save it we can, and save it we must, and then shall we earn the eternal thanks of mankind."

KEY TERMS

zero-sum	Fourth World	sovereignty
realism	state terrorism	nationalism
liberalism	ethnic cleansing	self-help
national security	self-determination	public good
security dilemma	failing states	sustainable development
hegemon	human rights	civil society
politics	displaced people	neotraditional realism
soft power	nonintervention norm	neoliberalism
preemptive war	doctrine	human security
military necessity	humanitarian intervention	end of history
ethnocentrism	collective security	high politics
clash of civilizations	globalization	low politics

SUGGESTED READING

Balkin, Jack M. *The Laws of Change*. New York: Pantheon, 2003.

Blyth, Mark. *Great Transformations*. Cambridge: Cambridge University Press, 2002.

Cornish, Edward. *Futuring: The Exploration of the Future*. Bethesda, Md.: World Future Society, 2004.

Denemark, Robert A., Jonathan Friedman, Barry K. Gills, and George Modelski, eds. *World System History: The Social Science of Long-Term Change*. London: Routledge, 2000.

Friedman, Thomas L. *Longitudes and Attitudes: Exploring the World after September 11*. New York: Farrar, Straus & Giroux, 2002.

Fukuyama, Francis. *State-Building: Governance and World Order in the 21st Century*. Ithaca, N.Y.: Cornell University Press, 2004.

Kegley, Charles W., Jr., ed. *The New Global Terrorism: Characteristics, Causes, Controls*. Upper Saddle River, N.J.: Prentice Hall, 2003.

Kegley, Charles W, Jr., and Gregory A. Raymond. *The Global Future*. Belmont, Calif.: Thomson/Wadsworth, 2005.

Lomborg, Bjørn, (ed.). *Global Crises, Global Solutions*. Cambridge: Cambridge University Press, 2004.

Mead, Walter Russell. *Power, Terror, Peace and War*. New York: Alfred A. Knopf, 2004.

Singer, Peter. *One World: The Ethics of Globalization*, 2nd ed. New Haven, Conn.: Yale University Press, 2004.

Snyder, Jack. "One World, Rival Theories," *Foreign Policy* (November–December 2004): 53–62.

WHERE ON THE WORLD WIDE WEB?

International Futures Programme
http://www1.oecd.org/sge/au/index.htm

The Organization for Economic Cooperation and Development (OECD) has designed a program to help decision makers in government and industry deal with the formidable challenge of assessing the long-term trends that shape our global future. Scan the website and read about conferences and projects now under way. Do you think this is a good model for other organizations that strive to understand the changes occurring in the international system? What suggestions can you give?

WHERE ON THE WORLD WIDE WEB? (continued)

World Citizen Foundation
http://www.worldcitizen.org/

As a student of international relations, you may ask yourself if there is a better way to organize international relations than the state system. The World Citizen website allows you to think about your world citizenship, asking how we, as world citizens, can collectively govern our world. The World Citizen Foundation believes that the Internet can help serve as a communication tool whereby the citizens of the world can vote on common global issues. Do you believe that one day soon we may be able to vote on world issues like we do national issues? Is it possible to form a world government?

World Future Society
http://www.wfs.org/

This last chapter of your text asks you to think about future global trends. To help with this task, visit the World Future Society website. The World Future Society is a nonprofit educational and scientific organization whose main interest is how social and technological developments are shaping the future. Its website is a neutral clearinghouse for ideas about the future. Peruse the "News" section to find current articles of interest. You can also participate in one or more of the several discussion forums.

INFOTRAC COLLEGE EDITION

Brown, Lester R. "A Planet Under Stress: Rising to the Challenge." *The Futurist* (November–December 2003).

Millett, Stephen M. "Tomorrow's Conflicts: Faster, Safer, and Casualty-Free." *The Futurist* (November–December 2003).

Maiti, Prasenjit. "Clash of Civilizations?" *The Humanist* (November–December 2001).

Friedman, Thomas L. "States of Discord." *Foreign Policy* (March 2002).

For more articles, enter:
"war" in the Subject Guide, and then go to subdivision "analysis"
"globalization" in the Subject Guide, and then go to subdivision "evaluation"
"United Nations" in the Subject Guide, and then go to subdivision "forecasts"

Go to http://politicalscience.wadsworth.com/kegley10 to access additional resources related to this chapter.

REFERENCES

Aaronson, Susan Ariel. (2001) *Taking Trade to the Streets: The Lost History of Public Efforts to Shape Globalization.* Ann Arbor: University of Michigan Press.

Abramowitz, Morton. (2002) "The Bush Team Isn't Coping," *International Herald Tribune* (August 20): 6.

Adelman, Kenneth L., and Norman R. Augustine. (1992) "Defense Conversion," *Foreign Affairs* 71 (Spring): 26–47.

Adler, Emanuel. (2002) "Constructivism and International Relations," pp. 95–118 in Walter Carlsnaes, Thomas Risse, and Beth Simmons (eds.), *Handbook of International Relations.* London: Sage.

Adler, Emanuel, and Michael Barnett (eds.). (1998) *Security Communities.* Cambridge: Cambridge University Press.

Albright, David. (1993) "A Proliferation Primer," *Bulletin of the Atomic Scientists* 49 (June): 14–23.

Albright, Madeleine. (2000) "Time to Renew Faith in the Nonproliferation Treaty," *International Herald Tribune* (March 7): 8.

Alesina, Alberto, and Enrique Spolaore. (2003) *The Size of Nations.* Cambridge, Mass.: MIT Press.

Allen, John L. (2002) *Student Atlas of World Politics*, 5th ed. New York: Dushkin/McGraw-Hill.

———. (2001) *Student Atlas World Geography*, 2nd ed. New York: McGraw-Hill.

———. (2000) *Student Atlas of World Politics*, 4th ed. New York: Dushkin/McGraw Hill.

Allen, John L., and Elizabeth J. Leppman. (2004) *Student Atlas of World Politics*, 6th ed. Guilford, Conn.: Dushkin/McGraw-Hill.

Allison, Graham T. (2004) *Nuclear Terrorism: The Ultimate Preventable Catastrophe.* New York: Henry Holt.

———. (1971) *Essence of Decision: Explaining the Cuban Missile Crisis.* Boston: Little, Brown.

Allison, Graham T., and Philip Zelikow. (1999) *Essence of Decision: Explaining the Cuban Missile Crisis*, 2nd ed. New York: Longman.

Al-Sammarrai, Bashir. (1995) "Economic Sanctions against Iraq," pp.133–39 in David Cortwright and George A. Lopez (eds.), *Economic Sanctions.* Boulder, Colo.: Westview.

Altman, Lawrence K. (2002) "AIDS Is Called a Security Threat," *International Herald Tribune* (October 7): 1, 10.

Altman, Roger C., and C. Bowman Cutter. (1999) "Global Economy Needs Better Shock Absorbers," *International Herald Tribune* (June 16): 7.

Angell, Norman. (1910) *The Great Illusion: A Study of the Relationship of Military Power in Nations to Their Economic and Social Advantage.* London: Weidenfeld & Nicholson.

Annan, Kofi. (1999) "Two Concepts of Sovereignty," *Economist* (September 18): 49–50.

Ardrey, Robert. (1966) *The Territorial Imperative: A Personal Inquiry into the Animal Origins of Property and Nations.* New York: Atheneum.

Arkin, William M. (1995) "The Pentagon's Blind Ambition," *New York Times* (May 10): A19.

Art, Robert J. (2005) "Coercive Diplomacy," pp. 163-177 in Robert J. Art and Robert Jervis (eds.), *International Politics*, 7th ed. New York: Pearson Longman.

———. (1999) "Geopolitics Updated: The Strategy of Selective Engagement," *International Security* 23 (Winter): 79–113.

A. T. Kearney/*Foreign Policy*. (2004) "Measuring Globalization" *Foreign Policy* (March–April): 54–69.

———. (2002) "Globalization's Last Hurrah?" *Foreign Policy* (January–February): 38–71.

Atwood, Brian. (1999) "Trade, Not Aid," *Christian Science Monitor* (July 6): 9.

Auguste, Byron G. (1999) "What's So New about Globalization?" pp. 45–47 in Helen E. Purkitt (ed.), *World Politics 99/00*, 20th ed. Guilford, Conn.: Dushkin/McGraw-Hill.

Avery, Dennis. (1995) "Saving the Planet with Pesticides," pp. 49–82 in Ronald Bailey (ed.), *The True State of the Planet.* New York: Free Press.

Ayoob, Mohammed. (2004) "Third World Perspectives on Humanitarian Intervention," *Global Governance* 10 (January–March): 99–118.

———. (1995) *The Third World Security Predicament.* Boulder, Colo.: Lynne Rienner.

Babai, Don. (2001) "International Monetary Fund," pp. 412–18 in Joel Krieger (ed.), *The Oxford Companion to Politics of the World*, 2nd ed. Oxford: Oxford University Press.

Babones, Jonathan, and Jonathan H. Turner. (2004) "Global Inequality," pp. 101–20 in George Ritzer (ed.), *Handbook of Social Problems.* London: Sage.

Bacevich, Andrew J. (ed.). (2003) *The Imperial Tense.* Chicago: Ivan R. Dee/Rowman & Littlefield.

———. (2002) *American Empire.* Cambridge, Mass.: Harvard University Press.

Badey, Thomas J. (ed.). (2005) *Violence and Terrorism 05/06*, 8th ed. Guilford, Conn.: Dushkin/McGraw-Hill.

Bagdikian, Ben H. (1992) *The Media Monopoly.* Boston: Beacon.

Baker, Raymond W., and Jennifer Nordin. (1999) "A 150-to-1 Ratio Is Far Too Lopsided for Comfort," *International Herald Tribune* (February 5): 6.

Baldwin, David A. (2000) "The Sanctions Debate and the Logic of Choice," *International Security* 24 (Winter): 80–107.

——— (ed.). (1993) *Neorealism and Neoliberalism: The Contemporary Debate.* New York: Columbia University Press.

Barber, Benjamin R. (2003) *Fear's Empire: War, Terrorism, and Democracy in an Age of Interdependence.* New York: Norton.

———. (1995) *Jihad vs. McWorld.* New York: Random House.

Barbieri, Katherine. (2003) *The Liberal Illusion: Does Trade Promote Peace?* Ann Arbor: University of Michigan Press.

Barbieri, Katherine, and Gerald Schneider. (1999) "Globalization and Peace," *Journal of Peace Research* 36 (July): 387–404.

Barkin, Samuel. (2003) "Realist Constructivism," *International Studies Review* 5 (September): 328–42.

———. (2001) "Resilience of the State," *Harvard International Review* 22 (Winter): 40–46.

Barnes, Joe, Amy Jaffe, and Edward L. Morse. (2004) "The New Geopolitics of Oil," *National Interest* (Winter/Energy Supplement): 3–6.

Barnet, Richard J. (1980) *The Lean Years.* New York: Simon & Schuster.

———. (1977) *The Giants: Russia and America.* New York: Simon & Schuster.

Barnet, Richard J., and John Cavanagh. (1994) *Global Dreams: Imperial Corporations and the New World Order.* New York: Simon & Schuster.

Barnet, Richard J., and Ronald E. Müller. (1974) *Global Reach: The Power of the Multinational Corporations.* New York: Simon & Schuster.

Barnett, Michael, and Martha Finnemore. (2004) *Rules for the World: International Organizations in Global Politics.* Ithaca, N.Y.: Cornell University Press.

Barnett, Thomas P. M. (2004) The Pentagon's New Map. New York: G. P. Putnam's Sons.

Baron, Samuel H., and Carl Pletsch (eds.). (1985) *Introspection in Biography.* Hillsdale, N.J.: Analytic Press.

Beckman, Peter R., and Francine D'Amico (eds.). (1994) *Women, Gender, and World Politics.* Westport, Conn.: Bergin & Garvey.

Beitz, Charles R. (2001) "Human Rights as a Common Concern," *American Political Science Review* 95 (June): 269–82.

Bennett, A. Leroy. (1988) *International Organizations,* 4th ed. Englewood Cliffs, N.J.: Prentice Hall.

Bennett, Scott, and Allan C. Stam. (2004) *The Behavioral Origins of War.* Ann Arbor: University of Michigan Press.

Berdal, Mats, and Mónica Serrano (eds.). (2002) *Transnational Organized Crime and International Security.* Boulder, Colo.: Lynne Rienner.

Berger, Peter L., and Samuel P. Huntington (eds.). (2002) *Many Globalizations: Cultural Diversity in the Contemporary World.* Oxford: Oxford University Press.

Bergesen, Albert, and Ronald Schoenberg. (1980) "Long Waves of Colonial Expansion and Contraction, 1415–1969," pp. 231–77 in Albert Bergesen (ed.), *Studies of the Modern World-System.* New York: Academic Press.

Berghahn, Volker R. (1995) *Imperial Germany, 1871–1914.* Providence, R.I.: Berghahn Books.

Bergsten, C. Fred. (2004) "The Risks Ahead for the World Economy," *Economist* (September 11): 63–65.

———. (2000) "Free Trade Is a Real Boon for the Developing World," *International Herald Tribune* (February 9): 9.

———. (1997) "American Politics, Global Trade," *Economist* 344 (September 27): 23–26.

Bernstein, Richard. (2003) "Aging Europe Finds Its Pension Is Running Out," *New York Times International* (June 29): 3.

Bertelsen, Judy S. (ed.). (1977) *Nonstate Nations in International Politics.* New York: Praeger.

Berthelot, Yves. (2001) "The International Financial Architecture—Plans for Reform," *International Social Science Journal* 170 (December): 586–96.

Bhagwati, Jagdish. (2004) *In Defense of Globalization.* New York: Oxford University Press.

———. (1999) *A Stream of Windows: Trade, Immigration, and Democracy.* Cambridge, Mass.: MIT Press.

———. (1993) "The Case for Free Trade," *Scientific American* 269 (November): 41–49.

Bienefeld, Manfred. (1994) "The New World Order: Echoes of a New Imperialism," *Third World Quarterly* 15 (March): 31–48.

Birdsall, Nancy. (2001) "Life Is Unfair: Inequality in the World," pp. 361–74 in Charles W. Kegley, Jr., and Eugene R. Wittkopf (eds.), *The Global Agenda,* 6th ed. Boston: McGraw-Hill.

Blainey, Geoffrey. (1988) *The Causes of War,* 3rd ed. New York: Free Press.

Blanton, Shannon Lindsey. (1999) "Examining the Impact of Arms Transfers on Human Development," *Journal of Third World Studies* 16 (Fall): 75–93.

Blanton, Shannon Lindsey, and Charles W. Kegley, Jr. (1997) "Reconciling U.S. Arms Sales with America's Interests and Ideals," *Futures Research Quarterly* 13 (Spring): 85–101.

Blechman, Barry M. (1995) "The Intervention Dilemma," *Washington Quarterly* 18 (Summer): 63–73.

Blinken, Anthony J. (2004) "From Preemption to Engagement," *Survival* 45 (Winter): 33–60.

Blumenthal, W. Michael. (1988) "The World Economy and Technological Change," *Foreign Affairs* 66 (No 3): 529–50.

Blustein, Paul. (1999) "Currencies in Crisis," *Washington Post National Weekly Edition* (March 1): 6–7.

Blyth, Mark. (2002) *Great Transformations.* Cambridge, U.K.: Cambridge University Press.

Boli, John, Michael A. Elliott, and Franziska Bieri. (2004) "Globalization," pp. 389–415 in George Ritzer (ed.), *Handbook of Social Problems.* London: Sage.

Boli, John, and Frank Lechner. (2004) *World Culture.* London: Blackwell.

Bolton, John R. (2001) "United Nations," pp. 871–73 in Joel Krieger (ed.), *The Oxford Companion to Politics of the World,* 2nd ed. New York: Oxford University Press.

Bolton, M. Kent. (2005) *U.S. Foreign Policy and International Politics: George W. Bush, 9/11, and the Global-Terrorist Hydra.* Upper Saddle River, N.J.: Prentice Hall.

Borenstein, Seth. (2003) "U.S. to Revive Dormant Nuclear-Power Industry," *Columbia (S.C.) State* (June 16): A5.

Borrus, Michael, Steve Weber, John Zysman, and Joseph Willihnganz. (1992) "Mercantilism and Global Security," *National Interest* 29 (Fall): 21–29.

Bostdorff, Denise M. (1993) *The Presidency and the Rhetoric of Foreign Crisis.* Columbia: University of South Carolina Press.

Boswell, Terry. (1989) "Colonial Empires and the Capitalist World-Economy: A Time Series Analysis of Colonization, 1640–1960," *American Sociological Review* 54 (April): 180–96.

Bowring, Philip. (2004) "Echoes of Panic over Global Disease," *International Herald Tribune* (February 18): 7.

———. (2001) "Thinking at Cross-Purposes about Globalization," *International Herald Tribune* (February 1): 8.

Boyle, Francis A. (2004) *Destroying World Order.* London: Clarity/Zed.

Bozeman, Adda B. (1994) *Politics and Culture in International History.* New Brunswick, N.J.: Transaction.

Braudel, Fernand. (1973) *The Mediterranean and the Mediterranean World at the Age of Philip II.* New York: Harper.

Braveboy-Wagner, Jacqueline Anne (ed.). (2003) *The Foreign Policies of the Global South.* Boulder, Colo.: Lynne Rienner.

Brecher, Michael. (1993) *Crises in World Politics.* Oxford, Eng.: Pergamon.

Brecher, Michael, and Jonathan Wilkenfeld. (1997) *A Study of Crisis.* Ann Arbor: University of Michigan Press.

Brecke, Peter. (1999) "The Characteristics of Violent Conflict since 1400 A.D.," paper presented at the annual meeting of the International Studies Association, Washington, D.C., February 17–20.

Brierly, James L. (1944) *The Outlook for International Law.* Oxford, Eng.: Clarendon.

Broad, Robin (ed.). (2002) *Global Backlash: Citizen Initiatives for a Just World Economy.* Lanham, Md.: Rowman & Littlefield.

Broder, David. (2002) "Senator Brings Vietnam Experiences to Bear on Iraq," *Columbia (S.C.) State* (September 18): A15.

———. (1999) "Global Forces May Change Balance between States and Federal Government," *Columbia (S.C.) State* (August 11): A9.

Bronfenbrenner, Urie. (1971) "The Mirror Image in Soviet–American Relations," *Journal of Social Issues* 27 (No. 1): 46–51.

Brown, Justin. (1999) "Arms Sales: Exporting U.S. Military Edge?" *Christian Science Monitor* (December 2): 2.

Brown, Lester R. (2002) "Planning for the Eco-economy," *USA Today* (March): 31–35.

Brown, Lester R., and Christopher Flavin. (1999) "A New Economy for a New Century," pp. 3–21 in Lester R. Brown et al., *State of the World 1999.* New York: Norton.

Brown, Lester R., et al. (1999) *State of the World 1999.* New York: Norton.

Brundtland, Gro Harlem. (2003) "The Globalization of Health," *Seton Hall Journal of Diplomacy and International Relations* (Summer–Fall): 7–12.

Brzezinski, Zbigniew. (2004) *The Choice: Global Domination or Global Leadership.* New York: Basic Books/Perseus.

———. (1998) "The Grand Chessboard," *Harvard International Review* 20 (Winter): 48–53.

Bueno de Mesquita, Bruce. (1975) "Measuring Systemic Polarity," *Journal of Conflict Resolution* 22 (June): 187–216.

Bueno de Mesquita, Bruce, James D. Morrow, Randolph M. Siverson, and Alastair Smith. (2004) "Testing Novel Implications from the Selectorate Theory of War," *World Politics* 56 (April): 363–88.

Bull, Hedley. (2002) *The Anarchical Society: A Study of Order in World Politics,* 3rd ed. New York: Columbia University Press.

Butterfield, Herbert. (1944) *The Englishman and His History.* Cambridge: Cambridge University Press.

Buzan, Barry, and Gerald Segal. (1998) *Anticipating the Future.* London: Simon & Schuster.

Buzan, Barry, and Ole Weaver. (2003) *Regimes of Power.* Cambridge: Cambridge University Press.

Byers, Michael, and Georg Nolte (eds.). (2003) *United States Hegemony and the Foundations of International Law.* New York: Columbia University Press.

Caldwell, Christopher. (2004) "Select All: Can You Have Too Many Choices?" *New Yorker* (March). 91–93.

Caldwell, Dan. (1977) "Bureaucratic Foreign Policy Making," *American Behavioral Scientist* 21 (September–October): 87–110.

Calvocoressi, Peter, Guy Wint, and John Pritchard. (1989) *Total War: The Causes and Courses of the Second World War,* 2nd ed. New York: Pantheon.

Campbell, Ian. (2004) "Retreat from Globalization," *National Interest* 75 (Spring): 111–17.

Caporaso, James A., and David P. Levine. (1992) *Theories of Political Economy.* New York: University Press.

Caprioli, Mary. (2004) "Feminist IR Theory and Quantitative Methodology," *International Studies Review* 6 (June): 253–69.

Carment, David. (1993) "The International Dimensions of Ethnic Conflict," *Journal of Peace Research* 30 (May): 137–50.

Carothers, Thomas. (2004) *Critical Mission: Essays on Democracy Promotion.* Washington, D.C.: Carnegie Endowment for International Peace.

———. (1997) "Democracy without Illusions," *Foreign Affairs* 76 (January–February): 85–99.

Carpenter, Ted Galen. (1991) "The New World Disorder," *Foreign Policy* 84 (Fall): 24–39.

Carr, E. H. (1939) *The Twenty-Years' Crisis, 1919–1939.* London: Macmillan.

Caruso, Guy F. (2003) "World Oil Market Status and Outlook," *Journal of Energy and Development* 23 (Autumn): 1–16.

Casetti, Emilio. (2003) "Power Shifts and Economic Development: When Will China Overake the USA?" *Journal of Peace Research* 40 (November): 661–75.

Cashman, Greg. (2000) *What Causes War?* 2nd ed. Boston: Lexington Books.

Caspary, William R. (1993) "New Psychoanalytic Perspectives on the Causes of War," *Political Psychology* 14 (September): 417–46.

Cassese, Antonio, and Andrew Clapham. (2001) "International Law," pp. 408–11 in Joel Krieger (ed.), *The Oxford Companion to Politics of the World,* 2nd ed. Oxford: Oxford University Press.

Cavallo, Alfred. (2004) "Oil: The Illusion of Plenty," *Bulletin of the Atomic Scientists* (January–February): 20–22, 70.

Cederman, Lars-Erik, and Kristian Skrede Gleditsch. (2004) "Conquest and Regime Change," *International Studies Quarterly* 48 (September): 603–29.

Center for World Indigenous Studies. (2002) *The State of Indigenous People.* Olympia, Wash.: Center for World Indigenous Studies.

Central Intelligence Agency. (2002) *Global Trends 2015.* Washington, D.C.: Central Intelligence Agency.

———. (2001) *Handbook of International Economic Statistics 2000.* Langley, Va.: Central Intelligence Agency.

Cerny, Philip G. (1994) "The Dynamics of Financial Globalization," *Policy Sciences* 287 (No. 4): 319–42.

Chaliand, Gérald, and Jean-Pierre Rageau. (1993) *Strategic Atlas,* 3rd ed. New York: Harper Perennial.

Chandler, Clay. (2004) "Can China Keep the Lights On?" *Fortune* 149 (February 23): 46–51.

Chase-Dunn, Christopher, and E. N. Anderson (eds.). (2005) *The Historical Evolution of World-Systems.* London: Palgrave.

Chase-Dunn, Christopher, and Thomas D. Hall. (1997) *Rise and Demise: Comparing World Systems.* Boulder, Colo.: Westview.

Chatterjee, Deen K., and Done E. Scheid (eds.). (2003) *Ethics and Foreign Intervention.* Cambridge: Cambridge University Press.

Checkel, Jeffrey T. (1998) "The Constructivist Turn in International Relations Theory," *World Politics* 50 (January 1998): 324–48.

Chen, Lincoln, Jennifer Leaning, and Vasant Narasimhan (eds.). (2003). *Global Health Challenges for Human Security.* Cambridge, Mass.: Harvard University Press.

Chernoff, Fred. (2004) "The Study of Democratic Peace and Progress in International Relations," *International Studies Review* 6. 49–77.

Choi, Ajin. (2004) "Democratic Synergy and Victory in Wars, 1816–1992," *International Studies Quarterly* 48 (September): 663–82.

Chomsky, Noam. (2004) *Hegemony or Survival: America's Quest for Global Dominance.* New York: Metropolitan Books/Henry Holt.

Cincotta, Richard P., and Robert Engelman. (2004) "Conflict Thrives Where Young Men Are Many," *International Herald Tribune* (March): 18.

Cincotta Richard P., Robert Engelman, and Daniele Anastasion. (2003) *The Security Demographic.* Washington, D.C.: Population Action International.

Clancy, Tom, and Russell Seitz. (1991–92) "Five Minutes Past Midnight—and Welcome to the New Age of Proliferation," *National Interest* 26 (Winter): 3–17.

Clapham, Andrew. (2001) "Human Rights," pp. 368–70 in Joel Krieger (ed.), *The Oxford Companion to Politics of the World,* 2nd ed. New York: Oxford University Press.

Clarke, Richard A. (2004) *Against All Enemies.* New York: Simon & Schuster.

Claude, Inis L., Jr. (1989) "The Balance of Power Revisited," *Review of International Studies* 15 (January): 77–85.

———. (1971) *Swords into Plowshares,* 4th ed. New York: Random House.

———. (1967) *The Changing United Nations.* New York: Random House.

———. (1962) *Power and International Relations.* New York: Random House.

Clegg, Liz. (1999) "NGOs Take Aim," *Bulletin of the Atomic Scientists* 52 (January–February): 49–52.

Cline, William. (2004) *Trade Policy and Global Poverty.* Washington D.C.: Institute for International Economics.

Clodfelter, Michael. (2002) *Warfare and Armed Conflicts: A Statistical Reference to Casualty and Other Figures, 1500–2000,* 2nd ed. Jefferson, N.C.: McFarland.

Clyburn, James E. (2001) "Global Action on TB Needed," *Columbia (S.C.) State* (March 24): A9.

Cobb, Roger, and Charles Elder. (1970) *International Community.* New York: Harcourt, Brace & World.

Cohen, Benjamin J. (2000) *The Geography of Money.* Ithaca, N.Y.: Cornell University Press.

———. (1996) "Phoenix Risen: The Resurrection of Global Finance," *World Politics* 48 (January): 268–96.

———. (1973) *The Question of Imperialism.* New York: Basic Books.

Cohen, Eliot A. (1998) "A Revolution in Warfare," pp. 34–46 in Charles W. Kegley, Jr., and Eugene R. Wittkopf (eds.), *The Global Agenda,* 4th ed. New York: McGraw-Hill.

Cohen, Joel E. (1998) "How Many People Can the Earth Support?" *New York Review of Books* 45 (October 8): 29–31.

———. (1995) *How Many People Can the Earth Support?* New York: Norton.

Cohen, Roger. (2000) "A European Identity," *New York Times* (January 14): A3.

Cohen, Saul Bernard. (2003) *Geopolitics of the World System.* Lanham, Md.: Rowman & Littlefield.

Coleman, Isobel. (2004) "The Payoff from Women's Rights," *Foreign Affairs* 83 (May–June): 80–95.

Conger, Lucy. (1999) "A Fourth Way? The Latin American Alternative to Neoliberalism," pp. 197–201 in Robert M. Jackson (ed.), *Global Issues 1999/00.* Guilford, Conn.: Dushkin/McGraw-Hill.

Cooper, Richard N. (2004) "A False Alarm: Overcoming Globalization's Discontents," *Foreign Affairs* 83 (January–February): 152–55.

Copeland, Dale C. (2000) "The Constructivist Challenge to Structural Realism," *International Security* 25 (Fall): 187–212.

Coplin, William D. (1971) *Introduction to International Politics.* Chicago: Markham.

———. (1965) "International Law and Assumptions about the State System," *World Politics* 17 (July): 615–34.

Cornish, Edward. (2004) *Futuring: Re-Exploration of the Future.* Bethesda, Md.: World Future Society.

Cortwright, David, and George A. Lopez (eds.). (2002) *Smart Sanctions: Targeting Economic Statecraft.* Lanham, Md.: Rowman & Littlefield.

Cortwright, David, and George A. Lopez. (1995) "The Sanctions Era: An Alternative to Military Intervention," *Fletcher Forum of World Affairs* 19 (May): 65–85.

Coser, Lewis. (1956) *The Functions of Social Conflict.* London: Routledge & Kegan Paul.

Cox, Richard W. (2003) Review of *Freedom and Finance,* by Mary Ann Haley, *Perspectives on Politics* 1 (March): 233–34.

Craig, Campbell. (2003) *Glimmer of a New Leviathan: Total War in the Realism of Niebuhr, Morgenthau, and Waltz.* New York: Columbia University Press.

Craig, Gordon A., and Alexander L. George. (1990) *Force and Statecraft,* 2nd ed. New York: Oxford University Press.

Crawford, Neta C. (2003) "Just War Theory and the U.S. Counterterror War," *Perspectives on Politics* 1 (March): 5–25.

Crenshaw, Martha. (2003) "The Causes of Terrorism," pp. 92–105 in Charles W. Kegley, Jr. (ed.), *The New Global Terrorism.* Upper Saddle River, N.J.: Prentice Hall.

Crook, Clive. (2003) "A Cruel Sea of Capital," *Economist* (May 3): 3–5.

———. (1997) "The Future of the State," *Economist* (September 20): 5–20.

Crossette, Barbara. (1995) "The Second Sex in the Third World," *New York Times* (September 10): E1, E3.

Crump, Andy. (1998) *The A to Z of World Development.* Oxford, Eng.: New Internationalist.

Daalder, Ivo H., and James M. Lindsay. (2003) *America Unbound: The Bush Revolution in Foreign Policy.* Washington, D.C.: Brookings Institution Press.

Dahrendorf, Ralf. (1999) "The Third Way and Liberty," *Foreign Affairs* 78 (September–October): 13–17.

Dai, Xinyuan. (2002) "Political Regimes and International Trade," *American Political Science Review* 96 (March): 159–69.

Daly, Herman E., and John B. Cobb, Jr. (1989) *For the Common Good.* Boston: Beacon.

D'Amato, Anthony. (1982) "What 'Counts' as Law?" pp. 83–107 in Nicholas Greenwood Onuf (ed.), *Law-Making in the Global Community.* Durham, N.C.: Carolina Academic Press.

Davidson, Keay. (1991) "Slashing U.S. Nuclear Arsenal Now Thinkable," *Baton Rouge Sunday Advocate* (November 10): E1.

Davis, Wade. (1999) "Vanishing Cultures," *National Geographic* (August): 62–89.

Dehio, Ludwig. (1962) *The Precarious Balance.* New York: Knopf.

Demko, George J., and William B. Wood. (1994) *Reordering the World: Geopolitical Perspectives on the Twenty-First Century.* Boulder, Colo.: Westview.

Denemark, Robert A., Jonathan Friedman, Barry K. Gills, and George Modelski (eds.). (2002) *World System History: The Social Science of Long-Term Change.* London: Routledge.

Dentzer, Susan. (1993) "Meet the New Economic Bogeymen," *U.S. News & World Report* (October 18): 67.

DeRivera, Joseph H. (1968) *The Psychological Dimension of Foreign Policy.* Columbus, Ohio: Merrill.

Desch, Michael C. (1998) "Culture Clash," *International Security* 23 (Summer): 141–70.

Deutsch, Karl W. (1974) *Politics and Government.* Boston: Houghton Mifflin.

———. (1957) *Political Community and the North Atlantic Area*. Princeton, N.J.: Princeton University Press.

———. (1953) "The Growth of Nations: Some Recurrent Patterns in Political and Social Integration," *World Politics* 5 (October): 168–95.

Deutsch, Karl W., et al. (2006) *Backgrounds to Community*. Columbia: University of South Carolina Press.

Deutsch, Karl W., and J. David Singer. (1964) "Multipolar Power Systems and International Stability," *World Politics* 16 (April): 390–406.

De Vecchi, Robert, and Arthur C. Helton. (1999) "The United Nations Requires an Upgrade," *International Herald Tribune* (September 20): 16.

Diamond, Jarad. (2003) "Environmental Collapse and the End of Civilization," *Harper's* (June): 43–51.

DiRenzo, Gordon J. (ed.). (1974) *Personality and Politics*. Garden City, N.Y.: Doubleday-Anchor.

Dogan, Mattei. (2004) "Four Hundred Giant Cities Atop the World," *International Social Science Journal* 181 (September): 347–60.

Dollar, David, and Aart Kraay. (2004) "Spreading the Wealth," pp. 43–49 in Robert Griffiths (ed.), *Developing World 04/05*. Guilford, Conn.: Dushkin/McGraw Hill.

Dorraj, Manochehr. (1995) "Introduction: The Changing Context of Third World Political Economy," pp. 1–13 in Manochehr Dorraj (ed.), *The Changing Political Economy of the Third World*. Boulder, Colo.: Lynne Rienner.

Dos Santos, Theotonio. (1970) "The Structure of Dependence," *American Economic Review* 60 (May): 231–36.

Dougherty, James E., and Robert L. Pfaltzgraff, Jr. (2001) *Contending Theories of International Relations*, 5th ed. New York: Longman.

Dowd, Maureen. (2004) *Bushworld: Enter at Your Own Risk*. New York: G. P. Putnam's Sons.

Downs, George W. (ed.). (1994) *Collective Security beyond the Cold War*. Ann Arbor: University of Michigan Press.

Doyle, Michael W. (1997) *Ways of War and Peace*. New York: Norton.

———. (1995) "Liberalism and World Politics Revisited," pp. 83–106 in Charles W. Kegley, Jr. (ed.), *Controversies in International Relations Theory: Realism and the Neoliberal Challenge*. New York: St. Martin's.

Doyle, Michael W., and G. John Ikenberry (eds.). (1997) *New Thinking in International Relations Theory*. Boulder, Colo.: Westview.

Drezner, Daniel W. (2002) "Bottom Feeders," pp. 44–49 in Robert J. Griffiths (ed.), *Developing World 02/03*. Guilford, Conn.: Dushkin/McGraw-Hill.

Drozdiak, William. (2001) "Protectionism in the Global Age," *Washington Post National Weekly* (May 21–27): 17.

———. (1999) "Germany Shifts Its Focus Eastward," *International Herald Tribune* (September 11–12): 1, 4.

Drucker, Peter. (2001) "A Survey of the Near Future," *Economist* (November 3): 3–19.

———. (1997) "The Global Economy and the Nation-State," *Foreign Affairs* 76 (October): 159–71.

Dupont, Alan. (2002) "Sept. 11 Aftermath: The World Does Seem to Have Changed," *International Herald Tribune* (August 6): 6.

Durbin, Andrea C. (1995) "Trade and the Environment," *Environment* 37 (September): 16–20, 37–41.

Durning, Alan Thein. (1993) "Supporting Indigenous Peoples," pp. 80–100 in Lester R. Brown et al., *State of the World 1993*. New York: Norton.

Dworkin, Ronald. (2001) *Sovereign Virtue*. Cambridge, Mass.: Harvard University Press.

Dyson, Freeman. (1997) *Imagined Worlds*. Cambridge, Mass.: Harvard University Press.

Easterbrook, Gregg. (2002) "Safe Deposit: The Case for Foreign Aid," *New Republic* (July 29): 16–20.

Easton, David. (1969) "The New Revolution in Political Science," *American Political Science Review* 63 (December): 1051–1061.

Easton, Stewart C. (1964) *The Rise and Fall of Western Colonialism*. New York: Praeger.

Eberstadt, Nicholas. (2004) "The Population Implosion," pp. 168–77 in Robert J. Griffiths (ed.), *Developing World 04/05*, Guilford, Conn: Dushkin/McGraw-Hill.

———. (1995) "Population, Food, and Income: Global Trends in the Twentieth Century," pp. 7–47 in Ronald Bailey (ed.), *The True State of the Planet*. New York: Free Press.

Eckes, Alfred E., Jr., and Thomas W. Zeiler. (2003) *Globalization and the American Century*. Cambridge: Cambridge University Press.

Economist. (2005) *The World in 2005*. London: Economist.

———. (2004) *The World in 2004*. London: Economist.

———. (2002) *Pocket World in Figures, 2002*. London: Profile Books.

———. (1999a) *Pocket World in Figures, 2000*. London: Profile Books.

———. (1999b) *The World in 2000*. London: Economist.

Edwards, Stephen R. (1995) "Conserving Biodiversity," pp. 212–65 in Ronald Bailey (ed.), *The True State of the Planet*. New York: Free Press.

Eichengreen, Barry. (2000) "Hegemonic Stability Theories of the International Monetary System," pp. 220–44 in Jeffrey A. Frieden and David A. Lake (eds.), *International Political Economy*. Boston: Bedford/St. Martin's.

Eisendrath, Craig, Melvin A. Goodman, and Gerald E. Marsh. (2001) *The Phantom Defense: America's Pursuit of the Star Wars Illusion*. Westport, Conn.: Greenwood.

Eizenstat, Stuart. (1999) "Learning to Steer the Forces of Globalization," *International Herald Tribune* (January 22): 6.

Eland, Ivan. (2004) *The Empire Has No Clothes: U.S. Foreign Policy Exposed*. New York: Independent Institute.

Elliott, Kimberly Ann. (1998) "The Sanctions Glass: Half Full or Completely Empty?" *International Security* 23 (Summer): 50–65.

———. (1993) "Sanctions: A Look at the Record," *Bulletin of the Atomic Scientists* 49 (November): 32–35.

Elliott, Michael. (1998) "A Second Federal Democratic Superpower Soon," *International Herald Tribune* (November 24): 8.

Elrod, Richard. (1976) "The Concert of Europe," *World Politics* 28 (January): 159–74.

Elshtain, Jean Bethke. (2003) *Just War against Terror: The Burden of American Power in a Violent World*, New York: Basic Books.

Emmanuel, Arghiri. (1972) *Unequal Exchange: An Essay on the Imperialism of Trade*. New York: Monthly Review Press.

Emmott, Bill. (2002) "Present at the Creation: A Survey of America's World Role," *Economist* (June 29): 1–34.

Engelhardt, Henriette, and Alexia Prskawetz. (2004) "On the Changing Correlation between Fertility and Female Employment over Space and Time," *European Journal of Population* 20 (No. 1): 1–21.

Enloe, Cynthia H. (2001) "Gender and Politics," pp. 311–15 in Joel Krieger (ed.), *The Oxford Companion to Politics of the World*, 2nd ed. New York: Oxford University Press.

———. (2000) *Maneuvers: The International Politics of Militarizing Women's Lives.* Berkeley: University of California Press.

Enriquez, Juan. (1999) "Too Many Flags?" *Foreign Policy* 116 (Fall): 30–50.

Eriksson, Mikael, and Peter Wallensteen. (2004) "Armed Conflict, 1989–2003," *Journal of Peace Research* 41 (September): 625–36.

Esbobar, Arturo. (2000) "The Invention of Development," pp. 93–96 in Robert M. Jackson (ed.), *Global Issues 00/01,* 16th ed. Guilford, Conn.: Dushkin/McGraw-Hill.

Etheredge, Lloyd S. (1999) "The Internet and World Politics," paper presented to the Columbia University Seminar on Human Rights, New York, May 10.

Evans, Gareth. (1998) *Human Rights Fifty Years On.* New York: Manchester University Press.

Evans, Peter B. (2001) "Dependency," pp. 212–14 in Joel Krieger (ed.), *The Oxford Companion to Politics of the World,* 2nd ed. New York: Oxford University Press.

Falk, Richard A. (2004) *The Decline of World Order: America's Imperial Geopolitics.* New York: Routledge.

———. (2003) "The Aftermath of 9/11 and the Search for Limits: In Defense of Just War Thinking," pp. 216–22 in Charles W. Kegley, Jr. (ed.), *The New Global Terrorism.* Upper Saddle River, N.J.: Prentice Hall.

———. (2001a) "The New Interventionism and the Third World," pp. 189–98 in Charles W. Kegley, Jr., and Eugene R. Wittkopf (eds.), *The Global Agenda,* 6th ed. Boston: McGraw-Hill.

———. (2001b) "Sovereignty," pp. 789–91 in Joel Krieger (ed.), *The Oxford Companion to Politics of the World,* 2nd ed. Oxford: Oxford University Press.

———. (1999) "Globalization Needs a Dose of Democracy," *International Herald Tribune* (October 5): 8.

———. (1970) *The Status of Law in International Society.* Princeton, N.J.: Princeton University Press.

Falk, Richard, and Andrew Strauss. (2001) "Toward Global Parliament," *Foreign Affairs* 80 (January–February): 212–18.

Fallows, James. (2002) "The Military Industrial Complex," *Foreign Policy* 22 (November–December): 46–48.

Feinstein, Lee, and Anne-Marie Slaughter (2004) "A Duty to Prevent," *Foreign Affairs* 83 (No. 1): 136–50.

Ferencz, Benjamin B., and Ken Keyes, Jr. (1991) *Planet-Hood.* Coos Bay, Ore.: Love Line.

Ferguson, Niall. (2004a) "A World without Power," *Foreign Policy* (July–August): 32–39.

———. (2004b) *Colossus: The Price of America's Empire.* New York: Penguin.

———. (2001) *The Cash Nexus.* New York: Basic Books.

———. (1999) *The Pity of War.* New York: Basic Books.

Festinger, Leon. (1957) *A Theory of Cognitive Dissonance.* Evanston, Ill.: Row, Peterson.

Fettweis, Christopher J. (2004) "Evaluating IR's Crystal Balls," *International Studies Review* 6: 79–104.

Fieldhouse, D. K. (1973) *Economics and Empire, 1830–1914.* Ithaca, N.Y.: Cornell University Press.

Fields, A. Beldon, and Kriston M. Lord (eds.). (2004) *Rethinking Human Rights for the New Millennium.* London: Palgrave.

Filson, Darren, and Suzanne Werner. (2002) "A Bargaining Model of War and Peace," *American Journal of Political Science* 46 (No. 4): 819–38.

Finnegan, William. (2002) "Leasing the Rain," *New Yorker* (April 18): 43–53.

Finnemore, Martha (2003) *The Purpose of Intervention: Changing Beliefs about the Use of Force.* Ithaca, N.Y.: Cornell University Press.

Flanagan, Stephen J., Ellen L. Frost, and Richard Kugler. (2001) *Challenges of the Global Century.* Washington, D.C.: Institute for National Strategic Studies, National Defense University.

Flavin, Christopher, and Seth Dunn. (1999) "Reinventing the Energy System," pp. 23–40 in Lester R. Brown et al., *State of the World 1999.* New York: Norton.

Flint, Colin (ed.). (2004) *The Geography of War and Peace.* New York: Oxford University Press.

Frank, Andre Gunder. (1969) *Latin America: Underdevelopment or Revolution.* New York: Monthly Review Press.

Frankel, Max. (2004) *High Noon in the Cold War: Kennedy, Khrushchev, and the Cuban Missile Crisis.* New York: Random House.

Freedom House. (2005) *Freedom in the World 2005.* Lanham, Md.: Rowman & Littlefield.

———. (2004) *Freedom in the World 2004.* Lanham, Md.: Rowman & Littlefield.

French, Howard W. (2002) "Japan Considering Nuclear Weapons," *New York Times* (June 9): A12.

Freud, Sigmund. (1968) "Why War," pp. 71–80 in Leon Bramson and George W. Goethals (eds.), *War.* New York: Basic Books.

Fried, John H. E. (1971) "International Law—Neither Orphan nor Harlot, Neither Jailer nor Never-Never Land," pp. 124–76 in Karl W. Deutsch and Stanley Hoffmann (eds.), *The Relevance of International Law.* Garden City, N.Y.: Doubleday-Anchor.

Frieden, Jeffrey A. (2001) "International Debt," pp. 404–6 in Joel Krieger (ed.), *The Oxford Companion to Politics of the World,* 2nd ed. Oxford: Oxford University Press.

Friedheim, Robert L. (1965) "The 'Satisfied' and 'Dissatisfied' States Negotiate International Law," *World Politics* 18 (October): 20–41.

Friedman, Thomas L. (2004a) "Dreadful Irresponsibility after 9/11," *Columbia (S.C.) State* (December 5): D3.

———. (2004b) "The Third Great Era of Globalization," *International Herald Tribune* (March 5): 9.

———. (2001) "Love It or Hate It, but the World Needs America," *International Herald Tribune* (June 16–17): 6.

———. (2000) "Corporations on Steroids," *Columbia (S.C.) State* (February 8): A9.

———. (1999) *The Lexus and the Olive Tree: Understanding Globalization.* New York: Farrar, Straus, Giroux.

———. (1993) "Friends like Russia Make Diplomacy a Mess," *New York Times* (March 28): E5.

Friedmann, S. Julio, and Thomas Homer-Dixon. (2004) "Out of the Energy Box," *Foreign Affairs* 83 (November–December): 72–83.

Frum, David, and Richard Perle. (2004) *An End to Evil: How to Win the War on Terror.* New York: Random House.

Fukuyama, Francis. (2004) *State-Building: Governance and World Order in the 21st Century.* Ithaca, N.Y.: Cornell University Press.

———. (2002) "The West May Be Cracking," *International Herald Tribune* (August 9): 4.

———. (1999a) *The Great Disruption: Human Nature and the Reconstitution of Social Order.* New York: Free Press.

———. (1999b) "Second Thoughts: The Last Man in a Bottle," *National Interest* 56 (Summer): 16–33.

———. (1992a) "The Beginning of Foreign Policy," *New Republic* (August 17 and 24): 24–32.

———. (1992b) *The End of History and the Last Man.* New York: Free Press.

———. (1989) "The End of History?" *National Interest* 16 (Summer): 3–16.

Fuller, Graham E. (1995) "The Next Ideology," *Foreign Policy* 98 (Spring): 145–58.

———. (1991–92) "The Breaking of Nations and the Threat to Ours," *National Interest* 26 (Winter): 14–21.

Gaddis, John Lewis. (2004) *Surprise, Security, and the American Experience*. Cambridge, Mass.: Harvard University Press.

———. (1997) *We Now Know: Rethinking Cold War History*. Oxford: Oxford University Press.

———. (1991) "Great Illusions, the Long Peace, and the Future of the International System," pp. 25–55 in Charles W. Kegley, Jr. (ed.), *The Long Postwar Peace*. New York: HarperCollins.

———. (1990) "Coping with Victory," *Atlantic Monthly* (May): 49–60.

———. (1983) "Containment: Its Past and Future," pp. 16–31 in Charles W. Kegley, Jr., and Eugene R. Wittkopf (eds.), *Perspectives on American Foreign Policy*. New York: St. Martin's.

Galtung, Johan. (1969) "Violence, Peace, and Peace Research," *Journal of Peace Research* 6 (No. 3): 167–91.

Gardels, Nathan. (1991) "Two Concepts of Nationalism," *New York Review of Books* 38 (November 21): 19–23.

Gardner, Richard N. (2003) "The Future Implications of the Iraq Conflict," *American Journal of International Law* 1997 (July): 585–90.

Gareau, Frederick H. (2004) *State Terrorism and the United States*. London: Clarity/Zed.

Garrett, Geoffrey. (2004) "Globalization's Missing Middle," *Foreign Affairs* 83 (November–December): 84–96.

Garrett, Laurie. (2000) *The Coming Plague: Newly Emerging Diseases in a World out of Balance*, rev. ed. London: Virago.

———. (1998) "Runaway Diseases," *Foreign Affairs* 77 (January–February): 139–42.

Garten, Jeffrey A. (1999). "Beware the Weak Links in Our Globalization Chain," *International Herald Tribune* (August 19): 8.

Gelb, Leslie H., and Morton H. Halperin. (1973) "The Ten Commandments of the Foreign Affairs Bureaucracy," pp. 250–59 in Steven L. Spiegel (ed.), *At Issue*. New York: St. Martin's.

Gelber, Harry. (1998) *Sovereignty through Interdependence*. Cambridge, Mass.: Kluwer Law International.

George, Alexander L. (2000) "Strategies for Preventive Diplomacy and Conflict Resolution," *PS: Political Science and Politics* 33 (March): 15–19.

———. (1992) *Forceful Persuasion: Coercive Diplomacy as an Alternative to War*. Washington, D.C.: United States Institute of Peace.

———. (1986) "U.S.–Soviet Global Rivalry: Norms of Competition," *Journal of Peace Research* 23 (September): 247–62.

———. (1972) "The Case for Multiple Advocacy in Making Foreign Policy," *American Political Science Review* 66 (September): 751–85.

German, F. Clifford. (1960) "A Tentative Evaluation of World Power," *Journal of Conflict Resolution* 4 (March): 138–44.

Gilbert, Alan. (2000) *Must Global Politics Constrain Democracy?* Princeton, N.J.: Princeton University Press.

Gilboa, Eytan. (2003) "Foreign Policymaking in the Age of Global Television," *Georgetown Journal of International Affairs* 4 (Winter): 119–26.

———. (2002) "Global Communication and Foreign Policy," *Journal of Communication* 52 (December): 731–48.

Gill, Stephen. (2001a) "Group of 7," pp. 340–41 in Joel Krieger (ed.), *The Oxford Companion to Politics of the World*, 2nd ed. Oxford: Oxford University Press.

———. (2001b) "Hegemony," pp. 354–86 in Joel Krieger (ed.), *The Oxford Companion to Politics of the World*, 2nd ed. Oxford: Oxford University Press.

Gilligan, Michael, and Stephen John Stedman. (2003) "Where Do the Peacekeepers Go?" *International Studies Review* 5 (No. 4): 37–54.

Gilman, Benjamin A., and Sam Gejdenson. (2000) "Preventing Disease," *International Herald Tribune* (July 4): 6.

Gilpin, Robert. (2001) "Three Ideologies of Political Economy," pp. 269–86 in Charles W. Kegley, Jr., and Eugene R. Wittkopf (eds.), *The Global Agenda*, 6th ed. Boston: McGraw-Hill.

———. (2000) *The Challenge of Global Capitalism*. Princeton, N.J.: Princeton University Press.

———. (1987) *The Political Economy of International Relations*. Princeton, N.J.: Princeton University Press.

———. (1981) *War and Change in World Politics*. Cambridge: Cambridge University Press.

Glaberson, William. (2001) "U.S. Courts Become Arbiters of Global Rights and Wrongs," *New York Times* (June 21): A1, A20.

Gleditsch, Kristian Skrede. (2004) "A Revised List of Wars between and within Independent States, 1816–2002," *International Interactions* 30 (July–September): 231–62.

Gleditsch, Nils Petter, et al. (2002) "Armed Conflict 1946–2001: A New Dataset," *Journal of Peace Research* 39 (September): 615–37.

Goertz, Gary. (2003) *International Norms and Decision Making: A Punctuated Equilibrium Analysis*. Lanham, Md.: Rowman & Littlefield.

Goldstein, Joshua. (2002) *War and Gender*. Cambridge: Cambridge University Press.

———. (1988) *Long Cycles: Prosperity and War in the Modern Age*. New Haven, Conn.: Yale University Press.

Gottlieb, Gidon. (1982) "Global Bargaining," pp. 109–30 in Nicholas Greenwood Onuf (ed.), *Law Making in the Global Community*. Durham, N.C.: Carolina Academic Press.

Graham, Bradley. (1995) "Revolutionary Warfare," *Washington Post National Weekly Edition* (March 6–12): 6–7.

Grant, Rebecca, and Kathleen Newland (eds.). (1991) *Gender and International Relations*. Bloomington: Indiana University Press.

Greenfield, Meg. (1997) "Back to the Future," *Newsweek* (January 27): 96.

———. (1995) "When the Budget Is Colonized," *Newsweek* (May 22): 78.

Greenstein, Fred I. (1987) *Personality and Politics*. Princeton, N.J.: Princeton University Press.

Grey, Edward. (1925) *Twenty-Five Years, 1892–1916*. New York: Frederick Stokes.

Grieco, Joseph M. (1995) "Anarchy and the Limits of Cooperation: A Realist Critique of the Newest Liberal Institutionalism," pp. 151–71 in Charles W. Kegley, Jr. (ed.), *Controversies in International Relations Theory*. New York: St. Martin's.

Grimmett, Richard F. (2004) *Conventional Arms Transfers to Developing Nations, 1996–2003*. Washington, D.C.: Congressional Research Service.

———. (2002) *Conventional Arms Transfers to Developing Nations, 1994–2001*. Washington, D.C.: Congressional Research Service.

Gugliotta, Guy. (2004) "Scientists Say Warming to Increase Extinctions," *Columbia (S.C.) State* (January 8): A6.

Gulick, Edward V. (1999) *The Time Is Now: Strategy and Structure for World Governance.* Lanham, Md.: Lexington.

———. (1967 [1955]) *Europe's Classical Balance of Power.* Ithaca, N.Y.: Cornell University Press.

Gurney, Kevin Robert. (1996) "Saving the Ozone Layer Faster," *Technology Review* 99 (January): 58–59.

Gurr, Ted Robert. (2001) "Managing Conflict in Ethnically Divided Societies," pp. 173–86 in Charles W. Kegley, Jr., and Eugene R. Wittkopf (eds.), *The Global Agenda,* 6th ed. Boston: McGraw-Hill.

———. (2000) *Peoples versus States.* Washington, D.C.: United States Institute of Peace Press.

———. (1993) *Minorities at Risk.* Washington, D.C.: United States Institute of Peace Press.

———. (1970) *Why Men Rebel.* Princeton, N.J.: Princeton University Press.

Gurr, Ted Robert, et al. (2002) *Peace and Conflict 2002.* College Park, Md.: Integrated Network for Societal Conflict Research, University of Maryland.

Haass, Richard N. (1997) "Sanctioning Madness," *Foreign Affairs* 76 (December): 74–85.

Haffa, Robert P., Jr. (1992) "The Future of Conventional Deterrence," pp. 5–30 in Gary L. Guertner, Robert Haffa, Jr., and George Quester (eds.), *Conventional Forces and the Future of Deterrence.* Carlisle Barracks, Pa.: U.S. Army War College.

Haggard, Stephan, and Beth A. Simmons. (1987) "Theories of International Regimes," *International Organization* 41 (Summer): 491–517.

Hall, Anthony J. (2004) *The America Empire and the Fourth World.* Montreal: McGill-Queen's University Press.

Hall, John A. (2001) "Liberalism," pp. 499–502 in Joel Krieger (ed.), *The Oxford Companion to Politics of the World,* 2nd ed. Oxford: Oxford University Press.

Hall, Thomas D. (2004) "Ethnic Conflicts as a Global Social Problem," pp. 139–55 in George Ritzer (ed.), *Handbook of Social Problems.* London: Sage.

Hanson, Victor Davis. (2003) *Ripples of Battle.* New York: Doubleday.

Hardin, Garrett. (1993) *Living within Limits.* Oxford: Oxford University Press.

———. (1968) "The Tragedy of the Commons," *Science* 162 (December): 1243–1248.

Harknett, Richard J. (1994) "The Logic of Conventional Deterrence and the End of the Cold War," *Security Studies* 4 (Autumn): 86–114.

Hartung, William, and Michelle Ciarrocca. (2005) "The Military-Industrial-Think Tank Complex," pp. 103–7, in Glenn P. Hastedt (ed.), *American Foreign Policy 04/05,* 10th ed., Guiford, Conn: Dushkin/McGraw-Hill.

Harries, Owen. (1995) "Realism in a New Era," *Quadrant* 39 (April): 11–18.

Harvey, David. (2004) *The New Imperialism.* Oxford: Oxford University Press.

Hausmann, Richardo. (2002) "Prisoners of Geography," pp. 9–15 in Robert D. Griffiths, (ed.), *Developing World 02/03,* 12th ed. Guilford, Conn.: Dushkin/McGraw-Hill.

Haynes, Jeff. (2004) "Religion and International Relations," *International Politics* 41 (September): 451–62.

Hedges, Chris. (2003) "What Every Person Should Know about War," *New York Times* (July 6): www.nytimes.com.

Hegre, Håvard. (2004) "The Duration and Termination of Civil War," *Journal of Peace Research* 41 (May): 243–52.

Hehir, J. Bryan. (2002) "The Limits of Loyalty," *Foreign Policy* (September–October): 38–39.

Held, David, and Anthony McGrew. (2001) "Globalization," pp. 324–27 in Joel Krieger (ed.), *The Oxford Companion to Politics of the World,* 2nd ed. Oxford: Oxford University Press.

Held, David, and Anthony McGrew, with David Goldblatt, and Jonathan Perraton. (2001) "Managing the Challenge of Globalization and Institutionalizing Cooperation through Global Governance," pp. 136–48 in Charles W. Kegley, Jr., and Eugene R. Wittkopf (eds.), *The Global Agenda,* 6th ed. Boston: McGraw-Hill.

———. (1999) *Global Transformations.* Stanford, Calif.: Stanford University Press.

Helmuth, Brian. (2004) "The Big Headache of Climate Change," *Columbia (S.C.) State* (November 28): H1.

Herbert, Bob. (2001) "Global Warming Is Already upon Us," *Columbia (S.C.) State* (February 26): A7.

Heredia, Blanca. (1999) "Prosper or Perish? Development in the Age of Global Capital," pp. 93–97 in Robert M. Jackson (ed.), *Global Issues 1999/00,* 15th ed. Guilford, Conn.: Dushkin/McGraw-Hill.

Hermann, Charles F. (1988) "New Foreign Policy Problems and Old Bureaucratic Organizations," pp. 248–65 in Charles W. Kegley, Jr., and Eugene R. Wittkopf (eds.), *The Domestic Sources of American Foreign Policy.* New York: St. Martin's.

———. (1972) "Some Issues in the Study of International Crisis," pp. 3–17 in Charles F. Hermann (ed.), *International Crises.* New York: Free Press.

Hermann, Charles F., Charles W. Kegley, Jr., and James N. Rosenau (eds.). (1987) *New Directions in the Study of Foreign Policy.* Boston: Allen & Unwin.

Hermann, Margaret G. (1988) "The Role of Leaders and Leadership in the Making of American Foreign Policy," pp. 266–84 in Charles W. Kegley, Jr., and Eugene R. Wittkopf (eds.), *The Domestic Sources of American Foreign Policy.* New York: St. Martin's.

———. (1976) "When Leader Personality Will Affect Foreign Policy," pp. 326–33 in James N. Rosenau (ed.), *In Search of Global Patterns.* New York: Free Press.

Hermann, Margaret G., and Charles W. Kegley, Jr. (2001) "Democracies and Intervention," *Journal of Peace Research* 38 (March): 237–45.

Hermann, Margaret G., and Bengt Sundelius (eds.). (2006) *Comparative Foreign Policy Analysis: Theories and Methods.* Upper Saddle River, N.J.: Prentice Hall.

Herrmann, Richard K., and Richard Ned Lebow (eds.). (2004) *Ending the Cold War: Interpretations, Causation, and the Study of International Relations.* London: Palgrave Macmillan.

Hertsgaard, Mark. (2003) *The Eagle's Shadow: Why America Fascinates and Infuriates the World.* New York: Picador/Farrar, Straus & Giroux.

Herz, John H. (1951) *Political Realism and Political Idealism.* Chicago: University of Chicago Press.

Hilsman, Roger. (1967) *To Move a Nation.* New York: Doubleday.

Hindle, Tim. (2004) "The Third Age of Globalization," pp. 97–98 in the *Economist, The World in 2004.* London: Economist.

Hirsh, Michael. (2003) *At War with Ourselves: Why America Is Squandering Its Chance to Build a Better World.* Oxford: Oxford University Press.

Hoagland, Jim. (1996) "Yes, Sanctions Can Be Effective, but You Have to Work at It," *International Herald Tribune* (February 8): 8.

———. (1999a) "At Present the Brutal Colonialists Aren't Westerners," *International Herald Tribune* (September 20): 12.

———. (1999b) "Is the Global Economy Widening the Income Gap?" *International Herald Tribune* (April 27): 6.

Hobsbawm, Eric. (2002) "War and Peace in the 20th Century," *London Review of Books* 21 (February): 16–18.

Hobson, John A. (1965 [1902]) *Imperialism*. Ann Arbor: University of Michigan Press.

Hodge, Carl Cavanagh. (2005) *Atlanticism for a New Century: The Rise, Triumph, and Decline of NATO*. Upper Saddle River, N.J.: Prentice Hall.

Hoebel, E. Adamson. (1961) *The Law of Primitive Man*. Cambridge, Mass.: Harvard University Press.

Hoffman, Eva. (2000) "Wanderers by Choice," *Utne Reader* (July–August): 46–48.

Hoffmann, Stanley. (1998) *World Disorders*. Lanham, Md.: Rowman & Littlefield.

———. (1992) "To the Editors," *New York Review of Books* (June 24): 59.

———. (1971) "International Law and the Control of Force," pp. 34–66 in Karl W. Deutsch and Stanley Hoffmann (eds.), *The Relevance of International Law*. Garden City, N.Y.: Doubleday-Anchor.

———. (1961) "International Systems and International Law," pp. 205–37 in Klaus Knorr and Sidney Verba (eds.), *The International System*. Princeton, N.J.: Princeton University Press.

Holsti, Kalevi J. (1996) *The State, War, and the State of War*. Cambridge: Cambridge University Press.

———. (1995) "War, Peace, and the State of the State," *International Political Science Review* 16 (October): 319–39.

———. (1992) *International Politics*, 6th ed. Englewood Cliffs, N.J.: Prentice Hall.

———. (1991) *Peace and War*. Cambridge: Cambridge University Press.

———. (1988) *International Politics*, 5th ed. Englewood Cliffs, N.J.: Prentice Hall.

Holsti, Ole R. (2001) "Models of International Relations: Realist and Neoliberal Perspectives on Conflict and Cooperation," pp. 121–35 in Charles W. Kegley, Jr., and Eugene R. Wittkopf (eds.), *The Global Agenda*, 6th ed. Boston: McGraw-Hill.

———. (1989) "Crisis Decision Making," pp. 8–84 in Philip E. Tetlock et al. (eds.), *Behavior, Society, and Nuclear War*. New York: Oxford University Press.

Homer-Dixon, Thomas. (2005) "The Rise of Complex Terrorism," pp. 220–26 in Thomas J. Badey (ed.), *Violence and Terrorism 05/06*, 8th ed. Guilford, Conn.: Dushkin/McGraw-Hill.

Hopf, Ted. (1998) "The Promise of Constructivism in International Relations Theory," *International Security* 23 (Summer): 171–200.

Hopkins, Terence K., and Immanuel Wallerstein (eds.). (1996) *The Age of Transitions: Trajectory of World Systems 1945–2025*. London: Zed.

Hottelet, Richard C. (1999) "Desertification: Forgotten Threat," *Christian Science Monitor* (December 15): 8.

House, Karen Elliot. (1989) "As Power Is Dispersed among Nations, Need for Leadership Grows," *Wall Street Journal* (February 21): A1, A10.

Howard, Michael E. (1983) *The Causes of War*. Cambridge, Mass.: Harvard University Press.

———. (1978) *War and the Liberal Conscience*. New York: Oxford University Press.

Howell, Llewellyn D. (2003) "Is the New Global Terrorism a Clash of Civilizations?" pp. 173–84 in Charles W. Kegley, Jr. (ed.), *The New Global Terrorism*. Upper Saddle River, N.J.: Prentice Hall.

———. (1998) "The Age of Sovereignty Has Come to an End," *USA Today* 127 (September): 23.

Hufbauer, Gary Clyde, Jeffrey J. Schott, and Kimberly Ann Elliott. (1990) *Economic Sanctions Reconsidered*, 2nd ed. Washington, D.C.: Institute for International Economics.

Hughes, Barry B. (2000) *Continuity and Change in World Politics*, 4th ed. Upper Saddle River, N.J.: Prentice Hall.

Hughes, Emmet John. (1972) *The Living Presidency*. New York: Coward, McCann and Geoghegan.

Huntington, Samuel P. (2004) "The Hispanic Challenge," *Foreign Policy* (March–April): 30–45.

———. (2001a) "The Coming Clash of Civilizations, or The West against the Rest," pp. 199–202 in Charles W. Kegley, Jr., and Eugene R. Wittkopf (eds.), *The Global Agenda*, 6th ed. Boston: McGraw-Hill.

———. (2001b) "Migration Flows Are the Central Issue of Our Time," *International Herald Tribune* (February 2): 6.

———. (1999a) "Big Powers Have Little Sway When Rival Civilizations Clash," *International Herald Tribune* (December 17): 10.

———. (1999b) "The Many Faces of the Future," pp. 15–18 in Robert M. Jackson (ed.), *Global Issues 1999/00*, 15th ed. Guilford, Conn.: Dushkin/McGraw-Hill.

———. (1996) *The Clash of Civilizations and the Remaking of World Order*. New York: Simon & Schuster.

———. (1991) *The Third Wave: Democratization in the Late Twentieth Century*. Norman: University of Oklahoma Press.

Hurwitz, Jon, and Mark Peffley. (1987) "How Are Foreign Policy Attitudes Structured?" *American Political Science Review* 81 (December): 1099–1120.

Huth, Paul K., and Todd L. Allee. (2003) *The Democratic Peace and Territorial Conflict in the Twentieth Century*. Cambridge: Cambridge University Press.

Ignatieff, Michael. (2004a) "Hard Choices on Human Rights," pp. 54–55 in the *Economist, The World in 2004*. London: Economist.

———. (2004b) *The Lesser Evil: Political Ethics in an Age of Terror*. Princeton, N.J.: Princeton University Press.

———. (2001a) "The Danger of a World without Enemies," *New Republic* 234 (February 26): 25–28.

———. (2001b) *Human Rights as Politics and Ideology*. Princeton, N.J.: Princeton University Press.

Institute of International Finance. (2004) "Capital Flows to Emerging Market Economies, (Press release, April 15): 1–18.

International Labour Office. (2004) *Working Out of Poverty*. Geneva: International Labour Office.

International Monetary Fund (IMF). (1997) *World Economic Outlook May 1997*. Washington, D.C.: International Monetary Fund.

Ip, Greg. (2004) "American Reliance on Overseas Cash May Ultimately Hurt," *Wall Street Journal Europe* (April 26): 1.

Isaak, Robert A. (2000) *Managing World Economic Change*, 3rd ed. Englewood Cliffs, N.J.: Prentice Hall.

Isenberg, David. (2001) "Combat for Sale: The New Post–Cold War Mercenaries," *USA Today* 129 (March): 12, 16.

Jackson, Patrick Thaddeus (ed.). (2004) "Bridging the Gap: Toward a Realist–Constructivist Dialogue," *International Studies Review* 6 (June): 337–52.

Jacobson, Harold K. (1984) *Networks of Interdependence*. New York: Knopf.

Jain, Subhash, and Chelminski Piotz. (1999) "Beyond Buzzwords—Defining 'Globalization,'" *International Herald Tribune* (April 25): 9.

James, Barry. (2002a) "Summit Aims, Again, for a Better World," *International Herald Tribune* (August 8): 1, 8.

———. (2002b). "Talks to Tackle Threat to Biodiversity," *International Herald Tribune* (August 23): 1, 9.

———. (2002c) "World Loses Ground to Deserts," *International Herald Tribune* (April 4): 1, 10.

———. (2001a) "Mischievous Species Capitalize on Globalization," *International Herald Tribune* (May 21): 1, 9.

———. (2001b) "Warming on Earth Raises New Alarm," *International Herald Tribune* (January 23): 5.

James, Patrick. (1993) "Neorealism as a Research Enterprise," *International Political Science Review* 14 (No. 2): 123–48.

Janis, Irving. (1982) *Groupthink: Psychological Studies of Policy Decisions and Fiascoes*, 2nd ed. Boston: Houghton Mifflin.

Jensen, Lloyd. (1982) *Explaining Foreign Policy*. Englewood Cliffs, N.J.: Prentice Hall.

Jervis, Robert. (2005) *American Foreign Policy in a New Era*. New York: Routledge.

———. (2002) "Theories of War in an Era of Leading-Power Peace," *American Political Science Review* 96 (March): 1–14.

———. (1999) "Realism, Neoliberalism, and Cooperation: Understanding the Debate," *International Security* 24 (Summer): 42–63.

———. (1992) "A Usable Past for the Future," pp. 257–68 in Michael J. Hogan (ed.), *The End of the Cold War*. New York: Cambridge University Press.

———. (1985) "From Balance to Concert," *World Politics* 38 (October): 58–79.

———. (1982) "Security Regimes," *International Organization* 16 (Spring): 357–78.

———. (1976) *Perception and Misperception in World Politics*. Princeton, N.J.: Princeton University Press.

Joffe, Ellis. (2001) "Don't Exaggerate the Military Threat from China," *International Herald Tribune* (July 28–29): 4.

Johansen, Robert C. (1991) "Do Preparations for War Increase or Decrease International Security?" pp. 224–44 in Charles W. Kegley, Jr. (ed.), *The Long Postwar Peace*. New York: HarperCollins.

Johnson, Chalmers. (2004) *The Sorrows of Empire: Militarism, Secrecies, and the End of the Republic*. New York: Metropolitan Books/Henry Holt.

Johnson, James Turner. (2005) "Just War, As It Was and Is," *First Things* 149 (January): 14–24.

———. (2003) "Just War Theory: Responding Morally to Global Terrorism," pp. 223–38 in Charles W. Kegley, Jr. (ed.), *The New Global Terrorism*. Upper Saddle River, N.J.: Prentice Hall.

Jones, Dorothy V. (1991) *Code of Peace: Ethics and Security in the World of the Warlord States*. Chicago: University of Chicago Press.

———. (2005) *International Law in the 21st Century*. Lanham, Md.: Rowman & Littlefield.

———. (2002) "The United Nations," pp. 147–72 in Peter J. Schraeder (ed.), *Exporting Democracy*. Boulder, Colo.: Lynne Rienner.

———. (2001) "The Reality and Relevance of International Law in the Twenty-First Century," pp. 243–56 in Charles W. Kegley, Jr., and Eugene Wittkopf (eds.), *The Global Agenda*, 6th edition. Boston: McGraw-Hill.

———. (1995) "Collective Sanctions as Peaceful Coercion," pp. 241–70 in *The Australian Yearbook of International Law 1995*. Canberra: Australian National University.

Judis, John B. (2004) "Imperial Amnesia," *Foreign Policy* (July–August): 50–59.

Juergensmeyer, Mark. (2003) "The Religious Roots of Contemporary Terrorism," pp. 185–93 in Charles W. Kegley, Jr. (ed.), *The New Global Terrorism*. Upper Saddle River, N.J.: Prentice Hall.

Kadera, Kelly M., and Gerald L. Sorokin. (2004) "Measuring National Power," *International Interactions* 30 (July–September): 211–30.

Kagan, Donald. (1995) *On the Origins of War and the Preservation of Peace*. New York: Doubleday.

Kagan, Robert. (2004) "America's Crisis of Legitimacy," *Foreign Affairs* 83 (No. 2): 65–87.

Kahneman, Daniel. (2003) "Maps of Bounded Nationality," *American Economic Review* 93 (December):1449–1475.

Kaiser, David. (1990) *Politics and War*. Cambridge, Mass.: Harvard University Press.

Kaminski, Matthew. (2002) "Anti-Terrorism Requires Nation Building," *Wall Street Journal* (March 15): A10.

Kane, Hal. (1995) *The Hour of Departure: Forces That Create Refugees and Migrants*. Washington, D.C.: Worldwatch Institute.

Kaplan, Morton A. (1957) *System and Process in International Politics*. New York: Wiley.

Kaplan, Robert D. (2002) *Warrior Politics: Why Leadership Demands a Pagan Ethos*. New York: Random House.

———. (1999) "China: A World Power Again," *Atlantic Monthly* 284 (August): 16–18.

Kapstein, Ethan B. (2004) "Models of International Economic Justice," *Ethics & International Affairs* 18 (No. 2): 79–92.

———. (1991–92) "We Are Us: The Myth of the Multinational," *National Interest* 26 (Winter): 55–62.

Kapur, Devesh, and John McHale. (2003) "Migration's New Payoff," *Foreign Policy* (November–December): 49–57.

Karns, Margaret P., and Karen A. Mingst. (2004) *International Organizations*. Boulder, Colo: Lynne Rienner.

Katzenstein, Lawrence C., and Stefanie Lenway. (2001) "Multinational Corporations," pp. 564–66 in Joel Krieger (ed.), *The Oxford Companion to Politics of the World*, 2nd ed. New York: Oxford University Press.

Kaufman, Stuart J. (2004) "Peace Means Saying You Are Sorry—And Meaning It," *International Studies Review* 6: 145–47.

Keegan, John. (1999) *The First World War*. New York: Knopf.

Keeley, Lawrence. (1996) *War before Civilization*. New York: Oxford University Press.

Keeny, Spurgeon M., Jr., and Wolfgang K. H. Panofsky. (1981) "MAD vs. NUTS," *Foreign Affairs* 60 (Winter): 287–304.

Kegley, Charles W., Jr. (ed.). (1995) *Controversies in International Relations Theory: Realism and the Neoliberal Challenge*. New York: St. Martin's.

———. (1993) "The Neoidealist Moment in International Studies? Realist Myths and the New International Realities," *International Studies Quarterly* 37 (June): 131–46.

Kegley, Charles W., Jr., and Margaret G. Hermann. (2002) "In Pursuit of a Peaceful International System," pp. 15–29 in Peter J. Schraeder (ed.), *Exporting Democracy*. Boulder, Colo.: Lynne Rienner.

———. (1997) "Putting Military Intervention into the Democratic Peace," *Comparative Political Studies* 30 (February): 78–107.

Kegley, Charles W., Jr., and Gregory A. Raymond. (2005a) *The Global Future*. Belmont, Calif.: Wadsworth/Thomson Learning.

———. (2005b) *The Imperiled Imperium*. Oxford: Oxford University Press.

———. (2004) "Global Terrorism and Military Preemption: Policy Problems and Normative Perils," *International Politics* 41 (January): 37–49.

———. (2002a) *Exorcising the Ghost of Westphalia: Building World Order in the New Millennium*. Upper Saddle River, N.J.: Prentice Hall.

———. (2002b) *From War to Peace: Fateful Decisions in World Politics*. Belmont, Calif.: Wadsworth.

———. (1999) *How Nations Make Peace*. Boston: Bedford/St. Martin's.

———. (1994) *A Multipolar Peace? Great-Power Politics in the Twenty-First Century*. New York: St. Martin's.

———. (1990) *When Trust Breaks Down: Alliance Norms and World Politics*. Columbia: University of South Carolina Press.

Kegley, Charles W., Jr., Gregory A. Raymond, and Margaret G. Hermann. (1998) "The Rise and Fall of the Nonintervention Norm: Some Correlates and Potential Consequences," *Fletcher Forum of World Affairs* 22 (Winter–Spring): 81–101.

Kelman, Herbert C. (1965) *International Behavior*. New York: Holt, Rinehart & Winston.

Kennan, George F. (1984a) *The Fateful Alliance*. New York: Pantheon.

———. (1984b) "Soviet-American Relations," pp. 107–20 in Charles W. Kegley, Jr., and Eugene R. Wittkopf (eds.), *The Global Agenda*. New York: Random House.

———. (1967) *Memoirs*. Boston: Little, Brown.

———. (1954) *Realities of American Foreign Policy*. Princeton, N.J.: Princeton University Press.

———. (1951) *American Diplomacy, 1900–1950*. New York: New American Library.

———. ["X"]. (1947) "The Sources of Soviet Conduct," *Foreign Affairs* 25 (July): 566–82.

Kennedy, Paul. (1987) *The Rise and Fall of the Great Powers*. New York: Random House.

Keohane, Robert O. (2002) "Governance in a Partially Globalized World," *American Political Science Review* 94 (March): 1–13.

———. (1989) "International Relations Theory: Contributions from a Feminist Standpoint," *Millennium* 18 (Summer): 245–53.

———. (ed.). (1986a) *Neorealism and Its Critics*. New York: Columbia University Press.

———. (1986b) "Realism, Neorealism and the Study of World Politics," pp. 1–26 in Robert O. Keohane (ed.), *Neorealism and Its Critics*. New York: Columbia University Press.

Keohane, Robert O., and Joseph S. Nye. (2001a) *Power and Interdependence*, 3rd ed. New York: Addison Wesley-Longman.

———. (2001b) "Power and Interdependence in the Information Age," pp. 26–36 in Charles W. Kegley, Jr., and Eugene R. Wittkopf (eds.), *The Global Agenda*, 6th ed. Boston: McGraw-Hill.

———. (2000) "Globalization: What's New? What's Not? (And So What?)," *Foreign Policy* 118 (Spring): 104–19.

———. (1989) *Power and Interdependence*, 2nd ed. Glenview, Ill.: Scott, Foresman/Little, Brown.

———. (1988) "Complex Interdependence, Transnational Relations, and Realism: Alternative Perspectives on World Politics," pp. 257–71 in Charles W. Kegley, Jr., and Eugene R. Wittkopf (eds.), *The Global Agenda*, 2nd ed. New York: Random House.

———. (1977) *Power and Interdependence*. Boston: Little, Brown.

Khripunov, Igor. (1997) "Have Guns Will Travel," *Bulletin of the Atomic Scientists* 53 (May–June): 47–51.

Kibbe, Jennifer D. (2004) "The Rise of Shadow Warriors." *Foreign Affairs* 83 (March–April); 102–15.

Kim, Dae Jung, and James D. Wolfensohn. (1999) "Economic Growth Requires Good Governance," *International Herald Tribune* (February 26): 6.

Kim, Samuel S. (1991) "The United Nations, Lawmaking and World Order," pp. 109–24 in Richard A. Falk, Samuel S. Kim, and Saul H. Mendlovitz (eds.), *The United Nations and a Just World Order*. Boulder, Colo.: Westview.

Kindleberger, Charles P. (1973) *The World in Depression, 1929–1939*. Berkeley: University of California Press.

Kinnas, J. N. (1997) "Global Challenges and Multilateral Diplomacy," pp. 23–48 in Ludwik Dembinski (ed.), *International Geneva Yearbook*. Berne, Switzerland: Peter Lang.

Kissinger, Henry A. (2004) "America's Assignment," *Newsweek* (November 8): 32–38.

———. (2001) *Does America Need a Foreign Policy?* New York: Simon & Schuster.

———. (1999) *Years of Renewal*. New York: Simon & Schuster.

———. (1994) *Diplomacy*. New York: Simon & Schuster.

———. (1992) "Balance of Power Sustained," pp. 238–48 in Graham Allison and Gregory F. Treverton (eds.), *Rethinking America's Security*. New York: Norton.

———. (1979) *White House Years*. Boston: Little, Brown.

———. (1969) "Domestic Structure and Foreign Policy," pp. 261–75 in James N. Rosenau (ed.), *International Politics and Foreign Policy*. New York: Free Press.

Klare, Michael T. (2004) *Blood and Oil*. New York: Henry Holt.

———. (2001) "The New Geography of Conflict," *Foreign Affairs* 80 (May–June): 49–61.

———. (1999) "The New Arms Race," pp. 139–43 in Robert M. Jackson (ed.), *Global Issues 1999/00*, 15th ed. New Guilford, Conn.: Dushkin/McGraw-Hill.

———. (1994) "Adding Fuel to the Fires," pp. 134–54 in Michael T. Klare and Daniel C. Thomas (eds.), *World Security*. New York: St. Martin's.

———. (1990) "Wars in the 1990s: Growing Firepower in the Third World," *Bulletin of the Atomic Scientists* 46 (May): 9–13.

———. (1988) "Low-Intensity Conflict," *Christianity and Crisis* 48 (February 1): 11–14.

Klare, Michael T., and Daniel C. Thomas (eds.). (1991) *World Security: Trends and Challenges at Century's End*, 2nd ed. New York: St. Martin's.

Kluger, Jeffrey. (2002) "The Big Crunch," pp. 25–27 in Robert M. Jackson (ed.), *Global Issues 02/03*. Guilford, Conn.: Dushkin/McGraw-Hill.

———. (2001) "A Climate of Despair," *Time* (April 9): 30–35.

Knickerbocker, Brad. (1999) "Who Rules Next? Where America Stands among World Empires," *Christian Science Monitor* (December 29): 1, 4.

Knight, W. Andy. (2000) *A Changing United Nations*. London: Palgrave.

Knorr, Klaus, and James N. Rosenau (eds.). (1969) *Contending Approaches to International Politics*. Princeton, N.J.: Princeton University Press.

Knorr, Klaus, and Sidney Verba (eds.). (1961) *The International System.* Princeton, N.J.: Princeton University Press.

Knox, MacGregor, and Williamson Murray. (2001) *The Dynamics of Military Revolution: 1300–2050.* Cambridge: Cambridge University Press.

Kober, Stanley. (1990) "Idealpolitik," *Foreign Policy* 79 (Summer): 3–24.

Kohli, Atul. (2004) *State-Directed Development: Political Power and Industrialization in the Global Periphery.* Cambridge: Cambridge University Press.

Korany, Bahgat. (1986) *How Foreign Policy Decisions Are Made in the Third World.* Boulder, Colo.: Westview.

Korten, David. (1995) *When Corporations Rule the World.* West Hartford, Conn.: Berrett-Koehler.

Krasner, Stephen P. (2004) "Sharing Sovereignty: New Institutions for Collapsed and Failing States," *International Security* 29 (Fall): 85–120.

———. (2001) "International Political Economy," pp. 420–22 in Joel Krieger (ed.), *The Oxford Companion to Politics of the World,* 2nd ed. New York: Oxford University Press.

Krauthammer, Charles. (2003) "The Unipolar Moment Revisited," *National Interest* 70 (Winter): 5–17.

———. (2002) "NATO Is Dead; We Should Not Work to Revive It," *Columbia (S.C.) State* (May 26): D3.

———. (2001) "The Bush Doctrine," *Time* (March 5): 42.

———. (1999) "The Limits of Humanitarianism," *Time* (September 27): 118.

Krepinevich, Andrew F., and Steven M. Kusiak. (1998) "Smarter Bombs, Fewer Nukes," *Bulletin of the Atomic Scientists* 54 (November–December): 26–32.

Krepon, Michael. (2002) "Weakening the Anti-Proliferation Regime," *International Herald Tribune* (October 20): 8.

Kristof, Nicholas D. (2004) "A New Ethnic Cleaning," *Columbia (S.C.) State* (March 25): A9.

———. (1993) "The Rise of China," *Foreign Affairs* 72 (November–December): 59–74.

Krugman, Paul. (2004) "An Oil-Driven Recession Is Possible," *International Herald Tribune* (May 15–16): 9.

———. (2003) *The Great Unraveling: Losing Our Way in the New Century.* New York: Norton.

———. (2000) "Some Don't Want to Be Saved from Globalization," *International Herald Tribune* (February 17): 7.

Kruzel, Joseph. (1991) "Arms Control, Disarmament, and the Stability of the Postwar Era," pp. 247–69 in Charles W. Kegley, Jr. (ed.), *The Long Postwar Peace.* New York: HarperCollins.

Ku, Charlotte, and Paul F. Diehl. (eds.) (2003) *International Law,* 2nd ed. Boulder, Colo.: Lynne Rienner.

Kugler, Jacek. (2001) "War," pp. 894–96 in Joel Krieger (ed.), *The Oxford Companion to Politics of the World.* 2nd ed. New York: Oxford University Press.

Kunz, Josef L. (1960) "Sanctions in International Law," *American Journal of International Law* 54 (April): 324–47.

Kunzig, Robert. (2003) "Against the Current," *U.S. News & World Report* (June 2): 34–35.

Kupchan, Charles A. (2003) *The End of the American Era: U.S. Foreign Policy and the Geopolitics of the Twenty-first Century.* New York: Knopf.

Kupchan, Charles A., and Clifford A. Kupchan. (1992) "A New Concert for Europe," pp. 249–66 in Graham Allison and Gregory F. Treverton (eds.), *Rethinking America's Security.* New York: Norton.

Landes, David S. (1998) *The Wealth and Poverty of Nations: Why Are Some So Rich and Some So Poor?* New York: Norton.

Laqueur, Walter. (2004) "The Terrorism to Come," *Harper's* (November): 13–20.

———. (2003) "Postmodern Terrorism," pp. 151–59 in Charles W. Kegley, Jr. (ed.), *The New Global Terrorism.* Upper Saddle River, N.J.: Prentice Hall.

———. (2001) "Terror's New Face," pp. 82–89 in Charles W. Kegley, Jr., and Eugene R. Wittkopf (eds.), *The Global Agenda,* 6th ed. Boston: McGraw-Hill.

———. (1986) "Reflections on Terrorism," *Foreign Affairs* 65 (Fall): 86–100.

Lauren, Paul Gordon. (1999) *The Evolution of Human Rights.* Philadelphia: University of Pennsylvania Press.

Lavin, Douglas. (2002) "Globalization Goes Upscale," *Wall Street Journal* (February 1): A18.

Lebovic, James H. (2004) "Uniting for Peace?" *Journal of Conflict Resolution* 48 (December): 910–36.

Lebow, Richard Ned. (2003) *The Tragic Vision of Politics: Ethics, Interests, and Orders.* Cambridge: Cambridge University Press.

———. (1981) *Between Peace and War.* Baltimore: Johns Hopkins University Press.

Legrain, Philippe. (2003) "Cultural Globalization Is Not Americanization," *Chronicle of Higher Education* (May 9): B7–B70.

Legro, Jeffrey W., and Andrew Moravcsik. (1999) "Is Anybody Still a Realist?" *International Security* 24 (Fall): 5–55.

Leitenberg, Milton. (2003) *Deaths in Wars and Conflicts between 1945 and 2000.* Ithaca, N.Y.: Cornell University Peace Studies Program.

Lemke, Douglas. (2003) "Development and War," *International Studies Review* 5 (December): 55–63.

Lentner, Howard H. (2004) *Power and Politics in Globalization: The Indispensible State.* New York: Routledge.

Leow, Rachel. (2002) "How Can Globalization Become 'O.K.' for All?" *International Herald Tribune* (February 15): 9.

Lesser, Guy. (2004) "War Crime and Punishment," *Harper's* (January): 37–52.

Levine, Robert A. (1999) "The Global Market Holds Poor Nations at Its Mercy," *International Herald Tribune* (October 17–18): 8.

Levingston, Steven. (1999) "Does Territoriality Drive Human Aggression?" *International Herald Tribune* (April 14): 9.

Levy, Jack S. (2003) "Applications of Prospect Theory to Political Science," *Syntheses* 135 (May): 215–41.

———. (2001) "War and Its Causes," pp. 47–56 in Charles W. Kegley, Jr., and Eugene Wittkopf (eds.), *The Global Agenda,* 6th ed. Boston: McGraw-Hill.

———. (1998a) "The Causes of War and the Conditions of Peace," *American Review of Political Science* 1: 139–65.

———. (1998b) "Towards a New Millennium," pp. 47–57 in Charles W. Kegley, Jr., and Eugene R. Wittkopf (eds.), *The Global Agenda,* 5th ed. New York: McGraw-Hill.

———. (1997) "Prospect Theory, Rational Choice, and International Relations," *International Studies Quarterly* 41 (March): 87–112.

———. (1990–91) "Preferences, Constraints, and Choices in July 1914," *International Security* 15 (Winter): 151–86.

———. (1989a) "The Causes of War: A Review of Theories and Evidence," pp. 209–333 in Philip E. Tetlock, Jo L. Husbands, Robert Jervis, Paul C. Stern, and Charles Tilly (eds.), *Behavior, Society, and Nuclear War.* New York: Oxford University Press.

———. (1989b) "The Diversionary Theory of War," pp. 259–88 in Manus I. Midlarsky (ed.), *Handbook of War Studies.* Boston: Unwin Hyman.

Lewis, Paul. (1999) "Corporate Conduct Code Is Proposed for Third World Nations," *New York Times* (April 29): A7.

Leyton-Brown, David. (1987) "Introduction," pp. 1–4 in David Leyton-Brown (ed.), The Utility of International Economic Sanctions. New York: St. Martin's Press.

Liberman, Peter. (2004) "Trade and Peace," *International Studies Review* 6: 139–41.

Libicki, Martin. (2000) "Rethinking War: The Mouse's New Roar?" *Foreign Policy* 117 (Winter): 30–42.

Lichtblau, Eric. (2004) "Bush Pushed for Iraq Link to 9/11, Rice Says" *Columbia (S.C.) State* (March 29): A1, A5.

Lifton, Robert Jay. (2004) *Superpower Syndrome: America's Apocalyptic Confrontation with the World.* New York: Thunder's Mouth Press/Nation Books.

Lilly, James, and Carl Ford. (1999) "China's Military: A Second Opinion," *National Interest* 57 (Fall): 71–77.

Lind, Michael. (1993) "Of Arms and the Woman," *New Republic* (November 15): 36–38.

Lindblom, Charles E. (1979) "Still Muddling, Not Yet Through," *Public Administration Review* 39 (November–December): 517–26.

Lindsay, James M. (1986) "Trade Sanctions as Policy Instruments," *International Studies Quarterly* 30 (June): 153–73.

Lipson, Charles. (2003) *Reliable Partners: How Democracies Have Made a Separate Peace.* Princeton, N.J.: Princeton University Press.

Lissitzyn, Oliver J. (1963) "International Law in a Divided World," *International Conciliation* 542 (March): 3–69.

Little, David. (1993) "The Recovery of Liberalism," *Ethics & International Affairs* 7: 171–201.

Lomborg, Bjørn (ed.). (2004) *Global Crisis, Global Solutions.* Cambridge: Cambridge University Press.

Longman, Phillip. (2004) "The Global Baby Bust," *Foreign Affairs* 83 (May–June): 64–79.

Lopez, George A., and David Cortwright. (1995) "Economic Sanctions in Contemporary Global Relations," pp. 3–16 in David Cortwright and George A. Lopez (eds.), *Economic Sanctions.* Boulder, Colo.: Westview.

Lorenz, Konrad. (1963) *On Aggression.* New York: Harcourt, Brace & World

Lumpe, Lora. (1999) "The Lender of the Pack," *Bulletin of the Atomic Scientists* 58 (January–February): 27–33.

Luterbacher, Urs, and Detlef F. Sprinz (eds.). (2001) *International Relations and Global Climate Change.* Cambridge, Mass.: MIT Press.

Lutz, Wolfgang. (1994) "The Future of World Population," *Population Bulletin* 49 (June): 1–47.

Mack, Andrew. (1996) "Allow the Idea of Nuclear Disarmament a Hearing," *International Herald Tribune* (January 26): 8

Mackinder, Sir Halford. (1919) *Democratic Ideals and Reality.* New York: Holt.

Mahan, Alfred Thayer. (1890) *The Influence of Sea Power in History.* Boston: Little, Brown.

Majeed, Akhtar. (1991) "Has the War System Really Become Obsolete?" *Bulletin of Peace Proposals* 22 (December): 419–25.

Malaquias, Assis V. (2001) "Humanitarian Intervention," pp. 370–74 in Joel Krieger (ed.), *The Oxford Companion to Politics of the World,* 2nd ed. New York: Oxford University Press.

Mandel, Robert. (2002) *Armies Without States: The Privatization of Security.* Boulder Colo.: Lynne Rienner.

Mandelbaum, Michael. (2002) *The Ideas That Conquered the World: Peace, Democracy, and Free Markets in the Twenty-First Century.* New York: Public Affairs/Perseus.

Mann, James. (2004) *Rise of the Vulcans: The History of Bush's War Cabinet.* New York: Viking.

Mann, Michael. (2003) *Incoherent Empire.* New York: Verso.

Mansfield, Edward D., Helen V. Milner, and B. Peter Rosendorff. (2002) "Replication, Realism, and Robustness: Analyzing Political Regimes and International Trade," *American Political Science Review* 96 (March): 167–69.

Mansfield, Edward D., and Brian M. Pollins (eds.). (2003) *Economic Interdependence and International Conflict.* Ann Arbor: University of Michigan Press.

Marx, Anthony W. (2003) *Faith in Nation: Exclusionary Origins of Nationalism.* New York: Oxford University Press.

Mastanduno, Michael. (1991) "Do Relative Gains Matter?" *International Security* 16 (Summer): 73–113.

Mathews, Jessica T. (2000) "National Security for the Twenty-First Century," pp. 9–11 in Gary Bertsch and Scott James (eds.), *Russell Symposium Proceedings.* Athens: University of Georgia.

———. (1997) "Power Shift: The Rise of Global Civil Society," *Foreign Affairs* 76 (January–February): 50–66.

Matlock, Jack F. (2004) *Reagan and Gorbachev: How the Cold War Ended.* New York: Random House.

May, Ernest R. (2000) *Strange Victory.* New York: Hill and Wang.

Mayall, James. (2001) "Mercantilism," pp. 535 and 540 in Joel Krieger (ed.), *The Oxford Companion to Politics of the World,* 2nd ed. New York: Oxford University Press.

Mazarr, Michael J. (1999) *Global Trends 2005.* London: Palgrave.

Mazur, Amy G. (2002) *Theorizing Feminist Policy.* New York: Oxford University Press.

McGranahan, Donald. (1995) "Measurement of Development," *International Social Science Journal* 143 (March): 39–59.

McGurn, William. (2002) "Pulpit Economics," *First Things* 122 (April): 21–25.

McKibben, Bill. (1998) "The Future of Population," *Atlantic Monthly* (May): 55–78.

McNamara, Robert S., and James G. Blight. (2001) *Wilson's Ghost.* New York: Public Affairs.

Mead, Margaret. (1968) "Warfare Is Only an Invention—Not a Biological Necessity," pp. 270–74 in Leon Bramson and George W. Goethals (eds.), *War.* New York: Basic Books.

Mead, Walter Russell. (2004) *Power, Terror, Peace, and War.* New York: Knopf.

———. (2001) *Special Providence: American Foreign Policy and How It Changed the World.* New York: Knopf.

Meadows, Donella H. (1993) "Seeing the Population Issue Whole," *World & I* 8 (June): 396–409.

Meadows, Donella H., Dennis L. Meadows, Jørgen Randers, and William W. Behrens III. (1974) *The Limits to Growth.* New York: New American Library.

Mearsheimer, John J. (2001) *The Tragedy of Great Power Politics.* New York: Norton.

———. (1990) "Back to the Future: Instability in Europe after the Cold War," *International Security* 15 (Summer): 5–56.

Mearsheimer, John J., and Stephen W. Walt. (2003) "An Unnecessary War," *Foreign Policy* (January–February): 50–58.

Melloan, George. (2002a) "Bush's Toughest Struggle Is with His Own Bureaucracy," *Wall Street Journal* (June 25): A19.

———. (2002b) "Meet Mr. Hu—Or Should It Be Mr. Who?" *Wall Street Journal* (April 30): A17.

Menand, Louis. (2002) "September 11th and the American Soul," *New Yorker* (September 16): 98–104.

Mendelsohn, Jack. (2005) "America and Russia: Make-Believe Arms Control," pp. 205–9 in Glenn P. Hastedt

——— (ed.), *America Foreign Policy 04/05,* 10th ed. Guilford, Conn.: Dushkin/McGraw-Hill.

———. (2002) "America and Russia: Make-Believe Arms Control," *Current History* 101 (October): 325–329.

Menkhaus, Ken. (2002) "Somalia: In the Crosshairs of the War on Terrorism," *Current History* (May): 210–18.

Michael, Marie. (2001) "Food or Debt," pp. 78–79 in Robert J. Griffiths (ed.), *Developing World 01/02.* Guilford, Conn.: Dushkin/McGraw-Hill.

Micklethwait, John, and Adrian Wooldridge. (2001) "The Globalization Backlash," *Foreign Policy* (September–October): 16–26.

Midlarsky, Manus J. (2003) "The Impact of External Threat on States and Domestic Societies," *International Studies Review* 5 (No. 4): 13–18.

———. (ed.). (2000) *Handbook of War Studies II.* Ann Arbor: University of Michigan Press.

———. (1988) *The Onset of World War.* Boston: Unwin Hyman.

Miller, Marian A. L. (1995) *The Third World in Global Environmental Politics.* Boulder, Colo.: Lynne Rienner.

Mitchell, Sara McLaughlin, and Brandon C. Prins. (2004) "Rivalry and Diversionary Uses of Force," *Journal of Conflict Resolution* 48 (December): 937–61.

Mitrany, David. (1966) *A Working Peace System.* Chicago: Quadrangle.

Mittelman, James H. (2000) *The Globalization Syndrome.* Princeton, N.J.: Princeton University Press.

Modelski, George (ed.). (1987a) *Exploring Long Cycles.* Boulder, Colo.: Lynne Rienner.

———. (1987b) "The Study of Long Cycles," pp. 1–15 in George Modelski (ed.), *Exploring Long Cycles.* Boulder, Colo.: Lynne Rienner.

———. (1978) "The Long Cycle of Global Politics and the Nation-State," *Comparative Studies in Society and History* 20 (April): 214–35.

———. (1964) "The International Relations of Internal War," pp. 14–44 in James N. Rosenau (ed.), *International Aspects of Civil Strife.* Princeton, N.J.: Princeton University Press.

Modelski, George, and William R. Thompson. (1999) "The Long and the Short of Global Politics in the Twenty-First Century," *International Studies Review,* special issue, ed. by Davis B. Bobrow: 20–40.

———. (1996) *Leading Sectors and World Powers.* Columbia: University of South Carolina Press.

Moisy, Claude. (1997) "Myths of the Global Information Village," *Foreign Policy* 107 (Summer): 78–87.

Møller, Bjørn. (1992) *Common Security and Nonoffensive Defense: A Neorealist Perspective.* Boulder, Colo.: Lynne Rienner.

Moon, Bruce E., and William J. Dixon. (1992) "Basic Needs and Growth-Welfare Trade-Offs," *International Studies Quarterly* 36 (June): 191–212.

Morgenthau, Hans J. (1985) *Politics among Nations,* 6th ed. Revised by Kenneth W. Thompson. New York: Knopf.

———. (1948) *Politics among Nations.* New York: Knopf.

Morris, Desmond. (1969) *The Human Zoo.* New York: Dell.

Morse, Edward L., and James Richard. (2002) "The Battle for Energy Dominance," *Foreign Affairs* 81 (March–April): 16–31.

Mount, Ian, Matthew Maier, and David H. Freeman. (2003) "The New Military Industrial Complex" *Business* 2 (March): 102–8.

Mowlana, Hamid. (1995) "The Communications Paradox," *Bulletin of the Atomic Scientists* 51 (July): 40–46.

Mulhollin, Gary. (1994) "The Business of Defense Is Defending Business," *Washington Post National Weekly Edition* (February 14–20): 23.

Muravchik, Joshua. (2002) "Democracy Is Quietly Winning," *International Herald Tribune* (August 21): 6.

Murdoch, James C., and Todd Sandler. (2004) "Civil Wars and Economic Growth," *American Journal of Political Science* 48 (January): 138–51.

Murithi, Timothy. (2004) "The Myth of Violent Human Nature," *Peace & Policy* 8: 28–32.

Murray, Williamson, and Allan R. Millett. (2000) *A War to Be Won.* Cambridge, Mass.: Harvard University Press.

Nankivell, Kerry Lynn. (2004) "Troubled Waters," *Foreign Policy* (November–December): 30–31.

Neack, Laura. (2004) "Peacekeeping, Bloody Peacekeeping," *Bulletin of the Atomic Scientists* 57 (July–August): 40–47.

Nelson, Stephan D. (1974) "Nature/Nurture Revisited: A Review of the Biological Bases of Conflict," *Journal of Conflict Resolution* 18 (June): 285–335.

Neuman, Johanna. (1995–96) "The Media's Impact on International Affairs, Then and Now," *National Interest* 16 (Winter): 109–23.

Newhouse, John. (2003) *Imperial America: The Bush Assault on World Order.* New York: Knopf.

Newland, Kathleen. (1994) "Refugees: The Rising Flood," *World Watch* 7 (May/June): 10–20.

Nichols, Bill. (2002) "After Two Years at the Top Russia's Putin Still an Enigma," *USA Today* (March 27): 1A–2A.

Niebuhr, Reinhold. (1947) *Moral Man and Immoral Society.* New York: Scribner's.

9/11 Commission. (2004) *Final Report of the National Commission on Terrorist Attacks upon the United States: The 9/11 Commission Report.* New York: Norton.

Nnoli, Okwudiba. (1993) "Ethnicity," pp. 280–84 in Joel Krieger (ed.), *The Oxford Companion to Politics of the World.* New York: Oxford University Press.

Nossel, Suzanne. (2004) "Smart Power," *Foreign Affairs* 83 (March–April): 31–142.

Nye, Joseph S., Jr. (2005a) *Power in the Global Information Age.* New York: Routledge.

Nye, Joseph S., Jr. (2005b) *Understanding International Conflicts,* 5th ed. New York: Longman.

———. (2004a) "America's Soft Learning Curve," pp. 31–34 in *The World in 2004,* London: Economist.

———. (2004b) *Soft Power.* New York: Public Affairs.

———. (2002a) "The Dependent Colossus," *Foreign Policy* (March–April): 74–76.

———. (2002b) *The Paradox of American Power.* New York: Oxford University Press.

———. (2001) "The Changing Nature of World Power," pp. 95–107 in Charles W. Kegley, Jr., and Eugene R. Wittkopf (eds.), *The Global Agenda,* 6th ed. Boston: McGraw-Hill.

———. (1990) *Bound to Lead: The Changing Nature of American Power.* New York: Basic Books.

———. (1987) "Nuclear Learning and U.S.-Soviet Security Regimes," *International Organization* 41 (Summer): 371–402.

Oatley, Thomas. (2004) *International Political Economy.* New York: Pearson Longman.

Oberdorfer, Don. (1991) *The Turn.* New York: Poseidon.

O'Brien, Conor Cruise. (1993) "The Wrath of Ages," *Foreign Affairs* 72 (November–December): 142–49.

———. (1977) "Liberty and Terrorism," *International Security* 2 (Fall): 56–67.

O'Brien, Richard. (1992) *Global Financial Integration.* New York: Council on Foreign Relations.

O'Brien, Robert, and Marc Williams. (2004) *Global Political Economy: Evolution and Dynamics.* London: Palgrave.

Odom, William E., and Robert Dujarric. (2004) *America's Inadvertent Empire.* New Haven, Conn.: Yale University Press.

Oneal, John R., and Bruce Russett. (1999) "Assessing the Liberal Peace with Alternative Specifications: Trade Still Reduces Conflict," *Journal of Peace Research* 36 (July): 423–42.

Onuf, Nicholas. (2002) "Worlds of Our Making: The Strange Career of Constructivism in International Relations," pp. 119–41 in Donald J. Puchala (ed.), *Visions of International Relations.* Columbia: University of South Carolina Press.

———. (1989) *World of Our Making: Rules and Rule in Social Theory and International Relations.* Columbia: University of South Carolina Press.

———. (1982) "Global Law-Making and Legal Thought," pp. 1–82 in Nicholas Greenwood Onuf (ed.), *Law-Making in the Global Community.* Durham, N.C.: Carolina Academic Press.

Opello, Walter C., Jr., and Stephen J. Rosow. (2004) *The Nation-State and Global Order,* 2nd ed. Boulder, Colo.: Lynne Rienner.

Organski, A. F. K. (1968) *World Politics.* New York: Knopf.

Organski, A. F. K., and Jacek Kugler. (1980) *The War Ledger.* Chicago: University of Chicago Press.

Ostler, Nicholas. (2003) "A Loss for Words," *Foreign Policy* (November–December): 30–31.

Ostry, Sylvia. (2001) Review of *The Challenge of Global Capitalism* by Robert Gilpin, *American Political Science Review* 95 (March): 257–58.

Owen, John M., IV. (1997) *Liberal Peace, Liberal War.* Ithaca, N.Y.: Cornell University Press.

Packenham, Robert. (1992) *The Dependency Movement.* Cambridge, Mass.: Harvard University Press.

Panagariya, Arvind. (2003) "Think Again: International Trade," *Foreign Policy* (November–December): 20–28.

Parry, Clive. (1968) "The Function of Law in the International Community," pp. 1–54 in Max Sørensen (ed.), *Manual of Public International Law.* New York: St. Martin's.

Paul, T. V., G. John Ikenberry, and John A. Hall (eds.). (2003) *The Nation-State in Question.* Princeton, N.J.: Princeton University Press.

Pease, Kelly-Kate. (2003) *International Organizations: Perspectives on Governance in the Twenty-First Century.* Upper Saddle River, N.J.: Prentice Hall.

Peirce, Neal R. (2000) "Keep an Eye on 'Citistates' Where Economic Action Is," *International Herald Tribune* (January 11): 8.

———. (1997) "Does the Nation-State Have a Future?" *International Herald Tribune* (April 4): 9.

Pells, Richard. (2002) "Mass Culture Is Now Exported from All Over to All Over," *International Herald Tribune* (July 12). 9.

Peterson, Erik. (1998) "Looming Collision of Capitalisms?" pp. 296–307 in Charles W. Kegley, Jr. and Eugene R. Wittkopf (eds.), *The Global Agenda,* 5th ed. New York: McGraw-Hill.

Peterson, John L. (1999) "Getting Ready for the Twenty-First Century," *USA Today* 128 (May): 56–58.

Peterson, Niels Helveg. (1999) "Place Priority on Human Rights in Applying International Law," *International Herald Tribune* (July 27): 7.

Peterson, V. Spike. (2003) *A Critical Rewriting of Global Political Economy: Retrospective, Productive and Virtual Economies.* London: Routledge.

Peterson, V. Spike, and Anne Sisson Runyan. (1993) *Global Gender Issues.* Boulder, Colo.: Westview.

Petras, James. (2004) *The New Development Politics.* Willison, Vt.: Ashgate.

Petras, James, and Henry Veltmeyer. (2004) *A System in Crisis: The Dynamics of Free Market Capitalism.* London: Palgrave.

Pettis, Michael. (2001) "Will Globalization Go Bankrupt?" *Foreign Policy* 126 (September–October): 52–59.

Pfaff, William. (2001a) "Anti-Davos Forum Is Another Sign of a Sea Change," *International Herald Tribune* (July 25): 6.

———. (2001b) "The Question of Hegemony," *Foreign Affairs* 80 (January–February): 50–64.

———. (2000) "Look Again: The Nation-State Isn't Going Away," *International Herald Tribune* (January 11): 8.

———. (1999) "Getting the Facts on a Bumper Century for War Crimes," *International Herald Tribune* (September 4–5): 8.

———. (1996) "Seeking a Broader Vision of Economic Society," *International Herald Tribune* (February 3–4): 6.

Pfetsch, Frank L. (1999) "Globalization: A Threat and a Challenge for the State," paper presented at the European Standing Conference on International Studies, Vienna, September 11–13.

Phillips, Nicola (ed.) (2005) *Globalizing Political Economy.* London: Palgrave.

Pickering, Jeffrey. (1999) "The Structural Shape of Force," *International Interactions* 25 (No. 4): 363–91.

Pieterse, Jan Nederveen. (2004) *Globalization or Empire?* New York: Routledge.

Pipes, Richard. (1977) "Why the Soviet Union Thinks It Could Fight and Win a Nuclear War," *Commentary* 26 (July): 21–34.

Pirages, Dennis. (1998) "An Ecological Approach to International Relations," pp. 387–94 in Charles W. Kegley, Jr., and Eugene R. Wittkopf (eds.), *The Global Agenda,* 5th ed. New York: McGraw-Hill.

Pomfret, John. (2002) "Taiwan Set Up Fund to Buy Global Influence," *International Herald Tribune* (April 6–7): 1, 7.

———. (1999) "China Maps Changes in Defense Strategy," *International Herald Tribune* (June 12–13): 1, 4.

Porter, Bruce D. (1994) *War and the Rise of the State.* New York: Free Press.

Porter, Gareth. (1995) "Environmental Security as a National Security Issue," *Current History* 94 (May): 218–22.

Porter, Gareth, and Janet Welsh Brown. (1996) *Global Environmental Politics,* 2nd ed. Boulder, Colo.: Westview.

Post, Jerrold M. (2004) *Leaders and Their Followers in a Dangerous World.* Ithaca, N.Y.: Cornell University Press.

Pound, Edward T., and Jihan El-Tahri. (1994) "Sanctions: The Pluses and Minuses," *U.S. News & World Report* (October 31): 58–71.

Powell, Colin L. (1995) *My American Journey.* New York: Random House.

Power, Jonathan. (2004) "United Nations—Much Maligned, But Much Needed," *International Herald Tribune* (February 26): 6.

Powers, Thomas. (1994) "Downwinders: Some Casualties of the Nuclear Age," *Atlantic Monthly* (March): 119–24.

Prestowitz, Clyde. (2003). *Rogue Nation: American Unilateralism and the Failure of Good Intentions.* New York: Basic Books/Perseus.

Price, Richard. (2003) "Transnational Civil Society and Advocacy in World Politics," *World Politics* 55 (July): 519–606.

Priest, Dana. (2003) *The Mission: Waging War and Keeping Peace with America's Military*. New York: Norton.

Putnam, Robert D. (1988) "Diplomacy and Domestic Politics: The Logic of Two-Level Games," *International Organization* 42 (Summer): 427–60.

Quester, George. (1992) "Conventional Deterrence," pp. 31–51 in Gary L. Guertner, Robert Haffa, Jr., and George Quester (eds.), *Conventional Forces and the Future of Deterrence*. Carlisle Barracks, Pa.: U.S. Army War College.

Quinn, Jane Bryant. (2002) "Iraq: It's the Oil, Stupid," *Newsweek* (September 30): 43.

Rapkin, David, and William R. Thompson, with Jon A. Christopherson. (1989) "Bipolarity and Bipolarization in the Cold War Era," *Journal of Conflict Resolution* 23 (June): 261–95.

Ravallion, Martin. (2004) "Pessimistic on Poverty?" *Economist* (April 10): 65.

Ray, James Lee. (1995) *Democracy and International Conflict: An Evaluation of the Democratic Peace Proposition*. Columbia: University of South Carolina Press.

Raymond, Gregory A. (2003) "The Evolving Strategies of Political Terrorism," pp. 71–105 in Charles W. Kegley, Jr. (ed.), *The New Global Terrorism*. Upper Saddle River, N.J.: Prentice Hall.

———. (1999) "Necessity in Foreign Policy," *Political Science Quarterly* 113 (Winter): 673–88.

Reardon, Betty. (1985) *Sexism and the War System*. New York: Teachers College Press.

Redfield, Robert. (1962) *Human Nature and the Study of Society*, vol. 1. Chicago: University of Illinois Press.

Regan, Patrick M. (1994) *Organizing Societies for War*. Westport, Conn.: Praeger.

Regan, Patrick M., and Aida Paskevicute. (2003) "Women's Access to Politics and Peaceful States," *Journal of Peace Research* 40 (March): 287–302.

Reid, T. R. (2004) *The United States of Europe: The New Superpower and the End of American Supremacy*. New York: Penguin.

Reinares, Fernando. (2002) "The Empire Rarely Strikes Back," *Foreign Policy* (January/February): 92–94.

Reinicke, Wolfgang H. (1997) "Global Public Policy," *Foreign Affairs* 76 (November–December): 127–38.

Reiter, Dan. (2003) "Exploring the Bargaining Model of War," *Perspectives on Politics* 1 (March): 27–43.

Reiter, Dan, and Allen C. Stam III. (1998) "Democratic War Initiation and Victory," *American Political Science Review* 92 (No. 2): 377–89.

Renner, Michael. (1999) "Arms Control Orphans," *Bulletin of the Atomic Scientists* 58 (January–February): 22–27.

Reuveny, Rafael, and William R. Thompson. (2004) "World Economic Growth, Systemic Leadership and Southern Debt Crises," *Journal of Peace Research* 41 (January): 5–24.

Revel, Jean-Francois. (2004) *Anti-Americanism*. San Francisco: Encounter.

Rice, Susan, and David Scheffer. (1999) "Sudan Must End Its Brutal War against Civilians," *International Herald Tribune* (September 1): 6.

Rich, Frank. (2004) "The Corporate-Military Whiz Kids," *International Herald Tribune* (January 24–25): 8.

Richardson, Lewis F. (1960a) *Arms and Insecurity*. Pittsburgh: Boxwood.

———. (1960b) *Statistics of Deadly Quarrels*. Chicago: Quadrangle.

Richardson, Neil R. (1995) "International Trade as a Force for Peace," pp. 281–93 in Charles W. Kegley, Jr. (ed.), *Controversies in International Relations Theory*. New York: St. Martin's.

Ridley, Matt. (2003) *Nature Vs. Nurture: Genes, Experiences and What Makes Us Human*. New York: HarperCollins.

———. (1998) *The Origins of Virtue: Human Instincts and the Evolution of Cooperation*. New York: Viking.

Rieff, David. (1999) "The Precarious Triumph of Human Rights," *New York Times Magazine* (August 8): 36–41.

Rifkin, Jeromy. (2004) *The European Dream: How Europe's Vision of the Future Is Quietly Eclipsing the American Dream*. New York: Tarcher.

Riggs, Robert E., and Jack C. Plano. (1994) *The United Nations*, 2nd ed. Belmont, Calif.: Wadsworth.

Riker, William H. (1962) *The Theory of Political Coalitions*. New Haven, Conn.: Yale University Press.

Ripsman, Norrin M. (2004) "The Political Economy of Hegemonic Decline," *International Studies Review* 6: 133–35.

Rosa, Jean-Jacques. (2000) *Euro Error*. New York: Algrera.

Rosecrance, Richard. (1997) "Economics and National Security," pp. 209–38 in Richard Shultz, Roy Godson, and George Quester (eds.), *Security Studies for the Twenty-First Century*. New York: Brassey's.

———. (1992) "A New Concert of Powers," *Foreign Affairs* 71 (Spring): 64–82.

Rosen, Jeffery. (2004) *The Naked Crowd: Reclaiming Security and Freedom in an Anxious Age*. New York: Random House.

Rosenau, James N. (1995) "Security in a Turbulent World," *Current History* 94 (May): 193–200.

———. (1990) *Turbulence in World Politics: A Theory of Change and Continuity*. Princeton, N.J.: Princeton University Press.

———. (1980) *The Scientific Study of Foreign Policy*. New York: Nichols.

Rosenberg, Shawn W. (1988) *Reason, Ideology and Politics*. Princeton, N.J.: Princeton University Press.

Rosenthal, Joel H. (1991) *Righteous Realists*. Baton Rouge: Louisiana State University Press.

Ross, Michael L. (2004) "What Do We Know about Natural Resources and Civil War?" *Journal of Peace Research* 41 (May): 337–56.

Ross, Philip E. (1997) "The End of Infantry?" *Forbes* (July 7): 182–85.

Rosset, Peter. (1999) "Biotechnology Won't Feed the World," *International Herald Tribune* (September 2): 8.

Rostow, W. W. (1960) *The Stages of Economic Growth*. Cambridge: Cambridge University Press.

Rothgeb, John M., Jr. (1993) *Defining Power: Influence and Force in the Contemporary International System*. New York: St. Martin's Press.

Rothstein, Linda. (2001) "After September 11," *Bulletin of the Atomic Scientists* 57 (November–December): 44–48.

Rowan, Carl. (1999) "U.S. Is on Right Side of History in Kosovo Campaign," *Columbia (S.C.) State* (March 30): A9.

Rubenstein, Richard E. (2003) "The Psycho-Political Sources of Terrorism," pp. 139–50 in Charles W. Kegley, Jr. (ed.), *The New Global Terrorism*. Upper Saddle River, N.J.: Prentice Hall.

Rubin, Nancy. (1999) "It's Official: All of the World Is Entitled to Democracy," *International Herald Tribune* (May 18): 8.

Ruggie, John Gerald. (1983) "Continuity and Transformation in the World Polity: Toward a Neorealist Synthesis," *World Politics* 35 (January): 261–85.

Rummel, Rudolph J. (1994) *Death by Government*. New Brunswick, N.J.: Transaction.

Rusi, Alpo. (1997) *Dangerous Peace*. Boulder, Colo.: Westview.

Russett, Bruce. (2001) "How Democracy, Interdependence, and International Organizations Create a System for Peace," pp. 232–42 in Charles W. Kegley, Jr., and Eugene Wittkopf (eds.), *The Global Agenda*, 6th ed. Boston: McGraw-Hill.

Sadowaski. Yahya. (1998) "Ethnic Conflict," *Foreign Policy* 112 (Summer): 12–23.

Sagan, Carl. (1989) "Understanding Growth Rates: The Secret of the Persian Chessboard," *Parade* (February 14): 14.

———. (1988) "The Common Enemy," *Parade* (February 7): 4–7.

Sagan, Carl, and Richard Turco. (1993) "Nuclear Winter in the Post–Cold War Era," *Journal of Peace Research* 30 (November): 369–73.

Sageman, Marc. (2004) *Understanding Terror Networks*. Philadelphia: University of Pennsylvania Press.

Sambanis, Nicholas. (2004) "What Is Civil War?" *Journal of Conflict Resolution* 48 (December): 814–58.

Samuelson, Robert J. (2002a) "'Digital Divide' Facing Poor Looks Like Fiction," *Columbia (S.C.) State* (April 3): A13.

———. (2002b) "The New Coin of the Realm," *Newsweek* (January 7): 38.

———. (2001a) "Better Energy Policy a Critical Need for U.S.," *Columbia (S.C.) State* (October 11): A17.

———. (2001b) "The Spirit of Capitalism," *Foreign Affairs* 80 (January–February): 205–11.

Sandel, Michael J. (1996) "America's Search for a New Public Philosophy," *Atlantic Monthly* (March): 57–74.

Sanger, David E. (1998) "Contagion Effect: A Guide to Modern Domino Theory," *New York Times* (August 2): Section 1, 4–5.

Saul, John Ralstom. (2004) "The Collapse of Globalism and the Rebirth of Nationalism," *Harper's* 308 (March): 33–43.

Saurin, Julian. (2000) "Globalization, Poverty, and the Promises of Modernity," pp. 204–29 in Sarah Owen Vandersluis and Paris Yeros (eds.), *Poverty in World Politics*. New York: St. Martin's.

Schelling, Thomas C. (1978) *Micromotives and Macrobehavior*. New York: Norton.

Schlesinger, Arthur, Jr. (1997) "Has Democracy a Future?" *Foreign Affairs* 76 (September–October): 2–12.

———. (1986) *The Cycles of American History*. Boston: Houghton Mifflin.

Schneider, Gerald, Katherine Barbieri, and Nils Petter Gleditsch (eds.). (2003) *Globalization and Armed Conflict*. Lanham, Md.: Rowman & Littlefield.

Schraeder, Peter J. (ed.). (2002) *Exporting Democracy*. Boulder, Colo.: Lynne Rienner.

Schroeder, Paul W. (1989) "The Nineteenth-Century System," *Review of International Studies* 15 (April): 135–53.

Schuler, Corinna. (1999) "Helping Children Warriors Regain Their Humanity," *Christian Science Monitor* (October 20): 1, 12–13.

Schulz, William F. (2001) *In Our Own Best Interest: How Defending Human Rights Benefits Us All*. Boston: Beacon Press.

Schwab, Klaus, and Claude Smadja. (1996) "Start Taking the Backlash against Globalization Seriously," *International Herald Tribune* (February 1): 1, 8.

Schweller, Randall L. (2004) "Unanswered Threats: A Neoclassical Realist Theory of Underbalancing," *International Security* 29 (Fall): 159–201.

———. (1999) Review of *From Wealth to Power* by Fareed Zakaria, *American Political Science Review* 93 (June 1999): 497–99.

———. (1992) "Domestic Structure and Preventive War," *World Politics* 44 (January): 235–69.

Scott, Shirley V. (2004) *International Law in World Politics*. Boulder, Colo.: Lynne Rienner.

Seck, Manadon Manosour. (1999) "Shrinking Forests," *Christian Science Monitor* (May 3): 9.

Selck, Torsten J. (2004) "On the Dimensionality of European Union Legislative Decision-Making," *Journal of Theoretical Politics* 16 (April): 203–22.

Sellers, M. N. S. (1998) "Separatism and the Democratic Entitlement in International Law," pp. 115–22 in *The Challenge of Non-State Actors*. Washington, D.C.: American Society of International Law.

Sen, Amartya. (1994) "Population: Delusion and Reality," *New York Review of Books* 41 (September 22): 62–71.

Serfaty, Simon. (2003) "Europe, Enlarged, America Detached?" *Current History* (March): 99–102.

Shah, Timothy Samuel. (2004) "The Bible and the Ballot Box: Evangelicals and Democracy in the 'Global South,'" *SAIS Review of International Affairs* 24 (Fall): 117–32.

Shambaugh, David. (2001) "Facing Reality in China Policy," *Foreign Affairs* 80 (January–February): 50–64.

Shannon, Thomas Richard. (1989) *An Introduction to the World-System Perspective*. Boulder, Colo.: Westview.

Sheehan, Michael. (1996) "A Regional Perspective on the Globalization Process," *Korean Journal of Defense Analysis* 8 (Winter): 53–74.

Sheffer, Gabriel. (2003) *Diaspora Politics: At Home Abroad*. Cambridge: Cambridge University Press.

Shultz, Richard H., Jr., Roy Godson, and George H. Quester (eds.). (1997) *Security Studies for the Twenty-First Century*. New York: Brassey's.

Shultz, Richard H., Jr., and William J. Olson. (1994) *Ethnic and Religious Conflict*. Washington, D.C.: National Strategy Information Center.

Siegel, Martin J. (1983) "Survival," *USA Today* 112 (August): 1–2.

Siegle, Joseph T., Michael M. Weinstein, and Morton H. Halperin. (2004) "Why Democracies Excel," *Foreign Affairs* 83 (September–October): 57–71.

Simmons, Beth A., and Zachary Elkins. (2004) "The Globalization of Liberalization: Policy Diffusion in the International Political Economy," *American Political Science Review* 98 (February): 171–89.

Simon, Herbert A. (1997) *Models of Bounded Rationality*. Cambridge, Mass.: MIT Press.

———. (1957) *Models of Man*. New York: Wiley.

Singer, Hans W., and Javed A. Ansari. (1988) *Rich and Poor Countries*, 4th ed. London: Unwin Hyman.

Singer, J. David. (1991) "Peace in the Global System," pp. 56–84 in Charles W. Kegley, Jr. (ed.), *The Long Postwar Peace*. New York: HarperCollins.

———. (1981) "Accounting for International War: The State of the Discipline," *Journal of Peace Research* 18 (No. 1): 1–18.

——— (ed.). (1968) *Quantitative International Politics*. New York: Free Press.

———. (1961) "The Level-of-Analysis Problem in International Relations," pp. 77–92 in Klaus Knorr and Sidney Verba (eds.), *The International System*. Princeton, N.J.: Princeton University Press.

Singer, J. David, and Melvin Small. (1974) "Foreign Policy Indicators," *Policy Sciences* 5 (September): 271–96.

———. (1968) "Alliance Aggregation and the Onset of War, 1815–1945," pp. 247–85 in J. David Singer (ed.), *Quantitative International Politics*. New York: Free Press.

Singer, Max. (1999) "The Population Surprise," *Atlantic Monthly* (August): 22–25.

Singer, Max, and Aaron Wildavsky. (1993) *The Real World Order: Zones of Peace/Zones of Turmoil.* Chatham, N.J.: Chatham House.

Singer, Peter. (2004) *One World: The Ethics of Globalization,* 2nd ed. New Haven, Conn.: Yale University Press.

Singh, Sonali, and Christopher R. Way. (2004) "The Correlates of Nuclear Proliferation," *Journal of Conflict Resolution* 48 (December): 859–85.

Sivard, Ruth Leger. (1996) *World Military and Social Expenditures 1996.* Washington, D.C.: World Priorities.

———. (1993) *World Military and Social Expenditures 1993.* Washington, D.C.: World Priorities.

———. (1991) *World Military and Social Expenditures 1991.* Washington, D.C.: World Priorities.

———. (1982) *World Military and Social Expenditures 1982.* Leesburg, Va.: World Priorities.

Siverson, Randolph M., and Julian Emmons. (1991) "Democratic Political Systems and Alliance Choices," *Journal of Conflict Resolution* 35 (June): 285–306.

Sklair, Leslie. (1991) *Sociology of the Global System.* Baltimore: Johns Hopkins University Press.

Slaughter, Anne-Marie. (2004a) *A New World Order.* Princeton, N.J.: Princeton University Press.

———. (2004b) "The Clear, Cruel Lessons of Iraq," *Financial Times* (April 8): 15.

———. (1997) "The Real New World Order," *Foreign Affairs* 76 (September–October): 183–97.

Small, Melvin, and J. David Singer. (1982) *Resort to Arms: International and Civil Wars, 1816–1980.* Beverly Hills, Calif.: Sage.

Smith, Alastair, and Allan C. Stam. (2004) "Bargaining and the Nature of War," *Journal of Conflict Resolution* 48 (December): 783–813.

Smith, Dan. (1997) *The State of War and Peace Atlas,* 3rd ed. New York: Penguin.

Smith, Jackie, and Timothy Patrick Moran. (2001) "WTO 101: Myths about the World Trade Organization," pp. 68–71 in Robert J. Griffiths (ed.), *Developing World 01/02,* Guilford, Conn.: Dushkin/McGraw-Hill.

Smith, Michael J. (2000) "Humanitarian Intervention Revisited," *Harvard International Review* 22 (April): 72–75.

Smith, Steve. (1997) "Bridging the Gap: Social Constructivism," pp. 183–87 in John Baylis and Steve Smith (eds.), *The Globalization of World Politics.* New York: Oxford University Press.

Snidal, Duncan. (1993) "Relative Gains and the Pattern of International Cooperation," pp. 181–207 in David A. Baldwin (ed.), *Neorealism and Neoliberalism: The Contemporary Debate.* New York: Columbia University Press.

Snider, Lewis W. (1991) "Guns, Debt, and Politics," *Armed Forces and Society* 17 (Winter): 167–90.

Snow, Donald M. (2004) *National Security for a New Era: Globalization and Geopolitics.* Boston, Mass.: Longman.

Snyder, Glenn H. (1991) "Alliance Threats: A Neorealist First Cut," pp. 83–103 in Robert L. Rothstein (ed.), *The Evolution of Theory in International Relations.* Columbia: University of South Carolina Press.

———. (1984) "The Security Dilemma in Alliance Politics," *World Politics* 36 (July): 461–495.

Snyder, Glenn H., and Paul Diesing. (1977) *Conflict among Nations.* Princeton, N.J.: Princeton University Press.

Snyder, Jack. (2004) "One World, Rival Theories," *Foreign Policy* (November–December): 53–62.

Sodaro, Michael J. (2001) *Comparative Politics.* Boston: McGraw-Hill.

Somavia, Juan. (2004) "For Too Many, Globalization Isn't Working," *International Herald Tribune* (February 27): 6.

Somit, Albert. (1990) "Humans, Chimps, and Bonobos: The Biological Bases of Aggression, War, and Peacemaking," *Journal of Conflict Resolution* 34 (September): 553–82.

Sommaruga, Cornelio. (1999) "Renew the Ambition to Impose Rules on Warfare," *International Herald Tribune* (August 12): 8.

Sørensen, Georg. (1995) "Four Futures," *Bulletin of the Atomic Scientists* 51 (July–August): 69–72.

Sorensen, Theodore C. (1963) *Decision Making in the White House.* New York: Columbia University Press.

Sorokin, Pitirim A. (1937) *Social and Cultural Dynamics.* New York: American Book.

Soroos, Marvin S. (2001) "The Tragedy of the Commons in Global Perspective," pp. 485–99 in Charles W. Kegley, Jr., and Eugene R. Wittkopf (eds.), *The Global Agenda,* 6th ed. Boston: McGraw-Hill.

Soros, George. (2003) *The Bubble of American Supremacy: Correcting the Misuse of American Power.* New York: Public Affairs.

Souva, Mark. (2004) "Institutional Similarity and Interstate Conflict," *International Interactions* 30 (July–September): 263–80.

Spero, Joan E., and Jeffrey A. Hart. (2003) *The Politics of International Economic Relations,* 6th ed. Belmont, Calif.: Wadsworth/Thomson.

Speth, James Gustave. (1999a) "Debt Relief, Yes, but Development Aid as Well," *International Herald Tribune* (May 7): 6.

———. (1999b) "The Neglect of Growing Poverty Poses a Global Threat," *International Herald Tribune* (July 17–18): 6.

Spykman, Nicholas. (1944) *Geography of Peace.* New York: Harcourt Brace.

Srodes, James. (2001) "Importing Economic Muscle," *World Trade* 14 (June): 13–15.

Stanley Foundation. (1993) *The UN Role in Intervention.* Muscatine, Iowa: Stanley Foundation.

Stephenson, Carolyn M. (2000) "NGOs and the Principal Organs of the United Nations," pp. 270–94 in Paul Taylor and R. J. Groom (eds.), *The United Nations at the Millennium.* London: Continuum.

Stern, Jessica. (2003) *Terror in the Name of God: Why Religious Militants Kill.* New York: Ecco/HarperCollins.

Stevenson, Richard W. (1997) "The Cost of 'Fast-Track' Setback," *International Herald Tribune* (November 11): 3.

Stock, Thomas, and Anna De Geer. (1995) "Chemical and Biological Weapons," pp. 337–57 in Stockholm International Peace Research Institute, *SIPRI Yearbook 1995.* New York: Oxford University Press.

Stockholm International Peace Research Institute (SIPRI). (2004) *SIPRI Yearbook 2004.* New York: Oxford University Press.

———. (2002) *SIPRI Yearbook 2002.* New York: Oxford University Press.

———. (2001) *SIPRI Yearbook 2001.* New York: Oxford University Press.

Stokes, Bruce. (2000) "The Protectionist Myth," *Foreign Policy* 117 (Winter): 88–102.

Stopford, John. (2001) "Multinational Corporations," pp. 72–77 in Robert J. Griffiths (ed.), *Developing World 01/02,* Guilford, Conn.: Dushkin/McGraw-Hill.

Stott, Philip. (2002) "Cold Comfort for 'Global Warming,'" *Wall Street Journal* (March 25): A18.

Strang, David. (1991) "Global Patterns of Decolonization, 1500–1987," *International Studies Quarterly* 35 (December): 429–545.

———. (1990) "From Dependence to Sovereignty: An Event History Analysis of Decolonization 1870–1987," *American Sociological Review* 55 (December): 846–60.

Streeten, Paul. (2001) "Human Development Index," pp. 367–68 in Joel Krieger (ed.), *The Oxford Companion to Politics of the World*, 2nd ed. New York: Oxford University Press.

Stross, Randall E. (2002) "The McPeace Dividend," *U.S. News & World Report* (April 1): 36.

Sutcliffe, Bob. (2002) *100 Ways of Seeing an Unequal World*, 2nd ed. London: Zed.

Sylvester, Christine. (2002) *Feminist International Relations*. New York: Cambridge University Press.

Talbott, Strobe, and Nayan Chanda (eds.). (2002) *The Age of Terror*. New York: Basic Books.

Tessman, Brock, and Steve Chan. (2004) "Power Cycles, Risk Propensity and Great Power Deterrence," *Journal of Conflict Resolution* 48 (April): 131–53.

Thakur, Ramesh. (1998) "Teaming Up to Make Human Rights a Universal Fact," *International Herald Tribune* (December 10): 10.

Thakur, Ramesh, and Steve Lee. (2000) "Defining New Goals for Diplomacy in the Twenty-First Century," *International Herald Tribune* (January 19): 8.

Thompson, Kenneth W. (1960) *Political Realism and the Crisis of World Politics*. Princeton, N.J.: Princeton University Press.

———. (1953) "Collective Security Reexamined," *American Political Science Review* 47 (September): 753–72.

Thompson, William R. (ed.) (1999a) *Great Power Rivalries*. Columbia: University of South Carolina.

———. (1999b) "Why Rivalries Matter and What Great Power Rivalries Can Tell Us about World Politics," pp. 3–28 in William R. Thompson (ed.), *Great Power Rivalries*. Columbia: University of South Carolina Press.

———. (1988) *On Global War: Historical-Structural Approaches to World Politics*. Columbia: University of South Carolina Press.

Thurow, Lester C. (1999) *Building Wealth*. New York: HarperCollins.

———. (1998) "The American Economy in the Next Century," *Harvard International Review* 20 (Winter): 54–59.

———. (1992) *Head to Head: Coming Economic Battles among Japan, Europe, and America*. New York: Morrow.

Tickner, J. Ann. (2002) *Gendering World Politics*. New York: Columbia University Press.

———. (1999) "Searching for the Princess? Feminist Perspectives in International Relations," *Harvard International Review* 121 (Fall): 41–48.

———. (1992) *Gender in International Relations*. New York: Columbia University Press.

Tilford, Earl H., Jr. (1995) *The Revolution in Military Affairs*. Carlisle Barracks, Pa.: U.S. Army War College.

Tillema, Herbert K. (2006) *Overt Military Intervention in the Cold War Era*. Columbia: University of South Carolina Press.

———. (1994) "Cold War Alliance and Overt Military Intervention, 1945–1991," *International Interactions* 20 (No. 3): 249–78.

———. (1989) "Foreign Overt Military Intervention in the Nuclear Age," *Journal of Peace Research* 26 (May): 179–95.

Tillema, Herbert K., and John R. Van Wingen. (1982) "Law and Power in Military Intervention," *International Studies Quarterly* 26 (June): 220–50.

Tilly, Charles. (2003) *The Politics of Collective Violence*. Cambridge: Cambridge University Press.

Timmerman, Kenneth. (1991) *The Death Lobby: How the West Armed Iraq*. Boston: Houghton Mifflin.

Tocqueville, Alexis de. (1969 [1835]) *Democracy in America*. New York: Doubleday.

Todaro, Michael P. (2002) *Economic Development*, 8th ed. Reading, Mass.: Addison-Wesley.

———. (2000) *Economic Development*, 7th ed. Reading, Mass.: Addison-Wesley.

———. (1994) *Economic Development in the Third World*, 5th ed. New York: Longman.

Todd, Emmanuel. (2003) *After the Empire: The Breakdown of the American Order*. Translated by C. Jon Delegu. New York: Columbia University Press.

Toner, Robin. (2002) "FBI Agent Gives Her Blunt Assessment," *Columbia (S.C.) State* (June 7): A5.

Toynbee, Arnold J. (1954) *A Study of History*. London: Oxford University Press.

Trachtenberg, Marc. (1990–91) "The Meaning of Mobilization in 1914," *International Security* 15 (Winter): 120–50.

Tuchman, Barbara W. (1984) *The March of Folly*. New York: Ballantine.

———. (1962) *The Guns of August*. New York: Dell.

Tucker, Robert C., and David C. Hendrickson. (1990) *Empire of Liberty*. New York: Oxford University Press.

Turk, Danilo. (2001) "Genocide," p. 316 in Joel Krieger (ed.), *The Oxford Companion to Politics of the World*, 2nd ed. New York: Oxford University Press.

Tyler, Patrik E. (2001) "Seeing Profits, Russia Prepared to Become World's Nuclear Waste Dump," *International Herald Tribune* (May 28): 5.

Underhill, Geoffrey R. D., and Xiakoe Zhang (eds.). (2003) *International Financial Governance under Stress: Global Structures versus National Imperatives*. Cambridge: Cambridge University Press.

United Nations Conference on Trade and Development (UNCTAD). (2004) "Global FDI Decline Bottoms Out in 2003," press Release.

United Nations Development Programme (UNDP). (2004) *Human Development Report 2004*. New York: Oxford University Press.

———. (2003) *Human Development Report 2003*. New York: Oxford University Press.

———. (2002) *Human Development Report 2002*. New York: Oxford University Press.

———. (2001) *Human Development Report 2001*. New York: Oxford University Press.

———. (1999) *Human Development Report 1999*. New York: Oxford University Press.

———. (1995) *Human Development Report 1995*. New York: Oxford University Press.

———. (1991) *Human Development Report 1991*. New York: Oxford University Press.

United Nations Environment Programme (UNEP). (2004) *State of the Environment and Policy Perspective*. New York: United Nations.

———. (2002) *Global Environment Outlook*. New York: Oxford University Press.

United Nations Population Division (UNPD). (2004) *World Population Prospects*. New York: United Nations.

Urquhart, Brian. (2002) "Shameful Neglect," *International Herald Tribune* (April 25): 12–14.

———. (2001) "Mrs. Roosevelt's Revolution," *New York Review of Books* 49 (April 26): 32–34.

———. (1994) "Who Can Police the World?" *New York Review of Books* 41 (May 12): 29–33.

U.S. Arms Control and Disarmament Agency (ACDA). (2002) *World Military Expenditures and Arms Transfers.* Washington, D.C.: U.S. Government Printing Office.

———. (1997) *World Military Expenditures and Arms Transfers 1995.* Washington, D.C.: U.S. Government Printing Office.

U.S. Department of State. (2005) *Patterns of Global Terrorism 2005.* Washington, D.C.: Department of State.

———. (2004) *Patterns of Global Terrorism 2004,* rev. ed. Washington, D.C.: Department of State.

Vaitheeswaron, Vijay. (2000) "Big Oil in Big Trouble," pp. 89–90 in the *Economist, The World in 2000.* London: Economist.

Vandersluis, Sarah Owen, and Paris Yeros. (2000a) "Ethics and Poverty in a Global Era," pp. 1–31 in Sarah Owen Vandersluis and Paris Yeros (eds.), *Poverty in World Politics.* New York: St. Martin's.

——— (eds.). (2000b) *Poverty in World Politics.* New York: St. Martin's.

Van Evera, Stephen. (1999) *Causes of War.* Ithaca, N.Y.: Cornell University Press.

———. (1994) "Hypotheses on Nationalism and War," *International Security* 18 (Spring): 5–39.

———. (1990–91) "Primed for Peace," *International Security* 15 (Winter): 6–56.

Vasquez, John A. (1998) *The Power of Power Politics: From Classical Realism to Neotraditionalism.* Cambridge: Cambridge University Press.

———. (1997) "The Realist Paradigm and Degenerative versus Progressive Research Programs," *American Political Science Review* 91 (December): 899–912.

———. (1993) *The War Puzzle.* Cambridge: Cambridge University Press.

———. (1991) "The Deterrence Myth," pp. 205–23 in Charles W. Kegley, Jr. (ed.), *The Long Postwar Peace.* New York: HarperCollins.

Vasquez, John A., and Colin Elman (eds.). (2003) *Realism and the Balancing of Power: A New Debate.* Upper Saddle River, N.J.: Prentice Hall.

Väyrynen, Raimo. (1992) *Military Industrialization and Economic Development.* Aldershot, Eng.: Dartmouth.

Verba, Sidney. (1969) "Assumptions of Rationality and Nonrationality in Models of the International System," pp. 217–31 in James N. Rosenau (ed.), *International Politics and Foreign Policy.* New York: Free Press.

Verbeek, Bertjan. (2006) "Can International Organizations Have a Foreign Policy?" in Margaret G. Hermann and Bengt Sundilius (eds.), *Comparative Foreign Policy Analysis.* Upper Saddle River, N.J.: Prentice Hall (forthcoming).

Vidal, Gore. (2004). *Imperial America.* New York: Nation Books.

Vital Signs 2005. New York: Norton, for Worldwatch Institute.

Vital Signs 2004. New York: Norton, for Worldwatch Institute.

Vital Signs 2003. New York: Norton, for the Worldwatch Institute.

Vital Signs 2002. New York: Norton, for the Worldwatch Institute.

Vital Signs 2000. New York: Norton, for the Worldwatch Institute.

Vital Signs 1999. New York: Norton, for the Worldwatch Institute.

Vital Signs 1997. New York: Norton, for the Worldwatch Institute.

Volgy, Thomas J., and Alison Bailin. (2002) *State Strength and the New World Order.* Boulder, Colo.: Lynne Rienner.

von Glahn, Gerhard. (1996) *Law among Nations,* 7th ed. Boston: Allyn & Bacon.

Wade, Robert Hunter. (2002) "America's Empire Rules an Unbalanced World," *International Herald Tribune* (January 3): 7.

Walker, William O. (1991) "Decision-Making Theory and Narcotic Foreign Policy," *Diplomatic History* 15 (Winter): 31–45.

Wallace, Brian. (1978) "True Grit South of the Border," *Osceola* (January 13): 15–16.

Wallensteen, Peter, and Margareta Sollenberg. (2001) "Armed Conflict 1989–2000," *Journal of Peace Research* 38 (September): 629–44.

Wallerstein, Immanuel. (2004) *World-Systems Analysis.* Durham, N.C.: Duke University Press.

———. (2002) "The Eagle Has Crash Landed," *Foreign Policy* (July–August): 60–68.

———. (1988) *The Modern World-System III.* San Diego: Academic Press.

Walter, Barbara F. (2004) "Does Conflict Beget Conflict?" *Journal of Peace Research* 41 (May): 371–88.

———. (1997) "The Critical Barrier to Civil War Settlement," *International Organization* 51 (Summer): 335–64.

Walters, Robert S., and David H. Blake. (1992) *The Politics of Global Economic Relations,* 4th ed. Englewood Cliffs, N.J.: Prentice Hall.

Waltz, Kenneth N. (2000) "Structural Realism after the Cold War," *International Security* 25 (Summer): 5–41.

———. (1995) "Realist Thought and Neorealist Theory," pp. 67–83 in Charles W. Kegley, Jr. (ed.), *Controversies in International Relations Theory.* New York: St. Martin's.

———. (1993) "The Emerging Structure of International Politics," *International Security* 18 (Fall): 44–79.

———. (1979) *Theory of International Politics.* Reading, Mass.: Addison-Wesley.

———. (1964) "The Stability of a Bipolar World," *Daedalus* 93 (Summer): 881–909.

———. (1954) *Man, the State, and War.* New York: Columbia University Press.

Walzer, Michael. (2004) *Arguing About War.* New Haven, Conn.: Yale University Press.

Ward, Michael D., David R. Davis, and Corey L. Lofdahl. (1995) "A Century of Tradeoffs," *International Studies Quarterly* 39 (March): 27–50.

Warrick, Joby. (1997) "How Warm Will It Get?" *Washington Post National Weekly Edition* (December 1): 6–7.

Watson, Douglas. (1997) "Indigenous Peoples and the Global Economy," *Current History* 96 (November): 389–91.

Wattenberg, Ben J. (2005) *Fewer: How the Demography of Depopulation Will Shape Our Future.* Chicago: Ivan R. Dee.

———. (2002) "Over-population Turns Out to Be Overhyped," *Wall Street Journal* (March 4): 10.

Weart, Spencer R. (1994) "Peace among Democratic and Oligarchic Republics," *Journal of Peace Research* 31 (August): 299–316.

Weidenbaum, Murray. (2004) "Surveying the Global Marketplace," *USA Today* (January): 26–27.

Weitsman, Patricia A. (2004) *Dangerous Alliances: Proponents of Peace, Weapons of War.* Stanford, Calif.: Stanford University Press.

Wendt, Alexander. (2000) *Social Theory of International Politics.* Cambridge: Cambridge University Press.

Wendzel, Robert L. (1980) *International Relations: A Policymaker Focus.* New York: Wiley.

Whitbeck, John V. (2004) "'Terrorism'—A World Ensnared by a Word," *International Herald Tribune* (February 18): 6.

White, Donald W. (1998) "Mutable Destiny: The End of the American Century?" *Harvard International Review* 20 (Winter): 42–47.

White, Ralph K. (1990) "Why Aggressors Lose," *Political Psychology* 11 (June): 227–42.
Whitney, Craig R. (1999) "European Union Vows to Become Military Power," *New York Times* (June 4): A1, A16.
Will, George. (2002a) "Bush Move on Steel Shows Soft Principles," *Columbia (S.C.) State* (March 8): A11.
———. (2002b) "Tough-Taking Administration Getting Soft on Trade," *Columbia (S.C.) State* (April 14): D3.
Wills, Garry. (2004) "What Is a Just War?" *New York Review of Books* (November 18): 32–32.
Wilmer, Franke. (1993) *The Indigenous Voice in World Politics: Since Time Immemorial*. Newbury Park, Calif.: Sage.
Wilson, James Q. (1993) *The Moral Sense*. New York: Free Press.
Wise, Michael Z. (1993) "Reparations," *Atlantic Monthly* 272 (October): 32–35.
Wittkopf, Eugene R., Charles W. Kegley, Jr., and James M. Scott. (2003) *American Foreign Policy*, 6th ed. Belmont, Calif.: Wadsworth.
Wohlforth, William C. (1999) "The Stability of a Unipolar World," *International Security* 24 (Summer): 5–41.
Wolf, Charles, Jr. (2002) "To Intervene or Not to Intervene?" *International Herald Tribune* (November 8): 8.
Wolf, Martin. (2001) "Will the Nation-State Survive Globalization?" *Foreign Affairs* 80 (January–February): 178–90.
Wolfensohn, James. (2004) "The Growing Threat of Global Poverty," *International Herald Tribune* (April 24–25): 6.
Wolfers, Arnold. (1962) *Discord and Collaboration*. Baltimore: Johns Hopkins University Press.
Woodward, Bob. (2004) *Plan of Attack*. New York: Simon & Schuster.
———. (2002) *Bush at War*. New York: Simon & Schuster.
World Bank. (2005a) *World Development Indicators 2005*. Washington, D.C.: World Bank.
———. (2005b) *World Development Report 2005*. New York: Oxford University Press.
———. (2004a) *World Development Indicators 2004*. Washington, D.C.: World Bank.
———. (2004b) *World Development Report 2004*. Washington, D.C.: World Bank.
———. (2003) *World Bank Atlas*. Washington, D.C.: World Bank.
———. (2002a) *World Development Indicators 2002*. Washington, D.C.: World Bank.
———. (2002b) *World Development Report 2002*. New York: Oxford University Press.
———. (2001) *World Development Report 2000–2001*. New York: Oxford University Press.
———. (2000) *World Development Report 1999–2000*. New York: Oxford University Press.
———. (1999a) *Global Economic Prospects and the Developing Countries, 1998/1999*. Washington, D.C.: World Bank.
———. (1999b) *World Development Report 1998/99*. New York: Oxford University Press.
———. (1996) *World Debt Tables 1996*, vol. 1. Washington, D.C.: World Bank.
———. (1995a) *Global Economic Prospects and the Developing Countries 1995*. Washington, D.C.: World Bank.
———. (1995b) *World Development Report 1995*. New York: Oxford University Press.
World Resources Institute (WRI). (2004) *SDI: Sustainable Development Index*. Washington, D.C.: World Resources Institute.
World Trade. (2002) *World Trade 14* (June): 13–15.
Worldwatch Institute. (2000) *The World in 2000*. New York: Norton.
Wright, Quincy. (1953) "The Outlawry of War and the Law of War," *American Journal of International Law* 47 (July): 365–76.
———. (1942) *A Study of War*. Chicago: University of Chicago Press.
Yardley, Jim. (2004) "China's Economic Engine Needs Power (Lots of It)," *New York Times* (March 14) 33.
Yearbook of International Organizations, 2003/2004, vols. 1–5. Munich: K. G. Sauer.
Yoder, Edwin M., Jr. (1991) "Isolationists Would Put America on a Dangerous Course," *Columbia (S.C.) State* (December 14): A10.
Zacher, Mark W. (1987) "Trade Gaps, Analytical Gaps: Regime Analysis and International Commodity Regulation," *International Organization* 41 (Spring): 173–202.
Zacher, Mark W., and Richard A. Matthew. (1995) "Liberal International Theory: Common Threads, Divergent Strands," pp. 107–49 in Charles W. Kegley, Jr. (ed.), *Controversies in International Relations Theory: Realism and the Neoliberal Challenge*. New York: St. Martin's.
Zagare, Frank C. (2004) "Reconciling Rationality with Deterrence," *Journal of Theoretical Politics* 16 (April): 107–41.
———. (1990) "Rationality and Deterrence," *World Politics* 42 (January): 238–60.
Zakaria, Fareed. (2004) "The One-Note Superpower," *Newsweek* (February 2): 41.
———. (2002a) "Europe: Make Peace with War," *Newsweek* (June 3): 35.
———. (2002b) "Stop the Babel over Babylon," *Newsweek* (October 16): 34.
———. (2002c) "The Trouble with Being the World's Only Superpower," *New Yorker* (October 14 and 21): 72–81.
———. (1999) "The Empire Strikes Out: The Unholy Emergence of the Nation-State," *New York Times Magazine* (April 18): 99.
———. (1998a) *From Wealth to Power: The Unusual Origins of America's World Role*. Princeton, N.J.: Princeton University Press.
———. (1998b) "The Future of Statecraft," p. 42 in *The World in 1999*. London: Economist.
———. (1992–93) "Is Realism Finished?" *National Interest* 30 (Winter): 21–32.
Ziegler, David. (1995) Review of *World Politics and the Evolution of War* by John Weltman, *American Political Science Review* 89 (September): 813–14.
Zimmerman, Tim. (1996) "CIA Study: Why Do Countries Fall Apart?" *U.S. News & World Report* (February 12): 46.
———. (1994) "Arms Merchant to the World," *U.S. News & World Report* (April 4): 37.

Photo Credits

Photos that appear on contents and part-opening pages are duplications of chapter photos.

Chapter 1: Page 3: Rajesh Kumar Singh/AP/Wide World; Page 7: AP/Wide World; Page 15: Greg Baker/AP/Wide World; Page 22: NASA

Chapter 2: Page 27: Charles Kegley; Page 30, left: The Granger Collection, NY; Page 30, right: The Granger Collection, NY; Page 34, left: Scala/Art Resource, NY; Page 34, right: Bridgeman Art Library; Page 45: Pedro Ugarte/AFP; Page 51: Arturo Mari/AP/Wide World

Chapter 3: Page 57: Luc Delahaye/Magnum; Page 64: Koji Sasahara/POOL/AP/Wide World; Page 73: Barbara Kinney/White House/Newsmakers/Getty Images; Page 80: White House/Getty Images; Page 90: AP/Wide World

Chapter 4: Page 95: FDR Library; Page 99: UPI Photo/Ali Khaligh/Landov; Page 108: Topham/The Image Works; Page 116: Biber/Sipa; Page 123: Stephen Shaver/AFP

Chapter 5: Page 132: Fred Chartrand/AP/Wide World; Page 139: Rene Burri/Magnum; Page 141, left: The Granger Collection, NY; Page 141, right: Bettmann/Corbis; Page 160: Robert Nickelsberg/Time Magazine

Chapter 6: Page 169: Rob Elliott/Agence France-Presse/Getty Images; Page 172: Jeff Katz/Earth Justice; Page 177: UN/DPI photo; Page 191: Audio Visual Library/European Commission; Page 195: Getty Images; Page 197: Allen Tannenbaum/Corbis-Sygma; Page 203: Peter Aventurier/Liaison/Getty Images; Page 215: Beth A. Keiser/AP/Wide World

Chapter 7: Page 220: Jerome Delay/AP/Wide World; Page 222: AP/Wide World Photos; Page 235: Scott Nelson/Getty Images; Page 236: Seamus Contan/FSP/Liaison/Getty Images; Page 242: AP/Wide World Photos; Page 245: Piers Benatar/Panos Pictures; Page 248: Fred Peer/Camera Press, London

Chapter 8: Page 261: Saleh RiFai/AP/Wide World; Page 264: Sally Wiener Grotta/The Stock Market/Corbis; Page 270: Glenn McLaughlin/Corbis; Page 271: Francois Guillot/AFP; Page 273: Richard Vogel/AP/Wide World Photos; Page 277: Patrick Lin/AFP/Getty Images; Page 287, left: Douglas Engle/AP/Wide World; Page 287, right: Eraldo Peres/AP/Wide World; Page 288: Peter Parks/AFP; Page 291: Frank Fournier/Contact; Page 293: Ritz Sino/New York Times; Page 296: Ira Wyman/Corbis-Sygma

Chapter 9: Page 301: Richard Vogel/AP/Wide World; Page 312: Angel Franco/New York Times; Page 321: Peter De Jong/AP/Wide World; Page 327: Greg Baker/AP/Wide World; Page 330, top: Anja Niedringhaus/EPA/AFP; Page 330, bottom: Louisa Gouliamaki/AFP; Page 331, left: Frederick Brown/AFP; Page 331, right: Eric Feferberg/AFP

Chapter 10: Page 349: Sherwin Castro/AP/Wide World; Page 358: Mike Hutchings/Reuters/Getty Images; Page 362: Robert Harbison/©1996 *The Christian Science Monitor* (www.csmonitor.com); Page 363: Isabelle Rouvillois/AFP; Page 365: NASA/AP/Wide World; Page 374: Yann Arthus Bertrand/Corbis; Page 379: Daniel Beltra/Greenpeace; Page 382: Wesley Bocxe/Photo Researchers; Page 384: Arko Datta/AFP; Page 391: Nik Wheeler/Corbis

Chapter 11: Page 399: AP/Wide World; Page 403: U.S. Air Force/Agence France-Presse/Getty Images; Page 408, left: Chris Hondros/Getty Images; Page 408, right: Les Stone/Corbis-Sygma; Page 416, left: Hulton Archive/Getty Images; Page 416, right: U.S. Army/AP/Wide World; Page 424: A. Yagsobzadeh/Sipa; Page 434, left: AP/Wide World; Page 434, right: Karim Sahib/AFP/Getty Images; Page 435: AP/Wide World

Chapter 12: Page 442: Corbis; Page 449: Reuters/Corrine Dulka/Archive Photos/Getty Images; Page 457: AP/Wide World; Page 458: Philip Wallick/Corbis; Page 459: Scott Peterson/Liaison/Getty Images; Page 461: Alain McLaughlin (alainm@mindspring.com); Page 469: Bernard Hermann/Liaison/Getty Images; Page 472: Andrea Comas/Reuters/Getty Images; Page 477: Charles Crowell/Black Star/Stock Photo; Page 484: Courtesy Lockheed Martin Corporation; Page 487: Chien-min Chung/AP/Wide World

Chapter 13: Page 499: Corbis; Page 502: The Granger Collection, NY; Page 519: Reuters/Archive/Getty Images; Page 522: Andreas Striglos/AFP; Page 525: Reuters/Archive/Getty Images

Chapter 14: Page 529: Reuters/Getty Images; Page 536: Getty Images; Page 538: Erich Lessing/Art Resource, NY; Page 544, left: Rubin Sprich/Reuters/Archive/Getty Images; Page 544, right: William Campbell/Time Magazine/Getty; Vienna Report/Corbis-Sygma; Kathy Willens/AP/Wide World; Corbis-Sygma; Matthiau/Potak/Corbis-Sygma, P. F. Gero/Corbis-Sygma; Page 546: Getty Images; Page 550: Maya Vidon/AFP; Page 551: Peter Morgan/Reuters/Archive/Getty Images; Page 557: Boris Grdanski/AP/Wide World

Chapter 15: Page 573: AFP/Corbis; Page 577: Noresen/Greenpeace; Page 580: Chuck Stoody/AP/Wide World; Page 582: Karel Prinsloo/AP/Wide World; Page 585: J. Van Hessel/Corbis-Sygma; Page 591: NASA; Page 592, left: Courtesy of INA/Getty Images; Page 592, right: Evan Vucci/AP/Wide World

INDEX

Glossary terms appear in **bold faced** type. Page numbers followed by italicized letters *f, m,* and *t,* indicate figures, maps, and tables, respectively.

Aaronson, Susan Ariel, 266, 274, 289, 320
ABC network, 271
Abramowitz, Morton, 83
absolute gain, 297, 308, 367, 557
Abu Ghraib prison, 536, 547
Abyssinia, 106
acid rain, 379–80
ACMs. *See* air-launched cruise missiles
acquired immune deficiency syndrome. *See* AIDS
actors
  emergence of the Global South, 137 (*see also* Global South)
  nonstate (*see* nonstate actors; nonstate nations)
  state (*see* states)
  types, 57
  unitary, 69, 196
adjudication, 533, 534
Adler, Emanuel, 44, 50
Afghanistan, 116, 233, 239
Africa, 355
African Charter of Human and Peoples Rights (1981), 246
agenda setting, 272
Ahtisaari, Martti, 566, 587
AIDS (acquired immune deficiency syndrome), 275, 276, 358–60, 359*m*. *See also* human immunodeficiency virus
air-launched cruise missiles (ACMs), 465
airports and security, 3
Albania, 70, 106
Alesina, Alberto, 213
Algeria, 143
Alien Tort Claims Act (1789), 547
alignments, 503
Allee, Todd L., 565
Allen, John L., 563
Allende, Salvador, 208
alliances
  advantages and risks, 501, 502
  balance-of-power theory
    concept of balance of power, 503
    counteralliances formation, 504
    managing the balance, 507
    objections to, 505–7
    rules for balancing process, 504–5
  collective security as an alternative, 502

  fundamental flaws, 501
Allied powers and World War II. *See* World War II
Allison, Graham, 70, 79, 467
Al Qaeda, 13, 83, 201, 435, 555, 576, 578
Alsace-Lorraine, 104
al-Sadr, Muqtada, 541
Altman, Lawrence K., 359*m*
Altman, Roger C., 331
America. *See* United States
America Online (AOL), 272, 274
Amnesty International, 194, 249
Amorim, Celso, 156
AMU. *See* Arab Maghreb Union
anarchy, 8, 39, 41, 44, 175, 415
Anastasion, Daniele, 409
anchoring, 76
Andean Group, 157
Anderson, E. N., 96
Andropov, Yuri, 116
Angell, Norman, 29, 30
Annan, Kofi, 3, 177, 179, 180, 244, 361, 392, 475, 510, 534, 550, 551, 567, 574, 575, 582, 583, 584
Anschluss, 106
anthrax, 466
Anti-Ballistic Missile Treaty, 513, 515
antibiotics, 276
antidumping duties, 310
antipersonnel landmines (APLs), 513
antisatellite (ASAT) weapons, 465
anti-Semitism, 108. *See also* Nazism
ANZUS, 555
AOL. *See* America Online
APEC. *See* Asia-Pacific Economic Cooperation
APLs. *See* antipersonnel landmines
appeasement, 106
Arab Maghreb Union (AMU), 193
Arafat, Yasser, 73*f*
Arbatov, Georgi, 117, 118
arbitrage, 280
arbitration, 31, 533, 534
ARCO Oil Company, 371
Ardrey, Robert, 405
Argentina, 4, 157, 336
Arias, Oscar, 451
Aristide, Jean-Bertrand, 4
Aristotle, 132, 576
armed conflict, 400. *See also* warfare

Armey, Dick, 81
arms control, 32
  bilateral agreements, 508, 509*f*, 510
  disarmament agreements, 508, 509*f*, 510
  multilateral agreements, 510, 511–12*t*
  obstacles to, 512–13, 514*m*, 515
  See also nuclear age
arms race, 117
arms trade, 154, 454–57, 454*f*
Art, Robert J., 475
ASAT. *See* antisatellite weapons
ASEAN. *See* Association of Southeast Asian Nations
Asian Tigers, 150
Asia-Pacific Economic Cooperation (APEC), 157, 192
Association of Southeast Asian Nations (ASEAN), 157, 192, 336, 555
asylum, 236
asymmetrical warfare, 473
Athens, 33
A. T. Kearney, 295
Atlantic Charter (1943), 532
atmosphere. *See* global warming
atrocities, 237
Augustine, St., 537
Austria, 106, 188
Austria-Hungary and World War I. *See* World War I
autocratic political systems
  foreign policy influences on, 65–67
  relation to human development, 230
autocratic rule, 65
Avian flu, 276
Axis powers in World War II. *See* World War II
Ayoob, Mohammed, 151, 251

Babai, Don, 331
Babones, Jonathan, 224, 231
Bacevich, Andrew J., 19, 120, 586
Baker, James A., III, 81
Baker, James D., 381
balance of power, 35
  after WWI, 100
  alliances and
    concept of balance of power, 503
    counteralliances formation, 504
    managing the balance, 507
    objections to, 505–7

I-1

balance of power—alliances and (*continued*)
 rules for balancing process, 504–5
 arms control and (*see* arms control)
 bipolarity period, 516–17
 collective security vs., 548, 549
 in Cuban missile crisis, 70
 multipolarity period, 517–18
 redistribution of power, 520, 521*m*, 522–24
 return to unipolarity, 518–19
 unipolarity period, 516
Baldwin, David, 41, 477
Ballador, Edward, 583
Baltic states, 109
bandwagoning, 486, 506, 520
Bank of Japan, 280
Barber, Benjamin R., 20, 263, 539
Barbieri, Katherine, 410, 559
bargaining model of war, 415
Barkin, Samuel, 50, 296
Barnes, Joe, 369
Barnet, Richard J., 210, 211, 295, 513, 559
Barnett, Michael, 44, 211
Baron, Samuel, 89
barter economy, 145
Basques, 58
beggar-thy-neighbor policies, 309
behavioralism
 armed conflict trends and, 400
 as a challenge to realism, 37
 defined, 377, 564
 theories of war, 413
behavioral science, 36, 37, 74
Beitz, Charles, 223, 246, 247, 248
Belgium, 143, 188
Bennett, Scott, 400, 564
Berdal, Mats, 278, 438
Berger, Peter L., 534, 584
Berger, Samuel R., 82, 592
Bergesen, Albert, 140
Bergsten, C. Fred, 316
Berlin Wall, 117
Bernstein, Richard, 355
Bertelsmann, 274
Berthelot, Yves, 329
Bevan, Aneurin, 462
Bhagwati, Jagdish, 151, 289, 305
Bieri, Franziska, 231, 266
Big Three, 110
bilateral, 157, 181
bilateral agreements, 508, 509*f*, 510
bilateralism, 481
Bin Laden, Osama, 82, 433, 435, 565, 578
biodiversity
 biogenetical engineering, 386–87
 biotechnology growth, 386
 environmental sustainability worldwide, 388*m*
 forests and plants and, 385–86
 implications of threats to, 386
biogenetical engineering, 386–87
biological weapons, 466–67
Biological Weapons Convention, 513

biotechnology growth, 386
bipolarity, 101, 115, 516
Bjola, Cornelia, 27
Blainey, Geoffrey, 419
Blair, Tony, 4, 132, 584
Blake, David H., 308
Blanton, Shannon Lindsey, 460
Blechman, Barry M., 541
Blight, James G., 586
Blix, Hans, 75
Boli, John, 231, 266, 274
Bolivia, 157, 336
Bolsheviks, 102, 103*m*, 112
Bolton, John, 553
Bonaparte, Napoleon, 488
Borenstein, Seth, 373
Bosnia, 544
Bosnian Serbs, 239
Bostdorff, Denise M., 75
Boswell, Terry, 142
bounded rationality, 72
Boutros-Ghali, Boutros, 400, 547, 574
Bowlin, Mike, 371
Bowring, Philip, 263, 276
boycotts, 476
Boyle, Francis A., 120, 539
Bozeman, Adda B., 534
brain drain, 235
Braudel, Fernand, 221
Brazil, 157, 287, 336, 384
Brecher, Michael, 473
Bretton Woods Conference (1944), 183, 186, 303–4, 317, 325–26
Brezhnev, Leonid, 116*f*
Brierly, James L., 537
brinkmanship, 468
Britain. *See* Great Britain
Brittan, Leon, 392
Broad, Robin, 289, 320
Broder, David, 71, 297
Bronfenbrenner, Urie, 111
Bronowski, Jacob, 591
Brown, Justin, 460
Brown, Lester R., 370, 373
Brundtland, Gar Harlem, 275
Brundtland Commission, 367
Brunei, 157
Brzezinski, Zbigniew, 20, 80*f*, 120, 343, 484, 519, 586
Buddhism, 203
Bueno de Mesquita, Bruce, 524
Bulgaria, 520
Bull, Hedley, 44
Bulletin of the Atomic Scientists, 467
Bunche, Ralph, 405
Bunn, Matthew, 464
bureaucracies. *See* bureaucratic politics
bureaucratic politics
 attributes of bureaucratic behavior, 82–85
 consequences of bureaucratic policy making, 85–86
 Cuban missile crisis example, 79–82
 efficiency and rationality, 78
 limits of, 78–82

 problems inherent to bureaucracies, 84
 properties of, 85
Burger, Julian, 198*m*
Bush, George W., 57*f*, 80*f*
 on Abu Ghraib abuse, 536
 decision-making process, 71
 decision to invade Iraq, 64*f*
 emigration from Mexico and, 233
 fast-track authority, 334
 on fighting terrorism, 433
 Kyoto Protocol stance, 380, 389
 loss of European support, 523
 pledge against terror, 4, 6
 on power, 447
 warning to Russia, 579
 See also Bush administration; Bush Doctrine
Bush administration
 attitude toward treaties, 513
 criticisms of pre-9/11 intelligence response, 83–84
 governmental politics in, 81
 nonrational impulses, 75–76
 See also Bush, George W.
Bush Doctrine, 87, 126, 483, 518, 540
Buzan, Barry, 44
Byers, Michael, 540

Caarlsson, Ingvar, 565
Cable News Network (CNN), 4, 272
CAEU. *See* Council of Arab Economic Unity
Caldwell, Christopher, 73, 74
Caldwell, Dan, 79
Calvocoressi, Peter, 107
Campbell, Ian, 341
Canada, 156, 296, 336–38
capital and economic growth, 147
capitalism
 as a cause of war, 409–10
 communism vs. in Cold War, 111, 112
 dependency theory and, 148
 imperialism and, 140–42
 Marxist view of, 29
capital mobility hypothesis, 281
Caporaso, James A., 148
Caprioli, Mary, 43
carbon dioxide (CO_2), 375, 378*m*
Cardoso, Fernando Henrique, 349
Caribbean Basin Initiative, 336
Caribbean Community (CARICOM), 192
Carnegie, Andrew, 29
Carpenter, Ted Galen, 118
Carr, E. H., 33, 575
carrying capacity, 349
cartel, 369
Carter, Jimmy, 13, 27, 116, 252, 399, 456, 567
Carter Doctrine, 116
cartographers, 10
Caruso, Guy F., 368, 369
Casetti, Emilio, 122
Cashman, Greg, 403, 408, 409

Caspary, William R., 405, 407, 413
Cassese, Antonio, 543
Castro, Fidel, 70, 519
Catholic Church. *See* Roman Catholic Church
caucuses, 79
Cavallo, Alfred, 369
Cavanagh, John, 211, 295
CBS network, 271
CCD. *See* UN Convention to Combat Desertification
CCL. *See* Contingency Credit Line
Cederman, Lars-Erick, 412
CEEAC. *See* Economic Community of Central African States
cellular phones use worldwide, 265
Center for World Indigenous Studies, 197
Central America, 117
Cerny, Philip G., 281
CFCs. *See* chlorofluorocarbons
CFE. *See* Conventional Forces in Europe
CFSP. *See* Common Foreign and Security Policy
Chad, 235
Chaliand, Gérald, 200
Chamberlain, Neville, 106
Chan, Steve, 418f
Chandler, Clay, 370
Chandra, Nayan, 435
chaos theory, 49
Chase-Dunn, Christopher, 96
Checkel, Jeffrey T., 50
Cheknomyrdin, Vickor, 525
chemical weapons, 466–67
Chemical Weapons Convention (CWC), 467, 510
Chen, Lincoln, 275
Cheney, Dick, 81, 82, 433, 580
Chernenko, Konstantin, 116–7
Chernobyl, 373
Chernoff, Fred, 565
children
  globalization and child labor, 291
  human rights of, 245
  NGOs supporting, 194, 408, 548
  victimization in war, 424, 449
Chile, 208, 336
Chiltelco, 208
China, 4
  coal use, 379–80
  economic projections, 122, 122f, 123f
  Falun Gong repression, 268
  friendship treaty with Russia, 520, 525
  geopolitics of, 61
  greenhouse effect contribution, 379
  human rights in, 239
  improvement in income inequality, 225–26
  improving economic status, 155
  invasion by Japan, 106
  membership in UN, 174
  membership in WTO, 15, 488
  military spending, 576
  national security strategy, 486–88
  nuclear weapons stockpiles, 461
  oil consumption, 370
  post-WWI status, 103
  sales to Wal-Mart, 206
  spheres of influence and, 140
China Investigation Report, 239
Chirac, Jacques, 99f, 523
chlorofluorocarbons (CFCs), 375
Choi, Ajin, 411
Chomsky, Noam, 20, 120
Christopherson, Jon A., 517
Churchill, Winston, 6, 95f, 110, 470, 505
Cincotta, Richard P., 409, 423
civil liberties, 4. *See also* human rights
civil society, 222, 584
Civil War, American, 412
civil wars
  casualty rates, 421
  causes of
    demographic stress, 422–23, 423m
    economic roots, 425
    failed states, 424–25
    nationalistic ethnic hatred, 423–24
    relative deprivation, 422
    secessionist revolts, 423
  characteristics and frequency, 420–22, 421t
  as diversions for leaders, 426–27
  international dimensions, 426–27
  UN's inability to control, 547, 554
Clancy, Tom, 462
Clapham, Andrew, 240, 246, 249, 543
Clarke, Richard A., 83
clash of civilizations, 144, 200, 239, 581
Claude, Inis, 143, 503, 506, 507, 549, 557, 559, 566
Clausewitz, Karl von, 400
Clegg, Liz, 214
climate change. *See* global warming
Clinton, Bill, 5, 40, 73f
  on democracies, 68
  Kosovo decision, 70
  on leadership, 88
  on nationalism, 423
  on national security, 574, 589
  on nonstate nations, 198m
Clinton Doctrine, 87
Clyburn, James E., 358
CNN (Cable News Network), 4, 272
CO_2. *See* carbon dioxide
coal, 379–80
Cobb, John B., Jr., 21
Cobb, Roger, 562
Cobden, Richard, 30
coercion, 442
coercive diplomacy
  described, 473–74
  economic sanctions, 476–81
  military intervention, 474–76
  OPEC's use of, 369
  tie to military capability, 447
coercive power, 543
cognitive dissonance, 12, 72, 84
Cohen, Benjamin J., 139, 140, 141, 280, 562
Cohen, Eliot A., 412
Cohen, Joel, 383
Cohen, Saul Bernard, 62
Cold War, 6, 8, 36, 40
  capitalism vs. communism during, 111, 112
  causes of, 111–12
  challenges after, 119, 589
  characteristic patterns during, 113–14
  coexistence to détente phase, 115–16
  confrontation phase, 114–15
  consequences of, 119
  end of, 89–90, 117–19, 471
  key events, 113f
  Non-Aligned Movement creation, 152
  renewed confrontation to reapprochement phase, 116–19
  standoffs during, 549
  UN and, 175
Coleman, Isobel, 242, 243
collective goods, 313, 387
collective security, 31, 127, 175, 502, 555, 583
Colombia, 157
colonialism, 106, 135
COMESA. *See* Common Market for Eastern and Southern Africa
Commando Solo, 466
commercial domino theory, 327–28
commercial liberalism
  comparative advantage principle, 305–7, 306t
  described, 281, 304, 305, 281
  economic and political benefits of trade liberalization, 307
  future prospects, 343–44
  hegemonic stability theory and, 316
  sustainable development and, 390
  theories of war and, 410
Common Foreign and Security Policy (CFSP), 560
Common Market for Eastern and Southern Africa (COMESA), 193
common security, 493
communism
  capitalism vs., in Cold War, 111, 112
  emergence after WWI, 102
  end of history and, 588
  imperialism and, 140, 410
  communist bloc, 519
communist theory of imperialism, 410
comparative advantage principle, 305–7, 306t
compellence, 468
complex interdependence, 42
Comprehensive Test Ban Treaty (CTBT), 462, 514m
computer use worldwide, 265–67
Comte, Auguste, 18
Concept of National Security (Russia), 485
concert, 127

Concert of Europe, 127, 507
conciliation, 533
confirmation bias, 74, 75
conflict, 400, 443
Congo, 143
Congress of Vienna, 507
Connally amendment, 547
constitutional democracy, 65
constructivism
  core perspectives, 47–48*t*
  decision making and, 77
  described, 28, 46, 49–52, 196
  gender politics and, 244
  interpretation of nonstate nations, 200–201
  mental maps and, 12
  theories of war, 400, 407
  view of Cold War, 112
  viewpoint of NGOs, 211
constructivist theory, 49
containment, 114, 488
Contingency Credit Line (CCL), 332
Contribution to the Critique of Political Economy, A (Marx), 303
Conventional Forces in Europe (CFE), 117
Convention on the Prohibition of the Use, Stockpiling, Production and Transfer of Antipersonnel Mines and Their Destruction, 513
Cooper, Richard N., 289, 540
cooperation, 547
Copeland, Dale C., 50
Coplin, William D., 77, 536
cornucopians, 361, 362, 364, 366, 367
Corporate Conduct Code for Third World Nations, 163
Cortwright, David, 480
Coser, Lewis, 400
Council of Arab Economic Unity (CAEU), 193
Council of Ministers, 190
counterfactual reasoning, 99, 471
counterterrorism, 434–36, 483
countervailing duties, 310
covert operations, 475
Cox, Richard W., 163
Craig, Gordon A., 473
Crawford, Neta C., 539
Crenshaw, Martha, 144, 428, 444
crimes against humanity, 532. *See also* just war doctrine
Croats, 239
Crook, Clive, 338
Crossette, Barbara, 243
Crump, Andy, 372*f*, 383
Crusades, 202
CTBT. *See* Comprehensive Test Ban Treaty
Cuba, 480, 519
Cuban Missile Crisis (1962)
  bureaucratic politics model example, 79–82
  bureaucratic sabotage during, 85–86
  decision-making process, 70
  nuclear deterrence and, 468

  threat to peace, 115
cultural conditioning, 407
cultural domains, 200–202
currency
  concepts and terms, 323*t*
  exchange stability, 304
  exchange system, 324*f*
  fixed exchange rates, 326–27
  floating exchange rates, 328–29
  monetary policy and, 322
  value of US dollar, 4
  See also monetary policy
current history approach, 29
Cutter, C. Bowman, 331
CWC. *See* Chemical Weapons Convention
cyberspace, 265
cycles, 9
cyclical theories of war, 417–19, 418*f*
Cyprus, 188
Czechoslovakia, 8, 102, 106, 109, 239
Czech Republic, 188, 239, 520

Daalder, Ivo H., 19, 20
Daly, Herman E., 21
Danube River Commission (1857), 559
Darwin, Charles, 404
Davis, Wade, 451
debt relief, 163
Decatur, Stephen, 414
decision making
  Cuban missile crisis example, 79–82
  intermestic, 60
  leaders' role in
    capacity to lead and, 88–90
    history-making individuals model, 86–88, 91
    human factor's importance, 87–88
    procedural vs. instrumental rationality, 87
  neorealism and, 90
  states' process
    discrepancy between theory and practice, 76–77, 77*t*
    opportunity cost considerations, 73–74
    psychological basis of, 74–75
    psychological propensities in, 75–76
    rational choice examples, 70–71
    rational choice impediments, 72–73
    realist view, 69
    steps taken by unitary actors, 69–70
  theory of, 45
Declaration on the Granting of Independence to Colonial Countries and Peoples, 143
decolonization, 137
deconstructionism, 37, 46
de facto recognition, 533
deforestation, 382–84, 385*m*, 386
De Geer, Anna, 466
Dehio, Ludwig, 505
de jure recognition, 533

Delay, Tom, 81
del Ponte, Carla, 544
democratic peace concept, 68, 411, 483, 564–65
democratic political systems
  end of history and, 588–89
  foreign policy influences on, 65–67, 66
  in the Global South, 144
  relation to human development, 230
  unlikelihood of warfare between, 411–12
  women's rights related to, 243
  world map of democracies, 67*m*
demographic transition, 356–57
demography, 349
Denmark, 188
density, population, 354*f*
Department of Homeland Security, 84
dependency theory, 45, 147, 148–49, 227
dependent development. *See* newly industrialized economies
dependentistas, 148
derivatives, 280
DeRivera, Joseph H., 89
Desai, Nitin, 153
desertification, 383, 385*m*
détente, 115
deterrence, 466, 468–70, 493, 501, 518
Deutsch, Karl, 414, 524, 562
DeVecchi, Robert, 554
developed countries, 145. *See also* Global North
developing countries, 145. *See also* Global South
development, 147
devolution, 195, 238, 563
Dhanapala, Jayantha, 153
Diamond, Jarad, 393
diasporas, 205
Diesing, Paul, 473
digital divide, 269–70
digital world economy, 280
diplomatic immunity, 532
diplomatic recognition, 533
DiRenzo, Gordon J., 89
disarmament agreements, 32, 508. *See also* arms control
Disney Corporation, 271, 274
displaced peoples, 424, 581–82
diversionary theory of war, 65, 426
divine right of kings, 532
Dixon, William J., 231
Doctors Without Borders, 195
doctrine, 154, 517, 564, 583
Dollar, David, 155
dollar convertibility, 326
domestic policy vs. foreign policy, 65, 76. *See also* foreign policy of states
domino theory, 112
doomsday clock, 467
Dougherty, James E., 51
Doyle, Michael W., 30, 40

Draay, Aart, 155
Drozdiak, William, 334
Drucker, Peter, 355
drug trade, 278
dualism, 148–49
Dubos, René, 573
Dulles, John Foster, 427, 468
Dunn, Seth, 371
Dupont, Alan, 71
Dworkin, Ronald, 221

Eagleburger, Larry, 81, 124–25
EAPC. *See* Euro-Atlantic Partnership Council
Earth Summit, 367, 383, 389
Easterbrook, Gregg, 226
Easton, David, 143
East Timor, 475, 581
Eban, Abba, 531
Eberstadt, Nicholas, 349, 363
Ebola virus, 275, 276
Eckes, Alfred E., Jr., 314
ecological fallacy, 405
Economic and Social Council, UN, 176
Economic Community of Central African States (CEEAC), 193
Economic Community of West African States (ECOWAS), 193
economic hierarchy, 8
economic nationalists, 308
economics
 classical liberal theory, 140
 commercial liberalism. *See* commercial liberalism
 contribution to WWII, 107
 currency exchange stability, 186
 as a determinate of foreign policy, 63–64
 development theories, 147–49
 environmental security, 366
 global economies projections, 122f
 GNP and foreign policy, 64
 human welfare and, 21–22
 impact of military vs. economic spending, 448–49
 laissez-faire, 140
 mercantilism *(see* mercantilism*)*
 MNCs and *(see* multinational corporations*)*
 politics and *(see* economic sanctions; international political economy*)*
 regulation by governments *(see* mercantilism*)*
 states' foreign policies and, 8
 states' systems as a cause of war, 409–11
 worldwide impact of 9/11 attacks, 312
economic sanctions
 deficiencies, 480–81
 effectiveness of, 480
 policy goals, 479
 popularity of, 476–77
 rationale for, 477–78
 vulnerability of countries, 478m

ecopolitics
 atmosphere and *(see* global warming*)*
 biodiversity
  biogenetical engineering, 386–87
  biotechnology growth, 386
  forests and plants and, 385–86
  implications of threats to, 386
 defined, 365
 of energy *(see* oil supply and consumption*)*
 environmental protection's importance, 365–66
 of forests, 382–85, 385m
 of oil *(see* oil supply and consumption*)*
 politics of scarcity, 366
 preservation and, 387, 388m, 389–90, 390f
 sustainability goal, 392–94
 sustainability vs. free trade, 390–93
 sustainable development and, 366–67
 water demand worldwide, 383
 See also population policy
ECOWAS. *See* Economic Community of West African States
ECSC. *See* European Coal and Steel Community
Ecuador, 157
Edwards, Stephen R., 386
EEC. *See* European Economic Community
Egypt, 62
Eichengreen, Barry, 328
Eide, Espen Barth, 585
Einstein, Albert, 460, 529, 556, 590, 592
Eisenhower, Dwight, 122, 449, 451, 458, 548, 576
Eizenstat, Stuart, 280
Eland, Ivan, 20, 82
el-Bashir, Omar, 582
Elder, Charles, 562
electoral process' influence on a political system, 65
electromagnetic pulse (EMP) bomb, 466
Elkins, Zachary, 296, 304
Elliott, Kimberly Ann, 477, 480
Elliott, Michael A., 231, 266, 491
Elman, Colin, 36, 503
Elrod, Richard, 507
El Salvadoran Battalion, 461
Elshtain, Jean Bethke, 539
El-Tahri, Jihan, 476
Emerson, Ralph Waldo, 86
Emmons, Julian, 66
enclosure movement, 386
end of history, 68, 119, 588–89
enduring rivalries, 13, 98
energy and ecopolitics. *See* oil supply and consumption
Engelhardt, Henriette, 356
England. *See* Great Britain
Engleman, Robert, 409, 423

Enlightenment, 30f
Enloe, Cynthia H., 43, 243, 407
Enriquez, Juan, 563, 581
entente, 127
Entente Cordiale, 99
environmental security, 366
environment and politics. *See* ecopolitics
epistemic communities, 366, 558
epistemology, 49
Eriksson, Mikael, 401, 419, 420, 421, 426
Eritrea, 563
Essay on the Principle of Population (Malthus), 362
Essence of Decision (Allison), 79
Estonia, 102, 109, 188, 520
ethics
 assessment of globalization, 289
 defined, 295, 537
 human rights and *(see* human rights*)*
 place in politics, 221
 of population growth, 350
 of preemptive war, 472
 See also just war doctrine
Ethiopia, 563
ethnic cleansing, 233–34, 581
ethnic groups, 196, 197
ethnicity, 196
ethnic nationalism, 196, 197
ethnic warfare, 424
ethnocentrism, 239, 581
ethnonationalism, 240
ethnopolitical groups, 196
Euratom. *See* European Atomic Energy Community
euro, 332
Euro-Atlantic Partnership Council (EAPC), 520, 521m
Euroland. *See* European Union
Europe, 355
European Atomic Energy Community (Euratom), 188
European Coal and Steel Community (ECSC), 188
European Commission, 190
European Court of Human Rights, 548
European Court of Justice, 190
European Economic Community (EEC), 188
European Parliament, 190
European Rapid Reaction Force (EU), 491, 557, 562
European Union, 8, 60
 challenges due to memberships, 188–89
 common currency, 332
 criticisms of protectionism, 342
 decision-making procedures, 191
 dislike of U.S. foreign policy, 523
 efforts to redistribute power, 520
 governmental structure, 189f
 membership, 188
 military spending, 576
 national security strategy, 491–92, 557, 562

European Union (*continued*)
  neoliberal viewpoint, 187–88
  organization and management, 189–90, 191*f*
  political integration, 560–62, 561*m*
  pooled sovereignty process, 191
Evans, Peter B., 148
exchange rates, 322, 323*t*
  fixed, 323*t*, 326–27
  floating, 323*t*, 328–29
export-led industrialization, 154–55
export quotas, 309
extended deterrence, 115, 518
externalities, 74, 160, 279, 391
extraterritoriality, 532
extreme militant religious movements, 203. *See also* religious movements

failed states, 153, 234, 279, 420, 475
failing states, 424–25, 581, 582
Falk, Richard A., 97, 211, 214
Fallows, James, 458
Falun Gong, 268
family planning, 360. *See also* population policy
FAO. *See* Food and Agriculture Organization
fascism, 29, 104, 106, 107, 108*f*, 588
fast-track negotiating authority, 334
FDI. *See* foreign direct investment
federalism, 556–58
Federal Republic of Germany, 60
Federal Reserve Board, U.S., 280
Feinstein, Lee, 222, 541
feminist theory, 42, 43, 223, 407
Ferdinand, Archduke, 98
Ferencz, Benjamin, 557
Ferguson, Niall, 19, 120, 438, 444, 499
fertility rate, 353
Festinger, Leon, 12
Fiat, 287
Fieldhouse, D. K., 140
Fields, A., 222
Filson, Darren, 415
financial globalization
  capital mobility, 281, 282*m*
  evidence of, 280–81
  key institutions, 280
  result of liberalization, 281
  undermining of state power, 281
Finland
  consequences of WWII, 109
  EU membership, 188
  geopolitics of, 61
  World War I and, 102, 107–8
Finnegan, William, 383
Finnemore, Martha, 211, 541
firebreak, 466
First World, 135. *See also* Global North
Fischer, Joschka, 523
Five Power Treaty, 102
fixed exchange rate, 323*t*, 326–27
Flanagan, Stephen J., 269
Flavin, Christopher, 370, 371

Flint, Colin, 408
floating exchange rates, 323*t*, 328–29
Food and Agriculture Organization (FAO), 547
food security, 364
Ford, Gerald, 80*f*
Foreign Affairs, 114
foreign aid, 157
  debt relief need, 163
  in Global South
    criticisms of programs' effectiveness, 159
    FDI inflows, 162*f*
    FDI need, 160–62
    goals of, 158
    practice of tying aid, 159
    ranking of world donors, 158*f*
    types, 157–58
foreign direct investment (FDI)
  financial globalization and (*see* financial globalization)
  impact on capital markets, 291, 292
  MNCs and, 160–62, 162*f*, 206
  See also International Monetary Fund
foreign investment, 148
foreign policy
  bureaucratic politics and (*see* bureaucratic politics)
  constraints on, 91
  defined, 58
  domestic policy conflicts, 65, 76
  global and domestic determinants
    conflicts between, 76
    conversions of governments to democracies, 67–68
    economic conditions, 63–64
    geopolitics, 60–62, 61*f*
    levels of analysis, 59–60, 59*f*
    military capabilities, 62–63
    type of government and, 65–67
  Global South's response to great powers
    arms acquisitions, 154
    insecurity concerns, 153–54
    nonalignment movement, 152–53
  leaders' role
    capacity to lead and, 88–90
    history-making individuals model, 86–88, 91
    human factor's importance, 87–88
    procedural vs. instrumental rationality, 87
  state economies and, 29
  See also national security
forest ecopolitics, 382–86, 385*m*
Fossil Free Energy Scenario, 372*f*
fossil fuel, 370. *See also* oil supply and consumption
Four Power Treaty, 102–3
Fourteen Points, 32, 102
Fourth Way, 164
Fourth World, 197, 237, 238–39, 581
Framework Convention on Climate Change, 375

France
  causes of WWII and, 106
  entry into WWI, 100
  EU membership, 188
  imperialistic occupations, 143
  nuclear weapons stockpiles, 461
Franco, Francisco, 106
Frank, Andre Gunder, 148
Frankel, Max, 468
Franklin, Benjamin, 13, 306
Frechette, Louise, 551
freedom fighters vs. terrorism, 428
Freeman, David H., 458
free riders, 313
Free Trade Area of the Americas (FTAA), 336
French, Howard W., 490
Freud, Sigmund, 403
Fried, John H. E., 531
Friedheim, Robert L., 535
Friedman, Thomas, 261, 268, 315, 411, 584, 586
frontier forests, 382
Frost, Ellen L., 269
Frost, Robert, 51
Frum, David, 120
Fukuyama, Francis, 40, 68, 118, 404, 584, 586, 588
Fuller, Graham E., 144
functionalism, 558–60

Gaddis, John Lewis, 111, 175, 176, 471, 586
Galtung, Johan, 535
Gandhi, Indira, 587
Gandhi, Mohandas, 393
Gardner, Richard N., 63
Gareau, Frederick H., 251, 539
Garrett, Geoffrey, 308
GATT. *See* General Agreement on Tariffs and Trade
Gaulle, Charles de, 462
G-8, 132*f*, 163, 329, 564
Gelb, Leslie H., 86
Gender Empowerment Measure (GEM), 240
gender inequalities, 242
gender politics
  challenges in protecting women's rights, 243
  conferences addressing women's issues, 240, 241*t*
  status of women worldwide, 241–43
  theories of world politics and, 43
General Agreement on Tariffs and Trade (GATT), 44, 181, 284, 317
General Assembly, UN, 176–77, 547
genetic engineering, 361, 363
Geneva Convention (1949), 244, 401
Geneva Protocol, 466–67
genocide
  indigenous peoples and, 237–38, 239
  international law and, 544
  nationalism and, 416
  Rwanda and, 233, 421, 544
  Sudan and, 235, 405, 421–22, 582

geo-economics, 21
geography distortions inherent in maps, 10, 11*f*
geopolitics, 29
  foreign policy of states and, 60–62, 61*m*
  geo-economics vs., 20–21
  geography as a cause of, 408–9
George, Alexander L., 44, 78, 473, 475, 592
Georgia, 4
German, F. Clifford, 443
German Bundesbank, 280
German Democratic Republic, 60
Germany
  consequences of WWII, 109 (*see also* World War II)
  EU membership, 188
  geopolitics of, 60
  hegemonic ambitions, 104
  Hitler's vision, 108–9
  national security strategy, 490–91
  Nazism and, 29
  population momentum, 355
  pre-WWII militarism, 106
  pre-WWI rise in global power, 100 (*see also* World War I)
Gilbert, Alan, 565
Gilboa, Eytan, 264, 272
Gill, Stephen, 46
Gilligan, Michael, 553
Gilpin, Robert, 28, 156, 305, 307, 308, 309, 311, 314
Glaberson, William, 547
Gleditsch, Kristian Skrede, 400, 412, 420
global agenda, 16
Global Dreams, 210
globalization, 6, 15
  child labor and, 291
  civilization clash and, 144
  controversial nature of, 262–63
  costs and benefits to peoples, 18–19, 288–89, 295–96, 583–85
  described, 60, 261–62, 515
  distribution of gains, 308
  financial (*see* financial globalization)
  forecasts for, 263
  global village image, 264–65, 297
  health and disease and
    ease of cross-country transmission, 276
    impact on public health, 275–76
    introduction of exotic species, 277–78
    narcotics trade, 278
    number of AIDS victims worldwide, 276
  human development controversy and, 231–32
  IMF and, 186
  information age
    cellular phones use, 265
    computers and the Internet, 265–67
    criticisms of electronic network, 268–69

  digital divide, 269–70
  pace of information technology, 268
  web bars, 271
  levels of, 294*f*
  media and
    agenda setting ability, 272
    concerns over concentration and power, 272–74
    diffusion of Western culture, 272
    domination by a few companies, 271–72
    liberalization's impact, 274–75
    migration crisis, 278–79
  MNCs and (*see* multinational corporations)
  neoliberalism and, 42
  probability of economic rivalries, 124–25
  states' powers and control impacted by, 296–97
  survival of the state and, 266–67
  theories of war and, 410
  threat to indigenous peoples, 197–98
  of trade (*see* trade globalization)
  WTO and (*see* World Trade Organization (WTO))
global level of analysis
  described, 15, 59*f*
  Global South and, 134
  IGOs and (*see* intergovernmental organizations)
  neorealism and, 38–39, 99
  realism and, 69
  warfare causes analysis
    cyclical theories, 417–19, 418*f*
    power transitions, 415–17
    question of violence breeding violence, 415
    reliance on self-help, 413, 415
Global North, 15, 21
  demographic divide between North and South, 353, 354*f*
  dimensions of, 135
  Internet use in, 266
  military spending, 452
  population momentum, 355
  South vs., in country characteristics, 136*m*, 144–45, 146*t*
global political system, 6
Global South, 15, 17, 21
  arms trade in, 454–55
  attempts at NIEO, 155–56
  basis of position with North, 134–35
  benefits from cross-border remittances, 279
  characteristics of emerging NIEs, 150–51
  civilization clash, 144
  colonial origins, 137–38
  demographic divide with North, 353, 354*f*
  digital divide and technology and, 269–71
  dimensions of, 135, 137
  economic interest in the tropics, 386

  emergence as an international actor, 137
  emerging NIEs examples, 150
  European imperialism, first wave, 138–40
  European imperialism, second wave, 140–42
  foreign aid
    criticisms of programs' effectiveness, 159
    goals of, 158
    practice of tying aid, 159
    ranking of world donors, 158*f*
    types, 157–58
  foreign direct investment inflows, 162*f*
  foreign direct investment need, 160–62
  foreign policy response to great powers, 152–54
  forest conservation opposition, 383
  geographic distribution, 133*m*
  globalization's impact on, 272, 289–90
  IGOs, 192–93
  Internet use in, 266
  lack of benefits from globalization of finance, 281, 282*m*
  legal migrants from, 235
  mandate system, League of Nations, 143
  market access difficulties, 157
  media coverage, dissatisfaction with, 273
  military spending, 452
  MNCs impact on, 206–7, 292–93
  new infusion of foreign investments impact, 162–63
  North vs., in country characteristics, 136*m*, 144–45, 146*t*
  pace of trade integration, 285–86, 286*f*
  population momentum, 355
  poverty and, 132–33, 226
  regional trade regimes, 156–57
  self-determination concept and, 142
  shift towards export-led industrialization, 154–55
  status at UN, 177–78
  underdevelopment explanations, 147–49
global structure, 515
global systems, 8
global village, 264–65, 297
global warming
  effects of continued temperature rise, 377
  greenhouse effect, 375
  ozone protection, 380–81
  rise in temperatures, 374–76, 375*f*, 376*f*
  sources of greenhouse gases, 378–80
Global Youth Connect, 194
GNI. *See* gross national income
GNP. *See* gross national product
Godson, Roy, 494

Goering, Hermann, 426
gold standard, 326
Goldstein, Joshua, 311, 417
good offices, 533
Gorbachev, Mikhail, 22, 89, 117, 118, 413, 583, 589
Gottlieb, Gidon, 532
Graham, Billy, 273
Great Britain
    Bretton Woods conference role, 304
    causes of WWII, 106
    decolonizations, 137, 139
    EU membership, 188
    former balancer role, 505
    geopolitics of, 60
    hegemon role, 417
    imperialistic occupations, 140
    nuclear weapons stockpiles, 461
    pre-WWI domination of world politics, 100
    support of U.S., 4
Great Patriotic War, 13
great-power politics
    economic projections, 122*f*
    emerging power centers, 121*m*
    first world war (*see* World War I)
    Global South's response to, 152–54
    hegemony quest, 96–98, 97*t*
    multipolarity challenges, 123–25
    options for dealing with security issues, 126–27
    rivalry between U.S. and Soviets (*see* Cold War)
    second world war (*see* World War II)
    unipolarity of U.S., 120–21, 122, 123*f*
great powers, 17
Great War, The. *See* World War I
Greece, 65, 188
green, 378–80
Greenfield, Meg, 82
greenhouse effect, 375, 378–80
Green Party, 373
Greenpeace, 363, 577
Greenstein, Fred I., 91
Grey, Edward, 492
Grieco, Joseph M., 40, 310
Grimmett, Richard F., 154, 454, 455, 456, 459
Grondona, Mariano, 159
gross national income (GNI), 145, 446. *See also* economics
gross national product (GNP), 21–22, 64. *See also* economics
Grotius, Hugo, 538
Group of Eight (G-8), 132*f*, 163, 329, 564
Group of Seven (G-7), 182, 329
Group of 77, 155, 177–78
groupthink, 85, 406
G-7, 182, 329
G-77, 155, 177–78
Gugliotta, Guy, 386
Gulf Cooperation Council, 555
Gulick, Edward V., 127, 505
gunboat diplomacy, 474

Gurr, Ted Robert, 196, 238, 240, 404, 422, 425, 563

Haass, Richard N., 480
Haffa, Robert P., Jr., 471
Hagel, Chuck, 71
Haggard, Stephan, 44
Hague, The, 251, 544
Hague peace conferences, 29
Haiti, 4
Hall, Anthony J., 226
Hall, John A., 37, 194, 215
Hall, Thomas D., 196, 197, 202
Halliburton, 208
halons, 381
Halperin, Morton H., 86, 565
Hamas, 427
Hammarskjold, Dag, 550
Hanson, Victor Davis, 406
Haq, Mahbub ul, 227
Hardin, Garrett, 350
hard power, 449
Harff, Barbara, 239
Harknett, Richard J., 469
Harries, Owen, 38–39
Harvey, David, 20, 120
Hausmann, Ricardo, 133
Havana Charter, 317
Havel, Václav, 214, 301
Haynes, Jeff, 203, 204, 427
HCFCs. *See* hydrochlorofluorocarbons
HDI. *See* Human Development Index
health and disease and globalization
    ease of cross-country transmission, 276, 357–60
    impact on public health, 275–76
    introduction of exotic species, 277–78
    narcotics trade, 278
    number of AIDS victims worldwide, 276, 359*m*
heavily indebted poor countries (HIPCs), 163
Hedges, Chris, 400
hegemon, 19, 96, 311, 417, 507, 577
hegemonic stability theory
    balance-of-power and, 518
    collective good and, 313
    commercial liberalism and, 316
    consequences of waning leadership, 316
    described, 46, 98, 311, 507
    hegemons' responsibilities, 311, 313
    need for hegemon-led order, 313–14
    U.S. economic vulnerability, 314–16
hegemony, 311
hegemony quest in great-power politics
    evolution of rivalries, 97*t*
    hegemonic stability theory, 98
    long-cycle theory, 96–98
Hegre, Havard, 402, 420
Hehir, J. Bryan, 575
Held, David, 18, 246, 289
Helton, Arthur C., 554
Hendrickson, David C., 564

Henry, Patrick, 590
Herbert, Bob, 377
Heredia, Blanca, 231, 232
Hermann, Charles F., 68, 79
Hermann, Margaret G., 46, 88, 89
Herrmann, Richard K., 118
Hertsgaard, Mark, 20, 120
Herz, John H., 31
hierarchies of states, 8
high politics, 17, 44, 212, 303, 366, 589
Hilsman, Roger, 77
Hindle, Tim, 207, 292
Hinduism, 203
HIPCs. *See* heavily indebted poor countries
Hiroshima, Japan, 109, 460
Hirsh, Michael, 20
history-making individuals model, 86–88, 91
Hitler, Adolf, 29, 60, 87, 106, 108, 108*f*, 416
HIV. *See* AIDS; human immunodeficiency virus
Hoagland, Jim, 286, 476
Hobbes, Thomas, 33, 34*f*, 226, 244
Hobson, J. A., 142
Hoebel, E. Adamson, 535
Hoffman, Eva, 278
Hoffmann, Stanley, 7–8, 482, 535, 586
Holjberg, Anne-Else, 556
Holsti, Kalevi J., 102, 107, 109, 423, 549, 555
Holsti, Ole R., 36, 44
Homer-Dixon, Thomas, 205, 437
Hong Kong, 150, 563
Hopf, Ted, 50
Hopkins, Terence K., 417
horizontal nuclear proliferation, 462
Hot Line Agreement (1963), 508
House, Karen Elliot, 524
Howard, John, 590
Howard, Michael E., 30
Howell, Llewellyn D., 266, 435, 584
Hufbauer, Gary Clyde, 477, 480
Hughes, Emmet John, 88
human agents
    dependency theory and, 227
    gender politics, 240–43, 241*t*
    globalization controversy and, 231–32
    human development measurement, 227–29, 228*t*
    human development preconditions, 229–31, 230*m*
    human rights (*see* human rights)
    indigenous peoples (*see* indigenous peoples)
    past ignoring of, 221
    poverty and (*see* poverty)
    quality of life measurement, 229*f*
    recognition of importance to world politics, 221–22
    refugee crisis (*see* refugee crisis)
human development, 360

Nasser, Gamal Abdel, 62
nation, 32, 58
national character, 405
national interest, 34
nationalism, 101, 196, 412–13, 414, 423, 557, 583
National Oceanic Administration, U.S., 381
National Security Council, U.S., 85
national security
   China's strategy, 486–88
   concerns over nuclear weapons, 373
   Cuban missile crisis and, 70
   defined, 237, 442, 451, 576
   environmental security, 366
   European Union's strategy, 491–92
   Germany's strategy, 490–91
   Japan's strategy, 488–90
   military capabilities and, 62–63
   military power and, 448
   military strategies for (*see* alliances; arms control)
   nonmilitary dimensions of, 494
   reconciling with human rights, 237
   Russia's strategy, 485–86
   September 11 attacks on U.S. (*see* September 11, 2001)
   U.S.'s strategy, 481–85
National Security Strategy of the United States of America (NSS), 471, 482–83, 505, 574, 578
National Snow and Ice Data Center, 379
nation-state, 58, 214–16
Native Americans, 58
NATO. *See* North Atlantic Treaty Organization
nature versus nurture, 404
Nauru, 139*f*
Naval Disarmament Treaties, 32
Nazism, 29, 104, 416
Neack, Laura, 553, 556
neem tree, 386
negotiation, 533
Nelson, Stephan D., 404
neocolonialism, 138
neofunctionalism, 560–63
neoimperialism, 138
neoliberal institutionalism, 491
   democratic peace concept, 564–65
   international law and (*see* international law)
   path from security to stability, 566–67
   political integration
      functionalism, 558–60
      neofunctionalism, 560–63
      political disintegration, 562–63
      preconditions for regional integration, 562–63
      world federalism, 556–58
   regional security organizations, 554–56
   United Nations and (*see* United Nations)
neoliberalism
   basis of, 40–42, 586

   concept of security in, 366
   core perspectives, 47–48*t*, 68
   emerging NIEs and, 150
   EU as viewpoint example, 187–88
   free markets and, 335*m*
   international regimes, 44–45
   neorealism vs., 41
   theories of war, 411–12
   transnational interdependence and, 42–44
   view of European Union, 187–88
   view of globalization, 263
neo-Malthusians, 361, 362, 364, 367
neomercantilism, 297, 308. *See also* mercantilism
neorealism, 38
   core perspectives, 47–48*t*
   on inevitability of war, 406
   neoliberalism vs., 41
   structuralism and, 99–100
neotraditional realism, 38, 586
Netherlands, The, 188, 417
Neuman, Johanna, 272
neutrality, 532
Newhouse, John, 20, 82, 120
New International Economic Order (NIEO), 155, 156
newly industrialized countries (NICs), 149
newly industrialized economies (NIEs), 149, 150, 287
News Corporation, 274
New World Information and Communication Order (NWICO), 273
NGOs. *See* nongovernmental organizations
Nicaragua, 529–30
Nicholas I, Pope, 537
NICs. *See* newly industrialized countries
Niebuhr, Reinhold, 33
NIEO. *See* New International Economic Order
NIEs. *See* newly industrialized economies
9/11 Commission (2004), 83. *See also* September 11, 2001
Nine Power Treaty, 103
Nixon, Richard, 80*f*, 90, 115, 116*f*, 328
Nixon Doctrine, 87
no first use, 486
Nolte, Georg, 540
Non-Aligned Movement (NAM), 152–53
nonalignment, 504
noncombatant immunity, 244, 250, 543
nondiscrimination rules, 339
nongovernmental organizations (NGOs), 17, 557
   balance process between opposing actors, 213
   collaboration with UN, 177
   constructivist viewpoint, 211
   description and scope, 172–73
   influence on international policy, 211–13

   international law and, 531
   multinational corporations (*see* multinational corporations)
   neoliberalism and, 42
   nonstate nations (*see* nonstate nations)
   possible impact on state sovereignty, 195–96
   purpose and scope, 194–95
   religious movements (*see* religious movements)
   states vs., 213–14
   WTO (*see* World Trade Organization)
nonintervention norm, 182, 475, 532, 542*f*, 582
nonlethal weapons, 465
nonproliferation, 510
nonproliferation regime, 462
nonstate actors
   challenge to nation-state system, 214–16
   defined, 17, 42, 151, 161
   IGOs (*see* intergovernmental organizations)
   NGOs (*see* nongovernmental organizations)
   number of states, IGOs, and NGOs, 170*f*
nonstate nations, 58
   ethnopolitical groups, 196–97
   indigenous peoples (*see* indigenous peoples)
   security concerns, 153
nontariff barriers (NTBs), 310
Nordic Council, 555
normal trade relations (NTR). *See* most-favored-nation (MFN) principle
North, Oliver, 85
North American Free Trade Agreement (NAFTA), 156, 296, 336–38
North Atlantic Treaty Organization (NATO)
   decision-making process and, 70–71
   described, 192
   evolution of, 520, 521*m*, 522–23
   transformations in, 555, 557
   type of alliance, 171, 517
   U.S. relationship with Russia and, 485
North Korea, 373
Nossel, Suzanne, 585
NPT. *See* Nuclear Nonproliferation Treaty
NSS. *See* National Security Strategy of the United States of America
Nth country problem, 461
NTR. *See* normal trade relations
nuclear age
   Cold War threat, 117
   military strategies
      compellence, 468
      deterrence, 466, 468–70, 493, 501, 518
   devastation possible from a nuclear war, 467

nuclear age—military strategies (*continued*)
  economic sanctions (*see* economic sanctions)
  frequency of international crises, 474*f*
  military intervention, 474–76
  preemption, 470–73
nuclear weapons, 373
  countries with, 463*m*
  deterrence and, 466, 468–70, 493, 501, 518
  incentives to acquire or develop, 462
  India/Pakistan dilemma, 464–65
  Japan's interest in, 490
  numbers worldwide, 460–61
  states' desire for, 462, 464
  steps towards nuclear disarmament, 464
  test ban treaties, 514*m*
  treaties concerning, 508, 509*f*, 510
  protests against weapons, 90
  realism and, 35
  weapons acquisition by Global South, 154
nuclear deterrence, 468
nuclear energy, 373
Nuclear Nonproliferation Treaty (NPT), 461, 510
nuclear utilization theory (NUT), 470
nuclear winter, 467
NWICO. *See* New World Information and Communication Order
Nye, Joseph S., Jr., 42, 44, 95, 119, 120, 122, 127, 181, 211, 297, 314, 443, 445, 448, 449, 484, 494, 505, 578, 585

OAS. *See* Organization of American States
Oatley, Thomas, 206, 208, 210, 290
OAU. *See* Organization of African Unity
Obasanjo, Olusegun, 132*f*
O'Brien, Conor, 429
O'Brien, Richard, 280
ODA. *See* official development assistance
OECD. *See* Organization for Economic Cooperation and Development
Office of Counter-Terrorism, U.S., 430
official development assistance (ODA), 157
Ogata, Sadaka, 425
Ohmae, Kenichi, 295
OIC. *See* Organization of the Islamic Conference
oil-exporting countries, 150
oil supply and consumption
  concentration of supplies, 370
  emergence of new energy sources, 371–73, 372*f*
  energy consumption worldwide, 368
  energy security concerns, 369–70

nuclear energy use, 373
  oil supply concerns, 369
  politics of scarcity, 374
Oklahoma City, U.S., 427
Olson, William J., 205
Olympics, Moscow, 116
OMA. *See* orderly market arrangement
Omnibus Trade Act, 333–34
Oneal, John R., 410
One World: The Ethics of Globalization (Singer), 289
On the Law of War and Peace (Grotius), 538
Onuf, Nicholas, 50, 535
On War (Clausewitz), 400
OPEC. *See* Organization of Petroleum Exporting Countries
Opello, Walter C., Jr., 212, 296, 584
Oppenheimer, Robert, 469
opportunity costs, 73, 448
orderly market arrangement (OMA), 309
ordinary 301, 334
organizational process, 79
Organization for Economic Cooperation and Development (OECD), 163, 564
Organization for Security and Cooperation in Europe (OSCE), 188, 555
Organization of African Unity (OAU), 555
Organization of American States (OAS), 171, 555, 564
Organization of Petroleum Exporting Countries (OPEC), 150, 369–70, 370
Organization of the Islamic Conference (OIC), 193
Organski, A. F. K., 416
orthographic projection, 11
OSCE. *See* Organization for Security and Cooperation in Europe
Ostler, Nicholas, 199
Ostry, Sylvia, 262
Our Common Future, 367
outsourcing, 150
overconfidence, 76
ozone layer, 380–81

pacifism, 404
pacta sunt servanda, 533
Pakistan
  decolonization of, 137, 143
  nuclear weapons possession, 464–65, 510
  nuclear weapons stockpiles, 461
Palestine, 13, 73*f*, 153, 432*m*
Palmerston, Lord, 501
Panagariya, Arvind, 308, 390
paradigm, 28, 223, 302, 366
Paraguay, 157, 336
Parry, Clive, 531
Partnership for Peace (PfP), 520
Paskeviciute, Aida, 43
patriotism, 414
Pattern, Christopher, 523

Patton, George, 416
Paul, T. V., 194, 215
Pax Americana, 524
Pax Britannica, 524
Pax Romana, 188, 524
peace building, 550
peace dividend, 448, 491
peace enforcement, 550
peaceful coexistence, 115
peacekeeping, 549
Peacekeeping Operations Bill (Japan), 489
peacemaking, 550
Peace of Paris, 104
Peace of Westphalia (1648), 58, 134, 169, 182, 213, 506, 532
peace operations, 550
Peffley, Mark, 12
Peirce, Neal R., 18, 266
Pells, Richard, 270
Peloponnesian Wars, 33
Pentagon, Washington, DC, 3
perceptual psychology, 10
Perez de Cuellar, Javier, 550
periphery, 149
Perle, Richard, 81, 118, 120
Permanent Court of International Justice, 31–32
permanent world criminal court, 544
Perpetual Peace (Kant), 68, 411
Persian Chessboard, Secret of the, 351–52
Persian Gulf War (1991)
  cause of, 368
  foreign policy of states and, 65
  military capabilities and, 63
  refugee crisis from, 233
  weapons trade in Middle East and, 459
Persson, Goran, 349
Peru, 157
Peterson, Erik, 343
Peter's projection, 11*f*
Petras, James, 302
petroleum. *See* oil supply and consumption
Pfaff, William, 250, 312, 543
Pfaltzgraff, Robert L., 51
Pfetsch, Frank L., 280
PfP. *See* Partnership for Peace
pharmaceutical companies, 386
Phillippines, 157
Pinochet, Augusto, 252, 545
Pipes, Richard, 117, 470
piracy, 430
Plano, Jack C., 143
Pletsch, Carl, 89
plutonium, 373
Poland
  consequences of WWII, 109
  EU membership, 188
  NATO membership, 520
  post-WWI, 102
  post-WWII, 106
polarity, 516, 517

polarization, 124, 516, 517
policy agendas, 74
policy networks, 79
political disintegration, 562–63
political economy, 107
political efficacy, 89
political freedom, 229
political hierarchy, 8
political integration
   functionalism, 558–60
   neofunctionalism, 560–63
   political disintegration, 563–64
   preconditions for regional integration, 562–63
   world federalism, 556–58
political systems
   autocratic, 65–67, 230
   democratic (*see* democratic political systems)
   types of governments, 65
politics, 16, 30, 79, 295, 307, 350, 400, 443, 578. *See also* ecopolitics; geopolitics; great-power politics; high politics; low politics; world politics
politics of scarcity, 366, 374
pollution
   from coal, 379–80
   See also ecopolitics; greenhouse effect
pooled sovereignty, 191
Pope, the, 51*f*, 169, 202, 204, 537, 565
population growth
   ethics of, 350
   global impact of, 21
   Global North vs. Global South, 145
   rate of, 350–52
population implosion, 357
population policy
   controversy over genetically engineered crops, 364
   controversy over sustainability, 361–64
   demographic divide between North and South, 353, 354*f*
   demographic transition, 356–57
   ethics of population growth, 350
   global impact of diseases, 357–60, 359*m*
   growth projections, 351*f*
   growth rates, 350–52
   international response to stabilization, 360–61
   life expectancy at birth, 357
   population density, 354*f*
   population momentum, 353, 355–56
   tragedy of the commons, 350
   world population, 349
   See also ecopolitics
Porto, Luigi Da, 419
Portugal, 143, 188, 417
positivist legal theory, 535
postbehavioral movement, 37
post-modern terrorism, 437
Pound, Edward T., 476
poverty
   as a cause of war, 407–8

consumption patterns, 226
depth of poverty worldwide, 226
digital divide and technology and, 269–71
division between rich and poor, 223–26, 225*m*
in the Global South, 132–33, 145
income inequalities in the world, 224–26
relation to conflict, 153
trade globalization and, 288–90
trends in, 225*m*
Powell, Colin, 81, 159, 392, 541
power
   balance of, 70, 100
   coercive diplomacy (*see* coercive diplomacy)
   defined, 443
   distinguishing from capabilities, 445–47
   elements of state power, 443–44, 444*f*
   geopolitics and, 62
   human vs. national security and, 450
   impact of military vs. economic spending, 448–49
   indications of emerging multipolarity, 523–24
   military capabilities and
     motives for arms trade, 457–59
     strategic consequences of arms sales, 459–60
     trends in military spending, 452, 453*f*
     trends in weapons trade, 454–57, 454*f*
   military spending per GDP, 450–51
   national security strategies
     China, 486–88
     European Union, 491–92
     Germany, 490–91
     Japan, 488–90
     Russia, 485–86
     U.S., 481–85
   neorealism and, 38
   nonmilitary dimensions of national security, 494
   in the nuclear age (*see* military strategy in the nuclear age)
   polarity's relationship to peace, 524
   realism and, 33
   redistribution of global, 520
   relative importance of factors, 444–45, 446–47*m*
   security dilemma of states, 492–93
   shifting geopolitical landscape, 520, 521*m*, 522–23
   soft vs. hard, 449
   weapons technology trends
     biological and chemical weapons, 466–67
     improvements to systems, 465–66
     nuclear weapons (*see* nuclear weapons)
Power, Jonathan, 180
Power and Interdependence (Keohane and Nye), 44

power balance, 123
power cycle of war, 417–19, 418*f*
power potential, 443
Powers, Thomas, 465
power transitions, 111, 124, 485, 518
power transition theory, 415–17
PPP. *See* purchasing power parity
preemption, 470–73
preemptive military action
   arguments against Iraq invasion, 81–82
   Bush Doctrine and, 63, 153, 540
preemptive war, 471, 473, 505, 579. *See also* just war doctrine
Prestowitz, Clyde, 20, 120, 314, 539
preventive diplomacy, 550
Price, Richard, 211
Principles of Political Economy (Mill), 303
Prins, Brandon C., 65, 426
Pritchard, John, 107
private international law, 531. *See also* international law
procedural rationality, 87
proliferation, 461
prospect theory, 74–75, 506
protectionism, 107, 309–10
Prskawetz, Alexia, 356
public good, 584
public international law, 531. *See also* international law
public opinion's influence on a political system, 65, 66
Puchala, Donald, 51
purchasing power parity (PPP), 231, 324*f*
Putin, Vladimir, 4, 485, 519, 523
Putin-Bush Strategic Offensive Reductions Treaty, 509*f*
Putnam, Robert, 76

Qaddafi, Muammar, 62, 87, 480
Qatar, 150, 477
Quester, George, 467, 494
Quinn, Jane Bryant, 369

Rabin, Yitzhak, 73*f*, 427
Rageau, Jean-Pierre, 200
rain forests, 382, 384–86
Rapkin, David, 517
rapprochement, 117
rational choice theory
   decision-making process examples, 70–71
   defined, 69, 406, 501
   impediments to, 72–73
   interpretation of cause of WWI, 100–101
   preemptive military action and, 471
   purpose of WTO and, 182
Ravallion, Martin, 224, 225*m*, 226
Ray, James Lee, 411
Raymond, Gregory A., 82, 120, 124, 134, 214, 314, 315, 406, 473, 483, 540
Reagan, Ronald, 87, 116, 118, 470
Reagan administration, 85

Reagan Doctrine, 87, 117
realism
  assumptions and propositions, 34–35
  balance-of-power theory and, 503
  concept of security in, 366, 500, 500*t*
  core perspectives, 47–48*t*
  ethics of war, 472
  extreme of machtpolitik, 104
  financial liberalization and, 281
  gender politics and, 243
  geopolitics school, 62
  global vs. national interests, 575
  human rights and, 244, 248–49
  intellectual roots, 33
  limitations of, 35–36, 38
  long-cycle theory, 311
  mercantilism and, 308–9, 310
  national security strategies (*see* national security of states)
  neoclassical extension of, 39–40
  neorealist extension of, 38–39
  nuclear age and, 35
  post-WWI, 102
  relevance today, 585–87
  state action and, 69
  structural, 134
  surprise end of Cold War, 117
  theories of war, 406–7, 409, 413, 415
  view of Cold War, 111
  view of international law, 531
  view of people as powerless, 221
  view of religious movements, 204
  view of states' power, 443
  viewpoint of NGOs, 212
  views on globalization, 297
  views on human aggression, 404
  WWII-era views, 108*f*
realpolitik, 33, 142, 174, 483, 493. *See also* realism
rebus sic stantibus, 533
reciprocity, 333, 339
recognition of a state, 533
Redfield, Robert, 221
reforestation, 383–84
refugee crisis
  countries' attitudes toward immigrants, 236–37
  ethnic cleansing and, 233–34
  legal migrants, 235
  motivation for becoming, 234–35
  numbers worldwide, 233–34, 234*f*
  refugee defined, 233
  Rwanda, 233, 421, 544
  Sudan, 235, 405, 421–22, 582
  xenophobia and, 236
Regan, Patrick M., 43
regimes, 157, 181, 195, 212, 247, 274, 380–81
regional collective defense, 555
regional currency union. *See* Contingency Credit Line
regional security organizations, 554–56
regional trade agreements (RTAs), 336–38

Register of Conventional Arms, UN, 456
Reid, T. R., 192, 332, 492, 523, 562
Reinares, Fernando, 436
Reiter, Dan, 415
relative burden of military spending, 450, 451, 452
relative deprivation, 422
relative gains, 297, 308, 367, 410, 557
religions, world
  end of secular authority of the pope, 169
  impact on world politics, 8
  numbers and locations worldwide, 201*m*
religious movements
  characteristics of radical factions, 205
  controversy over agendas, 204
  impact on international affairs, 202–3, 204, 205
  religion defined, 202
  state repression of minorities, 206
  types of international activities, 205
renewable energy sources, 371. *See also* oil supply and consumption
Renner, Michael, 461
replacement-level fertility, 353
reprisals, 543
Resolution 55/B (UN), 179
resource hierarchy, 8
Responsibility to Protect, The, 247
retorsion, 543
Reuveny, Rafael, 163
Revel, Jean-Francois, 20, 120, 519
revolution in military technology (RMT), 465, 539
Rhine River Commission (1804), 559
Ricardo, David, 305
Rice, Condoleezza, 433, 444, 472
Rich, Susan, 85
Richardson, Lewis F., 419
Ricupero, Rubens, 332
Ridley, Matt, 404
Rieff, David, 252
Rifkin, Jeromy, 562
Riggs, Robert E., 143
Riker, William H., 504, 506
Ripsman, Norrin M., 518
Robinson, Mary, 226
Rogoff, Kenneth, 132
Roh (South Korean president), 4
roles, 12, 242
Roman Catholic Church, 58
Romania, 109, 520
Roosevelt, Eleanor, 252
Roosevelt, Franklin, 95*f*, 107, 110
Rosecrance, Richard, 448, 507
Rosenau, James N., 18, 37, 77
Rosenberg, Shawn W., 12
Rosendorff, B. Peter, 410
Rosow, Stephen J., 212, 296, 584
Ross, Michael L., 409
Ross, Philip E., 466
Rosset, Peter, 363
Rostow, Walt W., 147

Rousseau, Jean-Jacques, 30*f*, 223, 492
Rowley, Coleen, 84
RTAs. *See* regional trade agreements
Rubenstein, Richard E., 435
Rubin, Nancy, 532
Ruggie, John Gerald, 38
Ruggiero, Renato, 274
Rummel, Rudolph J., 237
Rumsfeld, Donald, 80*f,* 81, 82, 84, 85, 188, 437, 448, 471, 536
Rush-Bagot Agreement (1817), 508
Rusk, Dean, 95
Russett, Bruce, 68, 410, 411
Russia, 13
  arms trade and, 456, 457
  bilateral arms control agreements, 508
  bipolar treaties with U.S., 516–17
  elections in, 4
  entry into WWI, 100
  friendship treaty with China, 520, 525
  national security strategy, 485–86
  nuclear energy and, 374
  nuclear weapons stockpiles, 461
  pre-WWI rise in global power, 100
  steps towards nuclear disarmament, 464
  See also Soviet Union
Rwanda, 233, 421, 544

SAARC. *See* South Asian Association for Regional Cooperation
SADC. *See* Southern African Development Community
Sadowaski, Yahya, 239
Sagan, Carl, 351, 467, 588
Sageman, Marc, 205, 434
Saldanha, Anil, 267
SALT. *See* Strategic Arms Limitation Talks
Salzburg Seminar, 266
Sambanis, Nicholas, 420
Samuelson, Robert J., 6, 159, 370
sanctions, 223, 476
sanctuary, 237
Sandler, Todd, 425
Sanger, David E., 328
Santayana, George, 5
Santos, Theotonio dos, 148
SARS (severe acute respiratory syndrome), 276
satisficing behavior, 74
Saudi Arabia, 65, 370
Saul, John Ralstom, 266
Saurin, Julian, 222, 226
Save the Children, 194
Scalfaro, Oscar Luigi, 239
scapegoat phenomenon, 65
Schelling, Thomas C., 468
schematic reasoning, 12
Schlesinger, Arthur, Jr., 471
Schlesinger, James, 28, 80*f*
Schmidt, Hans Christian, 393
Schneider, Gerald, 410
Schoenberg, Ronald, 140

Schott, Jeffrey J., 477, 480
Schraeder, Peter J., 564
Schroeder, Gerhard, 472, 491
Schroeder, Paul W., 507
Schulz, William F., 249
Schwab, Klaus, 263
Schweller, Randall L., 39, 310, 505
Scowcroft, Brent, 81, 514*m*
SDI. *See* Strategic Defense Initiative
sea power
  geopolitics and, 62
  of nineteenth-century Britain, 100
SEATO. *See* Southeast Asia Treaty Organization
secession, 205
Seck, Manadon Manosour, 385*m*
Second Lateran Council, 510
second-strike capability, 469
Second Vienna World Conference on Human Rights (1993), 246
Second World, 135
Second World Assembly on Aging, UN, 357
Secretariat, UN, 176, 547
Secret of the Persian Chessboard, 351–52
security, national. *See* national security of states
security community, 188, 562
Security Council, UN, 57*f*, 110, 174, 176, 547
security dilemma, 112, 113, 415, 465, 492–93, 499, 576
security regime, 114, 503, 537
Seitz, Russell, 462
selective engagement, 126, 551
Selek, Torsten J., 191
self-determination, 32, 142, 239, 563, 581
self-fulfilling prophecies, 111
self-help, 33, 413, 415, 442, 501, 534, 584
semiperiphery, 149, 150
separative revolts, 205
September 11, 2001, 3, 6–7, 7*f*
  Commission report, 82–84
  ethnocentrism and, 201, 239
  globalization and, 232
  impact of attacks, 312, 399, 433, 435, 578
  NATO's mutual defense principle and, 522
Serbia, 70, 100, 239
Serfaty, Simon, 188
Serrano, Monica, 278, 438
services, trade in, 287
severe acute respiratory syndrome (SARS), 276
Seville Statement, 404
Shah, Timothy Samuel, 204
Shannon, Thomas Richard, 148, 149
Sheehan, Michael, 591
Sheffer, Gabriel, 205
Shotwell, James T., 30
Shultz, George, 80*f*
Shultz, Richard H., Jr., 205, 494

Siegel, Martin, 587
Siegle, Joseph T., 565
Sikhs, 58
Simmons, Beth A., 44, 296, 304
Simon, Herbert, 72, 74
Singapore, 150, 157
Singer, J. David, 37, 409, 419, 420, 421, 524
Singer, Max, 144, 356
Singer, Peter, 289
Singh, Sonali, 462
Sino-Russian axis, 525
Sivard, Ruth Leger, 401, 405, 417, 452, 460, 537
Siverson, Randolph M., 66
Six Day War, 432*m*
size principle, 504
Sklair, Leslie, 155
Slaughter, Anne-Marie, 215, 216, 222, 250, 532, 541, 547, 567
SLBM. *See* submarine-launched ballistic missile
Slovakia, 188, 239, 520
Slovenia, 188, 520
Smadja, Claude, 263
Small, Melvin, 419, 420, 421
smart bombs, 465–66
Smith, Alastair, 415
Smith, Adam, 30, 140, 305, 308
Smith, Dan, 425
Smith, Jackie, 183
Smith, Michael J., 542
Snidal, Duncan, 39
Snyder, Glenn H., 473, 492, 501
Snyder, Jack, 587
Social Contract (Rousseau), 223
socialism, 29, 108*f*
socialization, 404
soft power, 449, 578
soil degradation, 383
Solomon, King, 414
Somavia, Juan, 279, 281, 289
Somit, Albert, 404
Sommaruga, Cornelio, 244
Sony, 274
SOPs. *See* standard operating procedures
Sorenson, Theodore, 72, 80*f*
Sorokin, Pitirim A., 419
Soroos, Marvin S., 375
Soros, George, 95, 123
SORT. *See* Strategic Offensive Reduction Treaty
South Asian Association for Regional Cooperation (SAARC), 193
Southeast Asia Treaty Organization (SEATO), 555
Southern African Development Community (SADC), 157, 193
South Korea, 4, 150
Souva, Mark, 411, 565
sovereign equality, 532
sovereignty, 58, 238, 406, 531, 583
Soviet Union, 8
  consequences of WWII, 109
  high politics and, 44

  invasion of Finland, 107–8
  post-WWII status, 110
  steps to rapprochement, 117
  veto authority in UN, 174
  See also Cold War; Russia
Spain, 36
  civil war and WWII, 106
  decolonizations, 139–40
  EU membership, 188
Spanish-American War (1898), 140
Sparta, 33
species extinction, 386
speculators, 322
sphere of influence, 61, 111
spillaround, 563
spillback, 563
spillover, 562
spiral model, 492
Spolaore, Enrique, 213
Sprinz, Detlef F., 377
Sputnik, 468
Spykman, Nicholas, 62
Srodes, James, 356
Stages of Economic Growth, The (Rostow), 147
Stalin, Joseph, 95*f*, 106, 110, 115
Stam, Allen C., III, 400, 415, 564
standard operating procedures (SOPs), 79
Stanley Foundation, 18
START. *See* Strategic Arms Reduction Treaty
statehood, 532–33
state level of analysis, 101
  cause of WWII and, 108
  described, 15, 59*f*
  globalization and, 263
  Global South and, 134
  states as a cause of war
    cultural determinants, 406–7
    duration of independence, 406
    economic system, 409–11
    feminist theory and, 407
    geography and, 408–9
    militarization, 409
    nationalism and, 412–13
    poverty and, 407–8
    type of government and, 411–12
states
  as a cause of war (*see* state level of analysis)
  challenges from nonstate actors, 214–16
  decision-making process
    discrepancy between theory and practice, 76–77, 77*t*
    opportunity cost considerations, 73–74
    psychological basis of, 74–75
    psychological propensities in, 75–76
    rational choice examples, 70–71
    rational choice impediments, 72–73
    realist view, 69
    steps taken by unitary actors, 69–70

states—decision-making process (*continued*)
defined, 8, 58
emergence of modern system, 58
foreign policy (*see* foreign policy of states)
globalization and, 266–67, 296–97
mercantilism and, 304
national security strategies (*see* national security of states)
nuclear weapons and (*see* nuclear age)
obligation to human rights, 244–46
possible obsolescence of, 17–18
power and (*see* power)
self-determination and, 32
sovereignty under international law, 18, 33, 58, 531–33
sponsorship of terrorism, 429, 545, 581
statehood components, 532–33
state sovereignty concept, 58
tension with markets, 341
undermining of power by financial liberalization, 281
as unitary actors, 69
states' attributes, 60
states' foreign policies, 32
state-sponsored terrorism, 429, 545, 581
Stedman, Stephen John, 553
Stephenson, Carolyn M., 173, 211
Stock, Thomas, 466
Stokes, Bruce, 316
Stopford, John, 210, 215
Stott, Philip, 379
St. Petersburg Declaration, 510
Strang, David, 143
Strategic Arms Limitation Talks (SALT), 116, 508, 512
Strategic Arms Reduction Treaty (START), 117, 508
strategic corporate alliances, 210, 290
Strategic Defense Initiative (SDI), 470
Strategic Offensive Reduction Treaty (SORT), 464, 508, 509*f*
strategic trade policy, 310
strategic weapons, 466
Strauss, Andrew, 211, 214
Stross, Randall E., 411
structuralism, 99–100
dependency theory, 148–49
world-system theory, 149
structural realism, 38, 134, 416
submarine-launched ballistic missile (SLBM), 510
sub-Saharan Africa, 355
Sudan, 235, 405, 421–22, 582
Sudentenland, 106
Sundelius, Bengt, 46
Super 301, 333–34
survival of the fittest, 404
sustainable development
defined, 21–22
ecopolitics and, 366–67

free trade vs., 390–92
goal of, 392–94, 584
Sutcliffe, Bob, 132
Sweden, 188, 405
Switzerland, 60, 65, 405
Sylvester, Christine, 223, 244

tactical air-to-surface missiles (TASMs), 465
Taiwan, 150, 174
Talbott, Strobe, 435
Tanzania, 544
tariffs, 333*f*. *See also* monetary policy
TASMs. *See* tactical air-to-surface missiles
TB. *See* tuberculosis
Tbilisi region, 4
Tenet, George, 84
territorial imperative, 405
Territorial Imperative, The (Ardrey), 405
terrorism
9/11 attacks, 3, 6–7 (*see also* September 11, 2001)
3/11 attack in Madrid, 4
Bush's response to, 71
changes in armed conflict due to, 401
characteristics of, 433–34
containing, 578–80
counterterrorism, 434–36
defined, 427, 428
due to international inequalities, 144
freedom fighters vs., 428
frequency in the world, 430, 431*f*
globalization and, 232
international law and, 542–43
just war debate, 436
Libya's support of, 62
Middle East and, 432*m*
by nonstate nations, 238, 239
persistant danger of, 436–38
religious roots, 204
state-sponsored, 429, 545, 581
subjective meaning of, 429–30
threat of acquiring WMD, 457
UN's inability to control, 547
U.S. intelligence failures, 82–83
Tessman, Brock, 418*f*
textiles and apparel exports, 309–10
Thailand, 157, 287
Thakur, Ramesh, 341
theories of world politics
constructivist conception, 28, 46, 49–52
core perspectives, 28, 47–48*t*
decision-making, 45
dependency, 45
evolution of theoretical inquiry, 29
feminist theory, 42
gender issues and, 43
hegemonic stability (*see* hegemonic stability theory)
to interpret national behavior, 37
liberalism (*see* liberalism)
long-cycle, 45

neoliberalism (*see* neoliberalism)
realism (*see* realism)
world-system, 46
theory, 29, 305
Third Way, 188, 231
Third World, 135. *See also* Global South
Thirty Years' War, 58, 134, 169, 202, 538
Thomas, Daniel C., 494
Thompson, Kenneth W., 33, 45
Thompson, William R., 96, 98, 163, 417, 517, 524
Thousand-Year Reich, 108–9
Three Mile Island, 373
Thucydides, 33, 65
Thurow, Lester C., 147, 280, 319
Tickner, J. Ann, 42, 43, 244, 407
Tillema, Herbert K., 475
Time Warner, 272, 274
Timmerman, Kenneth, 460, 592
TNBs. *See* transnational banks
Tocqueville, Alexis de, 22, 66, 110
Todaro, Michael P., 149, 151, 322
Todd, Emmanuel, 122
Tolstoy, Leo, 404
Toner, Robin, 84
Toynbee, Arnold J., 96
trade deficits in U.S., 4
trade globalization
impact of FDI on capital markets, 291, 292
poverty and, 288–290
production by MNCs and, 290–291
pursuit of MNC investment, 292–293
in services, 287
trade integration, 284–286, 285*f*, 286*f*
world gross product, 285*f*
worries about MNCs power, 293, 295
trade integration, 284–286, 285*f*, 286*f*, 339
trade regulation by WTO, 181–83
tragedy of the commons, 350, 367, 381
transformation, 6, 50
transgenetic crops, 361
transnational banks (TNBs), 207
Treaty of Augsburt (1555), 532
Treaty of Versailles (1919), 514*m*
Triple Entente, 101
tropical rain forests, 382, 383–84, 386
Truman, Harry S, 110, 114, 469
Truman Doctrine, 114
Trusteeship Council, UN, 176
tuberculosis (TB), 358
Tuchman, Barbara W., 72, 100
Tucker, Robert C., 564
Turco, Richard, 467
Turk, Danilo, 238
Turner, Jonathan H., 224, 231
Turner, Stansfield, 449
Tversky, Amos, 74
two-level games, 76, 341
Tyler, Patrik E., 374

Human Development Index (HDI), 227–29, 228t, 425
Human Development Reports, 227
human immunodeficiency virus (HIV), 358–60, 359m. *See also* AIDS
humanitarian intervention, 248–49, 583
human needs, 227
human rights
  categories of, 246–47
  children and, 245
  in China, 239
  conduct of war and, 244, 249–52
  controversy over humanitarian intervention, 248–49
  defined, 21, 223, 411, 542
  expanded legal protection, 252, 253–55t
  free trade and, 335–36
  fundamental principles, 244–46
  great powers' ability to protect, 581–83
  military intervention and, 475
  noncombatant immunity, 244, 250
  policy challenges, 247
  state authority vs., 250–51
human security, 233, 263, 450, 451, 452, 588
Hume, David, 30f
Hungary, 188
Huntington, Samuel P., 68, 144, 169, 200, 233, 239, 410, 534, 581, 584
Hurwitz, Jon, 12
Hussein, King, 73f
Hussein, Saddam, 57f, 62–63, 64f, 71, 368, 545, 546, 579, 592. *See also* Iraqi war
Huth, Paul K., 565
Huxley, Aldous, 413
hydrochlorofluorocarbons (HCFCs), 381
hydrogen bomb, 469

IBRD. *See* International Bank for Reconstruction and Development
ICBMs. *See* intercontinental ballistic missiles
ICC. *See* International Criminal Court
ICJ. *See* International Court of Justice
ICPD. *See* International Conference on Population and Development
ICT. *See* information and communications technology
IDA. *See* International Development Association
Idealism, 30
ideologies, 12, 112, 113, 175, 559
  capitalism vs. communism in Cold War, 111, 112
  in religious wars, 202
  theories of war, 413
  women's rights and, 243
  WWII fight over ethical values, 109
Ignatieff, Michael, 221, 232, 244, 250, 251, 252, 538

IGOs. *See* intergovernmental organizations
Ikenberry, G. John, 40, 194, 215
ILO. *See* International Labour Organization
IMF. *See* International Monetary Fund
imperialism, 62, 107
  capitalism and, 140–42
  dependency theory and, 148
  in the Global South, 138–42
  mercantilism and, 139
Imperialism (Hobson), 142
Imperialism, The Highest Stage of Capitalism (Lenin), 140–41
imperial overstretch, 122, 315
import quotas, 309
import-substitution industrialization, 154
In Defense of Globalization (Bhagwati), 289
India
  coal use, 379–80
  decolonization of, 137, 143
  enclosure movement and, 386
  improving economic status, 150, 155, 287
  nuclear weapons possession, 464–65, 510
  nuclear weapons stockpiles, 461
  population, 349
indigenous peoples
  cultural domains, 200–202
  defined, 135, 237, 563
  genocide and, 237–38, 239
  geographic spread, 198m
  irredentism rise, 240
  locations, 198m
  numbers in world, 197
  seeking of substate autonomy, 238–39
  threat of language extinction, 197, 199
individualistic fallacy, 405
individual level of analysis
  described, 14–15, 59f
  rational choice and, 100–101
  warfare causes analysis, 403–6
Indochina, 143
Indonesia, 157, 389
Industrial Revolution, 140, 142
infant industry, 310
infant mortality, 226, 425
inflation, 322
Influence of Sea Power in History, The (Mahan), 62
information age
  cellular phone use, 265
  computers and the Internet, 265–67
  criticisms of electronic network, 268–69
  digital divide, 269–70
  military power and, 446
  pace of information technology, 268
  sustainability and, 393
  terrorism and, 436
  web bars, 271

information and communications technology (ICT), 269–70
information technology (IT), 268
information warfare (IW), 466
infowar tactics, 466
instrumental rationality, 87
intelligence agencies in U.S., 82–83
Inter-American Court on Human Rights, 548
intercontinental ballistic missiles (ICBMs), 517
interdependence, 18–19, 304
interest groups' influence on a political system, 65, 66. *See also* nongovernmental organizations
intergovernmental organizations (IGOs), 17, 559
  global issues supported by, 171–72
  in the Global South, 192–93
  IMF, 186–87
  impact on world politics, 193–94
  international law and, 531
  membership and scope, 170–71, 171t
  OPEC (*see* Organization of Petroleum Exporting Countries)
  purpose of, 181
  regional example (*see* European Union)
  United Nations (*see* United Nations)
  World Bank (*see* World Bank)
  WTO (*see* World Trade Organization)
Intergovernmental Panel on Climate Change (IPCC), 376
intermestic decision making, 60, 514m, 559
International Bank for Reconstruction and Development (IBRD), 183, 326. *See also* World Bank
International Campaign to Ban Landmines, 513
International Chamber of Commerce, 194
International Civil Aviation Organization, 193
International Commission on Intervention and State Sovereignty, 247
International Conference on Population and Development (ICPD), 360
International Convention for the Suppression of Financing of Terrorism, 436
International Court of Justice (ICJ), 534, 545. *See also* World Court
International Criminal Court (ICC), 251, 544
International Development Association (IDA). *See also* World Bank
International Energy Agency, 369
International Labour Organization (ILO), 193, 279, 281, 547, 559
international law
  components of statehood, 532–33
  deference to state sovereignty, 531–33

international law (*continued*)
  dispute settlement procedures, 533
  divine right of kings, 532
  future role, 546–47
  inherent deficiencies, 534–35
  legal control of warfare (*see* just war doctrine)
  limitations due to state sovereignty, 533–34
  nationality and citizenship definitions, 532
  nonintervention norm, 532
  paths to international security, 530*t*
  private vs. public, 531
  prohibition against premeditated attack, 63
  relevance of, 535–37, 545–46
  rules for military intervention, 541–43
  rules for war's conduct, 543–44
  World Court's ruling against U.S., 529–31
international liquidity, 326
International Monetary Fund (IMF), 151, 183, 186–87, 326, 448, 564. *See also* foreign direct investment
international monetary system, 303. *See also* financial globalization
international organized crime (IOC), 278
International Peace Conferences, 510
international political economy
  Bretton Woods conference and, 303–4
  case for open trading system, 339, 340*f*, 341–42
  commercial liberalism (*see* commercial liberalism)
  described, 302
  domestic vs. foreign trade policies in countries, 334–35
  economic freedom's benefits, 334–36, 335*m*
  economic sanctions use (*see* economic sanctions)
  future prospects, 343–44
  global context, 302–3
  global free-trade regime emergence, 317, 318*t*, 319, 319*f*
  hegemonic stability theory and (*see* hegemonic stability theory)
  mercantilism (*see* mercantilism)
  monetary policy (*see* monetary policy)
  premises for future global economy, 342
  regional trade policies, 336–38, 337*m*
  tension between states and markets, 341
  trade growth trends, 339, 340*f*
International Red Cross, 194
international regimes, 44–45, 244, 316
international system
  criteria for defining a new system, 8

  liberalism and, 30
  neoclassical idealism and, 39–40
  neorealism and, 38–39
  realism and, 33
International Telecommunication Union, 193
International Telegraphic Union, 559
International Telephone and Telegraph (ITT), 208
International Trade Organization (ITO), 181, 317. *See also* World Trade Organization (WTO)
International Tropical Timber Organization (ITTO), 383
International Year of Mountains, 381, 409
Internet, 144, 265–67, 585
interspecific aggression, 404
intersubjective consensus, 28
intervention, 406
intolerance, 204
intraspecific aggression, 404
IOC. *See* international organized crime
Ip, Greg, 315, 328
IPCC. *See* Intergovernmental Panel on Climate Change
Iran, 467
Iran-Contra Affair, 85
Iraq, 36
  chemical weapons use, 467
  military capabilities, 62–63
  preemptive basis of U.S. attack on, 472
  UN embargo, 480
  UN ultimatum against, 551
  U.S. occupation of (*see* Iraqi war)
Iraqi war, 3
  Bush administration's nonrational impulses, 75–76
  European's view of, 491
  governmental politics in Bush administration, 81
  NATO opposition to, 523
  prisoner abuse by U.S., 536
  protests against, 99*f*
  questions on justness of, 541
  questions on legality of, 539
Ireland, 188
irredentism, 104, 205, 240
Isaak, Robert A., 317
Isenberg, David, 556
Islamic fundamentalism
  impact on world politics, 8
  terrorism and, 204
isolationism, 60, 106
Israel, 4, 13, 432*m*, 461
IT. *See* information technology
Italy
  EU membership, 188
  first world war and (*see* World War I)
  pre-WWII militarism, 106
  second world war and (*see* World War II)
ITO. *See* International Trade Organization

ITT. *See* International Telephone and Telegraph
ITTO. *See* International Tropical Timber Organization
IW. *See* information warfare

Jackson, Patrick T., 50
Jacobson, Harold K., 173, 560
Jaffe, Amy, 369
James, Barry, 278, 377, 388*m*, 392
James, Patrick, 40
Janis, Irving, 85
Japan
  comparative advantage in trade example, 306–7, 306*t*
  dependence on foreign energy, 477
  imperialistic occupations, 140
  national security strategy, 488–90
  nuclear energy use, 373
  Pearl Harbor attack on U.S., 107
  population momentum, 355
  pre-WWII militarism, 106
  U.S. atomic bombing of, 109
Jefferson, Thomas, 30, 66, 411, 479
Jensen, Lloyd, 66
Jervis, Robert, 3, 40, 492, 507
Jesus Christ, 414
Jews, 416
Joffe, Ellis, 487
Johannesburg World Summit on Sustainable Development (2002), 243
Johansen, Robert C., 471
John Paul II (pope), 51*f*, 204, 565
Johnson, Chalmers, 20, 82, 120
Johnson, James Turner, 539, 541
Jordan, 432*m*
Joyner, Christopher, 394, 531, 535
Judis, John B., 518
Juergensmyer, Mark, 203
just war doctrine
  basis of, 436, 537–38
  criteria for, 472, 538–39
  legal prohibition against initiating wars, 473, 540*f*

Kagan, Robert, 536
Kahneman, Daniel, 72, 74, 75
Kaiser, David, 101
Kaminski, Matthew, 435
Kane, Hal, 401
Kant, Immanuel, 30, 30*f*, 66, 68, 223, 411, 472
Kaplan, Morton, 504
Kaplan, Robert D., 120, 123, 483, 486
Kapstein, Ethan B., 208, 215
Kapur, Devesh, 279
Kashmir, 143, 464
Katzenstein, Lawrence C., 207
Kautilya, 33
Keegan, John, 99
Keeley, Lawrence, 584
Kegley, Charles W., Jr., 27*f*, 40, 68, 82, 120, 124, 134, 214, 314, 315, 406, 460, 473, 483, 540
Kellogg-Briand Pact (1928), 32, 102
Kelsen, Hans, 535

Kennan, George F., 33, 66, 114, 118, 249, 488, 501
Kennedy, John F., 70, 86, 90, 115, 399, 442, 469, 592. *See also* Cuban Missile Crisis (1962)
Kennedy, Paul, 122, 315, 453
Kennedy, Robert, 80f
Keohane, Robert O., 38, 42, 44, 119, 127, 181, 211, 445, 449, 585
Keyes, Ken, Jr., 557
Keynes, John Maynard, 304
Khalistan, 427
Khomeini, Ayatollah, 275
Khrushchev, Nikita, 115, 470
Kibbe, Jennifer D., 401
Kim, Dae Jung, 163
Kim, Samuel S., 535
Kindleberger, Charles, 313, 314
King, Martin Luther, Jr., 575, 576
Kinnas, J. N., 566
Kissinger, Henry, 57, 63, 70, 74, 80f, 86, 88, 115, 116f, 121, 125, 401, 425, 529, 548, 580
Klare, Michael T., 366, 394, 409, 455, 459, 494
Kluger, Jeffrey, 349
Knickerbocker, Brad, 524
Knight, W. Andy, 212
Knorr, Klaus, 37
Kober, Stanley, 40, 586
Korany, Bahgat, 78
Korean War, 114
Korten, David, 559
Kosovo, 70, 239, 272, 405, 475, 557
Kovanda, Karel, 554
Krasner, Stephen D., 302, 316, 547
Krauthammer, Charles, 119, 126, 453, 483, 518, 573
Krepinevich, Andrew F., 484
Krepon, Michael, 462
Kristof, Nicholas D., 235, 486
Kropotkin, Peter, 406
Krugman, Paul, 369
Kugler, Jacek, 416, 417
Kugler, Richard, 269
Kunz, Josef L., 539
Kunzig, Robert, 376
Kupchan, Charles A., 20, 122, 507, 518, 523
Kusiak, Steven M., 484
Kuwait, 63, 150, 368, 550
Kyoto Protocol, 378m, 380, 389, 513

LAIA. *See* Latin American Integration Association
laissez-faire economics, 140, 306, 410
Landes, David S., 147
landmines, 513
languages
  numbers worldwide, 240
  threat of extinction of indigenous, 197, 199
Laqueur, Walter, 427, 430, 436, 437
Larsen B ice shelf, 379
Latin America, 61–62, 164, 193

Latin American Integration Association (LAIA), 193
Latvia
  EU membership, 188
  NATO membership, 520
  post-WWI, 102
  post-WWII, 109
leaders' role in decision making. *See also* individual level of analysis
  capacity to lead and, 88–90
  history-making individuals model, 86–88, 91
  human factor's importance, 87–88
  procedural vs. instrumental rationality, 87
League of Arab States, 555
League of Nations, 13, 31, 32, 102, 104, 107, 143, 548
Leaning, Jennifer, 275
least developed of the less-developed countries (LLDCs), 137, 145
Lebovic, James H., 552
Lebow, Richard Ned, 12, 118, 567, 586
Lechner, Frank, 274
Lee, Steve, 341
Legrain, Philippe, 274
Legro, Jeffrey, 40, 586
Lemke, Douglas, 153, 407
Lenin, Vladimir, 102, 112, 140, 141, 148, 409
Lentner, Howard H., 560, 584
Lenway, Stefanie, 207
Leow, Rachel, 271
Leppnan, Elizabeth J., 563
Lesser, Guy, 544
level of analysis, 14–16, 59–60, 59f, 223. *See also specific levels*
Levine, Robert A., 148
Levingston, Steven, 405
Levy, Jack S., 62, 65, 74, 75, 101, 413, 415, 427
Lexus and the Olive Tree, The (Friedman), 584
Leyton-Brown, David, 476
Liberal International Economic Order (LIEO), 44, 155, 156, 304
liberalism, 223
  commercial (*see* commercial liberalism)
  core beliefs, 31, 500
  core perspectives, 47–48t, 481
  described, 30
  economics and, 140
  effectiveness of World Bank and, 185–86
  environmental security approach, 366
  global vs. national interests, 575
  human rights and, 244, 248–49
  reform program, 31–32
  relevance today, 585–87
  self-determination and, 142
  sustainable development and, 390
  theories of war, 411–12
  views on globalization, 297

WWI and, 29–31, 102
Libya, 87, 480
LIEO. *See* Liberal International Economic Order
life expectancy, 226
Lifton, Robert Jay, 20, 120
limits-to-growth proposition, 21
Lincoln, Abraham, 88
Lind, Michael, 407
Lindblom, Charles E., 303
Lindh, Anna, 567
Lindsay, James M., 19, 20, 479
linkage strategy, 116f
Lipson, Charles, 564
liquidity, international, 326
Lissitzyn, Oliver J., 535
Lithuania
  EU membership, 188
  NATO membership, 520
  post-WWI, 102
  post-WWII, 109
Little, David, 40
LLDCs. *See* least developed of the less-developed countries
Lloyd, William Foster, 350
Locke, John, 30
Lofdahl, Corey L., 451
long-cycle theory, 45, 96–98, 311, 417–19, 418f, 516
long peace, 401
Lopez, George A., 480
Lord, Kriston M., 222
Lorenz, Konrad, 404
loss aversion, 76
low politics, 17, 46, 212, 303, 361, 547, 589
Lula da Silva, Luis Ignacio, 180
Lumpe, Lora, 461
Luterbacker, Urs, 377
Lutz, Wolfgang, 356
Luxembourg, 188

Macao, 563
Machiavelli, Niccolò, 33, 34f, 426
machtpolitik, 104
Mack, Andrew, 575
Mackinder, Halford, 29, 62
macroeconomic policies, 311
MAD. *See* mutual assured destruction
mad cow disease, 276
Madison, James, 30, 411, 479, 564
Madrid, Spain, 4
Mahan, Alfred Thayer, 29, 62
Mahon, Alice, 472
Maier, Matthew, 458
Majeed, Akhtar, 447, 468
Malaquias, Assis V., 249
Malaysia, 157, 287, 383
Malta, 188
Malthus, Thomas, 350, 362
Manchuria, 106
mandate system, League of Nations, 143
Mandelbaum, Michael, 68, 151
Manhattan Project, 469
Mann, Michael, 83

Mansfield, Edward D., 410
Marshall Plan, 326
Marx, Anthony W., 413
Marx, Karl, 140, 141f, 221, 303
Marxism-Leninism, 8, 29, 140
massive retaliation, 468
mass media. *See* media and globalization
Mastanduno, Michael, 310
Mathews, Jessica T., 518
Matlock, Jack F., 118
Matthew, Richard A., 30, 42
May, Ernest R., 107
Mayall, James, 309
Mazarr, Michael J., 43, 144, 284
Mazzini, Giuseppe, 5, 590
Mbeki, Thabo, 349
McCarthy, Joseph, 112
McGrew, Anthony, 246
McGurn, William, 226, 232
McHale, John, 279
McKibben, Bill, 386
McNamara, Robert S., 80f, 86, 407, 586
Mead, Margaret, 575
Meadows, Donella H., 362
Mearsheimer, John J., 524, 539
media and globalization
  agenda setting ability, 272
  concerns over concentration and power, 272–74
  diffusion of Western culture, 272
  domination by a few companies, 271–72
  influence on a political system, 65
  liberalization's impact, 274–75
mediation, 31, 533
Melloan, George, 84, 488
Mendelsohn, Jack, 510, 515
Menkhaus, Ken, 437
mental maps, 9, 12
mercantilism
  described, 304, 308–9, 364
  future prospects, 343–44
  imperialism and, 139
  protectionist policies, 309–10
  relative gains issues, 310–11
Mercator projection, 11
Mercosur Agreement, 157, 336, 337
methane, 376
Mexico
  emigration to U.S., 233
  NAFTA membership, 156
MFA. *See* Multi-Fiber Arrangement
MFN. *See* most-favored-nation principle
Michael, Marie, 163
Micklethwait, John, 284, 320
Middle East
  monopoly power of OPEC, 369–70, 370
  territorial imperative as a cause of war, 405
  terrorism and, 432m
  weapons trade in, 459
Midlarsky, Manus J., 101, 403

migration, 278–79
military asymmetries, 8
military capabilities
  foreign policy and, 62–63
  as a function of economic capabilities, 63–64
  strategies for national security (*see* alliances; arms control; military strategy in the nuclear age)
military-industrial complex, 458
military intervention, 153, 474–76
military necessity, 539, 579
military strategy in the nuclear age
  compellence, 468
  deterrence and (*see* deterrence)
  devastation possible from a nuclear war, 467
  economic sanctions (*see* economic sanctions)
  frequency of international crises, 474f
  military intervention, 474–76
  preemption, 470–73
Mill, John Stuart, 30, 303
Millennium Challenge Account Initiative, 159
Millennium Round, 320
Millennium Summit, UN, 175
Millett, Allan R., 104, 109, 110
Milner, Helen V., 410
Milosevic, Slobodan, 70, 252, 544, 545
Minorities at Risk Project, The, 240
mirror images, 13, 111
MIRVs. *See* multiple independently targetable reentry vehicles
Mishra, Brajesh, 462
Mitchell, Sara McLaughlin, 65, 426
Mitrany, David, 558
Mitterrand, François, 587
Miyazawa, Kiichi, 489
MNCs. *See* multinational corporations
Modelski, George, 45, 57, 96, 417, 418f, 426
modernization, 147, 356
Moisy, Claude, 268
Møller, Bjørn, 494
monetarist theory, 322
monetary policy
  currency concepts and terms, 323t
  currency exchange system, 324f
  described, 322
  fixed exchange rates system, 326–27
  floating exchange rates, 328–29
  government intervention in currency markets, 323, 325
  interconnectedness of international system, 327–28
  reform prospects, 329–32
  tariffs and, 333f
  U.S. unilateralism, 333–34
monetary system, 321
money supply, 322
Monnet, Jean, 559, 560
Montevideo Convention (1933), 532
Montreal Protocol on Substances that Deplete the Ozone Layer, 381

Moon, Bruce E., 231
Moore, Mike, 283, 321
Moore's Law, 265
morality, 221
morals, 537
Moran, Timothy Patrick, 183
Moravcsik, Andrew, 40, 586
More, Thomas, 405, 538
Morgenthau, Hans J., 33, 35, 96, 515, 524, 535
Morris, Desmond, 426
Morse, Edward L., 369
most-favored-nation (MFN) principle, 339
Mount, Ian, 458
Mowlana, Hamid, 274, 275
MTV, 272
Mubarak, Hosni, 73f
muddling through, 77
Mueller, Robert, 580
Muhammad, 414
Müller, Ronald E., 210, 559
Multi-Fiber Arrangement (MFA), 309–10
multilateral agreements, 508
multilateral aid, 360
multilateralism, 127, 481
multinational corporations (MNCs)
  arguments for and against, 161
  defined, 206
  dependency theory and, 148
  dualism and, 149
  functionalism and, 559
  Global South's pursuit of, 292–93
  increasing influence of, 208, 209t
  involvement in political affairs of countries, 208
  outsourcing of management, 207
  production globalization and, 290–91
  states' difficulties in controlling, 210
  transnational banks and, 207
  world economic impact, 206
  worries over their power, 293, 295
multiple advocacy, 78
multiple independently targetable reentry vehicles (MIRVs), 465, 510, 512
multipolarity as a cause of WWII, 107
multipolar system, 123
Murdoch, James C., 425
Murithi, Timothy, 404
Murray, Williamson, 104, 109, 110
Mussolini, Benito, 104
mutual assured destruction (MAD), 470, 510
My American Journey (Powell), 81

NAFTA. *See* North American Free Trade Agreement
Nagasaki, Japan, 109
NAM. *See* Non-Aligned Movement
Nankivell, Kerry Lynn, 430
Narashimhan, Vasant, 275
narcotics trade, 278

Ukraine, 373, 374
ultimatum, 473, 551
UNCED. *See* United Nations Conference on the Environment and Development
UNCTAD. *See* United Nations Conference on Trade and Development
underemployment, 279, 291
Underhill, Geoffrey R. D., 328
UNDP. *See* United Nations Development Programme
UNEF. *See* United Nations Emergency Force
UNEP. *See* United Nations Environment Programme
UNESCO. *See* United Nations Educational, Scientific, and Cultural Organization
UN Framework Convention on Climate Change, 380
UNHCR. *See* United Nations High Commissioner for Refugees
UNICEF. *See* United Nations Children's Emergency Fund
unilateralism, 126, 481
Union of Concerned Scientists, 194–95
Union of Soviet Socialist Republics (USSR), 103m. *See also* Russia; Soviet Union
unipolarity, 114, 119, 518
unitary actor, 69, 196
United Arab Emirates, 150
United Kingdom. *See* Great Britain
United Nations, 15, 18
 agencies and conferences (*see specific agencies and conferences*)
 budget and cash flow problems, 178–80
 changing membership, 174f
 charter limitations, 549
 collaboration with NGOs, 177
 collective security and, 548
 conferences on population growth, 357, 360
 creation after WWII, 110
 emerging NIEs and, 151
 General Assembly, 143, 176–77
 global network, 178m
 global role, 180–81
 ideology and agenda, 175
 inability to control civil wars, 547, 554
 neoliberalism and, 42
 objectives, 175
 peacekeeping operations, 549–51, 552m, 553
 purposes, 547
 reliance on the U.S., 553–54
 Security Council, 57f, 110, 174, 176
 selective engagement accusations, 551, 553
 specialized agencies, 547
 standoffs during Cold War, 549
 structure, 176, 548
 Universal Declaration of Human Rights, 220, 246, 250, 252
 world conferences, 175–76
United Nations Children's Emergency Fund (UNICEF), 548
United Nations Conference of the Human Environment, 367
United Nations Conference on the Environment and Development (UNCED), 367
United Nations Conference on Trade and Development (UNCTAD), 155, 290, 548
United Nations Convention to Combat Desertification (CCD), 385m
United Nations Development Programme (UNDP), 227, 548
United Nations Educational, Scientific, and Cultural Organization (UNESCO), 273, 548, 559
United Nations Emergency Force (UNEF), 549
United Nations Environment Programme (UNEP), 381
United Nations High Commissioner for Refugees (UNHCR), 233
United States
 arms trade and, 455–56, 457, 460
 atomic bombing of Japan, 109
 bilateral arms control agreements, 508
 bipolar treaties with Russia, 516–17
 Bretton Woods conference role, 303–4
 Cold War and (*see* Cold War)
 comparative advantage in trade example, 306–7, 306t
 concern over media dominance, 272–274
 consequences of superpower status, 19–20
 criticisms of, 342, 586–87
 economic hegemon position, 311, 312, 314
 economic leadership cost, 326–27
 economic sanctions use, 480
 economic unilateralism, 333–34
 economic vulnerability, 314–16
 emigration from Mexico, 233
 entry into WWI, 100
 entry into WWII, 107
 foreign policy, 481–85
 geopolitics of, 60, 62
 governmental politics, 80–82
 greenhouse effect contribution, 378m, 380
 hegemon role, 417, 516
 high politics and, 44
 ignoring of humanitarian law, 251
 imperialistic occupations, 140
 Iraq and (*see* Iraqi war; Persian Gulf War)
 isolationism and WWII, 107
 loss of European support, 523
 military spending, 443–44, 444f, 448, 452, 576
 Millennium Challenge, 159–60
 NAFTA membership, 156
 national debt, 315
 national security strategy, 481–85
 nuclear energy use, 373
 nuclear weapons doctrine, 468
 nuclear weapons stockpiles, 461
 oil consumption, 370
 participation in GATT, 181
 population momentum, 355–56
 post-WWII status, 110
 preemptive military action use, 63 (*see also* Iraqi war)
 preemptive strategy, 471
 questions about future trade policies, 343
 ranking on human security indicators, 451
 reputation worldwide, 578
 steps towards nuclear disarmament, 464
 terrorism against (*see* September 11, 2001)
 trade deficit, 4
 UN debt, 179
 unipolarity of, 120–1, 122, 123f, 518–19
 UN reliance on, 553–54
 value of U.S. dollar, 324f
 veto authority in UN, 174
 withdrawal from World Court, 530–31, 544, 547
Universal Declaration of Human Rights, 220, 246, 250, 252
Universal Postal Union (1874), 193, 559
uranium, 373
Urban II, Pope, 202
Urquhart, Brian, 169, 180, 238, 252, 554
Uruguay, 157, 336
Uruguay Round, 182, 317, 318t, 319f
USSR. *See* Soviet Union; Union of Soviet Socials Republics

Vaitheeswaron, Vijay, 371
Vance, Cyrus, 80f, 575
Vandersluis, Sarah Owen, 222, 245, 246
Van Evera, Stephen, 108, 412
Vasquez, John A., 28, 36, 39, 40, 62, 171, 503
Vedrine, Hubart, 120
Veltmeyer, Henry, 302
Venezuela, 157
Verba, Sidney, 37, 69, 89
Verbeek, Bertjan, 169
Verizon Communications, 271
VERs. *See* voluntary export restrictions
Versailles peace settlement, 142
vertical nuclear proliferation, 462
Viacom, 271, 274
Viendt, 274
Vietnam, 157
Vietnam War, 14, 85, 90
virtual corporations, 290
virtuality, 268
virtual nuclear arsenals, 466

viruses, 276. *See also* health and disease issues
voluntary export restrictions (VERs), 310
von Glahn, Gerhard, 539

Wallace, Brian, 224
Wallensteen, Peter, 401, 419, 420, 421, 426
Wallerstein, Immanuel, 46, 122, 417
Wal-Mart, 206
Walt, Stephen W., 539
Walter, Barbara F., 415, 420, 422, 424
Walters, Robert S., 308
Waltz, Kenneth N., 19, 36, 38, 39, 40, 127, 310, 499, 505, 517, 524
war crimes, 250–52, 543, 545
Ward, Michael D., 451
warfare
  armed conflict defined, 400
  civil wars (*see* civil wars)
  common security concept, 493
  conduct of war and human rights, 244, 249–52
  containing terrorism, 578–80
  continuities and change in armed conflict, 400–401, 402*f*, 403
  global causes of
    cyclical theories, 417–19, 418*f*
    power transitions, 415–17
    question of violence breeding violence, 415
    reliance on self-help, 413, 415
  human rights and (*see* human rights)
  individuals as a cause of
    biological bases of aggression theories, 403–4
    influence of leaders, 405–6
    national character and, 404
    territorial imperative and, 404
    war as a learned cultural habit, 404
  as an instrument of national policy, 29
  legal control of (*see* international law; just war doctrine)
  long-cycle theory, 96–98
  military power's purpose, 575–78
  military spending, 576
  nationalism's linkage to armed conflict, 412–13, 414
  nonmilitary dimensions of national security, 493–94
  outlawing of, 32
  pervasiveness in history, 400
  possible obsolescence of, 575–78
  security dilemma of states, 492–93
  self-destruction potential, 587–88
  states as a cause of
    cultural determinants, 406–7
    duration of independence, 406
    economic system, 409–11
    feminist theory and, 407
    geography and, 408–9
    militarization, 409
    nationalism and, 412–13, 414
    poverty and, 407–8

  type of government and, 411–12
  terrorism (*see* terrorism)
  transforming nature of, 28
  trends in, 401
  war defined, 400
  WWII fight over ethical values, 109
Warrick, Joby, 381
Warsaw Pact, 517
war weariness hypothesis, 419
Washington Naval Conference (1922), 102, 510
Watson, Douglas, 239
Way, Christopher R., 462
Weakland, Rembert, 232
Wealth of Nations, The (Smith), 140, 308
weapons of mass destruction (WMD), 436, 457, 466, 499, 510
weapons technology
  biological and chemical weapons, 466–67
  improvements to systems, 465–66
  military capabilities and power
    motives for arms trade, 457–59
    strategic consequences of arms sales, 459–60
    trends in military spending, 452, 453*f*
    trends in weapons trade, 454–57, 454*f*
  nuclear weapons (*see* nuclear age)
  proliferation of, 8
Weart, Spencer R., 564
Weaver, Ole, 44
web bars, 271
Weber, Max, 78
Weidenbaum, Murray, 210, 291, 301
Weimar Republic, 60
Weinberger, Caspar, 80*f*
Weinstein, Michael M., 565
Weitsman, Patricia A., 502
Wendt, Alexander, 28, 49, 50
Wendzel, Robert L., 87
Werner, Suzanne, 415
West Bank, 432*m*
Westphalian system, 58
WFP. *See* World Food Programme
WGP. *See* world gross product
Whitbeck, John V., 428, 429
White, Donald W., 315
White, Ralph K., 101
Whitman, Walt, 5
WHO. *See* World Health Organization
Wildavsky, Aaron, 144
Wilhelm II, Kaiser, 60, 89
Williams, Jody, 513
Wills, Garry, 436, 537, 541
Wilson, James Q., 404
Wilson, Woodrow, 30, 32, 66, 102, 411, 501, 586, 588
Wint, Guy, 107
Winter War, 108
Wise, Michael Z., 532
WMD. *See* weapons of mass destruction
WMO. *See* World Meteorological Organization

Wohlforth, William C., 524
Wolf, Martin, 210
Wolfensohn, James D., 132, 159, 163, 184, 220, 226, 261
Wolfers, Arnold, 64
Wolfowitz, Paul, 81
women
  challenges in protecting women's rights, 243
  conferences addressing women's issues, 240, 241*t*
  feminist theory, 42, 43, 223, 407
  gender issues in world politics (*see* gender politics)
  status of women worldwide, 241–43
  victimization in war, 424
Woodward, Bob, 83, 541
Wooldridge, Adrian, 284, 320
World Bank
  administration, 184
  creation and purpose, 183–84, 326
  effectiveness of, 185–86
  Global South and, 151
  lending policies, 185
  organization, 184
  support of democracy, 564
  voting system, 184
World Biodiversity Day, 277
World Commission on Environment and Development, 367
World Commission on the Social Dimensions of Globalization, 289
World Conference on Sustainable Development, 360
World Conference on Women, 243
World Conservation Union, 277, 386
World Court, 529–30, 534
World Economic Forum, 169, 312
world federalism, 556–58
World Food Programme (WFP), 548
world gross product (WGP), 285*f*
World Health Organization (WHO), 547
World Meteorological Organization (WMO), 193, 376
world politics
  clash of civilizations, 581
  containing terrorism, 578–80
  criteria for defining a new system, 7–8
  cycles in, 9
  end of history, 588–89
  finding a new world order, 590–91
  global vs. national interests, 574–75
  great powers' ability to protect human rights, 581–83
  hierarchies of states, 8
  impact of changes to, 6
  key questions
    consequences of U.S. hegemony, 19–20
    geo-economics vs. geopolitics, 20–21
    globalization pros and cons, 18–19, 583–85
    human welfare and, 21–22

Ukraine, 373, 374
ultimatum, 473, 551
UNCED. *See* United Nations Conference on the Environment and Development
UNCTAD. *See* United Nations Conference on Trade and Development
underemployment, 279, 291
Underhill, Geoffrey R. D., 328
UNDP. *See* United Nations Development Programme
UNEF. *See* United Nations Emergency Force
UNEP. *See* United Nations Environment Programme
UNESCO. *See* United Nations Educational, Scientific, and Cultural Organization
UN Framework Convention on Climate Change, 380
UNHCR. *See* United Nations High Commissioner for Refugees
UNICEF. *See* United Nations Children's Emergency Fund
unilateralism, 126, 481
Union of Concerned Scientists, 194–95
Union of Soviet Socialist Republics (USSR), 103*m*. *See also* Russia; Soviet Union
unipolarity, 114, 119, 518
unitary actor, 69, 196
United Arab Emirates, 150
United Kingdom. *See* Great Britain
United Nations, 15, 18
  agencies and conferences (*see specific agencies and conferences*)
  budget and cash flow problems, 178–80
  changing membership, 174*f*
  charter limitations, 549
  collaboration with NGOs, 177
  collective security and, 548
  conferences on population growth, 357, 360
  creation after WWII, 110
  emerging NIEs and, 151
  General Assembly, 143, 176–77
  global network, 178*m*
  global role, 180–81
  ideology and agenda, 175
  inability to control civil wars, 547, 554
  neoliberalism and, 42
  objectives, 175
  peacekeeping operations, 549–51, 552*m*, 553
  purposes, 547
  reliance on the U.S., 553–54
  Security Council, 57*f*, 110, 174, 176
  selective engagement accusations, 551, 553
  specialized agencies, 547
  standoffs during Cold War, 549
  structure, 176, 548
  Universal Declaration of Human Rights, 220, 246, 250, 252
  world conferences, 175–76
United Nations Children's Emergency Fund (UNICEF), 548
United Nations Conference of the Human Environment, 367
United Nations Conference on the Environment and Development (UNCED), 367
United Nations Conference on Trade and Development (UNCTAD), 155, 290, 548
United Nations Convention to Combat Desertification (CCD), 385*m*
United Nations Development Programme (UNDP), 227, 548
United Nations Educational, Scientific, and Cultural Organization (UNESCO), 273, 548, 559
United Nations Emergency Force (UNEF), 549
United Nations Environment Programme (UNEP), 381
United Nations High Commissioner for Refugees (UNHCR), 233
United States
  arms trade and, 455–56, 457, 460
  atomic bombing of Japan, 109
  bilateral arms control agreements, 508
  bipolar treaties with Russia, 516–17
  Bretton Woods conference role, 303–4
  Cold War and (*see* Cold War)
  comparative advantage in trade example, 306–7, 306*t*
  concern over media dominance, 272–274
  consequences of superpower status, 19–20
  criticisms of, 342, 586–87
  economic hegemon position, 311, 312, 314
  economic leadership cost, 326–27
  economic sanctions use, 480
  economic unilateralism, 333–34
  economic vulnerability, 314–16
  emigration from Mexico, 233
  entry into WWI, 100
  entry into WWII, 107
  foreign policy, 481–85
  geopolitics of, 60, 62
  governmental politics, 80–82
  greenhouse effect contribution, 378*m*, 380
  hegemon role, 417, 516
  high politics and, 44
  ignoring of humanitarian law, 251
  imperialistic occupations, 140
  Iraq and (*see* Iraqi war; Persian Gulf War)
  isolationism and WWII, 107
  loss of European support, 523
  military spending, 443–44, 444*f*, 448, 452, 576
  Millennium Challenge, 159–60
  NAFTA membership, 156
  national debt, 315
  national security strategy, 481–85
  nuclear energy use, 373
  nuclear weapons doctrine, 468
  nuclear weapons stockpiles, 461
  oil consumption, 370
  participation in GATT, 181
  population momentum, 355–56
  post-WWII status, 110
  preemptive military action use, 63 (*see also* Iraqi war)
  preemptive strategy, 471
  questions about future trade policies, 343
  ranking on human security indicators, 451
  reputation worldwide, 578
  steps towards nuclear disarmament, 464
  terrorism against (*see* September 11, 2001)
  trade deficit, 4
  UN debt, 179
  unipolarity of, 120–1, 122, 123*f*, 518–19
  UN reliance on, 553–54
  value of U.S. dollar, 324*f*
  veto authority in UN, 174
  withdrawal from World Court, 530–31, 544, 547
Universal Declaration of Human Rights, 220, 246, 250, 252
Universal Postal Union (1874), 193, 559
uranium, 373
Urban II, Pope, 202
Urquhart, Brian, 169, 180, 238, 252, 554
Uruguay, 157, 336
Uruguay Round, 182, 317, 318*t*, 319*f*
USSR. *See* Soviet Union; Union of Soviet Socials Republics

Vaitheeswaron, Vijay, 371
Vance, Cyrus, 80*f*, 575
Vandersluis, Sarah Owen, 222, 245, 246
Van Evera, Stephen, 108, 412
Vasquez, John A., 28, 36, 39, 40, 62, 471, 503
Vedrine, Hubert, 120
Veltmeyer, Henry, 302
Venezuela, 157
Verba, Sidney, 37, 69, 89
Verbeek, Bertjan, 169
Verizon Communications, 271
VERs. *See* voluntary export restrictions
Versailles peace settlement, 142
vertical nuclear proliferation, 462
Viacom, 271, 274
Viendt, 274
Vietnam, 157
Vietnam War, 14, 85, 90
virtual corporations, 290
virtuality, 268
virtual nuclear arsenals, 466

viruses, 276. *See also* health and disease issues
voluntary export restrictions (VERs), 310
von Glahn, Gerhard, 539

Wallace, Brian, 224
Wallensteen, Peter, 401, 419, 420, 421, 426
Wallerstein, Immanuel, 46, 122, 417
Wal-Mart, 206
Walt, Stephen W., 539
Walter, Barbara F., 415, 420, 422, 424
Walters, Robert S., 308
Waltz, Kenneth N., 19, 36, 38, 39, 40, 127, 310, 499, 505, 517, 524
war crimes, 250–52, 543, 545
Ward, Michael D., 451
warfare
  armed conflict defined, 400
  civil wars (*see* civil wars)
  common security concept, 493
  conduct of war and human rights, 244, 249–52
  containing terrorism, 578–80
  continuities and change in armed conflict, 400–401, 402*f*, 403
  global causes of
    cyclical theories, 417–19, 418*f*
    power transitions, 415–17
    question of violence breeding violence, 415
    reliance on self-help, 413, 415
  human rights and (*see* human rights)
  individuals as a cause of
    biological bases of aggression theories, 403–4
    influence of leaders, 405–6
    national character and, 404
    territorial imperative and, 404
    war as a learned cultural habit, 404
  as an instrument of national policy, 29
  legal control of (*see* international law; just war doctrine)
  long-cycle theory, 96–98
  military power's purpose, 575–78
  military spending, 576
  nationalism's linkage to armed conflict, 412–13, 414
  nonmilitary dimensions of national security, 493–94
  outlawing of, 32
  pervasiveness in history, 400
  possible obsolescence of, 575–78
  security dilemma of states, 492–93
  self-destruction potential, 587–88
  states as a cause of
    cultural determinants, 406–7
    duration of independence, 406
    economic system, 409–11
    feminist theory and, 407
    geography and, 408–9
    militarization, 409
    nationalism and, 412–13, 414
    poverty and, 407–8
    type of government and, 411–12
    terrorism (*see* terrorism)
    transforming nature of, 28
    trends in, 401
  war defined, 400
  WWII fight over ethical values, 109
Warrick, Joby, 381
Warsaw Pact, 517
war weariness hypothesis, 419
Washington Naval Conference (1922), 102, 510
Watson, Douglas, 239
Way, Christopher R., 462
Weakland, Rembert, 232
Wealth of Nations, The (Smith), 140, 308
weapons of mass destruction (WMD), 436, 457, 466, 499, 510
weapons technology
  biological and chemical weapons, 466–67
  improvements to systems, 465–66
  military capabilities and power
    motives for arms trade, 457–59
    strategic consequences of arms sales, 459–60
    trends in military spending, 452, 453*f*
    trends in weapons trade, 454–57, 454*f*
  nuclear weapons (*see* nuclear age)
  proliferation of, 8
Weart, Spencer R., 564
Weaver, Ole, 44
web bars, 271
Weber, Max, 78
Weidenbaum, Murray, 210, 291, 301
Weimar Republic, 60
Weinberger, Caspar, 80*f*
Weinstein, Michael M., 565
Weitsman, Patricia A., 502
Wendt, Alexander, 28, 49, 50
Wendzel, Robert L., 87
Werner, Suzanne, 415
West Bank, 432*m*
Westphalian system, 58
WFP. *See* World Food Programme
WGP. *See* world gross product
Whitbeck, John V., 428, 429
White, Donald W., 315
White, Ralph K., 101
Whitman, Walt, 5
WHO. *See* World Health Organization
Wildavsky, Aaron, 144
Wilhelm II, Kaiser, 60, 89
Williams, Jody, 513
Wills, Garry, 436, 537, 541
Wilson, James Q., 404
Wilson, Woodrow, 30, 32, 66, 102, 411, 501, 586, 588
Wint, Guy, 107
Winter War, 108
Wise, Michael Z., 532
WMD. *See* weapons of mass destruction
WMO. *See* World Meteorological Organization

Wohlforth, William C., 524
Wolf, Martin, 210
Wolfensohn, James D., 132, 159, 163, 184, 220, 226, 261
Wolfers, Arnold, 64
Wolfowitz, Paul, 81
women
  challenges in protecting women's rights, 243
  conferences addressing women's issues, 240, 241*t*
  feminist theory, 42, 43, 223, 407
  gender issues in world politics (*see* gender politics)
  status of women worldwide, 241–43
  victimization in war, 424
Woodward, Bob, 83, 541
Wooldridge, Adrian, 284, 320
World Bank
  administration, 184
  creation and purpose, 183–84, 326
  effectiveness of, 185–86
  Global South and, 151
  lending policies, 185
  organization, 184
  support of democracy, 564
  voting system, 184
World Biodiversity Day, 277
World Commission on Environment and Development, 367
World Commission on the Social Dimensions of Globalization, 289
World Conference on Sustainable Development, 360
World Conference on Women, 243
World Conservation Union, 277, 386
World Court, 529–30, 534
World Economic Forum, 169, 312
world federalism, 556–58
World Food Programme (WFP), 548
world gross product (WGP), 285*f*
World Health Organization (WHO), 547
World Meteorological Organization (WMO), 193, 376
world politics
  clash of civilizations, 581
  containing terrorism, 578–80
  criteria for defining a new system, 7–8
  cycles in, 9
  end of history, 588–89
  finding a new world order, 590–91
  global vs. national interests, 574–75
  great powers' ability to protect human rights, 581–83
  hierarchies of states, 8
  impact of changes to, 6
  key questions
    consequences of U.S. hegemony, 19–20
    geo-economics vs. geopolitics, 20–21
    globalization pros and cons, 18–19, 583–85
    human welfare and, 21–22

obsolescence of states, 17–18
levels of analysis, 14–16 (*see also specific levels*)
liberalism's relevance to, 585–87
perceptions' influence on reality
  factors involved, 12–13
  mental maps and, 9, 12
  role of images, 13–14
politics defined, 16
possible obsolescence of war, 575–78
post-Cold War challenges, 589
realism's relevance to, 585
self-destruction potential, 587–88
theories of (*see* theories of world politics)
transformation points, 6
World Population Conference, 360
World Resources Institute, 374, 382
World Social Forum, 169
World Summit, 375
World Summit for Children, 408
World Summit for Social Development, 227
World Summit on Sustainable Development, 367, 392
world-system theory, 46, 141, 149
World Telecom Pact, 274
World Trade Center, NY, 3, 399
World Trade Organization (WTO), 8
  arguments for and against, 320–21
  China's membership in, 15, 488
  enlargement of membership, 283*m*, 284
  establishment and purpose of, 44, 181–83, 283–84, 317, 318*t*, 319*f*, 320

global communications and, 274
Global South and, 156
influence of, 183
neoliberalism and, 41
World Urban Forum, 573
World War I
  causes of, 99–101
  consequences of, 102–3, 103*m*
  international law and, 539
  liberalism and, 29–31
  ratio of soldiers to civilians killed, 543
  territorial changes following, 103*m*
  theories of world politics and, 29
World War II, 14
  causes of
    Germany's hegemonic ambitions, 104
    Hitler's vision, 108–9
    policy of appeasement results, 106–7
    psychological forces, 108
    reemergence of multipolarity, 107
  geopolitical consequences, 109–10
  German attacks on Poland and France, 106–7
  map of Europe during and after, 105*m*
  ratio of soldiers to civilians killed, 543
  rise in realism after, 35
  system-transforming impact of Allied victory, 109–10
  total deaths, 104
  U.S. emergence as hegemon, 516

Worldwatch, 366
World Wide Fund for Nature (WWFN), 384
World Wildlife Federation, 194
Wright, Quincy, 409, 419, 535
WTO. *See* World Trade Organization
WWFN. *See* World Wide Fund for Nature

"X" article, 114, 118
xenophobia, 236

Yalta Conference, 110
Yardley, Jim, 370
Yeros, Paris, 222, 245, 246
Yoshida Doctrine, 488–89
Yugoslavia, 8, 36, 70, 102, 233, 239, 409, 544, 563

Zacher, Mark W., 30, 42, 44
Zagare, Frank C., 87, 442
Zaire, 275
Zakaria, Fareed, 18, 40, 81, 288, 320, 491, 519
Zeiler, Thomas W., 314
zeitgeist, 90, 91
Zelikow, Philip, 70, 79
Zemin, Jiang, 525
zero-sum contest, 152, 313, 482, 574
Zhang, Xiakoe, 328
Ziegler, David, 417
Zimmerman, Alfred, 30, 425
Zoellick, Robert, 341, 342